Contributors

Dr John Alexander
University of Cambridge

Dr Peter Andrews
British Museum (Natural History),

Professor David Baerreis
University of Wisconsin

Dr G. N. Bailey
University of Cambridge

Iris Barry
Institute of Archaeology, London

Dr Donn Bayard
University of Otago

Dr Warwick Bray
Institute of Archaeology, London

Dr Bennet Bronson
Field Museum of Natural History,
Chicago

Richard Burleigh
Research Laboratory, British Museum

Dr Paul Cartledge
University of Cambridge

Dr Dilip Chakrabarti
University of Delhi

Dr Nikolai Dejevsky

Dr Robin Dennell
University of Sheffield

Dr D. Brian Doe

Professor Don E. Dumond
University of Oregon

Professor Clive Foss
University of Massachusetts, Boston

Professor Leslie Freeman
University of Chicago

Peter Garlake
University College, London

Dr Ian C. Glover
Institute of Archaeology, London

Professor James B. Griffin
University of Michigan

Dr J. W. K. Harris
Leakey Institute, Nairobi

Dr Georgina Herrmann
British Institute of Persian Studies

Dr Ian Hodder
University of Cambridge

Ray Inskeep
Pitt Rivers Museum,
University of Oxford

Dr G. J. Irwin
University of Auckland

Dafydd Kidd
British Museum

Professor Richard Klein
University of Chicago

J. G. Lewthwaite
University of Cambridge

Dr Michael Loewe
University of Cambridge

Dr Stephen Mitchell
University College of Swansea

Dr P. R. S. Moorey
Ashmolean Museum,
University of Oxford

Dr Craig Morris
American Museum of Natural History

Dr Daphne Nash
Ashmolean Museum,
University of Oxford

Dr Joan Oates
University of Cambridge

Dr David O'Connor
University Museum, Pennsylvania

Dr John O'Shea
Ashmolean Museum,
University of Oxford

Peter Parr
Institute of Archaeology, London

Dr D. W. Phillipson
Glasgow Museums and Art Galleries

Dr Colin Platt
University of Southampton

Nicholas Postgate
British Archaeological
Expedition to Iraq

Dr T. W. Potter
British Museum

Gary Presland
Institute of Archaeology, London

Professor Colin Renfrew
University of Southampton

Dr Derek A. Roe
University of Oxford

Professor C. Thurstan Shaw

Dr Stephen J. Shennan
University of Southampton

Dr Andrew Sherratt
Ashmolean Museum,
University of Oxford

F. Alayne Street
University of Oxford

David Stronach
British Institute of Persian Studies

Professor Romila Thapar
Jawaharlal Nehru University,
New Delhi

Dr Alan Thorne
The Australian National University,
Canberra

Professor Denis Twitchett
University of Cambridge

Professor Peter Warren
University of Bristol

Dr David Whitehouse
British School at Rome

Marek Zvelebil
University of Cambridge

Contents

THE
CAMBRIDGE ENCYCLOPEDIA
OF ARCHAEOLOGY

NOTE

Superior figures in the text indicate bibliographical references, which are to be found on pp. 453–65.

All dates based on radiocarbon determinations have been corrected according to the tree-ring calibration, to give estimates that correspond to true historical dates. To avoid inconsistency at the limits of the available calibration, radiocarbon determinations falling between 7000 and 10000 years ago have been adjusted upwards by decreasing amounts, using an extrapolation of the calibration curve. This provides the best available estimates of absolute age in this time range, though they may differ slightly from published dates based on uncorrected radiocarbon determinations.

All measurements are given in metric units. The following conversions may be helpful:

1 hectare = 2.47 acres	1 kilogram = 2.21 lbs
1 kilometre = 0.62 miles	1 gram = 0.04 ounces
1 metre = 1.09 yards	1 litre = 1.76 imperial pints

First published in 1980 by the Press Syndicate of the University of Cambridge, The Pitt Building, Trumpington Street, Cambridge CB2 1RP
296 Beaconsfield Parade, Middle Park, Melbourne 3206, Australia

First published in the United States in 1980 by Crown Publishers Inc. and the Press Syndicate of the University of Cambridge

First published in Canada in 1980 by Prentice-Hall of Canada Limited and the Press Syndicate of the University of Cambridge

ISBN 0 521 22989 8

Created, designed and produced by Trewin Copplestone Publishing Limited Advance House, 101-109 Ladbroke Grove, London W11

© Trewin Copplestone Publishing Limited 1980

Executive editor: Candida Hunt
Cartography: Swanston & Associates
Diagrams and plans: Martin Causer
Drawings: Michael Craig
Designer: Joanna Dale
Picture research: Angela Murphy
Indexer: Anna Pavord

Typeset in Great Britain by
SX Composing Limited, Rayleigh, Essex
Colour origination by Positive Plus, London

Printed and bound in Hong Kong by
Leefung-Asco Limited
Kowloon

THE CAMBRIDGE ENCYCLOPEDIA OF ARCHAEOLOGY

Editor
Andrew Sherratt, MA, PhD (Cantab.), FSA
Ashmolean Museum, University of Oxford

Foreword by
Professor Grahame Clark, CBE, MA, ScD, PhD (Cantab.), FSA, FBA
Master of Peterhouse, University of Cambridge

CAMBRIDGE UNIVERSITY PRESS
Cambridge   London   New York   New Rochelle
Melbourne   Sydney

Foreword

Archaeology has long ceased to be the preserve of experts or vulgarizers and has become part of the discourse of the educated man or woman. For accurate information it is natural to turn to works of reference. The *Cambridge Encyclopedia of Archaeology* is no mere dictionary or repository of facts. It treats of major themes opened up by archaeology, and it does so in a dynamic manner. The aim is to engage the reader in what is, by common consent, one of the major enterprises of the age: nothing less than a dramatic extension of the range of human awareness. The measure of the success of this volume is the fact that the authors are still active in their chosen fields and are as aware of what remains to be discovered as they are well apprised of the present state of knowledge. In a word, they stimulate our interest and engage our curiosity.

As the media have discovered, the appeal of archaeology is as broad as humanity. It attracts the interest of people of all ages and levels of education, and of every calling, culture and race. Moreover, it does this at the physical, sensual and conceptual levels, frequently at the same time. The physical pleasures of archaeology require no exposition for anyone who has shared in the camaraderie and hard labour of excavation, whether under temperate rain, tropical sun or arctic thaw – or even under water, exploring, wrecks, harbours or cargoes. For the older traveller few experiences can match the pleasure of exploration of ancient sites set in wild places. Aesthetically, the appeal of archaeology is primarily visual, to a lesser extent tactile. The most important impact is likely to be made by the works of art that for some thirty thousand years have been among the most revealing products of our species. This does not end the matter. Over a much greater time-span, going back well into the Middle Pleistocene, men have habitually shaped their artifacts, even those designed for basic needs, with a greater subtlety and finish than their function strictly demanded. The appreciation and practice of archaeology require, and pleasantly exercise, a sensibility to nuances of style that, more than anything, permit definitions and support attributions. The tactile qualities of some materials may heighten aesthetic appreciation, as the Chinese insisted in respect of jade, porcelain or bronze patina.

The supreme appeal of archaeology, however, resides in the story it can tell. As a disciplined method of recovering what happened in the unwritten past, archaeology first began to emerge from antiquarianism in western Europe during the last quarter of the eighteenth century, but its full scope and significance was not appreciated until the implications of Darwin's hypothesis became apparent for the descent and antiquity of man. The range of concern rapidly expanded from the antecedents of European man to the prehistory of mankind in general. This defined a challenging gap in knowledge. The first to step into the breach were the ethnologists who, from their armchairs on either side of the Atlantic, composed confident works of conjectural history based on the fallacy that the course of cultural evolution could be unveiled by the mere process of arranging the cultures of modern 'primitive peoples' in order of complexity. Archaeology, the only valid method of reconstituting the early history of man, was an arduous and much slower process: it took a century to establish even the main lines of human prehistory and the genesis of man's major civilizations. Even so, much remains to be learned about the course of cultural history, and the investigation of process is still in its infancy.

As so much remains to be achieved by archaeologists, it is all the more appropriate to reflect on the meaning and value of their endeavours. By enlarging the bounds of history to include the prehistory of humanity, archaeology allows us to view ourselves in a far wider perspective than ever before. In tracing the divergence of man from the other primates it defines our very humanity. It brings home to us, in the most concrete manner, the fact that we have become human to the extent that our animal appetites have been harnessed to increasingly artificial modes of behaviour. Archaeological artifacts are veritable fossils of our humanity. Whereas the products of the earlier types of men in the warmer parts of the Old World were marked by a notable degree of homogeneity and an extremely slow rate of change, those of sapient varieties underwent much more rapid development and displayed increasing diversity of expression, culminating in the distinctive high civilizations of recent millennia. It is well to remember, in the face of modern homogenizing trends, that we owe our humanity as much to this diversity as to our underlying community.

Grahame Clark

Introduction

Archaeology has come of age. While it began as a method of identifying places and objects already known from the historical record, it has become a powerful means of discovering new facts not only about the historical period but also about ages beyond the reach of written evidence. It is at last beginning to provide answers to some of the most fundamental questions about human origins and the development of human society. Dealing with the whole story of man's existence on Earth, it brings a fresh perspective to the study of past and present conditions.

Its evidence is the material imprint of man's activities on the landscape: the remains of his shelters, his tools and the facilities that he has created in order to exploit the natural environment. The methods of the archaeologist range from the microscopic examination of traces of wear on ancient tools to the reconstruction of whole landscapes through the use of aerial photography and field survey. Such methods are as valuable in investigating the recent past as they are in reconstructing the more remote periods of prehistory. They complement the documentary studies of the historian by providing evidence of aspects of life that frequently went unrecorded by the often narrowly based, literate elites whose concern was with the personalities and achievements of the powerful rather than with the broader development of human culture and technology.

One effect of archaeological research has been to direct attention to the basic material conditions of life in early societies – the means of production and livelihood and the distribution of durable goods. While there is a danger that this may lead to an over-simplifying materialism, it is a valuable counterbalance to the political and military accounts that often form the bulk of the historical record, which can lead to an anachronistic view of the past as a result of our projecting back to earlier societies the attitudes of our own time.

The methods of the archaeologist can also be used to give historical depth to peoples without their own written history. The societies studied by the ethnographer and anthropologist in Africa or Oceania, for example, can be put into context and given a past through the use of archaeological techniques. One of the most exciting spheres of current research is those areas where simple societies can be studied both through the analysis of their recent economies and social institutions and through the complementary reconstruction of their origins and background. The study of these living social systems gives valuable insights into the organization of early communities.

Perhaps the most valuable contribution of the archaeological perspective, however, is its time-scale. The study of human development begins as geology and evolutionary biology and ends as history. The earliest parts of this story are measured in millions of years, the historical part in hundreds or tens of years or even in months. In between, the constantly accelerating rate of change requires a time-scale that is increasingly refined as it gets nearer to the present. Archaeology demands a logarithmic imagination successively to encompass the massive scale of biological change in the Cenozoic, the hundred-thousand-year rhythms of the Pleistocene Ice Age, the ten thousand years of Postglacial development and the five thousand years of recorded history. The language of archaeology deals with processes rather than events; it stresses the regularities of change and its consequences rather than the unique impact of contingent circumstances. It forms a bridge between the types of explanation that characterize the biological sciences and those of the humanities; and it requires its own discipline and philosophy to produce explanations appropriate to the scale of its subject and material.

Archaeology is thus both a set of methods for the reconstruction of past states of society and a realm of inquiry dealing with the long-term development of human culture and its explanation. While it must be open to ideas and interpretations based on the study of existing societies, and while it makes use of generalizations about the organization and working of human societies as they can be observed by social scientists of today, its characteristic is that it deals with processes whose very scale precludes direct observation. The key to an understanding of this scale of development lies in controlled comparison – the recognition of regularities in the development of human societies in diverse circumstances and of the similarities and differences that have arisen among them.

The state of archaeological research in different parts of the world is still very uneven. Nevertheless, the progress of the last decades has produced striking advances in our understanding of global developments over the archaeological time-scale. This book is an attempt to summarize the present state of knowledge over the whole field of archaeological inquiry. It reflects a growing awareness of the contribution that archaeology can make in revealing the common history of mankind.

Andrew Sherratt

The craft of archaeology

Archaeological evidence

The raw materials of archaeology are the surviving traces of past human activity. Some of these are the accidental side-effects of everyday operations such as building houses or making stone tools; some are products involving symbolism and communication, like a wall painting or a gold ornament. While the latter may to some extent be studied as objects in themselves, all of them yield more information when considered in the contexts in which they occur. These may be accidental accumulations – in a rubbish pit, for instance – or they may have been deliberately deposited, as with objects in a tomb. In both cases there is some degree of *association* between them, in that they were used at more or less the same time and quite probably by the same community. In the case of a grave group, there is a direct association between a set of objects and a particular person. Such associated finds thus constitute an *assemblage*: these are the building blocks of archaeology.

The aim of archaeology is not merely to recover ancient objects but also to establish the patterned relationships among them. As such features are best preserved by burial (whether natural or deliberate), this process usually involves *excavation*. An archaeological *site* is any area where coherent traces of early activity may be systematically investigated, and archaeological research most frequently takes the form of uncovering and recording such remains (see Chapter 3). As many activities may have taken place on the same spot, however, they must be disentangled by working out the order in which they took place. The simple rule of superposition – that later deposits lie on top of earlier ones – is the basis of the discipline of *stratigraphy*, which archaeologists share with geologists, who first formulated it.

To interpret the meaning of the activities represented on a site, the archaeologist must interrogate his material further in terms of some coherent set of ideas or *model* that raises a series of expectations about what is involved. In the case of a building he can do this in the light of his experience of construction techniques; he expects to find traces of the digging of pits and foundations, the laying of floors, etc. In dealing with more complex questions about the organization of the society he is considering he must call on some more general ideas, for instance about ranking and the transmission of property, that can be tested by noting how wealth is distributed in a cemetery and whether infants are buried with rich grave goods. Most of these procedures involve *taxonomy* – the classification of the objects and features that he recovers. This usually consists of the definition of consistently recurring types (*typology*) and the analysis (often involving statistics) of patterns of association and distribution. A particular type of decorated axe, for example, may constantly recur with other weapons in the graves of adult males in a particular area. This leads on to further questions about where they were made and how they circulated in the social network (see Chapter 4).

In the early stages of research the dominant questions often concern *chronology* – the relative and absolute dating of finds. The former involves building up *sequences* by stratigraphy and association; the latter requires some kind of radiometric assay (see Chapter 62). In sorting his material into preliminary packages it is useful for the archaeologist to define *cultures* – consistent groups of contemporary types occurring within a restricted area. These have no necessary coincidence with racial or social units but form convenient entities for generalization from particular sites. They provide a framework within which to interpret changes in the way of life that can be reconstructed from monuments, artifacts and residues of food-gathering such as animal bones, shells, seeds and other organic remains (see Chapter 5).

From his analysis of the material record, the archaeologist goes on to define processes of change. Early investigators tried to interpret their results in purely historical terms – as evidence of invasions, movements of people, the diffusion of civilization from higher cultures. While this approach has some validity in certain circumstances, more fruitful models are now being explored, and archaeologists are beginning to exploit the unique properties of their evidence by reconstructing long-term patterns of development. The following chapters provide many examples of the results that are beginning to emerge from systematic programmes of research (see Chapter 7).

Terminology

The terminology used in archaeology has grown up haphazardly and thus contains anomalies and inconsistencies. Many regional sequences have been worked out independently and labels may have different meanings in different areas. It might be simpler to invent an entirely new set of terms, but it is necessary for present purposes to respect existing usage. (Further details of special terms and their usage are given in the appropriate chapters).

Geologists divide the history of the world into four stages (eras) related to the evolution of life: Primary (Palaeozoic), Secondary (Mesozoic), Tertiary and Quaternary (Cenozoic). The Cenozoic – the Age of Mammals – is divided into seven epochs, of which the latest are the Miocene, the Pliocene, the Pleistocene and the Holocene. The final division is somewhat arbitrary, as climatically it is only the latest warm phase in the series of cycles of warm and cold conditions that constitute the Ice Age, which began in the later Cenozoic era and dominated the Quaternary epoch. These cycles have been reconstructed from fragmentary traces of glaciation in several areas and have been given labels based on local names, such as Riss or Würm in the alpine region (see Chapter 8).

The development of human culture has been used to provide subdivisions of the archaeological record. Nineteenth-century European prehistorians devised the 'three-age' system of Stone, Bronze and Iron Ages. This is not the best basis for a worldwide scheme, if only because several continents did not go through an intermediate phase of bronze-using. However, it is enshrined in both specialist usage and popular parlance. The system was soon elaborated by the division of the Stone Age into three phases – Palaeolithic, Mesolithic and Neolithic – corresponding roughly to Pleistocene hunters, Holocene hunters and stone-using agriculturalists respectively. Further subdivision produced the Lower, Middle and Upper Palaeolithic – monstrosities that are now too deeply engrained to eradicate. Subdivision of the metal ages in the Old World began with the recognition of a simple, early phase of copper-using, distinguished as the Copper Age, Chalcolithic or Eneolithic period. In the New World an independent system is in use that is related to the development of the still largely stone-using civilizations of Mesoamerica. It is divided into Archaic (cf. Mesolithic), Formative (cf. Neolithic) and the Classic and Post-Classic phases of urban life.

The objects and monuments that first struck the imagination of early investigators have often been given specific names that have survived as technical terms, sometimes inappropriately (as with 'hillforts'). The custom of naming people after their artifacts ('Beaker folk' or 'mound-builders') has created an often odd-sounding shorthand. Foreign words, such as the Arabic *tell* (meaning the mound formed by a succession of ancient villages or towns), are often used in a wider context. World archaeology has added its quota of native terms for common objects (the American *atlatl* for the hunter's spear-thrower, and *metate* and *mano* for the farmer's concave quern and its grinder), while Classical archaeology has contributed literary terms like *megaron* or *depas* for particular types of building and object. Other words have been made up from Greek roots, such as 'megalith' to describe the monumental tombs of large, undressed stones erected by peasant communities in several parts of the world, or 'microlith' to denote the small, chipped flints that were part of composite tools for hunting or harvesting. Scientific terms, too, are appearing in increasing numbers to express concepts such as exponential growth or the various types of random sample, as well as words like 'trajectory', which has been given a derivative sense to describe pathways of cultural development. Fresh terms are still being invented to fulfil new needs: 'site catchment', meaning the economic hinterland of a settlement, is a good example. More fundamentally, the meaning of some common words, such as 'domestication', has been modified to apply to the different conditions of the past.

The accelerating rate of change in the last 100 million years: successive enlargements of the latest 10 per cent of the preceding column show the main divisions of later geological and archaeological time-scales.

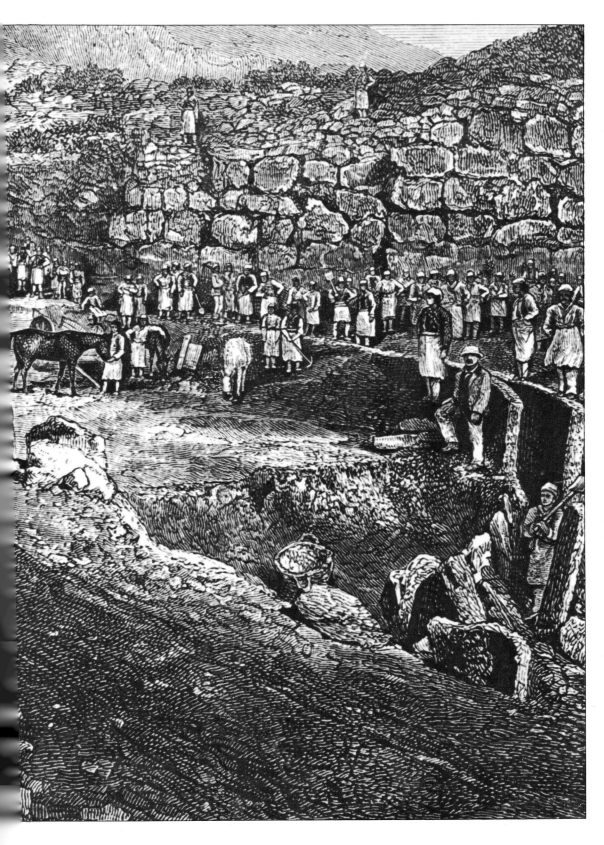

I: The development of modern archaeology

The interest in antiquities that was part of the Renaissance rediscovery of the European past was given a fresh impetus by the Industrial Revolution, when a new scale of construction and earth-moving brought to light many remains of early man and his works. Systematic study was at first largely concerned with stray finds of attractive objects, but opportunities were increasingly taken to investigate early sites by excavation, which yielded information about not only the contexts of such objects but also their relationship to each other. The new science of geology provided a time-scale beyond the scope of earlier imagination, while interpretations of early life were broadened by the colonial encounter with less developed peoples in many parts of the world. Exploration of the centres of early civilization in Asia and America also gave a new dimension to the historical record through the discovery and excavation of early towns and cities. Recently archaeology has been transformed by new scientific techniques and by further archaeological exploration of the more remote parts of the world. Modern archaeology deals not only with ancient artifacts and monuments but also with whole landscapes and their organization, as these can be reconstructed by increasingly sophisticated methods of analysis.

1. The origins and growth of archaeology

Speculation about the human past (including some striking anticipations of modern views) can be traced back into Classical Antiquity, but serious investigation of monuments and artifacts only began with the Renaissance, and the methodical analysis of large quantities of material was a development of the eighteenth and nineteenth centuries. Three sources in particular contributed to the rise of the systematic discipline of archaeology: the study of Classical and oriental antiquities; the discovery of the European past through monuments and ancient artifacts; and the study of human origins, which was an outcome of the developing sciences of geology and biology.

Renaissance antiquaries

The concern with Classical Antiquity emerged in Renaissance Italy, beginning in the fifteenth century. At first the interest was purely literary, but one consequence of this was a desire to identify the actual sites of places and events mentioned in the literary texts. By the middle of the century the first collections of coins, gems and statuary were being assembled by Cosimo I de' Medici in Florence and Pope Sixtus IV in Rome. By the sixteenth century architects were exploring the remains of Roman buildings, adapting ancient designs and removing statues to embellish their patrons' palaces. Andrea Palladio investigated the ruins at Palestrina and in Rome,[1] while his colleague Pirro Ligorio dug at Hadrian's Villa, Tivoli. Antiquarian research in Italy culminated in the excavation, under licence from the Bourbon kings of Naples, of Herculaneum and Pompeii, the former from 1709 and the latter from 1748.

By this time Classical Antiquity had aroused the intense curiosity of scholars and collectors all over Europe. Johann Winckelmann (1717–68), after studying Classical art in Greece, moved to Rome and wrote, between 1764 and 1768, *Kunstgeschichte der Antiken* (*The History of the Art of the Ancients*), one of the milestones in the history of art, while other scholars described the monuments and antiquities of particular regions.[2] Meanwhile, collectors like Sir William Hamilton exported case after case of Greek vases and other antiquities.

In England an interest in antiquities developed out of the topographical surveys of the sixteenth century. John Leland was appointed King's Antiquary in 1533 and toured England and Wales looking at ancient monuments. William Camden visited Stonehenge and Hadrian's Wall, incorporating descriptions of these and other monuments in his *Britannia* of 1586. Other writers, such as Robert Plot, who published natural histories of Oxfordshire and Staffordshire, included notes on artifacts and sites. Collections of curios and rarities began to be established – for example, that of John Tradescant, whose 'closet of curiosities' formed the nucleus of the Ashmolean Museum in Oxford. By the eighteenth century there was a flourishing tradition of field archaeology and antiquarian research, exemplified by the work of William Stukeley[3] and William Borlase.[4]

Elsewhere in Europe the study of ancient monuments and their contents was arousing interest in the early inhabitants of the continent. Ole Worm, a Danish antiquarian, published in 1643 an account of the early monuments of Denmark, especially stones with runic inscriptions and megalithic 'altars'. In Sweden a state antiquities service was founded by Gustavus Adolphus II (reigned 1611–32). In France archaeological imagination was fired by the discovery in 1653 of the grave of the fifth-century Frankish king, Childerich. Megaliths also attracted attention, and soon de Robien (1698–1750) was excavating sites near Carnac. The systematic study of ancient artifacts was greatly aided by the publication, between 1719 and 1724, of *L'Antiquité Expliquée et Répresentée en Figures*, by Bernard de Montfaucon.

1.1: *A bizarre discovery at Pompeii, described by Sir William Hamilton as 'the skeleton of the washerwoman' in 1777. The exploration of the Roman towns of Pompeii and Herculaneum on the Bay of Naples, both destroyed by an eruption of Vesuvius in AD 79, began in the eighteenth century. The earliest excavations were directed mainly towards recovering Classical statues for the Bourbon royal collections, and scholarly investigations did not begin until about 1860. The sites are extraordinarily well preserved beneath the volcanic debris, and they continue to provide invaluable information about Roman culture and daily life.*

Establishing order

The steady acquisition of antiquities, whether by chance discovery or excavation, soon posed the problem of classification. It was obvious that objects were not all of the same age, but how could the remains of one period be distinguished from those of another? The problem was particularly acute in north-west Europe, where the Romans had not penetrated and where, as a result, hardly anything was known of the inhabitants before the Middle Ages. In Denmark Rasmus Nyerup (1759–1829), who excavated an important collection of prehistoric antiquities from 'kitchen middens' (Mesolithic shell-mounds), was not alone in lamenting, 'Everything which has come down to us from heathendom is wrapped in a thick fog; it belongs to a space of time we cannot measure.'

The first move towards ordering the chaos came from Christian Jurgensen Thomsen (1788–1865). In 1806 the Danish Government set up a commission to look into the country's geology and natural history. Thomsen was secretary to the commission, and when a national museum was created in 1816, he became its first curator. Confronted by a large collection of antiquities, Thomsen arranged them according to the materials of which they were made; stone, bronze and iron. It was a short step to recognize the three groups of artifacts as representative of three chronological periods – a concept that was to be found in the work of the Latin poet Lucretius and that, by the end of the eighteenth century, was current in Germany. The 'three ages' became widely used: Sven Nilsson (1787–1883) adopted the system in a paper on the origins of hunting in 1834 and in a later book,[5] and Thomsen himself published a full exposition in 1836.[6]

Thomsen's assistant at the national museum was J. J. A. Worsaae (1821–85), who went on to become official inspector of antiquities and eventually director of the museum. Worsaae occupies an important place in the history of archaeology not simply because, encouraged by ethnographic parallels, he too

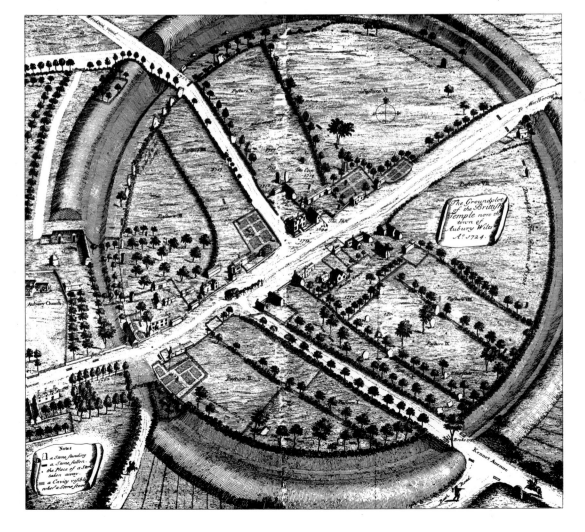

1.2: *A prospect showing the late Neolithic henge monument (ceremonial centre) at Avebury in Wiltshire, England, with its stone settings and embankment. The engraving is a good example of English topographic work of the early eighteenth century.*

adopted the 'three-age' system, but in particular because of his careful excavations. Instead of simply digging into shell-heaps or burial mounds to extract the more prominent objects, Worsaae noted carefully their position in relation to superimposed deposits and other features, making it possible to isolate closed groupings and to attribute finds to particular stages in the history of the site. In his excavations in peat bogs he was the first to realize that changes in the occurrence of different types of vegetation formed a consistent sequence, and in this respect he anticipated later palaeobotanical work.[7]

In the alpine lands, too, the pace of archaeological research was accelerating. In Switzerland the very dry winter of 1853–4 caused the water of Lake Constance to fall to abnormally low levels, revealing the first of the prehistoric lakeside settlements, Obermeilen. In the next twenty years this and other sites were investigated by Ferdinand Keller (1800–81). By 1875 more than two hundred lakeside sites had been recorded. In Austria the Iron Age cemetery of Hallstatt came to light in 1846 and was excavated by von Sacken over the next eighteen years.[8]

In 1865 John Lubbock (1834–1914) published *Prehistoric Times*, one of the finest archaeological syntheses produced in Britain in the nineteenth century. In this work he divided the Stone Age into an earlier phase of flaked stone tools (the Palaeolithic) and a later period of polished stone axes (the Neolithic). Typological analysis, pioneered by Thomsen, became one of the cornerstones of archaeological method. In Britain one of its chief exponents was Sir John Evans (1823–1908), who wrote on pre-Roman coins and stone and bronze implements. In Sweden Oscar Montelius (1843–1921) developed typological studies,[9] and his pupil, E. Salin, published the first systematic analysis of early medieval metalwork.[10] The use of typology in conjunction with the study of associated finds such as hoards of bronzework allowed Paul Reinecke (1872–1958) to provide a detailed sequence for the Bronze and Iron Ages of central Europe.

The 'three-age' system attracted a wider interest among both the educated public and scholars working in the growing field of ethnography. Encounters with less developed peoples in various parts of the world, and collections of items of their material culture, raised similar questions about classification. General Augustus Henry Pitt Rivers (born Lane-Fox; 1827–1900), who during his military career had been responsible for the development of the rifle, applied the idea of evolutionary development both to ancient and to ethnographic artifacts[11] and established the two large public collections of archaeological and ethnographical material that bear his name.

The notion of stages of culture was also broadened: from a technological scheme it developed into a postulated succession of modes of subsistence. Sven Nilsson, in the same work in which he applied the 'three-age' system,[12] argued from ethnographic evidence for a sequence of four socio-economic stages: savagery, nomadic pastoralism, settled agriculture, and civilization – the last characterized by the use of writing and money and the division of labour. Nilsson's comparative method was adopted by the Oxford anthropologist Sir Edward Tylor (1832–1917), who suggested a threefold division: savagery, barbarism and civilization.[13] Tylor's hypothesis was expanded by the American anthropologist Lewis H. Morgan, who postulated a sevenfold division in his book *Ancient Society* (1877): three stages of savagery (up to the discovery of fire, up to the invention of the bow, up to the invention of pottery); three stages of barbarism (up to the domestication of animals, up to the use of iron, up to the invention of the alphabet); and one stage of literate civilization. In Morgan's view, all human societies had passed or were passing through his seven successive stages of development. They did not all, however, pass through each stage simultaneously. 'The *condition*', he wrote, 'is the material fact, the *time* being immaterial.'

These ideas had a profound influence both on Karl Marx (1818–1883) and, more particularly, on Friedrich Engels (1820–95).[14] Together with the theories of biological evolution that culminated in the work of Charles Darwin (see below), they provided the foundation for a new view of the human past.

1.3: *Lower Palaeolithic handaxe from Hoxne, England, found by John Frere in 1797. Frere, a local squire and Fellow of the Royal Society, wrote a careful account of the discovery: the handaxes were, he thought, 'evidently weapons of war, fabricated and used by a people who had not the use of metals. They lay in great numbers at a depth of about twelve feet [3 metres] in a stratified soil....'*

The antiquity of man

Until the nineteenth century the main guide to the human past was the account given in the Bible. The Old Testament chronicles events from the Creation to the time of the civilizations recorded in Classical literature: ancient Egypt, Babylonia and Persia. Taking this account literally, Archbishop James Ussher (1581–1656) calculated in 1650 that the creation took place in 4004 BC. The Bible, therefore, seemed to show that the entire history of the Earth spanned less than six thousand years, half of which period was taken up by the ancient civilizations.

What, then, of fossils? Obviously, these were the remains of long-dead plants and animals: when did they die? *Genesis* provided the answer, describing how Noah's flood overwhelmed the Earth, destroying all creatures not in the Ark: hence the 'diluvial' theory, which explained fossils as products of the biblical deluge.

One man with a broader vision was John Frere of Norfolk. In 1797 Frere wrote to the Society of Antiquaries of London about flint implements recently found in a local brick-pit at Hoxne. They were, he suggested, 'fabricated and used by a people who had not yet the use of metals. . . . The situation in which these weapons were found may tempt us to refer them to a very remote period indeed, even beyond that of the present world.' Frere's conjecture, which seemed to cast doubt on the idea of a single act of creation, was extraordinarily adventurous in the 1790s. He was not, however, alone. In France Baron Georges Cuvier (1769–1832) concluded that there had been several catastrophes like the Flood before the creation of man and the modern fauna. While Cuvier and other 'Catastrophists' attempted to reconcile the great diversity of fossils with the Bible, James Hutton (1726–97) of Edinburgh maintained that geological deposits were the results not of catastrophes but of the same natural processes that were occurring in his own day.[15] Hutton's 'uniformitarianism' was elaborated by Sir Charles Lyell (1797–1875),[16] the father of modern geology, whose work implied the passage of a period of time far longer than six thousand years.

While geologists like Lyell began to think in terms of an Earth shaped by natural processes rather than divine intervention, biologists began to question the biblical account of the Creation. Although the theory of evolution is rightly associated with the name of Charles Darwin (1809–82), he was not the first person to postulate the transformation of one species into another. His grandfather, Erasmus Darwin (1731–1802), had written of 'perpetual transformations' that linked past and present species, while in France Jean-Baptiste de Lamarck (1744–1829) had suggested that species changed in response to changes in their environment. Herbert Spencer (1820–1903) was writing and lecturing on evolution before Darwin. For Darwin himself, a mechanism for the transformation of species was suggested during the voyage of the *Beagle* in 1831–6. On the remote Galápagos Islands in the Pacific Darwin observed that each island supported a different variety of finch; although clearly related, each variety had specific features adapted to local conditions. As a consequence

of reading Thomas Malthus's (1766–1834) *Essay on Population* in 1838, he concluded that such adaptations arose from the 'struggle for survival' that gave a selective advantage to certain individuals. In 1859 Darwin published his theory, with full documentation, as *The Origin of Species by Means of Natural Selection*. This had profound implications for human origins and for theologians. He waited until 1871 before stating clearly, in *The Descent of Man*, that evolutionary theory applied to mankind no less than to animals. By this time, however, geologists were convinced that artifacts occurred in deposits dating back to far earlier than 4004 BC and that the idea of human antiquity could be demonstrated from archaeological evidence.

From the 1820s onwards scholars in several parts of Europe arrived independently at the conclusion that man had coexisted with animals that are now extinct. In France Tournal reported human remains associated with the bones of extinct animals in the Grotte de Bize in 1828; in Belgium Schmerling found human bones and flint implements with the remains of mammoth and rhinoceros in a cave at Engis, which he published in 1833–4; in Britain Father J. MacEnery excavated in Kent's Cavern, Torquay, and discovered flint implements and the bones of extinct species, sealed by a stalagmite floor.

These early discoveries failed, however, to convince the Catastrophists; and it was not until 1859 – the year of *The Origin of Species* – that the antiquity of man was irrefutably demonstrated. William Pengelly, who succeeded MacEnery as director of the excavations at Kent's Cavern, began work in a newly discovered cave at nearby Brixham. The excavation, which took place in 1858–9, became a test case in the dispute about human origins. It produced precisely what progressive thinkers had expected: flint implements and the bones of extinct animals, sealed beneath a thick deposit of stalagmite. Meanwhile, Jacques Boucher de Perthes, a customs officer at Abbeville in the Somme valley, had collected a large number of flint implements (now attributed to the Lower Palaeolithic) in local gravel pits that, like the Brixham cave, also yielded the bones of extinct animals. In 1858 the British palaeontologist Hugh Falconer visited Abbeville with Joseph Prestwich, the geologist, and John Evans, the antiquarian; all of them were convinced of the antiquity of the flints. Lyell, too, added his strong support, and from then onwards few scholars seriously doubted the antiquity of man.

This idea was rendered more acceptable by general recognition of the fact that some kind of environmental change had occurred in the fairly recent past in the form of an ice age. By the 1820s it had already been realized that alpine glaciers must formerly have been more extensive, and by 1875 similar evidence had been recognized in many parts of Europe. Careful study of the glacial deposits in the Alps led to the definition of a series of phases of ice advance and retreat, which were named by A. Penck and E. Brückner after various alpine rivers in a classic study, *Die Alpen im Eiszeitalter*, published in 1909.

In 1860 the French magistrate Edouard Lartet (1807–71) investigated ancient remains at Aurignac (Haute Garonne). In 1863, with the English banker Henry Christy, Lartet began an investigation of the caves and rockshelters of the Dordogne, which led to the recognition of what is now known as the Upper Palaeolithic. The sites included Gorge d'Enfer, Laugerie Haute, La Madeleine and Le Moustier. Lartet and Christy published their classic monographs, entitled *Reliquiae Aquitanicae*, between 1865 and 1875. In these studies Lartet divided prehistoric sites into successive periods on the basis of the fauna, using periods marked by the occurrence of cave bear, mammoth, reindeer and bison, and Christy distinguished between an earliest period of flint implements from gravels like those of the Somme, a middle period of implements from caves and a latest phase of surface finds.

Neither system lasted long. In 1869 Lartet's pupil, Gabriel de Mortillet (1828–98), insisted that classification based on fauna would not work. In their place he proposed a system based on distinctive types of artifact that, he realized, were made in different periods. He named the various assemblages of implements after sites at which they occurred, recognizing four successive periods: the Mousterian (after Le Moustier), Solutrian (Solutré), Aurignacian (Aurignac) and Magdalenian (La Madeleine) (see Chapters 12 and 13). Although the classification was revised, the scheme remains a milestone in palaeolithic research.

More spectacular than the finds of flint implements, and for many far more difficult to accept, was the discovery of Palaeolithic art. Among the first to recognize its existence was a Spaniard, the Marquis de Sautuola, who in 1875 found the famous paintings in the cave of Altamira, near Santander. While he maintained from the outset that the paintings were as old as the Palaeolithic deposits on the floor of the cave, it was not until the beginning of the twentieth century that their antiquity was generally accepted.

As soon as evolutionary thinking was applied to man, questions arose about his ancestry and particularly about his relationship to the most closely related living forms, the apes. Discoveries of the bones of early man made before the 1860s were either ignored or misinterpreted. The famous skull fragment discovered in the Neanderthal, near Düsseldorf, in 1856 was interpreted first as a modern pathological specimen, although Thomas Henry Huxley correctly suggested in 1864 that it was an early form of man. From this date onwards, however, human fossils were more readily accepted. The Upper Palaeolithic burials uncovered at Cro-Magnon (1868), Grimaldi (1872) and the Grotte des Enfants (1874–5) were identified immediately as the remains of prehistoric man. These skeletons were, however, virtually identical with the bones of modern man and revealed nothing about the evolution of the species. Among the earliest fossils to be recognized as evidence of a possible evolutionary ancestor were a skull cap and a femur found in 1891 by Eugène Dubois at Trinil in Java. The bones had primitive features and were identified as the first evidence of an extinct species, *Pithecanthropus erectus* (*Pithecanthropus* meaning 'ape-man' and *erectus* indicating, as the thigh bone showed, that it walked erect). Similar remains were found between 1926

and 1941 at Choukoutien, 50 kilometres from Peking, that anatomists now attribute to a single early species of man, *Homo erectus*.

Meanwhile, excavations at Le Moustier (Dordogne) and La Chapelle-aux-Saints (Corrèze) brought to light bones that resembled the find from the Neanderthal. These bones of 'Neanderthal man' are now classified as those of an early variant of *Homo sapiens*. Marcellin Boule, a distinguished French anthropologist who studied the skeleton from La Chapelle, reconstructed a stooping creature with a low forehead, heavy brows and a receding chin – the cartoonist's caricature of 'Stone Age man'. Boule, however, was mistaken, as this skeleton was in fact chronically arthritic, and there is now no doubt that 'Neanderthal man' walked erect; unfortunately, the earlier image has survived.

In 1924 remains of another species of fossil man were discovered at Taung in South Africa, and additional specimens were found in the same region at Sterkfontein and at Swartkrans between about 1930 and 1950. These finds (named *Australopithecus* by the finder of the Taung specimen, Raymond Dart) represented a more primitive creature than *Homo erectus* and carried the story of human ancestry significantly further back into the realm of Darwinian evolution.

The development of Egyptian archaeology

Antiquarians of Classical Antiquity and the Middle Ages were fascinated by ancient Egypt, and its significance in relation to the Old Testament gave it a continuing interest. Scientific study began with Napoleon's invasion in 1798. The expeditionary force spent three years in Egypt and was accompanied by a scientific mission, the purpose of which was to compile a comprehensive survey of the country, which appeared between 1809 and 1828. The most important archaeological discovery was the Rosetta Stone, found in 1799, on which was a bilingual inscription in ancient Egyptian (in both hieroglyphic and demotic scripts) and Greek. In England Thomas Young, who knew the Coptic language, which is derived from ancient Egyptian, made a start on the task of decipherment, but credit for the first full translation, in 1824, goes to the French scholar, Jean-François Champollion.[17]

Egyptology became a popular pursuit, and antiquities were exported to Europe in increasing numbers. Among the early collectors in Egypt was Giovanni Battista Belzoni, who became an expert at heavy-handed collecting. Of one tomb exploration he wrote, without the slightest perceptible regret: 'I sank altogether among the broken mummies, with the crash of bones, rags and wooden cases. . . .' The loss to science through his depredations was immense.

In the 1830s, against a background of growing protest at the pillage of antiquities, Auguste Ferdinand Mariette (d. 1881) established a state antiquities service. He had been dispatched by the Louvre to collect papyri but, shocked at the indiscriminate looting of sites, he prevailed on the authorities both to set up an archaeological service and, in 1857, to appoint him conservator of Egyptian antiquities.

Egyptology reached a new level in the 1880s with the work of Gaston Maspero (1846–1910), who succeeded Mariette as director of the Service des Antiquités, and Sir Flinders Petrie (1853–1942). Petrie in particular initiated the painstaking study of *all* the artifacts from a site, not simply those of artistic merit. He was a prolific excavator and a prompt publisher; and at the Predynastic cemetery of Nakada he worked out the technique of 'sequence dating', a method of using closed tomb-groups to establish a firm relative chronology. Petrie's long series of excavations, which included Naucratis, Tell el-Amarna, sites in the Fayum and Abydos, transformed scholars' understanding of ancient Egypt, and his careful field techniques had a marked impact on archaeology generally.

Mesopotamia and the Near East

The early history of archaeology in Mesopotamia contains two principal strands: the identification and excavation of sites and the study of written records. The first steps towards the decipherment of ancient records were taken at the beginning of the nine-

teenth century, following Karsten Niebuhr's visit to Persepolis in 1765, when he copied several inscriptions. Achaemenian (ancient Persian) inscriptions, such as those at Persepolis, Naqsh-i Rustam and in particular Bisitun, may be trilingual, consisting of parallel texts in Old Persian, Babylonian and Elamite. The key to decipherment was Old Persian. The Zoroastrian sacred text, the *Zend Avesta*, preserves an early form of the Persian language; once Old Persian words could be translated by analogy with the *Zend Avesta*, equivalent words in the Babylonian and Elamite versions could be recognized and translated.

The first partial decipherment of Old Persian was achieved by Georg Friedrich Grotefend, using Niebuhr's transcriptions from Persepolis.[18] Grotefend presented his results at the Göttingen academy in 1802, but they were never published. For this reason, credit for decipherment usually goes to Sir Henry Creswick Rawlinson (1810–95), who transcribed the long, barely accessible inscriptions, high on the cliffs at Bisitun in western Iran, between 1835 and 1845, helped by a Kurdish boy who reached the least accessible parts 'by hanging on with his toes and fingers to the slightest inequalities on the bare face of the precipices' to make the vital copies. Rawlinson translated the Old Persian text and proceeded to the difficult task of translating the syllabic Babylonian version. His claims to have translated the cuneiform inscriptions were vindicated in 1857, when independent translations of the same text, based on Rawlinson's method, were submitted to the Royal Asiatic Society by three scholars, Fox Talbot, Hincks and Oppert; the translations were very similar.

The beginnings of practical archaeology in western Asia also date from the early years of the nineteenth century.[19] Claudius James Rich (1787–1820) became British Resident in Baghdad in 1808 and visited numerous ancient sites in Iraq. He surveyed Babylon in 1811, for example, and the results of his further reconnaissance, published in 1818, 'virtually exhausted the possibilities of inference without excavation'.[20] Rich's collection of antiquities passed to the British Museum in 1825.

Serious excavations began a generation later. Paul-Emile Botta began work at Nineveh in 1842 but the following year transferred his efforts to Khorsabad, where sculptures had come to light by chance. Almost immediately, Botta discovered the palace of Sargon II (721–705 BC) and its reliefs. Informed of the find, the French Government sent the draughtsman M. E. Flandrin to join the expedition. In 1846 many of the reliefs were removed to the Louvre, and Botta's *Monument du Ninève* appeared in 1849–50.

1.4: *The third (innermost) gold coffin of Tutankhamun, garlanded with flowers. The most spectacular archaeological discovery in Egypt was the tomb of the pharaoh, who died in about 1343 BC, excavated by Howard Carter in 1922.*

Meanwhile, an English expedition directed by Sir Austen Henry Layard (1817–94) began work at Nimrud. The excavations lasted from 1845 until 1847, when the most important finds were dispatched to the British Museum, which had sponsored the work. French and British expeditions continued to dig in Iraq until 1855, when the outbreak of the Crimean War put an end to their activities. This first phase of Mesopotamian archaeology (1808–55) was characterized by an almost indiscriminate scramble for antiquities, in particular sculptures and cuneiform tablets. It was a tragedy (but perhaps an instance of poetic justice) when in 1855 the entire French consignment sank in the Shatt al-Arab *en route* to the Louvre.

Mesopotamian archaeology resumed in the 1870s. British efforts were stimulated by the discovery, by George Smith of the British Museum, of the fact that a broken tablet from Nineveh contained part of an epic poem describing a deluge comparable with the biblical flood. An expedition to search for the missing portion of the tablet was successful – after only five days in the field. Smith died at Aleppo in 1877, and his place as director of the British Museum's expeditions was taken by Hormuzd Rassam, who had worked with Layard and had found the palace of Assur-ban-apli at Nimrud in 1852. Rassam now excavated widely in Syria, eastern Turkey and Mesopotamia, exploring, among other sites, Tell Balawat in 1878 and Tell Habbah (ancient Sippar) in 1880.

The French, meanwhile, were digging at Telloh in southern Iraq, under the consul at Basra, Ernest de Sarzec. Work began in 1877 and revealed for the first time a Sumerian city: Lagash. Among the finds was a spectacular series of sculptures in the round, including the portrait statue of the governor Gudea, now in the Louvre. In the last quarter of the nineteenth century German and (from 1884) American missions were also at work.

The early years of the twentieth century witnessed a series of systematic expeditions that initiated long programmes of excavation on a new scale. German work at Babylon began under Robert Koldewey (1855–1929) and at Assur under Walter Andrae (1875–1956); and the massive French campaigns at Susa started at the turn of the century under Jacques de Morgan (1857–1924). These produced material for the methodical application of the techniques of archaeological and philological analysis. Of the many succeeding excavations, only a few may be singled out here: the work of Sir Leonard Woolley (1880–1960) at al-'Ubaid and Ur indicated the wealth of the earliest Mesopotamian civilizations, while the sustained German campaigns at Uruk (modern Warka, biblical Erech) threw new light on the beginnings of urban life, and the French excavations at Mari revealed the detailed plan of an important royal palace (see Chapter 17). By the beginning of

1.5: *The monumental stairway of the Apadana at Persepolis, discovered and restored by Herzfeld Ernst, who led the German excavation of this centre of the Persian Achaemenian empire in the 1930s.*

1.6: *The site of Ur in southern Iraq was identified in 1854. The University of Pennsylvania and the British Museum worked on the site in 1918–19 and in 1922–34, sponsored a joint expedition directed by Sir Leonard Woolley. The most striking discovery was the royal cemetery, found in 1922. Sixteen royal tombs were found to contain a wealth of offerings, accompanied by the slaves of the deceased. This gold dagger is an example of the quality of Sumerian metalwork.*

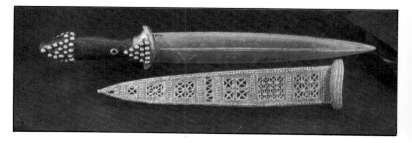

the Second World War rows of substantial excavation reports were available to sustain studies of early Mesopotamian society.

Archaeology in Palestine developed along the same lines as Mesopotamian research. After a period of exploration and survey, in the course of which the rock-cut Nabataean city of Petra was discovered (1809), excavation began in the 1860s. The Palestine Exploration Find, which (like its Egyptian counterpart) was greatly concerned with biblical archaeology, was founded in London in 1865 and began excavations in Jerusalem in 1867. Other early excavations were those of Petrie at Tell el-Hesi (1891–2) and R. A. S. Macalister at Tell Jezer (ancient Gezer). The Deutsche Orient Gesellschaft excavated at Megiddo in 1901–5, a site later investigated on a larger scale by the Oriental Institute of Chicago. Duncan Mackenzie, Evans's assistant at Knossos, worked at Ain Shems (ancient Beth-Shemesh) in 1911–12, by which time the broad lines of Palestinian later prehistory were becoming clear.

Aegean archaeology

Heinrich Schliemann (1822–87) has been justly hailed as the founder of prehistoric Aegean archaeology. After making a fortune in business, he retired to pursue his passion for archaeology, which had been fired by reading Homer. Regarding Homer's description of Troy as the literal truth, Schliemann identified the ancient city with the mound at Hissarlik, where he excavated from 1871. He also worked at Mycenae (1874–6), at Orchomenos (1880) and at Tiryns (1884–5). Throughout his archaeological career he remained convinced of the accuracy of the Homeric epics: hence his entirely fanciful identification of the graves of Agamemnon and Clytemnestra at Mycenae. Nevertheless, Schliemann's pioneer excavations paved the way for a long series of investigations of pre-Classical sites. The British School at Athens dug at Phylakopi (1894–5); Sir John Myres worked on Cyprus; the Greek archaeologist Tsountas excavated at Vapheio, Mycenae and Athens. Most spectacular of all, however, were Sir Arthur Evans's excavations at Knossos. Rapid clearance begun in 1899 revealed a hitherto unsuspected pre-Mycenaean civilization, which Evans named 'Minoan'. Knossos was demonstrated to be a palace with richly frescoed walls,[21] while the basis of a chronology from this and other sites was established through the discovery of imported objects from Egypt (now datable, thanks to the work of Petrie) in association with local material.

The archaeology of Classical Greece and Rome, following the tradition of scholarship established earlier, continued on an increasing scale. Activities included systematic study not only of standing monuments but also of new features revealed by excavation, such as the cemetery at the Dipylon Gate in Athens. Larger-scale investigations were conducted at Hellenistic sites such as Pergamon in Asia Minor. In Italy the background to the emergence of Rome was revealed by the excavation of Etruscan tombs and the town of Tarquinia. Detailed typological studies of metal objects were undertaken, while sophisticated methods of stylistic analysis were developed in the study of Greek vases.

Archaeology in the Americas

In the Americas, as in the Old World, field archaeology became firmly established in the nineteenth century through the classification and description of ancient material. One of the earliest active archaeologists in America was Thomas Jefferson (1743–1826), later third President of the United States, who excavated burial mounds in 1784 in order to establish their age. The prehistoric ceremonial earthworks of Ohio, Mississippi and elsewhere attracted considerable attention. Many were carefully recorded, notably by Ephraim G. Squier and E. H. Davis.[22] A second line of inquiry concerned the antiquity of man in the Americas. An important figure in this context was Frederick Ward Putnam, curator of the Peabody Museum at Harvard (1875–1909) and professor at the university from 1887. Under Putnam the Peabody Museum rose to prominence and became a leading centre for research, particularly into the earliest traces of man in America.

Meanwhile, the remains of pre-Columbian civilizations in Central and South America were visited, recorded and published. In Central America the pioneer explorers were J. L. Stephens and the draughtsman Frederick Catherwood, who discovered the lost Mayan centres of Uxmal, Copan, Palenque and Chichén Itzá between 1839 and 1842. Catherwood's meticulous drawings are justly famous as some of the finest pre-photographic records of archaeological monuments. The archaeological exploration of South America began in Peru in the 1850s with the researches of Max Uhle (1856–1944).

The early twentieth century was marked by continuing exploration, increasingly by stratigraphic excavation and by the first attempts at synthesis. Investigation of prehistory proceeded alongside ethnographic studies of recent Indian groups, which constituted a starting point for the study of earlier cultures. The Pueblos of the Southwest provided a focus for research into early farming groups in that region, as the shell-mounds of California concentrated attention on coastal hunters and collectors, and many of the ceremonial and burial mounds of the Southeast, which had interested earlier explorers, were excavated. The programme of relief work during the Depression of the 1930s brought new opportunities for archaeologists to employ labour on a larger scale. Detailed typological work increasingly involved quantification and the use of sequence dating (seriation), while comparative work led to syntheses of regional development. Alfred Kidder summarized progress in the Southwest,[23] as did Herbert Spinden for Mesoamerica.[24]

The Far East and Africa

The exploration of overseas regions naturally inspired accounts of local monuments and promoted the study of archaeology. Some of the most systematic work was carried out in India, where the Archaeological Survey of India was created in 1863. The Survey produced a detailed record of the monuments of the subcontinent and was responsible for the recognition of one of the half-dozen oldest independent civilizations, that of the Indus valley. The largest urban sites, Harappa and Mohenjo-Daro, were excavated in 1921 and 1922 respectively. The latter was further investigated by Sir Mortimer Wheeler (1890–1976).

The long prehistoric sequence that lay behind the emergence of Chinese civilization was revealed by Swedish work in China, notably that of J. G. Andersson (1874–1960), who discovered the Neolithic village of Yang-shao. The importance of this culture has been emphasized by the more recent Chinese excavations at Pan-p'o-tsun of 1953–5. A site of prime importance to Palaeolithic studies, the cave of Choukoutien with its remains of *Homo erectus*, was excavated by Davidson Black and Wen Chung Pei between 1927 and 1937.

The intervening region of central Asia was explored around the turn of the century by Sir Aurel Stein, who revealed its archaeological wealth and whose work complemented the growing body of information that was being gathered by Russian archaeologists.

In Australia and Oceania the study of archaeology emerged as an outgrowth of anthropological work. In Australia it not only provided time-depth for the study of rock art but also demonstrated the long prehistory of the Aboriginal tribes that reached back into the Pleistocene. In Polynesia, by contrast, archaeology disclosed the relatively recent date at which these islands were settled.

In Africa a variety of cultures, from that of the Bushman to the complex societies of West Africa, presented a fertile field for research. The study of Palaeolithic material in conjunction with finds of early man ensured international interest. Bushman rock paintings were another focus of attention, while the art of the later societies of Benin (Nigeria) attracted collectors before becoming the object of serious archaeological research. The ruins of Zimbabwe were investigated by several expeditions, and archaeological work clearly demonstrated their local Bantu context, dispelling earlier misconceptions about their exotic origins.

European archaeology in the early twentieth century

The typological study of stray finds that had dominated archaeological work in the nineteenth century gradually gave way to a more detailed study of individual sites as excavation was transformed from treasure-hunting into a systematic process of recovery of material from known contexts. The techniques of modern excavation were pioneered in England at the end of the nineteenth century by General Pitt Rivers, who inherited an estate in Dorset and retired to pursue his interest in archaeology. Not only did he devote himself to the collection of ancient artifacts, but he began the series of meticulous excavations for which he is most famous, during the course of which he devised and elaborated the art of precise recording. He wrote: 'Excavators as a rule record only those things which appear to them important at the time, but fresh problems are constantly arising. Every detail should, therefore, be recorded. . . .' Pitt Rivers observed this principle rigorously. He was one of the first excavators to record stratigraphy in detail, and his reports contain information about potsherds, animal bones and even clay tobacco pipes.

While his high standards were not to be widely emulated until well into the present century, the new emphasis on excavation produced more information not only about the stratigraphic succession of object types but also about house types and settlement plans. Excavations on *tells* in the Balkans (such as Vinča in Yugoslavia and Sesklo in Thessaly) provided a wealth of information that fleshed out the bare sequence of metal and pottery types.

As the picture of prehistoric development became clearer, disputes arose over the origins of early European cultures. Nationalistic authors with a detailed knowledge of north European prehistory, such as Gustav Kossinna (1858–1931), insisted on a local origin for the succession of early peoples; some, like Carl Schuchhart (1859–1943), who had a wider knowledge of eastern Europe and Near Eastern material, saw striking similarities over long distances and supported a Near Eastern origin for new forms of material culture. The scene was set for a protracted conflict between those who supported a local evolution of European societies and those who saw a process of diffusion from the centres of higher civilization.

Detailed local work in many areas of Europe provided the basis for syntheses of European prehistory. Schuchhart published his *Alteuropa* in 1919, in which he methodically described material from different areas in terms of *cultures* – distinctive and recurrent groups of artifacts that, by analogy with the ethnic groups of the Migration Period, were taken to represent separate peoples, whose wanderings could be reconstructed from the distribution of their material remains. His ideas were introduced to English-speaking scholars by V. Gordon Childe (1892–1957).

Born in Australia, Childe came to Oxford to study philology and Aegean archaeology, especially the work of Evans, and he undertook extensive study tours in eastern Europe. He summarized the state of research in two classic books, *The Dawn of European Civilization* (1925) and *The Danube in Prehistory* (1929), the first of which was regularly revised and reissued until his death. He wrote a comparable review of developments in western Asia, *The Most Ancient East* (1928), which was similarly revised. Accepting a moderate diffusionist outlook, Childe saw the prehistory of Europe as a process of continuing irradiation from the Near East. His concepts remained central to archaeological thinking until the 1960s.

The early years of the twentieth century therefore witnessed, both in Europe and elsewhere, a considerable increase in the amount of archaeological information available to scholars, which was assembled within a framework established largely in the preceding century. The systematic organization of the archaeological record – the progress made in the classification of material culture and the reconstruction of chronological sequences – provided a firm foundation for future developments in interpretation and technique.

2. The revolution in archaeology

The recent revolution in archaeology has stemmed from the rediscovery of its potential contribution to the wider study of human society. Renewed contacts with ethnology and anthropology have enlarged the scope of interpretation beyond studies of ancient objects and monuments to processes of economic and social change. In some respects this has restored the unity of these subjects, which existed in the nineteenth century under the umbrella of evolutionary theory.

Such studies, however, like those of L. H. Morgan,[1] the New York lawyer, were largely concerned with the reconstruction of past states of society by reference to existing tribal groups. While this approach produced useful definitions of the contrasts between hunter–gatherers, simple agriculturalists and urban societies, its assumptions about the 'primitive' character of non-Western societies and its failure to provide convincing accounts of working social systems brought such evolutionary views into disrepute. As more fieldwork was undertaken among tribal groups, they began to be studied in their own terms rather than as representatives of early stages of society. The flow of information from this work kept anthropologists busy, while archaeologists concerned themselves with the classification and chronological ordering of the hundreds of finds that industrial development was turning up. The main achievement of this period was to describe rather than to analyse, and the archaeological record was interpreted, in a simple 'historical' way, in terms of migrations, political and military events and influences disseminated by merchants or missionaries. Invasion or the diffusion of elements from higher cultures were seen as the main causes of change in material culture.

By the 1920s many areas, such as Europe, the Near East and North and Central America, were sufficiently well investigated for major synthetic studies of their cultural history to be written. Other areas of archaeology were also being opened up by expeditions that revealed new information, for instance on the early development of Indian and Chinese civilization. Some of the expeditions undertaken in the 1930s were on a scale never since matched: the Second World War brought conflict to many of these areas, as well as the destruction of museums and documents in Europe; paradoxically, it also produced technical innovations that were to have important implications for archaeology.

Seeds of change, 1945–65

In the early post-war years interest in wider questions began to revive among a few archaeologists and anthropologists. Notable among the former was Gordon Childe, an expatriate Australian, who held the first chair of prehistoric archaeology at the University of Edinburgh. Childe took up once again Morgan's evolutionary scheme and looked at the archaeological evidence that had accumulated since.[2] He saw prehistory as divided by two great turning points: the Neolithic Revolution, which saw the beginning of farming, and the Urban Revolution, which brought towns and economic specialization. Having identified these two key developments in the archaeological record, he sent post-war workers into the field to confirm or disprove his ideas.

The theme of evolution was revived in American anthropology in very different ways, by Julian Steward[3] of the University of Illinois and Leslie White[4] of the University of Michigan. Although both maintained that the importance of development through time was a significant question for anthropology, Steward's concept of multilinear evolution stressed the parallel development of human societies under similar conditions, while White's idea of unilinear evolution emphasized the general improvement of control over sources of energy as a determinant of social forms. Both of them used archaeological and historical evidence in studying the development of early states and, by their teaching, they influenced a rising generation of archaeologists.

A third central element was the work of Karl Polanyi[5] in economic anthropology. Starting from the importance of gift exchange in tribal society, Polanyi recognized that before the development of a market economy in Classical Antiquity, an important mode of economic organization had existed in which goods were collected and redistributed by a central authority. While the idea of redistribution was first elaborated in relation to the Bronze Age civilizations of Mesopotamia, it proved to be of general significance in interpreting the anthropology of chiefdoms and was used, for instance, by Marshall Sahlins in his study of Polynesia and elaborated in his later work, *Stone Age Economics*.[6] Relating this to Morgan's ideas of a scale of social complexity, Elman Service[7] produced a fourfold division of pre-industrial society: bands (small, mobile hunting and collecting groups), tribes (small-scale sedentary communities), chiefdoms (centrally organized, usually agricultural communities) and states. It did not evade the major criticism directed at Morgan's work – that it was more a classification of the end products of social evolution than an account of it – but this scheme has appealed to archaeologists as a useful framework within which to consider their evidence.

In America the dissatisfaction with archaeology as simply the study of ancient artifacts was well expressed by W. W. Taylor,[8] and both here and in Europe new approaches were pioneered. Gordon Willey,[9] working in the Virú valley in Peru, began to study whole settlement networks rather than single sites. A team of archaeologists and environmentalists led by Robert Braidwood[10] of Chicago, who had set out to search for evidence of early agriculture in Iraqi Kurdistan, looked at the natural setting of sites and evidence of subsistence in the form of bones and seeds. Comparable co-operative work was undertaken by J. G. D. Clark[11] at Star Carr in north-east England, using pollen analysis of peat deposits and careful three-dimensional recording of cultural debris to reconstruct a Mesolithic camp site and its lakeside environment.

Increasingly, archaeology came to be affected by technological developments, many of which were the result of the war. These ranged from the use of aerial photography and of heavy machinery in excavation, through devices for detecting metal and buried features, to the application of advanced physics and chemistry and the quantitative thinking that developed along with computer electronics. Archaeologists were able to examine new aspects of their material: completely uncovered sites, prehistoric landscapes revealed from the air, detailed analyses of ancient objects provided by chemical microanalysis and – most important – direct physical measures of age. It was the techniques described in Chapter 62, and in particular the development of radiocarbon dating, that had the most fundamental repercussions in archaeology. These were threefold. First, an external standard of dating removed the necessity for treating chronology as a primary goal of archaeological investigation: it freed archaeologists to tackle more fundamental questions. Second, it placed in doubt some of the cherished chronological equations that assumed all innovations to have been made in areas like the Near East and to have diffused into other regions. Third, it enormously expanded the archaeological time-scale, pushing developments such as the beginning of farming back by thousands of years. In so doing it demonstrated the slowness of many of the fundamental processes of change in prehistory, and how different they were from the rapid events of the historical time-scale. All these prepared the way for major rethinking about the nature of archaeology.

A decade of revolution, 1965–'75

Among the social and biological sciences as a whole the 1960s were a time of exciting new ideas. A change in attitude was indicated by the widespread adoption of quantitative techniques and the attempt to measure things that had previously been appreciated only intuitively. It led to an appreciation of basic factors such as population density and rates of growth, and of the complex and interconnected relationships that characterize ecological systems. This approach stressed the need to analyse systems as a whole; it also produced a new interest in ways of representing such patterned relationships and hence a concern with models – simplifying analogies that represent the main characteristics of a system.

In archaeology these new trends became apparent in the later 1960s, associated in America with the work of Lewis Binford[12] and in England with that of David Clarke.[13] They were reinforced by developments within archaeology itself, including a proliferation of archaeologists employed in universities and elsewhere. Especially in the United States, these changes took the form of a propagandist 'New Archaeology'. A fundamental idea was the notion of human culture as essentially adaptive, rather than simply the outcome of arbitrary choice and tradition. By examining assemblages of flint implements such as tool-kits, for instance, and looking for patterns representing activities at different places during a seasonal cycle, Binford sought to reinterpret this kind of evidence in the light of what was known about existing hunting and collecting

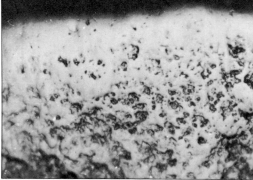

2.1: *Industrial expansion has introduced a new scale of excavation, necessitated and made possible by the existence of large earth-moving machinery. This photograph shows part of an extensive early Neolithic settlement area near Cologne being excavated in advance of brown-coal working.*

2.2: *The use of microscopic examination has revealed new sources of information from archaeological materials. These two microphotographs, at ×100 and ×200 magnification, show successive stages of polish on the edge of a flint artifact used for working wood.*

groups. Similarly, different types of pottery could not be taken automatically to represent different peoples, he suggested, but should be looked at in terms of their different functions, the way they were made and traded and the different contexts in which they were found. Cemeteries were particularly valuable in investigating the social structures behind the settlement evidence, as study of the age and sex of the skeletons could demonstrate 'social' personalities' and thus show the way in which artifacts were associated with social categories.

Binford urged that all archaeological evidence should be subjected to more rigorous examination by formulating specific hypotheses, drawing implications and testing these against specially collected data. This might involve recording certain aspects of excavated material in more detail than had hitherto been customary: for example, plotting the distribution of all pieces of flint on a settlement to identify activity areas, or looking at the different kinds of pottery within particular rooms to identify social groupings. Such analyses – especially where they involved quantitative treatment – necessitated a proper regard for the principles of sampling and the systematic collection of data for study within both the region and the site (see Chapter 3).

David Clarke's work began with a quantitative study of decorated Neolithic pottery, in which he applied techniques of computer-aided classification developed in biology under the general name of numerical taxonomy. He elaborated this approach to provide a theoretical basis for archaeological interpretation, taking as a starting point the idea of an archaeologically evidenced culture as a system with a particular line of development (trajectory), which was involved in various kinds of interaction with its neighbours and its natural environment. The use of systems theory (see Chapter 4), which had been developed in biology to describe complex phenomena with self-regulating behaviour, offered a way of describing ancient societies without making the specific assumptions associated with historical analogy. Patterns of material culture could thus be described and reconstructed before they were explained in terms of environmental relations, social classes or linguistic and ethnic differences. Useful ideas on spatial organization came from work being undertaken during this period as part of the 'New Geography'.[14] This also used the basic idea of the system to analyse settlement in terms of a hierarchy of sites with movements on different scales around different classes of settlement – cities, towns, villages and hamlets. Sites could thus be seen as the centres of territories: villages with their supporting areas, towns with their market areas, and so on. Archaeologically, this meant that useful information about important resources and economic organization lay coded in the locational pattern of former settlements, which reflected the ecological strategies of their inhabitants (see Chapter 5).

A major feature of this period was a renewed interest in environmental work and the use of ecological models in explaining cultural development. One of the first areas of archaeology to assert its new understanding of the subject matter, based on the integration of archaeological and ethnographic information, was the study of hunters and gatherers. A conference in 1968[15] drew together studies of population density and group size by physical anthropologists, of band organization and activities by social anthropologists and of Pleistocene problems by archaeologists. The picture that emerged was one of a stable and long-lived adaptation characterized by low population densities (often controlled by infanticide) and a relatively abundant supply of easily obtained food. By contrast to the popular picture of the generally harsh existence of hunting and gathering populations, which left little spare time for cultural pursuits, one participant spoke of 'the original affluent society'. This realization helped to bring about the replacement of an 'economic' view of the human past (one of steadily improving conditions and technological progress) by an 'ecological' one, in which innovations can be seen as having often been forced upon unwilling populations as the result of a balance being upset.

This change in thinking was also apparent for later periods, for example in Mesoamerica. Using Service's categories of bands, tribes, chiefdoms and states, William Sanders and Barbara Price[16] sought to relate these successive levels of social integration to increasing densities of population. They suggested that pressure of population led to more intensive land use, with increasing competition for good land – a theme that had also entered the literature of development economics.

The advantages of using a systems-theory framework for considering the network of ecological relations has been well exemplified in the work of Kent Flannery, especially in connection with the origins of agriculture.[17] In particular, the idea of large-scale change as the result of the amplification of small initial deviations proved useful in describing the minor alterations in selective pressure that created more productive varieties of early crop plants, which had increasingly important repercussions throughout the system.

A growing concern with the economic basis of early communities led to practical as well as theoretical innovations. Stuart Streuver in North America and Eric Higgs in Europe began to develop new methods of retrieving floral and faunal evidence through the sieving and flotation of excavated material. Direct evidence of on-site activities was supplemented by the technique of site-catchment analysis[18] that Higgs developed with the geographer Claudio Vita-Finzi, which consisted of a detailed examination of the resources accessible from the site. Such analysis demonstrated the often complementary character of contemporary sites in different ecological zones, which might be exploited either seasonally, by movement between the two, or permanently, through occupation and exchange of products. One result of looking more closely at prehistoric subsistence was that doubt was thrown on some of the traditional categories of thought, provoking a re-examination of the meaning of words such as 'domestication'.

The analysis of trade was complementary to the study of local production and became increasingly important for later periods with more complex societies. Notable work along these lines was carried out by Colin Renfrew,[19] who not only used evidence from trace-element analysis to identify ancient sources of the obsidian used for tools but also attempted to quantify the amounts of this material found as implements or debris on sites at varying distances from these sources. (As with the study of subsistence remains, excavation techniques are a crucial factor where quantitative treatment is used, demanding proper sampling and high-quality retrieval techniques such as sieving.) The study of trade connections, especially in the light of Polanyi's views on early forms of exchange and redistribution, opened up new opportunities for interpretation in which anthropological ideas played a major part. Significant among these was the concept of the 'interaction sphere', developed in eastern North America by Joseph Caldwell and Stuart Streuver,[20] to describe a phase of particularly intensive trade associated with the emergence of ceremonial centres and local elites who controlled imported items. Such reconstructions, involving social models of networks for the circulation of different items, have offered an alternative to the rather sterile interpretations of widespread features in terms of ethnic groups such as the 'Beaker folk' of European prehistory: indeed, explanations stressing indigenous, local factors have largely replaced diffusionist explanations in a range of contexts.

The emergence of complex societies, marked by urban centres, extensive trading, social elites and the apparatus of the state, provided a significant area of research to which archaeology began to make an important contribution. Outstanding among such studies has been the work of Robert Adams[21] on the reconstruction of ancient settlement patterns in the nuclear areas of Mesopotamian civilization. A combination of sustained fieldwork and penetrating analysis of archaeological material in the light of early written sources has transformed our understanding of early urbanization and its social consequences. This work demonstrated the power of the comparative method, which contrasts similar processes in different parts of the world. Integrated, multi-stage projects using the new techniques, such as Flannery's investigations in Oaxaca or the intensive survey of *pueblo* remains in Arizona and New Mexico, began to bear fruit. The systematic investigation of living hunter–gatherers, pastoralists and simple agriculturalists from an archaeological point of view began, under the name of ethno-archaeology, to observe directly the processes of site formation and the significance of cultural debris. Experimental archaeology (the reconstruction of ancient sites, for example, and the employment of ancient methods of agriculture and manufacturing) also provided fresh insights. At the same time archaeological activity in both urban and rural areas reached new levels in the face of redevelopment and the threat of destruction by industrial expansion, often commanding larger budgets than had been available before.

What was the net effect of these new approaches? One result of the application of new techniques was that many branches of archaeology were drawn together in a common quest, linked for the first time by a set of shared concepts and interests that facilitated comparison between developments in different areas. Another was that archaeologists became aware of basic factors of subsistence and population previously ignored. Sites came to be seen in the context of their hinterlands and trading areas and as parts of whole systems. Attitudes towards the raw material of archaeology changed: on the one hand, highly structured information obtained from a completely excavated settlement or cemetery was recognized as being infinitely more valuable than randomly rescued fragments; on the other, there was a more mature appreciation of the biases inherent in archaeological samples. Most important, however, was a new enthusiasm and optimism about what archaeology could do.

The present scene

The revolutionary decade around 1970 was an exciting time to be working in archaeology. Many of the insights gained in that period represent major advances in understanding. However, in the last few years certain aspects of the work of this period have been viewed more critically, and some new lines of interest are emerging. Although it was important to come to terms with ecological realities, there is now a greater urge to deal with social factors directly, without simplistic reduction to ecological terms. There is also a reaction against many of the systems models that assumed human societies to be static and saw all change as the result of environmental alterations. One symptom of this is the renewed interest in Marxist ideas, stressing contradiction and conflict. Such views are, however, in marked contrast to the technological emphasis that characterized the work of Gordon Childe and instead owe much to French anthropologists such as Maurice Godelier.[22] The theme of competition also recurs in the ideas of sociobiology, which have begun to interest students of the Palaeolithic; they deal with strategies of self-interest in the animal world that have a wider application to social analysis. The idea of population growth as an independent agent of change has also been critically appraised, and has been replaced by more sophisticated demographic arguments.

Anthropologists, too, have raised doubts about the validity of concepts such as 'band' and 'tribe' in aboriginal contexts, as these may be closely related to the effects of contact with more organized groups. Paradoxically, many of these problems devolve once more on the archaeologist, who alone has the opportunity to study original conditions; recognition of this should promote a much closer cooperation between archaeologists, anthropologists and historians, who are engaged on complementary aspects of the same quest. It seems likely that many of the advances of the next few years will be made in understanding protohistoric periods, in which the skills of all three disciplines can be brought together.

As always, however, the cumulative growth of archaeological information – through both planned research and accidental discovery – will have its own dynamic and will continually alter our picture of the past, rapidly making old controversies irrelevant in the light of wider knowledge. One thing is certain: there are still surprises in store.

3. Investigation in the field

The last two decades have seen dramatic changes in the scale and character of field archaeology. The spur for these changes has come from two different sources: the increased pace of industrial, urban and agricultural development on the one hand, and the changes that have taken place in archaeology as a whole, particularly in its aims and theory, on the other. Although these latter developments should logically take precedence, it is probably true to say that the pace of change has been forced by the external threat, and it is principally this that has attracted public attention to archaeology: the subject's current public image is that of the archaeologist digging desperately in the shadow of an advancing bulldozer.

The destruction of archaeological evidence by the processes of economic development is a world-wide problem, prevalent in both developed and developing countries. It has had a beneficial effect in that it has enormously increased the pace of discovery of archaeological evidence and in many places has completely revolutionized earlier ideas of the wealth of archaeological material potentially available, but these insights have generally been gained in the course of the total destruction of that evidence. Nevertheless, as a result of the changed climate of public opinion governments in many countries have felt obliged to bow to archaeological pressure and to provide funds and frame legislation to alleviate at least some of the difficulties. Such campaigns have probably been most successful in the United States, where huge sums of money are now being invested in archaeological projects as a result of recent legislation. Unfortunately, most other countries, and those of the developing world in particular, have no hope of matching this investment, although international agencies such as UNESCO have been able to play a part, and teams from various countries have also been invited to participate.

The effect of these pressures on archaeology cannot be overestimated, especially as the new influx of money has coincided with a decline in traditional sources of funding, but their main impact has been on field archaeology, because the threat has been to archaeological evidence in the ground. It has become both possible and necessary to carry out fieldwork on a larger scale than ever before, and this has meant major changes in the way field archaeology is organized. Summer expeditions led and staffed by members of universities have been replaced, in those countries that can afford it, by permanent field archaeology organizations. The change led initially to a divergence in outlook between academic archaeologists and those at work in the field. (On the whole it has been the universities that have been involved in the theoretical advances of the last two decades, while publicly financed field archaeology has been concerned with the 'saving' of threatened sites, usually by excavation.) Each side accused the other of betraying the best interests of archaeology: the universities by failing to respond to the enormously increased rate of destruction of archaeological evidence, public archaeology by its failure to produce results of any academic value. In the last few years, however, attitudes have begun to change and it has been more widely accepted that 'the crisis in . . . archaeology is not simply the need to save the endangered site but to meld method with theory in order to deal with the problems that archaeologists have said are their concern.'[1]

In practice, probably the two main areas of common interest are regional approaches to archaeology and the development of what has been called middle range theory, which is concerned with the relationship between our contemporary observations of the archaeological record and what went on in the past.

A hypothetical research design was proposed for investigating 'the structure and functioning of extinct cultural systems and how they relate to one another as regards processes of change and evolution'.[2] An essential aspect of this design was the fact that it was multi-stage. It was argued that the most satisfactory framework for field research was one that began by examining, in a preliminary way, the archaeology of the region as a whole and then focused on increasingly limited sections of it with increasing intensity. Often an attempt to initiate work on a project at all levels simultaneously and with uniform intensity leads to confusion – it certainly means that it is impossible for work carried out in the region as a whole to guide more intensive studies.

The indispensable initial phase of such a design is the acquisition of reliable and representative information about the location of the various sites of past human activity within the region, including their relationships with environmental variables and with one another. The next stage is the more intensive investigation of a number of the sites discovered in the first phase, by means of detailed surface examination and, possibly, trial excavation. Finally, on the basis of all the previous stages of work, perhaps only one of a whole group of sites will be selected for extensive excavation.

Such multi-stage approaches, in which each phase is guided by the preceding one, have been widely adopted in the years since they were first proposed, particularly in the United States, where they have made a considerable impact on conservation archaeology.[3]

Clearly, different methods are required at each stage and, equally obviously, as the intensity of study increases, so does the cost. Although in general more money is available for archaeology than ever before, resources have not kept pace with the increasingly stringent demands that are being made on archaeological data as a result of the theoretical and methodological advances of the last two or three decades – demands that range from the requirements of regional spatial analysis at one end of the scale to the recovery of minute plant remains for subsistence studies at the other (see Chapter 5).

Preliminary investigations: aerial and ground survey

For the first stage of work on the regional scale – the acquisition of reliable information about site location – only two approaches are practicable, remote sensing (especially aerial photography) and ground survey. Aerial photography has been especially important in Great Britain and north-west Europe, where one of its main achievements has been the demonstration of the large-scale laying out of field systems in the prehistoric landscape; knowledge of the later Bronze Age, Iron Age and Roman periods in particular has been transformed. At a very different scale satellite imagery has begun to be of considerable importance, especially for large-scale archaeological projects in more remote parts of the world; an example is the archaeological work now in progress in connection with the opening up of northern Alaska for oil exploration. Here satellite imagery is playing a variety of roles: it is being used to establish ecological subdivisions of the area prior to ground survey, to assist with logistical planning and mapping and to define areas of poor ground-survey visibility.

With aerial methods of survey it is obviously possible to cover large areas of ground very quickly. On the other hand, their results are considerably affected by the nature of the local surface geology and other ground conditions, while only certain types of archaeological feature are readily identifiable with the aid of such methods.

3.1: *The Roman temple on Hayling Island, Hampshire, England, revealed as a crop mark during the drought of 1976. The mark has been produced by the parching of the cereal crop immediately above the surviving stone foundations of the temple walls. Excavation has subsequently shown that the Roman temple overlay an Iron Age one not apparent from the photograph.*

For these reasons ground survey continues to play an essential part. As a technique it is straightforward; it simply involves covering a selected area on foot, looking for archaeological finds and features, and noting and mapping them when they occur. Adequate ground survey, however, is extremely time-consuming, and except in rare circumstances it is generally impossible to achieve total coverage of an area of interest, so that some form of sampling has to be used. In the past such selection tended to be carried out haphazardly, but in the last few years fairly extensive use has been made of probability sampling, especially in the United States. Such techniques have allowed the use of procedures of statistical inference for estimating the number of sites in an area and their association with ecological variables, but they have also served the important purpose of ensuring that the archaeologist's preconceived ideas about the nature of the population he is dealing with do not bias his results. Experiments on totally surveyed areas, using varying combinations of sampling unit sizes, shapes, layouts and numbers, have shown that the methods do produce acceptable results and have begun to establish guidelines for the best techniques.[4] The main limitation of these methods is the difficulties they present for the investigation of spatial patterning at the regional level; the sampling units are usually small landblocks scattered over fairly large areas, so that in general large, continuously surveyed areas are lacking. This is where aerial reconnaissance is particularly important, but in its absence it is possible to use sample ground-survey data to obtain a number of indices of spatial patterning, such as the extent to which settlement was clustered or dispersed.[5]

Surface survey

The next stage in the implementation of the regional research design is the detailed surface investigation of a number of the sites discovered during the first phase of the work; the preliminary investigations will have produced information about the overall chronological span of the sites discovered and an indication of their size, but little else. The current emphasis on the need to understand regional settlement patterns in order to be able to infer from them the nature of local social and economic organization means that it is necessary to know more than this, particularly about site function. Furthermore, if the aim of the work is to study changing patterns of settlement through time and to derive associated changes in the density and distribution of the known population – two of the most important parameters defining any regional system – then it becomes essential to establish not only the overall spatial and chronological span of the sites discovered, but also the exact spatial extent and density of occupation of particular phases. Full information can only be obtained by excavation, but this is generally precluded by the large amount of time and money that would be required for work on a large number of sites.

It is for this reason that attention is increasingly being paid to the possibility of extracting information from site surfaces: most sites will only ever be examined in this way, but even on those sites that are later excavated surface survey can provide an excellent guide to further work.

The aim of this type of site survey, whatever particular technique is adopted, is to use the surface to obtain a representation of the subsurface evidence that is as accurate as possible with regard to the nature, extent, distribution and chronology both of features

and of artifactual and other debris. At this scale too aerial reconnaissance can provide invaluable information in the right conditions,[6] to the extent of providing a virtually complete site plan. Even in circumstances in which aerial photography is precluded because of the nature of the local geology or vegetation cover, it is often possible to obtain a good plan of the archaeological features by means of geophysical survey, which in any event can often prove a useful supplement to air photography.

Two main groups of methods are employed: resistivity survey and magnetometry. They depend on the fact that the presence of buried walls or the disturbance of the subsoil by past human

3.2: *An oblique air photograph of an area of chalkland in western Hampshire, England, showing a variety of complex archaeological features in the form of soil marks, which result from the contrast between the disturbance caused by man-made features and the underlying subsoil. A pattern of prehistoric fields is visible as rather diffuse, lighter-coloured lines, with its main axis running from the top right of the picture diagonally to the left. Running from top left diagonally to the right is a boundary ditch, also prehistoric, which cuts through the field system and marks a later stage in the evolution of the landscape. In the upper part of the picture the ditch still survives as an earthwork, but in the lower part it remains only as a soil mark in the arable field.*

3.3: *Factors affecting the preservation and recognition of archaeological sites. The original distribution of sites may have been an even scatter, but differential preservation and discovery can create patterns such as clusters or associations with landscape features.*

- ● site discovered
- ● site surviving, not yet discovered
- ● site destroyed

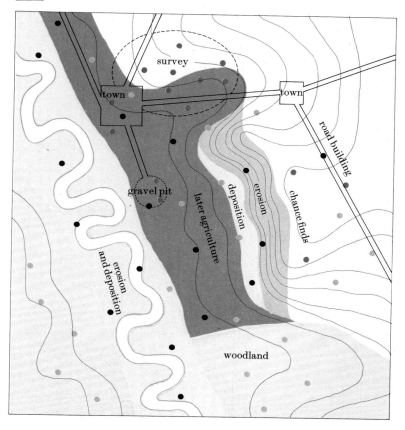

activity (for example, the digging of pits) leads to variations in the resistance of the ground to electric current and to changes in its magnetic field; these may be detected and mapped. In the field of magnetometry particularly advances have been made in recent years with the development of an instrument known as the flux-gate gradiometer;[7] this has resulted in a considerable increase in the speed with which magnetic surveys can be carried out and a consequent enlargement in the scale of projects on which they may be employed. The methods have also been considerably aided by the development of computer techniques that filter out the background 'noise' from archaeologically significant results and thus improve the resolution of the picture obtained. Geophysical survey reveals many of the same types of feature as air photography, and both pose the same problem: their failure to record an archaeological feature does not necessarily mean that none is present. In any individual case the precise reasons for failure still remain rather unpredictable.

Information of a different type is revealed by phosphate survey, which involves the testing of soil samples for their phosphorus content. The phosphorus present in organic refuse dumped in and around a settlement remains fixed in the soil; by collecting soil samples on a grid pattern it is possible to obtain a picture of spatial variations in phosphorus quantity and thus to define areas of settlement and other aspects of human activity. The method has had its problems in the past, particularly in distinguishing the effects of early human activity from those of modern fertilizers, but these are now being resolved. It has been used extensively in the study of early field systems in Scandinavia as well as in the Wessex and Dartmoor areas of England.

The surface-survey method that is probably most widely used, especially in the United States and also in countries where air photography for archaeological purposes is not encouraged or where geophysical equipment is not available, is the controlled collection of surface debris. Again, a grid system is employed that enables spatial patterns of variation to be recovered; depending on the size of the area involved, collection may be complete or some form of probability sampling may be used. Clearly, numerous factors affect the recovery of material from site surfaces and these are currently undergoing detailed investigation. Research is concentrating particularly on those surface properties that reveal what lies underneath.[8] Excavation has shown in many cases that the surface provides an excellent indication of subsurface patterning, but there are occasions when it does not, and deeply stratified sites present obvious difficulties for this type of approach.

Excavation

In any survey it is to be hoped that surface work will provide a basis on which to select the one or two sites in the region that can actually be excavated. Even in the context of a rescue project, where the choice of site to be excavated has been dictated by factors other than the interests of archaeology, a surface survey should always be carried out to provide the basis for determining the next stages of an excavation.

The demands made on excavation by modern archaeological interests and ideas are considerable. (It is perhaps paradoxical that the insistence on more and better information at this stage actually leads to a decrease in the amount of excavation because of contingent demands on time and money.) One of the most important is the interest of the modern archaeologist in reconstructing behaviour rather than in simply finding typical examples of artifacts and features. This requires an examination of spatial patterning within the site and demands that careful attention should be paid to the contexts in which items are found. It has led to the abandonment of the grid of small squares for excavation advocated, for instance, by Sir Mortimer Wheeler[9] and its replacement by open-area excavations on a large scale, so that spatial patterns may be clearly seen. This approach was pioneered in the 1930s and 1940s in Germany and Scandinavia, but it has only come to fruition since the late 1950s.[10] Its emphasis on the horizontal plan rather than the vertical section has been of considerable value, and the need for extremely rigorous control of excavation and recording (for example, by means of photogrammetry and new methods for describing stratigraphic relationships) has undoubtedly encouraged very high standards. Nevertheless, these can only be achieved at a price: two options face the archaeologist. Either excavation has to continue for decades while innumerable minute layers are successively peeled from one another, or much of the potential of the site has to be sacrificed in the attempt to recover a complete plan; in a 'rescue' context only the latter course can be adopted and the site is often simply stripped by mechanical means until the plan becomes visible. This approach has often been regarded mistakenly as total excavation: it tends to mean that other interests are ignored. Of particular relevance here are the studies that have developed as a consequence of the increasing importance of ecological and economic approaches to archaeology (see Chapter 5).

The gathering of information about subsistence activities, which is increasingly regarded as essential to the reconstruction of the past, requires the processing and meticulous examination of large numbers of soil samples in order to obtain representative samples of animal and fish bones, seeds, etc. (for instance, at the Koster site in Illinois about 5 000 000 such items have been retrieved, and that includes only the small-scale material, not the larger animal bones). Again, judicious use of probability sampling schemes in excavation and subsequent processing of the material will ensure that the different possible reasons for excavating a site are not mutually exclusive,[11] but even so, choices have to be made unless resources are unlimited. The need for explicit research designs is critical here, so that the archaeologist is aware of the choices he is making at every stage; the total recovery of all the evidence at a site is never possible.

A recent and important development in excavation is the use of microcomputers for site-recording purposes. This technique is still in its infancy, but it is already clear that its impact is going to be enormous, both on archaeological publication and documentation and on site analysis, and that ultimately it will lead to the integration, in a computer-based form, of information from all the different levels – region to site – that have been discussed. The associated tendency towards rigorous, standardized methods of recording is also certain to be beneficial in a discipline in which the validity of all-important inter-site comparisons is often vitiated by inconsistencies and a lack of comparability in the data presented and the ways in which they have been collected.

These are some of the aims of archaeologists, the problems they face and their methods of tackling them at different levels. A further – perhaps the most obvious – feature of the archaeological record deserves attention: its partiality. The archaeologist largely controls the way in which he investigates the archaeological record as it exists at present, but he cannot control the factors that may have distorted that record between the time of its deposition and the time at which he collects his data; he must also take into account distortions that may be introduced by the process of investigation itself. (A distinction is often made between what is available to the archaeologist to study and what he is interested in: the former is known as the 'sampled population', that which the archaeologist actually samples, and the latter the 'target population', that which he wishes to make inferences about.)

Reconstructing the past

Of course, the use of the archaeological record to reconstruct the past has always been at the very heart of the craft of archaeology. Nevertheless, the arguments that archaeologists advance in making their inferences at all scales, from the region to the site, have come under increasingly critical scrutiny in recent years. The reasons for this are the same as those suggested above in the context of archaeological investigation in general: the increasingly ambitious aims that archaeologists have set themselves and consequent demands for high-quality data. At the regional level, for instance, if an archaeological distribution map is being used as a basis for assessing the relationship between a settlement distribution and a particular soil type, it is essential that the archaeologist should understand the factors behind the compilation of the map. Does the patterning in the distribution of sites really relate to preferences for different soils, or does it reflect the presence of a keen local fieldworker who has done a lot of survey work in his own area? It may represent the fact that archaeological evidence is accessible in some parts of the region but not in others, because of the nature of local land use (especially arable as opposed to pasture), or because the evidence has been destroyed in some places by the building of towns, villages or roads, by gravel extraction or even by earlier agriculture. In many areas erosion and deposition can present severe problems; in some places sites will have been eroded away; in others they will be covered with metres of re-deposited eroded material. All these factors must be taken into account if valid inferences are to be made.

Similar problems are also present at the site level, and this whole issue has now become a topic of considerable interest affecting all archaeologists, whether or not they work in a 'rescue' framework. Explicit concern about the difficulties involved was first evident in an analysis of the Iron Age lake village of Glastonbury, England,[12] which showed that in order to understand the site, it was necessary to take into account the precise way in which different types of objects had found their way into the archaeological record (by loss, as rubbish, etc.), the disturbance that later occupation had caused in the patterns of earlier phases and, finally, all the factors that had intervened between the site's abandonment and its excavation. The approach has been developed and systematized, and three main areas of concern have been defined: correlates, C-transforms (cultural transforms) and N-transforms (non-cultural transforms).[13] The first of these areas, correlates, is concerned with the way in which artifacts reflect particular types of human behaviour. The second, C-transforms, deals with the patterns formed by the ways in which items drop out of circulation, and in which they are affected by different modes of rubbish disposal and then often disturbed or even recycled for different uses. In both of these areas ethnoarchaeological studies are playing a crucial role (see Chapter 4).[14] Finally, N-transforms are concerned with all the natural processes that affect the archaeological evidence once it is in the ground, acting both to destroy the original patterning imposed by human activities and, often, to impose a spurious patterning of their own.

If the study of site formation is an important area of development, another of increasing significance is archaeological investigation conducted in areas beyond the bounds of the conventional definition of a 'site'. Considerable emphasis has been given here to the discovery and examination of settlement sites as the principal aim of field archaeology. This remains of central importance, but archaeologists are increasingly acknowledging the fact that human activities ranged over the whole of the landscape in the past, as in the present, and traces of these activities can tell us a great deal. One of the best examples of work based on this assumption, for which aerial photography has been largely responsible, has already been mentioned – the study of the development of field systems in the landscape of north-west Europe.[15] In a very different area, the arid Great Basin of the western United States, the artifact rather than the site was taken as the unit of interest for fieldwork purposes, and the scattered distribution of stone tools, which would normally have been ignored, was shown to have much to tell us about the past exploitation of wild plants and their resources.[16]

It seems safe to say that in the foreseeable future the main pressure for fieldwork will continue to come from the destructive impact of development; but it is now far more likely than it was formerly that this challenge will be met by approaches designed to use fieldwork opportunities to answer interesting questions about the past.

4. Analysis and interpretation

During the last two decades there has been a dramatic increase in the range of analytical techniques to be applied in archaeology. Such techniques are important in the context of the broad theories and models that lie behind the current interpretation of archaeological data – systems theory, locational models and concepts derived from social anthropology – and complement the new ideas on subsistence economics discussed in Chapter 5.

Systems theory

An idea that has recently become popular in archaeology is that of systems theory,[1] according to which the total cultural system is analysed in terms of subsystems that are linked with each other and with the 'environment' – that is, with the social and physical context of the system. Systems theory concentrates on the 'connectedness' of these subsystems and of the variables within each of them. Many archaeologists use systems theory in a very simplified form; for example, they construct 'box' or 'flow' diagrams to illustrate the hypothetical way in which the components of a system are related. But systems theory also provides for more specific concepts and a detailed terminology.[2] Thus, positive feedback occurs when one subsystem stimulates another, which in turn stimulates the first one: it is a self-stimulating link that leads to growth and change (morphogenesis). Negative feedback occurs when one subsystem restrains another so that things remain as they are (homeostasis). Kent Flannery has applied these ideas to the beginning of agriculture in Mesoamerica and to the growth of states,[3] and Colin Renfrew has made systematic use of them in discussing the growth of Mycenaean civilization.[4]

General systems theory attempts to move on from the study of individual systems towards general statements about the workings of classes of systems. Systems, whether mechanical, biological or social, are classified according to the way in which their components are interrelated. The aim is to establish typical patterns of behaviour for each class of system, even if that class includes such diverse and apparently unrelated phenomena as motor cars and human social systems. Systems theory has had an important impact on archaeology, both because it has been a useful instrument for clarifying complex processes and because it has focused attention on the interrelated, multiple causes of change. A potentially important set of ideas are those of the branch of mathematics called catastrophe theory,[5] which shows how abrupt change and discontinuity may occur in certain types of system when a particular threshold is exceeded.

The application of systems theory in archaeology has, however, met some considerable difficulties. The archaeologist usually

4.1: *Regularities in the distribution of walled towns in Roman Britain, shown by plotting Thiessen polygons. The circles drawn around selected tribal centres (shown by a pecked line) indicate the radial distribution of lesser towns in relation to cantonal capitals. Three* coloniae *are also shown.*

4.2: *The structure of the basic unit in the Iron Age marsh settlement at Glastonbury in south-west England, showing its organizational and functional components. In varying numbers, this module recurs throughout the history of the site.*

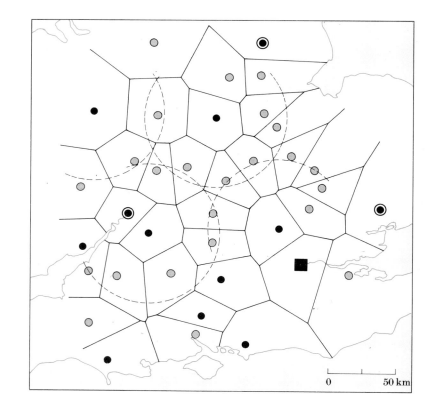

0　　　　50 km

knows very little about the links connecting subsystems, and he may not even know whether he has identified the components of the system correctly. The subsystems may be defined in different ways or may have differing types of links, and it is difficult to choose between the several possible arrangements of a systems model. This is especially the case since much of the early use of systems theory was concerned with very general and very large-scale events – the growth of states, for example, or the emergence of a civilization.

For smaller-scale systems there is some hope that experiments with the different possible arrangements of subsystems will show which could produce behaviour and output similar to those derived from archaeological evidence. One of the advantages of the theory and its application is that any system can be simulated on a computer; because of the great speed at which computers work many different arrangements of a system can be tested to see if the model produces acceptable results, and some general idea of the behaviour of the system in different conditions can be gained. Computer simulation has been used by archaeologists to mimic, for example, the spread of early Neolithic settlement across Europe, the spread of man into North America, the exchange of obsidian and other artifact types, and the peopling and abandonment of Polynesian islands.[6]

Computer simulation is important in archaeology because it enables experiments to be made with multiple hypotheses; however, even large computers have difficulty in coping with the many different variables that have to be examined. A further problem is that ideas about the working of a prehistoric system can usually be obtained only from the very archaeological data that are being simulated, and it is therefore difficult to devise independent tests of the hypotheses. Both systems theory and computer simulation (which can be seen as practical systems theory) provide a general framework for examining causal statements about the past. Information theory provides a very general set of related theories about the transmission of cultural information.[7] More specific models that have been used by archaeologists derive from human geography and anthropology. These models concern locational patterning, social structure and exchange mechanisms.

Locational models

The simplest model with which to compare the distribution of archaeological sites (or artifacts on a site) is a random pattern. If every point in an area has an equal and independent chance of receiving a site, then the process of settlement and the distribution of sites can be described as random. Of course, it would be unrealistic to assume that every location in an area were equally attractive to settlement. But if few constraints are placed on the choice of site location, so that each site is chosen for idiosyncratic reasons, then the resulting pattern will be largely random. Similarly, if the destruction or discovery of sites is unstructured, the resulting site distribution may appear random. It is only if strong constraints have been imposed on the location, survival or recovery of sites that clear non-random patterns may be identified.

Numerous methods have been used by archaeologists to determine whether the arrangements of points in space is other than random. For example, the statistical technique of nearest-neighbour analysis has been used to examine the distributions of different types of artifacts on living floors. The clustering of such artifacts on sites is often assumed to indicate areas of particular activity or of rubbish disposal. It is now clear, however, that the clustering and patterning of artifacts on sites cannot be assumed to be a direct reflection of the behaviour of individuals in settlements.[8] Numerous processes may distort and rearrange artifacts during or after deposition. The analysis of spatial distributions remains important, since it permits the structure of the patterns to be observed, but these must be subjected to sophisticated testing and interpretation. On the regional scale clustering in the distribution of settlements may result from two broad processes: first, settlers may have been attracted to particular locations because of water or good soil, or sites may have enjoyed unusually good chances of survival or recovery (in areas suited to the preservation of artifacts or subjected to intense research); second, clustering may occur as a consequence of the spread of 'daughter' settlements around early colonies (settlements spread outwards but tend to remain fairly close to established sites). While the results of these two processes may often appear to be identical, they can

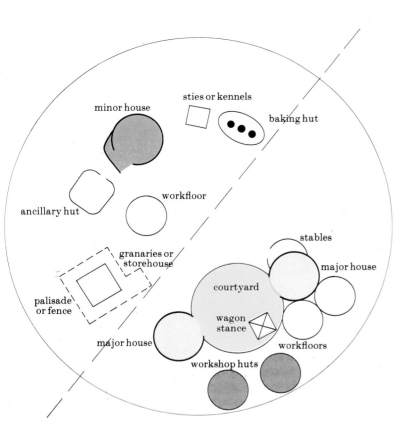

sometimes be distinguished by examining the statistical properties of the distributions at different scales of analysis. For example, settlements may occur in discrete units, within which the distribution of sites may be largely random. The grouping would only be apparent if a large enough area were included in the analysis.

Archaeologists are also interested in analyses of site distributions that indicate some uniformity of spacing, as this is often a sign of competition between sites in the mutual adjustment of their territories. If such competition can be identified, models derived from human geography may be relevant for the interpretation of settlement distribution. The geometrical pattern that allows for the most widespread and efficient contact between the centre and a dispersed population is a triangular placing of centres, with hexagonal service areas around each centre. If the centres vary in the range of goods they provide, central place theory[9] provides for certain expectations in terms of their spatial and hierarchical relationships. Such ideas have been applied to complex changes in settlement patterns in pre-contact times in the Valley of Mexico and to the interpretation of archaeological sites in the Early Dynastic period in Iraq.

There is a similar pattern in the distribution of Romano-British walled towns. In Figure 4.1 Thiessen polygons (produced by drawing perpendiculars at the mid-points between towns) have been used to define the hypothetical service areas around each centre, on the assumption that factors such as ease of access were uniform and that it was considered important to minimize movement. The suggested service areas can be tested by reference to the distributions of artifacts that were marketed from the towns.[10] Figure 4.1 also suggests a ring of dependent smaller towns around the major cantonal capitals. Although such a pattern may indicate that some aspects of central place theory are relevant, the same arrangement could have been produced by the application of other theories with a more military or 'tribal' emphasis. A major problem raised by the analysis of all spatial patterns is that different processes may produce very similar arrangements. In the case of Roman towns the predictions of a range of different hypotheses have been tested statistically against the observed distribution pattern, but it remains difficult to discern which hypotheses have provided the best fits. One reason for this is that locational decisions based on different criteria – for instance, military security as opposed to economic advantage – may produce similar patterns, as they reflect the underlying distribution of native populations. Several regional studies have looked for hierarchies of sites and the spatial arrangement of settlements of different rank.[11] But the archaeologist is often unable to demonstrate the exact contemporaneity of sites in regional distributions, and he cannot be sure that the rank of the site is directly reflected by its size – though this is often the only measure of the importance of sites that can be obtained.

Similar approaches have been adopted in analysing the layout and content of individual settlements. Archaeologists have been especially interested in estimating population size from the area of sites. Various figures or formulae have been proposed for the settlement area needed per person, but ethnographic data demonstrate that people are able to live at very different densities, so site population may not be reliably estimated from site size; there is evidence only of a constant limit to the densities that can be supported in a wide variety of settlement types.

Other techniques have been employed for analysing patterning within sites. One method that has been adopted is trend-surface analysis, which examines variations in the density of artifacts; another approach is graph theory, which draws on the degree of interconnection between rooms. Naturally, well-preserved buildings with plentiful finds – as, for instance, at Pompeii – provide greater opportunities for study and interpretation than sparse scatters of material in poorly preserved sites, although in both cases computers can be used to help with the sorting and arrangement of material. In a classic study Clarke[12] examined the distribution of structures, clay floors, hearths and artifacts on the Iron Age site of Glastonbury in south-west England, 'in order to attempt the recovery of the inherent rules of building followed by the inhabitants'. A search of the distributions was made in an effort to establish repeated locational regularities. Clarke suggested that the structures were frequently found on the site in particular associations, making up modular units (Figure 4.2). The comparative analysis of 'living' ethnographic settlements is an important check on the validity of such reconstructions: indeed, social anthropology is a major source of archaeological models.

Ethnographic models and ethnoarchaeology
Ethnography has made an important contribution to three aspects of archaeology; it has shed light on social structures and on exchange mechanisms, and it has stimulated the recent development of ethnoarchaeology.

General models of levels of social organization and the workings of bands, tribes, chiefdoms and states have been used by several archaeologists in their interpretations of the structures of past societies;[13] for example, the evidence of burials and settlements in the Early Bronze Age in southern England has been used to argue for the existence of chiefdoms. Ethnographic studies have also been used to build models that might account for variations in burial practices and cemetery patterning.[14] Such uses of ethnographic data increase the awareness of the archaeologist, but they remain of limited value because the archaeologist is making broad correlations and ethnographic associations often without understanding the precise function and significance of the features in question. For example, world ethnographic data may suggest that the majority of plough agriculturalists and pastoralists transmit property through the male line (patrilineal inheritance), but it would be wrong to interpret a past society with plough agriculture as necessarily patrilineal without having established in detail the mechanisms of inheritance and the factors that may have given rise to a patrilineal system.

Where ethnographically based generalizations and archaeological data can be most usefully united is in the analysis of the links between economic and environmental organization and pressures, attitudes to death and inheritance and cemetery structure. For example, the right of a corporate group to use a particular set of resources is likely to be legitimized by use over several generations and will be reflected in rituals stressing ties to ancestors that often involve reference to their physical remains. The development of such hypotheses about the process of cemetery formation has been accompanied by considerable progress in the analysis and measurement of cemetery structure; for example, computer-aided sorting and cluster analysis have been used to identify associations of artifacts with individuals of different ages and sexes in prehistoric cemeteries.[15]

Ethnography has also been a source of inspiration for ideas about exchange mechanisms. This area of study is extremely important in archaeology because certain developments in archaeological science are making it possible to assign a wide range of artifact types to their sources; the inclusions and clay in pottery can be examined by thin-sectioning and heavy-mineral analysis; the composition of the fabric can be investigated by microchemical analysis, using spectrometry and X-ray diffraction techniques, in order to identify their origin.[16] Similarly, petrological analysis of Neolithic stone axes has identified the major sources of these items. The archaeologist can thus ascertain the source of artifacts and is able to compile a distribution map illustrating their dispersal.

What process of exchange and dispersal could have produced the distributions? Statistical analysis, including the technique of regression analysis,[17] may be able to offer some clues by permitting the comparison of distributions with the patterns predicted by particular mathematical models (such as random dispersal from a point), but ethnographic work is necessary to provide fuller information about primitive exchange.[18] Sometimes ethnohistorical data can facilitate the interpretation of particular archaeological distributions in the recent past, as in the case of axe distributions in Australia. For earlier periods more general models are required, but even these indicate the general relevance of mechanisms such as ceremonial gift exchange – the obligatory giving and receiving of gifts among approximate social equals – which has informed the study of prehistoric material and its distribution in Europe.[19] Another form of exchange, redistribution, involves the pooling of goods in the hands of a chief or some other recognized central agency and their reallocation among the community. This second type of exchange is of fundamental importance in emerging social hierarchies, at the level of the chiefdom and the early state. Traditional market exchange occurs when exchange is fairly free from institutional kinship obligations,[20] and such considerations are important to the analysis of the early growth of towns.

One problem posed by ethnographic data is that initially much of the material was not gathered with the archaeologist in mind. More recently, archaeologists have felt the need to carry out their own ethnographies to enable them to answer particular archaeological questions; such work is often called ethnoarchaeology.[21]

Much of this type of archaeology has been concerned with the processes associated with site formation. For example, archaeologists have examined the rate at which deposits may accumulate as a result of pastoralist occupation in East Africa, and they have also studied the post-depositional movement of artifacts caused by trampling. Site size and duration of occupation may have an important effect on the relationship between activities and refuse – the longer and more intense occupation of larger sites often necessitated the removal of rubbish from areas of habitation.

Ethnoarchaeology has also been concerned with developing models for the interpretation of social organization within the site. So far, however, attempts to relate the patterning of material culture within settlements to the people who lived there have been only partially successful. On the one hand, ethnoarchaeology has encountered difficulties raised by the fact that buildings may have constantly changed function and may have been inhabited by several people for a variety of reasons; on the other, the study has enabled archaeologists to postulate certain provocative hypotheses. One such hypothesis (though it has its limitations) is that men joined their wives' households on marriage, the social organization may be reflected in localized pottery designs within settlements.

Until recently material culture was interpreted largely in terms of 'cultural relationships', inferred from similarities in the shape or style of artifacts. It was suggested that the greater the interaction or contact between individuals, the more typological similarity there would be among cultural items, and the more centralized the production of artifacts, the wider the cultural similarities. Ethnoarchaeology has demonstrated the limitations of this view. Material culture is now regarded not merely as a means of adapting to the environment, but as a kind of language through which individual needs and desires are expressed. The conscious and subconscious structures in the human mind impose their patterning on the external world created by man – they constitute his culture. If the archaeologist is to 'read' the past, he must understand more about the way in which material culture can be used as a vehicle for expression and about the patterns of thought that find expression in material form.

5. Economic archaeology

Economic archaeology has emerged as an important focus of development during the last twenty-five years. As with other young and rapidly changing subjects, there is considerable controversy over its aims. To some, economic archaeology is the study of the production, distribution and consumption of all commodities used by early communities; its main concerns are prehistoric trade and exchange systems between communities, and the production and distribution of goods and resources within human groups. Others envisage economic archaeology primarily as the study of the relationships between early populations and their resources. According to this definition, the discipline seeks to explain how communities utilized their resources and coped with seasonal and longer-term fluctuations; how population growth caused or resulted from changes in technology and subsistence strategies; and what factors regulated the size, density and longevity of settlements. Its central concern is thus subsistence, and its prime raw materials are food residues, supplemented by data on the location and environmental setting of ancient settlements. This definition of economic archaeology is accepted here.

The growth of economic archaeology has been most notable in the study of prehistory and has arisen through important changes in the goals of prehistoric studies. Radiocarbon and other dating techniques (see Chapter 62) have largely freed prehistorians from the need to construct chronological frameworks based upon typological comparisons of the artifacts shared by neighbouring cultural groups.[1] Because it is no longer necessary to regard settlement sites primarily as convenient sources of material for cross-cultural comparisons, or cultures as purely chronological devices, both can be viewed as indicating instead different aspects of prehistoric human behaviour. One reason for the rapid growth of economic archaeology over the last decade has been the realization that it is possible to find direct evidence of prehistoric subsistence instead of merely making inferences from ancient artifacts. This point has been especially relevant to studies of early agriculture in Europe and the Near East. Until only a few years ago the flintwork and pottery of early farming communities in these regions were frequently documented in far greater detail than their plant and animal resources. Much archaeoeconomic work over the last decade has been concerned with redressing this imbalance by augmenting the data on prehistoric plant and animal husbandry through the systematic recovery of animal bones and seed remains from excavations.

These shifts in emphasis in prehistoric studies from culture to community and from chronology to behaviour have considerably altered the type of information required from faunal and botanical data. A simple list of the plant and animal species associated with a prehistoric settlement is no longer adequate. Information is now required about the importance and usage of each animal resource, the age at which animals were slaughtered, the ways they were butchered and their sex ratios. Data on the health of animal resources and the role of secondary products such as milk, hides and dung are also needed. Archaeobotanical data are expected to indicate the relative importance of each plant resource, its usage and the methods employed in its preparation for storage and consumption. Investigations into early farming communities also require evidence of the type of crop system, the prevalence of weeds and other parasites and the use of technologies for irrigation or drainage.

More important, perhaps, than the change in the kind of data now required from each type of food residue is the trend towards integrating the components of a subsistence economy. One problem that has become highly important in recent years is the question of how the relative proportions of plant and animal foods in the diet of a prehistoric community can be evaluated. The use of prehistoric fodder resources and animal fertilizers are two further issues that affect both the animal and plant husbandry of a community and that have to be investigated by an integrated consideration of botanical and faunal data.

These developments in the usage of botanical and faunal data have both caused and resulted from some important improvements in the retrieval and analysis of prehistoric food residues. Faunal and botanical data were formerly recovered from excavations in the same way as artifacts; that is to say, with the aid of trowels and even of picks and shovels. Not surprisingly, much evidence was missed, however great the care and skill of the excavator. More important, the resulting samples were usually biased in their composition. The remains of small or immature animals were often overlooked, and the evidence for animal husbandry was frequently weighted in favour of large adult beasts.[2] The recovery of carbonized and desiccated plant remains was usually haphazard and often accidental. In most cases only those plant remains that were easily visible in the course of an excavation were collected, and these rarely provided an accurate account of the prevailing plant husbandry. Today many excavators sieve, and even wash, archaeological deposits through a variety of meshes to ensure the recovery of all faunal remains and artifacts, so that the samples obtained provide an accurate account of what was contained in the deposits before excavation. The most significant recent improvements in recovery techniques have affected the retrieval of carbonized plant remains. Over the last decade a variety of flotation techniques has been developed that enable excavators to recover macroscopic plant remains from up to a tonne of deposits a day.[3] Consequently, botanical evidence can be recovered from large areas of settlements, and from deposits where it is present in very low densities, without impeding the progress of an excavation.

The recent improvements in the quantity and quality of data on prehistoric food remains have engendered a considerable literature on the most appropriate ways to make use of the information provided by faunal and botanical samples. Techniques for estimating the numbers of animals and the weight of meat represented in

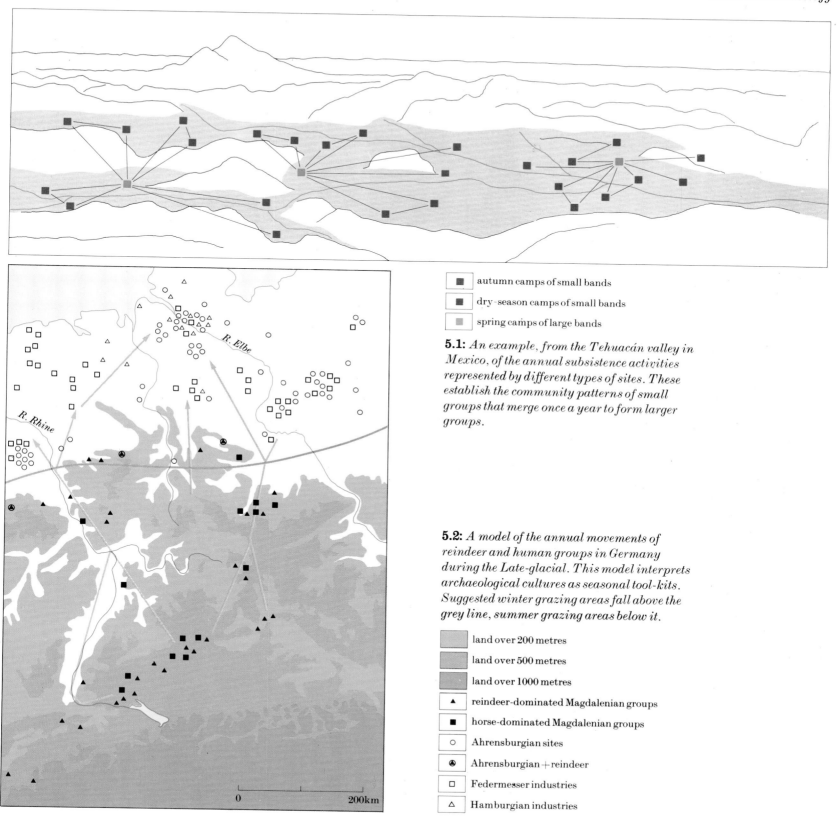

autumn camps of small bands

dry-season camps of small bands

spring camps of large bands

5.1: *An example, from the Tehuacán valley in Mexico, of the annual subsistence activities represented by different types of sites. These establish the community patterns of small groups that merge once a year to form larger groups.*

5.2: *A model of the annual movements of reindeer and human groups in Germany during the Late-glacial. This model interprets archaeological cultures as seasonal tool-kits. Suggested winter grazing areas fall above the grey line, summer grazing areas below it.*

land over 200 metres

land over 500 metres

land over 1000 metres

▲ reindeer-dominated Magdalenian groups

■ horse-dominated Magdalenian groups

○ Ahrensburgian sites

⬒ Ahrensburgian + reindeer

□ Federmesser industries

△ Hamburgian industries

R. Elbe

R. Rhine

0   200km

excavated deposits have received much attention and are based increasingly upon rigorous statistical procedures. The advantage of these techniques over earlier and simpler ones is that they can take fuller account of such factors as the size of the sample, differences in the numbers of bones and teeth and the different rate of destruction of each anatomical part.[4] Estimates of the age at which animals were slaughtered have also undergone extensive re-appraisal, and many criteria based on the fusion rates of bone and the growth and wear of teeth have been refined.

Less attention has been paid to the problem of analysing archaeo-botanical data in terms of prehistoric subsistence activities. This state of affairs only partly results from a shortage of flotation machines and of archaeobotanists. A more important cause is that the ways in which prehistoric plant resources were utilized are generally considered to be less important than their evolution and dispersal, particularly in the case of early farming communities. Attempts to discuss prehistoric plant husbandry in relation to individual settlements have encountered serious difficulties in overcoming the biases inherent in this type of data. The greatest obstacle is that the abundance of an archaeological plant species is not directly related to its importance; conversely, the scarcity of a plant species in archaeological contexts need not indicate that it was unimportant. This is because the preservation of archaeobotanical data depends largely on the characteristics and usage of each plant and the domestic activities with which it was associated. Although statistical techniques have been devised in recent years to over-come some of these problems, most are suspect because they are based upon the assumption that the abundance of a prehistoric plant resource is an indication of its importance. An alternative approach has been to identify the types of domestic activities that resulted in the preservation of plant samples and to use this information to assess the value of each plant species in a qualitative rather than a quantitative manner (as shown in Figure 5.3).[5] The quality of information from archaeobotanical data is unlikely to match that obtained by faunal analysts until more attention is paid to the archaeological factors that resulted in the preservation and composition of each sample.

The recent increases in the amount of data on prehistoric plant and animal husbandry have created new problems that will require extensive discussion over the next few years. One is the problem of cost-efficiency. The costs of large-scale excavations are rapidly becoming prohibitive and post-excavation analyses are both time-consuming and expensive. Beyond a certain critical and, at present, ill-defined point, the results of additional work do not justify the resources expended in obtaining them. What is not known yet in sufficient detail is how to minimize the amount of data obtained from excavation without endangering the reliability of the con-clusions drawn from them. The key variables in this problem are the objectives and funding of an excavation and the type of settle-ment under examination.[6] At present archaeologists lack the experience to predict with confidence the proportion of a settle-ment that needs excavation, the numbers of sampling units

required, the type and fraction of material in excavated deposits that can be safely disregarded, and the minimum range of faunal and botanical samples that is consistent with guaranteeing a successful outcome to different types of research programme. Further research is needed to ensure that funds, expertise and new techniques for recovering faunal and botanical data are used to full advantage.

Economic archaeology has made its greatest impact upon two areas of prehistoric studies, of which the first is the early develop-ment of agriculture. This now appears to have originated over a wider area and at an earlier date than previously supposed. In the Old World the concept of a short and highly localized 'Neolithic Revolution' has been replaced by one of a gradual and widespread evolution from hunting and gathering to farming. Previously crisp distinctions between hunters and farmers, and between wild and domestic resources, have become blurred. Many criteria used traditionally for identifying prehistoric plant and animal domesti-cates have been challenged; for example, some have argued that the decrease in the size of animals such as cattle and pigs during the early Holocene resulted from readjustments to the warmer condi-

5.3: *An example from two Bulgarian Neolithic sites of how samples of carbonized plant remains can be used to model prehistoric crop-processing activities.*

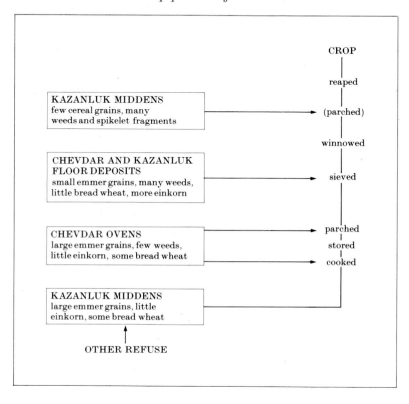

tions of the Postglacial rather than from domestication. Re-appraisals of pre-Neolithic faunal data have indicated that so-called hunting communities may have been as selective over the age, type and perhaps sex of animals they killed as many later agriculturalists. Some prehistorians have used this data, and recent successful attempts to domesticate such animals as red deer, saiga antelope and eland, to suggest that some Late-glacial communities may have domesticated ungulates such as reindeer, red deer and gazelle.[7]

The Near East has also lost some of its former pre-eminence as the area in which agriculture first developed and later diffused to adjacent territories. For example, by the early Holocene the dog appears to have been domesticated independently of the Near East in north-west Europe, North America and Japan; claims for the independent and early domestication of sheep have been made for southern France and the western Sahara; the earliest domestic cattle yet found are from sites in Greece and Crete. Early dates for the domestication of cattle in Thailand and the pig in New Guinea have also been suggested in recent years. Although positive evidence is so far lacking, it is likely that China and India will also emerge as areas where agriculture evolved at an early date. Finally, impressive sequences have been obtained that show the gradual and local domestication of plant resources from both Peru and Mexico.[8]

Our understanding of early plant domestication in the Old World is still greatly impeded by an almost total lack of information on the use and distribution of cereals in the Late-glacial and early Holocene. Present-day wild cereals provide inconclusive evidence; they too have probably evolved over the last ten millennia, and their distribution has been considerably modified by human activities. The discovery of wild barley grains in a Late Pleistocene context in southern Greece suggests that cereal domestication may have begun in areas outside the Near East. The discovery of grains of apparently domesticated emmer wheat from a similar context in Israel may also suggest that the evolution of domestic wheats is more complex than previously suspected. Most recent evidence of plant domestication in the Old World, however, concerns the last ten thousand years. Nevertheless, this has considerably lengthened the antiquity of many domesticates. Bread wheat (*Triticum aestivum*) is now claimed from sites of the seventh millennium BC in Crete and Turkey. Rye is evidenced from the eighth millennium BC in Syria and the fifth millennium BC in Romania; flax appears to have been fully domestic in the Near East by 6000 BC.[9] In the context of crop agriculture it is also noteworthy that the last decade or so has demonstrated that the simple plough, or ard, was known in north-west Europe by the fourth millennium BC, and irrigation techniques were used in the Near East by the late sixth millennium BC, and possibly even earlier.

The other area in which economic prehistorians have made notable progress is in the modelling of the subsistence strategies of small communities that were generally self-sufficient in their food resources. Most of these studies have been considerably influenced by recent ecological and anthropological accounts of how the density and distribution of animal and human populations are regulated by fluctuations in the abundance and location of resources throughout the year. Anthropological data have also been important in indicating that human groups can use a variety of tool-kits during the year to make the best use of available resources. As a consequence, many recent archaeological studies have tended to stress that a prehistoric settlement may provide only a partial account of the annual activities of a group, and that contemporaneous assemblages from adjacent areas could represent seasonally distinct tool-kits of one group and not distinct 'cultures' of separate communities.[10] The last decade has produced several studies of the annual movements of prehistoric groups based on their probable responses to seasonal fluctuations in food resources (see Figures 5.1 and 5.2). Studies of the use of shellfish have also yielded interesting insights into subsistence strategies. Although prehistoric coastal shell-mounds (middens) in many parts of the world often reach an impressive size, detailed examination of the rate at which they accumulated and of the amount of food they represent suggests that shellfish formed only one-fifth of the total quantity of food eaten by a community and that these middens were probably occupied for only a few weeks each year.[11]

Considerable attention has also been paid to reconstructing the subsistence bases of individual settlements with the aid of both excavated evidence concerning technology and resources and detailed study of their local environmental setting. In this context the technique of site catchment analysis has proved useful (see Figure 5.4). This evaluates the productivity of the resources contained within the area habitually exploited by the inhabitants of a prehistoric settlement. Radii of 5 and 10 kilometres (equivalent to one and two hours' walking) have been suggested as the probable maximum extents of the catchment areas of prehistoric agriculturalists and hunter–gatherers respectively on the basis of ethnographic data. The resources within this area can be assessed in various ways – in terms of, for example, soils, vegetation and modern land use. This technique is still at an experimental stage but should eventually become an important and integral part of archaeoeconomic studies.[12]

One particularly interesting result of some recent studies of prehistoric subsistence is the extent to which non- and pre-agricultural populations appear to have modified their environment. Like domestication, man's impact on the landscape seems to have a far greater antiquity than was suspected a few years ago. Widespread evidence of the clearance of forest by fire by pre-agricultural groups during the early Holocene has been obtained from north-west Europe; similar data have been collected from the Nile valley, and much of the aboriginal flora in Australia is now thought to have been modified by burning.[13] In all these instances it seems that firing was undertaken deliberately to encourage the growth of plant foods for man and browse fodder for his animals. Information of this kind has challenged the validity of earlier views that prehistoric hunter–gatherers lacked the technological means to raise the level of their resources and to increase their populations.

The main achievements of economic archaeology over the last two decades or so have been to increase the quality and quantity of data on prehistoric plant and animal husbandry; to reshape views of the origins of agriculture; and to develop ways of studying prehistoric subsistence in an integrated fashion. Economic archaeology has, however, two serious weaknesses that will require serious attention over the next decade. The first is that it is of very limited value in studying the economies of complex societies composed of hierarchical and interdependent communities. While economic archaeologists can provide piecemeal information about some aspects of the plant and animal husbandry of individual settlements, they have had little success in formulating models of their total economic structure. For this reason, economic archaeology has hardly affected the study of later prehistoric and early historic periods. The second major weakness of

economic archaeology is that it has been predominantly the study of subsistence and not of economy; some recent studies have rightly been accused of environmental determinism and of overstressing the role of subsistence in regulating the size, distribution and development of prehistoric communities. Its main concern has so far been the study of the interactions between prehistoric populations and their physical environments; it has yet to take into account the effects upon that relationship of the social environment and such factors as trade, social organization and craft manufacture. The challenge of the next decade is to develop economic archaeology into a study of both the physical and the social environments of prehistoric communities.

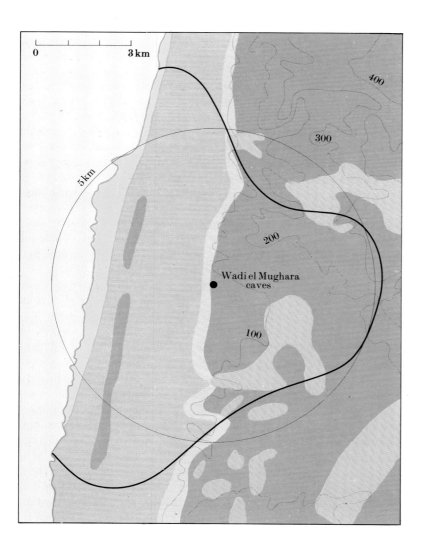

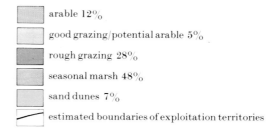

5.4: *Site catchment analysis. This site, in Israel, is early Holocene in date and lies in an area that appears to have a low potential for cereal cultivation.*

	arable 12%
	good grazing/potential arable 5%
	rough grazing 28%
	seasonal marsh 48%
	sand dunes 7%
——	estimated boundaries of exploitation territories

6. Historical archaeology

Knowledge of a past society that has left no documentary record must be derived from its material debris alone, but severe limitations are imposed on the scope of any such inquiry by the unrepresentative character of its surviving remains. The goods a society produces or acquires, deposits or loses, the nature of its buildings and settlements, imports, wealth goods and manufactures constitute evidence, some of which is discarded or accidentally lost and some of which is deliberately concealed or buried. Which components of this material survive is determined by the intervention of war or physical catastrophes, by soil conditions or by subsequent land use, all of which favour the survival of a community's least perishable goods, which are necessarily unrepresentative of its original debris as a whole. This poses acute problems in the case of a complex, stratified society, from which goods pertaining to the elite or ruling class tend to be disproportionately well represented. The same difficulties of interpretation are inherent even in those cases where contemporary histories of the society written by its own historians, have been preserved; in cases where no written accounts whatever survive, or where, as in later prehistoric Europe, contact with literate communities has resulted in a fragmentary literature that documents certain aspects of this contact, the difficulties are particularly pronounced.

The interests of archaeologists and their methods of detection and recovery further influence what portion of the debris of a society is available for study. They have concentrated in the past on monumental sites and well-stocked graves, so these have constituted an unreasonable proportion of the record and have influenced in turn the opinions archaeologists have formed of the societies they represent. One consequence of the increasing sophistication of current concepts of early societies, which generate questions to which the traditional archaeological record provides no answers, is that traces of more perishable remains – such as food residues and relatively flimsy constructions – are being sought and found whose existence was formerly unsuspected or which were not susceptible to investigation by traditional techniques.

The identification of the artifacts of a society and their interpretation are contingent on archaeologists' concepts of that society, which are themselves based on analogy with other, better documented societies with an apparently similar material culture. Direct evidence of a society's structure is not provided by its material remains: its language, its social stratification or class system, the organization of the production and distribution of food and goods – all these are lost to the archaeologist. If a model of the society is to be constructed that will account for the archaeological findings, some of these systems must be supplied conjecturally, because they form the context within which the artifacts functioned. For this reason the social or political history of a society known solely by its material remains is unlikely ever to be written.

Direct evidence of social structure, however, can be provided by more or less contemporary ancient documents, if these are available. They offer accounts based on observation or hearsay that can be used in conjunction with material debris to form the basis of social and political models more complex and more specific than those that can be constructed from evidence supplied by material remains aided by analogy alone. Yet documentary evidence also provides an unrepresentative record of ancient societies and, like archaeological remains, sheds most light on the ruling class or social elite. In this twilight only the outlines of a social and political history can be discerned, and the range of questions that may be answered with conviction remains very restricted. It is never possible to provide an account of an ancient society, even a Classical one, that would satisfy the requirements of an ethnographer of a living community.

Both material debris and textual accounts must be interpreted before they constitute evidence of the way of life of a past society, and the perspective from which they are viewed determines which elements are regarded as significant for a reconstruction of the society's social system and history. The evidential value of ancient accounts of barbarian societies is influenced by circumstances that include the degree of literacy of the society itself, the nature of the interest taken in it by its literate neighbours, the conceptual apparatus of observers, the incidence of surviving manuscripts and inscriptions and, finally, the percipience of the historian. The techniques used to interpret documentary sources naturally differ from those applied to material finds, and this has contributed to the unfortunate separation of much historical and archaeological inquiry. Yet even when the use of historical material is explicitly renounced, its influence persists, as archaeologists continue to use ethnic or place names and to make certain assumptions about the class structure of the societies whose remains they examine. None of these is a simple or uncontroversial matter capable of definitive study; the textual record therefore requires continual re-examination as the interpretation of archaeological findings advances.

Documentary evidence permits a more reliable account of social and political systems to be constructed than is possible in its absence, though in itself such evidence may not be wholly dependable. The difficulties associated with combining material and documentary evidence are aggravated when two societies have been in contact, but the records concerned give only one society's view of a neighbour. In spite of this one-sidedness, documents do offer unique insights into aspects of life and forms of social structure not otherwise recorded. As an example of such a situation, the archaeology and history of the western Celts in the later first millennium BC illustrates an important general point and is considered below in some detail.

On the fringe of Classical Europe

The evidence illuminates three aspects especially of the life of the western Celts of this period: material culture, language and social structure. In the first place, documents provide descriptions of the material aspects of their society, some of which have been preserved archaeologically, but many of which have perished. Descriptions of the appearance of people, their animals and their settlements are important sources of information, but even such apparently straightforward accounts are the products of interpretation by Classical observers and may be misleading. Second, Classical accounts preserve personal and place names and bits of vocabulary on the basis of which language and dialect and the ethnic composition of Celtic communities can be studied. Third, and most important, they provide accounts of the social structure and values of the society of the Celts, which cannot be obtained by any other means.

Four main types of document – inscriptions, administrative records, transcribed oral traditions and observers' accounts – survive to shed light on the development of western Celtic society in the later first millennium BC. The survival and interpretation of inscriptions is subject to constraints that affect the general archaeological record. Among barbarian societies of Europe literacy was a late development; most inscriptions date from after the Roman conquest and therefore provide only oblique evidence for pre-conquest communities. Many inscriptions consist of little more than the names of persons, places and deities, and their use as historical evidence for the society that produced them depends on the perspective from which they are interpreted. To take one example, personal names inscribed on coins have sometimes been regarded as the names of merchants, an assumption based on the erroneous belief that ancient coinage was produced to facilitate trade.[1] A model of European barbarian communities that places traders in a social position from which they could strike precious metal coinages cannot be made to account satisfactorily for the rest of the material and documentary record. Recent work has instead insisted on the function of gold and silver coinage as wealth fashioned for the purpose of making official payments and issued by individuals or authorities with at least an army to pay; the general interpretation of coinage is correspondingly affected.[2]

The second form of documentary evidence about past societies is that furnished by their later colonial administration. This is indirect evidence, but it is an important source of information about ethnic and place names and administrative boundaries. The central Gaulish *civitates* (states) that Caesar shows to have been politically most centralized in the fifties BC all possessed boundaries that the Roman provincial administration could assimilate more or less without change after the conquest; it is therefore evident that their governments already administered large territories before the conquest. In other areas of Gaul, where Roman boundaries coincided with earlier political units, they were rather small, as were some of the Belgic *civitates*; or new boundaries were drawn up to include an unspecified number of small communities whose identity and character are now lost.

This point raises a general problem of historical archaeology. Both inscriptions and ancient textual sources name a wealth of communities at widely different points in their histories, without ever specifying what sort of social units they constituted. Names do not always refer to cohesive political units. All Celtic communities had histories of formation and dissolution, and it is very unusual to be informed of the process[3] or to be given the names of the *pagi* (administrative subsections) of larger *civitates*. Foreign observers are notoriously prone to seeing unity where there is none and to creating 'tribes' out of socially disparate elements, while native informants for their part might exaggerate the extent of their own community's effective authority.

Yet, at the other extreme, attempts to reconstruct Celtic territories on the basis of archaeological finds alone inevitably fail, and provincial documentary evidence is therefore an indispensable guide to the political significance of settlement patterns. Even when the limits of a political territory are well established, as are those of the Gaulish Bituriges Cubi, for instance, the distribution of pottery or coins is never uniform throughout the territory and never stops cleanly at the borders. In this case the distribution of coins could reasonably lead to the conclusion that there were two independent authorities in the area, while settlement analysis would suggest four or five. However, within a framework constructed from historical as well as archaeological evidence it is possible to regard the territory of the Bituriges as a state with a central government and four or five subordinate *pagi* with responsibilities for their own defence and administration.

The third surviving type of document is transcriptions from oral traditions. Vernacular transcriptions of very ancient traditions survive in some areas and include Homer, the Irish and Welsh epics and Norse sagas; their use as historical information is unjustified in isolation from the archaeological record, although they help to provide a context for the interpretation of material findings. Continental Celtic and German vernacular tradition is almost irrecoverably lost, but Greek and Latin summaries of oral traditions, whether of recent events or of those of the more distant past, are of great value, despite the fact that they have been mediated through two different ethnic perspectives in the course of transmission. The first perspective is that of the Celtic narrative itself, which poses the difficulties of interpretation as historical evidence common to any oral tradition. These accounts were composed and transmitted by specialists closely associated with the aristocracy of each community;[4] according to the purpose for which an account was preserved, certain selected persons and events were accorded significance while others were ignored or dismissed. The second perspective is that of Classical excerptors, who had their own reasons for retelling stories whose full versions were certainly of considerable length. Their motives determined what they selected and how they chose to cast the material. In addition, their understanding of the meaning of ethnic names and other elements in the Celtic tradition influenced their interpretations of the accounts.

The fourth (and by far the most common) ancient accounts of the illiterate societies of Europe are those based on the observations of authors or on information acquired from their sources. These record, either deliberately or in passing, barbarians with whom Mediterranean communities came into contact. They document only those events that directly affected these communities – mainly migrations, the use of mercenaries and conquests – and have therefore been instrumental primarily in preserving material relating to the warrior class. It is only from ethnographical works and sustained narratives such as Caesar's that information about the overall structure of barbarian society and its politics may be obtained.

Ancient authors were not apparently aware of or interested in historical change within barbarian societies, except when it involved the adoption of Mediterranean institutions. Until fairly recently few modern historians looked for evidence of social and political change among the second-century Celts either, but instead discussed the evolution of their culture in terms of the contradictions that emerge from the accounts of Caesar and Poseidonios, as though only one of them could be 'right'. Yet on documentary grounds alone it can be demonstrated that barbarian communities experienced political development,[5] and archaeological evidence leaves no doubt that in Celtic Europe important changes in settlement pattern, imports, manufactures and the use of coinage took place during the late second and first centuries BC. The Celtic societies described by Poseidonios, Polybius and other early authorities closely resemble those of the early Irish epics but differ significantly from the emergent political states of central Gaul described by Caesar. In order to explain the emergence of the latter it is necessary to specify what changes took place, and to do this archaeological evidence is as important as documentary. It is possible, then, to discern the structural dynamics of Celtic society and the role played by relations between the Celts and their neighbours, and to construct a framework for an explanation of the social and political changes.

Some of the problems that have arisen in the development of historical archaeology have resulted from erroneous preconceptions about the relation of ancient texts to societies and to their archaeological records. The fact that certain events were important in the history of Rome's relations with the Celts does not mean that they were equally important for the Celts themselves. Even when they occurred at roughly the same date as archaeologically recorded phenomena, they cannot be regarded as causally related in the absence of further evidence; the written record cannot simply be used to 'interpret' archaeological 'facts'. Despite the difficulties inherent in their interpretation, when the historical accounts are re-examined in the light of recent archaeological work new concepts of social structure and historical change in barbarian societies may emerge that take account of both types of evidence.

The changes in settlement, ceramics, weapons and imports that occurred in most Celtic areas during the later second and first centuries BC may be seen not as reactions to invasions or other local catastrophes, but as social and political responses to prob-

lems posed by the development of new relationships between the Celts and their Mediterranean neighbours. Historical texts make it clear that Mediterranean imports into Gaul were scarce between about 400 and the mid-second century BC. The Romans, on the other hand, did not use mercenaries, and in the course of their unusually well documented conquest of the Mediterranean they put an end to their use by Macedon, Carthage and numerous Greek cities. Instead, the Romans required slaves for use in agriculture and industry, and Diodorus records[6] that Celtic slaves were bought for wine, a luxury commodity of which a surplus was produced in Italy and which played an important role in competition within the Celtic aristocracy. Archaeological finds of *amphorae* of first-century BC date are made throughout the area of central Gaul, which Caesar described as politically pre-eminent and which the archaeological record shows to have had the most highly developed urban settlements in Gaul.[7] The later phases of Celtic coinage developed in a way that presupposes increasing administrative complexity and suggests the institution of a new series of state coinages in the early first century.[8] Both documentary and archaeological evidence, therefore, suggest Celtic social and political change in response to a new relationship with Mediterranean neighbours, which enriched the aristocracy that conducted it and tended at the same time to encourage warfare whose principal aim was the seizure of captives and an increase in domestic exploitation to support the growth of towns and ever more complex state institutions.

Conclusion

Until recently, most of the important advances in methods of interpretation of an archaeologically attested society have been made by prehistorians, whose severely limited evidence has necessitated the development of sensitive analytical techniques, often drawing on work by ethnographers of recent or living communities to suggest models of social structure. Where documentary evidence relating to a past society has been preserved, further progress is possible, because greater certainty is introduced into concepts of its structure and external relations. Yet documentary evidence cannot be used in isolation to provide an adequate historical account of even the most literate of ancient communities. Historical documents may, for instance, provide invaluable evidence of the organization of an industry and of the social status and activities of some of those engaged in it, but only archaeological evidence can demonstrate the scale of production and geographical distribution of the product. Such combined evidence makes possible a deeper understanding of the relationships involved; it is in this area that some of the most important and fruitful work remains to be done.

7. Recent advances and current trends

Archaeology used simply to be a technique for recovering material from the past. Excavation took place and finds were made that were fitted together to form some coherent narrative picture – archaeologists 'pieced together the past', in Gordon Childe's memorable phrase. Today there are good grounds for believing that archaeology is on the road to becoming something more than this, a source of new ideas about the nature of man, his origins and the evolution of his culture, of insights into the great transformations – from hunting and gathering to food production, from simple, fragmentary society to complex state – that we are coming to recognize as the decisive steps in the human story.

Until two decades ago the thrust of much archaeological work was 'artifact-oriented', concerned simply with the efficient recovery of data. Archaeology today is, or should be, 'problem-oriented' – concerned with ideas, with hypotheses, with theory and, of course, with their relation to the available data. Seen in this perspective, the most important recent advances and the most exciting current trends are those that aid significantly this process of theory building and link theoretical work with empirical observation. Indeed, the ultimate goal is some general theory offering insight into the major transformations wherever they occur, so that from the general model predictions can be made that successfully explain many of the significant features of individual and specific cases. A necessary preliminary here is a clearer understanding of the way the archaeological record is formed, and a concern with formation processes, with the detailed explanation of artifact variability, marks some of the most interesting recent work.[1] But the task is not a straightforward one, and in practice it is often easier to speculate, to produce general theories at a rather high level of abstraction, than to apply such theories in the field or to show just how they may be investigated and tested. Between the abstract model and the 'working face' of archaeological field practice must come a coherent body of what Lewis Binford terms 'middle-range theory' – a theory that allows the construction of a bridge between the available (and, in this sense, contemporary) data that are gleaned from the archaeological record and whatever more general theories and models we may have at our disposal to express our understanding of the dynamics of past culture systems.[2] In many areas this bridge remains to be constructed: there is no ready-made way of doing this, and until the task is accomplished, many of the more theoretical pronouncements of the 'new archaeology' will continue to appear somewhat abstruse and their operational application elusive.

Research techniques

Real advances are being made, however, and at the practical level. For any significant advance in the efficiency of data gathering or in the quality of the data is of importance. In the field of dating (see Chapter 62) the continuing refinement of radiocarbon determination is enhancing the method that, more than any other, has made the construction of a 'world prehistory' an attainable goal. Indeed, in 1961 Grahame Clark was able to publish the first edition of *World Prehistory – An Outline*, which summarized the huge body of information suggested by the title, relying heavily on radiometric datings.[3] The statistical basis for the tree-ring calibration of radiocarbon dates has been set on a sure theoretical footing and, within the limits of its accuracy, the method harmonizes well with other dating procedures. Moreover, the use of a new technique for determining the amount of active carbon in ancient samples promises radiocarbon dates from exceedingly small samples – perhaps no larger than a carbonized cereal grain – and will probably permit the time-range for radiocarbon dates to be extended beyond the present effective limit of about 30 000 years and thus provide a chronology for the Middle as well as the Upper Palaeolithic periods, although the potassium/argon method will remain crucial for the Lower Palaeolithic (see Chapter 62).

The other analytical technique whose usefulness has been clearly demonstrated in recent years, producing accurate data in quantity on a routine basis, is trace element analysis employing the principle of neutron activation. Here the goal is characterization: the determination of features in a material, usually on the basis of trace elements, that allow its source to be identified and hence permit the documentation of trading patterns. This method has now effectively displaced optical emission spectroscopy, which was formerly in widespread use. Among many applications, those to obsidian, pottery and jade have been informative,[4] although for many stone artifacts, as for pottery,[5] traditional petrological methods remain more effective. Neutron activation analysis has established itself, alongside radiocarbon dating, as one of the really useful laboratory techniques in archaeology.

Progress in the environmental sciences has been particularly vigorous (see Chapter 5), and here it is the renewed attention paid to recovery techniques (flotation and sieving), as well as a more careful consideration of formation processes, that is proving rewarding. The same holds, in a sense, for the most significant recent development in field archaeology, the consistent and deliberate application of sampling procedures. Here, perhaps for the first time, the methods of quantitative archaeology are seen to yield immediate results in excavation and survey projects, in terms both of money saved and of an increase in the output of information.[6] The most important rewards have come from field survey. It is now being widely acknowledged that an intensive survey, by field walking, of a limited but carefully selected area of the terrain, carried out using a probabilistic sampling strategy, can yield results of greater utility than those supplied by a more extensive exercise. The impact upon project design – that is to say, the definition of the goals of the excavation, along with the problems to be investigated (or hypotheses to be tested), followed by a thorough consideration of the relevant methods – in rescue or salvage archaeology operations, as well as those conducted without such practical constraints, is considerable (see Chapter 3).

Field projects

Perhaps the greatest current problem in applied archaeology is that of relevance, of problem orientation in the field. For with increasing awareness of the significance of the archaeological record, and of the threats to it posed by urban and rural development, has come far greater public support for field archaeology. In Britain and in the United States more money is available to archaeology for rescue or salvage projects than is contributed by all other sources put together.

The reason for digging in such cases is clear: the sites are to be destroyed in the course of development, and as much information as possible must be recovered before it is too late. Sampling must be employed to help answer specific questions. But what questions are we to ask? Can we foresee now what information an archaeologist fifty years hence would like to retrieve from the site? In fact we cannot, and the central paradox of much rescue archaeology is that often no one is quite sure *why* he is digging, other than because the site is there (and will not be there much longer).

The most effective response has often been to begin with a real problem, and then to tackle it by choosing sites that, being threatened, are suitable for rescue archaeology. It is in this way that urban archaeology has developed in Europe, undoubtedly the most significant development there in field archaeology over the past thirty years. So it is that in Britain bodies such as the Winchester Research Unit, the York Archaeological Trust, the Norwich Survey and the Southampton Archaeological Research Committee have carried out excavations, and have then begun to develop models of urban development, that together with a few Continental counterparts have completely transformed the face of medieval archaeology. In continental Europe work conducted on some of the early Slav towns, such as Novgorod (USSR) and Mikulčice (Czechoslovakia), has been outstanding, as has research on the early trading towns of northern Europe, such as Dorestad (Holland), Hedeby (Denmark), Birka (Sweden) and Kaupang (Norway). Many of these, and a few more, such as the excavations at the Iron Age hillfort at Danebury in Hampshire, have succeeded in using the rescue opportunity in Britain as a means of tackling a larger problem, in the grand manner originally developed by some post-war archaeological expeditions, which had no concern with the rescue of threatened sites.

Professor Robert Braidwood's expedition to Iraqi Kurdistan was one of the earliest of these:[7] with its integrated use of environmental collaboration to focus on the early plant and animal domesticates, it was one of the first such projects to tackle a problem rather than simply a site. The same is true of its leading successor in the Near East, led by Professor Frank Hole, which is concerned with agricultural origins in the Deh Luran plain;[8] of the great projects organized by Richard MacNeish in the Tehuacán Valley of Mexico and the Ayacucho area of highland Peru;[9] and of Kent Flannery's project in Oaxaca, Mexico,[10] which has stimulated much interesting new work. Whether in a rescue context or not, it is the nature of the problem and the clarity of the theoretical response that principally govern the quality of the resultant work.

Developments in theory

General theory, however, remains the ultimate goal. And since mathematics has been the chief source of powerful theoretical formulations in other sciences, it is perhaps to mathematical models that the archaeologist should look first. One of the first of these, the Wave of Advance Model for the spread of farming in Europe,[11] encapsulates, like most good models, many specific implications within a very simple formulation. Population growth and small-scale migratory activity are seen here as instigating the spread of farming. The model specifies the set of quantitative relationships that are considered to hold among the variables (rate of growth, variance of migratory activity and velocity of spread), thus establishing a predictive framework that can be used for evaluating the adequacy of the model. System dynamics modelling, using computer simulation to follow the development of a culture system, built up on analogy with Jay Forrester's 'urban dynamics',[12] may soon prove effective. It has already been used to model both the pig cycle among the Maring of New Guinea and the collapse of the Classic Maya civilization.[13]

Other approaches are available for the consideration of the behaviour of whole systems and their transformations. Neo-Marxist archaeologists are now working constructively on this,[14] and the recently developed mathematics of catastrophe theory may yet offer some fruitful insights.[15] But perhaps there is a risk of trying to run before we can walk. Complex systems such as these are always culture systems, involving human beings and human interactions. The fact is not in itself any bar to modelling or to the use of mathematical methods, but it does require that we investigate such systems in order to learn what is special about their behaviour precisely because they are culture systems. We need to know more about modes of exchange in human societies[16] and the way different exchange systems mesh with the social system as a whole — about what the Marxist anthropologists term the 'relations of production'. A clearer insight is needed into prestige and ranking in human societies[17] and into the manner in which patterns of information flow determine their behaviour.[18]

All these questions are currently under active investigation, and already it has been possible to make stimulating attempts at generalizing about such issues as the origins of complex societies and of the state.[19] But so far all these have been preliminary attempts, often based as much on armchair theorizing (which does not deny their validity) as on empirical observation. Between the two must come the middle-range theory and a good deal of further work on how to relate the actual results of excavation and research in the field with such theoretical constructs.

This great enterprise is little more than a decade old and already good progress is being made. The next decade promises to be as exciting as the last.

PART TWO

II: Man the hunter

The problem of human origins involves an evolutionary time-scale that is much longer than was once thought. The divergence of human stock from that of the nearest living apes took place more than ten million years ago, and the emergence of man parallels that of other modern species of mammals. The most rapid developments took place during the Ice Age, one of the rare periods of unstable climate that have punctuated the history of the Earth. Beginning in Africa, early human populations colonized the whole of the globe except Antarctica before the beginning of agriculture. Small bands of hunters and collectors became adapted to a wide range of environments, including some of the harshest, through the elaboration of a material culture that included the use of fire, clothing and shelters. Important changes, leading to the emergence of fully modern populations, took place within the last 50 000 years. These included fundamental developments in social organization, subsistence and technology, which have provided the first evidence of both trade and artistic activity. By the beginning of the Postglacial period relatively dense, regionally differentiated populations of hunters and collectors were to be found throughout the world, with the exception of the Arctic and Oceania.

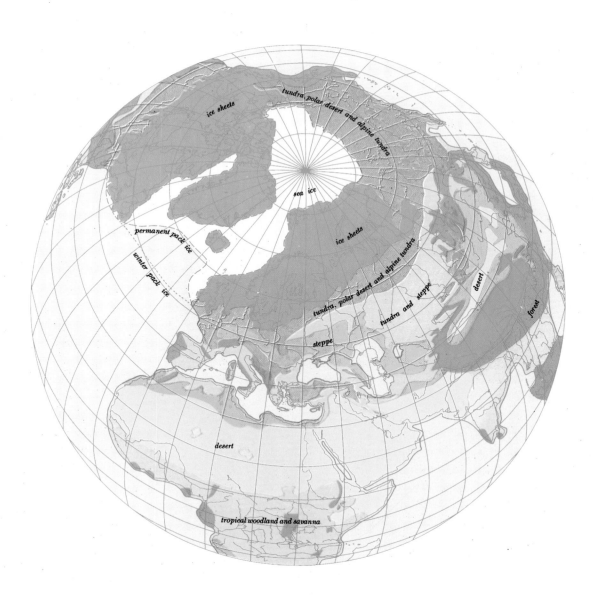

8. Ice Age environments

The later part of the Cenozoic Era – the age of mammals – was a period of rapidly changing and often cold climate, which culminated in the Late Cenozoic Ice Age.[1] These changes reached their peak in the most recent period of Earth history, the Quaternary, spanning the last 1.7 million years. Although brief by geological standards, it saw unusually rapid and large-scale changes, including major advances of the ice caps (up to 3000 kilometres beyond their present limits), with consequent adjustment of vegetational zones and changes in sea level.

The first signs of global cooling, after a long period of warm and equable climate, occurred about 38 million years ago in the Oligocene, when a belt of pack ice first became established around Antarctica. This was followed by a precipitous temperature decline between 14 and 11 million years ago, in the Middle Miocene, during which an extensive ice cap accumulated in the Antarctic; about 3.2 million years ago large ice sheets also built up on the northern continents.[2] The volume of water locked up in the ice during these early advances was sufficient to cause a drop in sea level of about 40 metres. The scale of glaciation increased about 2.5 million years ago, when the Earth entered its present phase of continually fluctuating climate.

During this last two and a half million years climates as warm as or warmer than the present one have been rare. Such episodes, known as interglacials, have lasted on average only 10 000 years each.[3] The glacial phases have not themselves been uniformly cold but have been punctuated by short phases known as interstadials, which, although somewhat milder, did not reach present-day temperatures. In fact, the temperature curve shows constant fluctuations, which caused shifts of varying magnitude in climatic and vegetational patterns.

The beginning of the Quaternary can now be seen as an arbitrary point within the phase of cold, fluctuating climate that produced extensive glaciation in the northern hemisphere. By international agreement it is defined in a section of marine deposits in Calabria in southern Italy, where it has been dated indirectly by the palaeomagnetic method (see Chapter 62). The use of this technique, especially on deep cores of sediment from the ocean bed, has revolutionized our view of the Quaternary period. It is now conventionally divided into a long Early Quaternary phase, lasting about a million years, a Middle Quaternary, lasting just over half a million years, and a Late Quaternary that includes the last glaciation and adjacent warm episodes and began 127 000 years ago.[4] The latest warm interval, which began 10 000 years ago and is still continuing, is conventionally referred to as the Holocene, by contrast with the preceding part of the Quaternary, which is called the Pleistocene. This distinction, emphasizing the uniqueness of the last 10 000 years, is more important in terms of cultural development than of climatic patterns, in which the present warmer, 'postglacial' episode is only one of many. To the archaeo-logist, however, the Pleistocene represents the significant phase of cultural development within the larger framework of the Quaternary, and is used in this sense in subsequent chapters. Various divisions of the Pleistocene have been proposed; those adopted here correspond to the Early, Middle and Late divisions of the Quaternary.

Recent discoveries

Our present understanding of Quaternary climates is based first and foremost on the study of deep-sea sediments. Continuous cores taken from the ocean bed have provided samples for chemical and palaeontological analysis. Pioneering work on the ratio of the two isotopes of oxygen ^{18}O and ^{16}O in tiny marine fossils has provided a means of reconstructing the sequence of climatic fluctuations in fine detail in many parts of the world.[5] The organisms used are planktonic foraminifera – microscopic animals that live close to the ocean surface. The composition of their limy shells reflects that of the sea water around them and their remains therefore provide a record of the $^{16}O/^{18}O$ ratio in surface ocean waters. Although it is also influenced by sea-surface temperature and salinity, this ratio chiefly reflects the total volume of water locked up in glacier ice. A time-scale for the entire Quaternary is provided by palaeomagnetic dating of the cores.

The pattern of oxygen-isotope variations has been confirmed by analyses of the changing abundances of foraminifera and other groups of marine microfossils, such as coccoliths and radiolaria, that are preserved in the sediments. More recently, scientists belonging to the largely American-based CLIMAP group (CLIMAP stands for Climate, Long-range Investigation, Mapping and Prediction) have developed statistical techniques for converting the percentage frequencies of different species into numerical estimates of sea-surface temperatures and salinity.[6] This method is based on the assumption that relationships between the abundance of each species and oceanic conditions in the past are similar to those of today. It can only be used in studies relating to the last few hundred thousand years, however, because of the slow rate of evolutionary change in the ecology of the organisms involved.

The climatic picture emerging from deep-sea core studies is highly complex. During the Early Quaternary, glacial–interglacial fluctuations were still relatively small. Their scale increased considerably after 0.8 million years ago. Since then, glacial maxima have tended to recur every 100 000 years on average, with smaller, superimposed oscillations on time-scales of roughly 20 000 and 40 000 years. There is a close correspondence between these three periodicities and the perturbations in the Earth's orbit around the Sun – the so-called Milankovitch variations – that affect the seasonal and latitudinal distribution of solar radiation received by the Earth. This has led many scientists to believe that glaciation and deglaciation are triggered by these long-term astronomical changes. However, many other internal factors, such as fluctuations in the amount of volcanic dust in the atmosphere, and interactions between the oceanic and atmospheric circulations, may also have played a part.[7]

Research into the history of the continents during the Quaternary period is less advanced, largely because the sedimentary record on land is generally patchy, discontinuous and difficult to date by radiometric (absolute) methods.[8] The classic sequence of four glacials (Günz, Mindel, Riss and Würm) and four interglacials, which was originally derived from the Alps and subsequently applied to areas as far afield as North America and China, has been shown to be seriously incomplete, and therefore misleading, and should accordingly be abandoned for general use. Unfortunately, it has not yet been replaced by a more realistic and up-to-date model. The current view is that correlations should be based on the longest and most continuous sedimentary sequences, of which there are two main kinds. First, there are deposits of the wind-blown dust known as loess, which blankets large areas, for instance in China and central Europe. The loess was laid down under cold and windy steppe conditions during the glacials and was later stabilized by interglacial soil formation under grassland or temperate forest. These deposits can be dated palaeomagnetically. The loess sequence confirms the complexity of the oxygen-isotope record, suggesting that there have been at least seventeen major glacial–interglacial cycles since the brief magnetic reversal about 1.7 million years ago known as the Olduvai event.

The second type of evidence comes from long cores taken from lakes or peat bogs. Analysis of fossil pollen grains and other plant remains preserved in these sediments provides a detailed picture of changing vegetation conditions. The celebrated pollen sequence from Lake Philippi (Tenaghi Philippon) in Macedonia is shown in Figure 8.1. This extends back approximately 600 000 years, and it can be readily correlated with ocean-core curves.[9]

A much wider range of techniques has been used to investigate the last 127 000 years, which constitute the Late Quaternary. Modern dating methods, which permit a precise time-scale to be established, are of crucial importance; radiocarbon dating, in particular, has revolutionized the study of environmental changes during the last 40 000 years. Continuous or near-continuous sequences of glacial, marine, windborne and lake deposits spanning this period are now available from many parts of the world.[10] Methods involving the measurement of different isotopes are being widely applied to derive long climatic records from ice cores, cave deposits like stalagmites (speleothems) and tree rings. It is likely that future research will concentrate increasingly on the techniques that are capable of yielding quantitative estimates of climatic variables such as temperature or precipitation.

Climatic oscillations of the Middle and Late Quaternary

During the last 700 000 years (the present phase of magnetic polarity), known as the Brunhes epoch, there have been eight glacial–interglacial cycles.[11] Many climatic curves for this interval show a characteristic 'saw-tooth' pattern, suggesting that the build-up of ice sheets took place in a relatively slow and fluctuating fashion – in contrast to deglaciation, which was sudden and spectacular. The phases of rapid ice retreat have been called 'terminations'. Each corresponded to a major rise in sea level, causing a 'marine transgression' in low-lying coastal areas. Lesser rises in sea level also occurred during the minor interstadial warm episodes, when the ice sheets partially melted. At their maximum the glaciers covered nearly a third of the entire land area of the globe. During interglacials their extent was similar to that of today, so the corresponding marine shorelines would have been within 5 to 10 metres of present sea level on stable coasts.

Beyond the limits of the ice sheets the abrupt changes in climate caused profound alterations in the distribution of vegetation and available surface water. In mid-latitudes interglacial phases were characterized by the expansion of boreal (northern) and temperate forests into areas previously covered by steppe, tundra and ice. This is clearly seen at the Tenaghi Philippon site, where moist interglacial oak forest gave way during the glacials to almost treeless steppes similar to those now found in central Asia. Less is known about events in low latitudes, though fluctuations in the content of wind-blown desert dust in deep-sea cores from the equatorial Atlantic suggest that recurrent, widespread desiccation of the southern margins of the Sahara coincided with glacial episodes.

The Late Quaternary began with a major marine transgression about 127 000 years ago (Termination II), at the start of an interglacial known in Europe as the Eemian. This lasted a mere 10 000 years. During this brief span global climate became 1°C to 3°C warmer than it is today. The area of perennially frozen ground (permafrost) in northern Eurasia shrank a long way behind its present limits, and the sea rose about 6 metres above its present level, suggesting that the ice on Antarctica and Greenland was less extensive than at present. Temperate forest expanded across Eurasia and North America, leading to the dominance of mixed-oak forest in north-east France and Macedonia. Pollen evidence from Queensland, Australia, indicates the existence of rainforest under high-rainfall conditions similar to those of the Holocene, and the scanty data from other parts of the tropics imply that many areas received amounts of precipitation equal to, or greater than,[9] those of the present day.

As the Eemian drew to a close the North American (Laurentide) ice sheet began to accumulate once more in its gathering grounds on the plateaux of Baffin Island and mainland Canada. By 115 000 years ago sea level had already fallen an estimated 70 metres. There was a correspondingly sharp deterioration in continental climate, which gave rise to open, grassy or shrubby vegetation in western Europe, and further east a continental steppe environment in which loess accumulated. The cooling trend was interrupted by two brief warm episodes centred on 105 000 and 82 000 years ago, which were first discovered through uranium–thorium dating of coral terraces in Barbados and New Guinea. These two mild interstadials permitted the partial recovery of the Eurasian forests.[12]

From 75 000 BP onwards glacial conditions generally prevailed, despite the occurrence of several cool interstadials. The Laurentide and Scandinavian ice sheets had already grown to substantial size, although they did not attain their greatest extent until 18 000 BP. This glaciation is known as the Weichsel or Würm in Europe and the Wisconsin in North America. The build-up of ice resulted in a sea-level drop of at least 130 metres, which exposed large areas of the continental shelves, especially in Australasia and eastern Asia. The Bering Strait between Alaska and Siberia became dry land, and Australia was linked to New Guinea by the emergence of the Torres Strait.

The glacial world: climate and vegetation patterns at 18 000 BP

At the last glacial maximum, large areas of the northern continents were effectively sterilized by ice or by extreme cold. The Laurentide ice sheet extended to 39°N, and the Scandinavian ice sheet to 52°N, while snowlines in most mountain areas were lowered by more than 1000 metres. Barren polar deserts occupied the unglaciated northern fringes of Siberia and Alaska on both sides of the Bering Strait.

Glacial climates, even in the habitable parts of the world, were generally harsh, dry and windy. Mean annual temperatures fell by 3°–8°C in the tropics and by as much as 16°C near the margins of the ice, resulting in a southward expansion of the limits of permafrost in Eurasia and Alaska. The increasingly widespread evidence of dry conditions, especially between the tropics, took many scientists by surprise, as glacials were traditionally believed to correspond to wetter conditions in low latitudes. It now appears that lower sea levels and cooler ocean temperatures combined to cause

8.1: *The repetitive nature of climatic fluctuations during the Middle and Late Quaternary is revealed by a deep-sea core from 54°N and by a long peat core from Macedonia. Variations in the abundances of planktonic foraminifera (curve A) reflect changes in North Atlantic sea-surface temperatures, and high frequencies of polar species indicate glacial conditions. Curve B shows the oscillations between interglacial oak forest and glacial steppe (high non-tree pollen) in Macedonia.*

- ■ warmwater species
- ▨ subpolar species
- ☐ polar species
- ☐ oak pollen
- ▨ pollen of other trees
- ▨ non-tree pollen

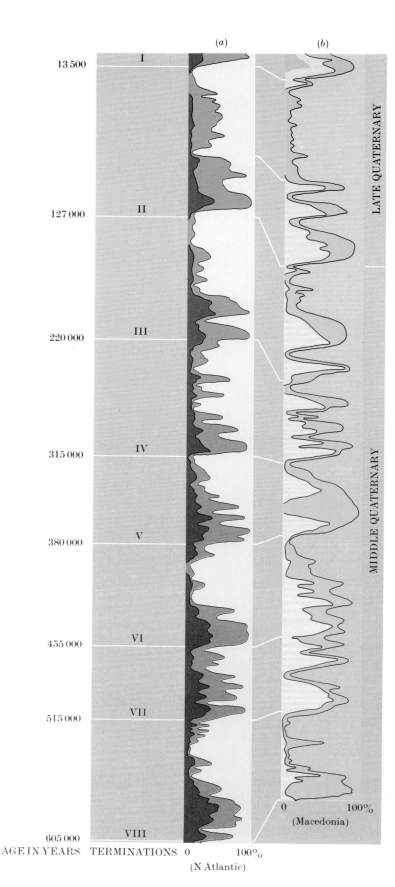

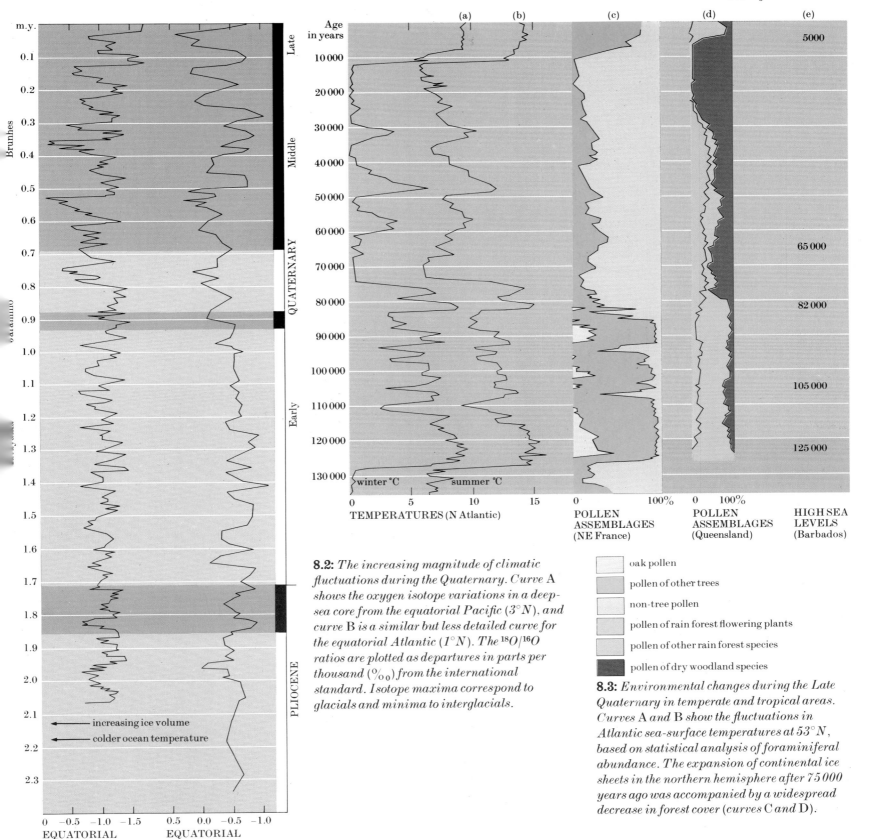

8.2: *The increasing magnitude of climatic fluctuations during the Quaternary. Curve A shows the oxygen isotope variations in a deepsea core from the equatorial Pacific (3°N), and curve B is a similar but less detailed curve for the equatorial Atlantic (1°N). The $^{18}O/^{16}O$ ratios are plotted as departures in parts per thousand (‰) from the international standard. Isotope maxima correspond to glacials and minima to interglacials.*

oak pollen

pollen of other trees

non-tree pollen

pollen of rain forest flowering plants

pollen of other rain forest species

pollen of dry woodland species

8.3: *Environmental changes during the Late Quaternary in temperate and tropical areas. Curves A and B show the fluctuations in Atlantic sea-surface temperatures at 53°N, based on statistical analysis of foraminiferal abundance. The expansion of continental ice sheets in the northern hemisphere after 75 000 years ago was accompanied by a widespread decrease in forest cover (curves C and D).*

an overall reduction in atmospheric moisture transport and precipitation.

South of the Scandinavian ice sheet, treeless tundra vegetation became established in maritime north-west Europe, merging into a great belt of cold continental steppe that stretched eastwards from Belgium into China and southwards from Siberia to the Mediterranean and Afghanistan. Forest trees appear to have survived in restricted refuges such as western Spain and Portugal. For reasons that are still not clearly understood, only a narrow strip of tundra developed between the much larger Laurentide ice sheet and a broad zone of coniferous forest to the south.

About half the land surface between 30°N and 30°S was occupied by deserts.[13] Savanna and open woodland encroached into the area at present occupied by equatorial lowland forest in Africa, south-east Asia and South America.[14] Along tropical coasts lowered sea levels and colder ocean temperatures probably resulted in a contraction in the distribution of coral reefs and mangrove swamps. In contrast to this generally bleak picture, certain mid-latitude deserts became more habitable at this time, as a result of adjustments in the atmospheric circulation because of glaciation. Notable examples are the American Southwest, southern Africa and the northern fringes of the Sahara. The lakes, springs and permanent streams that developed in these areas were often fed by melted snow running off adjacent high mountains; in addition, a general improvement in moisture conditions is indicated by the invasion of scrub and woodland.

Changing ecological opportunities during the Holocene

Following the last glacial maximum at 18 000 BP, severe climatic conditions persisted for another 4000 to 8000 years. A number of standstills and minor readvances of the ice occurred during this interval. The onset of postglacial warming in individual regions was determined by their proximity to the large, stagnating ice masses bordering the north Atlantic and by the breakdown of glacial circulation patterns in the atmosphere and the oceans.[15] This asynchronism is illustrated by events in the Atlantic and Indian Oceans. Radiocarbon estimates indicate that the Indian Ocean warmed up about 10 000 BP, whereas the north-east Atlantic, which initially became free of pack ice about 13 500 BP, experienced renewed cooling between 11 500 and 10 200 BP, when glaciers readvanced in eastern Greenland, Scandinavia and Britain. This short-lived but dramatic cold phase was brought to an end by a decisive warming shortly before 9300 BP.

By 13 000 BP sea level was rising fast. The Bering land bridge had been severed by about 10 000 BP, though levels close to those of the present were not attained until about 6000 years ago, when the last remnants of the Laurentide ice sheet disappeared. The sea penetrated particularly rapidly into recently deglaciated areas such as the Baltic and Hudson Bay, where the Earth's crust was still depressed by the former load of ice. There is considerable disagreement about the history of minor sea-level fluctuations since 6000 years ago; many geophysicists believe that it is not

possible to obtain a sea-level curve with worldwide validity for this period because of the elastic properties of the Earth's crust.

It appears that our present interglacial reached its peak several thousand years ago. The exact timing of the maximum varied from area to area, but temperatures generally rose about 1°–2°C above those of the present day. In eastern North America deciduous forest reached its northernmost limit about 7000 years ago; the pattern of change in western Europe is less easy to determine because of interference by men of the Mesolithic and Neolithic periods (see Chapter 15), but it is widely believed that temperate forest reached its fullest extent about 8000 to 5000 years ago, when almost the whole of the British Isles was covered by forest or woodland apart from the highest mountaintops and the outermost Scottish islands.

In lower latitudes fluctuations in precipitation were more important than fluctuations in temperature. It has been suggested that wild cereals and legumes migrated into the Near East about 11 000 BP, as the re-establishment of a Mediterranean pattern of rainfall brought about the rapid replacement of steppe by mixed-oak forest. Many areas between the tropics experienced phases of accentuated wetness between 12 500 and 5000 years ago, resulting in an expansion of the equatorial forest beyond its present limits and the conversion of the Saharan and Indo-Arabian deserts into a landscape of thorn scrub or grassland, dotted with lakes and marshes.[16] At the same time, desiccation set in in the American Southwest. As the large Late Pleistocene lakes in the Great Basin dried up one by one, competition for scarce ecological resources, combined with increasing hunting pressure, led to the extermination of many species of large mammals, including the elephant, the camel and the giant sloth.

The later Holocene has seen a partial reversal of the climatic trends that characterized the earlier Postglacial. Mountain glaciers and snowfields have increased in extent in many parts of the world, although it is difficult to discern a coherent pattern of readvance. Probably the most important change has been the widespread but intermittent desiccation of the present tropical deserts since 5000 years ago. In the rest of the world, and particularly in temperate and humid tropical areas, the increasing influence of man on the vegetation has become more significant than the natural processes of change.

9. Man and the primates

During the last seventy-five million years – the Cenozoic Era of geological time – mammals have dominated the animal kingdom. Evolving and diversifying from small, primitive forms, they have adapted to different habitats and different ways of life. Some (the ancestors of animals like the hedgehog of today) underwent a rather limited evolutionary development; others colonized new habitats, which involved much more pronounced adaptations – bats took to the air, for example, whales to the sea and primates to the trees. Some mammals became specialized herbivores, others their predators; each developed complementary specializations, becoming increasingly well adapted for flight and pursuit respectively. Among others, the primates were particularly flexible, and some families were able to put their tree-living skills to use in a wider range of habitats. These were man's ancestors, and he shares with other primates a common line of descent.

The primates are divided into two sub-orders: the Prosimii (prosimians), which include animals such as the tarsier and the loris, and the Anthropoidea (anthropoids) – monkeys, apes and man. The prosimians are the little-changed descendants of the ancestral primates that lived between forty and sixty million years ago; the anthropoids represent a more sophisticated development, in evolutionary terms – they are larger-brained and more intelligent. The comparison of living examples of these two sub-orders permits some conclusions to be drawn about the relationship between them, and it clarifies the distinction between primitive characteristics and later specializations.[1]

One group of anthropoids, the New World monkeys of the family Cebidae, retain certain primitive features, such as long fore- and hindlimbs. The proportions of the forelimb are also characteristic: the radius and the ulna, the bones of the lower part of the limb, are slightly longer than the humerus bone of the upper part. The hands and feet of these monkeys are adapted for grasping, for manipulating objects and for hanging or climbing while they move through trees. Their teeth are adapted for a vegetarian or fruit-based diet, with rounded cusps in a simple 4- or 5-cusped pattern. These features certainly indicate specialization, but by comparison with the other higher primates (of which man is one), the New World monkeys are primitive, in that they resemble more closely than the others the original common ancestor of the anthropoids. Although both man and the apes share many of their characteristics, there are significant differences between the specialized features that each acquired later.

Besides the New World monkeys, the anthropoids include the Old World monkeys (Cercopithecoidea) and the group that comprises man and the apes (Hominoidea: hominoids). Certain features of the dentition of Old World monkeys – such as molars with paired transverse ridges – are highly specialized and distinguish this family from the hominoids, which retain primitive tooth patterns as well as many other ancestral characteristics.

One group of the hominoids, however, has developed a form of locomotion that involves swinging through trees by the arms (brachiation). This group is the Hylobatidae (hylobatids: gibbons), which contains the siamangs and the gibbons. Brachiation was once thought to be typical of all apes and even of early man, but it is now known to be restricted to hylobatids, in which the forelimb, especially the forearm, has become greatly elongated and highly mobile, which enables them to brachiate with agility and speed. The other hominoids, man and the apes, are all able to swing by their arms as the result of at least one shared characteristic, the mobile forelimb, but as this is probably a primitive anthropoid characteristic, it should not be assumed that the larger apes and man are in any sense 'failed brachiators', as has been claimed.

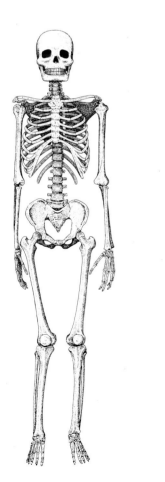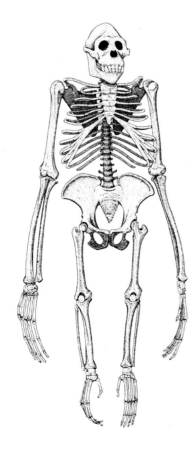

9.1: *Skeleton of man* (left) *and gorilla* (right), *showing the longer arms and shorter legs of the gorilla and its more heavily buttressed skull. In man the face is also smaller relative to the brain case.*

Man and the great apes

The great apes include two species in Africa, the chimpanzee and gorilla, and the orang-utan in Asia. They were formerly grouped (as Pongidae) in a separate family from man, but it is becoming clear that man, chimpanzee and gorilla had a common ancestor not shared by the orang-utan.[2]

Many apparent anatomical similarities between the great apes can be shown to be simply a consequence of their large size: for example, the long forelimbs, elongated hands and broad chest, and the shape and position of the shoulder blade, are all modifications of shape that are the product of increasing size and conform to a predictable pattern known as the allometric gradient. One significant way in which man differs from the great apes, however, is in his extra length of leg. For his size man has legs that are longer than would be accounted for by any allometric constant shared with other primates, and this feature must be related to his two-legged (bipedal) gait, which is very different from that of the four-footed (quadrupedal) apes. A number of other anatomical features are associated with bipedality in man: the structure of the hip and knee joints has completely changed; the vertebral column

has developed its S-shaped curvature to absorb the stresses set up through the movement of the legs during locomotion; the foot has reduced toes; the big toe is in line with the rest of the foot rather than being divergent as it is in the apes; and a transverse arch has developed on the foot in addition to the longitudinal arch present in apes. Fossil remains of early man going back at least three million years testify to the development of bipedality.[3]

Another difference between man and apes, perhaps even more significant, is brain size. In man the brain is at least three times the size of that of any non-human primates. The relative sizes of the different parts of the brain have also changed – the frontal lobes and cerebral hemispheres have expanded considerably. This accords with a general trend of increasing brain size apparent in all primates (the monkeys have larger brains than the prosimians, the apes larger brains than the monkeys and man a larger brain than the apes), but during the evolution of man brain size has increased in relation to increased body size even more than would be expected from the allometric constant present in the apes, for example, and the increase is much more dramatic than in any other primate.

The third major difference between man and apes concerns the teeth and jaws. (This is particularly important when fossil evidence is examined because these are the body parts most frequently preserved.) Many of the teeth, particularly the molars and incisors, are very similar in man and the apes, but the canines and premolars

9.2: *Simplified phylogeny of the Anthropoidea, showing the probable relationships between the living and fossil species.*

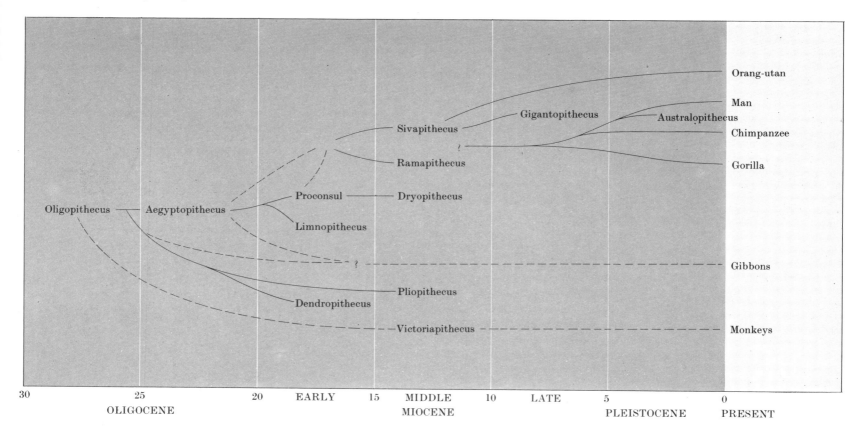

9.4: *Comparison of the lower jaw of the latest known* Ramapithecus, *dated to about 9 million years ago, and one of the earliest known species of* Australopithecus, *which is about 3 million years old. The* Ramapithecus *jaw is from Pakistan, while the* Australopithecus *comes from the territory of the Afar in Ethiopia.*

9.3: *Generalized vegetation maps of Africa, contrasting the present-day distribution of vegetation with that probably occurring during the early Miocene period. The early apes lived in the midst of the forest belt, which was formerly more widespread in East Africa than it is now.*

- desert
- macchia
- dry woodland and bushland
- moist woodland
- lowland forest
- montane forest

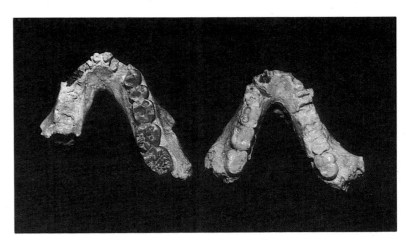

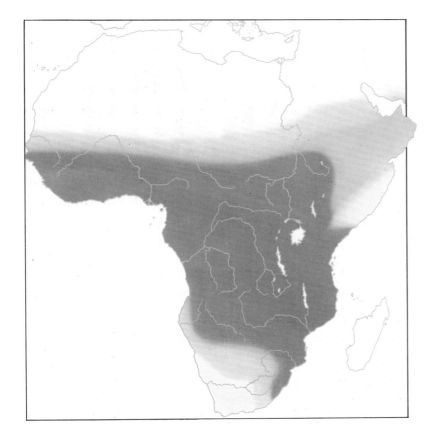

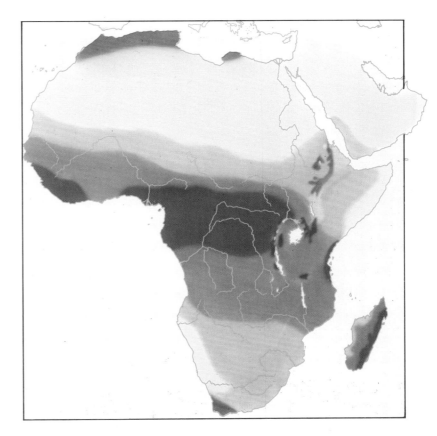

are different. Partly as a result of these differences, the apes have long straight tooth-rows, prominent canines and incisors, separated from the molars by a gap (diastema), and projecting jaws and snouts; in man, on the other hand, the reduction in the size of the front teeth has produced a much shorter and more rounded dental arcade, resulting in a flatter face. The canine teeth in apes are long and projecting, characteristics that reflect the shape of their primitive prototypes; the human canine is smaller and its function has changed – it is no longer a penetrating tooth but has assumed the role of an incisor. In the apes the front lower premolar, known as the P_3, closes up (occludes) against the projecting canine, while in man it has a second cusp that enables it to act as a grinding tooth.

When these changes are related to the expansion of man's brain case it will be seen that the face has become small in relation to the rest of the skull: it fits below the expanded frontal lobes of the brain rather than projecting in front, and the cheek (zygomatic) region expands sideways rather than forwards. This gives a mechanical advantage to the chewing muscles, which in man act in line with the molars rather than behind them, so that they are able to grind food more effectively. As a consequence the enamel on the teeth has become much thicker, the crown of individual cusps has been reduced and parts of the lower and upper jaws have become thicker and more heavily buttressed.[4]

The origin of man

The emergence of the hominoids was set against a background of continental change that has been clarified by recent work on plate tectonics. The geography of Africa and Eurasia has changed radically: in the early Cenozoic the continents of Africa and South America were separated from the northern landmass of Asia and North America. The last two formed a single entity at the begin-

9.5: *Reconstruction of the probable habitat of* Ramapithecus. *This may have been a mixture of woodland with open areas, and* Ramapithecus *probably used both the ground and the trees for feeding and shelter.*

ning of the Cenozoic, but were parted shortly afterwards. About sixteen million years ago, during the Miocene period, Africa and Arabia collided with the northern landmass, obliterating the intervening Tethys Sea and thrusting up the mountain chains from the Alps to the Himalayas, which enabled exchanges of fauna between previously separate realms to take place.

The anthropoid primates can be traced back to the Oligocene period (that is, over thirty million years ago), before the continental collision. The early ape-like primates, such as *Oligopithecus* and *Aegyptopithecus*, have been found in Africa. They appear to have had mainly primitive characteristics and fit well with the ancestral type suggested for the Old World monkeys and apes. The first hominoid, however, is not known definitely until the end of the Oligocene and the beginning of the succeeding period, the Miocene. At this time, between twenty-two and eighteen million years ago, there began a rapid evolutionary diversification of the apes, known collectively as the Dryopithecinae. At least six species of the genera *Proconsul* and *Limnopithecus* have been distinguished, and there was apparently a further group of species, which included the genus *Dendropithecus*. The apes flourished in the early Miocene, and some species survived into the middle Miocene (see Figure 9.2).

The most diverse genus at this time was *Proconsul*. Its species still retained many primitive characteristics of the skull and of dentition, but the presence of newly acquired specializations link them with living apes and with man. These innovations include the change in function of the P_3, which primitively had a honing function, maintaining a sharp edge on the upper canine. This characteristic is present in monkeys and gibbons as well as in the Oligocene anthropoids and *Dendropithecus*, but in *Proconsul*, as in the living great apes, the P_3 had developed a grinding function. A second characteristic is the broadening of the central incisor, primitively narrow and high-crowned and also seen in the groups mentioned above. Thirdly, *Proconsul* developed a frontal sinus in the skull, a feature characteristic of the great apes and man but not known in monkeys, gibbons or Oligocene primates or in *Dendropithecus*. One further specialized characteristic of *Proconsul*, which is shared by all the living hominoids but is not present either in *Dendropithecus* or in any of the other anthropoid primates, is the wrist meniscus, a pad of cartilage that gives increased mobility and stability to the wrist joint.

From this evidence emerges a picture of two groups of hominoids, one with derived characteristics shared with living apes and the other (of uncertain status) typified, in the main, by primitive characteristics. Both these groups are known almost exclusively from East Africa, where they lived in the forest habitats that covered most of this region during the early part of the Miocene. The extended area of forest is inferred from the evidence furnished by fossil flora and fauna; most species of the *Proconsul* and *Dendropithecus* groups are associated with indications of forest conditions. The fact that both retain the primitive tree-living features of the limb bones and also the primitive dental adaptations to a fruit-based diet mentioned earlier is consistent with this evidence.[5]

Following a separate line of inquiry, it can be shown that the palaeogeography of East Africa in the early Miocene also indicated the presence of forest. Today East Africa is a land of very varied habitats, largely because of the formation of the rift valleys, with wet montane forest in highland areas and dry bush and woodland in the rain-shadows of the highlands; at the beginning of the Miocene, however, the rift valleys had only just started to form and had not interrupted the equatorial zoning of the vegetation that is still present today in West Africa. The equatorial trough, a region of low pressure and high rainfall that produces the wet lowland forests of western and central Africa, today ends against the wall of the western Rift Valley highlands, but before the formation of the Rift Valley the equatorial trough would have extended at least to the continental divide that ran through central Kenya in the early Miocene and perhaps right across the continent. The Miocene localities in East Africa are all in the western half of Kenya and Uganda and would have been situated well within the postulated area of high rainfall (and hence of forest) (see Figure 9.3). It can be concluded with reasonable certainty, therefore, that these early Miocene apes were forest dwellers.[6]

For the middle Miocene and on into the beginning of the late Miocene (between fourteen and ten million years ago) there is evidence of an even bigger and more complex radiation of the hominoids. The origins of this radiation are largely unknown, although it is likely that a *Proconsul*-like group was involved. The sudden proliferation of new species at this time is almost certainly related to the expansion of the hominoid primates out of Africa into Asia when the land bridge connecting the two continents was formed. These middle Miocene hominoids were formerly included in the same sub-family as *Proconsul* and *Limnopithecus*, the Dryopithecinae (dryopithecines), but now the greater complexity of the radiation is better reflected by the division of the eleven known species into two groups: the dryopithecines, which include only *Dryopithecus*, and the Ramapithecini (ramapithecines), which are recognized as a fossil tribe of the sub-family Homininae (hominines) and include at least three genera, *Sivapithecus*, *Ramapithecus* and *Gigantopithecus*. The dentition of *Dryopithecus* retains many primitive characteristics, and this hominoid therefore appears rather similar to *Proconsul* in many respects; it is the second group that is of particular interest to the evolution of man.

There are at least nine known species of the three ramapithecine genera. They are all similar to each other and differ from the dryopithecines in respect of the thick enamel layer on their molars and premolars. The upper and lower jaws are also more stoutly built; it appears that the face projects less and that the zygomatic regions are positioned further to the side and are more heavily built (robust). All these characteristics distinguish man from the apes, and their presence in this lineage can be taken as evidence that the ramapithecines are more closely related to man than are the other fossil apes. This can be concluded with all the more confidence because it is clear from comparison with both living and early Miocene apes that these characteristics have all been derived from a primitive pattern that is retained in the apes.

The ramapithecines, in contrast to the early Miocene apes, are distributed almost exclusively in Asia. One species of *Ramapithecus*, *R. wickeri*, is known from East Africa, and some species of *Sivapithecus*, or species closely related to that genus, are known from eastern Europe and Greece, but apart from these the group has a distribution that extends across Asia from Turkey to China. This distinctive distribution pattern is of the greatest importance in establishing the geographical origin of man, and it appears that much of the early hominine radiation took place in Asia.

The habitats occupied by the ramapithecines also contrast with those of early Miocene apes; in at least four localities, in Kenya, Turkey, Hungary and Pakistan, it is possible to interpret the habitat of ramapithecines as a form of more open woodland. Both species of *Ramapithecus* and most of the *Sivapithecus* species are associated with faunas indicating this type of habitat, and at Rudabanya in Hungary there is also an associated flora that confirms the faunal evidence.

There is one supremely important ecological division among all the various tropical habitats – that between forest and non-forest. The vast majority of animal species are confined to one or the other, and only a small number can exist in both. The difference in habitat demonstrated between the forest-living apes on the one hand and the non-forest ramapithecines on the other is therefore of the greatest significance. The adaptation to a new habitat is nearly always accompanied by a change in diet, and in this also the ramapithecines differ from the earlier forest-living apes and resemble the later hominines. The thick enamel on the teeth of the ramapithecine species and their relatively more robust jaws suggest that they may have been omnivorous and better adapted than apes for a coarser and more varied diet. These adaptive changes are similar to those of undoubted hominines of the Pleistocene period, and as the distribution of modern and fossil man over the last three million years has also been a non-forest one, it becomes all the more likely that the ramapithecines are closely related to man.

It is not possible at present to speculate beyond the assumption that the ramapithecines are the group of primates most closely related to man. Although they have been classified in the subfamily Homininae, it cannot be concluded that any one ramapithecine species was ancestral to modern man, for the differences within the group are relatively minor. The most likely candidate, however, is *Ramapithecus punjabicus*. If this species is compared with the most primitive known australopithecine, Lucy, discovered in Ethiopia and dated to about three million years ago, the resemblances are striking (see Figure 9.4). The developments of the Miocene were the beginning of the path to man.

10. Early man

Ramapithecus punjabicus and related forms, which are likely to have been ancestral to man, are known to have existed as early as ten to fourteen million years ago in widely dispersed localities in Europe, the Near East, Asia and Africa. But for a few inconclusive fragments of teeth, the next five million years are a blank. It is not until the early Pliocene, some five million years ago, that further evidence continues the story of man's emergence; and this evidence shifts the focus of discovery to the continent of Africa. Here, for the succeeding three to four million years, there have been literally hundreds of early fossil hominid finds, which have been recovered from the east and the south. These remains, together with the earliest archaeological evidence for culturally patterned behaviour, justify Darwin's contention that Africa was probably the cradle of mankind.

The recent substantial advances in the knowledge of the earlier stages of human evolution are the result of cooperative work between biological anthropologists, archaeologists, geologists and others: the wealth of new hominid fossil finds has led to real progress in the reconstruction of evolutionary relationships, while the discovery of simple stone tool-kits has provided evidence of the early development of human culture. Together these have allowed an integrated view of human evolution from ecological, biological and cultural perspectives. Furthermore, recent advances in isometric dating techniques – notably potassium/argon age determinations, palaeomagnetic stratigraphy and fission-track dating (see Chapter 62) – provide the means by which environmental change as well as biological and cultural development may be assessed.

10.1: *The major geographical features and vegetation zones of the African continent. The detailed maps show the fossil hominid and archaeological sites, which are restricted to the southern and eastern regions of the savanna zone. Those in East Africa are open sites and are associated with the Eastern Rift Valley, while those in southern Africa are limestone cave sites.*

10.2: *In the East African landscape the banks of sandy stream courses were among the camp sites most favoured by early hominids. A nearby source of water, as well as a readily available supply of cobbles and boulders (found in the stream bed) for the manufacture of stone tools were obvious reasons for selecting these places. As the present-day analogy near the shores of Lake Turkana depicts, gallery forest lining the banks and bush cover extending out on to the open grassland also offered shady, sheltered places to camp. Furthermore, the fact that vegetation is thickest near well-watered places would have been an important factor to early hominids partly dependent on a vegetarian diet.*

Geographical and ecological range

The geographical range of the early fossil hominid and archaeological sites covers a wide area in eastern and southern Africa and indicates that the early stages of hominid evolution took place in a tropical to subtropical environment. It is especially significant that the distribution of finds falls within the zone of relatively open savanna that lies between the tropical forest and the desert. This vast area extends from West Africa south of the Sahara and sweeps in a broad are around the dense, heavily vegetated and forested region of the Congo basin to East Africa and the southern subcontinent. In this area, sites are naturally restricted to deposits of suitable age that have yielded fossil and hominid remains and artifacts, and this may explain apparent gaps in the distribution.

The savanna should not be viewed simply as open grasslands, for in fact it constitutes a rich mosaic of habitats that support an extraordinary variety of plant and animal life. The vegetation varies from forest fringe, through more open woodland and bushland, to stunted bush and dry, treeless grasslands. The savanna also supports the largest variety of species of any zone in Africa.[1]

The climate in Africa during the Pliocene and the Early Pleistocene was never subject to the dramatic changes apparent in Europe and Asia, particularly during the Pleistocene. Changes did occur, but they were mostly towards a relatively stable, warm, dry climatic regime. Earth movements and volcanic activity associated with the formation of the Rift Valley had a more drastic effect on the climate and vegetation patterns in East Africa, while in southern Africa the lowland tropical forest was replaced by dry (xerophytic) vegetation. The cooler upland regions where the early hominid sites are situated were relatively stable.

During the later Miocene and early Pliocene major earth movements (including rifting or fracturing, faulting and uplift) were associated with volcanic eruptions in the formation of the Rift Valley system in East Africa. A broad trough in the Earth's crust

was created that extended along the length of the subcontinent and was flanked by high volcanic mountains and elevated plateaux.[2] The effect of these geological processes was to disrupt the former vegetation and hydrological patterns (see Chapter 8) and to create a landscape with a broad range of palaeoenvironments. This volcanic activity also provided the rocks and ash that have made possible the radiometric dating of the important fossil- and artifact-bearing beds of this region.

Many of the East African hominid and archaeological sites are found preserved in sediments associated with lake basins situated along the floor of the Rift Valley. A wide range of habitats was occupied by early hominids. Lake-shore environments included lakeside grassland plains, more densely vegetated swampy areas and other areas with trees and bushes along the banks of distributary streams close to the delta margins. By contrast, the inland areas consisted of more open grassland environments. Here the sites were generally restricted to the silty floodplains and sandy channels lined with fringing bush and gallery forest that were formed by rivers flowing out across the broad alluvial plains. These sites were adjacent to the more heavily wooded and forested slopes of the volcanic uplands.

Koobi Fora and Olduvai provide good examples of well-investigated areas within sedimentary lake basins, where hominid remains and archaeological sites occurred in a variety of settings.[3] Another such locality is the Omo river valley at the north end of Lake Turkana. Here sites were located in a mosaic of floodplain, river bank and deltaic settings associated with a meandering perennial river that fluctuated according to the lake level.[4] Studies carried out at the important site of Hadar show that fossil hominid finds were restricted to the plains, stream and delta margins close to an ancient lake.[5] This is also a feature of less extensively studied lake-basin localities such as Lothagam, Kanapoi, Chemeron, Chesowanja and Peninj.

Sites that are not associated with lowland lake basins (400–500 metres above sea level) are rare. Laetoli lies in more elevated terrain at the foot of volcanic hills. Early hominids appear to have occupied or moved across a flat, barren countryside with a scattering of dry acacia bush, but there is little evidence of stream activity.[6] Finally, to the north, in Ethiopia, two archaeological localities, Melka Kunturé and Gadeb, were situated in river contexts in high plateau country (2000 metres) on the flanks of the Rift Valley. The evidence suggests that by at least 1.5 to 1 million years ago early hominids had extended their ecological range into the cooler, more evergreen, forested upland regions of East Africa.

In southern Africa several features that characterize the early hominid and archaeological sites contrast with those of East African sites. The sites so far discovered are restricted to the cooler, more open plateau environments at 1600–1800 metres above sea level. It has been suggested that Taung was located in a drier, scrub–grassland setting because of its proximity to the Kalahari Desert. On the other hand, Makapansgat, Sterkfontein, Swartkrans and Kromdraai are situated in wetter bush settings associated with grassland and nearby water.[7] Whereas the eastern African localities preserve open-air sites, all the southern African fossil hominids and artifacts have been recovered in deposits in limestone caves, though this does not necessarily mean that the caves were used as dwellings.

The shift from an arboreal to a terrestrial way of life, and especially the occupation of a broad range of savanna habitats by early hominids, brought about major changes in behaviour. The movement into less forested environments led to a completely different way of life from that of the anthropoid apes. Such changes should be seen as adaptations to the selection pressures of life in new habitats: the savanna not only offered opportunities for a higher-protein diet based on meat, but also favoured bipedal locomotion, tool-making, food-sharing and other related behaviour.

Evolutionary relationships and the chronology of the early hominids

Our understanding of the character and relationships of early hominids is based on fossil specimens recovered from eleven localities in eastern Africa and five localities in southern Africa. The sample is relatively small in relation to the great time-depth involved, and opinions on the classification and naming of these finds have varied widely.

Studies of the skeletal anatomy of our closest living relatives have been critical in demonstrating that the fossils recovered belong to the family of man and are not simply the remains of aberrant apes (see Chapter 9). Furthermore, behavioural studies of the apes and other non-human primates provide invaluable models on which to base interpretations of early hominid social and economic patterns of behaviour. However, it is crucial to our understanding of early evolutionary relationships to place the hominid finds in their correct order. In fact, the first known early hominid specimens were recovered from undated contexts in southern Africa, and because these became the reference specimens for future discoveries, misunderstandings have arisen.

While problems still exist and gaps in our knowledge remain, the abundance of new material, particularly from well-dated contexts in East Africa, show an emerging overall pattern of divergence and speciation among early populations of the Hominidae. Thus, rather than a single evolving line, there was differentiation and branching from the basal hominid stock. One lineage underwent processes that gave rise to *Homo*, whereas the other was subjected to evolutionary change of a different nature, which led towards evolutionary extinction.

Beginning with the reconstruction of events in the early Pliocene, it is generally recognized that the earliest dated finds belong to the basal hominid stock generally called *Australopithecus*. These finds are a partial lower jaw with one molar tooth from Lothagam, located near the western shores of Lake Turkana, which is dated to 5.5 million years ago, and the lower end of an arm bone (distal humerus) recovered just to the south, at Kanapoi, from deposits dated to about 4 million years. The fragmentary nature of these specimens provides few insights into the morphological character or the biological nature of the australapithecines.

The specimens (well over a thousand of them) recovered from the limestone cave deposits in southern Africa, however, allow a more complete description. The australopithecines have been variously referred to as 'ape-men', 'man-apes' and 'near men', because of the ape-like appearance of the first discoveries in the 1920s and 1930s: a projecting face, massive jaws and large teeth, but a small brain. These distinctive features contradicted what scientists at this time generally accepted as an early hominid ancestor, 'Piltdown Man'. This creature combined a large brain, an important distinguishing feature in contrast to the small, ape-sized brain, and ape-like jaws and teeth. However, not only was the Piltdown skull a composite fake, but detailed studies of the bones attributed to the australopithecines have demonstrated that their overall morphological pattern is hominid. The brain size is small, varying between 435 and 530 cubic centimetres – about one-third the size of the present-day human brain. However, studies of internal (endocranial) casts of the fossil finds indicate reorganization of the shape towards a human pattern, and the overall pattern of the dentition is man-like rather than ape-like, although the sizes, particularly of the back or cheek teeth, are much larger than those of *Homo sapiens*. To accommodate them, the jaws are relatively massive and, as a consequence, the face is projected forward.

The post-cranial skeleton shows further hominid characteristics. Details from well-preserved and fragmentary vertebral columns, pelves and limb bones indicate that the australopithecines adopted an habitually upright posture. Although there are certain features unique to the musculature and morphology of the hip and thigh bones, these creatures were capable of walking and running erect, though perhaps more clumsily than humans today.

Although opinions vary widely, there are thought to have been two species of australopithecines in southern Africa – a slender, smaller, more gracile form, *Australopithecus africanus*, and a slightly larger, more robust form, *Australopithecus robustus*. Estimates of their body weight range from 57 kilograms to 36 kilograms for the robust forms and 43 kilograms to 27.6 kilograms for the graciles.[8] Both forms stood about 1.5 metres high.

Brain size also differed between the two species. The brain of the robust type averaged about 500 cubic centimetres, while that of the graciles was slightly smaller, approximately 480 cubic centimetres, though this feature is more likely to have been correlated with greater body size than with any increase in intellectual capacity. More striking is the marked enlargement of the jaws and the cheek teeth of the robust forms, as greater musculature was required to move their larger jaws. The robust australopithecine had more rugged and robust facial and cranial features, designed to withstand chewing stresses, while bony crests along the skull provided attachments for strong chewing muscles.

A key to the problem of whether these two forms represented a single evolving lineage or were, instead, parallel contemporaneous hominid species is their chronological relationships. *Australo-*

pithecus africanus is found at three sites – Taung, Makapansgat and Sterkfontein, and *Australopithecus robustus* at two – Swartkrans and Kromdraai. So far the southern African cave deposits have not yielded ages determined by radiometric dating methods. Rather, faunal occurrences associated with these sites have been correlated with radiometrically dated faunal occurrences from East Africa. A variety of methods has been used to determine the relative chronologies of the two australopithecine species, from which it has been inferred that they were not contemporaneous but were representatives of early hominid populations covering different ranges of time: *Australopithecus africanus* 2.5–3 million years ago and *Australopithecus robustus* 1.5–2 million years ago. Most authorities agree, however, that they probably constitute a single evolving line.

One school of thought maintains that not only did *Australopithecus africanus* evolve and give rise to the robust form, but some gracile populations also underwent further radical changes, this time in a human direction, and probably generated *Homo*.[9] Unfortunately, there is little evidence for early *Homo* in southern Africa, and support is thus lacking for the hypothesis that the two forms represented contemporary hominid lineages. In southern Africa there is evidence at only one site (Swartkrans) for an early representative of the genus *Homo* occurring together with the robust australopithecines. In East Africa the evidence is more plentiful, and the fossil evidence from Laetoli in northern Tanzania and Hadar in eastern Ethiopia is particularly relevant. The hominid specimens so far recovered are important, as they fill in chronological gaps in the early record of the Hominidae. Laetoli and Hadar span a period between three and four million years ago and are therefore somewhat older than the southern African cave deposits bearing australopithecine remains.

The Laetoli finds comprise mostly jaws and teeth but also include the partial skeleton of a baby. Associated in the same strata are remarkable sets of footprints left by a wide variety of animals, including early hominids.[10] The hominid prints are the oldest evidence so far to indicate that a fully upright posture and a bipedal, free-striding gait had been achieved. At Hadar a superb collection of fossil hominids has been recovered in an excellent state of preservation and unusually complete.[11] A unique find was the partial remains of one individual skeleton, known as Lucy; it is estimated that about 40 per cent of the skeleton was recovered. Another major find was the recovery of over two hundred specimens representing at least thirteen early hominids from one locality. The preservation of such finds allows the assessment of the variations in a single population.

Because of their overall morphological similarities, the accumulated fossil remains from both Laetoli and Hadar have been lumped together and treated by some researchers as representative of one hominid lineage. When looked at from this perspective, several striking features emerge. Individuals appear to have varied considerably in size, and there were marked differences between males and females. This condition is seen in modern apes

10.3: *The most complete skeleton of an early fossil hominid (about 40 per cent of the remains) that has so far been discovered. The specimen belongs to a new species called* Australopithecus afarensis, *but it is commonly referred to as 'Lucy'. It comes from deposits at Hadar in Ethiopia that have been dated to 3 million years ago. This creature stood about 1.2 metres tall, and features of the pelvis and limb bones indicate that it was well adapted to bipedal locomotion. (See also Figure 9.4.)*

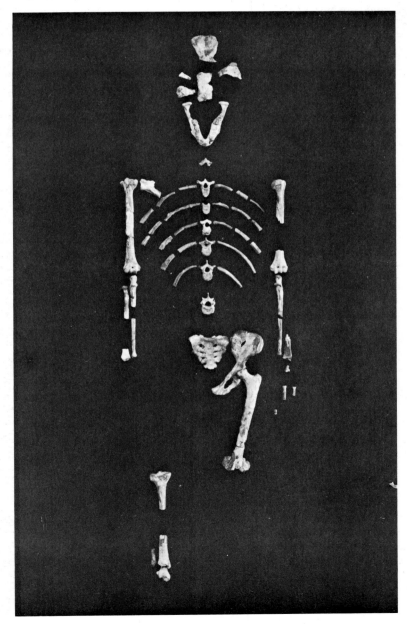

but is less pronounced in present-day human populations. Furthermore, there is a whole series of primitive dental and cranial characteristics. In the light of this set of morphological traits, which are primitive by comparison with *Australopithecus africanus*, and its relatively greater age, a new hominid species called *Australopithecus afarensis* has been proposed.[12] This would represent the ancestral australopithecine stock that later diverged, one branch leading on to *Homo* and the other to *Australopithecus africanus* and finally *Australopithecus robustus* (including the hyper-robust form *Australopithecus boisei*, as it is known in East Africa). While the naming of a new species has not been universally accepted, its status and this reconstruction of early hominid evolutionary relationships appears to fit best with the available fossil evidence.

Fossil remains of early *Homo* and unequivocal evidence for the

existence of two hominid lineages in the later Pliocene and the Early Pleistocene derive mainly from the Shungura Formation in the lower Omo valley and the Koobi Fora Formation located in the Lake Turkana basin, and from Olduvai Gorge. Hundreds of square kilometres in these areas have been surveyed and an abundance of fossil specimens representing almost the entire anatomy have been collected from known strata that have been dated radiometrically.

The earliest specimen attributed to *Homo* is an almost complete

10.4: *The temporal relationships of the Pliocene and Early Pleistocene localities in Africa that have yielded hominids (yellow) or artifacts (orange) or both in eastern and southern Africa. On the same time-scale is a suggested early hominid evolutionary tree.*

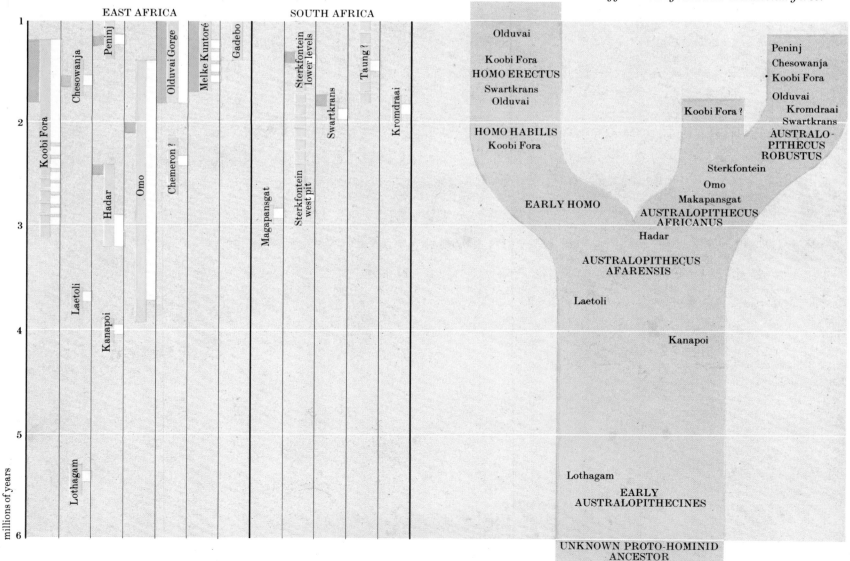

skull, known by its Kenyan museum accession number, 1470.[13] This remarkable find derives from strata dated to just over two million years ago at Koobi Fora. The most conspicuous feature is the substantial expansion of the braincase, which is nearly 800 cubic centimetres and fully two-thirds as large as that of the australopithecines. The forehead is well-developed, and the skull vault is round and lacks the bony crest along the top that is characteristic of the robust forms. Additional skulls, jaws, hips and limb bones

10.5: *A diagrammatic representation of the sequence of strata at Olduvai Gorge, indicating the major fossils and archaeological industries. These strata preserve a unique continuous record of man's presence and activities during the last 2 million years. Rivers and other erosional forces have cut into the strata and have exposed ancient sedimentary surfaces and in addition a whole complex of hominid and archaeological sites that extend over an area totalling about 240 square kilometres.*

have been recovered in strata of a similar age (approximately 1.5 to 2.3 million years ago) from various localities in the area of Koobi Fora and confirm the existence of early *Homo*. Living contemporaneously with early *Homo* at Koobi Fora was the hyper-robust australopithecine, *Australopithecus boisei*, perhaps a racial or geographical variant of the southern African form, *Australopithecus robustus*, or possibly a separate species. It has also been suggested that a third species was present, as several specimens resemble the gracile australopithecines of southern Africa, *Australopithecus africanus*.[14]

Further evidence of the coexistence of different species comes from Olduvai Gorge, probably the best-known early man site. Detailed studies of this unique area have produced the most thoroughly documented record of early man, his cultural activities and the environmental setting over the last two million years. In the lower strata of the gorge hominid evidence confirms the hypothesis of the existence of two hominid lineages. These are the hyper-robust *Australopithecus boisei*, which is found in the same strata – and in some instances at the same sites – and a more advanced hominid named *Homo habilis*.[15] This creature is characterized by a small skull but a relatively large brain. Associated

10.6: *Two of the most important and complete skulls to be found in the Early Pleistocene record of fossil man in Africa, recovered from sedimentary deposits on different parts of the landscape at Koobi Fora and both 1.5 million years old. The skull on the left provides unequivocal evidence for the presence of* Homo erectus *in Africa about half a million to a million years earlier than elsewhere. The skull on the right belongs to the robust australopithecine lineage, known in East Africa as* Australopithecus boisei.

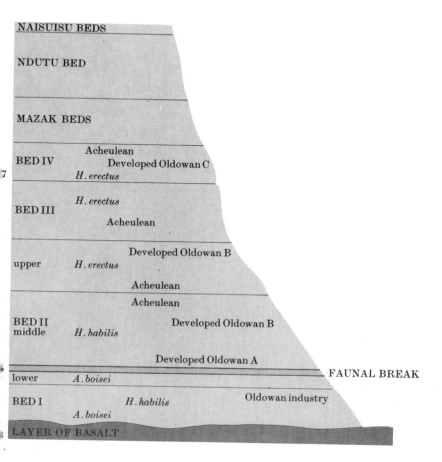

NAISUISU BEDS		
NDUTU BED		
MAZAK BEDS		
BED IV	Acheulean	
	Developed Oldowan C	
	H. erectus	
BED III	*H. erectus*	
	Acheulean	
upper		Developed Oldowan B
	H. erectus	
	Acheulean	
	Acheulean	
BED II middle		Developed Oldowan B
	H. habilis	
	Developed Oldowan A	
lower	*A. boisei*	FAUNAL BREAK
BED I	*H. habilis*	Oldowan industry
	A. boisei	
LAYER OF BASALT		

hand bones show that it was well adapted to the manipulation of objects and fully capable of manufacturing simple stone tools. Dr Mary Leakey, who has undertaken the archaeological analysis at Olduvai Gorge, suggests that this creature alone was responsible for the abundant stone artifacts found in the same strata.

Reassessment of the Olduvai early hominid material suggests the presence of a gracile australopithecine among the hominids, of which all specimens were formerly attributed to *Homo habilis*.[16] This tends to confirm the existence of three contemporary species, *Australopithecus boisei*, *Australopithecus africanus* and *Homo habilis*, though it serves to illustrate the problem facing researchers in recognizing valid species during a stage in human evolution characterized by highly variable populations. However, there seems to be no doubt about the presence of early *Homo* (*Homo habilis*) and its coexistence with robust australopithecines. If, as suggested, the gracile and robust forms of *Australopithecus* are parts of a single evolving lineage, the possible existence of a third 'species' at this time can be best explained by the survival of residual gracile populations after the divergence of robust forms from the ancestral gracile stock.

Finally, by 1.5 million years ago early *Homo* or *Homo habilis* had advanced to become *Homo erectus*. Dramatic confirmation of the early presence of *Homo erectus* on the African continent was the recovery of two well-preserved skulls at Koobi Fora[17] of this date, by which time residual populations of the gracile australopithecines had become extinct, although robust forms still occur in the fossil record in places such as Koobi Fora, Peninj and Chesowanja. By approximately a million years ago the robust australopithecine had also become extinct, leaving *Homo erectus* alone to spread out of Africa and populate other parts of the world (see Chapter 11).

The earliest occurrences of stone artifacts

The earliest well-documented stone artifacts occur in the Rift Valley of East Africa. Their appearance just over two million years ago marks an important threshold in human evolution: these stone artifacts, simple as they may appear, are the earliest preserved manifestations of culturally determined behaviour organized in a truly human pattern. It is thus highly significant that their appearance coincides in the geological record with a more advanced hominid that, on morphological grounds, has been attributed to the genus *Homo*.

The earliest stone artifact occurrences are called Oldowan, after collections of stone artifacts excavated from the oldest strata at the type-site of Olduvai Gorge. The Oldowan forms an 'industrial' complex, with a time-range from about 2.5 million years to 1.5 million years, preceding the advent of the Acheulean. The stone tool-kits are characterized by two kinds of stone objects: cobbles or blocks of stone from which chips or flakes have been removed (core tools), and the flakes produced by this process.

Fist-size water-worn lava cobbles found in nearby stream beds were frequently used for making this simple stone tool-kit. Repeated blows by one cobble on another removed flakes and a sharp edge was produced – a basic technique of stone-tool manufacture that remained stable over nearly a million years.

Sites represented by localized concentrations on the landscape of Oldowan stone tool-kits are fairly widespread in the Rift Valley. Possibly the earliest Oldowan site so far discovered is in the upper strata above the fossil-hominid-bearing levels at Hadar.[18] An age of 2.4 million years is suggested, but this awaits confirmation by radiometric dates. Several early sites, which date to about 2.1 million years, have been excavated in the Shungura Formation at the Omo.[19] The character of the stone tool-kits found at these sites differs somewhat from that of the tool-kits discovered at other Rift Valley sites. For making their artifacts early hominids chose to use small quartz cobbles, which tend to fracture or smash into small pieces. Many of the tool-kits comprise small flakes and fragments, but a few heavy-duty core tools are also present.

As the name suggests, the most comprehensive study of Oldowan sites has been undertaken at Olduvai Gorge.[20] Here there is an abundance of sites that range in age from about 1.8 to 1.5 million years. Some elaboration is noted over this time, leading to the Developed Oldowan, before the appearance of more variable tool-kits, including new types that characterize the Developed Oldowan B and the Acheulean (which is described in Chapter 11).

A similar situation is found in a well-documented series of sites around Koobi Fora. Local variants of the Oldowan technocomplex, called the KBS Industry and the Karari Industry, are found superimposed in strata radiometrically dated to 1.8 and 1.5 million years respectively. Several finds have been made to the north, in the basal strata at Melka Kunturé in Ethiopia, and to the south, in basal strata at Chesowanja on the east side of Lake Baringo.[21] While small occurrences of stone tools have been recovered at Swartkrans and Sterkfontein in southern Africa, their ages are uncertain, and the presence of new stone tool types suggests that they are best treated as belonging to the Acheulean.

There is no direct evidence of the function of these simple stone tools. However, the presence of stone tools at occupation sites implies some changes in the diet of these early hominids, which included food that required stone tools for its acquisition and preparation, and the recurring association of broken-up animal bones and simple stone tools to be found at many of the early hominid sites offers strong circumstantial evidence for their use in butchering and processing meat.[22] Such sites preserve either the fragmentary, broken-up bones of a single carcass or the fragmentary bone remains of a wide range of animals, from large species such as elephant, hippopotamus and antelope to smaller creatures like tortoises and rodents. To cut through the tough hide or skin of an animal requires a sharp cutting implement. Presumably, a thin, sharp flake was used for skinning and dismembering in much the same fashion as we use a knife today. Furthermore, a blunt, heavy-duty implement like a chopper was required to pound and break open rib cages, for example, or to crack open bones to get at the marrow.

However, this is not to say that early stone tools were used only for butchery and meat-processing purposes, or that the early hominid stone-tool-makers were primarily meat eaters. On the contrary, studies of present-day hunters and gatherers inhabiting the tropical zones indicate that vegetable products constitute 60 to 80 per cent of their diet.[23] Unfortunately, vegetable residue has not so far been found preserved on early hominid occupation sites; but sharp stone implements were presumably required to make pointed wooden digging-sticks to uncover succulent tubers and roots buried in the ground, and crushing implements would have been needed to crack open nuts and pound rough foliage to make it more palatable. The long, stable period of the Oldowan technocomplex signifies that simple stone tool-kits were quite adequate for the essential tasks required to sustain early hominid life on the savanna.

Simple stone tool-kits make their appearance relatively suddenly in strata dated to a little over two million years ago. The inception of stone-tool manufacture and use closely coincides with the differentiation of *Homo*, but the same strata also contain finds belonging to *Australopithecus*. There is no way at present to determine whether a hominid found in or near an archaeological site represents the remains of the tool-maker, an item of the tool-

maker's diet or a specimen that was fortuitously preserved at the spot after the site had been abandoned. However, several conclusions may be drawn. There are no visible signs of stone artifacts in strata that have yielded a large number of hominid specimens and other mammalian fauna at Laetoli, Hadar and the southern African deposits before about 2.5 million years ago. Admittedly, this is negative evidence, and there may well have been a rudimentary stage of simple tool use (the use of sticks and unmodified stones, for example) that has not been preserved or is no longer visible in the archaeological record.

The absence of stone tools prior to 2.5 million years ago, and their appearance at approximately the time of the emergence of *Homo*, seems good justification for linking the two. Stone tools indicate innovative, adaptive behaviour and signify changes in the subsistence strategies of early hominids to include the acquisition and preparation of food requiring their use. It may have been this addition to the behavioural repertoire that gave early *Homo* an advantage over his contemporaries. We do not know if the australopithecines were also tool-makers, but they presumably underwent different changes that ultimately contributed to their extinction.

Behavioural implications

During the Miocene the ramapithecines were already occupying the forest fringe and were probably exploiting food resources in more open woodland areas. On these ecological grounds, as well as on grounds of morphology, ramapithecines have been treated as possible hominid precursors. If this hypothesis is accented, then what selective factors gave rise first of all to *Australopithecus* and ultimately to the genus *Homo*?

During the late Miocene and early Pliocene more open country developed, following changes in vegetation patterns caused by climate and tectonic instability in Africa and Asia, in areas inhabited by hominoids. Within this framework of environmental change it is possible to envisage geographical isolation among groups of ramapithecine and related populations (who, on the basis of fossil evidence, were widespread in many parts of Eurasia and Africa), followed by reproductive isolation, speciation and the ultimate emergence of the basal hominid stock, *Australopithecus*. The particular selective agencies involved, however, are still unknown. What we can be sure of is that this was not a sudden event, particularly if we accept the time-scale for hominid divergence as being between five and eight million years ago.[24] At Lake Baringo, in northern Kenya, isolated hominid teeth found at Ngorora dated to about nine million years ago, and at Lukeino dated to six million years, offer tenuous links with the ramapithecines. However, until well-preserved fossil specimens are found in the crucial chronological gap between five and ten million years ago the date of divergence will remain speculative.

Environmental change and the occupation of new savanna habitats were accompanied by changes in hominid behaviour, though these did not take place all at once. For example, the fossil

10.7: *The spectacular discoveries of early hominid footprints by Dr Mary Leakey at Laetoli, dated to 3.7 million years ago, indicate that bipedalism was an early adaptation to life on the African savanna. The characteristics of the trail of the two sets of prints suggest that two hominids passed by at different times.*

evidence demonstrates that bipedalism preceded the expansion of the brain, which illustrates the concept of the mosaic nature of human evolution. Hominids adopted an upright posture and a bipedal means of locomotion early on. The fossil prints at Laetoli show that by at least 3.7 million years ago, and probably considerably earlier, hominids were well-adapted bipeds. The importance of bipedalism cannot be underestimated, for this unique trait was the basis for adaptation to life on the savanna. Hominids were able to range widely over more open terrain in search of food. With the hands free, food and raw materials for tool-making could be transported back to camp sites. Furthermore, fine manipulative practices involving simple tool manufacture and tool use could be accomplished. Through mutual reinforcement this range of behaviour, operating together with mental capacity, increased in complexity and scope.

Equally fundamental to life on the savanna was the development of cooperative group behaviour. Locality 333 at Hadar, where at least thirteen individuals, including infants, juveniles and adults, were recovered, provides striking evidence that early hominids congregated in groups.[25] In addition, studies of the eruption patterns of the teeth of fossil specimens indicate a delayed period of maturation, implying a long period of infant dependency on maternal care similar to that prevalent among present-day

10.8: *The earliest stone tool-kits comprise sharpened or shaped cobbles or blocks of stone produced by deliberate fracture, and small sharp stone fragments (flakes) that result from the percussion blows of striking one cobble against another. One of the earliest concentrations of stone tools comes from the KBS site at Koobi Fora, dated to 1.8 million years ago.*

human populations but unlike the pattern of dependency to be observed among the apes.[26] The maintenance of a cohesive group of adults, children and perhaps aged or non-productive members required cooperative subsistence strategies and food-sharing.[27] It is believed that early hominids were scavenger hunter–gatherers, for whom vegetable resources formed the greater part of the diet. Success in scavenging for meat, the incipient hunting of game and the gathering of vegetable and plant foods depended upon division of labour within the group. If we invoke modern ethnographic analogy, it is probable that the males usually engaged in hunting and scavenging activities, whereas the females were responsible for gathering plant and vegetable food. Furthermore, the procurement of food in this way indicates delayed consumption: wide-ranging hunting or scavenging, for example, presumably lasted for several days, which suggests the need for a central location or home base to return to. The home base was an important focus of early hominid life; at the site of DK, situated in the lowest strata at Olduvai, for example, a pile of stone was arranged in a well-defined circle, suggesting a semi-permanent shelter or windbreak.

The association of early hominid sites in East Africa with lake-basin environments, especially rivers or lake-edge and delta distributary streams, can be attributed to the fact that early hominids required water; their lack of containers or storage vessels may also have determined their choice of location close to a source of water. Proximity to exploitable food resources must have been another critical factor in the choice of location. Watering places along stream banks, where animals congregated, presumably provided excellent opportunities for hunting, as well as being likely localities for the scavenging of remains of animals killed by carnivores. In addition, plant and fruit resources are usually to be found in better watered areas, such as stream and river banks.

Archaeological studies of lake basins indicate that, in some instances, early hominids returned repeatedly to the same localities, which suggests prior knowledge and memory. Planning and cooperation were required to exploit a wide range of resources and thus support a cohesive group. A knowledge of the terrain, particularly in the light of the seasonal movements of game and the seasonal availability of fruits and plants, was essential to the survival of the group. These basic hominid traits can be regarded as responses to pressures in the exploitation of the local terrain.

The inception of stone-tool manufacture and stone-tool use marks the entry into a cultural domain. The rudimentary methods of manufacture and use were learned behaviours that were transmitted from one generation to another, and stone-tool use appears to have become habitual in the behavioural repertoire of some early hominids. The manufacture of stone tools was clearly linked with the emergence of a more advanced hominid attributed to the genus *Homo*. Thus by two million years ago a new adaptive strategy had become well-established: it included bipedal locomotion, stone-tool-making, food-sharing and the division of labour, adaptations that formed the fundamental characteristics of human behaviour.

11. The handaxe makers

The establishment of early patterns of distinctively human behaviour and the making of the first simple tool-kits seem, on present evidence, to have taken place wholly in Africa (see Chapter 10). The pace of these events was slow, the area vast and the human populations small; man's subsistence requirements were not sophisticated and the African environments offered abundant resources. It should not, therefore, be surprising if for hundreds of thousands of years there was no spread of population to other continents.

The long period known as the Lower Palaeolithic includes the story of this first great expansion and of the diversification of human material culture that kept pace with it. Partly, such diversification indicates growing technological competence and increased human ability in general, but much of it reflects man's arrival in new environments where fresh activities had to be pursued, often using a different set of raw materials: would precisely the same tool-kit be required or available in cool continental conditions in Europe as beside a Rift Valley lake in tropical Africa? With this background, the uniformity of many Lower Palaeolithic tools is in many ways more striking than regional differences.

During something like 1.5 million years before the beginning of the last glaciation, some 75 000 years ago, human populations spread throughout Africa and the southern half of Asia, and into Europe as far north as central Britain. Although it is possible that man reached the Americas during this period, there is as yet no wholly convincing evidence that he did so. Similarly, while important archaeological material of this period occurs in south-east Asia at least as far east as Java, it appears that the barriers to human movement from there to Australia were not surmounted.

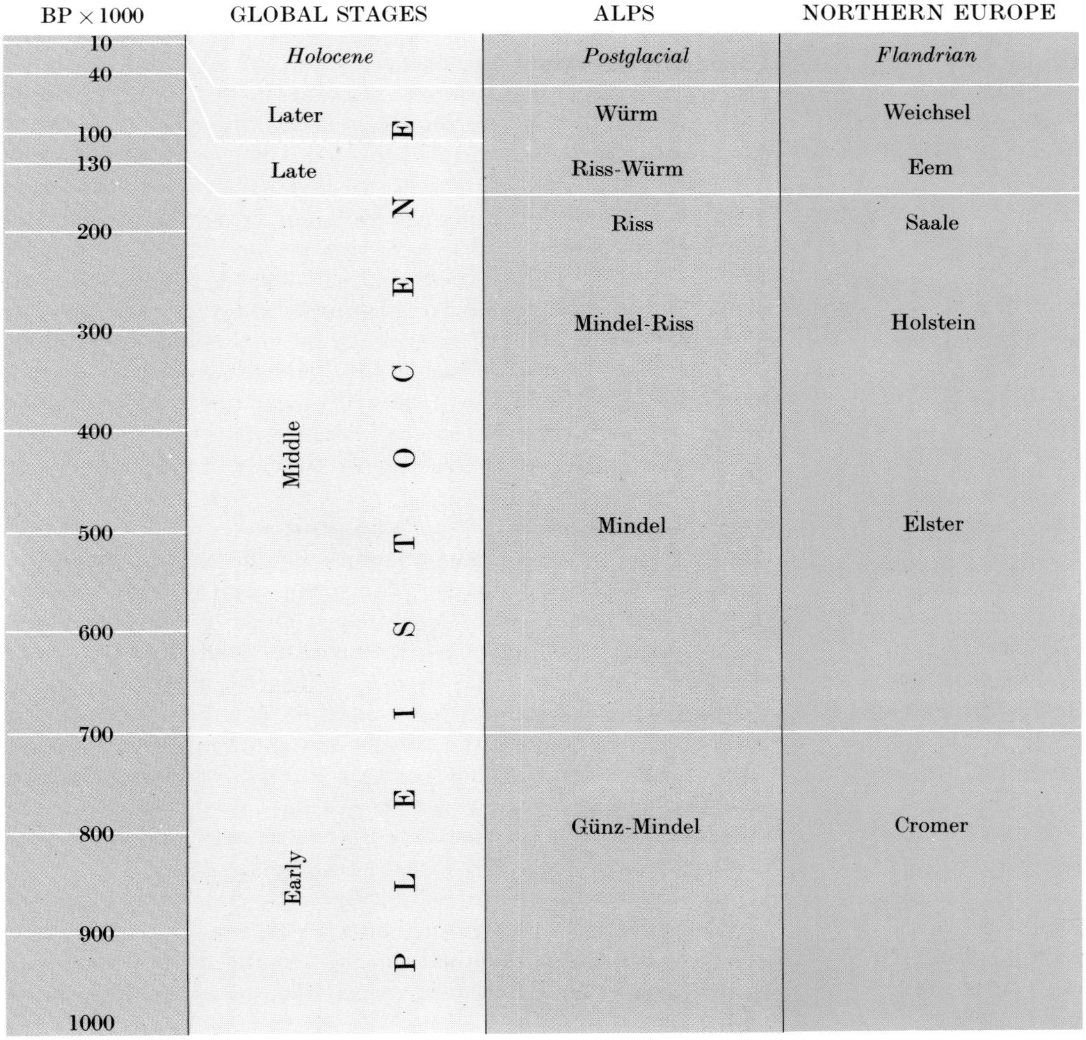

BP × 1000	GLOBAL STAGES		ALPS	NORTHERN EUROPE
10	Holocene		Postglacial	Flandrian
40				
	Later	E	Würm	Weichsel
100				
130	Late		Riss-Würm	Eem
		N		
200			Riss	Saale
		E		
300			Mindel-Riss	Holstein
		C		
400	Middle	O		
500		T	Mindel	Elster
		S		
600				
		I		
700				
		E		
800	Early	L	Günz-Mindel	Cromer
900		P		
1000				

11.1: *Regional terminologies for major glacial episodes. The various phases of ice advance in different areas are given local names, which are not necessarily precisely equivalent. Evidence from deep-sea cores (see Chapter 8) shows a more complex pattern of climatic changes than this schematic form based on the terrestrial record. Some of the divisions shown here may therefore require subdivision, and the suggested correlations and starting dates are thus tentative.*

On the basis of geological evidence, the vast span of time within which the Lower Palaeolithic period occurs can be divided into smaller units to provide local sequences. The succession of glacials and interglacials in the northern hemisphere, especially in Europe, offers the best-known set of subdivisions, although recent research is revealing an increasingly complex picture, particularly in the earlier phases. There are different sets of local names for the major climatic fluctuations, as the table shows (see Figure 11.1).

Human evolution and the Palaeolithic sequence

By about 1.5 million years ago (m.y.a.), the line of human ancestry (see Chapter 9) had passed a threshold marked by the emergence of the species designated *Homo erectus*. This form was distinguished by the first appearance of an essentially modern pelvis reflecting a fully upright posture and the ability to walk with a striding gait. Its brain was distinctly larger than those of its predecessors, in some cases even approaching the modern average. The most notable difference from modern forms of man lay in its massive jaws and teeth and in the still relatively robust character of the face. Perhaps as early as 250 000 years ago, the enlargement of the brain and development in the facial structure, lower jaw and teeth were sufficiently marked to justify the distinction of a new species, *Homo sapiens*. One subspecies, *Homo sapiens neanderthalensis*, was widely distributed by quite early in the last glaciation, but remains representing men of a completely modern type are not commonly found before about 40 000 years ago. These belong to the subspecies *Homo sapiens sapiens*, which includes all living humans.

Within this broad outline, many problems of detail remain. Such difficulties are inevitable, since we simply do not have enough fossil evidence to define the range of variation of these early human types. One has only to consider the variability of living man to realize the difficulty of classifying fragmentary hominid fossils at the species level. Accordingly, many specimens fall into intermediate positions, and their attribution is a matter of dispute. Furthermore, long periods of overlap between some of these early hominid types can now be demonstrated. Early specimens of *Homo erectus* were present 500 000 years before the genus *Australopithecus* was extinct, while late *Homo erectus* fossils have been attributed in Europe to the same interglacial (Holstein/Hoxnian) in which transitional *Homo sapiens* forms appeared, about 250 000 years ago.

The earliest known *Homo erectus* remains, notably a recent find (KNM-ER 3733) from east of Lake Turkana in the research area formerly known as East Rudolf, are dated to about 1.5 m.y.a. Hominid 9 from Bed II at Olduvai Gorge, discovered in 1960, is perhaps another example of not much later date. Opinions may differ about the respective roles of the australopithecines, of *Homo habilis* and of other as yet unnamed early *Homo* species during the earliest Palaeolithic, but the arrival of *Homo erectus* has always been regarded as marking an important stage of human evolution. Besides, he is associated with diverse and important archaeological occurrences in various parts of the world, many showing technological progress beyond the earliest stages of tool manufacture.

In the most general terms, this period includes a long phase dominated in many parts of the Old World by 'handaxe' industries, traditionally called Acheulean after a French type-site at Saint-Acheul, Amiens. Handaxes themselves are distinctive, bifacial, large cutting tools and visually rather striking, although they were only one element of the lithic industries in which they feature. In some areas there appear to be contemporary alternatives to the local Acheulean, while Acheulean industries themselves are scarce or absent east of India and east of central Europe. As the Lower Palaeolithic progressed, finely made flake tools increased in number and importance, and special knapping techniques were developed to produce flakes of predetermined shape and size, for direct use as tools or for further modification (the 'prepared-core technique'). In these ways a 'Middle Palaeolithic' technology grew gradually out of the Lower Palaeolithic one, reaching its classic expression in the finest 'Mousterian' industries of *Homo sapiens neanderthalensis*. The roots of the Mousterian, and the earliest Mousterian industries themselves, lie within our period, but its full development belongs to the first half of the last glaciation.

Palaeoanthropology and economy

Much of the evidence for human activities at this period is inevitably provided by the most durable remains: the stone tools themselves, their character and distribution. Only in exceptional circumstances are dwelling structures and living floors preserved along with environmental evidence to give a more vivid and detailed view of human life in its natural setting. The study of stone implements is still much concerned with their typology and technology, but techniques such as microwear analysis – the study at high magnification of the traces left by use on their working edges – increasingly offer the possibility of glimpsing specific human domestic activities. Lower Palaeolithic artifacts of perishable materials such as wood, bone or leather are extremely rare, but microwear analysis sometimes shows that these substances were worked.[1]

The distribution of Lower Palaeolithic sites in the Old World suggests that the men of this period could not maintain long-term settlements within the zone of freezing winter temperatures, despite their ability to use fire, for which good evidence survives at some sites (for example, Choukoutien in China). But they were necessarily hardy people, capable of lengthy local journeys to favoured sources of food or raw materials, and ultimately of long migratory movements in the warmer phases of the Pleistocene that took them as far north as western Europe, including Britain, where rich game resources were available. Unequivocal traces of them are, however, very scarce indeed north of the mountain barrier that extends from the Caucasus to Mongolia.

Many Lower Palaeolithic sites, especially Acheulean ones, are closely associated with stream channels or lakeside environments: several examples are mentioned in this chapter, from Olorgesailie in Kenya to Hoxne in eastern England. Open grasslands or savanna with good water and game resources were clearly favoured. Caves were sometimes used when they were available. It has been argued that at Grotte du Lazeret, near Nice, a hut structure was erected actually inside the cave.[2] It is extremely rare for structural traces to survive on open sites, but Terra Amata, also at Nice, provided traces of artificial dwellings of light but effective construction, with domestic hearths. Evidence has been claimed here for successive short-term occupations near the coast in spring or summer,[3] and it is likely that most Lower Palaeolithic populations regularly followed a pattern of seasonal movement associated with the varying availability of sources of meat and vegetable food.

In the quest for meat the men of this period regularly practised organized big-game hunting. At Torralba and Ambrona in Spain numerous elephants were killed and butchered; it is probable that fire was used to drive them into soft ground where they were killed, doubtless with the aid of long wooden spears like the one found with

elephant remains at Lehringen in Saxony. One of the Acheulean sites at Olorgesailie in Kenya[4] furnished probable evidence for the slaughter of a baboon troop. A wide range of Pleistocene mammals of all sizes was hunted in various parts of the Old World. A few sites have yielded fish bones among the food debris. In some areas vegetable food must have been at least as important as meat, but direct evidence is rarely preserved. However, remains of hackberries were recovered at Choukoutien and various fruit, seed and nut remains occurred on an Acheulean floor at Kalambo Falls, Zambia.

Where sites are well preserved it is sometimes possible to discern their nature – as, for example, living sites or home bases, kill and butchery sites or factory sites. Examples of the first two categories have already been given; the earliest known stone-implement factory site occurs at Olduvai Gorge, Tanzania, dating from about

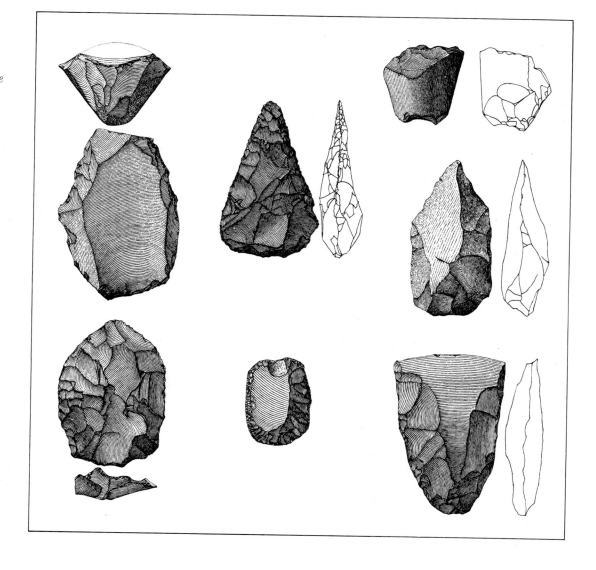

11.2: *A representative group of tools, shown one-quarter actual size.* Near right: *'Levalloisian' prepared core and flake from Baker's Hole, Northfleet, England. From the upper surface of the core* (above) *a single large flake like the one shown* (below) *was removed as the sole end-product. Note the carefully prepared striking platforms of both core and flake.* Centre right: *well-made Acheulean handaxe from Barnfield Pit, Swanscombe, England, found in the same layer as the hominid skull fragments; finely made flake tool (Later Acheulean) from L'Atelier Commont, Saint-Acheul, France.* Far right: *Crudely made implement from Choukoutien Locality 1, China, used for chopping tasks, associated in the deposit with* Homo erectus *remains; Early Acheulean handaxe from site EF-HR in Bed II at Olduvai Gorge, Tanzania; Later Acheulean cleaver from Kalambo Falls, Zambia.*

1.6 m.y.a. Particularly good rock sources were often subject to organized exploitation in Lower Palaeolithic times: European sites of this kind include Baker's Hole, Northfleet, England (for English chalk flint), and Reutersruh, Ziegenhain, Federal Republic of Germany (for quartzite). Throughout the period Lower Palaeolithic man showed considerable skill in fashioning stone implements for cutting, scraping, piercing and other such tasks. Quite apart from the development of tool types as time passed, his industries show considerable contemporary variation, which is probably most often related to the different activities carried out at individual sites by nomadic hunters in their seasonal cycle of movement.

Development of the Lower Palaeolithic in Africa

In the great sequence at Olduvai Gorge[5] typical Acheulean hand-axes and cleavers first appeared in Middle Bed II, some 1.2–1.4

m.y.a., the best site being EF-HR. No remains of *Homo erectus* are directly associated with these tools, but it is significant that they first appear at Olduvai at much the same level. Chronologically and technologically, the name Early Acheulean is appropriate for these Bed II handaxe industries, with their large, thick, bifacial implements, boldly and economically fashioned from heavy flakes, often side-struck. It has been argued that the ability to obtain such large flakes from the massive boulders of hard volcanic or other rocks was never possessed by the local Oldowan population, and that the first Acheulean groups must therefore be regarded as fresh arrivals at Olduvai; perhaps the Acheulean and Developed Oldowan traditions existed side by side in the Olduvai region from the period of Middle Bed II until the end of Bed IV times. Such a situation existed elsewhere in Africa, at Isimila, Olorgesailie, Gadeb and Melka Kunturé. If the Early Acheulean is indeed intrusive at Olduvai, we are

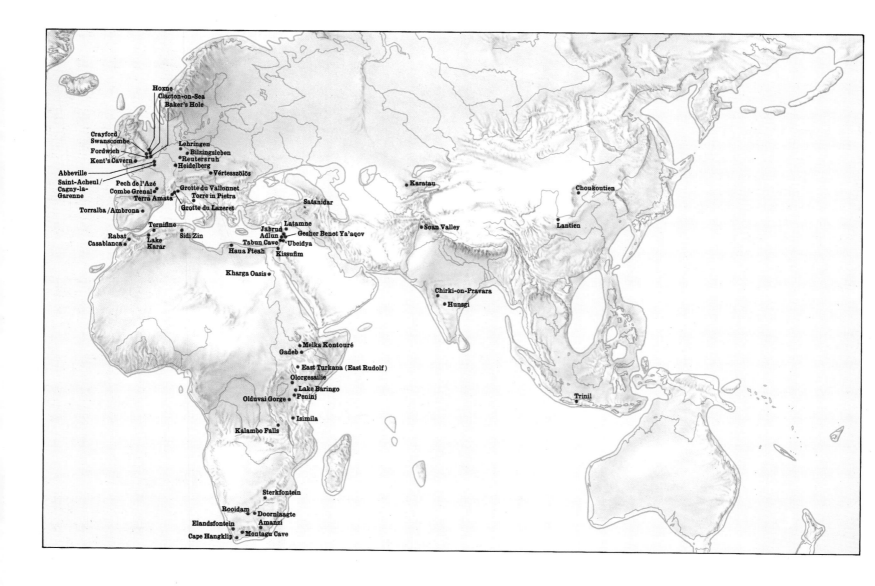

at present left to guess at its original source. A similar industry occurs in the Humbu Formation at Peninj, near Lake Natron, Kenya; potassium/argon (K/Ar) dates from above and below it make it broadly contemporary with the Olduvai Bed II occurrences. There are also Early Acheulean sites in Ethiopia (for example, Simbirro III at Melka Kunturé, and Gadeb 8D), for which no directly measured dates are yet available.

In north-west Africa a long and important Lower Palaeolithic sequence has been reported in Morocco, especially in the Casablanca area.[6] Present age estimates would suggest that the Moroccan Lower Palaeolithic stages are likely to be much younger than their East African counterparts – arguably, by some hundreds of thousands of years. Finds of Lower Palaeolithic artifacts far into the present Sahara demonstrate that viable routes across the arid area existed at times during the Pleistocene.

The full sequence in Morocco includes no fewer than eight Acheulean stages, occurring in known stratigraphic order over a long period of time in the Middle Pleistocene, showing technological progress in handaxe manufacture and the advent and development of 'prepared-core' flaking techniques. Several 'evolved *Homo erectus*' fossils have been found, some associated with Middle or Later Acheulean artifacts (as at Grotte des Littorines, Casablanca, and at Rabat). At Ternifine, in Algeria, *H. erectus* remains of more primitive character occurred with an Early or Middle Acheulean industry and a fauna of the early Middle Pleistocene.

In southern Africa[7] Acheulean material is abundant but rarely occurs in stratified or datable contexts. At South African sites like Cape Hangklip or Doornlaagte finished handaxes and cleavers occur in tens of thousands; how such concentrations have come about is hard to explain. Some sites are of better quality; Montagu Cave, Amanzi, for example, and perhaps one area of the Elandsfontein (Hopefield) site, near where the Saldanha skull was found, which some authorities consider may be of Middle Pleistocene age and possibly *H. erectus* or early *H. sapiens*. All these industries are technologically somewhat advanced, however, and there is no undisputed example of an Early Acheulean industry in southern Africa. The general absence of Pleistocene volcanic activity in southern Africa means that opportunities for direct dating are rare. It is thus on typological and technological grounds that one is left to conclude that the major Acheulean sites of southern Africa belong mainly to the Later Acheulean, with their fine, flat, symmetrical handaxes and their elegant flake cleavers.

In central-southern and East Africa[8] there are also Later Acheulean sites, often found in more accurately datable contexts.

11.3: *Map showing the world-wide distribution of Lower Palaeolithic sites mentioned in the text. The lowered coastline of the period of maximum glaciation is also indicated.*

At Olduvai Gorge such industries occur in Bed IV and the Masek Beds, in the time-range 0.8–0.3 m.y.a. Other famous examples include Olorgesailie in Kenya, Isimila in Tanzania and Kalambo Falls in Zambia, all in the time-range 0.5–0.19 m.y.a. There is no widespread indication of a technologically distinctive 'Middle Acheulean' stage in sub-Saharan Africa, such as can reasonably be claimed in western Europe.

Some industries at this time possess distinctive features: the so-called 'Fauresmith' variant in South Africa includes small, symmetrical handaxes as well as larger tools; in the epi-Acheulean 'Sangoan' development in certain parts of the south and west, perhaps mainly in forested zones, heavy pick-like 'core-axes' play a part alongside more ordinary handaxes, cleavers and flake tools; the technologically advanced Acheulean industry from the Kapthurin beds near Lake Baringo in Kenya has some remarkable prepared cores and a surprising proportion of blade-like pieces. A K/Ar date of about 0.23 m.y.a. was obtained here. At Kalambo Falls a Sangoan floor overlay the youngest of several Late Acheulean floors, dated to about 0.11 m.y.a. by amino-acid racemization (see Chapter 62). A Late Acheulean/Fauresmith occurrence at Rooidam, near Kimberley, gave a uranium/thorium (U/Th) date of about 0.115 m.y.a. (115 thousand years ago) and 0.167 m.y.a.

There are abundant Later Acheulean artifacts too in North Africa: Stages IV–VIII of the Moroccan sequence offer good examples, and other important sites include Sidi Zin (Tunisia), Lake Karar (Algeria) and Kharga Oasis (Egypt). No direct dates are available; in local terms, these occurrences are of late Middle and Late Pleistocene age.

The Acheulean forms a major part of what in sub-Saharan Africa is called the Early Stone Age. Over much (if not the whole) of this area it is followed, with no obvious transitional phase, by industries that specialize in flake and flake-blade tools obtained from prepared cores and referred to as Middle Stone Age. Until recently it was thought that the Middle Stone Age began rather less than 40 000 years ago, but it is now becoming clear that it began at least as early as the main 'last interglacial' marine transgression and perhaps earlier, that is, 120 000–150 000 years ago. In fact, it had probably ended in many regions by its formerly assumed starting date. These new limits make it broadly contemporary with the Middle Palaeolithic 'Mousterian' episode in Europe, parts of Asia and North Africa, with which it has much in common technologically (see Chapter 12). The present balance of evidence would suggest that its maker was *Homo sapiens*, perhaps an African subspecies equivalent to the Neanderthaloids of the northern hemisphere.

South-west Asia and Europe

In south-west Asia[9] a site belonging to the end of the Early Pleistocene, 'Ubeidiya, Israel, has living floors in a lakeside environment and stone tools not unlike those of the Developed Oldowan, which underlie lavas dated to about 0.64–0.68 m.y.a. Middle Acheulean sites in the Levant include Latamne in Syria and Gesher Benot

Ya'aqov in Israel, while important Late Acheulean sites include Tabun Cave and Mount Carmel in Israel, Kissufim in the Gaza Strip and Jabrud, Shelter I, in Syria, among many others. A Late Acheulean variant of Late Pleistocene age, with a great prolifera-feration of flake tools, is the Jabrudian, clearly seen at Jabrud and Tabun and at the Adlun sites in Lebanon. An interesting feature at these same sites is the occurrence, apparently during the last interglacial, of 'Amudian' or 'Pre-Aurignacian' industries, with a

11.4: *The Phase I surface at Ambrona in Spain, showing the distribution of elephant bones: fragments of scapulae (shoulder blades) and pelves, vertebrae, tusks and ribs and, in the right foreground, the radius and ulna of a single individual in near-anatomical position may all be seen. As well as bones, the occupation debris included considerable quantities of ash from domestic fires and traces of vegetable food remains.*

strong component of blade tools thought by many to foreshadow the Upper Palaeolithic technology seen in the same area at least 50 000 years later. A similar phenomenon has been reported at the Haua Fteah cave in Libya, and it is sad that none of these 'precocious blade industries' has associated hominid remains.

Unequivocal pre-Acheulean occurrences in Europe are relatively rare, but some interesting 'non-Acheulean' industries certainly exist. It has long been suggested that the Rhine valley marks an approximate frontier between a flake- and pebble-tool province to the east and the main area of Acheulean distribution in Atlantic Europe to the west. It is certainly true that handaxe industries are rare in central and eastern Europe, except perhaps in Germany, but Lower Palaeolithic material of any kind is sparse there, and the continental climate may often have been too harsh for early man during the Pleistocene. The famous Mauer mandible (found near Heidelberg, Federal Republic of Germany), of Cromerian or Inter-Mindel age, is generally accepted as a *Homo erectus* fossil, but was not associated with artifacts. The site of Vértesszölös in Hungary[10] yielded remains of living floors in travertine deposits, dated on faunal and floral grounds to a Mindel interstadial (see Chapter 8). The industry contained many flake tools, simple core tools and pebble tools of tiny size; the hominid remains have been classified as either developed *H. erectus* or early *H. sapiens*. A site that may prove similar in some ways, dated to the succeeding interglacial (Holstein), has recently been discovered at Bilzingsleben (German Democratic Republic), where both tools of minute size and much heavier implements were represented, along with *H. erectus* remains. Neither here nor at Vértesszölös is there any sign of classic Acheulean artifacts such as handaxes. Several other findspots in central or eastern Europe have yielded small quantities of broadly similar material.

In western Europe various small-scale pre-Acheulean sites have been reported, notably in France, and some, like Grotte du Vallonnet (Alpes Maritimes), or the Upper High Terrace of the Somme at Grace (Montières) are claimed as Early Pleistocene. In Britain the industries called Clactonian consist of heavy cores, choppers and rather crude flake-tools, with little or no sign of handaxe manufacture. Similar industries occur in northern France and in Belgium; there are no hominid fossil associations yet. The Clactonian and Acheulean traditions are regarded by most authorities as separate, though probably largely contemporary.

Atlantic Europe has produced abundant Acheulean material.[11] In Iberia, and sometimes in southern France, there are certain technological affinities with northern Africa, doubtless the main source area for the west European Acheulean. Further north the fine chalk flint was easier to work, and various elegant flaking methods developed there. Torralba and Ambrona, in Soria, Spain, are important Acheulean hunting and butchering stations, dating apparently to within the Mindel glaciation. Not many European Acheulean industries can be dated indisputably to Mindel or earlier, but examples of those that might be regarded as Early or 'Archaic' Acheulean, on geochronological and technological

grounds combined, include Terra Amata (near Nice), Torre in Pietra (near Rome), certain occurrences on the High and Middle Somme Terraces near Abbeville and Amiens in northern France, and perhaps a few British sites, including Kent's Cavern, Torquay, and Fordwich, Canterbury. There is no clear evidence, however, that these occurrences are anything like as old in absolute terms as their equivalents in sub-Saharan Africa.

The peak period of Middle Acheulean industries in Britain and France occurred during the later Middle and the Late Pleistocene. In France these are represented not only at open sites in the major river valleys but also by occupations in caves or rockshelters such as Combe Grenal, Grotte du Lazeret and Pech de l'Azé II. The best British Middle Acheulean sites include Swanscombe in Kent and Hoxne in Suffolk, but the findspots occur in thousands and the industries show considerable variety within the same general technological level. Fine Late Acheulean industries can also be identified in various parts of western Europe during the last interglacial, including the variant known as Micoquian, with elegant pointed handaxes, which is well represented in France and Germany.[12] Some Micoquian industries may even date from the mild opening phase of the last glaciation. In the later German Micoquian there appears to have been a technological overlap with some of the central European 'leaf-point' industries of the Middle Palaeolithic.

Sometimes, in European Middle or Late Acheulean industries, the flake-tools are numerous and finely made – those of L'Atelier Commont, Cagny-la-Garenne, France, and the Upper Industry at Hoxne are good examples. From the time of the penultimate glaciation onwards, especially in areas where high-quality flint was abundant, much use was made of the so-called 'Levalloisian' prepared-core technique, an effective if uneconomic method of obtaining large, flat flakes of predetermined shape and size by the careful shaping of a large core that was discarded after one or two good flakes had been obtained. A good British example occurs at Baker's Hole, Northfleet, Kent, a site of penultimate glacial age. Some later Acheulean industries used the technique freely, while others ignored it – sometimes, no doubt, because of limited raw material; a few almost purely Levalloisian industries are found (for example at Crayford, in north Kent, probably of last interglacial age).

The increase of flake-tools in quantity and quality, and the development of various prepared-core flaking techniques, form the basis from which the full Mousterian lithic technology developed during the last glaciation (see Chapter 12), evidently in the hands of *Homo sapiens neanderthalensis*. Various 'proto-Mousterian' or 'archaic Mousterian' industries, on occasion called 'Tayacian', appeared as far back as the penultimate glaciation, while the Acheulean tradition was still in full swing.

South and East Asia

Vast though the Asian landmass is, its Lower Palaeolithic sequence is perhaps somewhat impoverished by African and European standards. The USSR has little undoubted evidence for occupation earlier than the local Mousterian, except for a few Acheulean sites just north of the Caucasus, of which Satanidar is the best known,[13] and some ten findspots of non-Acheulean industries in Soviet Central Asia, notably Karatau I, near Dushanbe. It is fair to say that these probably represent the northernmost extremes of distributions that properly belong to the Levant and to northern India respectively.

In the Indian subcontinent[14] there is much Acheulean material, widely distributed. Until recently, well preserved sites have been lacking, but Chirki-on-Pravara and Hunsgi are examples of new discoveries helping to fill this gap. There are still, however, no chronometric dates and no hominid remains of Pleistocene age. In the north of the subcontinent an alternative to the Acheulean is offered by the Soan series of industries, which seem to begin in the Middle Pleistocene. They represent a long-lived pebble-tool and flake-tool tradition, probably unconnected with the Acheulean and perhaps adapted to particular local conditions. The later Soan was presumably the source of the groups that reached Soviet Central Asia.

East of India Acheulean industries or typical handaxes seem to be absent or extremely rare. In China, Malaya, Burma, Thailand and Java there are industries belonging to what has been called the 'chopper-chopping tool' group, to which the Soan may also be ascribed.[15] Often the artifacts are derived from gravels, probably of Middle or Late Pleistocene age, and in some industries the poor quality of the available raw materials, such as silicified tuff and fossil wood, imposed constraints on technology and typology. China and Java are the best areas, and both have produced abundant *Homo erectus* fossils. The famous Choukoutien caves near Peking (Locality 1 in particular) have yielded thousands of crude stone artifacts, many hominid remains (some with possible evidence for cannibalism), utilized bone, abundant traces of fire, and much faunal and floral evidence for a Middle Pleistocene age. Lower Palaeolithic findspots are in fact much more widely distributed in north and south China than is generally realized and Choukoutien is merely the most famous and prolific locality. Another important find of *H. erectus* remains associated with artifacts was made at Lantien in 1963–4. On faunal and geological grounds they appear to be older than the Choukoutien finds and are probably of Early Middle Pleistocene age.

In Java it is not easy to match the good *H. erectus* finds with the occurrences of artifacts, but *H. erectus* seems to be contemporary with the Trinil fauna, at about 0.7–0.8 m.y.a., and the apparently older Djetis fauna. The latter evidently spans a long period, perhaps extending back into the Early Pleistocene: one K/Ar reading was 1.8 ± 0.4 m.y., though the hominid presence may not go back as far as this. There are artifact occurrences of Trinil age, but not yet certainly of Djetis age. Some *H. sapiens* fossils of Late Pleistocene age are known from both Java and China. In east and south-east Asia there are some signs of improved technology in the Late Pleistocene stone tool-kits (for example, at Choukoutien Locality 15) but no obvious change in the overall local traditions. It is interesting that the earliest hominid remains from Australia, dating from a mere 30 000–40 000 years ago, are regarded as showing clear signs of the late *H. erectus* ancestry that one might predict for them.

Conclusion

The Middle Pleistocene thus saw the spread of human population over a wide area of the more hospitable parts of the Old World, from Britain to Indonesia. It was only in the following millennia, however, that man penetrated in appreciable numbers into the colder regions of central Eurasia, adapting his technology to the rigorous conditions that prevailed there.

11.5: *Middle Pleistocene hominid-bearing sediments at Choukoutien Locality 1, China. This is one of the most important sites of the East Asian Early Palaeolithic.*

12.The development of human culture

The earlier part of the Late Pleistocene period, between about 130 000 and 40 000 years ago, witnessed the development, spread and ultimate replacement of the types of industry that are labelled Middle Palaeolithic. This process took place during the Last Inter-glacial period (known as the Eem) and the first half of the Last Glacial (the Würm) (see Figure 11.1). Both these phases included shorter climatic fluctuations. The warm climate of the former was interrupted several times by colder episodes before the onset, about 75 000 years ago, of the period of cooler oscillations leading to a time of intense cold (called the Lower Pleniglacial Würm). This then gave way, about 40 000 years ago, to a more moderate climate, interrupted by short-lived cold events, before the return of harsher conditions in the last third of the glacial (see Chapter 8).

The climatic and erosional effects of continental glaciation were marked. Over much of temperate Europe mean annual tempera-tures were at least 10°C cooler than at present, displacing vegeta-tional zones towards the equator. The descent of permanent snow-lines pushed altitude zones downwards; the shift of northern vegetation zones into areas with less variable day length produced plant and animal communities not paralleled by any modern equivalent. Grasslands may have been even richer sources of nutrients for large ungulate populations than they are today,[1] and the worldwide fall in sea level and the emergence of the con-tinental shelves added much exploitable terrain to the habitats available to hunter–gatherers.

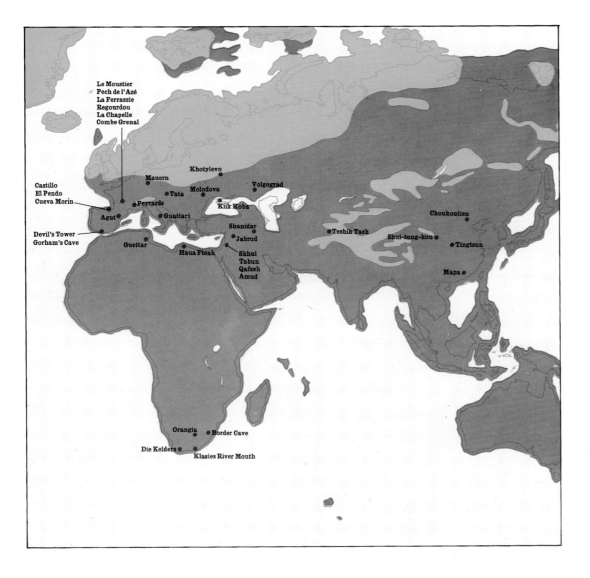

12.1: *Map showing the distribution of Middle Palaeolithic sites. A number of these have occupation levels representing periods other than those discussed in this chapter; compare, for example, with the sites shown in Figure 13.1.*

Hunters and gatherers making Middle Palaeolithic industrial assemblages were widespread throughout the Old World – from Die Kelders Cave, near the southern tip of South Africa,[2] to Khotylevo (53°15′N), near Bryansk in Russia,[3] and from Mauretania to Peking. The major difference between this area of dispersal and the region inhabited by Middle Pleistocene hunter – gatherers is the penetration of European Russia where, apart from a possible Lower Palaeolithic site in the Caucasus, the earliest stratified human occupations are all Mousterian.[4]

During this period humans occupied a great variety of environmental settings, from continental grasslands, Mediterranean scrub and desert oases and wadis to moist montane valleys, chill boggy heaths and steaming tropical forest. Although many of these environments were already colonized in the Middle Pleistocene, Middle Palaeolithic peoples do seem to have been better able to cope with cold, dry continental climates than were their Lower Palaeolithic predecessors.

Partly because of the drastic changes in the Earth's surface that have since occurred, the record of human history during the earlier part of the Late Pleistocene is scattered and partial, although it is better than that for earlier periods. Much evidence of the former presence of hominids in glaciated or resubmerged areas is now destroyed or lost. Open-air sites were especially liable to destruction by erosion or to deep burial under blankets of windblown loess or waterborne alluvium. Our record for the period is thus biased towards an over-representation of cave sites or of open-air sites along eroded gorges and dissected terraces in regions where Late Pleistocene deposition was especially rapid. Furthermore, Last Interglacial events are usually not well documented in the caves that provide the data for many European Late Pleistocene palaeoclimatic reconstructions.

Even taking the effects of erosion, site destruction and differential accessibility into account, however, there does seem to be a many-fold increase in the evidence of human presence in most inhabited Old World areas during the earlier part of the Late Pleistocene; and in many places where sites with long Palaeolithic occupation sequences are abundant, the majority of those sequences begin with Middle Palaeolithic residues. These facts would seem to speak for an actual increase in the numbers of hominids present during the earlier part of the Late Pleistocene.

Middle Palaeolithic industries

In already inhabited regions most evidence suggests the gradual development of Middle Palaeolithic assemblages from antecedent Lower Palaeolithic flake or biface complexes. In Europe and around the Mediterranean there are many assemblages whose assignment to Lower Palaeolithic or Middle Palaeolithic industries is quite arbitrary. In France, for example, the presence in small numbers of a single distinctive tool type, or current assessments of relative age, are often the only criteria used in differentiating the two kinds of complexes. Late ('Riss'-age) Acheulean industries in France are often identified on the basis of the appearance of

peculiar biface forms in association with flake-tool assemblages virtually indistinguishable from those considered characteristic of Middle Palaeolithic ('Mousterian') complexes: the replacement of the 'Micoquian' bifaces in some latest Acheulean assemblages with small triangular ones would lead to their reclassification as 'Mousterian of Acheulean Tradition'. With the exception of the European part of the USSR,[5] the case for a gradual Lower Palaeolithic/Middle Palaeolithic industrial transition can, in fact, be made for all of Europe.

Typological continuity has been claimed for the transition from Lower Palaeolithic to Middle Stone Age industrial complexes in sub-Saharan Africa.[6] Although the claim may be well founded, one of its strongest bases – the assumption that the Lupemban complex of the Congo basin and Angola and its antecedent, the more widespread, seemingly forest-adapted Sangoan, are Late Pleistocene outgrowths of the later Acheulean – while typologically reasonable, may be chronologically shaky. There is increasing evidence that the Sangoan and Lupemban may be much older than was previously thought, and that the former industry at least probably did not survive the Middle Pleistocene. Existing radiocarbon dates[7] for these complexes should be viewed as minimum age estimates and may be far younger than their true ages.[8]

In some parts of the world the earlier part of the Late Pleistocene allegedly witnessed no transition at all; there is little or no typological change in artifact industries. Complexes first identified as Middle Pleistocene seemingly continued relatively unaltered through the Late Pleistocene and even into the Holocene. This is said to be true for such chopper and flake complexes as the Late Soan from India, the Anyathian and Hoabinhian from mainland south-east Asia or the Javan Padjitanian, for example.[9] This assessment is based largely on comparisons of stratified later occurrences with undatable (surface) finds of supposedly Middle Pleistocene age, so that much more research is needed to prove the point. The situation is further complicated by the fact that geologically crushed pieces are confused with retouched tools in the artifact classifications used in some areas.

It is often asserted that Chinese Palaeolithic industries are very conservative,[10] but the observation is exaggerated. While it is true that some Late Pleistocene assemblages, such as those from Tingtsun on the Fen river, resemble earlier industries in some typological details, the Fen river localities also yielded types such as elongated bifaces and trihedral picks not reported in the Middle Pleistocene collections from Choukoutien or other sites.[11] One Chinese site that may well belong to the earlier part of the Late Pleistocene, Shui-tung-kou from the Ordos region, has been diagnosed as evolved Levalloiso–Mousterian (some 28 per cent of the tools found there are of so-called 'Upper Palaeolithic' types).[12] This assemblage, if it is as old as has been suggested, is far from 'conservative'.

The earlier part of the Late Pleistocene witnessed no striking innovations in stone tool typology: each Middle Palaeolithic artifact type has its Lower Palaeolithic counterpart. In some sites stone tool assemblages are not more carefully produced than their predecessors, and some Middle Palaeolithic assemblages are made up mostly of tools that look cruder than average Lower Palaeolithic collections from the same region. Most earlier Late Pleistocene stone tool assemblages, however, do seem to show greater control over shape and finish as compared with that of earlier industries. Nevertheless, even the most rigidly 'standardized' types recognizable by trained classifiers in a single collection are still quite variable in both size and shape, and there is less difference between comparable types from widely separated geographical regions than would be the case for most of the products of fully modern man; this suggests that considerable differences in thought and behaviour separate us from our Middle Palaeolithic relatives – even from those who were skeletally most like us.

In Europe and Africa the most common retouched artifacts are those made on flakes, rather than either bifacial implements or 'blade tools'. Most assemblages consist largely of pieces with long scraping edges, denticulated tools with serrated edges, notched pieces, perforators and more or less sharply triangular points. In some assemblages blunt-backed, sharp-edged 'knives' are quite numerous. Many occupations have yielded no bifacial implements (handaxes, cleavers, picks, disks) at all, while in others they are present and even relatively abundant. Tools and unretouched flakes made from prepared (Levallois) cores are often represented and are very numerous in some assemblages. Types such as burins and endscrapers, which are typical of, and abundant in, the Upper Palaeolithic, also appear in most Middle Palaeolithic assemblages, but usually in small proportions. Bifacially retouched, leaf-shaped spearpoints and pieces with tangs or stems (perhaps for hafting) occur in some regional Middle Palaeolithic contexts, often quite

12.2: *Types of stone tools commonly found in Mousterian sites. Although all the specimens shown here are from Cantabrian Spain, all but the cleaver flake are much more widely distributed.* Top row: *flint burin, two quartzite sidescrapers, Mousterian flint point ;* centre row: *quartzite notched tool, flint backed knife, quartzite endscraper ;* bottom row: *quartzite denticulate, flint perforator, igneous rock cleaver flake.*

early. Most tools are made of raw materials found very close to the sites, in outcrops or river gravels.

Bone implements are found in some Middle Palaeolithic levels. A common assumption that such artifacts did not exist prior to the Upper Palaeolithic has led most excavators to neglect to search carefully through collections of bone fragments for evidence of intentional alteration, and one suspects that such pieces may be much commoner than is generally supposed. The abundant Mousterian bone tools from the caves of Morín and El Pendo in Cantabrian Spain are mostly made on irregular long-bone fragments by direct percussion flaking. They include a variety of regularly retouched notches, denticulates and scraper edges that are perfectly analogous with stone-tool types from the same sites.[13] Certain bone-tool types such as compressors, hammers and sharp-ended punches or awls are frequently reported.

The interpretation of Middle Palaeolithic assemblages

Middle Palaeolithic industries are heterogeneous, exhibiting major regional differences and, in some areas, minor temporal trends; the latter, however, do not seem consistent from one region to another. Sometimes regional difference is manifest in the replacement of one or a few tool types known from one region by a set of local counterparts in another, the rest of the assemblages remaining similar. Small, finely finished triangular and heart-shaped hand-axes, present in parts of France, may be replaced in similar contexts by cleavers on flakes in parts of Spain. Large, crescent-shaped backed knives are a striking feature of some South African Middle Stone Age assemblages, and peculiar sharp, spire-ended points are found in some south-west Asian sites. Commonly, similar types may be represented in quite different proportions in two regions. Bifacially retouched sidescrapers, fusiform scrapers called 'limaces' and leaf-shaped points are rare in western European assemblages, but in some central and eastern European sites (Mauern, Kiik Koba, Volgograd, for example) they are much more abundant. In studies of regional or inter-assemblage differences it seems probable that the significance of peculiar local tool types may be quite different from that of discrepancies in the proportions of universally or commonly represented types in different regions. The first are far more likely than the second to mark stylistic distinctions (the boundaries between different social groups) of a conscious or unconscious kind.

European Middle Palaeolithic assemblages belong to the Mousterian, named after the cave of Le Moustier in the Dordogne. An important advance in the study of such material in recent years has been the analysis of entire stone artifact assemblages, rather than reliance on single distinctive types, to classify industries and to assess their relationships. The leading authority on Middle Palaeolithic industries, François Bordes, has used the relative abundance of different types of tools (particularly sidescrapers, denticulates, backed knives and bifaces) to define four major groupings (facies) within the Mousterian.[14] These he interprets as independent traditions – distinctive styles of tool-making practised by different, long-enduring social groups or tribes that coexisted, with varying degrees of contact between groups, in the French Late Pleistocene countryside. Although Bordes has recognized the contribution of 'stylistic' variation through time as a cause of change in some cases, most of the significant differences between facies are clearly not related to time, as they often alternate in long stratigraphic sequences.

Rival theories have been put forward. It has been suggested that the differences between the facies primarily indicate different chronological stages of development;[15] or that their differences mostly reflect different technological functions – that the facies are different sets of tool-kits each used for a different range of activities, such as slicing, abrading, perforating, wedging or rending.[16] Indeed, when Bordes defined the tool types most classifiers employ, he deliberately emphasized characteristics shared by tools from all regions, and these are more likely to be basic attributes essential to their function than stylistic features that reflect the existence of different social groupings or traditions in different areas. To take a present-day analogy: if one reduces the definition of a knife to 'a sharp edge opposed to a very blunt back', one can no longer expect to distinguish tool-kits made and used in the USA from those made in France or the USSR on the basis of the shape of the knives they contain. If this observation is correct, new kinds of typologies will be needed to detect stylistic variations in the Mousterian.

Those who advance these theories do not claim that they account for *all* differences between Mousterian artifact assemblages, but rather that they explain the most important contrasts; their

12.3: *Stone tools in a 1-metre square on the Mousterian level 15 living floor at Cueva Morín. Most of the tools are small scrapers and denticulates of flint, quartzite and volcanic rock.*

proponents admit that other explanations will hold true for minor variations. More recently the debate about Mousterian facies has moderated in the light of two new kinds of evidence.

First, research in Mediterranean France and Cantabrian Spain now suggests that the Bordes facies definitions may only fit a minority of Mousterian assemblages.[17] Even in south-west France, a certain number of 'blended' or 'intermediate' assemblages have always been known. The possibility that the Bordes facies may be at best scattered 'modal' tendencies in a background of continuous variation, or at worst totally arbitrary classificatory constructs, now deserves serious consideration.

Second, a rather large number of Mousterian occupations have now been subjected to multi-variate statistical tests, the results of which indicate that the Bordes types form discrete sets or constellations, each of which appears to be largely independent of the others, and that these constellations are found clustered in different places on single living floors.[18] In future, these discrete constellations of types may assume more importance than the facies in Mousterian studies.

During the Middle Palaeolithic possible 'style zones', defined by the geographically restricted occurrence of formally distinctive tool types, are generally very much larger than the largest areas occupied by single food-gathering societies today or the apparently stylistically distinctive regions of the Upper Palaeolithic. The characteristic Mousterian cleaver flakes, for example, are found from the French side of the Pyrenees, throughout the Iberian peninsula, and across the Mediterranean to Atlantic Morocco. To what extent this apparent stylistic continuity reflects parallel or convergent technological developments, as opposed to the continuous diffusion of information throughout the region, is unknown; but clearly the cultural processes responsible for the Middle Palaeolithic distributions and the very nature of the process by which new generations learned the behavioural skills essential to group survival must have been quite different from those at work in the cultural systems of fully modern man.

Subsistence and settlement
Our best evidence of Middle Palaeolithic subsistence comes from European and African contexts. Generally speaking, the food-gatherers of the earlier part of the Late Pleistocene are best defined as opportunistic; they seem to have made extensive use of the terrestrial resources in their immediate vicinity. In most parts of the world it seems that hunting practices concentrated on large and medium-sized mammals, especially (but not exclusively) ungulates. The species recovered vary with climate and local environmental conditions, but wild cattle, goats, equids and red deer,

12.4, 12.5: *Plan of the structural remnant and reconstruction of the dwelling at the open-air Mousterian site of Molodova I, in the Ukraine. The ring of large mammal bones, which encircled fifteen hearths and about 29 000 pieces of flint, is thought to mark the approximate limits of an ancient dwelling, the bones being used as weights to hold down skins that covered a wooden superstructure.*

0

10 m

with occasional rhinos and elephants, are usual components of archaeological faunal assemblages from western Europe, and mammoth and reindeer are common in sites on the central and eastern European plains. It is quite usual for such faunal assemblages to contain the remains of certain larger carnivores, particularly the hyena, the cave bear, the cave lion, the wolf and the fox, though these may have been exterminated as competitors as often as they were taken for food. Small nocturnal or burrow-dwelling carnivores are only sporadically recovered, and very occasionally birds are reported, which could have been taken at night from their nests. However, both bird and small mammal bones in Middle Palaeolithic levels may often be the remains of the meals of birds of prey or other carnivores that co-occupied sites with people or were present at times when people were not. Middle Palaeolithic hunters in Cantabrian Spain and South Africa seem to have made restricted use of certain obvious resources in their areas: in both regions wild pigs seem to have been avoided, perhaps because of their well-known ferocity, while in Cantabria alpine ungulates are poorly represented in most Mousterian faunal assemblages.[19]

The animals reported and their usual numbers suggest that most hunting was undertaken by individuals stalking or ambushing game, or by groups participating in game drives or surrounds. There is no evidence to suggest the existence of tools tailored to kill just one kind of animal, and those animals that could best be taken in traps and snares designed with the size and habits of the prey species in mind are conspicuous by their scarcity in Middle Palaeolithic occupations. Nor is there convincing evidence of the selective or disproportionate exploitation of particular prey species. Where one large mammal species dominates the faunal assemblage, it is usually the species that would have been most abundant or easiest to locate and hunt in the immediate area.

Middle Palaeolithic peoples used a relatively wide range of resources, however. At Abric Agut, near Barcelona, Spain, rabbits are more numerous than other animals, while mole rats, the Cape hare and tortoises are predominant species in the South African Middle Stone Age site of Die Kelders. Middle Stone Age peoples along the South African Cape seem to have pioneered the exploitation of marine animals: seals, penguins and shellfish are abundantly represented at Klasies River Mouth. At Devil's Tower and Gorham's Cave on Gibraltar there is also evidence of at least the sporadic use of marine birds and molluscs, but the Devil's Tower mussel midden may be in part a natural rather than a cultural accumulation.[20]

There is almost no available information about the extent of vegetable foods in diet during this period. However, most Middle Palaeolithic peoples must have eaten some vegetable foods, and in some habitats they probably consumed more plant foods than meat. Charred pine cones (which may only have been used for fuel) are reported from the Gorham's Cave Mousterian, and at Abric Agut carbonized seeds of a sea-beet (*Beta*) and a wild vetch (*Vicia* or *Lathyrus*) were recovered from a Mousterian horizon. The latter finds are almost certainly remains of hominid meals.

No complete Palaeolithic settlement has yet been described, but some suggestions may be made. Wherever several broadly contemporaneous sites are known from a particular region, they are usually divisible into at least three different kinds. First, there are extensive cave or open-air occupations in which, given good preservation, both stone and bone remains may be very abundant. Next, there are quite restricted scatters, sometimes in caves or rockshelters, sometimes in the open, in which artifacts of all kinds and bone remains are very rare. These two site types differ at least in the degree to which they were utilized, but little is known of the latter kind, partly because they are not considered rewarding to excavate. Evidence does not permit confident generalizations to be made concerning the range of activities undertaken at these two kinds of sites, although the smaller, ephemeral ones seem likely, as a rule, to have been more specialized. Even quite large sites may have been functionally specialized, however: at Cueva Morín, for instance, the dense accumulation of debris in one Mousterian level has been interpreted as the residue of hideworking processes.[21] Third, quarry or workshop sites are often recognizable by the presence of very large quantities of cores and flaking debris and 'unfinished' or obviously flawed pieces, and the relative scarcity of finished tools or bones. Such sites are often found along streams and on beaches, probably because stone cobbles provided the most readily accessible raw materials. Bone-rich open-air kill or butchery sites are also known in some areas.

In Cantabrian Spain sites tend to be found near the central sector of the long, narrow lowland zone exploited by Mousterian peoples, which may suggest that regular short forays by small, special-purpose teams were the rule, rather than periodic long-term shifts of population from one part of the range to another.

Cave sites tend to be substantially over-represented in western European site samples because they are the most evident potential living spots in the places where bedrock permits their formation. In cave-rich areas we have only recently become aware of the abundance of open-air Middle Palaeolithic occupations. On the other hand, open sites are abundantly documented on the eastern European plain, where caves are non-existent.

What may well be the first discovered ruins of Middle Palaeolithic dwellings have been found at open-air sites. At Molodova I these consist of an oval ring of mammoth bones, some 10 metres by 7 metres in exterior dimensions, containing extremely dense stone artifact and food-bone remains and fifteen hearths (see Figures 12.4, 12.5). The mammoth bones have been interpreted as weights to hold down a superstructure of stretched skins over a light wooden framework. More disturbed remains of what may have been a similar structure were found nearby, at Molodova V.[22] At Orangia, in South Africa, semi-circular rubble walls have been interpreted as supports for windbreaks. Deliberate structural modifications of cave interiors are also known in western Europe: for example, remnants of dry-stone walls were found in Mousterian levels at

Morín and Pech de l'Azé, and the paving of living floors with rubble or cobbles is known from several caves, including La Ferrassie and Combe Grenal. A single posthole was also recovered at the last site.[23] At La Baume de Peyrards an arrangement of large blocks may represent an elongated hut, some 11.5 metres by 7 metres in size, with a series of fireplaces along its centreline, the whole being constructed against the face of a rockshelter.[24] There are peculiar arrangements of debris in several other sites, but their interpretation is usually less certain. Especially striking is an artificial conical mound of stones battered into spherical shapes, bone splinters and stone tools, constructed by Mousterian peoples in an artesian spring at El Guettar, Tunisia.[25]

Art and ritual

Although it is generally supposed that the first vestiges of 'artistic endeavour' or 'notation' date from the Upper Palaeolithic, sporadic Middle Palaeolithic examples do exist. Fragments of mineral colouring matter, ground smooth or shaped into pointed pencils, have been found in many sites, although it is not known what kinds of surfaces they may have been intended to decorate. There are even more direct kinds of evidence, however. At the Mousterian site of Tata, in Hungary, a fossil nummulite with an incised cross on one surface was found.[26] What seem to be Mousterian 'tally-marked' bones have been recovered in the Charente and also in the deepest level at Cueva Morín, where a roe deer rib fragment with two pairs of regularly spaced curvilinear grooves and part of what seems to be a third was recovered. These decorated finds indicate prefigurations of the behaviour of fully modern man, but their production seems to have been confined to a few isolated and perhaps unusual individuals. On occasion Mousterian peoples collected striking minerals or rock formations, using them as raw material for tool manufacture, but sometimes, as in the case of quartz crystals, minerals and fossils from sites such as Castillo in Spain, the specimens were left unaltered, perhaps because they were regarded as curiosities.

There is even more direct evidence that the psychology of Middle Palaeolithic man was gradually becoming more modern. For the first time the dead were deliberately interred in specially prepared graves, sometimes with considerable accompanying ceremonial, to judge from the inclusion with the corpses of what seem to be mortuary offerings. Only a small proportion of the relatively numerous human remains from sites of the earlier part of the Late Pleistocene comes from such deliberate interments, however, and in France, where their chronology is clearest, true burials are mostly relatively late in the period. Burials of Middle Palaeolithic people have a wide geographical distribution, being reported from Uzbekistan (Teshik-Tash), the Crimea (Kiik-Koba), Iraq (Shanidar), Israel (Qafzeh, Skhul), southern Africa (Border Cave) and western Europe, especially France. To this list of ceremonially treated dead one must add the isolated cranium from Guattari Cave, in Italy, found lying on the ground surface surrounded by a circle of stones.

Most of the western European burials are of infants or small children, which is probably a reflection of natural mortality rates. However, some individuals reached the age of 45 (La Ferrassie I) to 50 (La Chapelle), and there are isolated remains of even older individuals. Although there are several cases of sites with burials of single individuals, the repeated reuse of a site for several burials is more common, at least in the Mediterranean region. Sometimes, as at La Ferrassie, a number of people who may well have been members of a single family were found in one occupation level.

The position of the body in the grave is quite variable. Grave offerings sometimes include specially arranged, particularly well-made stone tools (La Ferrassie V) or, more usually, joints of meat. There are some unique inclusions: a cup-marked slab of stone on a child's grave at La Ferrassie, for example. At Shanidar one individual is supposed to have been accompanied by offerings of flowers, but the case is problematical, since the excavator did not recognize the context as a burial or detect the limits of any artificial disturbance of the ground in its vicinity. It was only identified as a burial after pollen analysis suggested the presence of whole flower heads in the nearby earth. Where the sex of buried adults can be determined, the ratio of males to females is about two to one, and it seems that males were more frequently accompanied by grave offerings than females.[27] Sometimes, as at La Ferrassie, burials may be part of a larger structural complex. There, six individuals were variously interred in trenches or pits or under mounds, and the burials are related to a complex including nine regularly spaced earthen mounds and eight trenches of unknown function. At Regourdou, in a level that yielded numerous stone piles, trenches and stone-lined cists containing remains of several brown bears, there is a single human burial, in a trench capped by a tumulus; this individual was accompanied by stone artifacts and a bear humerus. As the construction of the tomb postdates the other structural remnants, their association is only a possibility.[28] Whatever their interpretation, these burials suggest a concern for the proper treatment and well-being of members of society beyond death's frontiers and the beginnings of complex ideological and social practices like those of fully modern men.

Human types and the transition to modernity

Human remains from the Last Interglacial are very rare, but their immediate predecessors seem to have been primitive members of our own species, *Homo sapiens*, often without the robust skeletal structures that characterize either *Homo erectus* or the Neanderthals. However, some more robust 'pre-Neanderthal' specimens, such as that from Tautavel, are known. During the rest of the earlier Late Pleistocene all human remains known from western Europe are Neanderthals, a group of humans with anatomical peculiarities that justify their distinction as a subspecies within the species *Homo sapiens*. The complex of skeletal features that distinguishes European Neanderthals extends as far as China (Ma-pa), and is found in the Near East and in south-west Asia (Shanidar, Tabūn, Amud) as well. However, there are examples of non-Neanderthaloid, fully modern man in association with Middle Palaeolithic cultural remains. At Border Cave in South Africa *Homo sapiens sapiens* is found associated with Middle Stone Age industries in deposits that may be between 90 000 and 105 000 years old.[29] At Qafzeh in Israel burials of skeletally modern *Homo sapiens* were found in convincing association with Levalloiso–Mousterian industries. The skeletally variable Mousterian inhumations at Skhul on Mount Carmel may represent two populations, the earlier more Neanderthaloid, the later more modern. The two Jebel Irhoud skulls from Morocco (whose age and associations are unclear) may belong to the very early part of the Late Pleistocene; they show an interesting mixture of primitive modern and more robust Neanderthal-like traits. After about 38 000 years ago all other human types were replaced worldwide by skeletally modern *Homo sapiens sapiens*, either by *in situ* evolution or by immigration and population replacement.[30]

This development was accompanied by major changes in material culture. The transition from the Middle to the Upper Palaeolithic is not yet fully understood. It did not happen all over the world at the same time, nor was it accomplished in the same way in each region. There is evidently extensive typological continuity between some South African Middle Stone Age industries (for example, Howieson's Poort) and Late Stone Age successors (see Chapter 24). Precocious, blade-rich assemblages with characteristic backed knives occur, apparently out of place, in the midst of Middle Palaeolithic sequences at the Haua Fteah in Libya and at Tabūn in Israel and Jabrud in Syria. In parts of Asia and North Africa the transition is said to have been gradual and continuous, but throughout Europe it seems to have been discontinuous.

In the Iberian peninsula the earliest Upper Palaeolithic industry, the Chatelperronian, appears, from the standpoint of typology and manufacturing techniques, to be intrusive. On the other hand, many French prehistorians favour a local origin for their Chatelperronian industries, pointing to the undeniable existence of similar types (sidescrapers, denticulates, points, curved-back knives) in both the earliest Upper Palaeolithic and the local Mousterian of Acheulean Tradition. But one might well ask what significance this sort of similarity has for the detection of cultural continuities and the local evolution of tool-making traditions: the presence of knives in two tool-kits needs indicate no more than a common need to perform the technological operation of slicing. True Upper Palaeolithic industries, with endscrapers, burins, backed knives and split-based bone points, are reliably dated in central and eastern Europe to between 40 000 and 45 000 years ago, well before the earliest dated western European Upper Palaeolithic levels of between about 33 000 and 35 000 years ago. Even in France radiocarbon dates suggest some local coexistence of the latest Mousterian and earliest Upper Palaeolithic assemblages. The youngest consistent dates from French Mousterian levels, those from Les Cottés and La Balme, are as late as 29 000–30 000 years old. It would thus seem that the replacement of Middle Palaeolithic industries was a complex process: there were evidently various kinds of Middle/Upper Palaeolithic transitions that took place at various times, rather than a single universal change.

Clearly, there is still much to be learned about this critical threshold of human development, and it will continue to be an exciting focus of research.

12.6: *Plan of a Mousterian burial and structural complex at La Ferrassie. It consists of groups of shallow excavated depressions, deeper trenches, and rounded mounds associated with six international human interments. (Red triangles indicate skeleton finds.)*

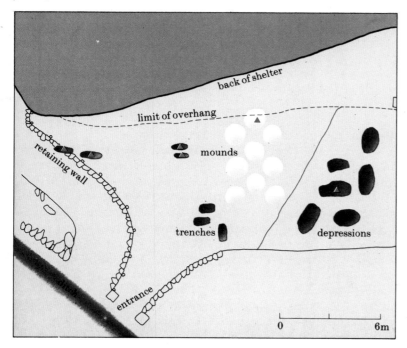

13. Later Pleistocene hunters

The later Pleistocene, as the term is used here, is the time between 40 000 and 10 000 years ago. The date 40 000 BP has been chosen to coincide with the first appearance in Europe of anatomically modern people (*Homo sapiens sapiens*) and their Upper Palaeolithic cultures; 10 000 BP has been chosen to coincide approximately with the end of the last glacial period, also regarded conventionally as the end of the Pleistocene epoch and the beginning of the succeeding Holocene. The focus here is on Europe, because it has provided far more information than other areas on prehistoric ways of life in the later Pleistocene.

Later Pleistocene artifact assemblages in Europe

European artifact assemblages dating from between roughly 40 000 and 10 000 years ago are generally referred to as Upper Palaeolithic. They are readily distinguishable from the preceding Middle Palaeolithic artifact assemblages (see Chapter 12), as they are usually characterized by a high proportion of tools made on elongated flakes called blades, and among the tools the most

13.1: *Map showing the distribution of ice sheets and the position of world coastline approximately 18 000 years ago, at the time of maximum cold during the last glaciation. Water incorporated in the glaciers came mainly from the oceans in the form of snow that failed to melt and was therefore not returned to them. As a result, during times of extensive glaciation the sea level dropped by more than 100 metres. The land thus exposed joined New Guinea and Tasmania to Australia; many islands off south-east Asia became part of the mainland; and, perhaps most significant, there was a land bridge up to 1000 kilometres wide connecting Siberia to Alaska, over which people may have first entered the Americas. The locations of sites mentioned in the text are also shown.*

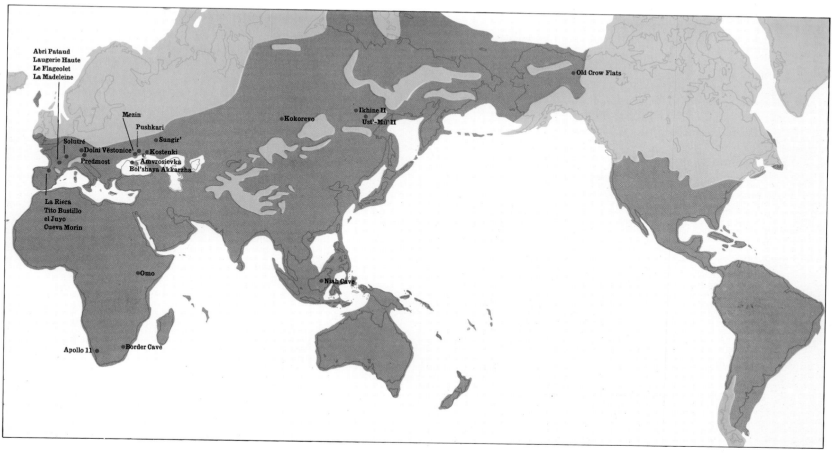

prominent types are various kinds of endscrapers and burins (the latter are chisel-ended pieces resembling modern engraving tools, which were perhaps used, among other things, to engrave bone). In Middle Palaeolithic assemblages blades are generally much less abundant than ordinary (non-elongated) flakes, and the most frequent tool types are various kinds of sidescrapers and denticulates (saw-edged pieces). Upper Palaeolithic assemblages also often contain well made, easily recognizable tools in bone, antler or ivory, including standardized types that suggest use as projectile points, awls, punches, sewing needles, hide-burnishers, shaft-straighteners, and so forth. Often the bone artifacts are engraved with geometric or naturalistic designs, and many Upper Palaeolithic assemblages include engraved or carved bone objects that prehistorians classify as 'portable art' (to distinguish it from the famous cave-wall art, which is probably also of Upper Palaeolithic origin). Bone tools are known in Middle Palaeolithic assemblages, but they are far rarer and more casually made, while objects that may reasonably be classified as 'portable art' are virtually unknown.

The makers of Upper Palaeolithic artifacts

Wherever diagnostic human remains have been found in association with Upper Palaeolithic artifacts in Europe, the people represented have turned out to be anatomically modern individuals. In contrast to the Neanderthals (*Homo sapiens neanderthalensis*) who preceded them and who apparently made Middle Palaeolithic artifacts, Upper Palaeolithic people generally possessed skulls with high, vertical foreheads, relatively small faces, flattish side walls and distinct chins.

Detailed study of the relatively large sample of Upper Palaeolithic skeletons now available suggests that their owners were robust, muscular people, who rarely, if ever, suffered from dental caries. As with modern Europeans, males were on average much larger than females. Demographic analysis of the Upper Palaeolithic skeletons indicates a pattern of mortality similar to that observed among historic hunter–gatherers.[1] Child mortality was high, and females apparently had a lower life expectancy than males, probably because of the risks associated with child-bearing. Females probably rarely reached 40 and males rarely 60 or even 50 years of age.

While Upper Palaeolithic people lived in Europe during the later Pleistocene, other people occupied Africa, Asia, Australia and the Americas. So far, their physical remains are not as well known to science as those of their European contemporaries, but enough bones are available to indicate that people outside Europe were also anatomically modern; in fact, in some areas anatomically modern groups may already have been present while Neanderthals still occupied most or all of Europe.

The origins of the Upper Palaeolithic

There are two conflicting theories about the origins of the Upper Palaeolithic in Europe. One is that it evolved in different areas at different times from various Middle Palaeolithic antecedents. The other is that it was an intrusion from elsewhere and replaced the Middle Palaeolithic rather abruptly.

In support of the theory of the local, multiple evolution of the Upper from the Middle Palaeolithic, authorities in various parts of Europe have cited artifact assemblages that they believe to be transitional. In every case, however, the similarities that link the supposed transitional industries with those of either the preceding Middle Palaeolithic or the succeeding Upper Palaeolithic, or both, are relatively weak; alternative explanations for such similarities are conceivable – for example, culture contact between Middle and Upper Palaeolithic peoples, or even chance. Although the matter has not been finally decided, the bulk of the evidence favours the contention that the Upper Palaeolithic intruded into Europe.[2] This is supported by the fact that there is no evidence to indicate the local evolution of Neanderthals into anatomically modern people, particularly in western Europe, where reasonably large samples of pertinent human remains are available. Conversely, there is skeletal evidence for the evolution of modern people from Neanderthal-like ancestors in south-west Asia, in a Middle Palaeolithic context predating 40 000 BP. Secondly, a combination of radiocarbon dates and stratigraphic extrapolation suggests that artifact assemblages similar to early Upper Palaeolithic assemblages in Europe appeared in south-west Asia 40 000 or more years ago, while in western Europe the earliest Upper Palaeolithic does not appear to be more than 35 000 years old. Dates of 40 000 years or more have also been tentatively established for the earliest Upper Palaeolithic of south-east Europe, from which putative movements from south-west Asia to western Europe could be inferred. Finally, there is the fact that there is a greater typological similarity among unquestionably early Upper Palaeolithic assemblages in various parts of Europe and south-west Asia than among later assemblages that succeed them in the same places. This suggests at least a single origin, if not necessarily a place of origin and direction of movement, for the early Upper Palaeolithic. New artifactual, skeletal and dating information is needed if more definitive conclusions are to be reached about the origins of the Upper Palaeolithic.

In discussions of this kind it has long been common to focus on Europe and south-west Asia. What has excluded other regions from detailed consideration is not the assumption that they are irrelevant but the scarcity of information. However, recent finds made in the Omo Valley in Ethiopia and at Border Cave in South Africa indicate that anatomically modern people may have existed in Africa south of the Sahara 90 000 or even 130 000 years ago.[3] Moreover, an anatomically modern skull found at Niah Cave in Borneo in south-east Asia may be 40 000 years old,[4] and anatomically modern people were certainly in Australia by 30 000 years BP (see Chapter 14). The accumulation of further discoveries in Africa, Asia and Australia may one day lead to a fuller and more certain understanding of the origins of modern people, which can be expected to rely far less on evidence of their appearance in Europe and of the Upper Palaeolithic cultures that they produced there.

The spatial and temporal variability of later Pleistocene cultures

Before the beginning of the later Pleistocene some 40 000 years ago, vast areas were characterized by remarkably uniform artifact assemblages that differed from one another mainly in the proportions they included of the different kinds of tools common to them all. Furthermore, the artifacts did not change much over the course of time; basic assemblage types lasted tens or even hundreds of thousands of years. During the later Pleistocene, however, the pattern changed. Broadly contemporary later Pleistocene artifact assemblages from neighbouring regions often differed qualitatively from one another, as did assemblages that succeeded each other within a single region. Readily discernible spatial and temporal variability characterizes not only stone artifacts of the later Pleistocene, but also the art objects and items of personal adornment that frequently accompany them. Overall, it is probable that these variations are essentially cultural, in the sense that the word is used by social anthropologists, even if the specific late Pleistocene 'cultures' isolated by archaeologists do not always correspond to those defined by social anthropologists. While it may seem peculiar to us that cultures should apparently have varied so little in different regions and at different times before the later Pleistocene, the variety that characterizes the cultures of the later Pleistocene world is reminiscent of that of more recent history. The extensive cultural variability of the later Pleistocene and successive periods presumably reflects the presence of modern people, with their seemingly infinite capacity for innovation.

Later Pleistocene technology

Later Pleistocene peoples in various parts of the world generally made a wider variety of artifact types than their predecessors, suggesting the expansion of the technological repertoire to encompass new kinds of activities, which probably included, particularly in Europe and northern Asia, the extensive working of bone, ivory and antler. More generally, the increase in the number of tool types in the later Pleistocene probably reflects a substantial increase in the use of tools to make other tools (rather than for use directly as projectile points, skin-scrapers, etc.) and also perhaps an increase in the manufacture of composite tools in which different kinds of stone bits were hafted in bone or wooden holders rather than held directly in the hand.

Later Pleistocene peoples must have had an intimate knowledge of the properties of different raw materials and, at least on occasion, they travelled long distances to seek them or acquire them through trade. Besides the numerous Upper Palaeolithic sites at which luxury items like amber or sea shells have turned up tens or even hundreds of kilometres from their point of origin, there are sites where much of the stone used to make tools was transported considerable distances. The most spectacular examples are the complex of Upper Palaeolithic sites at Kostenki on the Don river in the USSR, where large quantities of high-quality flint were probably brought from at least 130 kilometres away. No such movements of raw materials – whether 'luxury' or 'essential' – have ever been documented in a Middle Palaeolithic context,

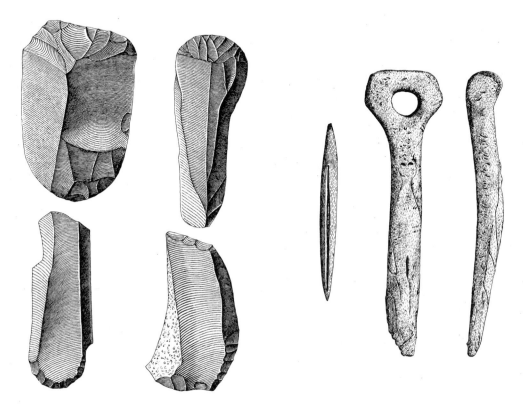

13.2: *Characteristic Upper Palaeolithic stone tools from Europe.* Above: *endscrapers from the Ukrainian site of Bol'shaya Akkarzha;* below: *burins from the Ukrainian site of Amvrosievka.*

13.3: *Characteristic Upper Palaeolithic bone artifacts from Europe.* Left: *a grooved 'projectile point' from the Ukrainian site of Mezin;* right: *two views of a 'shaft-straightener' from Molodova V, also in the Ukraine. Note the stylized engraving of a human figure on the handle of the shaft-straightener.*

which perhaps reflects the more primitive intellectual or social constitution of Middle Palaeolithic peoples.

In middle and upper latitudes in Europe and northern Asia later Pleistocene peoples were confronted by harsh climates with long, cold winters. Their sites have provided evidence of the technology they possessed to meet the environmental challenge. In several sites, dated to at least 19 000–18 000 years ago, bone artifacts occur that are so similar in appearance to modern sewing needles that it is hard to interpret them in any other light. They were probably used to manufacture well tailored, close-fitting clothing that helped maintain bodily warmth. The configuration of soil discoloration and of strings of beads surrounding, girdling and paralleling the skeletons of people buried 23 000–22 000 years ago at the Upper Palaeolithic site of Sungir', 210 kilometres north-east of Moscow, even suggest details of such clothing, consisting of a leather cap, a shirt, a jacket, trousers and moccasins. The super-abundant beads and other objects found with the skeletons were apparently sewn on the clothing as decorations or fasteners.

In addition to tailored clothing, later Pleistocene peoples also manufactured substantial dwellings or adapted natural shelters to meet the demands of harsh climates. Where caves and rock-shelters were abundant, as in south-western France and northern Spain, people regularly lived in these (near the mouth, in the case of deep caves). Modern excavations, like those at Cueva Morín and El Juyo in northern Spain, show that they sometimes built walls or otherwise modified natural shelters to make them more comfortable. In areas where caves did not exist, as, for example, in most of the European USSR, later Pleistocene peoples lived exclusively in the open air, and careful excavation at numerous sites has shown that they often built substantial structures. The evidence consists of large, artificial depressions in the ground, regular arrangements of postholes, patterned concentrations of large bones or stone blocks (serving as constructional elements), well defined concentrations of cultural debris, or a combination of these features. Almost always, apparent 'ruins' enclose or cover patches of ash and charcoal, which mark the positions of ancient fireplaces that heated the dwellings and were probably also used in cooking. Sometimes the fireplaces are relatively complex, with intentionally corrugated floors or small ditches leading out from the central ash accumulation. Modern experiments have shown that this modification increases oxygen flow and produces a hotter flame.

From the food debris found in their sites, we presume that at least until the very end of the Pleistocene, all later Pleistocene peoples were hunter–gatherers, and thus that a very large proportion (perhaps the majority) of artifacts found in their sites were used in hunting and gathering.[5] Many of the artifacts were probably used in processing meat, skins, plants, and so forth. The stone artifacts called endscrapers, for example, may often have served to scrape hides clean of hair and fat, after which the bone tools often called hide-burnishers may have been used to smooth them or impregnate them with softening agents or pigment. Many artifacts were probably used expressly for hunting. Some of the more enigmatic bone objects found at many sites perhaps served as trips or other parts of compound traps for snaring foxes, hares and other animals whose skins were valued for clothing. It is presumed that many of the stone and bone artifacts called points were in fact used to tip hunting spears or arrows whose perishable wooden shafts have long since vanished. Probable bone projectile points from European and Siberian later Pleistocene sites sometimes bear broad, shallow grooves that may have served as blood runnels to promote bleeding in a wounded animal (see Figure 13.3). One such grooved point was actually found embedded in a bison scapula at the Siberian site of Kokorevo I. Stone points, too, have been found still stuck in animal bones, as, for example, a flint point in a wolf skull at the Upper Palaeolithic site of Dolní Věstonice in Czechoslovakia.

Although it appears that the bow and arrow were later Pleistocene inventions, it remains unclear just how old they are. The oldest direct evidence for their presence, wooden arrow shafts from north German sites, comes from the very end of the Pleistocene, 11 000–10 000 years ago. The bow and arrow were probably in use in southern Africa at about the same time, if not before, judging by the occurrence in some sites of small stone bits very similar to ones that indigenous peoples used to tip arrows in historic times. Other important hunting weapons that were probably later Pleistocene inventions were the harpoon and the spearthrower, a device that permits a hunter to throw a spear harder and further. Both harpoons and spearthrowers have a demonstrable antiquity of about 14 000 years but may in fact have been invented earlier. Artifacts clearly interpretable as fishing gear also turn up in the very latest Pleistocene. The oldest known hooks have been found in European sites with dates of about 14 000 years ago, and objects believed to be 'fish gorges' – shaped bone slivers resembling double-pointed toothpicks – occur in South African sites that are only slightly younger. Fishing with spears, traps, etc., had probably been under way for some time before this, since fish remains occur in some more ancient later Pleistocene sites.

In conclusion, given their obvious capacity for innovation, the length of time later Pleistocene peoples were present (25 000–30 000 years) and the sheer number of groups that must have existed, it seems probable that virtually the entire range of hunting–gathering technology observed among historic hunter–gatherers was already present by the end of the Pleistocene. The Upper Palaeolithic people who occupied the Czech site of Dolní Věstonice 28 000–27 000 years ago had even discovered that soft clay, properly mixed with other materials (temper) and heated to a high temperature, hardens into a much more durable material. Both fired clay (ceramic) objects, especially fragmentary animal and human figurines, and the kiln that was used to fire them have been found at the site.[6] Near the end of the Pleistocene, 13 000–12 000 years ago, other hunter–gatherers living in Japan independently rediscovered ceramic technology, but this time applied it in the manufacture of the world's oldest known ceramic vessels.[7]

13.4: *Reconstruction of the Upper Palaeolithic structure found at the site of Pushkari I in the Ukraine. The 'ruins' consisted of a shallow, irregularly quadrangular depression about 12 metres long, 4 metres wide and 30 centimetres deep. Overlying the floor, which was littered with stone artifacts, bits of ochre and broken-up animal bones, were a large number of mammoth bones, especially tusks, which were perhaps part of a collapsed superstructure. The principal excavator of Pushkari, P. I. Borishkovskij, believes that the building was composed of three parts, each centred on a hearth.*

13.5: *Plan of excavation in an archaic Aurignacian (early Upper Palaeolithic) horizon at the site of Cueva Morín in northern Spain. The plans shows that this horizon contained a complex of hearths, postholes and graves, and the foundation of a semi-subterranean 'hut'. Such features have not often been reported from Palaeolithic cave sites, probably because most excavations have not been designed to identify them. The large black spots are rocks, placed in position by the ancient inhabitants for reasons that remain unclear.*

Later Pleistocene subsistence

Although the emphasis here has been on the differences between later Pleistocene peoples and their predecessors, there was one important respect in which they were certainly similar – they made their living through the hunting and gathering of wild resources. Only in the very latest Pleistocene, 11 000–10 000 years ago, is there good evidence for a significant change, when some people, in south-west Asia and perhaps elsewhere as well, began the process of domesticating animals and plants (see Chapter 15). Even these people, however, probably remained heavily dependent upon wild resources for centuries, if not millennia.

Ethnographic observations of present-day hunter–gatherers have shown that the gathered (mostly vegetal) component of the diet is generally more important, as far as bulk is concerned, than the hunted component. It is difficult to document the relative importance of gathered and hunted foods at later Pleistocene archaeological sites, because debris from the gathered part of the diet normally survives far less well than debris (bones) from the hunted part. This has perhaps led archaeologists to overemphasize the hunting aspect of later Pleistocene cultures, particularly in lower latitudes where it may be assumed that gatherable plant foods were readily available. In middle and upper latitudes the emphasis is probably less misleading, as potential food plants were probably not available in large supply, while large game animals were common.

Game was especially abundant in middle latitudes in later Pleistocene Europe and Asia, because the climatic conditions of the time favoured the formation of grasslands over vast areas where forests have predominated in the post-Pleistocene or Holocene period. The grasslands owed their existence to the same set of climatic features as did the great ice sheets of the time. The melting of the ice sheets and the expansion of forests at the end of the Pleistocene and the beginning of the Holocene went hand in hand.

The great grasslands of later Pleistocene Eurasia supported enormous numbers of woolly mammoth, reindeer, bison, horse and other hoofed creatures that could never have been as numerous in forest environments. Reindeer reached southernmost France, and some even penetrated the Pyrenees to northern Spain. In south-western France they were probably the most common large herbivores throughout most of the later Pleistocene, and their bones are conspicuous in many Upper Palaeolithic sites, including Abri Pataud, Laugerie Haute, La Madeleine, Le Flageolet I and II and numerous others. In broadly contemporaneous sites located elsewhere other species predominate; for example, red deer at La Riera, Tito Bustillo, El Juyo, and other sites in northern Spain, horse at Solutré in eastern France, mammoth at Dolní Věstonice, Předmost and other sites in Czechoslovakia, and bison at Amvrosievka and Bol'shaya Akkarzha in the southern Ukraine. In spite of differences between sites or regions, probably reflecting dif-

13.6: *Traced copy of an engraving on the wall of the famous Spanish Palaeolithic art cave of Altamira. It includes two bison, one mounting the other, in exactly the same positions as have often been observed among live bison. Close study of figures in this site has shown that other naturalistic compositions illustrating the same theme (reproduction) are present; re-examination of cave art at other sites would probably reveal that Upper Palaeolithic people often depicted characteristic facets of animal behaviour, not simply frozen and unrelated figures.*

ferences in local environments, there is a common emphasis on large gregarious herbivores with a known or probable preference for relatively open vegetational settings.

Besides food, it is clear that later Pleistocene peoples derived important raw materials from large mammals. They used bone, antler and ivory to manufacture numerous implements and art objects. Large bones, antlers and tusks apparently also served as constructional elements in dwellings – clearly patterned arrangements of bones often constitute the only remaining evidence for dwellings at Upper Palaeolithic sites. Some Upper Palaeolithic peoples, living in areas where trees were virtually unknown, apparently even used bone for fuel. Their fireplaces are especially rich in bone ash and 'charcoal'. It is possible that they also burned the dried dung of large herbivores.

It has been suggested that later Pleistocene peoples in various parts of the world exploited local resources more efficiently than their predecessors. This certainly seems likely in western Europe, where the number of known Upper Palaeolithic sites greatly exceeds the number of Middle Palaeolithic ones, suggesting that Upper Palaeolithic people were much more numerous. (There is no evidence to support the most cogent alternative argument – that Upper Palaeolithic sites generally represent shorter-term occupations than Middle Palaeolithic ones, that is, that Upper Palaeolithic people moved around more.) Since the basic resources available to Middle and Upper Palaeolithic groups were the same, Upper Palaeolithic people could only have been more numerous if they exploited these resources more effectively. Unfortunately, there is not much direct evidence for this. Bird and fish remains are certainly more common in Upper Palaeolithic sites than in earlier ones, and it may be that active fishing and fowling were unique to the Upper Palaeolithic. Increased reliance on fish may have been especially important in parts of northern Spain, south-west France and south Russia, where the knowledge that salmon run annually, combined with technological innovations for catching and preserving them, could have led to dramatic increases in human populations.

It may be that Upper Palaeolithic people hunted mammals more efficiently than their predecessors, but this cannot be shown at present. It has also been suggested that Upper Palaeolithic groups showed greater sophistication in opting to hunt just one or two species. However, there are Middle Palaeolithic sites in which the faunal remains are dominated by only one or two species, and on available information the proportion of such sites is not significantly smaller than in the Upper Palaeolithic. Further, wherever concentration on just one or two species has been found in a Middle or Upper Palaeolithic site, it is possible that this reflects a natural setting in which these species dominated. Obviously, the relative abundance of various species in an ancient environment must be known before concentration on one or two may be taken as evidence for specialization or for a change or advance in human hunting effectiveness. It is not even necessarily true, of course, that a species that is well represented at a site was regularly hunted, or

that remains at a site are those of animals killed by people. The outstanding example is the woolly mammoth, whose bones are common at many Upper Palaeolithic sites in central and eastern Europe, where they were clearly used for house construction or artifact manufacture. The possibility that such bones may often have been scavenged from long-dead animals is supported by chemical analysis of the mammoth bones among 'ruins' at Mezin. Analysis has shown that bones in a single ruin probably derive from individual animals who died generations apart.

So far southern Africa has perhaps provided the best evidence of a later Pleistocene advance in the exploitation of local resources.[8] The artifacts of the later Pleistocene people involved and their Holocene descendants are identified as Late Stone Age artifacts; those of their predecessors, living 40 000 or more years ago, are referred to as Middle Stone Age artifacts. In the southern Cape Province of South Africa Middle Stone Age peoples living in coastal habitats do not seem to have been actively engaged in fishing and fowling, while Late Stone Age peoples were. Both Middle and Late Stone Age peoples collected shellfish, but later Stone Age peoples may have done so more intensively, since the individual shellfish they collected were on average significantly smaller. Southern Cape Middle and Late Stone Age sites also differ in the remains of land animals they contain. These differences suggest that local Late Stone Age peoples killed a significantly higher proportion of the live animals available to them and that they were better able to deal with more dangerous prey, especially wild pigs. The greater efficiency of Late Stone Age hunters presumably reflects advances in technology, perhaps including the development of snares or weapons that could be dispatched from a distance (see Chapter 24). It is not possible to determine whether or not similar contrasts characterize Middle and Late Stone Age fauna from other parts of Africa, either because no pertinent faunal samples of adequate size exist, or because they have not been analysed in sufficient detail, or both.

Later Pleistocene non-material culture

While it is obvious that everything we know about later Pleistocene peoples must be based on the interpretation of their material remains, we can sometimes make inferences about non-material aspects of their behaviour. The presence of art objects and items of personal adornment in later Pleistocene sites and their absence in earlier ones clearly implies that there was more to later Pleistocene culture than a mechanical grubbing for existence. This is true not only in Eurasia, with its famous Upper Palaeolithic portable and cave art, but also in Africa, where ostrich eggshell beads similar to those used by historic hunter–gatherers make their first appearance in the later Pleistocene, and where paintings of animal figures on rock slabs buried in deposits at the Apollo 11 shelter in Namibia have been dated to between 27 500 and 25 500 years ago.[9] These Namibian paintings are perhaps as old as, or older than, any known in Europe.

In addition to the evidence provided by art, the widespread

custom of burial permits inferences to be drawn about non-material aspects of later Pleistocene culture. In Eurasia, and probably also in Africa, earlier people also buried their dead, but not with the quantity or quality of grave goods that have been found in many later Pleistocene burials. Such grave goods, often consisting of butchered portions of animals as well as stone and bone artifacts, probably testify to the respect of the living for the deceased, their concern for his welfare, and so forth. More generally, they suggest a burial ritual and notions about an afterlife of the sort that has often been recorded among historic hunter–gatherers. At some later Pleistocene sites graves were covered with large rocks or mammoth bones, perhaps as part of a ritual, perhaps to prevent wolves, hyenas, etc., from exhuming the body. Exhumation by

13.7: *The meticulously depicted head of a deer, from the cave of Lascaux near Montignac in south-western France.*

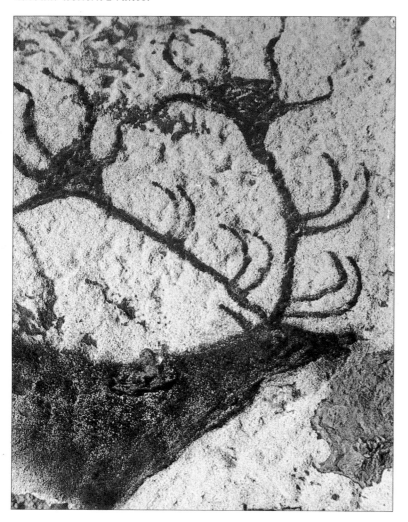

carnivores may account for the isolated and fragmentary human bones that are a relatively frequent occurrence in later Pleistocene sites. The common alternative explanation, cannibalism by the human occupants of the sites, cannot be ruled out, but it seems implausible as cannibalism has rarely been observed among historic hunter–gatherers.

Population expansion in the later Pleistocene

It has been noted that Upper Palaeolithic sites in Europe are much more abundant than Middle Palaeolithic ones in places where both are found, and that this probably reflects a substantial increase in population, a consequence of more efficient exploitation of natural resources by later Pleistocene peoples. It is possible – perhaps even probable – that similar increases in later Pleistocene populations occurred outside Europe. If nothing else, later Pleistocene peoples extended the geographical range of the human species, probably colonizing north-eastern Europe, Siberia, the Americas and perhaps Australia for the first time.

Middle Palaeolithic and earlier sites have yet to be found in the most northern and eastern parts of Europe (incorporated today in the USSR), and as each year passes, it seems increasingly likely that Middle Palaeolithic peoples simply did not live there, presumably because of the harsh continental climate that prevailed even in interglacial periods. Upper Palaeolithic peoples obviously did not find the climate an insuperable problem, and their sites have been found in the extreme north-east, virtually on the Arctic Circle, at the latitude of the Ural mountains.

Climatic conditions over most of Siberia are even harsher than in the adjacent part of Europe considered above. It is probably significant, therefore, that there is no evidence of human occupation of Siberia before 35 000 BP, although it is possible that evidence has not come to light because archaeological reconnaissance and commercial activity leading to site discovery have been less intense in Siberia than in the European USSR. In any case, the oldest known sites in Siberia, at Ust'-Mil' II and Ikhine II in the Lena basin, are 35 000–30 000 years old, and the record of occupation after that is documented at numerous sites.[10] The cultural remains from Siberian later Pleistocene sites have traditionally been assigned to the Siberian Upper Palaeolithic, which is distinguishable from the European Upper Palaeolithic in detail but shares with it the extensive manufacture of bone, ivory and antler artifacts, the presence of easily identifiable art objects and items of personal adornment, the construction of substantial dwellings, relatively elaborate burial of the dead, and so forth. By and large, Siberian Upper Palaeolithic peoples enjoyed a way of life very similar to that of their European contemporaries, subsisting largely on gregarious herbivores that had become even more numerous and widespread as a result of the shrinkage of forests.

During the later Pleistocene glaciers were relatively restricted in Siberia because there was not enough moisture to feed them, but the existence of very large glaciers in Europe and especially in North America led to lowered sea levels, as a consequence of which north-eastern Siberia was linked with Alaska by a dry-land bridge up to 1000 kilometres across. Alaska and adjacent ice-free areas of north-west Canada were parts more of Siberia than of North America, since most of Canada was covered by vast ice sheets that made movement south virtually impossible. It is likely that the first occupants of North America were in fact Siberian Upper Palaeolithic peoples, who would have extended their range as far as Alaska as naturally as did other typically Asian creatures such as the saiga antelope and the yak. Just how early the first Siberian Upper Palaeolithic groups arrived is uncertain at present, but it may have been as long ago as 35 000 BP. From Old Crow Flats in north-west Yukon there is archaeological evidence – mainly in the form of radiocarbon dates for animal bones believed to have been modified by human beings – that people were already there 27 000 or more years ago (see Chapter 55).[11]

The early occupants of ice-free Alaska and north-west Canada would have found their way south blocked either by continuous ice or by a long, narrow, inhospitable, ice-free corridor that perhaps extended along the eastern side of the Rocky Mountains. Movement south would have been greatly facilitated 14 000 years ago, when substantial shrinkage of the Canadian ice sheets began. It is perhaps no coincidence that the oldest compelling and universally accepted evidence of human presence in the forty-eight adjacent American states and areas further south dates from 14 000–12 000 BP. It is also possible that the ecological shock caused by the appearance of a powerful new predator, perhaps in combination with environmental change at the end of the Pleistocene, led to the dramatic disappearance of many large mammals from the Americas between 14 000 and 10 000 BP.[12] In any case, the association between the early Americans, commonly known as Palaeo-Indians, and long-extinct species like mammoth, native camel and native horse has been well established at a series of later Pleistocene sites located chiefly in the western United States.

The possibility that the Palaeo-Indians were at least partially responsible for the extinction of many large mammals is a potent reminder of the level of hunting–gathering competence that later Pleistocene peoples may have achieved. Similar, if less extensive, extinctions of large mammals occurred at or near the end of the Pleistocene in Eurasia and Africa, and here again it seems likely that people were involved, perhaps providing the final blow after environmental changes had restricted the numbers and areas of distribution of some prominent game animals. That environmental change alone does not adequately explain the extinction of these large mammals is indicated by the fact that the same species that disappeared roughly 10 000 years ago survived a comparable environmental change at the end of the glacial before last, roughly 130 000 years ago. What was different about the end of the last glacial period was the presence of much more advanced hunter–gatherers, whose ability to alter their environment was perhaps a harbinger of a problem that is so much a matter of concern today.

14. The arrival of man in Australia

The colonization of Greater Australia (embracing what are now the New Guinea and Australian landmasses) in the later Pleistocene took place, on present evidence, at least 30 000 and probably as much as 50 000 years ago. This movement of people has profound implications for the history of man in Australia; it is also extremely significant in the context of the development of man's capacity for sea voyaging.

While evidence is accumulating rapidly on the later phases of Australian prehistory, we do not know exactly when that prehistory began. It is less than twenty years since the human occupation of Australia and New Guinea was demonstrated to have occurred in the Pleistocene, and less ten years since a date of more than 30 000 years BP was obtained from an archaeological site in Australia; earlier sites may yet be found. Already, however, these discoveries have produced a revolution, not only in ideas about the physical and cultural development of the Aborigines, but also in assessment of the major geographical and biological changes that have occurred in greater Australia over the last 50 000 years.

The peopling of Australia has its origins in tropical south-east Asia, an area inhabited by human populations for the greater part of the Pleistocene period. While there is abundant skeletal evidence of these people, virtually nothing is known about their cultural life. From evidence of faunal sequences and of the hominids themselves, it appears the area was one of environmental and biological stability. This is to be expected, as the Malayo–Indonesian area was at all times part of the monsoon tropics and not a zone of major biological movements, other than those of human populations.

It is important to remember that Sunda Land, the area that in glacial phases was the single landmass fusing the Malay peninsula, the Indonesian islands of Sumatra and Java and Borneo, as well as parts of the Philippine archipelago, has always been separated by sea from Sahul Land, linking Australia and New Guinea. The area in between, Wallacea, forms a biological overlap zone, but until man himself passed across, no large land animals were able to spread from south-east Asia to Australia. Given the physiography of Sunda Land, and the sequence of Pleistocene phases that produced marked changes in sea level, it can be assumed that hominid populations were familiar with coastal environments over a long period. It is likely that many, if not most, human populations in the area practised a coastal economy, and by Late Pleistocene times these people had developed maritime technologies sufficiently sophisticated to enable them to travel by sea. Whether the watercraft were rafts or canoes made of bark and wood is unknown. On ethnographic and experimental evidence, it seems that the watercraft used by recent Australian Aborigines would not have been adequate for the much earlier voyages that were made across Wallacea. Tasmanian rafts, made of bundles of bark joined into a canoe shape, permitted sea passages of only a few kilometres. The bark canoes of southern Australia were suitable for riverine or sheltered coastal use only, and the Bentinck Islanders from the Gulf of Carpentaria, using rafts of wood, are known to have suffered major loss of life in short journeys of less than 20 kilometres. The dugout canoes of modern northern Australia are a recent introduction, but Pleistocene watercraft made of bamboo have been advanced as likely candidates.[1] The fact that suitable bamboos in south-east Asia are not present in Australia may explain why such craft were not used by Aborigines in the recent past.

The emphasis here on the use of adequate watercraft in the hands of competent mariners is important. It has been argued that the initial landings in Australia were the result of chance events, but simulations using various combinations of fertility, mortality and mating patterns suggest that viable founding populations based on small groups thrown up by accident on a foreign shore are highly unlikely, particularly along the extensive Pleistocene Sahul coast. The successful colonization of Australia is best seen as the product of a competent maritime technology, of a sort many prehistorians have found difficult to imagine was in use at least 50 000 years ago.[2]

Possible migration routes available to the first Australians have recently been explored in detail.[3] The shortest route involves an eastward movement from Java to Timor, and thence south to Australia. A more indirect path starts in Kalimantan (Borneo), moving eastward through Sulawesi to north-western New Guinea and then south to Australia. Whatever the route or routes taken by these colonists, the minimum water gap that they crossed during the course of their island-hopping was 80–100 kilometres, and then only if their passage was made at a time at which sea level was particularly low.

The initial human occupants of Australia's northern shores found an environment very similar to the one they had left. The coastlines of the Indonesian islands and Australia exhibit a similar range of marine resources based on sandy and rocky foreshores, and mangrove and estuarine areas. Animals such as the dugong, the crocodile, the turtle and a variety of sea birds are common to both areas. Shellfish and fish are similar and would have been procured by known methods. In the immediate area of the coast many plant and animal foods were recognizable – closely related fruiting trees, yams, palms, freshwater fish and turtles, and a wealth of similar birds, rodents, reptiles and small marsupials. Fresh water could be found in familiar places.

It was in exploration away from the immediate area of the coast that difficulties arose, because in this area the larger marsupials, flightless birds and vegetation were alien to the newcomers. The eventual occupation of these inland environments was to become the peculiarly Australian adaptation. How it occurred is still subject to debate, but the most persuasive argument postulates the conquest of the continent's environments via a coastal spread of population.[4] First, the familiarity of the northern coasts, par-

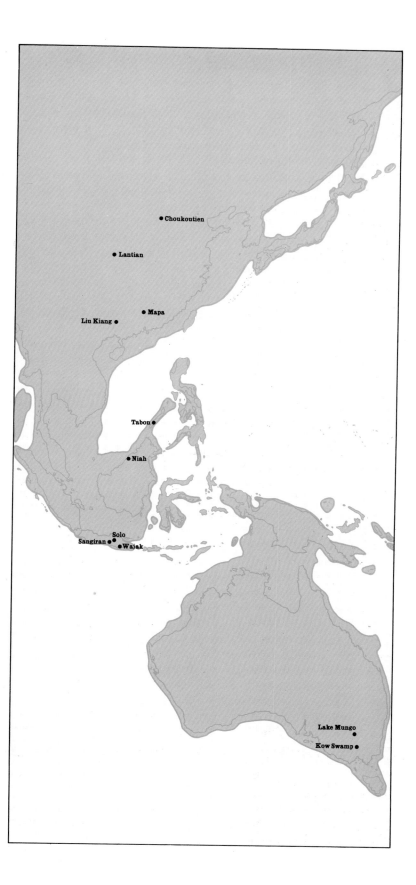

ticularly of their economy, implies that lateral movements down the west and east coasts of Australia represented minor and gradual cultural adaptations, as compared with a direct assault on the interior. Second, though still relatively unexplored archaeologically, the arid central third of the continent shows no evidence for a significant Pleistocene human presence, and the sorts of desert adaptations present in the central areas of Australia today first appear in the prehistoric record about 15 000 years ago. Finally, the earliest substantiated evidence for man in Australia comes from western New South Wales in an area of lake systems. It has been demonstrated that the economic activity evidenced around the lakes differs in no essential way from coastal technologies, and that the way into the southern and eastern heart of the country proceeded around the coasts to the southern outlet of the Murray–Darling river system.[5] Here simple changes took place, from saltwater through estuarine to riverine economies, which led Aboriginal groups to enter the continent by following the river systems north and east.

The archaeological evidence

Since 1969 research in the Willandra Lakes area of western New South Wales has produced the oldest Australian archaeological evidence substantiated by radiocarbon dates. A result of between 34 000 and 31 000 years BP was obtained from

14.1: *Map showing the major Pleistocene hominid sites in Australasia. The maximum extent of exposed sea floor about 18 000 years ago is also shown: this crèated a south-east Asian Sunda Land peninsula and an Australian–New Guinea Sahul Land.*

14.2: *The Lake Mungo III burial during excavation. This burial took place 28–30 000 years ago. The body of the man was placed in a shallow grave on the lee side of the dune bordering the lake. Red ochre powder and pellets were sprinkled over the body during the burial.*

freshwater mussel shells from a small midden exposed on the southern edge of the sandy lunette bordering Lake Mungo. There is additional evidence, based on the dating of charcoal, shell and bone, spanning the period 31 000 to 26 000 years ago, and several prehistoric remains there are probably 37 000 to 35 000 years old.[6] The oldest Australian human skeletal remains have been found at this site, the female (Lake Mungo I) being 26 000 to 24 500 years old and the male (Lake Mungo III) at least 28 000 and probably closer to 30 000 years old. The Willandra sites relate to a period when the lakes were full of water as a result of increased runoff from the eastern highlands rather than local rainfall. Although the lake system evolved much earlier, the human occupation there dates to a lake-full phase that began about 45 000 years ago and ended when the lakes began to dry up some 15 000 years ago.

The archaeological evidence dating from about 33 000 to 15 000 years ago indicates that economic activity in the area focused on lacustrine resources, with some contribution from local terrestrial faunas. Freshwater mussel-shell middens are scattered on shores throughout the lakes. The shellfish (*Velesunio*) were collected from the shallows along the lake margins. Crayfish and perch and cod fishes (*Plectroplites, Maccullochella*) up to 15 kilograms in weight were taken. Large scatters of emu eggshell fragments in middens and hearths attest to winter gathering from nests in the surrounding bushland. Other animals represented in food remains include wallabies, the burrowing rat kangaroos and wombats. The extensive stone-tool assemblages from these sites include notched and steep-edged scrapers as well as 'horse-hoof' cores.

A second prehistoric site of at least comparable age is Keilor, close to the city of Melbourne on the southern edge of the Australian mainland. Stimulated by the discovery of skeletal remains, excavations in the Keilor terrace have produced stone tools dating back to approximately 18 000 years ago. Underlying this terrace is a clay deposit that contains stone flakes and animal bones. Excavations are currently being carried out to define the extent and nature of the prehistoric evidence, but on radiocarbon dates and assessments of soil development the artifacts can be dated conservatively to between 36 000 and 25 000 years ago; the base of the deposit is probably as old as 45 000 years BP.

The sites at Keilor and the Willandra Lakes show that Aborigines were well-established in south-eastern Australia in the period 45 000 to 35 000 years ago. Situated far from the northerly entry points to the continent and man's likely movements after arrival, a minimum occupancy of Australia spanning 50 000 years is currently a conservative estimate. The apparent absence of archaeological remains from coastal dunes that mark the last interglacial high sea levels at about 120 000 years ago suggests that the initial colonization of the continent took place after that time. However, as the oldest sites known at present are situated on the side of the continent opposite to that on which the areas of the first landfalls are sited, a huge region only now being prospected archaeologically in any detail, substantially older evidence of Aboriginal presence in Australia can be expected.

Evidence of human occupation somewhat later than the lower prehistoric strata at the open-air sites of Keilor and Willandra is widespread. It indicates that adaptations to a wide variety of environments had been achieved quite early – certainly by 20 000 years ago. Man was demonstrably in Devil's Lair in the south-west corner of Western Australia by at least 25 000 years BP, and occupation of the far north of that state, in the Ord river valley, at the Miriwun rockshelter, began about 18 000 years ago. Shelter sites along the East Alligator river, in the Arnhem Land area of the Northern Territory, have revealed occupation levels dated to 24 000 years BP. On the east of the continent, but on the western side of the Great Dividing Range, Kenniff Cave was visited at least 19 000 years ago, and a shelter site near Laura on the eastern side of Cape York Peninsula may be of similar antiquity. A number of sites dating to 20 000 to 18 000 years BP have been excavated along Australia's eastern margin. Towards the southern extremity of the continent Cave Bay Cave has recently demonstrated a Pleistocene presence for man in high latitudes as early as 23 000 years ago. At the time of its earliest occupation the cave looked out over the Bassian Plain that linked Tasmania and mainland Australia more than 10 000 years before rising seas isolated Tasmanians from other Australians. Further west there is the unusual site of Koonalda Cave, close to the present cliffs of the Great Australian Bight. The flint bands in this cave, deep below the Nullarbor Plain, were mined for the raw material for stone implements between 22 000 and 15 000 years ago. Hand-impressed markings were made in the soft walls of the cave in this period, when the site lay some 180 kilometres from the coast. Finally, it must be remembered that while the Aborigines were busily occupying Australia, similar people had penetrated the New Guinea highlands by at least 26 000 years ago.

The ecological context

From this outline of early sites it is clear that much of Australia was occupied or being explored by Aboriginal people 20 000 years ago. Apart from the initial settlement of the tropics, populations were invading the rugged north-west, and the mountainous north-east, had followed the Darling, Murrumbidgee and Murray river systems in the south-east and had established themselves in Tasmania. The only blank was the arid core of the country and, as noted above, excavated evidence suggests that settlement of this largely inhospitable environment began at the end of the Pleistocene. Indirect confirmation of this comes from the Willandra Lakes, where about 15 000 years ago grindstones first appear in prehistoric sites. As these tools were used to mill grass seeds, one of the basic requirements for desert life, it appears that this adaptation was stimulated in part by the demise of the lake systems.

At the time that this last major environmental barrier was being broken, an equally important change occurred. As in other parts of the world, a number of animal forms are known to have become extinct in Australia some time during the Late Pleistocene. While this process is often regarded as the extinction of the megafauna, the most striking examples being large animals, many smaller animal species also disappeared at this time. The list includes several large kangaroo-like genera (*Procoptodon, Sthenurus, Protemnodon*) and much larger species of the living group *Macropus*. A giant monitor lizard, the flightless bird *Genyornis* that resembled the New Zealand moa, and the leopard-sized carnivore *Thylacoleo* also disappeared. The extinct group that left no living relatives are the diprotodons, a diverse group of herbivorous marsupials that included species similar in size to the living rhinoceros and hippopotamus. Until recently association of these extinct forms with man was tenuous, given the lack of well-dated animal fossils and their extreme rarity in archaeological sites. Association of man and the megafauna is now clear from a number of areas in south-eastern Australia, including western New South Wales, Kangaroo Island, southern Victoria and Tasmania. This area spans a range of environments from semi-arid to wet temperate. A most important discovery was made at Lancefield Swamp, near Melbourne, where the well-preserved bones of between ten thousand and twelve thousand animals are represented. Most are of the extinct kangaroo *Macropus titan. Diprotodon*, the kangaroos *Protemnodon* and *Sthenurus* and probably the bird *Genyornis* are also represented. The bones accumulated rapidly some time between 26 000 and 20 000 years ago. There is no evidence, however, that this was a hunting site.

Apart from confirming the coexistence of the Aborigines and a number of extinct marsupials for a minimum of 25 000 years, there is no clear evidence of the role (if any) that the Australians played in these extinctions, although hunting man and climatic change have both been advanced as causes. A review of palaeoclimatic data[7] indicates that the period between 18 000 and 16 000 years ago in southern Australia was one of marked aridity and significantly increased temperature variation. Although this situation provided the environmental instability that might account for the extinctions, Australia had experienced similar, if not more pronounced, glacial-related climates earlier, at about 55 000 and 150 000 years ago.[8] Moreover, the fluctuations in sea level on which these climatic changes were ultimately based did produce, for many of the extinct forms, an expansion of suitable habitats. The range of these larger mammals stretched from Tasmania to New Guinea. During parts of the Late Pleistocene both these islands were joined to Australia, and during periods of low sea level the ecological zones inhabited by these marsupials were considerably increased, both north–south and east and west of the then arid alpine areas. Thus it is difficult to account for the demise of the megamarsupials on purely environmental grounds.

On the other hand, there is little evidence that the Aborigines were responsible, either directly through hunting pressure or indirectly through environmental modification (the use of fire especially). It is extremely difficult to believe that Aborigines did not hunt or at least eat these animals, given evidence for hominid consumption of large animals in the Early and Middle Pleistocene and the opportunistic practices of contemporary Australian hunters and gatherers. As noted above, no so-called kill sites have been found in Australia, but for various reasons it is unlikely that the bones of animals the size of *Diprotodon*, for example, would be found archaeologically, other than in direct association with the place of death of the animals. The finding of such a site at present will be a chance event, as we remain largely ignorant of the behaviour of the animals as far as habitat and food preferences are concerned, and we do not know whether or not they were solitary.

Given the known period of man–megafauna association and the Lancefield evidence that at least some of the large extinct species were still plentiful at about the time that these extinctions occurred, it is unlikely that hunting predation alone was responsible. Aboriginal burning practices, however, particularly at a time of environmental stress, may have been more important. The importance to Aboriginal economies of fire-stick farming, as it has been called, is now being recognized.[9] Practised very widely by Tasmanian, Centralian and Arnhem Land people, regular burning of the landscape created a mosaic of environments that promoted both variety and richness of resources and facilitated their acquisition. When the practice of firebrand land management began is not known, or even whether it was part of the cultural life of the earliest colonists. As it is likely that much of the 'natural' Australian environment first seen by European settlers was, in fact, maintained and partly created by its original inhabitants, it is difficult to minimize the effect the Aborigines now seem to have had over a long period, of which the large animal extinctions may be but a small part.

The evolution of Aboriginal populations

Of all the questions dealing with the arrival of man in Australia, the central one concerns his own biology: what was the physical background of the colonists, and how did the high degree of contemporary Aboriginal variation come about? Naturally, discussion of the prehistoric biological evidence that bears on these issues is restricted to scattered and often fragmentary skeletal remains, and until the end of the 1960s such evidence was rare and poorly dated. What data there were, based on remains of skulls and teeth, suggested the existence of two morphological types. One of these was large and robust, exhibiting features reminiscent of early populations from Indonesia, while the other was, by comparison, small and gracilized, with a number of what were seen as recently developed characteristics. Recent extensive skeletal evidence confirms this picture and provides a basis for speculation about the areas from which the first Australians came.

Evidence for the robust morphology has dramatically expanded, since 1967, with the discovery of a large burial site at Kow Swamp in northern Victoria. A group of more than forty partial skeletons, including males and females, adults and juveniles, demonstrates features of generally increased size and rugosity compared with those of Aborigines of the recent past. The remains have been dated, by a variety of radiometric techniques, to between

15 000 and 9000 years ago. Adults of this group, which morphologically includes the Cohuna, Mossgiel, Lake Nitchie and Talgai crania, also possess characteristics of the face, forehead and dentition that are not seen in modern Aborigines. These have been regarded as archaic or osteologically primitive, as they reflect the features of Middle Pleistocene hominids from Java. By contrast, the considerably older skeletal remains from Lake Mungo, as well as a cranium from the Keilor site that is dated to about 14 000 years BP, appear ultramodern in form in relation to near-contemporary Aboriginal populations. Additional skeletal data from the Willandra Lakes region indicate that people of this form occupied that area between 30 000 and 20 000 years ago. Examination of these Pleistocene remains has shown that all of them lie outside the range of contemporary Aboriginal skeletal variation, but in two very different directions.[10]

Various hypotheses have been proposed to account for this morphological dichotomy. One is the notion that Australian variation, at all times, results from a single entry of people to the continent. From this viewpoint it has been suggested that variation in the past was wider than at present, due to the development of physical adaptations, and as a result of genetic drift, during Aboriginal expansion across the continent. If this were the case we would expect at least some of the Pleistocene remains to show a modern form, but they do not. It has also been argued that as the Lake Mungo remains are earliest, they represent the initial Aboriginal morphology, and therefore the robust and contemporary cranial forms are developed from them. This is highly unlikely, as too

little time has elapsed in south-eastern Australia for such major changes to have occurred. Further, explanation of robust groups along the Murray valley, close to Lake Mungo, as a local development is denied by the recent discovery of similarly large and robust remains from the coast of Western Australia, dating to mid-Holocene times. The alternative explanation, that the contrasting remains from the Pleistocene mark the movement of very different peoples to Australia at different times, is now seen as more likely. The robust Pleistocene remains, and the modern Australians in general, exhibit features that have been present in the Indonesian region for perhaps 500 000 years. Thus it seems the rugged Pleistocene remains reflect the earliest movement to Greater Australia. If this is the case, the gracile remains from Lake Mungo and elsewhere represent a later movement of people into Sunda Land and from there to Australia. Remains from Wadjak in Java, Niah Cave in Kalimantan and possibly Palawan Island in the Philippines show that Mungo-like people were present in the Indonesian area at the same period. Remains from sites in China, particularly at Liu-kiang and Choukoutien, suggest the possibility that the ultimate source of the gracile people of Australia and Indonesia is to be found there. The presence of edge-ground tools in Arnhem Land and Japan, more than 20 000 years ago, may be a cultural reflection of the spread of mainland Asian peoples in different directions. In Australia the complexity of contemporary physical variation, and to some extent cultural variation as well, could then be explained by the fusion of these people in different ways across the continent before the end of the Pleistocene period.

14.3: *The Cohuna* (left) *and Kow Swamp 5 crania, showing the characteristic forehead flattening and prognathism of the jaws that distinguish the robust group of Australian Pleistocene Aboriginal skeletal remains.*

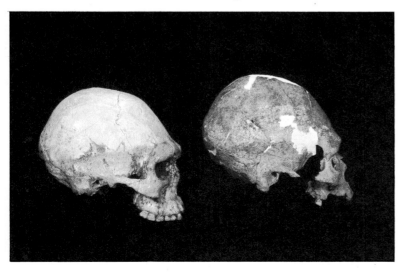

III: The Postglacial revolution

The changes towards present-day climatic conditions about ten thousand years ago accelerated developments already under way among advanced collecting and hunting groups in several parts of the world. Increasing interference with the natural environment and the deliberate movement of plants and animals beyond their natural habitats produced explosive consequences, as in several areas the density of population increased and larger permanent communities became possible. These changes were self-sustaining, as population growth encouraged outward migration and local changes in social organization. The most significant effect of this was an unprecedented increase in social inequality, culminating in the rise of socially differentiated communities that were engaged in extensive trade with neighbouring groups and lived in towns and cities that were the centres of defended territories. These early states set up a chain reaction that resulted in a spreading network of trade and conquest. Nuclear regions began to interact with each other, creating a zone of developed communities surrounded by simpler agricultural peoples, pastoralists and surviving groups of hunters and collectors.

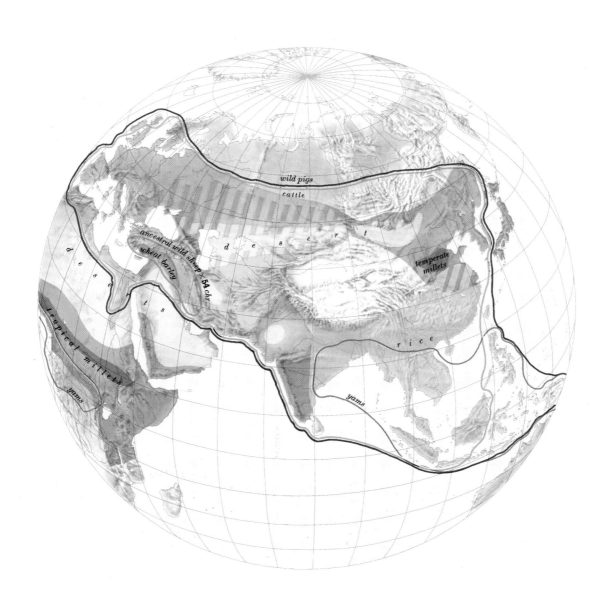

15. The beginnings of agriculture in the Near East and Europe

Of the four chief areas of the Old World where agriculture began, changes were first evident in the west Asiatic or Near Eastern centre. The major development of cultivation in this area was part of a wider series of adjustments to the onset of interglacial conditions some ten thousand years ago, but the roots of the process go back into the closing phase of the Late Pleistocene.

The last major cold period – the full-glacial or Pleniglacial phase – lasted from about 23 000 to 14 000 BP, when the temperature underwent a rapid increase. After some oscillations, marking a transitional Late-glacial phase, the temperature had settled down by shortly before 10 000 BP to the range known over the historic period. These last ten thousand years, from 8000 BC onwards, are known as the Postglacial or Holocene, though this phase is climatically no different from earlier interglacial phases.

The climate of the glacial period was not only cold but, because of the reduced evaporation from the oceans, also drier (see Chapter 8); sea levels were lowered by about 130 metres because of the amount of water locked in the polar ice caps. As a result of these cold, dry conditions, forests were restricted and steppe and desert areas more extensive. In Africa and across to north-west India the desert areas were extended in some places up to 200 kilometres beyond their present margins. In Eurasia the belt of coniferous forest between the tundra and steppe zones was squeezed eastwards as both of these treeless zones expanded in the cold, dry conditions. While northern Europe was affected by periglacial (tundra) conditions, southern Europe and large areas of the Near East were covered by dry steppe vegetation, dominated by sagebrush (*Artemisia*) and goosefoot (*Chenopodium*), and representing a westward extension of the Asian steppes. Trees survived only in restricted refuge areas, in a local montane belt at about 100 metres above sea level near the coast in Greece, and more widely in the coastal mountains of the Levant. With the probable exception of the south Caspian, there was little forest in the mountain belt further east, and pollen diagrams show that some parts of the Zagros mountains had a largely open vegetation until 5000 BC.

True 'Mediterranean' vegetation, the product of a winter-rainfall regime, would have been considerably restricted. One climatic model recently put forward[1] suggests that expansion of the polar high-pressure zone pushed the rain-bringing westerlies southwards so that their winter course no longer corresponded with the easy passage along the Mediterranean. Much of their moisture was probably absorbed by the coastlands of north-west Africa, and what rain they did bring fell largely in the southern half of the Mediterranean.

During the Late-glacial this pattern began to give way to fluc-tuating conditions leading towards the warmer and wetter conditions typical of interglacials. The reversion to a warmer climate caused a retreat of the ice margin and initiated a return of water the seas, which was taking place by 13 000 BP. Approximately half the total volume had been transferred by 10 000 BP, and the whole process was more or less complete by 6000 BP, depending on local topography. In Africa a relatively wet phase began about 12 000 BP as monsoonal rainfall increased, and this lasted well into the Postglacial. The cyclonic rainbelt would also have begun to shift northwards, allowing rain to penetrate further east along the coast of North Africa. Even though the north Mediterranean coastlands and the upland areas of Anatolia and Iran still remained dry (permitting only a local extension of pine) the Late glacial brought conditions of increased rainfall to the Levant, Sinai and western Arabia.[2] The area of 'Mediterranean' vegetation was thus able to expand again in the eastern Mediterranean, and indeed probably covered a greater area than at present, notably in the Negev.

These vegetational changes were significant because of the plant resources that became more widely available as a result. An important component of the more open 'sub-Mediterranean' oak woodland of hilly areas are the large-seeded annual grasses that were the ancestors of the cereals wheat and barley.[3] These plants quite often form extensive pure stands that ripen in the spring. With their stored food in the seed, they are well adapted to summer drought. The brittle head shatters when the seed is ripe, and the sharp spikelets help to implant the seeds in cracks in the dry ground, away from rodents and birds. Such an easily storable form of food was also attractive to human collectors; and as it increased in abundance, so its economic importance grew.

The hunting and collecting cultures of the Late-glacial

In Europe the reindeer-hunting cultures were reaching their climax with the Magdalenian culture, but signs of change are evident in the appearance of sites in the Alpine foreland, and the occurrence of many sites in shallow rockshelters beside rivers suitable for fishing. Reindeer-hunting groups such as the Hamburgian culture extended up into the North European Plain. The resumption of organic deposition in the morainic lakes of that region has preserved a pollen record of park-tundra characterized by the Mountain Avens (*Dryas octopetala*). A short oscillation towards warmer conditions (named after the pollen diagram from Allerød) allowed birch trees to spread up into this region, and reindeer hunters to move as far north as Denmark.

In North Africa the Late-glacial period is characterized by the culture known as Iberomaurusian, whose economy was based on hunting the Barbary sheep (*Ammotragus*). The main concentration of sites lies in a strip within 100 kilometres of the (present) coast. Further east, in Egypt and Nubia, the recently defined Quadan culture has given important evidence not only for the exploitation of fish and herd animals at this time but also for important use of several varieties of wild grain, including wild barley. This is reflected in a technology that included mortars, sickles and grinders set into the bedrock. This adaptation in fact lasted unchanged for long into the Postglacial, until the introduction of west Asian domesticates from the Levant about 5000 BC; the manipulation of wild grains did not lead to the kind of effective agriculture that emerged in Palestine during this period and had such explosive potential, though it did provide a subsistence base satisfactory enough to allow these west Asiatic innovations to be resisted for two thousand years after their spread to Cyprus, Anatolia and Europe.

In the area where wheat and barley were available, from Sinai to Syria and possibly beyond, these resources already had an important role in the economy. There are some indications that wild cereals were already being exploited in the Kebaran culture, between 17 000 and 14 000 BP. Recent work[4] has shown that a significant shift in the sizes and locations of sites took place, at least in the southern part of the Levant, between the Kebaran and the Late-glacial Natufian culture. Natufian sites are particularly common in areas such as the Judaean hills, where stands of wild cereals are most frequent, while their size and the presence of processing equipment strongly suggests exploitation from major base-camps. The equipment includes pounders and mortars – some made in the rock at the front of the caves themselves – and sickle-flints. These are most common in the larger, base-camp sites of the Natufian period, which have further indications of permanence in the traces of round huts and associated cemeteries. Examples of such sites are to be found not only in the caves and their terraces of the Mount Carmel area, but also in fully open sites such as Ain Mallaha on the shore of Lake Hula or underneath the remains of later agricultural villages in north Syria such as Mureybet and Tell Abu Hureyra on the Euphrates.[5] Despite the extensive use of cereals, the main animal staple at this stage remained the gazelle, which in the Natufian period formed approximately 80 per cent of the meat component of the diet.

Further east, in the mountains of the Zagros, such adaptation to plant foods is less apparent. A wider range of animals was used, however, which significantly included sheep and goats as well as cattle, deer and equids.

The early Postglacial and the origins of farming
After the false start of the Allerød, the renewal of warmer conditions about 10 000 BP marked the beginning of a more or less continuous retreat of the ice sheets and readjustment of the vegetational zones. Forests began to spread from their isolated refuge areas to cover large parts of Eurasia once again. Although the rise in temperature was rapid (as insect faunas indicate) the spread of forest was limited by the rate at which individual species of trees could disperse. Pioneer species such as birch moved most rapidly to occupy newly opened habitats, followed by conifers and then by the various components of the mixed oak forest. This

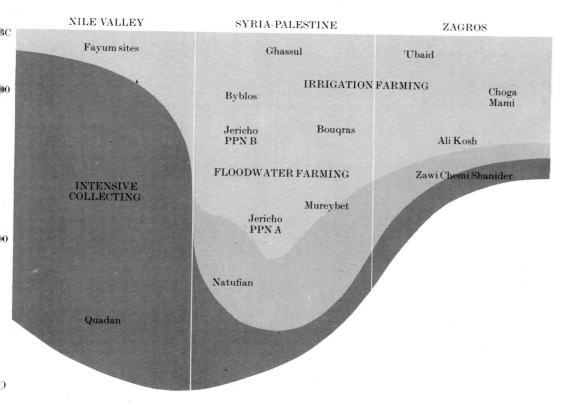

15.1: *The domestication and intensive cultivation of cereals was only the last phase of a long relationship between human populations and the large-seeded grasses. Seasonal harvesting of wild stands was increasingly supplemented by deliberate sowing and the unconscious selection of new varieties, leading to a dominant reliance on agriculture.*

NILE VALLEY   SYRIA-PALESTINE   ZAGROS

Fayum sites

Ghassul

'Ubaid

IRRIGATION FARMING

Byblos

Choga Mami

Jericho PPN B

Bouqras

Ali Kosh

INTENSIVE COLLECTING

FLOODWATER FARMING

Zawi Chemi Shanider

Jericho PPN A

Mureybet

Natufian

Quadan

☐ reaping of large-seeded grasses

☐ reaping and local cultivation of large-seeded grasses, especially cereals

☐ cultivation of domesticated forms of cereals

FULL GLACIAL   LATE GLACIAL   POSTGLACIAL

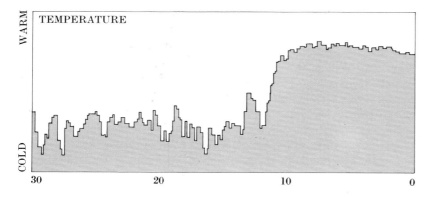

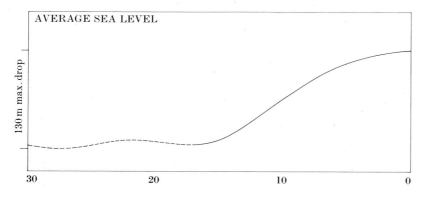

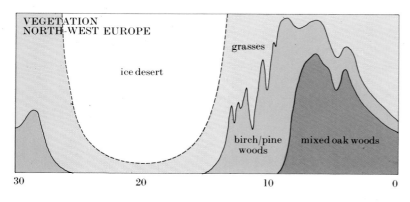

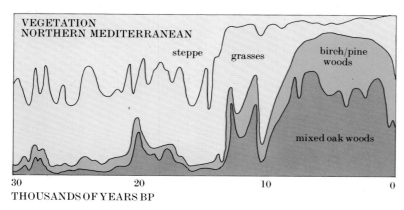

THOUSANDS OF YEARS BP

sequence was fairly rapid in the Mediterranean and oak woodland soon became widespread, but further north these stages of dispersal were more protracted. In consequence there was in temperate Europe a phase lasting for two to three thousand years with high temperatures when only the northern forest species (now characteristic of latitudes beyond 60°N) were present.

This open woodland, which soon included extensive growths of hazel, supported large numbers of red deer, elk and pig. With the many morainic lakes in recently deglaciated areas, still extensive coastal plains with plentiful migratory waterfowl and warm-water fish and molluscs, it represented a highly favourable habitat for human occupation. While it no longer supported the large migratory herds of reindeer, which followed the tundra areas northwards, it sustained dispersed but semi-sedentary hunting and collecting populations over wide areas, including some that had not previously been occupied.[6] This pattern characterizes the earlier part of the Mesolithic period in Europe. In northern Europe this is represented by the Maglemose culture, with its small composite (microlithic) flint tools, bone harpoons and also flint-core axes for woodworking: in southern Europe by the Sauveterrian cultures, which lacked the heavy tools.

In North Africa the onset of Postglacial conditions and the drowning of the coastal plain after 10 000 BP saw a general move inland to the bush–steppe zone, where the hartebeest (*Alcelaphus*) became the main source of food for the bearers of the Capsian culture. In the Sahara as a whole the wetter conditions offered rising lakes and areas of well-watered pastureland in the highland massifs that increasingly attracted population, though mainly after 6000 BC.

The most striking changes in economy were taking place at this period in the Levant. In this relatively moist phase, Mediterranean oak forest had continued to expand without interruption since the Late-glacial. However, this spread of woodland did not radically affect the hunting of herd animals in the still extensive steppe

15.2: *Climate and vegetation from 30 000 BP. The change from the conditions of the Glacial to those of the Postglacial, through an intermediate Late-glacial phase, is reflected in changes in oxygen isotope ratios in the Greenland ice cap (A). Melting ice returned more water to the sea, the level of which rose slowly (B). In northern Europe higher temperatures allowed grasses to spread into the former ice desert, followed by trees: first birch and pine, then mixed oak forest (C). In the Mediterranean wetter conditions permitted the extension of woodland into areas formerly characterized by dry steppe (D). The later decline in forest represents clearance by man.*

lowlands in the way that afforestation had affected the reindeer-hunters of Late-glacial Europe; gazelle remained the most widely hunted species. What the vegetational changes did do was to make more widely available the large-seeded grasses that were one component of the open-woodland community. Some pressure to make use of these new opportunities was presented by gradually rising sea levels, which ultimately removed about 10 kilometres of the coastal plain (and larger areas around the Red Sea and the Persian Gulf). Such pressure, especially in a heavily settled region like the Levant with few opportunities for outward expansion, may well have promoted an increasing use of wild cereals and experiments with cultivating them; and these species were able to respond by rapid evolutionary change.

Such genetic changes only occurred in certain circumstances where selective pressure was operating, and the cultivation of cereals may be very much older than the appearance of 'domesticated' forms. By the beginning of the Postglacial there are indications that cereals were not only being collected but also deliberately sown in some places where they would not naturally grow. Remains of cereals that are indistinguishable in form from wild varieties have been found at sites in the Euphrates valley in Syria in places well away from the natural habitats of the species. In wild cereal populations the head shatters when the seeds ripen. The evolution of non-shattering forms was not an inevitable result of cultivation. An obvious method of harvesting the seed of shattering forms is by tapping the stem with a stick and collecting the falling seeds in a bag. If the seeds are then sown, selective pressure in favour of the natural means of dispersal would be reinforced. If, however, seed were harvested with a sickle (when the head would be less likely to shatter), and then sown in a new area away from the wild, self-seeding population, there would be selection in favour of the tough, non-shattering heads. These conditions were fulfilled in the Natufian, where reaping-knives were in use and cereals were cultivated on mud-flats by rivers and springs.

Evidence of the results of this process is found at sites like Jericho, which developed from a hunting and collecting camp to a village settlement at the very beginning of the Postglacial, and where for the first time 'domesticated', non-shattering forms of emmer wheat (*Triticum dicoccum*) and two-row barley (*Hordeum distichum*) made their appearance.[7] This site, on the edge of the Jordan Rift, is only about 20 kilometres from one of the main present-day concentrations of wild wheat in the Judaean hills. Situated in an oasis in the semi-desert of the lower Jordan valley, it is not a location where wild cereals would have grown naturally; but its copious spring would have provided locally high ground-water where they could be sown. Such locations, by springs, rivers or lakes, are characteristic of the earliest agricultural sites, and suggest that the crops could be sown in the alluvium without extensive preparation of the ground, even though wild cereals would not under natural conditions be able to take advantage of such habitats. This restricted 'floodwater farming' represented a single, rare and highly localized form of intensified exploitation, which the successors of the Natufians followed in the early Postglacial. It was one facet of local opportunism in a community that continued its dependence on gazelle, and whose contemporaries in less favoured positions continued to subsist largely upon these animals. Other species cultivated or collected at Jericho included legumes such as lentils and field peas.

The importance of these developments – floodwater cultivation and the achievement of a domesticated cereal with greater harvesting efficiency and ease of handling – are reflected, as early as 10 000 BP, in the character of the settlement at Jericho, with its greatly increased size, permanent architecture and long occupation. The achievement of a stable agricultural base resulted in the establishment of larger, permanent communities living in village settlements, and in the emergence of a new type of site. A substantial village built in mud brick, repeatedly reconstructed on the same spot over many generations, eventually forms a considerable mound, known in Arabic as a *tell* and in Turkish as a *hüyük*. The appearance of such sites, which are common in the Near East, together with agricultural equipment such as small polished stone axes, marks the beginning of a characteristic Neolithic pattern. These developments preceded the first use of pottery. Because the earliest Neolithic remains at Jericho, those of the Pre-pottery Neolithic A (PPN A) period, underlie a massive later accumulation, they have been exposed only in small areas, but these reveal what may be up to 4 hectares of round houses made of 'hog-back' (convex) mud bricks, surrounded – at least in part – by a stone wall

15.3: *A view of the large, multi-period* tell *(left) and modern settlement of Jericho in the Jordan Rift, looking east to the mountains of Moab from the foot of the Judaean hills, habitat of the wild cereals.*

3 metres thick with at least one solid stone tower 9 metres high and 10 metres thick. While this size and scale of building is so far unique, it serves to demonstrate that such large, almost town-like agricultural settlements could be established, even at this stage of farming development and without fully domestic animals, in places of outstanding local potential.

Another important area at this time was north Syria, where Natufian deposits at the riverside site of Tell Abu Hureyra and the round houses of level II (post-Natufian) at Mureybet have yielded seeds of wild einkorn (ancestor of *Triticum monococcum*) – a somewhat less productive species of wheat, whose natural habitat was much wider than that of emmer.[8] While this was certainly introduced and deliberately cultivated, it had not undergone the transformation to a non-shattering variety. Animal remains show a continuing reliance on wild ass, aurochs and gazelle. By level III,

square constructions occur as well as round ones, forming a small *tell* of 2 hectares.

In the Zagros at this stage some open sites are known, though they have few traces of substantial architecture and may represent seasonal rather than permanent occupation. Both sheep and goat were exploited at such sites as Zawi Chemi Shanidar, lower Ganjdareh, and Karim Shahir. It is possible that cereals were also used, but probably not on the same scale as in the Levant.

By the end of the ninth millennium BC, therefore, fully agricultural communities had been established. In Syria and Palestine such sites supported a very much larger local population than their contemporaries by the cultivation of cereals – including specifically domesticated strains of both wheat and barley – in a narrow range of habitats where ground-water was available. It was not a large-scale agriculture, but rather resembled what elsewhere has

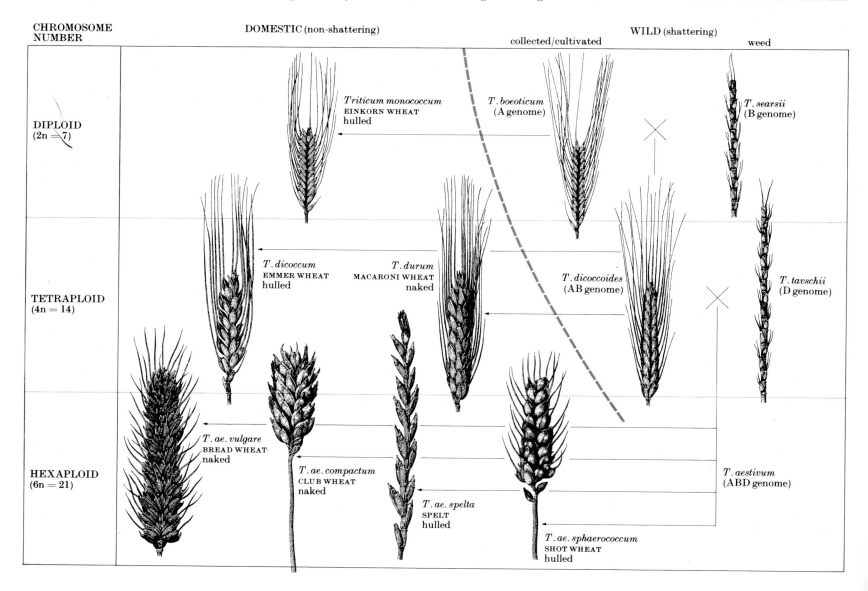

been called 'fixed plot horticulture' (see Chapter 56). This adaptation proved successful; during the eighth millennium BC agricultural villages spread over the whole of the area from southern Anatolia to Khuzistan, and by the end of the millennium were also to be found on the islands of the eastern Mediterranean.

The spread of farming and Neolithic village settlement

Developments in Syria and Palestine in the eighth millennium BC were characterized by the appearance of many more farming sites, marking the transition to a fully agricultural economy in what is known as the Pre-pottery Neolithic B (PPN B) period. A more effective architecture based on rectangular mud-brick structures with plaster floors had now developed, and *tell* sites became common. The goat took over from the gazelle as the main meat source at many sites in the south, such as Jericho and Beidha; not only does it occur in very high proportions but there are also examples of the twisted horncores characteristic of the domesticated form. This suggests further adjustments in animal exploitation to the sedentary pattern of settlement necessitated by a reliance on cereal crops. At contemporary sites in the north, such as Çayönü, sheep were present and were probably domesticated; while non-shattering varieties of both emmer and einkorn wheat were cultivated. Large numbers of new sites appeared in the Judaean hills and in the loess area of the northern Negev, south of Beersheba. Further north, the central Levantine sites of Munhatta and Ramad belong to this phase, as do El Kowm and Bouqras on the Syrian steppe. These encompass a greater diversity of locations but sites suitable for floodwater farming, using seasonally high water levels, remain common.

Mud-brick villages of similar character also appeared for the first time in the upland plains of southern Anatolia at this period, represented at the pre-pottery sites of Aşikli, Can Hasan III and

15.4: *The recent evolution of wheat illustrates two principles: hybridization between related species and human selection of non-shattering and free-threshing forms. The simplest wheats are diploid (i.e. they have two sets of seven chromosomes). Hybridization with a related species produced the tetraploid wheats, with four sets of chromosomes. Both these types occur wild and have corresponding domestic (i.e. non-shattering) forms, of which some are free-threshing. Further hybridization produced the hexaploid wheats, with six sets, and these are only known as cultivated forms – the modern bread wheats. The rapid evolution made possible by combining diverse genetic material (genomes) from different species enabled these wheats to adapt to new habitats.*

basal Hacilar, with many features in common ⟨⟩ ments to the south.[9] These sites are generally larger Syro-Palestinian settlements, or the su⟨ ⟩ Hüyük in the succeeding pottery-using phase. A ⟨ ⟩ herd animals was exploited at these sites, including ⟨ ⟩ equids in more open areas. Noteworthy among the ce⟨ ⟩ ⟨ ⟩ains are finds of *Triticum durum*, the first wheat with 'naked' seeds that could be easily separated from their enclosing husk by threshing.

As well as this westward extension into Anatolia, early agricultural sites appeared to the east in the intermontane valleys all round the oak–pistachio belt of the lower Zagros, and in the better-watered parts of its steppe fringe. As in the Levant, some of these were situated on top of older collecting and hunting camps, though they are distinguished by the solidity of their rectangular mud-brick architecture, and they are still mainly fairly small. From the beginning, sheep and goats were important animals, and some of the best evidence for the domestic status of the latter is the ubiquity of their hoofprints in mud brick at Ganjdareh. An extension of occupation to the Khuzistan steppe, perhaps seasonally at first, is indicated by the site of Ali Kosh, where goats and cultivated cereals were supplemented by a wide range of collected small seeds from uncultivated or waste land nearby. Such sites were probably economically complementary to settlements higher up in the mountains behind, both by the exchange of products and by the movement of flocks between seasonal pastures.

These sites all round the Fertile Crescent and in southern Anatolia were linked by trade in small quantities of desirable raw materials such as obsidian (which was traded southwards from Anatolia down both the Levant and the Zagros) and even luxury materials such as turquoise, malachite and native copper.[10]

The development of the Neolithic

The extension of the area occupied by farming villages provided much greater opportunities for exchange and cross-fertilization between regions, as communities in different areas solved their problems of adaptation to the new way of life with their own local resources. The pace of change began to quicken, and in the seventh millennium BC a number of notable new features appeared. These included the spread of sheep as an important domestic animal, the colonization of coastlands and islands, the development of agglomerative architecture at large and complex sites such as Çatal Hüyük, and the widespread use of pottery.

The Pottery Neolithic period in the Levant seems to have been a time of stress, for there was a radical alteration in the zones where settlement was concentrated, involving a move from the south and south-east – especially the Negev – towards the better-watered coastlands and the upper Jordan. It is possible that areas like that around Jericho went over to a more pastoral emphasis at this period, while the focus of development shifted to sites in the northern Levant like Byblos and Ras Shamra (both famous for their later cities) open to innovations from the north. It was in this context that settlements such as Khirokitia first appeared in us; a site that, although aceramic, is contemporary with the ceramic cultures of the adjacent coastlands, for instance the lower levels at Mersin. Khirokitia had emmer wheat, and sheep and goat had been introduced – indeed, it is likely that pig and Mesopotamian fallow deer were also Neolithic introductions, indicating that the artificial extension of the natural range of animals was as important an aspect of human interference as their day-to-day management.

This coastal expansion may have been a feature of southern Anatolia as well, for at the same time the earliest Neolithic settlements appear both on Crete at Knossos, on the Greek mainland at Franchthi cave in the Argolid, and at the base of several *tell* sites in Thessaly, such as Argissa and Achilleion.[11] While there may have been an initial aceramic phase, it was soon followed by the spread of the developed monochrome pottery typical of central and western Anatolia, and known also from the cave of Aghio Gala on Chios. There is little sign of any widespread inland penetration of northern Anatolia at this date, though sites like Fikirtepe near the Sea of Marmara suggest some coastal spread. Finds of Melos obsidian in the earlier layers of the Franchthi cave may indicate some measure of familiarity with seafaring among the pre-agricultural coastal peoples, whose economy included the catching of tuna fish. Both in Greece itself and on the islands sheep were introduced, while the Knossos evidence suggests that cattle, which as they were apparently not present there in the Pleistocene, were first introduced to Crete at this time. Cereals were also introduced, including both emmer and *Triticum durum*, which occurs at Knossos.

These developments in the Mediterranean coastlands were, however, peripheral to the major cultural achievements at this

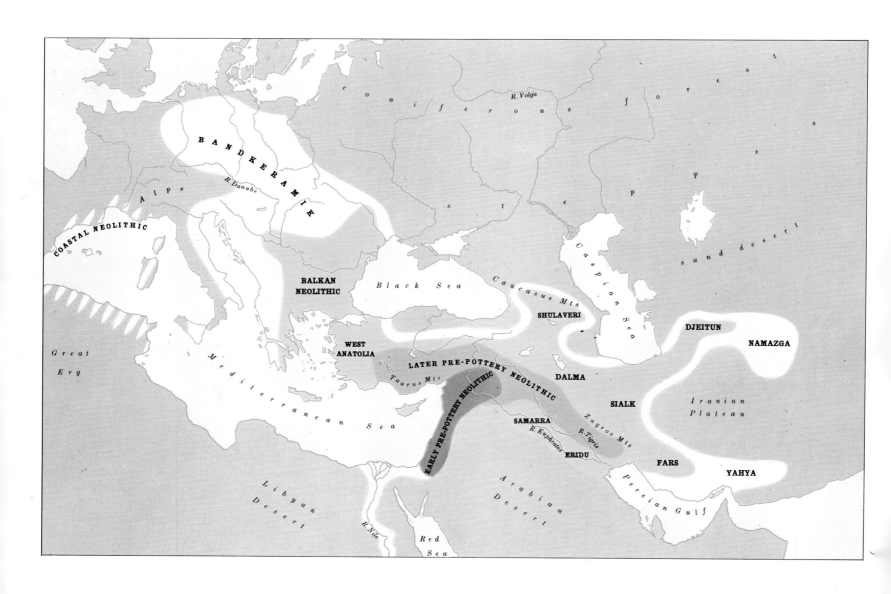

time on the Konya plain in south-central Anatolia. They were dominated by the 13-hectare site of Çatal Hüyük, on the junction of fan and backswamp where streams from the highland lakes enter this internal-drainage basin. Sustained by all three available wheat species, as well as some of the first examples of domesticated six-row barley, the protein requirements of the population were met by the exploitation of large herds of cattle, whose management was depicted in wall paintings. Architecture, now using moulded rectangular mud bricks, reached new levels of sophistication with agglomerated multi-storey dwellings, which must have been similar to recent *pueblo* villages in the arid southwest of the United States. Some contained rooms with spectacular cult fittings, including murals in relief and plastered bulls heads. Large quantities of materials such as obsidian show that Çatal Hüyük must have been supported by an extensive hinterland

15.5: *The spread of agriculture in western Asia and Europe, 8000 to 5000 BC. From its nuclear area in the eastern Mediterranean and the Taurus–Zagros mountains, agriculture spread both east and west. Eastwards its course was constrained by the mountain ranges and the deserts of the Iranian Plateau; southwards it was barred by the Arabian and Libyan deserts, while the plant-collecting groups of the Nile basin resisted agriculture for two millennia. The main area of rapid expansion was Europe, in the Balkans and the fertile loess-lands of central Europe. Pottery and sheep-rearing (though not cereal cultivation) also diffused rapidly among existing coastal groups in the western Mediterranean. There was little penetration of steppe areas or of the coniferous forest at this stage.*

extent of agricultural settlement

to 8000 BC

to 7000 BC

to 6000 BC

to 5000 BC

reaching beyond the plain, and many of the objects show high standards of craftsmanship.[12]

Çatal Hüyük is so far unique, and such supersites, like Jericho the result of unique conditions and local resources, are not known further east, though the trend towards greater architectural complexity is reflected in the small multi-room courtyard complex of Umm Dabaghiyah, situated in the Assyrian steppe. A large area of what were apparently storerooms gives some of the first evidence of central storage facilities and hints at wider socio-economic relations, especially as the buildings conform to a regular plan instead of being multiples of a single module. This site also has mural paintings, representing onagers, which were probably hunted for food by carefully placed drives and which provided two-thirds of the meat. This site, and others recently explored in this area, indicate the importance of the northern plain and of the relatively little-explored region where Iraq, Syria and Turkey meet.

By comparison, the continuing small sites of the Zagros intermontane valleys are less impressive; they include the ceramic levels at Jarmo in Iraqi Kurdistan, Tepe Guran and the later Ganjdareh levels in Luristan, and the parallel developments of the Mohammad Jaffar phase in Khuzistan. These rather restricted conditions were transformed by the development of simple irrigation techniques, allowing a proliferation of sites where mountain streams entered the flat steppe country, and of other techniques that gave the potential for further agrarian expansion well beyond the limits previously reached.

Irrigation and the expansion of Chalcolithic culture

The sixth millennium BC saw continuing growth among the communities of the Taurus–Zagros arc: simple irrigation allowed populations to expand along the mountain edges, and other developments carried agriculture further into the dry plains that lay on either side. Cattle, by now domesticated, became common on lowland sites. Agricultural development was matched by technical achievements in painted pottery and metallurgy; the widespread occurrence, by the end of the millennium, of pieces of hammered native copper, and even of pieces that were possibly smelted, has labelled the period 'Chalcolithic'. Trade in manufactured goods, for instance in fine pottery, linked well-connected chains of settlement along the steppe margins. For the Levant it was a time of relative recession; but fresh waves of settlement carried some of the innovations of this period to new areas of agricultural colonization in Balkan Europe, the area between the Black Sea and the Caspian, the Iranian Plateau, Turkmenia, and the south Iranian intermontane basins of Fars (the plain of Persepolis) and Kerman. Some of the most important developments of this period were taking place in Mesopotamia, where they formed the beginning of the process leading to urbanization. (See Chapter 16 for a more detailed account of this area.)

This period saw a major expansion of population in the steppe areas inside the Fertile Crescent associated with the Hassuna,

Samarra and Halaf cultures. On the plain margins, artificial water-spreading began, as evidenced at Choga Mami near Mandali, north-east of Baghdad.[13] Its position on an alluvial fan, where water enters the plain, was exploited by the villagers, who cut trenches across the branching streams to spread the water to a wider area and thus increase its effective use for agriculture. Beyond this zone, agriculturalists expanded on the fertile but dry brown soils of the Assyrian steppe, indicating some comparable advance in technique. Many sites are also known in the rather different environment of the Khabur catchment.

Sites occur along the main rivers of the Mesopotamian plain: on the Tigris, for instance, at Samarra and the nearby rectangular walled settlement of Tell es-Sawwan, with some ten or so modular multi-roomed complexes inside it. An outlier of this culture occurs at Baghouz on the Euphrates, immediately to the west. Further south there is evidence for the first time of agricultural communities on the lower Euphrates represented, for instance, by sites around Eridu. Largely buried under later extensive urban sites, these earliest settlements are little known; but they were in existence by the sixth millennium BC, and form the background for the more extensive occupation of the 'Ubaid period in the next millennium, when the influence of this area extended far up the Euphrates and Tigris to the Assyrian steppe.

Changes are evident not only in the distribution of sites but also from the artifacts. Ground stone hoes became common as greater field-preparation became necessary. Many kinds of flint leather-working tools disappeared, and woven cloth may have begun to replace leather for clothing. Pottery also improved, with chaff-tempered ware being replaced by well-fired grit-tempered wares painted in attractive designs. Styles such as that of Halaf were produced over wide areas.

In northern Iran, settlement extended from Kurdistan into the large intermontane plain occupied by Lake Urmia (Reziyeh), where simple villages of free-standing rectangular houses are known from Dalma, Hajji Firuz and Yanik Tepe. To the north these sites brought the extending range of village settlement into contact with a largely independent centre of sedentary collecting and cultivation in the isolated valleys, drained by the Kura and the Araxes, of the hill country south of the Caucasus. Groups of round houses in mud brick on stone foundations are typical of sites such as Shomu Tepe, Shulaveri, and Kültepe near Nachichevan. The first of these has produced evidence of a range of locally domesticated wheats and barleys with the characteristics of local wild species. This region continued to preserve its individuality, despite southern contacts.

There was also a wider occupation of the plateau to the east of the Zagros. At small oases on the western side of the dry, salt, inner plain of Iran sites began to appear: small ones like Tepe Zaghe and larger ones like Tepe Sialk, whose inhabitants kept goats and cultivated barley as well as hunting the local wild fauna. Early pottery was a low-fired soft ware, but characteristic local painted wares later developed, while the rich local mineral deposits were worked and traded for a variety of ornamental stones and native copper.

These sites in north-central Iran provide a geographical and cultural link with the group of settlements on the northern edge of the Kopet Dag in Turkmenia. Cultivation in this dry environment was made possible by irrigation, where the well-watered mountains meet their adjacent arid lowlands. Here the sites of the Djeitun culture provide good examples of the use of simple water-spreading on alluvial fans, and the extensively excavated villages show clusters of single-room, rectangular detached houses with standardized built-in ovens. More complex agglomerated structures are known from the more developed phase represented at Anau, Namazga, and the sites of the Geoksyur oasis: farming settlement had thus spread along this route almost as far as Afghanistan.[14]

Another route of eastward penetration, around the southern end of the central Iranian desert, led through the intermontane valleys of the southern Zagros such as Fars, past the upland lakes east of Shiraz and on to Kerman, on the threshold of Baluchistan. By the fifth millennium BC sites such as Tal-i-Iblis and Tepe Yahya were important manufacturing settlements for copper and steatite respectively, and are indicative of the role of these far-flung highland villages in supplying the growing demand for raw materials in the more populous lowlands.

In southern Anatolia the early Chalcolithic period is represented by sites like Çatal Hüyük west, Can Hasan I, and the upper levels at Hacilar. Settlements in the Konya plain show a pattern of proliferation, expanding from the backswamp edge back up the fans, where water-spreading may have been practised. In the later levels of Hacilar an enclosed settlement was constructed, with thick mud-brick walls surrounding three courtyards, and with domestic and workshop buildings that included a pottery. The local ceramics were of high quality, and the standard of pyro-technology is indicated by a spherical copper macehead from Can Hasan, possibly of smelted copper.

The spread of agriculture to Europe

There are many echoes of the material culture of Anatolia on the other side of the Aegean, in Thessaly; though as metallurgy is not known from European sites at this time they are labelled 'Neolithic' rather than 'Chalcolithic'. Sites of the Hacilar culture are known extensively in south-west Anatolia, spreading westwards down the Maeander valley towards the coast. No influence of this kind is discernible on Crete, but the appearance of red-and-white painted wares on the mainland at Sesklo and in the north Thessalian *tells*, along with a variety of small clay, stone and bone objects, suggests a measure of direct maritime contact across to the gulf of Volos in the sixth millennium BC.[15] The rectangular, free-standing mud-brick dwellings from Argissa, Otzaki, Tsangli and Achilleion, however, show a local tradition in architectural construction and layout, and the locations of sites of this phase in areas of naturally high ground-water does not suggest the need for water-spreading and irrigation. It was this complex, with its mixture of introduced and local features, that spread northwards to Macedonia and on up the Axios (Vardar) to the basins of the Maritsa, the Morava and the Danube, taking with it the cereals and domestic animals (predominantly sheep at this stage) to a new range of temperate environments.

The pre-existing maritime trading network among Mesolithic coastal groups around the Mediterranean, already distributing obsidian, carried some of these innovations further west. During the sixth millennium BC sheep began to appear in already occupied caves and in coastal shell-mound sites in western Greece, Italy, southern France, North Africa and Spain. They were carried by colonists who occupied Corsica and Sardinia for the first time, and crossed to North Africa where settlement began again in the coastal strip abandoned by the Capsian peoples. At all these sites the presence of obsidian shows continuing maritime contact.

15.6: *Reconstruction of a two-storied house at Sesklo in Thessaly, northern Greece (after Theocharis). This building belongs to the Middle Neolithic, about 5000 BC, and was one of two dozen occupied on the site during this period. The footings are of stone, surmounted by a mud-brick superstructure. The village was situated in a small valley between two streams and was surrounded by a wall.*

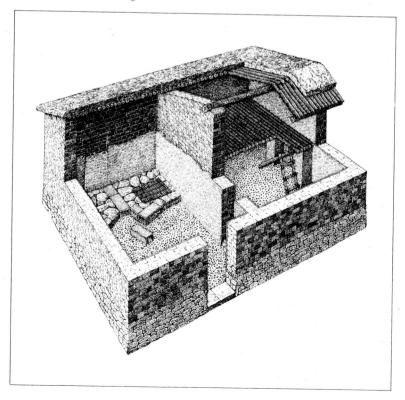

Pottery, too, was copied and characteristically ornamented with the edges of shells (especially the cockle *Cardium edule*), giving the name Cardial or Impressed Ware to these assemblages. There is no evidence of cereal cultivation from these sites, however, and these early assemblages are not known from agricultural villages: they occur in caves at Crvena Stijena in Dalmatian Yugoslavia, at Curacchiagghiu in Corsica and at Châteauneuf-les-Martigues in the south of France, and in coastal middens like Sidari on Corfu, or at Coppa Nevigata on the west coast of Italy. None of these shows any traces of substantial constructions.

In Macedonia Neolithic settlement is best represented at Nea Nikomedia, near the former shore of the Gulf of Salonika, and at Anzabegovo in the Ovče Polje near Skopje; in Bulgaria, where it arrived slightly later, it is well known from Kremikovci in the Sofia basin and at Azmak and Karanovo on a tributary of the Maritsa. Valley-edge sites near springs are common. When excavated, such sites have been shown to represent a group of a dozen or so identical square, free-standing houses with hearths and ovens.[16]

Contrasts are evident, however, between areas like the Vardar and Maritsa valleys, still within a climatically Mediterranean zone, and the Danube catchment with its central European climate. Nucleated *tell* settlements of houses with upright walls seem at this time to be characteristic only of the former, while linear hamlets of houses with sloping walls, positioned at some distance from each other along bluffs and river banks, seem more typical of the latter, and are known from southern Hungary. These belong to the culture named after the site of Starčevo on the Danube, or the Körös river in Hungary where such sites are particularly abundant.[17]

Connections between different parts of this area are indicated by the distribution of characteristic types of figurines, for instance the rod-head form, and the similar kinds of simple bichrome painted pottery produced over most of it. There was a tendency for painting to become less common with time, and there are rather few pieces of fineware in the peripheral northern assemblages, which by the time settlement had reached the Körös and the lower Danube in Romania were dominated by chaff-tempered wares with impressed ornament. The general impression given by most of these groups, especially to the north of Macedonia, is one of successive simplification from the rather higher levels of organization and technical skill that had been achieved further south and east, as pioneer settlers found a fertile landscape from which to gain a living without great effort or hardship.

16. The emergence of cities in the Near East

By the end of the fourth millennium BC society in Mesopotamia had reached a level of complexity that leads us to recognize it as the world's first urban civilization. Both archaeological and textual sources provide evidence of settlements of increasing size and diversity of function and of the differentiation of society into increasingly specialized groups. To explain this is a major task, especially from data that are often biased or incomplete. The fact that there exists extensive third-millennium textual documentation from Sumer has commonly led to an undue emphasis on what is, from the archaeologist's point of view, a relatively late phase of urban growth; archaeological evidence allows the process to be studied in a more realistic perspective.

The development of lowland settlement

Near Eastern civilization was based on indigenous crops and herd animals (emmer, einkorn, bread (? club) wheat, barley and pulses; sheep, goats, cattle and pigs). Indeed, once established, some time in the seventh millennium BC, the basic pattern of Mesopotamian farming persisted essentially unchanged down to the advent of modern mechanized agriculture, the only exception being the introduction in the first millennium BC of summer-grown crops such as rice and cotton.[1] Lowland areas probably played an important part in the domestication of cattle, as their remains are found on settlements of the seventh millennium such as Bouqras in eastern Syria and Umm Dabaghiyah in northern Iraq at a time when they were apparently absent in highland areas, where sheep and goats were predominant. Recent evidence points to the importance of the north Mesopotamian plain at this time, and the discovery of a pre-pottery settlement near Yarim Tepe (Maghzaliyah) with 8 metres of archaeological deposits, including circular stone-walled houses, promises to revolutionize existing interpretations of the origins of settlement in this area.

Among these seventh-millennium farmers the smelting of both copper and lead is known; at Yarim Tepe a massive lead bracelet and a number of copper objects have been found. The site is also noted for a large number of two-stage domed pottery kilns, the earliest yet discovered, situated in a clearly demarcated 'industrial' area. Investigations of contemporary pottery using a scanning electron microscope reveal kiln temperatures that approached 1100°C, sufficient to melt copper for casting. Metal was a valuable commodity, however, seldom carelessly lost, and the earliest cast copper so far recovered (from Arpachiyah) is dated to a millennium later. Multi-roomed storehouses of identical plan are found at seventh-millennium sites such as Yarim Tepe I and Umm Dabaghiyah, suggesting the likelihood of some communal economic activity. Thus, despite the small size (1–2 hectares) and early date of these settlements, the antecedents of the social and economic developments that were to be associated with urban life in Sumer several millennia later can already be discerned.

The most crucial innovation came in the Samarran phase (about 6000 BC) with the growth in central Mesopotamia of villages of greater size (4–5 hectares) and complexity, with an economy based on the simple irrigation technology that was to make possible the extensive agricultural settlement of Sumer itself (the southernmost part of the country). At the same time increasing evidence appears for specialized craftsmanship in the form of potters' marks, a growing trade in luxury goods such as copper and turquoise, and communal defensive works such as the wall and ditch that surround the level III village at Tell es-Sawwan and the massive mud-brick tower that guards one entrance to the town at Choga Mami. Seals and seal impressions – evidence of 'ownership' or 'authorization' – imply the concept of personal property and perhaps some form of central redistributive agency. At Sawwan the vast, indeed unique, cemetery in which the grave goods consist of exotic beads and beautifully carved objects in

16.1: *The names of various Sumerian cities appear among the pictographs on this tablet sealing from Jamdat Nasr. Such seals illustrate the 'collective' commercial activities of these late fourth-millennium cities.*

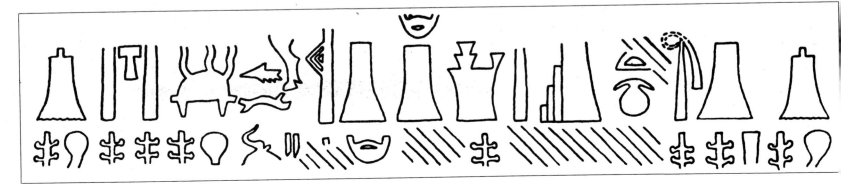

alabaster suggests that this was a site of specialized function.

The al-'Ubaid period

The culmination of these prehistoric advances is to be found in the 'Ubaid period of the sixth and fifth millennia, when the earliest settlements are known from Sumer. This area was characterized by the very great fertility of its alluvial soil and – outside local areas of marsh and lagoon where a specialized fishing, hunting and collecting economy could have been practised – an extremely arid environment that necessitated the use of irrigation for successful agriculture. The marsh environments probably already carried local non-agricultural populations, who adopted farming and irrigation techniques from central Mesopotamia.

The vast potential of irrigation farming, both in economic and in social terms, provides a sharp contrast to those areas of northern Mesopotamia, north of the average rainfall limit of 300 milli-metres a year, where villages of the Hassuna and Halaf cultures are to be found and where rain-fed cultivation of winter-growing crops such as wheat, barley and linseed was possible. In the south not only did the irrigated land produce more, but the necessity for cooperation among local farming groups, for example over such simple matters as the equitable distribution of water and the maintenance of irrigation systems, provided a cohesive social force unique to the irrigation environment. In Sumer, owing to the heavy silt content of the rivers, annual cleaning of water channels was an essential task that required not so much a large workforce as a level of cooperation that must certainly have influenced the structure of society.

One of the most important consequences of irrigation farming in the particular environment of Sumer was that land values inevitably varied with the availability of water. The consequent inequalities must have produced comparable inequalities in alienable, hereditary wealth and thus encouraged the emergence of a class society. Certainly in the historic periods the relationship of persons to property appears to have been the basic factor in Mesopotamian social structure, and Mesopotamia is unusual in that even in these later times there was a notable lack of non-economic status stratification.[2] Inequality of land holdings was less significant in areas of reliable rainfall, where land could be effectively tilled by simple family units and where, in the particular northern Mesopotamian environment, arable land was largely of equal value and did not require extensive clearance of forest. Even in the rain-fed north, however, access to water remained an important determinant of settlement patterns.

In the south dependence on irrigation also led to a greater level of agricultural stability, at least in the early periods of its development before the lack of drainage began to produce acute problems of salination. On the other hand, this agricultural potential was combined with the insecurity of a land where there were flash floods, violent dust storms, scorching winds, pestilence and un-

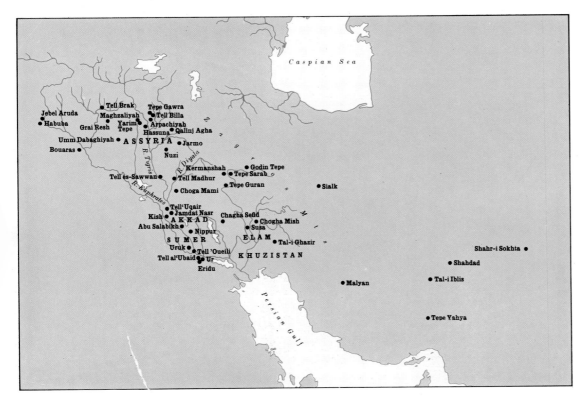

16.2 *Major sites giving evidence of urban development in Mesopotamia. The majority of settlements were situated in the more fertile areas – the alluvial plains between the Tigris and the Euphrates and the moist steppeland of the northern plain – where agriculture had been successfully established.*

predictable rivers whose regimes – unlike that of the more pre-dictable Nile – were a constant danger. The impact of these natural forces, which were no doubt a further incentive to social integration, is very clear in Mesopotamian religion, which seems to have become institutionalized for the first time in early 'Ubaid Sumer.[3]

The appearance, not long after 6000 BC, of the first Mesopo-tamian buildings that can be unequivocally identified as temples or shrines marks the beginning of a long, though not universal, religious tradition, of which one characteristic architectural feature was the preservation of the ruins of one shrine beneath the foundations of its successor. This is most strikingly illustrated at Eridu, in a remarkable series of temples, representing perhaps some 3500 years, which culminates in the great stepped tower or ziggurrat constructed at the end of the third millennium BC. This prehistoric architectural convention led to the construction of increasingly high platforms or terraces, the predecessors of the ziggurrats of later times.

One of the most important institutions in the rise of the Sumerian city was this central corporate body, which we call its temple but which was also extensively involved in farming and manufacturing activities. It also appears to have functioned as an economic institution engaged in the collection and distribution of surplus in the form not only of agricultural produce but also of the products of the specialized crafts and industries it sponsored. It is impossible to be sure how far such functions were also characteristic of the first prehistoric shrines, but the continuity of cult for which there is clear evidence at Eridu suggests a gradual development of the temple as an institution, including its economic activities.

Indeed, by the end of the 'Ubaid period (some time in the fifth millennium BC) the pattern of town and temple, so characteristic of the early Sumerian city, was well established. The recovery at Tepe Gawra in northern Iraq of a large number of seal impressions from a well connected with a late 'Ubaid shrine suggests the economic function of such 'religious' institutions. By this time, too, at Gawra there existed three separate shrines situated within an imposing precinct.

Such developments suggest an advancement of society that is otherwise ill documented. The distinctive monochrome-painted pottery that is characteristic of 'Ubaid Mesopotamia is found on most major sites in Sumer, yet we know nothing of the villages or towns that these sherds represent. Indeed, our perception of social and economic developments at this time is seriously limited by the absence of settlement excavation. By the late 'Ubaid phase some settlements, such as 'Uqair in northern Babylonia and Tell Awayli ('Oueili) near Larsa, already approached 11 hectares in area. Such developments emphasize the growing need for a central authority, but neither the few 'Ubaid houses that have been excavated nor the grave goods from the extensive cemeteries found at Ur and Eridu indicate any degree of social stratification.

Perhaps the most striking feature of 'Ubaid Sumer is the evidence for movements of people and for long-distance trade far beyond the geographical limits of the 'Ubaid homeland. This is most evident in the distribution of 'Ubaid pottery along the coasts of eastern Arabia, most of which can on analysis be shown to have been manufactured in Sumer.[4] In northern Iraq and adjacent areas of Syria a variety of 'Ubaid features is found, including not only pottery styles but also building techniques. Even religious

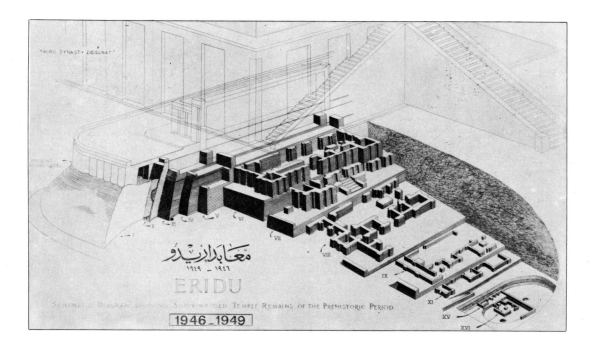

16.3: *This long sequence of temples, excavated at the site of Eridu, covers a period of almost four thousand years and provides one of the most striking examples of continuity of religious cult and tradition in Sumer. From the sixth-millennium BC levels onwards the remains of earlier shrines are actually preserved within the foundations of their predecessors.*

practices seem to have spread, and the temple plans of Gawra largely imitate or elaborate those of Eridu. This cultural intrusion, larger than anything previously attested, suggests that the inhabitants of Sumer were attempting to control the trade routes on which depended their acquisition of such raw materials as timber, stone, metal ores and (in the case of the Gulf) marine products, which were lacking in their own environment. Indeed, we know that even the pigments with which their pottery was so elaborately painted were imported over long distances. Although little metal has actually been recovered from sites of this phase, both gold and lapis lazuli are known by the end of the 'Ubaid period and the baked clay model shafthole axes from 'Uqair confirm the presence of cast-metal prototypes well before 5000 BC.

The Uruk period

While the complex processes that led to the growth of urban civilization are clearly evident in the 'Ubaid period in Sumer, it was in the succeeding Uruk phase, spanning the fourth millennium BC, that settlements of urban proportion and function first appeared. Unfortunately, despite the obvious importance of sites of this period, little excavation has been carried out. Most of our knowledge comes from the site of Uruk itself, from the meticulous German excavations in the area of the Anu ziggurrat and the monumental Eanna complex – a vast terrace surmounted by large and often elaborately ornamented public buildings. Regrettably, we know nothing of the contemporary town, estimated to have covered perhaps 30 to 50 hectares, a fact that has led many authorities erroneously to view Uruk at this time as little more than a 'ceremonial centre'. With the exception of a few limited soundings only the latest levels of the Uruk phase (from perhaps 3500 BC onwards) have so far been exposed. The earlier phases remain virtually undocumented, and we must turn to Susa in adjacent Khuzistan for more detailed knowledge of the level of development that must also have existed in contemporary Mesopotamia.

Geographically Khuzistan represents an extension of the alluvial plains of Mesopotamia, and at times it was controlled by Mesopotamian dynasties. Yet its native inhabitants were not Mesopotamian and it was to become the centre of an Elamite-speaking dynasty centred on its one great city, Susa. Mesopotamian influence is clear as early as the sixth millennium at sites such as Chagha Sefid and Chogha Mish, but the founding of Susa itself appears to have been an entirely local phenomenon. The earliest settlements so far identified at Susa, Period A on the acropolis (levels 33–27), cover an area of at least 10 to 15 hectares, and perhaps as much as 25 hectares. This phase is notable for an impressive terrace over 10 metres in height that presumably supported several public buildings, a cemetery in which it is estimated that some 2000 bodies were interred, the great quantity of metal deposited in these graves, including large numbers of copper axes and mirrors, and the extraordinarily fine quality of the associated pottery, thrown on some type of potter's wheel. Although the necropolis burials generally contain grave goods of some value, no single grave stands out as clearly richer than the others. The elaborate public architecture, the large number of seals and sealings and imported luxuries, especially metal, all point to increasing organization and differentiation of wealth.

While this growing complexity might have led in Khuzistan, as

16.4: *One of two dark shale plaques (16 centimetres wide) known as the Blau monuments, originally thought to be forgeries but now recognized as the earliest known objects on which writing and pictures are combined. The inscription, in the archaic style of the Uruk III tablets, remains obscure but may record dedications on behalf of craftsmen depicted on the reverse. The so-called 'man in the net skirt' on the left, bearded and wearing a headband, commonly appears as a figure of authority in Late Uruk narrative scenes.*

in Mesopotamia, to the creation of a local urban state, the evidence at Susa shows that the high terrace was abandoned, and there followed a period of such close association with Sumer as to suggest some form of control from the west in the phase represented by levels 22–17 on the acropolis. This 'Uruk interlude' in Khuzistan saw a further increase in settlement complexity, and by the mid-fourth millennium Susa had certainly grown to some 25 hectares in area. At the same time the appearance of smaller sites on which clay cones – elements of mosaic wall decoration associated with religious or other public buildings – are found suggests not only a growing economic or political authority but also an increasingly hierarchical patterning of settlements.[5]

In Mesopotamia the beginning of the Uruk period in the late fifth millennium BC is characterized by the introduction of mass-produced pottery, for the most part undecorated. This development coincides with the widespread use of a true potter's wheel, perhaps the single most important reason for the apparently abrupt change from the painted pottery of the 'Ubaid period to the largely plain Uruk wares. By 4000 BC a distinctive open bowl with a bevelled rim, cheaply produced in enormous quantities from moulds, is found both in Mesopotamia and in Khuzistan. This has been plausibly interpreted as a 'ration measure'.[6] By the end of the Uruk period it is found throughout much of western Asia and suggests not only some form of central economic authority but also the spread of the Sumerian and Elamite administrative systems.

At Tepe Gawra, a peripheral and in many ways atypical site, a number of mud-brick or stone-built tombs with rich grave goods belong to this period. Three tombs were especially rich, and contained unusually large quantities of gold, electrum, lapis lazuli and ivory. One tomb alone yielded over 200 objects in gold and some 450 lapis lazuli beads. While there has been less excavation on Uruk period sites in Sumer itself, contemporary cemeteries there have not so far revealed such major differences in wealth until the Early Dynastic period, some time after 3000 BC.

By the beginning of the Late Uruk period, not long after 3500 BC, a monumental ceremonial and administrative complex had developed at Uruk itself (levels V–IV). Level IV produced the world's first written documents, and at the same time representational art appeared, with the portrayal of priestly or 'king-like' figures. The presence of writing provides new insights into contemporary society. Although the language of the essentially pictographic Uruk IV texts cannot be read, the meaning of individual symbols is often clear or can be determined from the later cuneiform signs that were derived from them. The scribes of the Uruk IV period possessed a repertoire of some 1500 separate signs, including the words for carpenter, smith, donkey, chariot (two- and four-wheeled), boat, copper (already in the form of an ingot), two types of plough, the socketed axe and the harp or lyre. The sense 'to buy' is implicit in one ideogram, while another signifies 'road' or 'expedition'. For the most part these early clay tablets appear to be lists of commodities, business transactions and land sales. There are lists of, or receipts for, dairy products, including milk and

cattle, wheat and barley, bread, beer, items of clothing and, above all, flocks of sheep, which must have constituted a major source of income.

Most interesting among a number of largely undeciphered Uruk IV ideograms are the sign for 'assembly' (*unken*) and the titles *en*, often translated as 'lord' and in later times the head of the temple community, and *sanga*, later the chief administrator of the temple complex. Despite such indications of growing central authority, the existence of the *unken* leads us to assume that there was a basically democratic political structure at this time, an assumption in keeping with the lack of archaeological evidence for a markedly structured society.[7] The words for 'king' and 'palace' do not appear until early in the third millennium, while the vocabulary for warfare appears later still in Early Dynastic Mesopotamia.

Although the language of the earliest tablets cannot be specifically identified, the existence of the Sumerian sexagesimal system of numerical notation strongly suggests that the Sumerians were indeed the inventors of this earliest writing system. Moreover, the long sequence of religious buildings at Eridu and at Uruk, culminating in the White Temple on the Anu high terrace, reveals not only the early association of temple and town but an uninterrupted religious tradition that argues convincingly for a substantial continuity of population until Sumerian times. The tablets from Uruk level III are more informative and include a Sumerian personal name. A ration list records a day's bread and beer allocation for some fifty individuals; other similar fragments refer to the issue of barley and fish.

Levels III and II at Uruk are paralleled by the nearby site of Jamdat Nasr, at which polychrome pottery once thought to represent a distinct period was found. At Uruk itself the great Eanna precinct, which by now had been extended to enclose the last temple on the Anu terrace, was entirely redesigned to create a new central sanctuary, built on a high terrace and surrounded by many administrative or storage rooms. At Jamdat Nasr there is evidence for an impressive administrative building,[8] from which perhaps the most revealing discovery is a sealing found on several tablets that appears to represent some form of validation on behalf of a group of Sumerian cities, among them Ur, Uruk and Larsa. Similar 'collective' sealings have been found at Ur (Early Dynastic I) rolled on clay lumps, presumably from jars or bales conveying various commodities. On the basis of this evidence the existence in Sumer of an early league of cities has been proposed.[9] Whether or not this represents a 'political' unification cannot be determined at present, but there can be no doubt about the close commercial relationships between the various cities of Sumer at least as early as the end of the Uruk period, together with an increasing centralization and elaboration of administration within each individual city. It would also appear that these economic links may have been complemented from a very early period by wide intellectual contacts, seen in the circulation of scholarly texts; even the word lists by which the scribes learned the new script were already set down in identical order at Jamdat Nasr and Uruk.

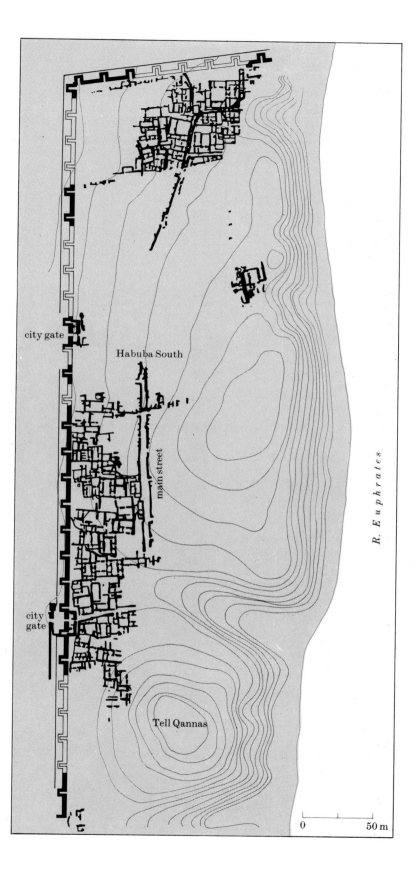

city gate

Habuba South

main street

R. Euphrates

city gate

Tell Qannas

0 ——— 50 m

Uruk trade and administration

Related to this late fourth-millennium evidence for organized economic activity within Sumer itself is a rapidly increasing body of evidence for the establishment of long-distance trading contacts, if not political domination, in Syria and Iran. The widespread occurrence and specific association of such administrative items as 'notational' clay tablets (i.e. those inscribed solely with numbers), cylinder seals and sealings identical to those from Sumer and Susa, bevelled-rim bowls and, in Iran, Jamdat Nasr-like polychrome jars, suggest a world in which people and ideas, and probably also merchandise, circulated freely. One of the most impressive new sites is Habuba South/Qannas, a large walled town on the upper Euphrates east of Aleppo, where virtually the entire range of pottery resembles that from levels V–IV at Uruk, some 800 kilometres away. Even the brick used in the construction of its buildings is identical to that of the same period in southern Mesopotamia. Here and at a contemporary religious sanctuary on Jebel Aruda just to the north notational tablets, seals and sealings identical to examples from southern Mesopotamia and Khuzistan have also been found. At the least, here is a merchant colony that originated in Sumer, but it is difficult not to suspect that Habuba and Jebel Aruda may represent an actual Sumerian provincial administration.

In Iran the pattern is slightly different in that the common repertoire of administrative items occurs generally in association with an otherwise local tradition. At Godin Tepe, near Kermanshah, for example, a proto-Elamite administrative complex or trading post coexists with the local town.[10] By the Uruk III ('Jamdat Nasr') phase and continuing into Early Dynastic I similar evidence comes from a number of distant Iranian sites including Sialk, Tal-i Ghazir, Malyan and Shahr-i Sokhta. One of the most informative is Tepe Yahya, 1000 kilometres south-east of Susa, where proto-Elamite tablets, seals, sealings, bevelled-rim bowls and Jamdat Nasr-type jars have been recovered from a

16.5: *Plan of the German excavations at Habuba Kabira South in northern Syria, showing the large walled settlement of the Late Uruk period that extends over and to the south of both Habuba South and the mound of Tell Qannas, excavated by a Belgian expedition. The objects and building techniques found here closely resemble those at Uruk in Sumer, suggesting that Habuba South/Qannas may have been a Sumerian merchant colony or administrative centre. Some of the buildings resemble in plan the tripartite temples found by a Dutch expedition at nearby Jebel Aruda but are undoubtedly secular in function.*

large administrative building; 85 per cent of the pottery is of indigenous types, however, and domestic houses on the opposite side of the mound contain none of the official paraphernalia of the administrative centre.[11] Funerary vessels of Jamdat Nasr type are also found along the Persian Gulf and as far south as Oman, but the role of the Sumerians in this area is less easily ascertained. Whether the establishment of these far-flung connections represents merely the activities of merchant communities based at Susa and the cities of Sumer, or the actual exercise of Sumerian and Elamite political hegemony remains a matter for investigation. Yet another pattern may possibly be represented by the vast site of Tell Brak in north-eastern Syria, where a long sequence of 'Jamdat Nasr' temples, purely Mesopotamian in conception, has been identified.

Here too, bevelled-rim bowls and a Late Uruk notational tablet have been recovered, but it remains possible that the great city that flourished at Brak in the fourth and third millennia BC is characteristic of a parallel development of urbanism in northern Mesopotamia for which we have as yet little evidence.

At a number of these early administrative centres numerous clay *bullae* have been found. These are hollow, spherical objects containing clay 'counters' of various shapes that represent particular consignments of goods. The *bullae* are sealed on the surface, presumably as validation by the producer and transporter of the merchandise concerned. The tokens are thought by some to represent an early stage in the development of the pictographic scripts of Sumer and Elam,[12] but it is equally possible that they

16.6: *Two seal impressions, illustrating* (above) *a ritual scene before a temple façade and* (below) *the high level of late fourth-millennium BC technology, domed pottery kilns on a sealing from Susa. The ritual seal (height 4.2 centimetres) is identical in style to those from Uruk but was found at Tell Billa, near Nineveh, some 650 kilometres to the north: it is one of many examples of the widespread influence of Late Uruk Sumer.*

16.7: *One of the most famous objects of Sumerian art, this alabaster vase (height 1.05 metres) from Uruk depicts the produce of fields and herds being presented to a deity in a ritual procession led by the 'man in the net skirt', the tassel of whose belt is held by an attendant* (upper right).

represent no more than a method of accounting used in transactions with distant and/or illiterate peoples. Such *bullae* have been found at Nuzi as late as the second millennium BC.

In recent years a number of archaeological surveys have served to illuminate the changing patterns of settlement that led to the urban growth documented above. Those in the regions of Uruk itself, Nippur and Susa have been most extensive, and thus most informative,[13] even though they are based on fairly crude chronological divisions and rough estimates of site size. Difficulties in dating individual sites make calculations of populations at different periods very problematic but, recognizing these limitations, results so far indicate a variety of patterns of urban growth. Although important, Uruk was not unique in its rise to urban status. Survey data at Nippur appear to demonstrate an earlier pattern of settlement clustering and the more rapid growth of Abu Salabikh and Nippur itself, a city we know from historical sources as Sumer's most important religious centre, perhaps even the focus of the league of cities hinted at in the collective seals. Moreover, excavated data from Late 'Ubaid sites such as 'Uqair and Gawra suggest that there was already some simple hierarchical pattern of settlement well before the end of the fifth millennium, and indeed before such trends can be detected on the basis of survey data alone.

Uruk seems to have attained its maximum size (? 400 hectares) during the Early Dynastic I period, not long after 3000 BC, and it is thought that Uruk, and perhaps also Susa and Kish, an ancient city-state in Akkad (the northern part of southern Mesopotamia), which appears at an early period to have been of much greater political importance than Uruk, may have grown not so much through population increase as through depopulation of the countryside. Susa presents a very different picture in that all the resources of Elam were concentrated in this, its one major city; in Sumer, by contrast, a number of city-states are attested by Early Dynastic times.

The reasons for the very early growth of urban society in Sumer and Elam are certainly complex, and are possibly beyond the perceptions of archaeology. Such processes, however, had their roots in the unique combination of agricultural potential and lack of resources that encouraged not only an early development of trade and consequent contact with an ever-widening world, but also specialization and centralization. The urban process in Mesopotamia, however it began, was self-sustaining, while Sumer and Elam can be said to have 'exported' the urban concept as their trading activities stimulated growth in surrounding regions.

16.8: *The ritual hunting of lions is associated with royalty throughout Mesopotamian history. This basalt stela from Uruk (height 78 centimetres) provides the earliest example, although whether the bearded figure – identical to the 'man in the net skirt' depicted in ritual scenes on cylinder seals – represents a 'kingly' or 'priestly' figure is impossible to determine. A similar figure before a horned temple on a high terrace can be seen on the seal impression from Susa in Elam* (right).

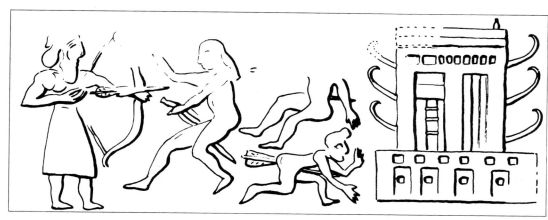

17. Mesopotamia and Iran in the Bronze Age

From about 3000 BC, in what archaeologists term the Early Dynastic period, study of the recently formed Sumerian city-states in southern Iraq increasingly involves both archaeological data and textual evidence. Some of this is contemporary, but many of the 'historical' texts were composed later and need careful analysis to distinguish the real course of events from myth and legend.[1] Excavations have long concentrated on temples, large administrative buildings and graves; but in the last twenty years surface surveys have played an important part in extending the range of archaeological research.[2]

It is customary to think of Mesopotamia at this time as Sumerian-dominated. This view may be seriously misleading, since it owes so much to a concentration of excavation and survey in the south and to texts in the Sumerian language. Although Sumerian influence was at times considerable, there were regions north and east of modern Hillah (close to Babylon) already populated by Semitic Akkadian-speaking peoples and others, who were later to make major contributions to Mesopotamian civilization.[3] Here villages, with nomadic peripheral populations, were more common than the towns that distinguished Sumer, and they have yet to receive systematic archaeological investigation.

During the Early Dynastic period, as its name indicates, the Sumerian city-states passed into the control of individual rulers and court establishments increasingly independent of the theocratic authority taken to characterize their government in the later prehistoric period. By Early Dynastic II/III (about 2750–2350 BC) actual palaces are known at Eridu, Kish and Mari, and texts reveal them elsewhere. Although Sumerian kingship may originally have been an *ad hoc* device for electing war leaders, and traces of elective bodies survived long after its establishment, it soon became a permanent institution sanctioned and legitimized by a strong relationship between the ruling families and the cults of city gods. There are many points in the early history of such city-states as Lagash (Al-Hiba), Ur and Uruk that suggest that Sumerian rulers were politically expansionist, even imperialist,

long before the Akkadian dynasty (see below).

The emergence of kingship was the most obvious of many signs of increasing social stratification and more diversified sources of economic control within towns. These complex developments are tentatively reconstructed from such material indicators as growing differentiation in the wealth of grave furnishings and marked distinctions in the size and equipment of town houses, and from administrative texts whose special terminology is often not yet fully understood. Even if the old idea of the monopolistic Sumerian temple economy has been rejected as a gross oversimplification based on a single archive of tablets,[4] the extent of temple-controlled land was considerable. The city temples, the manor houses of the gods, with their richly endowed mud-brick shrines, offices, stores, workshops and, in some places, staged towers (*ziggurrats*) dominated the towns. Temple bureaucracies controlled many agricultural and mercantile enterprises, supervising the supply and flow of goods and services. Under temple patronage – for most of what are now called 'works of art' were made for the service of the gods – craftsmen showed much inventiveness, technological progress was marked and literary skills outstanding. The unique status of Nippur, seat of Enlil (head of the Sumerian pantheon) but never a political capital, ensured a remarkably unified Sumerian culture by associating all temples in a complex economic and scribal interdependence.

By the later Early Dynastic period the evolving institutions of

17.1: *Fragment of the so-called 'Stela of the Vultures' from Telloh (ancient Girsu), showing Eannatum, ruler of Lagash c. 2450 BC, leading his troops both on foot (in the upper register) and in his chariot (in the lower), against a neighbouring Sumerian city-state. This is an unusually elaborate illustration of Sumerian arms and armour in action.*

monarchy matched those of the temple, at times to the point of friction, as rulers began to take temple lands and activities under crown control. An aristocracy of ruling families, each with extensive property, had clients bound to them in varying degrees by allotments of land or the distribution of rations; in some cases this control amounted to slavery. In what was predominantly an agricultural economy based on household units there also survived what may be the oldest element of all: kin-based communities with considerable, if declining, areas of land under corporate control, that were represented by popular assemblies and councils of elders. Although state establishments largely controlled both the circulation of goods within Sumer and foreign trade, there is increasing evidence for private individuals participating in profitable business enterprises.

The urgent need for raw materials lacking at home, and agricultural surpluses more than sufficient to secure them, took Sumerians abroad. In these foreign undertakings there was a strong, if still obscure, interaction of military and commercial factors – the flag followed trade. Archaeological evidence for Sumerian cultural penetration, usually art objects, is most conspicuous in regions vital to the maintenance of supplies of metals, of building and semi-precious stones and of timber, as at Mari and Tell Chuera in Syria, Assur in north Mesopotamia and Susa in south-west Iran. Contacts varied in intensity, as the surviving evidence varies in distribution and significance; but the security of lines of supply

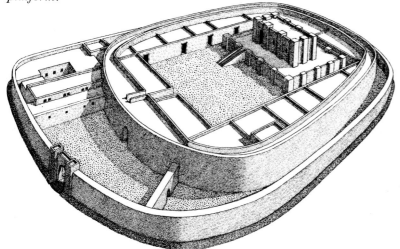

17.2: *Reconstruction of the mud-brick Oval Temple at Khafaje, in the Diyala valley, about 2500 BC. The conjectural raised shrine, the house of the god, is set in an enclosed unit including accommodation for priests, stores and workshops, whose foundations had survived on a massive oval platform.*

from the Gulf to the Mediterranean shores underlay the most ambitious military enterprises. The recently discovered palace archives at Tell Mardikh (ancient Ebla) in Syria[5] have opened up many new perspectives. Here was a major city-state involved in a network of military and commercial enterprises, already embracing Assur and possibly Kültepe in Anatolia (see Chapter 26), whose armies were capable of imposing its authority and exacting tribute from rich cities, such as Mari, within the Sumerian orbit. Sumerian contacts are evident in the artistic and documentary finds at Ebla. The Sumerian language was used there; the local Semitic language (Eblaite) was written in the cuneiform script; and links with the scribal traditions of central Mesopotamia, as represented at Abu Salabikh and Kish, are manifold, suggesting a common ancestry through earlier Sumerian 'colonial' activities in Syria (see Chapter 16).[6]

The empires of Akkad and the Third Dynasty of Ur, c. 2350–2000 BC

During the Early Dynastic period personal names of private individuals, and a handful of gods and rulers, indicate a progressive infiltration of Sumer by Akkadian-speaking Semites from the north, who adopted the cuneiform writing system of the Sumerians for their own language. As so often in ancient Mesopotamia, it needed the drive of one man to turn this into a political supremacy. Sargon, rising to power at Kish, overthrew the dominant Sumerian ruler of Uruk to bring the Akkadians to power. As it is a period for which archaeological information is meagre and 'historical' textual sources modest (often later legends), the emergence and structure of this Akkadian hegemony remains unclear.[7] Even the location of the new capital, Akkad, somewhere near Babylon, is still unknown. Sargon established a dynastic tradition in one family over four generations and used his extended family to secure and stabilize royal authority. His 'empire' was little more than an unprecedented territorial expansion, in which few of the organizational characteristics of later empires may yet be detected. On the one hand, Sargon's armies struck to the north-west, through Syria, deep into Anatolia to secure control of long-established lines of supply previously manipulated by Syrian rulers (as at Ebla, which Sargon overran and his grandson Naram-Sin later sacked). On the other hand, in the south and south-east armies opened up the way to trade with Dilmun, the modern island of Bahrein in the Gulf, and to Magan and Meluhha, lands of unknown location along the sea route through the Straits of Hormuz and around Iran to the Indus valley (see Chapter 31). Inscriptions record the arrival of their ships at the quays of Akkad, and distinctive Gulf and Indus valley seals and etched carnelian beads began to reach Mesopotamia from these regions, as well as the raw materials previously brought overland to Sumer from Iran (see below).

Sargon's sons, the successive kings Rimush and Manishtusu, and particularly his grandson Naram-Sin, pursued comparable policies of military aggrandizement and profit. Their objective continued to be the acquisition of raw materials, while the booty and tribute dedicated to temples were predominantly metals, timber and semi-precious stones. Though merchants are evident in the internal economy of Mesopotamia at this time, their role in foreign trade is uncertain. In Syria, at Tell Brak, and in the Assyrian heartland around Assur and Nineveh, Akkadian domination is evident in strongholds designed for the collection and storage of goods and in the foundation of temples and towns. At Susa in Khuzistan (ancient Elam) an army of occupation ensured allegiance. Relations with the Sumerian city-states were unpredictable: apparently good under Sargon, who carefully respected their religious institutions and involved his family with them, but increasingly hostile thereafter. The standardization of official documents, private letters and economic texts, now written in cuneiform in Akkadian, reflects a strong element of centralization in the bureaucracy. In art, monumental and minor, it was an era of outstanding achievement. Royal prestige and patronage is clear from rock-cut reliefs and from surviving statuary in stone and in cast copper, which, like the miniature scenes cut on cylinder seals, show a new interest in portraying physical reality. Seals are unusually rich in mythological imagery, much of it fantastic but imagined and depicted more concretely than under the Sumerians.[8]

The insecurity of the Akkadian dynastic system is evident from revolts in the reigns of most of its rulers and royal assassinations in palace conspiracies. When combined with constant pressure from neighbours provoked by their expansionist policies, and with the need to maintain ill-defined frontiers and long lines of supply, weakness at the centre was fatal, as so many of Mesopotamia's most ambitious rulers were to find. In this case diverse foreign elements, such as the Elamites, mountain tribesmen from the Zagros like the Guti and Lullubi, Hurrian-speaking peoples from the north and Amorites from the west, eroded and finally destroyed the Akkadian empire. Then the Sumerian towns, secure in their agricultural self-sufficiency and strong unified local traditions, again emerged as enduring political centres. Cities such as Uruk and Lagash (under its famous ruler Gudea, immortalized in his statuary) took the initiative; but it was Ur, furthest from the sources of Akkadian power, closest to rich trading routes and richest in accumulated religious and political authority, that gained more enduring advantage under a series of kings known as the Third Dynasty of Ur.

Two kings especially, Ur-Nammu and Shulgi, established a wide dominion reminiscent of Akkad's; governors in cities as far apart as Byblos in the Lebanon, on the Mediterranean coast, and Susa in Iran acknowledged their authority.[9] Again, an extended royal family briefly provided a number of able rulers, a reservoir of manpower to staff the main religious and administrative offices and royal ladies for diplomatic marriages and important temple appointments. The legitimacy and authority of the kings, some of whom now aspired to divine status, were secured by massive expenditure on the rebuilding of the ancient sanctuaries of Sumer, as archaeology has revealed at Ur. There the impressive royal mausolea have also been excavated, though the kings may actually

have been buried at the holy city of Nippur, where they were crowned.[10] A vassal ruler at Eshnunna (Tell Asmar) in the Diyala valley dedicated a temple to the deified king of Ur, Shu-Sin (about 2037–2029 BC).[11] Foreign trade, in which royal control still played a major part, involved the well-documented export of wool, grain, dates, dried fish, skins and some manufactured goods, in return for both traditional raw materials and exotic foods, plants and animals. Numerous documents, only slowly being processed, survive from the internal administration of this time, promising to make it eventually one of the best known. Many others attest to a renaissance in Sumerian language and literature in the great temple scribal schools and libraries. They particularly benefited from strong government and in turn promoted the status of the monarchy and the unity of its authority around Nippur, long the heart of Sumerian civilization.

Elam and highland Iran, c. 3000–1200 BC

It is clear from the earliest historical records from Sumer that the inhabitants of Elam, a state in south-west Iran that united in a federation the plains of Khuzistan and the adjacent highlands, were often in conflict with the Sumerian city-states.[12] But it was a strife moderated by economic and cultural contacts vital to both regions. Although they had developed urban societies at about the same time, each had drawn on strong local traditions that survived to distinguish them. Campaigns in the Early Dynastic period were sporadic. Sumerian rulers penetrated deep into Elam, while according to the Sumerian King List the rulers of Awan, an Elamite city of unknown location, established a brief supremacy over Sumer. Excavations at Susa, whence most of the present archaeological information comes, have revealed corresponding fluctuations in the extent of Sumerian cultural influence, more

17.3: *A simple mud-brick house, of the type occupied by prosperous citizens of Ur, contemporary with the palace at Mari (see Figure 17.6). The structure is organized around an open court in which many household activities would have been pursued; the family probably lived on the first floor.*

17.4: *A carved chlorite bowl, probably from Khafaje in the Diyala valley, imported to Mesopotamia from a manufacturing centre in south-central Iran in the first half of the third millennium BC. The designs are foreign to the tradition of the Sumerians, but must have appealed to them as many such vessels were traded.*

often from central Mesopotamia (Kish and the Diyala region) than from heartland Sumer.[13] The Elamites still used their own script ('Proto-Elamite'), as yet only debatably deciphered, to write an unknown language that some have claimed to be related to Dravidian.

At this time, unlike the later prehistoric period (see Chapter 16), there is no real sign of Elamite authority eastwards beyond Khuzistan and Fars (notably the site of Tepe Malyan, ancient Anshan). Yet there is clear evidence that trans-shipment centres (such as Shahr-i Sokhta, far to the east, which handled lapis lazuli) and production centres (such as Tepe Yahya in the Kerman region, which manufactured carved chlorite vessels) played some part in trading relationships involving Elam and Sumer, though they did not necessarily use Elam as an intermediary. Indeed, Sumerian legends relating to the east Iranian state of Aratta indicate direct economic and diplomatic contacts. In one of them, after much diplomatic activity, the king of Aratta sends gold, silver, lapis lazuli and precious stones to the king of Uruk in exchange for large quantities of grain.[14] It may have been the Mesopotamian demand for the natural resources of the Iranian plateau that stimulated the development there of urban societies with wealthy elites and specialist craftsmen.[15] Such societies are archaeologically attested in the rich tombs of Shahdad, with their wide range of metalwork and vessels in alabaster, chlorite and lapis lazuli, and in graves and buildings away to the north-east, at Tepe Hissar on the frontiers with central Asia.

The conquest of Elam by the rulers of Akkad in about 2300 BC had profound and enduring consequences for Elamite society. At first, inscriptions in the Akkadian language, using the cuneiform script, appear side by side with developed 'Proto-Elamite' texts; but soon thereafter no inscriptions seem to have been composed in the native language for hundreds of years. Akkadian took over. Strong local traditions were now only to be detected in distinctive scribal practices, and an Akkadian that differs in language and content from the Mesopotamian mainstream. Relations with Babylonia continued to ebb and flow: the Elamites devastated Ur in about 2000 BC and installed rulers in Larsa for sixty years, while Hammurabi of Babylon and some later Kassite kings subsequently exercised authority over Susa.[16] Within Iran the second millennium BC is still very much an archaeological dark age, with the appearance first of the Indo-Aryans, who penetrated westwards into Mesopotamia and Syria (Mitanni), and then of the Iranian-speaking peoples, only roughly and tentatively traced through pottery distributions and a few linguistic indicators.[17]

Hittites, Hurrians and Mitannians, c. 2000–1200 BC

Identification of the native Anatolian peoples with whom the armies of Akkad contested and the merchants of Assur negotiated (see Chapter 26) is a long-standing problem. Its resolution turns on whether or not the Hittites, who spoke an Indo-European language (the linguistic family to which English belongs) later to be written in the cuneiform script, were already established in central

Anatolia in the middle and later third millennium BC. Indo-European personal names have been detected in the documents from Kültepe (Karum Kanesh) in the twentieth century BC, and later records identify Hittite centres of power by that time at two cities, Nesha (?Kanesh) and Kushshar, on the central plateau. In about 1650 BC a ruler claiming to come from Kushshar set up his capital at Hattusha, modern Boğazköy, and changed his name to Hattushili. Most current knowledge of the Hittites, until the fall of their empire about 1200 BC, is derived from objects and tablets found in excavations at Boğazköy.[18] Among the tablets are some in a language called 'Hattic', a non-Indo-European language, which is commonly supposed to be that of the inhabitants of the Anatolian plateau before the arrival of the Indo-European Hittites from the north-west or north-east some time in the third millennium BC. The 'Hattic' legacy was particularly strong in Hittite cult and mythology, in court protocol and perhaps also in religious art.

Under the Hittite Old Kingdom (about 1750–1550 BC) two kings, Hattushili and his successor Murshili, established military and diplomatic patterns that were to endure, although their own achievements were ephemeral. Their priorities were strikingly like those of the Mesopotamian rulers eager to secure supplies of raw materials from mines and forests in Anatolia. The Hittite kings also sought to stabilize centres of power within a realm that lacked secure natural frontiers and was threatened on all sides,

and to ensure control of profitable trade routes south-eastwards through Syria to the heart of Mesopotamia. In a lightning campaign in about 1595 BC Murshili even succeeded in sacking Babylon and ending the dynasty of Hammurabi. Throughout the period of the New Empire (about 1400–1200 BC) the Hittites vied with the Egyptians and the Mitanni (see below) for control of the Euphrates trade route. When the Hittites were in the ascendant a viceroy ruled from the fortress city of Carchemish (Djerablus). Little that was achieved by force of arms, diplomacy or international royal marriages endured without the initiatives and energy of individual kings, not all of whom were as dynamic as Shuppululiumà I (about 1380–1346 BC), who established the Hittites firmly in Syria for over a century. The Hittite empire collapsed in about 1200 BC from complex internal and external causes that involved, among others, the 'Sea Peoples' (see Chapter 28), though its cultural legacy persisted in the Neo-Hittite states of Syria.[19]

To distinguish it from other contemporary forms of government and social structure, Hittite society is regularly termed 'feudal', though the implied medieval analogy is not precise. It was a complex, multi-lingual, ethnically mixed society, which had evolved slowly and did not attain the form best known from tablets until the New Empire period. It incorporated administrative organs developed by the age-old Anatolian village communities of peasant farmers that underpinned the whole Hittite economic and social

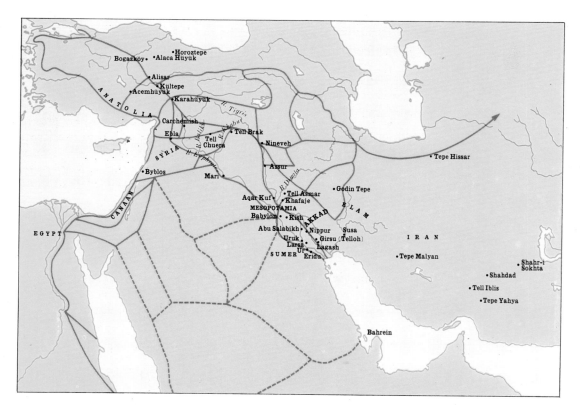

17.5: *The major sites of Mesopotamia and Iran, with the principal overland trade routes including those crossing Arabia, which were dependent on the camel.*

17.6: *Plan of the great mud-brick palace of King Zimri-Lim at Mari in Syria about 1800 BC. The various elements of the building are evident, each arranged around a courtyard, with separate provision for royal public and private life, administration, and food storage and processing.*

system. The king, who was viceroy on earth of the supreme storm god, owned the land, which he distributed as he willed under ties of homage to nobles, whose followers in turn owed them services. Periodically the king held great courts in the capital to which the nobles were summoned for ceremonial, judicial and advisory duties. As in all feudal societies, they were bound to supply contingents of chariotry and infantry to the king when he required them. Although never regarded as divine in his own lifetime, the king had special status as chief priest, in which role it was vital for him to preside over all the important festivals of the gods. These were various in origin and very numerous, the local cults particularly offering a microcosm of the Hittites' diverse cultural heritage. The chief gods of the state religion of the later New Empire are spectacularly shown in processional reliefs in the rock-cut sanctuary of Yazilkaya, near Boğazköy (see Figure 17.6).[20]

Among the most elusive, but most interesting, of the peoples of the ancient Near East are those who spoke the Hurrian language, perhaps of Caucasian origin, written in cuneiform script.[21] Having entered from the north in ever-increasing numbers from the Akkadian period (about 2350–2100 BC), the Hurrians may be recognized by their distinctive personal names in Mesopotamia. Texts in their language were found in the palace at Mari, in about 1800 BC, at a time when they were first referred to as a people and their penetration of Syria intensified. It was probably the Hurrians who pioneered construction of the light horse-drawn chariot with spoked wheels, the training of horses to draw it, its use as a platform for firing the composite bow, and the development of scale-armour for men and horses as a counter to it. Before that, heavy war-wagons with solid wheels had been drawn by asses and related equids. From about 1650 BC the Hurrians were regularly in conflict with the Hittites, particularly when they briefly formed a coherent state in north-east Syria known as Mitanni, ruled by an intrusive Indo-Aryan minority (about 1500–1350 BC). The kings of Mitanni bore Indo-Aryan names, and among their gods were the well-known Indo-Aryan deities Mitra, Varuna and Indra, as well as the Hurrian Teshup and Hepa. Their society was distinguished by a military aristocracy (*maryannu*), which used chariots and received royal land grants in return for services. Until their capital, Washshukkanni, is located and excavated, their material culture will remain unknown, though certain types of decorated pottery have been loosely attributed to them. For a time the Mitannian state controlled much of Syria, Assyria and towns east of the Tigris, such as Nuzi, and maintained friendly diplomatic relations with Egypt to counter the strength of Assyria and the Hittites in Syria. The Assyrians eventually superseded and absorbed the Mitannian kingdom.

Amorites, Babylonians and Kassites c. 2000–1200 BC

One of the main preoccupations of the Ur III kings had been a military threat from Amorites (Amurru) in the north-west. This was so serious that they built a great line of fortifications between the Tigris and the Euphrates to keep them out. Such defences are only appropriate as long as they may be adequately manned by central government; once that was affected by crisis, as under the last king, Ibbi-Sin, this inflexible defensive system collapsed.[22] City-states on the periphery of the Ur III empire reasserted their independence and looked to their own interests, while Amorites penetrated deep into the south and Elamites took advantage of a serious dislocation of agricultural supplies to sack Ur in a manner long remembered for its ferocity. Isolated Amorites, living peacefully in Sumerian towns, may be recognized in Mesopotamian texts by their distinctive names as early as the later Early Dynastic period;[23] by early in the second millennium they were more conspicuous, with individuals attaining high positions and even royal authority.

A very large archive of clay tablets from the palace at Mari has provided a unique opportunity for the study of the economic and social background of the various tribes of Amorite origin.[24] The royal officials at Mari in the eighteenth century BC were regularly in contact with the tribal societies west of the Euphrates in Syria. The desert peoples constantly threatened well-watered land and lines of communication; displaced members of tribes often sought employment as mercenaries or labourers at Mari; and palace officials tried to impose forced labour, military duties and taxes on the tribes. It is not surprising, therefore, that current opinion tends to reject the old idea that Semitic nomadism involved large movements of peoples and periodic large-scale invasions into

kitchens and storerooms

palace offices

royal private apartments

royal ceremonial apartments

courtyard

courtyard

royal audience hall

main gate

0   50 m

adjacent urban societies. Strife between interdependent elements of the same society was endemic, arising as much from urban attempts to impose political systems on village–pastoral economies, including transhumant nomads (a 'dimorphic' society), as from the relentless pressure of 'barbaric' nomads. (This last description owed much to texts written by city-dwelling scribes, whose experience of the situation was neither direct nor happy.)

If such social pressures produced a basic instability outside the immediate confines of urban Sumer that might at any time have precipitated major changes in the balance of power, so increasingly, it seems, did the environment of southern Mesopotamia.[25] Textual studies and surface surveys have revealed a progressive ecological problem in the later third and early second millennia BC. A decline in crop yields, a shift to the cultivation of more salt-tolerant crops like barley and explicit records of increasing stretches of land ruined for cultivation by salt together indicate a highly damaging process of salination at this time. Irrigation agriculture, upon which southern Mesopotamia was dependent, is inevitably associated with progressive salination of the soil in areas of high summer heat and aridity combined, as here, with minimal surface slope and sub-surface drainage. Although individual cities remained long in occupation, there was an increasingly sharp contraction in urban settlement in the south in the second millennium BC, as the frontiers of cultivation retreated. Political factors certainly played their part in the northward shift of power centres at this time, but they were complemented by this developing agrarian problem in the south.

After the fall of Ur in about 2000 BC the towns of the south contended for independence, as they had a millennium earlier, in struggles that polarized around the rival cities of Isin and Larsa, after which the period is named. Culturally there was little evident change; Neo-Sumerian traditions endured. Trade flourished at cities like Ur,[26] where a group of seafaring merchants took textiles to Bahrein (Dilmun) in order to acquire large quantities of copper, ivory and perhaps pearls, brought there, in some cases, from sources higher up the Gulf. It seems that the initiative now had to be taken by the Mesopotamian traders not, as before, by foreigners from Magan and Meluhha. A century or two later even Bahrein had lost touch with them and for a millennium or so copper, precious stones and rare woods no longer came up the Gulf to Ur; Mesopotamian trade depended on its traditional sources to east and west.[27]

In the eighteenth century BC Babylon emerged as the dominant city under Hammurabi (about 1792–1750 BC) of the Amorite First Dynasty of Babylon. His reign is relatively well documented and his enduring fame indicates his achievements. His own administrative letters reveal great energy and attention to detail; the palace archives at Mari show the effects of his somewhat cynical diplomacy; and numerous economic and literary texts assist with the reconstruction of contemporary Babylonian life and society.[28] Hammurabi profited from a securely established dynasty, and the struggles of rulers elsewhere, to impose his authority throughout Mesopotamia. Within a decade of his death much of his realm had broken away and it was over a millennium before Babylon achieved comparable status again. Hammurabi's law code has long been regarded as presenting a unique view of Mesopotamia in

17.7: *View of the east wall of rock chamber B in the Hittite sanctuary of Yazilkaya, showing the god represented by a dagger 3.3 metres high, with a hilt formed of lions and the god's head as the pommel. Behind is a smaller group, with the massive god Sharruma embracing King Tudhaliyas IV (c. 250–1220 BC) in a protective gesture.*

his time. It is not strictly a legal document, like the Roman or Napoleonic codes, but rather a literary expression of the king's conception of his social responsibilities and his awareness of the discrepancies between what exists and what is desirable in his realm. Seen in these terms, it finds a ready place in a period distinguished by the range of its writings in Sumerian, which endured, like Latin in medieval Europe, as the appropriate language for learning and literature. The latter is often nostalgic, with many legends of the past achievements of Sumerian gods, heroes and kings, as well as hymns to their glory, associated with a large body of cultic texts.

Archaeological evidence for the Neo-Sumerian and Old Babylonian periods[29] supplements the very varied written record at many points, though levels of this period at Babylon itself have yet to be explored. At cities like Eshnunna (Tell Asmar) in the Diyala valley, at Isin and Larsa and at Ur and Uruk, temple, palace and town architecture is well represented. The Mari palace, above all, ravaged by Hammurabi's sack, retained vestiges of its luxury fittings, wall paintings, mosaics and sculpture, as well as the more mundane fittings of its kitchens, offices and storerooms.[30] Much of the art of the period in precious materials, in paint on plaster and in terracotta has perished, and what survives is a pale shadow of what the texts describe. The art of the seal cutter was now increasingly unadventurous, using restricted religious imagery and often poor technique. Fortunately, a range of baked-clay mould-made plaques, characteristic of this period, are more varied and include scenes of daily life.

When a sudden Hittite raid on Babylon in about 1595 BC finally destroyed the weakened dynasty of Hammurabi, it was a people known as the Kassites who profited locally.[31] It has usually been assumed that they came from highland Iran, but evidence for their presence there is much later. Before Babylon fell they were already established on the middle Euphrates and are mentioned in documents as foreigners on the western outskirts of Babylon. The century and a half after 1595 BC is one of the most obscure in Mesopotamian history: a documentary and archaeological dark age, during which, to judge by subsequent events, the Kassites steadily took control of most of Babylonia. From about 1460–1150 BC the Kassite kings held their place with the great rulers of the day, those of Egypt, of the Hittites and of the Mitanni. Their relations with Egypt were characterized by royal marriages and lavish gift exchanges. Babylon sent horses and chariots, silver and lapis lazuli, bronze and oil; Egypt, most often gold, but occasionally fine furniture and garments. In the thirteenth century a doctor was sent from Babylonia to the Hittites, and from Babylon a Hittite king requested lapis lazuli, fine horses and a carver of stone reliefs. Relations with Assyria were always more equivocal. Although the Assyrian armies were probably the stronger, it was not until the mid-twelfth century BC that simultaneous assaults by Assyrians and Elamites destroyed the Kassite supremacy. At its height, Babylonia was involved with caravans (still of donkeys, not yet of camels) trading deep into Egypt, Canaan, Syria and Anatolia.

Documents suggest that the Kassites were traditionalists, maintaining the great Babylonian scribal schools and fostering preservation of the existing literary legacy. Art and architecture, in the rare instances where they have survived, as at Aqar Quf (Dur-Kurigalzu), Uruk and Ur, do not entirely support this conservative picture. The well-known Kassite 'boundary stones' (*kudurrus*) do not represent the most original aspects of Kassite art, which are best seen in small objects of polychrome glass and faience, in finely cut cylinder seals and in naturalistically modelled terracottas.[32] Here traces of Egyptian and Syrian, perhaps even Aegean, inspiration may be detected. The architecture of the palace at Dur-Kurigalzu, newly founded as the capital, has individual features, and the painted dados anticipate, in function at least, the use of sculptured slabs in later Assyrian royal palaces.

17.8 *Top of a basalt stela on which is carved the law code of King Hammurabi of Babylon (c. 1792–1750 BC). The king is shown to the left, standing before the seated god Shamash, the horned crown denoting divinity and the rays on his shoulders his role as sun god. In his right hand he extends to the king the 'rod and ring', believed to symbolize divine power delegated to the monarch.*

pt and the Levant
Bronze Age

Recent discoveries have shown that between 15 000 and 5000 BC the rich flora and fauna of the Nile valley were exploited by a number of groups of hunter–gatherers who possibly attempted the domestication of some local grasses and large mammals. However, the fully developed agriculture of the Neolithic is associated with the introduction of superior domesticates from the north-east (the Levant) or north-west (Africa), either brought by intrusive groups or imported by some of the indigenous Mesolithic populations.

In the prehistoric period two major groupings are evident. A northern one is represented in the Cairo–Fayum area and by a single site in the Delta, at Merimde. An archaeologically empty zone about 250 kilometres wide separates this group from a southern group in Upper Egypt, though this gap may be only accidental, a result of intrusive sand dunes covering sites on the west bank. The extreme rarity of sites in the Delta and of major settlement sites in southern Egypt is due to the fact that these were for the most part located on the alluvial plain and have either been destroyed or not yet recovered through survey and excavation. The Upper Egyptian group, however, is represented by many cemeteries on the low desert adjacent to the plain and can be divided into several phases on the basis of this material. These phases are labelled, in chronological order, Badarian, Amratian (Nakada I), Gerzean (Nakada II) and Nakada III (formerly called Semaienean). This relative chronology is based on the association of objects in graves, with some confirmation from vertical stratigraphy. Radiocarbon dates for both the northern and Upper Egyptian groups span the fifth and fourth millennia BC.

How did the Egyptian state, which appeared rapidly at the close of the fourth millennium, evolve from these Neolithic communities? National effort demanded by the draining and irrigation of the valley was not significant, for the annually inundated flood plain, divided by old river levees into natural basins, responded well to disparate local efforts. The earliest phases of farming culture, Badarian and Nakada I, although they did not necessarily constitute a politically cohesive entity, show a uniform material culture that was restricted to the area between latitudes 26° and 27°N. Nakada II, however, is characterized by a gradual spread of distinctive material culture northwards to the Fayum and southwards into Lower Nubia, presumably absorbing, or being absorbed by, surviving Mesolithic communities. This expansionism need not reflect the infusion of foreign elements, as is sometimes argued. All the Upper Egyptian phases are marked by typological change and innovation, but each one is preceded by transitional phases, and strong continuities link each phase or sub-phase. Thus the characteristic slate palettes, ivory carvings, red-polished and red-polished, black-topped pottery of Nakada I is anticipated in the Badarian and continues into Nakada II. The innovative light-

coloured 'desert' wares (often with red-painted decoration) and 'rough' wares of Nakada II draw upon local materials, shapes and decorative motifs and are part of a complex of technological changes that may be explained by indigenous developments and discoveries. Substantial copper implements begin to complement the stone-tool industry in Nakada II, and an expansion of riverine transport was perhaps accompanied by craft specializations and greatly expanded trade. Monopolization of, and competition for, raw materials (by no means uniformly distributed), skilled craftsmen and trade routes may have been the origins of the marked social and economic inequalities that begin to appear in the Nakada II cemetery record, crystallizing in Nakada II–III in apparent 'chieftains' graves' at Hierakonpolis, Abydos and Tarkhan.[1]

Egyptian culture was conservative, characterized by strong continuities derived from a world view that dominated society until Christian times. The fundamental belief was that a creator god had established a specific and unalterable universal and social order (*ma'at*). Egyptian society had to conform to this order and to participate, through both ritual and 'secular' actions, in the process of ensuring the conformity of the supernatural and natural worlds. However, there were inevitably changes and limited innovations over the millennia, particularly as long periods of centralized rule and national cohesion were punctuated by phases of internal disintegration and disorder, the 'intermediate' periods.

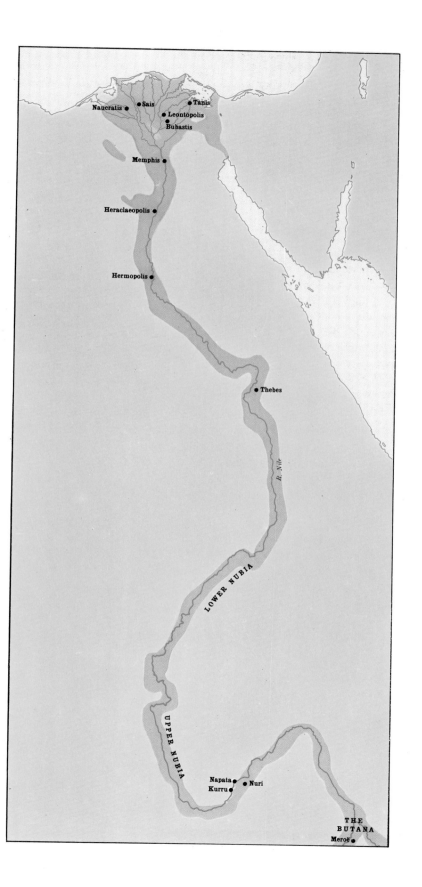

Each of these created problems whose solutions (always in the traditional conceptual framework) gave a distinctive character to the succeeding period. Textual and archaeological data in the historical periods clearly reflect these interwoven processes of conservatism and innovation.

The Early Dynastic period

Archaeological data and later written tradition indicate the existence in the late prehistoric period of several states, which finally merged into two competitive kingdoms, north and south. Military conflict is documented, for the first time, in Nakada III– Early Dynastic times by narrative reliefs on ceremonial ivory knife handles and gigantic stone cosmetic palettes and mace heads. The culminating document is the Narmer palette, commemorating Egypt's unification under a king who was probably Meni, the 'founder' of later Egyptian tradition. The highly abbreviated texts and richer pictorial art of Early Dynastic (Dynasties I and II) Egypt reveal that kingship, without the support of council or assemblies, was the dominant political institution. The other important political element was the king's servants, the developing civil and priestly bureaucracy that is discernible in numerous jar-sealings and other documents. Future political life would always revolve about king and bureaucracy. The general level of political organization and also of technology was much higher than in prehistoric times, and writing was a major innovation.

The hypothesis that these developments were stimulated by an intrusive 'dynastic race' of exotic (perhaps Mesopotamian) origin or by itinerant foreign merchants and artisans is an unnecessary one. Many of the chief features of the Early Dynastic cultural assemblage – for example, styles and techniques of relief art and carving in the round, the ubiquitous ceramic styles descending directly from those of late Nakada II and Nakada III – are clearly derived from prehistoric Egypt. Innovations are either distinctively Egyptian in content (the hieroglyphic script, for instance) or excavation may be expected to show their indigenous origins (monumental mud-brick architecture with panelled façades was a natural decorative progression from earlier strengthening buttresses). Specific Mesopotamian elements are certain relatively uncommon pottery types, a few cylinder seals and artistic motifs probably derived from cylinder seals. All these were probably secondary imports and influences, derived from trade with the

18.1: *Proto-dynastic ceremonial macehead (c. 3000 BC) of King Narmer (Menes), probably the first ruler of both Upper and Lower Egypt. He is shown viewing a parade of captives.*

18.2: *Map of the Nile, showing the narrow fertile strip on which Egypt and Nubia depended.*

Levant (not Mesopotamia) and culturally of minimal significance.

Archaeology documents the nature of Early Dynastic society. The large-scale building and planning evident in some of the cemeteries indicate that substantial towns probably existed, but evidence is scanty; traces of such towns have been located at Abydos and elsewhere, however, and recently, more revealingly, at Elephantine (with enclosure wall) and Hierakonpolis (a possible palace). Cemeteries are more informative and indicate clearly the king's dominant position. All the known royal graves are at Abydos and consist of schematized, square 'mound' superstructures with underlying pits and chambers and, some distance away, large walled enclosures, perhaps containing funerary temples. The combined economic and organizational effort required for these complexes was far greater than that needed for any other burial; the architectural plan is unique and the grave goods, badly plundered, comparably rich. Members of the royal family and the court were buried around the royal tomb in neat rows, while elsewhere elite members of the bureaucracy were buried in larger, imposing brick tombs with panelled façades. Many of these are located at Saqqara, near Memphis, traditionally the Early Dynastic national capital, while others (perhaps those provincial governors) are found in the provinces. Other tombs are conspicuously poorer and smaller. Throughout Egypt the archaeological assemblage is a uniform one. Luxury objects are chiefly in metal and stone, the once-decorative ceramic having been relegated to utilitarian functions.[2]

The Old Kingdom (Dynasties III–VI)

The names and chronological sequence of Old Kingdom rulers are known, but the few surviving historical records provide very inadequate glimpses of the processes that shaped society. The kings ruled through a complex and literate bureaucracy (headed by a *tjaty*, a vizier or prime minister), the structure of which is revealed by numerous official titles preserved upon tomb walls and, more rarely, in sealings and papyri. With rare exceptions (for example, the Abusir papyri, documenting the administration of Dynasty V funerary cults), little information is available on actual methods of government. Much history must therefore be inferred from art and archaeology, which are dominated by the extraordinary royal funerary complexes, all roughly in the Memphite region.

In a way not yet fully understood, these evolved from the royal tombs of Abydos (mentioned above) and from contemporary stepped mounds hidden inside elite tomb superstructures at Saqqara, the transitional monuments being the first examples of large-scale Egyptian stone architecture, the stepped pyramids of Dynasty III. King Zozer's at Saqqara (62 metres high) is the only substantial surviving monument of this kind. The true pyramid, with smooth faces, developed under King Snefru (Dynasty IV) in his two pyramids at Dahshur (each just over 100 metres high) and culminated in the enormous Khufu pyramid at Giza (nearly 150 metres high). Thereafter Old Kingdom pyramids declined steadily in size and quality of construction.

Like all royal tombs until about 1000 BC, the pyramids were located in the desert. Zozer's complex was large and elaborate, combining a dummy festival palace with functional cult buildings, but the final traditional plan, first attested in the Meydum pyramid of King Huni, was much simpler. The funerary temple lay in the eastern part of the pyramid and was also (pictorially rather than architecturally) identified as a symbolic palace. A causeway linked it to a valley temple at the cultivation's edge. Within the complex, small pyramids marked burials of queens and perhaps of royal viscera. Technology was simple. Raw materials were obtained locally, although finer stone (some blocks 49 tonnes in weight) were shipped in by river and canal, and building blocks were dragged up enormous ramps to be positioned.

The power of the kingship was evident. Labour was forcibly recruited in large numbers during the slack of the agricultural year; an administrative system was set up to organize the building, the supply operations and the subsequent cult; and materials, drawn from areas as distant as Lebanon, Sinai, Aswan and Nubia, were used on a scale far grander than that of the enterprises of other Egyptians. The shrinking size of later pyramids parallels a decrease in royal power. This was linked to weakening control over the bureaucracy, which grew increasingly complex as the role of the government expanded (and, for reasons of dynastic stability, royal relatives had been excluded from high office after Dynasty IV). Centrality decreased as provincial governors, formerly easily transferable officials who ended their careers at the royal capital, became hereditary local lords with strong provincial economic and power bases. These centrifugal developments, exacerbated perhaps by social distress caused by a sustained period of low inundations, led to the collapse of the centralized kingship in the First Intermediate Period.

However, the basic functions and symbolism of the royal funerary complexes survived. The complexes provided the physical setting for burial rituals, the burial itself and a permanent offering cult, each administered and serviced by a permanent community housed in a nearby 'pyramid town'. The cults were supported by incomes from estates scattered throughout Egypt, the growth of which may have reduced royal economic power. The complex probably symbolized the core of the universe. The pyramid linked the concepts of the primeval mound upon which the creator (sun god) stood to initiate creation, the sun god's rays (life-giving force) shining down upon Egypt and the universe thus created; the solar aspects of the complex were reinforced in Dynasty V by the building of nearby solar temples. The human battles depicted in the funerary temples were a reflection of the eternal struggle to protect the order of the universe from supernatural evil, while a gigantic, king-headed lion (sphinx) guarded the sacred realm. Into this realm the dead kings passed, while from it emanated the power activating the universe in which their living successors ruled.

In all probability Old Kingdom Egypt was urbanized, although the excavated sites are small, essentially peripheral workers' towns and pyramid cities. All pyramids were surrounded by the tombs of contemporary officials, and the Giza elite cemetery, laid out along a rectilinear grid and carefully zoned according to the size of the tombs and the status of their occupants, may reflect the plan of the contemporary royal capital, divided between the royal palace, the palaces of the royal family and an 'official city' staffed and lived in by the bureaucracy. Cemeteries in general remain the best indicators of the social and economic hierarchy and of historical change: elite tombs in the provinces grew in number and ostentation as power diffused from the centre; tombs had rectangular superstructures or were rock-cut depending on local topography; art was modelled upon the styles and techniques established in the royal cemeteries. Even outside the royal and provincial capitals, socially stratified cemeteries show that local elites existed in communities of every size.

Foreign relations

In prehistoric and early historic times Egypt's strongest direct contacts were with adjacent regions, which were easily accessible, contained valuable resources and trade routes and were a potential threat to the security of the frontier, and with more remote regions, which produced otherwise unobtainable items and were, with some difficulty, directly accessible. Archaeological evidence, the only available data for prehistoric times, are equally important in historic times as a corrective to the surviving textual and pictorial references to foreign contacts. These are mostly symbolic and religious in nature; details of contacts with foreign regions are omitted, and recorded events are equated with the triumph of supernatural order (Egypt) over chaos (foreigners). Specific dated events were even copied in their entirety by later kings.

Prehistoric Egypt, lacking political and military cohesion, engaged primarily in trade abroad, mainly during Nakada II and III. Pottery from northern Palestine in its 'Proto-Urban' phase occurs in Nakada II, as does Sinaitic turquoise and copper (?) and coniferous products, probably from Byblos (Lebanon), where a Nakada II–III palette was found. Presumably as yet unknown Egyptian products were exchanged for these. Southern contacts were different at first, for northern Lower Nubia completely absorbed Nakada I material culture, but thereafter the culture of the indigenous Nubian A-group became typologically distinct, though rich in trade goods from Nakada II or early Dynasty I Egypt, which were received in exchange for exotic items (ivory, ebony) from further south.

After unification Egypt became more aggressive towards adjacent regions. During Early Dynastic times the A-group was driven out of the Lower Nubian trade corridor, and during Dynasties III to V the area was peacefully exploited by Egypt for diorite and copper. By Dynasty III (and perhaps earlier) Sinai was under Egyptian control and until Dynasty VI the turquoise

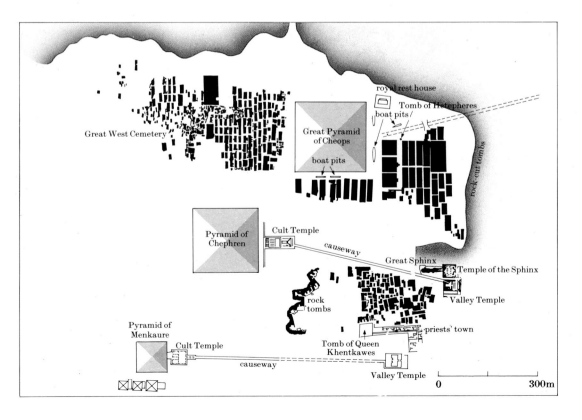

18.3: *Plan of the royal pyramid city at Giza, Dynasty IV. Note the obvious differences in size between the royal family's tombs east of the pyramid and those of officials and courtiers on the west.*

(and perhaps copper) mines of southern Sinai were worked by the Egyptians. A large amount of pottery brought by traders from the urbanized regions of Palestine or Syria occurs in Early Dynastic royal and elite tombs, and relations with cedar-producing Byblos were close throughout the Old Kingdom; several Egyptian kings sent inscribed votive objects there. Punt, a source of incense on the Red Sea coast, was periodically visited until late Dynasty VI, and there were occasional clashes with intrusive Libyans.

This vigorous pattern of contact began to change in the late Old Kingdom. Lower Nubia was occupied by a new people, the C-group, who interfered with Egyptian trading parties despite periodic punitive action by Egypt. As Egypt's internal troubles grew, it retreated entirely from Nubia, while in the Levant the urbanized natives collapsed into semi-nomadic cultures, and Egyptian contact contracted sharply.[3]

The First Intermediate Period (Dynasties VII–XI)

After the collapse of Old Kingdom government the provinces were forced to rely on their own resources, and the governorates became competitive petty kingdoms, each with its own army and fleet, often fighting alone or in alliances of two or three provinces. Nevertheless, the force of tradition permitted the development of a northern kingdom, ruled successively by Dynasties IX and X of Heracleopolis, and of a roughly contemporary Theban kingdom (Dynasty XI). The Heracleopolitans, once relatively secure, concentrated upon stabilizing the eastern Delta, which had become heavily infiltrated by Asiatics. However, once Thebes had pacified southern Egypt, it attacked and eventually overthrew Dynasty X, reuniting Egypt under Nebhepetre Mentuhotep. Formal unity left the provincial lords, especially those in Middle Egypt, with considerable independence, and the national government was still provincial in character, being centred upon Thebes (rather than the more central site of Memphis) and, in its upper ranks, staffed mainly by Thebans.

This was a period of considerable internal stress, vividly reflected in literature and archaeology. Written records indicate that the old order collapsed violently and was replaced by insecurity, injustice and even famine; archaeology testifies to the fact that fortified towns became characteristic (although so far only one example has been located by excavation) and weapons became a more frequent funerary gift. A rise in the death rate due to famine may be indicated. In architecture the formerly dominant royal funerary complexes disappeared from the archaeological landscape, except for the Dynasty XI tombs at Thebes, which typically developed out of a local elite tomb-type and were little influenced by the Old Kingdom form. The uniform 'court' art style characteristic of the Old Kingdom was replaced by a more varied pattern; in the numerous and sometimes elaborately decorated tombs of local rulers Old Kingdom traditions survived in some areas, while in others a less sophisticated but vivid provincial style was the rule.

As a whole the archaeological assemblage, while descended from earlier ceramic and artifact types, has a distinctive character of its own; particularly striking are regional differences in pottery that indicate a breakdown in the national trading or redistribution system. The resulting emphasis on local resources is indicated by contemporary funerary texts, which emphasize the self-reliant, aggressive character and private entrepreneurial activity of the deceased, in contrast to earlier evidence of discretion, submission to authority and wealth derived from government service. Only with unification in Dynasty XI does national uniformity begin to dominate the archaeological assemblage again.

The Middle Kingdom (Dynasties XII–XIII)

Dynasty XI was replaced by a new Theban line, founded by its last vizier; this line, as Dynasty XII, recreated genuine national unity. An essential part of the revitalization of Egyptian society was a new concept of kingship, which emphasized its responsibilities to men and the creator god as well as its power; the Dynasty XII rulers skilfully exploited this concept in subtly propagandist literature that simultaneously stressed royal awareness of responsibility, the power granted the ruler by the gods as a result and the desirability of serving in an efficient, loyal bureaucracy. Combined with a shrewd administrative policy, this led to the gradual suppression of the provincial lords and the appearance of a fully centralized governmental system controlled from Itj-Towy, a new capital near ancient Memphis. The kings were once more buried under large and ostentatious pyramids; court-inspired art tended to become the national norm; and the fortified towns of the earlier period disappeared. From the Middle Kingdom comes the earliest substantial urban component yet excavated in Egypt, the pyramid city of King Senwosret II, at Kahun, originally occupying over 1000 square metres and laid out in a grid plan, carefully divided into elite and lower-class segments. This social inequality was characteristic and is clear also in the cemeteries, although it has been suggested that a 'middle class' emerged as the result of royal governmental policy.

Foreign relations

A natural expression of internal stabilization was renewed expansion and aggression in foreign contacts. The Lower Nubian C-group had supplied mercenaries to the local armies of the First Intermediate Period but enjoyed independence until the region was 'annexed' by Nebhepetre Mentuhotep (Dynasty XI). Dynasty XII made the conquest permanent by building a chain of great mudbrick fortresses from Aswan to the Second Cataract. With massive towered walls, originally perhaps 11 metres high, lower ramparts with bastions, dry defensive moats and interior towns constructed to a rigorous design, these fortresses are outstanding examples of military architecture and town planning. From them the Egyptians both raided and traded with Upper Nubia. The C-group survived to follow its traditional culture, but it was deprived of the many trade goods of Egyptian origin found in its earlier cemeteries. Similar fortresses existed along the Asiatic frontier of the east Delta, and the army organization required for garrisoning was also, no doubt, an important support for royal internal power. Punt once again became a trading partner and Sinai was vigorously exploited. Relations with the Levant are less clear. Byblos was certainly in close contact, its rulers receiving many Egyptian royal gifts, and the Execration Texts (ritual lists of Asiatic and Nubian places at least theoretically subject to Egypt's control) show an extensive knowledge of the small, urbanized city-states of Palestine. However, many Middle Kingdom statuettes and other objects found in Palestine and Syria may be booty acquired during the Second Intermediate Period and may therefore not indicate Middle Kingdom contact. Occasional Minoan artifacts in Middle Kingdom indicate an even wider trading network.[4]

18.4: *Chart showing the chronological sequence of the dynasties of Egypt.*

PERIOD	DATE	DYNASTY
Early Dynastic Period	c. 3100–2890 BC	I
	c. 2890–2686 BC	II
Old Kingdom	c. 2686–2613 BC	III
	c. 2613–2494 BC	IV
	c. 2494–2345 BC	V
	c. 2345–2181 BC	VI
First Intermediate Period	c. 2181–2173 BC	VII
	c. 2173–2160 BC	VIII
	c. 2160–2130 BC	IX
	c. 2130–2040 BC	X
	c. 2133–1991 BC	XI
Middle Kingdom	1991–1786 BC	XII
	1786–1633 BC	XIII
Second Intermediate Period	1786–c. 1603 BC	XIV
	1674–1567 BC	XV
	c. 1684–1567 BC	XVI
	c. 1650–1567 BC	XVII
New Kingdom	1567–1320 BC	XVIII
	1320–1200 BC	XIX
	1200–1085 BC	XX
Third Intermediate Period	1085–945 BC	XXI
	945–730 BC	XXII
	817?–730 BC	XXIII
	720–715 BC	XXIV
	751–668 BC	XXV
Late Period	664–525 BC	XXVI
	525–404 BC	XXVII
	404–399 BC	XXVIII
	399–380 BC	XXIX
	380–343 BC	XXX
	343–332 BC	XXXI

The Second Intermediate Period (Dynasties XIII–XVII)

During Dynasty XIII the orderly succession of rulers broke down; the unusual shortness of many reigns indicates either an 'elective' kingship or, more probably, vigorous competition for the kingship amongst the bureaucratic elite. National government slowly disintegrated. Increasingly the authority of Dynasty XIII came to be limited to the Theban region, while an independent dynasty (XIV) may have developed in the north-west Delta. More significantly, Asiatic invaders expanded through the north-east Delta, to emerge in about 1670 BC as Dynasty XV, which held substantial if qualified power throughout Egypt for over a hundred years. These people were called 'foreign rulers' by the Egyptians, a term mistranslated as 'Hyksos' (Shepherd Kings) by later Greek writers. They came from Palestine, then heavily urbanized. Experienced in the construction of fortified towns, in siege techniques, and in the use of chariotry, which they introduced to Egypt, the Hyksos were well equipped to take advantage of Egyptian weakness and adopted those elements of Egyptian ideology and custom that were essential to effective rule.

Elsewhere the frontiers also proved permeable. The Egyptian colonies of Lower Nubia came under the rule of an intrusive 'Kingdom of Kush', based on Kerma in Upper Nubia, while eastern desert nomads began to settle in significant numbers in Upper Egypt. Middle Kingdom traditions were best maintained by a Theban dynasty (XVII) that eventually threw off its vassalage and began, under its last kings, a war of independence resulting in the expulsion of the Hyksos and the reconquest of Lower Nubia.

Archaeology confirms the complex cultural picture implied by the written sources. The dominant archaeological assemblage is purely Egyptian and includes new types of artifacts descended directly from those of the Middle Kingdom. However, recent excavations, such as those at Tell el Da'aba and Tell el Maskutah, have shown that in the eastern Delta there were enclaves of Syro-Palestinian material and culture, while many trade objects of Syro-Palestinian origin were distributed and copied throughout Egypt and Nubia, implying a widespread trade network. 'Pangrave' cemeteries (named after the shape of the characteristic grave) that occur in Upper Egypt are those of the nomads from the eastern desert; while Egyptian, C-group and Kushite ('Kerma-Group') cemeteries are all found in Lower Nubia. The general standard of art and architecture was low, and the only surviving royal tombs are the small brick pyramids of Dynasty XVII at Thebes.[5]

The New Kingdom (Dynasties XVIII–XX)

The Egyptian state was revitalized by the shocks of the occupation period and the triumph of the Hyksos' expulsion; it began the longest and most expansive phase of foreign contact in Egypt's history and simultaneously a strongly centralized government developed that was both necessary to expansion and reinforced by it. Foreign relations were of unprecedented importance. During early Dynasty XVIII Egyptian control extended over Upper

'ourth Cataract), much of Palestine, Lebanon and
n Syria. Tuthmosis III gave these conquests per-
tting up an efficient imperial system of regional
eaucrats, garrisons and indigenous vassal rulers
throughout the conquered countries. These were the effective
limits of permanent control. The northern Sudan had a diffused
population that would have required dangerously long and exposed
lines of communication to control, while the city-states of Syria
were normally dominated by other Near Eastern powers that were
Egypt's equals in military strength. Typically, long periods of
conflict with Mitanni (earlier Dynasty XVIII) and the Hittites
(end of Dynasty XVIII to mid-Dynasty XIX) were followed by
treaties establishing long periods of peace, while Egyptian trading
and diplomatic contacts extended not only to Punt, but also to
Mitanni, the Hittites, Babylonia, Assyria and the Minoan and
Mycenaean worlds. In Dynasties XIX and especially XX, however, serious problems occurred. Libyans exerted increasing
pressure upon the western Delta, while the 'Sea Peoples', an
assortment of marauding Asiatic warriors, forced a gradual
Egyptian retreat from Lebanon and Palestine.

New Kingdom government was geared in large part to the maintenance of an efficient military machine, but it also provided
strong and effective civil government. The chief political problems
involved internal relations in the dynasties and fluctuations in
the balance of power between the king and powerful bureaucrats.
The kingship was extremely wealthy (partly because of the empire)

and often very strong. Akhenaten, for example, successfully
imposed the innovation of monotheism upon his pantheistic
country, although it was detested and abandoned soon after his
death. Serious disputes over the succession arose in late Dynasty
XIX, while in Dynasty XX royal economic and political power
seems to have been eroded, to the advantage of the great officials.
Ultimately the state was divided between two lines of military
origin, with Dynasty XXI effectively controlling the north and a
line of Theban military commanders and high priests ruling the
south.

The culture of the New Kingdom

Society, more richly documented than in any other period, was
dominated by the king. While the real power of individual kings
certainly fluctuated, it was often very great and was sustained by
the king's unique role as chief mediator between men and the gods.
Although on a level lower than theirs, the king was believed
literally to be of divine birth and had a quasi-divine status clearly
reflected in court ceremonial and royal architecture: All kings
built or expanded temples dedicated to the different gods – large
rectangular structures in stone, constructed according to a uniform
plan with forecourts, columned halls and sanctuaries. Fronted by
pylons, surrounded by pseudo-fortified walls and covered with
scenes and texts, the temples were settings for ritual, fortresses
protecting the divine images from supernatural evil and reproduc-
tions of the setting for creation, for which each god could be con-

18.5: *Village of the royal artisans, Dynasties
XVIII–XX at Deir el Medineh, western
Thebes. For many generations the sculptors
and painters of this village cut and
decorated the nearby royal tombs in the Valley
of the Kings. The brick and rubble houses are
extraordinarily well preserved, some still
containing their owner's name.*

sidered responsible. Akhenaten's temples, dedicated to the Aten or sun disk, broke with tradition and were open to the sky. They were later demolished, but thousands of their re-used building blocks are now being studied and the original appearance of Aten temples is being reconstructed. The royal funerary temples, very similar to gods' temples, were grouped at the base of the cliffs of western Thebes, the kings being buried in rock-cut tombs in a nearby desert valley. Of these, the wealthy, largely intact tomb of Tutankhamun is the most famous, but most of the rest were much larger and more elaborately decorated. The built pyramid was now replaced by a towering natural peak. Parts of royal palaces excavated at Tell el Amarnà, Thebes and Memphis show that these elaborate complexes combined throne rooms deliberately modelled on temple architecture, with extensive suites of private chambers for the royal family, harem, court officials and servants. The kings normally divided their time between Thebes and Memphis, although the latter was increasingly preferred and an additional royal residence, Pi-Ramesses (east Delta), was founded in Dynasty XIX.

The elite was essentially that created by the government structure, in which power was carefully divided up among leading officials who, under the general supervision of the vizier, respectively administered the extensive royal estates, economic affairs, justice and the priesthoods. Military officials also ranked highly but had little direct involvement in internal government, while the army was under the control of the king and the crown prince. Although documents on the actual working of government have survived (for Egypt, an unusually large number), the most vivid impression of this elite is conveyed through their decorated tombs, particularly those cut into the cliffs of Thebes and Amarnà. Brightly coloured reliefs, often well preserved, document the social life, official duties and religious beliefs of the elite and incidentally offer a great deal of information about the lower classes too. Actual houses have been excavated, mainly at Amarnà; though spacious, they do not contain many rooms, indicating a comparatively simple life style that was enhanced by artifacts in rare or expensive materials,' often made by highly competent craftsmen. Such items are best preserved in the tombs of the elite, of which a number have survived intact.

As before, socio-economic inequalities were strongly marked, as the many comparatively poorly equipped tombs of the lower classes attest. Texts show that the principal occupations were those of scribe (official), soldier (chariotry and infantry), priest, herdsman and, most common of all, 'cultivator'. Artisans and members of the more specialized professions were important but there were few of them. Private landownership existed, but most land belonged to the royal domain, government offices and temples, the bulk of the population being tenant farmers, while many artisans were fed and paid directly by the government. The economy was largely redistributive and controlled through the government, but officials did invest in land and trade in grain and other commodities, as did the temples, while even state artisans also made items for the market. Internal conditions were relatively tranquil, and the settlement pattern seems to have consisted of a number of substantial unwalled towns, spaced along the valley and through the Delta. They were surrounded by fairly dense agglomerations of rural villages, thinning away into more open, pastoral areas.

Although many towns expanded at this time and new ones were founded, only two are documented archaeologically in any detail. At Akhenaten's new capital at Amarnà, despite the absence of a rigorous plan, the city was divided into zones, with a comparatively remote royal residence and an 'official city' in which were sited the main temples, a ceremonial palace and many government offices. Flanking the official city were extensive residential zones. At Thebes the urban plan is much less clear, but special note must be made of Deir el Medineh, a small brick village occupied by generations of royal artisans for over four hundred years. Thoroughly excavated, this village is rich in textual and archaeological data and provides unique insights into the life of the more prosperous segment of the lower class.[6]

In the four thousand years between 5000 and 1000 BC, therefore, Egypt grew from a series of tribal communities into a unified state with extensive external trade, and finally into an imperial power. Throughout the historical period, despite episodes of anarchy and disorganization, it nevertheless remained strongly conservative and maintained a remarkable continuity of culture and world view.

19. The Aegean and western Anatolia in the Bronze Age

The Aegean Sea, dotted with islands, forms the centre of a well defined physical region. Indented with extensive coastlines and easy beaches, it is surrounded by fertile coastal plains and river valleys reaching into the neighbouring landmasses. With an abundance of Mediterranean crops and fish, it lies open to the Anatolian land routes and the sea lanes from Cyprus and the Levant, as well as offering contacts westwards to the Adriatic and southern Italy.

The development of effective shipping, as well as the cultivation of such crops as vine and olive, allowed this region to emerge during the Bronze Age as a major focus of economic and social change. From the pattern of peasant communities of the Neolithic period in lowland areas, such as the Thessalian plain, more complex societies grew up in the third and second millennia BC in what had hitherto been relatively peripheral regions, especially on the coasts and islands. These new centres showed from the beginning a wider range of contacts and economic relationships with the older-established urban communities of the eastern Mediterranean.

The Early Bronze Age

Early in the third millennium major developments took place in north-western Anatolia. At Troy,[1] Poliochni on the adjacent island of Lemnos, Thermi on Lesbos and elsewhere walled towns appeared, characterized by streets and longhouses in rows and by metal-working. By the mid- to late third millennium, urbanization had

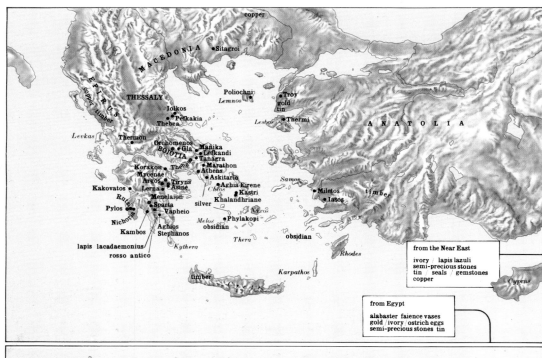

19.1: *The Aegean in the Bronze Age, showing major sites, raw material resources and luxury imports from Egypt and the Near East. The Minoan and Mycenaean civilizations had access to lead and silver within the Aegean, but needed to import copper, tin and gold from external sources. Their structured societies, with a class of artist-craftsmen of the highest skills, also made use of many luxury materials from the east. Fine pottery and scented oils were the main goods known to have been given in exchange. Before and during the palace periods (1900–1200 BC) there were uninterrupted and expanding exchange systems within and beyond the Aegean region.*

- ● site of palace
- tin exports

19.2: *Myrtos living system. The economies of Aegean Bronze Age villages may be seen as systems; the distinct aspects of their way of life, such as food production, craft specialization or external exchange, were the subsystems whose interaction promoted the success of the village. Phounou Koryphe at Myrtos is one of many Cretan villages from whose economies and societies the Minoan palace system was to emerge.*

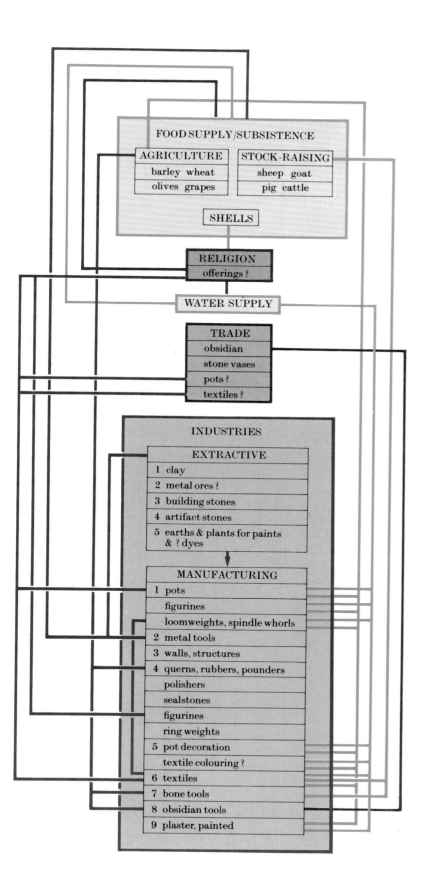

FOOD SUPPLY/SUBSISTENCE

AGRICULTURE	STOCK-RAISING
barley wheat	sheep goat
olives grapes	pig cattle

SHELLS

RELIGION
offerings ?

WATER SUPPLY

TRADE
obsidian
stone vases
pots ?
textiles ?

INDUSTRIES

EXTRACTIVE
1 clay
2 metal ores ?
3 building stones
4 artifact stones
5 earths & plants for paints & ? dyes

MANUFACTURING
1 pots
figurines
loomweights, spindle whorls
2 metal tools
3 walls, structures
4 querns, rubbers, pounders
polishers
sealstones
figurines
ring weights
5 pot decoration
textile colouring ?
6 textiles
7 bone tools
8 obsidian tools
9 plaster, painted

advanced in scale, with larger towns and an implied social hierarchy, for whose dominant members superlative gold jewellery and vessels were made.

These north-west Anatolian towns may have had metallurgical links with sites further east, such as Alaca Hüyük, and their supplies of metals very probably derived from the rich metal sources of north-central Anatolia. One possible reason for the wealth of Troy and Poliochni is that they served as outlet points for the transmission to the Aegean of eastern gold (and perhaps tin). There were no sources nearby for ores of these metals, though both towns have yielded many more gold objects than the contemporary Aegean villages of the Early Bronze Age; the pieces, some of which contained tin, were also more skilfully worked. On present evidence, urban development was clearly more advanced in north-west Anatolia.

In the Aegean itself herding, stock-raising and cereal agriculture persisted as in Neolithic times, though with important modifications. The innovations of the later fourth and early third millennia BC were at least partly the work of the existing Neolithic population, but they were on a scale that suggests that newcomers too may have been involved; there is a clear ceramic connection

19.3: *Troy II, the second city in the sequence, dates to the third millennium BC. Its impressive stone walls were crossed by a great paved ramp, leading in to the longhouses (megarons), which may have been occupied by prominent families. These families enjoyed conspicuous wealth in jewellery, vessels and weapons, created by highly skilled metallurgists. Schliemann found his famous treasure near the base of the wall seen here.*

with north-western Anatolia and its offshore islands. The domestication of the vine took place at this time; later, metallurgy became more widespread. At the beginning of the Early Bronze Age north-west Anatolian pottery forms appeared at Sitagroi and elsewhere in northern Greece, and in the Cyclades and Crete. The Cretan circular tomb emerged and cultivation of the olive began, and the island experienced, for the first time, the foundation of large numbers of open settlements, many on fairly high ground. The numerous cemeteries of the Cyclades also imply initial settlement on a substantial scale.

By the mid-third millennium important developments had taken place and many proto-urban villages had been established.[2] Examples are Pefkakia near Volos in Thessaly; Eutresis, Lithares and Thebes in Boeotia; Askitario in Attica; Asine, Lerna and Tiryns in the Argolid; Akovitika in Messenia; Aghia Eirene on Kea and Kastri on Syros; and Khania, Knossos, Lebena, Mallia, Mochlos, Myrtos, Palaikastro, Phaistos and Vasilike on Crete. Cemeteries with rich grave goods, such as the island of Lefkas, Khalandhriane on Syros, and Arkhanes, Koumasa and Platanos in Crete, also imply substantial settlements. Fully developed mixed farming, based on olives, vines, cereals and stock-keeping, was combined with a wide range of crafts. In addition to industries that have left few or indirect traces, such as woodwork and textiles, these crafts include pottery-making, among which the dark-surfaced, incised wares of the Cyclades and the painted wares of Crete stand out; seal-carving in stone, bone and ivory; sculptured figurines and stone bowls of white marble on the islands; vessels in a wide range of shapes and coloured stones on Crete; jewellery and vessels in precious metals and beads and pendants; and, above all, the manufacture of hundreds of tools and implements made either of copper or of bronze (consisting of copper alloyed with arsenic or tin).[3] The distribution of obsidian, pottery and marble figurines indicates intra-regional exchange, in which the products of the Cycladic islands seem to have predominated. The 252 chamber tombs and the island character of much of the pottery suggest a Cycladic settlement at Aghia Photia on the north-east coast of Crete. But the island had itself established a settlement on Kythera in the mid-third millennium, and the gold used in Cretan jewellery, the island's faience bead technology, ivory for seals and imported Egyptian stone bowls demonstrate that contacts had already been established with cultures outside the Aegean region.

In the Cyclades, and on Crete particularly, tombs have yielded many of the finest artifacts. Burial was communal everywhere, but burial places are very varied. The pit graves at Zygouries, the elaborately constructed graves at Marathon, the large cist-grave cemeteries in the Cyclades, the circular stone tombs,[4] rectangular ossuaries and built tombs and caves on Crete were all used over long periods. The burial of grave goods with the bodies of the dead implies a belief in existence after death, but the pushing aside or heaping up of bones and skulls indicates that the material needs of the dead were believed to be finite.

The Aegean Early Bronze Age villages – sometimes fortified, always involved in farming and trading – give a distinct impression of having been small, independent units. However, Lerna in the Argolid, with its central building and clay seal impressions indicating the organized storage of goods, hints at a larger control of territory and a redistributive economy in which, later in the Bronze Age, all goods and raw materials were issued by the palaces, to which finished articles had to be returned, so that all transactions could be recorded; the House of the Tiles may represent a microcosm of the later Aegean palace systems.

About 2200 BC this pattern of successful development was arrested temporarily on the Greek mainland, and altered at Troy and in the Cyclades, though it was seemingly unaffected in Crete. Lerna and many other mainland sites were destroyed about the same time[5] or a little later (Eutresis, Berbati), to be replaced and over-built by longhouses with or without apsidal ends. New types of pottery, notably grey wares, appeared. At some sites, particularly the new foundations at Lefkandi and Manika in Euboea, Aghia Eirene (Kea), Lerna, Aigina and Pefkakia, some of the pottery was of west Anatolian character, as it was at Kastri on Syros, before the destruction or abandonment of the settlement about 2100 BC. The first real town was founded at the same period at Phylakopi on Melos. On Crete, although Myrtos and Vasilike were burnt in about 2200 BC, there is no sign of cultural intrusion; the island displays total artifactual and burial continuity on into the First Palace Period.

It has been suggested that this clear break on the Greek mainland and offshore islands marked the first arrival in the Aegean of Indo-European, proto-Greek-speaking peoples; at Troy the contemporary or slightly later break, the change in ceramic tradition and the introduction of the horse marked a similar Indo-European arrival there.

The Cretan palace civilization

The uninterrupted expansion of settlement, population and culture in Crete during the third millennium (nearly 200 sites of the Early Minoan II period are known) seems to suggest one centralizing or cohesive development towards the end of the millennium; sanctuaries were built on mountain peaks (for example, at Vrysinas near Rethymnon, on Juktas at Knossos, at Petsopha above Palaikastro and at Traostalos in the Zakros district), probably to serve villages in surrounding lowlands. Terracotta votives of human figures or parts of them imply that these were believed to have a healing function; those of animals indicate, perhaps, hopes for success in hunting and the fertility of stock. A mountain Mistress of Animals and Master of Animals, both represented on later engraved seals, may have been worshipped.

Further centralization soon becomes apparent in the foundation of the palaces. This happened in the twentieth century, perhaps about 1930 BC on the stratigraphical ceramic evidence, and the palaces lasted until about 1450 or, in the case of Knossos, the early

1300s BC. The palaces of Knossos, Mallia, Phaistos and Zakros, as they survive today, consist of a large, rectangular, central courtyard surrounded by a cell-like structure of groups of rooms, corridors and magazines on several floors, the whole having been carefully measured and planned in advance and divided into well defined, functional areas for religion, storage, reception, domestic life and craft production. Knossos, the largest palace, occupies about 19000 square metres. The first three palaces also have a large western courtyard providing access to the building. The palaces underwent major reconstruction after destruction, probably by earthquake, about 1700 BC. Their architectural form before that is uncertain, although it is of crucial importance to the solution of the complex question of their initial foundation. Knossos and the great construction of the newly excavated area Mu at Mallia seem to have started as separate blocks, though they were later remodelled as a single unit. Phaistos, with its dozens of small Middle Minoan rooms and corridors, may have been a single construction from the start. Zakros had an earlier central court than that visible today, but the full form and exact date of an earlier palace are not known. It is possible that the basic plan was derived from foreign models such as distant Mari, but the cellular group of small rooms, western court and central open area is like those found at Early Minoan Mallia, Myrtos and Vasilike, and the palatial economic system was already present on a small scale, to judge from evidence of agricultural production and storage and the range of craft products of the Early Minoan villages.

Knossos, Mallia and Phaistos had been large and important settlements in the Early Bronze Age. It seems as if one or more powerful families or clans at each site came to realize the economic and political advantages to be gained through the control of large territories centred on a well organized place. The degree of organization necessary to mobilize the raw materials, to design and build the first palaces was considerable. The evidence we have of the control of production and the storage of food for the dependants of these large units implies that the palaces had authority over more territory than that of an Early Minoan village, and within the palaces themselves the wide range of highly skilled crafts again suggests well organized leadership. The production of exquisitely decorated pottery, sometimes eggshell-thin, skilled goldwork, including granulation (especially at Mallia), the first carving of hard stones for seals and the production of big vases of serpentine for domestic use all flourished. By the close of the First Palace Period, around 1700 BC, a system of writing, the Linear A script, had been devised to facilitate administration. The system may have derived from or run parallel to the earlier Hieroglyphic Script, known from stone prism seals, clay bars and labels.

External trade began to play a larger part. Goods were carried in sailing ships that seals show to have been an improvement on the mastless long boats of the Early Bronze Age. Pottery and stone vessels were exported all over the Aegean, to places as far north as

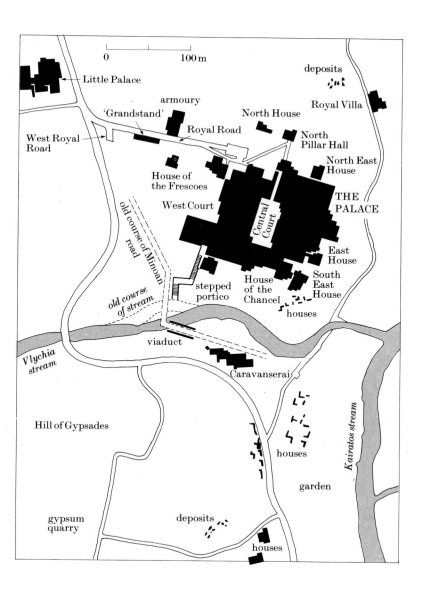

19.4: *The Bronze Age town of Knossos comprised the palace, large surrounding mansions and smaller houses linked by a system of paved roads dating from about 1900 BC. The buildings probably housed a hierarchy of functionaries for the complex economic system centred on the palace. A Neolithic village was founded in the seventh millennium near the two streams; its Early Bronze Age successor has been revealed at several points. From this large proto-urban community the palace was created about 1900 BC.*

Pefkakia in Thessaly and to Samos, Miletos and Iasos on the Anatolian coast. Links with Cyprus, the Levant and Middle Kingdom Egypt are indicated by the fine Middle Minoan pottery discovered at a string of sites, a recent find being made as far south as Aswan. One vital import was tin; an eighteenth-century BC tablet from Mari records its transport westwards to the Syro-Palestinian ports and ultimately to a recipient who was probably from Crete. Copper must have come from Cyprus, lapis lazuli from Afghanistan, amethyst, carnelian and gold probably from Egypt. Timber and resin may also have been exported.

The Second Palace Period, 1700–1450 BC, saw the finest flowering of civilization in Crete.[6] Besides the four palaces,[7] there are dozens of small towns with different forms. The palaces were surrounded by large houses and streets; Gournia and Myrtos Pyrgos had a dominant central building or small palace surrounded by small cobbled streets and blocks of houses with small rooms; Palaikastro and Pseira had more imposing blocks and streets but (so far) no palace; Mochlos and Tylissos seem to have consisted of free-standing mansions only, an arrangement closely mirrored at Thera. A new type of site also arose, the individual country villa as the centre of an estate;[8] examples are coastal Amnisos and Nirou Khani, inland Sklavokampos and Vathypetro, the villas of the Seteia valley and Epano Zakros in east Crete. The buildings and their contents look like the palace system on a smaller scale, and they may well have been under economic obligation to the palaces. While each palace would have controlled its own territory, there are at least two factors that exercised a unifying influence on all Minoan culture. These are writing and religion.[9] The Linear A script was in use throughout the island, both as an aid in the compilation of the detailed inventories essential to a redistributive economy and for inscriptions on ritual or votive stone vessels in peak sanctuaries.

The workshops of both palace and town produced an amazing range of beautiful objects, which combined a deep understanding of form with technical skill. Among them are vessels in obsidian, rock crystal, Egyptian alabaster, Peloponnesian *rosso antico* and *lapis Lacedaemonius*; animal-headed *rhyta* (vessels for liquids);

serpentine vases on which scenes of Minoan religious life and sports were carried in relief; gold rings and seals in semi-precious stones, exquisitely carved with abstract patterns, images of worshippers participating in religious rites and the flora and fauna of the natural world; figurines in terracotta, bronze, ivory and faience; bronze vessels ranging in size from huge cauldrons to small bowls; cups in silver and gold, including two with relief scenes of bull capture from Vapheio and one with a siege scene from Mycenae; bronze tools, including two-man saws and swords a metre long; wall frescoes in palaces, towns and villas; and everywhere pottery, ranging from tall *pithoi* (storage jars) to fine wares decorated with floral and marine motifs.

Most of these objects have been found among the destruction debris of inhabited sites, especially the shrine treasuries of the palaces. Some, however, especially bronze and terracotta figurines and swords, were found in sacred caves and mountain sanctuaries, and others among the relatively few known burials of the period. Grave forms were varied. Circular tombs persisted (Arkhanes, Kamilari, Knossos); chamber tombs were common at Knossos; cist graves occurred at Pseira; caves were used everywhere; and at Myrtos Pyrgos an elaborate form of house-tomb was used for burials within the village. Bodies were buried in pits, *pithoi* or *larnakes* (terracotta chests).

Minoan culture extended northwards into the Aegean. Minoan settlements or sites under strong Minoan influence are known on Kythera, Kea, Melos, Naxos, Thera, Karpathos and Rhodes, and at Iasos on the Anatolian coast. Goods were exported to these places, to the mainland, especially the Peloponnese, and the east Aegean, to Troy, Cyprus, the Levant coast and Egypt. The magnificent three-storeyed houses of Thera, with their wall paintings, each of which is unique,[10] were destroyed about 1500 BC, the settlements in Crete about 1450 BC. The great volcanic explosion of Thera may have been responsible for the later period of destruction, but Mycenaean invaders cannot be exempted from responsibility, as Mycenaeans were in control at Knossos in the second half of the fifteenth century BC.

19.5: *Aegean mariners had established sea routes since at least the eighth millennium, transporting obsidian from Melos to the Peloponnese. In the Early Bronze Age the Cycladic islanders incised on pottery pictures of long boats with a high prow. Models, too, were made in the islands and on Crete; Cretan engraved seals from about 2000 BC show that masted sailing ships had been created.*

The Greek mainland: the Middle Bronze Age and the Early Mycenaean period

After the disruptions of about 2200–2000 BC, the Greek mainland passed through a period of little distinction. The farming villagers lived in apsidal or rectangular megarons (long houses with a porch leading to the main room), used attractive grey burnished pottery (Minyan ware) descended from the brown and grey wares of about 2200–2000 BC, and dark-on-light painted ware. Bronze tools were rare. The bow was in common use for hunting. Wheat, barley, oats, peas, chick peas, lentils and beans were grown, and almost certainly the figs and grapes that were cultivated in the Early Bronze Age. Burials were frequently within the settlement, in pits or stone cists. Tumuli with pit, cist and jar burials have also been found, especially in western Greece. There are hints of prosperity and probably social hierarchy in the graves with pottery and metalwork on Lefkas, in the horses at Lerna and in gold diadems in burials at Asine and Corinth. These sites, and places like Aghios Stephanos, Eutresis, Lefkandi and Nichoria, were major local centres. Coastal sites, such as Lerna and Pefkakia, imported fine Minoan pottery, as did the islands of Aigina, Kea and Melos. But Middle Helladic life seems altogether poorer than that of contemporary Crete or even of the Sixth City at Troy, where the earliest fortifications had been built.

Towards 1600 BC prosperity spread throughout central Greece and the Peloponnese. Evidence is provided by a number of burial sites: large built graves at Eleusis, shaft graves at Lerna, tumuli containing built graves with a sacrificed horse at Marathon, the first stone *tholos* tombs (corbelled, with beehive vaults) on the mainland in Messenia (a form probably adopted from contemporary Crete) and the burials of Grave Circle B at Mycenae, with pottery, weapons, vases of precious metal and an electrum death mask. Richer social groups or powerful families emerged, soon to be eclipsed themselves by those who owned the incomparable wealth of the six shaft graves of Schliemann's Circle at Mycenae, dating to 1550–1500 BC.[11] The objects found at these nineteen burials are heterogeneous: a decorated ostrich egg; stone, faience, silver and bronze vessels and bronze swords from Crete; amber beads from north-west Europe; boars' tusks from helmets; inlaid daggers; gold cups; engraved rings; death masks; and scores of thin disks and jewels, all gold, which were probably of local manufacture.

How is this wealth to be explained? The burials reflect the general rise in mainland prosperity and social distinctions at this time, stimulated by contacts with the long-established palace civilization of Crete. But more is needed to explain Mycenae's predominance. The number of weapons shows that these were warrior rulers, their skeletons that they reached nearly two metres in height. Heterogeneous warrior wealth of this kind simply does not look like the wealth of merchant princes, but it has many parallels in European (including Homeric) epic; gift exchange or raiding for booty are as likely as other forms of commerce.

Mycenaean palace civilization

The fifteenth century was a time of complex transition for Mycenaean culture. At first it was under the artistic domination of Crete (Minoan civilization being at its zenith) and of a society organized under warrior rulers, whose burials at Rutsi near Pylos and at Vapheio have a weapon-rich character like those of the shaft graves of an earlier period. Besides these sites, other important local centres were developing, such as Kakovatos, Korakou in Corinthia, Nichoria, the Menelaion site at Sparta, Kambos with its magnificent *tholos* tomb, Thermon in Aitolia and Iolkos in Thessaly. Cultivation of the olive, so rich in food value, is documented for the first time on the mainland. At some stage there was a military change, the creation of a class of organized warriors armed with metal corslets, helmets and greaves (corslets are known from Dendra and Thebes about 1400 BC). The warriors must have played an important part in the most momentous advance of the Mycenaeans of this century, the takeover of Crete after about 1450 BC.

19.6: *Stone-corbelled, beehive-shaped tombs with long entrance passages* (tholoi) *were built from about 1600 BC onwards in Mycenaean Greece. They were the burial places of the chief person or family in a given territory. The tomb at Orchomenos in Boiotia, one of the largest and finest in Greece, was built c. 1400–1350 BC. Like the so-called Treasury of Atreus at Mycenae, it has a side chamber, in this case with a magnificent sculptured ceiling in an elaborate spiral pattern.*

Centred at Knossos, the Mycenaeans learned from the Minoans, adapted their system and created a complex economy based on written records, the Linear B (Mycenaean Greek) tablets. The records took the form of a detailed quota system of foodstuffs, animals and craft products owed to the palace; some eighty-five place names on the tablets suggest control of the whole island. Bureaucratic expertise would have been derived from the older Minoan palace system, but control must have been exercised with the aid of the uniformly armed warriors whose corslets are recorded on the tablets. These warriors were buried north of the palace, without corslets but with weapons and helmets. Rich graves of the same date, though not of military character, are known at Aghia Triadha (with its famous polychrome sarcophagus) and at Kalyvia, both near Phaistos. The artifacts of many rich graves at Knossos and Arkhanes about 1400 BC have parallels at Athens, Dendra and Thebes and demonstrate the close links between the Cretan and mainland workshops at this time. However, by about 1375 BC Knossos had been destroyed by earthquake, Cretan revolt or other Mycenaean invaders. Thereafter it ceased to be an international centre, but it remained until the twelfth century an important local centre, like Kydonia (modern Khania) in western Crete.

Despite the mainland developments of the fifteenth century, no palatial administrative centre has been found. The earliest phases of the existing palaces at Mycenae, Pylos, Thebes and Tiryns seem to date to the fourteenth century. While mainland society and economic progress must have been sufficiently advanced to sustain a complex, centralized economy, a second factor, the Mycenaean adaptation of the palace system during their rule on Crete, must have been equally important for the eventual establishment of a palatial economy on the mainland itself.

Our evidence comes chiefly from the palaces[12] and their contents – remains of frescoes, pottery, metalwork, semi-precious stones and, above all, the Linear B tablets of the time of the destruction of the palaces in the thirteenth century. The tablets testify to the complex redistributive economy controlling the production and social organization of the villages of each kingdom, ruled by its *wanax* (king), officials and army.[13] The few Theban tablets are concerned with sheep and those from Mycenae with spices, while the great collection from Pylos deals with a wide

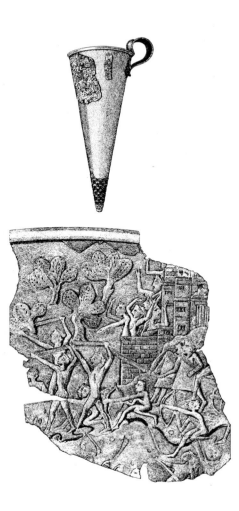

19.7: *Vessels in hard stones were among the finest products of the Cretan palaces. Breccia, calcite, red, white and mottled marbles, obsidian, porphyry, rock crystal and serpentine were used from 1700–1450 BC. Many vases were used in palace shrines; others were exported, perhaps in systems of prestige gift exchange.*

19.8: *This famous silver* rhyton, *from Shaft Grave IV at Mycenae, is a Minoan product whose surviving fragments depict a battle before a town. The defenders comprise naked slingers and archers and men with body shields. Several figures have crested hairstyles. All these features indicate that the scene could be Crete, and fragments from the lower part suggest a setting near the sea shore.*

range of crafts, including bronzework. Occupations recorded on the Pylos tablets include those of bakers, bronze-workers, carpenters, fullers, heralds, masons, messengers, potters, shepherds and unguent-boilers. Mycenaean artifactual evidence reveals skill in superlative ivory carving, metal inlay work, fresco painting and the production of excellent decorated pottery, to which must be added the building skills of the great corbelled *tholos* tombs and of the palaces themselves, and the vast drainage works of Lake Kopais.

The importance of religion is clear. The Pylos tablets record offerings to most of the gods and goddesses known in Classical Greece and to priestesses who controlled religious property. Mycenae had a cult centre near the palace; shrines here and within settlements on Kea and Melos housed male and female terracotta statuettes, perhaps representing divinities, to whom were offered jewellery and seals. A fresco from Mycenae shows a Mistress of Animals.

Society was markedly hierarchical, from the king down to female slaves (some of the latter at Pylos apparently came from towns on the Anatolian coast). Villages included common land and there were also private estates. Burials, too, suggest social ranking, from the great *tholos* tombs (nine have been found at Mycenae and many others all over the mainland) to family chamber tombs, which were often reused and have yielded offerings that are very varied in quality. The chamber tomb cemetery at Tanagra in Boeotia is unique in Mycenaean Greece, with its *larnakes* painted with scenes of mourning and ritual (*larnax* burial was the standard mode in contemporary Crete).

From the start of the fourteenth century the Mycenaeans expanded their foreign trade. Its surviving evidence is mostly pottery – wine *kraters* (deep, two-handled bowls) with chariot and bull scenes and small closed vessels that probably contained scented oils – that was exported to Italy and Sicily in the west and throughout the Anatolian coast and the Levant, appearing on nearly a hundred sites in the area from northern Syria to beyond southern Egypt. Special pieces, like the inlaid silver bowl from Enkomi on Cyprus, may have been the gift exchanges of rulers. Metals, ivory and perhaps slaves seem to have been the chief imports, and the styles of ivory carving show clear connections between Megiddo, Cyprus, Delos and mainland Greece. The cargo of a ship wrecked off Cape Gelidonya in about 1200 BC exemplifies the commercial trade of the time; it was carrying scrap bronzes and imports of copper and tin.

The collapse of Mycenaean civilization

At the height of Mycenaean power in the thirteenth century certain citadels were fortified; Mycenae, Tiryns and Gla in Boeotia, with its 3000-metre circuit, are the best instances. The final great walls of Troy were built at this time. But Pylos had no walls and none is known at low-lying Orchomenos. Fortifications imply wealth worth guarding and the anticipation of raids. In this century sites began to be destroyed: Pylos, Zygouries and the

houses outside the citadel of Mycenae apparently well before 1200 BC, then most of the big sites about 1200 BC (Berbati, Eutresis and Prosymna were abandoned, not burnt). Others such as Argos, Asine, Athens, Iolkos, Korakou, Lefkandi and Nichoria escaped destruction until the twelfth century. Culture was by then no longer based on palaces, but was still wholly Mycenaean. Mycenae and Tiryns were extensive and vigorous towns; the peaceful coastal settlements of the Ionian and Cycladic islands and Crete flourished. Mycenaeans colonized Cyprus. Foreign features are not found in the palace destructions, but dark-faced pottery that looks non-Mycenaean appears here and there in Greece and across the Dardanelles in contemporary Troy. Towards the end of the twelfth century cemeteries of cist graves with single burials, brooches (*fibulae*), rings and incised terracotta figurines of Balkan or Epirote origin appeared in central Greece.

These are the facts in bare outline. Any explanation of the collapse of the Mycenaean palace civilization must take them into account. As Mycenaean village culture persisted after the collapse, an invasion by non-Mycenaean peoples seems out of the question. So does the drought and famine advocated by some, because the tablets, from Thebes to Pylos, indicate a flourishing agriculture. Destructions at different times and in different regions might imply earthquakes, but earthquakes would not have prevented the rebuilding of palaces in subsequent reinhabitation. One plausible explanation is inter-state rivalry and warfare within the Mycenaean world, perhaps exacerbated by pressure on land in the preceding florescence of these small kingdoms. Such conflict (known as *stasis*) was to be endemic in later Greek civilization, and the ancient writers clearly believed that it accounted for the downfall of the Mycenaeans. Later, perhaps from the end of the twelfth century, newcomers came from north-west Greece; they were probably the Donians, later the main speakers of the West Greek dialect (see Chapter 29).

In the eleventh century Athens emerged as the most important new Early Iron Age centre, and the towns of Euboea soon followed. Cremation, which began before 1100 BC, replaced inhumation. Iron technology had arrived from Cyprus after the collapse of the Hittite empire in about 1200 BC, and soon the Greeks were producing iron knives and swords. Contact with Cyprus, especially through traders from Athens and Crete, was never lost. But the most important legacies of the Bronze Age world of Minoan Crete and Mycenaean Greece were non-material – religion, heroic legends in oral tales, and language.

20. Early agricultural communities in Europe

In the period that saw the emergence of the state and urban life in the Near East and the eastern Mediterranean, temperate Europe continued to be organized largely along tribal lines. While substantial changes are evident in the archaeological record, they do not show the strong tendency towards centralization that elsewhere produced towns and palaces. Only in the Aegean, where there was contact with Anatolia and the Levant, were hierarchically organized societies present by the second millennium BC (see Chapter 19).

The most basic change perceptible during this period was the continuing colonization of the European landmass. By comparison with later periods, population was still scattered in isolated pockets separated by large areas of woodland and marsh; but these pockets of settlement multiplied and grew in size, creating new patterns of contact and corridors of communication. A wider range of environments brought new opportunities for trade, while technical development produced fresh skills and new materials (notably metals) for production and exchange.[1]

An important factor in spatial expansion and economic development was the package of innovations that spread across Europe in the third millennium BC, involving the use of animals for traction and transport and the first use of secondary products such as milk and wool.[2] The light plough assisted in the opening up of the European forests and went along with an increase in the numbers of beasts that could be kept for their meat and milk and for other purposes. Travel and transport on land were thus facilitated as the ox cart, horse and chariot came successively into use, and this phase saw also the beginnings of extensive maritime contact. But increased mobility – and raiding, which was one of its consequences – brought greater insecurity and metal armaments underwent a rapid development.

The first agricultural penetration

The beginning of cultivation in the Balkans and the southern fringes of central Europe in the sixth millennium BC (see Chapter 15) took place as new forest species such as oak, elm and lime were slowly spreading from their southern refuges to replace the light birch and pine woods that had covered much of Europe in the early Postglacial. The closed canopy of this dense woodland reduced the amount of light reaching the ground and thus hindered the growth of grasses and shoots that supported the animals hunted for food; consequently such animals became less plentiful. The spread of mixed oak forest also reduced the numbers of important food-bearing plants such as hazel. At the same time the multitude of morainic lakes began to be obliterated by infilling with sediment and vegetation, while the continuing postglacial rise in sea level drowned large areas of productive coastal low-

lands. All these factors placed an increasing stress on the indigenous hunting and collecting populations of Europe, causing the reduction or displacement of their numbers and concentrating their attention on open uplands, coasts, meres and rivers where newly arrived species like salmon offered an attractive source of food.

The agrarian communities that appeared in the southern part of the Carpathian Basin in the latter half of the sixth millennium BC (the Starčevo–Körös group) derived their crops, livestock and basic equipment from farming groups already established in the Balkans, but they used riverine resources in the same way as their contemporaries further north. Sites in eastern Hungary, along the Danube, Tisza and Körös rivers, indicate a pattern of linear hamlets situated by streams, with plentiful remains of fish, shellfish and waterfowl, as well as the bones of domestic livestock (mainly sheep) and traces of grain. This adaptation to the opportunities offered by large river basins, however, was limited in area, and the further spread of agriculture required a larger adjustment to the conditions of central Europe.

The most fertile soils of central Europe are those developed on the deposits of wind-blown silt, known as loess, laid down on the margins of the glaciers during the last ice age. These occupy large areas of the main basins between the Alps and the North European Plain. As settlement spread to the smaller streamcourses in the rolling loess-covered country of western Hungary, it crystallized into a form that could be transferred throughout the loess-land habitats of central Europe, from Belgium to the Ukraine. The economy was based on cattle rather than sheep and on the hoe cultivation of cereals and other large-seeded grasses (such as *Bromus secalinus*) in narrow strips of land near rivers and streams. As clearings were small, the cattle were probably partly stall-fed, and they were kept in the longhouses characteristic of this period. These structures, which were 6 metres wide and varied between 8 and 40 metres in length, represent the beginnings of timber-framed architecture in Europe. The characteristic woodworking tool was the wedge, especially the long stone 'shoe-last' form that developed at this time. Techniques of carpentry were still rudimentary; the joints of these structures were primitive and the uprights self-supporting rather than acting as parts of frames. In consequence, the posts had to be deeply sunk, and excavated houses show a large number of massive postholes, traces of which have survived despite heavy subsequent erosion (see Figure 20.5).

About 5000 BC this pattern of pioneer village farming spread with great rapidity into Moravia, and thence in three great streams north-eastwards into southern Poland and the Ukraine, north-westwards to Bohemia and central Germany, and westwards along the upper Danube to the Rhine and beyond. Everywhere it was characterized by small clusters of longhouses along streams running through the loess, whose occupants used simple round-based forms of pottery decorated with incised (and later punched), linear, ribbon-like ornament – the so-called Bandkeramik. Although the houses themselves were rebuilt once every generation or so, as typological studies of their pottery indicate, the settlenents were very stable, and some sites were occupied more or less continuously for nearly a thousand years. The cemeteries of such communities show that men had a higher life expectancy than women and that older males received special respect, being buried with stone woodworking tools and ornaments of prized *Spondylus* shell that occur throughout the Bandkeramik zone. The first agrarian penetration of the temperate forest zone thus produced a very uniform culture and economy, resulting from the occupation of a very similar series of habitats by related groups with a common economic and technical base. Although it carried farming populations into the heart of Europe, it was nevertheless only a small-scale penetration of a narrow range of environments, none of which supported dense Mesolithic populations.[3]

In contrast to this movement of colonization into a relatively empty zone, the spread of pottery and domestic animals in the Mediterranean took place largely among pre-existing local populations. This spread was not accompanied by the development of village-based farming: there is little evidence of cereal cultivation before the fifth millennium, and many of the settlements continued to be in caves, usually previously occupied. Population was already concentrated on the coasts where maritime resources were abundant; fishing expeditions brought different groups into contact with each other and encouraged the distribution of valuable resources like obsidian. Such networks also disseminated new elements such as domesticated sheep and the manufacture of pottery, and they maintained the stylistic unity of the latter product, which is named Impressed Ware, or Cardial Ware, after the characteristic cockle (*Cardium*) impressions with which it was decorated. Sites with this pottery, associated with shellfish, hunted ungulates and a few sheep, are known from Dalmatia, southern Italy and Sicily, Corsica and Sardinia, southern France, the Balearic Islands and coastal Spain. Many of these islands were occupied for the first time, and the general distribution is conspicuously coastal.[4]

This Cardial Ware complex can thus plausibly be regarded as one of a number of sub-Neolithic groups that used pottery and kept domestic animals and that grew up on the fringes of the area of fully agrarian settlement in areas where Mesolithic populations were able to survive and expand their numbers. Similar phenomena occurred all around the fringes of the Balkan–central European agricultural salient, especially where Bandkeramik populations lived next to areas of abundant natural resources. Along the rivers of the Ukrainian steppes, for instance, beyond the easternmost Bandkeramik villages, there developed communities that kept cattle and made impressed, point-based pots that define the Bug–Dniester culture. On the northern fringes of the Bandkeramik distribution, around the lakes of the North European Plain and the shallow fjords of Jutland, there developed the Ertebølle–Ellerbek culture, best known on the coasts for the heaps of oyster shells that accumulated at littoral base camps. These have yielded coarse, point-based pottery and the bones of domestic stock, as well as plentiful remains of local wild deer.

However, temperate-forest Mesolithic cultures unaffected by incoming Neolithic influences survived in the British Isles, which were now effectively insulated. Some measure of expansion, or at least adjustment to the loss of North Sea territories, is indicated by the increased occupation of highlands and islands.

Consolidation and advance
As the Bandkeramik groups were spreading over central Europe, the *tell*-based communities of the Balkans were multiplying and

20.1: *Plan of an excavated Copper Age village at Polyanitsa in north-eastern Bulgaria. In this fifth-millennium village there were nearly two dozen houses, all densely packed within an enclosing palisade. The houses were built of mud on a timber framework.*

- hearths
- mud and timber walls
- trench with palisade
- postholes

0   15 m

expanding. New areas of limestone basin fringes were occupied in central Yugoslavia, and many substantial sites came into existence in the valleys of the lower Danube and the Maritsa in Romania and Bulgaria, and also in Thessaly. Largely undefended by anything more than wooden fences, these long-lived sites occur in large numbers in the lowland plains. Communities of between fifty and a few hundred people lived in villages of rectangular wood and mud huts with a uniform house plan, which divided the huts into living space and cooking area with hearths and ovens. Excavations at deeply stratified sites like Vinča (Yugoslavia), Karanovo and Polyanitsa (Bulgaria) and Boian and Gumelnitsa (Romania) have provided a wealth of information.[5] These nucleated villages testify to a lively trade and to craftsmanship in the domestic arts of potting and the manufacture of woven fabrics whose designs are reflected in the pottery. These include intricate maze patterns and swinging, curvilinear designs. Other ceramic products are the notable female and animal figurines in schematic forms. Attractive stones for finely polished axes, shells for dress ornaments and pigments for painting were traded over hundreds of kilometres. Among the traded stone items were lumps of malachite, a rich ore of copper that can be smelted by simple techniques,[6] and that was mined by sinking narrow shafts that followed the veins of ore from surface outcrops. By 4000 BC such mines, at places like Rudna Glava in north-east Yugoslavia, were already supplying raw material for the manufacture of copper axes, including types with shaftholes, that imitated existing forms made in stone. Such early applications of metallurgy were largely concerned with ornament and display, for the metal, as yet unalloyed, was very soft by comparison with true bronze. Simple manufacturing techniques, based largely on casting in open moulds and on hammering, were used to produce pins and arm rings. These innovations define a localized Copper Age in south-east and central Europe, though these communities differed little in other respects from the formally Neolithic groups that surrounded them. The easy accessibility of simple ores of copper in the Balkan and Carpathian mountains, in conjunction with limited trade and simple technical skills, produced the beginnings of a metallurgical industry that was to grow into a major technological achievement of the Old World.

While these technical advances were taking place in the Balkans true agricultural villages had begun to appear in the western Mediterranean. They were based on cereal farming and manufactured similar finely decorated pottery, which in some areas was also painted. Stone axes and querns became plentiful. Conditions uniquely suitable for aerial photography, in the dry plains of Apulia in southern Italy, have revealed traces of some hundreds of villages belonging to this period, with clusters of ditched hut enclosures gathered within single or multiple outer ditches. Some sites have only a few hut enclosures; others, such as Passo di Corvo, have more than a hundred. Away from these rich lowland areas, however, cereal cultivation and stock-keeping only slowly displaced native economies based on the hunting of red deer. In the west Mediterranean as a whole the unity of early *Cardium*-

decorated pottery gave way to regional styles using new forms of decoration. Open-air sites, appearing by lakes and as coastal settlements, increasingly supplemented the use of caves. From the fifth millennium BC onwards settlement began to spread beyond the littoral zone, and the Chassey culture appeared widely in southern and central France, including the plateaux of the Grands Causses. Sites spread up the Rhône and are especially frequent on river terraces.

The main spread of population into western and northern Europe, however, stemmed from the loess areas of central Europe and the Bandkeramik tradition. This expansion during the fourth millennium was the result both of natural population growth and of changes in the loess itself as a result of cultivation, which made it less tractable. But as the areas suitable for cultivation beyond the loess margins already carried Mesolithic populations clustered around the coasts and the morainic lakes of the North European Plain and the Alpine Foreland, penetration of these areas took place slowly, at first avoiding the main centres of indigenous population.[7]

By the mid-fourth millennium BC agricultural sites had appeared in a broad arc from western France to the British Isles, Scandinavia and the North European Plain, as well as in the circumalpine zone, where settlements took the form of small nucleated villages situated by lakes (and where waterlogged conditions have preserved rare evidence of organic materials such as wooden tools and textiles). In northern and western Europe a more scattered pattern of settlement appeared, in which monumental tombs – small stone chambers with an earth or stone mound – played an important part. Such mortuary shrines appeared independently in a number of areas, and in northern Europe particularly the long mounds imitated the earlier tradition of house plans. Agriculture formed the basis of the economy, and limited numbers of stalled cattle were kept in the small clearings in the forest. Pollen diagrams from Denmark demonstrate the introduction of both cereals and weeds of cultivation at this time, and also the limited scale of attack on the forest, which often regenerated after its first clearance. The pottery of these groups was still round-based and mostly plain: in northern Europe the characteristic flaring rim has given the name Funnel-beaker (Trichterrandbecher, TRB) culture to these groups.

Another area of agricultural penetration at this time was the belt of forest–steppe to the north of the true steppe area in southern Russia. Villages related to those of the Balkan *tells* spread from river valley to river valley around the north of the Black Sea, where their remains are found on terraces and promontories, as at Cucuteni in Romania and Tripole in the Ukraine. Painted, curvilinear-decorated pottery indicates their affiliation to neighbours in Romania and Bulgaria.

Around these agricultural communities, in a belt along the middle Dnieper and in the forest zone of European Russia, a basically Mesolithic economy based on hunting and collecting was augmented by Neolithic techniques of stone polishing and pottery manufacture and by small numbers of domestic animals. Coarse pottery vessels with pointed bases were ornately decorated with comb impressions and pits. Such features are known from Estonia and Lithuania in the fifth millennium BC, from where they spread along the Volga and Kama rivers to the Urals (see Chapter 49).

The plough and the transformation of European agriculture

In about 3000 BC a decisive change took place in the European way of life, which is apparent from artifacts and settlement patterns as much as from direct evidence of subsistence. Present evidence indicates that important innovations were introduced from further east,[8] probably from the steppe region to the north of the Black Sea, though ultimately from the Near East. Among the most important of these was the use of animal traction to pull ploughs and carts, but it is probable that this was only part of a wider complex of animal husbandry that included the regular use of milk.

20.2: *La Panetteria, a Neolithic village in southern Italy, showing two phases of an enclosed settlement, with ditches around the settlement and individual hut compounds.*

One of the first indications of a new economy is the expansion of population in the true steppe area, marked among other things by the appearance of fortified settlements and the spread of circular burial mounds ('kurgans') constructed over pit graves containing skeletons covered in red ochre. In some cases the dead were buried with two- or four-wheeled carts with solid wooden wheels. Although the vehicles were drawn by oxen, the use of the horse is first indicated among these groups, and sheep-herding began to play a more important part on the open plains (see Chapter 38). These characteristic burial mounds appeared as far west as the Carpathian Basin, especially on the open saline soils east of the Tisza. These changes produced repercussions among the *tell* villages of the Balkans: many were abandoned, and those that remained were often fortified with stone walls, as at Ezero in Bulgaria. There are also striking changes in the pottery: the elaborate painted wares disappeared, and in their place came a wide range of coarse pottery pails and buckets and dark burnished finewares, among which jugs and cups were prominent. The appearance of such forms in a wide range of cultural contexts argues for a widespread dietary change rather than simply for new traditions or methods of production, and it is possible that they were used for the preparation and consumption of milk products. Another aspect of material culture that underwent significant change was metallurgy. As a result of influences from the Caucasian school, new techniques were introduced that included the use of arsenical alloying and the two-piece mould. This allowed the casting of more complex forms, and the earlier tradition of hammering largely disappeared.

In the eastern Mediterranean (see Chapter 19) similar changes were accompanied by a notable expansion of contacts by sea and a shift of population to coasts and islands. Not only were fruit crops such as olive and grape brought widely into cultivation at this period, but sea fishing was also increased through the use of effective boats. This is reflected in the expansion of trade between the islands, with their metal and stone deposits, and in the contacts with the western coast of Anatolia that resulted in the spread of new forms and techniques, especially in fine metalwork. The regular use of arsenical alloys and tin bronze defines the beginning of the Bronze Age here. Fortified sites and castles illustrate the effects of this new wealth and its attendant insecurity and mark the beginnings of the path to urban civilization in the Aegean.[9]

Comparable developments, though less advanced, can be traced in the central and western Mediterranean at this time, in the monumental architecture, metallurgy and long-distance trade in rare materials. Copper was used, though still without the addition of tin, but metal was plentiful only near sources such as the rich deposits of southern Spain. This period, known as the Chalcolithic, saw the construction of elaborate stone tombs and fortified stone villages in Iberia and in southern France, the growth of a considerable megalithic temple architecture in the more isolated location of the Maltese islands, rock-cut tombs in Sardinia and Sicily and fortified hilltop settlements in mainland Italy. In the

20.3: *The third-millennium megalithic temple of Ggantija on the west Mediterranean island of Gozo, looking out through the main entrance. Such temple centres contrast with the later, Bronze Age fortified settlements such as that of In-Nuffara, on the flat-topped hill that can be seen in the distance.*

20.4: *Diagram of the Early Bronze Age cemetery of Mokrin in northern Yugoslavia. Differences in wealth and status in this early second-millennium community are indicated by the presence of imported metal items.*

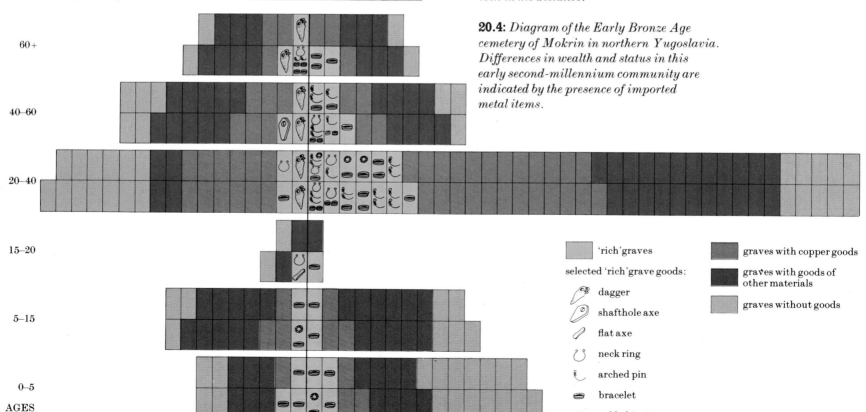

'rich' graves	graves with copper goods
selected 'rich' grave goods:	graves with goods of other materials
dagger	graves without goods
shafthole axe	
flat axe	
neck ring	
arched pin	
bracelet	
gold object	

60+

40–60

20–40

15–20

5–15

0–5

AGES
AT
DEATH

MALES   FEMALES

Central European Neolithic

Balkan Neolithic

1:40 000 000

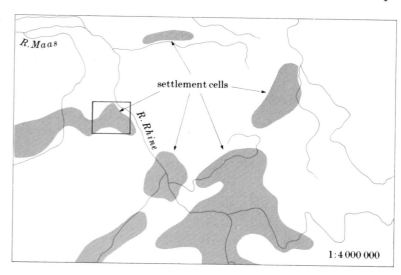

R. Maas

settlement cells

R. Rhine

1:4 000 000

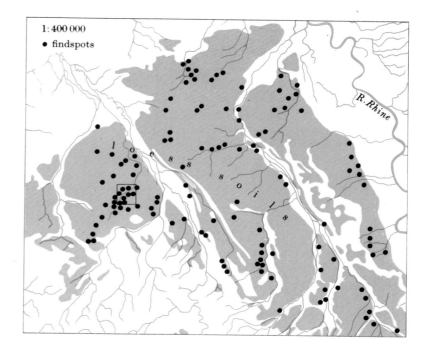

1:400 000

• findspots

l o e s s   s o i l s

R. Rhine

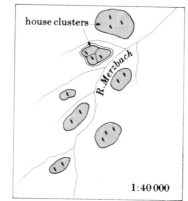

house clusters

R. Merzbach

1:40 000

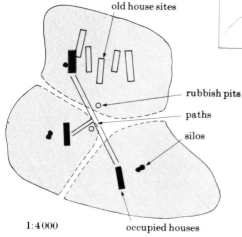

old house sites

rubbish pits

paths

silos

occupied houses

1:4000

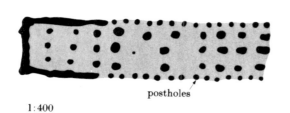

1:400

postholes

20.5: *Early Neolithic settlement in Europe. Successive enlargements of scale (by a factor of ten) show the characteristic patterns of fifth-millennium settlement, from the continental spread of agriculture to the individual house plan. Intensive fieldwork in north-west Germany has allowed a detailed reconstruction of these riverside villages of the Bandkeramik group.*

drier areas of Spain irrigation may have been practised. Pottery assemblages, at least in the central Mediterranean, included jugs and cups with ribbon-shaped handles like those found in central Europe, though here the pottery was decorated by painting. In Spain schematic human representations are found on pots, schist plaques (plates formed by the splitting of layered rock) and anthropomorphic *stelae*. Metal objects included pins, flat axes, daggers and, in Italy, rarer battle-axes. Metal forms influenced the flintwork, whose elaborate arrow- and lance-heads recall copper prototypes. Beads in various materials were widely traded, including characteristic 'winged' forms made of calcite, which are found from Italy to Spain. These are typical of the richer items found in tombs, some of which had corbelled chambers with passage entrances for collective burial. The famous cemetery of Los Millares in Almeria contained nearly a hundred of these tombs.

In northern Europe the introduction of the plough permitted cultivation to spread from the river valleys,[10] and ox traction allowed the construction of more complex megalithic tombs, built with large boulders cleared from the fields. Traces of criss-cross furrows, made by cross-ploughing with the simple ard or scratch-plough, can sometimes be traced under these monuments. In Britain and adjacent parts of continental Europe larger settlements were surrounded by low banks with discontinuous quarry ditches. These are well preserved, especially where thin loess soils overlie chalk. More elaborate fortifications are known from central Germany,[11] and in northern Europe stone battle-axes were made in elaborate shapes, some imitating the rare copper axes that were exported northwards. The increased scale of attack on the forests is reflected by the deep flint mines that were opened up from the southern British Isles to White Russia to supply the demand for efficient axes: flint and other suitable rocks were widely traded over hundreds of kilometres. Burial was still largely communal, and there is only limited evidence of social differentiation and the concentration of wealth. Small family groups were still the basic economic unit.

The area of farming economy continued to expand eastwards in the strip of deciduous woodland between the Russian steppe and the northern coniferous forests, at the expense of hunting-and-gathering groups using pit- and comb-marked pottery. The latter became confined to the lakes and rivers of the coniferous zone, and the central Russian plain around Moscow was incorporated in the cultural province covering Poland and northern Germany.

Expansion and social change

With population growth and environmental deterioration during the course of the third millennium, settlement in northern Europe spread increasingly to the poorer soils, especially the light, sandy ones that could withstand cultivation for shorter periods than those previously in use. A more flexible family structure evolved in these conditions, as is indicated by the new form of individual burial in small mounds, which were used for shorter periods than their monumental predecessors and imply a rapidly changing pattern of small homesteads. The various regions of settlement were connected by contacts along rivers and coasts and by the new potential for overland travel and transport afforded by the spread of the horse. The growth of a pastoral sector was promoted by increasing proportions of open land made available as the forests were cleared and soils deteriorated, together with the possibilities offered by milk-based stock-raising. Male status became more important, and richer individuals were buried with fine drinking vessels and weapons – especially battle-axes, daggers and archery equipment. Trade in these items, and probably also in textiles (for the first time in wool), linked settlements over wide areas. This is shown by the wide distribution of certain pottery types, particularly drinking vessels elaborately decorated with impressions of twisted cord. The climax of these developments was the emergence of a standardized inter-regional style, linking parts of northern, central and south-western Europe and characterized by a standardized set of male status-objects, of which the most prominent is the decorated drinking cup, the so-called beaker.[12] Pottery in this style appears both in the Rhine and Danube basins and also down the Rhône to the western Mediterranean, where it is known from later Chalcolithic contexts in the south. This internationalism seems to have been at its most intense in the later third millennium, and it facilitated the spread of metallurgical techniques to new areas in northern Europe, notably the British Isles and central Germany, where the local production of copper objects began.

While inter-regional contact and trade continued to increase during the second millennium, the peculiarly international flavour of the Beaker period was short-lived and individual regions pursued a less uniform course. However, many new features, such as the burial practices, continued and developed. In some areas – central Germany in particular – differences in social status are shown by one or two spectacularly rich burials with gold objects, such as that at Leubingen, near Halle. There was also a marked increase in the scale of metal production in this area, based on the ores of the Harz mountains. A characteristic feature of the early second millennium is the hoards of metal objects, notably axes and neck rings, that were widely traded and accumulated as indicators of personal wealth. This probably reflects the trading activity of enterprising individuals – like the 'big men' of Melanesia – rather than a hereditary aristocracy. The neck rings were worn mainly by women, who were the vehicles for such display. Both sexes fastened their loosely woven woollen cloaks with pins (see Figure 20.4).[13]

Vigorous new developments began to take place in the Carpathian Basin towards the middle of the second millennium. On the terraces and foothills to the north large numbers of fortified villages appeared that were associated with major advances in metallurgical techniques and the production of fine decorated black pottery. Elaborate individually produced and decorated weapons are characteristic. Among the new features that appeared at this time was the chariot, introduced from the steppe regions to the north of the Black Sea. Decorated bone and antler harness elements indicate the social significance of horse-rearing, and it is probable that influences from this region reached as far south as Greece, where they are reflected in the richly equipped shaft graves of the growing aristocracy of Mycenae (see Chapter 19). An expansion in the volume of trade in metals, and the development of new skills based upon it, is indicated in several parts of Europe by the rise of bronze industries in lowland areas away from metal sources. This is true of the metal products of Wessex in southern Britain, and it is spectacularly evident in Scandinavia, where a skilful school of bronzeworking grew up that was entirely dependent on imported material. Alloying with tin both produced a harder edge and allowed the production of more complex mouldings. Forms quickly developed that were designed to take advantage of the potential of bivalve casting. This is especially apparent in the rapid advances made in weaponry: daggers gradually lengthened into rapiers and solid-hilted swords, axes with improved forms of hafting evolved and halberds and spears appeared. These advances were quickly shared between regions, though in Spain the new forms were still produced by rather old-fashioned techniques.[14]

In the Mediterranean the sites of this period are often nucleated hilltop settlements defended by walls and ditches. Population was notably high in coastal regions and often concentrated on fortified promontories, reflecting the importance of maritime trading and raiding. The Baltic also provides evidence of the increased importance of seafaring. While some examples of defended sites are known from central Europe, large areas of the continental interior offer no evidence of nucleated settlement but instead indicate steady forest clearance by homesteaders on lighter soils, where their round burial mounds – now often on heathland or under forest – document the impact of techniques of extensive farming on the temperate forest environment. Nevertheless, vast areas of heavier soil or more mountainous terrain remained untouched, and settlement still had the overall appearance of small pockets of population surrounded by forest.

The main change was increasing mass production in the metal industries, shown by larger quantities of more uniform weapons and, increasingly, working tools. Poorer quality alloys, to which lead was added, became common in some areas, and metal was no longer squandered in such quantities on personal equipment for graves. Women continued to be buried with ornaments of imported metal or of rare substances such as amber, but massive contrasts in wealth are less apparent. Hoards of metalwork look increasingly like scrap for recasting rather than personal treasures.

This somewhat stagnant picture, in sharp contrast to the dynamic developments in the Aegean world at this time, was transformed towards the end of the second millennium by new economic forces and external contacts. The continuing deterioration of lighter soils forced an attack on fertile but more demanding soils such as clay and alluvium. To cope with such soils a heavier form of ard came into use, along with winter-grown cereals and new crops such as rye. The landscape was reorganized, and large-scale field systems were laid out. Defended centres and hillforts came into being, with a new elite whose rich graves contained the products of craftsmen skilled in the manufacture of armour and horse gear. New breeds of horse made cavalry superior to chariotry, which continued to be used in warfare only in remote regions like the British Isles. New rituals for burial and religious observance appeared to suit the changing social order. As Mediterranean trade quickened after the 'dark age' recession, fresh contacts across the Alps provided stimuli to development and trade. Expansion led to conquest and folk movements, and the map of modern Europe, bearing the names of familiar peoples such as the Celts (see Chapter 33), began to take shape.

20.6: *Bronze battle-axe from north-east Hungary, typical of the elaborately decorated weapons of the early second millennium in Europe.*

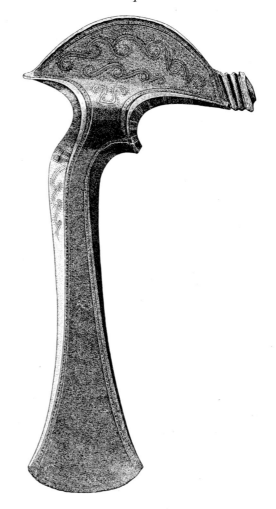

21. Agricultural origins in East Asia

Until a few years ago explanations for the development of settled village farming societies in East Asia were almost invariably given in terms of diffusion and migration from other centres of cultural innovation, ultimately from western Asia. Over the past fifteen years there has been a sustained attempt to investigate the early stages of these societies. In recognition of the many differences in environment and the distinct groups of plants and animals on which East Asian agriculture depended, it has become more common to interpret the emerging archaeological sequences as the product of internal evolutionary forces, without denying that movements of people did sometimes take place and that ideas and techniques would also have spread.

East Asia contains almost the full range of natural environments found in the world, from arctic tundra to tropical lowland forests, from high mountains and cold deserts to coral atolls and great lowland river valleys, seasonally flooded. Early societies were thus able to exploit many different combinations of plants and animals for food. It has been found useful to divide the region into a number of broad natural and cultural zones, where the particular combination of climate and resources provided distinct opportunities for human groups.

Within these zones, three 'centres' (north-central China, the lower Yangtze valley and north Thailand east to Vietnam) can be recognized, on present evidence, where various hunting and collecting societies intensified, at the end of the Pleistocene, their dependence on a narrow range of plant and animal species. The removal of these from their natural habitats into increasingly man-made surroundings induced genetic and morphological changes that led in turn to their dependence on man.

A number of important plants and animals provided the staple foods for these early Asian Neolithic communities. In north China, on the inland loess tablelands, broomcorn and foxtail millet were of overwhelming importance; many fruit trees, especially those of the genus *Prunus*, were cultivated; and of the leafy vegetables, mention should be made of the Chinese cabbage. In south China and the northern part of the mainland of south-east Asia, rice was the main cereal brought into cultivation, but roots and tubers, several water-loving vegetables and many of the citrus fruits were domesticated there. In island south-east Asia cereals may have been introduced by later Neolithic immigrants but, as on the mainland, many roots and tubers were domesticated, and an impressive range of tropical tree fruits were cultivated, such as coconut, bread and jack fruits, mango, mangosteen, rambutan and durian. Bananas were first domesticated here, and perhaps also sugarcane.[1]

Domesticated animals were less important in early East Asia than in the west. Dogs have been found at the end of the Pleisto-cene in Japan and are common in north Chinese Neolithic sites. Varieties of pig are found throughout the mainland of East Asia and appear to have been the first domesticated animals taken into the islands of eastern Indonesia and to New Guinea. Remains of cattle, sheep and goats, however, are not common until the later Neolithic cultures and indicate contacts with central Asia. But in Thailand a variety of small cattle occurs in the early villages of the north-east in the fourth millennium BC and was probably locally domesticated from the wild zebu.

Environmental changes

The effect of the global warming at the beginning of the Holocene brought readjustments in East Asia, as elsewhere. Over much of the Soviet Far East and in the interior of Siberia the climate prevented human settlement until just before 20 000 years ago. In continental areas such as inland north China, temperature, precipitation and land forms changed markedly, and the Late Pleistocene saw the creation of the great loess tablelands that were to be the scene of an indigenous development of agriculture in the Holocene. In the tropical south climatic changes were less extreme; the increase in mean annual temperatures of 3°–8°C produced altitudinal shifts of vegetational zones that, though locally important, could probably have been accommodated within the existing foraging ranges of Late Pleistocene bands. However, in coastal regions, and especially in island south-east Asia and around Japan, the rising sea levels that can be recognized after about 16 000 years ago inundated large tracts of low-lying land and subjected the occupying communities to stress. Japan was probably linked to the mainland of Asia through most, if not all, of the Pleistocene, its present coasts being established – with some variations due to local tectonic and volcanic activity – between 10 000 and 7000 years ago. The climate became more maritime in character and the proportion of productive coastline to lowland forest markedly increased.

In Indonesia and the Philippines a similar process took place; vast areas of lowland in the South China Sea were drowned, and the length of coastline increased as islands were formed. Between about 18 000 and 5000 years ago the ancient landmass uniting western Indonesia and the mainland of south-east Asia was reduced from 1.7 to 1 million square kilometres, and the length of coastline increased by a factor of 1.8, giving a more than threefold increase in the ratio of coast to land.[2] Changes on this scale undoubtedly helped to stimulate the process of adaptive evolution in human culture that took place at the end of the Pleistocene, leading to the regional intensification of food gathering and the parallel, and almost contemporary, development of plant and animal domestication in so many parts of the world.

Eastern Manchuria, Korea and the Soviet Far East

Human occupation of Siberia and the Soviet Far East came late. The taiga, the great northern steppe forest that extended in a continuous belt westwards from the Sea of Okhotsk throughout

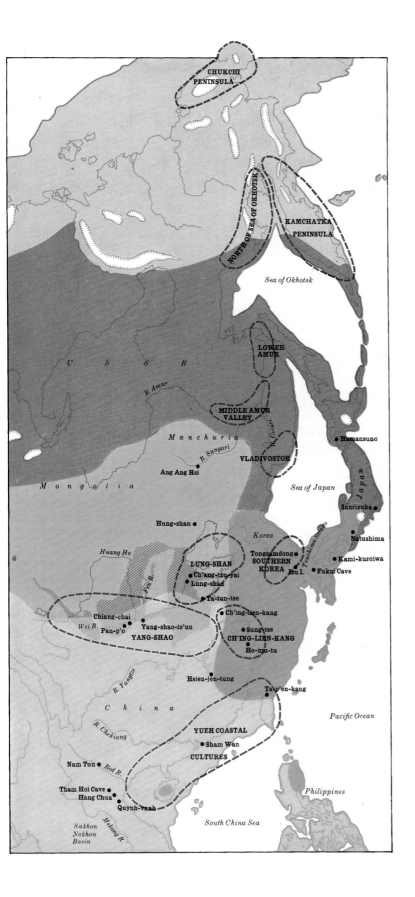

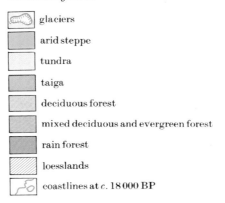

21.1, 21.2: *East Asia, showing the archaeological sites and culture areas mentioned in the text and the broad natural vegetation zones and coastlines at the end of the last glaciation. The extent of the main north–south vegetation zones has varied with climatic fluctuations over the past ten thousand years, and they have been much modified by clearance for farming during the last seven thousand years.*

- glaciers
- arid steppe
- tundra
- taiga
- deciduous forest
- mixed deciduous and evergreen forest
- rain forest
- loesslands
- coastlines at *c.* 18 000 BP

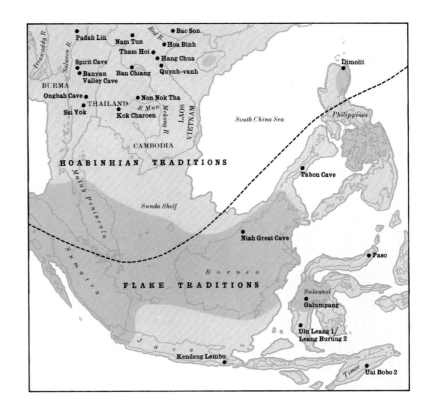

the Pleistocene, was poor in game and vegetable foods and was sparsely inhabited, if at all. Only a little before 20 000 years ago did man develop the techniques and equipment that permitted him to colonize the richer tundra further north, and the next 10 000 years saw the rapid diversification of a blade and burin tradition as empty niches were filled. The mixed forests of eastern Manchuria, Korea and the Amur river were occupied earlier, probably by groups from the south, but remains of Palaeolithic occupation are few, and it seems probable that most Palaeolithic sites were submerged by the Late Pleistocene rise in sea level. Pottery appeared in this region in the fourth millennium BC and is used by Soviet archaeologists to define the start of a 'Neolithic' phase that continued until the establishment of effective metallurgy in about the first millennium BC in the more accessible regions, though in some areas, such as north of the Sea of Okhotsk, metal tools came only with the Russian colonial expansion. The presence either of pottery or of metal does not indicate any basic change in the economy of hunting, fishing and collecting, though these technical innovations may have permitted larger populations to lead a more settled life and to exploit food sources previously unavailable or unappetizing.

The Pacific coast of Siberia continued in relative isolation from the interior through the Neolithic period, except along the Amur, and contacts, such as they were, followed a north–south direction. Seven Neolithic cultures have been recognized. On the middle Amur, by the middle of the third millennium BC, there is some evidence of farming from settlements on Lake Osinovo. Remains of millet were recovered, together with grinding stones, and the communities lived in large pit houses following a more or less sedentary life, thanks to the rich fish resources.

In the lower Amur seasonal fish runs were the basis of permanent village life – a situation similar to that on the north-west coast of America and perhaps in Jōmon Japan. This regional Neolithic culture is poorly dated but is believed to belong to the middle or even the early third millennium BC. Poor preservation of organic material limits the possibility of economic analysis, but it does appear that the specialized deep-sea fishing and seal hunting that characterized much of the far north-east in historic times only developed in the last centuries BC.[3]

The earliest pottery in Korea occurs in the Chodo phase at Tongsamdong site, near Pusan, and may be contemporary with the Early to Middle Jōmon wares of Japan. At Tongsamdong, where the long ceramic sequence demonstrates contacts with Japan across the Tsushima Straits from the earliest times, the economic emphasis was on fishing, seal hunting and shellfish collecting.

Japan

As Siberia and the Soviet Far East were devoid of human occupation, it must be assumed that the colonization of Japan took place via Korea, to which southern Japan was connected through-

21.3: *Fukui Cave, Kyushu, Japan has yielded the world's earliest dated pottery. Above: sherds with finger and nail impressions from Horizon 2, dated to about 10 000 BC. Similar pottery has been found at Kami-kuroiwa Cave and at other sites in southern Japan. Below: sherds with linear relief decoration from Horizon 3, dated to 10 500 BC. Despite its antiquity, this pottery is quite sophisticated, and Japanese archaeologists believe that the tradition has still earlier beginnings on the north Asian mainland.*

21.4: *Early Jōmon flared rim pot of Jusanbodai type from Hanatoriyama, Yamama-nashi prefecture. Late Jōmon pots are more elaborately decorated than this, with incisions and applied fillets of clay, but the Jōmon pottery tradition shows great continuity as well as much regional variation for over 8000 years.*

out the Pleistocene, for virtually all the faunal changes of mainland north-east Asia are found also in southern Japan. Occasional edge-ground tools occur in early contexts and one edge-ground axe from Sanrizuka site, east of Tokyo, is dated to about 30 000 years ago, earlier even than the edge-ground axes of northern Australia. After 20 000 years ago there is evidence for larger populations in southern Japan, and for an increasing tempo of cultural change with the development of microblades by about 15 000 years ago and pottery by 12 000 years ago.

The best evidence for this final Palaeolithic occupation comes from Fukui Cave in northern Kyushu, where in Horizon 3, dated to 12 500 years ago, pottery appears associated with the assemblage of microblades. This pottery is relatively sophisticated, decorated first with linear relief technique, later by nail stamping, and is believed to represent a distinct tradition earlier than, and different from, the cord-impressed pottery that gives its name to the succeeding Jōmon or, in Japanese terms, 'Neolithic' stage. Kamik-uroiwa rockshelter on Shikoku Island has also produced linear-relief pottery at a level dated to about 12 000 years ago.

About 11 000 years ago microblades were abandoned, and bifacial tanged arrowheads of chert and obsidian became common, together with flaked and edge-ground adzes and, occasionally, cord-impressed pottery of the Jōmon period, which is conventionally dated to between 10 000 and 2300 years ago. Rather than seeing the continuity and stability of Jōmon culture as a sign of cultural stagnation and isolation, Japanese archaeologists view the Jōmon as a remarkably successful adaptation to the temperate forests and the coasts, whose diverse marine and littoral resources enabled populations to be relatively sedentary and to develop a rich and idiosyncratic material culture in relative isolation from developments on the Asian mainland. This cultural isolation, which is undeniable, is the more unusual because it is clear from the evidence of deep-sea fishing at Natushima site on

Tokyo Bay, and the initial Jōmon occupation of Izu Island in Tsushima Strait, that Jōmon people had developed effective boats.[4]

With the stabilization of sea levels in the Holocene, many coastal settlements and shell-middens with well preserved food debris have survived, and for the first time in Japanese prehistory there is good evidence of subsistence patterns, site location, size and planning, domestic structures, and also of the physical remains of the people themselves. In addition to making sophisticated pottery, terracotta figurines, stone tools and ornaments, Jōmon people had canoes, the bow and arrow and elaborate fishing techniques, and they lived in substantial pit houses with upright posts and thatched roofs. Settlements, which were usually of three to ten dwellings, were relatively permanent, situated close to rivers, lakes or the sea. It has traditionally been held that the Jōmon societies were not food producers but hunters and collectors who acquired domesticated dogs about 7000 BC. Bone debris suggests that in addition to fish and shellfish, pigs, deer, small mammals and birds were important food sources. It is only recently that plant remains have been sought, but already rice, barley and gourd remains have been identified at Late Jōmon sites, and buckwheat and wild grains have been found in the Early Jōmon site of Hamansuno, in southern Hokkaido, dating to 7500–5000 years ago. Millet cultivation is also claimed for Late Jōmon sites in Kyushu. Thus the orthodox view that food production, in the form of wet rice cultivation, was only brought to Japan by the Yayoi culture about 300 BC is now being challenged. Nevertheless, it is probable that all Jōmon groups depended on wild foods until at least the middle of the first millennium BC, when prehistoric Japanese culture underwent a swift and dramatic transformation that marked the beginning of the Yayoi period.

North China and the Manchurian plain

Although much is known of the Middle and Late Neolithic cultures of China, the process of their formation is still obscure, for there are few sites in the north dated to the crucial period between 8000 and 5000 BC. Until about twenty years ago it was believed that agriculture in China developed in the third millennium BC as a result of the diffusion of ideas and materials from western Asia. However, hundreds of Neolithic sites are now known, many dated to the fifth millennium BC. It is clear that, from the start, their artifacts and structural arrangements had a distinctively Chinese character, and it is significant that they were based on the cultivation of millets in the north and rice in the south, in contrast to the wheat and barley of western Asia.[5] Two groups of Early Neolithic cultures have been distinguished in north China: the Yang-shao culture of the middle Huang Ho valley and its important tributaries, the Fen and the Wei: and the Ch'ing-lien-kang culture of the lower Yangtze. There are now preliminary reports of pre-Yang-shao Neolithic sites in Hopeh and Honan provinces with rocker-stamped pottery dated to the sixth and even the late seventh millennium BC.

Yang-shao

In 1921 the Swedish geologist Andersson excavated at the village of Yang-shao-ts'un in northern Honan, after seeing finds of stone knives, axes and black-and-red pottery made earlier by local villagers. It is now realized that Yang-shao-ts'un is a Late Neolithic site, not typical of the culture to which it gave its name, which developed around the junction of the Wei, Fen and Huang rivers – an area often referred to as the 'nuclear area' where Chinese civilization emerged from its prehistoric past.[6] The best-known site, because it is preserved as an example of 'primitive society' for the education of today's Chinese, is Pan-p'o, near the city of Sian. Yang-shao sites are usually situated on lower terraces of loess on tributaries of the Huang Ho. The principal field crop was millet. Hoes, spades and digging-stick weights have been found in great numbers, as well as lenticular-section polished stone axes and stone knives. Dogs and pigs were domesticated; cattle, sheep and goats, though known, were of lesser importance than in west Asian Neolithic sites. Hemp was grown, probably as a fibre plant, and

on the evidence of one carefully sliced silkworm cocoon, it is believed that silk production was already known. There is disagreement about whether Yang-shao villages were in permanent use, or whether shifting agriculture led to a cyclical pattern of abandonment and reoccupation of settlements.

Sites were large and well organized and the houses substantial. The best evidence comes from Pan-p'o and the nearby site of Chiang-chai. Pan-p'o extended over an area of about 50 000 square metres surrounded by a ditch and bank, and contained about a hundred houses in the two main phases of occupation. Houses were 3 to 5 metres in diameter, round or square in plan, and dug into the loess with timber supports for the steeply pitched thatched roofs. In the last phase a large rectangular house in the centre of the village is interpreted by Chinese archaeologists as a communal clan or club house in which to display surplus production, rather than as an indication of developing social inequalities. Pan-p'o was divided into three areas: the residential area, a cemetery at the north end and a series of pottery kilns to the east. At Chiang-chai

21.5: *Surrounding ditches and postholes of two successive Middle Jōmon pit dwellings, with fireplace (Locality 24A, International Christian University, Tokyo-to). The diameter of the outer ditch is about 6 metres. Settlements of between three and ten such houses were usually located close to lakes, rivers or the sea, and each probably housed a single family. It is thought that the roof was conical in shape and thatched with reeds. By partly sinking the houses into the earth, it was possible to build larger houses than could otherwise have been erected without substantial timbers or elaborate carpentry joints.*

21.6: *Chiang-chai, in southern Shensi, was excavated in 1972–4 and provides the best evidence yet of the layout of a Yang-shao village. As at Pan-p'o, both square and round houses were built, but here at least four large square houses face into the village centre, which was not excavated. The burial ground was to the east, and the pottery-making area lay beyond the village boundary ditch on the north-east side.*

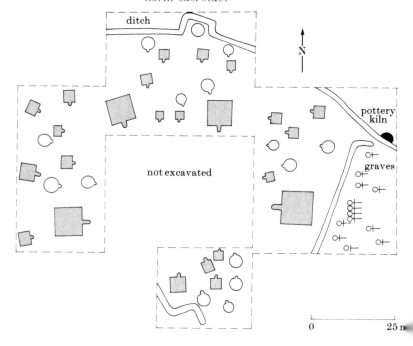

ditch

N

pottery
kiln

not excavated

graves

0   25 m

the houses were arranged in roughly concentric circles facing the centre of the village, the residential area of which was again marked by a ditch and separated from the burial ground by another ditch.

Yang-shao pottery is generally hand-made and finished on a slow wheel. A distinctive form, with a long history, is the hollow-leg tripod (*li*) used for cooking; there are also pointed-based water jars, narrow-necked bottles and a range of red burnished bowls and platters with geometric and curvilinear designs in black paint. Occasionally, stylized fish and animals are represented, and rare stylized human figures give us an idea of how the Neolithic inhabitants of north China thought of themselves. Pottery marks are common and suggest that the distinctive Chinese script that appears in the oracle bone and bronze casting inscriptions of the second millennium BC was already in the process of formation. Through the fourth millennium BC the Yang-shao culture spread to the west and south and diversified. In the third millennium it was absorbed into, and largely replaced by, the Late Neolithic Lung-shan culture.

Manchuria
In the river basins of central Manchuria several Neolithic groups have been distinguished. In the south, in Jehol province, the Hung-shan culture includes black painted and impressed grey ware vessels that suggest influences from both the later Yang-shao and the Lung-shan cultures, whereas the distinctive stone plough-shares and grinding stones are local forms. In the more arid western uplands of Manchuria and in the north, as at Ang Ang

Hsi in Heilung Kiang, both pottery and small flaked stone tools link these cultures with the pastoral peoples of Mongolia. Another Neolithic culture has been identified in the Sungari valley, where the pottery and jade beads and arm rings are paralleled at the Neolithic shell-mounds of the Amur and Ussuri rivers, between Khabarovsk and Vladivostok? The Manchurian Neolithic cultures are not well dated; most of the excavations were made many years ago, the recording was inadequate and plant and animal remains were not systematically collected. One important field crop of historic times in East Asia, the soya bean, is thought to have been first domesticated in Manchuria, reaching the north Chinese plain only about 1000 BC; however, no details are known of its role in these Neolithic cultures. As far as can be judged at present, these cultures represent an expansion northwards of north Chinese millet farming from the fourth to the third millennium BC.

The Ch'ing-lien-kang culture of the central eastern lowlands
Finds now attributed to this culture have been known for thirty years, but it is only in the past decade that some coherence has been recognized and their stratigraphic position resolved. Although the black-on-red pottery has affinities with Yang-shao, there are more differences than close similarities, and the Ch'ing-lien-kang culture represents an adaptation to the moist, marshy region of the lower Yangtze valley. It was once thought to post-date Lung-shan and to belong to a late surviving 'Lungshanoid' horizon of the first millennium BC, but radiocarbon dates from sites such as Sung-tse, Ta-tun-tse and Ho-mu-tu now show that the beginning of the Ch'ing-lien-kang culture was contemporary with

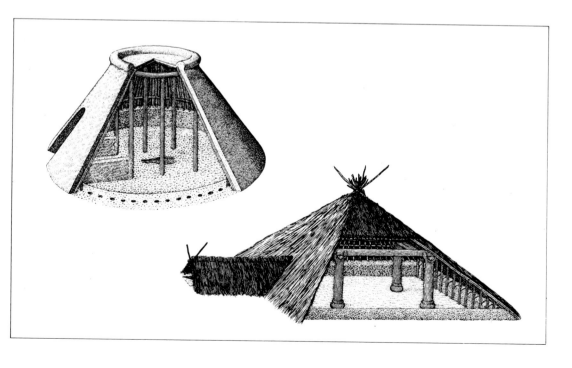

21.7: *Reconstructions of two houses at the Neolithic Yang-shao culture site of Pan-p'o, Shensi province. Round houses of this type (far left), some 3 to 5 metres in diameter, are believed to have housed a single family. They were built on low mounds of packed earth, with the floor sunk below ground level. Floors and interior walls were plastered with clay and straw, and the posts often rested on stone bases. Inside the door low plastered walls marked off a porch and there was usually a central hearth sunk into the ground. House I (near left), situated in the centre of the village and measuring about 11 by 10 metres, was the largest structure and is thought to be a communal clan house. The sloping walls and use of light poles suggest that the carpentry skills necessary for the jointed post and beam structures of later Chinese architecture had not yet been developed.*

the earliest Yang-shao of the fifth millennium BC. There were two main regional variants, to the north and south of the Yangtze. In the south rectangular houses of timber were constructed on low mounds near the banks of lakes, rivers and marshes, although apparently not right on the coast, and reed and woven matting walls and partitions were used. Single burials, oriented with the head towards the north, were placed away from the settlements. Painted pottery is rare; tripods are common forms, as are red-slipped, round-bottomed beakers, large-mouthed bowls, tall pedestal bowls and spouted tripod vessels. Ho-mu-tu is the most important Early Neolithic site to have been excavated since Pan-p'o, and shows the emergence of the characteristic Ch'ing-lien-kang culture. Waterlogged conditions favoured preservation in the lower layers and many remains of buildings and wooden artifacts were found, as were many unusual hoes made from the shoulder blades of cattle and the remains of gourds, water chestnuts, fruits and nuts. Rice stalks, grains and husks were spread over 400 square metres, in some places 25–50 centimetres thick. Perhaps a threshing floor, this is the richest find of early plant remains in China, and possibly in the world. Preliminary results indicate that both wild and domesticated rice were present, the latter said to be mainly of the *indica* variety. Bones of wild deer, turtle, rhinoceros and elephant, as well as those of domesticated dog and buffalo, suggest that the early farmers of the lower Yangtze still depended on hunting.

The origins of the Ch'ing-lien-kang culture are unknown; no Palaeolithic or Mesolithic habitation has yet been recognized in the north-east between the Huang Ho and the Chekiang river, and it must be assumed that in the early Holocene still undiscovered Mesolithic communities intensified their collection of naturally occurring wild rice in the Yangtze delta plains, bringing it into systems of cultivation that led to the genetic and morphological changes by which we can recognize the appearance of plant domestication.

Middle and Late Neolithic cultures: 'Lungshanoid' and Lung-shan

In 1928 a quite different Neolithic tradition was found at the site of Ch'ang-tzu-yai, near Lung-shan in Shantung. This was characterized by a hard, thin, lustrous black pottery, unlike the painted black-on-red Yang-shao wares; and the stone tools included many new types, some with drilled circular holes for securing hoe blades in their hafts, a technique also found on the stone tools of the Ch'ing-lien-kang culture.

For a long time Yang-shao and Lung-shan were seen as contemporary regional Neolithic traditions, but at a number of sites in northern Honan, Lung-shan levels were found overlying Yang-shao and were themselves followed by the Bronze Age Shang culture. Later still, Neolithic cultures with some Lung-shan characteristics were found in eastern and south-eastern China, and it was argued that these 'Lungshanoid' cultures marked the spread

21.8: *A bone hoe or spade* (ssu) *from Ho-mu-tu, Chekiang province* (near right). Ssu *were made from the shoulder blades of cattle, with the median ridge cut away before the blade was hafted to a wooden handle. Many of them are heavily worn and broken by use, and Chinese archaeologists believe that they were used for rice cultivation. The large numbers at Ho-mu-tu suggest that fixed field agriculture had already developed in the fifth millennium BC in the lower Yangtze valley. Far right:* A *polished stone hoe from a Chi'ing-lien-kang culture site near Nanking, Kiangsu province, dating to the late fourth or early third millennium BC. Below: A Neolithic polished stone knife with seven hafting holes, dating from the late fourth to the third millennium BC, from near Nanking, also of the Ch'ing-lien-kang culture. Stone knives were common in all the Neolithic cultures of north and central China, and in some areas were in use late enough to be copied in iron.*

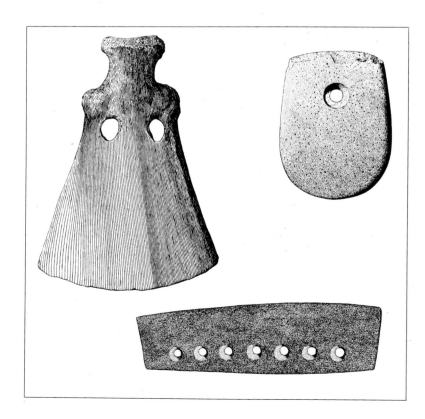

of Neolithic life down the south coast and up the major river valleys of southern China.[8] With the application of radiocarbon dating, it can be seen that the picture is more complicated than this, and in some ways reversed. Many of the cultures formerly called 'Lungshanoid' (including Ch'ing-lien-kang) were found to be older than the Lung-shan culture of Shantung, which can be dated to between 2500 and 1800 BC. Five regional Lungshanoid cultures are now recognized between roughly 3500 and 2500 BC. The third millennium BC saw the consolidation and cultural unification of the northern Lungshanoid cultures, which gave rise to the classic Lung-shan at about 2500 BC. Lung-shan settlements were larger than those of the earlier cultures. Many were defended by ramparts of beaten earth or mud brick, and some bronze or copper artifacts have been found in Late Lung-shan sites. These developments were accompanied by a transformation, in the mid-second millennium BC, of the earlier independent, seemingly peaceful and egalitarian village cultures into a warlike, territorial and ranked society that emerged in the central part of the Huang Ho valley under rulers of the Shang clan.

South China and mainland south-east Asia

At the end of the Pleistocene China south of the Yangtze shared a common prehistoric tradition with Indo-China, Thailand, Burma and west Malaysia, where the stone industries were dominated by pebble choppers, often with unifacial and unidirectional working. Stone mortars and pounders, bone spatulas and, in the later stages, cord-marked pottery and edge-ground stone tools were also common. Collectively, this tradition is known as the Hoabinhian culture, from the province in northern Vietnam where it was first recognized.[9]

With the exceptions of the slightly earlier Son Vi industry of the Red River valley and the Han-yuan assemblage of Szechwan, this is the only stone-working tradition present at this time on the south-east Asian mainland. The earliest stage of the Hoabinhian may not yet have been recognized, but sites such as Padah Lin in eastern Burma, Spirit and Ongbah Caves in western Thailand, Nam Tun, Tham Hoi and Hang Chua Caves in northern Vietnam, have been dated to between 12 000 and 8000 years ago. Hoabinhian sites are usually found in three locations – in limestone caves, in coastal and estuarine shell-middens, particularly on both sides of Malacca Straits, and on low, hilly terraces behind the coastal plains. With its emphasis on river pebbles of basic and volcanic rocks, the Hoabinhian contrasts with the contemporary small-flake industries of island south-east Asia. Only in north-east Sumatra and Luzon are Hoabinhian and flake industries found in the same territory, and these cultural interfaces have not yet been studied.

Perhaps the best-known Hoabinhian site excavated in recent years is Spirit Cave, near Mae Hong-Son in northwest Thailand. The sequence spans the period 10 500–7500 years ago and there was a cultural change about 8800 years ago, when the Hoabinhian pebble industry was enriched with ceramics, quadrangular adzes and polished slate knives – a change interpreted as the arrival of an alien farming culture.[10] The wide range of animal species in Hoabinhian sites suggests a broadly based foraging economy, and although some plant remains from the Hoabinhian levels at Spirit Cave have been tentatively identified as beans and peas, most of the plant specimens are from wild forest trees and perennials and need demonstrate no more than the harvesting of species that have remained useful and are often cultivated today.

In some areas of south-east Asia Hoabinhian occupation of mountain forests continued into the first millennium AD with little change, although rice husks at the Late Hoabinhian site of Banyan Valley Cave, in north-west Thailand, suggest that lowland farmers and some forest groups had become interdependent. By the middle of the fourth millennium BC there were certainly village settlements on the easily worked soils of the seasonally dry Sakon Nakhon basin in north-east Thailand, and over the next two millennia they expanded south into the Mun river basin and on to the margins of the wetter central plain of Thailand. Two thousand years, from about 5500 BC to 3500 BC, of which little is known beyond the continuing Hoabinhian forest culture, separate the end of the Spirit Cave sequence from the basal levels of sites such as Ban Chiang and Non Nok Tha. As in north China, it is still not possible to recognize in any detail the processes that transformed small, mobile collecting societies into sedentary farmers. The early graves at Ban Chiang, for instance, have a striking black-burnished pottery with incised designs above cord-impressed bases that, though generally south-east Asian in style, has no obvious local antecedents. It has been called 'Neolithic', but the most recent excavations at Ban Chiang make it clear that tin-bronze ornaments and weapons were present in the earliest phase of Ban Chiang, as at Non Nok Tha (see Chapter 23).

In south China also it is difficult to link the Hoabinhian cave occupation with the later Neolithic cultures, and only at Hsien-jen-tung, in north-east Kiangsi, are Hoabinhian tools (dated to the seventh millennium BC) associated with the cord-marked pottery characteristic of local Neolithic cultures. It has been suggested that the wide distribution of such pottery in south China and northern south-east Asia represents another primary Neolithic culture.[11] Although the pottery is widespread, extending even to Japan and Indonesia, it has not been established that it is everywhere contemporary and it cannot be the product of a single archaeological culture. From Sham Wan (Lamma Island, Hong Kong) and Ta-p'en-keng (northern Taiwan) there is information about two of a series of Neolithic cultures of south China, known as the Yüeh Coastal Neolithic cultures, which can be roughly dated to some time between the fifth and third millennia BC and which share a common ceramic tradition. Sites are generally positioned by or close to coasts and rivers, and shellfish gathering and fishing were clearly important. There is also evidence for bark-cloth making, and cordage was produced, presumably for nets and lines as well as for decorating pottery. However, little is known of the context of the finds: no structural evidence from settlements has been presented; no plant remains are known. In the main we have only the pottery, which is often coarse, gritty, buff-brown in colour, cord-marked below and incised on the upper part of the body with bold geometric and curvilinear designs.

In northern Vietnam cultures of the middle Holocene are better known, and continuity from the end of the Pleistocene is well demonstrated. After the Son Vi and Hoabinhian phases, two complementary Early Neolithic cultures have been identified, named Bac-son and Quynh-van after the type localities. The former is found primarily in caves north-east of the Red River delta. It was the first prehistoric material recorded from Vietnam over seventy years ago and, in many respects, is a development of Hoabinhian culture, with the addition of edge-ground tools and pottery. The Quynh-van culture is found at shell-mounds south of the delta. Cord-marked pottery first appears in these sites with edge-ground adzes and ceramic net weights. The Bac-son culture is dated, on the basis of a few radiocarbon dates, to between 8000 and 6000 BC. Hill rice agriculture and the domestication of dog and buffalo is claimed but not clearly demonstrated. A Middle Neolithic Da-but culture of 6000–4000 BC has yielded more substantial evidence for settled village life.[12]

Island south-east Asia

Apart from Japan, perhaps no part of eastern Asia was more affected by the environmental changes at the end of the Pleistocene than island south-east Asia. Sumatra, Java, Bali, Borneo and Palawan were southerly extensions of the mainland until isolated by rising seas at various times between 16 000 and 12 000 years ago. There were major changes in the proportion of lowland to mountain, and coastlines, with their rich resources, increased by more than three times in relation to the land area. Vegetational successions through these changes are known only from pollen cores taken from Sun-Moon Lake, Taiwan, from the mountains of eastern New Guinea and from Sumatra. All suggest that temperatures were about 3°–8°C lower 20 000 years ago, depressing the altitudinal forest zones. It has been argued that Late Pleistocene rainfall in the Indonesian region was lower and more seasonal in its occurrence than at present, because lower temperatures and the extensive plains on the Sunda and Sahul shelves would have weakened the effects of the rain-bearing monsoons.[13]

Despite these environmental dislocations, continuities in adaptive patterns and in material culture through the Pleistocene–Holocene boundary can be seen, and the broad contrast mentioned above between the pebble chopper traditions of the mainland and the flake traditions of island south-east Asia persist through the dissection of the Sunda Shelf. Archaeological sequences dated to the Late Pleistocene and the Holocene are known from Tabon and nearby caves on Palawan in the Philippines, Niah Great Cave in Sarawak, Borneo, Leang Burung 2 and Ulu Leang 1 Caves near Maros in south Sulawesi, and Uai Bobo 2 Cave in east Timor. At Tabon the sequence is apparently complete from before 30 000

21.9: *A Hoabinhian shell-mound at Sukujadi, near Medan on the east coast of northern Sumatra. Shellfish from the river estuaries were an important food in prehistoric, as in modern, south-east Asia, and such refuse heaps preserve much evidence of past ways of life as well as providing lime for modern industrial processes. Here an archaeological site is being dug out commercially.*

21.10: *Maros points from Ulu Leang 1 Cave, south Sulawesi, Indonesia. These points were probably arrowheads for hunting small mammals and are one of the many specialized stone tool types that were developed in or introduced to the islands of eastern Indonesia about 6000 years ago.*

down to 9000 years ago, and there is continuity in a simple industry of large unretouched flake tools made of chert from unprepared cores. At Niah, where the preceramic levels are roughly contemporary, the few illustrated artifacts are similar, but details of the sequence are obscure. In Sulawesi a dated sequence spans the periods 30 000–16 000 years ago at Leang Burung 2, and 8000–1500 BC at Ulu Leang 1, where backed blades, geometric microliths and hollow-based points are added, from about 4000 BC, to a little-changing tool-kit of scrapers, bone points and knives with silica gloss on the cutting edges. Pottery first appears in this sequence about 2500 BC, and while plant remains at Ulu Leang are mostly of wild grasses, sedges, herbs, shrubs and fruit trees, some rice grains were recovered from the middle and late levels.

In Timor, Uai Bobo 2 Cave has a sequence from 14 000–2000 years ago, which again shows continuity, through the Pleistocene–Holocene boundary, of an idiosyncratic flake industry. However, in Timor, more isolated than Sulawesi, food production does appear to have been introduced about 2500 BC and is recognized by the sudden appearance of fine, hard, red-burnished pottery and domesticated and exotic wild animals, such as pig, monkey, civet cat and cuscus; the more frequent use of sites perhaps reflects consequent demographic changes. This small-flake tool tradition of the early to middle Holocene has also been recorded at the Paso shell-midden in north Sulawesi, at Leang Tuwo-Mane'e in the Talaud Islands, at many sites in Sumatra, Java, the Philippines and in the eastern islands of Indonesia.

Earlier interpretations of the development of food-producing societies in island south-east Asia were invariably made in terms of migration and diffusion from centres of cultural innovation and growth on the mainland to the north.[14] A common postulate was that Austronesian speakers, with quadrangular-sectioned adzes, developed pottery, boats and timber-framed houses, brought suites of already domesticated plants and animals into the southern

and eastern islands of Indonesia, where small populations of hunters and gatherers had been isolated since the Late Pleistocene. Other groups with lenticular-sectioned axes were thought to have entered the islands from the Philippines, Taiwan and Japan. Such theories were formulated by European and American scholars working within the various schools of diffusionism prevalent in academic archaeology in the first half of the twentieth century. Today the fashion favours internal, systemic explanations of cultural change rather than those that posit multiple episodes of population and cultural replacement. Nevertheless, it is difficult satisfactorily to refute diffusionist models with our present limited knowledge of island south-east Asian prehistory. Neolithic sites – that is to say, open-air sites with abundant pottery, ground stone tools, perhaps some domesticated animal bones, and evidence of relatively stable occupation and the cultivation of domesticated plants – have barely been investigated, and some researchers doubt whether true Neolithic cultures comparable with those of China existed in the region. Village sites believed to be Neolithic include Kendeng Lembu in east Java, Galumpang in west-central Sulawesi[15] and Dimolit in north-east Luzon, but only at the last have plans of structures been recognized and acceptable excavation and recording methods used. Elsewhere there are surface collections and burials with pottery, stone tools and little or no metal that have a 'Neolithic' aspect but are for the most part undated.

Regional patterns

In East Asia, as in other parts of the world, rapid climatic and environmental changes at the end of the Pleistocene provoked adaptive responses among the many cultures of the region. Generally these led to the intensified exploitation of limited territories and a concentration on fewer food sources, which were encouraged to yield more than they did in natural conditions by clearing, the firing of woodlands and the suppression of competitors. This required a more sedentary life, which was accompanied by demographic expansion and accelerated technological change as previously unoccupied habitats were filled and intercourse between different cultural groups became more sustained. In both the subarctic and the equatorial zones only the rich resources of the sea permitted a substantially increased rate of exploitation. Elsewhere certain food plants, especially annual grasses such as the millets and rice, and roots and tubers able to survive seasonal deficiencies of water through the development of underground storage, provided dependable and high-yielding food sources. In at least three areas of East Asia, the inland loess plains of northern China, the lower Yangtze valley and the deciduous forest zone of northern south-east Asia, this process of intensified and selective collecting led to the domestication of key food plants increasingly dependent on cultivation by man, and ultimately to the appearance of sedentary farming communities whose way of life necessarily involved expansion and colonization to bring wider areas into the new economic system.

22. Early agriculture and the development of towns in India

Present evidence suggests that the earliest agriculture in India spread from west to east. Wheat and barley were introduced into north-west India, where the Indus civilization had already emerged by the time that farming spread to inner India. Behind this simple picture, however, lie the varied cultures and the great diversity of food crops that contributed to the intricate pattern of Indian agriculture.

Some indication of how complex this pattern was is given by recent finds from various parts of India.[1] Pollen profiles from lake beds in Rajasthan show pollen grains of cereal type, together with quantities of charcoal, dated to the seventh millennium BC, though there is no archaeological evidence here of cultivation at this date. At Bagor in Rajasthan, however, as well as at Adamgargh in Madhya Pradesh, domesticated sheep or goats and cattle have been claimed before 5000 BC. Remains of rice, including both wild and domesticated forms, are said to have occurred at Koldihawa in the Belan valley in Uttar Pradesh in the fifth or sixth millennium BC, and similar finds have been claimed for the third millennium at Chirand in Bihar. In Assam the presence of handmade, cord-marked pottery at a number of sites indicates contacts with the early food-producing zone of south-east Asia. Millet appeared in south India from the mid-third millennium onwards in the form of *Eleusine coracana* – supposedly developed from *Eleusine africana*. As there is no positive evidence of links with Africa, where the latter species is native, it is possible that it was domesticated independently in southern India.

The background to the Indus civilization

The earliest settled villages in India are represented by the aceramic levels at Mehrgarh in the Sibi plain, Kile Gul Mohammad in the Quetta valley, Anjira in the Kalat plateau, Rana Ghundai in the Zhob–Loralai area and Gumla in the Gomal valley.[2] All of these lie along the eastern margin of the Baluchistan arc. To what extent this fact can be related to the emerging picture of a continuous Stone Age sequence in the area, particularly in Sind, is not yet clear. The southern part of Soviet Central Asia, eastern Iran, Afghanistan, Baluchistan and the Indus valley constitute, on the historical and ethnographic evidence, a single political and economic interaction zone; the growth of agriculture in Baluchistan and the Indus region should thus be seen as a part of the beginnings of agriculture in this wider region. Radiocarbon dates from the relevant levels of Rana Ghundai and Kile Gul Mohammad suggest a spread during the sixth and fifth millennia BC, but at Mehrgarh, in the cliff section of the Bolan that flows past the mound, there is a 9-metre section of unexcavated aceramic deposit

that, when dated, may indicate a much earlier spread.

Baluchistan developed its regional ceramic styles, such as Quetta, Nal, Togau, Kulli and others, on this basis, but the interest soon shifted eastwards to the Indus region as a whole. Here the major excavated sites and relevant levels are Saraikhola I and II in the Potwar plateau, Gumla II and III and Rehman Dheri in the Gomal valley, Lewan in the Bannu plain, Jalilpur I and II in west Punjab or the upper Indus valley, Kot Diji I and Amri I in Sind or the lower Indus valley, Bala Kot I in the Las Bela plain west of Karachi, Kalibangan I in the dried-up Ghaggar valley in Rajasthan and related sites further east in Haryana. The earliest dates from the upper level of Bala Kot I, Amri I, Kot Diji I and Kalibangan I range from 4000 to 3000 BC and indicate that the eastern extension is later. However, the recent report of a still undefined earlier Jalipur-related complex called the Hakra complex in the Bahawalpur region raises doubt on this issue too. This all suggests a long history of agricultural growth in the Indus and the peripheral regions to the west and the east, much of which awaits further research. The data indicate the following basic achievements: the establishment of a plough-based agricultural

system (plough marks have been uncovered at Kalibangan I), along with extensive craft specialization (including metallurgy) and the knowledge of planned nucleated settlements within walls (as at Kalibangan I and Kot Diji I, and at Rehman Dheri where a regular grid plan has been reported); inter-site exchange, which is reflected in the distribution of pottery types and the discovery of sites such as Lewan, which was apparently devoted to the manufacture of various stone objects for trade; long-distance trade (suggested by the occurrence of turquoise from north-east Iran, lapis lazuli from north-east Afghanistan and terracotta female figurines typical of the craft of contemporary south Turkmenia); and the evolution of ceramic forms like dishes-on-stands, terracotta 'cakes', fish and *pipal* leaf designs, which suggest a continuity in artifact types and perhaps religious belief between this stage and the succeeding Indus civilization.

There is no doubt that this level (designated variously as 'pre-Harappan', 'early Harappan' and even 'early Indus') formed the technological, economic and perhaps, to some extent, ideological base of the Indus civilization.[3] But the form of this civilization, as reflected in its grid-planned cities, the copper-bronze metal-lurgy, its monumental architecture and sculptural idiom, its wide trade network and, above all, the art of writing, cannot be satisfactorily explained by this base. If the present impression is correct, the Indus civilization developed its form with considerable rapidity. As there is no reason to attribute its growth and development to diffusion from Mesopotamia or elsewhere, it must be assumed that the Indus civilization evolved from the social organization and context of pre-Harappan society.

The Indus civilization

Since its identification at Harappa in 1921 and the beginning of excavations both here and at Mohenjo-Daro more than 250 settlements of this civilization have been listed between Sutkagen-dor on the western edge of the Pakistani Makran coast and Alam-girpur, near Delhi, in western Uttar Pradesh, on the one hand, and between Manda in Jammu and Bhagatrav/Malvan in the Kim estuary in Gujarat on the other. The size of the settlements varies from about 850 000 square metres at Mohenjo-Daro and Harappa, both of which had populations of 30 000–40 000 people, to about 47 500 square metres at Lothal, with a population of perhaps 2000–2500. Some settlements are smaller. But even modest settlements such as Lothal and Ahladino possessed considerable artifactual wealth, and they bear witness to rigorous planning and literacy. The distinction between urban and rural settlements is not easy to discern in the Indus context and definition will depend on a much larger sampling of sites.[4] It is equally difficult to draw a line between 'mature' and 'late' settlements, mainly because of the lack of detailed comparative stratigraphical studies, but a good number of sites in east Punjab, Rajasthan, Haryana, western Uttar Pradesh and Gujarat are considered 'late', primarily as a result of ceramic considerations. Inter-site variations in planning and other details are detectable, but there is always considerable uniformity.

The planning of the Indus settlements[5] may be made clear with reference to the two mounds of Mohenjo-Daro, where the lowest deposit (14.8 metres) lies unexcavated because of the subsoil water, with which other major excavated sites may be compared. In the western mound at Mohenjo-Daro buildings were constructed inside a fortified enclosure, above a mud and mud-brick platform, with civic complexes like the 'granary', the 'great bath', the 'pillared hall' and two massively built structures arbitrarily called 'residence for priests' and 'collegiate building'. The eastern mound

22.1: *Bust in steatite of a priest king recovered from Mohenjo Daro, on of the few stone sculptures to have been found.*

22.2: *A group of Indus seals depicting, as do many of the thousands of seals that have been found, animals of a variety of species.*

perhaps also lay within an enclosing wall and was divided into a number of house-blocks by principal streets about 10 or 11 metres wide. The houses, sometimes with an upper storey, were mostly of burnt brick at Mohenjo-Daro, and were equipped with arrangements for soakage linked to the drains in the streets. The houses inside the fortified western mound at Harappa were destroyed by brick robbers, but in the northern shadow of the citadel were found, among other things, a granary, working men's quarters and circular, brick-lined platforms with hollows for pounding grains. The eastern mound at Harappa, which was also destroyed by the brick robbers, could not be excavated, but south of the habitation area is a burial ground.

At Kalibangan the western mound had two separate but interconnected sections – one presumably for the residence of the elite and the other for a number of high platforms that provide evidence of ritualistic fire pits. There is a burial ground to the west of the site, and to the east there is evidence of an apparently separate ritual structure. The layout of the eastern mound at Kalibangan resembles that of the eastern mound at Mohenjo-Daro, with the difference that the houses here are of mud brick and there is no noteworthy household or civic drainage system. Surkotada reflects the planning of the western mound at Kalibangan; it does not have an eastern mound. The entire settlement at Lothal is within one enclosing wall. Its eastern sector is dominated by a 'dockyard', an identification that, even if accurate, is not based on convincing archaeological arguments. The Lothal cemetery lies to the west of the site.

It is not necessary to postulate a climatic change to account for the growth of the Indus civilization in the modern Indus valley and its adjacent areas, which receive a limited amount of rainfall. The ancient appearance of the lower Indus valley, or Sind, is supposed to have resembled the valley before the advent of modern irrigation canals – jungle cover along the river banks and the alluvial flood plain, interspersed with subsidiary river channels and occasional waste patches. To the east, in Bahawalpur, Rajasthan, east Punjab and Haryana, the Ghaggar–Hakra combine constituted an almost parallel system with its own network of tributaries. In the Kutch and Kathiawar peninsulas of Gujarat the basic drainage is radial, emanating from a central knot of hills. The settlements followed the alignment of the riverine alluvium. In mainland Gujarat the Indus people showed a similar preference for the coastal alluvial stretch. The upper Indus valley, or west Punjab, was virtually an arid waste before the implementation of the modern irrigation system, but then only two or three Indus sites (the most important of which is Harappa, on a dried-up bed of the Ravi) have been reported in this region.

There is no evidence of a systematic irrigation system, nor is such irrigation necessary, given the seasonal cycle of river floods. Nine crops have so far been identified: rice (*Oryza* sp., but only at eastern sites such as Lothal and Kalibangan), two varieties of barley (*Hordeum vulgare*, var. *nudum*, *Hordeum vulgare*, var. *hexastichum*), three varieties of wheat (*Triticum sphaerococcum*,

Triticum vulgare, *Triticum compactum*), sesame, cotton, date palm, water melon, pea and a variety of brassica called *juncea*. The domesticated animals included both humped and hump-less cattle, pig and buffalo; elephant and horse are also known. Terracotta models of carts and boats indicate that these were the methods of transport used. The stone technology included the mass production of parallel-sided blades, the art of bead-making and the manufacture of rectangular seals in steatite. Only a small percentage of pottery was painted, with geometric, floral or rare naturalistic designs, generally in black on rich red slip. The copper-bronze objects show developed metallurgical techniques such as closed casting and the lost-wax process, but the types remain simple; an Indus spearhead without a strengthening mid rib is likely to buckle at the first impact.[6] The standardization of measurements and weights is noteworthy because of its similarity to later Indian systems. Both foot (33.5 centimetres) and cubit (approximately 52 centimetres) seem to be known. The cubical chert weights follow the binary system in the lower level and the decimal in the upper. For surveying there was a device made of shell, found both at Lothal and Mohenjo-Daro. Both circular and true saws and fine tubular drills have been reported. Specific art objects are few, the most famous of them being a priest's head and a bronze 'dancing girl' from Mohenjo-Daro and two stone male torsos, one presumably that of a dancer, from Harappa. The similarity between the style of these objects and the historic

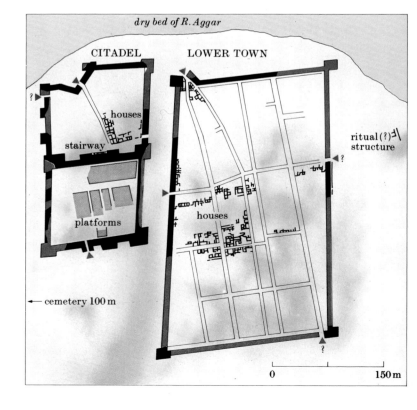

Indian sculptural idiom is unmistakable. Many elements of religion, such as the representation of a *yogi* figure on a Mohenjo-Daro seal, phallic stones, the profusion of terracotta mother-goddess figurines, and the evidence of rituals in fire-pits, can be matched in modern Hinduism. Approximately 400 signs of the Indus script are known. The inscriptions are invariably short and the general direction of writing is from right to left; the system is generally considered syllabic. Claims notwithstanding, the script has not yet been deciphered, and attempts to identify it as proto-Dravidian have as much validity as attempts to identify it as an early form of Sanskrit.

The evidence of Indus long-distance trade, in the form of seals, two types of beads (etched carnelian and long, barrel-cylinder carnelian) and a few other miscellaneous items, is found in varying proportions in the Persian Gulf, Mesopotamia (both north and south), Iran (both north and south), Soviet south Turkmenia and Afghanistan (in the north, where an Indus settlement at Shortu-ghai was perhaps a response to the lapis lazuli and tin trade). Two noteworthy items that reached the Indus people are a Persian Gulf seal from Lothal (a surface find) and a cylinder seal with an Indus motif from the Indus level at Kalibangan. Chronologically this trade goes back to the mid-third millennium BC, the Early Dynastic III period (see Chapter 17), as evidenced by the discovery of etched carnelian and long, barrel-cylinder carnelian beads in the Royal Graves at Ur, but its main spread belongs to the late third and the second millennia BC, between the Sargonid and Isin–Larsa periods in Mesopotamia. The routes followed were both maritime and overland, as the distribution of sites and finds clearly indicates. It is not clear what items were exchanged, but turquoise, lapis lazuli, jade and tin were surely flowing into the

22.3: *Plan of the Harappan metropolis at Kalibangan (Period II), built of mud brick. The change in background colour gives an indication of the rising land level on which the settlement was sited.*

22.4: *Map of the Indian subcontinent, showing the regional topography and major sites mentioned in the text.*

Indus valley. Whether the term 'Meluhha' in Mesopotamian literature meant the Indus valley alone is a debatable point, but presumably the term embraced the Indus valley. Specific data on the internal trade are limited, but there is no doubt that the civilization was successfully exploiting the internal sources of raw materials. Very little can be inferred about the social organization of the Indus civilization, except that its rigorous planning and uniformity suggest a state mechanism that, if the dominant impression of conservatism is correct, possessed a strong theocratic element. The burials (mostly flexed, although there are also some urn burials) do not reveal any significant class differentiation. Calibrated radiocarbon dates for the Indus civilization fall within the third millennium BC, although in the peripheral areas to the east the civilization may have survived longer. Its end is still uncertain, but there is no reason to attribute it to the Aryan invasions.[7] On the other hand, the hypotheses that a permeable dam was tectonically thrown up downstream of Mohenjo-Daro, resulting in a rising deposit of silt that gradually engulfed the city, or that the Indus civilization ended because of the over-exploitation of the landscape would need the support of more positive data if either were to be generally accepted. (Incidentally, no theory has yet been offered to account for the end of the Indus civilization as a whole over its entire distribution area.)

Cultures outside the Indus orbit

Within its distribution area the end of the Indus civilization brought cultural fragmentation, amply evidenced from such regional phenomena as the Jhukar culture in Sind, Cemetery H occupation in west Punjab and Bahawalpur, Ochre Coloured Pottery and other ceramic varieties in Rajasthan, east Punjab, Haryana and western Uttar Pradesh, and Lustrous Red Ware and associated ceramics in Gujarat. The link between these and the Indus civilization is not fully understood, but there is no reason to postulate a time break.

In the rest of the country a number of well-developed farming cultures are known.[8] In Kashmir in the north the excavated site of Burzahom, with its pit dwellings, hand-made mat-impressed pottery, stone 'harvesters' of Chinese affinity along with more usual bone and polished stone tools and burials, including those of dog, wolf and ibex, suggests a northern Neolithic, which at Burzahom itself emerged between about 3000 and 1600 BC. In Swat and adjacent areas in the north-west a grave complex of central Asian affinity, called the Gandhara Grave Culture, appeared about the middle of the second millennium BC.

The area between south-east Rajasthan and Maharashtra has three Chalcolithic groupings: the Ahar culture of south-east Rajasthan, identified at Ahar and dating from about 2400 BC; the sequence of Kayatha (2400–2100 BC), Ahar and Malwa (2000–1600 BC) cultures discovered at Kayatha in Malwa; and the sequence of suggested 'late Harappan', Ahar, Malwa and Jorwe (from about 1600 BC) cultures discovered at Daimabad in Maharashtra. Differentiated partly by stratigraphy and partly by

regional variations in pottery and a few other details, the three basic components of this zone (south-east Rajasthan, Malwa and Maharashtra) had much in common and emphasize picture of settled farming communities going back to well bef 2000 BC. The technology included a stone-blade industry an generally limited use of copper, although the Ahar culture ma se of the Rajasthan ores. The settlements were quite large r itself measured 450 by 250 metres, and Navdatoli (of the   culture on the river Narmada) was roughly 200 metres e. The houses, rectangular in south-east Rajasthan and rec lar and/ or circular in Malwa and Maharashtra, used loc vailable materials. The crops (with regional variations) in wheat, barley and rice, apart from a wide variety of legumes x (from Nevasa of the Jorwe culture). Cattle, sheep and g ccur at every site. The Jorwe culture has urn burials below e floors, and at Inamgaon of the same culture there is an nkment (240 metres long and 2.25 metres wide and high) igation. A stylized terracotta mother-goddess figurine fou ociated with a bull suggests a ritualistic continuity with the   , just as house types, the use of animals and crop patterns   strate a link between Chalcolithic and modern villages in th

A long developmental sequence of the Neolithic ring the third and second millennia BC, during which perio tal-free assemblage of ground-stone industry, a rudimenta ke-blade tradition and a predominantly hand-made ware is su d by an increasing use of metal, blade tools and painted pot as been isolated in the Karnatak plateau, south of Mahar and its periphery at the excavated sites of Brahmagiri, Pi , Utnur, Hallur and others. Information on crops is meagre hey are known to have included millet (*Eleusine coracana*) a legume known as horse gram (*Dolichos biflorus*). The ar remains indicate the presence of cattle, sheep, goat and horse Hallur). In the first phase the people were pastoralists rather farmers.

Except for sporadic surface finds there is very litt umenta- tion further south, and the same may be said of the   section of Andhra, although here both Neolithic and Chalc sites are known to have existed. Orissa in the east does not h y dated Neolithic site. In west Bengal there are Chalcolithic   lages at sites such as Pandu Rajar Dhibi and Mahishdal, w haps an earlier metal-free horizon. The west Bengal Chalcol es back to about 1600 BC and is linked to the corresponding ments in Bihar (or the middle Gangetic valley), of which Ch perhaps going back to the third millennium BC) shows w nd rice. West Bengal sites show only rice. Evidence of the   opper is limited, which is surprising in view of the genera imity of these sites to Bihar ores. In the extreme east As s so far revealed nothing specific except a wide variet undated polished stone axes.

In the upper Gangetic valley the prehistoric cultu uation is not fully understood. The post-Indus Chalcolithic is a suc- cession of Ochre Coloured Pottery and a black d ware, succeeded by the Painted Grey Ware that is assoc with the use of iron. This composite stratigraphy is worked out at sites like Hastinapur, Atranjikhera and Noh, but apparently there is an earlier, pre-iron Painted Grey Ware that forms a direct sequel to that of the late Harappans at some sites in Haryana and east Punjab. The earliest date of the Ochre Coloured Pottery of the early third millennium BC is from a Rajasthan site, Jodhpura, whereas at Atranjikhera, in the upper Gangetic valley, thermoluminescent dates place the pottery in the first half of the second millennium BC. At Saipai a harpoon that is a diagnostic type of the upper Gangetic valley 'copper hoards' (hitherto found unstratified) is said to have been found in association with the Ochre Coloured Pottery, thus apparently resolving an old controversy regarding the stratigraphic position of these copper hoards.

The beginning of iron

The earliest radiocarbon dates for iron in India are from Eran IIA in Madhya Pradesh at the end of the second millennium BC and from Hallur in Karnataka at the very beginning of the first millennium BC. Eran IIA is a continuation of the earlier Malwa Chalcolithic level at the site, with the addition of iron, and the relevant level at Hallur marks the transitional phase between the Neolithic and the iron-using Megalithic phases. From this period onwards Megalithic monuments of different kinds continued to occur all over the southern peninsula, continuing well into the historic period. The other dated early iron horizons are the Painted Grey Ware level of the upper Gangetic valley, generally dated to about 800–400 BC; the post-Chalcolithic levels of sites like Mahishdal and Chirand in eastern India, dated to about 750 BC; the post-Chalcolithic level of the site of Pirak in the Kachhi plain adjoining Sind, dated to about 800 BC; and the Gandhara Grave Culture in Swat, which shows just one fragment of iron, of perhaps about 1000 BC. It seems that by about 1000 BC the use of iron was well established in India, at least in Madhya Pradesh in the centre of the subcontinent and in the Karnataka plateau in the south.[9] Iron gradually became more widely used, and all over India the Iron Age was to merge into the early historic period.

22.5: *Reconstruction of the settlement of Ahar in south-east Rajasthan, centre of the Ahar culture dating from about 2400 BC. The rectangular houses of this substantial settlement were built of locally available materials.*

23. East Asia in the Bronze Age

The results of recent intensive research in China and south-east Asia, coupled with the impact of absolute dating methods,[1] have led to radical and still controversial reinterpretations of the region's prehistory. These entail the discarding of diffusionist and monogenetic models to explain the rise of advanced technology and civilization, and their replacement by models emphasizing local development and evolution. Nevertheless, the evidence remains unevenly distributed, and the picture is a complicated one. As well as contrasts between complex and simpler societies, there are also important technological differences among the latter, notably in metallurgy.

The rise of civilization in north China

Until relatively recently the sudden appearance of urbanism, writing and bronzeworking on the central plain of the Huang Ho was commonly ascribed to diffusion from western Asia. However, research over the past twenty years[2] has refuted this view and provided archaeological evidence for the roots of Chinese civilization in the Honan variant of the Lung-shan culture (see Chapter 21). Technological advances and an increase in craft specialization and social stratification (indicated chiefly by burials), as well as signs of inter-village warfare, show a move away from the earlier, relatively egalitarian and peaceful conditions towards the stratified society and endemic warfare of the Shang. A wide variety of pottery forms were made, many of them with the aid of the fast wheel; *li* (hollow-legged), *kui* (handled) and, less commonly, *ting* (solid-legged) tripods presaged the appearance of these forms in bronze during the Shang.

The Shang civilization itself arose in a relatively small area of western Honan province. At Erh-li-t'ou and Cheng-chou excavations have documented the transition from the Lung-shan to the earliest stage of the Shang. Erh-li-t'ou has yielded evidence of bronze metallurgy, a highly stratified society, craft specialization and the presence of large structures with pounded earth (*hang-t'u*) foundations. Radiocarbon dates indicate that this phase of Shang civilization began about 1850 BC. The middle Shang period, or Erh-li-kang phase, is represented not only at Cheng-chou and Lo-yang, but also at a number of other sites on both sides of the Huang Ho. During this period (1650–1400 BC) the Shang state expanded rapidly, and Shang civilization spread well beyond the

limits of the state's political control. Middle Sha[ng] although more dispersed than Near Eastern or cities, can truly be called urban.[3] The casting of el[aborate] ritual vessels, which had begun in the early perio[d] more common and bronze technology more advance[d]

The shifting of the capital to An-yang in about [the] beginning of the late Shang or Yin period, durin[g] civilization reached its highest point. The Shang c[ity] some 24 square kilometres, with a clearly defin[ed] centre inhabited by the royal household, worksho[ps] in bronze, bone and pottery industries, and the spe[cial] tombs at Hsi-pei-kang, where the Shang kings we[re] accompanied by sacrificed retainers, slaves and chariots. The casting of many kinds of ritual ves[sels] bronze artifacts reached a pinnacle of artistic and skill rarely if ever surpassed in the ancient world. Chinese ideographic script also makes its first a[ppearance] quantity at this time on bones used for scapuloman[cy] using 'oracle bones'), as well as occasional inscripti[ons] and pottery. The Shang capital continued to flou[rish] conquest by the Chou peoples to the west in about 11[00 BC]

The nature of Shang civilization

The roots of Shang civilization were thus firmly fixe[d in the pre-] ceding cultures of the north Chinese Central Plain;

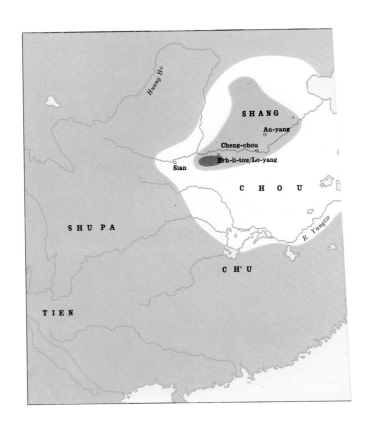

23.1: *Map of Shang China, showing the area of Shang origins and its later extent and the area of the Chou civilization, as well as the locations of the other early states and sites.*

Shang period represents the achievement of a level of organization and sophistication in society, religion and technology that is fully comparable with the Bronze Age civilizations of western Asia and Europe. Moreover, the Shang was a purely indigenous Chinese phenomenon; with the exception of the horse-drawn chariot, there is no evidence for any significant influence from the West. Like most Old and New World civilizations, the Shang state was organized along the lines of a theocracy, with power flowing from a divine king down through the nobles and court retainers to the common people. In Shang society social classes were clearly defined and ranked, but although society and government were highly stratified, textual evidence suggests that some degree of upward mobility was possible for the exceptional commoner.

The Shang economic pattern represents an intensification of earlier Lung-shan farming. Millet remained the staple grain crop, now supplemented by rice, barley and wheat; the last two were apparently introduced from the West during early or middle Shang times.[4] Two crops of millet and rice a year were grown, which would seem to imply the presence of irrigation and/or fertilizer; however, no evidence exists for the extensive use of these techniques until well after the Shang period. Fishing continued to supplement the diet of the masses, but hunting had become the preserve of the nobility and contributed only a negligible amount of the everyday diet.

The pinnacle of Shang technology is without a doubt its bronze-working. During the first half of this century many Western scholars attempted to show that this technology was derived from western Asia and Europe; however, the absence of such Western techniques as hammering, annealing and lost-wax casting, and the presence of the highly complex piece-mould method of casting, destroy these diffusionist arguments and clearly indicate an indigenous origin for Shang metallurgy.[5] Moreover, the centrifugal spread of bronze from the Central Plain outwards in post-Shang times also indicates an indigenous development, although the relatively late date of its appearance in north China *vis-à-vis* its fourth-millennium manifestation in mainland south-east Asia is puzzling; when south China has been surveyed as intensively as the north, an answer may be forthcoming. The roots of Shang bronze-working lie in the advanced ceramic technology of the late Lung-shan and early Shang periods; by this date pottery kilns were able to attain temperatures high enough to smelt tin and copper ore and to melt the resultant metals for casting. Adequate supplies of copper and tin ores were available within some 300 kilometres of An-yang, and it appears that these were exploited rather than the much more extensive deposits to the south. In contrast to the lost-wax method, Shang bronzeworking used a model or a core of clay with the segmented pieces of the fresh clay mould applied around it. After firing, the pieces of the mould were removed and the clay model was scraped or broken away from the remaining core to a depth corresponding to the thickness of bronze required. The baked clay mould segments were then reassembled around the core and the molten bronze poured in. This method had the great

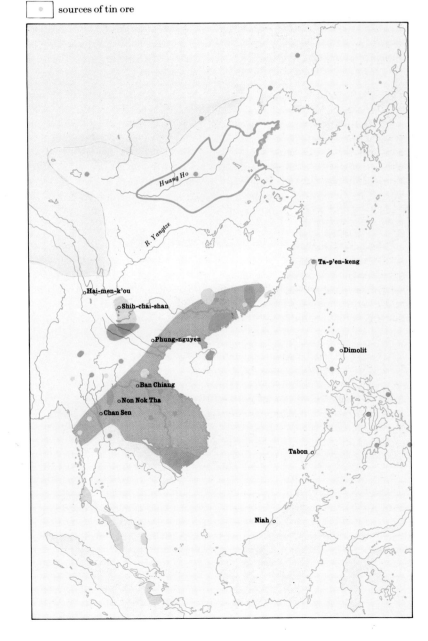

23.2: *East Asia, showing the area of the Lung-shan cultures, and the sources from which copper and tin ore required by the bronze-using cultures were obtained.*

◯ area of Lung-shan cultures

▨ probable extent of bronze-using cultures of 4th and 3rd millennia BC

▨ probable extent of bronze-using cultures of 2nd millennium BC

• sources of copper ore

• sources of tin ore

advantage over lost-wax techniques of enabling a number of artifacts to be cast from a single mould; and it made possible the manufacture of vessels of great complexity.

The Chou period

About 1100 BC the Shang state was conquered by a people living to the west, in the vicinity of Sian; little is known about the nature of Choud society before the conquest, but it is likely that it had a social organization, economy and technology similar to those of the state it conquered. The major social innovation of the Chou period was a shift from patrimony towards 'feudalism', though the Chou system lacked the complex legal and contractual machinery of Western feudalism.[6] In 771 BC the Chou state lost its western capital to 'barbarians' and shifted to Lo-yang, beginning the Ch'un-ch'iu, or 'Spring and Autumn' period (often referred to as the Eastern Chou). During this period urbanism spread far beyond its original Shang boundaries, and in central as well as north China city-states sprang up that were at least nominally under Chou authority; in effect, these were more or less sovereign entities 'federated' by ritual loyalty to the imperial Chou court. By 500 BC the larger city-states were in the process of absorbing many of the smaller ones, and 480 BC marked the end of the Ch'un-ch'iu period and the beginning of the Chan-kuo or 'Warring States' period. The pattern of inter-state warfare continued until the end of the Eastern Chou period, with the unification of much of what is now modern China under the Ch'in 'First Universal Ruler', Shih Huang Ti, in 221 BC.

Technologically speaking, the two centuries 600–400 BC saw two major advances. The first was the appearance of iron tools and a complex iron-casting technology clearly based on indigenous bronze-casting techniques. By 500 BC iron agricultural tools were in relatively common use, and this may have had its consequences in the second major development: the elaboration and intensification of irrigation systems for the cultivation of wet rice and other staple crops that enabled China's population to continue to expand (see Chapter 37).

Late Neolithic and bronze-using cultures of south China

In connection with what is now central and southern China (from the Yangtze valley southwards) there are two problems. Although this region is well over twice as large as north China, it has seen markedly less archaeological research; and many archaeologists have tended to view south China as an appendage of the north, advancing largely, if not wholly, through influences from the Central Plain region. While it is undoubtedly true that various cultural and technological traits did spread southwards from Shang times onwards, evidence is accumulating that indicates that the cultures of south China – like those of mainland south-east Asia – were innovative and advanced in their own right, and the metal-using civilizations that developed there during the first millennium BC owed at least as much to local creativity as to north Chinese influence.

At some time during the first millennium BC – o[r] earlier – pottery with distinctive stamped geometri[c] its appearance over most of the Yüeh area of coast[al] (the so-called Geometric horizon, once thought Shang and Chou influence). However, some evide[nce] gests that it may have been an independent dev[elopment] dating the middle Shang.[7] The occasional finds Geometric contexts may also indicate an earlier d[eve] lurgy in the area than was previously thought likel[y] even its independent invention there; certainly, the[y] were present and more abundant than they were i[n] (see Figure 23.2).

On the other hand, some tentative evidence for a[n] development is also available from the Yüeh-related adjacent regions of Vietnam. Chief among these i[s the] nguyen culture, represented by several sites on th[e] plains, west of Hanoi. This culture features sophisti[cated] with a wide variety of incised designs, many of which related to designs on the later Dong-son bronzes. The in its earliest levels, dated to the mid-third millenniu[m] the middle of the second millennium BC bronze artifa[cts] ploughshares, socketed axes, weapons and orname[nts] tively common. Connections with the early metal mainland south-east Asia (see below) are probabl[e] early metal also occurs in south-western China, wh[ere] mid-second millennium date, called Hai-men-k'ou, [has] artifacts of hammered copper. The distance from Plain, the foreign nature of the hammering techniqu[e] of copper rather than bronze all tend to make a Shan[g] unlikely; although the hammering technique and the alloyed copper is equally foreign to south-east Asi[a] limited evidence tentatively suggests that some of th[e] south China had made the move into the 'Bronze A[ge] significant influence from Shang and Chou civilization

By the middle of the first millennium BC a num[ber of] developed states had appeared in the areas to the s[outh of] Chou. Chief among these was the state of Ch'u, cen[tred in the] middle Yangtze valley. Although it had close ties wi[th] immediately to the north, many features of Ch'u cu[lture set it] apart as a distinctive entity. To the west, in Szechuan, Shu and Pa were well established by the beginning of th[is] period, with distinctive artifact types and design m[otifs and a] peculiar pictographic script. Finally, Shih-chai-shan sites in Yunnan have revealed much about the largely civilization of Tien.[8] It was this civilization, exten[ding from] Yunnan into northern Vietnam, that produced the Dong-son bronzes (in particular, the elaborately o drums) that found such a wide distribution over most o and island south-east Asia. While evidence of conta[ct] Chou state is certainly present, the distinctive art metallurgical techniques of Tien set it clearly apart fro[m] Chinese civilization. The use of lost-wax casting in made possible the production of the wealth of representative art recovered from Tien tombs; these artifacts portray a highly stratified society with distinctive rituals and an apparently matriarchal orientation alien to north China), which, fused with Chinese elements by the Han conquest, underlay later Vietnamese civilization.

During the two millennia prior to the Han expansion there were thus a number of distinctive cultures (and later civilized states) present in the area of what is now south China. But the extent to which this area can be called Chinese in pre-Han times is an open question. While the Ch'u state was most probably occupied by peoples speaking a Sinitic language, most of the other cultures and states were made up of peoples speaking languages affiliated to modern Tibeto-Burman, Tai, Vietnamese and possibly even Austronesian language groups. Though in some sense constituting a 'greater China', many of the cultures of south China were quite distinct from the Chou north and would appear to have had close economic and technological links with mainland south-east Asia.

Rice farmers and early metallurgists in mainland south-east Asia

In mainland south-east Asia bronzeworking had even earlier origins. Until recently it was believed that bronze and iron made a late entry into this area from India and China between 800 and 300 BC, but present evidence now supports an independent development of bronze some three millennia earlier – far earlier than in China or much of India. Although this involves a major change in accepted views, it is less surprising in the context of the abundant deposits of copper and tin ores that exist in this area and the scarcity of suitable stone resources in much of the rolling lowlands zone. Ceramic technology, although well behind that of Shang China, and based on open firing rather than on kilns, was sufficiently advanced to reach temperatures capable of smelting both copper and tin ores; simple piston bellows provided the higher heat necessary to melt the resultant metal.

South-east Asia is still very far from adequately investigated. Sites excavated according to modern standards are few and are unevenly distributed because of political factors. Thus Thailand has seen relatively extensive excavation, and the sporadic efforts of French archaeologists in Vietnam have been massively supplemented in recent years by the work of the Vietnamese themselves. West Malaysia has seen a moderate number of excavations (none to date with early metal), but very little is yet known about the pre-Indianized cultures of Cambodia, Burma and Laos. It must also be emphasized that here, as in China, by no means all cultures took up metallurgy. Its distribution appears to have been limited to peoples inhabiting the rolling lowland zone between the mountains and the flat alluvial plains of the great rivers. We lack evidence of major human occupation of any sort on the alluvium itself until considerably later. On the other hand, peoples practising an essentially Hoabinhian way of life (see Chapter 21), with little reliance on agriculture, persisted in the mountain zones well after the spread of bronze and iron, and even after the rise of the Indianized civilizations; archaeological evidence supports their

presence in the mountains of northern Thailand until AD 1000 or even 1500, and several Malayan aboriginal (Orang Asli) groups were non-agricultural until very recently.

Much of our knowledge of the economy and technology of the early bronze-using peoples of the area comes from only two sites: Non Nok Tha and Ban Chiang, both located on the rolling lowlands of north-eastern Thailand. Non Nok Tha was the first site to give a clear indication of a distinct bronze period in south-east Asia. Its chronology poses many complex problems,[9] but the absolute dates from the site, taken in conjunction with ceramic and burial typology, suggest the following sequence. An Early Period, dating from about 4500 BC to about 3500 BC, was followed by a Middle Period, which lasted until about AD 200; after a gap in the sequence the site was reoccupied in about AD 1000 (the Late Period) and

23.3: *A drum-shaped container of bronze cast by the lost-wax method from a Tien culture tomb at Shih-chai-shan in Yünnan. Note the ensemble of bronze drums, the south-east Asian style of house on piles, and the possible human sacrifice in the foreground.*

abandoned some 150 years ago. The economy of the Non Nok Tha culture was apparently based on rice from the outset, as suggested by the use of rice chaff as a tempering material in pottery from the beginning of the Early Period. Domestic cattle, dogs and, very probably, pigs are also present from the earliest level; however, the presence of deer and other wild species indicates a significant reliance on hunting and gathering as well. A variety of pottery was recovered in burials of the Early Period, most of it round-bottomed and cord-marked; some of the vessels had elaborate incised designs. A few fragments of bronze from the bottom level and a socketed axe from the top level indicate that bronze was in use, but rare, throughout the Early Period. It became relatively abundant at the onset of the Middle Period, which is marked by an elaboration of pottery types and finds of sandstone moulds, coarse ceramic crucibles and bronze artifacts, indicating the casting of bronze at the site. Greater variations in wealth and burial style tentatively suggest increasing social stratification, perhaps the result of a growing trade in bronze, but the economic pattern of the Early Period continued. Some evidence for intermittent occupation may indicate that rice was being grown by swidden (slash-and-burn) methods rather than in wet fields. The Late Period inhabitants of the site used iron tools and cremated their dead, and appear to have been similar to wet-rice farmers of the area.

More recent excavations within the modern Chiang have yielded a similar sequence and rela artifacts.[10] Initial occupation of the site also 4500 BC, and cast-bronze spearheads, bracelets found even in the basal layers; the pottery of the reminiscent of Early Period pottery at Non Nok the faunal remains indicates reliance on hunting well as rice cultivation. At about 2000 BC an in occurred; water buffalo bones and a decline in dwelling species indicate the clearance of fore swamps for wet-rice cultivation.

At the same date iron began to appear at the s form of bimetallic iron-bronze artifacts (an iron s cast-bronze tang). The appearance of iron at this earlier than in China) is in some ways even more s early dates for bronze and strongly suggests an ind ment of iron as well. This hypothesis is supp thermoluminescence dates associated with iron sites varying between 600 and 1300 BC. The te casting appears to have grown out of the bival

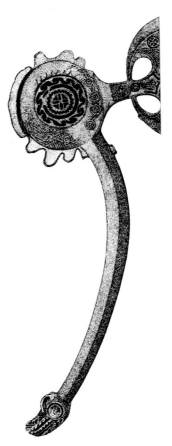

earlier used for bronze. The techniques employed in both cases were probably relatively simple: a charcoal fire, piston bellows (still in use throughout south-east Asia), pottery crucibles and moulds of sandstone. However, coldworking and annealing of bronze were also known, and some of the more elaborate bracelets at both sites may have been cast by the lost-wax process, a technique that reached China only at a much later date.

Some time before 1000 BC the development of wet-rice cultivation, in conjunction with the water buffalo for ploughing and the use of iron tools, made possible one of the major population shifts in the region's prehistory: the movement from the rolling lowlands to the hitherto unsettled alluvial plains that now support the vast majority of south-east Asia's people. Perhaps stimulated by population pressure, groups began to move on to the deltas of the Red and Chao Phraya (and probably Mekong) rivers early in the first millennium BC. This is seen in Phase I of the Chan Sen site on the Chao Phraya plain, where there was a sizeable village of wet-rice agriculturalists using both bronze and iron. The investigation of one of a large number of moated and walled sites on the Chi alluvium in north-eastern Thailand indicates that these were probably occupied by iron-using rice farmers shortly before 500 BC. Finally, sites of the Go Mun culture on the Red River delta dating from before 1000 BC indicate that a similar phenomenon was taking place there. The overall picture is one of movement to, and agricultural intensification on, the alluvial plains, and the growth of large villages and, later, towns. The growth of population, incipient urbanization, the control of water resources and the spread of waterborne trade all combined to produce a situation ripe for the introduction of Indian religio-political concepts at the beginning of the Christian era. The evidence suggests that the south-east Asians themselves took an active part in acquiring a number of cultural traits from India that enabled them to produce their own civilizations in the first few centuries AD.

The spread of agriculture and metallurgy to island south-east Asia

It is likely that some form of horticulture – perhaps indigenously developed – flourished in the islands of south-east Asia prior to the arrival of rice agriculture. In any event, by the mid-fourth millennium BC or earlier some form of agriculture was very probably being practised by the Ta-p'en-keng culture of Taiwan, and developed pottery appears at a slightly later date in the Philippines, at sites such as Dimolit on Luzon. Pottery appears only in the second millennium BC at the cave sites of the Tabon area (Palawan) and Niah (Sarawak), but probably developed earlier in the area. The rapid spread of ceramics (and presumably agriculture) is demonstrated by finds of pottery in the Talaud Islands and Sulawesi by about 3000 BC,[11] and it seems safe to assume that food production was well established throughout island south-east Asia by the end of the third millennium BC. However, some groups retained a hunting-and-gathering economy until the recent past – for example, the now well-known Tasaday. Intensive rice cultivation spread only slowly eastwards through the islands and is still spreading today at the expense of economies based on sago and root-crop horticulture.

The spread of bronze and iron appears to have begun shortly after 1000 BC and continued through the first millennium. From about 500 BC onwards bronze artifacts of Dong-son style, in many cases locally made, were distributed throughout Indonesia, even reaching the coast of Irian Jaya. This obviously does not reflect the spread of a Dong-son (or Tien) 'culture', but rather widespread trading contacts maintained by people with an advanced maritime technology. By the first half of the first millennium AD the stage was set for the rise of Indianized civilizations in western Indonesia that paralleled those emerging on the mainland.

23.4: *Socketed bronze axes from Ban Chiang. These were cast at the site, using bivalve moulds made of local sandstone, although the metal itself was apparently smelted elsewhere and imported.*

23.5: *An ornate cast bronze axe from the island of Roti, Indonesia. While distinctive Dong-son motifs are present, the axe is almost certainly of local manufacture rather than an import from the Dong-son/Tien region.*

24. The final stages of hunting and gathering in Africa

Until recently it was thought that the beginning of the present (Holocene) era 10 000 years ago was marked by major changes among hunting and collecting groups in Africa. Up to the mid-1960s the evidence did indeed suggest that the microlithic industries of the Late Stone Age in Africa (best known in the south and east) made their appearance about 8000 or 9000 years ago as logical successors to 'transitional' industries (the Magosian and Howieson's Poort cultures) that bridged the gap and marked the transition from the Middle Stone Age to the Late Stone Age. It was generally thought that they disappeared while farming and metallurgy spread through the continent.

The sudden upsurge of archaeological research in Africa since the early to mid-1960s has drastically modified this rather simple picture. The beginning of the Middle Stone Age, once thought to lie between 30 000 and 40 000 years ago, has been pushed back to upwards of 100 000 years ago, while in the south the so-called 'transitional' industries are now shown to represent a phase of Middle Stone Age development some 35 000 to more than 50 000 years ago.[1] Some of the elements thought to herald the appearance of microlithic Late Stone Age industries in fact took place within the Middle Stone Age at a very early date. The particular elements involved are the production of small blades and the presence of a blunting retouch on small flake and blade tools. Such developments are seen not only in the industries described as Magosian and Howieson's Poort, but also in Middle Stone Age industries in Lesotho in which 'sophisticated blades' are present.

Several sites in South Africa have yielded an industry that consists very largely of tiny ribbon-like bladelets together with the cores from which they are struck, but with very few formally shaped tools. Dates for this industry, which in the southern Cape Province has been named the Robberg industry, range from 29 000 to about 11 000 years ago. And yet this industry cannot, at present, be shown to have given rise in a simple way to the microlithic industries (known as Wilton in eastern and southern Africa) of the early to mid-Holocene. This is because at several sites in the southern Cape Province, where the period has been most closely studied, it is found that another, totally different industry intervened between the Robberg and the Wilton industries. This is the so-called Albany industry, characterized by the production of flakes (as distinct from bladelets) and with large scrapers as virtually the only formal stone tools, though in one coastal site there is an assortment of associated bone tools. The dates for this industry range from about 12 500 BC to between 7000 and 6000 BC. Somewhat similar industries, apparently occupying broadly the same time range, have been noted from the inland plateau area

as far north as the Transvaal (South Africa) and

In the Cape Folded Mountain range the Alban ceeded by the Wilton, which passed through gra changes from its formative stage about 8000 y its climax some 6000 years ago and finally losi to 2000 years ago, to give rise to a quite differe not well understood. On the inland plateau ar the situation is less clear. It looks as if much of t or only sparsely inhabited between 8000 BC and the numbers began to increase at about the industries north of the Cape Folded Mounta ficantly from those in the mountains and to the s northern edge of the mountains may thus rep historic cultural (perhaps linguistic) divide, sep (Smithfield) people from those of the eastern Ca later Holocene.[2] Further north still, in the T Holocene industries (from 3300 BC), while rela field of the Orange Free State, nonetheless s ferences, particularly in the absence of small l bladelets.

Elsewhere in Africa information on the late early Holocene is less detailed, but a few sites, wh important differences from the south, point to microlithic industries. In central and northern Z lithic Nachikufan culture is traceable through se a few centuries ago to upwards of 16 000 years ag

24.1: *A selection of Wilton ar convex scrapers and the segm especially characteristic, the l (bottom left) less so. Ostrich-very common in many Holoce but also occur in earlier times.*

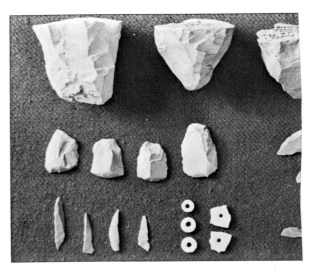

⌐ fully microlithic industries in the cave of
M⌐   ⌐ack to at least 32 000 years ago, and possibly up-
wa⌐   ⌐ years ago.

W⌐   ⌐ the technological advantages of microlithic tools over
macrol⌐ .ic ones, their adoption cannot be explained by the beginning of the Holocene. Microliths, which were surely parts of
composite tools and/or weapons, have a long and varied history
in Africa, and while there is evidence of an unbroken tradition
from parts of central Africa this is clearly not the case in southern
regions. The hunter–gatherer cultures of the Holocene in Africa
are probably best seen simply as the latest in a series of cultural
developments, often local or regional, that occurred with increasing frequency during about the last fifty thousand years. There
were probably several different factors involved, operating at
different times and places and in different combinations: environmental changes, cultural heritage, invention and diffusion may all
have played a part.

Environmental factors

At several sites in the southern Cape region the replacement of
the Albany industry by the microlithic Wilton industry about
6000–5500 BC is marked by a change in emphasis from the hunting
of the larger, more gregarious animals of the open grasslands to a
concentration on the smaller, solitary antelopes found in a more
confined bush or wooded environment.[3] In this most southerly
region there is good evidence that a change from an open to a more
closed habitat took place, but the development of the Wilton culture cannot be seen simply as a reflection of the change, for the
microlithic Robberg folk were hunting the open-plains animals in
the same region 10 000 years earlier, while at Boomplaas the
change from open-plains animals to closed-habitat antelope occurred *within* the Albany period.

Unravelling the effects of environment in this southern region
is made more difficult because the changes in temperature (and
thus in vegetation and fauna) that occurred at the end of the
Pleistocene were accompanied by the submersion of a vast coastal
plain up to 70 kilometres wide as the sea rose with the melting of
the ice sheets of the last glaciation. This not only robbed great
herds of animals of their grazing lands, but must also have set in
train considerable population movements. It has already been
noted that much of the inland plateau of southern Africa seems to
have been unoccupied in the early Holocene, and it is likely that
this too was linked to the temperature rise at that time.

Throughout central and much of eastern Africa it is harder to
point to evidence of environmental change that might have had a
significant effect on hunting societies in this time range. The
abundant fauna from the Matupi cave indicates a savanna habitat,
though the cave is now in the forest zone; but it seems that any
shift in the boundary between savanna and forest was not great.

In West Africa and the Sahara it was different. The evidence is
not abundant, but at Iwo Ileru in Nigeria an evolved microlithic
industry is present by 10 000 BC. Most other occurrences are dated
rather later, but there is a general distribution of microlithic industries in the savanna regions that contrasts sharply with sites in
the forest areas to the south, where microliths are absent.[4] The
implication is that microliths are related to the hunting of savanna
game, and formed the armature of arrows and perhaps spears,
while subsistence methods in the forest produced a different technological response.

The situation in the Sahara is even more interesting, for in a
broad swathe embracing desert and semi-arid areas across the
southern Sahara and southwards along the Eastern Rift of East
Africa are found a group of sites with bone fish-hooks, harpoon-
heads and quantities of fish bones.[5] The sites range in date from
8000 to 2500 BC, but it is clear that the climax period was about
7000 BC, and that they represent a widespread hunting-and-
gathering economy in which fishing played an important, and often
a dominant, part. It is hard to escape the conclusion that this widespread exploitation of the lakes' resources was stimulated by a
period in the early Postglacial when lake levels throughout Africa
were much higher than at present and the Sahara was 'a land of
lakes and marshes', with a rainfall up to 300 per cent greater than
it is now. With plant food and the animals of the adjacent savanna
to supplement their diet, these communities must have enjoyed
a life of relative security and abundance that only diminished with
the onset of drier conditions (desiccation) from 2000 BC onwards
and the incursions of pastoralist groups into these more favourable
areas.

The exploitation of resources

Africa was a land of great abundance in its natural state: contemporary ethnographic observations and the accounts of early
travellers leave us in no doubt about this. The mixed savannas and
grasslands teemed with game, and if the thicker bush of the valley
sides and 'bushveld' areas were lacking in vast herds there were
still the small nocturnal antelopes to be trapped, and often herds
of buffalo and solitary kudu (another antelope species). The coastal
waters and estuaries abounded in fish, the rocks in shellfish and
the cliffs in sea fowl. Everywhere there was an abundance of
seemingly insignificant creatures that were all nevertheless potential sources of food: insects and their eggs and larvae, birds and
their eggs (an ostrich egg is the equal of a dozen hen's eggs),
rodents, lizards, snakes, frogs, and the much-loved honey of the
many species of bees. All these things are known to have been
exploited.

Advantage could be taken of much of this potential wealth of
food with the aid of very little specialist equipment and relatively
little social organization. Much of it could be gathered merely with
the fingers. If any quantity was to be carried collecting bags would
be needed, and these are attested both ethnographically and in
prehistoric rock art: they were often made from a small antelope
skin slit along the belly and carefully removed from the carcass,
with a sling attached to the legs. Digging-sticks were used for
grubbing out roots, tubers and burrowing creatures, and although

few survive in the archaeological record they are widely attested by the bored stones that often weighted them. The simple throwing-stick would have been effective against many smaller mammals and birds.

These aids to the acquisition of food are probably extremely ancient, but there are other devices that are likely to have evolved more recently, some of them very recently. The bow and arrow is widely depicted in the rock art of Africa, from the Sahara to the southern tip, but it is difficult to know just when it was first used. Certain delicately retouched and symmetrical 'points' from the Middle Stone Age could well have been arrowheads, and the occasional microliths from similar contexts add strength to the

24.2: *Map of Africa, showing some of the major features, peoples and sites referred to in the text.*

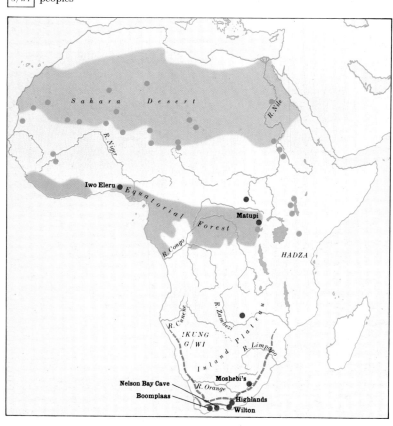

	Cape Folded Mts
	Great Escarpment
●	bone harpoon sites
●	archaeological sites
G/WI	peoples

suggestion. But the earliest clear evidence is prob[...] late Predynastic palette engravings from Egypt[...] heads and a possible bow fragment from Gwisho[...] about 2500 BC, and a fine piece of bow stave fro[...] Cape dates from a little over a thousand years ag[...]

There is no doubt that the bow and arrow must[...] sented a drastic leap forward in the technology o[...] effectiveness would have been greatly enhanced[...] of poisons that could be applied to the arrows.[...] poison is certainly widespread in Africa today, bu[...] apparently specializing in its use seem to be[...] southern Africa (represented today by the !Kun[...] the Kalahari), whose tiny bows and delicate arro[...] ineffectual without it. The Ovatjimba of north-[...] also use poison with their arrows, but the bow i[...] arrow lacks the specialized composite construct[...] used by the Bushmen. In East Africa the Hadza[...] bow with a variety of arrow types, only one of w[...] poison.[6] If the Bushman bow and arrow repres[...] commitment to the use of poison, it may be that[...] poisons evolved in southern Africa during the la[...] early Holocene. Certainly the use of poison is att[...] years ago at Gwisho, where wooden arrowhe[...] imitating the bone heads of the modern and his[...] composite arrows.

Traps of various kinds are widely used today in[...] small game, and where faunal remains reveal a[...] the small solitary and nocturnal antelopes their[...] ably be inferred. Such traps are so simply cons[...] parts might be impossible to identify in archaeo[...] though it is likely that they are represented amo[...] cordage found at a variety of sites in southe[...] specialized, and at the same time more localized,[...] found at many points along the southern coast o[...] Helena Bay in the west to the Zululand coast in[...] devices call for careful construction and regular[...] they can be enormously productive. They carry[...] group cooperation, and even if they did not pro[...] permanent residence they must certainly ha[...] regularly in the course of seasonal movements.[...]

Evidence of more conventional approaches t[...] the form both of artifacts and of rock paintings[...] early examples of harpoons and hooks already[...] Sahara and East Africa, grooved sinkers (app[...] fishing) and fish-gorges have been found at sev[...] sites, and fish-hooks from a site in Lesotho. The u[...] is widespread in Africa and good representations a[...] rock art, as are examples of fishing with both line[...] as the inland hunter may scavenge meat from[...] dators, so may the coastal dweller occasionally b[...] consumed shark kills that wash ashore, or fro[...] mammals. On the south coast too he may reap[...]

24.3: *Tidal fish traps on the south coast of Africa. The device relies on fish entering during high tide and becoming trapped in the pool as the tide recedes.*

24.4: *Rock paintings provide ample evidence of fishing with various aids in inland waters. Here spears or harpoons are being used from rafts or boats, one of which is anchored. This painting is to be found in the mountains of the Great Escarpment in Lesotho.*

24.5: *4000-year-old arrowheads from Gwisho, compared with a modern Bushman head (near left) of the same kind, also in wood. All these wooden heads are patterned on the composite type of head (far left) comprising a bone tip joined to a bone linkshaft by a reed collar, bound with sinew to prevent splitting. The end of the linkshaft was seated in the hollow end of a reed arrow shaft, also bound to prevent splitting. This delicate device would be effective only if used with poison, and the Gwisho specimens imply the early use of arrow poison.*

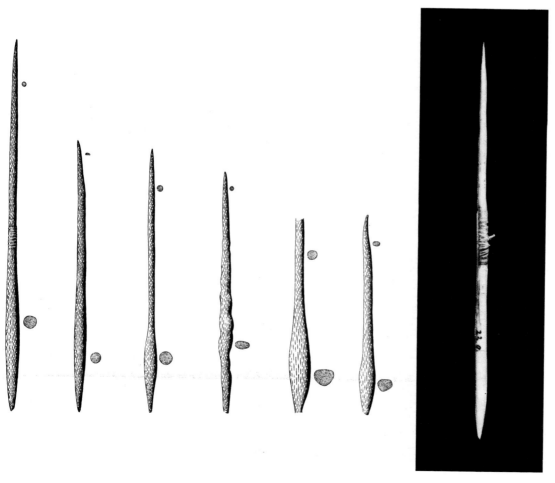

fish stunned by the sudden welling up of cold water in the summer months.

Subsistence strategies

If nature is generous she is also fickle, and hunter–gatherers are generally found to have evolved appropriate strategies to help them minimize the effects of drought or disease or any vagaries in the movements of game. The avoidance of rigidly structured social groups clearly helps, and among both the Bushmen and the East African Hadza people there is considerable movement of individuals between groups, which may as a result vary in size quite considerably from day to day.[7] This flexibility may to some extent be geared to local variations in the food supply; it also helps to maintain contact between groups and plays a part in the securing of mates.

While band sizes may fluctuate, the average size of the band will depend to some extent on the abundance and reliability of the food supply. The G/wi of the Kalahari occupy a territory at the rate of about 11 square kilometres per person, with band sizes varying from forty to sixty people. They are obliged to move frequently, and in late summer, when the plant foods that form the staple part of their diet (60 to 70 per cent among both the G/wi and the !Kung) are very hard to find, the group splits up and the men stop hunting to join the women in the quest for plant foods.[8] Their !Kung neighbours to the north might share the same experience were it not for the groves of highly nutritious mongongo nut trees, which quite transform their lifestyle. The nut forms 50 per cent of their vegetable diet, and it keeps all the year round. The population density of the !Kung is higher at one person per square kilometre; they move camp only five or six times a year, mainly because of the seasonality of the water supply. In East Africa the Hadza live in groups of around eighteen adults at a density for the total population of about 3 square kilometres per person; they move about once a fortnight.

These figures provide some idea of the probable organization of prehistoric hunter–gatherers at a similar technological stage of development. It is, of course, very difficult to arrive at figures for prehistoric times, or for different environmental settings. Historical records suggest that Bushman band sizes in the Cape and the Namib desert were smaller than for the present-day Kalahari, while for the Karoo, eighteenth-century records suggest band sizes varying from 5 to 55, with a mean of around 18. Analysis of group sizes depicted in the rock art of the south-west Cape suggest a mean size of 13, and the excavated site of de Hangen, in the same area, suggests occupation by a group of 12 to 15. It seems, therefore, that the prehistoric Bushmen of the Cape did indeed live in smaller bands than their Kalahari counterparts.

A detailed knowledge of the regional food supplies at all seasons is essential to an understanding of the pattern of livelihood of the Holocene hunters, as mobility is another strategy that may be adopted to ensure the success of the food quest. It may be of two kinds. An example of the first is provided by the G/wi, who are highly mobile but move within a uniform territory: the range of foodstuffs remains very much the same from place to place, varying only with the seasons. It is impractical for the G/wi to move seasonally to a different ecological zone as the distances involved would be too great. There is a different kind of mobility in regions within trekking distances of the coast, and the changes in zones are even greater where mountain ranges or a plateau scarp parallel the coast at no great distance. Such a situation exists in the southern and south-western Cape, and there is good archaeological evidence to indicate seasonal movement across several zones. In the south-western Cape the evidence points strongly to groups exploiting plant foods as a staple in the Cape Folded Mountains in summer and wintering at the coast where shellfish replaced plant foods (scarce in winter) as the dependable staple.[9] The hunting and trapping of game was supplemented by the rich resources of the coastal waters: fish, crayfish, whale, dolphin and sea fowl. The fact that this is a winter-rainfall area strongly influenced the details of the pattern. Six hundred kilometres to the east, in the summer-rain zone, there is evidence that the pattern was reversed; coastal sites were occupied in summer, and winter was spent in the mountains.

Conclusion

There is nothing about the activities of hunter–gatherers in Africa that is unique to the Holocene. Almost all the elements of their material culture were present, even widespread, well before the end of the Pleistocene. In some parts of Africa there is little evidence of culture change at the end of the Pleistocene, and where such change did occur it has yet to be shown that it was an inevitable response to environmental change rather than simply evidence of the increasing tempo that seems to have characterized the late stages of the later Pleistocene. Even such events as the rise of the fishing economies of the Sahara and East Africa represented temporary and to some extent local adaptations or specializations of pre-existing culture.

The populations of the Holocene were entirely modern both physically and in terms of intellectual capacity. Their material culture was highly developed, and their lives were well organized to cope with the business of staying alive. Leisure time was often devoted to the production of ornaments for personal decoration, and surviving groups show the high degree to which fine skin clothing and accoutrements might be developed. There is no reason to suppose that the hours of storytelling, games and dancing enjoyed by some of the survivors of this highly successful way of life have not been a part of it for thousands of years. The few bands of hunter–gatherers that remain in Africa today can hardly survive much longer; but while the emphasis has shifted to agriculture and stock-raising, hunting and gathering often remain prestige pastimes and may still make a valuable economic contribution. The old way of life did not pass quickly in Africa: after at least six thousand years of encroachment, the farmer has still not entirely ousted the hunter.

25. Agricultural origins in Africa

Recent work on African crop plants has transformed our understanding of the origins of agriculture in Africa. North Africa and the Nile valley form part of the agricultural province centred on south-western Asia, with wheat, barley, sheep and goats; but the area immediately south of the Sahara produced its own grain- and root-crops and characteristic forms of cultivation. While these developments took place later than in south-western Asia and were less explosive in their effects, they too can be seen as part of a pattern of response to environmental change.[1]

Cereals

The crops first domesticated in south-western Asia, wheat and barley, are winter-rainfall crops adapted to the Mediterranean climatic pattern (see Chapter 15), and first cultivated by dry-farming methods. Both crops spread widely in sub-tropical areas, and could be grown with the help of irrigation in the Nile and Indus valleys. In the summer-rainfall areas of the tropics, where no wild ancestors of wheat or barley have ever grown, it is virtually impossible to grow them by dry-farming methods. Cereal agriculture in sub-Saharan Africa thus had to develop in its own way, and could have been achieved by one of three methods: the growing of wheat and barley by irrigation; the introduction of crops already domesticated in the tropics outside Africa; or the domestication of wild African grasses.

There is no evidence that the first of these possibilities – an ancient diffusion of wheat and barley outside the Nile valley and Ethiopia – was realized. Wheat and barley were introduced in ancient times into Ethiopia, where they succeeded in adapting to the highland climate, and varieties proliferated in the widely differing conditions there. It is possible that barley was grown as far south as the latitude of Khartoum in the ancient kingdom of Meroë, although it is sorghum (the Guinea corn type of millet) rather than either wheat or barley that is shown in a Meroitic rock engraving dated to the first century AD (see Figure 25.1).

There are nowadays no serious candidates for the second category before the introduction of maize from the New World in the sixteenth century AD. Finger millet was once thought to have been domesticated in India, but botanists now declare it to be African in origin, so it must be considered as belonging to the third category. Until recently there was no direct archaeological evidence for finger millet before the eighth century AD, but examples of grains have now been found at Gobedra, near Axum in Ethiopia, occurring in a layer that produced a single radiocarbon date in the sixth millennium BC, below a layer dated to the later part of the second millennium BC. At Kadero, a few kilometres north of Khartoum, pots bearing impressions of (?) finger millet seeds are dated to about 4000 BC. The likely areas of domestication of finger millet are Ethiopia and northern Uganda.

Besides finger millet, eight other wild African grasses were domesticated. The most important of these is sorghum. Its original area of domestication is regarded as the sahel, the strip between the desert and the savanna stretching from Lake Chad to the Nile, and the process may have had more to do with an imbalance between population and food resources, occasioned by the Saharan area becoming drier, than with any cultural stimulus from growers of wheat and barley in north-eastern Africa. From its original area of domestication it diversified and spread out in all directions. There is archaeological evidence for domesticated sorghum from Jebel Tomat, south of Khartoum, in the third century AD, though the only early date so far is, again, from pot impressions at Kadero about 4000 BC.

Two grains of pollen from the Hoggar highlands of the Sahara, dated to the sixth millennium BC, are claimed to be derived from bulrush millet, but the next archaeological evidence for it is more than four thousand years later at the Dhar Tichitt sites in Mauretania. Here there were settlements spanning from early in the second millennium into the middle of the first millennium BC,

25.1: *A Meroitic rock engraving at Jebel Qeili, dated to the first century AD, which features a sorghum plant. (The king, Sherkerer, appears about 1 metre high.)*

divided into seven phases. Impressions on pottery revealed the use of a number of different kinds of desert grasses: in the first three phases there were many seeds of bur grass, still collected to some extent as a famine food, and a single grain of bulrush millet, though it is impossible to tell whether this was wild or cultivated. In the fourth phase two other grass seeds appeared, and bulrush millet rose to 3 per cent of the total. In the fifth and sixth phases bulrush millet accounted for 60 per cent and 80 per cent respectively, rising to nearly 90 per cent in the seventh phase, when it had all the characteristics of a cultivated grain. It looks as though the Tichitt people were experimenting with wild grasses and hit upon bulrush millet as the best, or that it was introduced from outside to a community already practising cereal eating and among whom it rapidly gained popularity over all others. South of the equator bulrush

25.2: *Map showing the spread of domesticated sorghum (Guinea corn) and its different varieties through Africa. DB = durra-bicolor, C = caudatum, ½C = half-caudatum, K = kafir, GK = Guinea-kafir.*

→ early movements

► later movements, 1st century AD and later

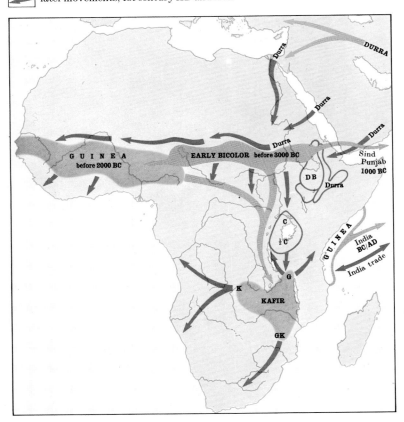

millet had not until recently been recorded at dates earlier than the ninth century AD, but now a sherd bearing impressions, dated to about AD 300, is reported from the site of Silverleaves Farm in the Transvaal. The area of domestication of bulrush millet was most of the sahel strip stretching from the Atlantic in the west to the Darfur in the east.

Four other types of millet have been domesticated in Africa, though there are no archaeological data about any of them: two types of 'hungry rice' grass or 'fonio', one belonging particularly to the Hausa areas of Nigeria, the other widespread throughout the savannas of western Africa; 'animal fonio' (the grass whose botanical name is *Brachiaria deflexa*), nowadays only cultivated in the Fouta Djallon; and 'jungle rice' or 'chindumba', endemic as a cultivated cereal in the highlands of eastern Africa.

The middle Niger delta is considered the home of African rice domestication, perhaps with secondary centres in the lower Gambia river valley and in the Republic of Guinea. Rice replaces yams (see below) as the staple in the western half of West Africa, but it is only since the Second World War that African rice has been recognized as a separate species. Few archaeological occurrences of African rice have yet been recorded, but on botanical grounds it must be added to the list of locally domesticated species.

The last of the nine indigenously domesticated African cereals is teff. Its cultivation is confined to Ethiopia, and it has been suggested that the Cushitic inhabitants of Ethiopia who introduced emmer wheat there also domesticated local plants such as teff. However, in the absence of any archaeological information, it has been argued that teff must have been domesticated before wheat and barley had been introduced to Ethiopia or it would not have been thought worthwhile to cultivate such a tiny grain; on the other hand, if wheat and barley are superior to teff, why is the latter not restricted to areas where wheat and barley will not grow well? Although we have no archaeological evidence for teff in Ethiopia, it is known from a sherd impression in a southern Arabian context dated to the first centuries BC/AD. This should also serve as a reminder that if agricultural ideas entered sub-Saharan Africa from outside and were not entirely independent innovations, they could have done so from Arabia as well as from the lower Nile valley.

Root crops

Yam cultivation was probably very important in the development of indigenous African agriculture, but because tubers, unlike cereal grains, leave no archaeological evidence, its antiquity cannot be established. Until recently it was believed that domestication of the indigenous African yams was a result of the introduction of Asian forms. It was speculated that various Asiatic food plants entered Africa via the Ethiopian lowlands and travelled westwards along what was erroneously called the 'yam belt'.[2] Nowadays it is generally believed that the Asian food crops, including plantains, bananas, one type of cocoyam and the citrus fruits, reached Africa from Indonesia via Madagascar or the adjacent parts of the

25.3: *Map showing the area in which it is believed, principally on botanical grounds, that the indigenous African crops were domesticated. The banana was introduced from Asia and may have displaced a formerly more widespread cultivation of ensete.*

natural distribution

- teff
- shea butter
- ensete
- ensete cultivation
- bananas (intensive cultivation)
- limit of area of exploitation of aquatic resources
- northern and southern limits of date palm

probable areas of domestication

- Guinea corn
- bulrush millet
- finger millet
- African rice
- hungry rice
- yams
- oil palm

25.4: *Isochronic chart of the spread of cattle in Africa. This is composed from a limited number of sites and dates, and further research may alter the picture, especially in East Africa. In Africa north of the equator there were in fact two distinct phases, rather than a single, long, progressive movement from north to south (as the chart would seem to indicate). The earlier spread was to take up grazing lands in what is now the Sahara desert, which was then better watered than now; the later movement was to escape the progressive desiccation of the Sahara after 3000 BC.*

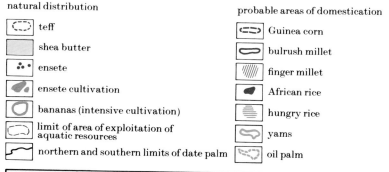

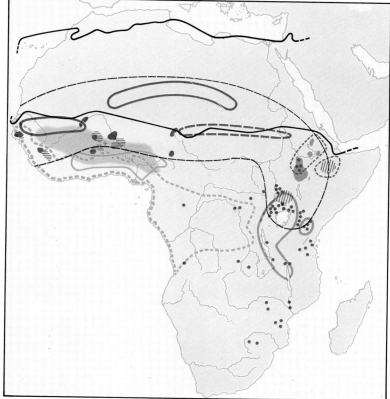

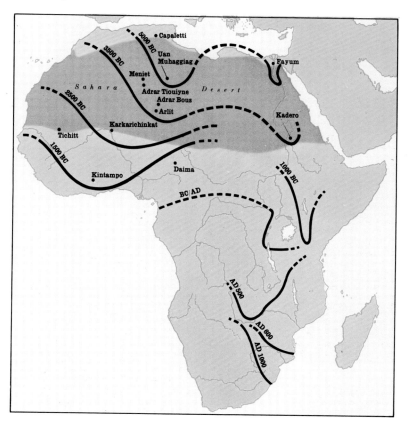

east coast in the earlier part of the first millennium AD, whereas indigenous yam cultivation in West Africa may go back four or five thousand years.

No other indigenous tuberous crop has the same importance as the yam, but the 'Hausa potato' is a cultivated crop, although the area of its domestication remains uncertain – both Ethiopia and West Africa have been suggested. Just as it is likely that many different tropical grasses were at one time grown for their grain, so it is probable that a number of African tubers, the Hausa potato among them, were formerly much more widely cultivated than they are now, having been displaced by more successful crops such as cassava, sweet potato and the second type of cocoyam, all

introduced from America by Europeans. The African banana, or ensete, which bears no edible fruit but whose stem and root provide a staple diet in south-western Ethiopia, must have been indigenously domesticated in that country. At one time it too may have been more widely used as a food source, but outside Ethiopia it was replaced by the bananas and plantains introduced from Asia.

Pulses, vegetables and tree crops

The indigenously domesticated pulses include two kinds of African groundnut and cowpea, which was probably domesticated in Nigeria. None of these had the same importance as staples that millets and yams had. The same can be said about okra,

CEREALS	
Sorghum bicolor	Sorghum, Guinea corn
Pennisetum americanum	Pearl millet, bulrush millet
Eleusine coracana	Finger millet
Digitaria exilis, D. iburua	Hungry rice, 'fonio'
Oryza glaberrima	African rice
Brachiaria deflexa	Animal fonio
Eragrostis tef	Teff
Echinochloa colona	Jungle rice, 'chindumba'

PULSE CROPS	
Vigna unguiculata (V. sinensis)	Cowpea
Caianas caian	Pigeon pea
Voandzeia subterranea	Bambara groundnut
Kerstingiella geocarpa	Kersting's groundnut

ROOT CROPS	
Dioscorea cavanensis, D. rotundata	Yams
Plectranthus esculentus	Hausa potato
(Coleus dazo, C. esculentus)	
Sphenostylis stenocarpa	Yam bean

BUSH AND TREE CROPS	
Elaeis guineensis	Oil palm
Buterospermum paradoxum	Shea butter
Cola nitida, C. acuminata	Kola
Musa ensete (Ensete ventricosa)	Ensete, false banana
Coffea arabica	Coffee

VEGETABLES	
Hibiscus esculentus	Okra
Hibiscus sabdariffa	Roselle
Amaranthus spp.	Spinach
Telfairia occidentalis	Fluted pumpkin
Cucumis melo	Melon
Citrullus lanatus	Watermelon
Cucumeropsis edulis	Pumpkin, squash
Lagenaria siceraria	Gourd
Aframomum maligueta	Malaguetta pepper, 'Grains of Paradise'

OIL SEEDS	
Guizotia abyssinica	Niger seed, 'noog'
Ricinis communis	Castor
Polygala butyracea	Beniseed

amaranthus spinach, roselle, gourd, melon, castor and niger-seed or 'noog', all of which have an African origin – how ancient we do not yet know, though seeds are beginning to be obtained in archaeological contexts.

There remain the important tree crops – shea butter, kola and, above all, the oil palm. Remains of palm nuts were found at the site of Shaheinab, north of Khartoum, dated to about 4000 BC, which may have come from Jebel Marra where there is evidence that oil palms were growing at the time. At a site in Ghana dated to about 1600 BC oil palm was found associated with cowpea and domestic cattle. At another rockshelter in Ghana it was found that the fruit of the incense tree had been used from before 4000 BC;

later the oil palm was also used, and later still it entirely supplanted the incense tree. The securing of a supply of palm oil as an ingredient in the diet may have been an important element in population growth.

Domestic animals

The only three indigenous creatures domesticated in Africa are the ass, the cat and the guinea-fowl, and only the last as a food source. The guinea-fowl was formerly to be found further north than today down the Nile valley; it was known in Predynastic Egypt, and as a table bird in ancient Rome, but it became lost to medieval Europe and acquired its name only when it was rediscovered by

25.5: *The principal indigenously domesticated African food crops.*

25.6: *Some of the major domesticated crops of Africa (various scales). From right to left: Guinea corn or sorghum. It is probably the most important of Africa's indigenously domesticated cereals. There are several different varieties, and botanists have a fair idea of how each of these spread.*
Finger millet, which is grown most in East Africa and was probably domesticated there and/or in Ethiopia.
Pearl millet or bulrush millet. Probably the second most important cereal (domesticated in Africa, in spite of its misleading Latin botanical name), it is faster-growing than Guinea corn and can thrive in a drier climate.
Cowpea, an important African pulse, was probably domesticated in Nigeria.
Yam, the most important and nutritious tuber. D. cayenensis and D. rotundata are the African-domesticated forms; other species were later introduced from Asia.
African banana, false banana or ensete. This type of banana bears no fruit; instead it is cultivated (in Ethiopia) for the lower part of the stem and for the tap root, from which a staple food is prepared.
Oil palm has its natural habitat along the fringes of the forests, in clearings and along watercourses in the forest, or in gallery forests in the savanna. It provides valuable vegetable protein and vitamins.

the Portuguese at the end of the fifteenth century.

Whereas sub-Saharan Africa had to find its own local equivalent for wheat and barley, and in fact found other food crops for itself as well, the four domestic animal species introduced – cattle, sheep, goats and pigs – were able to adapt to tropical conditions, and succeeded so well that it was unnecessary to domesticate local species; the plentiful supply of game may have been an additional disincentive.

The evidence for cattle suggests a generally southward movement of cattle-keeping from central North Africa that went on for a period of three or four thousand years. They are known in the Aures mountains of Algeria before 5000 BC and not long after in the Acacus, the north-easterly outlier of the Hoggar in south-west Libya; in the Fayum of Egypt by 4800 BC and at Adrar Bous in the Republic of Niger by 4500 BC; at sites in the Hoggar highlands about 4100 BC and at Kadero, just north of Khartoum, at about 4000 BC; in the Wadi Tilemsi, north-east of the Middle Bend of the Niger, by 2400 BC; in central Ghana by about 1600 BC; and in the Rift Valley area of Kenya from about 1000 BC onwards.

To begin with, this southward movement was simply to take up grazing grounds in the central Saharan highlands, which in the moister climate before 3500 BC were suitable for cattle; but after about 3000 BC it would have been to escape the severe desiccation then setting in. These cattle were traditionally thought to have come originally from south-west Asia, but there are two other possibilities. First, as cattle occur in Greece and Crete at an earlier date than in Anatolia and south-west Asia, it is possible that Neolithic herdsmen emigrated along the northern shores and archipelagos of the Mediterranean, making landfall in Tunisia and thence spreading south and into the interior. The second possibility is that cattle were native to North Africa and were domesticated in that area.

The increasing desiccation of the third millennium BC, which impelled the pastoralists to move south out of the Sahara, is likely also to have shifted southwards the tsetse fly barrier to cattle, making it easier for them to penetrate the East African highlands. There are now a number of dates from 1000 BC onwards for cattle bones associated with the Late Stone Age people of that area, who are characterized also by their making of bowls and platters of stone. In Zambia cattle did not appear until the fifth century AD; they were introduced by the earliest iron-using people, who spoke Bantu languages (see Chapter 52).[3]

Until recently it seemed that goats might have spread more rapidly into Africa than cattle, but it now looks as though sheep, goats and cattle must in many cases have been spread together. In common with other parts of the Old World, the archaeological record in Africa for the domesticated pig is much more scanty than for the other three domesticates. It was known in Egypt by 4800 BC, but it seems never to have been an important food source in Africa, and this independently of Muslim inhibitions in the later periods.

Why was agriculture and stock-keeping adopted?

The African evidence poses once again the general question of why agriculture came about. Gatherers of wild food were well aware that a seed stuck into the ground would grow into a plant, but why bother if abundant supplies grown by nature were available?

Conventional explanations stress diffusion of the idea of agriculture, either via the Nile valley or across the Red Sea from Arabia. South-west Asiatic crops did not spread further because the summer-rainfall area does not suit their growth requirements. It is possible that when attempts to grow wheat and barley proved unsuccessful these were replaced by local grasses that were at first regarded as weeds. On the other hand, local factors may have contributed to an independent process of domestication.

An important element in this is the partly sedentary character of life in the Late Stone Age even before agriculture was practised, especially where it was based on fishing. This was the case not only in the southern Sahara and the sahel, where watercourses had more water than now, but also in the Great Lakes of East Africa. It was precisely in such areas that the African cereals were domesticated. Increasingly arid conditions would gradually have dried out the lakes, making the collection of wild grain more important and its conservation a matter for intervention. Pressure on pastoral communities at the same time may have had a similar effect, either directly or because of competition for shrinking resources.

The cultivation of yams and oil palms in the woodland savannas could also have been an independent development in Africa rather than an introduction from elsewhere. Their natural habitat is the forest margin (ecotone), beside streams and in clearings. The yam is a vine, adapted by its evolution to a severe dry season, but needing something to climb up; it is therefore suited neither to grassland savanna nor to high forest. Similarly, the oil palm needs plenty of moisture at its roots but cannot propagate itself unless it receives adequate sunshine, which it cannot do under a high rain-forest canopy. These ecotonal foods were doubtless important for Late Stone Age hunters, and the conservation of such resources, leading to intentional planting, may have had its origins at an early stage, whenever pressure forced savanna populations southwards.

In a number of areas of the world the adoption of agriculture ultimately resulted in a population build-up that in turn provided the circumstances for urbanization and state formation. In sub-Saharan Africa factors such as human and animal diseases or poor soils hindered agricultural expansion; also an abundance of both land and game offered alternative sources of subsistence. Some peoples retained a hunting-and-gathering way of life into the twentieth century; elsewhere, by the end of the first millennium AD agriculture was able to support populous kingdoms.

IV: The early empires of the western Old World

The earliest states were often based on individual cities; the differential growth of certain centres produced larger units of organization that incorporated several of these cities. The quest for raw materials, and the military conquests that accompanied it, led to the formation of competing power centres, each with its zone of client states. Within these empires the greater concentration of resources allowed further investment in production and communication. For instance, large-scale irrigation and the construction of roads and caravanserais became possible. The existence of a regionally administered urbanized zone linked by effective transport allowed the spectacular growth of empires such as that of Alexander of Macedon, who gained control of the greater part of the developed world as far east as the Indus. The supply routes of this zone stretched out into the surrounding arid areas of central Asia and Arabia, bringing luxury goods over long distances. The extension of the commercial network along the Mediterranean opened up routes into temperate Europe, where local states had a brief florescence before being incorporated into the expanding empire of Rome.

26. The Assyrian empire

The Assyrians are justly famous as the creators of the first of the succession of empires that dominated the entire Near East. This empire, however, lasted scarcely more than a century and accounted for only the final tenth of the long history of the Assyrian state. The name 'Assyrian' is derived from the city of Assur (Aššur or Ashur), a site that was occupied from at least the mid-third millennium and whose importance at that date is now confirmed by the archives of Ebla (Tell Mardikh). The identity of the Assyrian state was in its early centuries (the 'Old Assyrian' period) closely associated with the city itself, and the god of both city and state was also called Assur. The concept of a 'land of Assur' (i.e. Assyria) is first encountered in the written sources only in about 1350 BC. The people of Assur spoke and wrote a distinctive variant of the Akkadian language, which continued to develop independently of the southern, Babylonian, dialect from the time of its earliest attestation in the merchants' documents and royal inscriptions of about 1800 BC until the end of Assyria in 605 BC. By that time, as the language of empire, it had spread far from its home at Assur, and had ousted the spoken and written traditions of Hurrian and Babylonian in the north of Mesopotamia.

In its early days Assur owed its importance to its role as a trading post. Strong Sumerian influence in Early Dynastic times points to trade southwards down the Tigris, but there was also an important overland route, which came from the east and struck out north-westwards from Assur to the Khabur basin and beyond. The archives of Ebla now give documentary confirmation that Assur was involved in trade with the west as early as 2400 BC, and the nature of the venture may reasonably be reconstructed by comparison with the thousands of cuneiform tablets unearthed at Kültepe (near Kayseri in central Anatolia), which belonged to a flourishing trading colony established there by merchants from Assur some five hundred years later. The basis of this trade was the transport by donkey caravan of tin (which probably came from Elam or beyond to the east), supplemented by quality textiles, from Assur to Kanesh (Kültepe), where the consignments were received for distribution within Anatolia. Recent research indicates that the considerable profits were brought home as silver and gold; copper was not carried except as a medium of exchange within Anatolia.[1]

The emergence of Assyria

The overland trade between Assur and Anatolia continued until the political chaos that overtook northern Mesopotamia after the reign of Hammurabi of Babylon (about 1792–1750 BC) effectively blocked the trade routes. During the inevitable recession Assur came under the domination of the kings of Mitanni in the Khabur basin, but the city nevertheless retained its identity, and during the fourteenth and thirteenth centuries BC its kings embarked on a policy of expansion in their turn. Spectacular marches were made to the Mediterranean in search of cedar logs for ambitious building projects; the remnants of Mitannian hegemony were stamped out; and for a short while Babylon was even annexed. Assur became a major power, and its kings corresponded on equal terms with Egyptian pharaohs and the Great Kings of the Hittites.

Although many of its more distant conquests were impermanent, Assur now ruled a land we may call Assyria, lying almost all to the north, up the Tigris and into the foothills of the Zagros, in the fertile north Mesopotamian plains that had earlier been fragmented into small Amorite and Hurrian principalities. Assur itself, now Qal'at Sherqat on the Tigris, was close to the limit of the rainfall zone, and relied much on irrigated crops in the alluvial riverbed. Further to the north, however, in the newly acquired territories, the reliability of the rainfall increases rapidly as one approaches the mountains; these prime agricultural lands could support a much denser population than the vicinity of Assur, and the geographical nucleus of Assyria was now to be found at cities like Arbil, Nineveh and Kilizu, with their associated lands. Although they too had been subject to the Mitannian kings, Nineveh and Arbil at least had been major centres since prehistoric times, and the result was a decisive shift in the country's centre of gravity.

When the small merchant community found itself with other cities and lands to administer, some transformation was needed. Although the kingship was hereditary, the king seems all along to have been only the first among equals, and it was the traditional merchant families that took over the functions of government: administrative responsibility was couched in terms of commercial liability, and accordingly the least action or instruction was painstakingly documented. The most important 'houses' acted as ministries or provincial governorates, and although these were still based at Assur, archives of the thirteenth century BC illustrating their activities, both public and private, have been found at widely scattered sites: Tell Billa, Tell al-Rimah, Tell Fakhariyah and, most recently, Sheikh Hammad on the middle Khabur.

Transition to the first millennium

At the end of the second millennium there was widespread unrest in the Near East, from which Assyria was not exempt: its long southwestern flank lay exposed to the desert lands between the Tigris and the Euphrates, the traditional homeland of sheep and goat nomads. Incursions from this quarter are a recurrent feature of Mesopotamian history, and from about 1100 BC onwards Assyria suffered intense pressure from a vigorous wave of Aramaean tribes. Years of famine caused by drought weakened the settled population, and the same conditions forced the nomads to press further and further through the countryside towards the hills in search of the grazing they lacked. It seems that at times they had a free run of the heartlands of Assyria, and it was probably only their traditional scorn for and mistrust of urban life that kept them out of the cities and enabled the nucleus of the Assyrian state to survive.

Although nomads do not leave much trace in the archaeological record, site survey west of Nineveh has demonstrated that wide tracts of arable land were abandoned at this time, and the extent of the Aramaean takeover can be gauged from the campaigns by which the Assyrian kings of the tenth and ninth centuries restored Assyria to its former supremacy. The foundations of this success were laid by the tenth-century kings. The first necessity was obviously to re-establish control of the cultivable lands and to promote agricultural prosperity. Their royal inscriptions describe a regular four-pronged plan: 'palaces' (i.e. military and administrative headquarters) were built at strategic points, ploughs were supplied, grain reserves accumulated and draught-horses acquired for the army's chariots. The resettlement of the abandoned territories was thus accomplished, with guaranteed security, agricultural equipment and seed-corn.[2]

Consequently, when Assur-nasir-apli II came to the throne in 883 BC he inherited from his predecessors a flourishing economy with a rich reserve of manpower for his military ambitions. Assyrian rule was acknowledged as far west as the Khabur, and south-eastwards beyond Arrapha (Kerkuk). There was the usual interminable skirmishing in the mountainous terrain on the northern and eastern frontiers, but the tribes offered no serious threat to Assyrian hegemony. Babylon remained weak and disjointed, and the only serious military opposition lay westwards, where a series of vigorous young Aramaean states flourished. The major part of Assyria's military efforts over the ensuing century – and indeed later – were devoted to the progressive defeat of these tenacious Aramaean dynasties. As a result of their assimilation, by the end of the ninth century the whole of the fertile belt from Nineveh west to the Euphrates had irreversibly become part of the Assyrian state, and it was this zone that gave the empire the economic basis for its subsequent expansion.

The only state that rivalled Assyria at this time was the kingdom of Urartu, which had its core in the upland plains of eastern Anatolia around Lake Van (historical Armenia). Urartu was renowned for its metal-working, especially in armour and widely

26.1: *King Assur-nasir-apli II is shown hunting lions (a traditional activity of the Assyrian kings) on this relief from his North-West Palace at Kalhu. Such reliefs are the principal source of evidence for the chariots that were a crucial component of the Assyrian army.*

exported luxury objects of fine craftsmanship, and for its horses and horsemanship. Its provincial capitals, such as Karmir Blur in Soviet Armenia, were defended by massive fortifications, and the mountainous terrain that separated Urartu from Assyria virtually excluded any direct confrontation between the two states. However, at its greatest extent Urartian territory included Lake Rezaiyeh (Urmia) as well as Lake Sevan, and in western Iran as well as northern Syria Urartian and Assyrian spheres of influence did overlap during the eighth century, which led to some hostilities.

The army and the countryside

The Assyrian army, like any other army of its day, depended on three staples: men, corn and transport animals – horses and mules. Because the fighting season coincided with harvest time, the kings continually faced the problem of how to raise troops

without damaging agriculture. One solution to the shortage of agricultural manpower was to deport conquered populations, and this policy was so successful that as the years went by the limits of cultivation were pushed steadily southwards into the 'desert', where renewed political and economic stability made areas of marginal rainfall productive once more. Both in the newly settled areas and on well-established farming lands the majority of the farmers were probably deportees, tied to the land and 'owned' by longer-standing Assyrian families, who were thereby freed for civil or military service – or perhaps simply for the life of absentee urban landlords.

Archaeological and documentary sources agree in giving a picture of barley and some wheat as the predominant cereal crops, mixed in suitable areas further north with a variety of fruits, including large vineyards. Sheep were present in large numbers,

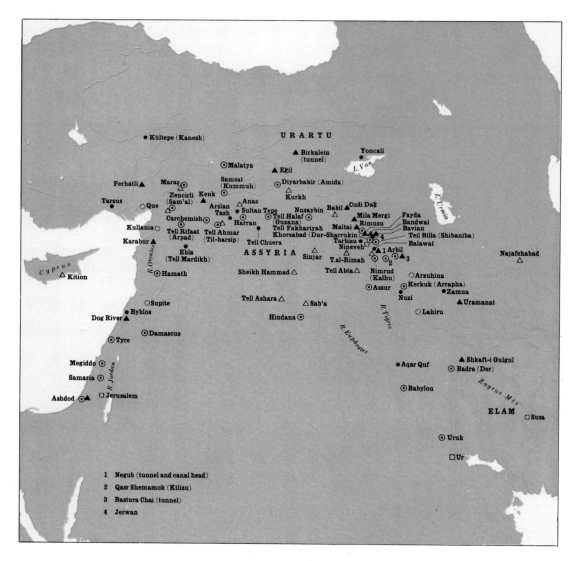

26.2: *The Assyrian empire, with the main towns and monuments to illustrate the archaeological evidence for the extent of the empire.*

□	major towns
⊡	provincial capitals (site fairly certain)
○	provincial capitals (location uncertain)
•	other sites
▲	rock reliefs
△	stelae

1 Negub (tunnel and canal head)

2 Qasr Shemamok (Kilizu)

3 Bastura Chai (tunnel)

4 Jerwan

and there were some goats; donkeys and oxen were the draught animals. Horses and mules formed no part of the average agricultural household, and it is quite likely that there was a virtual government monopoly of these animals. Certainly, from the earliest days of the first millennium kings were concerned to build up their holdings of horses, which were used principally for chariotry and later also for cavalry; the mules, of course, provided equally essential baggage transport. Evidence suggests that the chariotry at least was an exclusive Assyrian wing of the army. They operated in cohorts of fifty, and during the winter months the animals could be billeted in the villages with their own men. From their correspondence it is clear that the kings were much concerned about the sheltering and feeding of the army's animals. As for the infantry, from the eighth century BC the enlargement of the standing army was achieved by recruiting auxiliaries from well-disposed Aramaean tribes, or by enrolling units *en bloc* from the armies of conquered states.[3]

Cities and palaces

The most convenient starting point for the Neo-Assyrian empire is the reign of Assur-nasir-apli II (883–859 BC). Early in his reign this king took the practical step of moving the effective capital of Assyria from its traditional home at Assur to a point nearer the geographical centre of the state. Kings had already taken to launching their campaigns from Nineveh, but Assur-nasir-apli

decided to build his new capital at the ancient but by then decrepit site of Kalhu (modern Nimrud). The capital remained here, and here the kings resided until the reign of Sargon II (721–705 BC); its archaeological remains are correspondingly complex and varied. Khorsabad, on the other hand, which was founded by Sargon to the north-east of Nineveh, did not survive its founder's death as a capital city. His son, Sennacherib (704–681 BC), adopted Nineveh as his capital, and it remained so until its final sack in 612 BC.

The selection of a new capital did not involve merely the construction of a yet more glorious palace for the king. Successive kings also ensured that the city as a whole was worthy of their residence and of its status as capital of the empire. Old temples were restored or new ones built, fortification walls and gates were strengthened and the area they enclosed was greatly enlarged, while subsidiary palaces were built for high officials and close relatives of the king. The construction of temples and city walls was included among the traditional obligations of a Mesopotamian king, as was irrigation work. In the south the maintenance of an efficient irrigation system was of crucial importance; even at Assur the availability of river water on the valley bed was a virtual agricultural necessity. There is plenty of evidence from inscriptions of the relatively simple canalization of Tigris water, and a similar project is attested about 1000 BC for a semi-independent ruler on the middle Khabur. In general, though, the

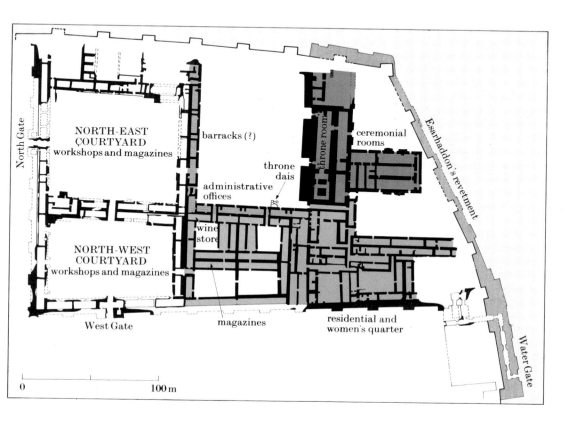

26.3: *'Fort Shalmaneser' is the name given by its excavator, M. E. L. Mallowan, to the great arsenal-palace constructed by Shalmaneser III at the south-east corner of the city of Kalhu (Nimrud). More than in any other palace it is possible, from the architectural design and the cuneiform tablets found in the rooms, to establish the functions of the different parts: the great courtyards enabled the marshalling of men, animals and vehicles; in the south-east courtyard a dais was placed for the review of the troops; in the storerooms were found arms and armour as well as huge quantities of the spoils of war, especially ivory. While the king used his Throne Room only occasionally, the palace had a regular population, including slave girls who were presided over by a 'housekeeper', some of whose archive was found.*

Assyrian kings undertook canal building not so much to meet agricultural needs but in order to improve the amenities of their cherished cities. Assur-nasir-apli II took a canal off the Upper Zab to water orchards and a botanic garden of his creation at Kalhu. Sennacherib undertook very extensive canalization of the streams and springs in the hills north of Nineveh, and although this work certainly benefited the people of the metropolis, it was the artificial swamp and game reserve that caught the royal imagination. Engineering works on this scale leave traces: the canals themselves, sometimes cut out of the rock, can often be detected today, and associated structures have frequently also survived. Sennacherib's activities have left us at least two weirs or dams, and a superb aqueduct at Jerwan, where the main canal was carried on masonry arches across a seasonal wadi bed. At the head of Assur-nasir-apli's Kalhu canal, Esarhaddon (680–619 BC) found it necessary to cut a tunnel and some new sluices out of the natural conglomerate, while Sennacherib was also responsible for a tunnel and a system of *qanats* (see Chapter 30) designed to carry water from a mountain river to the city of Arbil. Such projects were generally commemorated by an inscription at the site that has often survived. Sennacherib alone was in the habit of having scenes carved on the rocks at the head of his canals, and four such reliefs are known.[4]

Most excavation in Assyria has concentrated on the capital cities, and inevitably, because of their sheer size as well as the natural preoccupations of earlier excavators, the palaces dominate the Neo-Assyrian archaeological record, with temples a rather remote second. Each of the major palaces excavated – those of Assur-nasir-apli at Kalhu,[5] of Sargon at Khorsabad,[6] and of Sennacherib and his grandson, Assur-ban-apli, at Nineveh – is a huge complex of interconnecting courtyard units, in which the walls of the public and ceremonial suites are decorated with sculptured bas reliefs. Before the time of Assur-nasir-apli II in the ninth century BC no Assyrian building with this sort of decoration is known, although in the previous millennium there were elaborate wall paintings in reception chambers at Nuzi and at Kar-tukulti-ninurta (near Assur), while painted processions of courtiers are known from a Kassite palace at Aqar Quf. Assur-nasir-apli's own palace at Assur has no reliefs, only glazed plaques fixed to the wall from which the excavators reasonably suppose tapestries may have been hung.[7] Stone relief carving of excellent quality is known from the Middle Assyrian period, but nothing remotely foreshadows the incredible quantity of reliefs in Assur-nasir-apli's palace at Kalhu, which may have been inspired by Neo-Hittite architectural traditions, for example at Carchemish and Tell Halaf.[8]

The palace was more than a royal residence. It acted as treasure-house, audience chambers and administrative centre. The North-West Palace at Kalhu still housed some of the ivory and bronze spoils of war that were so lovingly listed by the kings in their campaign accounts, but it is clear that before long the volume of business became inconvenient, and Shalmaneser III built a special 'review palace' in the lower town of Kalhu for the marshalling and

administration of the army. This was a functional building, in which reliefs and the accompanying huge winged beasts that guarded the gateways were not considered necessary; nevertheless, some older and less prestigious forms of wall decoration remained in use, and as well as simple wall paintings, a magnificent arched panel composed of multi-coloured glazed bricks was installed, with a carved throne-base for the royal throne. More than a century later Shalmaneser's example was followed in the construction of subsidiary palaces and temples of Khorsabad, which included a separate 'review palace' in the outer town. This in turn provided the example for Sennacherib's and Esarhaddon's second palace at Nineveh (Nebi Yunus).

In its capacity as a treasure-house, 'Fort Shalmaneser' has yielded rooms stacked with ivory furniture; like other Assyrian palaces, however, it also housed archaeological treasure of another kind, in the shape of cuneiform tablets. To perpetuate their martial exploits, their prowess in the hunt and their building and engineering achievements, the kings of Assyria left for posterity long inscriptions that provide an invaluable framework of historical events. For obvious reasons, periods of Assyrian recession are less well documented, and even the liveliest of these stereotyped texts tells us next to nothing of the country's internal life, not even of the processes of government. Fortunately, from the palaces of Nineveh and Kalhu in particular there are in compensation three less formal types of document: private legal contracts of loan or sale, reflecting the affairs of those who lived and worked in the palaces, official administrative documents and official correspondence. Thus it is that we have a large body of original letters to (and sometimes from) the Assyrian kings from the time of Tiglath-pileser III (745–727 BC) to Assur-ban-apli (668–627 BC). They deal with military and civilian affairs, the problems of architects without bricks and quartermasters without straw, or report on the state of the harvest or the significance of astrological portents.

The Assyrian provinces

The cuneiform sources make it possible to build up a picture of both the military and the civil administrations. A system of provincial governorates had been inherited from the Middle Assyrian period of the fifteenth to the thirteenth centuries BC, but by the early eighth century BC a weak monarchy seems to have allowed some governors a considerable measure of independence. On his accession in 745 BC Tiglath-pileser III initiated reforms that included the creation of much smaller provincial units and, presumably, a tightening of central control. Each province had a capital town that was often the only one of any size; the majority of these can be at least approximately located. Some of them are ancient cities of north Mesopotamia, others were gradually added to Assyria with the advance of the armies. The texts maintain a strict distinction between various degrees of submission by foreign states and the final abolition of independent status and incorporation within the provincial system. Many of the later provincial capitals of the west had once been the seats of local Aramaean or Neo-Hittite dynasties, and these, like Carchemish or Damascus, are usually easy to identify. It is mainly in the Zagros region to the east and north-east that the extent of Assyrian direct rule is not accurately known.

The provincial governor was directly answerable to the king, and although in every province he was entrusted with the collection of taxes and the conscription of soldiers, the particular demands made by the central government and the extent of the governor's administrative reach would naturally have varied according to the political and geographical situation of the province. The royal archives reveal some of the points of contact between province and palace: reports from the north-eastern provinces on Urartian military manoeuvres, requests to the governors nearest Nineveh for labour to help with the construction of Sargon's new capital at Khorsabad, information on the movement and welfare of deportees, and news of tribal affairs on the Median frontiers. Most im-

portant of all was the defence of the empire, which required both the maintenance of an adequate and vigilant standing force and participation on request in any major or minor campaigns beyond the existing frontiers. Sometimes, as once in Cilicia, the royal annals admit that a governor was sent out alone to undertake a foreign campaign, but more often major undertakings were at least nominally under royal command.

Outside the centre excavated traces of Assyrian administration are rather sketchy. Within an area bounded by the Euphrates at

26.4: *Relief sculptures often illustrate campaigns in the manner of a cartoon strip: here a city is captured with siege engines (lower left), the population deported, and the spoil carried off, while scribes (one cuneiform, one Aramaic) dutifully record it. This relief dates from the reign of Tiglath-pileser III.*

Carchemish and by the Zagros various small townships have been investigated, and they yield recognizably Assyrian levels. Legal and administrative documents have turned up at Sultan Tepe (Huzirina), Tell Halaf (Guzana), Tell Billa (Šibaniba) and Balawat (Imgur-Enlil), and a single tablet each at Tell al-Rimah and Carchemish. Sultan Tepe remains the only site apart from the capital cities to have produced a proper library. At Tell Ahmar (Til-Barsip) to the south of Carchemish, the governor's palace was decorated with wall paintings in imitation of the stone reliefs of the metropolis,[9] and other characteristically Assyrian architectural elements have been unearthed at Sherikhan (Tarbisu) and Arslan Tash (Hadattu). Some of the most important provincial capitals (for example, Harran, Arbil and Arrapha) are still untouched, often because of heavy later overburdens or modern occupation.

Almost all the towns mentioned so far had been within Assyrian borders from the time of Shalmaneser III (858–824 BC), and by the seventh century they had long since lost any pretensions to independence. Further afield, however, there were much less thoroughly Assyrianized provinces. Levels coinciding with Assyrian rule have been excavated at Palestinian, Syrian and Anatolian sites such as Gezer, Samaria, Tell Rifaat (Arpad), Zencirli (Sam'al), Tarsus and Malatya, but apart from the occasional cuneiform tablet or fragmentary royal inscription, such sites have yielded little to betray Assyrian influence.

The Assyrians, of course, also left traces of their presence beyond their frontiers: in the mountains from the Lebanon eastwards to Khuzistan one may still visit the carved images and boastful inscriptions of the Assyrian conquerors, chiselled on the rock in a tradition of victory monuments that stretched back two millennia. In mountainous areas their control was at best fitful, so care was generally taken to make such carvings inaccessible to unsympathetic natives. On other occasions a free-standing monument might be erected, usually in a gateway, a temple or an open space within the city, to commemorate either a military success or the completion of a building project. Various *stelae* have been found in the capital and the provincial cities of Assyria as well as further afield.

Assyrians and foreigners

Assyrian influence may sometimes be hard to detect in the more remote provinces, but there is no lack of evidence for the reverse process. As well as the material testimony supplied by the plunder found stacked in the palaces of Nineveh, Kalhu and Khorsabad – such as Phoenician ivories and Egyptian vases – there is ample textual evidence for contact with distant lands. During the seventh century Nineveh became increasingly cosmopolitan. Quite apart from the visits of client kings or their emissaries, who often came to greet the Assyrian king at a New Year ceremony in his palace, and of their sons, who might be brought up as hostages in the Assyrian court, Egyptians and Iranians lived permanently in the capital. Some of these may have been deportees, many of whom had been settled in the heart of Assyria, but even high

offices of state were filled by men with Aramaean or even Phoenician names. Foreign merchants are occasionally mentioned, but the question of trade is debated: it has been suggested that the administrative control of commodity movements within the empire made trade as such superfluous, while for political reasons the longer-distance routes skirted the imperial borders. However, it seems unlikely that all the trading instincts of the Assyrians had perished, and there is sufficient evidence to indicate that privately organized trade, at least in luxury and semi-luxury items, did persist.[10]

As the monopoly of the traditional Assyrian families in government had been eroded, so their language was fighting a losing battle against Aramaic, which had the double advantage of being written in the simpler alphabetic script and of being spoken and understood from southern Babylonia to Palestine. The royal palace had a chief scribe proficient in both Assyrian and Aramaic, at least from the reign of Sargon (721–705 BC), and this was no doubt the origin of a chancery style adopted by the Persian empire, where Aramaic was used as an official *lingua franca*. Assyrian culture seems to have consisted predominantly of Babylonian artistic and written traditions mixed with influences from the west.

In so far as Assyria left a legacy, it was in the sphere of imperial administration: although it had no direct geographical successor, the methods of military and civil organization developed during the last century of Assyrian rule were inherited by the component parts of the empire and reappeared recognizably in the Neo-Babylonian and Achaemenian empires.

27. Late Period Egypt and Nubia

By the first millennium BC Egypt was no longer a semi-isolated and autonomous state that periodically extended imperial control over neighbouring areas, but was forced to take part in wider international power struggles with emerging forces such as those of Assyria and, later, Persia. As periods of foreign domination alternated with intervals of independence, not merely were strong continuities with the past evident in art and culture, but a deliberate archaism provided a refuge from contemporary troubles.

However, relations with newly important areas such as Greece increasingly introduced new elements into the Egyptian world, especially in the north, while the continuing urbanization of areas to the south created independent neighbours that were no longer under Egyptian domination.

The Third Intermediate Period (Dynasties XXI–XXV)

During this period internal political cohesion gradually disintegrated, and massive foreign intervention followed. Dynasty XXI of Tanis claimed formal authority throughout Egypt but in practice ceded control of middle and southern Egypt to a hereditary line of rulers who were also high priests of Amen, the Theban god formerly the state deity of the New Kingdom. The two lines were succeeded by Dynasty XXII of Tranis-Bubastis, who was descended from a long series of acculturated Libyan army commanders. Within a century and a half centrifugal tendencies had intensified. A formally recognized collateral dynasty (XXIII) emerged, with authority over Egypt from Leontopolis southwards; Tanis retained loose control over the Delta. The hereditary rulers of Thebes, Heracleopolis and Memphis were already semi-independent and increasingly claimed variable degrees of royal status. They were joined less than a hundred years later by further lines centred on Sais, six other Delta towns and Hermopolis. Interrelations were complex and periodically hostile. Sais was achieving dominance when the divided country fell relatively easily (728–715 BC) to the army of the Kushite Dynasty XXV, the first truly 'national' dynasty for two hundred years.

External pressure had not, however, caused this period of disintegration. The sharp decline in royal power and prestige in the late New Kingdom had enabled provincial nobilities and local army commanders to increase their regional power and influence. From Dynasty XXI onwards the royal solution was the same: the delegation of combined military, civil and ecclesiastical powers to royal relatives installed as governors of different regions. This inevitably generated competitive collateral dynasties, contributing to further disintegration.

The Kushites left the political system fragmented so that Egypt could not threaten their home kingdom in the Sudan and focused Egypto–Kushite efforts upon resisting Assyrian expansion into the Levant. Several clashes showed Assyria that Kushite Egypt, while peripheral to Assyrian interests, would always destabilize its Levantine conquests, and it soon conquered Egypt (674–663 BC). Assyrian efforts to keep its Egyptian vassals sufficiently divided so that they could not threaten the Levant, yet sufficiently cohesive to prevent Kushite reoccupation, created circumstances favourable to the renewed expansion of Sais, which gradually developed a centralized national government while Assyria was distracted elsewhere.

The Late Period (Dynasties XXVI–XXXI)

The 140-year period of 'Saite' (Dynasty XXVI) rule was the last long period of independence combined with stability. Although there were several military rebellions, in general the period was later reported to be that of Egypt's 'greatest prosperity'.[1] Reunification had been achieved by Psamtik I (664–610 BC), who combined Carian and Ionian mercenaries with *machimoi*, the Egyptian military class, to conquer the Delta and to reinforce the skilful diplomacy through which he negotiated the gradual relinquishing of power by the southern Egyptian dynasts. Thereafter Greeks were encouraged to settle permanently in landed military colonies in Egypt, and an aggressive foreign policy developed against Babylonia, the new 'great power' in the Levant. Increasingly this was maintained through sea power, as the army proved unreliable abroad.

By the late sixth century BC Persia had become the principal threat, and Saite opposition provoked the transformation of Egypt into a Persian province ruled by a satrap. During more than a century of increasingly harsh Persian control several rebellions were attempted, and in 405 BC Egypt became independent (Dynasties XXVIII–XXX). The sixty years of this period of independence are not yet well documented; a centralized system of government certainly existed and extensive royal building programmes indicate a prosperous economy, but there were serious dynastic disputes that involved depositions and sometimes civil war, while vigorous Persian attempts at reconquest imposed severe military strains. Eventually Egypt fell to Persia in 343 BC, and shortly after to Alexander and his heirs, the Macedonian Ptolemaic dynasty.

Egyptian society and archaeology in the first millennium BC

During these frequently disturbed periods there were major fluctuations in the character of Egyptian life, so far best documented in texts, art and monumental architecture. The systematic excavation of contemporary town sites has begun only very recently, while few representative cemeteries have yet been adequately recorded. During the Third Intermediate Period the centrifugal political system and the recurrent civil wars and foreign invasions stimulated the growth of many heavily fortified towns, often referred to in texts and sometimes still visible archaeologically. There was probably a marked contraction of the comparatively expansive rural settlement pattern of the New Kingdom. The prevalent world view also changed, emphasizing the interventionary role of the gods in human affairs, minimizing that of the discredited kingship and stressing local patriotism and cults. Land values fell, which reflected the physical insecurity of exposed farmland and the need to produce surpluses only for regional needs, not for those of a national redistributive system.

Recentralization in the Late Period brought prosperity, stability and a deliberately cultivated 'archaism' to counteract the negative effects of former distress. Textually, society is better documented in indigenous documents and in the valuable descriptions of Herodotus and later Greek writers, but the archaeology of urban life is virtually unknown. Presumably, under the Saites and Persians fortified towns were not permitted and rural expansion probably recurred, but the disturbances of Dynasties XXVIII–XXX may have led to refortification and concentration. A number of massive temple enclosures, defining areas large enough to include substantial towns, apparently belong to this time.

The general archaeological assemblage is also less comprehensively defined because the custom of depositing secular items in tombs largely ceased, itself an indication of an important shift in funerary beliefs. The funerary items (coffins, figurines, canopic jars and amulets) do, however, show marked typological changes that must have been paralleled in the secular realm.

The archaeology of kingship has survived best, though we are deprived of most royal tombs because the desert cemeteries, exposed to robbery, were abandoned in favour of burial within or close to royal cities. At Tanis some royal tombs of Dynasties XXI–XXII (not in pyramidal form) have been excavated, but those of Sais and later dynasties are perhaps irrecoverable. Similarly, apart from a dubious example of Apries at Memphis, royal palaces have not been explored. Temples, the other chief expression of royal architecture, are better known. During the Third Intermediate Period Tanis and (intermittently) Thebes were the chief beneficiaries, but later new temples were built and others enlarged throughout Egypt. Unfortunately, many are known only through fragments, but clearly the traditional plan and decorative schemes were still being followed.

In the Third Intermediate Period a fairly high level of art and technology was maintained at royal centres, to judge from the well-made coffins (silver in some cases), jewellery and artifacts from the Tanis tombs, and occasional statues in stone and even bronze with silver and gold inlay. The standard of provincial art, however, was very low, as many crudely carved *stelae* attest. From Dynasty XXV onwards quality improved nationally, as fragments of temple and tomb decoration and a series of grandees' tombs (Dynasties XXV–XXVI) at Thebes show. Technically accomplished reliefs and paintings reveal a fascinating amalgam

27.1: *Map of Egypt and Nubia, showing the major sites mentioned in the text.*

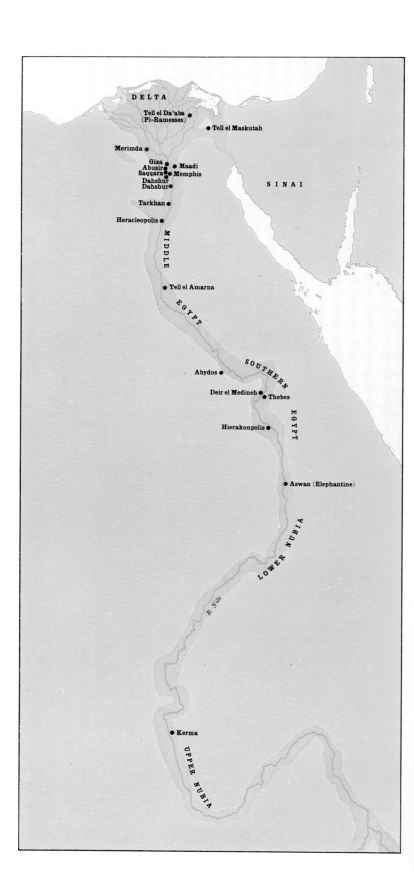

of Old and New Kingdom styles and even subject matter with a fashionable new 'realistic' style. Archaism, evident in royal names and bureaucratic titles, was deliberate policy. In religious art especially it opened up channels of communication with, and the transfer of power from, a supernaturally potent past. Statuary, royal and private, adhered variously to traditional canons, to a sometimes striking realism and, increasingly, to a mannered style leading to the softly modelled characteristics of Ptolemaic art.

Foreign relations

Despite periodic bouts of aggression in the Levant between Dynasties XXI and XXX, Egypt never rebuilt its New Kingdom empire, partly because the region was dominated by powers of superior strength, partly because the indigenous political units – for example, Israel and the Phoenicians – were stronger and more cohesive than before. There were strong diplomatic and commercial links. In the tenth century BC Israelite government followed pharaonic models, while the Phoenicians, inspired by the jewellery, ivory carvings and decorated metal bowls and faience cups from Third Intermediate Period Egypt, created an 'Egyptianizing' style that diffused over much of the New East. Relations with Ionian, island and mainland Greeks were also important. Greek military settlers aided the Saites, and later the armies of Dynasties XXVIII and XXX included many Greek soldiers. The presence of these soldiers was disturbing, however; as they were mercenaries hired for money or troops sent by Greek states in temporary alliance with Egypt against Persia, lack of money or political change could lead to their abrupt withdrawal, while their leaders became unduly influential in internal affairs. Egyptian kings sent aid to Greek allies and votive gifts to famous Greek shrines, and an extensive trading network developed. Greek traders probably entered the west Delta in the seventh century BC. Later (by Dynasty XXVI) they were concentrated at Naucratis, where they had their own temples, and later still they probably enjoyed freer access to Egyptian markets. Egypt was little influenced by Greece, but Greek architectural styles, building technology, possibly vase painting and above all statuary were strongly influenced by Egyptian knowledge and models. At a lower level many 'Egyptianizing' decorative artifacts were made by Greek craftsmen in Egypt and the east. Despite a romantic view of Egypt as the source of all knowledge, the philosophy, science and mathematics of the Greeks in fact owed little to Egypt.[2]

Nubia and Sudan

This region – Kush – was more strongly influenced by Egypt than any of the other contact areas, the critical period being the ninth to seventh centuries BC and the seminal region Upper Nubia; Lower Nubia was practically uninhabited for most of the first millennium BC. Kushites were ethnically and linguistically different from Egyptians, and their earliest royal tombs (at Kurru) show little trace of the Egyptianization that had characterized Upper Nubia in the New Kingdom. However, New Kingdom temples survived as visible monuments and perhaps as functioning cult centres in the area, while the early Kurru tombs (ninth to eighth centuries BC) reveal trade with Egypt and possibly the presence of imported Egyptian builders. Cultural contact naturally intensified during Dynasty XXV, when Egypt came under Kushite control. Egyptian became an official language; the Kushite pantheon was made up of Egyptian gods; and temples were built in Kush by Egyptian artisans guided by Egyptian scribes. The successors of Dynasty XXV ruled Kush (including the Butana) for many centuries, based first at Napata ('Napatan' period, mid-sixth to fourth centuries BC) and later at Meroë ('Meroitic' period, fourth century BC to fourth century AD). Court culture remained heavily Egyptianized, despite the absence of documented 'official' contact, apart from a raid on Napata by Psamtik II (595–589 BC); trade, and the occasional use of Egyptian artisans, continued.

Although archaeological data on Napatan Kush is very incomplete, the cemeteries in which kings and queens were buried, first at Kurru and later at Nuri (both near Napata), are well documented. The earliest tombs (ninth to eighth centuries BC) are non-Egyptian, with earthen tumuli covering pit and chamber tombs, but later rectilinear superstructures, sometimes constructed of stone masonry, indicate the use of Egyptian artisans. Piankhy (747–716 BC) built the first pyramid after the conquest of Memphis, and pyramids remained typical of Napatan and Meroitic royal burials. The stone pyramids are small and their angle (60° to 70°) like that of non-royal pyramids of New Kingdom and later Egypt, but their use was surely inspired by the Old Kingdom royal pyramids, symbolic of the famous past now being revived. Unlike the earlier Egyptian royal cemeteries, Napatan ones were restricted to kings and queens, the elite being buried elsewhere, although at Nuri royal chariot horses were buried in neat rows. Royal burial chambers were sometimes decorated in Egyptian style, but the offering chapel on the east side of each pyramid was undecorated. Royal grave goods were very rich and strongly Egyptian in style, but the few excavated non-royal cemeteries show that while a substantial portion of the population was heavily Egyptianized, many people preferred distinctively Kushitic graves and burial customs and had funerary gifts of non-Egyptian types.

Wealth derived from trade and manufacturing, and the example of urbanized Egypt, led to the growth of major towns. Usually evident from surface remains, these have rarely been excavated, and then only partially. Better-known are several Napatan temples, adhering to Egyptian tradition in plan and decoration and showing the mixture of archaizing and realistic styles that is seen in Egypt.[3]

During the first millennium BC, despite fluctuating political fortunes, the population of Egypt rose to two or three times its level in the Old Kingdom. Nevertheless, although rich, Egypt was no longer unique; and as neighbouring areas developed both economically and politically, it was forced to take its place as merely one element in a wider regional configuration.

28. The Levant in the early first millennium BC

The disturbances in the eastern Mediterranean at the end of the Late Bronze Age (about 1200 BC), which led to the collapse of the Egyptian and Hittite empires, left a power vacuum in the Levant that new population groups were quick to exploit. The earliest of these were the Israelites. Some of their tribes may already have begun to settle in southern and central Canaan in the preceding centuries, but their main impact was felt after the Exodus of Moses and his followers from Egypt, probably in the mid-thirteenth century BC.[1] At this time the Egyptians were engaged in defending their country from attacks by, among others, the so-called Sea Peoples,[2] refugees and marauders from the Mediterranean islands; at the beginning of the twelfth century at least one group of these, the Philistines (Peleset), were able to occupy the southern coastal plain of the land to which they gave their name, Palestine. Meanwhile, in inland Syria, warlike pastoral tribes from the fringes of the desert, known first as Akhlamu and then as Aramaeans, were exerting pressure on the more fertile regions surrounding them and were beginning to establish states of their own.[3] Yet, despite these disruptions and incursions, not all of the Late Bronze Age cities were destroyed. In northern and central Syria centres such as Carchemish, Aleppo and Hamath managed to survive the overthrow of the Hittite empire, of which they had once been part, and played an important role in transmitting the culture of that empire to its first-millennium successors. Of even greater importance was the survival of an independent Canaanite population along the coast north of Mount Carmel, where, unaffected by the Philistine and Israelite invasions farther south, and protected by the high Lebanese mountains from the Aramaean hordes to the east, they were able to preserve their Late Bronze Age culture almost intact and, in the course of time, to spread it westwards throughout the Mediterranean basin.

Lack of texts and of reliable archaeological evidence makes the actual course of events during the first (and most formative) two centuries of the Iron Age difficult to follow, but from the beginning of the first millennium the picture is clearer. In coastal Palestine the five city-states of the Philistine federation – the Pentapolis – had already passed their heyday and by the late tenth century BC were on the eve of defeat at the hands of David, king of Israel, though they were to retain some form of independence until their incorporation into the Assyrian empire three centuries later. The Canaanites on the Syrian coast – or Phoenicians, as the Greeks called them took advantage of the local natural resources of good harbours and fine timber to develop those skills in shipbuilding and seafaring for which they became famous. Particularly after the decline of the Philistines, Phoenician towns such as Aradus, Byblos, Sidon and Tyre flourished on the profits of overseas trade, which took their merchants as far afield as Spain (and possibly Cornwall)

in the west and Arabia in the south, and which even their gradual incorporation into the Assyrian empire in the eighth and seventh centuries did little to diminish.[4] As for inland Syria, little is known in detail of the fortunes of the Aramaeans, though it is clear that not only did they form states of their own in the south but, during the tenth and ninth centuries, they also took control of most of the neo-Hittite towns that had survived since the Late Bronze Age. However, the Aramaean states were exposed in the east to the resurgent power of Assyria, and despite some initial successful resistance (as, for example, at the battle of Qarqar, near Hamath, in 853 BC, where a coalition of Aramaean rulers forced Shalmaneser III to halt his advance), they gradually succumbed, and by the end of the eighth century had all been included in the Assyrian empire.

Politically, the most remarkable and best-known development in the Levant in the early first millennium BC is the establishment of the Israelite state – remarkable, because it was the most successful of the various attempts by the new Iron Age populations to achieve independent nationhood; best-known, because despite problems of interpretation, the Old Testament still forms the best historical source for the period.[5] By about 1020 BC the original tribes of Israel had been forced by the pressure of hostile neighbours (of whom the Philistines were the most dangerous) to unite under one leader, Saul, and the monarchy was thus created. It was left, however, to the next two kings, David (c. 1010–970) and Solomon (c. 970–930), to take the new state to the apogee of its power. Essentially a soldier, David was able, by a series of brilliant campaigns, to extend his rule not only over the whole of Palestine (with the exception of Philistia) but also over most of the country east of the river Jordan and parts of southern Syria. His more peaceful son, Solomon, consolidated these gains by administrative reorganization on the one hand and by cultural and economic alliances with neighbouring states, especially the Phoenicians, on the other. For a few brief decades the United Kingdom of Israel was certainly the most powerful and probably the most prosperous state in the Levant. It was a short-lived achievement, however. On Solomon's death tribal jealousies, fuelled by resentment of oppressive taxation and forced labour that had marred the king's achievements, led to a division of the realm into two separate kingdoms, Israel in northern Palestine and Judah in the south. Rivals more often than not, the Divided Kingdoms faced external threats as well, from a re-emergent Egypt in the south, from the Transjordanian states of Ammon and Edom in the east and from the Aramaeans in the north – but also increasingly, and inexorably, from Assyria (see Chapter 26). The political history of the Levant in the ninth and eighth centuries, as far as we know it, is little more than a tedious recital of Assyrian campaigns and destructions of cities. Inevitably Israel fell; in 722 BC the capital, Samaria, was ravaged by Sargon II and its inhabitants deported. The southern kingdom, Judah, survived for another century or more, but only as a vassal state. In 587 BC, after a series of rebellions, it too was destroyed by Nebuchadnezzar, the Babylonian heir of

Assyria. With its collapse the entire Levant was once more part of an empire and entered a new chapter of its history.

Cultural development

The outline of political events given above is based mainly upon textual evidence; archaeology in the strict sense has added little to our knowledge and has served only to add a touch of vividness to our understanding of events already known – as is the case, for example, with the fall of Samaria, where the ferocity of the Assyrian destruction is amply confirmed by the excavated remains. Of the material culture of the Levant during these centuries, however, archaeology has revealed a great deal, although even here the evidence is very unsatisfactory.[6] In the first place, both the excavation techniques and the interpretative methods used by archaeologists in this area until very recently fell far short of what are now regarded as acceptable, and the emphasis was all too often simply on the recovery of monumental architecture, art objects and inscriptions. For the period with which we are concerned, the study of settlement patterns, ancient agriculture, the sources of raw materials and the problems of environmental change – to name but a few aspects of the ancient world that now concern the archaeologist – has hardly begun. In the second place, archaeological research has been largely concentrated in the area of ancient Israel, and comparatively few Iron Age sites have been investigated in Syria or Lebanon. This geographical imbalance in the evidence makes it possible that any generalizations based upon it will eventually be proved wrong.

One generalization that is surely accurate, however, is that the Iron Age inhabitants of Syro-Palestine, whether Israelites, Phoenicians or Aramaeans, were culturally the heirs of their Late Bronze Age ancestors. This is clearly demonstrable in architecture, for example. The most famous building of the Iron Age Levant is probably the temple of Solomon at Jerusalem; and although nothing of this remains, it is described in some detail in the First Book of Kings.[7] The descriptions are detailed enough to show that its plan, of three rooms one behind the other, must have resembled closely the temple excavated at Tell Ta'yinat, near Antioch, which dates to the ninth century. The Old Testament indicates that the temple at Jerusalem was adjacent to Solomon's palace, and this is also true of Ta'yinat and of other sites, where temple–palace complexes have been uncovered. Many of these palaces conform to a design in which a wide, columned portico forms the main entrance, leading to a broad, shallow room that served as the official audience chamber of the king. Prototypes for this distinctive plan have been found in northern Syria in the Late Bronze Age (the palaces of Ras Shamra and Alalakh IV, for instance), but the earliest known true example is that built by Solomon in the tenth century as part of his fortified administrative centre at Megiddo.[8] The plan was adopted by Assyrian architects and became a standard feature of palaces throughout the empire.

The military architecture of the period also demonstrates both the debt of the Iron Age Levant to the Late Bronze Age and the basic cultural homogeneity of Palestine and Syria. Fortifications built by Solomon and his successors at Hazor, Megiddo, Gezer and

28.1: *Sarcophagus of Ahiram, king of Byblos. The inscription on the lid, which gives the name of the king, is one of the earliest examples of the use of the Phoenician alphabet, later borrowed and adapted by the Greeks. Most scholars date the sarcophagus to c. 1000 BC. The carved scenes on the sides and ends are typical of Canaanite and Phoenician art, with its mixture of Egyptian and Asiatic motifs. Some experts believe the carving to indicate a thirteenth-century date, in which case Ahiram must have reused it, but such precise dating of this eclectic, derivative style is not really possible.*

Samaria, for example, and by their contemporaries in Syria at such sites as Carchemish, typically comprise a casemate system – parallel walls with rooms between – and a multiple-entry gateway, both features that were widespread in the Levant and Anatolia in the second millennium.[9] Masonry and construction techniques were perhaps rather more varied, but at their best, in the 'royal quarters' at Megiddo (tenth century) and Samaria (ninth century), they are characterized by extremely fine ashlar work (in which stones are square-cut), often with a distinctive marginal drafting, again derived from the styles of Late Bronze Age Canaan and again influencing the Assyrian builders of, for example, Nimrud.

The highest achievements of Levantine craftsmanship are to be seen not in architecture, however, but in the decorative arts, especially ivory carving and fine metalwork. Ivory carving was an ancient craft that had its roots, perhaps, in woodworking; the

Levant was a forested region, and elephants also were to be found there until the first millennium BC. Copper and silver were also readily available, though gold and tin had to be imported. Examples of finely decorated metal vessels and jewellery are not common in the Levant itself; they are better represented by finds from the Phoenician colonies in the western Mediterranean. Ivories, however, have been better preserved in Levantine sites, for example at Samaria, where pieces made for the decoration of the palace of Ahab, king of Israel (*c.* 874–853 BC), have been found.[10] Some of these ivories from Phoenicia and Israel found their way eastwards as booty in the wake of the Assyrian military campaigns; they stimulated similar production by Aramaean and Assyrian craftsmen, examples of whose work have been found at Nimrud and elsewhere. Many fine ivory objects have also come from the Phoenician colonies of the west. From these finds it can be seen

28.2: *The Levant in the early first millennium BC, showing political and ethnic groups, major towns and trade routes.*

28.3: *Ivory plaque from Samaria, probably part of the wall or furniture decoration of the palace of Ahab. The plaque, which is about 7 centimetres high, shows a sphinx in a lotus thicket, a motif of Egyptian origin that was popular with Phoenician craftsmen.*

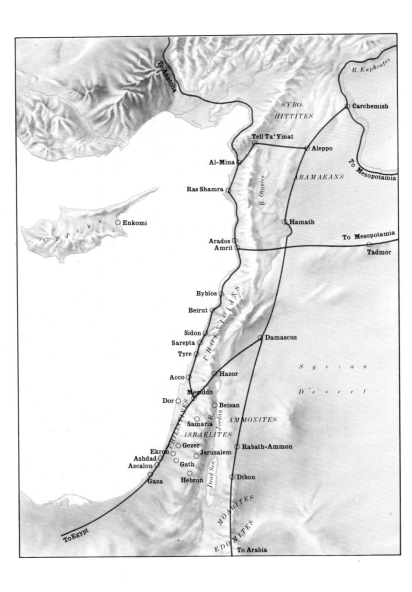

that in essence Phoenician and Aramaean art was little different from Canaanite art of half a millennium earlier. It was eclectic and syncretic, based on motifs and conventions derived from elsewhere – Egypt, Mesopotamia and Anatolia – but it used them in uncanonical and original ways that would have been anathema to the more conservative artists of other countries, yet gave Levantine art the freshness and vitality that is its special merit.

The wide distribution of Levantine art objects throughout the Mediterranean basin is illustrative of what must be considered the most important role played by the Phoenicians in the history of civilization – the diffusion of culture as a consequence of trade. From early times trade had played a large part in the economy of the Levant, a region richly endowed with certain natural resources – timber, copper and silver ores, precious stones, olives and grapes – and situated astride major natural routes. The Canaanites

28.4: *Plan of Megiddo, with (in red) the buildings attributed to Solomon (c. 970– 930 BC) and (in black) those attributed to Ahab, ruler of the northern kingdom of Israel c. 875–854. Megiddo was probably a royal administrative centre rather than a town in the strict sense, and the buildings are mostly monumental in character.*

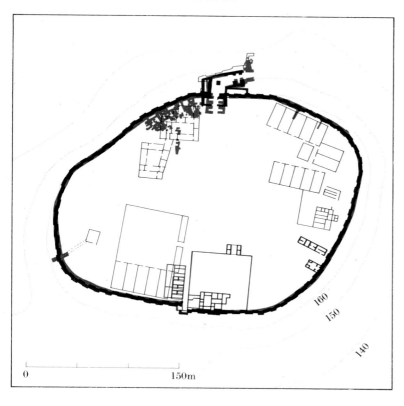

had been pre-eminently traders (the word itself possibly means 'merchant'), and their first-millennium successors were no different. Israelite commercial ventures in the south, towards the incense-producing regions of Arabia (see Chapter 31), are best known from the biblical story of the visit of the Queen of Sheba to Solomon's court, and much of the later conflict between the kingdoms of Israel and Judah with their neighbours in Transjordan probably stemmed from a need to control the main route south. Further north, the Aramaeans were among the first to use the camel, recently domesticated,[11] in opening up routes across, rather than around, the steppes and deserts of inland Syria. But it was the Phoenicians who ventured furthest. With timber for building ships and harbours for sheltering them, they were ideally suited to replace their Canaanite ancestors and the Mycenaeans on the seaways of the Mediterranean. The earliest Phoenician settlements overseas were not colonies in the true sense but were simply trading centres, established wherever a good anchorage and a friendly reception were to be found. Only later, when Phoenicia itself came under the threat of Assyrian aggression, did a real emigration movement develop. Despite the accounts of the Classical historians, who place the foundation of Phoenician settlements at Lixus and Utica (in north-west Africa) and Gades (in Spain) in the twelfth century BC, the archaeological evidence suggests that the earliest centres (in Cyprus, where the attraction was the rich copper deposits) in fact date back only to the tenth century, and that the expansion to the west, in search of the tin and gold of Spain, did not begin until the late ninth century, with the founding of Carthage in 814 BC.[12] Many of these western colonies, especially Carthage, did found daughter settlements in their turn, so that in the course of time the western Mediterranean basin was almost as 'orientalized' as the eastern.

The trading networks established by Phoenicians, Aramaeans and Israelites were responsible not only for the diffusion of Canaanite art but also for the spread of something much more vital to the growth of civilization – an alphabetic script.[13] The alphabetic principle – according to which one sign represents one sound – had been invented in Canaan during the second millennium, probably as a response to the merchants' need for a system of recording that was simpler and easier to learn than that provided by the cumbersome hieroglyphic or cuneiform signs of Egypt and Mesopotamia. Various 'alphabets' were devised, but the most successful was that adopted by the Phoenicians towards the end of the second millennium and best known from the inscription on the sarcophagus of King Ahiram of Byblos (see Figure 28.1). The Aramaeans adopted this script, and within a few centuries it became the standard form of writing throughout the Assyrian, and later the Persian, empire. In similar fashion, the Phoenician script was transmitted to the west, although with greater modification, and became the vehicle of writing for, in turn, the Greeks, the Etruscans and the Romans. Between them, the Phoenician and Aramaic scripts are the progenitors of every alphabet in use today throughout the world.

29. Iron Age Greece and the eastern Mediterranean

In 1000 BC the Greeks were few, isolated and impoverished, and almost all of them lived in mainland Greece or on the adjacent islands. By the time Alexander the Great ascended the Macedonian throne in 336 BC their settlements stretched from Spain to Turkey, from Russia to Egypt, and this enlarged world had undergone unprecedented economic growth and structural alteration. For the Greeks had established the stock of productive techniques that was to remain basically unchanged until the Middle Ages. They had created some 1500 political units linked within a shipping distance of forty to sixty days. They had invented, in the Peiraeus of Athens, a focus for Mediterranean exchange where something like a market economy first appeared. They had evolved a way of seeing that, filtered through the vision of the Renaissance, still influences ours today. Finally, and not least, they had inaugurated the process of Hellenization, the absorption of Greek culture by non-Greeks, that was to be dramatically accelerated in the wake of Alexander's eastern conquests.

The Greek dark age, c. 1100–800 BC

The period 1100–800 BC is a 'dark age' partly because it is opaque to us, and partly because the scanty archaeological remains betoken a cultural recession between the Mycenaean era and the 'renaissance' of the eighth century. Population shrank drastically at first, by up to 90 per cent in previously prosperous areas like Messenia. Communications were reduced. The level of material technique dropped sharply. However, these dark centuries were also in two fundamental respects the formative period of historical Greece. First, the political and linguistic map was redrawn by population movements – that of Doric speakers from backward north-west Greece to the Peloponnese, the southern Aegean islands and south-west Anatolia, and that of Aeolic and Ionic speakers from central Greece to the northern and central coastlands of western Anatolia respectively. Second, the more progressive areas of the Greek world achieved the technological breakthrough implied in an alternative title for the period, the Early Iron Age.

The most significant legacies of Mycenaean civilization were non-material. Yet the legatees were not merely passive recipients. New gods, for instance, joined or supplanted the old, and new sanctuaries were founded, sometimes on the site of a Bronze Age cult (though nowhere has continuity of worship been demonstrated archaeologically), more often on a virgin site or one that had been used for settlement in Mycenaean times. The most abundant, though partial, witness to such developments is painted pottery. By 900 BC the Protogeometric style had spread to most parts of the Greek world from Thessaly to Caria, but its leading producers and probable inventors were the potters and painters of Athens.[1] However, the modest scale even of Athenian production and the impoverishment of the eleventh and tenth centuries generally are conveyed by the grave goods from Athens's main dark age cemetery: a little over two hundred Protogeometric vases and, apart from bronze finger-rings and pins, fewer than twenty other objects.

Nevertheless, in a period without written records, or indeed writing of any kind, the Protogeometric and subsequent Geometric (ninth–eighth centuries) pottery does provide a chronological framework for cultural changes. Most significant by far was the introduction of iron technology, probably via Cyprus, so that by 800 BC the crucial edged implements were typically of iron rather than bronze.[2] This advance seems to have been forced on the Greeks by a shortage of bronze (or rather, tin) in the years around 1000 BC. But from the early ninth century there are further signs of a cultural awakening, particularly in areas with eastern – that is, probably Phoenician – connections. Ivory, gold and faience were imported once more, and long-forgotten techniques like filigree, granulation and inlaying were relearned. In Crete and Attika oriental master-craftsmen came to settle, but by 800 Greek traders had responded in kind by establishing themselves at Al Mina in Syria and perhaps Tarsus in Cilicia, no doubt to obtain the metals the Greeks lacked.

The Greek renaissance and Phrygia, c. 800–700 BC

The eighth century was an era of rapid and extensive movement, prompted apparently by demographic increase.[3] The explanation is to be sought in the agrarian development hinted at by the model granaries deposited in richly furnished Attic tombs, a development facilitated by iron technology. Greece and coastal Asia Minor, however, were relatively poor in arable land, poorer even than today, as the fertile coastal lowlands built up by river alluvium had not yet formed. So population pressure motivated a further sustained wave of migration from about 775 to 550 BC. This 'colonizing' movement was mainly confined to the familiar climatic zone between 35° and 45° of latitude.

Traders led the way, above all Euboian islanders who, after taking the initiative at Al Mina, had by 750 also settled in Italy (see Chapter 34). Their example was soon followed by agrarian colonists, mainly from the Peloponnese. This western trade and colonization not only relieved social tensions in the motherland but also promoted fruitful contact with urnfield Europe (see Chapter 33). By 720 Greek bronzeworkers under European influence could produce masterpieces like the two-piece corslet excavated in an aristocratic burial at Argos.

However, the greatest stimulus to the eighth-century Greeks came from the east. In about 775 they created the world's first fully phonetic alphabetic script out of the Phoenician non-vocalic sign system and soon used it to write obscene graffiti as well as poetry. By 700 BC the 'orientalizing' phase of Greek art, Greek in spirit but oriental in flavour, had begun. Even in the conservative medium of painted pottery, the Geometric tradition, which had been most richly expressed at Athens and Argos in about 750 BC, was losing its vitality; and in about 720 Corinthian painters developed an orientalizing black-figure style, favouring animal friezes and floral ornament drawn in silhouette with incised details.[4] Perhaps the most striking orientalizing artifacts, though, are the great bronze cauldrons with siren handles or griffin heads (*protomai*) dedicated at Olympia, Delphi and lesser sanctuaries.

Immediate oriental influences on eighth-century Greece emanated chiefly from the Levant. Relations between the Greeks and the great oriental power of Anatolia, the Phrygian kingdom centred on Gordion, are harder to interpret. The Aeolian Greeks, who alone shared a frontier, were perhaps prevented by Phrygia from settling within the Propontis. On the other hand, the Phrygian alphabet and painted pottery both reveal Greek influence, and the Greeks imported or copied Phrygian types of bronze dish, cauldron, belt and brooch (*fibula*). Phrygian textiles perhaps accompanied the *fibulae*, but they would not be expected to survive in the Greek soil and climate. Consistent with this peaceful intercourse is the tradition preserved in Herodotus that Midas of Phrygia was the first philhellenic oriental ruler to make lavish offerings at Delphi.

In two important related areas, town planning and architecture, oriental practice did not exert a fundamental influence. The *polis* or city-state was a quintessentially Greek creation of the eighth century BC, which aimed at eliminating the opposition between town and country. Our evidence for town life is extremely limited before the sixth century, but urban centres in old Greece seem typically to have grown outwards from a central refuge of the acropolis type. By contrast, colonial foundations provide the earliest examples of planning, both in the town and in the country. A fortified enclosure wall was an isolated phenomenon in the eighth century (there are examples at Halieis, Siphnos, Zagora, Phaistos, Methymna, Smyrna and Troy) and, indeed, not a normal feature of the Greek city before the fifth century. Of domestic architecture as opposed to houses it is hardly possible to speak until the Classical period (the later fifth and fourth centuries). Best preserved of eighth-century dwellings are the clusters of one-roomed houses at Zagora. These owe their preservation to the customary Cycladic use of stone, whereas on the Greek and Anatolian mainlands house walls were characteristically of mud brick on a stone base.

The temple, however, was singled out for monumental elaboration from the eighth century. Early in the century the Samians constructed a *hecatompedon*, or 'hundred-foot' temple, for their patron goddess Hera, and some time after 750 BC they surrounded it with a wooden colonnade, thereby creating the first peripteral temple. Half a century later the Corinthians erected for their patron Poseidon a temple whose stone walls were faced with painted stucco panels and whose surrounding colonnade and upperworks may represent the prototype of the Doric architectural order. By 700 the building of a temple to a recognized patron deity could be the outward and visible sign that a community had graduated to the status of city-state.

The Archaic Greeks and Lydia, c. 700–750 BC

Early in the seventh century the Phrygian kingdom was swept away by the marauding Cimmerians, and its Anatolian role was assumed by the kingdom of Lydia, whose capital, Sardis, lay just 100 kilometres inland from Smyrna. It was fortunate for the Greeks that by 650 BC technological improvements had made the hoplite, or heavy-armed infantryman, the best-equipped warrior in the eastern Mediterranean. He was therefore very desirable as a mercenary, and by 600 BC Greek hoplites had been hired by rival oriental potentates in Lydia, Syria, Egypt and Palestine and had been settled in semi-permanent camps within their territories.

The earliest such mercenary settlement was perhaps at Dasky-

29.1: *Attic black-figure* pelike (*oil or wine jar*) *of the early fifth century BC from Rhodes, by the Eucharides Painter. One of the rare vase scenes of craftsmen at work, this depicts a cobbler cutting leather around the foot of a young customer whose father looks on. Cobblers occupied an important position in Athenian political and social life: they had a reputation for radical politics, their products were necessaries, and their shops were favourite haunts for conversationalists.*

leion in the Propontis, where Greek pottery occurs from about 675 BC. But it was not long before the Greeks founded their first independent, agrarian settlement in that region, at Kyzikos. The metropolis was Ionian Miletos, to which tradition ascribed the inflated number of ninety colonies in the Black Sea area. As in the west, trade and other contacts preceded the flag, but the gap in time between the two colonization movements indicates the greater difficulties posed by the north, especially the navigational hazards of the Hellespont (Dardanelles) and Bosporus bottlenecks. Not before the seventh century did the Greeks build specialized merchantmen, wind-powered and capable of speeds up to six knots.[5] Only then did *emporos* acquire the technical meaning of long-distance trader. It was towards the end of the century that Greek traders founded the important emporium of Naukratis as a port of trade linking the dissimilar Greek and Egyptian economic systems.[6]

In both Egypt and the Black Sea area the prime movers, whether as settlers or traders, were eastern Greeks. Thus the status of Corinthian as the leading fine-pottery export fabric was challenged by Rhodian and Chiot ware, while of pots exported for their contents, the Athenian oil or wine *amphorae* of 'SOS' type were matched by the wine *amphorae* of Chios and Lesbos. At home the wealth and taste of the eastern Greeks are best displayed on Samos and at Smyrna. Following a flood in about 660 BC, the Samian Heraion received its eighth successive altar, its third temple, one of the earliest examples of the Greek *stoa*, or multipurpose covered colonnade, and many handsome dedications, of which those in wood deserve special mention. Smyrna offers a rudimentary gridiron town plan, rectangular houses with porch and two rooms, an elegant corbelled fountain house and a remarkably thick city wall of small stones packed in clay behind a facing of massive blocks.

Not even this wall, however, was proof against a Lydian assault (attested by a siege mound) in about 600 BC. Yet although by 550 all the Asiatic Greeks except Miletos were Lydian subjects, cultural relations were less one-sided. The best Greek architects and craftsmen were employed by philhellenic Lydian monarchs and may have been paid, like the mercenaries, in the medium of coinage invented by Lydia in the later seventh century.[7] Conversely, when the Ephesians constructed their gigantic (115 by 55 metres) Ionic temple to Artemis in about 560, Croesus paid for some of the forest of marble columns. This temple was the largest edifice in the Greek world (though fiercely rivalled by the near-contemporary temples of Hera on Samos and Apollo at Didyma), and the weight and disposition of its marble entablature strained to the utmost the limited resources of Greek technology, which were always more readily applied to religious than to secular improvements.[8]

The economic and cultural development of mainland Greece and the islands since 700 BC had been independent but equal. Continued close contact with the Levant led to the borrowing of the Syrian mould, which from about 675 was employed to mass-

29.2: *The Athenian* agora *in the late fourth century BC. Athens' earliest* agora, *or place of assembly, probably lay west of the acropolis, but the present site in the Kerameicos district was set aside as the civic centre from c. 600. By 500 the eastern foot of Kolonos Agoraios hill was flanked by half a dozen public buildings, both secular and sacred; to the east lay the Altar of the Twelve Gods, the Ash Altar, the South-East Fountain House and the Great Drain; the remainder is an archaeological blank. By 400 the Agora looked much as it did a century later.*

- 6th century BC
- 5th century BC
- 4th century BC

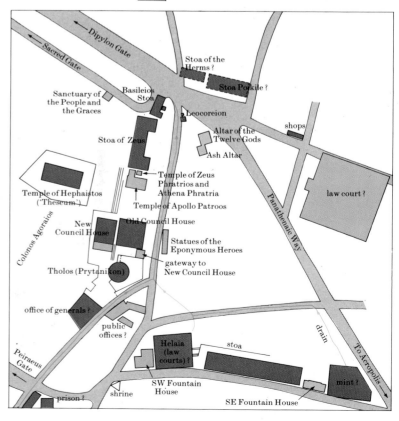

29.3: *The eastern Greek world in the fourth century BC. The Black Sea lay beyond the olive-growing zone, but otherwise the Greeks who spread out in waves from the mainland during the first half of the first millennium chose to settle in the familiar environmental surroundings produced by the Mediterranean climate.*

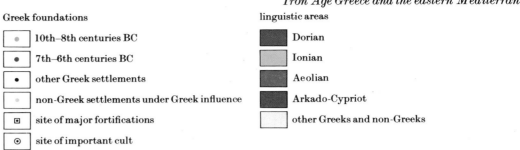

Greek foundations

- · 10th–8th centuries BC
- ● 7th–6th centuries BC
- ● other Greek settlements
- ● non-Greek settlements under Greek influence
- ⊡ site of major fortifications
- ⊙ site of important cult

linguistic areas

- Dorian
- Ionian
- Aeolian
- Arkado-Cypriot
- other Greeks and non-Greeks

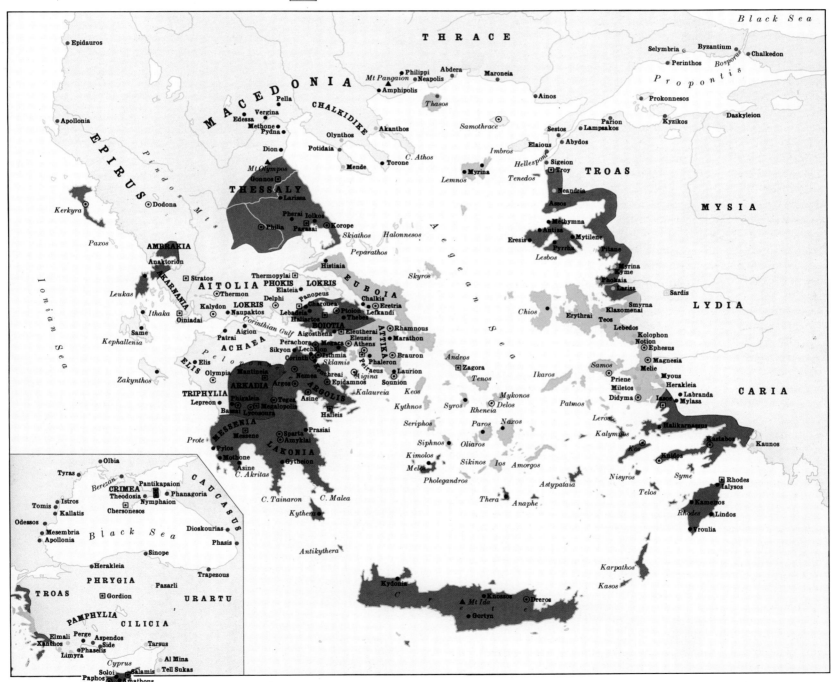

produce cheap terracotta figurines in the orientalizing Daedalic style. One of the leading Daedalic centres was the island of Crete, and it was here, in about 650 BC, that the style was adapted to create monumental statues of limestone. Shortly afterwards the first known lifesize *kore* (clothed female figure) in marble was dedicated on Delos by a girl from the marble island of Naxos. By 625 the *kore* had her nude male counterpart, the *kouros*, and it was principally through the medium of the *kouros* that Greek artists felt their way, by 480 BC, to the representational style that dominated Western art for almost 2500 years.[9]

Marble working also required new and improved tools such as the claw chisel, which was invented by 550 BC. This is a useful reminder that although by modern (and even medieval) standards the Greek world was backward in agriculture, transport and manufacture, the Greeks did make great strides in some aspects of production. The provisional statistics of temple building and monumental statuary indicate that the expansion that took place in the sixth century was greater by a factor of three or more than that of the seventh century.[10]

Megara was the only state outside eastern Greece to colonize in the Black Sea area (at Byzantium and Chalcedon in about 650), Aigina the only such state to participate in the foundation of Naucratis. But both continued to be outshone materially by Corinth. To the latter is to be credited the major share in the development of the Doric style of temple building, the establishment of the first truly industrial quarter in a Greek city, the erection of the first treasury in the panhellenic sanctuary of Delphi, and the promotion of commerce through the construction of a stone slipway across the isthmus of Corinth and the great harbour at Lechaion – all in the later seventh or early sixth century BC. Thus Corinth in 600 occupied the cultural position held by Athens in the fifth century; it was an omen that by 550 Corinthian fine pottery had been virtually driven out of production by its Athenian rival.

Persia and the Greeks, c. 550–480 BC

In the 540s Cyrus the Great forcibly incorporated Lydia and the eastern Greeks into the fast-growing Persian empire (see Chapter 30). The flourishing cities of Phokaia and Teos were abandoned, but in general the Persian conquest did not bear more oppressively on Greek material culture than had the Lydian, nor did it halt the Hellenization of the Near East. In about 540, for instance, Knidos erected the first all-marble Greek building in the form of a treasury at Delphi, which, like Olympia, was coming to resemble a city more than a sanctuary. Samos in the 530s and 520s enjoyed its maximum splendour under Polykrates, whose piratical Aegean empire is most impressively commemorated in the water tunnel designed by Eupalinos of Megara. Greek artistic influence spread eastwards to Lycia, most conspicuously in the two painted tombs near Elmali and the 'Harpy' tomb at Xanthos, and even to Persia itself, where Greek stonemasons and sculptors were employed at the capitals of Pasargadae, Susa and Persepolis.[11]

Politically, however, the eastern Greeks failed against Persia, and after their revolt had been crushed in 494 BC the leading Ionian city, Miletos, was destroyed. Much more successful, however, was Athens, whose role in resisting the subsequent Persian invasions of mainland Greece in 490 and 480–79 BC was based on a solid economic foundation. Poor in grainlands, which could feed only an estimated 75 000, and with an urban population of less than 10 000, Attika was admirably suited to the olive, whose product was widely exported from 600. The import of necessities, above all wheat, further promoted Athenian industry and commerce, which was in the hands of non-Athenians and non-Greek slaves as well as Athenian citizens. From about 550 and 530 BC respectively Attic black-figure and red-figure pottery cornered the Mediterranean markets, as may be seen most clearly in the cemeteries of Italy and the Black Sea area.[12] The impressive marble *kouroi* and *korai* on the Athenian acropolis mark the beginning of Athens's role as the artistic school of Greece. Besides these natural and manufactured products, Attika possessed a 'treasure of the earth' (Aeschylus), the argentiferous lead of the Laurion district. It was a rich strike of Laurion silver in the 480s that enabled Athens to build the largest Greek fleet of triremes (propelled by some 170 oarsmen, disposed in three banks, and capable of 11.5 knots) and so repel the Persians.

The Athenian empire, 478–400 BC

After the Persian Wars Athens built up an anti-Persian empire whose subjects embraced most of the Aegean and extended from Byzantium to Cyprus. The mainly Athenian imperial fleet cleared the seas of pirates and convoyed merchantmen bringing wheat from Egypt, Cyprus and especially the Crimea to feed Athens's growing urban population, although, as in the other Greek states, the majority of Attika's perhaps 300 000–400 000 inhabitants still lived in the country. The Peiraeus became the focal point of Mediterranean commerce, and Athenian writers and politicians were apt to stress the variety and abundance of the commodities passing through the port and the specialization of retail trades in the Athenian *agora* (market place).[13]

Most of these goods and services have left no archaeological trace – or none yet identified. In the sharpest possible contrast, the Parthenon, Propylaia, Erechtheion and temple of Athena Nike, built of local Pentelic marble on the Athenian acropolis during the second half of the fifth century, are among the most familiar images of the Western world. What may be less well known is that they were paid for out of imperial tribute, and that the Erechtheion at least was fashioned by 'barbarian' slaves as well as by free Athenians and resident aliens.[14] Apart from the acropolis, the *agora* and, indeed, the countryside of Attika were also splendidly adorned with monumental buildings. The Stoa of Zeus in the *agora* is a worthy contemporary of the Parthenon, as is the temple of Hephaistos on Kolonos Agoraios, which was perhaps designed by the same architect as the temples of Poseidon at Sounion and Nemesis at Rhamnous. Far less time and money were expended on domestic structures.

From about 460 onwards the Persian threat receded, and the Athenians and their allies spent most of the rest of the fifth century fighting against, and eventually being defeated by, the other main multi-state grouping of the Greek world, the alliance headed by Sparta. To this fact we owe the many fortifications of the period, which include some of the finest examples of Greek drystone masonry. Especially noteworthy are the frontier forts of Attika and the enclosure walls of Oiniadai in the otherwise still backward north-west of Greece. Equally important was the

29.4: *The workshop of Pheidias at Olympia, and the chryselephantine (gold and ivory) Zeus, c. 430 BC. One of the seven wonders of the ancient world, and over 13 metres high, the statue is irretrievably lost and this artistic reconstruction depends on an ancient description, but the workshop and its debris have been excavated. The plentiful pottery shows that the statue was made in the 430s, after Pheidias' chryselephantine Athena for the Parthenon at Athens.*

general fifth-century concern with urban planning.[15] The Hippodamian gridiron system had existed rudimentarily since the seventh century, but it takes its name from Hippodamos of Miletos, who allegedly planned not only the rebuilding of his own city after 479 but also the rationalization of Peiraeus after 450 and the new foundation of the city of Rhodes in 408.

The rise of Macedon, 400–336 BC

By the end of the fourth century a Greek city was defined architecturally by government offices, a *gymnasium*, a theatre, an *agora*, public fountains and reasonably solid houses. Among cities with some or all of these characteristics the most spectacular is Priene as rebuilt after 350, but the best preserved is Olynthos, to whose destruction in 348 and subsequent abandonment we owe our clearest picture of Hippodamian planning.

The man who destroyed Olynthos was Philip II of Macedon. A decade later, after the decisive battle of Chaironea in Boiotia, he forcibly united the defeated Greeks in a league formed ostensibly to conduct a crusade against the waning Persian empire. It used to be argued, in excessive reliance on the pottery evidence, that the political and military weakness of Aegean Greece was due to economic decline, but architectural evidence from Messene, Megalopolis and Epidauros sufficiently disproves this. Rather, the outlying areas of the Greek world raised themselves to economic parity with the heartland. Particularly instructive is the evidence from the Black Sea colonies. At Pantikapaion, for example, the urban area covered 100 hectares, while at Chersonesos not only the city but also the surrounding country (more than 10 000 hectares) was given the Hippodamian treatment.

Pantikapaion, capital of the Bosporan kingdom, also illustrates well how, after the democratic flowering led by Athens in the fifth century BC, the Greek world came increasingly under the sway of powerful monarchs, whether Greek or, like Mausolus of Caria, Hellenized. Philip was himself technically a Greek, but Macedon had only recently been introduced to Greek high culture and was still mainly of interest to the Greeks as a source of timber. Under Philip, however, who unified his kingdom, seized the strategically crucial Amphipolis and exploited the gold and silver mines of Mount Pangaion, Macedon became the arbiter of Greece.

Philip's victory at Chaironea in 338 received monumental commemoration at Megalopolis, Olympia and perhaps Nemea. But by far the most illuminating commentary on Macedonian power and Hellenic taste in the fourth century is provided by the sumptuous royal tombs recently discovered at Vergina, the ancient Aigai. If one artifact were to be singled out for mention from the mass of gold, silver, iron, bronze and other valuable grave goods, it would be the gold diadem (from the so-called Tomb of Philip) built up of delicate flowers, many of which have tiny golden bees sipping nectar at their centres. A diadem is an entirely appropriate symbol of the Macedonian might and Greek culture that Philip's son, Alexander the Great, was to extend throughout the Near East and as far as the Indian subcontinent.

30. Iran under the Achaemenians and Seleucids

The rise of the Achaemenian empire in the sixth century BC was in part the outcome of new influences on the ancient kingdoms of the Near East. The domination of the Indo-European-speaking peoples on the steppe lands west of the Tien Shan and the development there of pastoral economies based on horse riding (see Chapter 38) brought successive waves of invaders into the more fertile regions to the south. Even before 2000 BC the Bronze Age communities south-east of the Caspian were subject to external attack; little more than a thousand years later the main body of the Iranian tribes would seem to have taken possession of a substantial part of the upland country that today bears their name. Among such invaders it was the Medes, themselves close relatives of the Persians, who assumed the dominant role in the earlier part of the first millenium BC.

Three excavated sites in the Median heartland (that is to say, in the central western Zagros) have so far produced substantial remains of eighth- to sixth-century date.[1] The Medes chose to place their main settlements either on dominant *tells* or, as in the case of the strongly fortified capital, Ecbatana (modern Hamadan), on the heights of an isolated rock outcrop. Mud brick was the outstanding medium of construction. Baked brick was seldom employed, and finely dressed masonry was unknown. The main impact of this architecture came from soaring façades, massive mud-brick walls and lofty columned halls. Slim window openings and arrow slots 2 metres tall added further definition to the buttressed external walls. Together with these traditional features are to be found, in the singular design of the Central Temple at Tepe Nush-i Jan and in the shape of its associated fire altar, certain of the first expressions of Median belief and religious practice.

Recent surveys have shown that the monumental administrative and religious centres of the Medes were complemented by modest but nonetheless permanent villages. The economy of such seventh- and early sixth-century settlements was based on crops such as hulled six-row barley, emmer, bread wheat, rye, lentils and grapes; and while hunting in the forested mountains was an active pursuit, animal husbandry played a major role in daily life. The domestic bone sample from one excavated site reveals the presence of nine species, the most common of which were sheep and goats (with the former outnumbering the latter by a ratio of more than 2 to 1), pig and cattle.

Persian settlement in Fars

When at the end of the eighth century BC the main mass of the Persians thrust south to reach the broad valley floors and bold limestone hills of Fars (the area around Shiraz), they encountered a land where a predominately nomadic existence (and, in particular, a system of transhumance incorporating seasonal migrations between summer and winter pastures) had repeatedly presented an alternative to a sedentary pattern. The present state of

30.1: *The fortified eighth–seventh century BC Median site of Tepe Nush-i Jan in western Iran. The tall mud-brick walls of the fort dominate the east end of the mound.*

field research suggests, for example, that the scale of permanent settlement in Fars was far from intensive during the first four centuries of the first millenium BC; at the very least we know that the once great city of Anshan, 50 kilometres west of Persepolis, was never seriously reoccupied after the collapse of Middle Elamite power in about 1100 BC. In the virtual absence, therefore, of pre-existing fortified strongholds at the natural focal points of political power, the growth of new permanent centres would seem to have been a slow process at best.

The etymology of local names is instructive. In the fertile valley of Fasa, 130 kilometres south-west of Shiraz, we know that the principal town went under the name of 'Pasa' until at least the beginning of the Islamic period. As has recently been suggested,[2] the Old Persian form of the name could originally have identified an 'encampment' or 'settlement' of Persians on the plain of Fasa. Equally, there is more than a hint of the nomadic condition of the forbears of Cyrus the Great (559–530 BC) in the name that was given to his capital, Pasargadae. The most probable Old Persian forms of the name, *parsa-argada* or *parsa-rgada*, may each be taken to mean 'the Persian settlement' – a designation that would suggest that for a time it too was one of the few permanent places of residence within the bounds of the new homeland.[3]

From kingdom to empire

In the annals of the Neo-Assyrian kings, who remained a dominant force in the Near East from 885 to 612 BC, the Persian tribes merit little more than passing notice. Shortly before 640 BC Ashurbanipal of Assyria states that one 'Cyrus of Parsumash', on hearing of the Assyrian destruction of Elam, offered his submission and sent his son Arukku as a hostage to Nineveh. There is evidence to suggest, nevertheless, that the line of Achaemenes, the eponymous founder of the Achaemenian dynasty, was fast gaining in significance. Cambyses I, possibly a second son of Cyrus of Parsumash, was

permitted to marry the daughter of his Median suzerain, Astyages; and from this union Cyrus the Great was born.

The astonishing conquests of Cyrus, which were to bring him a far larger and more powerful empire than the Assyrians had known, began in 549 BC, when he accomplished the overthrow of his grandfather, Astyages. Next, within the span of a single decade, he brought all the eastern Iranians under his rule, effected the capture of Sardis, the well-appointed capital of Lydia, and secured Babylon (whose subject rulers, as far as the borders of Egypt, then submitted to him). To these possessions his son and successor, Cambyses II, added the rich prize of Egypt, while under Darius the Great (522–486 BC), a member of a collateral branch of the Achaemenian family, the empire grew to its greatest extent, stretching from Libya to the Jaxartes and from south-eastern Europe to the Indus (see Figure 30.2).

Achaemenian palaces

Parallel with such conquests came a vigorous programme of royal construction. As lords of a vast realm who had fallen heir to older Near Eastern concepts of universal kingship, Cyrus and his successors found the need to express their new-found position in monumental form. East of the riverine plain of Mesopotamia there were no adequate models to draw upon; and the site of Pasargadae, founded by Cyrus in 546 BC as the formal seat and permanent residence of his line, may be said to illustrate a number of striking departures in the architectural history of Iran. The massive, finely jointed masonry of the tomb of Cyrus and the equally impressive panelled ashlar blocks of the Tall-i Takht both indicate the borrowing of advanced stone-working techniques from sixth-century Ionia and Lydia. Cyrus did much more, however, than simply import skilled masons from the newly conquered western provinces. On the one hand, Iran's traditional mud-brick walls and partly wooden roofs came to be combined with stone pavements, stone

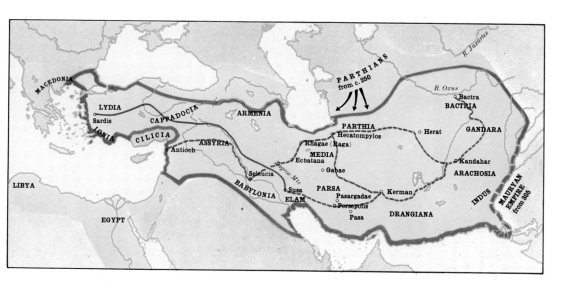

30.2: *Map indicating the approximate limits of the Achaemenian and Seleucid empires, and the core territory of the Persians, the region of Parsa. Both empires improved and protected the immemorial trade routes that traverse this immense area.*

maximum extent of Achaemenian empire under Darius the Great (*c.* 500 BC)

maximum extent of empire of Seleucus I (*c.* 300 BC)

principal trade routes in Seleucid times

Persian Royal Road

wall footings and stone columns; on the other hand, the centuries-old plan of the Iranian columned hall – with two rows of four columns, a fixed throne seat and a single entrance portico – was almost immediately transcended by a new, more open design. Palace S at Pasargadae could be entered from four directions; and in place of the solid outer walls so common in Near Eastern mud-brick architecture, we find a series of long open colonnades. In creating this harmoniously balanced structure Cyrus may be said to have combined the architectural traditions of Ionia and Iran with uncommon success.

Remarkably enough, Cyrus' close successor, Darius, was to reveal a parallel aptitude for architectural selection and synthesis: his standards and choices created the firm, almost unchanging mould of fifth-century and later Achaemenian art and architecture. At Susa (where he no doubt first enlisted the skills of the cuneiform scribes of Elam as an important adjunct of his administration) he erected an extensive royal residence. This was graced above all by his majestic throne hall or Apadana, a building that illustrates an elegant evolution from the earlier palace plans of Cyrus.

The most ambitious building project of the time, however, came to be centred on a new foundation called, like the region of Fars itself, Parsa. This notable site, known to the Greeks as Persepolis, embraced a partly fortified palace precinct raised on a high stone terrace, the rock-cut royal tombs at Naqsh-i Rustam and, most probably, a separate township standing some 7 kilometres to the north of the terrace. This singular creation, which engaged much

of the building energies of Darius and his immediate successors, served both as a counterpart to Pasargadae (that is, as the formal dynastic home of Darius' branch of the Archaemenian family) and also, it would seem, as a ceremonial expression of Iran's imperial power.

Most of the major buildings on the Persepolis terrace were decorated with relief sculptures.[4] These not only celebrate the role of the monarch but also provide an interesting insight into the Achaemenians' perception of world empire: of the relationship, conceived if not actual, between ruler and ruled. At Persepolis there is no record of martial triumph and pillage; rather, as in the case of the sculptured reliefs of the Apadana (where the enthroned king was originally shown receiving twenty-three delegations bearing valuable and exotic gifts), we find, in stark contrast to many of the reliefs of the Assyrians, each of the subject peoples depicted with conscious dignity and respect.[5]

Local administration in Fars

The swift rise of the Achaemenians necessarily had far-reaching effects on social and economic conditions in late sixth-century Fars. Apart from the great programmes of construction that were launched at Pasargadae and Persepolis, further royal palaces or pavilions came to be built at Fasa, Firuzabad, Jinjin and Borazjan, not to mention the still unidentified Taoce of Classical accounts. More important still, the recently deciphered Elamite administrative texts from Persepolis[6] provide details of a network of urban centres and well travelled roads that were to be found throughout late sixth-century and early fifth-century Fars.

Although there are references to such distant centres as Sardis and Kandahar, the texts refer in the main to three local regions: the Persepolis area, the Susa area and the lightly populated area between Persepolis and Susa. Only six of the twenty-seven place names that can be attributed to the first of these regions can be accurately located: Persepolis, Pasargadae, Fasa, Shiraz, Niriz and Anshan. Fasa stands out in this post-Cyrus period as the second settlement of Fars. It was a focus of royal construction; it was an active religious centre, as we learn from a reference in one text to a Custodian of the Fire; it harboured a larger work force than any reported from either Shiraz or Pasargadae; and it was, after Persepolis, the most common destination for travellers from Susa. Elsewhere in the province, not only Shiraz but also Niriz, 160 kilometres to the east, stood at the hub of an apparently well-populated region.

30.3: *An imaginative reconstruction of the tomb of Cyrus at Pasargadae. With its massive, finely jointed stone blocks and smooth, plain surfaces with only a minimum of decorative detail, the tomb creates a singular impression of dignity, simplicity and strength.*

As most travel rations only sufficed for a single day, and as most travellers journeyed on foot, the distance between wayside stations cannot have exceeded 30–40 kilometres. Such stations were not only able to supply fresh rations, but also had resident scribes who duly recorded the details of the provisions made over to each travelling group. In certain cases the texts seem to refer to 'caravan leaders' or 'caravan guides'.

The widespread distribution of such early caravanserais recalls Xenephon's claim that Cyrus was the original builder of such road-side stations. However that may be, local traffic was heavy by the beginning of the fifth century, and many of the texts refer to the export, delivery and deposit of large quantities of grain and other goods. Prominent in the records too are the mounted couriers of the express service, who plied not only the 2300-kilometre Royal Road from Susa to Sardis, with its 111 supply stations,[7] but also the eastern extension of this highway from Susa to Persepolis.

The Elamite texts from Persepolis may also be said to reflect a new, more rigorous approach to problems of agricultural production. To mention only one of many topics, it is now possible to re-construct the probable chain of command as it affected the always important husbandry of sheep and goats.[8]

Agricultural policies

In their determination to expand available food supplies – a policy not to be interpreted merely as a means of increasing land revenues – the Persians were probably responsible for transmitting the irrigation techniques of ancient Elam and Mesopotamia to the distant riverine plains of central Asia. They also possibly borrowed, and at all events greatly developed, the ingenious irrigation system of the *qanat*, which would seem to date back at least to the second quarter of the first millennium BC. In this distinctive system, underground gravity-flow channels, often of great length and depth, each marked at 10- to 20-metre intervals by vertical in-spection shafts, are used to bring a continuous flow of ground water, almost without evaporation, from some adjacent high point in the water-table to those low-lying areas of fine soil that most invite cultivation. While a slight fall in the level of the water-table is often enough to render the 'mother-well' of the *qanat* dry, and while maintenance of such underground channels is both time-consuming and dangerous, the *qanat* can be seen to have remained a familiar feature of the agrarian scene, not only in Iran and neigh-bouring Pakistani Baluchistan, but also in Cyrenaica, at what was once the western limit of the Achaemenian realm. Parallel with this interest in the techniques of irrigation, we know, both from Classical records and from excavated evidence,[9] of the creation of carefully planned, luxuriant gardens.

More important still, the Achaemenians were interested in the propagation of new types of food. Rice, which was probably first cultivated in India, was found by the Greeks who accompanied Alexander to be growing already in Bactria, Khuzistan, Babylonia and Syria. Sugar-cane was possibly also brought to Iran from India in Achaemenian times, and it has been plausibly suggested

that such originally Chinese fruits as the peach (*Persicum*) and the apricot (*Armeniacum*) found their way to Iran in this same period.[10]

Settlement patterns

It is only recently that controlled excavations at such sites as Susa and Pasargadae have begun to demonstrate in detail the types of pottery that were in use in Achaemenian and immediately post-Achaemenian times. Accordingly, the surveys of surface remains that were undertaken in the Diyala region and in Khuzistan in the 1960s cannot yet be assumed to have told us all that there is to know of local Achaemenian settlement in these two areas (see Figure 30.4). While there can be no quarrel with the general con-clusion that Achaemenian settlement in the Diyala region was notably less dense than in the Parthian period, let alone in the Sasanian period (see Figure 43.4),[11] some doubts must attach to the claim[12] that nearly all Achaemenian villages in Khuzistan were restricted to dry farming areas in the eastern part of this last, extremely fertile region.

Elsewhere, both on the Iranian plateau and in Afghanistan, recent fieldwork provides clear evidence that Achaemenian pot-tery, like Parthian pottery, was subject to intense regional variation. There is, moreover, a further problem: the Achaemenian period only lasted for just over two centuries, and within this relatively brief span of time we should not necessarily expect to find too many new, diagnostic forms of pottery. In short, we cannot yet hope for more than a fragmentary picture of Achaemenian settlement over the greater part of Iran – let alone in the wide borderlands to the east.

Stagnation and decline

As they were conceived at first, the administrative provisions of the Achaemenians were unusually enlightened and the subjects of Iran were probably more favourably placed than those of Assyria or any earlier imperial power. Side by side with a common code of law, gold currency, royal measures of weight and the use of Aramaic as the official language of the empire, we witness within each major province, or satrapy, the continued observance of old local laws, customs and traditions. In particular, the still ill-defined religious beliefs of the Achaemenians do not appear to have been systematically imposed on the polyglot, heterogeneous peoples of the empire. Each satrapy, in other words, remained to a surprising degree an independent social and political unit.[13] From the reign of Xerxes onwards (486–465 BC), however, there is evidence that discontent in the provinces was on the increase. Nowhere does this state of affairs emerge more plainly than in Egypt and Babylonia, two of the richest (and, by the same token, two of the most heavily taxed) regions under Persian domination.

The range of burdens that came to afflict the inhabitants of Babylonia can be gauged in part from the *Histories* of Herodotus and from extant cuneiform records. In addition to having to meet a high annual tax and tribute, Babylonia was obliged to provide food for the army and the court for four out of the twelve months of the year. Other revenues came from a wide variety of specific taxes on land, on natural resources and on different commodities; and, as elsewhere, the satrap was entitled to levy his own taxes in order to support his personal court. A problem of yet another kind was that much of the best land was still retained by the powerful Babylonian temples or was parcelled out to members of the Persian aristocracy, who held it, often as absentee landlords, in the form of large estates. If we add to this catalogue the scale of local inflation, which saw a constant rise in the cost of land, seed and draught animals, it is not surprising that local unrest became a pervasive mark of the time.

The impact of the West

At the height of Iran's power, early in the fifth century BC, the city-states of Greece combined to resist successfully the invading forces first of Darius the Great and then of Xerxes. Little of note served to disturb the subsequent *status quo* until Philip of Macedon, soon to be succeeded by his son, Alexander the Great (336–323 BC), began to unite the greater part of mainland Greece by conquest. The Achaemenian leadership, weakened by internal feuds, was slow to respond to this turn of events, and in 334 BC, at the age of twenty–two, Alexander was able to cross the Hellespont unopposed and to begin his unique career of conquest in Asia.

Against a less redoubtable foe the empire's vast resources of

manpower could conceivably have been made to count for more. If nothing else, the Iranians might have made a more vigorous attempt to defend a new border along the line of the Zagros chain; but – with momentous consequences for the future – this was not to be the case.

Notwithstanding those strands of insecurity or romantic impulse that can be shown to have clouded Alexander's judgement on occasion, he emerges above all as a supreme pragmatist – able to take full advantage of situations as he found them. Time and again, not only his military but also his political successes were ensured by careful planning, followed by a bold and ruthless stroke delivered precisely when the opportunity offered.[14]

In assessing the achievement of Alexander it is appropriate to remember that he owed at least part of his seemingly easy success – far beyond the scale of anything that Rome was ever able to achieve in the East – to the often belittled polity that he overthrew. For although the Achaemenian empire undoubtedly suffered from the restive ambition of its powerful satraps, who on occasion more closely resembled independent monarchs than dutiful governors, and although it lacked to a large extent any clear national, religious or cultural unity, it had succeeded in drawing the greater part of western Asia into one political system. In terms of this inheritance, Alexander was able to govern in through existing administrative units; the long-established boundaries of Cyrus and Darius served to define the outer limits of Greek rule in the East; and, on the death of Darius III in 330 BC, the care that Alexander took to pose as the successor to the last ruling Achaemenian may have done more than a little to buttress his rule.

There is even an intriguing possibility that the Iranians might have salvaged certain advantages from their new situation. Alexander was more than mildly seduced by the pomp and splendour of the oriental monarchy to which he found himself heir; and if only because he recognized the need to recruit substantial numbers of Iranians for military purposes, we know that he was prepared to countenance successive, not unimportant concessions to the aristocracy. But how far this policy would have been pursued

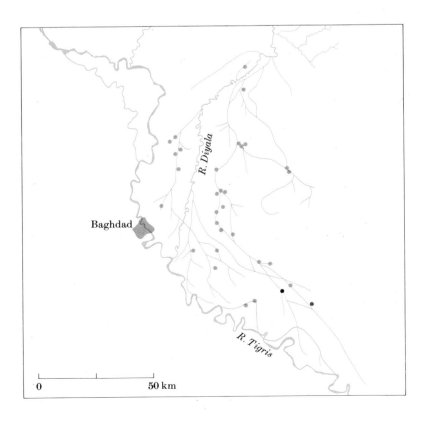

30.4: *Settlements and watercourses on the lower Diyala plains of Iraq in the Achaemenian period (537–331 BC). In this period almost all settlements lie along the course of artificial canals. (See also Figure 43.4.)*

•	village or hamlet, less than 4 hectares
•	town, 4–30 hectares
•	small urban centre, 30–100 hectares
•	city, more than 1 sq. km

had Alexander survived his thirty-third year is far from clear. The Egyptian and Babylonian priests proved willing to accommodate the conqueror's claims to native kingship, but the religious groups, the Magi, appear to have been unbending in their opposition. The Iranian priesthood might have been bound in any case to reject an impivous invader as king, but the fact remains that a single, totallly implitic act – the burning of Persepolis in the early summer of 330 BC – did fundamental violence to the pragmatic policies of conciliation that were usually favoured by Alexander. And it is at least arguable that this same act served to strengthen Iran's resistance to the inroads of the West down to Sasanian times. Only one surviving monument from Alexander's brief rule in Iran is known: the famed 'lion of Hamadan', which was probably erected as a cenotaph to Hephaestion, Alexander's close friend and companion, who died at Hamadan in 324 BC.[15]

30.5: *A side view of the reclining Heracles found at Bisitun and dated to c. 147 BC. This sculptural type was particularly popular in the Hellenistic Near East; there is also strong evidence to suggest that the cults of both Heracles and Dionysus continued to flourish in Iran for several centuries.*

Seleucid Iran

Under Seleucus I (312–281 BC), one of the former commanders of Alexander's army, whose own rise to power began in Babylonia, the power and wealth of the new Seleucid state moved firmly westwards.[16] In Iran itself a blending of cultures is suggested by various monuments, not least by the roadside shrine to Heracles that stands at the base of the great cliff at Bisitun. Here an inscription in Greek indicates that the powerful figure of Heracles, depicted reclining, bowl in hand, beneath an arbour of vines, was made in about 147 BC. Strongly provincial as this last work undoubtedly is, it serves to remind us of the extent to which Greek art, religion, language and law came to penetrate the western valleys of the central Zagros. Such influences were no doubt equally at home in lowland, south-western Iran. Lying firmly within the commercial nexus of Seleucia-on-the-Tigris (the great political capital of the east Seleucid world, with an estimated population of 600 000), this region witnessed an unusually active policy of settlement. Here Susa, one of the chief administrative seats of the Achaemenians, was refounded as Seleucia-on-the-Eulaeus, and a significant number of other cities and states came to be founded around the headwaters of the Persian Gulf.

To the north and east the fortresses and the few cities of the Iranian plateau, with populations probably not in excess of 30 000 to 100 000, were chiefly sited on the main arteries of trade and military movement.[17] Seleucus I founded (or rather refounded) the city of Raga (Rhagae), which he named Europos, and it seems probable that he also refounded the city of Hecatompylos, which stood further east on the great Khorasan Road. During the last years of Seleucus' reign his son Antiochus I (born of an Iranian mother) was also active in establishing new settlements. But in many parts of Iran that stand at some distance from the principal east–west route the Seleucid impact is hard to detect, and areas such as inland Fars were probably not long in falling under the effective control of local dynasts. Indeed, with the limited Greek population congregated in cities or military colonies, there was little that the Seleucid monarchs could do after the middle of the third century BC either to prevent distant Bactria from pursuing a separate course or to protect the eastern provinces of Iran from the latest nomadic intruders from the north – the Parthians.

A methodical search for sites of Seleucid date, based on the available early sources as well as on the results of numerous recent surveys, may still yield useful results within upland Iran. It is only in the past few years, for example, that Afghanistan, in the wake of more extensive fieldwork, has become the 'new frontier' of contemporary Greek studies. Already a number of excavations in Iran have allowed us to begin to define the characteristic local pottery of the third and second centuries BC,[18] and, given the availability of such diagnostic markers, it cannot be long before more is known of this short but intriguing moment in the history of Iran, when Greek and Iranian culture had to contend on the same ground.

31. The emergence of Arabia

Lying between the Persian Gulf and the Red Sea, the Arabian peninsula falls entirely within the arid zone. Less than a quarter of its area is habitable, and settlement is distributed mainly along its edges. The two major concentrations of population are in the east, on the shores of the Gulf, and in the west – especially the south-west – on the shore of the Red Sea and the adjacent Arabian Sea. The population of the east coast was the first to develop, as a result of maritime contacts in the Gulf in the third millennium BC, while the western part developed most rapidly in the first millennium BC as a result of the camel-borne incense trade.[1]

Eastern Arabia

From the early third millennium to the second millennium BC the countries on both sides of the Gulf to the Indian Ocean were involved in trading, both with each other and with southern Mesopotamia. The lack of natural resources and the need for wood, stone and metals in Mesopotamia laid the foundations for commercial intercourse with those regions known as the 'lower sea'. In the Uruk-Jamdat Nasr period (see Chapter 16) limestone, basalt, timber and semi-precious stones obtainable from Iran were traded for Sumerian wheat and barley. While some of this trade took place overland, the Gulf was an important route for seaborne trade. Navigation along the Iranian coast was impracticable, as it had few sheltered anchorages, so the sea trade would have operated along the Arabian coast, where there were natural harbours and fresh water. In the cuneiform texts of the third and early second millennium it is recorded that the boats trading with Sumer were those from the trading centres of Dilmun, Magan and Meluhha. Sargon of Akkad recorded that he had caused the ships from these countries to anchor at the quay in front of Akkad.

Dilmun was apparently a political and cultural federal union in the north-west of the Gulf.[2] It comprised several islands as well as coastal strips on the mainland of Arabia. The two principal islands were Failaka and Bahrain, which had political and economic domination over portions of the mainland. The position of Bahrain, with its sheltered anchorages and freshwater springs, provided ideal conditions for an important entrepôt. Thus Dilmun traded with inland Arabia as well as with Magan and Meluhha, acting as middleman in the forwarding of raw materials to Mesopotamia. Situated half-way between the Indus and Mesopotamia, the Dilmun federation, with its urban and temple architecture and a necropolis of many thousands of large burial mounds, was apparently a sophisticated civilization. The distinctive circular Dilmun 'Persian Gulf' steatite stamp seals differ in shape from both the cylinder seals of Mesopotamia and the square steatite seals found in the Indus (Harappan) civilization; but the architecture and masonrywork, pottery typology and metalwork all show influence from both these centres.

At Qala'at al-Bahrain the massive city wall is dated to about 2300 BC, and there are also 'warehouse' structures of this date. The temple at nearby Barbar, built of finely cut masonry, belongs to the same period. This Early Dilmun period lasted until about 1750 BC and also saw the construction of thousands of grave mounds, and settlements on Tarut and later on Failaka.

Magan, the second of Sumer's trading partners, was an important source of copper, stone – including the special diorite used for carvings – and wood, particularly timber for boat building. The evidence indicates that Magan may be identified as a 'country' whose people inhabited both sides of the entrance to the Gulf. The great number of distinctive burial tombs on the Arabian side suggests that this was the territorial homeland.

Pottery styles found at inland sites in Baluchistan, particularly Sistan, Shahr-i Sokhta and Bampur, have been identified at sites on the Arabian coast and in inland Oman.[3] Probably the earliest connections are to be found in the 'Jamdat Nasr' horizon pottery found at Tepe Yahya in southern Iran (see Chapter 16), dated to the last half of the fourth millennium BC, and at Shahr-i Sokhta. Similar biconical jars with everted rims and low necks datable to about 2700 BC have been found in the cairn tombs of Hafit in

31.1: *One of a large group of beehive tombs at the necropolis near Bāt, north of Ibri in Oman. The triangular entrance passage, 1 metre high, faces south and leads to a paved chamber. The tomb is built of two ring-walls of hewn stone with an encircling plinth of flat stones about half a metre wide. Tombs such as this may contain between two and five burials. They appear to be a development between the 'Jamdat Nasr' period and the more elaborate and spacious Umm an-Nar tombs in Oman; they may be dated to between the third and second millennium BC.*

Oman, south of Buraimi. Blue-green faience beads and cube-shaped bone beads in Hafit tombs may also indicate links with Mesopotamian Jamdat Nasr.[4] Circular 'beehive' tombs and cairns are found on rocks and hills throughout northern Oman, extending to the Musandam peninsula, and indicate an extensive occupation of the country from the early third millennium.[5] The beehive tombs are constructed of flat stones, usually arranged in two concentric walls sloping inwards over a single paved chamber, often with a lancet-shaped entrance. They may be a development from the Jamdat Nasr tomb, which was of rougher construction.

Tombs and stone houses on the island of Umm an-Nar near Abu Dhabi provide evidence of cultural links with Bahrain, Dilmun, Magan in Iran at Shahr-i Sokhta, and at Bampur and Tepe Yahya during the third millennium.[6] From its location at the nearest point on the coast to the Oman mountains and the copper-mining areas, the island settlement may have been a trading station; this appears to be confirmed by the scatter of copper fragments there as well as camel bones. On the island there are about fifty tombs of a unique type, circular with cross walls forming compartments for collective burials. Built on kerb stones and paved, they are about 7 metres in diameter with wall heights of about 1.5 metres. The walls are constructed of flat stones with courses corbelled internally to form roofs.

There are similar tombs and a settlement at Hili near Buraimi, a well-watered oasis in a key position for the inland caravan routes.[6] A large mud-brick Umm an-Nar defence tower has been excavated here, where the trade routes extend inland in two directions. One track crosses the mountains to the Batina coast, where there are tombs in Umm an-Nar style in the Wadi Jizzi area, and the other leads south and round the edge of the mountains. North-east of Ibri there are two important Umm an-Nar settlements, Bāt and 'Amlah. At Bāt, in addition to several large ring-wall structures, there is a large defence tower with a well, similar to that at Hili but constructed with massive blocks of masonry. The necropolis, with beehive and Umm an-Nar tombs, is close to the area of habitation.

The Umm an-Nar culture covers the period from the second quarter of the third millennium to about 1800 BC. It extended from present-day Abu Dhabi to the Batina coast and as far as Ras al-Hamra, near Muscat. In the south, within the wadis near the lower slopes of the ranges of Jabal Akhdar, the area covered was from Buraimi to Bāt and 'Amlah, near Ibri, north-east to al-Banah and eastwards to Wadi Samad. The culture had strong connections with south-east Iran, and the canister jars at Hili indicate connections with Bampur and Shahr-i Sokhta in Baluchistan from about 2400 to 1800 BC. Steatite or chlorite articles, often compartmented boxes decorated with the encircled dot motif found in an Umm an-Nar context, have also been associated with an industry at Tepe Yahya. A plain concave-sided steatite hut pot, together with an *amphora*-shaped jar found on Umm an-Nar island, suggest an earlier date for trade with Mesopotamia, as similar pottery has been found in the Royal Cemeteries at Ur. This would have been before the end of the Early Dynastic III period in the late third millennium BC.

The earliest copper-mining and smelting sites have been dated to the end of the third millennium, in the Wadi Samad, close to water-courses. They are settlement sites with irrigated crop-growing areas, beehive tombs and the remains of small rectangular structures that were probably houses. Copper ore for smelting was found locally, forming a village industry, unlike the industry of the larger combined mining and smelting sites in the north and west of the Jabal Akhdar mountains. An abundance of copper in Iranian Baluchistan, with a similar technological level and smelting sites dated to the mid-third millennium, indicates a common cultural convergence of southern Iran and Oman from the late fourth millennium.

Meluhha is now generally identified with the Harappan civilization in the region of the Indus river, which matured before 2400 BC. It is assumed from clay ship models that seagoing vessels were used, and similar ships may have been used by Magan. Direct trade with Mesopotamia as well as with Dilmun is shown by finds of square steatite Indus stamp seals identical in shape and decoration to seals found at Mohenjo-Daro and Harappa, but it is not known whether they travelled only by sea or whether the overland route through southern Iran was also used. The trade with Mesopotamia ended after the Akkadian period and after the Ur III period in the early centuries of the second millennium BC, when Magan was also no longer mentioned in cuneiform texts. Dilmun remained, probably through trade connections on the mainland, the entrepôt of the Gulf.

In the mid-first millennium BC, during Achaemenian times, Persians in Oman settled principally on the western side of the mountains, where the earlier Magan had been concentrated. They introduced the *qanat* system of water collection and conservation for field irrigation (see Chapter 30). Following the Parthian conquests in the third century BC, little is known of Oman until the third century AD. Migrating Arabs from the west, descendants of earlier Persian settlers, and the indigenous population and fishing communities – probably the Sabae, Macae and Ichthyophagi of the Classical authors – then formed the three main groups of people inhabiting Oman.

Following the overthrow of Parthia by the Persian Ardashir I in AD 226 the Persians gained control of part of the Arabian coast of the Gulf, an area they designated Mazun, later 'Uman, centred on present-day Sohar. The majority of the Arabs in Sasanian times were the Azd from western Arabia, who migrated through western Hadramawt. The Persians controlled the coastal areas to the south and the centres of maritime trade as well as a large part of the best agricultural land. As the result of a treaty with the Persians in the sixth century the Azd were allowed to control the mountain pastures, the deserts and other areas surrounding 'Uman. Then Khusrau I (AD 531–79) reorganized and developed the country, building roads, forts, *qanats* and other irrigation works. With the coming of Islam the Persians were evicted and the Arabs gained control of Oman.

South-west Arabia

The wealth of south-west Arabia came from the trade in frankincense and myrrh, grown inland and also imported from the Horn of
Africa; these are the only places where incense grows naturally.
Their early trade, probably from the third to the first millennium
BC, seems to have been to north-east Arabia, to Egypt and to the
developing countries of the Mediterranean. At a later period the
south Arabians, acting as middlemen, obtained luxuries and
spices from India and the East, principally destined for the
markets of Egypt and Rome.

   Sea trade routes were established early, from the time of the
expedition of Queen Hatshepsut in the mid-second millennium BC.
The trading fleets of Solomon in the early first millennium BC, and
the Roman traders from Egypt and the head of the Red Sea,
sailed as far as Eudaemon Arabia (? Aden) for direct trade. Shortly
before the beginning of the Christian era the sea traders learned to
use the monsoon winds and were able to sail direct to and from
India. The collapse of the imported trade affected the internal
caravan trade, and incense was obtained from the ports of Muza
and Moschca in Dhufar, where the best frankincense grew.

   The cultures of south Arabia developed in the first millennium

31.2: *Trading and supply routes in Arabia
from the third millennium BC to the early
centuries of the Christian era developed by sea
and by land. Dilmun, Magan and Meluhha
traded with Sumer and southern Mesopotamia
through the Arabian Gulf in the third and
second millennia; expeditions from Egypt in the
mid-second millennium and later Solomon's
trading fleets from the Gulf of Aquaba led to
overland trade by the south Arabians both to the
north and across Arabia from the incense-
growing areas of south Arabia and the Horn of
Africa. The discovery in the first century BC
of monsoon winds and sea routes to India made
the northern land routes redundant.*

	trade and supply routes
	sea routes in first millennium BC
	Egyptian expeditions
	Roman trading fleets
	states in third millennium BC
	states in first millennium BC

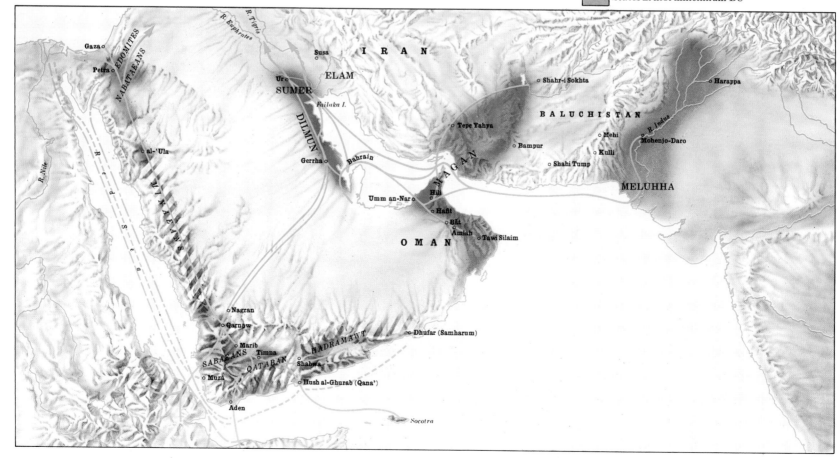

BC from the farming people who lived in the valleys that front the inland Sayhad desert, the Ramlat Sabatayn. The mountain ranges form a natural division between the inland area and the country facing the sea. The coastal side of the mountains, which was relatively less developed and where there were no monuments or irrigation works, was occupied by the tribes of Himyar, who traded at Muza after the first century, and were for a time subordinate to Qataban. All the principal centres were on the inside of the mountains, facing towards the desert region. Four regional groupings, corresponding to the main dialects of southern Arabian, had a political structure involving a *mlk* or king, and also *mkrb* rulers in Saba' and Qataban. These people were described by Classical authors.[7] The northernmost was Ma'in, land of the Minaeans, with its centre at Qarnaw in the Wadi Jawf.[8] They were nomads and herdsmen who became the principal traders of incense through the land later held by the Nabataeans. Immediately to the south lay Saba', a federation in the highlands of present-day Yemen. The Sabaeans, once conquerors of the country as far as the coast, were centred on Marib in the Wadi Dhana, where they had a large oval-shaped temple. They were supported by trading and irrigation farming, and their great dam across the wadi once watered an area of some 65 square kilometres. To the south-east lay Qataban, with a number of walled settlements of which the capital was Timna', in the Wadi Baihan, which had a large temple. The Qatabanians produced myrrh and traded in incense. Ancient canals and sluices that irrigated their farmland can be seen in the areas bordering the main wadis. At one stage Qataban extended to the coast for the import and trade of frankincense and myrrh. The Hadramawt, with their capital and temples at Shabwa, occupied a large area inland from the south coast. Their territory extended eastwards from the port of Qana' as far as Dhufar. It included extensive frankincense-growing areas, principally on the mainland but later also on the island of Socotra, some 480 kilometres offshore.

All these groups produced finely cut masonry, especially for their temples.[9] The Sabaeans appear to have introduced the carving of inscriptions in south Arabia, using well-proportioned characters probably developed from the emergence of a 'geometric' style found in the Fertile Crescent, during the sixth to fifth centuries BC. These texts have made significant contributions to our knowledge and understanding of these ancient peoples.

The Nabataeans

Originally from the area now known as Transjordan, the Nabataeans established their centre at Petra, once an Edomite stronghold. From here they controlled the incense trade from south Arabia to Syria and Palestine after the fourth century BC. They became agriculturalists skilled in irrigation and water-conservation techniques. Following the Minaean withdrawal from their trading station at Dedan (al-'Ula) in the first century, the Nabataeans established a commercial centre at al-Higr (Mada' in Salih) in the northern Hejaz.

During the first century BC, as allies of Rome, the Nabataeans provided cavalry for the Alexandrian War and assisted in the invasion of Arabia (25–24 BC), when the outskirts of Marib were reached. At the beginning of the Christian era the Nabataean kingdom extended from the Hejaz as far north as Damascus and included parts of Sinai and the Negev. From this period to the second century AD the Nabataeans built temples, and carved the façades of their rock-cut tombs with Hellenistic architectural features, the finest of them at Petra. Nabataean autonomy ended under the Roman emperor Trajan in AD 106, when their territory became a Roman province, and from the third century their importance declined as the emphasis on trade moved away from Arabia.

31.3: *The south Arabians were skilled in the carving of alabaster and marble statuettes, offerings dedicated to temples, portrait heads, jars, bowls and cosmic palettes, inscription tablets and architectural designs and mouldings. The bull and the ibex held religious significance and formalized designs were frequently used as a decorative moulding or panel: these two fragments each formed part of a frieze.*

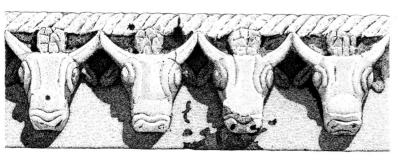

32. The Hellenistic world

In Classical times the focus of the Greek world had been Greece itself and the cities of the eastern Aegean seaboard such as Miletus, Smyrna and Ephesus. During the later fourth century BC the centre of gravity underwent a shift to the east: to Asia Minor, northern Syria and Egypt.

The historical basis of these developments was the unification of the divided city-states of Classical Greece by the most northerly of the Greek states, the kingdom of Macedon, and the struggle to free the Greeks in Asia from Persian domination. Although begun by his father, Philip II, the completion of this task and the great eastward expansion of Greek culture and political control that followed were the work of Alexander the Great, whose reign covered the years 336–323 BC. Alexander's conquests set the style for and began the process of Hellenizing the entire Near East.

The archaeological evidence for this process is rich but unbalanced. Hellenistic cities contained splendid and elaborate public buildings, many of which have survived to the present or can easily be recovered by excavation. As a result, Hellenistic city life is well documented and has been frequently described. However, the humbler quarters of these cities, and less conspicuous settlements such as villages and farmsteads, have been more or less neglected, with consequent damage to our understanding of many of the social and economic realities of Hellenistic life. The material record is complemented by excellent documentary evidence for social and institutional history in the letters and edicts of kings, the decrees passed by cities to regulate internal policy and relations with other cities, and very numerous inscriptions honouring individuals for their achievements and benefactions. Inscriptions and papyri also tend to throw light on the literate and wealthier sections of the community at the expense of the rest of the population. We know much about the wealthiest 5 per cent of the population but too little about the remainder.

The role of cities

The empire conquered by Alexander corresponded roughly with the furthermost limits of the Persian Achaemenian empire. It was thus a territory that was already developed both economically and politically; the Greeks could never have maintained control of this area if they had not taken over and exploited the administrative infrastructure established by the Persians. These had governed their provinces through satraps, who were installed in palaces at strategic points that now served as the centres of political power. The Hellenistic kings, especially in the east, simply inherited this method of government. They also relied on the communications network of caravan and post routes that held the Persian empire together, routes that Alexander himself had followed on his march of conquest.

The most important feature to spread was the Greek form of city. Greek civilization stretched from the Mediterranean to central Asia; the region in which it established the firmest hold was Asia Minor (modern Turkey), where dozens of new cities, with Greek-style institutions, came into being under Alexander's successors. The same tendency can be detected almost as clearly in Syria and Palestine, Mesopotamia, Persia and the Bactrian kingdoms in Afghanistan, although the distribution of cities is inevitably sparser in the east than in the west.[1]

The notion of a Greek city is a complex one, and any definition must seek to characterize not only its physical form but also the social and political institutions that it enshrined. Its physical form was, in the first instance, largely dictated by social needs, and certain visible features were common to most foundations and reflected characteristics shared by most cities. Buildings whose presence almost serves to define the community as a city included the temple of the chief city god or goddess, the fortification wall, especially necessary in the age of the autonomous city-state, and a central meeting place for the whole citizen body, sometimes taking the form of a large open square (agora), at others that of a building such as a theatre. Most Greek city constitutions included a council, much smaller than the total number of citizens, which would play an important part in government; this council, and also other administrative officers and committees, would meet in specially designed buildings such as the prytaneion (town hall), bouleuterion (council chamber) or odeion (small theatre). Education of the young men, both athletic and musical, was a fundamental element in Greek life, and was commonly provided by the state. This fact is reflected in such characteristic public buildings as the gymnasium and the palaestra (wrestling ground). Athletic games and competitions, also central to Greek life, would be held here or in a stadium, while musical and cultural activities, often competitive, would take place in the theatre or the odeion.

Economic factors were no less important in determining the physical nature of the Greek city-state. Each city aimed to support itself from its own resources, and indeed the high cost and difficulty of land transport encouraged self-sufficiency. To each city was attached a territory, usually containing villages, estates owned by private landowners, extra-mural temples and other settlements, and this area of dependent countryside was as important a part of the city-state as the town itself. The crops grown in the territory would be brought to town and sold in a central market place (agora) where the prices of essential goods were regulated by city officers.[2]

In Greece and in the areas of western Asia Minor that received Greek settlers at an early date the territories of cities were usually adjacent to one another, but in the interior of Asia Minor and places further east the new Greek cities by no means supplanted the existing pattern of settlements. Large stretches of countryside, no doubt settled with villages and farmsteads, were controlled by wealthy and powerful landowners, while other areas, notably in central Anatolia, Pontus, Cappadocia and Syria, can be designated temple-states. Here the land was technically owned by the god, represented by his high priest; the inhabitants of the land were regarded as slaves of the god. This native system of land tenure resisted the tide of Hellenism until the onset of Roman rule, when most of the temple-states were secularized, and usually transformed into Greek city-states of the familiar kind.

The circumstances behind the foundation of new cities in the Hellenistic period naturally varied greatly. Alexander himself was responsible for settling contingents of his Macedonian or Greek troops along the route of his victorious march. These cities served two purposes: the troops were rewarded with land and potential wealth on a scale they could not hope to attain in their native country, and the cities acted as administrative centres and defensive strongpoints inside newly conquered territory. For the most part, Alexander's cities were not established on completely virgin sites but supplanted important existing settlements. The most famous of these foundations was, of course, Alexandria in Egypt, a site chosen by Alexander himself on the sea at the western edge of the Nile delta. The choice of site was more than justified by the subsequent prosperity of the city, which by the first century BC had become the largest in the ancient world, with a population of perhaps a million inhabitants.[3]

Recent excavations at Ai Khanoum on the banks of the Oxus in northern Afghanistan have provided a striking demonstration of the spread of Hellenism to even the most remote areas of the known world. Ai Khanoum was a large city built to a Classical Greek model and inhabited by a Greek-speaking population. Its excavated buildings are grouped round a peristyle courtyard or *atrium*, and include a *temenos* (a shrine dedicated to a notable city benefactor, probably its founder, Kineas), administrative quarters, a theatre and a *gymnasium*. The architecture of the city buildings still made extensive use of mud brick (good building stone was not readily available in the area), but in overall design and in ornamental detail it is purely Greek. The original settlers both wor-

shipped the Classical Greek gods (a dedication to Hermes and Heracles was found in the *gymnasium*) and adopted local cults, as is shown by two temples, one inside and one outside the city wall, built on an oriental pattern.

The most remarkable discovery of the excavations to date is an inscription commemorating the visit of a certain Clearchus, a pupil of the philosopher Aristotle, who brought with him a copy of moral maxims from the sanctuary of Apollo at Delphi for the instruction and edification of the colonists. One could ask for no more dramatic demonstration of the unity of the Hellenistic world than this. Ai Khanoum appears to have been abandoned in the first century BC, perhaps two and a half centuries after its foundation, and this was probably the case with many of the more easterly foundations of Alexander and his Seleucid successors. However, the Greek settlements in central Asia and towards north-west India played a vital role in influencing the culture of the area. Further to the west, in Persia and Mesopotamia, several of the Greek cities founded by the Seleucids survived and flourished into the Roman period, notably Seleucia on the Tigris, the eastern headquarters of the Seleucid empire, and Seleucia on the Eulaeus, the ancient Elamite capital of Susa.[4]

Military settlement was not the only basis for new cities. Another frequent mechanism was the synoecism, the forced or voluntary uniting of several smaller settlements into a new large city. A typical example of this occurred a generation before Alexander, between 370 and 365 BC, when the Carian king, Mausolus, united six small towns of the modern Bodrum peninsula of southwest Turkey into his royal capital of Halicarnassus. Halicarnassus had always been the most important city of the area but now it was immensely expanded, acquiring a defensive fortification wall 7.5 kilometres long, an elaborate harbour and dockyards, new public buildings and its best-known monument, the funerary

32.1: *A view of Pergamum from the south. This was the royal capital of the Attalid dynasty, which came to power in north-west Asia Minor and challenged Seleucid supremacy in the later third and second centuries BC. The city occupies a strategic site at the edge of the Mysian highlands, overlooking the river Caicus. The royal palace, several important temples, a library and a theatre were all situated on the acropolis, seen in the background. To the south the paved road led to more public buildings, including the largest gymnasium in the Greek world, and from here to the lower town, underneath modern Bergama, where most of the population lived.*

temple of the royal dynasty, known as the Mausoleum, one of the seven wonders of the ancient world. This lavish building programme following a synoecism shows the use of wealth on a large scale to improve the public buildings of even quite modest cities.

Military colonies and forced synoecisms provide examples of city foundations imposed by the decision of a ruler, but Hellenization was also a voluntary process. Greek civilization was generally recognized by both Greeks and non-Greeks as superior, in cultural terms, to any of its rivals. It was therefore natural for those on the fringe of Hellenized areas to take on Greek customs and aspire to similar ideals. Native aristocracies were the first to be influenced in this way. The process began in areas adjacent to old-established Greek settlements, for instance in Lycia and Caria in south-west Asia Minor. In fact, Mausolus of Halicarnassus came from a native Carian family, though he became thoroughly Hellenized. More remote regions, such as Mysia and Pisidia, show signs of Greek influence much later and were never as strongly affected. The activities of Mausolus and of his contemporary Pericles in Lycia provide an example of the complex interrelationship between Greek and native that was to be found all over the Levant. Both established monarchical control over non-Hellenized regions of south-west Anatolia, and in the style of their rule showed a mixture of Greek and native influences. Both were eventually buried in elaborate funerary temples at Halicarnassus and at Limyra, an idea native in origin but realized in Greek architectural terms.

Furthermore, the custom of erecting such monuments to outstanding individuals implanted itself and was taken over by Hellenistic monarchs and Greek cities. The relationship between Greek and native was reciprocal. In general it appears that the coastlands and the main river valleys, representing the routes of penetration into the hinterland, sooner or later received Greek and Macedonian settlements and achieved a more or less uniform Greek culture; in the mountainous areas, away from major routes, the native aristocracies eventually took on Greek ways and adopted the Greek language, but most of the inhabitants of the countryside continued to use their native languages until the third or fourth century AD, and show little sign of having been affected by Greek culture in other respects.

The distribution of city sites through Anatolia and the Levant naturally echoes geographical realities. Along the west coast of Asia Minor and up the valleys of the Caicus, Hermus and Maeander a combination of settled political conditions and fertile land allowed a high concentration of sites, almost all of which prospered.

32.2: *The route chosen by Alexander of Macedon took him almost to the limits of the known world in pursuit of conquest. He not only conquered but also encouraged the adoption of Greek customs and culture among those who came under his domination.*

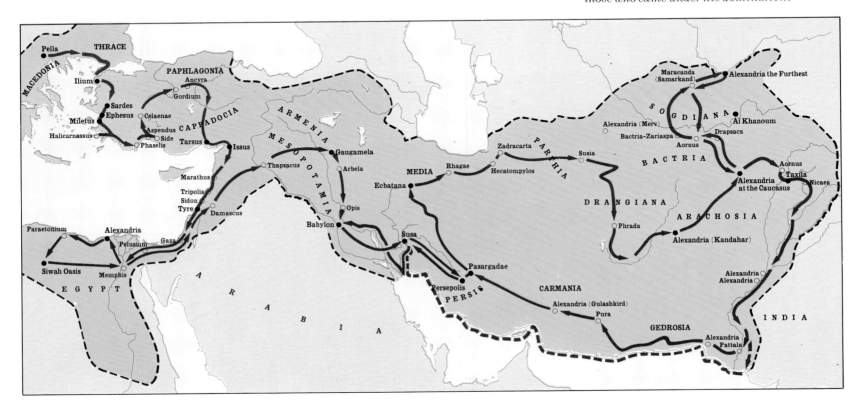

32.3: *Hellenistic Asia Minor and Syria.*

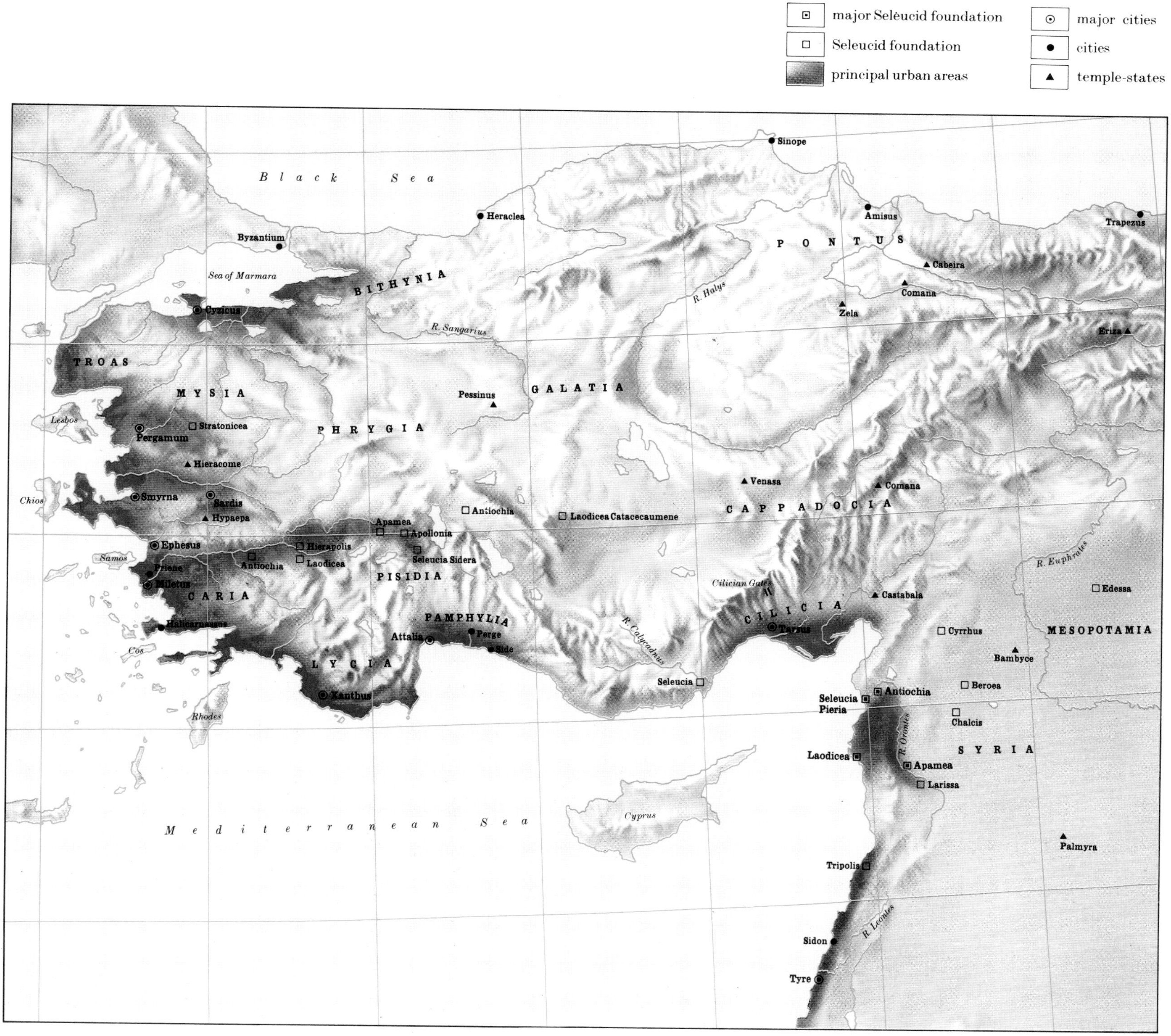

- ⊡ major Seleucid foundation
- □ Seleucid foundation
- principal urban areas
- ⊙ major cities
- ● cities
- ▲ temple-states

Black   Sea

● Sinope

● Heraclea

Sea of Marmara

● Byzantium

⊙ Cyzicus

B I T H Y N I A

R. Halys

R. Sangarius

P O N T U S

● Amisus

● Trapezus

▲ Cabeira

▲ Comana

▲ Zela

Eriza ▲

T R O A S

M Y S I A

P H R Y G I A

Pessinus ▲

G A L A T I A

Lesbos

□ Stratonicea

⊙ Pergamum

▲ Hieracome

Chios

⊙ Smyrna

⊙ Sardis

▲ Hypaepa

▲ Venasa

▲ Comana

C A P P A D O C I A

Samos

⊙ Ephesus

□ Antiochia

Priene

● Miletus

C A R I A

□ Antiochia

□ Hierapolis

□ Laodicea

□ Apamea

□ Apollonia

□ Seleucia Sidera

P I S I D I A

□ Laodicea Catacaecaumene

R. Euphrates

□ Edessa

● Halicarnassus

Cos

P A M P H Y L I A

Attalia ⊙

● Perge

● Side

L Y C I A

R. Calycadnus

Cilician Gates

C I L I C I A

⊙ Tarsus

▲ Castabala

M E S O P O T A M I A

□ Cyrrhus

▲ Bambyce

⊙ Xanthus

Rhodes

Seleucia ●

□ Beroea

Seleucia Pieria ⊡ Antiochia

□ Chalcis

Laodicea ⊡

R. Orontes

⊡ Apamea

□ Larissa

S Y R I A

Cyprus

▲ Palmyra

M e d i t e r r a n e a n   S e a

Tripolis □

R. Leontes

Sidon ●

Tyre ⊙

The Seleucids attempted to link this area with north Syria, first by a string of new cities in the Maeander valley (Antioch on the Maeander, Laodicea and Apamea) and then by a sequence of garrison cities across the less hospitable regions of Pisidia and Lycaonia (Seleucia Sidera, Apollonia, Pisidian Antioch and Laodicea Catacecaumene). From here routes led across the Taurus mountains to the port of Seleucia on the Calycadnus and to the Cilician plain, which the Seleucids controlled.

In Syria the most important of the new settlements became Antioch, Seleucia, Apamea and Laodicea, while other cities took the names of towns in Macedonia and northern Greece: Pella, Aegae, Edessa, Cyrrhus, Beroea, Amphipolis, Chalcis and Larissa. These cities were confined to the coastal belt and to the depression formed by the Orontes and Jordan valleys, separated from the sea by a mountain range. Further to the east the waterless land of the desert was peopled, as it always has been, by nomads as far as the Mesopotamian basin, where more permanent settlements could be established. Further east again the few cities were situated along the major routes, which were used both by armies and by the caravans of traders.[5] While a political or military purpose can be detected in most of these foundations, commercial and economic factors had a part to play in the development of many of them. The expense and difficulty of land transport meant that most of the important trading cities of the Hellenistic world were sea ports such as Cyzicus, Rhodes and Alexandria, but cities on important overland routes form an exception to this rule – Apamea, for example, at the head of the Maeander valley, and the caravan cities of the Syrian desert.[6]

Another feature of the Hellenistic city was a tendency towards uniformity of design. The cities of Classical Greece had usually emerged by a gradual process of organic growth, often after the synoecism of two or more adjacent villages, and this resulted in a disordered plan. Formal town planning had its origin in the fifth century BC, but it became much more prevalent in the fourth century and later as new foundations, and the authority of a single ruler, provided the opportunity to create cities on a unified plan.[7] An outstanding example is Priene in the lower Maeander valley, which has been almost completely excavated. The city, which lies on a sloping terrace some 200 metres below a fortified acropolis, was conceived as an entity and was built during the reign of Alexander the Great.

It is almost impossible to give accurate figures for city populations in the Hellenistic world, despite the considerable quantity of detailed documentation available. Literary sources yield a few random figures: 300 000 for Alexandria in Egypt in the first century BC, a figure that probably excluded the non-citizen element of the population, which might have swelled the total to a million; 600 000, a startlingly high figure, for the eastern Seleucid capital, Seleucia on the Tigris; 140 000 for Pergamum in the mid-second century AD; perhaps 200 000 for Syrian Antioch. In general it

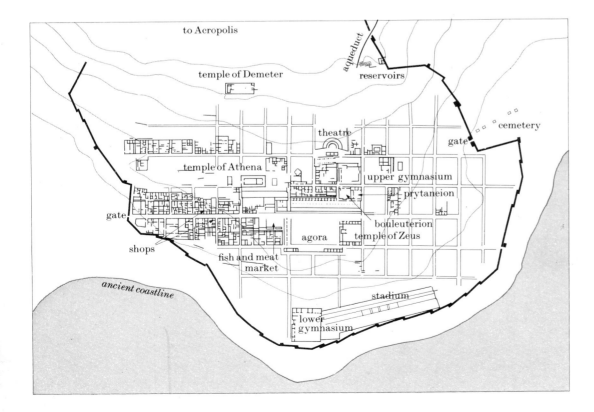

32.4: *The plan of the city of Priene, which is better preserved than at any other Hellenistic foundation. The fortification wall encloses a rectangular grid of streets, incorporating the temple of Athena Polias at the highest point of the town, a theatre, government buildings, and a stadium and gymnasium away from the central area. The shops and private houses are also remarkably well preserved.*

32.5: *The Mausoleum at Halicarnassus. Little more than the rock-cut foundations of this famous building can be seen today. Various reconstructions have been proposed, based on descriptions found in the writings of ancient authors, surviving fragments of sculpture and the plans of later buildings that were modelled on the Mausoleum. The reconstruction by E. Krischen shown here may need to be modified as a consequence of recent research, which suggests that the columns on the upper part of the building were differently spaced and that the three steps of the podium at the base of the building carried a sculptured frieze.*

seems likely that only Alexandria would be classed as a great conurbation by modern standards, with a population in the region of a million (to be matched later in antiquity only by Rome and Constantinople). Below this there was a handful of cities whose total population might have approached a quarter of a million, Pergamum, Miletus, Syrian Antioch and Athens among them, and then perhaps thirty or forty cities with between thirty and a hundred thousand inhabitants.

City and country

We should not be so blinded by the importance of cities in the Hellenistic world as to ignore other forms of settlement. Despite the spread of city life, most of the Near East beyond Mesopotamia and the mountainous and desert areas of Asia Minor and Syria were not directly affected by Hellenization; local traditions of political power and patterns and types of settlement continued unchanged. Furthermore the cities, as has already been emphasized, were almost entirely dependent on the countryside for their livelihood. Although coastal towns could and did import foodstuffs and other bulky imports relatively cheaply, this was impossible for land-locked cities, especially in the absence of good roads, which were extremely rare before the Roman period. Each city was dependent on its own resources. A recent survey of Troas in north-west Turkey suggests that there at least the tendency was to centralize the population, and thus political control, in the city rather than

to disperse it through the countryside. In this relatively small area there were about twenty cities in the Hellenistic period, many of them very small, with only four or five recognizable village sites among them. We may assume that not only landowners but also the majority of the peasants lived in the city itself, travelling out daily to work the fields. This pattern was perpetuated in the early Roman Empire, but changed in the Byzantine age when the number of cities decreased sharply and village sites became common again.[8]

Despite the interdependence of town and country there was a great gulf between the two. The mountains and forests were still peopled by native tribesmen owing little loyalty to the inhabitants of the cities; banditry was common, travel difficult and dangerous except in large caravans or under military escort. The alienation between town and country was made greater by another fact. In Classical Greece, with some notable exceptions, the inhabitants of the countryside generally possessed the same rights and privileges as the inhabitants of the cities. In Asia, settlers in Greek cities generally excluded the native population from citizenship rights, providing ample opportunity for class conflict. However, the dependence of towns upon the country must have brought some changes to the latter. With the foundation of a city the population in a given area almost certainly increased, bringing the need for more intensive exploitation of the land: a greater area was brought under cultivation and improved agricultural methods were introduced. At Ai Khanoum a whole plain that had been left as pasture or used for dry farming before the foundation of the city was irrigated with canals and intensively cultivated by the Greeks. Classical archaeologists have hitherto paid too little attention to this aspect of Hellenistic city life, but there is little doubt that detailed investigation would reveal a similar state of affairs in many other areas.

Although a considerable amount of scientific experiment was carried out in the main centres of learning, notably in Alexandria, the Hellenistic age shows relatively little technological advance over the Classical period. A great deal of attention was paid to the techniques of warfare, especially siegecraft, resulting in greatly improved torsion catapults and very sophisticated designs in defensive fortifications, but these military advances were an exception to the rule.[9] Buildings in Hellenistic cities tended to be larger and more lavish than their Classical predecessors as a result of the greater wealth available to the city notables who built them, but construction techniques remained unchanged. One thing that this building does demonstrate is the continuing availability of cheap labour. Agriculture apart, the construction industry gave employment to more people in the ancient world than anything else, and this may help to explain why the wealthy classes of the cities spent so much of their surplus wealth on erecting public buildings.

33. First-millennium Europe before the Romans

In the course of the first millennium BC Europe experienced the fastest and most dramatic changes it was to undergo before those of the eighteenth century AD. The cultural pattern that developed in Europe during the first millennium BC, with its mixture of iron-using peasant farmers and pastoral groups, its urban communities, its manufacturing and commercial ingenuity, its social adaptability and artistic originality, formed the basis of subsequent developments through to modern times.

Europe at 1000 BC

In about 1000 BC there was little hint of the changes to come; the whole of Europe, including the Mediterranean coastlands, was occupied by bronze-using farmers who, while prosperous, showed no sign of developing urban civilization and were apparently little affected by the sophisticated societies of western Asia, which were already using iron. Even in Greece, where Mycenaean civilization had recently been destroyed (see Chapter 19), little use was made of iron, and there was little technological advance over the rest of Europe. Indeed, no evidence of trade or influence from the Aegean at this time can be detected, even in Italy or the Balkans.[1]

Two areas of Europe seem to have been more highly developed than elsewhere: east-central Europe from Switzerland to Hungary, and southern Scandinavia. Both had flourishing and highly original metallurgical industries in gold and bronze, based in central Europe on well-organized mining and in Scandinavia on imported metals. Both had distinctive artistic traditions,[2] and numerous inhabitants who were engaged in efficient mixed farming and (in central Europe) used metal tools.

To the south-east of Europe lay the sophisticated, literate, iron-using communities of the eastern Mediterranean, engaged in maritime trade. In the case of the Phoenicians of the Levant, this reached as far as the opposite end of the Mediterranean, and such traffic affected the whole southern coast of Europe.[3]

In central Europe the final phase of the Bronze Age was a time of expansion and the crystallization of a pattern of social and political organization, expressed in hillforts and warrior burials, that was to characterize 'barbarian' Europe for centuries. Besides innovations in armour and weaponry, this period also saw changes in religious practice, marked by burial in 'urnfields' and the presence of cult objects decorated with symbols of the wheel, sun and water birds. The large cemeteries of this time, some of which – notably those on important transalpine routes – persisted into the iron-using period, may contain thousands of graves. Sites such as Hallstatt in Austria and Glasinac in Yugoslavia form the backbone of the older chronological schemes.

The spread of iron-using in Europe (for, in the absence of any evidence of local discovery, it must be seen as the result of diffusion) has long served as an archaeological marker, and the concept of an 'Iron Age' is deeply ingrained. This is unfortunate, for although iron-using spread rapidly during the ninth and eighth centuries, it was a long time before iron became common, and in its early stages the metal did not greatly affect communities. It is important to date its initial spread, however, for this preceded the great trading dispersal from the Aegean (see below) and must be seen as a diffusion of technology and ideas through many different communities; it was similar to the exactly contemporary spread of iron-using through North and West Africa. Nowhere in Europe did iron replace bronze; its use as a superior alternative metal for weapons supplemented that of bronze, and as it became more plentiful iron was also used for tools, harnesses and expendables such as nails and cartwheel rims.

The iron long-swords, spears and battle-axes, and contemporary bronze objects beloved of central Europeans, were widely adopted between the eighth and sixth centuries and have, rather unfortunately, been named 'Hallstatt' (a designation that signifies a period and a culture) after the site where they were studied in the nineteenth century.[4]

The acceptance of iron technology

During the eighth and seventh centuries the acceptance of iron technology, which included the smelting of local ores, and greater contact with the pastoral peoples of the south Russian plains occurred simultaneously in central Europe. Although suggestions of a spread of iron-using from the Caucasus through the Ukraine to central Europe earlier than the eighth century is not supported by recent research, it seems likely that the increased use of horses for riding and driving in central Europe owes much to steppe influence. The appearance of horse bits, often made of iron, of other items of harness and of four-wheeled, iron-tyred carts in the richer burials can be attributed to this contact, although an actual migration westwards of steppe horsemen (the Thrako-Cimmerians of past

writers) into the forests is unlikely.

Another contemporary phenomenon was the continued spread of 'urnfield rites' westwards into France and northwards across the European Plain. As changes are discernible in both the styles of ceramic and metal objects and religious practices, this spread has often been seen as the result of invasions or migrations. Folk movements can be identified from archaeological and literary evidence later in the millennium, so migrations may have taken place, especially in two regions: south-west Germany, eastern France and the Rhineland; and south-west France and northern Spain.

Mediterranean developments

In the Mediterranean coastlands south of the Alps a major cultural divergence from the development of the rest of Europe occurred during the eighth and seventh centuries. This was a consequence of Phoenician and Greek commercial enterprise. Present evidence suggests that few of their ships or traders had reached even Italy or Iberia in the centuries immediately before 800 BC, but that a sudden expansion then drew all the shores of the Mediterranean into one exchange network. The Phoenicians of Tyre and Sidon were the most adventurous (see Chapter 34), establishing trading and supply posts (Carthage, the predecessor of Tunis, became the most important of those along the North African coast and among the islands). Recent work in Huelva Bay (near the Riotinto region of south-west Spain) shows that the Phoenicians were active in the copper workings there from the ninth century, and through Gades (modern Cadiz), their trading emporium on an island at the mouth of the river Guadalquivir, they came to influence all southern Iberia.

33.1: *Scene on a situla from Grave III, Barrow I, Vače, in northern Yugoslavia. It shows a scene of equestrian combat, and depicts in great detail the different equipment of the two riders and their horses. The workmanship is northern Italian of the seventh or sixth century.*

33.2: *Europe in the first millennium BC, showing the spread of Celtic-speaking peoples that profoundly affected central and southern Europe in the fifth to third centuries. The major trade routes and the furthest advance westwards of the Persian empire are also indicated.*

spread of Celtic-speaking peoples

- before 400 BC
- 400–200 BC
- western limits of Persian empire

trade routes

- Greek
- Phoenician
- Etruscan

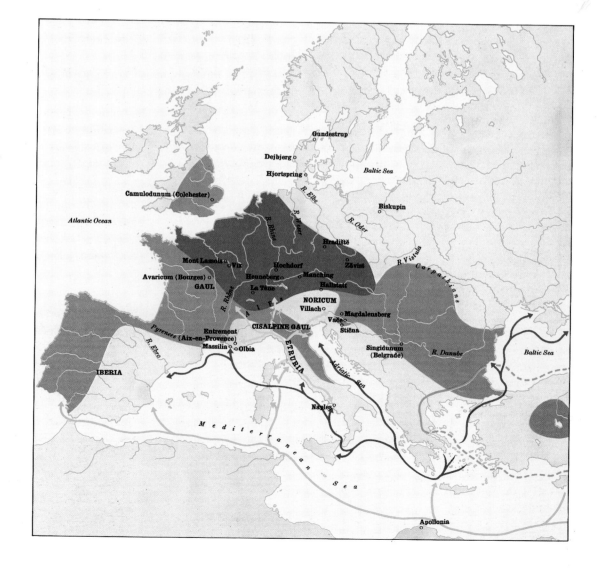

The central Mediterranean was much more quickly affected by the new developments than Iberia, for the copper of Sardinia, the iron of Elba and the varied minerals of Tuscany attracted both Phoenicians and Greeks, and they inspired the first native Italian civilization, that of the Etruscans. The beginnings of Greek expansion are better documented than the early stages of Phoenician enterprise. The Greeks of Euboea settled on the island of Pithecusa, opposite Naples, between 780 and 770 BC;[5] in the following century a whole series of trading posts and agricultural colonies were founded by different Greek states in Sicily, southern Italy and as far west as north-eastern Spain and southern France, where Massilia (modern Marseilles) was the most important.[6] Although their exports are found there, neither Phoenicians nor Greeks set up colonies in the rich regions of northern Italy. Presumably this was because of the rapid rise to power of the Etruscan city-states, which dominated Italy from the Alps to the Bay of Naples from before 600 BC and traded widely on land and sea.[7] For the next two centuries the Phoenician, Greek and Etruscan states fought each other for spheres of influence and slowly extended their power – the Phoenicians over North Africa and southern Iberia, the Etruscans over central Europe from eastern France to Yugoslavia, and the Greeks over both northern Spain and southern France, and the Black Sea coasts.

The effects on central Europe

The effects of this expansion on the indigenous peoples of Europe have been much studied, and were not unlike the effects of European maritime trade on West Africa when it developed so suddenly in the sixteenth and seventeenth centuries AD. Long-established exchange networks were upset, new resources of raw materials were located and exploited, and local social systems and settlement patterns were greatly changed. The inland exchange networks were the most affected, for entrepôts were established on the coasts of the western and central Mediterranean, from which long-distance caravans set out. The routes along which the luxuries of the civilized Mediterranean states moved were the Guadalquivir,[8] the Ebro and the Rhône valleys, and the alpine passes (such as the Austrian Brenner or the Yugoslav Knin). Archaeological evidence of the trade is widespread in central Europe: finds include fine table ceramics, coarser containers for wine or oil, metal vessels, jewellery and weapons.[9] Local copies naturally appeared at once, providing archaeologists with excellent typological sequences, now confirmed by radiocarbon dates. In central Europe these have been named Hallstatt C (750–600 BC), Hallstatt D (600–450 BC) and La Tène I (450–350 BC). Changes in social and political organization are suggested by the development of fortified hilltop settlements, often with graves nearby containing extravagant offerings and covered by enormous mounds. One mound, discovered in 1978 at Hochdorf near Stuttgart, was 30 metres high and covered an intact and rich male burial upon a wheeled bed surrounded by many costly objects. From Mont Lassois (Chalon-sur-Sâone) in France, with its nearby 'royal' burial at Vix, to the

Heuneberg on the Danube in Bavaria,[10] with the nearby Hohemichele burial, to Lovošice in Czechoslovakia, the elaborately defended settlements contain riches and indications of southern inspiration not previously found in central Europe. It may well be that they were the seats of 'high kings' (paramount chieftains), and that preliminary steps towards the formation of states and confederations were taking place. The finds from settlements also show that a vigorous and increasing population, using iron for its implements, was clearing and farming large tracts of central Europe with greater efficiency and was growing new crops such as winter wheat.

Northern Europe, from Scandinavia to the British Isles, followed a different pattern of development at this time. As yet too far away to be greatly influenced by the Mediterranean states, during the first half of the millennium it suffered severely from climatic deterioration, which led to the spread of great bogs in Ireland, northern Germany and Denmark and reduced crop-ripening seasons everywhere.

The military empires and the Celtic dispersal

From the sixth century another major change affected western and central European development: a steady decrease in Greek and Etruscan interest in the regions. Greek enterprise had taken traders into the Black Sea as well as the western Mediterranean, and in the wheat-rich river valleys of the Ukraine (although these were dominated by the semi-pastoral Scythians) Greeks found the granary they needed to feed their urban populations at home.[11] By the end of the fifth century some seventy settlements, including cities like Apollonia and Olbia, had been founded, and Greek interest in central and western Europe had dwindled.[12] Greek attention was also increasingly concentrated on the Persian empire of the Achaemenian dynasty (see Chapter 30), which, having absorbed all western Asia and Egypt, was turning its attention to south-eastern Europe. Its campaigns in Europe between 492 and 479 BC, of which those of Darius I and Xerxes are best known, failed; in the next century Alexander of Macedon was to overrun Asia as far as India. Greek energies were now diverted eastwards, and interest in western and northern Europe waned still further. In the same period Etruscan influence in central Europe declined. Defeated in southern and central Italy by Greeks, and in the Po valley by Celtic tribes from the north, the Etruscans and their cities were to be conquered piecemeal by Rome in the fourth century. Carthage and the other Phoenician settlements in the west confined their interests to Africa, southern Iberia and the Mediterranean islands, and most of western and central Europe was therefore left to absorb such ideas as it could from the still relatively distant civilized states in the south. The extending involvement of Mediterranean states with mainland Europe, which would probably soon have resulted in military conquest (as, in fact, it did in Spain), was postponed for several centuries.

This breathing space (500–55 BC), traditionally known to archaeologists in western Europe as the La Tène period (La Tène

I – 450–350; II – 350–150; III – 150–55 BC) encouraged stability and prosperity: on the northern periphery of the Mediterranean, to a depth of some 800 kilometres, flourished a variety of new political entities, new hierarchies of settlement culminating in proto- and fully urban communities, new industries and new artistic traditions.[13] Broadly contemporaneous development can be traced, through the increasing literary as well as archaeological evidence, in Spain (known as Iberian), France, western Germany and Czechoslovakia (known as La Tène), the north Balkans (Illyrian) and the south-east Balkans (Geto/Dacian). These developments were accompanied by folk movements and plundering raids that took large hordes of northerners southwards through the Pyrenees, the Alps and the Balkans and anticipated the movements of the fifth century AD. The best documented are those of the Celtic-speaking bearers of La Tène culture,[14] who had conquered northern Italy by 400, much of the Balkans by 290 and much of Iberia by 250 BC.[15] They were themselves to be attacked by Germanic-speakers, of whom the Cimbri (the 'Champions'), who roamed Europe from Hungary to Spain about 100 BC, and the Teutones were the most fearsome. South of the Rhine and the Danube at least, these wanderings were halted by Roman armies between 125 and 53 BC. In the process Roman control of central and western Europe increased, until by 27 BC half the continent lay within Augustus' empire.

The development of civilization in central Europe

During the last two hundred years of western Europe's independence Italian and Greek commercial interest in the area revived, resulting in closer trading and political ties. In Romania and Bulgaria states (as opposed to tribal confederations) were established, with cities like Seuthopolis (near Kazanluk, Bulgaria) and all the refinements of emerging civilization.[16] In Yugoslavia tribal groups were found – Celtic-speaking like the Scordiscii, with their fortified settlements (*oppida*) such as Singidunum (now Belgrade) and Siscia (near Zagreb), or Illyrian, with great settlements like Stična and Vače. In the Alps in eastern Austria a relatively well-known state also emerged in this period: this was the kingdom of Noricum, with its capital at Magdalensberg near Villach, which contained a Roman trading community and was connected to Italy by a road passable for wheeled traffic.[17] Similar *oppida* are found in Czechoslovakia (for example, Závist and Hradiště) and in southern Germany, where one of the best excavated is beside the Danube at Manching in Bavaria. Here timber-framed town walls enclosed an area some 6.5 kilometres in circumference and were held together, it is estimated, by about 300 tonnes of iron nails. In central and southern France urban development was also taking place; at Entremont (modern Aix-en-Provence), a city virtually indistinguishable from Italian ones although it was inhabited by Celto-Ligurians, has been extensively excavated.[18] Avaricum (Bourges), the capital of the Bituringan state, is known at present only from literary evidence, but it was said to be the 200 BC much of Iberia had already been conquered by the Romans

in the Punic Wars, but in the south and east urban communities flourished and preserved their Punic traditions in their religion, civil organization, script and art forms.

From the Black Sea to the Atlantic there was increasing social and cultural sophistication after 150 BC. Rome was now the dominant southern power, and its diplomatic and trading relationships penetrated most of the continent except the north-east. Coinages, used for a variety of purposes, became common; highly organized wheel-made ceramic, glass and metal industries were developed; and efficient agriculture supported larger populations than ever before. Even the British Isles were drawn into the Mediterranean orbit: in the south-east this was through links with the Belgic tribes of northern France and the Low Countries, and even through trans-Channel kingdoms; in the south-west it was through links – and a tin trade – with Brittany (especially the Venetic tribe) and Aquitaine. As a result, large fortified settlements appeared at Camulodunum (Colchester) and elsewhere. State formation was taking place, and new arts and crafts developed.[19]

33.3: *The Late La Tène* oppidum *of Manching in Bavaria, where large-scale excavations have taken place in recent years. These have demonstrated the presence of closely packed houses in the central area as well as manufacturing areas.*

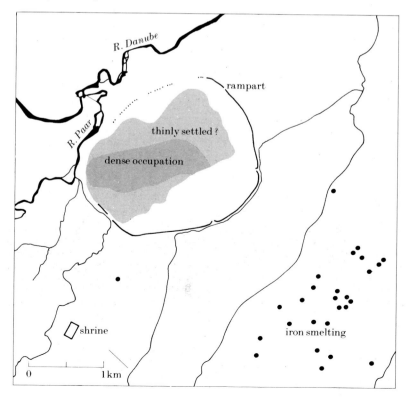

The isolation of eastern Europe

Three areas of Europe stood apart from these changes: northern Germany and Scandinavia; Poland and western Russia; and southern Russia and the neighbouring Black Sea coastlands. The first of these had been much affected by deteriorating climatic conditions, and its inherited, if impoverished, independent cultural traditions were only slowly affected by southern ideas; neither rich graves nor fortified proto-urban settlements have been found.[20] The relatively unstructured religious confederations recorded by the Roman historian Tacitus in the first century AD can be inferred from the archaeological evidence. Religious observances included human burial (or sacrifice) in bogs (as at Grabau) and votive deposits of boats (as at Hjortsprung), cauldrons (as at Gundestrup) and wagons (as at Dejbjerg). It is especially interesting – as this is the only part of Europe in which it can be observed – to see the first impact of iron-using on the circumpolar hunters and reindeer-keepers of northern Scandinavia, Finland and Russia.

In the coniferous forests of eastern Poland and western Russia, where iron had been in use (as at Biskupin) since the sixth century, relatively little change took place, although attempts have been made to identify the Slav-speaking peoples who were here in the first millennium AD. Finally, on the steppes of southern Russia the predominantly pastoral societies of Scythians and others, although in direct contact with Greeks and Asiatics, deliberately preserved their traditional ways of life. Their rulers were burned with extravagantly rich offerings (as at Chertomlyk and Altin Oba). They had accepted the luxuries of the Hellenistic and Roman worlds, so their very original art styles synthesized elements both from these and from Central Asia. The pressure brought to bear on them by other horse-riding pastoralists from beyond the Urals, such as the Sarmatians, is known from both archaeological and literary sources and was to increase in the first millennium AD.[21]

Thus by the end of the millennium Europe was divided into three main cultural areas, which were very different from those of a thousand years before. South of a line from the mouth of the Rhine to the shores of the Black Sea a common cultural tradition was developing under the *Pax Romana*. North and east of this line the steppe dwellers of the Ukraine and the forest dwellers of the North European Plain and Scandinavia, although influenced by the south, were pursuing their own independent evolutions. This new pattern was to endure for many centuries.

33.4: *The north-east European Plain in the first century AD: archaeological and tribal groupings. Symbols show the different groups that can be isolated archaeologically by their distinctive material culture; the names of tribes are those recorded in Roman literature and do not correspond directly to cultural groupings.*

major archaeological regions

▪	Rhine/Weser
○	North Sea
◻	Jutland/south Scandinavia
●	Elbe/Danube
•	lower Oder
△	upper Oder/Vistula
·	lower Vistula/east Pomerania

34. The western Mediterranean and the origins of Rome

During the eighth century BC the foundations were laid of a complex and extensive trading empire in the west Mediterranean. It was organized around a network of colonies, founded principally by Phoenicians and Greeks. Many important Mediterranean towns of today originated as colonies: among the Phoenician foundations were Valletta, Cagliari and Palermo, while Syracuse, Taranto, Naples and Marseilles were first settled by Greeks.

The factors that prompted this overseas expansion are complex and not fully understood. One important factor was undoubtedly the sharp increase in population that took place in the east Mediterranean from the late second millennium. Literary tradition asserts, and archaeological evidence confirms, that there was a growing shortage of land during this period. In an age when migration was a well-established response to such pressures, the foundation of new cities overseas was a logical response. An additional catalyst was the search for raw materials, especially to make the luxury goods that became increasingly common in graves of the eighth century onwards. In particular, the discovery and extraction of metal ores seems to have had a high priority from the earliest phases of the 'Age of Colonization'. Many of the original sites were selected not for their agricultural potential but for their proximity to raw materials. Only later did other factors, such as the presence of good arable land, begin to play a more important part in shaping the pattern of expansion and determining which settlements rose to prominence.[1]

Phoenician colonies

Literary tradition places the beginnings of Phoenician movement into the west Mediterranean as early as the late second millennium, but it is clear from archaeological evidence that the main period of expansion belonged to the eighth century. Carthage, destined to be the leader of the western Phoenician (Punic) colonies for over five hundred years, was one early foundation.[2] The Punic site (which is close to modern Tunis) lay at the head of a spur flanked by coastal lagoons. As yet little is known of the archaic town, but it was apparently enclosed by a wall 33.5 kilometres in extent. It was later provided with elaborate docks and came to control a territory that extended at least 150 kilometres into the fertile Tunisian hinterland. A great ditch is supposed to have demarcated this region, which soon became populous with towns and farms.

Despite its coastal position, Carthage was by no means typical of the setting of many of the more important Punic colonies. For example, Gades, modern Cadiz, lay at the tip of a long island where

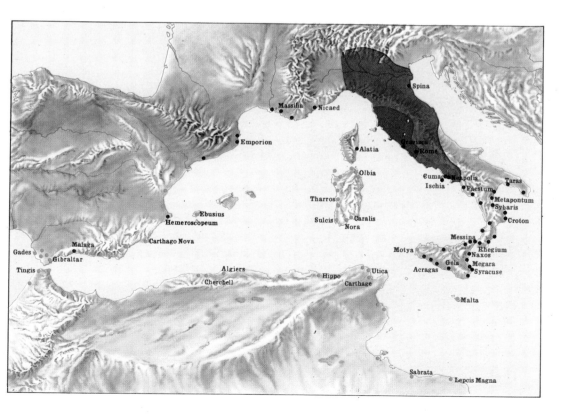

34.1: *The central and western Mediterranean in c. 500 BC. Phoenician colonies controlled the north coast of Africa, Malta and parts of Spain, Sardinia and Sicily, while Greek colonies commanded the trade routes up the western coast of Italy. The metal-rich land of the Etruscans is also shown, together with the territory that they held in the Po valley and in Campania.*

- · Phoenician colonies
- • Greek colonies
- ▓ Etruscan heartland
- ▓ extent of Etruscan expansion

strong natural defences were combined with a fine sheltered anchorage. Similarly, the principal colonies in Sardinia were all situated in promontory or island positions, where access from the land could be closely controlled.[3] For the west Sicilian colony of Motya, too, a small island was the site selected.[4] Protection from the sea was afforded by a long land bar, while the settlement itself lay on an island in the bay; a causeway linked the town with the shore. These natural defences were strengthened in the mid-sixth century BC by the provision of a massive stone wall enclosing the entire island, an area of some 50 hectares. There were two main gates and some twenty external towers. Inside the town (which was destroyed by Dionysius of Syracuse in 397 BC) excavations have disclosed small stone houses, some preceded by structures of mud brick; these were constructed early in the seventh century and converted into stone some 150 years later. A house with pebble mosaics depicting animals is also known, as well as a temple complex near the north gate. One intriguing feature is a rectangular basin, 51 by 35.5 metres, which in the early period of Motya's history seems to have been a dock or harbour.

Sites such as Motya, Carthage, Tas Silg̣ on Malta, and the Sardinian, southern Spanish and Moroccan colonies gave the Phoenicians tight control over some of the major trading routes in the west Mediterranean. That trade was the primary motive for the earliest phase of colonial settlement seems clear enough. At Riotinto in Spain, for example, the silver deposits were extensively worked in the eighth and seventh centuries by people whose houses contained large quantities of Phoenician pottery.[5] The silver was presumably transported in the form of ingots down the valley to the coast at Huelva and thence to Cadiz. Certainly Phoenician metal products were widely distributed over the Mediterranean, even in areas that were Greek and Etruscan preserves. For example, the very rich Bernadini tomb at Praeneste, east of Rome, has yielded two fine Phoenician silver dishes, with elaborate decoration

of seventh-century style. Other types of metal vessels, jewellery and earthenware vessels (*amphorae*) containing wine and oil were also widely traded, as were scarabs and objects of ivory and bone. Among perishable goods, textiles appear to have been an important item, some dyed with the renowned violet and purple shades produced from *murex* shells. Just how rapidly the Phoenician trading network became established is, however, still unclear. Occasional finds have been attributed to the ninth century, epitomized by an inscription from Nora in southern Sardinia,[6] but it is still difficult to envisage much very extensive activity before the second half of the eighth century.

Greeks in the west

Whereas the Phoenicians directed their main colonizing efforts towards the coasts of North Africa, Spain and some of the islands, the Greeks chose primarily to develop southern Italy and Sicily. Their settlements clustered along the southern and western shores of the mainland and also along the fertile coastal belt of Sicily. More than forty towns are known, whose size and architectural magnificence underline the importance of what came to be known as *Magna Graecia*, Greater Greece.

The earliest phases of this colonizing movement are now becoming much more closely documented as a result of recent excavations. Archaeological evidence shows that the first Greek settlements were being established on the coasts of Asia Minor during the tenth century. By the late ninth century the east Mediterranean trading routes were being opened up, with the foundation of sites like Al Mina, at the mouth of the Orontes river in Syria. Here warehouses were built in a native town, probably to house metalwork and other goods from some of the hinterland kingdoms such as Urartu (see Chapter 26). The rather later Greek emporium of Naucratis on the Nile provides a parallel example.

The first western colonies came rather later, in the first quarter

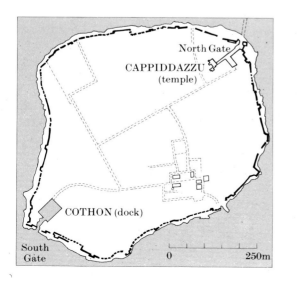

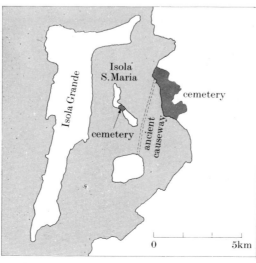

34.2: *The Phoenician colony of Motya in western Sicily. It was first settled in the seventh century BC, and the fine natural defences and excellent harbour facilities typify the setting of many Phoenician sites. The stone wall was added in the mid-sixth century.*

34.3: *Late Geometric painted vase of the eighth century BC from the cemetery at Pithecusa on the island of Ischia, Italy. The scene shows a shipwreck with sailors being eaten by sharks; it may well record an actual incident in the early days of Greek colonization.*

of the eighth century. The Greeks had already had a good deal of contact with Italy and elsewhere in Mycenaean times, between about 1500 and 1200 BC; but this trade had lapsed with the decline of the Mycenaean towns (see Chapter 19). Initially there seem to have been voyages of exploration, identifiable by sporadic finds of Middle Geometric pottery in native tombs of the early eighth century. Permanent settlement soon followed. The first known colony in the west lay at Pithecusa upon the island of Ischia.[7] Although Strabo described Ischia as particularly fertile, this small volcanic eminence situated in the Bay of Naples was a far from ideal choice. Much of the island consists of rugged upland terrain, while the coastal belt is mostly narrow and difficult to farm. The main reasons for selecting this site clearly lay elsewhere: Ischia was well placed to command the sea route up the western shores of Italy; there was a fine harbour and a small natural acropolis. Recent excavations have in fact demonstrated that by the acropolis, on the Mazzola site, there was a complex of small stone houses where the principal activity was the processing of metal, especially iron. Spectographic analysis has shown that the source of the ores was Elba, indicating that from the foundation of the settlement, in about 770 BC, the Greeks exploited the rich metal deposits of Etruria. The contents of the immensely rich graves in the Valle San Montano cemetery confirm both this contact with central Italy and the widespread nature of eighth-century Mediterranean trade. There were not only typical vases and brooches from Etruria but also an enormous range of objects from various parts of Greece and elsewhere: scarabs from Egypt, seals from Syria, jars for perfume (*aryballoi*) from Rhodes and a wide variety of Late Geometric pottery wares. One example shows the consequences of a shipwreck, a reminder of the Homeric legends, many of which may have been based upon these early voyages to Italy.

The first settlers of Pithecusa were Greeks from Chalcis on the island of Euboea, and it was the Euboeans who laid the first main network of colonies in *Magna Graecia*. In about 750 BC a settlement was founded at Cumae on the mainland opposite Ischia. Nearby was Lake Avernus, venerated as the entrance to the Underworld, and there was rich farming land around the acropolis.

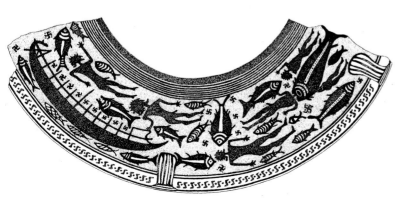

Control of the sea routes, however, seems to have been the principal factor in the choice of sites. Thus the first colony on Sicily lay at Naxos, a rocky headland on the east coast south of Taormina, and Reggio Calabria (Rhegium) and Messina (Zancle) were also soon settled. The evidence suggests that by about 740 the Euboeans were in complete control of the passage between Sicily and Italy.[8]

Other cities in Greece were also beginning to appreciate the importance of these new markets, and before long towns like Syracuse (one of a number of Corinthian colonies), Gela and, in southern Italy, Sybaris (an Achaean city) and Taranto (a Spartan settlement) had been founded. Subsidiary settlements were also established, such as Agrigento (founded from Gela) and Selinunte (created by Megara Hyblaea), as part of a process of infilling along the more fertile sections of the coast of *Magna Graecia*. Curiously, though, Apulia, which had been a major target for Mycenaean traders, was apparently left without colonies, indicating perhaps that the native tribes in this area were sufficiently strong to resist the Greeks. On the other hand, there was some attempt to establish settlements in Corsica and, more important, in southern France, where towns like Marseilles (Massilia) served as emporia for the produce of temperate Europe.

That *Magna Graecia* was aptly named is clearly confirmed by the surviving remains of temples, other public buildings and works of art. The colonies in Italy maintained close ties with their homeland, and in many respects achieved a comparable level of creativity. It was often the newer colonies that became preeminent. For example, Naples (Neapolis), founded by Cumae, soon eclipsed its parent city in importance. There was also much in the way of innovation. Recent work has shown, for example, that the concept of town planning can no longer be attributed entirely to the fifth-century architect, Hippodamus of Miletus.[9] At Megara Hyblaea, in eastern Sicily, the houses of the late eighth century were aligned with the space later to be occupied by the market place (*agora*); by the second half of the seventh century there was a regular grid of streets with wide east–west avenues and narrower north–south roads, resulting in long rectangular blocks. Most of the colonies demonstrate a similar pattern, in many cases preceding by a century or more the Hippodamian model that was eventually adopted in Greece itself. One of the most remarkable examples is to be found on the wide coastal plain in the instep of mainland Italy. Here, at Metapontum and Heraclea,[10] aerial photography and excavation have disclosed not only regularly planned cities but also a landscape several hundred square kilometres in extent with fields laid out as orthogonal blocks, each measuring 325 by 205 metres. The land was worked from small farms that date to the early fifth century, as do the first boundaries between them. Nearby Sybaris, where the archaic city that was buried beneath some 10 metres of river silt has now begun to emerge, must in part have acquired its fabled affluence through exploiting the same fertile terrain. Colonization was followed by consolidation: the conversion of trading posts into a coastal empire where urbanization achieved an unparalleled level of sophistication.

Colonies and native settlement

While many of the colonial settlements were founded upon virgin ground, it was inevitable that some sites should already be occupied. Cumae in the Bay of Naples and Tas Silġ in Malta provide instances of flourishing native centres whose occupants were displaced by the Greeks and Phoenicians. In general, however, the colonists seem to have forged good relations with the indigenous peoples. This is best reflected in the adoption by many native tribes of Greek traditions, with the result that some centres became almost as Hellenized as the colonies themselves. At Morgantina, a Sikel centre in eastern Sicily, for example, public buildings laid out on a Greek model and areas of native housing existed side by side from the sixth century. Similarly at Segesta in north-western Sicily the Elymian town developed into an important medical sanctuary, and possessed a fine Doric temple and, from the third century, a theatre. The hinterland of regions like southern France also became strongly Hellenized so that the houses of native towns (*oppida*) such as Ensérune closely resemble Greek models, and the material remains of the native inhabitants are almost indistinguishable from those of nearby colonies like Massilia. Even in areas that resisted colonial settlement, such as the east coast of Italy, the large native towns became heavily influenced in their architecture and artifacts by Greek styles. There can be no doubt that this was a direct consequence of close political and economic ties between colonist and native.

The Etruscans

Ancient Etruria, as later defined in the administrative code of Augustus, was demarcated to the north and south by the Arno and Tiber rivers, to the east by the Apennine mountains and to the west by the Tyrrhenian seaboard. It consisted of a fertile volcanic landscape, rich in metal ores, and was therefore a region with much to offer the settler, especially in a period when metal deposits were to become exceptionally important.

The essential features of its urban topography developed in the ninth century with the foundation of numerous Villanovan settlements (named after the Bronze Age urnfield cemetery near Bologna). Most of these sites developed into Etruscan centres, underlining the strong element of continuity between Villanovan and Etruscan. Thus, while there may be some truth in the assertion of Herodotus, Hellanicus and other ancient historians that the Etruscans came to Italy as a result of a migration from the east (Lydia in some versions), most scholars would now agree that the bulk of the Etruscan population was made up of indigenous peoples (as Dionysius of Halicarnassus, writing in the first century BC, believed); there may have been some new settlers, but they were not very numerous. The Etruscan language is a rather different problem. The earliest inscriptions, written in a variant of the Greek alphabet derived from Cumae, date to about 690 BC. Despite the claim that they cannot be read, there is no difficulty in making out their content: mostly very short, they are primarily concerned with

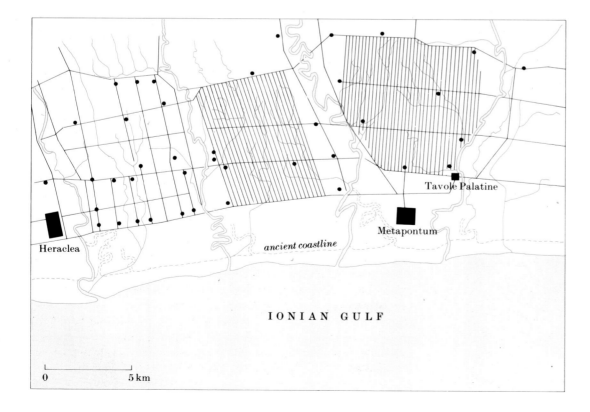

IONIAN GULF

Heraclea

ancient coastline

Metapontum

Tavole Palatine

0   5 km

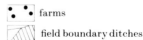

⊡ farms

▨ field boundary ditches

34.4: *The centuriated landscape on the coastal plain in the territories of the Greek colonies of Metapontum and Heraclea. The land boundaries of this field system, which consist of ditches, date to c. 470–460 BC, but replace an older system of regularly laid out drove roads and fields.*

34.5: *The Tomb of the Bulls, Tarquinia. An underground Etruscan chamber tomb dating to c. 550–520 BC, it shows an episode from the Trojan Wars in which Achilles lies in wait for Troilus. The tomb takes its name from the two bulls above the mythological scene; such scenes are extremely rare in the painted chambers of the later sixth and fifth centuries BC at Tarquinia.*

religious or funerary matters. Linguistically they appear to belong not to the Indo-European group (as do Latin and most other ancient dialects of the Italian peninsula) but to a quite different branch. There are some affinities with inscriptions of the pre-Greek period from the island of Lemnos in the Aegean, but otherwise there are no close analogies from outside Etruria. In short, we do not know whether it was an indigenous language or was perhaps introduced or adopted from elsewhere in the early seventh century.[11]

Apart from the question of Etruscan origins (now seen increasingly as an irrelevance), a great deal of attention is currently being paid to the remains of the settlements. The twelve principal cities of Etruria were grouped into a loose confederation, and among them were the great coastal towns such as Cerveteri (Caere), Tarquinia and Vulci as well as hinterland sites such as Veii, Chiusi, Perugia and Volterra. Within the territory of each city were smaller towns and villages, and numerous farms. Most of the larger settlements were located in positions of considerable natural strength, either on a hilltop or on a promontory surrounded by deep river gorges. Subsequently, the decision was taken at most sites to increase these defences by the addition of a stone wall, often of massive dimensions. The earliest known example is at Rusellae, dated to about 600 BC; but most towns and cities appear to have been walled during the fifth century, usually with elaborate gates. Within the walls, the towns of Etruria were seldom laid out with a regular street plan. While there may have been a centre with civic or religious buildings, as on the Piazza d'Armi at Veii, the present evidence reveals a loosely conceived layout of buildings reflecting an *ad hoc* development from Villanovan villages. House plans varied from the tight cluster of terraced stone buildings, as at San Giovenale in the Tolfa Hills, to the three-roomed houses, fronted by a veranda, common at Aquarossa near Viterbo. Courtyard buildings are also found, which foreshadowed the Roman *atrium* house of the Republican period.

Outside Etruria, within the Po plain (colonized by the Etruscans between the sixth and fourth centuries BC) and in Campania (occupied from the late seventh to the fifth centuries), the towns took a rather different form. In both areas they display a marked degree of formal planning. At S. Maria Capua Vetere near Naples, and at Marzabotto near Bologna, for example, there are cities whose layout of broad north–south avenues and narrower east–west streets is virtually indistinguishable from models to be found in the Greek colonies of southern Italy.[12] Even more remarkable, however, is the site of Spina on the Adriatic coast, where instead of the grid of streets there was a regular network of canals. A 'grand canal' gave access to the sea and, as in medieval Venice, the buildings rested on wooden piles driven deep into the alluvium. Two cemeteries are also known, with burials rich in imported objects, particularly Attic vases of about 480–360 BC; Spina was clearly an entrepôt of considerable importance until its demise after the Gallic invasion of the fourth century.[13]

The engineering skills displayed by the Etruscans at Spina can be widely matched in Etruria itself.[14] For example, we now know that an extensive road network, involving huge cuttings, viaducts and bridges, was slowly developed from the seventh century. In addition, underground tunnels (*cuniculi*) were devised to drain waterlogged ground, and even to carry roads beneath massive natural obstacles, as with the Pietra Pertusa road north of Veii. Comparable ingenuity was also applied both to public buildings and to funerary monuments. The massive circular *tholos* tombs with corbelled roofs, as at Quinto Fiorentino, or the underground chambers covered with huge tumuli, best represented at Cerveteri, are just two examples of the remarkable range of burial monuments that became common in Etruria from the seventh century. Although unified by the richness of the artifacts (which reflect very widespread trading contacts throughout the Mediterranean), the tombs display considerable regional variations in form. In the hinterland of Etruria around Blera, Norchia and Castel d'Asso, for example, the preference was for tombs with façades carved into the valley wall. Further north, the tombs were generally constructed above ground, while at Tarquinia the richer burial chambers were in many cases painted with scenes of hunting, sport and festivity. Such painted scenes were by no means uncommon in the Greek world and it may be, given the presence of a nearby Greek sanctuary at Gravisca,[15] that Greek artists were involved in their production.

The quantity of foreign goods in these graves emphasizes the importance of commerce for the Etruscans. Rich in metal ores, Etruria prospered greatly through this trade. The Etruscan cities were able to exercise control over the Tyrrhenian Sea and to drive the Greeks out of Corsica. But their prosperity was comparatively short-lived. Convincingly defeated in a sea battle off Cumae in 474 BC by the Greeks, and unable to put up any properly concerted front, they were no match for Rome when the Republican army began to annex the territories of Etruria.

35. Rome and its Empire in the West

The city of Rome lay half-way down the west coast of Italy, commanding major land routes both to the north and south and into the mountains in the east. Harbour facilities existed a few kilometres down the Tiber, and in the environs of the city there was fertile farming land as well as natural resources such as the Tiber valley salt beds. In combination, these natural advantages gave Rome an edge over virtually any other site in central Italy. Although only 10 kilometres from its Etruscan rival Veii, it rose first to local dominance and then to become the pre-eminent city of the ancient world.

The first settlement of importance dates to the Apennine Bronze Age in the mid–late second millennium BC, a period when many nucleated settlements were coming into existence in peninsular Italy. By the eighth century there were timber buildings on the Palatine Hill, and houses soon spread both onto other hills and over some of the lower ground. The Etruscan episode in Rome's history saw the conversion of these huts into rectangular buildings with mud-brick walls, as well as the construction of public works such as the *Cloaca Maxima* (great sewer), streets and the temple dedicated to Jupiter Optimus Maximus on the Capitoline Hill. Rome had in effect been transformed into a major urban centre.[1]

In about 510 BC a major phase of expansion began, coinciding with the expulsion of the last Etruscan ruler and the creation of a republic. By the early third century Rome was effectively in command of the peninsula, and before long the first war with the Carthaginians began in Sicily (264–241 BC). When the conflict was finally over in 146 BC Rome had acquired control of Sicily and Tunisia and also of a large part of Spain: the growth of empire was thus firmly established.

Republican Italy and the establishment of empire

Despite the rapid pace at which Rome brought new territories into the Italian alliance, it would be wrong to assume that there was immediate change in these areas. Some land was confiscated, but most of the towns and cities were brought into the confederacy by means of grants of citizenship, treaties and truces. As a result, the pre-existing pattern of urbanization was not at first subject to any substantial modifications, and many pre-Roman sites retained considerable importance throughout Classical times.

A measure of control over these newly conquered territories was achieved in two principal ways: first, by the construction of an efficient long-distance road system and, second, by the planting of colonies of Roman citizens at carefully chosen, strategically advantageous places. Much of the technology of road building was derived from the Etruscans; to their skills the Romans added the use of a proper paved surface and bridges constructed with arches. During the third and second centuries BC the basis of a comprehensive road network was laid down that provided Rome with direct and efficient links with all parts of Italy. These roads[2] often bypassed many of the old centres, as if emphasizing their growing redundancy in the new settlement patterns. They did, on the other hand, take careful account of the new *coloniae* such as Cosa on the Via Aurelia.

The model for the *coloniae* was developed at an early stage in Rome's expansion. At Ostia, for instance, where the port of Rome was developed from the late fourth century, the settlement was laid out in the form of a rectangle covering some 2 hectares. Two principal streets, the *cardo* and *decumanus*, divided the area into four equal quarters, and the *forum* was placed at the central intersection. As the town expanded, much of the street plan, and hence the public and private buildings, was aligned with this original layout. An identical rectangular arrangement was selected at Piacenza, a *colonia* founded in 218 BC. The two principal roads of the region, the Via Aemilia (which linked the Adriatic coast with north-western Italy) and the trunk route up through the Po valley, formed the *cardo* and *decumanus* of the town. The walls of the *colonia* were laid out in the form of a rectangle and the interior was divided into square blocks (*insulae*). This pattern of land division was carried on into the surrounding flat landscape, where fields measuring 720 by 720 metres marked individual allocations of land. Each square was in theory supposed to be equivalent to a hundred smallholdings, explaining the term 'centuriation' that is applied to such landscapes.[4]

Outside the area of the *coloniae*, the Roman conquest initially made little difference in the countryside. Disruption in the life of individual farms has been recorded by field survey over large parts of southern Etruria but seems to have been only temporary. Before long the size of the rural population began to increase sharply as more land came into cultivation.[5] But there was little change in the economy – viticulture and olive-growing, combined with cereal cultivation and animal husbandry – and only gradual modifications to the architecture of the buildings. By the period of the late Republic the countryside was more densely settled than at any previous period, underlining the falsity of the assumption that wars such as Hannibal's invasion of Italy laid waste large parts of rural Italy.

The history of the late Republic and early Empire is dominated by the remarkable generals and statesmen who, by conquest or diplomacy, combined to bring vast areas of the known world under Roman control.[6] The final demise of Carthage in 146 BC gave Rome Sicily, part of North Africa and some of Spain, and by the late second century BC a toehold had been established in southern Gaul with the foundation of a *colonia* at Narbonne. Caesar's campaigns in the mid-first century brought most of Gaul under Roman control – the first direct move into temperate Europe – and soon afterwards Roman towns were established in the already Hellenized regions of southern France. Here it was easy and profitable to set up Roman colonies, whereas in the north it was more practical to exercise control by means of treaties and diplomacy than by direct Italian settlement.

The major period of consolidation, however, came during the principate of Augustus (27 BC–AD 14). While in the east it was a question of integrating Hellenic and Roman culture, in the west the main concerns were the establishment of firm military control and the spread of Roman tastes and traditions. Major reforms in the provincial structure, combined with the reorganization and careful deployment of the army and its veterans, brought security and a large measure of peace. At the same time, the foundation of new towns and the gradual Romanization of old centres demonstrated to the provinces the Classical way of life. The Augustan age[7] was a period of massive propaganda, introduced through the media of architecture, coinage, artifacts, language and dress. The success of this strategy may be judged both from the peace that, with minor exceptions, endured in the western Roman world down to the late second century, and also from the extraordinary degree to which Romanization permeated town and country in the provinces. Only in the remoter hinterlands of countries such as Britain and the provinces of Africa did the Roman way of life become no more than a shallow veneer, making it necessary to maintain a continual military presence.

Urbanization and the economy

Roman law recognized a clear hierarchy for towns. There were distinct advantages to be enjoyed by the residents of a *colonia* (a settlement of Roman citizens, usually retired army veterans) or a *municipium* (where the inhabitants normally possessed Latin rights). Lower down the scale were the *civitates peregrinae*, which were communities of non-citizens but with the right of self-government, and then *vici*, minor centres of no constitutional importance. Promotion could be achieved, as with Avenches (Aventicum) in Switzerland, which eventually became a *colonia*; but this was a rare privilege and few towns changed their status.

In terms of distribution, the larger urban centres showed a clear preference for the regions bordering the Mediterranean. There were more than 300 towns with Latin rights in North Africa, forming a densely settled coastal belt. Provence and Languedoc (Gallia Narbonensis) was another favoured area, with a number of affluent *coloniae*, among them Arles, Orange and Nîmes. Here, as in Africa, the high level of urbanization in the pre-Roman period presented a structure that was easily adapted to Roman needs. Further to the north, on the other hand, both the density and the size of the major settlements tended to diminish. Britain[8] had just four *coloniae* (one, York, was only promoted to that status in the early third century) and probably not more than three or four *municipia*, St Albans (Verulamium) being the only certain site. London, the largest town in Britain with an area within its walls of about 135 hectares, was not much more than half the size of many *coloniae* in Provence, and only one-fifth the area covered by Pompeii. This was partly a question of investment. Romans preferred to put their money into the immensely rich grain-producing areas of Africa, Sicily and the Po valley or into the vine and olive

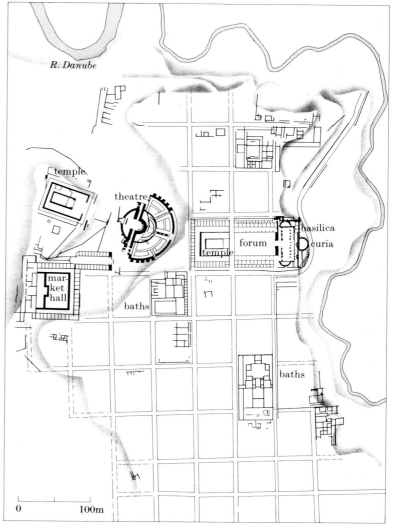

35.1: *The town of Augusta Raurica (Augst), Switzerland, founded in 43 BC. The town overlooks the Danube valley and was built on an irregular spur; nevertheless, the grid of streets was laid out with careful regularity. The public buildings included the* forum, basilica *and* curia *(where the town council met), as well as two baths and a large covered market. Private houses filled the other town blocks.*

regions of Campania, Etruria or Provence rather than into the undeveloped north. Moreover, while large settlements were very common in Celtic Europe, there was little about them that approached Mediterranean ideas of urban life: awkwardly situated on hilltops and spurs, they lacked a regular street plan, stone public buildings and proper drainage facilities. As a result, the first Roman settlements in many parts of northern Europe tended to be forts or fortresses, sited in positions where communications were good and the surrounding area fertile. Civilian settlements, attracted by a captive market, soon grew up around these forts, and as Romanization advanced and a permanent military presence became unnecessary the towns each received a civilian charter. Many northern *coloniae* originated in this way, such as Cologne and Colchester (Camulodunum), and in Britain the units of local government, the *civitates*, almost all developed from military

35.2: *The Roman Empire developed from a small Latin enclave in the area of Rome. By early in the third century BC Rome had extended its dominion over much of central and southern Italy. Soon afterwards the first foreign territories were annexed, and these were gradually extended during the period between the late first century BC and c. AD 100. Coloniae, towns peopled by legionary veterans, were used to Romanize these newly conquered lands.*

territory conquered by Rome

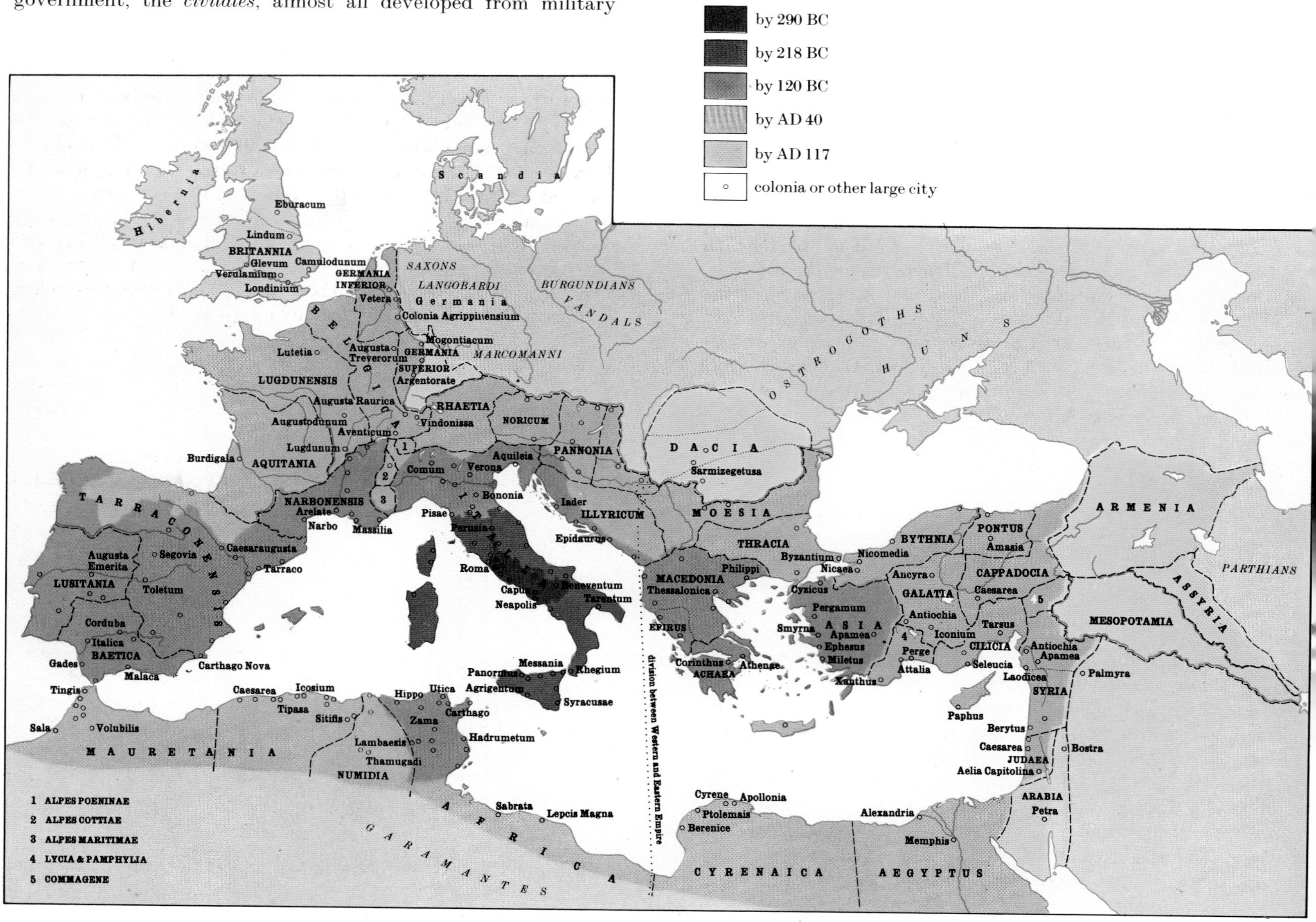

by 290 BC

by 218 BC

by 120 BC

by AD 40

by AD 117

○ colonia or other large city

1 ALPES POENINAE
2 ALPES COTTIAE
3 ALPES MARITIMAE
4 LYCIA & PAMPHYLIA
5 COMMAGENE

foundations. Similarly, the layout of new towns such as Aosta in northern Italy (founded 25 BC), Timgad in the hinterland of Algeria and Xanten in Germany (both laid out about AD 100) displayed explicit military influence in their rectangular plan and rigid grid of streets.[9] In central and northern Gaul, which was conquered before permanent forts were much used to control newly acquired provinces, a rather higher proportion of the pre-Roman centres survived as Classical towns. Lyon, Besançon and Alesia may be cited as instances. However, other towns such as Autun (which replaced pre-Roman Bibracte) and Clermont Ferrand (which succeeded Gergovia) illustrate Roman reorganization at work: there is little doubt that in terms of urban development the landscape of northern Europe saw quite fundamental changes during the period between the late first century BC and about AD 100.

The plan of the Roman town, once its main features had been developed during the mid–late Republic, was to achieve an extraordinary degree of standardization through the Roman world. The focus was provided by the *forum* and *basilica*, the main administrative and judicial buildings. As with other public buildings, these tend to show some regional preferences in their design but such differences are on the whole unimportant: much more significant are variations in scale. In poorer provinces such as Britain the public buildings tend to be small and utilitarian, whereas in the Mediterranean provinces they are notable for their lavishness. The Augustan period in particular[10] saw the construction of an enormous variety of prestigious monuments ranging from the Pont du Gard to the theatres of Lyon (Lugdunum), Orange, Mérida and elsewhere and the sumptuous *fora* and *basilicae* of the North African cities. The discovery of an efficient concrete introduced a new range of engineering possibilities – these vast, costly monuments both helped to promulgate Roman propaganda and served as architectural models for the indigenous population. Public works to be found in provincial towns included bath houses, amphitheatres, temples and often large market halls. The last are important; they underline the crucial part played by commerce in the life of the towns and cities. As well as serving as a marketing centre for agricultural produce from the region, however, these towns were also deeply involved in manufacturing. The Roman world was not geared to industrial production in the form of factories, but some towns did develop specialization based on particular local commodities.[11] Thus towns like Arezzo made and exported enormous quantities of pottery; Cologne specialized particularly in glass, and the Campanian cities in bronze and silverwork. Other towns were involved in the extraction of metal ores (which were largely state-owned), especially in Spain and Noricum, and there was widespread trade in commodities like wine, olives, *garum* (a kind of fish sauce) and grain. In most towns, however, there was a variety of industries: Trier (Augusta Treverorum), for instance, which prospered as an entrepôt supplying troops on the nearby German frontier, was concerned with the manufacture of pottery, glass, cloth, leatherwork, bricks and tiles; the processing

of local deposits of lead, copper and iron; stone-carving, millstones and the laying of mosaics; the building of ships, the making of barrels and other carpentrywork; the production of wine and honey; and of course cereal-growing and animal husbandry. The goods were sold in small shops, where much of the work was done on the premises and the artisan lived in rooms on the first floor.[12] Such arrangements seem to have been typical of the Roman world: while there was a monetary economy (prey in some periods to inflation and price controls), it depended principally upon agriculture and small-scale industry operating mainly for local consumption.

The urban pattern established during the late Republic and early Empire endured to a varying degree. The upheavals that affected France and Germany from the late second century encouraged the construction of massive town walls, which in the fourth century were provided with external towers for the mounting of artillery. Similar defensive measures were also adopted in Italy, Britain and elsewhere. In Italy, however, the effects of a declining population and a slow collapse in the administrative structure is reflected in the history of many towns from as early as about AD 200: public buildings lapsed into decay and private residences were increasingly abandoned. By contrast, in northern Europe the vigour of urban life seems to have been maintained much more strongly through the third and fourth centuries. Even so, after about AD 400 most urban life in the provinces gradually disappeared. Of the Western Empire only small parts of Italy and the African provinces retained to any significant degree the Classical way of life into the sixth and seventh centuries, when political and social disruption finally caused its demise.

Rural settlement

A number of textbooks giving advice to the farmer were produced during the Roman period, but there was on the whole little technical innovation.[13] Some attempt was made to improve both agricultural equipment (including the invention of a mechanical harvester, the *vallus*) and the quality and range of crops. But the most significant achievement of the period was undoubtedly to bring into cultivation large tracts of marginal land and thus to raise the level of production very considerably. It has been calculated, for example, that Rome alone imported 17 million bushels of corn a year, mainly from Egypt, Africa and Sicily: the grain was unloaded at Ostia and then brought up the Tiber in barges, each of which held some 2500 bushels. (A bushel is a capacity measure, the equivalent of 36 litres.) A surplus of this order illustrates how very successfully the Roman agricultural policy worked in a period when there was a steep rise in the size of the population.

The farming unit, the *villa*, ranged from a very modest smallholding to a large estate with an elaborate courtyard house. In lowland Italy, where statistics from field survey are now available for some areas, there was roughly one site per square kilometre; of these, about one in four represented a rich *villa rustica*, while the remainder consisted of small farms or other minor buildings.[14] Figures showing similar densities are now beginning to emerge from survey work in parts of Gaul,[15] though in North Africa the farming units seem to have been somewhat larger. The rural population reached a numerical peak at rather different times in different provinces, however. In Italy and many parts of Gaul it was the first and second centuries AD that saw the most intensive cultivation of the land. Thereafter, the number of sites in occupation began to fall, partly as smallholdings were reconstituted into larger estates but also as a result of a declining population. In Africa, where the cultivation of grain, vines, olives and figs produced an enormous surplus, the country estates maintained their prosperity well into the fifth century and perhaps later. In Britain, on the other hand, where some 650 villa estates situated mainly in the fertile lowlands are known, it was in the fourth century that villas were at their most numerous and affluent: it is possible that many of these farmers came from Gaul to escape the Germanic invasions of the third century.

We do not yet understand in detail how these fluctuations in the size of the rural population came about and what the economic consequences may have been. Much more evidence is becoming available, however, for the layout and evolution of the villa itself. The arrangement of rooms around a court was a layout that evolved during the second and first centuries BC and was widely adopted throughout the Roman world. There was usually a suite for the owner, with a private bath house, and often an elaborate formal garden. The rest of the complex was devoted to agricultural purposes and service areas. Similar arrangements, varying according to the main agricultural produce of the region, have been found throughout the provinces, emphasizing the fact that the villa was a commercial enterprise rather than a country retreat.[16]

If the villa estates were the norm in the Romanized parts of the Empire, it is important to bear in mind the continued existence of native-style farms in some of the provinces. In the hinterland of North Africa, for example, the indigenous tribes became only very superficially Romanized. Similarly, outside the lowland zone of Britain there is little apart from a few Roman artifacts to distinguish a pre-Roman farm from a native site inhabited during the period of the occupation. On the frontiers of the Western Empire, the graft of Mediterranean and native culture had only limited success.

The army, forts and frontiers

The conversion of a campaigning army of citizens supported by allies into a professional force of legionaries and auxiliaries was one of the great achievements of the Republic in the first century BC. It gave Rome both near-invincible military strength and the means of controlling a disparate empire. Moreover, the system of *coloniae*, created for retired veterans, meant that there was both a body of trained men on call and a recruiting area for new legionaries. The legions themselves were distributed between the provinces largely according to the requirements of campaigning. Thus in AD 23 Tacitus lists eight legions on the Rhine, three in Spain, two in Africa and twelve in the more easterly provinces. Many of the

fortresses and forts[17] of this period present a surprising contrast to the civilian architecture of the early imperial age: built with turf ramparts, wooden buildings and tentage for the men, they had little permanent about them. They were, however, intended to serve as campaign bases, and were often in full garrison only in the winter months. It was during the reign of Claudius (AD 41–54) that a more standard plan for auxiliary forts and legionary fortresses began to emerge. In Germany many of the military bases were reconstructed in stone, reflecting the abandoning of the abortive and costly campaigns east of the Rhine. In the newly annexed province of Britain, on the other hand, timber was still widely used. Here a combination of insurgency beyond a temporary frontier line, the fast pace of Romanization within the conquered area, and imperial ambition meant that the army was almost continually pushing north. As new regions were overrun, a network of auxiliary forts was laid down, linked by an efficient road system and focusing upon a number of legionary fortresses whose sites were altered as military priorities changed.

The concept of fixed frontiers (*limites*) emerged only at a fairly late date in the history of the Empire. The word *limes* originally meant a path or road, and the first boundary took the form of a line of communication, together with signal stations, through the disputed Taunus and Wetterau region of Germany. It was built in Domitian's principate (AD 81–96) and was intended to supplement the *ad hoc* defence-in-depth that had come into existence along the

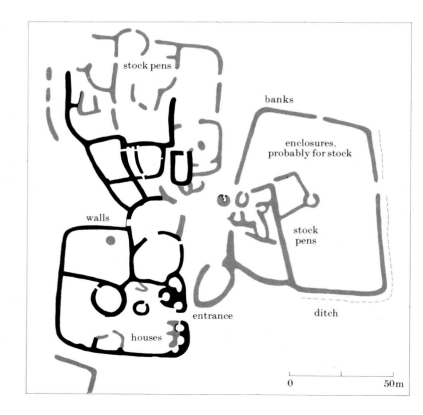

Rhine and Danube since the time of Tiberius and Claudius. The system was extended early in the second century by Trajan, but it was really Hadrian (117–38) who developed the concept of a solid frontier. In Germany a wall made of heavy timbers, each 30 centimetres in diameter and 30 centimetres apart, and with a regular arrangement of turrets and forts along its course, was constructed across some of the tangled countryside between the Rhine and the Danube. Special frontier troops (*numeri*) were recruited to patrol this *limes*.[18]

In Britain a wall, built of stone and turf, was constructed to divide the Romans from the barbarians. It extended for some 120 kilometres between the Tyne and Solway estuaries. There was a system of 80 fortlets, 160 turrets and 17 forts along this frontier, and similar defences, probably with a wooden palisade rather than a wall, extended 100 kilometres or more along the Cumbrian coast. Similarly, in Africa Septimius Severus and his son Caracalla constructed a buffer zone of forts, roads and fortified farmhouses garrisoned by soldiers along the zone between native tribes and the provinces of Mauretania, Numidia and Tripolitania. These frontiers were mostly to prove of limited success, especially in Germany, but they nevertheless provided some stability at a time when it was realized that the Empire had to have finite boundaries. The defended forts that became a feature of the shores of southeastern Britain and northern Gaul in the later third and fourth centuries reflect the decline in control: piracy had become rampant,

and the migration of the Germanic tribes was proving catastrophic for both northern Europe and Italy. Formal frontiers and a network of forts had proved temporarily successful; but in the end even these measures were insufficient to prevent the collapse of an over-large and far too complex imperial structure.

The collapse of the Western Empire

The pressures that contributed to the fall of the Western Empire can be detected from early in its history.[19] As far back as the first century AD there was population growth and consequently tribal movement in the regions east and north of the Rhine–Danube frontier. Trouble on the *limes* itself began in the later second century and gradually increased during the next two hundred years. Although there were attempts to absorb the barbarians into the Roman world – principally as federate troops – the scale of the migrations was far too great for any real measure of success. The invasions of different groups of Goths, Vandals and Huns during the late fourth and the fifth century was the decisive factor in the collapse of the economic and political structure of the Western Roman world. Even so, it is important to remember that internal factors also contributed to the process of decline. The anarchy and economic chaos of the third century demonstrated all too clearly the difficulties of controlling so extensive and complex an empire. Moreover, from the later second century there was a significant fall in the size of the population in some areas. The countryside

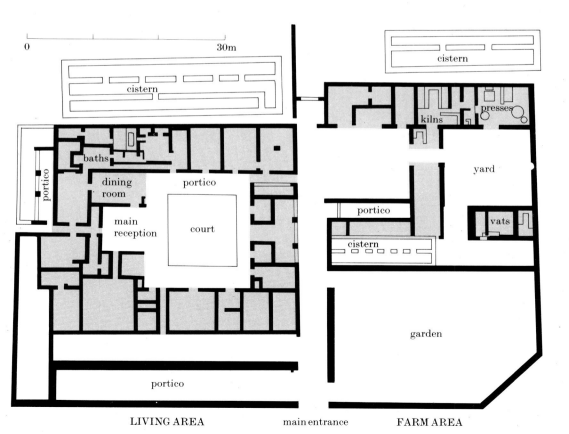

0   30m

cistern

cistern

kilns

presses

baths

portico

dining room

portico

yard

main reception

court

portico

vats

cistern

garden

portico

LIVING AREA   main entrance   FARM AREA

35.3: *The village of Ewe Close in Cumbria, England, a small farming community of peasants who lived in round houses of Iron Age type, situated in one enclosure. The other earthworks consisted of stock pens and small fields devoted to market gardening. Although occupied in the Roman period, the economy and architecture of the settlement differed little from those of an Iron Age village.*

35.4: *A villa built c. 50 BC at San Rocco, near Capua in Campania, Italy. The building combines the yards, presses, vats and storage areas of a working farm with the elegant and comfortable rooms of a country residence. The villa was widely adopted throughout the Empire by the Romanized part of the population.*

main roofed areas

became much more sparsely inhabited, many towns fell into decay, and trade and production were increasingly disrupted. An effective opposition to the vast folk movements of the later fourth century onwards was impossible. Surprisingly, however, invasion did not always mean the end of the 'Classical' way of life.[20] Ostragothic Italy, Visigothic Gaul and Spain, and Vandal North Africa all saw attempts to perpetuate features of Roman urban and rural organization. For many regions it was the Arab invasions of the seventh and early eighth centuries that finally extinguished the last traces of the Roman Empire.

35.5: *The Roman army maintained permanent garrisons in the less secure provinces; the soldiers were accommodated in forts and fortresses built initially of timber and later mainly of stone.*

Plan of the auxiliary fort at Pen Llystyn in north Wales (left), *built c. AD 80. The timber barracks provided accommodation for 1000 infantry. In the central range are the administrative buildings, granaries and commander's house. The defences consisted of a turf rampart, beyond which were two ditches.*

Fortress at Novaesium (Neuss) in Germany (right). *This was designed for a legion of 5000 men who, unlike the auxiliary troops, were Roman citizens. Constructed in the reign of Claudius (AD 41–54), this stone-built fortress was a permanent military base.*

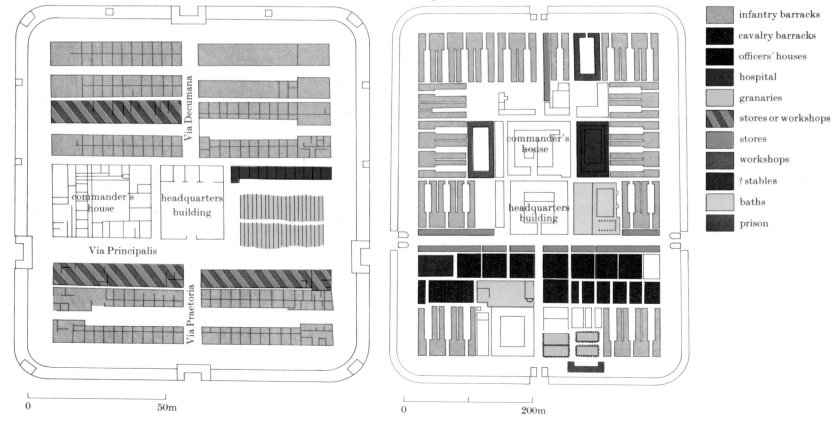

infantry barracks
cavalry barracks
officers' houses
hospital
granaries
stores or workshops
stores
workshops
? stables
baths
prison

36. The Roman Empire in the East

Roman interest in the affairs of the Greek world dates from the end of the third century BC. By this time Rome had overthrown the Carthaginian empire of Hannibal and had become the dominant power in the western Mediterranean. The militaristic structure of Roman society and the competitive ambitions of the ruling oligarchy rapidly led to intervention in the affairs of eastern cities and kingdoms, either at a personal or at a national level. Between about 200 and 150 BC a combination of cynical diplomacy and open intervention enabled Rome to manipulate the balance of power in the eastern Mediterranean to its own advantage and profit. Substantial indemnities were demanded from rivals defeated in war, and by the middle of the second century a regular tribute was imposed on much of the Greek east, ensuring that a large part of the financial surplus accruing in the Greek city-states was diverted to Rome. This had a profound economic effect both on Rome and on the newly subjected territories. The economic vitality of the Greek city-states and the Hellenistic kingdoms rapidly drained away, making them increasingly dependent on Rome in all political matters, while Rome itself was completely transformed by the enormous influx of wealth from the Empire.

Grandiose public buildings, often Greek in architectural inspiration, were erected at Rome in increasing numbers from the second quarter of the second century BC onwards. Furthermore, conquering generals used statues and other works of art looted from Greece and Asia Minor to adorn the city. The scale of this building activity was immense by the standards of the ancient world: the cost of an aqueduct at Rome built between 140 and 130 BC has been estimated at about four times the total cost of the Parthenon at Athens, the most expensive building of fifth-century Greece.[1]

The growth of the Empire

From 146 BC onwards Rome began to assume direct rather than indirect jurisdiction over the Levant, eventually extending the Empire as far as the Euphrates and to the shores of the Red Sea. The total area annexed to the Empire amounted to over 1 126 000 square kilometres, an enormous addition to the 160 000 square kilometres of Italy and roughly equal to the total area of Rome's western provinces, excluding possessions in Africa. The actual position of the boundary was only one aspect of frontier defence, which also included the use of allied dynasties or client kingdoms to act as buffer states against hostile territory or to control notably unruly and mountainous areas within the boundaries of the Empire. The rulers of these client states, among the most important of whom were the Herods of Judaea and the tribal rulers of Galatia in central Asia Minor, received financial and technical aid and in return were expected to act in Roman interests, though they were not liable to taxation or subject to direct jurisdiction. They predictably showed signs of Roman influence in their culture: their armies were often organized along Roman lines and their cities named after Roman emperors.

Relations with the provinces

During the late Republic (second–first centuries BC) the governing oligarchy of Rome paid scant heed to the welfare of the provinces or to the rights of the provincials. Direct and indirect taxes were collected with notorious harshness, and extortion and other forms of corrupt and oppressive behaviour were rife. Rome and the Italian peninsula were seen as the privileged centre of an empire, living off the profits drawn from subject territories; the provinces

36.1: *The frontier of the Eastern Empire, showing the disposition of legions and the major military roads during the second and early third centuries AD.*

- ■ legionary fortresses
- ● major cities
- ○ lesser cities
- 〜 military roads (schematic)
- ⨝ main crossing-points

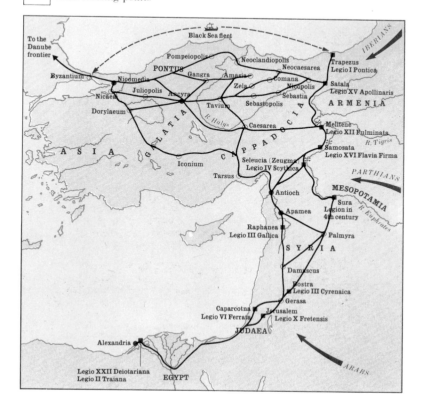

were treated largely as sources of revenue.[2]

Under the Empire (after 31 BC) the older-established provinces started to acquire the same privileges and status as Rome and Italy. Provincial communities and individuals began to receive the full rights of Roman citizenship, and by the principate of Augustus (27 BC–AD 14) members of the provincial aristocracies were making their way into the Roman governing elite. The Roman world gradually came to be treated as a unified whole consisting of many interdependent parts, in which the provinces were as important as the capital city. The Latinized regions of the west, Spain and southern France, were the first to produce Roman senators in the first half of the first century AD. The Greek-speaking eastern provinces followed at the end of the century and soon eclipsed the western areas as a source of administrative personnel for the government of the Empire. In the second century the aristocratic families of Asia Minor and Syria had established marriage connections not only with the western senatorial aristocracy but also with the imperial household, and the third century saw the first easterner to become emperor, Elagabalus, from a priestly dynasty in northern Syria (reigned AD 218–222).

This change is clearly reflected in the extraordinary uniformity of Roman civilization throughout the Empire. A bath building in Roman Britain can be compared in design and function to one in the Negev desert. Cities developed an even more uniform repertory of public buildings than was evident in the Hellenistic period, and local artistic traditions, while not disappearing altogether, became subordinated to a single imperial culture. This process was aided and advanced by the movement of materials such as quarried marble from one part of the Mediterranean to another, and by the migration of skilled craftsmen between provinces and cities. A city such as Lepcis Magna in North Africa in the second and third centuries AD could be transplanted to the west coast of Asia Minor or to northern Syria without seeming in any way incongruous.

This fundamental change in the relationship of government completely altered the attitude of the provinces to Rome. Under the Empire, Rome succeeded in winning the wholehearted support and loyalty at least of the provincial upper classes by offering them the rewards of office and wealth within the Roman system. The eastern provinces enjoyed a long period of peace and prosperity, briefly interrupted in the third century AD but resumed in the fourth. Disturbances were confined to relatively minor disputes between or within cities, which were quickly suppressed if they threatened the security of the provinces as a whole, and to a few abortive uprisings by the lower classes, who benefited little from the pact between Rome and the provincial aristocracies and continued to be exploited by them.[3]

The eastern frontier

Roman government in the east was principally concerned with three things: military security, the administration of justice and the collection of revenue. The biggest military threat to Rome came from internal uprisings on the one hand, and from the Parthian empire based in Persia and Mesopotamia on the other. During the reign of Augustus troops to contain these threats were stationed in Galatia (one legion), Syria (three or four legions) and Egypt (two or three legions), a total of some 40 000 first-class infantry soldiers supplemented by a similar number of auxiliaries. The first and last were mainly intended to control local disturbances, while the Syrian garrison was expected to prevent Parthian invaders from crossing the Euphrates where the river comes closest to the Mediterranean and attacking Roman territory over the relatively short stretch of desert country east of Syrian Antioch. Further

36.2: *The ruins of Palmyra, a magnificent city founded by the Aramaeans near an oasis on the edge of the Syrian desert. The city lay on the great caravan routes between east and west, a position that brought it great wealth. It came under Roman overlordship in the early first century AD, though it retained its right to self-government until the late third century, when it was destroyed by the Romans after a rebellion.*

36.3: *Ancyra was the nodal point for several important military roads linking the eastern frontier with the Danubian provinces. During the Empire small towns developed along these roads, acting as local market centres for the collection and sale of grain and other agricultural products. To the south there were few roads, and instead of towns there were large estates owned by wealthy magnates – including the emperor himself – and devoted largely to stock-raising.*

+	estate, with owner's name where known
▲	location of inscription suggesting land owned by citizen of Ancyra
	roads
	land over 1000 metres

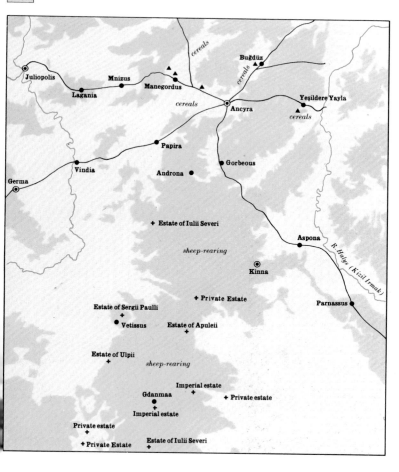

36.4: *The imperial temples and assize districts of Asia. Asia was the wealthiest of the eastern provinces, and the major cities competed with one another in building large numbers of imperial temples for which they could claim the title of 'temple warden'. Many were also assize centres for the province: the main duties of a governor were judicial, and assizes were regularly held at the main provincial cities. In Asia there were thirteen such centres, to which litigants would flock when a visit by the governor was scheduled. An assize centre gained not only considerable prestige from this but also economic advantages, as the throng of important visitors stimulated a healthy market in the city.*

⊙	assize cities
•	other cities
▲	imperial temples
	district boundaries
----	major roads

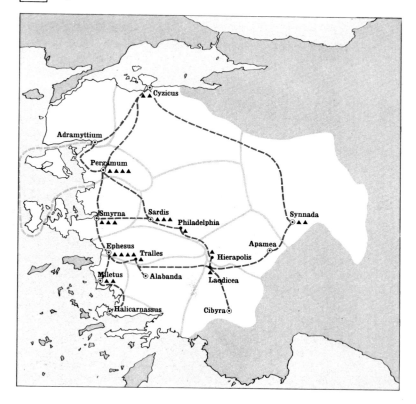

south the broad expanse of the Syrian desert provided sufficient protection without a major garrison. Invasion through the mountainous country of eastern Asia Minor could be contained by allied client kings and by the use of native levies.

The danger of uprisings receded as Rome established a firmer grip on the eastern provinces and put down pockets of resistance in mountainous territory, but the overall system of defence was judged inadequate by the emperor Vespasian (reigned AD 70–79) after a diplomatic agreement had allowed a Parthian nominee to take control of Armenia. He accordingly reorganized the eastern frontier by incorporating the client kingdoms of Armenia Minor and Commagene into the Empire, and stationing legionary garrisons at Satala in Armenia Minor, Melitene in Cappadocia, Samosata in Commagene, and Zeugma and Sura in northern Syria. Other legions were stationed behind the frontier line in Syria and Palestine. Two legions were maintained in Egypt, and one was transferred to Arabia Felix in AD 106. The legionary fortresses of the frontier were linked by paved highways, and auxiliary forts were positioned between them at roughly regular intervals. This *limes* formed the spine of the eastern defence system; the frontier was also designed in depth. Garrisons were stationed in the far north-east to control the Darial and Derbend passes through the Caucasus, and other contingents controlled the valley of the Hejaz and the Wadi Sirhan in the Arabian desert to maintain order in the south-east. Such outlying forces could contain minor disturbances and give advance warning of any serious trouble threatening the frontier. Other contingents were placed in the interior of Asia Minor behind the front line, notably at Ancyra (modern Ankara) in Galatia, an important nodal point in the communications network, and at Eumenia in Asia. In addition, several of the cities of Syria, among them Palmyra, Gerasa and Bostra, received fortification walls, originally erected in the early 70s AD against the Parthian threat.

This whole complex system was welded together by an enormous network of military roads covering the whole of Asia Minor and Syria, built in the reign of Vespasian and his immediate successors and completed by the beginning of the second century AD. It was designed to make the movement of men and supplies within the area, and troop transfers from the Balkans and the Danube frontier, as simple and efficient as possible, and was maintained in a good state of repair until the fourth century. The most important routes in the road system were those running from the Bosporus through the east–west valleys of Bithynia and Pontus to Satala, and across Anatolia to Ancyra and the Cilician Gates leading to Syria. There were also important roads linking Ancyra and Caesarea in Cappadocia with the Anatolian frontier, and the cities of northern Syria with the *limes*. It must be stressed that these and all other major Roman roads were constructed primarily for the use of Roman armies and officials, not to foster communications and trading links between provincial cities. However, it is clear that the existence of excellent all-weather paved roads facilitated travel and transport, a fact that should not be underestimated.[4]

Settlements and cities

Military establishments in the form of fortresses, roads and other installations were clearly the most substantial Roman introduction to the archaeological landscape of the eastern provinces. Other innovations in communications included the system of rest houses and post stations (*mutationes* and *mansiones*) erected for the use of official travellers along the main roads in the second and third centuries AD, and the buildings known as *praetoria* designed to accommodate governors and their staff. In terms of settlement, a major Roman contribution to the eastern provinces was the foundation of *coloniae*, settlements of veteran soldiers for whom the emperor was obliged to provide land after they had completed their legionary service. The majority of these colonies in the east date to the period of Julius Caesar and Augustus, when there was a drastic need to pay off the soldiers who had fought in the civil wars. There was an important group along the coast of the Sea of Marmara and the Black Sea (including Lampsacus, Parium, Apamea, Heraclea Pontica, Sinope and Amisus), and another in the mountainous district of south-west Asia Minor known as Pisidia. This latter group of about a dozen colonies was expected to contain the native tribesmen of the region in their mountain strongholds until they could be effectively subdued by a legionary force. The most important of them, Pisidian Antioch, may originally have received about 9000 settlers; it was designed as a miniature Rome in which each ward of the city was named after a ward of Rome itself. Settlers in these colonies also received parcels of land in the surrounding

countryside, the new foundations thus effectively supplanting any pre-existing conditions of land tenure. At first the colonies maintained their distinctly Roman identity among the Greek and native population (indeed, one of the few eastern examples of the building technique known as *opus reticulatum* occurs at Amisus), but through intermarriage and an increasingly complex network of social and economic relationships with their neighbours they gradually became absorbed into the local culture, and Greek had supplanted Latin as the chief language by the third century at the latest.[5]

Apart from the introduction of *coloniae* Rome did little to alter the pattern of settlement in the Near East, except to encourage and promote the tendency towards urbanization that already existed. Roman emperors followed the fashion of Hellenistic kings in giving their names to new cities and refounding old ones. Many of the more mountainous areas of Asia Minor were first urbanized under Roman rule. The history of the northern part of the province of Asia, south of the Sea of Marmara, shows this clearly. The chief cities of the plain, with ready access to the sea – Cyzicus, Apollonia and Miletupolis – had been founded by Greek colonists in the eighth and seventh centuries BC. Further inland, but still in the plain, there were a number of Classical and Hellenistic foundations. However, cities did not appear in the mountainous regions of Mysia before the Roman period: Phrygian Ancyra and Synaus are both Augustan cities (though the actual settlements there probably date back to an earlier period), Tiberiopolis dates to

36.5: *The transport of marble, shown on a tombstone of the third century AD carved in the local style. It comes from the region of Afyou Karahisar in central Turkey. There was an important ancient marble quarry at Docimeum nearby, and the stone depicts two methods of transporting quarried blocks. A lectica (stretcher) supporting a block of stone is shown along the upper border, and a cart with two spoked wheels drawn by a pair of oxen occupies the right-hand side of the lower panel. Behind it stand a man and a woman. The two upper panels depict a woman with a mirror, a basket and a comb for carding wool, and a man standing beside a small table. The owner of the grave was presumably a contractor or was otherwise employed in the business of transporting marble, a major task from this remote and landlocked quarry.*

Augustus' successor Tiberius (reigned AD 14–37), and the three cities of Hadriani, Hadriania and Hadrianutherae were founded by Hadrian between AD 117 and 138.

For the Romans as well as the Greeks civilization was to be found in cities. They relied on the well-established cities of Asia Minor and Syria to carry out much of the business of government on their behalf. Roman governors travelled with only a small staff and were not equipped to regulate minor details of civic affairs; local authorities were generally responsible for the smooth running of their cities and territories, for the erection of public buildings and for the collection of revenue, though much of this was paid over to the Roman government in due course. It was thus in Rome's interest for as much provincial territory as possible to be included in city territories, for which local magistrates were responsible.[6]

City architecture and design

The buildings of a Roman city in the Greek east were not radically different from those of the Hellenistic age, though architectural and artistic styles changed, and usually showed signs of coarseness by comparison with the earlier period. Marble was used on a wider scale than before, thanks to extensive quarrying in many parts of Greece, the Aegean islands and Asia Minor. The transport of large quantities of quarried marble from the important quarries at Docimeum in central Turkey to the coast was a major technological achievement, perhaps only possible because quarries were owned by the emperor, who could afford the huge expense involved.[7] Some new types of buildings reached the Greek east under Roman rule: one was the amphitheatre, of which examples are known at Cyzicus, Pergamum, Nysa and Pisidian Antioch, following the spread of Roman gladiatorial games throughout the east; another was the Roman bath house, distinct in style and much more extensive than Greek bath houses.

As before, wealthy private individuals bore most of the expense of erecting new public buildings in the cities, and clearly gained status from doing so. This was a trend that Rome encouraged, despite occasional concern about wasteful spending, as it allowed individuals to indulge in a form of rivalry and competition with one another that by and large benefited the cities and posed no threat to Rome.

An important way to secure the allegiance of local aristocracies was through the organization of provincial councils (*koina*). These *koina*, one in each province, comprised representatives from all the cities, and expressed their loyalty through the worship of Rome (the personification of the city) and the divine emperor Augustus. The major cities secured the right to dedicate provincial temples to this cult, earning themselves the title of Temple Warden. There was always rivalry between provincial cities; this expressed itself in many forms, but the most remarkable example was in the claims of cities to build more and more imperial temples conferring this title. Such behaviour was the product of an age in which the aristocracy had a huge surplus of income, mostly derived from landholding and moneylending activities rather than from trade and industry, and few means of spending it. However, it is noticeable that during the third and fourth centuries, when the demands of the Roman government for higher taxes and contributions became greater, this tradition of public generosity diminished.[8]

City and country

The bulk of our evidence for the eastern Roman provinces concerns the life of the cities and their inhabitants, in spite of the fact that the cities were almost entirely dependent on the agricultural surplus of the countryside for their livelihood.[9] Literary sources, inscriptions and some archaeological evidence yield more information about the relationship between town and country than do the sources for the Hellenistic period, but our knowledge is still very imperfect. An analysis of the evidence relating to the territory round Ancyra, the chief city of the Anatolian province of Galatia, is revealing in a number of ways. The city lies in rolling upland country mainly devoted to cereal cultivation and to pasture. Within easy reach of it, at a distance of 40 kilometres or less, are a number of broad valleys (of the Ankara Çay, the Ova Çay, the Cubuk Çay and the Yeşildere) devoted today, and presumably in antiquity, to cereal cultivation, and there is little doubt that most of the city's food was produced here. This inference is partly confirmed by inscriptions indicating that members of Ancyra's middle class (the city council) owned land here. Further afield, to the south of the city in the great expanse of rather barren country between Ancyra and Iconium (Konya), the pattern of land ownership changes. Here there is evidence for very large estates, devoted to sheep-rearing and other forms of stock-raising, which were owned in the Roman period by the wealthy elite of Asiatic cities, by Roman senators residing as far away as the west and south coasts, if not outside Asia Minor altogether, and in the second century AD by the emperor himself. These landowners were clearly not interested in cultivating grain for Ancyra or any other city but rather in producing wool or hides, which could be sold at a profit. The presence of perhaps 80 000 troops on the eastern frontier provided a ready market for such products.

The five Roman roads that met at Ancyra also affected the pattern of settlement there. Although these roads were originally constructed for military purposes, they clearly dictated the movement of all types of traffic in the area, and settlements appeared along them. Spaced at roughly equal intervals along the main routes, 25 to 40 kilometres apart, these served as local market centres for the villages around them. The pattern of settlement in fact closely resembles the modern one, but contrasts with the earlier Hellenistic and later Byzantine arrangement in the region. Much of rural Anatolia has not been carefully explored, and many of the smaller settlements have not yet been identified. It is clear that when they are an analysis of the settlement pattern will contribute much to the understanding of the rural economy of the region.

The exploitation of land

The pattern of exploitation of rural areas suggested here already

indicates a possible conflict of interests that is confirmed by the literary and epigraphic sources. Wealthy landowners would not necessarily be interested in growing the cereal crops needed to feed the population of the cities. In fact the cash return on cereals was considerably lower than it was on other crops, notably vines and olives, and there is plenty of evidence to show that the wealthy often preferred to grow these where the terrain and other circumstances permitted. The results of this became all too clear at the end of the first century AD, when a disastrous famine following on crop failure struck the whole of central and western Anatolia. The emperor Domitian tried to break away from the customary non-interventionist policy of the Roman government by instructing Asian landowners to uproot their vines and plant grain in their place. He was, however, eventually persuaded against taking this action by a delegation from the provincial council of Asia. The *status quo* was thus maintained and the interests of the wealthier classes prevailed.

Despite intermittent famine, which could cause severe hardship to cities unable to import food to make up for the deficit, the eastern provinces, above all those in Asia Minor, prospered throughout the Roman period, and served as a great reserve of resources for the Empire as a whole. Natural products such as timber and minerals were regularly exported, and the traffic in marble has already been mentioned. Even grain was occasionally sent overseas when the other great cereal-growing areas of the Empire, Egypt and North Africa, failed to produce their normal quota. Asia Minor and Syria also produced a constant stream of recruits for the Roman armies, and members of the educated upper classes were admitted in large numbers into the Empire's administrative network. When the Empire effectively broke into two in the fourth century and the imperial capital was transferred to Constantinople, Asia Minor continued to serve as the main source of strength and economic resilience to the Byzantine empire until it eventually fell to the Ottoman Turks in the fourteenth century.

V: Empires in the eastern Old World

The earliest states in the eastern part of the Old World grew up in the Indus valley, at the far eastern end of the belt of developing communities stretching across western Asia. A completely independent nucleus began to form in northern China, in the valley of the Yellow River. While the Indus civilization collapsed, perhaps as a result of local environmental changes, that of China showed a pattern of more or less continuous expansion. Important new links across Eurasia came about through the development of mobile societies adapted to the arid environment of the steppes. These carried to China western innovations such as the wheel and were the source of Indo-European populations that moved into northern India. Although other regions of south and south-east Asia were by no means backward, except in their remoter parts, local states did not begin to form over a wider area until a later date. Nevertheless, evidence for craftsmanship in metals shows that technical skills were not limited to the early civilizations. Shifts in the centres of Indian and Chinese civilization, to the Ganges and the Yangtze valleys respectively, were part of a wider pattern of development in south-east Asia. Increasing contacts through trade resulted in the formation of local states in Indo-China, although between these flourishing communities there were extensive tracts of land in which earlier ways of life persisted.

37. The growth of a Chinese empire

A distinct stage in China's evolution took place between the introduction of iron in about 600 BC and the re-establishment of a long-lasting empire under the house of T'ang in AD 618. In the intervening centuries diversity yielded place to political unity and cultural standardization, and the area of the Yellow River valley in the north acquired a growing dominance over the southern area of the Yangtze valley and beyond. In the Chou period (traditionally 1122–256 BC) parts of China had been governed by the kings of that house, but from about 800 BC a number of estates or states had grown up, each giving rise to its own institutions, organs of government and economic practices. By the fourth century BC these states had been reduced to seven major kingdoms (Ch'in, Ch'i, Ch'u, Yen, Wei, Chao and Han). A new era opened in Chinese history in 221 BC, when one of the seven, Ch'in, succeeded in forming a single unit of its rivals' territories. Thereafter the more effective government of a single empire extended a common way of life and an accepted set of values ever more widely, imposing its will by instruments such as a census, a standardized coinage and regular systems of taxation and conscript labour. Imperial officials attempted to organize the transport and distribution of staple goods along waterways and roads that lay under central control. New materials for writing were coming into fashion – such as silk and paper in place of bronze, stone or wooden tablets – together with a simplified standard script instead of the regional variations that had prevailed earlier. China's traditional religious beliefs and practices were sublimated by the ethics of Confucius (551–479 BC) and his followers, which were to have a marked effect on China's literature, education and official style of life; they were also enriched by the mysticism of Taoism in the fifth and fourth centuries BC, and by the impact of Buddhism on the whole of Chinese culture.

Regional diversities persisted, despite repeated attempts to impose the political discipline, social hierarchies and economic management of the north upon the more remote areas of the south and the west. Local characteristics are seen in the exuberant art and mythology of the pre-imperial kingdom of Ch'u, situated along the Yangtze river; in the geographical isolation and economy of the Valley of the Four Rivers to the west (modern Szechuan); and in the practice of aboriginal customs in the old kingdom of Tien (Yunnan). Towards the north-west, in the Ordos region, the land lay open to penetration by Scythian nomads and their culture, while the different terrain and climate of the south-east (the old kingdoms of Wu and Yüeh, or Viet, south of the Yangtze) gave rise to a characteristic lifestyle among forest, mountain and swamp.[1]

The evidence of tombs

The main body of archaeological evidence is drawn from tombs. The contents of Chinese graves, from before the Iron Age until the institution of the T'ang empire, comprised a wealth of funerary furnishings interred as articles to be treasured, as equipment to be used or as stores to be consumed. Artifacts of jade and stone, of bronze and iron, were buried with the dead, along with wooden or lacquered wares; in addition to skeletal remains, some of the tombs also included animal or vegetable matter. The tombs were built in a variety of styles, reflecting both regional diversities and social distinctions. There were deep pit-burials in central China; many-chambered mansions of brick or stone in the east and the north; and rock-hewn tombs in the west. They ranged from the richly decorated and furnished tombs of emperors, kings and noblemen to the serried ranks of convicts' graves.

In the earliest periods burial was accompanied by animal or human victims, but by the sixth century BC or earlier these were being replaced by models in bronze, clay or wood, by paintings, or by the inclusion of valuables and furnishings. By perhaps 200 BC attempts were being made to preserve the body intact, and strikingly successful examples have been found. Other practices, such as the burial of jewels, equipment or figurines, were intended to provide the souls of the dead with the necessities of life. Paintings or bronze mirrors were buried as talismans, whose function was to escort the soul to paradise; some graves include guardian figures of hybrid creatures, designed to scare away evil influences from the dead. These practices were often modified from the third century AD with the adoption of Buddhism, which enshrined radically new concepts of life, death and eternity.

37.1: *Cross-section (south–north) of tomb number 2 at Wang-tu in east China. The inner walls of this elaborate stone-built structure, which is some 20 metres in length, were decorated with frescoes, and in one case with a painted inscription, the text of the contract for the sale of the land, dated AD 182.*

The land and its people

The great majority of the Chinese people lived and worked in the country; intensive agriculture was one of the characteristics that distinguish the Chinese from their neighbours of the steppes. The main crops were millet, barley and rice. Changes were effected in agricultural practices by four technological innovations: the emergence and gradual spread of iron; the introduction of the ox-drawn plough; the adoption of a system of crop rotation; and the introduction and spread of semi-mechanical means of raising water.[2]

Cast-iron ploughshares and their moulds are known from sites that may be dated to at least 400 BC, if not earlier. Although the majority of early iron wares were agricultural tools, it is unlikely that such equipment was available on a general scale for some centuries, and the farmer's traditional methods of working doubtless persisted together with the use of bronze or stone, horn or wood. The ox-drawn plough had certainly been introduced by the first century BC, and in all probability earlier; it has been suggested that with its adoption there also emerged a new standard measurement for areas of arable land. Successful experiments in using lengths of land alternately year by year, first as ridge and then as furrow, were undertaken in about 100 BC in order to control the sowing of seed and as an attempt to use the soil more evenly. Written records found in the north-western extremity of the Han empire provide evidence of the application of these methods in state-sponsored colonies.

By the first century AD Chinese farmers were using pedal-operated chains of buckets to raise water from one level to another; more complex systems of large water-driven wheels were evolved for the same purpose. Such devices were of particular value in mountainous terrain such as that of Szechuan. Dykes were also erected to limit the effects of inundation or to retain supplies of water in natural reservoirs.

Early in the fourth century AD the imperial court and a large number of officials fled to the south in the face of invasion by non-Chinese northerners. The attention of the more highly organized and disciplined Chinese of the north was now directed to the working conditions of a southern climate and the problem of raising rice crops in the valley of the Yangtze. In succeeding centuries, before the imperial reunification of AD 589, some progress was made in methods of irrigation. In addition, there was a new urge for more frequent contact, exchange and transport between north and south. By about 600 the new imperial government of Sui had set its conscript labourers to the task of uniting a number of waterways into a single system, known subsequently as China's first 'Grand Canal', which constituted a major advance in economic development.

China was probably the first country in the world to provide census data on the size of its population. The first surviving count is for the year AD 1–2; the census records 12 400 000 households or 57 700 000 individuals, a measure of the spread and intensity of government and its provincial organs, which derived from the establishment of some 1500 administrative divisions, each including at least one walled town. A high proportion of these settlements had probably existed in some form (of unknown size) for centuries; many of them survived to give rise to religious, administrative, industrial or commercial centres in the centuries that followed the Han empire.

The towns

In the centuries before imperial unification towns had arisen as the seats of minor kings and their courts, as repositories for the protection of religious shrines and treasures, as centres of communications and as industrial workshops. Some of the features that marked China's later cities were already apparent. They were planned in a rectangular form, sometimes surrounded by two sets of concentric walls built of stamped earth, with formal gateways incorporated at set intervals along each side; originally the space between the two walls may have been sown with cereal crops to enable the defenders to withstand a siege.

Perhaps a tenth part of China's registered population lived in towns, which varied greatly in size from a few thousand inhabitants to between 100 000 and 250 000. As the buildings were constructed mainly of wood, the only surviving remains of pre-imperial or early imperial buildings are in the form of stamped earth foundations, or possibly walls, and the tiles that were used for roofing. Much may be learned of the structure of Han buildings from the ceramic models that were often buried in graves and from reliefs. A map of 168 BC found recently in central China is reported to include plans of a city.

The palace of the first Ch'in emperor (d. 210 BC) and a religious building lying to the south of the former Han capital of Ch'ang-an (before AD 25) are among sites that have been identified. Literary and material evidence combine to show that the Later Han capital city of Lo-yang (AD 25–220), while less splendid than its predecessor at Ch'ang-an, was probably the largest city in the world, with an estimated population of half a million.[3] Lo-yang was carefully oriented on a north–south axis, with its quarters planned as separate wards. The layout of the city's main buildings and of utilities such as waterways was designed as much to satisfy prevailing cosmological theory as to suit the convenience of the population. When Lo-yang was rebuilt as the capital of the Wei dynasty (495) it became subject to more highly developed planning; special zones were set aside for particular purposes and imperial buildings were clustered in one quarter. By now the city housed a large number of Buddhist temples and towers, which had proliferated in the fourth and fifth centuries. Literary descriptions testify to the splendour of these richly decorated buildings, long since perished in China but perhaps surviving in part in some Japanese imitations.

Coinage

The use of cowrie shells as a medium of exchange and as a means of estimating value in the Shang period was followed by the introduction of bronze spades and knives as items of barter, which were employed in various ways in different parts of China.[4] The real objects were replaced by replica tools that were gradually reduced in size, given some measure of stylization and decorated with a brief inscription recording their place of origin. Initially the distribution of different types of coin followed the political divisions of the time, but finds show that with the growth of trade, 'coins' of both spade and knife type mingled over large areas of northern China. Such finds testify to the spread of Chinese trade to Korea by the third century BC, when these early coins were replaced by the more convenient disk coin, which had a hole in the centre so that it could be threaded on a hempen or leather thong. In the southern state of Ch'u stamped gold pieces were in circulation, but they had fallen out of use by perhaps 300 BC.

With imperial unification there opened a new era in Chinese

coinage. The many different forms of coin used by individual states gave way to a bronze piece of a single denomination, whose size and weight was specified by the central government; from 112 BC minting was officially restricted to government workshops. Coins were sometimes supplemented by gold or silver ingots or, at times of dynastic instability, by a return to barter with silken bales.

There was a distinct contrast between the light, small coin produced regularly by the Han mints and the heavier piece circulated during the T'ang dynasty.

Transport and trade

Models buried in tombs, reliefs carved on stone, a few inscriptions and the decorations of impressed brick illustrate methods of transporting both staples and luxury goods. Natural waterways were

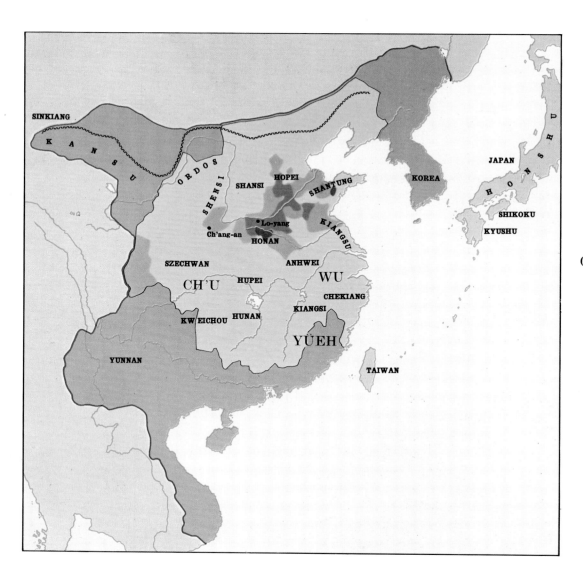

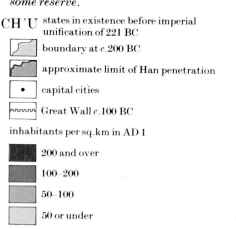

37.2: *By AD 1–2 the Han empire had been extended deep into central Asia and to the west. The administration was most effective in the valleys of the Wei and the Yellow River, and precise boundaries cannot always be shown to mark the limits of government at the periphery. The census of AD 1–2 was derived from the lists of registered households, but as registration brought with it obligations to pay taxes and provide conscript labour, false information was sometimes given or registration deliberately avoided, and the resulting figures must be regarded with some reserve.*

CH'U states in existence before imperial unification of 221 BC

⬡ boundary at *c.*200 BC

◼ approximate limit of Han penetration

• capital cities

〰 Great Wall *c.*100 BC

inhabitants per sq.km in AD 1

◼ 200 and over

◼ 100–200

◼ 50–100

◻ 50 or under

supplemented by canals from at least the fifth century BC; conscripts were put to the work of transporting commodities by water or land, to the maintenance of bridges and roads and to the construction of perilous causeways to surmount the hazards of mountain or torrent. Riding horses and light, horse-drawn curricles were available for officials, and horse-drawn wagons were perhaps used by wealthy merchants;[5] but a high proportion of Chinese goods were carried in ox-drawn carts or in single-wheel barrows pulled by men. Much of Han decorative art is given over to representations of horses, riders and carriages, and models and reliefs show the evolution of a more efficient type of harness that was brought into use from the first century AD.

Warfare

The wars fought between the pre-imperial states both before and in the course of the foundation of the early empires are reflected in a number of types of object: dagger-axes, short swords used by mounted infantry and chariot fittings. About China's defensive warfare of the following centuries material evidence is more informative: remnants survive of the earthwork frontier built as a defensive measure in the north and extended into central Asia to protect the trading caravans that were setting out to the west. This was the origin of China's 'Great Wall'. Sun-baked bricks and stamped earth were used to build the causeway, military quarters, square look-out towers and command posts, which were equipped to send signals along the line by fire, flag or smoke. The posts were subject to routine inspection by officers who examined the state of the buildings and their equipment and the weapons of the troops.[6] These were mainly crossbows, made to precise specifications and fitted with an intricate trigger mechanism of bronze; parts of sighting devices attached to the walls have also been found.

Industry and crafts

In contrast with other parts of the world, China probably evolved the use of cast iron before that of wrought iron. To attain the necessary heat, double-cylinder bellows were in use by the fourth century BC; these were supplemented by dual-action cylinder bellows in the second century BC, and by the first century AD these bellows were worked partly by water power. Steel was evolved in the Han period.[7]

Material evidence of China's early iron industry is provided by iron wares themselves, by the moulds in which they were cast and

37.3: *Bronze fittings, inlaid with gold and silver, believed to have formed parts of a heavy device for shooting arrows; they date from the fourth or third century BC.*

by a few workshop or foundry sites. Tradition has it that a local kingdom in eastern China tried to establish a state monopoly over ironworking in the seventh century BC, but this is not certain. As with the production of salt, however, a monopoly was introduced in 119 BC by the Han imperial government.

The work of the iron foundries was directed mainly at the manufacture of certain agricultural tools and weapons of war such as swords or spears. At this time bronze casting was also being practised for the production of finer wares such as sacred vessels, incense burners, ornaments and carriage fittings, together with domestic items such as lamps or wine-warmers.[8]

The wealth of funerary equipment found in tombs illustrates the range of the skills of Chinese craftsmen and the technological developments that accompanied changing fashions and tastes. A whole series of bronze mirrors can be traced, beginning with those of low-relief, curvilinear or geometric patterns of the fourth century BC, of which one example reached Pazyryk in the high Altai steppeland. By the first century AD mirrors were decorated with the highly symbolic imagery of contemporary religion and philosophy, but by about AD 150 this style was replaced by designs chosen solely for their decorative effect, culminating in the exquisite inlaid mirrors of the T'ang dynasty.

For the greater part of the population rough clothing was made from hemp, of which scant remains survive. For the higher levels of society, and as a valuable commodity for export, silk served as a luxury item. Sericulture is known to have been practised in China since about 1500 BC, and recent discoveries show how far Chinese skills had advanced by about 200 BC. At least eight representations of Han looms on decorative bricks have survived; some of their output has been found in the form of monochrome, polychrome and patterned silks, both in the bale and made up into clothing.

Glazed pottery[9] appears among the ceramics of Ch'u in the fourth century BC. In northern China ceramic vessels were being made in different shapes and styles at this time, sometimes in imitation of bronze pieces. Han potters turned out jars ranging from coarse unglazed wares to painted stonewares and high-fired glazes whose quality is close to that of porcelain. Figurines, animal figures and models of waggons exemplify the skills developed in the centuries after the Han dynasty, as do the gaily coloured platters and vessels designed for the tables of the rich. It is principally to the Han potters that we owe the miniature models of farms, well-heads, houses and boats that provide such excellent evidence of the daily life of the times. Some of the most beautiful examples of carving are seen in Buddhist statues of the fifth century AD. The state's patronage of Buddhism also led in time to the carving of massive statues in the rock in sites such as the caves and cliffs of Yun-kang and Lung-men (fifth to sixth centuries).

Before the imperial age carvers in jade had been producing delicately cut circular disks, rectangular pillars and other objects used for ritual purposes.[10] By the Han period they were also shaping

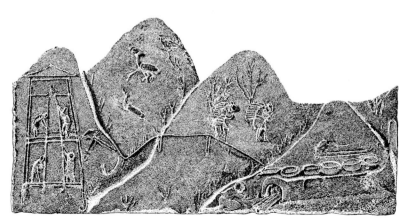

37.4: *The production of salt became a monopoly of the state in 119 BC. Thirty-four commissioners were posted at the mines and at the salt-producing areas of the coast to supervise the work of drilling for deposits, processing and transporting the finished product, as this relief (dated to between about 100 BC and AD 100) shows. The monopoly was only sporadically operated in succeeding centuries.*

ornaments used in dressing a corpse prior to burial; for the most highly privileged members of society they prepared tailor-made suits of shaped pieces of jade, intended to protect the corpse from decay. The art of lacquer painting, a characteristic feature of the pre-imperial state and culture of Ch'u, is well represented in pots, dishes, containers and articles of ladies' toilet sets found in graves from the fifth and fourth centuries BC onwards. These brilliant scarlet and black wares were produced for some centuries to come; their persistence is a reminder of the native romanticism and sense of mystery of the southern culture, which contrasts with the traditional and more regular styles of art associated with the northern kingdom of Chou. The lacquer wares of Ch'u also contrast sharply with the somewhat dull, routine work that is evident in many examples of Han pottery.

The spread of Chinese influence to Korea and Japan

For the earliest periods little is known about the continuity of human settlements in Korea. Two distinct types of Neolithic culture can be distinguished through pottery types and their distribution; and there was a particular type of burial, in pairs of facing jars, that was probably reserved for local chieftains. Metal goods were first brought to Korea from northern China and Mongolia, where the leaders of the Hsiung-nu confederacies were dominant, but it is unlikely that metal was cast there until the end of the third century BC.[11]

Chinese administration was established in the peninsula from 108 BC. Evidence of such colonial settlements over the next two centuries is provided by brick-built tombs of Han type, whose contents are comparable with those of contemporary tombs in China and reflect the adoption of a Chinese lifestyle and the material prosperity enjoyed by officials. With the decline of the Han dynasty in the second century AD and the weakening of Chinese political strength and stability, local native kingdoms, such as Koguryŏ in the north and Mimana in the south, were established.

Archaeological evidence from Korea includes a few *stelae* inscribed in Chinese characters, and it is mainly as a bridge that permitted cultural influences to move from China to Japan[12] that Korea played a significant role at this time. Finds of the Middle Yayoi period in Japan (*c.* 100 BC to AD 100) include wheel-made pottery and locally made bronzes; some sites have yielded the highly characteristic mirrors and coins of the period AD 9–23 from China. A large number of Chinese goods, principally bronze mirrors of the third century AD, are also found in the tombs of Japan. After the third century Japan established direct links more with Korea and its southern kingdoms than with the imperial courts of China; Japanese expeditions brought the living presence of Japan to Korea by armed force. In the fourth century Buddhist cults were taken from Korea to Japan, where they received official recognition in the sixth century. But a change came in the seventh century, when Japan attained a new measure of nationhood.

37.5: *Clay models of a two-storied house (28 centimetres high) and a granary (30 centimetres high), excavated from tombs in Kwangtung. Models not only of buildings but also of wells, farmyards, carriages, horses, etc., were buried in tombs to provide the necessary furnishings for a future life. The granary includes apertures for ventilation and four columns that raise it from the ground as a precaution against damp and rodents.*

38. The rise of the nomads in central Asia

Central Asia forms part of the vast arid zone that extends from West Africa to Manchuria. It is the edges of this zone that are most productive, though the mountains that punctuate it offer valuable seasonal pasture. Rainfall in the zone may have varied over the centuries, and there is evidence that conditions were even drier between 2000 BC and AD 700. Nomadic pastoralism arose as the result of man's adaptation to such a difficult environment.

Before the spread of nomadic pastoralism four separate areas of settlement were already established in central Asia. In the fourth millennium BC small villages and larger settlements of about 14 hectares were engaged in irrigation farming and the husbandry of sheep and goats in the foothills of the Kopet Dag.[1] To the north the desert–steppe area between the Caspian Sea and the Jaxartes river (Syr Darya) belonged to people of the Kelteminar culture, who lived by hunting, fishing and shellfish gathering. A number of groups in this area, such as the inhabitants of the Djebel, Damm-Damm and Kamarbant caves, developed a form of husbandry (seen by some scholars as indigenous goat domestication) as early as the seventh millennium BC. After 4000 BC the bones of cattle, goats and sheep are found with some frequency, while pomegranate and apricot fruits, as well as bone- and flint-bladed sickles, indicate gathering and perhaps cultivation.[2] The other early centres of cultural development were the Ferghana valley and lower Tadzhikistan. The northern fringes of central Asia were inhabited by groups of Forest Zone origin (see Chapter 49) who settled on the taiga–steppe border and made use of both environments through hunting, farming and the herding of cattle, sheep, goats, and horses.

In the third millennium BC a number of developments took place on the steppes, including riding, wheeled transport, a novel form of burial and possibly the use of animals for the provision of milk. Remains of horse-handling gear – for riding and for traction –

38.1: *Phases in the development of prehistory in central and northern Eurasia. (For the development in the northern and eastern parts of the European Forest Zone, see Figure 49.1.)*

Mesolithic: hunting and fishing economy without pottery use

Forest Neolithic: hunting and fishing with pottery use and probably greater concentration on plant resources

Farming and animal husbandry: in northern and eastern Europe usually combined with extensive hunting and fishing

Mounted nomadic pastoralism with simple farming as a secondary activity

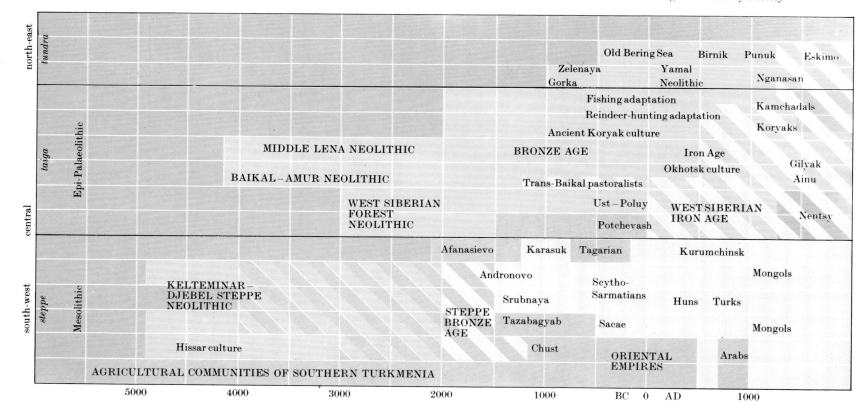

are found in their earliest contexts in the Srubnaya and Andronovo burials and do not antedate the second millennium BC. Horse remains commonly make up between 15 and 20 per cent of the bone sample of sites of this period, although at Khotor Riepin in the Don valley horse comprised as much as 80 per cent. It has also been established that the camel, another animal used for riding, was present in the early Andronovo, Karasuk and late Srubnaya cultures. During the second millennium BC horses began to play an important part in burials and religious life. Horse skulls were found in burial mounds in the Poltavka phase of the early Srubnaya culture (1800–1500 BC), and burials of whole horses have been discovered in the Andronovo culture and in later Srubnaya phases. Although they are rare, horse remains also appear in the burials of the Karasuk culture.

Wheeled transport, in the form of two-wheeled carts and later also of four-wheeled wagons, came into use on the Pontic steppes in the mid-third millennium BC and somewhat later in central Asia. This is clear from rock carvings, from clay models of wheeled vehicles and, more sporadically, from actual remains of wheels.

As in earlier periods, settlements continued to be located in the river valleys dissecting the steppe and along the forest–steppe margin. After the mid-third millennium BC burial mounds (kurgans) are found on the steppe as well as in areas adjacent to valleys. Kurgans are found over the entire steppe by about 1500 BC.

It is hard to define exactly when pastoralism became dominant,

38.2: *The steppe Bronze Age. Before about 2000 BC there were only small areas of intensive cultivation in the southern part of central Asia, while most of the rest of the region was occupied by people engaged in hunting, herding and simple plant cultivation. In about 2000 BC mounted nomadic pastoralism was gradually developed by the people of the Srubnaya and Andronovo cultures who occupied the steppe; from about 1500 BC dispersal took place, resulting in the emergence of secondary centres of nomadic pastoralism.*

- areas of intensive cultivation, mostly using irrigation systems
- hunting, herding and simple plant cultivation
- areas of initial transition to mounted nomadic pastoralism, 2000–1500 BC
- secondary centres of nomadic pastoralism
- main routes of dispersal of nomads

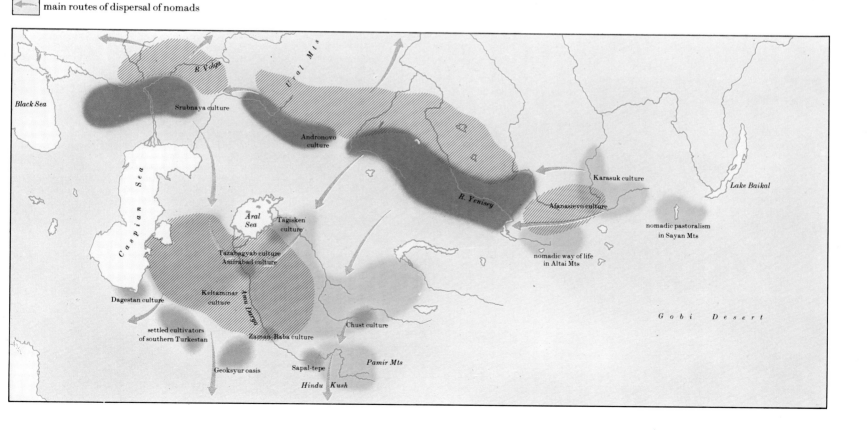

but settlement evidence suggests that independent pastoral economies existed on the steppe between the Dnieper and Ural rivers from about 2500 BC. About 2000 BC pastoral societies formed to the east of the Ural river.

The emergence of nomadic pastoralism

The rise of nomadic pastoralism appears to have been stimulated by three developments: an increase in the size of herds beyond the grazing capacity of the land around settlements; the practice of horse-riding; and increasingly dry conditions. These three factors together supported the trend towards greater mobility among the peoples of central Asia, who turned from sedentary farming and herding to seasonal migrations in search of grazing and then to mounted nomadic pastoralism.

There is a tendency among nomadic pastoralists to augment the numbers of their herds beyond subsistence needs. This may be to ensure the long-term survival of the herds or for social reasons, but if it is unchecked it leads to an overtaxing of the environment and eventual catastrophe for the economy. Nevertheless, careful herd management and the nomadic way of life usually enable nomadic pastoralists to keep more livestock and to exploit more marginal habitats than is possible in the two other economies that have been practised at one time or another in central Asia – the broad-based economy, and irrigation farming with associated stock-keeping. There are disadvantages to nomadic pastoralism, however: because the resources of the nomads have only one restricted base, with a simple food web, and because they exploit marginal habitats, there tend to be great fluctuations in the availability of food supplies.

The introduction of one innovation went some way towards minimizing these fluctuations – the nomads adopted the practice of milking their herds. Indeed, milk rather than meat production was the principal concern of pastoral nomadism: because the maintenance of large herds of mature animals was uneconomic unless they provided dairy products, milking greatly facilitated the development of nomadic pastoralism.[3] However, the management of herds was not without its problems. There was an advantage in keeping several kinds of animals because this ensured a steady supply of milk and meat throughout the year, but the risks inherent in a pastoral economy increased if the nomads relied too much on sheep and goats, because these animals are more susceptible to drought and disease than are cattle.[4]

The nomadic social system is generally characterized by a hierarchical structure and organization based on the herding group. Male dominance in social and economic life is commonly associated with nomadic pastoralism, but there are significant exceptions, such as among the present-day Tibetan nomads or, in the past, the Sarmatians, among whom women had claims and obligations comparable with those of men. In the latter case this is evidenced not only by the writings of Classical authors but also by frequent burials of armed women.[5]

The emergence of nomadic pastoralism to the east of the Ural river in about 2000 BC appears to have been influenced by the Yamnaya and Catacomb cultures of the Dnieper–Ural steppe. The similarities in the pottery that has been found in the two regions testifies to this. The change to nomadic pastoralism, which was superimposed on a number of culturally and economically distinct local groups, took place at the same time as the development of the bronze industry based on the mining of the Ural and the Altai ores, and resulted in the formation of the Andronovo culture. Early in the second millennium BC the steppe groups of this culture developed or adopted horse-riding, which facilitated the rapid expansion of mounted nomadic pastoralism.

The migration and dispersal of the nomads

The progress of nomads into the southern parts of central Asia was associated with two further developments. The irrigation-based, proto-urban communities of southern Turkmenia disintegrated, rather because of the failure to obtain an adequate supply of water than as a result of nomadic movements. Simultaneously, however, new settlements appeared in the Zeravshan valley, Khoresm, Ferghana and elsewhere, which showed clearly the blending of the Steppe Bronze Age and farming elements from southern Turkmenia.[6] Pastoral groups also penetrated into the Tien Shan to make use of seasonal grazing up to 3000 metres.

Nomadic movements in central Asia have frequently been identified with the migrations of Indo-European peoples. Attempts to match archaeological, linguistic and historical data have produced widely differing opinions about the original area, time of dispersal and archaeological cultures identifiable with the Indo-Europeans. Comparative studies of historical linguistics and archaeological records have led some scholars to believe that the Yamnaya culture of the lower Volga steppe was the earliest archaeologically perceptible equivalent of the Indo-Europeans. There is little doubt that at least some groups of the Srubnaya and Andronovo, both cultures succeeding and related to the Yamnaya, were Indo-European. There are obvious parallels in burial rite, art form and symbolism between the Steppe Bronze Age and the Ancient Aryan hymns of the *Rig-Veda*, dated to between 1500 and 1200 BC. Less obviously, there are parallels in social structure and in the form of economy, attested archaeologically as a pastoralist one. Finally, the Aryan penetration of India, linguistically postulated at 2000–1500 BC, is chronologically compatible with the events in central Asia and with the demise of the Indus valley civilization, for which the intruding Indo-Aryans may have been partly responsible.

From about the seventh century BC a number of separate nomadic groups or tribal confederations were recognized by ancient authors: the Scythians by the Greeks, the Saka (Sacae) by the Persians, the Wu-sun by the Chinese. They represent an ethnically divergent people who nevertheless spoke principally Iranian languages and had a 'Europoid' physique. Archaeological evidence favours the view that these pastoralists were descendants of the local Andronovo and Srubnaya groups whose culture became more elaborate under the influence of the cultures of the northern Caucasus and of ancient civilizations.

Archaeological data, obtained almost entirely from burials, support the observations of Classical authors on the nomadic life of these people. Apart from temporary encampments, no settlements have been found on the steppe, but burials testify in remarkable detail to the social habits, organization and mythology of the ancient nomads. This is seen best at Pazyryk, perhaps the most spectacular among the rich nomad tombs.[7] The wood-lined burial chambers remained encased in ice for twenty-four centuries, enabling the tattooed bodies of buried chieftains and a complete range of grave goods to be recovered. Despite the enormous distance between the Pazyryk and the Pontic Scythians, there is a remarkable similarity in their customs: the scalping of enemies, the embalming of corpses, the hemp-smoking ritual and other habits were practised by both, as described by the Greek historian Herodotus and as confirmed centuries later by the Pazyryk discovery.

Contacts between the nomads and the settled farmers of the central Asian oases or the civilizations of the ancient world took the form of keen trade or of armed conflict. The latter became more evident in the first millennium BC as successive groups of nomads, Scythians, Sarmatians and Parthians, pressed one another towards the fringes of the steppe and further into Europe and the Near East. This tendency, inherent in the nomadic system and the geographical setting of central Asia, was fostered by advances in technology that favoured nomadic warfare. Some scholars believe that horse-riding existed in the early Yamnaya culture (about 3000 BC), while others credit the Scythians with its development, placing its beginnings between the tenth and the eighth centuries BC. The latter regard the military success of the Scythians in Asia Minor and on the steppe itself as a result of the superiority of mounted archers over chariot-borne opponents. Later the Sarmatians, a kindred nomadic people, displaced the Scythians from the Pontic steppes largely because of the novel employment of armoured cavalry and the use of heavy lances. They were in turn dislodged by the Huns, who invented a more effective compound bow that could penetrate armour.

Hunnic migrations dominated central Asia from about the third century BC until the mid-first millennium AD. (The term Hunnic is used to describe a variety of people of mixed ethnic background, with the Turkic element predominating.) Three separate groups emerged from the proliferation of nomadic tribes in this period. The Hsiung-nu created a confederacy in the third century BC that included most of the nomad groups in Mongolia. Their conflict with China is well attested in Chinese chronicles, and their attacks on the Tien Shan nomads generated a series of collisions across the steppes resulting in the Sarmatian displacement of the Scythians.

The Ephthalites, or White Huns, were based in the south-eastern part of central Asia. From here they penetrated India and Iran in the mid-first millennium AD. A confederacy of Turkic and Mongolic nomads, known as the Black Huns, formed in the Altai in the first centuries AD. Their advance across the steppe, and the subsequent invasion of Europe in the fifth century AD led by Attila, heralded the end of the Roman empire and the beginning of the period of migrations.

Hunnic migrations initiated a new stage in the nomadic dispersal. The nomads who invaded the west arose to the east of the Tien Shan, marking the end of Indo-European domination of the steppe and the beginning of the dispersal of the Turkic and Mongolic peoples. Turkic tribes rose to prominence in the sixth century AD, as leaders in a nomadic confederacy that extended from the Altai to Manchuria, and subsequently migrated into central Asia. Peoples displaced by the Turkic expansion – Hungarians and Bulgars – entered Europe and settled where they are today. In the eleventh century the Turks themselves occupied Asia Minor.

The original homeland of the Mongols lay between Lake Baikal and the Amur river. They rose to power in much the same way as the Turks had before them. Through the organizing genius of Genghis Khan and the loyalty and endurance of his soldiers, the Mongols were able to establish the most effective of the nomad empires, which was eventually to extend from the Mediterranean to the Pacific. However, the social structure of nomadic society, with its emphasis on personal relations, a simple hierarchy and tribal loyalty, prevented them from maintaining the extensive empire that they had won. Rather, this structure contributed to the early demise of the empire, despite attempts by Genghis Khan to augment the power of the state. There were other obstacles, too: notably the mobility inherent in the nomadic way of life and the difficulties of integrating disparate peoples and different economies under a centralized government.

The nomads of central Asia passed through three stages of development. The initial formative stage can be dated to about 2000 BC. It may have been influenced by over-grazing of resources by unmounted pastoralists, environmental change or, in more southerly areas, the demands of irrigation farming. All these may have encouraged the development of wheeled transport and the use of animals for milking, both of which may be regarded as essential elements in mounted nomadic pastoralism. The adoption of pastoralism made it difficult to maintain the crucial balance between resources and population, and resulted in a disequilibrium that generated conflict and dispersal.

The second stage of development, which took place in the second millennium BC, saw expansion southwards, perhaps directed by climatic change. In general, nomads migrated to areas as yet unaffected by pastoral nomadism, including the Tien Shan, the Altai and the Sayans, while the people of Transbaikal adopted stockkeeping in the thirteenth century BC. This process continued in the first millennium BC.

The third stage, beginning with the rise of the Huns, is characterized by two important developments. Nomadic groups in the mountains extending eastwards from the Altai were developing their own form of pastoralism. With horse-breeding and the husbandry of sheep and goats rather than cattle, these groups were still more volatile and more prone to dispersal. The shift to this form of pastoralism did not take place only in the uplands of central Asia: among the lowland settlements of Khoresm the proportion of sheep and goats rose steadily from 50 per cent in the sixth century BC to 90 per cent in the tenth century AD.[8] Improvements in equestrian warfare – the Sarmatian armour and lance, the Hunnic bow, the Turkic stirrup, the Mongols' organization and tactics – further encouraged expansion and the adoption of riding. From the time of the Huns, the mountains and plateau between the Altai mountains and the Amur river came to serve as nomadic breeding-grounds in the centre of the arid zone from which the expansion originated.

Seen in this light, the mounted nomadic pastoralists of central Asia resolved their failure to adjust to situations they themselves helped to create by resorting to emigration and armed competition elsewhere. However, the rise of modern states gradually deprived them of this recourse, and when they were not absorbed into wider economic systems, they encountered the problems associated with the need to balance resources and population that still plague many nomadic societies today.

38.3: *Ecological zones and the pattern of migrations, 500 BC to AD 1300. The map shows the relationship between grazing potential and the movements of nomads. Steppe areas can produce up to ten times as much as those of semi-desert, and forest steppe three times as much again. Nevertheless, the forest was not able to support nomadic pastoralists, and although the mountainous central area could encourage the development of pastoralism, its potential was limited, and the nomads were eventually forced to disperse.*

- desert and semi-desert
- steppe
- steppe/forest
- forest

SACAE   Indo-European peoples

TURKS   non-Indo-European peoples

→ movements of Indo-European groups of Scytho-Sarmatian period

→ movements of Hsiung-nu and Huns

→ Turkish expansion

→ Arab expansion

→ Mongol expansion

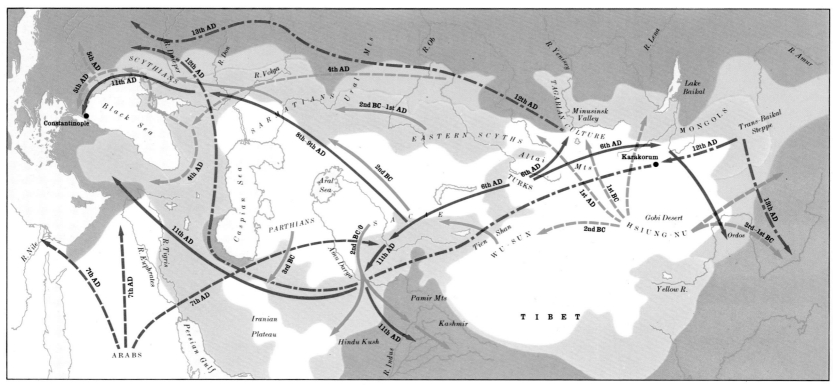

39. India before and after the Mauryan empire

The first millennium BC saw a shift of focus to the Ganges river system, due partly to ecological changes in areas settled earlier, during the Harappan period (see Chapter 22), and partly to new technologies such as the use of iron and the cultivation of rice, which made possible the settlement of new areas.

A variety of archaeological cultures are evident in the Indian subcontinent, some isolated and others overlapping with earlier ones. The Gandhara Grave Culture in the Swat valley continued, but with the introduction of new elements such as iron implements, the domesticated horse and the use of grey pottery. A grey pottery has given its name to the sites of the Painted Grey Ware along the Sutlej valley in northern Rajasthan, the watershed between the Indus and the Ganges systems and the western Ganges valley. This culture dates from the first millennium BC. The distinctive grey-ware pottery was generally decorated with black floral and geometrical designs and was different from that of the Gandhara Grave Culture. Another major culture is named after Black and Red Ware, so called because of the double colour derived from inverted firing. This ware seems to have had its genesis in the white-painted Black and Red Ware of Gujarat, whence it appears to have spread along the Aravalli hills in Rajasthan and, skirting the Yamuna valley to the west, along the Narmada valley into central India. From there it spread into the middle Ganges valley (at sites such as Chirand), with outliers into west Bengal, at Pandu Rajar Dhibi and Mahishdal, for instance. During this period the peninsula

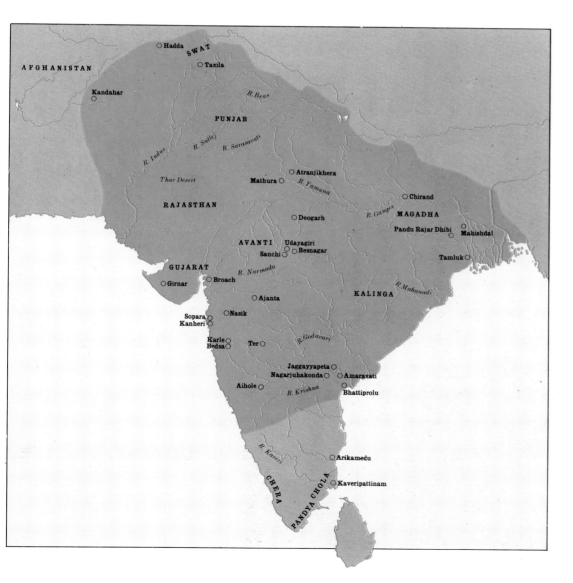

39.1: *The Indian subcontinent: sites and settlements c. 1000 BC to AD 500. The darker shading indicates the approximate extent of the Mauryan empire.*

gave rise to a variety of Megalithic cultures.

Attempts have been made to identify the north Indian cultures with tribes and territories mentioned in literary sources, but the suggestions remain tentative. These sources are the compendia of Vedic literature composed in Sanskrit, an Indo-Aryan language; for this reason the people who spoke it have been described as Aryan. The earliest *Veda* had a geographical focus confined to the area included in the Indus system and the valley of the Saraswati (which has since disappeared in the desert of Thar). This was followed by a movement of peoples eastwards into the Ganges valley. The texts suggest a mixed pastoral and agrarian economy, in which priority was given to the rearing of cattle, and this has prompted an identification with the Painted Grey Ware culture.[1] The Painted Grey Ware and the Black and Red Ware indicate mixed farming with a gradual emphasis on agriculture. The site of Atranjikhera in the western Ganges valley has provided evidence of the double-cropping of wheat or barley and rice. The former were more common in the north-western areas of the subcontinent, whereas rice and millets were more frequent in western India, while rice was grown predominantly in the middle and eastern Ganges valley.[2]

The introduction of iron goes back to the beginning of the first millennium BC, but its frequency increased by the middle of the millennium. However, the use of copper and bronze continued into this period, the most impressive remains being the copper hoards of the Ganges valley, whose date is uncertain as they are generally found in an unstratified context. It has been argued that iron technology led to urbanization in the Ganges valley, as it was the more efficient technology for clearing monsoon forests and for ploughing the heavy alluvial soil. However, weapons rather than agricultural implements constitute the greater part of the earlier finds, and in the absence of extensive horizontal excavation, the argument remains inconclusive.

Literary evidence suggests social stratification, and there are references to the emergence of caste distinctions (*varna* and *jati*).[3] The rise of oligarchies and the formation of small kingdoms indicate the shift of tribal identity to territorial states. The scarcity of religious monuments is partly due to the fact that sacrificial ritual (*yajna*) did not require permanent structures. The absence of burials suggests that by this stage cremation may have been the more common funeral rite. Reference is made to the worship of trees, pillars and sacred enclosures, and to tumuli (*chaitiyas* and *stupas*).

By the mid-first millennium BC a new ceramic industry is noticeable, with its genesis in the middle Ganges valley: the Northern Black Polished Ware ranged in colour from charcoal grey to black with a metallic sheen. Its spread to other areas seems to have followed river and land routes and is generally linked with the growth of urban centres, as it is more prolific in these. Two major routes are referred to: the northern route, with the city of Taxila as a nodal point linking Iran and Afghanistan with the Punjab and the Ganges valley, and the southern route, linking the Ganges valley via Avanti (the Malwa plateau) and the Narmada valley with the ports of the west coast (such as Broach – ancient Bhrigukaccha – and Sopara) as well as a route going further south into the peninsular region. Items of trade included textiles, woollen goods, pottery, precious and semi-precious stones and metals.

Urbanization has also been linked with the rise of new religious sects described as heterodox inthe context of Vedic brahmanical orthodoxy. These were the Buddhists, the Jainas and the Ajivikas, and a variety of other groups professing a generally materialist philosophy who were referred to as the Charvakas and Lokayatas. Many of the latter groups derived from the oligarchies (such as the Sakyas and the Vrijjis) and had a large following in the towns. The Buddhist and Jaina sects, which evolved into major religions, built their organizational strength on monastic institutions.[4]

One notable aspect of the urban ethos, as it is reflected in the literature of these sects, is the high status accorded to merchants and traders, whose wealth was computed in coined money (the use of punch-marked coins first occurred in this period). The coins were either small, bent bars or flat pieces of silver with symbols punched on both sides.[5] The symbols could be those of governmental authority, whether of the monarchies or of the oligarchies, or those of traders and bankers. The coins ranged in weight between ten and a hundred grains. The use of a script is indirectly referred to in the mention of letters of credit and promissory notes.

The same sources provide evidence of stratification at the lower levels of society. Mention is made of slaves and hired labourers (*dasa-bhritaka*), who worked on the fields of landowners, as domestic slaves in the houses of the wealthy and with artisans. The latter were gradually being organized into guilds (*shreni*) to facilitate both commodity production and trade.[6]

Of the states contending for domination, Magadha, located in south Bihar, emerged as a major power. It had access to agricultural wealth, forest resources and deposits of iron ore, and it had a strategic position from which to control the river trade on the Ganges. Trade was established eastwards, along the river to the Ganges delta, with its port at Tamluk. This provided links with the rich coastal area of Kalinga (the Mahanadi delta) and eventually with the kingdoms of south India. In the fourth century BC the Ganges valley became the base for the Nanda kingdom, believed to be the Xandrames of the Greek accounts, whose large army may well have been one of the reasons why Alexander's soldiers were deterred from undertaking further campaigns in India.[7]

By this time north-western India had been drawn into the politics of the Achaemenian empire (see Chapter 30). Having conquered the area once held by the Achaemenians Alexander continued across the Indus into the Punjab. He reached the Beas river, where he turned back and, having followed the Indus to its delta, sent part of his army by sea while he took the rest along the difficult coastal route back to Babylon. Alexander's campaign had little direct impact on India, but in the period after his death northern India had diplomatic links with the Hellenized kingdoms of western Asia.

The Mauryan empire

By the end of the fourth century BC a new dimension was apparent in Indian history, with the establishment of the Mauryan empire. During the reigns of the first three kings, Chandragupta, Bindusara and Ashoka, the empire was consolidated, and the distribution of the inscriptions of Ashoka indicate that it included virtually the entire subcontinent (except for the region south of Karnataka), as well as parts of eastern and southern Afghanistan.[8]

The empire was characterized by a differentiated economy, including food-gathering tribes, pastoralists, various categories of peasant cultivators and traders. The main economic thrust was in the extension of agriculture, and the state took the initiative in settling new areas for agricultural production (the major concern of the state seems to have been the collection of revenue). The famous edict of Ashoka, which expressed remorse for the suffering caused by the Mauryan campaign against Kalinga, refers to the deportation of prisoners of war, who are believed to have been used in the cultivation of waste land. In fertile areas double-cropping was a normal feature and some emphasis was given to irrigation facilities. Although there is evidence of only one instance of state-organized irrigation – the construction of a dam at Girnar in western India – it is clear that the state recognized the importance of irrigation and encouraged private irrigation works maintained by individual cultivators.

The subcontinental network of administration and the roads that connected various parts of the empire resulted in an extension of trade. This is also reflected in the wider distribution of Northern Black Polished Ware, in the emergence of urban centres and in the detailing of items manufactured and exchanged in various parts

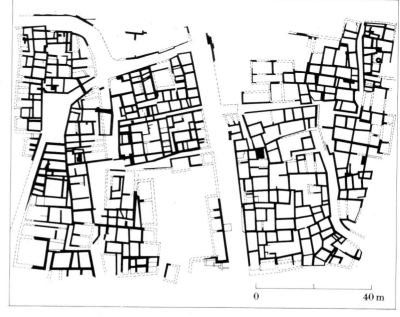

39.2: *Plans of two cities at Taxila, part of a larger complex of urban settlements and monuments excavated there. Bhir Mound, of the Mauryan period, provides evidence of the evolution of an urban centre from what appears to have been a pre-urban settlement; the city of Sirkap nearby dates to the post-Mauryan period and indicates a more carefully planned city.*

0   40 m

0   100m

of the empire. Guilds came under a measure of state control. Mauryan terracotta art provides an insight into the everyday urban life of the times.

The Mauryan kings were patrons of heterodox sects. Ashoka is particularly remembered for his doctrine of Dhamma – an ethical code that seemed necessary in a multi-cultural society. The edicts in which he elaborates on the Dhamma were inscribed on rock surfaces and on finely polished pillars located at places where people were likely to congregate. The pillars were frequently crowned by animal capitals, and these provide the earliest examples of art for the historical period, which have been compared with possible Achaemenian prototypes. The inscriptions constitute the earliest actual evidence for the use of a script during this period. They are inscribed mainly in the Brahmi script, although a few in the north-west testify to the use of the Kharoshthi script, influenced by Aramaic. In both cases the language is Prakrit, an Indo-Aryan language used extensively in the subcontinent. A few Ashokan inscriptions found in the north-west and in Afghanistan (Kandahar) were composed in Aramaic and Greek.[9]

The post-Mauryan period

The Mauryan empire declined in the second century BC and was replaced by a number of smaller kingdoms that attempted to build empires from time to time but generally failed. Northern India saw a succession of dynasties, most of which originated across the borders in Bactria and in central Asia. The Bactrian Greeks conquered the Punjab, penetrated as far as the fringes of the Ganges valley and founded the Indo-Greek dynasty. They were followed by the Scythians (Shakas in Indian sources) and the Parthians, who were in turn ousted by the Kushans (see Chapter 43). The latter extended their power over both central Asia and northern India, and this was crucial to their control over trade in these regions. The Kushan king, Kanishka, founded a dynasty that is believed to have spanned nearly two centuries, from AD 78 to 244 though the exact dates are uncertain.

The Indo-Greeks introduced finely minted coins that became the standard type for much subsequent north Indian coinage. The coins were based on the die-striking technique and carried the portrait of the king, the representation of a deity, perhaps a symbol of worship and a legend, usually incorporating an elaborate royal title.[10] The Kushans issued gold coins as trade expanded, although the more common issues were in silver and copper. The inscriptions of the period were chiefly donatory. Objects inscribed in Kharoshthi were presented to the Buddhist monasteries, and commemorative texts on relic caskets have been recovered from Buddhist *stupas*. An inscription in Brahmi at Besnagar in central India records the statement of Heliodorus, a Greek ambassador to a local court, who had been converted to an early form of the Bhagavata religion and the worship of Vishnu. The majority of the religious monuments were associated with Buddhism. Sculptured forms in the north-western regions were commonly of stucco and conformed to the Gandhara style, which illustrates the influence of Greco-Roman norms as typified by finds at Hadda.[11] Mathura and Sanchi, both important commercial and religious centres, provide evidence of Buddhist and Jaina sculpture in stone with a distinctly Indian style. Excavations at Taxila have revealed the cities of Bhir Mound, Sirkap and Sirsukh, which remain the most significant horizontal excavations of the historical period.[12]

The Shungas in the Ganges valley and the Chedis in Kalinga were successors to the Mauryas. Gujarat provides evidence of Kshatrapa rule, which was associated with the adoption of brahmanical ritual and the use of Sanskrit in inscriptions. The northern Deccan came under the control of the Andhra, or Satavahana, dynasty. Many of the local inscriptions record donations to the Buddhist order, often at caves, as cave monasteries became common in the hills of the western Deccan. These were

39.3: *The edicts of Ashoka inscribed on a polished sandstone pillar.*

39.4: *The stupa at Sanchi is among the earliest and more important Buddhist monuments. It is surrounded by a railing with four gateways, each elaborately decorated with a variety of low-relief panels and sculptured forms. The railing carries a large number of brief inscriptions referring to those who contributed towards its construction.*

often located at strategic points (Nasik, Bedsa, Ajanta, Karle, Kanheri) that linked the coast with the plateau. Guilds of artisans, identified by individual seals and insignia, are known to have financed the sculptural embellishments on *stupas*, many of which were enlarged during this period (Bharhut, Sanchi, Amaravati, Jaggayyapeta, Bhattiprolu). Trade with Rome via Egypt and western Asia is attested to by Roman finds in many areas of the peninsula, including Sopara and Ter. Exports consisted of spices, textiles, semi-precious stones, ivory and peacocks and were paid for in gold coin. Not surprisingly, local gold coins carry the name of *dinara*, and both these and a large variety of other coins were finely struck. However, despite Roman contacts the early coins of the Andhras had more in common with the punch-marked coins, since many of the symbols were retained. Some carried a brief legend in Brahmi.[13]

Among the inheritors of the Satavahana kingdom in the third century AD were the Ikshvakus, who ruled the Krishna–Guntur region from their capital at Nagarjunakonda. (This was recently extensively excavated and the monuments shifted to a hill when the area was flooded owing to the building of a dam.)[14]

Prior to the emergence of kingdoms in the Deccan and further south, there is evidence of large numbers of settlements whose megalithic funerary monuments include a range of menhirs, standing stones, multi-stone structures, cairns, stone circles with burial chambers, passages and rock-cut chambers with terracotta sarcophagi and urn burials.[15] The pattern of distribution is still under discussion, although the western coastal area appears to have a larger concentration of passages and rock-cut chambers, possible because of the softer rock. The origins of these settlements remains controversial, but many scholars associate them with Dravidian-speaking peoples. Superimposed on either Neolithic or Chalcolithic cultures, the megalithic pattern was not entirely unrelated to the past. The settlements indicate a growth in population and are associated with the cultivation of rice and millet, one variety of the latter being *ragi*, which suggests possible East African connections. There is reason to believe that catchment areas may have had embankments providing a kind of tank irrigation. Major artifacts at burial sites consist of black and red ware (its links with the northern Black and Red Ware are uncertain) and iron objects such as hoes, sickles, arrowheads, knives, daggers and horse-bits. At some sites there is a continuity from megalithic levels to early historical periods, as at Nagarjunakonda and Amaravati.

The earliest literary sources (largely heroic poetry, ballads and religious hymns, collected in an anthology known as the Sangam literature) reflect the transition from chiefships to kingdoms. Among the important kingdoms were those of the Cheras (Malabar), the Cholas (Kaveri valley) and the Pandyas (the Madurai region).[16] Coastal contact between western India and the south was early. Contact overland with northern India dates to the Mauryan period and was established by the second century BC, as is evident from the many brief inscriptions in the Brahmi script –

which was adapted to Tamil speech – recording donations to Buddhist and Jaina sects. The earliest urban centres were located in the maritime kingdoms, and some of the initial economic stimulus for urbanization was provided by maritime trade, which was accelerated by Roman traders using the regular, seasonal monsoon winds for mid-ocean routes. Excavations at Arikamedu have revealed a Roman trading station,[17] and elsewhere large hoards of Roman coins in the peninsula have superseded the punch-marked coins. Other Roman objects include pottery, beads, intaglios, lamps and glass, and these are found at sites such as Kaveripattinam, which was a port of the Cholas. The trade was at its peak during the first centuries BC and AD. With the gradual decline of Roman trade, south-east Asia provided new commercial avenues.

The Guptas

The Gupta kingdom, which arose in the fourth century AD and was restricted to northern and central India, was a watershed in early Indian history. The grandiose titles of the Indo-Greek and Kushan kings were adopted, but the political system gradually gave way to a decentralized agrarian structure that some historians see as the origin of a form of feudalism. Archaeological evidence suggests a gradual decline in urban centres and even, in some cases, a desertion of towns.[18] Nevertheless, the economic momentum of the Kushan and Andhra kingdoms played its part in stabilizing the economy. Royal patronage was expressed in a variety of ways. The earliest Hindu temples belong to this period (Sanchi, Deogarh, Ladh Khan at Aihole), as do Vaishnava and Shaiva icons, although Buddhist sculpture drew the finest craftsmen. Mural painting of this period survives on the walls of caves at Ajanta. Gupta inscriptions providing biographical information and claims to conquest were composed in elegant Sanskrit and echoed the language of court poets. The excellence of artistic and aesthetic achievement is demonstrated even by the technical proficiency of Gupta coins,[19] which far excelled earlier issues, and terracotta sculpture now assumed the status of a major form of artistic expression.[20] Royal patronage of heterodox sects declined and was replaced by the distribution of largesse to those sects associated with what came to be called Hinduism.

40. South-east Asia: civilizations of the tropical forests

The concept of civilization must be applied with caution in ancient south-east Asia, a region whose more recent history contains such disconcerting paradoxes as cannibals and collecting groups with alphabets of their own (the Batak of Sumatra and the Tagbanwa of Palawan), hunter–gatherers with the ability to make excellent steel (some Punan groups in Borneo) and even (as in nineteenth-century northern Vietnam) complex and populous states without settlements that can readily be called cities. Similar anomalies are evident in the prehistory of the region. The discoveries at Ban Chiang and other Thai sites show that several of the traits often associated with civilization – bronze and iron metallurgy and developed agricultural systems – antedated by many centuries the first appearance of other civilized traits such as literacy, monumental art, cities and states.

Civilizations with all these elements did indeed exist in south-east Asia in ancient times. Some were spectacularly successful by any standards: the empire of Angkor is hardly surpassed by Egypt or even Rome in the splendour, number and sheer size of its remains. Yet although archaeological study has concentrated on such city-building, monument-erecting societies, it should also be remembered that these are probably only part of the story. In south-east Asia, perhaps more than in most other regions, peoples uninterested in large, durable memorials may have made critical contributions to the fields of politics, technology and art.

When one examines the remains of those early societies of the region that did possess temples, cities, inscriptions and the rest, several facts stand out. For one thing, all were surprisingly late in spite of the early technological progress made in those same areas. For another, they were distributed most unevenly, even though good agricultural land and locations adjacent to major trade routes were available. Third, they were to a significant and perhaps unusual extent influenced by foreign ideas and models. All these facts pose major problems for archaeologists working in the region.

Early states in south-east Asia

Specialists have long recognized that priority in time belongs to northern Vietnam, thanks to its early (about 200 BC) contacts with, and only slightly later (about 100 BC) conquest by, China under the Han dynasty. Recent research[1] may extend this chronology. The site of Co Loa on the outskirts of Hanoi is now said to have possessed urban characteristics such as fortifications by the early third century BC, and still older sites (like those of the Phung-nguyen complex of the seventh to fifth centuries BC) are thought by Vietnamese archaeologists to have been associated with de-veloped states. This idea is rendered plausible by the rich assemblages of bronze artifacts found at Phung-nguyen and elsewhere, usually named after the type-site, Dong-son, which dates mostly to the Han period.

These northern developments seem, however, to have had little direct influence on the rest of the region, except to produce a lasting vogue for the large bronze musical instruments known as Dong-son drums.[2] While in the past these were often interpreted as evidence of a civilizing mission on the part of an advanced bronze-using northern society, the present tendency is to think that nothing much diffused southwards apart from the drums themselves. Finds showing other northern influences, whether from the pre-Chinese or the Han period, are extremely rare even at sites in southern Vietnam, and even rarer at those in Thailand, Malaysia and Indonesia. It is significant that the ancient peoples of those areas, when they began to feel the need for civilizing, turned not towards Dong-son and China but rather to the west, to India.

This did not take place immediately. No part of south-east Asia outside northern Vietnam can yet be shown to have possessed the defining elements of civilized society until well into the first millennium AD. The primary evidential support for this conclusion has until recently been historical.[3] Chinese (and, less decisively, Greco-Roman and Indian) sources begin in the first and second centuries AD to hint at the presence of substantial settlements and political units somewhere in south-east Asia. Historians are fairly certain of the existence of several relatively civilized sea ports along the trade routes between China and India by the end of the third century. These societies were reported to have dark-skinned inhabitants, cities, kings and what seem to be Indianized religions. The locations and dates of most of them remain highly controversial, but one, the kingdom known as Fu Nan to the Chinese, is well enough documented for it to be dated, on purely historical grounds, to the third–seventh centuries AD and for its location to be identified as close to the southern tip of Vietnam.

The oldest known materials showing direct contact with India – 'Rouletted Ware' sherds from southern India or Sri Lanka, found at Buni Complex sites near Jakarta and at Tengku Lembu Cave in north-west Malaysia – are not earlier than the first century AD. The oldest cities and towns – Oc Eo[4] in southern Vietnam (probably part of Fu Nan), Beikthano[5] and Winka in Burma, and U Thong, Chansen[6] and perhaps Si Thep[7] in Thailand – can only with difficulty be pushed back as far as the early second century. Some of the more urbanized features of these sites may, in fact, be rather later than the carbon and small finds on which their early datings depend. The fortifications at Chansen date to the seventh century. The fortifications and small structures at Oc Eo, the most famous of all such sites, need not be older than the sixth.

The first states in the region cannot be shown by archaeological evidence to be even as old as the first cities. Inscriptions[8] mentioning kings and kingdoms are non-existent until the fourth and fifth centuries. The earliest is that of Vo-Canh in central-southern Vietnam; some epigraphers place this as early as AD 300 on the basis of palaeographical comparisons with the styles of dated scripts found in India. The next oldest are inscriptions of the late fourth century from the Cham area in central Vietnam, of the early or middle fifth century from Java and (extraordinarily, in view of the complete absence there of later remains of this sort) eastern Borneo, and of the late fifth century from southern Cambodia (Kampuchea). All these were issued by kings who had taken Indian names, and most are in Sanskrit. None bears an actual date, so they must be dated stylistically.

Monuments and other public works large enough to require a state's capital and managerial resources are also possible indicators of a high level of political development. But here again the first known instances are late. It seems that none of the early engineering works of south-east Asia was beyond the capacities of a well-organized village. It is not until about 600, with the appearance of such sites as Sambor Pre Kuk in Cambodia and perhaps Nakhon Pathom in Thailand,[9] that monuments grew large enough to demonstrate convincingly the existence of a supralocal state.

Thus, according to the archaeological evidence, the flowering of civilization in south-east Asia was neither early nor rapid. By 1000 BC the region was already well-populated and technologically advanced; as late as AD 500 there had been little change. Although small towns, minor kings and a degree of literacy (in foreign languages) existed here and there, the average south-east Asian of the sixth century still lived much as had his ancestors a thousand years before.

The urban revolution of the seventh century
Within the next century and a half, by contrast, the south-east Asian world was to alter out of all recognition. Towns and cities had appeared in large numbers by AD 700 – more than a hundred are known in central and north-eastern Thailand alone. Monumental art and architecture, in several distinctive and seemingly mature styles,[10] were present in quantity. A number of true states controlling large tracts of land had come into being. Unlike earlier shadowy polities known mainly from historical sources, these states of between the late sixth and early eighth centuries left abundant and conspicuous physical remains: of the Burmese kingdom of Pyu, at Sriksetra/Hmawza;[11] of Dvaravati in Thailand, at Nakhon Pathom, Ku Bua, U Thong, Chansen, Muang Bon, Si Maha Pot and many other known sites;[12] of Chenla in Cambodia and north-eastern Thailand at Banteay Prei Nokor and Sambor Prei Kuk;[13] of Champa in central Vietnam at Mi-Son;[14] and of an unnamed kingdom (Ho-ling?) in Java at Dieng. The sea empire

of Srivijaya also usually appears on such lists, but prominent though it is in the historian's eye, Srivijaya is far from conspicuous to the archaeologist. So few are its remains, in fact, that its approximate location is still in serious doubt.[15]

All of the above-named sites have produced statues and reliefs, mostly of Buddhist or Hindu subjects, and all were furnished with substantial public buildings made of brick or stone. Many also contained much residential debris – sherds, animal bones, charcoal and so forth – and most were fortified. Although not as vast as the great Cambodian sites of the eleventh to thirteenth centuries, the walled and moated areas of these seventh-century sites are relatively extensive.

The effects of the seventh-century revolution are, however, much clearer on the mainland than in the southern peninsular and island areas. A scattering of statues and inscriptions from the Malay Peninsula, Borneo and Java testify to the presence of Indianizing tendencies and local literacy as early as 400–500, and the seventh century did see the appearance of a number of small stone temples in Java. Identifiable settlements, however, are absent and remain scarce until well after the period 700–900, the golden age of central Javanese civilization. Although one or two small villages from these centuries have been found in Java, none – and very few architectural remains of any kind – has been identified anywhere in Sumatra, the Malay Peninsula or elsewhere south of the Thai–Malaysian border. The earliest substantial settlement

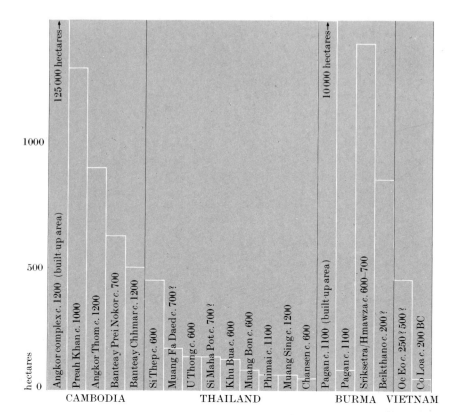

40.1: *The sizes of early cities and towns in south-east Asia. The largest sites were not necessarily densely settled, but little doubt exists that some were truly urban in terms of population as well as function.*

known thus far in the south is Kota Cina, an eleventh- to twelfth-century town in northern Sumatra. The earliest recognizable true city dates to as late as the fourteenth and fifteenth centuries: Trowulan in east Java, the capital of the empire of Majapahit.

Thus we find ourselves faced with one of the chief puzzles of south-east Asian archaeology. The south did not lag noticeably behind the north in acquiring most of the attributes of civilization.

40.2: *South-east Asian cities before AD 1200. Archaeologically known settlements, of substantial size and with fortifications and residential debris, are common in the northern part of the region. In seeming contradiction to the historical evidence, they are very rare in its southern part.*

- ■ excavated or well-explored urban and semi-urban sites
- • partially explored sites with urban characteristics
- ○ non-urban temple complexes, cemeteries, etc.

It even became a leader during the eighth and ninth centuries, when its monumental architecture, notably that at the famous sites of Borobudur and Prambanan,[16] attained a size and richness of decoration that far exceeded anything that yet existed on the mainland. Yet in spite of this, and although the neighbourhoods of the great Javanese monuments have by now been carefully examined for habitation refuse and other evidence of settlement, cities everywhere in the southern region remain exceedingly hard to find.

This is not the case in the north, where cities and towns continued to proliferate throughout the two or three centuries of consolidation that followed the revolutionary seventh century. Central Thailand suffered the worst setback during this period. While some settlements continued to be built (perhaps Si Maha Pot) and modest quantities of art in local styles were produced, the area had clearly become a backwater by the time it was absorbed into the expanding empire of Angkor in the early eleventh century. Burma, on the other hand, after a similar decline during which the Pyu kingdom was greatly weakened and its centre at Hmawza abandoned, witnessed a renaissance after 1000. Its capital at Pagan[17] became a moderately sized city and a gigantic religious centre, a walled nucleus of less than a square kilometre surrounded and almost buried by thousands of brick Buddhist *stupas* and extending over a total area of 60 or more square kilometres. Pagan's enormous capital investment in monuments

40.3: *The temple of Shiva at Prambanan, central Java, AD 800–850. Three towers of similar size once stood at this site; only one of these, and a few of the hundreds of subsidiary temples that once accompanied them, have been reconstructed.*

during the eleventh and twelfth centuries was exceeded only by that of its still more wealthy and powerful contemporary, Angkor.

Little archaeological information is available on urbanization in northern and central Vietnam during the first millennium AD. In central Vietnam the high level of political organization of ancient Champa is attested by a long series of inscriptions, as well as by Champa's remarkable success in its protracted wars with the much larger Chinese and Vietnamese kingdoms to the north and the Khmer kingdoms to the west. Its cultural achievement is displayed in distinctive styles of plastic art and monumental architecture found at such centres as Mi-Son. But local resources were small, and no site with Cham architecture is reported as showing evidence of a large, dense population.

No such doubts exist with regard to Cambodia, whose capitals – most of them located within the group of sites known collectively as Angkor – represent urbanization on a scale unmatched anywhere between India and China. At its height the city covered an area of 100 square kilometres with temples, canals, causeways and huge quantities of residential debris. In sheer bulk, in cubic metres of carved stone, the monuments of the Angkorean period greatly exceeded those of all other south-east Asian civilizations. Even the intensity of Angkor's political and cultural influence on distant places was remarkable. Other early civilizations have left at most a few statues and inscriptions in areas outside their immediate heartlands. The characteristic artifacts of Angkor, ranging from city plans to pottery, are found in large numbers everywhere between southern Thailand and Vietnam. They are so conspicuous and numerous, in fact, that Angkor might be recognized as the greatest of the region's civilizations even if Cambodia had never been archaeologically explored.

The interpretation of urban development

At this point we should return to the three issues raised earlier. Why were all these south-east civilizations late? Why were they so unevenly distributed? And why were they based, to such an unusual extent, upon foreign models, specifically those of India? None of these questions can yet be confidently answered.

The problem of lateness is especially intractable. We know that several parts of the region possessed at an early date what most theorists regard as the preconditions for the emergence of civilization: efficient methods of food production, an environment favourable to the large-scale use of those methods and a developed manufacturing technology. By 500 BC, and perhaps by 1500 BC,

40.4: *The city of Angkor. Except for vast quantities of potsherds, little evidence survives of residences, but enough reservoirs, walls, causeways and temples exist to show that Angkor in its day was one of the largest cities of the ancient world.*

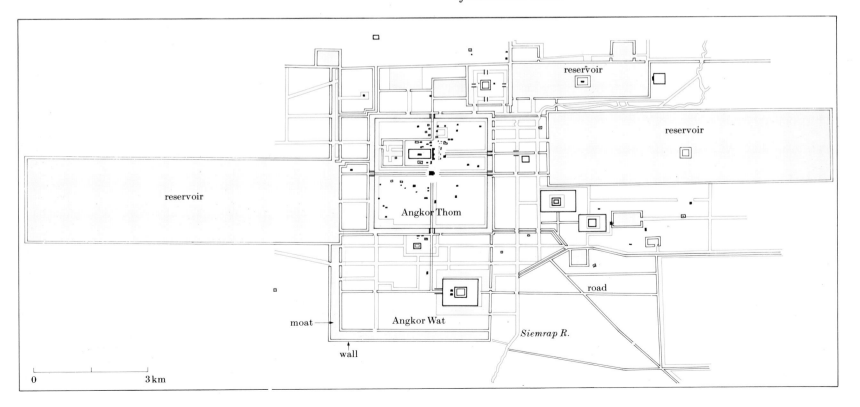

there were bronze- and iron-working, weaving, pottery manufacture, uniquely adaptable engineering materials such as bamboo
and rattan, excellent ships, developed skills in long-range navigation, numerous kinds of domesticated animals, many potentially
high-yielding protein and carbohydrate crops (including rice) and,
in all probability, irrigation systems. The emergence of an Angkor
was possible in the second millennium BC; yet it did not happen.
Why? Perhaps we must look for efficient causes, specific stimuli,
without which the precipitation of cities and states is unlikely to
occur. But what was absent in prehistoric times? One major missing
factor was long-distance trade. The initial period during which
civilizations emerged in the region does coincide chronologically
with the inception of intensive seaborne commerce between
China and the regions to the west, and in this instance could indeed
have stimulated the formation of states and cities. The details of
this process, however, are still unclear. Much research remains to
be done on the exact timing of events as well as on models of the
interaction of commercial and political development before the
emergence of states and cities can be confidently attributed to
trading.

The uneven distribution of the civilizations of the region raises
equally puzzling issues. Most sites are located in areas with extensive tracts of land suitable for growing rice with the aid of simple
techniques of water and soil management. The mountainous parts
of the region were too constricted; the central parts of the river
deltas were too deeply flooded (as in the cases of the Mekong, the
Menam and the Irrawaddy) or too infertile (as in the cases of the
Sumatran and Bornean rivers); and the eastern islands were too
dry for large-scale rice-growing, which is the reason why most
such places (with the exception of the recently drained and highly
productive mainland deltas) have remained thinly settled down to
the present day.

This explanation is clearly attractive, but it must be qualified.
First, a number of suitable rice-growing areas exist that seem not
to have supported early civilizations. The plains around Manila in
central Luzon, which now support a very dense rural population,
are a prime example. Second, some civilizations are thought to
have existed in places where rice-growing is very difficult. The outstanding example is Srivijaya, which all authorities agree must
have been located somewhere on the infertile shores of the landmasses bordering the Straits of Malacca. Perhaps we should conclude that in reality there were two kinds of civilization in the
region, one based on areas with good rice land and on revenues
extracted from large rural populations, and the other supported by
taxes levied on long-distance commerce and hence relatively independent of the quality of local soils and water supplies.

Later historical instances of such states are known, and it has
often been suggested that mercantile, coastal civilizations in the
region constitute a distinct and early type. But if they existed at
all, why were there not more of them? Why should they not have
arisen on the Spice Islands in eastern Indonesia, or in the southern
Philippines, or in any of the other areas located on or near major
routes of ancient trade?

A last insoluble problem concerns Indianization. Why did the
early south-east Asian states (with the exception of northern
Vietnam) turn to India rather than to China, which was much
closer, when they sought religious and political ideas, writing
systems and so forth? And why did they so completely adopt those
Indian ideas? Although indigenous contributions to the emerging
pattern of regional civilizations were undoubtedly important, the
fact remains that south-east Asia was dependent on foreign models
to an extent unusual in history, in that most comparable known
cases involve straightforward military conquest and subsequent
periods of imperialist rule.

Such conquest at the hands of Indian invaders was at one time
believed to have occurred, but historical sources preserved in
India make no mention of such invasions, and real Indian artifacts,
as opposed to artifacts strongly influenced by those of India, have
proved to be rather rare in south-east Asia. Many other explanations have therefore been proposed, ranging from evangelization
by Indian missionaries and traders to efforts initiated by the
south-east Asians themselves to find and import elements of
civilized society.

The answers to these questions are not yet known. Very little
research has been done in the region, and even less that would be
regarded as relevant research by modern archaeologists working
elsewhere. However, local archaeological capabilities in most
south-east Asian countries are now expanding rapidly and the
information needed to answer many such questions should be
available within the next decade.

41. Imperial China and its neighbours

In the centuries following the final disruption of the Han empire in AD 220, China passed through a period of political and cultural fragmentation during which the south and north followed very different courses. The country was divided into three independent regional kingdoms, each with a central government whose power was challenged increasingly by the generals and their armies on the one hand and by the many local magnates on the other. These trends were to characterize the next four centuries.

China was briefly reunified under the Chin in AD 280, but from the end of the third century internal weakness led to the first incursions of border peoples from the north. From the beginning of the fourth century northern China was overwhelmed by a succession of non-Chinese invaders. The Turkic Hsiung-nu in the north, the proto-Mongol Hsien-pei from the north-east, a variety of Tibetan tribes, the Ch'iang and Ti from the north-west overran what had been the most populous and productive regions of Han China. During the fourth century the whole of northern China, containing well over three-quarters of the country's people, suffered repeated invasions, constant warfare, social disruption, instability, physical devastation and depopulation.

The Chin, after being driven from the north, set up a separate southern regime at modern Nanking, where they were succeeded by a series of purely southern dynasties. At this time southern China was still very largely in the hands of various aboriginal peoples, known collectively to the Chinese as the Man. The Chinese settled population was largely confined to the region around the Yangtze delta, the Huai and Yangtze valleys, parts of modern Kiangsi and Hunan provinces and the Pearl river delta around Canton. Only gradually was the rest of south-eastern China brought under Chinese government and settled by Chinese. Much of the south, especially the hill lands, and all of the south-west remained border territory, in which tribal peoples were only gradually assimilated to Chinese culture. As late as the seventh century the Yangtze valley and the south contained less than a quarter of China's people, and the rate of increase during the centuries of division was very slow.

Both north and south shared some major problems. The southern courts were weak and unstable, and real authority lay in the hands of the generals and the great families. In the north the constant succession of non-Chinese tribal chieftains who found themselves rulers were without experience of civil government, and to control the large sedentary Chinese populations living in their territories they were forced to adopt Chinese administrative techniques and to employ Chinese officials with the necessary skills and experience. The north, like the south, was dominated by groups of powerful families, each with its local base. These great families, who had many retainers and adherents and considerable numbers of slaves, retained control of their home district even when they were involved in court politics. In the north-west the local Chinese families intermarried widely with the tribal nobility to produce an aristocracy of mixed blood whose lifestyle was very different from that of the purely Chinese great families of the north-east and south. Many of them spoke both Chinese and Turkish; they lived active, open-air lives; they were as much soldiers as administrators; and their women enjoyed great freedom and influence. Vivid evidence of this is offered by the mural paintings preserved in recently excavated tombs of members of the T'ang royal family,[1] which show court attendants of very varied ethnic origin and scenes of hunting and games such as polo. It was from this group of families of mixed blood that there arose the two dynastic houses of Sui and T'ang, which were to restore China to political unity, to bring about lasting peace and stability, to achieve a new level of political influence throughout East Asia, and to preside over a new flowering of Chinese culture.

Economic development, third to seventh centuries

The invasions of the fourth century caused vast loss of life, massive migrations of population and the depopulation of large areas that fell out of cultivation, especially in the north-west. The population gradually recovered in the late fifth and sixth centuries but by the early seventh century it was still below that of AD 2 (see Chapter 37). The cohesive commercial network of Han times, already disrupted by the disorders of the late second century, disintegrated. China split up into a great number of small, locally self-sufficient areas. Overland trade with western Asia was disrupted. Even the use of metallic coinage declined and bronze coin became scarce. Gold virtually disappeared, and its place was taken by commodity money, usually in the form of silk cloth. Within the local regions the great families held estates large enough to provide for almost every need and maintained many retainers and cultivator families as dependents. Slavery, especially common among the foreign conquerors of the north, increased throughout China.

However, there were many more positive aspects of Chinese development. In the Huai and Yangtze valleys a great deal of new land was brought under cultivation, and a multiplicity of small irrigation schemes were set up. The characteristic form of paddy-rice agriculture, using the transplantation system, that was to underlie China's prosperity in later times was perfected in this period. Already a given population in the Yangtze area could produce more grain than would be possible in the north, and paddy-rice farming could support far more intensive cultivation than could northern dry farming. But even in north China the techniques of dry farming were being perfected. By the sixth century a large number of specialized strains of the different grains had been developed for use in special environments; three grain crops in two years were being produced in some areas, and an enormous variety of vegetables was commonly cultivated. In technology, too, there were important advances: iron technology was greatly improved during this period by the use of coal as a fuel and by the development of water-powered blast for furnaces. The improved co-fusion process of steel making was perfected. By the seventh century China was producing copious quantities of cast iron, which was even used in building. The stirrup, first shown on a *stela* of 301, gradually became widespread and gave a new dimension to cavalry warfare; a more efficient draught harness was developed; while the nomadic occupations of the north made the use of the horse more general than ever before.

One new, large-scale institution was also introduced into north and south alike during these centuries. The Buddhist religion entered China during the later Han period, at first as a minority cult among the metropolitan elite, introduced by missionaries from central Asia, but later among the whole population. By the sixth century Buddhism was enjoying both royal patronage and mass support, and the establishment of Buddhist communities and the building of temples went on throughout China. Buddhism was not only an all-pervading religious faith that, for centuries to come, was to overshadow the native systems of belief; it was also a powerful economic institution, whose monasteries formed closed, perpetual corporations disposing of vast wealth. With their huge resources, lands, dependent families and slaves, the monasteries exerted considerable influence on society and the economy. They built up huge estates, opened up much land to cultivation, established mills, acted as a source of credit and provided lavish

patronage for artists and artisans of every type.

Sui and T'ang China

The Sui royal house, which reunited China in 589, was founded by a member of the part-Chinese, part-Turkic north-western aristocracy and brought order and stability to its empire by adapting the legal and administrative institutions that had developed in the north.[2] After consolidating its position in north China, it easily overwhelmed the last southern dynasty and proceeded to encompass the south firmly within its control through the patronage of southern Buddhism and the incorporation of the southern elite into the Sui system of government. The second Sui emperor gave a new physical unity to the empire through the construction of a major canal system linking Hang-chou with the Yangtze, the Huai and the Huang Ho, which was later extended to near modern Peking. This linked the three Sui capitals, Ta-hsing-ch'eng (later Ch'ang-an), the huge north-western metropolis, Lo-yang in Honan and Yang-chou (Chiang-tu) on the Yangtze, and enabled the administration, whose major centre remained in the north-west, to derive revenues and supplies from the Great Plain and the Huai and Yangtze valleys. Much of the Sui canal system either incorporated earlier waterways or canalized rivers. Some very ambitious engineering feats were involved, however. One of these was an attempt to make passable the rapids at San-men on the Huang Ho, where a bypass canal was constructed. This

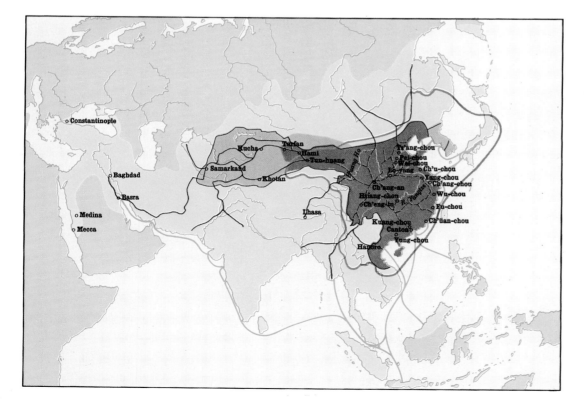

41.1: *T'ang China, showing the principal internal transport routes, both canals and roads, and also the major international trade routes and the extent of the world known to the Chinese.*

- extent of area known to the Chinese
- T'ang empire
- under Chinese control
- area of Chinese cultural influence
- principal canals
- major post roads

proved unsuccessful, but the remains of this and other projects were investigated and the findings published some twenty years ago. The canals also served a strategic need, enabling supplies to be shipped cheaply to the northern borders. Canal transport was cheaper and faster than carriage by road. The building of the capital cities, which were populated by means of the forcible resettlement of vast numbers of people from other areas, the construction of the canals and the reconstruction of long stretches of the Great Wall to protect the northern borders against the extremely powerful T'u-chüeh Turks required constant levies of conscript labour and caused widespread mortality, suffering and unrest, but they provided an essential foundation for the strong, centralized state of T'ang times.

During the period of division the Chinese had lost control over various marginal areas that had formed peripheral parts of the Han empire. In the Tarim basin and the far north-west, in southwest China and in northern Vietnam Chinese influence had either disappeared entirely or had been much reduced. The Sui reestablished control over Vietnam and conducted expeditions against the Turks. They then attempted to recover southern Manchuria and northern Korea, former Han colonies that were now the territory of a very powerful native kingdom, Koguryŏ. Repeated campaigns in this area, all ending in disaster, led to the mobilization of vast numbers of troops and conscript labourers. This led to widespread rebellions; the Sui were forced to abandon

north China and were replaced in 618 by the T'ang.[3]

The T'ang royal house was closely related to that of the Sui and supported largely by the same elements of the population. It continued to employ the system of government and institutions set up under the Sui, with few innovations, and enjoyed the benefits of the public works the Sui had completed at such a high cost. After a decade or two of consolidation, a policy of expansion began. This was made possible by the collapse of the very powerful Turkish empire that had dominated the northern steppelands and had even intervened in China during the Sui collapse. In 630 the Turks were decisively defeated by the Chinese, and for fifty years China had no powerful neighbour to threaten the northern borders. Chinese civil administration was soon extended westwards along the Silk Route as far as Turfan and Hami, and protectorates were set up to govern the native kingdoms of the Tarim basin and the tribal peoples of Dzungaria. Some of the earliest archaeological work on sites in this area was undertaken by British, German, Russian and Japanese scholars before the First World War. Most important was the discovery in the arid northwest, at Tun-huang and near Turfan, of large numbers of manuscripts dating from the Han to the Mongol periods. These include Chinese, Uighur and Tibetan manuscrips and works in Sanskrit and other Indian and central Asian languages. Many discoveries continue to be made in this region; they are essential to our understanding of everyday life during those periods.[4]

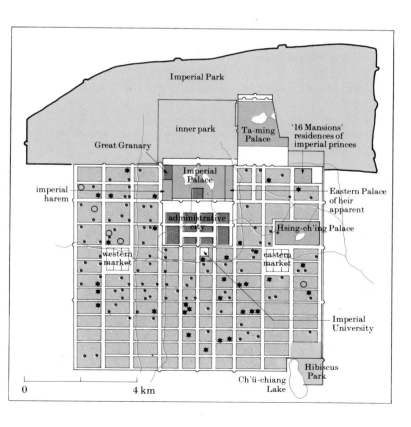

41.2: *Ch'ang-an c. 750 was the world's largest metropolis. Excavations show the main walls to have been 9.5 kilometres from east to west and 8.5 kilometres from north to south. Each of the markets and residential wards was surrounded by a wall with gates. All the houses, except those of the highest nobility, faced inwards. The great streets running from north to south of the city were 150 metres wide; those running east to west varied from 70 to 150 metres wide. The north-east of the city was the most exclusive area, while that around the western market had a large foreign population. Parts of the southern wards were probably never built up.*

▨ residential wards

✷ Taoist monasteries

• Buddhist monasteries

○ temples of foreign religions (Manichaean, Nestorian, Mazdean)

The Chinese advance into the Tarim and central Asia coincided with the emergence of two rival political powers. The first was Islam, whose armies were sweeping through the remains of the Sasanian dominions. The second was Tibet. A weak collection of nomadic tribes until about 600, Tibet began to grow into a powerful, well-organized and aggressively expansionist kingdom. It spread from its origins around Lhasa into Yarlung in western Tibet and threatened the petty kingdoms of the Pamir, key trade routes between India and central Asia. It also influenced Nepal and the tribes of south-west China and moved into the rich grasslands of modern Tsinghai province, formerly occupied by the T'u-yü-hun people, who were overwhelmed by the Tibetans in 663. From then on they threatened the Kansu corridor, which gave access to the Chinese outposts in inner Asia, and until the mid-ninth century Tibet was to remain China's major foreign enemy. During this period China gradually lost its cultural influence in Tibet, in the face of influence from India.

T'ang armies finally defeated Koguryŏ in 668, but it proved impossible to establish Chinese control over Korea and they soon withdrew. The result was the emergence of the first unified Korean state, Silla, which was organized on Chinese lines and remained on good terms with the T'ang. In southern Manchuria another powerful and prosperous Chinese-style state, Parhae, emerged and dominated eastern Manchuria and the Amur region until the tenth century.

Along their northern borders the Chinese continued to have problems with the Khitan of western Manchuria and with the Turks who, after half a century of eclipse, at the end of the seventh century again developed a powerful tribal confederation controlling the steppe from the borders of Manchuria to Lake Balkhash. In the 740s, however, riven by internal strife, their power suddenly collapsed. They were replaced as the predominant power in the northern steppe by the Uighurs, who remained generally well-disposed towards the Chinese, with whom they carried on extensive and profitable trade, selling horses for tea and silk. In the mid-ninth century, driven out of the steppe by the Kirghiz, the Uighurs settled permanently in the oases of modern Sinkiang and Kansu, abandoning their nomadic lifestyle.

During these crucial centuries China's international setting gradually took the shape that would persist for centuries to come. In the sixth century, apart from Koguryŏ, China had no literate neighbour. By the eighth century the East Asian oikumene was emerging, in which Chinese served as the language of culture, diplomacy and administration alike. By 750 the states of Silla, Parhae and Japan were all organized on Chinese models and were using the Chinese written language; in spite of being politically quite independent, each was under heavy Chinese cultural influence. The south-western state of Nan-chao, in spite of its enmity with China and its increasing involvement in upper Burma and Laos and along the Vietnamese border, was also a marginal part of this Chinese cultural world. China had become the centre of a cultural system that extended to Korea, Japan, Manchuria, south-west China and northern Vietnam.

This change among China's sedentary neighbours in the east was paralleled by changes among its western neighbours. By the mid-eighth century the Tibetans, the Turks and the Uighurs had in turn progressed from rather primitive tribal confederations into far more stable, well-organized and, above all, literate societies. Unlike the eastern neighbours, however, these societies proved unresponsive or resistant to Chinese culture. Although Chinese political power could sometimes be exerted among them, they remained part of an alien cultural world.

Economic development, eighth to thirteenth centuries

Major changes in China's internal structure followed the rebellions of the eighth century. Authority was delegated to a new tier of provinces. Those in the former rebel heartland of the north-eastern plain, which contained some thirteen million people (a quarter of the population), became semi-independent, beyond the effective control of the central power. Many other border provinces were heavily militarized and needed constant subsidy. Only central and southern China remained under firm civilian administration from the capital, and the government became increasingly dependent upon the Yangtze valley and the south for its revenues. As uniform local administration was allowed to decline, the resulting fragmentation of power had its social and economic effects. Many of the new provincial governments were run by the military, who even held control of civil affairs. The abandonment of a state system of land allocation and the growth of a free market in land made it possible for these rising groups to become landholders. The old aristocracy slowly declined and merged into a far more broadly based gentry of landowners and office-holders.

Until the eighth century the government had made a serious, and largely successful, attempt to control trade and commerce. In the provinces commerce was restricted to officially controlled markets in the prefectural and county cities. Important evidence of the close government control over trade has been discovered in manuscripts excavated at Turfan, which show extremely detailed price lists for an extraordinary variety of commodities on sale in the local markets in the 740s. The movement, business activities and even the lifestyle of merchants were surrounded by restrictions. In the countryside there seem to have been rather few small towns without administrative status. The government also, by collecting most taxes in the form of grain or textiles, effectively handled the circulation of these bulk commodities. Most government expenditure was centred in the capital, Ch'ang-an, a vast cosmopolitan metropolis of well over a million people, each of whose two chief markets was larger than London in the sixteenth century. Ch'ang-an represented an enormous concentration of the empire's wealth and commercial activity. Extensive excavations at Ch'ang-an, including the palace area and the western market, were carried out in the 1950s. As the city was built almost entirely of tamped earth and timber constructions, virtually nothing of the Sui–T'ang city survives about ground, apart from two stone pagodas of the seventh century. The city was practically razed in the 880s.

The new system of provincial government brought about some very important changes. Money taxation began to replace taxes levied in kind and hired labour the system of conscript duties by which much minor government business had been done. Each of the provincial capitals became the seat of a provincial 'court', with a great concentration of officials, troops and people engaged in services, and each developed into a major centre of official expenditure, where provincial revenues were spent to procure services and local needs. Many became centres of manufactures and handicrafts; often the provincial officials themselves were engaged in industry and trade. Some of these cities grew very large. Some of the larger provincial centres, such as Lo-yang, the secondary capital, Pien-chou (modern K'ai-feng) and Yang-chou, the main ports on the canal system, Ch'eng-tu, Chiang-ling and Canton certainly had populations numbered in six figures. Some preliminary findings related to excavations of medieval Yang-chou have recently been published, which establish the size of the city and the position of its port-suburb, Yang-tzu-hsien.

The eighth-century rebellions were also followed by further movements of population from north to south. Between 609 and 742 the Great Plain, the most densely populated area of China since Han times, lost 30 per cent of its people through warfare, repeated climatic disasters and plague. For the next five centuries it steadily declined in importance. The north-west, the traditional seat of government, also declined as the climate grew colder, the irrigation system was neglected and the cumulative effects of long periods of military pressures and over-exploitation took their toll. By the early eighth century Ch'ang-an was heavily dependent on huge shipments of grain and other commodities from the Huai and Yangtze regions, and only administrative inertia kept the T'ang administration there. (There have been recent excavations of the huge trans-shipment granary at Ho-yin, where the canal joined the Huang Ho, and of several other granary sites.) After Ch'ang-an's destruction in the rebellions and civil strife of the late ninth century, the north-west steadily declined into an economic and political backwater.

The loss of population in the north was counterbalanced by migration to the more favourable environment of the south, which by the end of the tenth century held more than half China's people, compared with less than a quarter in 609. The south steadily overtook the north, not only in population and productivity but also in education, in technical skills and in culture. In the warmer, fertile lands of the Yangtze valley a given number of people could produce far more in the rice-based system of agriculture than in the wheat- and millet-growing regions of the north, and they were much less vulnerable to crop failure and climatic disasters. As productivity rose, trade boomed. Many handicrafts and manufactures previously centred on the north (sericulture, for example) were established in the Yangtze cities. Moreover, this burgeoning of trade stimulated the emergence of a far denser urban network. Many small rural market towns grew up, at first

to serve local needs. Periodic markets became common in the countryside, and gradually a whole system of commercial towns with no administrative status emerged, parallel to, but independent of, the administrative network of county and prefectural cities. The urban structure of China from this time onwards thus became far more varied and complex, as well as far denser, than in earlier times.

Commerce was now organized on a very large scale. Credit institutions and proto-banks emerged in the eighth century. Discoveries of new silver mines in southern China gradually led to the use of silver in place of silk cloth as a form of currency for large transactions, and as silver was never minted into a coinage, control of the currency passed largely into the hands of silversmiths. The invention of printing in the eighth century, and its widespread use from the mid-ninth century, led both to a massive increase in the dissemination of information and to the use of paper money, which began in Szechwan and soon spread throughout the empire.

As the government relaxed its traditional restraints on trade and also its attempts to restrict the lifestyle of merchants, the government itself became increasingly involved in monopoly trading in such items as salt, tea, wine and alum, and became dependent upon taxes levied on commercial activities and on mining. By the twelfth century the Chinese state depended upon such revenue sources rather than upon the traditional taxes on land, poll-taxes and labour levies.

In this more commercial atmosphere the Chinese were no longer rivalled by foreigners to the same extent as in the eighth century. After 755 the trade routes across central Asia were cut off and largely replaced by seaborne trade from Canton, Yang-chou and Hanoi. Much of this was carried in Arab ships or ships from India, Ceylon or south-east Asia, and there were large Arab settlements in the Chinese coastal ports. Gradually, however, Chinese ships began to sail to India and the Persian Gulf, and by the eleventh century China was a major sea power. Recent excavations have discovered several medieval ships, showing among other things their division into watertight compartments, though no ocean-going ship has yet been found.

With the breaking of direct overland contacts with central Asia, the exotic influences that had pervaded every aspect of Chinese culture, and had been re-exported from China to Japan and Korea, began to fade. Only Buddhism remained, but cut off from its Indian and central Asian roots Buddhism in the Far East was now thoroughly naturalized as part of Chinese culture. While the schools of the seventh and eighth centuries had developed on Indian foundations, later movements such as Ch'an (Zen) were purely Chinese in origin.

In some respects the Sung period (960–1278) represents the high point of Chinese culture. But it was an inward-looking period, during which China was militarily beleaguered, with increasingly large areas under alien control; the easy confidence, the openness, the innovativeness and the cosmopolitanism of the T'ang had been lost for ever.

42. Forest cultures of south and south-east Asia

With the exception of the Indus valley civilization, the earliest evidence in south Asia for political organization at the level of the state comes from the Ganges river valley in the sixth century BC. Political control quickly spread over the whole of India (see Chapter 39). In some parts of the subcontinent, however, particularly in the forested areas in south and central India, and often in close proximity to urban centres, some peoples continued to practise a simple economy of hunting, collecting and shifting agriculture, and lived essentially outside the orbit of the states. Culturally these forest groups varied greatly, as do present-day peoples, and there is a wide range of economic practices among tribal groups in south Asia: from the exclusively hunting and gathering groups such as the Malapandaram, Chenchu and Vedda, through simple hand cultivation by slash-and-burn farming supplemented by some forest collection as practised by Reddi groups in the Bison Hills, to a predominately agricultural economy using ploughs as followed by Bhils and Gonds of Central Province.

The creation of 'islands' of tribal groups occurred in a similar way in south-east Asia, though at a later date. At the beginning of the Christian era the highest level of political organization throughout the region was that of the village chiefdom, supported by an economic base of simple agriculture, hunting and forest collection. From the first millennium AD, however, the lowland coastal areas of both the mainland and the islands saw the activities of a number of trading and political states (see Chapter 40). These developments left the forested highland interior of the region largely free to groups of people living in traditional ways.

Although nominally controlled by the political organization of the states, most forest dwellers throughout south and south-east Asia operated independently of administrative networks. Their seasonal movements and the relative remoteness of their situation made controls such as the exacting of taxes or the exercise of juridical power a difficult task. But it would be wrong to suggest that they were unaffected by the presence of urban settlements or unconnected with the commercial interests and activities of the traders. Although the forest peoples were culturally separate from those of the settled areas, there was nevertheless what often amounted to an economic interdependence that linked the two ways of life and was mediated through exchange or barter. All forest dwellers would have relied (as they do today) on trade as a means of obtaining resources and material to which they had little or no direct access. In return for salt, cloth, metal and cereal grains, for example, they could offer the very products often sought by the traders – 'jungle goods' such as resins, gums, rattan, fruits and lumber from the forest. Such business might be transacted

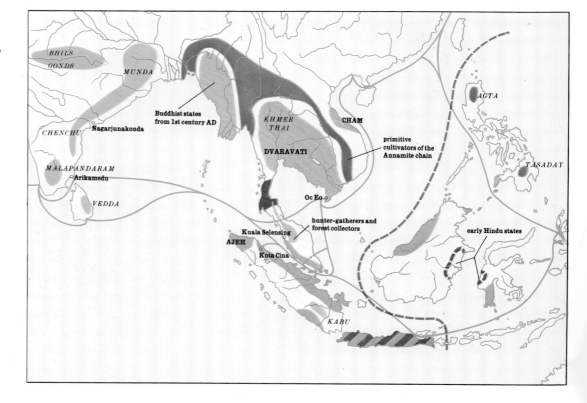

42.1: *South and south-east Asia, showing the approximate location and extent of forest cultures and early states and the trade routes by which local products reached the West.*

Muslim coastal trading states

Indianized coastal trading states

Hindu, Buddhist and later Muslim trading and island states

area of primitive cultivators and occasional collectors

mainland states

major tribal groups

trade routes

through a middleman, often on terms unfavourable to the forest people, but it was ultimately a mutually beneficial relationship and one that allowed them to maintain their way of life substantially unhindered.

The archaeology of these forest groups is not well known, partly because the major emphasis of research in this region has been on the trading states and their settlements and on the monuments they left behind. The scant archaeological evidence of hunter–gatherers, collectors and simple farmers can, however, be supplemented by reference to ethnological studies of present-day or recently existing groups. Peoples such as those mentioned above from the Indian subcontinent, as well as others in south-east Asia like the Tasaday and Agta (also called Aeta) in the Philippines, Semang and Senoi in Malaysia, and various forest collectors of the Annamite Chain of Vietnam, have maintained a way of life that has a long continuity in these forested areas. Sufficient ethno-

graphical data have been accumulated on these and other groups to allow the construction of a general picture of the way in which they live; a picture not significantly different from that of those analogous groups who lived on the peripheries of the great trading states in the past.

Archaeological evidence

Although these earlier forest cultures are not well represented archaeologically, there is nonetheless good evidence from a number of places of their economic interaction with the expansive trading states of the lowlands and coastal areas of south and south-east Asia. The trading networks were often complex and wide-ranging. Trade in cinnamon, cloves and other 'exotic' jungle products bound ultimately for Rome necessitated the sea links between remote Indonesian islands and regional collecting centres from where the goods were despatched to the West.[1] In India the site of

42.2: *Some important products from the forests of south and south-east Asia. The Moluccas (or Spice Islands) in Indonesia were the original home of a number of economically important forest products. For example, cloves (Eugenia spp.) (above left), the dried flowerbuds of a tropical tree, and nutmeg and mace (above right), both products of the tree* Myristica fragrens, *were collected in the interior and traded, ultimately to the West. A range of spices was also indigenous to south Asia. Cinnamon (below left) was produced, before modern cultivation, by stripping the bark from the young tree as it grew wild in the forests of south India and Sri Lanka. Cardamoms (below centre), though not traded on a large scale, were – and still are – an exchangeable commodity for forest dwellers in south India who harvested the capsules with a special tool and bartered them locally. In historic times the product of the pepper vine (below right) has been widely traded in bulk, but it also was collected initially by forest peoples in south India.*

Arikamedu on the Bay of Bengal, about 3 kilometres south of Pondicherry, has long been known as an Indo-Roman trading station, and Oc Eo in the Mekong delta had a similar function. At Arikamedu spices gathered from the forests of south and central India, as well as precious stones, pearls and muslin, were traded in return for Roman pottery wares, manufactures and gold for perhaps a hundred years from the beginning of the first century AD.

A similar role was played by Kota Cina on the east coast of Sumatra in Indonesia. This was the site of a trading settlement associated with the Malay kingdom of Aru in middle to late Sung times (twelfth to thirteenth centuries AD).[2] Considerable quantities of resins, including damar and kemanyan (*Styrax* spp.) were found during excavations; these and many other forest products are still collected in Sumatra and in the Malay Peninsula today. The resins are used for varnish and sealing wax and for medicinal and ritual purposes. Iron slag, copper spillage and a mould for an ornament were found at Kota Cina, and these suggest the presence there of metal-working artisans who would probably have traded their artifacts for the produce of the forested interior. Two stone statues of the Buddha, of central Indian or Sinhalese origin, were also found at the site. As a collection point Kota Cina was well situated. Resources from the forest had to be brought to the coast, perhaps from a subsidiary collection point inland,[3] and in this area there was easy access by river to the coast.

Another example of this type of entrepôt is Kuala Selensing, a settlement of pile-dwellings on a small island off the west coast of the Malay Peninsula, not far from the modern town of Port Weld. This was a collecting base for products of the hinterland and was linked to other Indianized entrepôts on the peninsula. Finds of some Chinese stoneware and a few pieces of blue-and-white ware suggest occupation of the site during Sung times.[4] During excavation enormous quantities of beads were unearthed, and it is likely that some were made locally of material obtained from another entrepôt nearby. It was the output of this local bead factory that was traded for the produce of the forested interior. One such product, a local kind of resin, has been found in numerous pieces in the deposit at Kuala Selensing.

By later prehistoric times a variety of cultural types, each exploiting a particular environmental area, coexisted throughout south and south-east Asia. That a stone-using hunter–gatherer tradition persisted over a long period of time, and in some cases literally alongside the settlements of urban-based peoples, can also be seen at a number of sites in this area. At the Buddhist city of Nagarjunakonda in southern Andhra Pradesh, for instance, quartz microliths characteristic of cultures of the Late Stone Age in India have been found, reportedly lying on top of ruined monastic buildings,[5] which suggests a reoccupation of the site by these hunter–gatherer groups. This evidence raises interesting questions about the longevity of such cultures. On the mainland of south-east Asia pebble-tool traditions of Hoabinhian type have a long duration: tools of this type can be seen at some sites stratified

above, and post-dating evidence of, the expansion of Buddhist states. At Gua Tampaq in Kelantan, Malay Peninsula, Hoabinhian tools were collected on the surface, while a Buddhist votive tablet of the historic period was found 30 to 40 centimetres lower in the deposit.[6] And at the Banyang valley site in north-west Thailand the recovery of husks of rice (*Oryza* spp.) in the upper two levels points to a connection between the Hoabinhian residents and lowland rice-growing groups. Radiocarbon dates from this site give a range of occupation of about 3000 BC to AD 700, attesting to the comparatively recent nature of the interaction and to the continued survival of these stone-using traditions into the late prehistoric period.

Contemporary forest cultures in south Asia

A number of cultural groups are still found in the forested parts of south India. The Chenchu, for example, are a well-studied group of hunter–gatherers who live in the hilly country north of the Krishna river on the Amrabad plateau in Andhra Pradesh.[7] The economic unit of Chenchu society is the local group, composed of one or more families, which varies in size according to the season and at times can be equated with the total village community. Villages typically contain between three and thirteen bamboo houses thatched with grass; these may last from ten to fifteen years. Most Chenchu groups move in a seasonal round. During the cool season, from about October to February, the groups live in their villages. An annual migration begins in mid-February, when temperatures rise and the people leave the permanent settlements to make temporary camps in the forest. Simple huts of bushes and leaves are con-

42.3: *Chenchu women digging for edible roots.*

structed or rockshelters are used. This movement is in preparation for the flowering of mohua trees, from which the Chenchu make liquor, which takes place at about the end of March. Between June and the end of September the wet season brings an average of 50 centimetres of rain, and the Chenchu move back to their permanent villages. During these movements an individual is free to join any group he wishes.

Men hunt deer, wild goats and pigs and even rodents in the open deciduous forests of the Amrabad plateau, using bamboo bows and arrows. Hunting contributes only irregularly to the food supply, however. Most groups on the upper plateau live entirely on wild plants. These are gathered by both men and women, usually working separately, using a digging-stick of bamboo tipped with iron. The mainstays of their diet are various tubers, but seasonally available fruits such as tamarind and fig have a significant place, and honey is collected in a special basket. The Chenchu have some contact with people on the plains, with whom they trade goods derived from the forest – mohua flowers, fruits, samber horns, honey, resin and bamboo baskets. In return they acquire cloth, and metal for weapons and implements. These exchanges are often made on terms unfavourable to the Chenchu; like many other tribal groups, they are poorly regarded by the lowland people.

The Reddi are another forest-dwelling people from the same area of south India.[8] The name refers to a number of groups inhabiting a large area, some of whom in the past achieved a local political importance and have an intensive agricultural economy based on the use of the plough. The Reddi of the Godavari region and the Northern Hills in the Eastern Ghats, however, practise a simple

42.4: *Reddi men dibbling millet seed.*

food production using dibble sticks, which they supplement with some collection of wild plants and sporadic hunting. They are essentially hill people, living in the high valleys of the main ranges and on slopes and spurs of foothills where they cultivate land to which modern agricultural methods cannot be applied. Their settlements are of two kinds: very small hamlets of up to four houses, perched on a ridge between 600 and 1000 metres above the plain, and larger villages of ten to forty houses in a river valley. In both cases the houses are of square construction and consist of a single room, about 2.5 metres square, with a veranda on two sides. Building materials are wattle and grass.

The area in which the Reddi live is subject to the south-western and south-eastern monsoons, and receives 85 to 100 centimetres of rain between June and September. The vegetation ranges from mixed deciduous forest interspersed with stands of bamboo on the lower slopes lining the Godavari river, to thick forests of shady trees, rambling creepers, high grasses and wild bananas with orchids and ferns of various types in the area of the Northern Hills. South of Godavari evergreen flora, including mangoes, jackfruit and rattan, is restricted to deep ravines with perennial streams. The fauna throughout these areas includes gaur (*Bos gaurus*), large cats, deer, nilgai and wild pigs. Of these animals the deer and pig in particular are hunted with bow and arrows by men from the Northern Hills groups, but in other areas little time is spent hunting; fishing by line and hook and hand nets is done in the main rivers. All Reddi groups engage in slash-and-burn agriculture, which they call *podu*. Small areas of the forest are cleared by men using axes and billhooks before the dry season between February and March, and in April the dried vegetation is burned. Millets of different types are sown by broadcasting or dibbling following the first rains in May. Techniques of cultivation vary from area to area: hoes are used by Reddi groups in the Northern Hills but not by those in the Godavari region; some groups on flatter land use ploughs. In addition to the food produced in this way many Reddi groups make use of wild plant resources. The most important of these is a sago-like palm (*Caryota urens*) of which they eat the pith and from which palm wine is made. Mangoes and tamarinds are only slightly less important, and women also dig for taro and other tubers and collect bamboo shoots. Villagers who live on the valley floors need to rely less on wild resources because of greater productivity, but often their entire agricultural produce is traded and they have to fall back on these foods.

South-east Asian forest cultures

A similar subsistence strategy – slash-and-burn agriculture with hunting and gathering – is to be found among some cultural groups in south-east Asia, such as the Senoi of the Malay Peninsula.[9] These people inhabit areas of primary jungle growth in the mountains and foothills of Main Range and are pejoratively known as Sakai or 'slaves' by the coastal Malays. One group, the Che Wong, are semi-nomadic hunter–gatherers, but others, such as the Semai and Temiar, subsist primarily on slash-and-burn agriculture, which they augment by hunting, collecting and fishing. A Semai group operates within a well-defined territory called a *sakaq* in which fairly permanent clearings lasting three to eight years are made; settlements typically comprise 50 to 200 people living in stilt houses. A *sakaq* is exploited by an extended family household, but ownership of individual fruit trees is hereditary and often maintains a person's loyalty to the *sakaq*. Initial clearing is the work of a male, although friends and relatives assist with planting in return for a feast. The usual crops are rice, maize, manioc (which the Senoi despise), and some pumpkin and taro.

The forest offers these people a variety of resources, both for their own consumption and for purposes of trade. Fish are caught mainly in basket traps but poison, spears and hooks are also used. The bulk of animal food comes by trapping in various ways, though blow-pipe hunting with poisoned darts also contributes to the bag. As well as collecting mushrooms, bamboo shoots and ferns for their own use, the Senoi gather jungle products for trade to Malay and Chinese middlemen. In exchange for rattan, lumber and fruits, together with some goats, chickens and ducks, they receive the commodities they need – salt, tobacco, sugar, cloth and metal tools.

The Semang, a neighbouring people in the foothills of Main Range, also engage in trade with Malays and Chinese as well as with the Senoi themselves. These Negrito hunter–gatherers have seven major subdivisions, each with a territorial area, in the Malay Peninsula and in Thailand, where in the lowland jungles they live in an economic symbiosis with Malays. Moving nomadically through the forest a band of up to fifty people will make use of caves, rockshelters or groups of trees for short stays, or for longer periods will construct a circle of between three and seventeen leaf shelters. The bulk of food is obtained by the women's gathering of wild resources, predominately roots and tubers; there is also some fishing using nets, spears and poison, and agricultural produce is obtained by trade with Senoi groups. Other collected sources of food are bamboo shoots, larvae, termites, honey and molluscs. Bamboo is a particularly valuable resource that is put to many uses, including being turned into cooking implements and other artifacts. Some iron is worked by pounding, and metal tools are acquired – along with cloth and tobacco – from Malays and Chinese in exchange for rare woods, gums, resins and rattan.

Isolated groups with economies similar to those of the Senoi and Semang still exist or have recently existed in other parts of southeast Asia.[10] In Sumatra, for example, in the swampy areas of the east coast lowlands and the foothills of Barisan Range, various groups of people such as the Mamak, Batin and Akit – all lumped together under the pejorative name of Kubu – live in largely traditional ways. Although many now live permanently on the fringe of rural Malay villages, some groups still lead a nomadic existence in the forested areas. After planting maize and tubers in cleared areas they move off on a seasonal round of hunting and gathering that eventually brings them back to harvest. The Kubu travel in bands of related families led by the oldest physically able

man. Using nets, spears and poisoned blow-gun darts, the men hunt elephants, monkeys and wild pigs. Their economy has however, always relied on their being able to trade forest produce for salt and metal.

In the Philippines scattered populations of hunter–gatherers and simple farmers can still be found today. The Tasaday of Cotabatu province, Mindanao, are perhaps the most famous example of an isolated stone-using group, but recently a hitherto unknown group of thirty-odd families of Tobatu were 'discovered' on Palawan Island. These people live in caves on the crater of an extinct volcano where they practise a simple agriculture. Also in the Philippines, in northern Luzon, scattered Negrito groups collectively called Agta ('black' in a local language) live predominately from slash-and-burn agriculture. Cultivated sweet potato cassava and maize provide 85 per cent of their diet, the rest being obtained equally from collected wild plants and hunted deer and pig. The game is driven by dogs and fire and killed with bow and arrows.

The Western Agta of the lower slopes of Zambales Mountain Luzon, are heavily acculturated, but some groups of twenty to forty people still live in scattered, semi-permanent settlements near the coast and, in even smaller groups, in the interior. There is a sexual division of labour in these local groups: women do the agricultural work and collect wild plants; the men hunt. Men also spend lengthy periods away from home arranging marriages negotiating trade and visiting relatives. As with all the forest dwelling groups, trade is an important factor in the Agta economy.[11] In this instance, trade with lowlanders brings the Agta ceramics, cloth and metal, in return for which they give beeswax and tobacco. The long-standing nature of this relationship is shown by the discovery of Dimolit, a Neolithic settlement dated to 3500 BC, which is contemporary with cave sites on the same coast

The surviving forest cultures of south and south-east Asia may be only the remnants of a once more general way of life, but by studying such groups it is possible to gain at least a general picture of their lifestyle in the past. With the aid of the archaeological record it has also been established that then, as now, these forest cultures were integrated into a wider economic system.

VI: Old empires and new forces

The continuing expansion of the developed zone of the western Old World and the growth of internal links – especially across deserts and by sea – resulted in a realignment of trade routes and political forces. The new importance of previously peripheral regions – northern Europe on the one hand and Arabia and North Africa on the other – truncated the Mediterranean-based empire of Rome, which shrank to the west Mediterranean trading node centred on Byzantium. Temperate Europe was split into smaller developing states, while the political integration of nomadic and town-dwelling communities in the arid zone produced a belt of formerly diverse societies, now unified by the culture and religion of Islam, that stretched from the Iberian peninsula to the Indus. The rise of powerful societies on the central Asian steppes also had a continuing effect on areas to the west. The long-distance trade routes of the Vikings, both overland via the Dnieper and along the sea lanes of the Baltic and the Black Sea, gave rise to a string of towns and trading centres that opened up northern and eastern Europe. But it was the steady extension of the agricultural basis of temperate Europe, checked by the Black Death but soon transcending the limits set on earlier population levels, that made possible the continuing growth of the medieval West, taking it along the path to overseas expansion on a global scale.

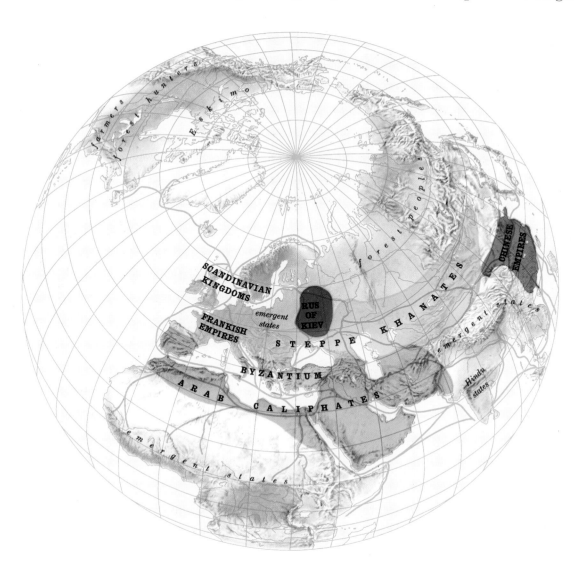

43. Parthian and Sasanian Iran

The Parthian and Sasanian periods lasted from about 240 BC–AD 224 and from AD 224–641 respectively. Their empires included all of present-day Iran and Iraq, and parts of Syria, Anatolia, central Asia, Afghanistan and northern India. Because there were no satisfactory physical boundaries, the extent of these empires depended on the relative strengths of the contending powers and fluctuated considerably during the eight centuries. In the early Parthian period the western boundary extended as far as the curve of the Euphrates in Syria and included the kingdom of Armenia, while later its borders were drawn further to the east. The siting of the eastern boundary is much less well established – indeed, we have little information about events there. The city of Merv in central Asia was usually under Iranian control: Shapur II (309–79) held Kabul, and Bahram V (421–39) was given some ports in the Indus delta as part of a marriage dowry. Much of the area was, however, lost by the Parthians in the first and second centuries AD, during the ascendancy of the Kushans, and by the Sasanians in the later fifth century to the Ephthalite Huns.[1]

Study of the Parthian and Sasanian periods is still in its infancy. Although so late in date, they are essentially protohistoric, for few internal written records have survived, and their history has to be reconstructed from a study of the coins, from rare inscribed monuments or labels, and from external records, both contemporary and later. Unless such records have survived and are discovered, the internal organization of these vast empires will have to be built up from the archaeological evidence. This is, however, already beginning to suggest a major growth of population and urbanization, together with the development of large-scale irrigation projects.

To document this long time-span and large area there is today still only a handful of sites, many of which were excavated before the Second World War and most of which concentrate on major public buildings. This paucity of information is partly caused by the time-scale of settlement in the area being so long, the area so large and the cultural cross-currents so complex that no one scholar could hope to cover more than a section of it. Each has therefore been forced to specialize, a necessity reinforced by the astonishing amount of recovered information that belongs to some periods, notably that of the Assyrian civilization. Because attention has been focused on the earlier periods, there has been relatively little interest, until the last twenty-five years, in the eight centuries of Parthian and Sasanian rule – centuries that show the impact of Greco-Roman civilization on the ancient Near East. To the Orientalist these centuries were too late and decadent; to the Classicist they presented too debased a form of Hellenism.

Serious interest is now being taken as the significance of these periods has been recognized, and there has been a massive increase in the number of archaeological expeditions working in the area. Not only have more sites been selected for excavation, but this has been accompanied by large-scale, comprehensive surveys of some areas being undertaken. The early Parthian period is represented by excavations at the first Parthian capital, Nysa, near Ashkabad,[2] which have demonstrated how strongly the Parthians were influenced by Hellenistic art and architecture. Recent work on numerous important sites in central Asia has documented the northern limit of the Kushans, as well as illuminating the archaeology of the Parthians and Sasanians.[2] Another early Parthian capital, Shahr-i Qumis, near Damghan,[3] probably to be identified with Seleucid Hecatompylos, has revealed remarkable three-storey structures dating to the early Parthian, Sasanian and early Islamic periods. Unfortunately, much of the site is totally eroded and no Seleucid construction has yet been observed. The Seleucid and Parthian periods are represented by a number of temples on the terraced platforms of Masjid-i Sulaiman and Bard-i Nishandeh in Khuzistan.[4]

In Mesopotamia excavations have taken place at Seleucia-on-the-Tigris and Dura Europos, two cities founded by Seleucus I (312–281 BC), a ruler credited with founding more than seventy-five cities. These fortified foundations were essential as garrison towns from which the small colonies of Greek settlers could administer the surrounding areas. They were run on Hellenistic lines, with numerous public buildings and a regular town plan. This Greek concentration on the foundation of cities was to have a profound effect on settlement patterns in the area. The Greeks maintained their privileged position in the early Parthian period, and Seleucia-on-the-Tigris maintained its autonomy until the first century AD. The earliest level revealed at Seleucia[5] belongs to the early Parthian period and shows a crowded area filled with houses whose plans illustrate an adaptation of the typical Greek porticoed dwelling to the indigenous courtyard style of life. Seleucia revolted in the first century AD, and this resulted in the city being brought under direct Parthian control. In the latest level, dated to about AD 120–200, the crowded houses had been replaced by a monumental Parthian palace with large *iwans*, barrel-vaulted halls opening out on to courtyards.

The best illustration of late Parthian architecture and town planning is provided by excavations at the Assyrian capital of Assur, Parthian Labbana, where large areas have been meticulously recorded.[6] These include ordinary houses as well as the famous palace and numerous temples. The excavator's careful study of Parthian building techniques has revealed the method by which the distinctive Parthian *iwan* could be built without scaffolding: this was one of the major technological innovations of the day, which revolutionized contemporary architecture. By this time the *iwan* formed a central feature not only of palaces and temples but also of the typical courtyard houses, as can be seen both at Assur and at nearby Hatra, another late Parthian city.

Excavations have begun recently at a remote fortress located in the Zagros, not far from Sar Pul-i Zohab and the main east–west highway, the great Khurasan road. This fortified mountain top, known today as Qaleh-i Yazdigird,[7] was only occupied for a short time, perhaps as little as fifty years, at the very end of the Parthian period and was probably the hideout of some robber baron who profited from the anarchy of the time to plunder passing caravans with impunity. He lived in a palatial residence richly decorated with gaily painted stucco plaques. These were carved with a bewildering variety of motifs drawn from the Parthian and East Roman repertoire as well as from indigenous traditions. When excavations have been completed this site will provide a wealth of information about the art and architecture at the time of transition between the two dynasties, as well as illustrating the layout

and daily equipment of such a fortress, and an invaluable corpus of closely dated pottery.

A bare outline of the development of Sasanian court architecture[8] in the west is provided by buildings recorded and excavated at various sites, including Firuzabad, built by Ardashir I (224–41), and Bishapur, founded by Shapur I (241–73), of the early Sasanian period; Paikuli, Aiwan-i Kerkha and Kish of the mid-Sasanian period; and Ctesiphon, Qasr-i Shirin and Damghan of the late Sasanian period. The great stone platform at Kangavar also belongs to the Sasanian period, as does the walled oval city of Takht-i Sulaiman in north-west Iran. A large area of the Takht has been uncovered and many of the buildings in the Sacred

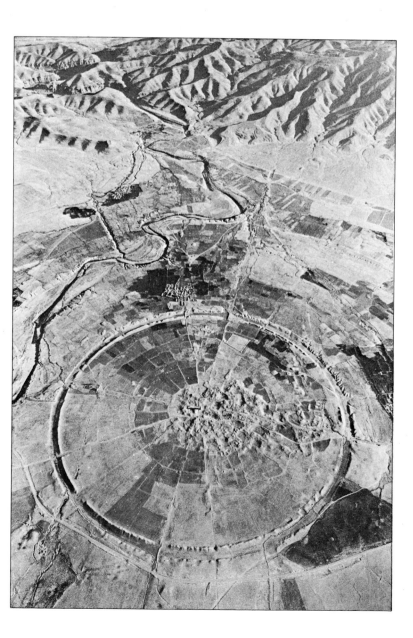

43.1: *The great circular city built in the plain at Firuzabad, south-west Iran, by the founder of the Sasanian dynasty, Ardashir I (AD 224–41). The huge double ramparts of clay formed a perfect circle enclosing an area nearly 2 kilometres in diameter. The city was divided into four quadrants by the two principal axes, which crossed in the centre at right angles and led to the city's four main gates.*

43.2: *Ardashir I, from a rock relief carved on the mountain near his city at Firuzabad. In this scene, 18 metres in length, three Sasanian knights are shown defeating their Parthian opponents, and the relief thus commemorates the moment that the Sasanian empire was founded.*

Precinct, which served as the principal shrine of the empire, have been planned. Parthian and Sasanian material has also been reported from many other sites, including Tureng Tepe and Daila-man in northern Iran, Haftavan Tepe in north-west Iran, Malyan in Fars, Tepe Yahya near Kerman, Susa, Siraf on the Persian Gulf, Nippur, Babylon, Warka (Uruk), Nineveh and Tell Mahuz in Iraq and Nush-i Jan near Hamadan, where a small Parthian village with an important corpus of pottery has been recorded.

Settlement and economy

The major development in Near Eastern archaeology in the last twenty-five years has been the comprehensive survey of large areas throughout their time-range, with the aim of documenting changing settlement patterns throughout the millennia. Such surveys have so far principally taken place in the Diyala region[10]

43.3: *Map of western Asia in the Parthian and Sasanian periods. The borders of the two empires changed considerably during these 800 years: the nucleus consisted of present-day Iraq and Iran, but at times the empire extended into central Asia, Afghanistan and northern India, and in the west often included part of Syria and the kingdom of Armenia.*

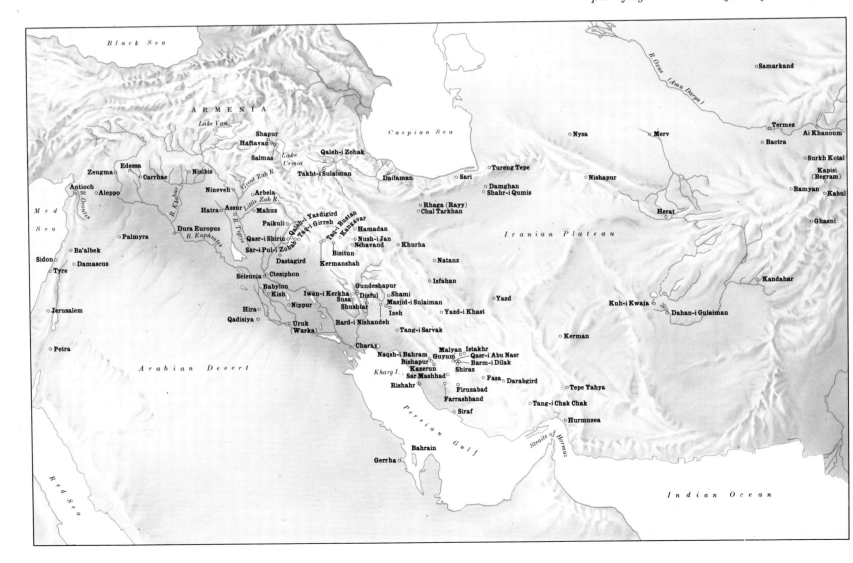

and around Warka[11] in Iraq and in Khuzistan,[12] and around Kermanshah, Kangavar, Malayer and Kerman in Iran. This work has been hampered by the fact that little is known about the pottery sequence, particularly that of the common wares, for nearly a millennium, from the Achaemenian to the early Islamic periods; and the precise dating of sites from surface survey, particularly within the four centuries of each of the Parthian and Sasanian periods, is almost impossible. The evidence of the surveys has, however, been overwhelming; this millennium was one of massive urbanization, supported by an essential increase in agriculture, itself made possible by ambitious irrigation schemes. This remarkable development is best documented to date in the Diyala, an area adjacent to the Parthian and Sasanian winter capital of Ctesiphon and on an arterial highway up to the Iranian plateau.

In the Seleuco-Parthian periods settlement in the Diyala increased more than fifteen-fold over the Achaemenian period and was three times greater than the previous period of maximum density, the Isin-Larsa period. For the first time there were truly urban centres. This urbanism is in complete contrast to Achaemenian settlement patterns and illustrates one of the effects of the Hellenization of the Orient. Both Alexander and the Seleucids are famed as founders of cities, a tradition carried on by the Parthians and Sasanians. The emergence of these urban centres depended on new methods of imperial organization. In the alluvial areas the first problem to be solved was that of the water supply, for

43.4: *Settlement in the Diyala valley near Ctesiphon increased greatly in the Parthian period and reached its maximum in the following Sasanian period, as can be seen by comparing the pattern of Parthian sites* (left) *with those representing Sasanian settlement. Numerous urban centres were founded in addition to villages and hamlets.*

- village or hamlet, less than 4 hectares
- town, 4–30 hectares
- small urban centre, 30–100 hectares
- city, more than 1 sq. km
- capital cities

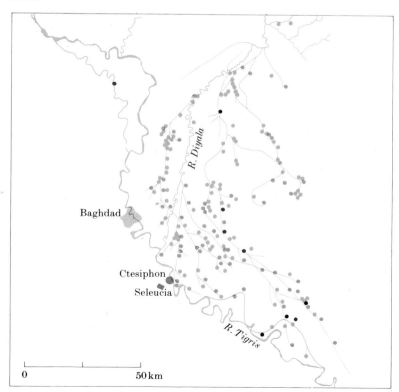

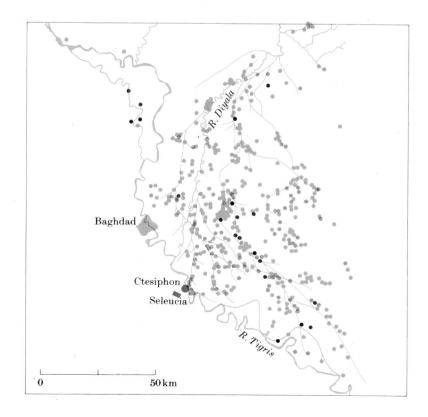

with adequate water supplies whole new districts could be brought into cultivation, to provide food for the new cities. Major programmes of planned canal construction, paid for by the state, were undertaken, including both the construction of new gravity-flow canals and the improvement of existing ones. Keeping these canals at maximum efficiency required regular routine maintenance and annual dredging, all of which had to be organized and paid for by the state, for local efforts were no longer sufficient to maintain the system. Because the new irrigation systems were so large and complex, alterations to or collapses of canals in one area could drastically affect local supplies elsewhere. This reorganization of water supplies required a complete change in government attitudes: central government had to provide large sums of money to achieve the agricultural expansion that in turn provided increased taxes and revenue for the state.

While there was a considerable increase in state-sponsored irrigation, agriculture and settlement in the Seleuco-Parthian period, this trend reached its peak in the following Sasanian period. Surviving settlements in the Diyala were at least thirty-five times as dense and widespread as in the Achaemenian period: settlement had, therefore, more than doubled since the Parthian period, though this impression may be slightly exaggerated, as heavy Sasanian settlement may have masked earlier Parthian sites. There was a new and comprehensive approach to the use of land and water, and virtually the entire land surface of the Diyala was brought into cultivation for the first and only time. These developments produced the greatest density of settlement ever achieved in the area. A massive programme of state-initiated irrigation works made maximum settlement possible: numerous small and prosperous manor houses have been found throughout the Diyala river basin; the number of villages increased and cities grew in size.

This remarkable growth in population was partially achieved by the forcible resettlement of prisoners of war and of the entire populations of captured cities, and it can be partly accounted for by natural increase under such favourable conditions. However, the density of population may not be accurately reflected by settlement size, because not only were towns and cities more spaciously planned than in the past but in the long time-span of each of these periods it is possible that not all sites were in continuous occupation. Even so, the size of these cities, the largest of which measured on average some 200 hectares, is proof of the large populations of the time, and the very size of the sites provides a daunting challenge to the archaeologist.

This picture of great cities set in a well-watered and fertile landscape suggests a long period of peace and stability: the essential annual canal maintenance required efficient organization and assured finance. However, both the Seleucid and the Parthian periods were politically unstable. There were frequently two or even three contenders for the throne – it was, indeed, during just such a period of anarchy that Seleucia had revolted in the first century AD. The feudal organization of the Parthian state was another contributory factor to this political instability, for when the monarch was weak the nobles and sub-kings asserted their independence. That the irrigation systems were maintained despite this probably reflects the fact that the various contenders for power had an active interest in their preservation and in the maintenance of a healthy agricultural base for the economy. Some damage was suffered in the second and third centuries AD, when the Romans reached Ctesiphon four times, but this was confined to a relatively narrow corridor west of the Tigris. Even the changes of dynasty, from Seleucid to Parthian and from Parthian to Sasanian, were achieved swiftly and apparently with little dislocation or destruction.

A variety of factors made possible the massive increase in irrigation, agriculture and settlement under the Sasanians. First, they had inherited an advanced, state-controlled irrigation system, which formed a satisfactory foundation for expansion. Second, Shapur's wars against Rome were immensely successful, and he captured thousands of prisoners, including Valerian's entire army with all its camp followers, as well as large quantities of treasure. This not only provided a considerable addition to the labour force but also made available new techniques, as can be seen in the great barrage bridges built by Roman prisoners in Khuzistan. Another important factor was the organization of the Sasanian state, which was much more strongly centralized and bureaucratic than the Parthian. The framework of the new state had been laid down by the founder Ardashir and his son Shapur and remained essentially the same until the sixth century, when wide-ranging reforms were initiated after a period of near-anarchy and weakness. Kavad (488–531) and Khusrau I (531–79) completely reorganized the tax system, which they based on a careful assessment of land and resources. As a result state revenues were greatly increased, and Khusrau undertook ambitious irrigation works.

Some of the effects of the initial reorganization under Ardashir and Shapur and the final phase in the sixth century can be documented in the Diyala. Traces of a canal that supplied the city of Buzurg Shapur, or Ukbara, founded by Shapur I, can still be seen: as the canal must have preceded the city, it can be dated to the early Sasanian period. It continued in use until it was cut by an even more ambitious irrigation project, the giant canal known as the Cut of Khusrau, which, by taking water directly from the Tigris, greatly increased water supplies to the Diyala region. Among much else, this canal fed the new city founded by Khusrau I for the citizens he had deported from Antioch, and can therefore be dated to the late Sasanian period.

Khusrau's reform of the tax system was, however, to lead to the downfall of the Sasanians, for Khusrau II (591–628) increased the tax burden to an intolerable level, not for reinvestment in the land but to finance an almost unbelievably extravagant court. Revenues from ancient Babylonia increased by more than 60 per cent in less than a century, from the reign of Kavad to that of Khusrau II. The strains on the system were exacerbated by a breakdown in central authority after the murder of Khusrau, when ten weak kings reigned in nine years. The Arabs, who overthrew the dynasty, were unable to overcome the crisis and restore the old prosperity. In the Diyala some 58 per cent of the sites occupied in the Sasanian period were abandoned and nearly half the land went out of cultivation, probably because the breakdown of annual canal maintenance led rapidly to silting up and to the salination of some of the land. As local inhabitants were no longer able independently to control and maintain their own water supplies, collapse at the centre rapidly led to the collapse of the whole complex system. Sasanian levels of settlement have never been regained.

A similar pattern of urbanization and increased settlement has so far been observed, with local variations, in parts of Mesopotamia and in the Khuzistan plains of Iran. Where surveys have been undertaken elsewhere, for instance in the Kangavar–Kermanshah and Malayer regions in western Iran, a considerable rise in Parthian sites has been reported, together with evidence of increased exploitation of the agricultural potential. The identification of Parthian sites in western Iran is relatively simple because of the appearance, in about 150 BC, of a distinctive red ware known as Clinky ware, which continued in use until the third century AD.[13] No such obvious guide ware has been pinpointed for the Sasanian period, and it is not yet possible to separate Sasanian from early Islamic sites. There were, however, numerous Sasanian–Islamic sites in the areas surveyed.

The study of Parthian pottery has been based on recent excavations at such sites as Shahr-i Qumis, Nush-i Jan and Susa. It has been established that Parthian Clinky ware was confined to western Iran, and that there was no uniform 'Parthian' pottery covering Parthian sites in Iran. Instead there were pottery 'provinces', not all of which have yet been defined. In these provinces – seven have been noted so far – there was both a continuity of pottery traditions from early times and considerable originality in creating new forms and wares. This regionalization is not altogether surprising, for Parthian control of the various areas of the empire was loose and feudal in style, and some vassal kingdoms enjoyed virtual autonomy at times. Furthermore, the various regions of the Parthian empire had formed part of a unified empire for only a relatively short time. The Assyrian and Babylonian empires had not extended into eastern Iran, and Iran had first been united by the Achaemenians (550–330 BC), who themselves had to fight to hold it together. Alexander had also had to fight to conquer former Achaemenian territories in the east, and his Seleucid successors had failed to maintain their hold there for long.

Although they were directly controlled by Greek rulers for less than two centuries, the impact of Greco-Roman civilization on the Parthian and Sasanian empires was considerable. There was an important artistic debt, particularly in the early Parthian period, but the most decisive result of Hellenization was the entirely new system of imperial organization and state finance. The state planned and maintained large-scale irrigation networks that led to much greater agricultural exploitation of the land and to mas-sive urban expansion. This urban revolution has only begun to be documented in the last twenty-five years. If the current pace of exploration can be maintained for the next twenty-five years, we may by then have a more accurate picture of court art and architecture, of city design and of regional variations in settlement patterns and land use during the eight centuries spanned by the Parthian and Sasanian empires.

44. Byzantium: an empire under stress

The Byzantine age is conventionally marked by the transference of the capital of the Roman Empire from Rome to Byzantium, but this era is in fact divided into two periods, whose society, economy and archaeological record are substantially different. Late Antiquity (AD 284 to about 610) was a time of prosperity, separated by war, plague and population decline from the Byzantine period proper, which lasted from the early seventh century until 1453 and was distinguished by shrinking territory and a declining economy.

Late Antiquity[1]

The Eastern Roman emperors ruled the rich provinces that stretched in an arc from the Danube through the Balkans, Greece, Asia Minor, Syria, Palestine and Egypt to Cyrenaica. The autocratic, Christian character of this state and the location of its capital at Constantinople were the results of the fundamental reforms of Diocletian (284–305) and Constantine (306–37). Diocletian reorganized the government and established a complex hierarchy of officials that ranged from the emperors to the governors of numerous small provinces. Each province was made up of the territories of cities, whose councillors were responsible for local administration and tax collection. The military formed a separate branch of the government, headed by generals in the

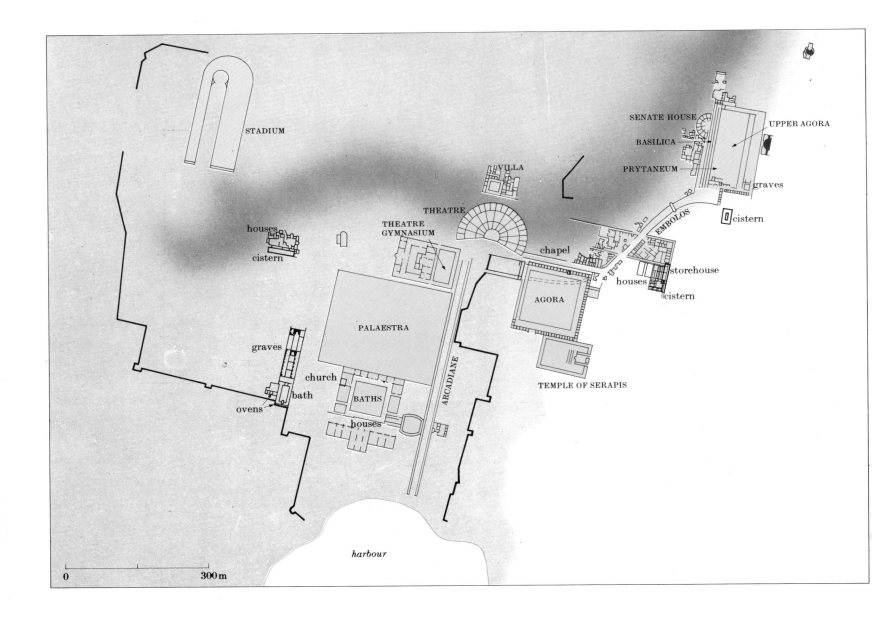

STADIUM

SENATE HOUSE

BASILICA

UPPER AGORA

PRYTANEUM

graves

cistern

VILLA

THEATRE

houses

THEATRE GYMNASIUM

cistern

EMBOLOS

chapel

storehouse

houses

AGORA

cistern

PALAESTRA

graves

church

bath

BATHS

ARCADIANE

TEMPLE OF SERAPIS

ovens

houses

harbour

0   300 m

capital. The system was designed to provide security after the anarchy and invasions of the third century. It succeeded at the price of a heavy burden of taxation, which compelled much of the population to remain in its place or profession. Constantine, converted to Christianity, established the new capital and patronized the Church, which grew phenomenally. The Church imitated the organization of the state and provided social services, such as hospitals, poorhouses and inns. Except for the Balkans, which were overrun by Goths and Huns, the eastern empire was generally peaceful and prosperous throughout the sixth century. The cities flourished, despite the frequent civil violence that arose from doctrinal disputes within the Church or the fanaticism of the fans in the hippodrome. The reign of Justinian (527–65), however, brought major changes. His grandiose projects of reconquest and construction created a strain that was answered by administrative reforms and increased taxation or met by open revolt. During the whole period municipal councillors became increasingly hard to recruit because of their personal responsibility for the taxes; Justinian finally put an end to the millennial autonomy of the cities by turning their administration over to the bishops and landowners, supervised by the governors. With this, one of the distinct characteristics of Antiquity came to an end. Finally, in 542, a devastating plague decimated the population, and recovery was precluded by the invasions of Slavs, Persians and Arabs that marked the end of the ancient world.

The cities and settlements of Late Antiquity

Abundant surviving remains in every province reflect the prosperity of Late Antiquity. This archaeological record may be considered by type: cities, villages, fortresses, palaces and monasteries.[2]

Late Antique cities were of two types: the new foundations, built on a regular plan, and the ancient cities, organic growths that were modified in typical ways. The cultural uniformity of the age appears in its urban remains, which show similar types and styles everywhere.[3]

The greatest of the new cities was Constantinople; ancient Byzantium was completely transformed by Constantine and his successors.[4] The new capital was built as a Christian city, with churches instead of temples. Its centre was the Augusteum, a large square on to which faced the Cathedral of St Sophia, the senate house, the imperial palace, the hippodrome and a large public bath. These symbolized the forces that formed the state: the emperor, the Church, the army (the headquarters of the imperial guard was next to the palace gate), the senate, which represented the land-owning aristocracy, and the people, who had no formal power but could make their influence felt by acclamation and riot at the games. The cathedral, rebuilt by Justinian after one such riot, is still the most magnificent building of the age; it rises over 45 metres to the dome, and its vast interior space is carpeted with marble and mosaic. The palace was an irregular complex of reception and ceremonial halls, churches and pavilions that stretched

44.1: *Plan of Ephesus, a Late Antique and Byzantine city. The areas marked in red show the extensive construction and restoration that took place in Late Antiquity, when the ancient metropolis still flourished. The smaller areas (in black) reflect the shrinkage and decline that took place in the Middle Ages, when the town by the harbour was eventually abandoned and replaced by a fortress.*

44.2: *The centre of Late Antique Ephesus. On the left the theatre, agora and the beginning of the Arcadiane can be seen; in the centre are residential quarters, a temple and a bath; and on the right, at the top of the Embolos, the buildings of the civic centre. The slopes of the hills were lined with houses, only partially excavated. The structures shown were extensively rebuilt and received substantial additions in Late Antiquity.*

down to the seashore; little of it remains. The hippodrome accommodated over 50 000 people and was decorated with works of art plundered from the whole empire. Such reuse of material, whether for adornment or for construction, was a characteristic of the age.

A broad, colonnaded boulevard led westwards from the Augusteum through a series of squares (*fora*) to the city walls. Each *forum* contained a column, triumphal arch or monument and each served as a market and centre of a district. In most cities commercial activity shifted from open squares to bazaars along the streets; Constantinople, the greatest market of the empire, had both. Finally, a massive rampart protected the city successfully for 900 years. On the landward side this consisted of a wall 4.2 metres thick with towers 18.3 metres high, further protected by a lower wall and a ditch. A very few new towns, notably Justiniana Prima in southern Yugoslavia (the birthplace of Justinian), followed a regular rectangular plan, with broad colonnaded streets, but the vast majority had grown irregularly from Classical times. All of them, however, were modified in significant ways that reflect the spirit of the age and the triumph of Christianity. Ephesus is an outstanding example.[5] Most of its public buildings had been built on a grandiose scale in earlier centuries. Many of them, notably the theatre, the stadium, the central market, the senate house and several baths, were rebuilt and continued to fulfil their ancient functions. Others show change or decline. A vast exercise ground with a *gymnasium* in the centre was abandoned and covered with houses, but the adjacent bath was restored. Changing social customs brought the end of the Greek *gymnasium*, but the baths continued to be a valued public service. Nearby a wide, colonnaded street lined with shops was built in about 400, in a straight line between the theatre and the harbour. A similar street, the Embolos, which led from the *agora* to the civic centre, was the heart of the city; it was lined with honorific statues, decrees, public and private buildings, and fountains. Numerous fountains adorned the city, some of them constructed from ancient buildings; they were a favoured building type of the age. Another new structure was the palace of the governor, a domed reception hall with antechambers and an attached bath. The people enjoyed a high standard of living. The city provided many free public services, such as baths and market buildings, as well as entertainments, and houses were large and comfortable. A group of apartments excavated on the Embolos contains suites of rooms decorated with cut marble, mosaics and frescoes, frequently arranged around open courts.

Ephesus illustrates the continuity of ancient urban life as well as the transformations that were taking place. Markets shifted to streets, *gymnasia* were abandoned, open spaces became cluttered with shops and houses; but it was Christianity that brought the greatest change. The remains clearly show that Ephesus was one of the great centres of the Church. A long building housing a market near the harbour was turned into the Cathedral of the Virgin, with its baptistery and bishop's palace; the temple of Serapis became another church; while the temple of Domitian and the building that housed the sacred fire of Vesta were de-

molished and their stones carted off to be reused elsewhere. The triumph of Christianity was manifest everywhere: crosses were set up or carved on ancient buildings and statues, the name of Artemis was erased from inscriptions, and chapels were added to public and private buildings. Outside the city walls the temple of Artemis, one of the wonders of the ancient world, was destroyed, to be replaced by the grandiose basilica of St John, which crowned the adjacent hill. The ancient metropolis became a Christian city, hardly diminished from Antiquity.

While the capital no doubt consumed far more than it produced, Alexandria, Antioch and Ephesus were major centres of trade and manufacture.[6] Industry was generally on a small scale, with the notable exception of the imperial factories that produced weapons and uniforms for the army and the civil service. In the cities artisans produced and sold their products in small shops along the main boulevards, or worked in booths in the colonnades. Tradesmen were organized in guilds, which were responsible for paying taxes to the government but left considerable freedom to individual workers.[7]

However impressive their remains, the cities formed a small part of the empire, whose economy was based primarily on agriculture. The bulk of taxes were levied from the land, and the mass of the population was composed of peasants. Most of these were tied to the land under the domination of large landlords who exercised an overwhelming influence on the society and on government, but independent smallholders always existed. In the eastern provinces the peasants lived in villages and worked the land in the same way as had their ancestors of the Classical period. The only major technological advance seems to have been a growing use of water-mills, which would have made possible a larger production of flour.

Although most ancient villages have disappeared through continuous occupation, Syria and southern Asia Minor preserve abundant remains that give a striking impression of rural prosperity, especially in the sixth century.[8] Typical villages stand in the hills above Antioch, centred on a meeting-house, a bath and a three-aisled basilical church, all built of neatly cut stone. Houses were usually solid structures of two storeys, with few rooms and a long veranda; along with storehouses or stables, they faced on to walled courtyards. The olive groves and presses on which the local economy depended were scattered through the village, while cemeteries lay on the outskirts. In southern Asia Minor, where research is only beginning, some villages had stone houses arranged close together in blocks along streets. The less permanent materials used in other regions have naturally left little trace.

Fortification was widespread in Late Antiquity.[9] Most cities were surrounded by walls, some hastily constructed from reused materials, others built of regular stones with bands of brick. The eastern frontier was protected by a series of rectangular castles, which typically contained a church, the commander's headquarters and barracks. Frontier towns, there and elsewhere, resembled large fortresses. The Justinianic town of Troesmis, on the Danube, for example, formed a rectangle of about 120 by 160 metres. Behind its heavy walls with round towers, the town was divided into two parts: on the north, the basilica, the governor's palace, the council hall and associated dwellings; on the south, the barracks.

The palace of Diocletian at Split, on the Adriatic coast of Yugoslavia, is similar. It forms a powerfully fortified square divided by two colonnaded streets. The focus of the complex was the court, which gave access to the imperial throne rooms and dwellings. Beside it stood the temple of Zeus and the mausoleum of the emperor; quarters for the troops and staff occupied the other half of the enclosed area. Most palaces were laid out on less rigid lines, and contained suites of courts, reception rooms, baths and habitations laid out in a hieratical order. They were usually built within city walls and served as homes and offices for emperors, bishops, governors and generals.

A spectacular growth of monasticism accompanied the rise of Christianity and has left many remains.[10] These range from a simple collection of reed huts, as in the Egyptian desert, to vast complexes of rooms arranged around courtyards next to a church. Monasteries were built both in cities and in the countryside and generally reflected domestic architecture. In remote areas they were usually fortified.

The Byzantine age[11]

The seventh century brought disaster to the empire. The Persians so devastated Asia Minor that urban life there never recovered.[12] They were soon followed by the Arabs, who permanently removed the rich eastern provinces and posed a dangerous threat to the lands that remained. In Europe, Avars and Slavs overran and occupied much of the Balkans, and the Bulgars established a powerful state south of the Danube. The empire, reduced to Asia Minor and parts of Greece, was forced to develop new forms of government and society on which to build. New provinces, governed by generals, were created, while the towns were ruled by their subordinates and the bishops. At the head of the state stood the emperor, his despotic power tempered by the influence of his councillors and generals.

After the crisis of iconoclasm, during which imperial policy dictated the destruction of the sacred images and religious art, stirring bitter internal dissension, the empire recovered and moved on the offensive. By the time of Basil II (976–1025) Byzantine armies were successful on all fronts: the empire stretched from the Danube to Armenia and Syria. In 1071, however, a new enemy, the Turks, crushed the imperial forces and overran Asia Minor. As only the coastal region was recovered, the Balkans became the base of Byzantine power under the Comneni (1081–1185). Finally, in 1204, the Fourth Crusade captured Constantinople. Although the government in exile, the Lascarids of Nicaea, managed to regain the capital in 1261, the restored empire was enfeebled by foreign attacks and civil strife. It was of little consequence when the Turks ended the city's history by conquering Constantinople in 1453.

Churches and fortresses form the most widespread and characteristic remains of the Byzantine period, reflecting the predominance of religion and the army in the society. Urban life, shattered by the invasions, survived in only a few centres, while most ancient cities were reduced to small towns and castles.[13] This phenomenon is of the greatest importance in differentiating the two periods and has far-reaching implications. The reduction of city life indicates a drastic decline in population, which is partly to be explained by the long centuries of invasion and devastation. In many regions decline had probably been provoked by the great plague of 540, but a more universal explanation may be at hand. Evidence (as yet scattered and uncollated) may suggest that a gradual climatic change, in which rainfall diminished and agriculture suffered, afflicted the empire at a time when resources were no longer available to counter its effects. The common phenomenon of deltaic formation and the silting of harbours was also of major importance for coastal settlements.

Although the detailed causes of these changes remain to be explained, their consequences were obvious in the cities.[14] Constantinople, still the greatest city of Europe, astounded medieval visitors by its magnificence. It preserved its ancient size and plan, although its appearance changed as buildings became dilapidated and large areas were abandoned or converted to gardens. Many new churches were built, all on a far smaller scale than before; in fact, churches all over the empire were tiny compared with their Late Antique forbears, a phenomenon to be explained in part by the decline in population. The capital was adorned with palaces even in its last days; the latest, next to the walls, is a simple structure with characteristic decorative brickwork. It shows considerable western influence, as do the roughly contemporary palaces at Nymphaeum, near Smyrna, and Mistra. Urban decline may be clearly traced at Ephesus, where a Persian attack caused the Embolos and the civic centre to be ruined and abandoned.[15] Subsequently about half the area of the ancient city was enclosed by a new fortification, which used the theatre and the stadium as bastions. Within it, the basilica dedicated to the Virgin was replaced by a smaller, domed church; crowded houses covered the Arcadian street and former public buildings; and cisterns were built into the ruins of other ancient structures. As the harbour gradually silted, the centre of the town shifted to the church of St John, where a massive wall of ancient marble encircled the hill. It protected the houses and small industrial installations that clustered around the church. The site by the harbour was abandoned, and the cosmopolitan coastal metropolis became an inland fortress.

Many Byzantine cities show a similar development – or a more extreme one, as a consequence of which they were reduced to hilltop fortresses or enclosed by walls built across an ancient theatre or market place. Some survived and flourished, however. Thessalonica, the greatest port of the Balkans, was decorated with numerous churches, and the Anatolian ports of Trebizond,

Smyrna and Attalia in Asia Minor retained their former extent. But in these cases little is known of secular buildings or an urban plan; in such circumstances, cities and fortresses were virtually synonymous. Fortresses are found everywhere. The most imposing, perhaps, is Ancyra (Ankara), the headquarters of a general and 8000 troops.[16] Its fortifications had numerous towers, a double circuit of walls facing the ruins of the ancient city and a citadel on the highest point. Other forts are less elaborate. In general, they have no regular plan but follow the contours of a hill and lack the sophistication of similar works in Europe or the Middle East. During the Dark Ages walls were often built of large stones from ruined buildings. (Later, smaller stones and brick were employed, and those of the twelfth and thirteenth centuries are usually marked by brick arranged in decorative patterns.) Few detailed studies have been made of the fortresses that defended Asia Minor against the Arabs and Turks; they were especially numerous in the western regions under the Comneni and Lascarids.

With the reduction of urban life, the Classical distinction between city and country became blurred. The towns of the period continued to function as regional economic centres, but they were less important than their Classical forebears. Village life is well known from a variety of sources, although it has left little trace in the archaeological record. In the Byzantine period peasantry and landlords alike lived in clustered villages and, in more secure regions and periods, in isolated holdings. Large landlords constantly attempted to add to their property to the detriment of the peasantry, and by the twelfth century they completely dominated the state. The population seems to have remained at a relatively low level until at least the tenth century, after which a gradual expansion took place. For the Byzantines this process was interrupted by the arrival of the Turks, under whom, however, a high level of prosperity was maintained for some centuries.

The remains of the reduced cities give an idea of town life and of the fortresses in which the population could take refuge, but few traces of actual villages have survived, or at any rate been recognized as such. A notable exception may be found in the inland region of Cappadocia, a port of central Anatolia exposed to constant attack, where churches, monasteries and entire villages were excavated in the local soft volcanic rock.[17] The villages, however, have yet to be studied or dated. In the same region a series of underground towns, built on several levels and with great millstones to block their entrances, provide a striking illustration of the conditions of life at the time of the invasions.

A second great age of monasticism began in the ninth century, when many establishments grew up in remote regions where hermits had taken refuge.[18] The most famous are those of Mount Athos in northern Greece. A typical monastery there features a church constructed on the domed-cross plan, with extensive cells and associated structures around a court. Most are surrounded by high walls. Few traces remain of similar communities on Mount Olympus in Bithynia and Mount Latros in Caria. The churches in Cappadocia, although hewn out of the rock, follow the plans of free-standing structures, complete with domes and interior colonnades, and preserve a remarkable collection of provincial Byzantine painting.

44.3: *The Byzantine walls of Ancyra, a city that was transformed into a major fortress against attack by Arabs and Turks.*

44.4: *Byzantine rock-cut houses in Cappadocia. Many monasteries, churches and entire towns were excavated into the soft volcanic rock of this part of the Anatolian plateau.*

45. The expansion of the Arabs

On the southern fringes of the Roman and Persian empires the peoples of Arabia had been best known as spice traders (see Chapter 31), whose overland caravan routes supplied the cities of the eastern Mediterranean. Caravan cities such as Petra, Palmyra and Mecca rose to prominence as a result of such trade. The increasing domination of this traffic by camel-breeding nomads, who gained control from the trading states, produced a powerful new political force.

The city of Mecca lay on the main route parallel to the west coast of Arabia, halfway between producing areas in the south and urban consumers in the north, and controlled the flow of commodities. From this nucleus not only was Arabia itself united, but Arab power was extended to take over the Persian empire and to expand across North Africa, creating a new axis of trade and political influence. This process is associated with the equally remarkable spread of the religion of Islam. Its founder, the prophet Mohammed, was born in Mecca in about AD 570. His religious writings, the *Qur'an* (Koran), along with the collection of sayings and deeds attributed to him, the *Hadith*, form the basis of Islamic belief, which prescribes the five duties of faith in God (Allah), daily prayer, fasting, payment of a welfare tax and the pilgrimage to Mecca (*Hajj*).

By the death of Mohammed a large part of Arabia had been united, and military expansion continued under his successors. The Arabs occupied Syria and Iraq in 636 and Egypt in 641, and had soon overrun Iran. By 714 Arab armies were in Spain, and the Umayyad dynasty ruled a territory stretching from the Atlantic to central Asia. Damascus became the capital of a huge empire in which the Arab population was a privileged minority, supported by the taxes levied on their subjects.

The Umayyad dynasty was overthrown by the Abbasids (750–945), who moved the capital to Baghdad in 763. Surviving members of the Umayyad family formed a breakaway state in Spain, with the capital at Córdoba. Other frontier regions saw the rise of quasi-autonomous vassal states. In the tenth century further fragmentation took place: the Fatimids seized power in Tunisia (909) and eventually conquered Egypt (969). In Iran the Buyids created a powerful state and from 945 also controlled Iraq, with Baghdad as their capital.

The political geography of the Islamic world was disrupted in the eleventh century by large-scale invasions of Turkic peoples from the furthest parts of central Asia. The Ghaznavids, who ruled from Ghazna in eastern Afghanistan, established a short-lived empire that extended from Khorasan to northern India, and the Seljuqs made even greater inroads into western Asia. Seljuq expansion began in 1040. By 1044 they controlled the Iranian plateau; in 1055 they occupied Baghdad, and in 1071 they annihilated a Byzantine army at Manzikert and occupied the greater part of Anatolia.

Meanwhile, in the Maghreb ('the west': Tunisia, Algeria and Morocco), a Berber dynasty, the Almoravids (from *murabitun*, 'the *ribat* dwellers' – see below) imposed militant Sunnism on Morocco, where they established themselves at Marrakesh in 1058, and later on Algeria and southern Spain. Other Berber groups seized power further east, filling the vacuum left by the Fatimids when they moved to Egypt.

A second wave of invaders from the eastern steppes broke over western Asia in the thirteenth century. The Mongols, united under Genghis Khan, conquered northern China in 1215 and then advanced westwards. Nomadic pastoralists without a tradition of urban civilization, the Mongols captured – and destroyed – the cities of western Asia, beginning with the lands of the Khoresm shah (Khorasan and Transoxiana) in 1220 and continuing through Iran and Iraq, where they sacked Baghdad in 1258. The invasion was stopped in 1260 when an Egyptian army defeated the Mongols at Ain Jalut. The successors to the Mongol invaders, the Ilkhans, re-established a flourishing urban society in Iran.

Cities and settlement

Islamic civilization is essentially urban, despite the widespread existence in Asia and North Africa of Muslim nomads. The cities were the centres of political and economic power; the traditional administrative unit was the town and the countryside that surrounded and supplied it – indeed, a place name such as Kerman refers to either the city itself or the surrounding territory. Towns have thus played an important part in Islamic studies.[1]

Islamic cities had diverse origins. In the west medieval Islamic cities developed out of the towns of the Greco-Roman world; at Aleppo J. Sauvaget explored the topographical changes that took place in Classical and Islamic times in the course of more than a millennium. In Iran and central Asia Sasanian cities provided the prototypes. The only specifically Islamic buildings in such cities are the mosques and religious schools. Other features, such as the permanent markets (*suqs* or *bazaars*), are typical of Islamic countries, but not themselves specifically Islamic. As far as institutions are concerned, cities as such had no legal function. *Shari'a* law, derived mainly from the *Qur'an*, applied equally to all Muslims and bye-laws scarcely existed: unlike medieval Europe, Islam had remarkably few corporate institutions.

Urban historians often distinguish between the towns that were the result of organic growth, perhaps over centuries (*villes spontanées*) and new towns or planned settlements (*villes créées*). Such new dynastic or administrative centres, established to emphasize the break with the past, had been created in Sasanian Iran, but were quite common in medieval Islam and have even been considered characteristic.

The Arab conquest of the area of Mesopotamia formerly under Sasanian control caused a vast redistribution of population in which, for instance, most of the major Sasanian towns in the

Uruk area disappeared and large areas of the countryside were abandoned, while new urban centres were founded at Kūfa, Basra and Wāsit.

Samarra is a medieval Islamic new town, a vast mushroom city founded by the Abbasid caliph al-Mu'tasim, who transferred the court from Baghdad in 836. It was abandoned as a royal capital before the end of the ninth century, and although occupation continued, the city suffered a sharp decline. Today the ruins of Samarra extend intermittently along the Tigris for more than 30 kilometres, dominated by the remains of two of the largest congregational mosques in Islam. The site was explored in 1912–14 and again in 1936–9, and has proved to be a unique source of information about ninth-century architecture and architectural ornament. In addition to the mosques, archaeologists have examined palatial and domestic buildings and have recovered a large quantity of carved and moulded stucco. The pottery, glass and other artifacts found during the earlier excavations provided the principal raw material for studies of the minor arts for almost fifty years, although none of the finds was properly stratified and some are known now to be later in date than the ninth century.

Islamic Siraf, in southern Iran, on the other hand, seems to have grown spontaneously out of a Sasanian settlement, and although whole quarters were put up in ambitious individual building programmes, the city expanded continuously throughout its period of great prosperity in the ninth and tenth centuries, when it was a major entrepôt for maritime trade.

Overland and maritime trade

The Islamic world was united by a series of elaborate caravan routes that supplied the cities with both raw materials and manufactured goods. Transport was mainly by animal, rather than by carts, with the dromedary in the west and the Bactrian camel in central Asia. Both are capable of supporting heavier loads than the horse or mule, and both have an exceptional capacity for surviving on poor fodder and little water. The routes were simply tracks, with revetments or stretches of paved road in only the most difficult mountain country. At intervals there were caravanserais, walled compounds that provided food and shelter for travellers, their animals and their merchandise. In some areas, such as southern Iran, routes might be marked at intervals by towers.

The most famous medieval caravan route was the so-called Silk Route (a name coined in the nineteenth century by Ferdinand von Richthofen), which connected the cities of western Asia with China.[2] The Silk Route was in fact not one but a series of caravan routes connecting adjacent cities and forming a network that extended from the Mediterranean to China. Few travellers made the entire journey, and most merchandise would pass through a

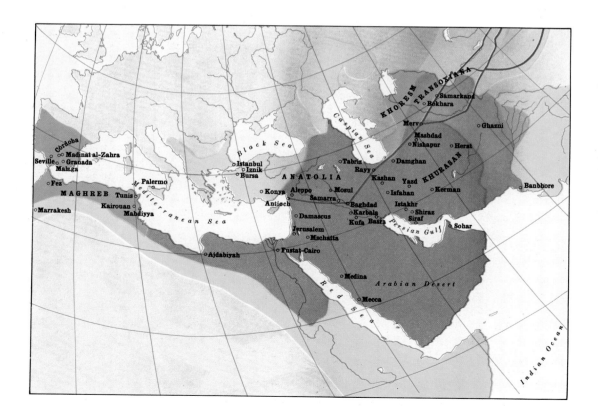

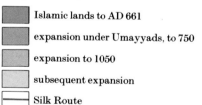

45.1: *Medieval Islam, showing the principal cities and sites mentioned in the text and the rapid territorial expansion that took place from the time of Mohammed to the twelfth century.*

- Islamic lands to AD 661
- expansion under Umayyads, to 750
- expansion to 1050
- subsequent expansion
- Silk Route

series of middlemen between one end of the network and the other. From Antioch, however, the traveller might journey to Palmyra, Baghdad, Rayy (Rhagae, south of modern Tehran) and then take either the northern route through Soviet Central Asia, or the southern route through Afghanistan. The northern route led through Samarkand to Turfan, Tun-huang, Ch'ang-an, Lo-yang and Yang-chou; the southern alternative took one to Balkh and across the Pamirs to Kashgar, Khotan, Lou-lan and Tun-huang. The terminal at the eastern end of the route was Ch'ang-an (modern Sian), the capital of China during the T'ang dynasty (see Chapter 41) and a large-scale producer of silk.

Trade between western Asia and China had already begun in the

45.2: *Chart showing the political history of Islam.*

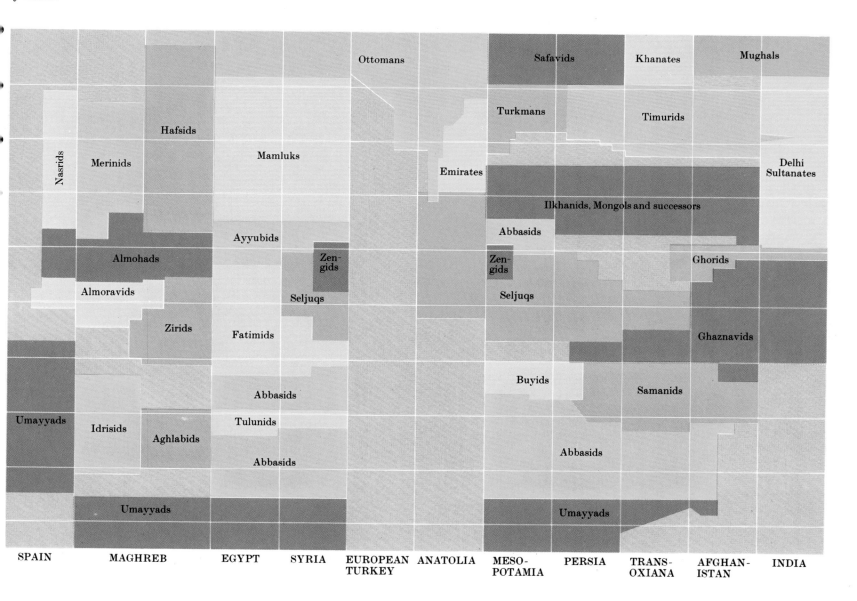

Roman period. It expanded in the Middle Ages and perhaps reached a peak in the Ilkhanid period, when the establishment of Mongol authority over a vast tract of Asia (the *pax tartarica*) afforded a greater measure of security than had existed previously. The best-known description of the Silk Route, the *Divisament dou Monde* of Marco Polo (about 1254–1324), usually known as the *Travels*, belongs to this period.

The importance of the Silk Route did not reside simply in its function as a trade route but also in its role as a vehicle for the diffusion of ideas and techniques; the westward spread of Buddhism, for example, owed much to the existence of an established network of communication. Maritime trade was also of great importance, especially in the Indian Ocean.[3] Indeed, when Vasco da Gama entered these waters in 1498 he encountered a network of trade that linked East Africa, western Asia, India and Sri Lanka, with regular voyages to China. This network developed over millennia, but in one period it underwent an explosive growth: in the early Islamic period, for the first time, we learn of ships from western Asia visiting ports as far away as Sofala in Mozambique and 'Khanfu' in China. As in earlier periods, captains made use of the monsoon winds, which provided optimum conditions for transoceanic voyages from western Asia to India in the summer and for return voyages in winter. Their ships, in the words of Vasco da Gama, were 'held together with cords'; manuscript illustrations and other eye-witness accounts corroborate his report. Nail-fastened vessels, like those of medieval Europe or China, were unknown; the ships that sailed regularly from the Persian Gulf to China (a round trip of 18 000 kilometres) were held together with coconut-fibre twine.

Maritime trade was already well developed in the Red Sea, the Persian Gulf and the Arabian Sea in pre-Islamic times. Early Islamic seafaring, therefore, developed on a firm foundation, stimulated by a demand for commodities and exotic luxury goods in the cities of western Asia and facilitated by the establishment of Muslim communities, linked by a common language and religion, along the coasts of the Arabian Sea.

The archaeological evidence for maritime trade has accumulated rapidly in the last twenty years, with the excavation of Siraf, Banbhore in the Indus delta and Kilwa and Manda in East Africa. These excavations have added substance to the lists of imports from China (e.g. silk), south-east Asia (spices) and Africa (gold, ivory and slaves) in medieval documents and the finds of Chinese porcelain at sites such as Fustat and Samarra.

Siraf, on the Persian Gulf, midway between Sohar and Basra, was excavated in 1966–73. Written sources refer to Siraf as a wealthy entrepôt in the ninth and tenth centuries, when the city covered 4 kilometres. Among the excavated buildings are the congregational mosque, a palace, a group of houses, the potters' quarter – and the bazaar. The bazaar, on the waterfront, stood next to the principal mosque. It contained blocks of one-roomed lock-up shops, at least one small mosque and a public bath. The pottery and small finds from Siraf include abundant Chinese coins

and ceramics, while seeds recovered by flotation include a clove from south-east Asia. The overall impression is that of a wealthy city, as the documents maintain. This is surprising only in the context of Siraf's environment: a barren coast with low soil potential, an arid climate and poor overland communications. The income derived from trade, however, was clearly enormous, and when for political and economic reasons Siraf ceased to serve as a major port the city rapidly declined.

Banbhore, 60 kilometres from Karachi, was excavated on a large scale from 1958 onwards. Like Siraf, it stood in a desolate environment; as the only major site in the region it is often identified as Debal, the first town in Sind to fall into Muslim hands, in 711. Medieval Banbhore contained several elements: the walled town, just over 500 metres across; extra-mural suburbs, and a pool that might have been an enclosed harbour. In the early Islamic period a port in the Indus delta was the outlet for commodities from the hinterland such as indigo, lapis lazuli from Afghanistan and musk from the Himalayas. Banbhore thus owed its existence to the profits of trade with the interior, which produced commodities, and the cities of India and western Asia, which provided markets and manufactured goods.

In East Africa there is evidence of Muslim settlers from the ninth and tenth centuries. The most detailed account of trade was written in the early tenth century: the furthest ports of call were Sofala and 'Waq Waq' (Madagascar, the Comores or some other place in Mozambique). The archaeological information comes chiefly from Kilwa in Tanzania and Manda in Kenya. Kilwa was the most important trading city on the East African coast when the Portuguese arrived. The nucleus of the town had an area of some 100 hectares, outside which were scattered stone buildings and perhaps also shanty dwellings. Manda, built among mangrove swamps in the Lamu archipelago, was a much smaller settlement: stone buildings occupied only 10 hectares. However, there is a wall that contains blocks weighing more than 1 tonne – a scale of construction unmatched elsewhere in sub-Saharan Africa – and imports accounted for 30 per cent of all the pottery. Manda evidently had a special function, perhaps the export of mangrove poles to the treeless regions of Arabia and the Persian Gulf, where the traditional building style employs poles for roofing.

One incidental effect of international shipping in the Indian Ocean should be mentioned: the introduction of the banana from south-east Asia to Africa some time in the first millennium AD. The importance of this event is comparable with the arrival of the potato in Europe in the sixteenth century.

Architecture

Architecture was among the first elements of Islamic civilization to attract attention in the West, initially through an appreciation of the Alhambra palace at Granada in Spain. Much more recently, Umayyad and Abbasid architecture was the subject of a lifelong study by Sir Archibald Creswell.[4] Strictly speaking, very few building types are specifically Islamic; indeed, it might be argued that the mosque (*masjid*) is the only one. The followers of Mohammed worshipped in the Prophet's house at Medina, and the mosque was subsequently developed as the focal point not only of cummunal prayer but also of other social activities. The largest mosques are the congregational mosques, built to accommodate the entire community for worship on Friday. We know from descriptions of buildings at Kūfa, Basra, Cairo and elsewhere that the standard plan evolved in the seventh century: a large rectangular closure with a central courtyard (*sahn*), a covered prayer hall at the end facing Mecca, and covered arcades (*riwaqs*) around the other three sides. Such is the plan of the eighth- and ninth-century mosques at, for example, Wāsit, Samarra and Siraf. This was not the only possible plan and several variations occur, especially when Muslim architects adapted existing buildings, as happened at Damascus and Jerusalem. In the Maghreb the distinctive 'T-plan' was developed for the prayer hall, with a broad axial 'nave' in front of the *mihrab* (the niche in the end – *qibla* – wall, marking the direction of Mecca) and broad 'transepts' in front of the *qibla* wall itself, as at Kairouan in Tunisia. This arrangement of the sanctuary was adopted by the Fatimids, and occurs in the al-Azhar (begun in 970) and al-Hakim (about 1002–3) mosques at Cairo. In Seljuq Iran another distinctive form of congregational mosque evolved, with prominent vaulted open-fronted halls (*iwans*) halfway along the sides of the courtyard. In addition to the great congregational mosques there are several types of smaller mosque such as the square, nine-dome type (e.g. at Balkh) and the small, rectangular mosques of Siraf.

Mosques apart, the *ribat*, mausoleum and *madrasa* should also be mentioned. The *ribat* was a frontier fort, erected on the edge of Islamic territory at times of expansion and used as a springboard for raids into hostile country. Each was manned by volunteers who spent much of their time in prayer and other religious activities. Only two early examples survive, at Sousse and Monastir, both in Tunisia. Mausolea, of course, are not exclusively Islamic. At the beginning of the Islamic period they were proscribed, but there were mausolea at Samarra in the ninth century. The Samanid rulers erected a mausoleum at Bukhara some time before 942, and both the Fatimids and the Seljuqs erected numerous chamber tombs, often with elaborate ornament. The *madrasa* was a religious school, often attached to a mosque, but no early Islamic example survives – at least, none has been recognized.

45.3: *Stucco from Uskaf Bani Junayd, Iraq, of the ninth century. The demand for stucco decoration, notably in the huge building programmes of the Abbasid caliphs, stimulated a rapid development of style and technique.*

45.4: *Bowl with blue painted decoration on opaque white glaze (diameter 25.5 centimetres), of a type that became popular in Iraq in the ninth century, when potters imitated stoneware bowls imported from China. Similar wares were made in Iran and Egypt.*

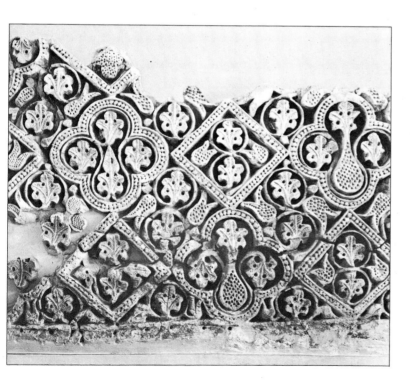

Islamic architects often decorate their buildings, using marble (and occasionally mosaic), stucco, brick patterns or glazed tiles. Although pictorial ornament occurs, especially in Umayyad decoration (for example, the mosaics in the Dome of the Rock, Jerusalem, or the stucco at Khirbat al-Mafjar near Jericho), geometric or vegetal motifs were more common. The development of moulded stucco and later of glazed tiles made it possible to cover large surfaces with repetitive ornament quickly, employing relatively few skilled craftsmen.[5]

Industry and crafts

Islamic pottery, especially the finest glazed pottery, has attracted collectors for a hundred years. Large collections exist both in the West and in the countries of origin. Most of this material was looted from sites by clandestine diggers who frequently inflated their prices by giving pieces well-known provenances such as Rayy or Nishapur. Fortunately, the study of Islamic pottery is now being put on a sound footing by controlled excavation to provide dates and field survey to establish distribution patterns.[6]

Most Islamic pottery is earthenware, although from the twelfth century a 'frit' (soft paste) body was also used. There was a variety of glazes (both lead and alkaline) and methods of decoration (moulding, painting, scratching, etc.). Depending on date and economic circumstances, production might be organized as the small-scale, semi-professional output of unglazed pots in rural areas to industrial production in towns. The most elaborate wares were traded over large distances.

Interest in medieval Islamic pottery has focused on western and central Asia and Egypt (not least because many of the major developments took place in these regions), although recently the wares of the Maghreb have received attention. In the ninth and tenth centuries, stimulated in part by the importation of Chinese ceramics, potters in Iraq produced a wide range of tablewares: moulded pots, vessels with opaque white glaze and painted decoration and others covered with green and yellow splashes and sometimes accompanied by scratched ornament, and lustre ware. Lustre ware is decorated over the glaze with metallic oxide, a technique borrowed from the glass-painter that is held to be one of the great achievements of early Islamic potters. It is generally believed that lustre ware came into use in Iraq in the ninth century, and it was being made in Egypt by the end of the tenth century. Meanwhile, potters in Khorasan were making tablewares painted with elegant epigraphic or vegetal motifs under transparent glazes. Pottery of this type is associated with Nishapur and Samarkand (Afrasiab), though there were many other places where it was produced: similar wares have been found in southern Iran at Sirjan and in Afghanistan (Ghazna and Lashkari Bazar).

In the twelfth century Iranian potters developed a white soft paste by adding ground quartz to the clay. Copying T'ang porcelain, they produced thin-walled 'Seljuq white ware' vessels and pots with aubergine, turquoise and bright blue glazes. Decoration was carved or painted under the glaze in bright blue or black. Overglaze ornament, using either lustre or coloured enamels (the so-called *minai* wares, which have meticulous polychrome decoration resembling illuminated manuscripts) was also used. The best-known place of production in Iran was Kashan. Underglaze painting was also popular in Syria (for example, at Raqqa) and in Egypt. Following the Mongol invasion, which terminated production in many places, including Raqqa, Chinese motifs such as the phoenix were introduced. At this time, too, the quality of glazed tiles for architectural ornament reached new standards of excellence.

Like pottery, medieval Islamic glass has attracted the attention of collectors for generations, but it is only recently that material has been recovered from datable archaeological contexts, notably at Fustat and Siraf. In the early Islamic period (between the eighth and the eleventh centuries) we find diamond-incised, wheel-cut, carved and, rarely, *millefiori* decoration, often applied to forms that were already current in the pre-Islamic period. Some of the most distinctive types – for example, the molar flask – have a wide distribution, and it is often difficult to assign unprovenanced pieces to a particular region. A rare decorative technique was painting in lustre. Between the twelfth and the fourteenth centuries the most spectacular Islamic glass was made in Syria (at Aleppo and Damascus) and Egypt. It consisted of drinking vessels, bottles and lamps decorated with polychrome enamel and (perhaps only in Syria) gilding. Some examples are extremely large and elaborately decorated with arabesque motifs and inscriptions.

Metalwork is easier to identify, because a higher proportion of metal objects bear inscriptions, sometimes with dates, than do either pottery or glass. Once more there was considerable continuity from the pre-Islamic period. Indeed, a group of vessels, mostly bronze, from northern Iran combine Sasanian forms and motifs with occasional Arabic inscriptions. A new repertoire of forms appeared in the Seljuq period, when engraved and later inlaid ornament became very elaborate. (Inlaid decoration is produced by hammering metal into prepared grooves in the surface of the vessel.) Examples of later Islamic metalwork in western Asia are uncommon, but the numerous illustrations in contemporary manuscripts confirm that delicate arabesque motifs were extremely common, often combined with small panels containing inscriptions.

Conclusion

The archaeology of Islam is still less developed than the study of written sources, despite the considerable contribution of numismatics, architectural history and the decorative arts. Many of the lands that adopted Islam already had ancient civilizations, and archaeological studies have often concentrated on these earlier periods. The increasing number of later finds from excavated contexts, however, offer new opportunities for detailed analysis and interpretation.

46. Barbarian Europe in the first millennium

The later Iron Age societies of Europe that lay outside the Roman Empire and its major political successors were seen from the Mediterranean as a barbarian hinterland. Recent archaeological research has revealed the complexity of social and economic development behind this traditional description.[1] Some aspects of the period are illuminated by documentary evidence. External observers, such as the military historians and geographers of Late Antiquity, Byzantine historians or Arab travellers of the Viking Age, recorded their impressions of contacts with Germans, Slavs, Avars and Scandinavians. Documents in Latin served the needs of the Christian Church; and chronicles, tribal histories and charters appeared after the conversion to Christianity. Monastic *scriptoria* preserved Antique literature, leading to a renaissance of learning among Franks and Northumbrian Anglo-Saxons from the late seventh century, when monks also edited traditional Germanic law codes and secular poetry. Scandinavian inscriptions first record complex secular information in runic characters in the later Viking Age. The documents help to provide a general chronological and ethnic framework for archaeological material.

Until recently the main sources of archaeological information about the period were studies of cemeteries. Depositing the dead in costume, with possessions reflecting their status, was a common pagan practice. Coins or luxuries imported from areas with a fine, historically based chronology provide chronological fixed points when associated with native material. But such combinations are

46.1: *Europe in the early ninth century: a schematic map showing ethnic consolidation following the migrations of the fifth to seventh centuries. A central bloc of Germanic population, with a Celtic fringe in the north-west, is expanding; the expansion of Scandinavian population in the Viking Age is also shown. To the east a Slav bloc is giving way along its western frontier, but is itself in the process of displacing Finns and Balts to the north and east. In the Danube basin the Eurasian Avars will be replaced politically by the Magyars.*

	boundary of Roman empire 2nd century AD
	boundary of Byzantine empire c.628
	boundary of Carolingian empire c.814
	Germans
	Scandinavians
	Scandinavian settlement
	Celts
	West Slavs
	East Slavs
	South Slavs
	Balts

largely restricted to graves of an upper social class, and their representative character is debatable. Unscientific discovery produced great quantities of artifacts, and only recently have demographic and social studies been undertaken on large excavated cemeteries. Artifacts in regular combinations, especially dress ensembles, provide the basis for studying chronological change, tribal groupings and trade contacts. In cremation burials the effects of fire and the selection of surviving fragments for burial systematically distorts our view of the wealth available to communities practising this rite. After conversion to Christianity, both cremation and the deposition of grave goods were forbidden, which changed the basis of the material evidence for such groups.

Many excavated settlements represent failures on marginal land lacking stratigraphy and finds, while the more successful lie inaccessible under their successors. Systematic excavation of deep, stratified urban sites and of open settlements is an important post-war development, especially the study of naturally defined settlement areas (*Siedlungskammern*) combining excavation, sampling and environmental investigation. Notable research has been carried out on such processes as the fifth-century abandonment of parts of northern Germany; changing settlement hierarchy in northern Poland associated with the tenth-century rise of the Piast dynasty; and the long development of urban communities such as Winchester and York.

Population history

Between the first and the early fifth centuries Roman frontiers based largely on the Rhine and the Danube were a barrier to the kind of folk movements from the north that had occurred in the earlier Iron Age. In Free Germany – broadly, a bloc of land between the rivers Rhine, Oder and middle Danube, including Scandinavia – there were Germanic groups who shared a common language. Tribes of different size formed ephemeral confederations; from the third century such groups as Franks and Saxons are known. Population expanded in a phase of favourable climate and developing economy. Migration occurred: the Goths, for example, moved from the Baltic in the second century and established control of the lower Danube and south Russia in the fourth; in the later third century the Alemanni occupied Roman territory between the upper Rhine and the Danube. Further east, in present Poland and the Ukraine, were groups later known as Slavs, while the Danube plain had a mixed population, including Eurasian nomads, Germans and Celtic groups. In the later fourth century pressure from Eurasian nomads caused a western movement of the Goths, who broke the Danube frontier to escape; one such group, the Huns, established an ephemeral empire and threatened western Europe until the 450s. The Rhine frontier broke irreparably in 406, and in 410 Rome was sacked by Vandals. In the fifth century western Europe was a mosaic of allied tribal armies, tribes occupying and settling new territories, and local sub-Roman administrations that often employed Germanic mercenaries. In areas such as southern Gaul land was divided between provincial

landowners and newcomers who preserved local organization. Oases of peace and local prosperity occurred, and in some areas the takeover from local administration was more political and relatively peaceful, and the local population survived. During the fifth to seventh centuries Germanic tribes progressively abandoned some areas, moving to occupy the territories of the former Roman Empire and to establish tribal kingdoms. Their numbers and relations with the native population varied. In southern and eastern Britain the Germanic takeover was a relatively slow, peasant land-taking, extending into the ninth century and opposed by shrinking Celtic kingdoms in the west and north. In Gaul, by contrast, takeover was rapid. Areas of the north-east had been settled from the mid-fourth century by Franks acting as land-based defensive troops within the Empire. Where Germanic troops were settled, here and in other provinces, more Roman institutions survived. By the early sixth century the Franks were dominant, having conquered the other Germanic tribes in Gaul; co-operation with the Romano-Gallic aristocracy and the adoption of Catholicism made them powerful. Dynasties of Merovingian, then Carolingian, kings conquered the other Germans and created an empire based on the power of a land-holding aristocracy and its followers. An aggressive foreign policy brought them into conflict, in the late eighth century, with Slavs, Avars, Danes and Muslims. The Vandals in North Africa were a short-lived military caste who also became pirates; in Italy the Byzantine empire held the southern part of the peninsula after struggles with the Ostrogoths from 476 and the Lombards from 568; in Spain the Visigoths, long harassed by the Byzantine empire, were conquered by Muslim Arabs in the early eighth century.

During the fifth and sixth centuries Slavs moved westwards from present Poland and the Ukraine because of pressure first from Huns, then from Bulgars and Avars. Occupying agricultural areas abandoned by the Germans, they rapidly reached the Elbe, Saale and Maine rivers, absorbing relict Germanic populations in some areas in the west and north-west. Their initial uniformity disintegrated as peasant groups consolidated into tribes and federations, developing economically and politically at different rates. As in western Europe, advanced states based on military conquest developed: in Moravia (Czechoslovakia) in the eighth and ninth, and in Poland during the ninth and tenth centuries. In the mid-sixth century Avars moved from the steppe and settled in the Danube plain, forming a wedge between the western Slavs and those who had migrated southwards into the Balkans (see Chapter 49). Their semi-oriental state was broken up by Charlemagne in the 790s and the remnants conquered by another Turkic group, the Magyars, in the late ninth century.[2] These horsemen raided deep into western Europe in the early tenth century and subjugated Greater Moravia. After they were crushed in 955 they settled largely in present-day Hungary.

Scandinavia developed internally as population expanded, leading to colonization on the east Baltic coast before a massive population explosion westwards in the late eighth to tenth centuries. Peasant populations migrated to Iceland and the Scottish islands, and to northern and eastern England, often settling on secondary land in populated areas and increasing their prosperity, while small, permanent settlements were established as far west as Greenland. Petty kingdoms based on towns of craftsmen and traders were founded or extended by Scandinavians, from Dublin and York to Ladoga and Kiev. As they settled and became amenable to political influence from outside, Christianity was increasingly introduced into Scandinavia. While reconquest by local political forces soon occurred in some areas, the linguistic effects and the widespread economic stimulus of the new population remained.[3]

Social and economic development

Because of its own weakness, the Western Roman Empire progressively lost territory to Germanic tribes who were transformed both socially and economically from the third century. The subsequent folk migrations disrupted these developments, and removed the broad economic stimulus provided by the Empire. Influenced by Byzantine policies, political consolidation in northern Europe led to the formation of petty kingdoms among Celts, Germans and Slavs. Based on agricultural potential and good communications, areas of wealth and political power began to be established that were later to dominate medieval Europe. Populations gradually ceased to be tribally based, and national states started to emerge. Social stratification became more formalized and hierarchies of obligation controlled by king and warriors developed. Deep raids by land and sea into western Europe, from the late eighth to late tenth centuries, tended to consolidate the power of magnates who acted for the king in levying taxes and defending local districts.

A steady population pressure following the redistribution of the migrating peoples increased the extent of agricultural settlement and woodland clearances; settlements became more fixed and local continuity more common.[4] Artificial fields were built up on some poor soils; systematic improvement by dunging became more widespread; and crop rotation made fields more productive. Rye introduced progressively northwards was suitable for the wetter, colder climates. Iron was increasingly extracted from local bog ores, and tools for hunting, fishing and agriculture became more widely available and more effective. The heavy plough was more widely used in opening up heavier soils that the ard could not cultivate. Animal traction, especially that of the horse, made ploughing faster and land transport more efficient. Improvement of fords and roads occurred at the very end of the period.

The rural population became fixed to the land. Social and economic development proceeded in a mosaic pattern with increasing rapidity from the eighth century. Increasing aggregations of population, in craft-working or marketing centres, developed into towns under royal control.[5] The definition of a town based on historical criteria is inadequate to describe the archaeological evidence of the long, complex development of historically known centres. Long-distance, luxury trade based on towns, through which great profits could be made, increased in volume. The economy of northern Europe, which had been stimulated by Roman and Byzantine gold into the seventh century, was increasingly influenced by silver traded from the east, then looted from Anglo-Saxon England, which circulated widely from the ninth century and facilitated local trade as well as high-value transactions. By AD 1000 native silver commercial coinages had been widely adopted. Craft activities became more specialized as the range of natural resources worked into consumer products increased. Mass production of pottery, costume jewellery and other accessories developed, as well as the manufacture of luxuries.

The defence of the kingdoms of Denmark and of Mercia in England from the eighth century, by great earth ramparts and the creation of defended towns as strongpoints, reflects the concentration of resources of early states. By the early eleventh century Catholic Christianity dominated western and central Europe, supporting the Church's secular organization. Ecclesiastical buildings in stone often appeared soon after conversion.[6]

The Roman Iron Age to c. 425

Provincial Roman artifacts circulated widely beyond the frontiers in Free Germany, with growing effects on the expanding native population and developing economy. The period takes its name from this cultural influence, which greatly increased from the later second century. Diplomatic activity created buffer states along the frontiers and allies beyond; technical assistance was provided for friends and hospitality for exiles from hostile tribes. As the provinces weakened, Germanic raids increased – from the later third century, lands between the upper Rhine and the Danube were occupied by an Alemannic confederation. The numbers of Germans in Roman service increased, and individuals reached high administrative positions. In the army German mercenary troops were used increasingly, sometimes based on town garrisons, while groups of prisoners or communities of refugees were settled to cultivate and defend depopulated territory.

Roman provincial styles of coiffure and armament, military belt sets and hoards of Roman gold coins appeared in Free Germany, while costume jewellery testified to strong connections between north-eastern Gaul and north-western Germany from the later fourth century.

The prestige of rich farmers and local chiefs was expressed by the rich provincial Roman imports deposited in their graves, and imported gold and silver were melted down for native jewellery. In the early phase sets of items came from Mediterranean workshops, while after about AD 200 an increasing volume of mass-produced material came from Danubian and Rhineland provinces and the Eastern Empire. Trade was associated with the river systems flowing northwards and eastwards from key frontier entrepôts to the Baltic. Sea transport across the Baltic or North Sea led to Scandinavia, where boat-houses along the Norwegian coast date from the fourth century onwards. Objects spread widely from hand to hand, while the political situation dictated changes in the direction of major trade routes. The rich Baltic islands were transit areas as well as great consumers, as were areas of Czechoslovakia. In the later Roman period trans-shipment centres emerged in strategic locations where craftwork was also practised. Trade was associated with rich families and with their control of agricultural surplus and craft production. Near the frontiers there was short-distance bulk trading; Roman coins circulated as exchange units. Lava quernstones, fine pottery and cheap jewellery were traded, presumably in exchange for foodstuffs, leather and cloth. Internal production for trade was stimulated. In southern Jutland iron-working settlements exploited bog iron to satisfy the increasing demand for tools and weapons. Cloth appears to have improved in quality and leather-working to have intensified. Settlement in Scandinavia expanded, associated with the exploitation of iron and fur, and its wealth in the late Roman and Migration periods reflects special contacts. At Helgö in east-central Sweden, a redistribution centre for luxury imports, iron from a variety of Swedish sources was worked in a

46.2: *Schematic development of the Roman Iron Age village-mound of Feddersen Wierde, near Cuxhaven, in the German Federal Republic. The original linear arrangement expanded to a radial plan around an open area. After a slow decline, caused by increasing salinity of the soil through flooding, the village was abandoned in the early fifth century. The latest phase of metal and pottery here can be paralleled in south-east England.*

initial settlement, mid 1st century BC

early 1st century AD

early 2nd century AD

3rd century

early 5th century before abandonment

8th/9th century resettlement

water channel

peat deposits

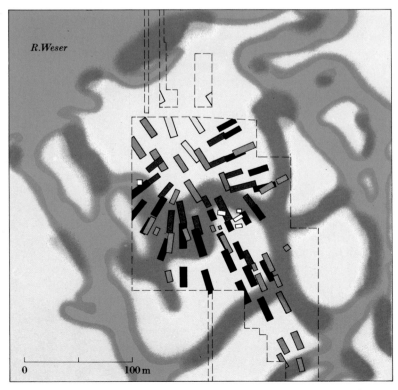

46.3: *The Slav village of Tornow, Brandenburg, German Democratic Republic. The plan shows the first phase of occupation, which took place in the seventh to eighth centuries. The open village has a defended burg attached.*

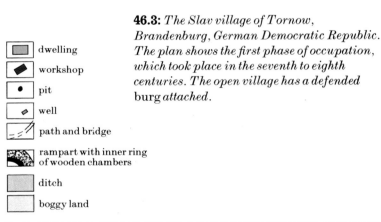

dwelling

workshop

pit

well

path and bridge

rampart with inner ring of wooden chambers

ditch

boggy land

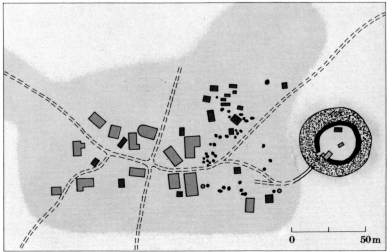

non-agricultural settlement.

Settlement was rural, in individual farmsteads or hamlets. One basic unit consisted largely of timber-built dwellings, outbuildings, some of which might be partly dug into the ground (*Grubenhaüser*), post-built rectangular granaries, hayricks, wells and ovens. One type of building, the 'three-aisled longhouse' had dwelling space, working area and cattle stalls placed laterally under one roof, which was carried on pairs of weight-bearing posts. Some units were stockaded, while others were isolated and unenclosed. Village-like communities developed, mainly from the third century, when regular, block-like dispositions developed in some communities from less complex units. In Jutland mounds occupied over many centuries have settlements successively stratified, showing a stable, dense population. On the southern coastal marshes of the North Sea basin settlement mounts (*Wurten* or *Terpen*), built against the encroachment of the sea, adopted a radial arrangement, which suggests local organization. Marked differences in wealth developed, apparent from the varying numbers of cattle stalls and granaries and the appearance of dwellings whose occupants partly

engaged in craft activity. On poorer soils settlements 'wandered' randomly over several hectares during the whole period, while others shifted position regularly in one direction or were abandoned. (In the late fourth and early fifth centuries political factors led to widespread abandonment in many areas.) In southern Scandinavia unrest is reflected in the overshadowing of bog 'sacrifices' of an agricultural nature – tools, vessels, costume jewellery – by massive dumps of mutilated weapons, riding equipment and their gold or silver fittings.

A similar pattern emerges from cemetery evidence – a gradual population expansion, further stratification of society, creation of new settlements, then the widespread impoverishment of some communities and the abandonment of many. Cremation predominated in the early phase, and in areas of north Germany, where it persisted, great flat urnfields with characteristic pottery define tribal groupings. According to the size of the community and the length of use, some cemeteries exceeded ten thousand burials. From the Christian Roman provinces and southern Scandinavia the rite of inhumation spread. In some Germanic groups it was associated with high-prestige burials, of men, women and children, in elaborate chambers or mounds containing rich imported goods or weapons. An internationalism of taste can be seen in outstandingly rich early Roman burials from Slovakia to southern Norway, while in the later phase more local groups emerged with preferred variants, who were buried in small

46.4: *One of a pair of shoulder clasps from the baldric (a belt or girdle worn across the chest) of King Redwald of East Anglia, buried c. 625 in a ship at Sutton Hoo, Suffolk, England. Millefiori glass squares, garnet translucent with hatched gold-foil backing, filigree and granulation all contribute to the rich polychrome effect. Profiled, interlaced or biting animals form a profusion of cryptic zoomorphic decoration. The obvious command of craftsmanship and wealth of imported materials all contributed to the prestige of the wearer.*

46.5: *Rich Roman provincial imports of the third and fourth centuries from a cemetery of prosperous farmers at Himlingøje, Sjaelland, Denmark. The drinking of imported wine was accompanied by sumptuous silver, bronze and glass tableware and specialized vessels such as strainers.*

cemeteries, sometimes separate from the general community.[7]

Migration and early consolidation, c. 400–50

The social effects of the migration westwards of whole tribes and their contact with relict populations accentuated the earlier appearance of the rich warrior. Society was highly stratified, and laws codified later indicate the monetary value attached to each level. Status was reflected in the range of costume jewellery and accessories buried with the dead, and sharp differences between communities appeared. Cemeteries ranging from tens to hundreds of burials record changes in fashion for glass, pottery and metal vessels, and in male and female costume, while regular assemblages define rank as well as tribal affinity. Status cannot be automatically related to riches, although rich graves must have belonged to leaders of society. These may have formed the focus of a regular cemetery or of a separate family group attached to an estate, while others appear entirely isolated, sometimes under mounds. Cemeteries such as the Frankish were regularly laid out in rows (*Reihengräberfriedhöfe*), copying late Roman practice. Rich graves were sometimes robbed in Antiquity, although translations to hallowed ground occurred. Christians were not allowed grave goods, but a series of burials with rich accessories in churches reflects the ambiguity of the early conversion of magnates. The Church's urban organization often persisted, and churches and cemeteries in some Gallic areas survived in use. The conversion of Germanic kings, often for political reasons, was the result of aggressive proselytization. The monasteries, many of which were endowed with land by kings and nobles, flourished as centres of learning from the seventh century. Considerable population survival accounts for the continuity of Late Antique traditions within some Frankish areas.

Settlement was largely rural, ranging from village-like communities to small groups of dwellings, each with its cluster of working huts or outhouses. A seventh-century royal site at Yeavering, Northumberland, revealed a complex of carefully constructed timber halls, assembly area and hillfort. House plans varied widely in construction and size, reflecting different social or economic conditions. Many settlements are known only from their cemeteries: some were noble estates; others, apparently inferior, had very little outside contact or wealth.

The Anglo-Saxon poem *Beowulf* suggests how some famed weapons and precious objects passed from kings and among the warrior caste according to complex social relationships. Exile, marriage gifts and baptismal presents account for the transport of others, while foreign costume jewellery ensembles in a community indicate exogamy. Luxury trade brought Indian ivory, Red Sea cowrie shells and Byzantine bronze vessels over the Alps and down the Rhine, even to northern Norway. Red garnet, cut to complex shapes that enriched Germanic polychrome jewellery, was imported for a time, perhaps from Persia. From the later fourth century Roman and Byzantine bullion was the source of the richness of such jewellery. Imitative gold coinage used for high-value transactions was struck in the Germanic kingdoms of Gaul and the Mediterranean. The exhaustion of imported noble metals in northern and western Europe marks the end of the long transition from the Late Antique period. Coinage began to be heavily debased from the early seventh century, while Arab pirates disrupted high-value trade across the Mediterranean. Within the territories of the former Western Empire some towns were deserted; others functioned as local refuges inhabited by squatters or were farmed within the walls. Some were seats of royal and ecclesiastical power and became centres for craftsmen, who often carried on the luxury industries for their new masters, while early documents refer to foreign traders in such old towns. These activities, limited in area and scale, partly preserved the sites and certain of the functions of some Roman provincial towns until economic, administrative and religious complexity led to their development. It was prosperity during the late seventh and eighth centuries that encouraged the growth of new, undefended trading settlements along the English Channel, the North Sea and in southern Scandinavia, which acted as entrepôts at strategic points. In Anglo-Saxon England the need to resist Viking raids and to reconquer

46.6: *An intricately carved and elaborately constructed wooden waggon from the early ninth-century royal ship burial at Oseberg, Norway. Among the motifs are scenes that can be identified from Scandinavian mythology. The wealth of artistic expression in organic materials now perished can only be guessed at from rare surviving complexes such as that found in this burial.*

occupied territory was a further stimulus in the creation of a net-work of defended refuges (*burhs*) that served as mints, markets and administrative centres.

Ireland and Pictish Scotland lay beyond the Empire, and the Celtic uplands of Wales and Cornwall were not deeply Romanized. In the post-Roman period there were migrations from Ireland eastwards, and from Cornwall to Brittany. Anglo-Saxon invaders precipitated some westward movement, but the local population was increasingly absorbed as they progressed further north and west. Local war leaders dominated a stratified society, some developing petty kingdoms. Grave memorials inscribed in native Ogham script or barbaric Latin record some of their names. Their seats were centres of craftworking and sporadic trade in wine, oil, and exotic pottery from the Mediterranean and south-western France. Based on hillforts, some of which were refortified pre-historic structures, their timber gates and superstructures some-times copied Roman models. Some preserved a sub-Roman existence in former provincial towns. Exotic contacts may have been partly connected with the Church, which had developed a regional form from Roman origins. Isolated stone cells, monas-teries and chapels in dry-stone forms are characteristic. Surviving material culture is relatively poor and simple around the Irish Sea, while little is known of rural farmsteads, except in areas where stone enclosures and small huts are preserved. Of the Picts little remains except their pictorial art on grave memorials.[8]

Scandinavia, c. 400–1000

In southern Scandinavia piracy and warfare in the late fourth and fifth centuries were characterized by unclaimed hoards, the abandonment of farms and the creation of refuges or regularly defended settlements away from the coast. Continuing population growth led to internal expansion, the exploitation of resources and exploration eastwards, across the Baltic. Centres of political power and wealth emerged where international contacts in prestige jewellery and foreign trade were maintained. Styles of animal art developed independently and vigorously throughout the period, and from the mid-eighth century craft and trade centres developed. In the later eighth century western Norwegian popula-tions began to settle Atlantic islands and to raid Britain, while silver coins from the Muslim East appeared in eastern Sweden. In the ninth and tenth centuries Vikings penetrated eastern and western Europe across the open sea and along deep rivers. Their tactics exploited the opportunities of the moment. In the west military defence was weak: raids developed in populated areas, from hit-and-run infiltrations to the creation of bases for system-atic looting, sometimes followed by large-scale permanent settle-ment. In Dublin and York urban trading communities ruled by Viking kings dominated the countryside, while in Normandy and eastern England a Viking population settled densely on the land. Scandinavians prospected the western Atlantic as far as New-foundland and Greenland, and established rural colonies there and

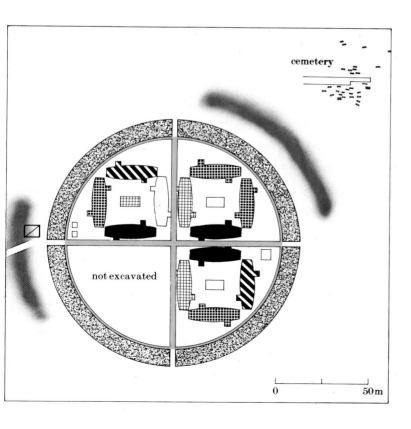

46.7: *The late tenth-century ring-fort of Fyrkat, near Hobro, Jutland, Denmark. The variety of functions undertaken on these strategically situated sites (there are four of very similar construction) perhaps reflects their use as royal strongpoints for administration. The command of resources for their construction, and the need for their services in controlling the country, are marks of a growing centralized power in Denmark.*

dwelling

smithy

fine-metal workshop

store, stable

use uncertain

ditch

rampart

guardhouse

wooden roadway

in Iceland. Lacking military superiority in the east, Swedes exploited the great Polish and Russian waterway systems to trade as far as Byzantium itself. For furs, swords and slaves they obtained silks, luxury manufactures and, above all, silver in vast quantities. In bazaars such as those at Bolgar and Itil they came into contact with the Far East and raided into the Caspian. With Finns and Slavs, Scandinavians catalysed existing trade routes and, where possible, took over local institutions. The extent of Scandinavian political influence in the innovation of political units, particularly among the eastern Slavs, has been contested in the 'Normanist controversy', but there are similarities in the opportunism of Scandinavian activity in east and west, as well as in their ready adoption of native fashions.

The introduction into Scandinavia of mobile silver wealth accentuated economic and social change leading to political centralization. Towns developed under royal protection from earlier trading settlements, notably Birka in east-central Sweden and Hedeby (Haithabu) in southern Denmark. Harbour palisades, and massive earthworks enclosing areas of 12 and 24 hectares respectively, defended them from the tenth century onwards. A range of specialized craft activities developed here, exploiting local resources and imported materials and stimulated by silver hacked into fragments for small transactions. Densely packed and regularly arranged, the towns housed workshops of traders and craftsmen producing standardized goods in bulk. Cemeteries show the density of population of these towns and their wealth in luxuries, imports and weapons, compared with rural settlements. Birka so relied on the east that when trade routes were interrupted in the 970s it collapsed. The rich and free farmers of Gotland exploited its central Baltic position in trade with east and west. Settlements in small units was overwhelmingly agricultural; only from the eleventh century did widespread village-like communities appear, associated with specialized activities such as fishing or manufacturing. Rural subsistence activities were supplemented by furs, skins for ropes, walrus ivory for carving and other tradeable material such as feathers, soapstone and wax. Exploitation of bog-iron deposits to meet the growing demand for tools and other equipment encouraged new settlement in harsh regions, and iron blanks were widely traded, leading to great improvements in

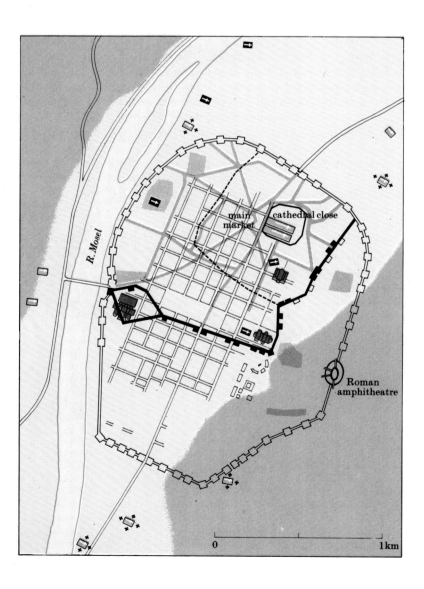

46.8: *Schematic summary of the survival of the Roman walled city of Trier, German Federal Republic, into the early medieval period. While the street pattern changed to meet the new utilization of land within the walls, some administrative and religious buildings retained their status and formed a new nucleus.*

Roman town wall
Roman street plan
church founded in Roman period
major Roman buildings reused in early medieval period
extent of town *c.*1100
medieval town wall
principal medieval roads
early medieval settlements
church founded in early medieval period
graves of early medieval period

technology. Surplus foodstuffs were needed to support urban communities, and quality grain may have been traded from the southern Baltic to supplement taxed or traded local produce.

In the Viking period regular sea and river communications were maintained over greater distances than ever before. The development of long ships resulted in keeled, clinker-built bodies strengthened by frames and propelled by sail as well as oars. Long, open-sea crossings were possible, and the shallow draft of these boats permitted both beaching on open shelving coasts and deep river penetration. The range of vessels found in an early eleventh-century blockade at Skuldelev, Denmark, put into context boats found in important Viking burials. The late development of broad, deep, cargo vessels required deep-water anchorage, making former harbours inadequate.[9]

The western Slavs, c. 500–1000
The issue of the early origins of the Slavs, and the archaeological groups that can be identified with them during the Roman Iron Age, is controversial. Much of Poland and the western Ukraine may then have been occupied by proto-Slavs, identifiable with groups who buried their dead in cremation pits and whose homeland may have been the Warthe–Dnieper region. These groups were stimulated by trade in provincial Roman imports: in southern Poland iron was mined in large quantities; wheel-turned pottery was produced; and from the third century there was considerable prosperity. The first identifiable peasant groups pressing north and west appear in Slovakia from the early fifth century. Some early migrants are associated with simple pottery in cremations whose lack of metalwork makes their chronology obscure. In general, identifiable Slav burials are poorly furnished and inhumation was widely practised even before conversion. Cultural groupings are based largely on pottery and settlement forms, while tribal attribution rests on a broad continuity of occupation until names are recorded historically. Geographically, the western Slavs were open to foreign influence and attack, which especially affected the development of border tribes: Franks and Germans, with their aggressive Catholic religion, pressed along the western frontier; Byzantine diplomacy and Orthodox religion came from the south and strongly influenced the culture of Greater Moravia, which lay between the two; Scandinavians settled in towns along the south Baltic coast; and commercial warfare as well as peaceful trade between the emerging states occurred from the early ninth century.

A widespread settlement form was the *burg* or defended settlement (also characteristic of the Balts), which often lay at the centre of a group of open, agricultural, village-like settlements that remained largely undifferentiated in wealth and complexity until the eleventh century. Their timber-built houses, or structures partly dug in the ground, varied according to tribal affinity. The long-house of Germanic tradition, related to the extended family group, was absent. Early *burgs* were protected by a palisade, later by a more substantial earth-and-timber rampart, even stone-faced. They vary in size from 30 metres in diameter to an area of 3 to 5 hectares. The size and function of the *burg* were determined by its level of social and economic development and its local topography, as well as by its relationship with other *burgs* and with its hinterland. No chronological development is applicable to the morphology of *burgs* over wide areas. A hierarchy is generally visible, from large tribal centre, to agricultural community, to noble seat. Rapid political change may be seen, for example, in the replacement of a large defended settlement by a small military enclosure dominating open settlements. Development is evident from the elaboration of defences and the extent of the area enclosed. Often a *vorburg*, or subsidiary area, defended less important social elements. Within the mosaic of political and economic development in western Slav areas the earliest advanced state was Greater Moravia. The central settlement of Mikulčice contained five stone churches and a stone 'palace', while a *vorburg* contained well-built wooden houses for retainers and craftsmen engaged in luxury production. At Staré Mesto settlement peripheral to the centre covered over 400 square kilometres, involving specialized subsistence activities and metalworking. Rich burials around and in stone churches show in jewellery and weapons the eclectic styles of craftsmen in the service of the ruling families.

The concentration and protection of craftsmen making prestige goods and the domination of long-distance luxury trade began in the eighth century. On the south Baltic coast *burgs* on protected river estuaries near the coast developed early, some exploiting salt production and Baltic trade. The range of crafts developed in their workshops is similar to that in Scandinavia, and links are represented by Scandinavian traders, sometimes buried in separate cemeteries. From the ninth century trade with the east in furs and slaves, which took traders up the Polish rivers to Kiev and beyond, brought silver in increasing quantities. Hoards of hack-silver, especially cut-up jewellery and beads or Kufic coins, indicate the commercial importance of silver in small transactions. As trade expanded, a network of towns developed to serve marketing and administrative needs both along the main international trade routes and in hinterland areas. Local trade involving furs, foodstuffs, millstones and iron blanks developed in intensity, and craftsmen acquired greater expertise in the production of pottery, iron and steel items and silver jewellery. Transport by dug-out canoe is evidenced, and clinker-built boats are known from the ninth century. The major overland route, Kiev–Krakow–Prague–Mainz, brought increasing urbanization to southern Poland and central Europe.[10]

Conclusion
By the early eleventh century centralized kingdoms, with defended towns as centres of trade, tax and administration, were developing strongly in northern Europe. The power of the Christian Church too, often adopted for political reasons, supported the secular political hierarchy. This mosaic development was the prelude to the institutions of the developed European medieval period.

47. The rise of temperate Europe

Considered overall, the economy of Europe during the Middle Ages was certainly one of expansion. Nevertheless, medieval economies were no more immune than their modern equivalents to pronounced fluctuations of fortune; and while many of these were merely temporary, with a regional impact alone, a longer-term cycle can also be recognized, from expansion through recession to recovery. The charting of this cycle has been a preoccupation of economic historians since the days of that great Belgian scholar, Henri Pirenne. Both in outline and in some of its details, scholarly conjecture is now finding confirmation in archaeology.

Economic growth

A population recovery was essential to the emergence of the West from its barbarian 'Dark Ages'. Already detectable in the late seventh and early eighth centuries, it became especially pronounced some four centuries later and reached its peak about 1300.

At no point is this recovery easy to quantify; yet it is clear even as early as the late eleventh century that certain of the more favoured areas in western Europe were showing signs of progressive overcrowding. The Domesday Survey of Anglo-Norman England, compiled in 1086–7, establishes that this was already the case in parts of East Anglia and in Kent, with another concentration along England's southern coast. Domesday Book, moreover, recorded a population not at the end of its cycle of growth but very much nearer the beginning.

It is not yet certain what brought about this growth, but some of the answers are probably to be found in improvements in agricultural technology. The heavy quadrangular-framed wheeled plough, with a refined fixed mould-board for turning the furrow, had made an appearance in northern Europe by AD 700 at the latest. It required a large plough-team to pull it, making it better suited to the broader sweeps of land that had been newly enclosed than to the small square fields of existing settlements. Yet forest clearance and the reclamation of waste were just then beginning to characterize European society. As settlement spread outwards and open-field farming was more generally adopted, with such additional improvements as three-field crop rotation and the development of a more efficient fixed-collar harness for horses, the opportunities for the production of a marketable surplus on the land continued to multiply through the centuries.

These surpluses were, of course, by any modern standards, still far from adequate. Crop yields were diminutive, and a single bad season could leave the peasant cultivator with little more than his seed for the next year. Nevertheless, there are other signs of a conjunction of circumstances in these centuries that was uniquely favourable to growth. Throughout early medieval Europe the plagues and other epidemics of Late Antiquity had either retreated or died out altogether. Leprosy, it is true, had only lately found a home there, and leper houses, constructed for the isolation of its victims, became in due course an essential adjunct of every major European town. However, the heavy mortalities of the sixth-century plagues were not to be repeated in the medieval West before the 'Great Dying' of the mid-fourteenth century, otherwise known as the Black Death. Moreover, these relatively disease-free years through the early and the central Middle Ages coincided fortuitously with what is now recognized by historians of climate as a warm epoch, characterized by some centuries of seasonal stability. At best, the dry summers and mild winters of the period before 1250 brought temperature rises of little more than between a half and one degree centigrade, with a reduction in rainfall of approximately 10 per cent.[1] Yet the generally favourable conditions of the climatic optimum were sufficient to encourage archaeologically verifiable settlement in, and cultivation of, such naturally harsh environments as Iceland in the late ninth century and Greenland before the end of the tenth. Overall, the advance of the plough in medieval Europe over areas previously uncultivated has not been equalled since.

Beyond the frontiers of modern farming, on exposed hillsides and in those regions now given over to woodland and to scrub, traces of medieval cultivation are still obvious. Most eloquent of these are the forest-swamped churches of the middle and lower Rhineland, overgrown and long since abandoned. Surrounded by the ridges and furrows of former open-field arable farming, they are all that survives of a medieval movement of clearance and enclosure that lasted only as long as population pressure forced men to put their labour into the less productive soils. Throughout Europe these forgotten Black Forest settlements have many parallels in the thousands of deserted or shrunken villages that confirm a wholesale retreat from the margin. They mark the furthest extent of the colonizing drive that had accompanied population expansion.

From the beginning, clearance and colonization frequently resulted from the deliberate initiative of a lord. Thus the resettlement of the north of England after William the Conqueror's ravages was at least in part the work of great landowners like the Anglo-Norman priors of Durham,[2] while seigneurial pressure in its early stages is the most likely explanation of the first clearance and cultivation of the Black Forest.[3] In just the same way, heavy capital expenditure on major projects of drainage and irrigation – in Flanders, on the south and east coasts of England, along the Po valley in northern Italy and elsewhere – required both resources and a capacity for planning that put them beyond the reach of the peasant. Inevitably, it has been these large-scale works that have left their mark most obviously on the landscape, whether in the irrigation channels of the Naviglio Grande in Lombardy or in the surviving embankments on the Pevensey Levels in coastal Sussex, erected contemporaneously by the English monks of Battle to protect their estates from the sea. However, the public works of the late twelfth and the thirteenth centuries, impressive though some of them are, preserve little more than the surface expression of a very much more general movement of enclosure and reclamation in which the individual peasant, with his small-scale assart (arable land won from the forest or marsh), was then just as likely to be engaged.

Place-name evidence from those many regions of medieval Europe where a living could still be won by forest clearance establishes the foundation, between the eleventh and thirteenth centuries, of a mass of satellite settlements, which recruited originally from existing villages and contributed a new element of their own to the cultivated land stock of the West. An exact measurement of the expansion is impossible; however, it has been suggested that this outward drive, by peasant and lord, increased the cultivable area of northern Europe by something like a third. Nor does this total include the substantial contribution that woodland won from the forest or marsh), was then just as likely to be made to the thirteenth-century economy.

In part, the peasant drive to cultivate the waste may be seen as an act of desperation: there was nowhere else that a man of slight means might go. Yet it reflects too the social pressures that had intensified with the development of a lordship clearly definable in law and with the spread of manorialization. The aristocracy of Europe is not as old as it sometimes claims to be, and in France, for one, the formation and definition of the seigneuries was still in progress well into the eleventh century. What the assarting peasant could hope to avoid, in the relative freedom of the forest, was the tightening control of a new race of landowners, professionally organized for war.

The knight, with his lance, his armour and his horse, has a secure place in every schoolboy's medieval mythology. Yet in fact he emerged somewhat late in the day, when the feudal society with which he is usually associated in the myth was neither young nor particularly effective. The social acceptability of the mounted warrior, in effect the ennoblement of the knight, can now be dated with some precision to the century between 950 and 1050.[4] And it was in those years, both in France and in Germany, that a local dynastic aristocracy, much engaged in the practice of private war, developed at the expense of the crown. Essentially, the product of warfare at this level was the private fortress, or castle, the contemporary diffusion of which over the whole face of Europe was to become the symbol of a major reordering of society.

Earthwork fortresses, characterized by their steep castle mounds and their enclosed lower courts, or baileys, have been identified and excavated in many parts of what was formerly the medieval West. On occasion the mounds have been shown to have enclosed structures of some elaboration, securely founded on the original ground surface below. Nevertheless, the essential characteristics of castles such as these remained simplicity of design and cheapness of construction, which brought them within the reach of a very broad sector of the nobility. They required only those

47.1: *Château Gaillard, Normandy, France, built for Richard I of England between 1196 and 1198, is one of the earliest of the great concentrically planned castles that were beginning to be built in the West, usually under royal patronage, towards the end of the twelfth century. Based on the lessons of Richard's own experience while on crusade in the Holy Land, Château Gaillard embodied many of the latest ideas in castle building, chief among these being the virtues of multiple defences and the reduced importance of the keep.*

resources readily available to a landowner, and they could be put up quickly to defend an estate, to meet the crisis of the moment.

The so-called 'motte-and-bailey' earthwork castle of eleventh- and twelfth-century Europe reflects very precisely the social chaos of its times. It belongs, along with the quarrelsome aristocracy with which it is usually associated, to a period of loose-reined government, postdating the collapse of the remnants of royal authority in the West and preceding the emergence of strong national kingdoms, particularly the kingdom of France. Of course, such an aggressive manifestation of wealth without responsibility could not be allowed to last. In the eleventh century the Church had found alternative outlets for warlike energies in the crusade against Islam, while doing its best, by example and instruction, to outlaw private war. A century later the national kings – the Angevins in England, the Capetians in France, the Hohenstaufens

in Germany and in Italy – were in a position to take the initiativ for themselves. The expensive stone fortresses of the late twelft and the thirteenth centuries were usually, though not exclusively royal works. If not built by the king or by members of his family they could be put up only with the explicit permission of th crown. Castle building had been brought, however imperfectly under government control.

The increasing cost and sophistication of castle building, now accessible only to the magnates, found its parallel throughout th propertied classes in more elaborate domestic provision. I became common, from quite early in the thirteenth century, fo the domestic quarters (even those on a modest estate) to be con structed of stone, with a roof of slate or tile. Private chamber might be floored with tiles and lined with wainscot; they could b furnished with side-wall fireplaces and with screens and glaze

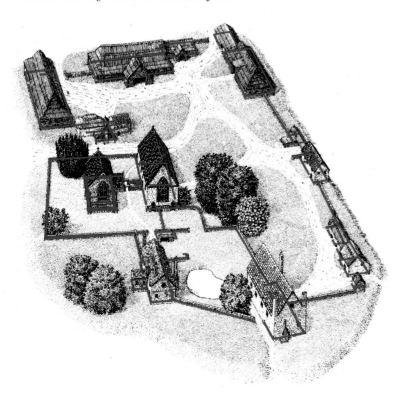

47.2: *One of the consequences of agricultural expansion in thirteenth-century Europe was heavy investment in farm buildings. The Templar estate-centre at South Witham, England, reconstructed here from excavated evidence, was abandoned early in the fourteenth century. It has preserved with unusual completeness the plan of a large thirteenth-century manorial demesne farm.*

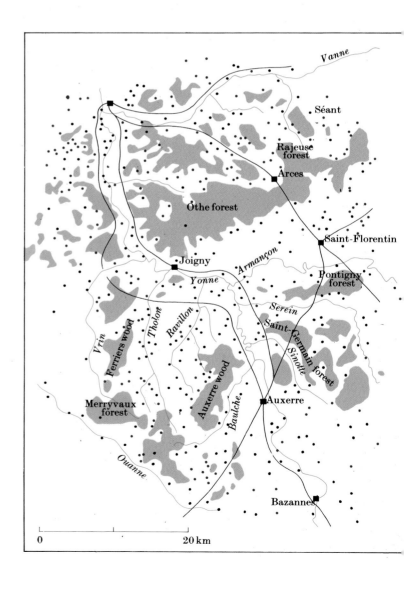

windows to keep out the worst of the draughts. Out in the farm-yard, the improvement of farm buildings was recognizably a product of thirteenth-century agricultural expansion, as rising prices and falling wages (both the consequence of excessive population growth) promoted considerable seigneurial invest-ment in the land. Chief among its monuments are the great cathedral-like barns – Ter Doest in Flanders, for example, or Great Coxwell and St Leonard's in England – with which the wealthier of the monastic houses saw fit to equip their estates. Indeed, the monks themselves were at the heart of the expansion, from which they drew their essential support.

As it happened, a new wave of monastic reform and renewal had begun before the end of the eleventh century, inspired by the radical changes then taking place in the papacy under the funda-mentalist Gregory VII (1073–85). However, what allowed the majority of the new foundations to establish themselves so suc-cessfully was less the militancy of papal leadership at Rome than the almost universal onset of prosperity that at last gave a surplus to those willing to pass some of it on to the Church. With-out question, the most successful of the new monastic orders was the Cistercian, which carried the austere precepts of the charis-matic St Bernard (1090–1153) all over Europe from the principal Burgundian mother houses at Cîteaux, at Clairvaux (St Bernard's abbey) and at Morimond. But other orders of monks and canons became well established during the period as well, among them the Carthusians, the Augustinians and the Premonstratensians. And all were great builders in their day.

Indeed, a heavy and continuous investment in building, per-sisting especially through the twelfth and thirteenth centuries, characterized the Church throughout western Europe in each of its many branches. Parish churches, along with manor houses, were usually rebuilt in stone during these years, and although such rebuilding might continue to be resisted in areas like Norway, where a carpentry tradition remained strong, its attraction for patrons as a permanent memorial to their piety was too powerful for the majority to resist. In the cities the rebuilding of the north European cathedrals, of which Chartres is probably the most cele-brated example, was undertaken at just this time. The wealthy merchants, the artisans and the guildsmen who played such an important part in the reconstruction of Chartres Cathedral after the fire of 1194 were proud of their new church and their city. They put their signature on the building in commemorative win-dows, recording the cooperative effort of the crafts. And they were clearly engaged in a civic enterprise that, within the decade, had become openly competitive. Bourges and Soissons in the late 1190s, Reims from 1211, Amiens from 1220, Beauvais after the fire of 1225 – each of these buildings was more than a cathedral: it was a monument to urban self-confidence and wealth.

Both wealth and self-confidence were the more influential for being comparatively new. Of course, urbanization had made

47.3: *Western Europe everywhere experienced an expansion of settlement during the eleventh, twelfth and thirteenth centuries. In the middle Yonne valley, France, as elsewhere, this took the form of the reclamation of waste and hitherto uncultivated lands, and the area of land covered by forests was reduced through campaigns of woodland clearance and new settlement.*

- places for which there is documentary, archaeological or place-name evidence for a date of origin earlier than the 12th century

- places settled in the 12th century and later

- Roman roads

- forest

47.4: *Aigues-Mortes, in Provence, France, on which work began in 1245 in preparation for Louis IX's departure on crusade to the Holy Land, is among the best preserved of the many new towns built throughout the West during the course of the thirteenth century. Its grid-like plan and strong defences are characteristic of the late foundations of this period.*

appreciable progress in northern Europe some centuries before the rebuilding of Chartres. However, the foundation of new towns and the further expansion of old ones that came to characterize the European economy during the twelfth century reflected an unprecedented regeneration of trade. It was from early in the twelfth century that the great international fairs of Champagne and Brie (at Troyes and Provins, Lagny and Bar-sur-Aube), first came into their own; before long almost every large town had its fair, and even villages commonly had markets. Something of this revival can be measured by the grants of market that occur in contemporary records. But another way of viewing it has recently been pioneered in the charting of artifact distribution patterns, in particular the distribution of pottery.[5] It may well be that the distinctive regional cultures of the earlier Middle Ages were already breaking down. Industry itself had become more specialized – in iron working and glass making as much as in pottery – and transport, though crude, was scarcely worse overland than it continued to be until the eighteenth century. Nevertheless, one of the more hopeful departures in medieval archaeology today is the study, at a local level, of an entire material culture almost wholly inaccessible through the records. There is no other method of reaching it.

Another departure, certainly as important, is recent work on the archaeology of towns. Economic growth, though most evident in the great urban centres of Flanders and the north Italian plain, was by no means confined to these regions. It is traceable, for example, in the stage-by-stage expansion of many city defences to take in former suburban areas that had developed outside earlier walls. And it is particularly clear in the proliferation of new towns on virgin sites throughout the West, one of the later and more spectacular of these being Louis IX's Aigues-Mortes. Significantly, it also affected a port as remote as Bergen, on the west coast of Norway, where, on the pottery evidence alone, a widening of trade links on an entirely new scale occurred from the late twelfth century. Well before its further development as an element in the late medieval Hanseatic trading system, Bergen had become included in an active north European commercial network that brought to it the products of England and of Flanders, as well as those of the distant north.[6] Among the ports with which it had dealings was the small but prosperous English town of Lynn, in Norfolk, deliberately extended in the mid-twelfth century by its lord, the bishop of Norwich, in a successful effort to capture at least part of this trade. Both at Bergen and at Lynn, through the central and later Middle Ages, the line of the waterfront crept steadily forward as demand for access to the quays increased and as new wharves were added to the old.[7] In each case the stages of growth have been identified and charted in systematic programmes of archaeological research.

One of the artifacts recovered in the Bergen excavations was a scratch-carving on wood of a fleet of Viking ships – forty-eight in number, and longships in the traditional style. Yet the trade that brought prosperity to Bergen is more likely to have been carried in another sort of ship altogether. It was in the thirteenth century that the cog, a sturdy merchantman with high sides and a broad beam, was introduced in the northern waters to which it was obviously well suited, and it was on ships of this type that the success of such major trades as the Bordeaux wine trade and the salt trade from the Bay of Bourgneuf later came to depend. The cog itself had been equipped, for the first time, with a stern-post rudder in place of the simple steering oar that, before the beginning of the thirteenth century, had been usual in the shipping of the north. And this modification was in itself of considerable importance in the evolution of a ship capable of handling the burgeoning trade of the west European seaboard.

Other still more vital advances in medieval technology were undoubtedly those concerned with a more effective harnessing of power. Little of this is closely datable, for the first recorded use of a machine rarely coincides with its earliest introduction. However there are good prospects for an accumulation of new archaeological evidence to supplement that of the documents. On an English site at Tamworth, for example, the very considerable remains of a horizontal-wheeled watermill have been dated by radiocarbon to the eighth century.[8] Together with the vertical-wheeled watermill at Old Windsor, probably of the ninth century, and similar material from Ireland, these excavated mills have now provided important independent evidence to support the long-established historical hypothesis of a diffusion of the watermill across western Europe from either the south or the east, particularly between the eighth and the tenth centuries. Without doubt, water power in eleventh century Europe was already very widely exploited. In addition to its use in the grinding of grains, it had also been applied to the driving of hemp mills and fulling mills in the cloth-working industries, as well as hammer mills and stamping mills in iron working – the first real signs of that widespread mechanization that was to be so vital to the recovery of the West. Truly large-scale mechanization, even then very rarely applied, would have to await the first water-powered silk-throwing mills of thirteenth century Italy, where the work of hundreds could at last be done by a handful of machine-minding operatives. In that same century another important source of power began to be widely exploited: the windmill came increasingly into use, bringing an appreciation of elementary mechanics, often for the very first time, to areas that until then had had to do without it. At one level a simple device like the wheelbarrow, another thirteenth-century invention, serves to demonstrate the increasing application of such mechanical principles; at another, the challenge of High Gothic could not have been met without sophisticated architectural engineering.

The late medieval crisis
Growth had its problems, however, and technology by itself could provide few of the answers. Essentially, the overcrowding of the better lands, already evident as early as the eleventh century, had spread to the poor lands as well. Throughout Europe property

holders, whether rural or urban, had rarely lived as comfortably as they did in the thirteenth century, for labour was cheap and rents were high as the growth of population forced down wages and drove up the price of land. Yet the penalty to be paid for the depression of the poor and the increasing desperation of the landless was a rising tide of social discontent, which erupted regularly in violence.

One of the centres of the growing class struggle was northern Europe's industrial heartland in Flanders, and this struggle, together with the militant emergence of the craft guilds in large cities such as London, has long attracted the attention of historians. However, the association of violence with harvest failures and rural famines, so obvious in the crime statistics of the early fourteenth century, left its mark on the countryside as well – in castle-building programmes and refortifications, and particularly in the phenomenon of the moat. Only recently the subject of archaeological study, the moat has sometimes been explained, both in Flanders and in England, as a status symbol, owing its common appearance in village society of about 1300 to the emergence of a new class of prosperous peasant land-holders.[9] But this, if true at all, can surely be no more than a partial explanation of ditch-digging works, sometimes on a considerable scale, for which a defensive purpose is easy enough to establish. It was the relative prosperity of the main peasant families, whether freeholders or

dependent villeins, that gave them something of value to protect; simultaneously, the swamping and near-breakdown of the state legal system made them especially vulnerable to attack.[10]

Very much more is now known of the so-called 'agrarian crisis' in early fourteenth-century England, dating especially to the years 1315–22, when the harvest failures of 1315–16 were either accompanied or followed by the sheep and cattle murrains (epidemics) of 1313–17 and 1319–21 respectively.[11] Over northern Europe generally the famine years of 1315–17 took their savage Malthusian toll. The extension of arable by reclamation and enclosure had reduced the land available for pasture; with fewer livestock there was less manure and crop yields fell still further. Thus, half a century before the Black Death population growth was levelling off, although for some decades it maintained a precarious stability, with the poor on the edge of collapse. It was the spread of bubonic plague, from Constantinople in 1347, through western Europe and the north to Russia in 1353, that finally established a new balance.

Of course, the cost of the adjustment was terrible. Not all regions were affected equally; some escaped the plague altogether. However, the overall loss of population, taking the Black Death and its recurrences in the 1360s together, is likely to have amounted to at least a third of the pre-plague total in the West, and may have risen in some areas to a half. For the survivors this was no bad

47.5: *Marginal illustrations in late medieval manuscripts quite commonly depict familiar agricultural scenes. Among those decorating the English Luttrell Psalter, an East Anglian manuscript of c. 1340, is this scene showing a windmill of the post-mill type.*

47.6: *Over-population had made England calamity-sensitive by the early fourteenth century. The high foodstuff prices of famine years were followed immediately by steep increases in crime, as recorded in the Norfolk delivery rolls for the period.*

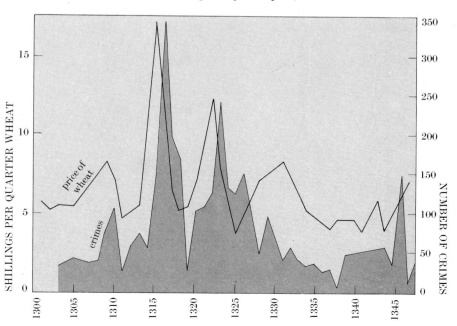

thing. At a stroke the damaging population surplus had been eliminated; good land was plentiful and wages were certain to rise. But the recovery of population, which in circumstances like these could have converted disaster into boom, was delayed for a century and more. The social injustices righted by the plague have thus to be seen in the context of a depressed economy, the withdrawal of settlement and a persisting stagnation of trade.

An obvious consequence of this semi-permanent population shrinkage in late medieval Europe was a very general regrouping on the land. In Germany, it has been estimated, somewhere between a fifth and a quarter of the settlements occupied in 1300 were abandoned within the next two centuries. Moreover, this followed a retreat from the margin in medieval agriculture that, in the Rhineland at least, had plainly begun some decades before the end of the thirteenth century. Rhineland desertions – of villages,

47.7: *Lawlessness increased in late thirteenth-century England as the demand for land exceeded the supply. Many manor houses and isolated farmsteads were provided with defensive moats at this time; the map shows a concentration of such works in East Anglia and the Midlands, where criminal gangs are known to have been especially active. (Land over 1000 metres is shown in brown.)*

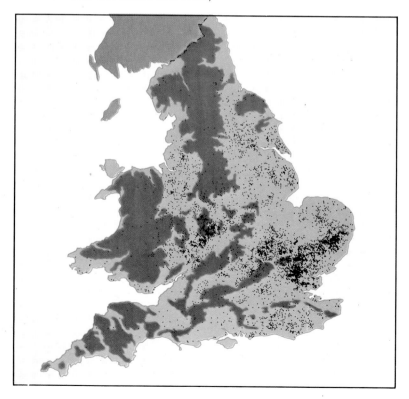

47.8: *The growing importance of Bergen, Norway, as an international port in the Middle Ages led to increased demand for the more valuable waterfront properties and a steady pushing forward of the quays. Similar reclamation on the harbour frontage has been charted recently at King's Lynn, England, one of the ports with which Bergen had dealings.*

main settlement areas of medieval town

medieval churches and religious houses

original medieval waterfront

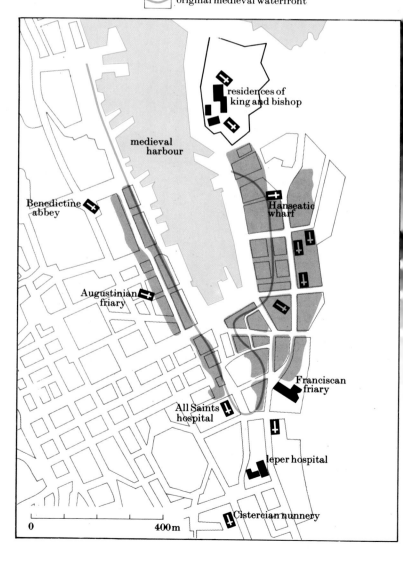

isolated farmsteads and mills – peaked in the period 1250–1300. And while the contemporary preference for the greater security of the towns may have been a response to the collapse of public order, it resulted also from the sheer impossibility of scratching a living on the poorer and less hospitable soils. In some areas the deterioration in the climate, which perhaps became obvious for the first time in the notably unsettled weather conditions of the later thirteenth century, further encouraged the retreat. In the fourteenth and fifteenth centuries in particular, repeated crop failures on the less fertile lands persuaded many to abandon them to pasture.[12] Such adjustments, of course, became easier after the Black Death, when land was available once again. The *Wüstungen* of Germany, and the many equivalent deserted villages of England and of France now the subject of archaeological research, can only rarely have lost their inhabitants as a result of enforced depopulation. If lands were waste and settlements deserted in the late medieval West, this was almost always the inevitable outcome of a chronic

47.9: *It is thought that the Black Death was brought to eastern Europe along the caravan routes from India and China. It reached Constantinople in 1347 and by the middle of 1348 had spread through Italy, much of France and eastern Spain. A year later it had reached northern Europe, moving into Russia in the early 1350s. In the more populous areas the Black Death and its succeeding plagues in 1361–2 and 1368–9 probably carried off between them something like a third of the pre-plague population, although the toll in thinly settled areas of eastern Europe was certainly very much smaller.*

inhabitants per sq.km in early 14th century

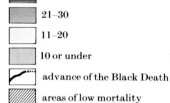

- over 31
- 21–30
- 11–20
- 10 or under
- advance of the Black Death
- areas of low mortality

47.10: *Gunpowder and cannon from the late fourteenth century were revolutionizing military technology in the West, this representation of a hand-cannon from Conrad Kyeser's* Bellifortis *being one of the illustrations in a manual of weaponry in which guns and grenades figure prominently.*

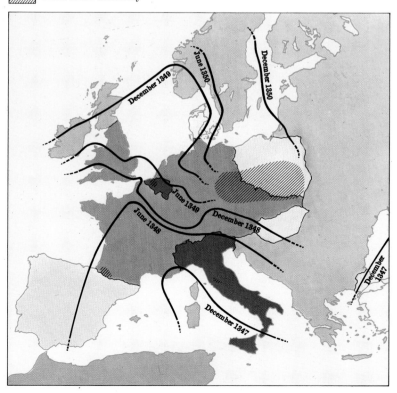

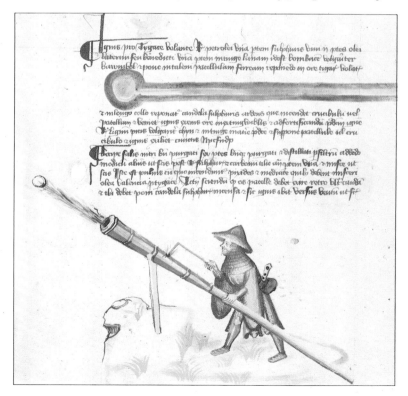

shortage of tenants.

In many village desertions the onset of plague would clearly have resulted rather in the confirmation of existing trends than in revolutionary new beginnings. But this is not to say, as is sometimes suggested by revisionist historians, that the Black Death was without real importance. One of its most obvious consequences was that the role of the independent, freeholding peasant farmer developed at the expense of the great landowner. And it was this growing status and wealth of the peasant freeholder that would be reflected, as often as not, in an archaeologically verifiable consolidation of holdings and in the greater size and quality of his farmstead.[13] Following the Black Death, the houseplots and gardens of a much larger pre-plague community were subsequently redistributed among a mere handful of more substantial farmers. Similarly, it is from the late Middle Ages that the first peasant houses have come down to us intact, the handsome timber-framing of the English 'Wealden' house being adequate at last to ensure its continuing preservation and use.

For the yeoman farmer who survived the plagues their tragedy had provided an opening. However, in the bacteria-infested towns of late medieval Europe this was scarcely a time of hope. In many of these towns the wall-building programmes of the thirteenth century, in which so much money and civic pride had been invested, came to an abrupt halt with the Black Death. Areas that had been enclosed within the last ring of walls, built in the expectation of continuing growth, remained unsettled and vacant, and one major investment of late medieval municipal authorities was more likely to be in public health. The organization of municipal water supplies, the paving and drainage of streets, the regulation (and sometimes banishment) of the more noxious trades, and even the provision of public lavatories are not confined to the late Middle Ages. But although certainly anticipated in some major cities before the

first visitations of the plague, they were to become much more evident during the decades after it – manifestations of a contemporary concern with mortality that quite quickly became an obsession. Characteristically, this obsession took the form of works of public piety, occasions for extravagant display. The colleges, almshouses and hospitals of the later Middle Ages were almost all commemorative in purpose. In addition to providing succour for the poor and the infirm, their functions included the maintenance in perpetuity of a pious round of memorial masses, easing the passage through the discomforts of Purgatory of the founder, his noble ancestors and his kin. Throughout Europe contemporary belief in the efficacy of the memorial mass encouraged an investment in the paraphernalia of death that gave employment to both builder and artist. Chantry chapels, whether financed by individuals or through the cooperative associations of the guilds, were to become the most familiar late medieval additions to both cathedrals and parish churches. And the skills of the sculptor were everywhere in demand for the screens of these chapels and for the tomb-chests and effigies that they housed.

Recovery

There is still disagreement among historians over when the recovery of population began. Some claim that the pre-plague population totals were restored and even slightly exceeded by 1500, while others prefer a later date for this restoration, perhaps as much as a full century later. Nevertheless, all would agree that, in some respects at least, Europe was already gathering itself before the late fifteenth century for the great surge forward it certainly experienced in the sixteenth. And although the control and retreat of disease was probably the most important single element in this recovery, another important factor that encouraged the climb was significant new advances in technology.

47.11: *One of the most sombre and dramatic of the fifteenth-century Burgundian funerary monuments is the effigy, supported by eight hooded mourners, of Philippe Pot, Grand Seneschal of Burgundy (d. 1493). The tomb, commissioned for the abbey church at Cîteaux, is probably the work of Antoine le Moiturier, who was noted for his memorial sculptures.*

The most remarkable technological breakthrough of the fifteenth century, and undoubtedly the most influential in the long run, was Gutenberg's development, in mid-fifteenth-century Mainz, of commercially viable printing. However, important though this was, it should be seen in the context of a more general revolution in mechanics, of which Leonardo da Vinci (1452–1519) was the principal theoretician and of which the instrument-makers of Nuremberg and Augsburg were the most experienced and practical exponents. Printing itself would probably not have been possible without the successful experiments in the use of oil-based paints undertaken by the earlier fifteenth-century Flemish masters, for these gave Gutenberg the recipe for his inks. Nor would Leonardo, perhaps, have been the innovator that he was without the solid foundation in applied mechanics that he had derived from the works of the great Florentine architect, Filippo Brunelleschi (1377–1446), to whom he was deeply and openly indebted. Such were the antecedents of the movement in the arts and of the intellect that we have come to call the Renaissance. From the 'Nuremberg egg' (the first portable spring-driven clock) to refinements of the hand-gun and of ships' rigging, Renaissance experimentalism had immediate and far-reaching applications.

This was particularly true of the drive, which had already begun quite early in the fifteenth century, to discover and to colonize a hitherto unknown world. The movement had started as a part of the Iberian *Reconquista*, inspired by the ambition of the Portuguese prince, Henry the Navigator (1394–1460), to penetrate beyond the Muslim lands of North Africa to the fabled sources of African gold and to potential allies in the perennial Christian struggle with Islam. It was spurred on by Ottoman expansion in the eastern Mediterranean, by Mehemmed the Conqueror's successful storming of Constantinople in 1453, and by his subsequent engulfing of the Balkans. Nevertheless, the European voyages of discovery in the late Middle Ages could not have taken the form (or achieved the success) that they did without the backing of the new technology. The motive may have been the protection and propagation of the Christian faith. The means were the ship and the gun.

Henry the Navigator himself was a scientist. His captains, penetrating ever further down the west coast of Africa, were hydrographers as much as they were military men and sailors, dependent always for the accuracy of their observations on the improving quality of the instruments they used. In shipping also it was from lessons learnt on the Portuguese caravel, combined with those of the north European cog, that the fully rigged carrack of the mid-fifteenth century assumed a form – with square sails, lateen sails and jibs – that would be instantly recognizable among seafaring men from that day through to the present. Carracks such as these carried the rich fifteenth-century trade between the Mediterranean and Flanders that was to prove such a spur to the economic recovery of the West. Christopher Columbus, setting out for the Americas in 1492, sailed in a ship that was fully rigged in the style first perfected on the carrack,

Of course, Columbus went armed as well. His ships carried the guns that, within a few decades, would bring the Aztecs and the Incas to their knees. It was guns that opened coastal Africa and then parts of India and the Far East to the Portuguese. And it was guns that, for well over a century, had been an abiding passion of the West. One of the earliest and most useful representations of a cannon in action was published in that remarkable manual of military technology, the *Bellifortis* (*c.* 1405) of Conrad Kyeser. The *Bellifortis* belongs to a class of such manuals that included the anonymous *Feuerwerkbuch* of not much more than a decade later, and in its emphasis on fortification and siege-works in the pre-artillery mode it was still distinctly old-fashioned. However, where Conrad Kyeser displayed his modernity was first in the space he allotted to the gun and then in the quite separate interest he evidently took in the varied applications of hydraulics. Here especially, in such inventions as the water-supply system for a nobleman's bath house, some foretaste is given of the experimental mechanics that, combined very often with military engineering, became so characteristic of the Renaissance. Leonardo da Vinci, Leon Battista Alberti (the fifteenth-century architect and writer) and Rodolfo Fioravanti (the Bolognese engineer of Ivan the Great's artillery fortress in the rebuilt Kremlin at Moscow) were as interested in the design of up-to-date fortifications as in the construction of the churches and the palaces they protected. They were builders of bridges, of locks and canals; they were mathematicians, painters and architects.

Achievements like these are a useful reminder of the distance that Europe, despite all reverses, had travelled since the days of its post-Dark Age re-emergence. For the future, progress would be scarcely smoother than it had been over the past centuries. But politically the states of Europe were now defined; economic systems were comparatively sophisticated; technology continued to make good progress. Before 1500 the essential groundwork had been laid for the age of European expansion. Europe's bid for world domination was especially soundly based.

48. The urbanization of eastern Europe

Since the Second World War the archaeologists of eastern European countries have concentrated much of their work on towns and settlements. The war caused extensive damage to countless cities, towns and villages, thereby creating unprecedented opportunities for investigating the remains of earlier settlements normally buried beneath living communities. The eastern European governments encouraged archaeological study of their nations' past, especially of the medieval period, and the pace of post-war reconstruction allowed such study to develop extensively. From the late 1940s onwards urban archaeologists were able not only to excavate on a great scale, but also to develop new methods and techniques that became standardized in some countries, especially the Soviet Union, and today guide most urban excavations. The most valuable accomplishment of urban archaeology in Eastern Europe has been to provide an understanding of the physical and topographical development of towns and of the different forms of urban growth that emerged. It is now clear that the rise of towns in Europe's eastern regions accompanied the rise of medieval nation states throughout this vast area, except for rare exceptions along the Baltic and Adriatic coasts and in the Crimea.

Western Slav lands

The earliest Slav state with distinct urban centres was Greater Moravia, which prospered in the ninth century. Its main centres

48.1: *The main towns of eastern Europe, c. 700–1500, occur principally along coastal and inland routes. The earliest towns developed in coastal regions and near to lands with an older urban culture: by the late Middle Ages urban networks extended to the subarctic and Asian peripheries of eastern Europe.*

48.2: *The unplanned growth of Moscow was confined through most of the Middle Ages to the promontory and plateau formed at the confluence of the Moscow river and the Neglinnaia stream. In the early sixteenth century the old town was separated from the rest of the settlement by a moat; the administrative stronghold thus formed survives today as the Kremlin.*

settlement

▨	11th–12th centuries
☐	12th–13th centuries
▨	13th–14th centuries

fortifications

••••	oldest
▦	14th century
■—■	15th century (Kremlin)
☐	principal churches

were Stare Mesto and Mikulčice, both of which developed from earlier tribal settlements. Neither was a fully integrated town; residential areas, which later fused to form a single, continuous, built-up area, were still separated by open spaces. Mikulčice, which has been studied in more detail, consisted of a princely fortress, from which an open suburb extended, and some smaller forts, scattered both within and beyond the residential area. A contemporary urban centre nearby, Nitra in western Slovakia, comprised four small fortresses, between which an open settlement stretched. These towns perished when Greater Moravia was overrun by the Magyars in the tenth century, but similar urban centres gave rise to great medieval towns in the same area soon afterwards.[1]

Prague, the capital of the Czech kingdom, grew from a loose urban centre into an integrated medieval town between the tenth and the thirteenth centuries. The town began as two fortresses situated diagonally opposite one another on a bend in the river Vltava. Separate open suburbs grew around each stronghold and gradually expanded, merging eventually into a single town in the fourteenth century. (Curiously, the first town wall had already been erected around the still discontinuous suburbs in the thirteenth century.) The growth of Prague was certainly due to its importance as a trading centre and to the relative stability of the early Czech state. The latter factor was probably the more important: this can be deduced by comparing the urbanization process in the lands of the Baltic Slavs and in Poland.[2]

By the early tenth century large, early urban centres had developed along the Baltic Slav coast and in Poland. Wolin, Szczezin, Kolobrzeg and Gdansk grew into great Baltic trading centres, but important as they were, these places were somewhat peripheral to eastern Europe; they are best understood as part of the Baltic area and northern Europe (see Chapter 46), and are probably most aptly compared with non-Slav centres of the time such as Birka and Haithabu.

The small local princedoms that controlled the Baltic Slav coast were apparently unable to create the conditions that could promote the development of these early urban centres into proper medieval towns. However, by the thirteenth century increasing German influence and, eventually, direct rule had transformed these centres into replanned and rebuilt German towns.

The growth of towns in Poland began slightly later than along the Baltic coast: its pattern shows clearly the connection between urbanization and the rise of a medieval state. The earliest great urban centre in Poland was Krakow, in the south of the country: it was already a large town by the end of the tenth century. A great trading centre, it began as a castle with a separate lower town nearby, surrounded by a cluster of smaller settlements. By the thirteenth century this group had grown together into a single urban network: its central and newest area was laid out as a grid, with a great market-place at its heart. This regular plan is clear evidence of the influence of German town planning on the western Slavs during the Middle Ages, as illustrated especially by the town charter of Magdeburg, the *Magdeburg Recht*. Apart from Krakow, however, the Polish south gave rise to no great towns; the urbanization of Poland was most pronounced in the central regions of the country, the heartland of the medieval state.

The main area of town growth in Poland lay between and in the basins of the rivers Warta and Vistula, along the great river routes connecting the Baltic with inland eastern Europe. The first capital of Poland, Gniezno, was established on the Warta in the tenth century. It developed as a chain of fortified enclosures; the walled royal residence was adjoined on one side by a fortified cathedral close, from the other side of which a fortified suburb extended. A great trading centre nearby, Wroclaw, developed in a way that recalls Krakow; its focal point was a central area laid out regularly in the German manner. The same German influence can be detected in the shaping of Warsaw, later to become Poland's capital on the Vistula. This town was at first little more than an early medieval castle: when a suburb began to grow by its walls in the thirteenth century, the new district was laid out according to the now familiar grid pattern.[3]

The Balkans

If orderly town planning came relatively late to those lands of eastern Europe discussed above, it provided the original inspiration for urbanization in the Balkans. Throughout the lowlands here, and especially along the Adriatic and Black Sea coasts, many Roman and early Byzantine planned towns thrived until the

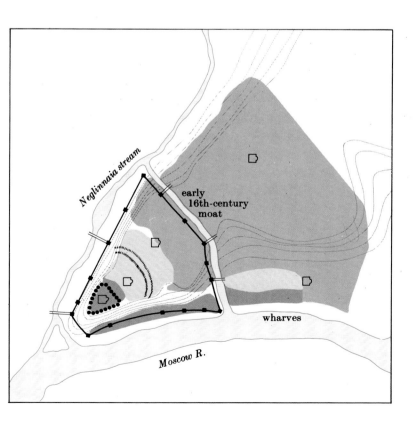

early
16th-century
moat

Neglinnaia stream

wharves

Moscow R.

second half of the first millennium. Most of these declined after the Slav invasions of the Balkans: very few of the old towns north of the Danube survived this upheaval, and those south of the river became less numerous and less prosperous. But even in this state the old towns inspired the Slavs to build new towns modelled on their plans. This adoption of an urban tradition is remarkable, as previously the Slavs had had no such tradition of their own.

The rise of the first Slav state in the Balkans, the first Bulgarian empire, was marked by the construction of the entirely new capital, Pliška, in the late seventh century. The plan of this town was inspired entirely by Classical and Byzantine examples. The town was contained within a precisely rectangular town wall and had at its centre a square citadel. Straight, symmetrical streets led from the citadel's four gates to a central square, where a great palace complex stood. Pliška's fortifications and water-supply systems, domestic architecture and general building techniques were all exactly like those found in the Roman-Byzantine towns of the Balkans. The first Bulgarian empire grew, and in the late ninth century it acquired a new capital, Preslav, again built entirely in the traditional mould. Preslav was also fortified and was basically rectangular in plan, having at its centre a citadel containing the royal palace. The plan, however, was somewhat less precise than that of Pliška, and the new capital was smaller than the first one. During the late tenth and early eleventh centuries the first Bulgarian empire was conquered by Byzantium, and the two capital cities, like many other Balkan towns, contracted under Byzantine rule, reviving noticeably only when local states emerged again. This regression can be shown by comparing Pliška and Preslav with Turnovo, the newly built capital of the revived Bulgarian state that emerged in the late twelfth century. Placed on high, naturally defended terrain, Turnovo consisted of a fortress housing a very compressed palace complex and an open suburb that clustered around the stronghold. The building technique was consistently inferior to that found at Pliška and Preslav, and the new capital had none of the regular planning that distinguished its predecessors. In general, the medieval towns of the Balkans were small; the more prosperous were located on major trade routes, above all along the Black Sea coast.[4]

The greatest area of urbanization in the Balkans lay along the eastern coast of the Adriatic. The large towns here all developed directly from Roman ones: they included Dubrovnik, Split, Zadar, Kotor and others. The most remarkable example of continuity occurred at Split, where the medieval town was contained almost entirely within the walls of the Roman emperor Diocletian's great palace, and where the imperial temple and mausoleum were converted into the town's baptistry and cathedral respectively in the thirteenth century. The Adriatic towns grew from the twelfth century onwards, either as autonomous political entities or as dependencies of Venice. These towns thrived on Adriatic and Mediterranean trade and had close ties with Italy, especially Venice: their urban institutions and architecture were derived directly from Italy.[5]

48.3: *Pliška, the first Bulgarian capital, was built as a new town in the late seventh century: its precise layout shows it to have been modelled after Classical and Byzantine towns common along the Black Sea coast. The town walls were built of earth ramparts, while the citadel and palace were constructed in dressed stone.*

churches

secular buildings

barrows

wells

stone funeral monuments

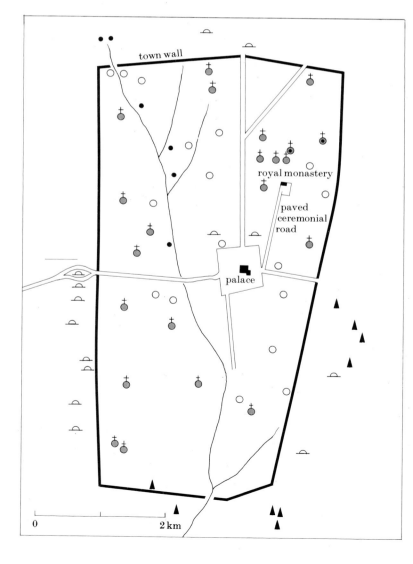

Russia

In contrast to the rest of eastern Europe, urbanization in Russia was affected only marginally by foreign models. Towns began to develop here in the tenth century, when the first Russian state took shape. A few relatively large international trading centres did exist a century or two earlier along the country's northern periphery: the best known of these are Ladoga and Gnezdovo, near Smolensk. These centres were populated predominantly by Balts, Finns and Varangians, and they were already in decline when the Slavs began penetrating northwards in growing numbers from the tenth century onwards. The proliferation of Russian towns is clearly linked with the growth of the medieval Russian state. A great many towns appeared during the later eleventh and the twelfth centuries, when the early medieval state was thriving; when the centralized state faltered between the thirteenth and fifteenth centuries urbanization contracted. Towns began to grow in size and number again in the sixteenth century, when the Muscovite state established its control over the whole of Russia. Without exception, Russia's medieval towns developed from non-urban beginnings. The main types of Russian urbanization are exemplified by three great medieval towns – Kiev, Novgorod and Moscow.

Kiev, the capital of early Russia, took shape as a town when the nation was converted to Christianity in 989. Earlier, its general location had been occupied by a number of unconnected settlements scattered along the eastern bank of the river Dnieper and the bluffs above it. A particularly defensible bluff was chosen as the site for a fortified town with churches and palaces: this was completed in the last years of the tenth century. In the first decades of the eleventh century a large, fortified outer town was erected on the inland side of the original nucleus. Some open and discontinuous suburbs grew up in the vicinity of the fortified centre and on the river bank below. This layout, at once centralized and

scattered, remained essentially unchanged until Kiev was devastated by the Mongols in the middle of the thirteenth century, never to recover fully during the Middle Ages.[6]

Novgorod's beginnings resemble those of Kiev, but the northern town developed differently from the capital on the Dnieper. In the tenth century Novgorod consisted of a cluster of three neighbouring settlements, two on one side of the river and the third facing them. The original inhabitants were probably of different stock. In the mid-eleventh century a small fortress was built by the river between the three communities: this housed the cathedral and bishop's palace. The original three settlements gradually grew together into a single open suburb around the fortress, which was expanded in the early twelfth century. The planning and architecture of the suburbs remained essentially rural, and a continuous town wall was not erected around them until the early fifteenth century, only half a century before the town lost its independent status to Moscow.[7]

In contrast to Kiev and Novgorod, Moscow developed gradually from a single nucleus. The town began in the eleventh century as a small promontory fort controlling a major junction of river and land routes. As the princes of Moscow gained power in Russia, so the town grew larger, though it remained a small strategic town, contained entirely within its ramparts, until the fourteenth century, when its land-side wall was relocated further inland, and a small open suburb appeared next to it. In the fifteenth century, when Moscow rose to prominence in Russia, the wall was moved still further inland: many old buildings (and even monasteries) were levelled in order to transform the walled area of the old town into a great princely and ecclesiastical compound. This enlarged administrative precinct survives today as the Kremlin. The town's suburb increased enormously in size as a result of this change but remained unfortified until the sixteenth century.[8]

Moscow's development anticipated the rise of Russian frontier

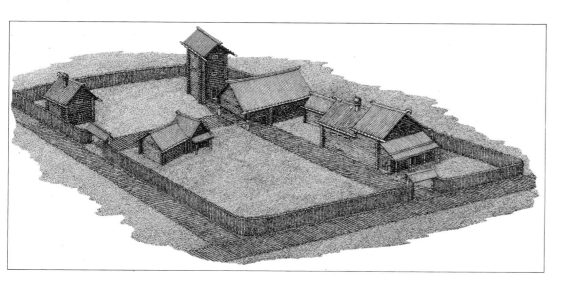

48.4: *A Novgorod estate of the thirteenth to fourteenth centuries. Built entirely of wood, a typical Novgorod estate housed within the stockade a diverse population. The lord (a noble, official or merchant) with his family and domestics occupied the larger and better buildings, seen here grouped on the right. The unfree and indentured dependants, mostly craftsmen, lived and worked in lesser buildings, as those clustered on the left.*

towns in the Urals and Siberia during the sixteenth and seven-teenth centuries. Most of these began as strategic fortresses and grew slowly into compact towns. In some frontier areas Russian towns displaced early medieval ones built by other peoples: in the Volga basin especially a number of Islamic towns, the greatest being Bulgar, had existed throughout the Middle Ages. The furthest extension of east European urbanism thus overlapped for a time with the northernmost extension of Islamic urbanism.

Russian towns were not influenced by eastern ones, but they may at first have been affected to some degree by the late Classical and early Byzantine towns of the Crimea. The latter towns, above all Korsun and Kerch, had persisted as great trading centres, much like those of the eastern Adriatic, except that they were under the dominant influence of Byzantium. It seems very likely, for example, that the fortified centre of Kiev, built in the late tenth century, as well as its early eleventh-century extension, were constructed by architects from the Crimea.

Conclusion

The overall pattern of urbanization in eastern Europe that emerges from recent archaeological studies reveals the close relationship between the rise of towns and the rise of medieval nation states. Towns grew and developed with these states: when the states faltered, urbanization decelerated and existing towns declined. The few regions in which towns thrived independently – the Baltic coast, the eastern Adriatic and the Crimea – were coastal areas dependent on the seas and thus peripheral to the continental mass of eastern Europe.

VII: On the edge of the Old World

While the belt of developed societies in the middle of the Old World was forming and expanding, the outer margins were also undergoing important changes. Two parts of the world – the Arctic and Oceania – were occupied for the first time. Others were receiving their first agricultural populations and practices such as milking, which allowed the formation of pastoral economies in areas as far apart as eastern Africa and Siberia. These new economies made it possible for more complex societies to form, as in the parts of Africa where native states grew up. Some of these became linked by long-distance trading contacts with the heartlands of Eurasian civilization. One of the most spectacular dispersals of agricultural population was the colonization of the remote islands of Polynesia as far east as Easter Island and as far south as New Zealand. Further maritime movements across the Indian Ocean carried Malayo-Polynesian languages to Madagascar, making this the most widely scattered language group in the world. This massive dispersal made no impact on Australia, whose hunting populations continued to develop in isolation at the same time as equally specialized but technologically more advanced hunting groups penetrated the Arctic wastes from Greenland to Alaska.

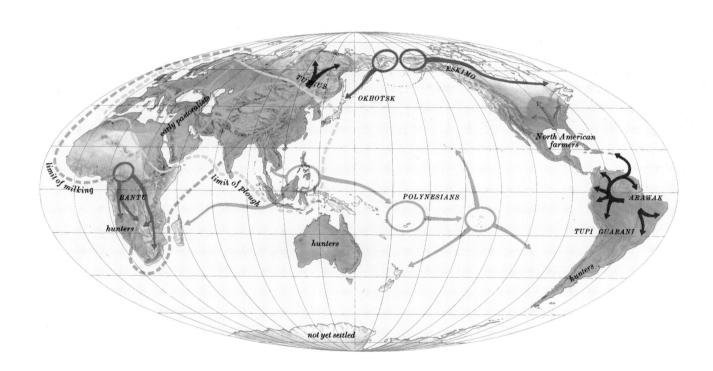

49. Northern forest cultures and the Arctic fringe

Northern Eurasia consists of three types of habitat: coniferous forest (taiga), arctic steppe (tundra) and the maritime zone. The environment is highly seasonal, with land and water remaining frozen, snowbound and deprived of light for four to six months each year. The largest area is that covered by the taiga, a uniform expanse of conifers and birch dotted by open spaces of marshlands, lakes and rivers, and the region is thus generally referred to as the Forest Zone.

The spread of settlement in this zone during the Holocene created a distinctive cultural unit that has been called the Circumpolar Stone Age.[1] The striking uniformity of this pattern was not necessarily due to contact and diffusion within the zone, however, as there are significant regional differences in artifact types; cultural homogeneity may have resulted largely from similar adaptive responses produced independently in different parts of a relatively uniform environment.

During the early Holocene there was little differentiation in material culture between the coastal and inland areas. Sparse as they are, remains belonging to this period indicate a highly mobile pattern of settlement, based on unspecialized fishing, sealing and hunting. The tool assemblages differ from nearby Palaeolithic ones in the diversification of tools forms and their adaptation to lacustrine and forested environments. Some sites, such as Kunda, Narva and Ust-Belaya, which show evidence of repeated occupation, may have served as focal points for surrounding groups. Characteristic tools included bone harpoons, fish-spears (leisters) and fishhooks. Bone played an important part in composite tools, and microblades were used as tips for projectiles or insets for cutting and scraping tools. Heavy stone tools included edged and hollow (gouge) chisels, axes, adzes, picks, spearheads and indented or perforated sinkers or maces; some were shaped by pecking, and occasionally by polishing, along the working edges. Organic remains from the north-east Baltic include bark floats, nets and sledges.[2]

The introduction of pottery in the fifth millennium BC was not accompanied by any abrupt change either in tool-kits or in the economic base, and sites continued to cluster around lakes, rivers and along coasts. The main form of pot was a wide-mouthed jar with a round or pointed base, decorated by incised strokes and impressions. Such pottery developed among several groups. The Pre-Jomon phase in Japan, the Keltaminar culture of central Asia, the Bug–Dniester Neolithic and the Sperrings phase in Finland have all been credited with the independent development of pottery. From its beginnings in the fifth millennium BC, the making of pottery spread to more remote parts of the Forest Zone over several thousand years. Many earlier sites throughout the area continued to be occupied in this phase: they range from 1000 to 10 000 square metres in area. At Sarnate in Latvia, dating to the mid-fourth millennium BC,[3] semi-subterranean wooden dwellings were found, along with remains of skis, dugout boats, paddles, nets, bark floats, wicker traps, wooden bowls, spoons, digging sticks, hammers and bark containers. Seals comprised half the animal remains, along with wild pig and beaver, birds and fish; while water chestnuts (*Trapa natans*) were intensively collected.

Economic diversification and cultural change, 3000 BC–AD 1000

There is evidence for a diversification of the economic base, the development of social stratification and increasing contact with areas to the south during the third millennium BC. This process lasted into the historical period. There was greater specialization in local resources, such as the hunting of sea mammals, anadromous fish and reindeer, while cereal farming and animal husbandry were adopted from the south. Agriculture, however, was only one component of the general trend towards increased productivity. While domestic stock is first evidenced only in the late third and cultivated plants in the second millennium BC,[4] changes in artifacts and site locations suggest an earlier date.[5] The earliest farmers belonged to the Corded Ware group, but the economy was hazardous at its ecological limit, and agriculture underwent several periods of advance and retreat, notably in the eastern Baltic and the Kama regions in the first millennium BC.

Maritime hunting, especially of seal, developed earlier in Scandinavia than on the Pacific coast. At Varanger in Finmark, from 3000 BC onwards,[6] people congregated along the coast, living from November to May in stone and turf villages of between 100 and 150 inhabitants, where they engaged in sealing and fishing. They dispersed for the summer to outlying islands for waterfowling, or inland for reindeer hunting. Bone remains, as well as specialized harpoon forms and slate knives for catching and processing sea mammals, indicate the importance of marine hunting, while the large number and duration of settlements bear witness to the success of this adaptation. Sealing was also one of the principal food resources of the Pitted Ware people of central Sweden in the third millennium, of the east Baltic coastal settlements in the second millennium and of the inhabitants of the islands in central parts of the Baltic during the same period.

The shift to a marine-oriented economy along the Pacific is well illustrated in the development of the Ancient Koryak culture along the Okhotsk Sea coast.[7] During the first millennium BC these people began to specialize in marine hunting with harpoons, including toggling forms, and shifted their settlements from inland to coastal sites. This process produced a characteristic marine culture, which in the first millennium AD included a variety of harpoon types and the use of large wooden boats equipped with oars. Other groups included the Okhotsk culture on the southern shore of the Okhotsk Sea and the Old Bering Sea culture – predecessors of modern Eskimos – on the Chukchi peninsula.

The earliest evidence of societies whose subsistence was based on salmon and other anadromous fish comes from the valley of the

Amur river. The inhabitants of Lake Osinovo in the middle Amur led a sedentary life based on millet farming and fishing. These settlements date to the third millennium BC. Further downstream large, permanent settlements formed at the same time around Kondon on the lower Amur.[8] Subsistence based on the fishing of anadromous species, with some reliance on simple farming, persisted on the middle and lower Amur throughout the Iron Age and into the historical period, and three-thousand-year-old remains of a salmon-fishing culture have also been found on the Kamchatka peninsula.

49.1: *Reindeer husbandry began to develop during the last five hundred years BC, and still plays an important part in the economy of such groups as the Samoyeds of northern Siberia. This whale-ivory model, thought to be Samoyed, shows a reindeer-herding camp.*

Reindeer breeding, encouraged perhaps by contact with the surrounding steppe pastoralists, developed in the Sayan mountains during the last five hundred years BC.[9] With the northward advance of the Samoyed people during the first millennium AD, reindeer husbandry spread into western Siberia and northern Europe, and at the same time penetrated north-eastwards into eastern Siberia with advancing Tungus groups. After the penetration of the taiga interior by these reindeer-herding groups, a merging of southern immigrants with the indigenous population occurred, in the course of which different types of reindeer husbandry developed.

The adoption of reindeer pastoralism was a gradual process, and reindeer domestication among the indigenous Forest Zone population was preceded by a period of reindeer husbandry that could be called neither domestication nor hunting in the conventional sense. Domestication progressed because of, and parallel to, the over-exploitation of wild reindeer. This is evidenced by the keeping

of reindeer as decoy animals among the Ust-Poluy[10] and other groups, and by the reluctance of the Lapps, the Nentsy and the Nganasans to change to reindeer breeding as long as wild reindeer herds were available. Specialized reindeer breeding became a more effective way of utilizing the taiga environment. Mounted and harnessed reindeer provided a means of transport that was an alternative to the dog-pulled sledges already in use; reindeer husbandry also served to emphasize social stratification, as it represented a form of wealth and status display.

Metal came into use during the third millennium BC. Following a period when copper was imported from the Caucasus, a number of copper-smelting centres developed in the Volga–Ural region early in the second millennium BC. About 1500 BC a bronze industry developed in the southern Urals. This was the distinctive Seima–Turbino industry, whose objects were distributed over wide areas of the Forest Zone. The other centre of metallurgy was in eastern Kazakhstan and the Altai mountains. Expanded by the Karasuk nomadic pastoralists after the thirteenth century BC, their bronzes penetrated into the Urals, western Siberia and the north-east as far as the middle Lena basin. While copper artifacts were too soft to be used for weapons and tools, the practical use of bronze was limited by the lack of tin in northern Eurasia.

Iron came into use during the first millennium BC. In the Kama–middle Urals region the Ananino industry arose, whose products were distributed beyond the area of the culture itself. The southern areas of the Forest Zone were affected by Scythian metallurgy, but in parts of European Russia and Scandinavia the technology for making iron did not become generally available until the first millennium AD. In the Siberian interior local metallurgy was eventually abandoned in favour of imported wares, made available by the development of beaten metal technology and of permanent trade systems between the taiga zone and the more advanced cultures to the south-west. This change, characterized by the disappearance of pottery and its substitution by vessels made of sheet copper, took place within the last thousand years.

Apart from the Samoyed and Tungus migrations, it is reasonably certain that two other large movements took place in the Forest Zone: the dispersal of the Uralic peoples and the Yakut migration. Information made available by linguistic palaeontology places the primeval home of the Uralic peoples in the middle Volga–Kama region. This original period, according to historical linguistics, should be dated to before 2000 BC. If this is true, it means that the Kama–Ural Forest Neolithic groups can be identified with the Proto-Finno-Ugrians. From about 2000 BC penetration of northern Europe and western Siberia by the Proto-Finno-Ugrians left material traces that can be seen in a number of cultures.[11]

The parent culture of the Yakut, a Turkic-speaking people, was located around Lake Baikal. The horse- and cattle-breeding, farming and hunting people of the Kurumchinsk culture were displaced by Mongolic pastoralists about AD 1100. Many of them migrated

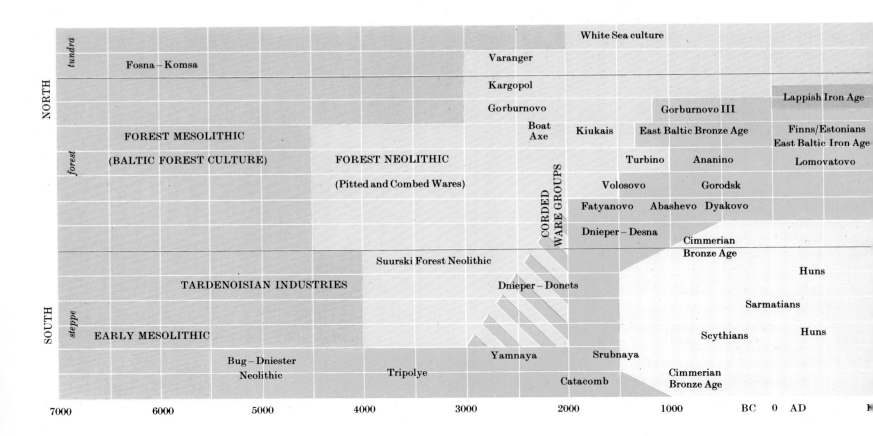

northwards along the Lena river, until in its middle reaches they found a habitat resembling their own. After the initial displacement of the indigenous population over wide areas, they were unable to maintain their old form of economy, despite the favourable relic steppe vegetation and the unusually low snow cover. When the Russians arrived in the seventeenth century, they found the Yakut in the process of transition to reindeer breeding and the indigenous fishing and hunting technology.[12]

Conclusion

Various factors, including population increase, environmental change and contact with more complex cultures to the south, influenced the development of northern Eurasia in the Holocene. All these factors played some part in upsetting the equilibrium between population and resources, or within different elements of the population itself. Readjustment usually demanded an intensified use of the available resources, such as the development of marine hunting or combined hunting–farming societies. In cultural terms this resulted in remarkably similar economic, social and technological developments that spanned a large geographical area and a considerable range of time. This uniformity was also promoted by direct contact. Skis, watercraft and – from 500 BC onwards – dog-harnessed and eventually reindeer-drawn sledges provided transport that could rapidly cover long distances in the flat and treeless tundra terrain or upon the frozen rivers that dissected the taiga. The contact between groups is reflected in the material culture: skis made of Siberian pine, which does not occur west of the Urals, have been found in Finland, for instance, and many distinctive forms of artifact are distributed over wide areas of northern Eurasia. Nevertheless, it is the parallelism of different parts of the area that is most striking. The uniformity of Forest Neolithic pottery, the combination of marine hunting and swine herding among such disparate groups as the Pitted Ware, the Saaremaa islanders and the Okhotsk culture, or the development of maritime adaptations about 3000 BC in a number of unrelated historical contexts are impressive examples of the regularity of cultural development within comparable environmental constraints.

49.2: *Phases in the development of prehistory in the northern and eastern parts of the European Forest Zone. The Forest Neolithic phase saw a more intensive use of resources, especially of marine and plant foods, and the homogeneity of the preceding period was replaced by a more varied range of specialized economies. (For northern Asia, see Figure 38.1.)*

Mesolithic: hunting and fishing economy without pottery use

Forest Neolithic: hunting and fishing with pottery use and probably greater concentration on plant resources

Farming and animal husbandry: in northern and eastern Europe usually combined with extensive hunting and fishing

Mounted nomadic pastoralism with simple farming as a secondary activity

50. The prehistory of Oceania: colonization and cultural change

The prehistory of Oceania, which comprises the regions of Melanesia, Micronesia and Polynesia, began 50 000 years ago, but the most remote islands received their first human colonists barely a thousand years ago. The prehistoric period ended gradually between the first arrival of Europeans in the sixteenth century and their final penetration of the New Guinea highlands during the last half-century.

There are five major themes to be considered in the prehistory of these regions: the peoples and initial settlement of the Oceanic islands; the early development of agriculture in Melanesia; the colonization of Oceania, where a large number of islands scattered over a vast expanse of ocean were settled with great speed by small founding populations; the processes that led to the diversification of local populations following initial colonization, well illustrated by New Zealand and a group of islands known as the Polynesian Outliers; and the economic and social systems of Oceania.

The Oceanic islands and their people
The islands of the Pacific offer diverse habitats for man. There is an important distinction between the islands of the partly submerged continents west of the Andesite Line (see Figure 50.1) and those further east, where submarine volcanic mountains penetrate the surface to form volcanic islands or indicate their presence by a cap of coral. The largest high islands west of the line are, in terms of geology and climate, as diverse as continents. Papua New Guinea, for example, has a snow-capped central cordillera within 6° of the equator, high plateaux, swampy lowlands and coastal plains. Such islands are rich in resources for human settlement. Inside the Andesite Line there are many high, volcanic islands, which generally offer fewer resources. They often have a windward–leeward climatic distinction, which is reflected in the pattern of rainfall. Most high islands have large, deep valleys with alluvial soils, fringing reefs along the shores or barrier reefs lying offshore. There is a large number of low islands that consist of reefs lying near sea level, while others have been elevated by volcanic activity. Low islands are often short of good soil and sometimes of water. The most extreme habitats are atolls, which comprise a rim of coral reef enclosing a lagoon without a central island. Along the reef are sandy islets rarely more than a metre or two above high-tide level. Maritime people have lived in such places for thousands of years.

Pacific islands occur both in groups and in isolation. From west to east there are general (though by no means regular) trends that have importance for human settlement. There is a tendency for island size to diminish and for the islands themselves to become more remote, and there is a progressive impoverishment of their flora and fauna, although marine life remains rich. The increasingly difficult environments further east prevented hunter–gatherers who arrived in New Guinea in Pleistocene times from penetrating far into Oceania. This was only accomplished late in prehistory, by people who developed a highly sophisticated maritime technology, a portable economy and adequate means of harvesting the sea.

Oceanic people had a technology without metal. Some societies, especially in sago-rich areas of New Guinea, maintained a considerable dependence on gathering and hunting, but agriculture developed early, dispersed widely and, in some areas, became intensive. Among the large number of cultivated plants were taro, sweet potato, yam, coconut, banana and breadfruit. In Melanesia tubers were often dominant; in Micronesia and Polynesia both tree crops and tubers were important. Swidden (slash-and-burn) agriculture was general, but there were widespread instances of intensification that included monocropping of sweet potato in the New Guinea highlands and taro irrigation elsewhere. A very large number of 'wild' plants were used as industrial materials – for medicine, cosmetics, fish poison, etc. Domesticated animals included pigs, dogs and fowl. Marine resources were important for coastal peoples.

Settlement patterns ranged from dispersed households to nucleated villages. Melanesian society was typically small-scale and egalitarian, without a formal hierarchy based on status, though within local groups certain men, known as 'big men', achieved considerable influence in their lifetime. This social structure contrasted with that of Polynesian society, which was not only on a larger scale, but was also stratified and characterized by hereditary leadership, a system seldom found in Melanesia and never in a highly developed form.

Origins of agriculture in Melanesia
The earliest known site in New Guinea is Kosipe, dated to about 26 000 years ago. It lay 2000 metres above sea level, on the boundary between forest and montane grassland. Seasonal occupation for the gathering of *pandanus* nuts is inferred, and hunting in the grasslands is also likely.

There is growing evidence for the presence of agriculture in the highlands early in the post-Pleistocene, even before the severance of Australia and New Guinea by rising sea levels. Indeed, the evidence for agriculture follows so rapidly after climatic amelioration that it may already have been developing at a lower altitude. The climate began to warm after 15 000 years ago, and the tree line rose considerably between about 11 000 and 8500 years ago, greatly diminishing the area of grassland surrounding the dwindling ice.

Archaeological evidence of agriculture within this period occurs in the intramontane basins of the highlands. Ground and polished axes (or adzes) were present at the site of Kafiavana after 11 000 years ago[1] and may have been used for bush clearance. A solitary pig tooth is reported from each of two rockshelter sites, Kiowa and Yuku, in levels that date to about 10 000 years ago.[2] Pigs reached Melanesia from south-east Asia, which was the source of many of the plant staples and domesticated animals of Oceania. It is believed that pigs were commonly fed with cultivated food, so it seems possible that some of the imported plant crops had been carried across the Wallace Line by this early date, although horticulture based on plants indigenous to New Guinea may have occurred independently of outside stimulus in the period immediately following the Pleistocene,[3] or even before. Likely candidates include sugar cane, some of the yams, sago, the *Australimusa* section of bananas and *pandanus*.

The best evidence for agriculture comes from the highland swamp site of Kuk, which at 1550 metres lay above the altitudinal limit for tropical species until the end of the Pleistocene.[4] Some 9000 years ago a distinctive deposit of grey clay began to form in the swamp, which has been interpreted as the result of erosion in the catchment caused by land clearance for gardens. It seems that this deposit formed because of the abandonment of a system of agricultural management of the swamp using large drainage channels. A number of subsequent and increasingly sophisticated phases of agricultural activity and water control in the swamp have been identified, whose history is closely related to that of the surrounding region.

Important developments are recorded in the swamp. By approximately 2500 years ago deposits indicate the practice of tillage in the catchment, suggesting that the sustained pressure of slash-and-burn agriculture by an expanding population had led to the widespread destruction of forest and the creation of grassland. This inference is supported by pollen evidence and also by the hoe-like stone implements known from several locations by this time. After 2000 years ago intricate drainage grids similar to recently recorded ones may represent a change from mixed cropping to monocropping of taro in the swamp. It is likely that intensified agriculture, supporting high local populations of people and pigs, predates the arrival of the sweet potato about 300 years ago. This crop, which reached the western Pacific by the agency of Spanish and Portuguese navigators, later became dominant in the highlands because of its greater productivity and altitudinal tolerance.

The colonization of Oceania

Settlement of the greater Australian continent (the area linked by low sea levels that includes New Guinea and Tasmania) occurred by 50 000 years ago, although the earliest evidence from New Guinea dates to 26 000 years ago. It has been calculated that the shortest route through Wallacea involved a sea voyage of 87 kilometres: at this time marine technology was rudimentary, but computer simulations suggest that founding groups of only a handful of people could have been sufficient. In coastal New Guinea, the Bismarcks and the northern Solomons there are glimpses of early activity in the form of surface artifacts. However, the earliest

deposits, dated to about 4000 BC, are from New Ireland, where at Balof Cave there is evidence that small quantities of obsidian were transported 600 kilometres from the Talasea source. Long-distance movements of goods remained a feature of subsequent cultures. It is useful to distinguish the region of Near Oceania, comprising large islands and short water gaps down the Solomons chain as far as San Christobal, from the more isolated archipelagoes and islands further east, known as Remote Oceania.[5] In the latter there is no evidence of human occupation before 1500 BC, with the possible exception of the enigmatic mounds of New Caledonia and the Isle de Pins, which are of uncertain age and origin.[6]

After 1500 BC a rapid spread took place, which is marked by the material of the Lapita culture. Known sites are distributed from Mussau in the west to Samoa in Western Polynesia (see Figure 50.4). The only obvious gap is in the main Solomons chain, but this is probably due to patchy fieldwork. The Lapita Cultural Complex has been described as a maritime, horticultural adaptation, characterized in places by a pattern of long-distance exchange.[7] Lapita sites occupy a specialized niche on small offshore islands or similar locations on the coast of large islands. These sites are conspicuous by their pottery. Other colonizing groups in island Melanesia are less obvious; where these overlapped with Lapita, they generally emerged a little later. This is the case in the northern and south-east Solomons, and it is also true of cultural sequences in the central and southern New Hebrides. In New Caledonia a tradition of paddle-impressed pottery was contemporary with the earliest Lapita ware, but the nature of their association is unclear. In short, there is no evidence that Lapita people were influenced by contemporary populations at the time of their initial spread.

Lapita sites are widely separated, which suggests that their distribution was not the product of ecological factors alone. People were not expanding simply to find more land, because they travelled very much further than was necessary. Some communities on remote low islands, for example, had to be supplied with stone by long-distance trade. Although Lapita sites spread rapidly, occupation continued in the areas settled. The implication is that some of the colonists became settlers while others continued their voyage.

This raises the question of the origins of the colonizing populations. There is no evidence to suggest that a continuous supply of settlers moved down the line to provide reinforcements at the voyaging frontier. It is more likely that initially there was a small population with the ability to reproduce fast enough to supply its own recruits and the capacity to equip them.

The Lapita colonization can be compared with the spread of early pottery sites in the first century AD in south coastal Papua, and also with the string of Archaic sites of the twelfth and thirteenth centuries AD that stretch down the east coast of New Zealand. These three distributions have several points in common. The sites are conspicuously alike in material culture in each case; there was widespread dispersal by sea and it was so rapid that on an archaeological time-scale it was instantaneous; in each case

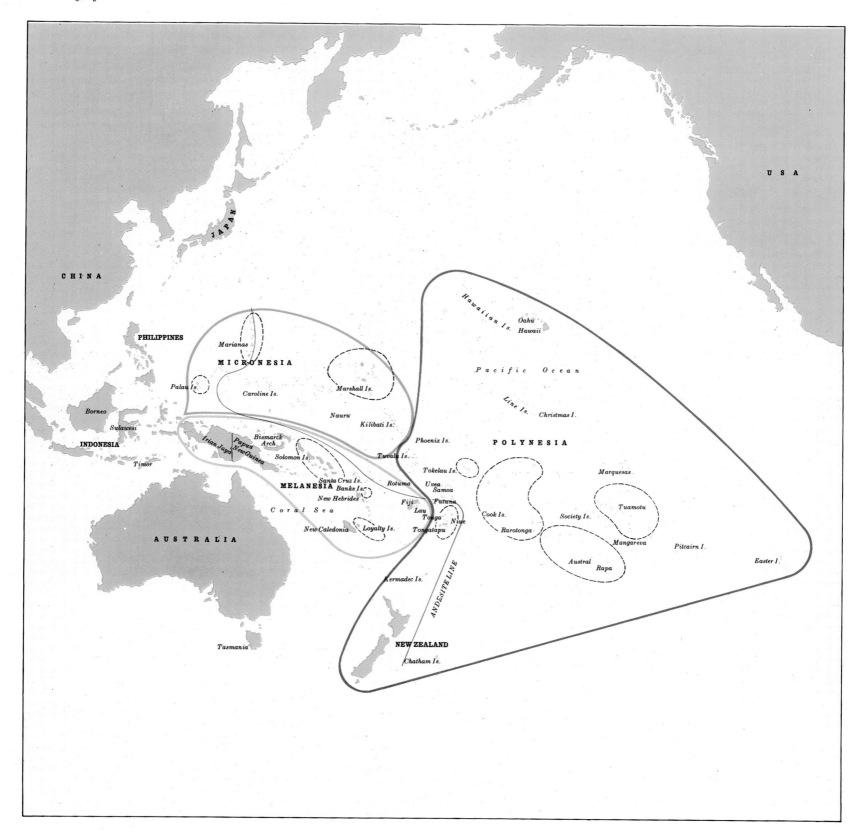

there was widespread movement of industrial stone from identified sources; and the colonists practised agriculture. The New Zealand evidence has usually been interpreted in terms of settlers whose founding population is thought not to have been large, although the early sites are widespread.

What, then, happened in Western Polynesia? Was there an interruption in the eastward movement of Lapita populations, during which characteristic Polynesian features emerged?[8] If so, why did this standstill occur, and why did these populations isolate themselves and differentiate from their Melanesian origins, given their known seagoing ability? Less than ten years ago it was thought that there were progressive west–east steps of settlement in Western Polynesia, in parallel with the pattern of linguistic sub-grouping. At that time Lapita sites had not yet been found in Samoa, but it is now known that settlement of the whole area took place at approximately the same time. Recent archaeology has also raised problems for the isolation theory. The pottery sequences of Fiji, Tonga, Samoa, Uvea, Futuna and the Lau are similar throughout the first millennium BC, which argues against local isolation. With the exception of Fiji, where pottery-making continued, there was a parallel development (and subsequent extinction) of Polynesian Plain Ware. One theory able to accommodate the evidence is that language and some elements of material culture diverged within the context of continuing communication. There are many ethnographic instances of regular contact between different culture groups – the specialized traders of Melanesia are good examples: some speak the languages of neighbours, while others use trade languages. Isolation in Western Polynesian prehistory was of a selective kind and occurred among interacting populations.

Eastern Polynesian prehistory is now generally considered to have begun in about AD 300, but there is a strong possibility that further fieldwork will extend it back well into the first millennium BC. Eastern Polynesian cultures share linguistic traits and artifacts without exact parallels in the west; however, the evidence indicates that island groups such as the Marquesas have early material, while other areas at the margins, like New Zealand, have later material. A model of successive dispersals seems appropriate.[9]

One problem associated with the identification of dispersal centres is that there is such similarity among known Eastern Polynesian sites dating to before AD 1000 that archaeologists are unlikely to be able to identify any one centre. All that can be said is that the area, of unknown size, was one within which the frequency of communication was sufficient to maintain homogeneity during the time of divergence from the Western Polynesian ancestor. Another difficulty encountered in reconstructing the sequence of dispersal to various islands stems from the probability of multiple settlement. The distribution of islands, some of which were much easier to reach than others, makes it likely that some islands received a second settlement before others received their first.[10] Secondary contacts would have left no linguistic trace if they were very slight, but if secondary settlers were numerous they probably overwhelmed their predecessors. Given the character of archaeological samples, many episodes of colonization may be inaccessible to us. Nonetheless, the evidence that is available shows that by AD 1000 the colonization of Oceania was complete.

50.1: *The island groups of Oceania and its major cultural divisions. From west to east the Pacific islands become both more remote and increasingly impoverished in resources. Colonization of the region was achieved by people with a maritime technology, a portable economy and sophisticated means of harvesting the sea.*

50.2: *A Mailu canoe of south-eastern Papua New Guinea similar to ones that made long voyages in Oceanic prehistory. The canoes were fast, navigators had sophisticated systems of dead-reckoning and islands could be detected from considerable distances offshore.*

The settlement of Remote Oceania took only 2500 years. Some general points are clear: the process was very rapid, given the vast area concerned, and there was a lot of purposeful colonization. One argument for this is that many islands are very difficult to reach by chance; for instance, it has been calculated that the probability of a drift to New Zealand is less than 1 in 100. Preparation is evident, in that domestic plants and animals were carried on voyages. Nearly all the important tropical food plants that could grow in a temperate climate were carried on board the canoes to New Zealand. Those that could not grow, such as coconut, bread-fruit and banana, were probably taken too but did not survive. This may explain the surprising absence of the pig, as may the fact that New Zealand was exceptional in having a wild terrestrial alternative, the moa, a large, flightless bird.

There is no doubt that colonization was deliberate, which raises the question of motivation. One common idea is that Oceanic people had a passion for exploration, or were habituated to it; another view is that the journeys were voyages of exile. There are arguments against the interpretation of early migrations as the result of pressure of population in the islands of source. First, the people who left took with them large capital items such as canoes and stores: expensive voyages can only have been supported by surplus production, and other population controls are cheaper than this. Second, voyages left island groups much earlier than the stress of numbers is attested archaeologically. Moreover, the voyages did not continue until large islands such as New Zealand had been filled by successive groups of migrants: the peripheral parts of Polynesia received a founding population and the process soon stopped. The evidence for this is that in Polynesia there is early widespread similarity in material culture, followed by deep-ening isolation and divergence. In the early period there was no expansion of land-eaters, simply an episode of pure colonization.

New Zealand was settled with the aid of multi-hulled craft by AD 1000, and the distribution of Archaic settlement implies a mobile, maritime people. However, that culture soon marooned itself, as at the time of contact, although large single canoes were extensively used, they were poor boats for sea-going. (Captain Cook's ship was overtaken by a double canoe, but these were rare.) Elsewhere, the Mangarevans were reduced mostly to sailing rafts and the Chatham Islanders to reed boats. Overall, the evidence from Polynesia suggests that the exercise was intended simply to place founding populations on all islands; with very rare exceptions, this aim was achieved. Once done, the strategy changed. Oceanic cultures expanded rapidly in a phase of settlement and subsequently entered a phase of local adaptation and diversification in the various island groups.

There is a continuing argument about voyaging skills. Until about twenty years ago many scholars favoured the notion of navigated return voyages of exploration, such as were thought to be recorded in indigenous tradition. Then it became accepted that the Pacific was settled by relatively uncontrolled drift voyages; but the reputation of Oceanic peoples as navigators has recently

been restored. One of their feats may have been to collect the sweet potato from America and carry it to Eastern Polynesia more than 1000 years ago. Despite this, current opinion maintains that they could not regularly travel beyond 600 kilometres and subsequently undertake a second outward voyage to the same place. Yet we are faced with the situation that once virtually every scrap of land in the Pacific had been settled, the process stopped. That is a remarkable coincidence. Unless there was some wide-spread underlying reason for the ending of voyages, it suggests that information that the islands had been successfully colonized was transmitted back to the sources.

The most important issue in relation to voyaging is not the question of one- or two-way voyages, or deliberately navigated voyages as against accidental drifts; it concerns the early high frequency and later low frequency of voyaging. The distinction has been obscured by the exceptional cases. It is well known that voyages continued where inter-island distances were short, as

among the Society Islands and north-western Tuamotus, or within Western Polynesia and Fiji. Another case is exemplified by Micronesia, whose scattered islands were too small to be viable in the long term without a continuing flow of trade goods and information. Communication was also necessary to restore local populations that were periodically extinguished or reduced as a result of tidal waves or other natural disasters. In cases such as these there were ecological reasons for the persistence of maritime skills that were formerly more widespread. However, the functional context was now different. In remote areas, where islands were larger, such continuing reinforcement became impossible and, in the long term, was also unnecessary.

It has often been said that to the people involved the sea was more a bridge than a barrier. Because there had always been more islands to find before, the voyagers could continue to assume that it was worth going to look for others, although there may have been some uneasiness among crews when distances between islands became very great. But by this stage the idea of a sea of islands would not have been critical because colonizing voyages clearly had great range. The ethnographic evidence indicates that canoes were fast; islands could be detected from a considerable distance; and navigators had sophisticated systems of dead-reckoning. Although there is no way of knowing how many lives were lost in these exploratory voyages, it is arguable that had the strategy of colonization been too costly, it would not have succeeded. The number of successful early voyages was sufficient to settle all of Oceania at a time when the total population was not nearly as large as it was later to become.

What colonizing populations thought they were doing and what they were actually doing are two separate questions. Geographical expansion, however it has been perceived, has been part of a general cultural strategy of human beings for at least two million years. It is possible to trace the progressive expansion of successive grades of hominid and to associate technological innovations with the occupation of certain environments. Oceania was the last part of the Earth to be settled (apart from the ice caps). In the Pacific people were able to colonize smaller and more remote islands, increasingly impoverished in natural resources. This was achieved by the adoption of a maritime culture and a portable economy.

Diversification and the Polynesian Outliers

After the colonization of Oceania there followed changes that led to the patterns of diversity observed at the time of European contact. The basic elements of change include the nature of initial migrants, the influences for change within and beyond the area settled and the time-depth of settlement. In the case of Melanesian prehistory, many explanations of change have invoked discrete migrations, invasions, intrusions and diffusions,[11] some of which do not stand up to close inspection, and local archaeological sequences can generally be explained in terms of continuous models where the processes at work are similar to those described ethnographically. These can be reduced to three general processes: adaptation to variable circumstances; the relative isolation of populations; and events whose occurrence can be predicted only in probabilistic terms, such as the chances of inter-island drift.[12] The following example illustrates this approach to problems in Pacific prehistory.

50.3: *Modern pottery making in Mailu is the current stage of an unbroken tradition that extends back a thousand years. These potters have a monopoly in the district and produce a standardized trade ware. Earlier, when potting was a widespread skill, the ware was more variable, reflecting the domestic context of production.*

The Polynesian Outliers are communities on small islands along the windward fringes of Melanesia and Micronesia (see Figure 50.4). Their inhabitants have sometimes been identified as Polynesian on the basis of their physical appearance, but the main criterion is language. Some fourteen languages found on nineteen islands all belong to the Samoic-Outlier group. Because the consensus view is that Polynesian language and culture developed within Polynesia itself, settlement of the Outliers is seen as a subsequent backwash movement. Results of initial excavations on the Outliers were puzzling to archaeologists, who had expected to find evidence of cultural replacement there. On Nukuoro a 600-year sequence revealed no Polynesian replacement in what was materially a Micronesian culture. Similar situations were encountered in the New Hebrides. On Rennell and Bellona in the Solomons Outlier sequences go back 2000 years, without clear evidence for replacement. On Taumako in the Duff Islands continuous occupation for over 500 years until the present was marked by artifacts characteristic of that part of Melanesia. The 3000-year prehistory of Anuta does not reveal a Polynesian takeover either, although it may have been discontinuous. It began to seem that either cultural replacements were stealthy processes or Outlier populations had perhaps previously adapted to Melanesian or Micronesian conditions on other unidentified islands.

Given a multiple settlement model, it appears that Polynesians moving down from the east with prevailing winds and currents upon the target arcs of the Melanesian island chains would reach the Outliers and would also pass through them to the larger islands. The proportions of voyagers doing one or the other would presumably vary according to whether voyages were navigated or drift. However, Outlier communities have not been found on

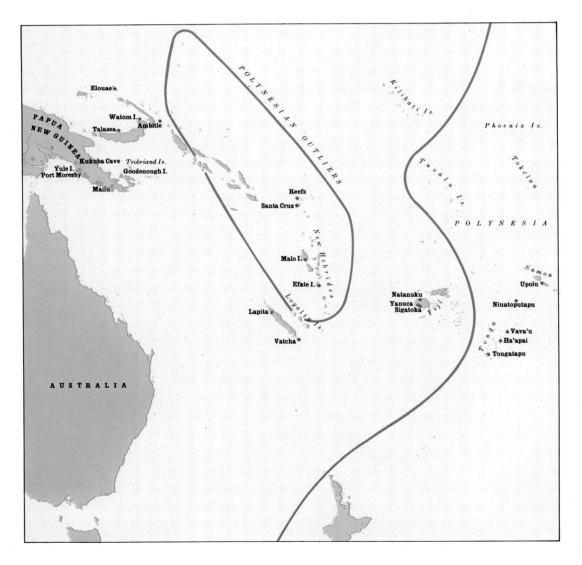

50.4: *Early Papuan sites, Lapita sites and the Polynesian Outliers. After 1500 BC colonists of the Lapita culture swept through Oceania to Western Polynesia, where they became ancestral to the Polynesians. A later backwash movement carried Polynesians into Melanesia and Micronesia, where they survived on the remote Outliers but were absorbed elsewhere.*

- • Lapita sites
- • early Papuan ceramic sites

the large islands. A likely explanation is that the smaller the island, the greater the impact of the migrants. In Melanesia there is a gradient of Polynesian influence that roughly corresponds to island size. The essence of the question, therefore, is not arrival but survival: Outlier communities once existed that now do not. One of these, somewhere among the large islands of the southern Solomons, gave rise to the community on Rennell and Bellona, which on geographical grounds could hardly have been reached from any known Outlier.

The Outlier problem now can be seen in a different light. Paradoxically, cultural replacement usually occurred not on the islands themselves but elsewhere, where such communities are still unknown. The Outliers have Melanesian or Micronesian artifacts well adapted to local environments and indicate one component of cultural input. Biologically, Polynesian traits occur in the Outliers but not alone. Elsewhere in Melanesia a Polynesian contribution has been made to an already diverse genetic inventory. There is almost a case for renaming the Outliers. The survival of Polynesian traits, notably language, occurred entirely because they outlie from Melanesia and Micronesia, and their spatial relationship to Polynesia is immaterial. They may be regarded as Melanesian or Micronesian Outliers (of Polynesian speakers).

Economic and social systems

The diverse cultures that evolved in Melanesia included many instances of remarkable specialization, among them the central places that developed within the specialized trading systems of coastal Papua.

The emergence of one such system, that of the Mailu in southeastern Papua, is known in detail.[13] At the close of prehistory Mailu had a population four times the average size of those of local villages. It was the only place in a wide area to make pots, which were usually traded for the food that the small island could not produce itself. Mailu was a point of articulation of local trade and of another, long-distance, network. Archaeology indicates that this area was first settled by pottery-making people some 2000 years ago. They practised a general gardening and fishing economy and lived in villages distributed along the coast and on offshore islands. At this time all villages were about the same size and were functionally unspecialized. Mailu developed as it gradually became central to the pattern of regional communication. Mineralogical study of pottery and clay sources shows that while pottery was made in a number of villages at first, all sources except Mailu dropped out. The monopoly became established at the precise location where pots could be distributed most efficiently from a single source to a wide area; with its establishment the Mailu ware became more standardized in form and decoration until finally a mass-produced trade ware evolved.

The emergence of Mailu at the same time as other Papuan trading systems, such as the Kula ring and the Hiri, is of particular importance to an understanding of the rich ethnographic literature of this area. There are various reasons why this should have

happened to some settlements and not to others. Ecological factors were partly responsible. Mailu, for example, had good clay deposits and little gardening land, and it relied on sea transport; but this combination of resources was also to be found in many places that lacked specialized centres. Their occurrence is related also to locational factors, as in the case of Mailu and also in the Kula, where the small but central island of Tubetube was the home of the most developed community of sea traders at the end of the prehistoric period. Other causal factors may be involved too. With a larger than normal population supported by the developing pottery trade, possession of seagoing canoes and the natural defences of their island, the Mailu may have become dominant in local warfare. However, this hypothesis has yet to be validated, for while there is evidence for some inter-village fighting during late prehistory, at the time of European contact the Mailu were partly supported by the sale of pots to villages to whom they were traditionally hostile. Trade and skirmishing were simply different aspects of one interaction system.

The Mailu Island community also exhibited a sociological difference from others in the area. While remaining egalitarian, it was internally more segmented, probably because of its greater size. However, had Mailu prehistory continued for longer, a degree of social stratification might have developed, and the factors that led to the emergence of Mailu may be similar to those associated with the rise of stratified societies in other parts of the world.

The difference between egalitarian societies and those based on hereditary inequality is a key distinction between Melanesia and Polynesia. Ancestral Polynesian culture incorporated a form of chieftainship, and during prehistory social stratification developed to different levels in different island groups. Tongan, Samoan and Tahitian society became markedly stratified, while Hawaii approached the formation of a primitive state. A range of theories has attempted to explain this variability. While a relationship between the distribution of resources and the degree of stratification has been proposed,[14] some regard status rivalry, not ecology, as the basis of social evolution.[15] Stratification has also been related to irrigation, a practice that developed not as a response to population pressure but (as in Hawaii) as a means by which chiefs gained competitive advantage over their rivals.[16] This theory could not hold for Tonga, however, where archaeological evidence of stratification is associated not with irrigation but with shifting cultivation.

Recent studies in Melanesia suggest that other variables may be involved. The celebrated case of chieftainship in the Trobriand Islands provides an example.[17] A local Trobriand subclan had only one recognized village leader; the many subclans and their leaders all had their different ascribed ranks. There were several economic districts, each with a senior chief. In the north Kiriwina was renowned for agriculture. However, the villages of Kuboma lay inland on stony lands, and although they were famous for their craft specialists, their status was lower. The village of the district chief was centrally located within each district; the village of the 'paramount' chief of the Trobriands ranked as the most central of all.[18] Chiefs managed unusually large quantities of resources, and the basis of this wealth was polygamy. While most people's income and outgoings were similar, chiefs received gifts of greater volume, and a high proportion of these originated from beyond the village and, sometimes, the district. The central locations of villages of ranking chiefs were ideal, given their role as centres for both the collection and the redistribution of goods – not only did chiefs accumulate wealth, they also disbursed it in a range of social activities.

A further point may be made about rank and the district economy. From north to south the strength of the district economies tended to decrease. Villages towards the south also became less well connected within the island network, a pattern that corresponds to the decreasing rank of leaders. In the far south they were no longer chiefs but just headmen. This pattern is the result of the interrelated factors of ecology, demography and centrality.

Conclusion

In Oceania there is direct continuity from prehistory into history. The descendants of prehistoric people are still alive, and the distinction between ethnography and late prehistory is often arbitrary. There is similar continuity in the ecological context of human behaviour, so archaeology in the region is generally anthropological in approach and the scope for inference is unusually broad. Because of the great range of sizes, environmental circumstances, degrees of remoteness and time-depth of settlements, the many thousands of islands in the Pacific provide a particularly valuable opportunity to study social change.

51. Holocene Australia

One of the most striking features of recent archaeological research has been the discovery that early Australians between 30 000 and 20 000 years ago possessed knowledge and skills at least as highly developed as those of other cultures elsewhere in the inhabited world of the time. The early immigrants must have been fairly accomplished navigators, as Greater Australia (including New Guinea) would always have been separated from the south-east Asian mainland by water-crossings of at least 60 kilometres, even at the maximum lowering of sea level during the last glacial period. The earliest human fossils, those from Lake Mungo, are fully representative of anatomically modern man and were also associated with evidence of cremation burial. Artistic designs were being traced on the walls of Koonalda Cave, while evidence of the use of ochre colouring material has been recovered from a number of early deposits, including Lake Mungo.[1] By contrast, the stone-tool technology is relatively unsophisticated in comparison with, say, the contemporary Upper Palaeolithic blade technologies of Eurasia. Flake scrapers and steep cores are the principal tool types, and their use has resulted in relatively uniform assemblages that are usually grouped together as the Australian core-tool and scraper tradition. Whether the crudity of the primary stone-working technique should be attributed to the available stone or, perhaps, to a dependence on perishable raw materials, it is in any case counterbalanced by evidence of grinding techniques for the sharpening of stone axes and of bone-tool manufacture, the former dated to 25 000 BP at Malangangerr in the Northern Territory.

This emerging body of information has added chronological

51.1: *These meandering grooves, incised by fingers in the soft limestone of Koonalda Cave in South Australia, cover large areas of the walls of this ancient flint quarry. The motifs have been dated to at least 20 000 years ago.*

51.2: *A tula adze from South Australia. These adzes (or chisels) were set into a wooden handle and used for a variety of tasks.*

depth and perspective to the later episodes of prehistory. What ethnographers have taken to be a classic example of the stable hunter–gatherer way of life is being increasingly demonstrated by archaeological research to have been the end-product of tens of thousands of years of cultural existence. While it was characterized in some respects by continuity of traditions, certain of its important features were marked by change and development.

The environmental background

Australia is renowned through geography textbooks as the arid continent, a land of desert or semi-desert plains and dissected plateaux ringed by better watered and occasionally, as in the southeast, more mountainous peripheries. The vegetation is mostly a fire-adapted one, ranging from eucalypt woodlands and savannas in the coastal regions to acacia scrub in the more arid interior.

Patches of rain forest occur in the high-rainfall areas of the Queensland coast and Tasmania. Over half the continent receives less than 50 millimetres of rain per year, and the water regime everywhere is marked above all by its unpredictability from year to year. The skilful, flexible, eclectic responses of Aboriginal society to such difficult and variable environmental conditions is one of the outstanding features of Australian ethnography. For the archaeologist the question arises of the course of environmental change during preceding millennia and the antiquity of economic adaptations that have been observed only recently. The question of the impact of human activity on the landscape and its contribution to environmental change, especially through the manipulation of fire, also needs to be considered, even for the earliest periods of human settlement.

The more general effects of global climatic change during the

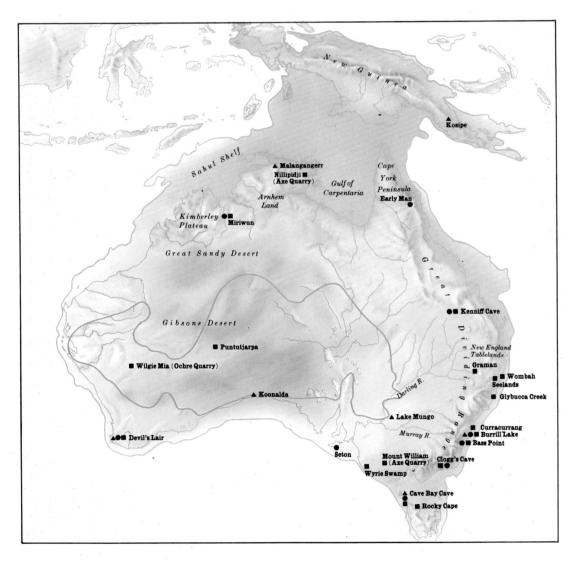

51.3: *Map of Australia showing the distribution of archaeological sites mentioned in the text. The Pleistocene coastline indicates the maximum extent of land at the height of the last glacial period about 18 000 years ago.*

	approximate coastline during the Pleistocene
	250 mm annual isohyet
▲	sites earlier than *c.* 20 000 BP
●	sites of 20 000–10 000 BP
■	sites from 10 000 BP to the present

51.4: *Aerial photograph of the southern end of Lake Mungo, taken from the south-west. The eroded dune surface in the foreground and upper right surrounds the dry lake floor. The lake was full of fresh water from about 40 000 to 15 000 years ago, but has since then been dry. Human occupation of the lake margins is dated to 36 000 years ago.*

last glacial period would have had a widespread effect on human populations in two principal ways: through temperature change and through changing sea levels. For much of the last glacial period conditions in Australia were both cooler and moister than they are now. Temperatures were between 5°C and 10°C lower than at present, and the extensive lake systems of the south-east, now completely dry, were filled with water. This may have been due to greater rainfall, but high lake levels may equally have resulted from lower evaporation rates because of cooler temperatures. Pollen sequences from north-east Queensland indicate a reduction of rain forest during the last glacial period, which suggests lower rainfall. A further drop in rainfall is indicated by the development of dry eucalypt woodland from about 38 000 years ago, though this could also have resulted from the firing of the landscape by human populations. At about 10 000 BP (8000 BC)

a sharp increase in rainfall is indicated by the return of the rain-forest vegetation, which persists in the area today.[2] There is thus some uncertainty about the interrelationship of different climatic indicators in different regions. What does seem certain is that the freshwater lakes in the south, so attractive to the early Australians, were already undergoing fluctuations of water level from about 30 000 years ago; by some 15 000 years ago they had dried out completely, indicating conditions of maximum aridity.

The lowering of sea level to more than 100 metres below the present level, which coincided with the maximum extent of the last glacial some 18 000 years ago, exposed areas of continental shelf, and land bridges linked New Guinea and Tasmania with the Australian mainland, creating a landmass a third larger than that of today. The progressive loss of these coastal lands, as the sea level rose to reach approximately its present level by 3000 BC,

would have altered the shape of the continent considerably. However, this may not have been quite the catastrophe for human settlement that it at first appears. Investigation of the now submerged Sahul Shelf off the northern coast of Australia suggests that, when exposed, this was an arid, albeit easily traversed, tract of land. Moreover, it is probable that the effects of the monsoon, which brings heavy rains to the northern coasts during summer and contributes to the high seasonal productivity of coastal areas, were restricted at this time by the cooler climate and the blocking of the warm ocean currents from the east by the sea bed that had emerged. Thus it is possible that the more convoluted (and hence longer) profile of the present coastline, and the stabilization of coastal habitats as the sea reached its present level, increased the potential supply of aquatic food resources, offering some compensation for the loss of land.

A number of changes in technology, subsistence and settlement distributions are discernible in the wake of these environmental changes, and in many cases they may represent indirect, if not direct, responses to them. An enigmatic aspect of late Pleistocene environmental change that should be mentioned is the extinction of the marsupial megafauna. Although the survival of large creatures such as the rhinoceros-sized *Diprotodon* overlapped the presence of man in time, there is as yet no unequivocal evidence to suggest that they were hunted for food or that they owe their extinction to human over-kill. The extinction of these large marsupials may be due rather to climatic change or to more subtle encroachments upon their habitat and can hardly be invoked as a significant factor in subsequent cultural developments.

Technological change

The changes that are most evident to the archaeologist are the modifications to be observed in artifacts. A new technology of blade production and a range of new artifact types began to be used increasingly alongside the older, traditional ones. Tools already in use at an earlier period, such as the edge-ground axe and the tula adze (a broad endscraper with a steeply flaked margin), became more frequent. The latter occurred in some numbers at the base of the Puntutjarpa rockshelter sequence in the western desert about 10 000 years ago. Most of the innovations of the 'Australian small-tool tradition', however, date from about 4000 to 3000 BC. At Kenniff Cave in Queensland, for example, a number of the new tool types, including geometric microliths, backed blades, small unifacial 'Pirri' points, eloueras (thick, backed blades, triangular in section) and a burin, appeared between 5000 and 2500 years ago in levels stratified above earlier deposits with assemblages of the core and scraper tradition. Similar assemblages are recorded throughout Australia, although the distribution of specific tool types is by no means contiguous. Backed blades, absent from sites in the north and north-east, occur in greatest concentrations in the south-east. Unifacial 'Pirri' points are distri-

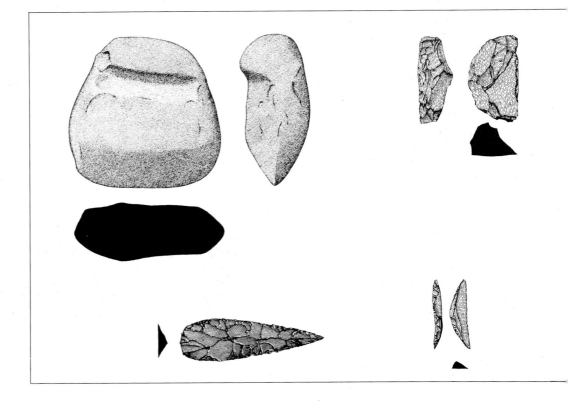

51.5: *A group of tools of the Australian small-tool tradition, drawn to half actual size. Near right, above: Pleistocene edge-ground axe from Malangangerr; below: unifacial 'Pirri' point from Mulka, South Australia. Far right, above: Elouera from Merewether, New South Wales; below: geometric microlith from Kenniff Cave (layer 9).*

buted in a broad swathe through the centre of the continent but are absent from eastern and western seaboards, while bifacially worked points are confined to the northerly part of this general area of distribution. Tula adzes appear to be most common in the desert regions in the centre of the continent.

The boomerang may also have been introduced during this period of technological change, although its antiquity is obscure because of the vagaries of wood preservation. Finds from Wyrie Swamp in South Australia dated to 8000 BC do at least give Australia a lead of five thousand years over the Braband specimen from Mesolithic Denmark.

The general similarity of the small-tool tradition, especially the microlithic component, with finds outside Australia suggests that it may have been introduced from elsewhere either by diffusion of ideas or through the immigration of new peoples. Backed-blade assemblages, known from suitably early contexts in the Celebes, India and Ceylon, support the hypothesis; the inundation of the Sunda Shelf as a consequence of rising sea levels, and the probable displacement of population that followed, render it plausible.

The persistence in Tasmania of the core and scraper tradition and the absence of the new artifact types offer further support to the hypothesis. In the absence of raw materials suitable for the construction of seaworthy craft capable of travelling more than 10 kilometres offshore, Tasmania's isolation from the Australian mainland was complete by about 8000 BC. However, isolation seems to have made the culture of the Tasmanians more susceptible to simplification than innovation, for the manufacture of bone tools and even the catching of fish had dropped out of use by the time Europeans reached the island.[3] The Tasmanian example, therefore, is not convincing refutation of the case for local development on the mainland.

Another significant indicator is the Aboriginal dog, the dingo. It must have come originally from south-east Asia, and its absence from New Guinea and Tasmania suggests that it was introduced after the submergence of the land bridges. This contention is also consistent with dated dingo remains in Australia, which are not recorded with certainty before about 6000 BC. Some movement between south-east Asia and Australia at about the time of the new developments in technology seems likely.

The principal drawback of an all-embracing diffusionist hypothesis is that the earliest fully developed backed-blade assemblages in north-west Australia are some three thousand years later than those in the south-east. Undated spear points in Indonesia are comparable with Australian examples but might argue for movement in either direction; other types, such as the tula adze, seem to be a distinctively Australian invention.

Alternative explanations look to the relationship between technological development and adaptation to changed environmental conditions. The greater frequency of tula adze flakes is perhaps most easily accounted for in this way. These were almost certainly hafted implements used principally for woodworking, which would have been in demand particularly for hard woods, such as

mulga, which are commonly found in desert areas. Similarly the elouera, commonly recorded in the south-east, seems to have been used in many cases for working soft woods.[4] The function of microlithic backed blades is rather more obscure. These are found in large numbers on all types of sites, from coastal dunes and shell middens to inland rockshelters. Recovery of specimens with traces of gum on the blunted edge indicates hafting. However, production of microliths had largely ceased by the time of European contact, regrettably depriving the archaeologist of the opportunity to make ethnographic observations of the manufacture and use of this ubiquitous artifact.

The disappearance of the microlithic backed blade is a reminder that technological change continued into the more recent prehistoric period. In the south-east, scene of the most prolonged and intensive archaeological investigations, with many dated sites and detailed sequences, eloueras and fabricators (*outils écaillés*) gradually superseded microlithic backed blades during the course of the last two thousand years. There is also evidence of an increase in the numbers of bone and shell artifacts. Although this may be the continuation of a tradition obscured by the poor preservation of organic materials in earlier deposits, the suggestion that fabricators may have been used for splitting bone used in tool manufacture is consistent with the evidence as it stands.

Economic change

Information about the economies practised by the early Australians is restricted by the scarcity of sites, the scantiness of traces of occupation and, in many cases, the poor preservation of dietary remains. Only the Mungo deposits have yielded a comprehensive picture of subsistence. A variety of resources was exploited, including freshwater mussels and golden perch taken from the lake, and small marsupial animals, such as the rat kangaroo and the hairy-nosed wombat, on land. Plant foods do not appear to have been collected in any quantity, to judge from the absence of grinding stones, but in other respects the pattern is very similar to that observed ethnographically among Aboriginal groups of the Murray-Darling basin in recent times.[5]

The absence of plant-food remains may be significant. Taken with other evidence, it suggests a relatively sparse population at an early stage of adaptation to the variable opportunities of the Australian environment. It is possible that the earliest routes of immigration from south-east Asia into Australia were along the coastlines, where the sea would have offered familiar food supplies in an otherwise alien environment and a line of least resistance in terms of economic adaptation. The relatively scanty evidence of occupation provided by deposits of this period at inland caves and rockshelters could indicate sporadic visits by settlers to the edge of territories whose principal settlements were located on the now submerged coastline; the Mungo sites, easily reached from the coast via the Murray-Darling river system, would then represent the inland equivalent of this early coastal economy.[6]

A number of native plant-food species would have been familiar to newcomers from south-east Asia, particularly in the north of Australia.[7] The presence of animal bones on the earliest known sites also suggests that the early Australians were already capable of hunting the marsupial fauna. Ignorance or inexperience in coping with an unfamiliar environment seems unlikely to have inhibited migration into the desert interior from a landfall somewhere on the north-west coast of Greater Australia, especially in view of the cooler and probably better watered conditions that are likely to have been found in many areas in the centre of the continent. The evidence, however, provides no indication of the development of intensive plant-food exploitation or of settlement in fully desert regions until the period beginning about 15 000 years ago, a period that coincides paradoxically with conditions of maximum aridity. The drying out of the lakes in the south-east would probably have had a detrimental effect on the economy. Subsequent occupation of middens in the Murray-Darling basin is also characterized by the introduction of grinding slabs. These could indicate a broadening of the diet to include previously neglected plant foods (probably the seeds of native millet) in response to local environmental pressure, or at any rate a more intensive exploitation of plant resources. The expansion of the population in the desert interior soon afterwards is indicated by sites such as Puntutjarpa, which was first occupied in about 8000 BC. Once established, these desert-adapted, plant-based economies seem to have survived almost without change until the ethnographic present.[8] The development of desert-adapted economies may have taken place slightly earlier to the north, in the Kimberleys and Arnhem Land, where grinding stones are dated to about 18 000 BP.

Other evidence of the expansion of populations and the increasingly diverse and determined exploitation of resources comes from the south-east. Intensive occupation from about 4000 BC onwards is recorded at a number of sites in a broad area extending from the New England Tablelands in the north to the rocky shores of Tasmania in the south, and in environments ranging from temperate sea shores and subtropical estuaries to the cooler upland regions of the Great Dividing Range.

The rockshelter of Graman, near the headwaters of the tributaries draining into the Darling river, has yielded evidence of grinding stones and crushed seeds, together with artifacts of the small-tool tradition and bones of possum and grey kangaroo, and suggests a successful extension of the seed-gathering adaptation. In contrast to the contemporary economies of the Murray-Darling basin, which seem to have been associated with considerable mobility prompted by seasonal variations in the water supply, archaeological evidence from Graman has been interpreted as

indicating almost year-round occupation. To the east of the mountain escarpment, rockshelters such as Seelands indicate a regular exploitation of resources in the coastal hinterland. Seasonal indicators, together with marine shells brought in from the coast over 40 kilometres away, suggest that the site may have been the winter resort of populations who spent the summer on the coast at large oyster middens, such as the Wombah oyster mound.[9]

Coastal shell middens of great variety, ranging from surface scatters to immense mounds, abound on many coastlines and appear to be confined to recent millennia. The earliest coastal middens, such as the one at Rocky Cape, are in Tasmania and are about eight thousand years old. A similar date for the start of intensive coastal occupation is indicated at Curracurrang, and many other coastal sites are recorded along the coastline of southern New South Wales, usually in rockshelters or as scatters

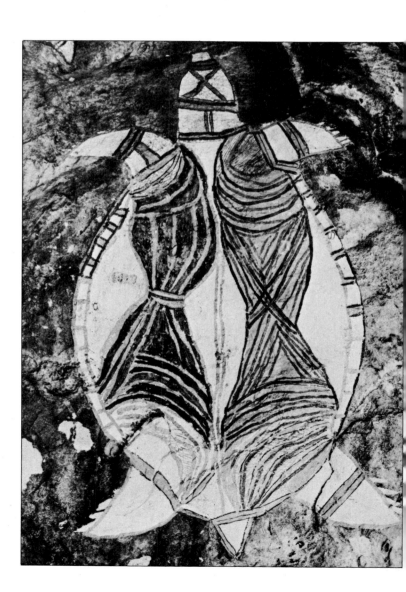

51.6: *Aboriginal rock painting of a turtle, found by wildlife scientists in the remote Arnhem Land, Northern Territory.*

on open sand dunes. Shell middens are rarely recorded along this coastline before about two thousand years ago, apparently because the conditions do not favour preservation. More substantial mounds of shell are found on the river estuaries of northern New South Wales. Early sites, dated to 2000 BC at Clybucca Creek, are located on an ancient shoreline abandoned because of the subsequent infilling of sediments and now situated some 10 kilometres inland from the present outlet of the Macleay river. The most spectacular coastal sites are the massive, steep-sided shell-mounds clustered around the shallow bays and large estuaries of Cape York and Arnhem Land, which seem to have accumulated mainly within the past two thousand years and many of which were in use up to the time of European settlement. It is possible that the beginnings of midden accumulation coincided with the formation of the extensive, shallow mud-flats and thick mangrove barriers that support the prolific shell beds of cockles and clams.

Other remains are sparsely recorded within these midden deposits, but it is clear that they were often associated with a wide range of subsistence activities – for example, the collection of plant foods such as yam tubers, water-lily rhizomes and nuts of the cycad and burrawang plants; the hunting of kangaroos, wallabies and paddymelons (a type of kangaroo); fishing for perch, mullet and snapper; sealing, the hunting of dugong (a large herbivorous mammal) or turtle and fowling; egg-collecting; and exploitation of a great many lesser resources besides, according to the opportunities offered by each locality. The sites were used in some cases only at certain seasons or for occasional meals, in others as more established foci of semi-sedentary settlement. Although molluscs form the bulk of the archaeological remains, they rarely constituted a substantial part of the diet, though they were clearly important during lean seasons and as a day-to-day supplement. The sites testify rather to the repeated use over centuries of specific localities offering favourable and diverse resources.

The correlation of these changes in settlement distribution and subsistence with the stabilization of sea levels at about their present level appears to provide another example of economic response to environmental pressure, in this case the removal of coastal territory by the encroachment of the sea, which forced coastal peoples back into the hinterland and into competition with their inland neighbours. Alternatively, the more intensive exploitation of previously peripheral inland resources during the postglacial period may have come about as a result of their increasing proximity to the coastal focus of settlement and the correspondingly greater ease with which they could be incorporated into the economy. Decisive evidence in favour of either hypothesis is not yet available, but coastal middens do seem to appear in the archaeological record at about the earliest moment when local conditions would have permitted their formation and preservation, which suggests that they are simply the truncated remnant of a longer sequence. Another factor that was probably of local importance in facilitating more intensive exploitation of upland resources in the south-east of the continent is the temperature rise that followed the retreat of the snowline.

An example of the way in which previously marginal resources became progressively integrated into human economies is the exploitation of bogong moths.[10] Large numbers of them spend the summer on the high peaks of the Snowy Mountains, where they provide a concentrated, nutritious and easily collected seasonal resource. They were first exploited during seasonal visits from the coastal lowlands from about 1000 BC onwards, perhaps earlier; such visits eventually led to permanent occupation of the highland zone between about seven hundred and three hundred years ago, suggesting that economic change was in progress even on the very eve of European contact.

The effect of the new technology on changes in population distribution and subsistence also needs to be considered, given that these various developments were nearly contemporary. The Tasmanian evidence provides a useful test case and shows, perhaps unexpectedly, that the absence of the small-tool tradition had very little noticeable impact on population densities and economic practices, both of which compare favourably with those of the mainland. The main effect of the new technology seems rather to have been to increase the efficiency of tool manufacture and use, and therefore to release more time and energy for the ceremonial and ritual activity that is so well attested in ethnographic accounts of mainland Aboriginal society but was less prominent among the Tasmanians.[11] If this link can be verified, it will provide a most interesting archaeological marker for the development of some of the less tangible features of Aboriginal society, as well as a

51.7: *Ethnographic evidence provides useful additional information for archaeologists. These Aboriginal stone axes, some hafted on to wooden handles, come from Western Australia and from Victoria.*

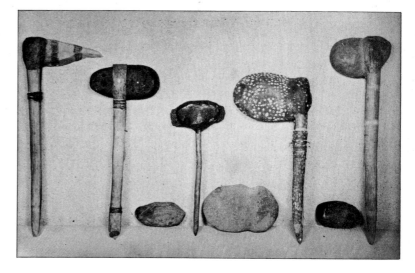

suggestive analogy for one of the traditional landmarks of Old World prehistory: the transition from the Middle Palaeolithic to the Upper Palaeolithic period.

Recent developments

The overlap of archaeological and ethnographic data offers many opportunities for enriching archaeological interpretation, particularly in the fields of technology and subsistence. It is, however, increasingly obvious that Aboriginal society was not static, and that contemporary observations and analogies cannot be extrapolated indefinitely into the past but must be complemented by independent archaeological evidence.

A promising focus for the integration of the two types of data is offered by the study of trade and exchange networks. Anthropology and ethnohistory are able to furnish details of the social context and motivations of exchange and the involvement of perishable objects, while archaeological research can specify the sources of raw materials, routes of distribution and the antiquity of such movements.

In recent times pressure-flaked bifacial spear points and axe blades were distributed far from sources of favoured stone such as the outcrop on Mount William in Victoria or the Nillipidji quarry in Arnhem Land. Ochre was quarried on a large scale at Wilgie Mia in Western Australia, and the removal of flint nodules from Koonalda Cave provides an early archaeological example of mining activity. Other materials that circulated over wide areas were the narcotic pituri plant (*Duboisia hopwoodii*), wooden tools and weapons and sandstone grinding slabs. Some of the most widely dispersed objects were baler shell ornaments, which were distributed from the Gulf of Carpentaria over distances of 2000 kilometres to the south and west.

Some of this distribution was accomplished through the agency of individuals or small parties travelling within the confines of their tribal territory; such journeys sometimes involved distances of up to 500 kilometres. Objects were also exchanged at intertribal ceremonial gatherings, when five hundred people or more, from different tribal territories, might come together for short periods. In the more arid regions, which were relatively unproductive and whose populations were consequently obliged to journey far and wide each year in search of food, the catchment

51.8: *A rock painting from Nourlangie. The elaborate headdresses are typical of Aboriginal art, much of which was imbued with religious significance.*

area from which the people and artifacts at a single gathering were drawn might be as large as 128 000 square kilometres.[12]

Anthropologists stress that the ritual and social aspects of gift exchange had an important part to play in the distribution of artifacts. Ceremonial gatherings would also have had long-term consequences, as they maintained inter-group contacts over large areas as an insurance against famine and unpredictable shortages of raw materials in local territories; they ensured the circulation of mates and consequently of genes; and they were a means by which new ideas and techniques could be rapidly disseminated. (At the end of the nineteenth century, for example, the Molonga dance ceremony apparently spread from north-west Queensland to southern Australia within a period of twenty-five years.)

How far back in time can these ceremonial exchange networks be traced by archaeological means? The implications of the introduction of the small-tool tradition at about 4000 BC have already been noted, and the production of delicately worked spear points, possibly of ceremonial significance, and the more frequent use of axes from about the same period offer similar hints. Petrological analysis of axes, already under way, should provide further information.

A puzzling point about Aboriginal society is the question of why the Aborigines never developed agriculture to any great extent. There is certainly widespread evidence of husbandry, but only on a small scale. Cereal seeds and cuttings of rootstocks were occasionally replanted to ensure the following year's crop, and other practices were aimed at increasing the productivity of a range of resources from emus to witchetty grubs. Fire was also used extensively to alter vegetation patterns and to improve conditions for game and plant resources. In the tropical north, where environmental conditions are most amenable to the development of rootstock horticulture on the New Guinea pattern, the rich coastal habitats offered an abundance of natural resources that supported some of the largest populations in Aboriginal Australia. These advantages may have offset that of the possible increase in plant-food productivity to be gained from agricultural development. In the more arid interior the risks associated with a highly unpredictable water supply probably more than outweighed the benefits of investment in large-scale cultivation of the available seed plants.

These matters deserve further investigation. It is perhaps fruitless to speculate about the developments that might have taken place in Aboriginal society if the disruptive effects of European contact had been delayed for another few hundred years. But it seems likely from archaeological evidence that developments in subsistence techniques and other aspects of Aboriginal life were already in train at least in recent periods of prehistory. To regard Aboriginal society as one isolated from the mainstream of developments elsewhere in the world is misguided and does less than justice to the archaeological and ethnographic evidence of repeated, if intermittent, contacts with areas to the north. What does seem clear from an archaeological point of view is that when further development did come about as a result of European intervention, it was but the latest episode in a cumulative process of at least 30 000 years' duration. It is only the ethnocentrism of an essentially European tradition of study that has endowed this latest stage with special significance.

52. Iron Age Africa and the expansion of the Bantu

Towards the end of the first millennium BC, and especially in the early centuries of the Christian era, important changes took place in sub-Saharan Africa that cut across existing ways of life. They involved not only the spread of new forms of economy from the north but also widespread movements of population. The integration of archaeological evidence with the results of linguistic research allows a tentative reconstruction of the processes of expansion.

Early Iron Age expansion

There can be little doubt that knowledge of iron technology was introduced to sub-Saharan Africa from the north. Unlike most other regions of the Old World, there is no indication here of pre-Iron Age working of copper or bronze. Instead, methods of smelting and forging iron appear in a developed and complex form, with no apparent local antecedents, in areas where metallurgy was previously completely unknown. It is generally suggested that two centres could have transmitted iron technology to more southerly latitudes: at both of these ironworking is attested from about the fifth or sixth century BC onwards. At Nok, which is situated to the north of the Niger–Benue confluence, extensive early iron-working was practised at the settlements of people who produced remarkable terracotta sculptures (perhaps derived from a wood-carving tradition), which are regarded as stylistically ancestral to the celebrated art school of Ife. Meroë, to the south of the fifth Nile cataract, is discussed in Chapter 27.

In the territory now occupied by the Bantu-speaking peoples the earliest evidence for Iron Age occupation has been recovered in the region of the great lakes of East Africa (including parts of Uganda, Kenya and Tanzania). In the Haya country of Tanzania, on the western side of Lake Victoria, extensive settlement and iron smelting sites such as Katuruka certainly date to at least the very beginning of the Christian era and may be several centuries older. They have yielded pottery of a type generally known as Urewe ware – after a site near the north-eastern shore of Lake Victoria – which is widespread between the Ruwenzoris and Mount Elgon, although it shows considerable local stylistic variation.

The antecedents of the Urewe settlements are hard to discern. They present a marked contrast to their predecessors in the region. It appears most likely that the formative processes of the Early Iron Age complex took place in the country to the north-west, in the 'sudanic' belt of open grassland savanna on the northern fringes of the equatorial forest. Although the archaeological support for such a view remains slender pending further fieldwork in this area, it has some linguistic support, which will be discussed below.

Ceramics typologically related to Urewe ware are found on more than five hundred sites of the first millennium AD distributed through almost all the more southerly regions of Africa as far as Natal, except the most arid areas and those covered by equatorial forest. They represent the earliest known Iron Age occurrences (in every area beginning in the first five centuries AD) in a vast tract of country extending south of the equatorial forest right across the continent from the Atlantic to the Indian Ocean coasts, and as far south as the Kalahari and the south-west African arid regions. There is little doubt that the sites indicate a rapid spread of ironworking agriculturalists into territory that was previously occupied by stone-tool-using hunter–gatherers. The archaeological assemblages display such homogeneity that they have been attributed to a single 'Southern African Early Iron Age Industrial Complex' in which there are, nevertheless, regional and temporal variations.

Two main geographical subdivisions may be recognized in these

52.2: *Groups and streams of the Early Iron Age. The Kalambo group shows features ;f both the eastern and western stream; the attribution to the western stream of sites south of the Limpopo remains tentative. The scarcity of Early Iron Age sites in what is now Angola and southern Zaire reflects the poor coverage of archaeological research. The lines demarcating groups are shown on the map for labelling purposes only: they do not represent actual boundaries, which are often ill defined.*

▲	Urewe sites
●	western stream sites
○	eastern stream sites
⌀⌀	named groups

52.1: *A Nok terracotta of a kneeling human figure (10.6 centimetres high) found at Bwari, Nigeria. The fine detail, especially of the triangular eyes, is characteristic of Nok art, which probably dates to between 400 BC and AD 200.*

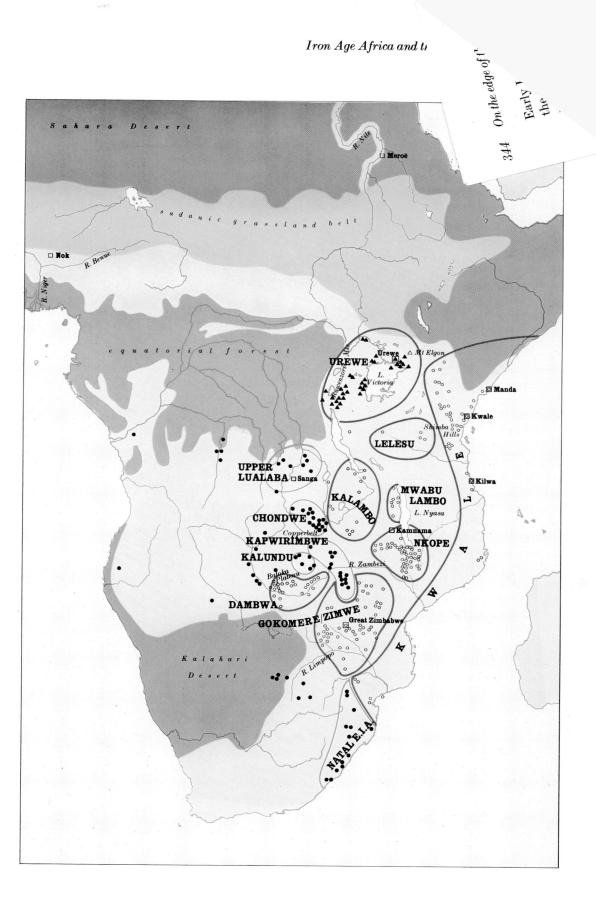

..on Age occurrences: they have been named provisionally ..astern and the western streams.[1] To the south of approximately latitude 6°S, the Early Iron Age settlements are quite distinct from those of their predecessors, for they provide the first evidence in the local archaeological record not only of metallurgy but also of agriculture and domestic stock, of settled village life and of the associated technological traits of semi-permanent house construction and pottery manufacture. In this southerly region, where the previous population had been exclusively stone-tool-using hunter–gatherers, there is little doubt that the introduction of Early Iron Age industries, already fully developed, can be attributed to population movement on a scale adequate to maintain the new lifestyle and its technology, despite the migrants' initially limited contact with the indigenous Late Stone Age population. In most other areas there is good evidence that the latter people continued their traditional way of life for several centuries after the advent of the Early Iron Age.

Within the eastern stream two distinct aspects may be recognized, most readily differentiated by the typology of the pottery associated with them. By the second century AD, Early Iron Age settlement had taken place in the Shimba and adjacent coastal hills south-west of Mombasa, where its local form is named after a site at Kwale. Pottery markedly similar to that from Kwale, typified especially by bowls with elaborately fluted inturned rims, is also found along an enormous stretch of the eastern African coastlands from the equator to beyond the mouth of the Limpopo – through no less than 26 degrees of latitude. It is effectively restricted to the coast and the adjacent lowlands and may be regarded as representing a distinct coastal manifestation of the Early Iron Age's eastern stream. The related material from the inland plateau regions is broadly contemporary; it is known best from the areas between Lake Nyasa and the Luangwa and also from what is now Rhodesia, where the earliest occupation at Great Zimbabwe is of this type.

Eastern stream Early Iron Age pottery occurs in two distinct archaeological contexts. It is found on village sites up to several hectares in extent – such as Kamnama in eastern Zambia – where the houses were evidently circular or sub-rectangular, built of mud applied over a wooden framework of the same general type as that still common among local rural communities. The inhabitants of these villages were predominantly agriculturalists growing millet and squash; they also herded small stock and, at least latterly, cattle. Evidence for ironworking is generally present, and chipped stone tools, where found at all, are usually rare. Identical pottery also occurs in small quantities in caves and rockshelters associated with concentrations of chipped stone artifacts of the Late Stone Age microlithic type, and there is evidence that the inhabitants of these sites were hunter–gatherers. It may safely be concluded that the Early Iron Age people were themselves mixed-farming village dwellers and that their artifacts, notably their pottery, were on occasion obtained by the Late Stone Age indigenous population whose technology and lifestyle at first seem

very similar to those of pre-Iron Age times.

Archaeological data relating to the western stream are very scanty. The only areas where there is a coherent body of excavated material are central Zambia, the Copperbelt, and the Upemba depression in the valley of the upper Lualaba. Here, close to the eastern limit of the western stream's distribution, the arrival of the Early Iron Age is not attested before the fifth century AD, but there are indications that it reached the west considerably earlier. It may also tentatively be suggested that the southernmost Early Iron Age settlements – those of the south-western Transvaal and Natal – may be more closely related to the western than to the eastern stream.

The rapid agricultural expansion of the first five centuries AD lies behind one of the major linguistic distributions of sub-Saharan Africa. The geographical distribution of the Early Iron Age complex is almost identical with that of the area occupied in more recent times by peoples speaking languages of the closely inter-related Bantu group, and this has led to the widely held belief that this complex represents the archaeological manifestation of the initial southward dispersal of the Bantu-speakers. The Bantu languages, which are today spoken by over 130 million people spread over an area of almost 9 million square kilometres, display a remarkable level of inter-comprehensibility, and there can be no doubt that they have reached their present extensive distribution as a result of dispersal from a common localized ancestral language within the comparatively recent past – certainly within the last three or four thousand years. Linguists are virtually unanimous in believing that this ancestral Bantu language was spoken close to the north-western border of the present Bantu-speaking area, in what is now Cameroon and eastern Nigeria. To the south and east of the equatorial forest, in the areas where the Early Iron Age complex is archaeologically attested, the modern Bantu languages fall into two major groups. These have been named the Western Highland Group, which is centred in Angola and northern Namibia, and the Eastern Highland Group, which is of far greater extent and covers virtually the whole of the eastern half of the subcontinent. Of these two groups, the Western Highland languages show considerably more internal diversity than do their Eastern counterparts, and the dispersal of the Eastern Highland Group may thus be assumed to have been significantly later than that of the Western Highland Group. The boundary between the two language groups does not coincide with that between the eastern and western streams of the Early Iron Age, but the general picture that emerges from linguistic studies is nevertheless strikingly similar in several ways to that put forward by archaeology.

The consensus of linguistic opinion suggests that the dispersal of the Bantu languages from their north-western homeland followed roughly this course: from the pre-Bantu homeland expansion initially took place both eastwards along the northern fringes of the forest towards the region of the Great Lakes and southwards to the country around the mouth of the Congo river. In this latter area a second dispersal took place that gave rise to the Western Highland languages. Subsequently, and from a westerly source, the Eastern Highland languages were dispersed – most probably from somewhere in the vicinity of the Zambia–Shaba Copperbelt. It is from this third dispersal that virtually all the Bantu languages spoken today in the eastern half of the subcontinent are derived.

The Western Highland Bantu languages may have developed in an Early Iron Age context, eventually giving rise to the Eastern Highland languages whose dispersal coincided with the advent of the later Iron Age in the eastern regions. This assumption involves acceptance of the view that there had been a previous, Early Iron Age, Bantu speech in eastern Africa, derived from the north-west via the region of the East African lakes.

Economy and society in the Early Iron Age

Throughout the area of the Early Iron Age complex the general nature of society, economy and technology seems to have been remarkably similar, which supports the hypothesis that local customs had been influenced by those of peoples further north. The metallurgical techniques that were practised were ultimately derived from a common source in the sudanic belt to the north of the equatorial forest, though several refinements, such as the use of pre-heated air in smelting furnaces, may well have been local developments south of the equator. (The latter technique led to the production of what was technically a mild carbon steel, though many of the advantages of this were lost through subsequent forging.) Most of the crops available to the Early Iron Age agriculturalists were indigenous African species, such as sorghum and squash, apparently first brought under cultivation in pre-Iron Age times in the sudan and sahel (see Chapter 25).[2] A single exception, which was probably available before the end of the Early Iron Age, is the banana, attested by documentary evidence on the East African coast as early as the tenth century. The large number of local varieties of banana that had developed by the nineteenth century in the region of the Great Lakes and beyond strongly suggests that this crop was introduced into the interior at a relatively early date. It was presumably brought to Africa from Indonesia by trans-Indian Ocean traders whose presence on the coast is attested archaeologically from at least the ninth century.

Further evidence for Indonesian influence comes from Madagascar. The island was apparently uninhabited until the early centuries of the Christian era, when it was settled by people who introduced languages akin to those still spoken in parts of Malaysia and Indonesia. Several other cultural traits may have been brought to the African mainland at this time, although those that may have spread beyond the coast and its immediate hinterland (such as xylophones and sewn boats) are only attested ethnographically, and their antiquity cannot be demonstrated. Indeed, for a long time there has been a tendency to overestimate the influence of Indonesian and Malagasy contacts on the Iron Age cultures of the interior of eastern Africa. It should be emphasized that no pottery or other artifacts of undoubted Indonesian manufacture have been found in Africa, and linguistic evidence suggests that the contacts

52.3: *Near life-size terracotta head, one of several recovered from an Early Iron Age site at Lydenburg, Transvaal, South Africa. Dated to c. AD 500, these objects are without parallel in the archaeological record of eastern and southern Africa; their affinities may prove to be with more westerly regions.*

that were established were not widespread or permanent. (Conversely, the impact of Bantu influence in Madagascar was considerable.)

The towns and settlements of the East African coast are often considered in isolation from the later Iron Age Bantu-speaking societies of more inland regions. However, there can be little doubt that these coastal communities were for the most part Swahili-speaking (Swahili is one of the many languages of the Bantu group); and much of their material culture – notably the local pottery – has strong affinities with the contemporary products of more inland regions. On the other hand, contact with traders and settlers from other lands bordering the Indian Ocean led to the early adoption of Islam and the development of a local urban architecture and lifestyle that formed a unique blend of African and foreign elements. At Manda, on the north Kenya coast, a rich trading settlement had been established by the ninth century AD; by the thirteenth century Kilwa, some eight hundred kilometres further south, had become a centre of major importance, probably as an entrepôt for the gold trade.

In the plateau regions between the Zambezi and the Limpopo several local technological developments took place during the Early Iron Age that were of considerable importance for later developments in that region. The weathered granite hills of Matabeleland and Mashonaland provided readily available raw material for the construction of drystone walls: field walls, terraces and stone enclosures were the earliest examples of this apparently indigenous architecture, which reached its finest expression at Great Zimbabwe in later Iron Age times. It seems likely that gold deposits were exploited in the same area before the end of the Early Iron Age. This coincides with the time at which objects, notably glass beads derived from the coastal trade, first occur at sites on the interior plateau. Whether the elaborate mining methods that may have been developed at this time (but are only firmly attested during the later Iron Age) were of local inspiration, or whether they owe their origin at least in part to contacts beyond the Indian Ocean, cannot yet be determined, but opencast copper mines on a small scale were being worked by Early Iron Age peoples on the Zambia–Shaba Copperbelt at an earlier period.

Localized raw materials such as copper, gold and particularly salt stimulated the development of inter-regional trading networks. As in more recent times, it appears that the general pattern was for people to travel far afield to obtain the raw materials they required.

Little is yet known about the art styles of the Early Iron Age. In Zambia and Malawi red schematic rock paintings are probably correctly attributed to people of the Early Iron Age.[3] A site near Lydenburg in the south-eastern Transvaal has yielded a series of near life-size terracotta heads[4] for which no reasonably close parallels are at present known.

The later Iron Age
Early Iron Age settlement as outlined above seems to have continued for several centuries. In some regions a significant increase

in site density and expansion of occupation into areas that were not settled initially is apparent during this time. By about the eighth century AD several local archaeological sequences began to diverge from this relatively homogeneous picture, as for example in the Victoria Falls region, on the Batoka Plateau and in central Malawi.[5] Over the greater part of eastern Bantu Africa, however, the main break did not occur until about the eleventh century. Taking this great region as a whole, the eclipse of the Early Iron Age pottery traditions is remarkable both for its suddenness and completeness and for its essential contemporaneity. This break is now attested virtually throughout the territory occupied by the eastern stream, as well as possibly in the Transvaal and Natal and also in some western-stream areas of central and southern Zambia. Further to the west the scanty archaeological data seem to indicate a much higher degree of continuity through this period. In the eastern region the later Iron Age pottery traditions show a certain homogeneity: it is only rarely that continuity may be detected with the local Early Iron Age industries.

The Early Iron Age pottery showing most features in common with the general typology of the later Iron Age is that of the Zam-

52.4: *Schematic map showing the main probable directions of expansion of the Bantu-speaking peoples in sub-equatorial Africa, as indicated by both archaeological and linguistic evidence.*

movements of Bantu-speakers

pre-Iron Age

Early Iron Age

Later Iron Age

present area of Bantu-speakers

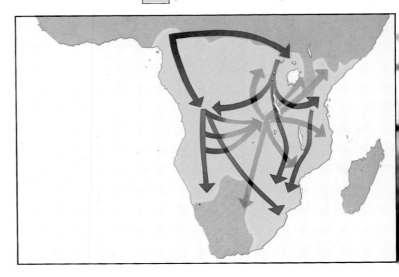

bian Copperbelt. It may be that the cultural developments that ultimately led to the development of the later Iron Age societies took place in this general area. To the north, in East Africa, the corresponding events are hard to interpret, not only because of the relatively sparse coverage of later Iron Age archaeological research, but also because it is here that the Bantu-speakers lived in close contact with peoples of other cultural and linguistic groups.

The greatest influence was probably that exerted by the Nilotic-speakers, who originated in the plains surrounding the White Nile and its tributaries in what is now the southern Sudan. This was the area where their characteristic pastoral lifestyle developed, possibly in pre-Iron Age times. At several periods in the course of the last three thousand years Nilotic-speaking groups have penetrated southwards into East Africa. At the present time many East African Bantu-speaking peoples, particularly those of the Great Lakes region but also several groups extending far southwards into Tanzania, make pottery bearing characteristic rouletted decoration that has almost certainly been adopted through contact with Nilotic-speaking peoples: this process of acculturation is still continuing. By contrast, further to the north-east, in the semi-arid plains surrounding the southern and eastern flanks of the Ethiopian highlands, some of the largely pastoral Cushitic-speaking peoples may not have adopted iron technology until the present millennium.

Elsewhere and further to the south, there is good evidence that the later Iron Age Bantu-speaking peoples depended considerably more than their predecessors had done upon the herding of domestic animals for their livelihood. Inter-regional trade, including the dispersal of goods derived from the coast, was also on a greater – and expanding – scale. Exploitation of the copper de-

posits north and south of the Zambezi was considerably extended, as was the working of gold in the latter area. Several of these developments may be traced back to an Early Iron Age origin, especially in the Shaba region, where the best archaeological evidence has been found in the Upemba depression at sites such as Sanga.[6] These economic developments were associated with a considerable expansion of population, which eventually (though perhaps not until about the sixteenth and seventeenth centuries in some areas) resulted in the final demise or absorption of the last of the stone-tool-using hunter–gatherers, except for those who lived in the arid regions of the far south-west, which were unsuited to Iron Age settlement.

The greatly increased population density and economic activity of the later Iron Age led in due course to the establishment of more complex and centralized political systems. These developments are hard to discern in the archaeological record, but recent interpretations of the oral traditions that survive among many Bantu-speaking peoples suggest that their centralized state-systems began at a significantly earlier date than was previously supposed. It is now clear that the presence of such state-systems among the later Iron Age peoples of the southern savanna predates considerably the period of the first European contacts at the end of the fifteenth century.[7] Traditionally, many of these states trace their origin to that of the Luba people in what is now southern Zaire, but no single influence can be credited with initiating the process of state formation in Bantu Africa with certainty. It seems more likely that the formation of states was a response to an interlocking network of local developments, typified by increasing population, pressure on land in the most favoured areas and increasing long-distance trade.

52.5: *A village of Bantu-speaking farmers in south-western Zambia. Modern villages such as this preserve architectural forms that were introduced to most Bantu-speaking areas in the Early Iron Age. The cylindrical houses have walls of mud applied over a wooden framework, and conical thatched roofs.*

53. Early states in Africa

Recent work on the formation of states in Africa has radically altered earlier views. Theories that attributed the rise of stratified societies to the invasion of 'Hamitic' peoples or the diffusion to Black Africa of 'divine kingship' on an Egyptian model have been discarded in favour of interpretations that stress the stimuli towards change generated within the societies concerned.

The West African sahel

Ghana, the earliest known Black African state, was described by Arab geographers in the early ninth century AD. Because the first West African states were known to the outside world only through the writings of their trading partners, commerce naturally features prominently in accounts of them and therefore in current historical interpretations of their development. But some sudanic states developed before links with the Muslim world were established; according to a tradition recorded in the seventeenth century, twenty kings of Ghana were said to have reigned before the time of Mohammed. Both these kings and their successors, all of whom belonged to the northern Mande or Soninke ethnic group, were buried beneath great earth tumuli. In the inland Niger delta cemeteries of great numbers of such tombs, many of enormous size, yielded rich grave goods, including copper and gold, to excavators at the beginning of the twentieth century. In Senegal and Gambia over 6000 tumuli and 1000 megalithic stone circles surrounding graves have been identified. Excavated tumuli dated to the eighth century AD contained bodies decked in gold, copper and carnelian beads. Megaliths were erected around graves throughout the first millennium. Though the context of these tombs is almost entirely unknown, they are convincing indicators of the antiquity of social stratification and centralized authority in West Africa.

Copper and salt, produced from mines in the Sahara desert, were traded southwards. Copper was used in the manufacture of the jewellery and regalia that signified status and thus provided an essential underpinning of these societies. Imported textiles served a similar function. Salt was not only essential as a foodstuff but, in its crystalline form as it came from the mines, was permanent enough to become a currency. Imports of horses allowed the sudanic states to form cavalry armies, which consolidated the power of the groups who could afford the horses, trappings and arms. Their speed and range in the savanna facilitated slave raiding and lay at the basis of the territorial expansion that formed the great 'empires' of West African history. However, authority was seldom directly exercised or permanent enough to warrant such a description. There was a gradation of control from the capital, through tributaries, to the groups on the periphery, who only acknowledged their obligations when confronted with punitive expeditions.

Gold, slaves and ivory were exported across the desert. Gold was mined in the tropical forests south of the Sudan, probably through the communal efforts of villagers during the agricultural slack season. Mines were not privately owned and their output was not directly controlled by any central authority. The centralized authorities of the sudanic belt did not create their wealth, nor were they the carriers of the trade – this was done by Saharan nomads; rather, they stood between the producers and the consumers. As middlemen, they grew rich through their political control over markets and entrepôts, where goods were trans-shipped from camels to donkeys and human porters.

Arab writers described the capitals of the early states in some detail. Many were 'twin cities', in which Muslim merchants' quarters were set some distance away from the indigenous town. At Kumbi Saleh, in southern Mauretania, the merchant quarter of the capital of Ghana has been excavated; the densely clustered complex of stone-built merchants' houses covers three square kilometres. Nothing of the indigenous town has been uncovered. Three hundred kilometres into the desert to the north lay Tegdaoust,[1] where excavations have uncovered the commercial centre of the peoples who controlled the caravan trade, dating from the ninth to the fifteenth centuries. It shows a sequence of substantial stone houses. Cultural connections with the Maghreb and direct evidence of the gold trade – in the form both of gold ingots and of glass weights, which were used in weighing the metal – were revealed.

Ghana was overrun by the Almoravids in the eleventh century. In their wake desert nomads pressed south, and their herds turned the northern savanna into the degraded scrub country that now forms the sahel.

States of the sudan

New centres of power arose in richer agricultural land nearer the sources of gold to the south. The best-known state was Mali, in the territory of the southern Mande peoples, the Malinke. An important site at Niani, probably Mali's capital, is in the process of extensive excavation. The first permanent settlements can be placed in the thirteenth century, while the final destruction of a building that has been identified as the royal palace occurred in the seventeenth century.[2] With Mali, the northern reaches of the Niger river grew in importance as a transport artery linking eastern and western trans-Saharan caravan routes. In the great inland flood plain of the river foreign commerce gave new impetus to an area of very high agricultural potential. The trading cities of Gao, Timbuktu and Jenne rose to power along the Niger.

Investigation of the *tells* of medieval Gao has started.[3] At Jenne a *tell* has revealed stratified deposits demonstrating continuous occupation for almost two thousand years, from the third century BC onwards. Preliminary tests indicate the transformation of camps based on hunting, fishing and cattle-herding into substantial permanent settlements, reflecting the introduction of rice cultivation in the early first millennium. Fieldwork over a wide area around Jenne has shown it to have been only one of many such settlements – many of them its equal in size and each the centre o several dependent villages. The local agricultural exchange network that this represents probably played as important a role in Jenne's rise to power as did long-distance trade.[4]

The central sudan

Far to the east, artificial mounds rise above the seasonally inundated black clay soils (*firki*) of the flood plain of Lake Chad, an area with as high a potential for intensive agriculture as the inland Niger delta. The Daima mound was occupied from the end of the second millennium BC to the sixteenth or seventeenth century AD.[5] Despite its strategic position at a communication node where the savanna is squeezed into a narrow gap between Lake Chad and the Cameroon highlands, Daima shows no evidence of long-distance trade, urbanism or social stratification. This may reflect the central sudan's lack of resources, especially the gold of the west. Similar mounds in Chad – so far poorly excavated – are dated to the fourteenth and fifteenth centuries AD. They have been attributed to the 'Sao civilization', which, tradition asserts, was the precursor of the central sudanic states of Kanem and Bornu.

As it developed over the centuries, the African end of the Saharan trade became almost a monopoly of Mande-speaking converts to Islam, the Dyula. As the original goldfields of the west became exhausted, they were supplanted by those of the southern forests. Dyula traders moved south and the town of Begho grew up on the edge of the forest. Excavation of a representative sample of the hundreds of distinct house mounds that are visible has confirmed the northern economic and cultural connections of Begho, particularly with Jenne.[6]

The West African forest

Small enclaves of Mande traders survive far down the Niger river below Gao, at the river's nearest point to Ife, the 'sacred' city of the Yoruba people, in the tropical rain forest of south-western Nigeria. Here, excavation – predominantly small-scale rescue work on restricted and incomplete town sites – has established the outline of a chronological and cultural framework. Ife flourished between the thirteenth and the fifteenth centuries. Houses with rectangular, mud-walled rooms were set around courtyards paved in intricate geometric patterns of sherds and pebbles, the walls often faced with mosaics of cut sherd disks. Each court contained altars, which were often surrounded with offerings, including magnificent, near life-size sculptures of human figures.[7] The economic basis of

Ife's extraordinary artistic flowering is still the subject of surmise. The town's location on the most direct route between the Niger river and the system of lagoons that permits canoe traffic from the Niger delta to the lagoons of Benin (Dahomey), as well as the presence of Dyula settlements on the river close to Ife, suggest that it may once have been an important link in trade between the northern Niger towns, the tropical forest and the coast.

If Ife raises problems of political and economic context, even greater difficulties are associated with attempts to interpret three hoards of elaborate bronzework that were excavated from shrines

53.1: *Terracotta head from the excavation of a shrine on Obalara's Land, Ife, dated to the fourteenth century. The facial markings represent scarifications, some of whose patterns can be matched among the Yoruba people today. Ife and its ruler remain the fount of all Yoruba regal authority.*

53.3: *Plan of Husuni Kubwa, an early fourteenth-century palace, administrative and warehouse complex on sandstone cliffs dominating the entrance to the harbour of Kilwa. Its ordered sequence of standardized domestic suites, its courtyards, elaborate domes and ornamental pools are a distinctive local adaptation of Islamic architectural principles.*

53.2: *The early states of West Africa.*

- ● copper
- ◌ gold
- ● salt
- ▨ tumuli and megalithic graves

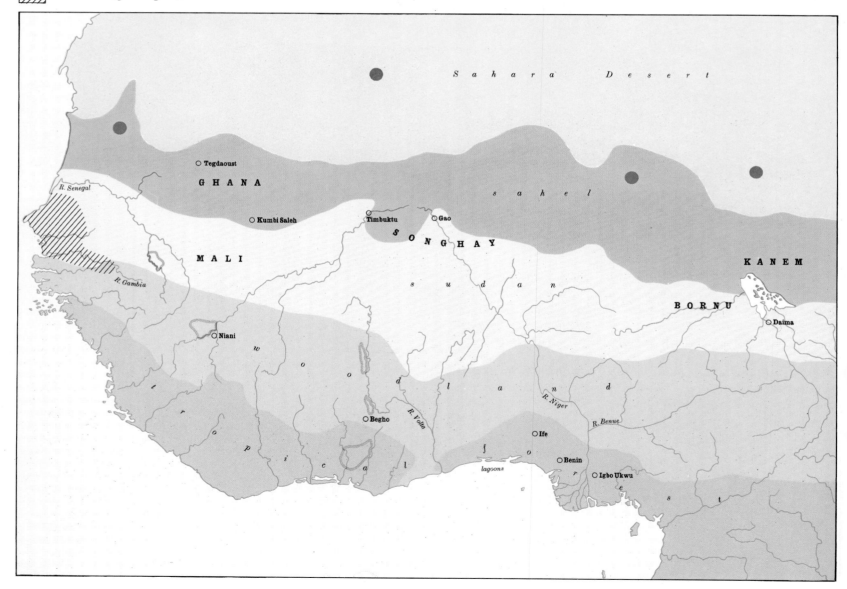

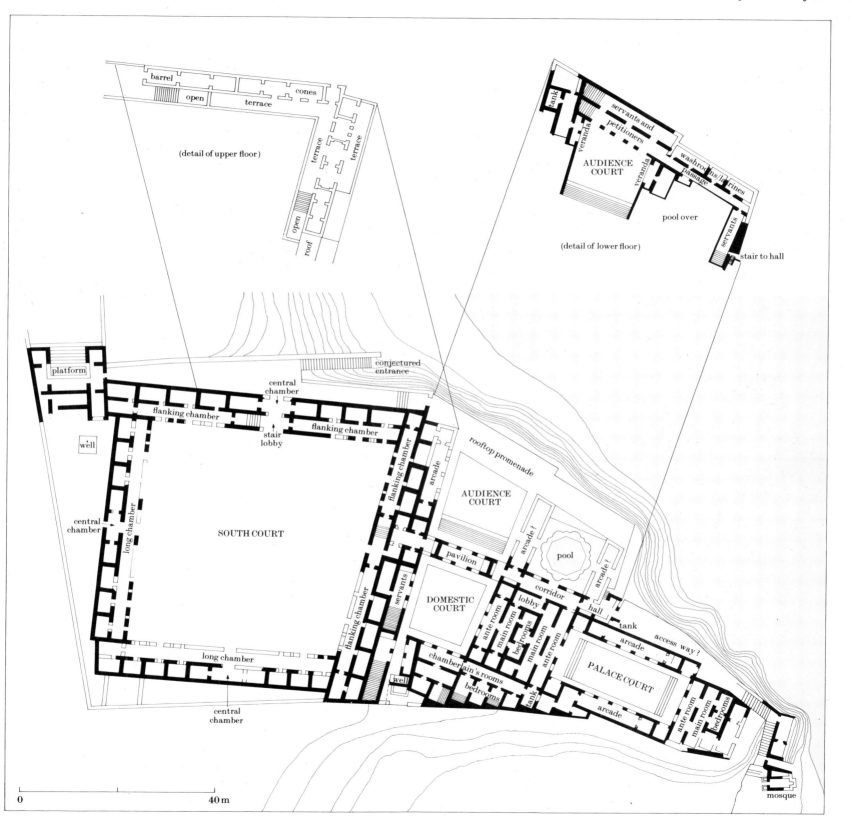

barrel

open

terrace

cones

(detail of upper floor)

terrace

terrace

open

roof

tank

veranda

servants and

petitioners

AUDIENCE
COURT

veranda

washrooms/latrines

passage

pool over

(detail of lower floor)

servants

stair to hall

platform

conjectured
entrance

central
chamber

flanking chamber

flanking chamber

stair
lobby

well

flanking chamber

arcade

rooftop promenade

AUDIENCE
COURT

central
chamber

long chamber

SOUTH COURT

arcade ?

pool

arcade ?

flanking chamber

servants

pavilion

corridor

hall

DOMESTIC
COURT

lobby

ante room

main room

bedrooms

main room

ante room

tank

arcade

access way ?

long chamber

flanking chamber

chamberlain's rooms

well

bedrooms

tank

PALACE COURT

arcade

central
chamber

ante room

main room

bedrooms

0   40 m

mosque

and graves at Igbo Ukwu, deep in the tropical forest east of the Niger river.[8] On the evidence of three radiocarbon dates – none of them obtained from entirely satisfactory samples – Igbo Ukwu is dated to the ninth century AD. The metalwork demonstrates sophisticated craftsmanship within an established artistic tradition at the service of a small group able to accumulate enormous wealth in bronze and ivory. Imported glass beads, as well as the bronze, point to distant trade connections. It seems inconceivable that the natural resources controlled by Igbo Ukwu could have attracted foreign trade so early. There are no metals nearby, and Saharan traders could obtain slaves and ivory more easily on the forest fringes. The fish and sea salt that were available would have been an inadequate substitute. We are thus left with hints of powerful integrating forces transforming traditional village societies that are otherwise quite unknown to history.

Benin, capital of the Edo people, lies between Ife and Igbo Ukwu. According to tradition, largely confirmed by archaeological excavations,[9] the Benin kingdom was founded in the fourteenth century. The hypothesis of direct connections with Ife, proposed from studies of sculpture, has been seriously weakened by detailed stylistic and technological analyses.[10] The metalwork and sculpture of Benin are certainly the manifestations of court patronage.

The East African coast

Although an account of seaborne trade in the Indian Ocean during the early second century AD describes ports in and voyages to East Africa, the earliest archaeological evidence of trading settlements on the coast is provided by Sasanian–Islamic ceramics of the eighth or ninth century from excavations on Manda Island, off northern Kenya.[11]

By the thirteenth century the towns of Mogadishu and Kilwa were minting their own coinage. In the early fourteenth century the most grandiose complex of buildings in sub-Saharan Africa's pre-colonial history was erected outside Kilwa town. The palace of Husuni Kubwa[12] and the nearby fortified 'factory' of Husuni Ndogo demonstrate ostentatious luxury under the highly centralized, even autocratic, control of an economic system that extended far down the coast to Sofala and inland to Great Zimbabwe. This system was short-lived. From the mid-fourteenth century, when towns were established on almost every island and all along the coast from Somalia to Mozambique, the core of each settlement was a small group of houses built of coral and lime to a standardized plan – dwellings of groups of merchants linked by common interests and kinship. They represent a small commercial oligarchy that had grown wealthy from the trade of gold and ivory from the interior to Arabia and India.

Populous centres, often on small, infertile islands, depended for their agricultural produce on a network of small mainland settlements. Here agents maintained contact with traders from the interior and, during year-round coasting voyages in small craft, collected exports for despatch to the main entrepôts to await the annual arrival of the overseas dhows that were dependent on the

monsoon for their ocean crossings. The coastal towns produced little or nothing themselves. Some beads were reworked and cotton textiles woven, but there were no local markets; plantation agriculture, using slave labour, was only instituted in the eighteenth century. Economic links did not result in political dependence – each town always retained a considerable measure of autonomy. The original stimulus and first settlers may have come from outside Africa, from Persia, Arabia and Somalia, but the society that developed, like the bulk of the population in every town, was African. The religion and many of the political institutions were Islamic, but the language was a Bantu one, Swahili. The complex relationships between urban merchants, their agents and the mainland farmers and tribesmen have yet to be investigated. The cultural diversity of the coast is best demonstrated by the enormous variety of artifacts and pottery styles revealed in excavations at Kilwa, but these have not yet been studied outside traditional chronological and typological frameworks.[13]

The East African interior

The West and East African states so far discussed all had strong links with overseas markets, to which the dominant sector of the economy was geared. In the interior foreign influence was much slighter. Throughout eastern Africa there was an abrupt and widespread change in pottery styles in about the eleventh century, marking the end of the Early Iron Age. This change is generally ascribed to population changes, with the source of the new populations in either southern Zaire or Natal (see Chapter 52). This is an unsatisfactory hypothesis, as the origins, growth and patterns of spread of the new societies are obscure and transitional stages are entirely absent. It is more helpful, and perhaps more accurate, to regard the changes in pottery styles as reflecting economic rather than ethnic changes. A considerable increase in cattle-herding probably played a key role in the process. As in many traditional African societies today, cattle were a means of converting a grain surplus into a permanent and increasing source of wealth; they were probably also a sign of status and a source of patronage; they were the main form of bride wealth; they tied a community together. Interaction between herders and farmers also gave rise to the sort of tensions whose resolution went far towards introducing more elaborate political systems.

The new forms of society were typified by changes that took place in the extensive grazing lands of south-western Zimbabwe. Here Early Iron Age villages were replaced by large settlements, often on fortified hilltops. Within these settlements different forms of dwelling and burials, some associated with gold grave goods, indicate pronounced social stratification. From this milieu, fully-fledged states developed in the twelfth and thirteenth centuries, represented most clearly by the 'Zimbabwe culture'.[14] Its most distinctive feature is the dry-stone masonry walls that surround dwelling huts and courtyards. The earliest and by far the largest stone-walled settlement was Great Zimbabwe. The first walls were built in about AD 1200, and the buildings were progressively extended until the settlement covered some 40 hectares before its abandonment in about 1450. Over a hundred much smaller stone enclosures, many housing no more than a single family, extended over the plateau and down to the sea. These were the dwellings of the ruling class of the Shona. They were, in essence, the symbols of its power: political statements. They also formed the points of control of the diversified economy of the plateau. Faunal remains from Manekweni, close to the sea in central Mozambique, demonstrate that cattle slaughtered in their prime provided the bulk of the meat diet of the ruling group.[15] Village herds have never been exploited in this way in traditional African societies. Intensive meat production points to the highly centralized control of herds, which were grazed at some distance from the stone courts. The distribution of courts suggests that they were deliberately sited at the nodes of a transhumance system, which was governed by the fluctuating limit of fly-borne cattle disease. Ownership or control of the cattle herds was a significant and perhaps formative stimulus, but not the only source of economic and political power of the Zimbabwe states.[16]

The importance of the gold trade from the plateau to the East African coast has already been discussed. Little is known about how gold was mined because the ancient workings that exploited every reef on the plateau were largely destroyed during colonial mining operations. Mining was probably a communal and seasonal affair conducted by primarily agricultural villagers who were perhaps indirectly stimulated and controlled by the exchange of state cattle for gold – as some historical records hint. Certainly, at Great Zimbabwe and other major courts far from the mines craftsmen worked the metal into jewellery, as they did the copper that was imported in ingots from the northern edge of the plateau. To judge by the great numbers of spindle whorls, textiles were also woven in considerable quantity at Great Zimbabwe. Trade with the coastal towns introduced foreign imports: porcelains, glass and a wide variety of trinkets. These were prestige goods, with a limited circulation and essential to demonstrate rank. Such items were found in a single hoard at Great Zimbabwe in the 1890s; with them were the iron gongs, hoes and sea shells that are still recognized as the attributes of chiefly authority by the Shona.

Specialized craftsmen and traders and regional trade networks are now discernible archaeologically. The copper ores of Urungwe were traded over the plateau and down the Zambezi river. The cemetery of Ingombe Ilede contained burials associated with copper ingots, tools for working the metal and copper rods in various stages of manufacture into wire jewellery. With them were gold jewellery and the hoes, gongs and shells that circulated as prestige goods.[17] Communities of self-sufficient farmers – known to archaeologists as the Harare and Musengezi cultures – added a further element to the plateau's social and economic diversity.

The Zimbabwe culture demonstrates the centralized control of a complex economy in a region with rich resources. It is a situation so different from any existing north of the Zambezi that it is perverse to regard the Zimbabwe states as evidence of the diffusion of

53.4: *Great Zimbabwe, capital of a Shona state between the thirteenth and the fifteenth centuries. The granite walls now appear to be a meaningless jumble, for the clay-walled huts and courtyards with which they were integrated to form a series of domestic dwellings have long been destroyed. The elliptical enclosure in the background, with walls some 10 metres high, contained the ruler's abode and formed the political and ritual focus of the whole settlement.*

political institutions from the north.

The Great Lakes region of East Africa

In the lands around the lakes of East Africa other states grew up. Early evidence for the control of large labour forces is best seen in the earthworks of Bigo, in the Nkore grasslands west of Lake Victoria. Here 11 kilometres of ditches and banks, presumably built to protect cattle herds, enclose an area of 5 square kilometres. Evidence of occupation was found only in a small central complex of mounds and banks, whose form closely resembled the remains of the traditional capitals of Nkore rulers. Radiocarbon dates place the occupation of Bigo between the mid-fourteenth and the end of the fifteenth century.

Bigo is associated with the Chwezi dynasty in the traditions of several Ugandan groups. These semi-mythical rulers are generally identified as a group of conquering Nilotic pastoralists from the southern Sudan, who established a short-lived hegemony some twenty generations ago. Further conquests by another Nilotic group, the Luo, in the late fifteenth and sixteenth centuries are associated, according to tradition, with the Bito dynasty and have been seen as the origin of the interlacustrine kingdoms of Nyoro, Nkore, Rwanda and Buganda, formerly depicted as conquest states in which an intrusive pastoral aristocracy ruled the original farmers. However, this model is becoming increasingly doubtful: several states now appear to be older than the Bito invasions. Their basis seems to have been the integration of pastoralists and agriculturalists, for whom the ruler was regarded as neutral arbiter rather than as conqueror. Integration was social (cattle promoted systems of clientage) and economic (cattle manure formed the basis of an intensified agriculture).

Because their origins are comparatively recent and well known, the early states of Africa illustrate vividly the complexity and the variety of the processes that contribute to the development of state institutions. There is no single, simple model for their origin, and their study integrates oral traditions, historical records and archaeology. In studying complex prehistoric societies in Africa, however, most archaeological research is in its infancy. It still has to break free from the old concern with tribes, migrations and external agents of diffusion and to come to terms more realistically with processes of change.

VIII: The New World

As the origins of the human species lay in the Old World and the route to the Americas lay through the periglacial tundras of Siberia and Alaska, the diverse environments of the New World were not colonized until the later part of the last glaciation. It is all the more striking, therefore, that by the time that European populations reached the Americas in the sixteenth century there had developed completely independently not only a native agriculture but also complex societies organized into states and empires. The parallelism of postglacial development in North America and in Eurasia demonstrates a comparable reaction to the onset of modern climatic conditions. In Central America, as in the central part of the Old World, the cultivation of a cereal crop – maize – accelerated economic and social development. The two main centres of early crop domestication, Mesoamerica and Peru, not only produced a variety of useful plants but also gave rise to indigenous civilizations based upon them. These flourished in diverse environments, from the semi-arid plains of Mexico and the tropical forests of Guatemala to the montane valleys of the western Andes. Significant development also took place in the tropical forests of South America, the setting for large-scale dispersals of agricultural populations.

54. North America in the early Postglacial

In North America, as in Europe, the effects of Pleistocene glaciation had been to displace the vegetational belts southwards. Lake Bonneville in western Utah maintained a generally high level in the Late Pleistocene, and grasslands prevailed in present desert areas of the west and south-west as a consequence of changes in rainfall. But, unlike Europe, much of the area immediately south of the ice sheet was covered with a northern coniferous forest rather than by tundra, which was extremely limited in extent.

The decisive onset of postglacial conditions 10 000 years ago produced a reversal to the present-day pattern. The south-west became more arid and prairies extended into areas of former woodland, while in the east the forest belts readjusted northwards. Just as with the southward movement of the boreal forest during the full glacial phase, when patches of temperate trees remained on favourable sites, differential rates of northward tree migration produced forest assemblages that have no precise modern analogues. Economic adjustments to this vegetational mosaic were equally complex and regionalized. There are some broad common features, however. The sharp and pronounced climatic adjustment accompanied by over-hunting resulted in a dramatic decline in big-game animals, leading to the extinction of the mammoth, mastodon, large long-horned bison, horse, camel, tapir, dire wolf and giant ground sloth. In any case, except on the expanding Great Plains of the western states it brought to an end the mobile hunting adaptation based on communal game-drives. Instead, as with the Mesolithic of the Old World, a new pattern emerged that characterized the societies known as Archaic. This was based to a large extent on sedentary resources such as nuts, seeds and shellfish, and a closer adjustment to forest or desert environments.

Nevertheless, such reactions were not uniform, and it is convenient to divide a description of the Archaic into Western, Plains and Eastern sections. The evidence for processes of change is rather better in the east than in the west, despite the unique insights offered by western dry caves. This eastern evidence demonstrates a pattern of population growth and ecological specialization integrated by the extension of trading systems.

Western Archaic traditions

The stratigraphic sequence at Danger and Hogup caves in Utah's eastern Great Basin provide a sustained record of a pattern of life initiated at least by 7000 BC and still maintained by Shoshoni-speaking bands in this same region in historic times.[1] While designated the 'Desert' culture – and indeed located within a region of remarkably low rainfall (less than 50 centimetres a year) – the topography consists of alternating mountain ranges and valley basins and maintains a considerable variety of habitats. The diversity of environmental zones, containing a number of different

plants usable as important sources of food, were harvested on a regular annual cycle. Waterfowl, shore birds of marshland habitats bordering desiccated lakes, rabbits, antelopes and mountain sheep supplemented plant resources. The wealth of food lay in the diversity of species, and the Archaic adaptation rested on the tight scheduling of the exploitation of these resources over the course of the year. In this pattern plants formed an essential part of the economy, for they did not fluctuate in abundance from year to year as much as did the animals. Further, unlike animals, plants are fixed in position, will normally fruit at about the same times each year, and their harvesting does not usually jeopardize the resource base. It was this predictability, and hence security, that led to the rise of the Archaic traditions.

A people whose life involves frequent seasonal movements accumulates minimal quantities of material possessions, unless these items can be safely left at base camps to which regular visits are made or are constructed of materials that are light and easily transported. The wealth of the latter category is well illustrated in the dry caves of the Desert culture: there is a variety of basket shapes made first by twining, then by coiling, which quickly became the more popular method. Mats, bags, carrying nets and large nets with a coarse mesh (probably used in rabbit drives) are also a part of the inventory. The manufacture of such items, together with moccasins, rabbit-skin robes and various kinds of cords, required an extensive range of stone and bone artifacts. Chipped stone projectile points, knives and choppers were carried and needed for hunting; heavier equipment such as millstones, grinders and hammerstones may well have been stored at stations on the seasonal round where the equipment was required.

While these features characterize Great Basin–Oregon developments, in California there is evidence for a later shift from hunting to the collection of seed resources between 6000 and 3000 BC. In southern California a number of regional variants of food-collecting cultures have been grouped into a Milling Stone horizon with dates in the sixth millennium BC.[2] Evidence indicates that similar food collectors had established themselves in central and northern California as well. Tools found at the sites seem scanty in number and lack diversity, comprising rare projectile points, cores reused as tools and a few polished stone disks and charmstones, but the dry conditions that preserved perishable materials in the Great Basin are lacking here. A few items of bone and shell are present, and twined and wicker basketry are known from Santa Cruz Island. Contemporary with this economy, there is also evidence at Santa Rosa Island of middens that contain remains of fish, sea mammals and shellfish, especially red abalone.

It has been suggested that about 3000 BC conditions of increased rainfall encouraged an enhanced subsistence efficiency involving a wider exploitation of available food resources. The Santa Barbara hunting culture provides faunal collections that reveal a dependence upon both land and sea through the procurement of shellfish, fish, sea mammals and large and small land mammals. As mortars and pestles match the earlier abundance of milling stones, they suggest an important reliance on vegetable food as well. Further to the north, beginning perhaps about 2500 BC, the Windmiller culture of the Sacramento river valley demonstrates a great wealth of artifacts reflecting a more advanced technology and a concern with artistic elaboration. Most conspicuous are polished charmstones or plummets, including phallic forms, while burials were frequently accompanied by shell necklaces, pendants and other objects. Hunting and fishing may have been of primary importance for this group, though seeds and nuts were doubtless also essential. In other localities the balance in the economy shifted as adjustments were made to the diversity of regional resources. From this period onwards archaeological evidence of rapidly evolving traditions based upon hunting, the gathering of acorns and other seeds and fishing is modifying the traditional ethnographic interpretation of Californian society as simple and highly fragmented, comprising hundreds of small, autonomous polities. On the contrary, there are indications of impressively high levels of cultural elaboration, with dense population, sedentary village life and political-economic arrangements on a considerable scale.[3] Such developments carried

54.1: *Charmstones, a distinctive artifact of the Archaic of California, are rather large and heavy to be worn habitually as pendants, and show little evidence of extensive use. They presumably had a magical function.*

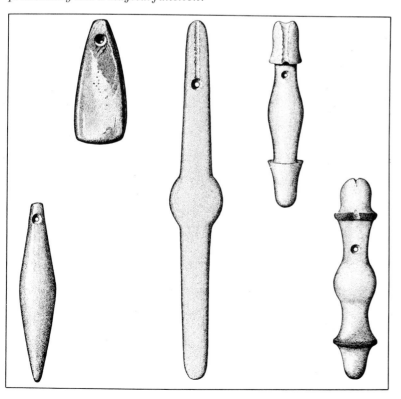

the region beyond the level of the Archaic, despite the absence of horticulture based upon domesticated plants.

In Arizona and New Mexico long Archaic sequences have been defined, though initially in their history there is a strong survival of Palaeo-Indian elements. Early in the fourth millennium BC there seems to have been a change to greater seasonal movements and an increase in the use of plant foods, including the introduction of a primitive maize towards the end of the phase.

Plains Archaic

The region most difficult to describe in terms of the shift from a primarily hunting economy to a diverse Archaic economy is the North American Great Plains area. Despite considerable topographic diversity, once the coniferous forests of Pleistocene times had been progressively replaced by grasslands, the bison formed the major resource throughout the region. Holocene Archaic adaptation is thus a shift from generalized big-game hunting to more specialized bison hunting. While there is no reason to deny that antelopes, mule-deer, white-tailed deer, elks and black bears, as well as smaller mammals, were important from earliest times, these reflect only the hunting component of the diet of the Plains peoples, and little is known of the importance of plant foods until the documentation of late prehistoric cultures. Indeed, for the times equivalent to Archaic developments elsewhere, much information comes from marginal locations.[4] Thus the suggestion that bison were scarce or absent between 5000–3000 BC and AD 500–1300 relates to the southern periphery and may simply reflect shifts in the locations of the major herds. In any event, until the introduction of horticulture and the accompanying sedentary villages, it was the bison that permitted the build-up of human population density; a shortage of bison must have prompted an exodus from the region. The native plant foods of the Plains did not provide the diversity of ecological niches that permitted the tightly scheduled seasonal movements that obtained in other regions with more diversified plant resources. Thus the Cherokee Sewer site of northwest Iowa, with occupation ranging from the beginning of the Holocene and spanning two millennia, demonstrates the early appearance of Archaic technology without necessarily indicating an Archaic economy of the kind characteristic of other regions. The presence of the domesticated dog, grinding slabs, bone artifacts, a ground-stone grooved axe at the nearby and related Simonsen site, and a shift in the style of projectile points, mark the beginning of the evolution of the Archaic pattern elsewhere. While evidence may be limited to sites from only a portion of the annual economic cycle, the Plains people may have persisted in an older pattern of life until the revolution produced by horticulture.

Eastern Archaic traditions

The postglacial vegetation of the eastern United States changed slowly, and with considerable local variation, in response to climatic changes. A dry interval is inferred for the south-east about 8000–4000 BC, in the northern Middle West from 6000–2000 BC and still later in the north-east from 2000 BC–AD 500.[5] Such different (and often local) responses complicated the gradual northward movement of the sequence of spruce parkland followed by a pine–hardwood forest and then an oak-dominated deciduous forest. Further complexity was introduced by the differential migration of some plant species. Hickory and chestnut, for example, potentially important sources of food, migrated more slowly than other elements of the modern deciduous forest. Archaic peoples adjusted primarily to this changing mosaic of plant assemblages and secondarily to an increasing human population density that seems to have reached a peak in the late Archaic.

As elsewhere, the basic rhythm of early Archaic life in the east was a movement according to the seasonal availability of resources. Only recently have recovery techniques that permit an evaluation of nut and seed exploitation been used on deeply buried sites. The Koster site in Illinois, Rodgers Shelter in Missouri, St Albans in West Virginia, Hardaway in North Carolina and Icehouse Bottom and Rose Island in Tennessee highlight this new development. This information casts doubt on the oft-repeated assertion that the Archaic cultures appear to be earliest in the west. It now seems that by 7500 BC the Tennessee region had already seen a shift from side- to corner-notched projectile points and the appearance of twined textiles and grinding basins for the exploitation of acorns and hickory nuts in their economy. The lag in the

spread of artifacts similar to the south-eastern Early Archaic types into much of the north-east has been explained as a consequence of the presence of a dense coniferous forest as opposed to the deciduous forests that dominated the south-east.[6] The gradual change in subsistence patterns that characterize the Eastern Archaic is shown in Figure 54.2. Just as vegetation changes gradually moved northwards, so that resources such as hickory nuts, walnuts, butternuts, acorns and pecans could be found in their modern mid-western distribution only by about 5000 BC, so too shellfish and many species of fish could only have reached their northern limits as the postglacial aquatic habitat approximated to modern conditions.

A series of regional Archaic traditions finds its clearest expression late within the sequence. The Lake Forest assemblage found primarily in the area of the Great Lakes contains both the distinctive copper tools long known as the Old Copper culture and characteristic burial offerings, including the use of red ochre. The Maritime Area, covering the coastal portions of northern New England, the maritime provinces of Canada, Newfoundland and Labrador, has a distinctive combination of caribou and sea mammal exploitation. Like the Lake Forest assemblage, the inclusion of axes, adzes and gouges among the artifacts reflects an extensive woodworking industry. Differences in technology and subsistence base characterize a Riverine Archaic, a Shield Archaic in Canada

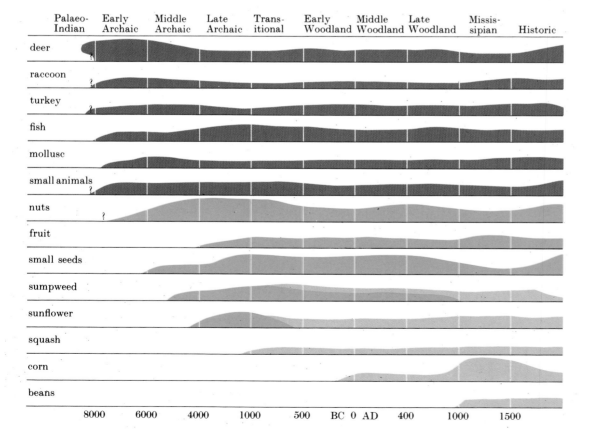

54.2: *Subsistence changes in the eastern United States. Cultivated plants are distinguished from uncultivated ones by a lighter shade of green.*

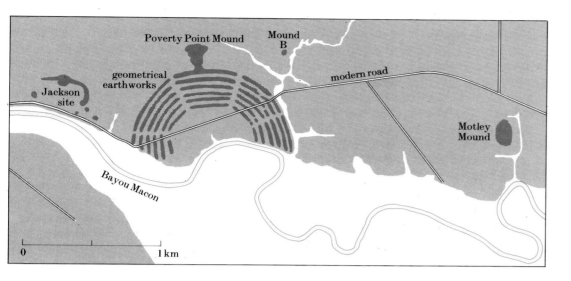

54.3: *Plan of the Poverty Point site. The geometrical earthworks are believed to have been used as dwelling sites; the large mound immediately to the west of them has a high ridge aligned north–south with a lower platform area to the east. Extensive erosion makes conjectural the suggestion that it was constructed in a bird form.*

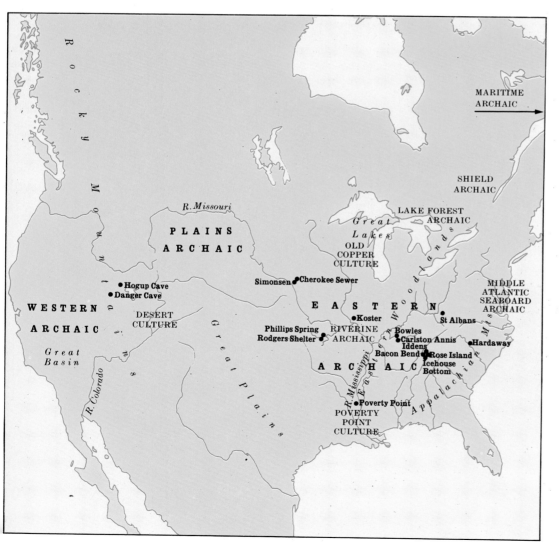

54.4: *Map of North America, showing site locations and the areas covered by both major regions and local cultures.*

and a Middle Atlantic Seaboard Archaic. All were linked, however, by a long-distance trade in durable but portable valuables – copper ornaments, shell beads and a variety of exotic lithic materials. This flowering of regional cultures and the presence of trade goods occurs in a context where the evidence for higher population densities is also clear. It has been suggested that this increasing population density obliged these groups to adapt their subsistence strategy. Previously, if subsistence were concentrated upon a single resource at one point in the annual cycle, fluctuations in annual yield would be compensated for by the harvesting of the same species at several alternative locations. But as increasing population density reduced the option of foraging widely, additions were made to the subsistence base, which culminated in the use of fruits and small seeds of pioneer annual plants. Finally, when even a great variety of plant and animal foods was not always sufficient for the population levels attained, trade provided the ultimate means of maintaining the high population density. The exchange of exotic trade items for food between neighbouring groups in effect created a more efficient distribution system that overcame natural fluctuations in food supply.[7]

There is evidence for cultigens in the Woodlands area as early as perhaps the third millennium BC. Specimens from five sites in Kentucky (Carlston Annis and Bowles), Missouri (Phillips Spring) and Tennessee (Iddens and Bacon Bend) document the presence of a tropical variety of domesticated squash. Sunflower and marsh elder are among the local domesticates, and other plants, including chenopods, knotweed and may-grass, were intensively used. Seeds thus came to rival nuts as the predominant plant food at the time

when indications of cultivation first appear.[8] Fibre-tempered pottery also makes its appearance in the south-east in this context.

These developments reached a climax in the Poverty Point culture of the lower Mississippi valley, which began in the early second millennium BC. The Poverty Point site itself, the type-site of the culture, includes a large earthen mound resembling a bird that is nearly 23 metres high and approximately 200 metres in diameter. Associated with the mound is a series of six concentric ridges with an outer diameter of 1208 metres. The one million or so cubic metres of earth used in the construction of the site, combined with an impressive site size of more than 5 hectares, indicates the existence of a major ceremonial centre.

Yet associated with these impressive construction features is a material culture not inappropriate for any of the Late Archaic complexes. Baked clay balls in a variety of forms, known as Poverty Point objects, simply serve as a substitute for stone (a scarce commodity in this alluvial habitat) in boiling and baking techniques. These, together with an elaborated microlithic industry, are among the hallmarks of the culture. Small figurines were also made of clay, but these are not abundant and fragments of ceramic vessels are equally scarce. Extensive trade networks are suggested by steatite vessels, a limited use of copper, haematite plummets and the wide variety of stone materials used for chipped tools. Evidence from other Poverty Point sites documents the importance of hunting and the exploitation of river resources, with mere indications of plant foods. Whether the rise of this great ceremonial centre represented an organizational achievement or an economic transformation is disputed, but, whatever the basis, this structure was abandoned, and nearly a thousand years passed before the Woodlands region again saw such evidence of elaborate ceremonial organization. Perhaps this great monument was one of the products of the population peak before its economic base proved inadequate for further growth.

54.5: *These distinctive Old Copper Culture tools, manufactured from native copper by cold hammering and annealing, are one of the technological achievements of the Archaic.*

55. The colonization of the Arctic

The permanent presence of humans in most of the true Arctic region of America came relatively late in prehistory – probably later than the occupation of any area of comparable extent save for the far-flung islands of the mid-Pacific. It followed long after an initial exploitation of the Late Pleistocene tundra of Alaska had given way to a successful adaptation to the open coasts of north-western America, and considerably after the successful colonization of the boreal forests that were to develop across North America upon the final recession of the massive glaciers of the Pleistocene.

Earliest evidence

The first absolutely positive indications of human settlement in any part of the Arctic are confined to portions of Alaska and are dated to the very end of the last glacial period. Evidence of a possible earlier occupation in the same general region, however, comes from the Old Crow river basin in northern Yukon Territory, Canada, where a fairly extensive collection of supposed artifacts fashioned from bone has been made from among the remains of a Late Pleistocene fauna, repeatedly eroded and redeposited, that has been dated to 25 000 – 30 000 years ago.

The first indisputable evidence of the presence of man is later, appearing in the heterogeneous set of Alaskan stone artifact assemblages that have been referred to collectively as the Palaeo-Arctic tradition and that date by radiocarbon from as early as 11 000 years ago to as late as about 8000 years ago. These assemblages are dominated by microlithic blades and wedge-shaped cores, some bifacial knives, scrapers and – in a few sites – more specialized projectile points, occasionally fluted. Sites are either in unglaciated regions or on the edges of glaciated areas that would have been freed from ice relatively early. In one site (Dry Creek) remains of bison, mountain sheep and elk are clearly preserved, and at another (Trail Creek caves) bones of horse and bison, as well as of elk and caribou, may represent debris from a camp site. Of these animals bison, horse and elk are now extinct in interior Alaska. Other sites of similar age (for example, Onion Portage and Carlo Creek) have yielded elements only of a fauna still present in the region – including caribou, moose, sheep, wolf, fox, hare, ptarmigan and duck.

These artifact assemblages resemble contemporary collections from Siberia, and it seems evident that they represent remnant Pleistocene hunters who were following a dwindling livelihood and a vanishing way of life on the fringes of wasting glaciers, pursuing shrinking numbers of such large grazing animals as remained at the end of the Pleistocene.[1]

Movement to the ice-free southern coasts of Alaska and beyond

Sites of the Palaeo-Arctic tradition were present in recently deglaciated areas of the Alaska Peninsula by 7000 BC, and at its Late Pleistocene tip – now Anangula Island, off Umnak Island in the eastern Aleutians – by 6000 BC. At the same date related people were present on the coast of south-eastern Alaska near

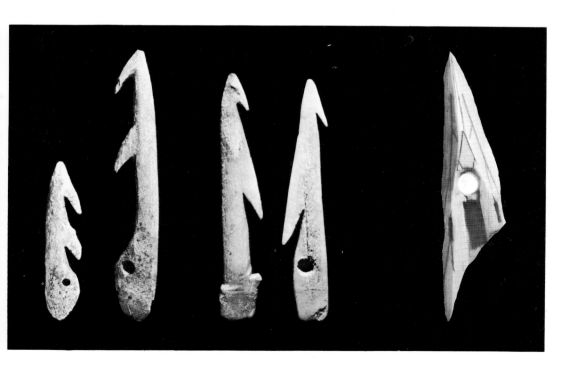

55.1: *Barbed harpoon dart heads of bone. Two (far left) are from the Alaska Peninsula, 76 mm and 130 mm in length, dating from about AD 1000; two (centre left) are from the Aleutian Islands, 72 mm and 70 mm in length, date unknown. The squared and projecting base on one of these implements is a more archaic means for attaching the lines than are the cut or drilled holes on the others.*

55.2: *An early Punuk culture toggling harpoon head (near left) from St Lawrence Island. Dating from about AD 500, the harpoon head is 87 mm in length, and is made of ivory with engraved decoration. The open socket and the small slots through which thongs were inserted to tie the head to the end of the shaft can be seen.*

Juneau (Ground Hog Bay) and as far south as the central coast of British Columbia (Namu), where they made use of land mammals such as deer and bear, and also of seal, porpoise and sea otter. After about 5000 BC apparently related microblade assemblages appear on the Queen Charlotte Islands, as well as in the southern interior of British Columbia. About two thousand years later they reached a southern limit in the south–central part of the state of Washington.

By 4000 BC descendants of the Palaeo-Arctic people were living on Kodiak Island, as well as on the southern coast of the Alaska Peninsula, where faunal remains include those of sea mammals – harbour seal, sea lion and sea otter – and of fish such as Pacific salmon, halibut and cod. Microblade technology survived in the earliest of these sites, before being replaced completely by an industry emphasizing the production of large, chipped, bifacial knives and a variety of specialized projectile heads of chipped stone, which was in turn replaced by an industry based on the polishing of slate. Shortly after 3000 BC this series of techniques developed alongside a bone technology that emphasized barbed harpoon dart heads. By this time reflections of the same technological continuum had appeared along the American coast as far south as Vancouver Island. It is likely that a significant proportion of the people on this coastal strip were Palaeo-Arctic descendants, who continued regular, if sometimes indirect, contacts along the north-west coast, leading ultimately to the development of the spectacular North-West Coast culture in the south and of the so-called Pacific Eskimos around Kodiak Island to the north.[2]

Further west other descendants of people of the Palaeo-Arctic tradition had moved into the Aleutian Islands, completing the colonization of that chain, 1700 kilometres long, no later than the middle of the first millennium BC. There they maintained a remarkably stable way of life, involving a rich technology of bone and chipped stone, that lasted until the arrival of the first Europeans in the eighteenth century.

Northward movement in the interior

As the last remaining hunters of the Palaeo-Arctic tradition haunted the glacier edges of Alaska, the recession of Pleistocene ice in Canada was accompanied by a northward movement of people already present in North America, who in their expansion showed a steady development of the use of post-Pleistocene resources as an interval of warmer climate brought the northward expansion of the boreal forest.

In the east people of Maritime Archaic culture had focused their activity on the coast of central Labrador, and by about 3000 BC they had reached the northern portion of that peninsula. In central Canada a related northward spread by southern Indians about 6000 BC brought caribou hunters north as far as the Thelon river, presumably as the tree line shifted northwards. Still further west, after about 4000 BC the newly forested zone of the Alaskan interior was inhabited by people of what has been called the Northern Archaic tradition. Although some of these used stone techniques

(in particular the production of microblades) that seem to link them with their Palaeo-Arctic predecessors, most of their material culture seems more clearly reminiscent of developments further south, as they evolved techniques for the harvest of forest fauna of modern character – caribou, moose and lesser animals.[3]

Throughout this time the true Arctic regions east of Alaska were uninhabited.

Occupation of the Arctic

At some point in the third millennium BC the first known representatives of the Arctic Small Tool tradition appeared in north-western Alaska. These people, makers of small and delicate stone sideblades, endblades and burins, lived primarily on the strip of tundra inside the coastline, where they focused their interest particularly upon caribou, but in some seasons they also visited the coast to take seals. Some prehistorians consider them to have descended from people of the much earlier Palaeo-Arctic tradition somewhere in the vicinity of the Brooks Range in northern Alaska; others see them as a third-millennium BC migration from Siberia. Most agree, however, that these pioneer Arctic folk represent the ancestors of modern Eskimo-speaking peoples.

By shortly after 2000 BC these people had spread as far south as the southern shore of the Bering Sea, to approximately the southern limit of sea ice on the Alaska Peninsula. By this time they had also expanded throughout hitherto unoccupied portions of Arctic Canada to Labrador, and as far north as Pearyland in northernmost Greenland. Making use of the resources both of the coast and of the tundra, these people used the bone toggling harpoon – a harpoon with a detachable head that twists sidewise or 'toggles' in the wound – as well as the bow. The degree to which they employed either dog traction or boats is uncertain, though it appears that some form of efficient transport would have been necessary for their explosive spread.

In west Greenland and around northern Hudson Bay the aspect of the Arctic Small Tool tradition known as the Pre-Dorset culture evolved steadily, and by about 800 BC the derivative Dorset culture can be recognized. Dorset people lived on the coasts, subsisting chiefly upon sea mammals and other products of the shoreline. They had a kit of bone hunting implements, including an impressive range of toggling harpoon heads, lances and spears, and a similarly impressive set of stone implements, of which most were chipped but a few were polished. The small stone lamp was in use, and the presence of the snow block house seems certain, although it may already have been used during Pre-Dorset times. A few skeletal remains indicate that these people were similar to modern Eskimos in physical type.[4]

In Alaska the evolution of later cultures from the Arctic Small Tool tradition cannot be so clearly demonstrated. A hiatus appears in most of the local sequences about 1000 BC, although not long after this date a people was present whose stone artifacts strongly suggest derivation from those of the Arctic Small Tool tradition, despite the obviously Asian source of their ceramics, which were the earliest in Alaska.

These later assemblages have been called the Norton tradition, and the sites yielding them are spread along the coast from the Alaska Peninsula in the south-west to a point on the northern coast near the modern boundary between Alaska and Canada, indicating the first heavy reliance upon coastal resources north of the Alaska Peninsula. Many coastal sites are large, and all include square, semi-subterranean houses.

In the north the earliest of these Norton tradition assemblages have been termed the Choris culture and date from after 1000 BC. Some time after 500 BC this variant gave way to assemblages of what were originally termed the Norton culture, in which stone artifacts were still related to those of the Arctic Small Tool tradition and pottery was characterized by check-stamped decoration. Shortly after the beginning of the Christian era there appeared the third northern Norton variant, which has been termed the Ipiutak culture and which persisted beyond the middle of the first millennium AD. Pottery and stone lamps disappeared, but the stone assemblage offers clear evidence of continuity with the preceding Norton culture; a highly developed burial art is associated with organic specimens from the major Ipiutak site at Point Hope.[5]

South of the Bering Strait the earliest Norton tradition sites date from about the middle of the first millennium BC; by the end of that millennium they were distributed as far south as the mid-portion of the northern edge of the Alaska Peninsula – about as far

as earlier people of the Arctic Small Tool tradition had penetrated. Around the Bering Sea the Norton tradition persisted with clear, although steadily evolving, continuity in stone implements, ceramics and settlement patterns until about AD 1000,[6] as part of a broadly north Pacific development of coast-oriented economies that also included the Ancient Koryak and Okhotsk cultures of the fringes of the Okhotsk Sea (see Chapter 49).

Background of recent Arctic peoples

Not long after the beginning of the Christian era the Bering Strait region saw the development of what has been termed the Northern Maritime, or Thule, tradition. The Old Bering Sea and Okvik phases of local culture involved an especially heavy dependence upon sea mammals, in particular the walrus and the seal. They were marked by the evolution of pottery and stone artifacts in a direction that diverged somewhat from that of the still vital Norton tradition of the American shores, although the early Thule tradition clearly had its origins either in the Norton tradition itself or in a similar combination of roots both Asian and American. Among organic implements, bone and ivory toggling harpoon heads were especially elaborate, and an art style of pleasing symmetry appeared in engraved lines on harpoon heads and other implements and on the bodies of numerous ivory figurines. Stone artifacts began to emphasize the polishing of slate in a manner reminiscent of that long known around Kodiak Island, although the

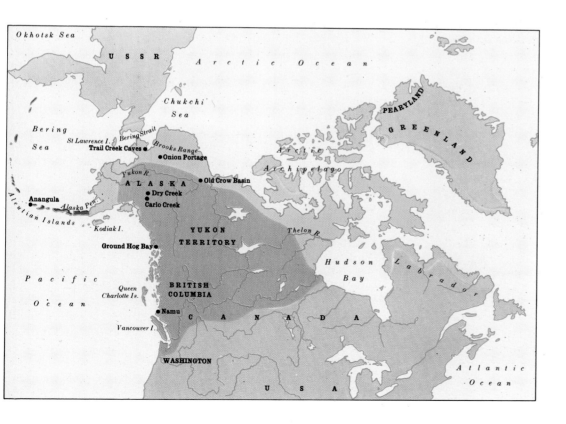

55.3: *Northern North America, showing the extent of the areas occupied by some recent native peoples and the location of some archaeological sites.*

extent of occupation in 19th century

Aleuts

Eskimos

Athapaskan and Northwest Coast Indians

• archaeological sites

intervening regions of the Bering Sea shore give no clear indication that the impetus was actually from that region.[7]

With the steady development of sea-hunting gear and techniques (including whaling) into the Punuk culture of the late first millennium AD, aspects of the Thule tradition began to appear around the northern Alaskan coastline in the whale- and seal-hunting villages of Birnirk and related cultures. By about AD 1000 characteristic tool assemblages of the Thule tradition were clearly present not only along the Siberian and the American coasts of the Chukchi Sea, but also around the American shore of the Bering Sea. They had penetrated across the Alaska Peninsula to the north Pacific around Kodiak Island and had made an impact noticeable in the polished slate implements that were to spread throughout the Aleutian chain of islands during the next few centuries.

It has been suggested that the generally warmer conditions that prevailed at about the end of the first millennium AD resulted in a reduction in sea ice in the Arctic Ocean and a change in the migration habits of large sea mammals – in particular, the larger whales – so that these passed the Alaskan coast far out to sea, nearing land only when they approached the Arctic Archipelago. It has also been suggested that the response of Thule people was a rapid movement from Alaska through the Arctic islands of Canada, and that they spread their new maritime techniques as far east as Greenland, displacing or absorbing the resident Dorset people along the way.[8]

Thus by about AD 1100, as the result of a second explosive expansion across North America, the immediate ancestors of modern Eskimo-speaking Inuit people had spread throughout northern Canada and Greenland, while their western cousins continued the steady developments in Alaska that culminated in the culture of the modern Eskimo peoples of those regions.

Some prehistorians presume that the historic Athapaskan Indians, whose northern representatives are distributed from the Alaskan interior through the northern interior of Canada to Hudson Bay, developed from people of the Northern Archaic tradition, who were in Alaska by about 4000 BC.[9] However, information about the transition from that early period to later events in the interior is limited, and the direct Athapaskan ancestors can nowhere be identified with real confidence earlier than the beginning of the Christian era and in many places not before the end of the first millennium AD.

56. Early agriculture in the Americas

Before the European conquest more than one hundred different plants had been brought into cultivation by the native Americans. The list includes major international food crops (maize, potato, manioc/cassava, peanut, many varieties of beans, and plants of the squash–pumpkin family), as well as chili peppers, vanilla, sunflower (grown for its oily seed), sweet potato, avocado, tobacco, coca (the source of cocaine), pineapple, tomato and cacao – these last two still travelling under their Mexican names, *tomatl* and *chocolatl*. In addition, American cottons are the basis of all modern commercial varieties.

Wherever seed crops predominated in aboriginal America, the combination of maize and beans was particularly important from the dietary point of view. These two plants complement each other, maize being rich in starch but deficient in total protein and in certain essential amino-acids, while beans are protein-rich and also contain precisely those amino-acids lacking in maize. In the high Andes quinoa seeds serve much the same function as beans, providing a rich source of protein in an economy dominated by starchy tubers.

Amerindian farming systems are not based on a random collection of crop plants, but are designed to provide not only a balanced diet but also the necessities of everyday life: containers, net floats, fish poisons, dyes, fibres, medicinal plants, stimulants and hallucinogens, gums and resins, ornamental flowers and materials used in ritual activities. It was in such a setting of generalized, multipurpose plant use that the first experiments with horticulture took place, and the earliest garden plots of the sixth millennium BC were probably very like Indian house gardens of today, with all kinds of useful plants growing side by side.[1]

With the diversity of plants goes a sophisticated understanding of their properties. Some foods need elaborate processing before they are edible at all. The leaves and hearts of the maguey cactus have to be roasted in pits for up to five days; acorns, quinoa, certain potatoes and the Andean lupin (*tarwi*) must be washed in water to remove the bitter toxins. In the high Andes potatoes are freeze-dried to convert them into *chuño*, hard lumps of nearly pure starch that can be stored almost indefinitely and are used to thicken soups and stews.

These techniques, like the crop plants themselves, have a long history, though its earliest stages are often difficult to identify. Domestication, whether of plants or animals, can only be recognized some time after the process has started, when the genetic make-up of the species has been so modified under human selection that the domestic forms are morphologically different (in size, shape or colour) from their wild progenitors. The earliest generations of cultivated, or merely 'tended', crops are indistinguishable from their wild forms (chili peppers the size of peas, maize cobs no longer than a thumb joint: see Figures 56.1 and 56.2) and give no hint of what they will eventually become. There is, inevitably, some botanical uncertainty about the status of plants in this initial stage of domestication, and it would be impossible to recognize the legendary 'oldest cultivated maize' even if the archaeologist were lucky enough to find it.

Animal domestication in the Americas

In contrast to their wealth of plant foods, the Americas are poor in domesticated animals. Of these, the dog is the first to appear in the archaeological record, and may even have accompanied man on his initial migration into the New World. Dog bones have been found at Jaguar Cave, Idaho, in deposits of the ninth or tenth millennium BC, and at caves in the Junín region of the Peruvian Andes by about 6000 BC. In some parts of America the dog was an important source of food. Sixteenth-century Spanish chronicles describe how the Mexicans fattened edible dogs on maize and household scraps, and analysis of the animal bones from archaeological sites in Veracruz, dated to between 1500 BC and AD 300, indicates that dogs provided up to half of the total meat supply.[2] Otherwise the repertoire of Mesoamerican domestic animals is small: the muscovy duck, the stingless bee and the turkey – 'birds with great dewlaps', as one Spanish *conquistador* described them – found on Mexican sites from 300 BC onwards.

It was only in the central Andes that domestic animals played a significant role in the economy, forming part of a mixed subsistence strategy that combined pastoralism with crop cultivation. The high and treeless *puna* grassland of the Andes, between 4000 and 5000 metres above sea level, is not well suited to cultivation, though some potatoes and quinoa may be grown there. In this environment the most productive sources of food are the large grazing animals, deer and camelids (llama, alpaca, and their wild relatives, the guanaco and vicuña), and the *puna* has at all times been a region of hunting and herding camps.

The llamas and alpacas that are the mainstay of the *puna* economy are all-purpose animals.[3] Their wool is used for cloth, sacks and cordage; the meat is eaten fresh or is dried in the sun to make *charki*; viscera, blood and crushed bones are used in soups; and the tallow is employed for candles. Pelts, hides and leather have a multiplicity of uses; sinews serve for binding; and the dung provides fuel and also an essential fertilizer for the potato fields. In addition, llamas will carry loads of 10–60 kilograms for up to 20 kilometres a day.

Archaeological evidence from *puna* sites shows a gradual drift away from deer-hunting towards an increasing reliance on the camelids, leading eventually to herding and to the emergence of domesticated breeds. Because of the difficulty of distinguishing, on purely anatomical grounds, between llamas, alpacas and guanacos in an early stage of domestication, the archaeologist is forced to look for other criteria: increasing dependence on camelids, indicated by the relative abundance of their bones at archaeological sites; regular occurrence of these animals outside their natural range; and unnatural population structures of a kind that would not be found in wild herds and that imply control or manipulation by man.

Employing these criteria, the process of domestication can be tentatively reconstructed from the bone samples preserved in Andean caves.[4] In the earliest strata at Lauricocha (8000–6500 BC) deer bones outnumber those of camelids, but in the more recent levels at the cave (6500–3800 BC) these proportions are reversed. The same phenomenon is recognizable in the *puna* of Junín,

56.1: *The development of domesticated chili peppers* (bottom row) *from their wild ancestors* (top row). From left to right: Capsicum annum, C. baccatum, C. chinense. *Evolution under cultivation has led to an increase in size, to variations in flavour, to a change from deciduous to non-deciduous fruits, and to loss of the natural means of seed dispersal by birds.*

56.2: *Increase in the size of Mexican maize cobs between 5700 BC and AD 1500. These specimens come from archaeological excavations in the dry caves of the Tehuacán valley. The oldest cob is less than 3 centimetres long, but belongs to a form of maize that may be separated by a thousand years or more from its wild ancestor. The first maize yielded no more than 60–80 kilograms of shelled kernels per hectare, rising to 90–120 kilograms by 3700 BC, and to 200 kilograms by about 2000 BC.*

where deer and camelids were hunted in roughly equal numbers from 10 000 to 6000 BC, after which camelids increase until they constitute over 80 per cent of the food bones. This high figure suggests either specialized hunting or some degree of control over the movement and breeding of the wild herds. Between 5000 and 3200 BC camelids also make a significant appearance in the lower Peruvian valleys.

After 5400 BC the existence of distinct large and small domestic breeds can be recognized at sites in the Ayacucho basin, and at about the same time the cave of Pachamachay (Junín) provides evidence for the selective culling of camelid herds. Between a half and a third of the animals at Pachamachay were killed at the age of eighteen months, which coincides with the dry season on the *puna* and with the best time to make *charki*. By about 3200 BC or shortly after, llamas were found on the coast at Chilca, far below their natural altitude range, and a fully developed herding economy (often involving transhumance) had come into being on the *puna* by 1000 BC at latest.

The domestic guinea pig derives from the wild guinea pig of the Andes. Today, these animals are household scavengers, and each family normally keeps fifteen to twenty of them for food. While llamas and alpacas do best in *puna* conditions, the natural home of the guinea pig is the Andean valley zone, below 4000 metres. This difference of habitat is reflected in the archaeological evidence. Guinea pig bones rarely occur on *puna* sites, but first appear soon after 7500 BC in great abundance (up to 40 per cent of the meat bones) in highland basin sites in two separate centres: near Bogotá (Colombia) and at Ayacucho in Peru. The great abundance of these animals between 6500–4600 BC is not accompanied by any increase in their size, and there is no proof of domestication — though the concentration on this single species hints that guinea pigs may already have been tamed or managed, attracted to the

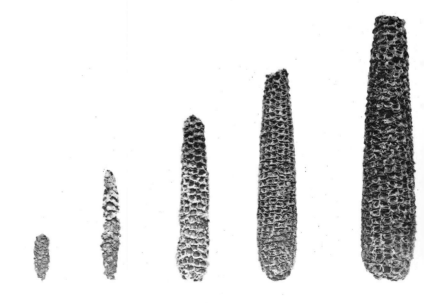

household by warmth and food. By the end of the second millennium BC larger size, greater variability and certain skeletal changes indicate domestication. After that date the domestic guinea pig was dispersed over a wide area of South America, reaching coastal Peru (Culebras) before 2000 BC, Ecuador by AD 700, and the Orinoco basin and the Antilles just before the arrival of the Spaniards.

The beginnings of farming in Mexico
The search for long archaeological sequences with good preservation of plant materials has led to a concentration of research on caves and rockshelters in dry, mountainous regions. In Mesoamerica our most complete evidence comes from the Tehuacán valley of central Mexico,[5] Tamaulipas in the north-east[6] and the valley of Oaxaca in southern Mexico.[7]

At the end of the Pleistocene Ice Age, Oaxaca and Tehuacán were slightly cooler and drier than they are today, but the transition from Pleistocene to modern conditions was not accompanied by any drastic changes. The horse and mammoth became extinct, but other species (deer and many smaller mammals) persisted, and still others were replaced by equivalent modern forms.

The archaeological evidence suggests not a sudden break in the mode of subsistence, but rather a series of fairly minor readjustments. In the Tehuacán valley, shortly before 7500 BC, the inhabitants of the rockshelters hunted the occasional horse and

prong-horn antelope, but the bulk of their meat came from small game: fox, skunk, coyote, ground squirrel, turtle, birds, lizards and rodents, with rabbits as the most important food animal. As part of their annual cycle, the Tehuacanos also harvested the seeds and pods of the mesquite, a leguminous tree that grew wild on the valley floor. By 7000 BC the horse was extinct and the antelope had left the valley. Conditions were approximately those of today, and in this new post-Pleistocene environment the Tehuacanos continued their old ways, hunting a wide variety of small animals and collecting wild plant foods: setaria (a small-seeded grass), amaranth, prickly pear, avocado and chupandilla fruits.

In the valley of Oaxaca the story is much the same. The climate was a little cooler and drier than at present, and from the rockshelter of Guilá Naquitz (with radiocarbon dates ranging from about 8800 to 6800 BC) comes archaeological evidence for occupation, during the rainy months of September to November, by small groups of people who hunted white-tailed deer and cottontail rabbits, collected mud turtles, and gathered acorns, pinyon and susi nuts, mesquite pods, maguey, prickly pear, tree fruits and berries, pumpkins, squashes and beans, and a plant which was either primitive maize or else teosinte, a weedy grass that is its closest wild relative. It is possible that the squashes, beans and maize-like plant were in an early stage of domestication.[8]

Tehuacán, Oaxaca and Tamaulipas are regions of low rainfall, where some of the major food resources are markedly seasonal.

SW Tamaulipas

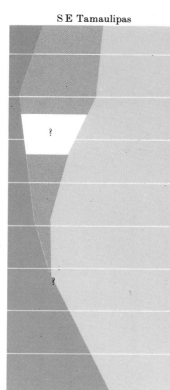
SE Tamaulipas

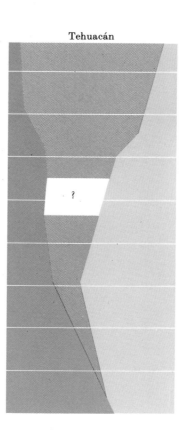
Tehuacán

56.3: *The relative importance of agriculture compared with hunting and plant-collecting in three areas of Mexico. At the time of the Spanish conquest the Tehuacán valley had large towns and cities, whose inhabitants obtained most of their food from irrigated farmlands. In the harsher conditions of Tamaulipas, on the north-east frontier, agriculture was less reliable and never contributed more than about 50 per cent of the total food supply. In all three areas, however, the adoption of farming was slow and gradual.*

☐ hunting
☐ agriculture
☐ wild plants

Cactus fruits, wild cereals and mesquite pods, for example, are rainy-season products. In good years these seasonal foods are available in great abundance, though they must be harvested quickly, before they spoil or are eaten by birds and animals. During the rainy months the scattered family groups were able to congregate into larger camps, of up to a hundred people, to enjoy the temporary abundance. Other resources, notably game and the less appetizing plant foods, are available all the year round, but are not abundant at any single place or at any one time. During the dry season, therefore, the large camps broke up and the population scattered in smaller groups for the months of scarcity. The excavated camp sites of the dry season are small, with no permanent structures and no more than two or three hearths, suggesting a group of fifteen people or so. The food debris consists mainly of year-round resources: deer bones, cactus leaves and the edible roots of the pochote tree (Ceiba parvifolia).

Gradually, some of the plants that had been collected in the wild were brought into cultivation (i.e. deliberately sown, sometimes in places where they would not grow naturally in the wild), though this rudimentary horticulture at first made only a small contribution to the diet (see Figure 56.3). The contents of human faeces from the caves make it very clear that people were eating whatever they could get, long after the first experiments with cultivation. Besides plant foods and meat, the faeces contain charred bits of snail shell, bones of mice, lizards, snakes and birds,

feathers and fragments of egg shell, grubs and bits of uncooked grasshoppers.

The archaeological material from Tehuacán and Tamaulipas accurately reflects this way of life. Deer and peccary (a pig-like mammal) were brought down by stone-tipped wooden darts, hurled with the aid of a spear-thrower. Meat was roasted in pits filled with heated stones, and the larger bones were smashed to obtain the marrow. Small animals were taken with wooden spring traps or by means of fibre snares, while rabbits were killed in communal drives by hunters equipped with nets, sticks and clubs. Plant foods were collected in net bags and in carrying baskets; seeds were crushed in mortars or ground on milling stones.

Because of the good preservation of organic materials in dry caves, we can build up a fairly complete picture of life during the period of incipient agriculture. Woodworking tools (gouges, spokeshaves, knives and scrapers) made of chipped stone were used to manufacture tool handles, spear shafts, traps, fire drills, flutes, digging sticks, rabbit clubs and tongs for picking spiny cactus fruits. Hides were cleaned with the aid of stone scrapers and then were cured by smoking. Plant fibres were rolled by hand into yarn for nets, carrying straps and kilts. Other perishable items include gourd bowls, baskets, textile fragments, bags and sleeping mats woven from the split leaves of palms or cactus plants. Trade brought in a little obsidian and a few ornaments made of sea shells.

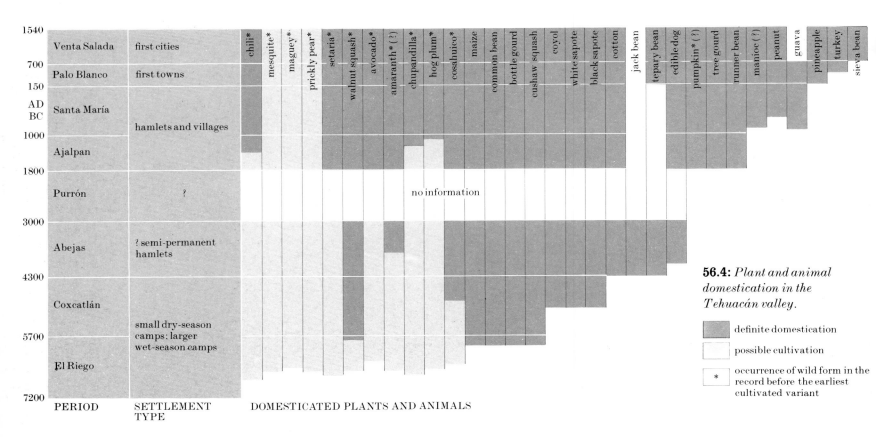

56.4: *Plant and animal domestication in the Tehuacán valley.*

■ definite domestication

□ possible cultivation

* occurrence of wild form in the record before the earliest cultivated variant

The earliest attempts at plant cultivation made little difference to the overall way of life. Domesticated races of plants are clearly recognizable by 5700 BC but the changeover from hunting and gathering to an agricultural way of life represents a slow evolution rather than a sudden revolution.

The general characteristics of this process can be studied in Figure 56.4, which summarizes the archaeological data from the Tehuacán valley. During the El Riego period all the cultivated plants were native to Tehuacán and had previously been collected in the wild. At this very early stage of domestication the plants were virtually indistinguishable from their wild ancestors; in fact, their cultivated status is in doubt. By the Coxcatlán period there is unambiguous proof of domestication, with the arrival of new crops whose wild forms did not grow in the valley. Some of these new arrivals were the ones that later became staple crops (maize, beans, squashes), and their centres of origin lay in other regions of highland Mexico, where they had already undergone some genetic improvement before being introduced to Tehuacán in fully domesticated form. By AD 850 cultivated plants of South American origin (peanuts, guava and perhaps manioc) had been carried northwards, to appear in the Tehuacán archaeological record.

Between 6000 and 2500 BC a number of interrelated developments ultimately brought about the emergence of settled village life based on full-time farming: the population grew until it exceeded the figure that could be supported by hunting and gathering alone; under human selection, certain plants – notably maize – became larger and more productive until it became increasingly worth while to clear away the wild vegetation in order to plant crops; as crop plants made a greater contribution to the food supply, communities were able to remain in one place for longer periods, and the camp sites were larger and more permanent; improved farming technology increased productivity still further, and settlements were located with an eye to agricultural needs rather than for hunting and foraging.

Of all these factors, the most critical one may be the increase in size and productivity of the maize plant (see Figure 56.2). As late as 3800 BC cultivated maize produced no more calories than an equivalent area of wild mesquite, but in about 2000 BC a critical threshold was reached. With a yield of some 200 kilograms per hectare, maize was now more productive than any wild plant and was capable of supporting settled life.[9] It was at just this time that the first villages of pottery-making farmers appeared in highland Mexico.

In arid regions sedentary life was impossible until the development of high-yield crops and efficient farming techniques overcame the need to move around in search of scattered, seasonal resources. In other environments, where food was available in one place throughout the year, settled life emerged much earlier and indeed preceded agriculture.[10]

Some of the coastal shell-mounds may possibly have been occupied on a year-round basis, though this has still to be demonstrated, and most of them are no older than the fourth millennium BC. The most convincing evidence for early sedentism comes not from the coast but from the site of Zohapilco in the Basin of Mexico, some 2240 metres above sea level.[11]

Today the Basin is deforested and much eroded, but between 6000 and 4500 BC it was one of the most favourable environments in Mexico. Pollen grains, animal bones and plant fragments preserved in peaty deposits show what foods were eaten by the people who lived around the freshwater lake that occupied the valley floor. The lake itself provided three species of fish and also some waterfowl throughout the year, while deer and rabbits were permanently available on the forested slopes. During the rainy months from April to October these foods were supplemented by snakes, turtles, axolotls (small amphibians with eel-flavoured flesh), and by plants (teosinte, amaranth, physalis and squash) from the alluvial soils of the lake shore. Just when the supply of rainy-season foods was running short, a new source of food became available as huge flocks of migratory ducks and geese arrived to spend the winter months on the lake.

In these conditions of abundance there was no need to roam in search of food, and sedentary life seems to go back to about 6000 BC. With later developments in mind, it is significant that seed-grinding stones were prominent in the tool-kit, and that the natural flora included potential domesticates. Pollen-grain measurements suggest that the protection and selection of teosinte/maize may have been practised from the start.

Herding and early farming in the Andes

In the Andes considerable ecological diversity is compressed into a relatively narrow space. The mountainous topography gives rise to a series of elongated, ribbon-like ecological zones, stacked one above the other, following the contours along the Andean spine of South America. Because of the steepness of the slopes, a journey of a few hours may take the traveller through four or five different environments, each with its own characteristic range of plants and animals.

Today maize, cotton, squashes, coca and other crops requiring a long growing season are planted at low altitudes. Above 3000 metres these begin to give way to the hardier, high-altitude seed crops (cañihua, quinoa, tarwi) and to the Andean tubers (potato, oca, ulluco and mashua). At still higher elevations, above 3900–4000 metres, the number of frost-free days is too small to allow cultivation, but these high-altitude grasslands are prime grazing territory for llamas and alpacas.

Each community tries to maintain access to all the resources it will need for the year. To achieve this, it must own lands – sometimes in a continuous bloc, but often in widely separated 'islands' – in all the different altitude zones. This pattern of 'vertical control' exists today,[12] was practised on an imperial scale in the fifteenth and sixteenth centuries,[13] and must have been a basic fact of life from earliest times. Camp sites of pre-agricultural hunters and gatherers are found in all zones from coast to *puna*, and may have formed part of a single annual cycle of migration or transhumance designed to harvest the seasonal resources of the different altitude zones.

The earliest evidence for plant domestication in the Andes comes from one of these sites, Guitarrero Cave, which may have served as a seasonal base camp in the thorn-scrub zone at 2600 metres. There, by 6500 BC at the latest (and perhaps as early as 8500 BC), the inhabitants were cultivating chili peppers and two species of beans, and were eating tubers and rhizomes (possibly wild) related to oca and ulluco. Maize does not appear at the cave until after 4800 BC.[14]

Making allowances for the different environment and for the importance of herding in the Andes, the general process of becoming agricultural was broadly similar to that of highland Mexico.

The most complete story comes from the Ayacucho Basin of

Peru.[15] The early post-Pleistocene groups of the ninth to seventh millennia BC hunted deer and camelids in the humid woodland zone, coming down to lower altitudes in the dry season to collect wild plants and small game, including guinea pigs. This pattern continued for several thousand years. Grinding stones, for processing seeds, are present from about 7500 BC, and there is evidence for the import of bottle gourds and achiote (*Bixa orellana*) seeds from the tropical forest east of the Andes.

Circumstantial evidence hints that the early stages of both plant and animal domestication in Ayacucho go back to about 6300 BC, but it is not until the fifth millennium BC that there is firm evidence for the cultivation of chilis, cotton, lúcuma, and also maize and beans. By the end of this period the economic system linked together all the altitude zones from the *puna* (hunting, herding and probably some root-crop cultivation) to the thorn forest, where the emphasis was on seed crops and the raising of guinea pigs. Some of the base camps along the rivers had by now grown into permanent or semi-permanent villages with circular houses on stone foundations. In Ayacucho this point marks the transition to settled agricultural life.

Coastal Peru

The desert coast of Peru and northern Chile is an anomaly: a region with no rainfall and no indigenous crop plants that nevertheless became a centre of great civilizations based on productive farming.

Although the desert itself is barren, the cold waters of the Humboldt Current support one of the world's richest fisheries, as well as large numbers of shellfish, water birds and sea mammals. Most of the molluscs and small fish are available at all times of year and can be obtained without any complex technology. The coastal zone is crossed by about forty river valleys, separated by infertile desert. In later periods these rivers were the source of the irrigation water on which the coastal civilizations depended, but from earliest times the valley bottoms and floodplains supported small trees and plants with edible fruits, pods and tubers. It was here that the first local experiments with cultivation took place.

The other niche useful to man is the *lomas* zone at elevations between 200 and 800 metres. At this altitude fog banks develop during the winter months, and the condensation of moisture

56.5: *Map of the Americas, showing sites where early evidence for the domestication of plants and animals has been found. The approximate northern limit of maize cultivation at the time of the first European contact is also indicated.*

·	single sites
●	areas containing several sites
⌐	northern limit of maize cultivation at the time of European contact

(possibly with some help from underground water) supports a seasonal vegetation of shrubs, mosses and plants with edible seeds, bulbs or tubers, as well as the snails and browsing animals that feed on these plants.

Early agricultural sites have been found along the Pacific coast from Ecuador to Chile, but the most complete evidence comes from the Chillón valley, near the town of Ancón, on the central coast of Peru. Some 3000 archaeological sites have been mapped in the valley, and the changing pattern of subsistence and settlement is well documented.[16]

A few quarries and workshops for the manufacture of chipped stone tools are dated 12 000–8000 BC, but it is not until about 6500 BC that there is evidence of settlements, in the form of temporary, seasonal camps, in areas of former *lomas* vegetation a few kilometres inland from the coast. These camps have no permanent structures, and consist of shallow patches of sand, ash and rubbish left behind by hunters and collectors of wild plants. The debris includes bones of deer and land mammals, together with the remains of birds, fish, shellfish, grasses, wild seeds and the milling stones used to crush them. The presence of bottle gourds

56.6: *Excavations near Ancón, on the central coast of Peru. The buildings belong to the period 2200–1100 BC. In an area without any rainfall, the unirrigated land is pure desert; in these dry conditions preservation of organic materials is unusually good, and the rubbish heaps of ancient villages are full of food debris (shells, bones and plant fragments) that make possible a fairly precise reconstruction of prehistoric diet.*

(which require a good deal of water and will not grow in the *lomas*) and of marine shell indicates that the *lomas*-dwellers also exploited the valley bottom and the coast.

Between 5000 and 3300 BC a change of emphasis can be recognized. Hunting became less important, and there was an increasing reliance on sea foods and on plants from the nearby valley. Large quantities of wild grass seeds indicate systematic harvesting and storage, and at the end of this period seeds of cultivated squashes made their appearance.

This interest in plants and marine resources foreshadowed a new pattern of subsistence and settlement that emerged suddenly at about 3300 BC and corresponded with a deterioration of the *lomas* as a result of either worsening climate or over-exploitation by a rapidly growing population. Whatever the cause, the outcome was a shift of settlement to the coast, with the establishment of the first permanent village at Pampa on the shores of the bay. The refuse at the Pampa site includes abundant shellfish, shore birds and sea lions, various wild seeds, tubers and rhizomes and a wider range of cultivated plants than before.

As farming made a greater contribution to the diet, attention turned more and more to the floodplain of the Chillón valley. Although some of the coastal villages continued in occupation, from about 2500 BC new settlements were founded away from the shore but close to the prime farmland of the valley bottom. Some of these villages were some distance upstream, and their inhabitants practised small-scale irrigation, but the main population centre was strategically placed near the mouth of the valley, within easy reach of the coast but also beside the rich floodplain soil that could be cultivated without irrigation. Here, at El Paraiso (Chuquitanta), was a town covering 50–60 hectares and with a population of between 3000 and 4000.

At El Paraiso there are at least six enormous rock piles, 3–6 metres high and up to 250 metres long, formed by the collapse of masonry rooms. More than 100 000 tons of quarried stone make up the ruins, and their construction implies a well-organized labour force and a degree of political coercion or direction. The one excavated mound consists of a platform topped by a series of rooms, courtyards and corridors.

Similar developments were taking place all along the Pacific coast. By 4000–3400 BC, at sites like Real Alto and San Pablo, there were large, stable farming villages in the coastal lowlands of Ecuador, with low earthen mounds, ceremonial architecture and formal layout, and there is evidence for the cultivation of maize.[17] In coastal Peru maize arrived later, but was present by 2200 BC at Huarmey, Culebras and Aspero, and by 1550 in the Ancón region. Predictably, maize in these coastal sites belonged to highland Andean races.

During this final preceramic period (3300–2200 BC) the pattern of future Peruvian coastal civilization began to emerge. All the major food crops were grown; the techniques of irrigation were understood; trade networks connected the different regions of the Andes, bringing highland obsidian and vicuña skins to the coastal towns, sea shells to sites high in the Andes, and motifs taken from Ecuadorian pottery to the gourd carvers of Huaca Prieta in Peru.

Burials have been found at most of the larger sites, some of them in graves constructed in the middens, others in cemeteries outside the settlement altogether. At Rio Seco between 2500 and 3000 interments were found in the midden rubbish, and a series of forty-nine graves is reported from the site of Asia on the south-central coast.[18] At Asia the skeletons were wrapped in rush mats, and all the tombs contained funerary offerings: textiles, necklaces and pendants, baskets and bags, jet mirrors in baked clay holders, slate tablets, combs, gourd dishes and the tools used in everyday life. All the different activities are represented – weaving (cotton and other plant fibres, spindles and spindle whorls), fishing (nets, lines, hooks and harpoon parts), hunting (spears and spear-throwers, chipped stone points, slings) and plant collecting (mortars and milling stones). In addition, there were trays and tubes for taking hallucinatory snuffs and also coca leaves, together with gourds for the powdered lime that was chewed with the leaves to aid absorption of the active agent. As some skeletons had three times as many offerings as the ordinary burials, there are signs that society was neither homogeneous nor egalitarian.

Above all, the late preceramic period was a time of increasing social and political complexity. At intervals along the coast there are large archaeological sites that must have served as centres of government. They had large, close-packed populations and monumental architecture – in short, all the signs of centralized control that usually accompany the practice of agriculture – though it was not until some thousand years later, in about 1500 BC, that cultivated plants came to equal marine products in dietary importance.

Origins and dispersals

The crucial question is whether agriculture in the New World was a completely independent discovery, or whether in some way the idea was introduced from the Old World.

Proponents of an Old World origin[19] note that, on present evidence, the first experiments with cultivation and animal domestication took place earlier in Asia than in America, and that boats or rafts capable of making a short ocean crossing were available in Australasia 30 000 years ago. The botanical controversy centres on the origin and early distribution of the bottle gourd (*Lagenaria siceraria*), which is used for dishes and containers, net floats and rattles. It is one of the earliest plants to appear in the American archaeological record, though from rind fragments alone it is impossible to tell whether these gourds were cultivated or wild. Since *Lagenaria* has no known American ancestor, and all the wild species are native to Africa, the plant was presumably carried across the Atlantic, either by the agency of man (though not necessarily as a cultigen), or by natural means as a wild plant. Experiment shows that *Lagenaria* remains viable after floating for a long time in salt water, though it will not readily propagate itself on sandy beaches without human intervention. And there, until we can establish the precise date and status of the first American

56.7: *Artifacts from a summer camp in the Ancón region of the Peruvian central coast, 4450–3300 BC. The textile was made by hand without the aid of a loom. The chipped stone spear point is of a size suitable for hunting deer and large animals, while the shell fish-hooks and the net-sinkers, made of stone, indicate the economic importance of fishing. The container is made from a gourd.*

56.8: *The botanical origins and first archaeological occurrences of the more important American cultivated plants.*

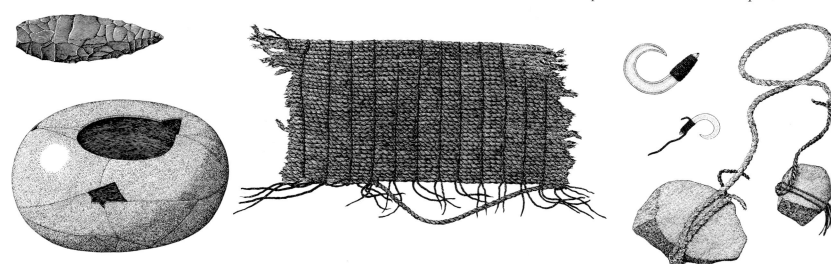

POPULAR NAME	BOTANICAL NAME	BOTANICAL CENTRE OF ORIGIN	EARLIEST ARCHAEOLOGICAL OCCURRENCES AS A DOMESTICATED PLANT
achira	*Canna edulis*	Caribbean or lower eastern slopes of the Andes (?)	Ancón 3300–3100 BC
amaranth	*Amaranthus hypochondriacus* *Amaranthus cruentus* *Amaranthus caudatus*	Mexico/south-west USA Mexico/Guatemala South America	Tehuacán AD 700 Tehuacán (?)4900 BC/4400 BC Argentina 50 BC
avocado	*Persea americana*	Mexico (?)	Tehuacán 1800 BC/Ancón 1150 BC
common bean	*Phaseolus vulgaris*	multiple origins in Central & South America	Tamaulipas & Tehuacán 5000 BC, Guitarrero Cave 8000–7000 BC, Ancón 1150 BC
runner bean	*Phaseolus coccineus*	Mesoamerica	Tamaulipas (?wild) from 7500 BC, Tehuacán 1800 BC
tepary bean	*Phaseolus acutifolius*	Mesoamerica	Tehuacán 4300–3000 BC
sieva bean	*Phaseolus lunatus*	Mesoamerica	Tamaulipas/Tehuacán/Yucatán AD 100–850
lima bean	*Phaseolus lunatus*	South America (? east of Andes)	Guitarrero Cave 8500–6500 BC, Chilca 4200 BC, Huaca Prieta 3300–3220 BC
bottle gourd	*Lagenaria siceraria*	Africa (?)	Ayacucho 11 000 BC (?wild; may be intrusive), Oaxaca & Tamaulipas 7500 BC, Tehuacán c.5700 BC, Ancón 6700 BC
chili pepper	*Capsicum annuum* *Capsicum baccatum* *Capsicum chinense* *Capsicum pubescens*	Mexico South Andes (?) Bolivia lowland South America, probably Amazon basin South America (?)	Tehuacán 7000–5700 BC (?wild) 1170–400 BC (cultivated) Huaca Prieta 3300 BC coastal Peru 400 BC–AD 600 no archaeological specimens
coca	*Erythroxylon coca*	South America, below 1200 metres	lime gourds: Culebras 3300–2000 BC, Valdivia 2500 BC leaf: Ancón 2180–1700 BC
cotton	*Gossypium hirsutum* *Gossypium barbadense*	Mesoamerica South America	Tehuacán 4300 BC coastal Peru 3300–3100 BC
guava	*Psidium guajava*	tropical/subtropical South America	Huaca Prieta & Ancón 3300–3200 BC
jack bean	*Canavalia plagiosperma* *Canavalia ensiformis*	South America Mesoamerica	Ancón 3300–3100 BC Dzibilchaltún, Yucatán 430 BC
maize	*Zea mays*	Mexico to Honduras (if teosinte is wild ancestor)	pollen of maize or teosinte: Guila Naquitz 8800–7500 BC, Gatún Lake 1450 BC cobs of cultivated maize: Tehuacán 5700 BC, Tamaulipas 3700 BC, Ayacucho 4350–2850 BC, Bat Cave c.3700 BC (?), Huarmey, etc. 2200 BC, Ancón 1550 BC
manioc	*Manihot esculenta*	tropical lowlands, South America/Mesoamerica	pollen (?) Gatún Lake c. AD 150; pottery manioc griddles in lowland South America by 1300 BC; Ancón 1150 BC
oca	*Oxalis tuberosus*	Andean South America	Ancón AD 1476 (?)
peanut	*Arachis hypogaea*	lowland South America below 2000 metres, (?) foothills of Bolivian Andes	Ancón 2500 BC, Tehuacán AD 150
potato	*Solanum tuberosum*	southern Andes	Chilca caves (?) 8000 BC, Chiripa 600 BC, north coastal Peru (pottery models) early centuries AD
pumpkin	*Cucurbita pepo*	South Mexico/Guatemala	Guilá Naquitz (?wild) 8800–8100 BC, Tamaulipas 7500 BC, Tehuacán 1800 BC, Kentucky/Missouri 2900 BC·
quinoa	*Chenopodium quinoa* *Chenopodium nuttalliae*	Andes over 2400 metres Mexico (?)	Ayacucho (?) 6300–5100 BC, Argentina 50 BC, Chiripa AD 300, Ancón 15th century AD grown at time of Spanish conquest
setaria	*Setaria*		Tamaulipas 4400 BC, Tehuacán 1800 BC
squash	*Cucurbita mixta* *Cucurbita moschata* *Cucurbita maxima* *Cucurbita ficifolia*	south Mexico/Guatemala south Mexico/Guatemala South America South America (?)	Tehuacán (?) 5700 BC, 3700 BC Tamaulipas 1900–1700 BC, Tehuacán (?) 6000 BC, Ayacucho 3600–2150 BC, Ancón 3300–3100 BC, south-western USA AD 950 Ayacucho 3600–2150 BC, coastal Peru AD 640 Ancón 4400 BC, Oaxaca (?) AD 700
sweet potato	*Ipomoea batatas*	tropical lowlands of South America (and perhaps Mesoamerica)	Chilca caves (? wild) 8000 BC, Ancón 2500–2200 BC (?)
sunflower	*Helianthus*	south-western and south-eastern USA	Riverton & Higgs sites 1250 BC, Tamaulipas 400 BC
tobacco	*Nicotiana tabacum*	South America	Niño Korin (Bolivia) AD 400, Valle de Chaviña (south coastal Peru) 5th century AD, Arizona AD 650
ulluco	*Ullucus tuberosum*	high Andes of South America	Chilca caves (?) 8000 BC

bottle gourds, the argument must rest.

Lagenaria excepted, all subsequent development was based on plants and animals native to America. The geographer Carl Sauer[20] has drawn a distinction between seed agriculture (maize, beans, squash, amaranth, etc.), which he believed originated in Mesoamerica and from there spread to South America, and agriculture based on vegetatively propagated crops (manioc and other starchy tubers), with its centre in the tropical lowlands of South America. Not only are the techniques of planting and harvesting quite distinct, but the two systems have completely different dietary potential. The Mesoamerican seed crops include sources of protein, carbohydrate and oil, providing a self-sufficient and balanced diet, whereas the lowland crops are high in carbohydrate but low in protein, and must therefore be supplemented by fish or wild game.

The primacy of one system over the other is impossible to demonstrate, mainly because of the poor preservation of plant materials in the tropical forest, but there are several lines of evidence that suggest multiple and independent centres of origin for cultivation within the New World.

Botanically, the wild ancestors of the major cultivated crops come from widely separated regions of America and from every environmental zone (see Figure 56.8). Where the same crop was cultivated in both Mesoamerica and South America, the plants are often of different species. This is true of cotton, squashes, *Phaseolus* beans, *Canavalia* beans, amaranth and chili peppers. For some of these plants the early botanical ancestry is still unclear, but for cotton and chili the evidence clearly demonstrates independent, parallel domestication in Central and South America. The same probably applies to the amaranths and some of the beans.[21]

The most problematic of the crop plants is maize, whose botanical ancestry is still the subject of controversy. One group of botanists maintains that domestic strains of maize are descended from teosinte, which is genetically very close to maize and was collected as a food in its own right by pre-agricultural foragers.[22] As teosinte does not grow south of Honduras, this theory implies that all maize is ultimately of Mesoamerican origin. Other botanists argue that the ancestor of domesticated maize is a hypothetical wild maize, which is now extinct. If this is so, and teosinte is not the progenitor of maize, a separate and independent centre of maize domestication may have existed in South America.[23]

Like the botanical evidence, the archaeological data also favour multiple centres of domestication. In each regional sequence the crop plants appear in a different order, starting with those that were locally available in the wild. After this initial period of experimentation, useful plants were exchanged between one region and another; certain races of maize were transferred from Mesoamerica to South America and vice versa, while tobacco, peanuts, guava, pineapple and tomato eventually reached Mexico from their South American homeland.

By a process of secondary spread, the knowledge of agriculture was transmitted to areas outside the zone of primary experimentation. One of these secondary recipients was coastal Peru; another was North America.

The hunter–gatherers of the American Southwest adopted maize agriculture from their Mexican neighbours to the south, and tiny, primitive cobs in an early stage of domestication occur at Bat Cave in the mountains of New Mexico. The radiocarbon dates for this site are rather ambiguous, but – accepting the oldest figures – maize cultivation might go back to 3700 BC. By 1200 BC farming based on maize and beans was fairly general in the Southwest.

In the Eastern Woodlands of the United States the sequence of events is different, and horticulture began with the introduction of the Mexican pumpkin (*Cucurbita pepo*). By 2900–2500 BC cultivated squash occurs at the Bowles and Carlston Annis shellmounds in Kentucky, and at Phillips Spring in Missouri, where it appears alongside the local wild food plants: grape, pokeweed, bullrush, elderberry, blackberry, amaranth, acorns, walnuts and hickory nuts. Under the stimulus of Mexican contacts, the people of the Eastern Woodlands began to domesticate indigenous North American plants – the sunflower (found at the Riverton and Higgs sites by 1250 BC) and sumpweed or marsh elder (*Iva annua* L.) – no later than 1800 BC.[24] By 600 BC the prehistoric inhabitants of Salts Cave, Kentucky, were obtaining 40 per cent of their food, at least on a seasonal basis, from cultivated crops. For reasons still not understood, maize did not spread to the Southeast until just before the time of Christ, and beans later still.

The final, and greatest, dispersal of native American plants came about as a result of the European conquest, when the returning *conquistadores* took home with them many of the crops they had learned to appreciate in the New World. Maize, potatoes and many other plants were soon naturalized in Europe, and from there were carried throughout the world. Today crops of American origin form 40 per cent of global food production.

57. Agricultural groups in North America

The agricultural activities of the North American Indians transformed the populations of the Eastern Woodlands, the Southwest and the Plains from bands of hunting–gathering societies to sedentary town and village dwellers, with populations of between 1000 and 5000 or more in the larger aggregates. This transformation took place slowly, over a considerable period of time, with the introduction of tropical cultigens from Mexico. The earliest known introductions were of gourd and squash, found at late Archaic sites in Missouri, Kentucky and Tennessee, which date to about 2500 BC, with the implication of a somewhat older appearance in states closer to north-eastern Mexico. These plants were used as containers, and their seeds rather than their pulp were consumed. The planting procedure evidently stimulated the domestication of sunflower and perhaps several varieties of *Iva* such as sumpweed and marsh elder. Considerable use was also made of *Chenopodium ambrosia* and *Polygonum*, but whether these were ever domesticated is doubtful.

Early eastern agricultural societies

The major agricultural plant in the East was, of course, maize. The crop was introduced into the area at about the time of Christ, probably from the Southwest, which had had maize for about a thousand years. This introduction seems not to have had much effect upon the eastern societies, which continued to depend for food on their old-established hunting and gathering skills, developed over many millennia.[1] At one time many archaeologists believed that the several eastern societies of the period between about 100 BC and AD 400 must have been agriculturalists because some of these populations (named Hopewellian after the type site) had major population concentrations at strategic locations, with extensive geometric earthworks and many burial mounds. The Hopewell sites of south-central Ohio are outstanding in this regard, with their house structures and extensive village debris both within and outside the walls of the earthworks.[2] The Hopewell site in Ross County, Ohio, covered 45 hectares and contained some thirty-eight burial mounds, most of which were small, dome-shaped structures, although Mound 25 was 9 metres high, 152 metres long and 55 metres wide. It contained over 250 burials, most of which were on the floor of the mound, as well as concentrations of offerings of manufactured items and exotic raw materials not directly associated with burials. The Ohio Hopewell society had a marked interest in foreign raw materials, which were made into artifacts employed in various social and ceremonial activities, and also served to indicate the status and supernatural power of the owner. Almost pure copper was obtained from the Lake Superior deposits on Isle Royale and the Keweenaw peninsula; silver from near Cobalt, Ontario; obsidian from the Yellowstone

Park area of Wyoming; galena from north-western Illinois; mica from south-western North Carolina; marine shells, barracuda jaws and shark and alligator teeth from the south Atlantic and Florida Gulf coasts; Knife River chalcedony from North Dakota; hornstone from south-eastern Indiana and meteoric iron from a number of different meteor falls. It is not clear how the acquisition of these materials was accomplished. Expeditions from Ohio may have obtained the obsidian from Yellowstone and various items from the Florida Gulf coast; in the case of the southern connection, there may have been a series of exchanges at population centres on the trails and water routes between Ohio and Florida. A small number of items manufactured in Ohio were taken to village leaders along the southern route and to centres in Illinois. Other items that could have been or were exchanged from Ohio are mica, copper earspools and prismatic blades of Flint Ridge flint.

In many of the burial mounds an adult male or males are accompanied by grave goods indicating their status in the society. Occasionally children have an unusual amount of burial furniture. Tomb construction varies considerably but the mounds often have a sub-floor chamber with logs placed along at least two sides, and the burials are covered by bark or other organic sheeting

57.1: *Outline of the cultural sequence in the agricultural traditions of North America.*

	SOUTHWEST	PLAINS	THE EAST
1500	CLASSIC	PLAINS COALESCENT	Fort Ancient
			MISSISSIPPIAN
1000	SEDENTARY Pueblo	PLAINS VILLAGE	Cahokia
	COLONIAL Basketmaker		LATER
500		PLAINS	Effigy Mound Coles Creek
	PIONEER	WOODLAND	WOODLAND
AD			
BC			Hopewell Marksville
	Initial Basketmaker	LATER	EARLIER
500		ARCHAIC	Adena Poverty Point
1000			WOODLAND
	ARCHAIC	ARCHAIC	ARCHAIC
1500			

Other mounds have limestone slabs incorporated into a floor covering or as a crypt to enclose a burial.

Some floors in the larger burial mounds were divided into three areas, each of which contained male burials with accompaniments indicating the man's status as an individual or as a social and political leader. There were large caches of cremated manufactured items and raw materials, which were perhaps destroyed because they were the personal possessions of a deceased leader and represented his personal power. The threefold division of the mounds may reflect social distinctions or may represent successive periods of time.

Another significant enclave of these Hopewellian societies was situated in the Illinois river valley, where the distinctive Havana Hopewellian developed and spread to western Michigan, southern Wisconsin, eastern Iowa and up the Missouri river valley as far as eastern Kansas and north-western Oklahoma. Some of the distinctive Hopewellian features appeared first in the Illinois valleys. The interaction or diffusion between these several regional populations is reflected in almost every phase of their material culture, with changes taking place at approximately the same time, although several regional developments reflect the existence of distinct societies in the various geographical areas.

The Havana sites do not, with rare exceptions, have geometric earthworks. Village size varies from 0.1 hectare to some 6 hectares, but most of them are between about 0.5 and 1.2 hectares. There probably would not have been more than a few hundred people at even the largest sites at any one time, and between thirty and a hundred at most of the sites. Population density was less than one per 2.5 square kilometres. House forms were ovoid to circular and sub-rectangular.

While maize has been found in excavations at a small number of villages, most of the food comprised locally harvested seeds, nuts and tubers, along with fish, birds and mammals obtained primarily from the river-valley environment in which they were located. Little use was made of prairie fauna or river molluscs for food. Local chert sources were adequate in most areas, but a nodular blue-grey hornstone from south-western Illinois, near Cobden, was buried in mounds from Havana south as far as Pike County. Fewer ornaments and implements were made of copper, and galena was seldom deposited with the dead.

Contemporary societies throughout most of the eastern United States and lower Canada participated to some degree in many of the behavioural patterns of the Hopewellian groups. However, the strong hold of prior traditions and the basic social relations were contained within their own territories throughout the lower Mississippi valley and the Southeast. Some of these were the Marksville–Issaquena of Louisiana and Mississippi, the Copena of northern Alabama, and the Santa Rosa Swift Creek of the northwest coast of Florida and its adjoining area to the north. Village and mound-site sizes and population densities were not as large as those of many groups in the north. To some extent, these southern groups traded and exchanged with the north as well as with each other, but artifactual remains demonstrating this are not very common.[3] There were also distinctive regional cultural units east of the Appalachians and north and east of the Great Lakes.

Late eastern agricultural societies

Following the gradual disappearance of the Hopewellian artifacts, art styles and burial procedures, and the trade and exchange of exotic raw materials and specialized status items after about AD 400, there was a period of some three hundred or four hundred years during which cultural groups in the east bore witness to a decline in those features that made the Hopewellian societies outstanding. As these changes took place gradually in every eastern area, regional developments, distinctive in detail yet indicating continuing interaction and exchange between contiguous bands, permitted recognition of their essential contemporaneity even before radiocarbon dating established it on a fairly firm footing. One of the cultural additions was the spread of the bow and arrow, which replaced the *atlatl* (spearthrower) and made a more effective hunting aid and aggressive weapon. The construction of flat-topped earthen mounds was initiated; buildings used as political and religious structures were placed on them and an area in front of the mounds was set aside for community activities. Fortified villages developed, with housing structures surrounding a central courtyard. There are also indications of an increasing emphasis on maize as a storable food supply; a shift toward rectangular houses; changes in a variety of implements; and different vessel forms for cooking, eating, storage and water containers.

Between AD 700 and 1000 these changes gradually produced societies whose economic base and social and religious orientation were quite distinct from previous ones. These may be called the Mississippian cultures of the Mississippi valley and its major tributaries and of the Southeast. They were complex societies characterized by a hierarchy of sites with a major town, smaller villages in fairly close proximity and subsidiary farmsteads, hunting or fishing stations, quarries and other extractive camps. In the major population centres there were clear differences in status between the majority of the people and the social and political leaders of the towns and associated communities. The farm lands were fine-grained silty loams of abandoned meander levees in the Mississippi valley south of Illinois, or similar fertile and workable soils in the river valleys of the east. The older known food resources of these same villagers, together with increased production of maize, squash and the common bean (which was added to the diet about AD 1000, probably from the Southwest), gave a more reliable year-round subsistence. The larger population concentrations were located not only in areas of good agricultural soils, but also where there was opportunity for the exploitation of more than one environmental zone and where water and land routes provided ready communication to both neighbouring and distant contemporary settlements. The major population centres and associated cultural developments occurred in the interior rather than on the coast.

The principal Mississippian concentration extended from the Cahokia area, in the flood plain of the Mississippi river opposite St Louis, approximately to Vicksburg. Various developments appeared early in this area, and the complexes of the middle Mississippi and its major tributaries had the largest towns, mounds and populations. The term Appalachian Mississippian has been applied to similar settlements in Georgia and North Carolina; Caddoan Mississippian to contemporary societies in the contiguous areas of Arkansas, Louisiana, Texas and eastern Oklahoma.[4] Middle Mississippi populations developed in the Illinois and upper Mississippi valley, west along the Missouri to Kansas City, in the Lower Wabash and in the Ohio valley, and populations in southern Ohio, northern Kentucky and West Virginia adopted many of the Mississippian cultural traits.

Mississippian towns were planned settlements, with rectangular, single-family houses arranged in an orderly manner around an open, central square, where the town meeting-house, the chief's house and a charnel house were built on adjacent earthen platform mounds.[5] These communities varied in size from a few hundred to a thousand or so; a few of the largest eastern centres, such as Moundville in west-central Alabama, and Cahokia in the East St Louis area, had significantly larger populations. A hierarchy of officials and priests – from community chiefs, war and peace leaders and mortuary priests to clan heads – directed the activities of the people of the larger centres in town and mound construction, planting, weeding, harvesting, hunting, gathering, dances and political and religious affairs.

Indian populations along the Atlantic coast, in the St Lawrence valley and in the Great Lakes area retained many of their established patterns and their relations with the world of the supernatural (see below), even though they were successful in adapting maize to conditions as far north as Nova Scotia, the middle Ottawa river area and the south shore of Lake Superior. Populations were not as dense as those in the interior, and most of the villages and towns were not as large. The growth and supremacy of the Iroquois in the New York area occurred after AD 1400 and was paralleled or exceeded by the several Iroquois groups in Huronia in southern Ontario. These Iroquoian-speaking groups had long houses with multiple family occupancy, and some Huron villages were reported to have over 200 such structures, with an estimated population of over 2000.[6]

Accompanying, and integrated with, the developing social and political ranked structures was an increasing concern with ceremonial observances connected with the supernatural. These represented expressions of ancestral obligation, celebrations of successful harvests, hunts and warfare and burial rites for social leaders. These activities, and no doubt others, were recorded on several kinds of surviving objects, such as thin copper plates and shell, by various symbolic embossed and engraved designs and representations of males engaged in the ceremonial activities. Many of these symbols and the costume items portrayed are found on and with adult males, whose place of burial within or near charnel-house mounds also reflects their importance as community leaders. Some artifact styles, such as specific types of circular shell gorgets, were made in central and eastern Tennessee, and a few of them were traded as far west as eastern Oklahoma. Copper plates with human and bird effigies and symbolic designs have a wide distribution from northern Florida to Oklahoma and as far north as central Illinois. The widespread iconographic distribution reflects a basic similarity over much of the East of religious and magical concepts and an acceptance of the designs and symbols because they were compatible with local beliefs. Various items of this Southeastern Iconographic System begin to appear about AD 1000 and reached a climax between 1200–1400; but the complex was still in existence in a changed and muted form in the late seventeenth century. Some of these art styles, and the platform mound topped by civic and religious buildings, were formerly thought to indicate a direct Mexican intrusion into the Southeast. While some of the religious symbolism seems to express ideas similar to certain late prehistoric Mexican ones, it does not suggest any direct transmission during the long, slow growth of Mississippian societies. There are no identified Mexican items in the Southeast.

Many of the representations of crosses, hand and eye, sun symbols, serpent, cat, woodpecker, falcon, raccoon and others, and ceramics modelled on animal and human forms, can be related to the belief systems of the Southeast and to their verbal expressions as folk tales, myths and religious statements recorded by ethnographers. Their production may well have been linked as closely to these aspects of the culture of local groups as to their economic or subsistence systems. Many of the early historic tribal groups of the Southeast were the descendants of Mississippian societies. These would include most of the Muskogean-speaking Creeks, Chickasaw, Choctaw, Apalachie, Alabama, Cherokee, Tunica and Natchez, and the Caddoan-speakers of Louisiana, Arkansas, eastern Oklahoma and north-east Texas. Some of the Algonkian and Siouan groups in the lower Ohio and upper Mississippi valleys also participated as Mississippian societies.

The Plains agricultural societies

In the eastern Plains, from North Dakota to northern Texas, and in the western Plains area from Montana to New Mexico, there appeared complexes that are collectively called the Plains Village Tradition.[7] Several variations of these developed over much of the area between the ninth and eleventh centuries, from more sedentary societies in eastern South Dakota and the adjoining areas of Minnesota and Iowa and in western Missouri and eastern Nebraska, to smaller, semi-sedentary village groups in south-central Nebraska and north-central Kansas. These groups had a significant dependence on maize and other tropical cultigens. They worked the alluvial soils of the Missouri and its tributaries with hoes made from bison scapulae. In addition, along the eastern Plains, native vegetal foods and fauna, including bison, formed a substantial part of the diet. The latter became more important in the central and western Plains, a region prone to droughts that made agriculture hazardous; the shifting eastwards of the boundary between the long- and short-grass prairie allowed the bison herds to expand.

Many of these eastern Plains villages were fortified to protect the several hundreds of inhabitants, who lived in the Dakotas in rectangular structures, and in the central Plains in smaller, square to rectangular houses with four centre-post supports.[8] The southern Plains groups had a close relationship with the central Plains groups; in the west groups interacted with Puebloan peoples and adopted some of their practices and in the east contact was made with Caddoan complexes.

The introduction of horses in historic times from the Southwest, where they had been obtained from the Spaniards, led to greater mobility and provided a more efficient form of transport that permitted an expansion of bison-hunting, along with a pattern of warfare and horse-thieving. Firearms, spreading from the east, led to a progressive migration from the Eastern Woodlands on to the Plains, where some groups such as the Omaha adopted Plains agricultural practices, while others, such as the Sioux, developed a fully nomadic way of life dependent on bison-hunting and raiding. This adaptation was, however, short-lived, as its base was increasingly eroded by the extermination of the bison. Many of the village tribes retained their farming practices into the eighteenth and nineteenth centuries, to be gradually destroyed by European and American diseases, spirits, trade, war and treaties.

Agricultural groups of the greater Southwest

The American Southwest – New Mexico, Arizona and sizeable portions of Colorado and Utah – is a dry region, varying from desert conditions to plateau and highland areas with coniferous forests and the sources of permanent streams that rise and fall with fluctuating rainfall patterns. Maize had been introduced into this area from Mexico by about 1000 BC, followed by beans and cucurbits considerably later. These tropical cultigens, together with the transmission of substantial cultural developments from north-west Mexico, gradually helped to transform the resident hunting–gathering populations into sedentary village dwellers. The several environmental areas assisted in producing major adaptations with recognizable subdivisions in both time and space within those areas.

In the southern Arizona desert a long sequence of cultural phases, dating from shortly before AD 1 to the early historic and contemporary Pima-Papago Indians, is known as Hohokam. The earliest phase is recognized by the presence of maize, beans and squash, all cultivated by irrigation canals; the first simple ceramics and figurines; the shaped *metate* (maize-grinding slab); clay figures; sub-rectangular pit-house buildings in small village clusters; and a significant dependence on native plants such as mesquite and screw-beans, deer and rabbits.[9] As the population increased during the Colonial and Sedentary periods, between about 500 and 1100, this desert adaptation spread north and east

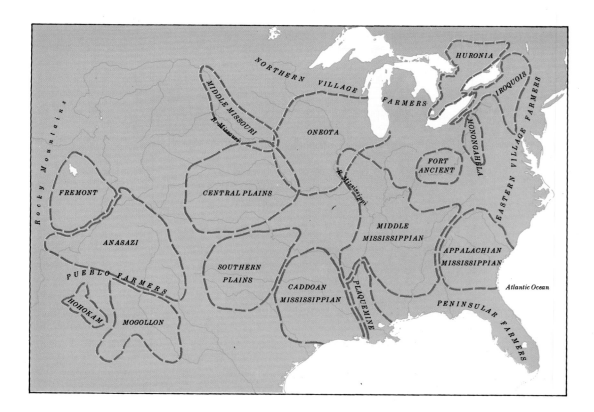

57.2: *The geographical locations of the major agricultural groups.*

up the tributaries of the Gila river. Village size increased with the continuing development of irrigation practices that permitted two plantings and harvests each year. There were important introductions from north-west Mexico, such as ballcourts, platform mounds, painted and effigy ceramics, legged vessels and shell artifacts made from Gulf of California molluscs, cotton, macaws for ceremonial activities and probably feathers and, almost certainly, religious concepts associated with crop fertility. House forms shifted to a somewhat more rectangular shape, with the long axis at right-angles to the short, covered entrance midway along one side. A distinctive red-on-buff pottery has varied geometric and effigy figure patterns, some of which reflect hunting activities and other aspects of economic life and ideology.

The Classic Period, about 1100–1450, witnessed a number of cultural changes that resulted from introductions from Puebloan Anasazi complexes, north-east of the Hohokam. Where earlier Hohokam societies were distinctive in the Southwest, as cremation was the normal burial procedure, inhumation became common. Instead of single, separate homes, there were contiguous rooms and surface and multi-storey buildings made out of adobe inside walled compounds. There were also hilltop sites and some located on hill slopes with stone construction features. Pottery vessels featured new polychrome styles.

In the mountainous region east and north of the Hohokam area, the introduction from Mexico of agriculture, and subsequently of pottery and other items and ideas, resulted in complexes that archaeologists call Mogollon, after the name of a physiographic feature, the Mogollon Rim.[10] By about AD 300, with the spread of pottery-making, probably from the early Hohokam, and the adoption of pit-house structures with circular or D-shaped form and projecting entrances, basin *metates* and *manos* (short, bone-stemmed, cylindrical pipes), the early Mogollon complex of small villages with a few houses and a larger ceremonial structure was on its way. Many sites of the early Mogollon were located in defensible positions on low hills, but after AD 700 these were moved to better land in river valleys for more stable crop production. At about this time designs on the brownish pottery were painted in red, and there was a distinctive treatment of the coiled-clay construction of pottery called Alma Neck-Banded. The villages grew somewhat larger, as houses tended to become rectangular and somewhat smaller, to accommodate single-family units. From 850 to 1000 the Mogollon societies began to receive concepts developed further north in the Anasazi area, such as corrugated external elements on pottery vessels, and a new black-on-white pottery developed, associated with the earlier red-on-white local ware. The pit house, with its rectangular outline and entry ramp, continued. Some of these ceremonial structures had entrances in their flat roofs, however, and some had masonry walls.

After about 1450 the Mogollon area resembled increasingly the more dominant Anasazi groups, so that the societies of this period are called western Pueblo. The majority of the population lived in multiple-room above-ground buildings, some with several hundreds of rooms, squares and rectangular *kivas* (semi-subterranean structures used exclusively by men for ceremonial activities). Pottery was primarily black-on-white, though bowls and painted jars were polychrome, while corrugated ware was decorated with pinching and incising. In the southern Mimbres area of southwestern New Mexico a striking portrayal of human, animal, bird and fish designs on bowl interiors was a unique art style, reflecting religious and other concepts. It is thought that with a gradual abandonment of the northern Mogollon area, some of the population moved north to Zuni and Hopi Pueblos, while others may have joined groups in the central Rio Grande area of New Mexico.

The 'classic' Southwestern prehistoric culture tradition is called Anasazi. It covers by far the largest territory and has many regional and temporal variants. This is the region of the 'cliff dwellers' and the large multi-room and multi-storey *pueblos* that caught the imagination of both scholars and the public in the latter half of the nineteenth century. This is also the area of the most refined work in dendrochronology (see Chapter 62), which began about fifty years ago and has developed to the stage where the dating of cultural events and the identification of both weather patterns in specific areas and the effects of climatic fluctuations on prehistoric populations are very accurate. The area comprises the north-western quarter of New Mexico, much of south-western and western Colorado, the northern half of Arizona and much of Utah. Most of this area is called the Colorado Plateau; the Rio Grande on its eastern border and the Colorado and its major tributaries as far west as the Grand Canyon provide most of its drainage.

Knowledge of crop production reached and spread through this area between AD 1 and 500. Maize production was an important addition before pottery was also introduced from the south and its local manufacture was initiated in the eastern Plateau areas. This initial period, called Basketmaker II, is characterized by the transition from hunting and gathering to the beginning of maize–squash cultivation. The occupied areas were normally located where the crops could be grown in valleys or on slopes with favourable drainage. Houses were built in the form of both circular pit houses and surface structures. Living and storage areas were also situated in rockshelters in cliff walls. Baskets and bags made with considerable skill were the major containers; the *atlatl* and the dart were the hunting and offensive weapons. Deer, rabbits and turkeys provided most of the protein, as well as leather and material for fur and feather cloaks.

With some hundreds of years' experience in cultivating maize in the Plateau, these people were able to produce crops in more varied locales and at some distance from substantial local food resources. Villages were larger, some with as many as fifty circular to rectangular pit houses. Turkeys were penned; beans were added to the diet; pottery became common over a wide area; and the bow and arrow was adopted toward the end of the Basketmaker III period, between 500 and 750. Most of the pottery was a grey ware, typified by simple bowls and jars on which a small amount of black paint was used to produce linear patterns. Some red-on-brown pottery was also made in a limited area, with similarities to contemporary Mogollon styles. Basketry continued to be important, and troughed *metates* and larger *manos* reflected the increased corn production.

It is customary to recognize two prehistoric populations between about 750 and 1150: Pueblo I in the first half of that period, and Pueblo II in the latter half. It was a period of growth in a variety of material items: in the style of architecture and building construction, in ceramic products adapted to a wide range of uses, whose decoration was more skilful and was applied to different vessel forms. Cotton was introduced from Mexico and was manufactured into cloth on a true loom, presumably primarily by men in the *kivas*. These preserved the basic form of the older style of house; most houses of this period, however, were surface structures of one room or several rooms joined in a linear fashion. Some large villages had up to a hundred rooms. Early dwellings were made of wattle and daub (often called jacal in the Southwest) and were rectangular. In the early part of this Puebloan development a cradle board with an added wooden support for an infant's head was adopted, which flattened the occipital area of the skull. For a time the effect of this was not recognized; it was thought that a new population had moved into the Anasazi area, bringing with it new cultural attainments.

In the latter half of this period populations continued to increase, to judge from geographical expansion, the construction of large cliff dwellings, multi-room and multi-storey masonry *pueblos* and an increase in the number of farming communities that occupied areas without adequate rainfall today. While the Anasazi did not develop a fully fledged irrigation system, they did make use of slope wash, small dams, terraces and other devices to conserve and distribute rainfall. *Kivas* persisted as major centres of religious activity; in some areas they were of considerable size and probably served a whole town or sizeable segments of a town. Arrowpoints became triangular, with side notches. Pottery styles continued to emphasize black paint on a white slip and carried more complex designs that were similar to those in the Hohokam Mogollon area. Most vessels were in the form of jars and bowls, but beakers, mugs, stirrup-neck bottles and effigy forms similar to those that appear in the developed Mississippian societies were also made.

A major area of development was Chaco Canyon, in north-west New Mexico, about 110 kilometres south of the Colorado line. This canyon has a remarkable group of large masonry constructions located on either side of the alluvium-filled canyon. While Pueblo Bonito, located where rainfall from the plateau drained into the canyon, is the largest, there are also three or four other constructions of unusual size. There are also more than a hundred smaller, apparently contemporaneous, Pueblo units. It is difficult to be certain about how many rooms in these several communities were actually occupied at any one time, but the population concentration here was unusually large and suggests that some political controls were necessary to regulate water rights and to maintain cooperative practices. Roads connected

these canyon communities and have also been found on the plateau leading north to the San Juan and Mesa Verde area, where there were also considerable population aggregations.

The next 200 years (1100–1300, known as Pueblo III), saw a continuation of the trends of the preceding period in much material culture, but there are indications of substantial population movements. Chaco Canyon became less important and was gradually abandoned. The Mesa Verde had an early period of growth, but lost most of its population towards the latter half of this period. Another area with large Puebloan units was north-eastern Arizona, where there are a number of large and small Puebloan cliff dwellings, now preserved by the National Park Service – as are Mesa Verde, Chaco Canyon and other Southwestern sites. In this period the best black-on-white pottery was produced and it was distributed, through trade, to the west and south. By AD 1300 these areas of concentrated populations were largely abandoned, while the population of towns along the Rio Grande in New Mexico, in west-central New Mexico and in the Hopi area of north-eastern Arizona began to expand. A combination of climatic factors, erosion patterns, inter-group conflict and other less easily identified influences produced these demographic changes. The Plateau populations were not driven out by invading hunters and gatherers, for evidence of such groups does not appear for at least a hundred years in the abandoned areas. The Rio Grande Puebloan populations were numerous and erected large, multi-room structures in several areas, as did the Hopi and Zuni to the west. These societies were in existence when the Spanish came into New Mexico in the mid-sixteenth century.

In north-central and north-western Arizona pottery was adopted from Hohokam groups to the south, and distinctive cultural changes took place that were derived from, and shared with, the Anasazi and Hohokam. These prehistoric complexes, riverine groups following a fishing, farming, gathering and hunting life in the lowland areas, have been called Hakataya. Their houses were of brush or jacal, rectangular in plan and strung out along a river bank, and larger structures were built for the community's religious, social and political activities. The river floodplains were used for farming maize, beans and squash. Cooking was done in stone-lined pits or ovens. Rubbish was rather carelessly scattered in the village area instead of in designated refuse areas. In the upland areas a somewhat different adaptation was followed, with shallow pit houses, and some use of stone for the lower walls of structures finished above with jacal. There were few large population concentrations. Hunting was important, while farming production varied according to area and climatic conditions. Where these were favourable, sizeable towns developed with features similar to those of the Anasazi Pueblos to the east. Some villages near Flagstaff, however, indicate a stronger connection with Hohokam culture to the south. The western Hakataya societies were almost certainly the ancestors of modern Yuman speakers, but whether the same is true for the highland Hakataya is not known.[11]

The small and scattered farming societies in Utah from about 700 to about 1300 are collectively known as Fremont. These developed by adopting the agriculture, ceramics and several other features of Anasazi cultures. The pit house was the most common structure, although in late Fremont sites closest to Anasazi settlements some above-ground masonry buildings were constructed. The villages were often located along valley sides, where runoff from the mountains formed alluvial fans. (Rainfall in much of Utah is more dependent on westerly winds carrying Pacific moisture, while the Plateau to the south relies on summer thunderstorms generated from Gulf moisture, in a pattern similar to that of highland Mexico.) Regional variants of Fremont can be recognized that were affected by their proximity to or distance from Puebloan and Hakataya groups to the south, local resources, soil fertility and the amount of water available for crops. Among the distinctive features of Fremont were an emphasis on the incising and punctating of pottery vessels, the production of clay figurines, the development of Fremont dent maize, apparently as a result of the distinctive environment, the absence of *kivas* and the use of leather moccasins instead of fibre sandals. Identification of modern descendants of the Fremont remains inconclusive.

Some fifty years ago the Southwest was regarded as a typical example of an area of hunting–gathering societies that received agricultural plants from Mexico and then developed their different regional cultural complexes without further introductions of any consequence. However, recent work at the Casas Grandes site and environs, some 200 kilometres south-west of El Paso, Texas, has revealed a major town with satellite communities that was a northern outpost of Mexican high culture to the south. The influence of the area in connection with the passage of Mexican materials and concepts into the Southwest had been suspected, but the strength of those transmissals and the degree of organization and complexity of the Casas Grandes society have only been recognized in the last fifteen years. Trade with the Southwest flourished – in marine shells and decorations made from them, ceramics, exotic birds, minerals and other items. It is believed that a variety of Mexican religious observances were also carried into the South-west and were there modified and transformed into the dances, decorative motifs and observances that came to play such a large role in Southwestern prehistoric and historic societies. The Casas Grandes area was most influential from about 1000 to 1350.[12]

The Plains and Mississippi valley agricultural societies expanded during the same period, from about AD 700 until the time of the Spanish and other disastrous contacts with European explorers, priests, colonists and traders. They did not grow in isolation from each other, for both societies had wattle-and-daub ground-level houses or slightly depressed, rectangular buildings. The introduction of the arrowpoint into both areas took place at about the same time, and subsequent stylistic changes were quite similar. Both areas used a mushroom-shaped pottery anvil to stabilize the walls of ceramic vessels as they were being thinned while still in a plastic condition. Painted pottery was produced in eastern Arkansas,

with designs similar to some of those in the Southwest. In Middle Mississippi there was a strong development of human and other effigy ceramic forms, as well as forms such as stirrup-neck bottles that were comparable with some in the Southwest and northern Chihuahua. The elbow pipe form, which developed in the Mississippi valley, spread to the Southwest; neck-banded pottery and corrugated vessels moved east into northern Texas. In late prehistoric times south-western turquoise reached as far east as the Mississippi valley near Clarksdale, Mississippi, and near Starved Rock in the Illinois river valley. Some archaeologists believe that the iconography of the Mississippian societies of the Southeast, and some part of the belief system associated with it, received the Mexican stimulus by way of the Southwest, which had modified its concepts and observances. These were in turn modified in the Southeast.

Summary

It has been the intention here to suggest that all North American agricultural developments were interrelated historically and that they were derived from prior appearances in central Mexico and further south. The Southwestern United States received and benefited from this spread before there was a significant impact in the Plains, in the Mississippi valley and in other eastern areas. The developments of the Mississippi valley and the Southeast grew and culminated, as did those of the Plains, at about the same time as the great expansion and regional climaxes of the Southwest. In terms of population growth, both in the eastern area as a whole and in favoured Southeastern regions, and in terms of socio-political development, the Southeast seems to have progressed to higher or more complex levels than did the Southwest or Plains, or the coastal, north-eastern and Great Lakes societies. The similarities and differences between all of these societies, products of their diverse historical backgrounds and environmental influences, can be compared with those that characterized various Neolithic and Bronze Age societies of the Old World in Europe and the Near East.

58. Mesoamerica: from village to empire

The cultural and geographical region referred to as Mesoamerica includes all of central and southern Mexico and extends into the Central American states of Guatemala, Belize, Honduras and El Salvador. The diversity of the region's landscape – which includes zones of recent volcanic activity, two great mountain chains that extend the full length of the area, broad tropical lowlands and rain forest – was at least partly responsible for the cultural diversity of the region, but it was also a factor in the unified development of Mesoamerican civilization from 2500 BC until its sudden collapse after 1519. Despite the emergence of such distinct regional manifestations as the Aztec of the Valley of Mexico, the Maya of the Yucatán, the Mixtec of Oaxaca and the Tarascans of Michoacan, widespread trade connections and, later, military conquest and expansion contributed to the unity of Mesoamerican civilization.

Mesoamerican prehistory is generally divided into three periods: the Formative era (2500 BC–AD 300), the Classic period (AD 300–900) and the Post-Classic (900–1520). Although the pace of cultural development varied in different localities, this chronological division accurately reflects the developmental stages of Mesoamerican civilization as a whole.

The Formative era

The concept of a formative period, during which the foundations of future cultural development were laid,[1] is especially appropriate to a discussion of the origins of Mesoamerican civilization. This period saw the emergence of nearly all of the features that are associated with that civilization, including hieroglyphic writing, calendrics, astronomical observation, monumental architecture, planned ceremonial and religious centres, specialization in art and craft and intensive irrigation agriculture.

The origins of the Formative era lay in the increasingly sedentary nature of Mesoamerican agriculture, a consequence of the spread of maize from the highlands and improvements in the strains, which resulted in higher yields. Settlement in the highland areas was concentrated at first beside rivers and lakes, in areas of high rainfall and on well-drained soils with a high water-table. Occupation of more marginal areas followed (the piedmont area of Oaxaca, for example, and the higher zones and alluvial valleys of the Basin of Mexico), where the application of water-control techniques, such as the diversion of slope-wash and modest canal irrigation, was necessary.[2] Water control was not a sudden innovation. In the Tehuacán valley the channelling of slope run-off may date to 4000 BC, and the Purron Dam complex has provided clear evidence of water capture and diversion from about 2000 BC.[3] Various forms of irrigation in the valleys of Oaxaca and Mexico are known to be of similar antiquity.

1 OAXACA – GUERRERO HIGHLANDS – SIERRA MADRE DEL SUR
2 VALLEY OF TULANCINGO
3 BASIN OF MEXICO
4 MORELOS – PUEBLA ESCARPMENT (AMACUSAC BASIN)
5 CENTRAL VALLEY OF CHIAPAS

58.1: *Mesoamerican culture area. This map shows the principal regions of Mesoamerica and the locations of the most important pre-Columbian sites discussed in the text. The 1000-metre contour line is indicated by the change in background colour.*

58.2: *Table of selected Mesoamerican centres and the span of their occupation in the Formative, Classic and Post-Classic periods.*

Although the identification of early sites without substantial architecture is hampered by the dense tropical vegetation cover, there is evidence to suggest that communities of sedentary agriculturalists were occupying the Maya lowlands before 2000 BC; comparable dates can probably be assumed for the whole of the lowland region. It has been suggested that maize and root crops were cultivated simultaneously by these lowland communities,[4] who also exploited local forest and riverine resources. In the Pacific coast lowlands, too, early settlers occupied coastal and riverine sites whose resources were an important supplement to agricultural produce. (In some sites the cultivation of root crops may have been abandoned with the introduction of higher-yield strains of maize, as at the site of Altamira, in coastal Chiapas.) Sites on the Pacific coast tended to retain this estuarine orientation until the emergence of the Izapa ceremonial complex in late Formative times.

The warm, well-watered Maya lowlands of Guatemala and the Yucatán, and the Mexican Gulf coast, provided an ideal environment for sedentary agriculture. Two crops of maize a year could be produced, and it is possible that root crops were also grown. The river levees and flood plains were particularly productive, because annual flooding rendered fallowing unnecessary; this meant that groups cultivating these lands were afforded both higher productivity and a greater degree of sedentism than those cultivating the loam soils that, although also capable of producing two crops annually, required fallowing at frequent intervals. Agricultural intensification was normally limited to a shortened fallow cycle, though there is evidence of modest swamp drainage and the artificial raising of fields.

The richness of these lowland areas both promoted and hindered cultural development. The groups who cultivated these lands enjoyed levels of productivity substantially higher than those of contemporary highland groups, a fact that may help to explain the precocious cultural developments of the Mexican Gulf coast in the Formative period.[5] On the other hand, further intensification could not significantly increase productivity, with the result that population densities of the kind later observed in the highlands were never achieved.

The beginnings of high civilization first occurred in the Olmec culture in the Gulf coast states of Veracruz and Tabasco in about 1200 BC. It was to the Olmec that pan-Mesoamerican culture owed the introduction of monumental sculpture, planned religious and ceremonial centres, a cosmology based on the were-jaguar and an intensive regional exchange system.

58.3: *Olmec colossal head. Sculptures of this kind, depicting individuals with some type of helmet or headgear, are common from all three of the principal Olmec centres – San Lorenzo, La Venta and Tres Zapotes.*

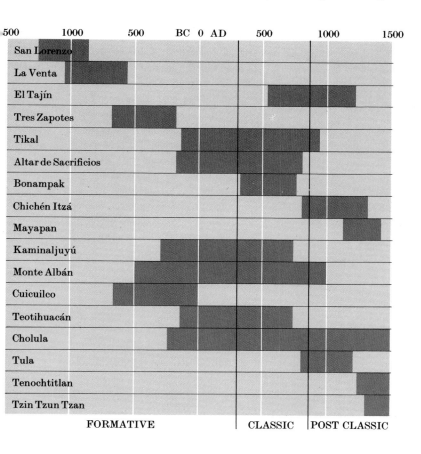

	1500	1000	500	BC 0 AD	500	1000	1500
San Lorenzo							
La Venta							
El Tajín							
Tres Zapotes							
Tikal							
Altar de Sacrificios							
Bonampak							
Chichén Itzá							
Mayapan							
Kaminaljuyú							
Monte Albán							
Cuicuilco							
Teotihuacán							
Cholula							
Tula							
Tenochtitlan							
Tzin Tzun Tzan							

FORMATIVE   CLASSIC   POST CLASSIC

From about 1200 to 600 BC Olmec culture focused on a series of ceremonial centres inhabited by no more than about a thousand people (the resident elite, their families and perhaps a few specialized craftsmen) and served by much larger populations who lived in small, dispersed hamlets throughout the lowland area. Olmec society could not be classified as a state, as it lacked the complexity, the population density and the monopoly of force that were to characterize later state formation in Mesoamerica, but it was rigidly structured and was able to mobilize considerable manpower for the construction and maintenance of the ceremonial precincts and other public works.

The earliest of these ceremonial centres, located about 80 kilometres inland, on the Coatzacoalcos river in southern Veracruz, was the site of San Lorenzo, an immense, artificially raised platform on which was erected a ceremonial court, house mounds and an elaborate system of drains and lagoons. Over sixty stone monuments have also been recovered from San Lorenzo, including colossal heads, massive altars and large, free-standing sculptures. It is evident that the Olmec participated in long-distance exchange, as great quantities of obsidian, magnetite (used in the production of mirrors), serpentine and mica have also been recovered. The most impressive import, however, was the basalt used by the Olmec for their sculpted monuments. These huge blocks, weighing as much as 34 tonnes, were quarried from volcanic deposits in the Tuxtlas region around Lake Catemalco, about 60 kilometres to the north-west.

San Lorenzo was abandoned in about 900 BC. The great basalt monuments were defaced, toppled into specially prepared trenches and buried. It is not clear whether the abandonment of the site was precipitated by an insurrection against the elite of Olmec society, as the mutilation of the monuments suggests, or whether it was related in some way to Olmec cosmology.

The second great Olmec centre, and the one that represented Olmec culture at its height, was La Venta, located on a small, swampy island about 18 kilometres from the coast in western Tabasco. It was built on a north–south axis with a deviation of 8 degrees to the west, and comprised a large, conical, fluted pyramid, a complex of raised earthen mounds and platforms, buried pavements with mosaics of were-jaguars and an elaborate tomb constructed of columnar basalt. Its monumental sculpture was a continuation of that found at San Lorenzo, and the centre was also associated with a flourishing long-distance trade network that, in addition to the exotic goods known at San Lorenzo, transported large quantities of jade from the Rio Balsas region of western Mexico. Olmec iconography was represented on bas relief sculpture and on artifacts of serpentine and jade (in artistic terms, the working of jade constituted the finest achievement of Olmec civilization). La Venta was abandoned in 600 BC, when the focus of Olmec culture shifted to Tres Zapotes in the Tuxtlas, although from this time the importance of the Olmec was clearly on the wane.

The Olmec were responsible for the creation of a regional exchange system that unified the diverse areas of Mesoamerica. Smaller-scale exchange networks are known to have existed in many areas before this – in the Maya area, in the central Mexican highlands, even on the Gulf coast – but the system that crystallized under the Gulf coast Olmec integrated these into a single pan-Mesoamerican network, which encouraged the diffusion of Olmec iconography and cosmology and its incorporation into culturally distinct regional complexes. The intensive exchange contact also tended to accelerate the process of social differentiation in areas beyond the Gulf coast, particularly those in which social complexity was already developing, such as the Valley of Oaxaca and the Basin of Mexico, where the local elite adopted the symbols and trappings of the Olmec as a means of signifying and legitimizing their own privileged position.[6] Inter-regional contact also led to the rapid dissemination of regional innovations, including hieroglyphic writing, the 260-day Mesoamerican calendar, the planning and orientation of ceremonial centres, and a cosmology that incorporated the were-jaguar and the flaming serpent. These traits formed a coherent package of elite or priestly knowledge that formed the basis for future cultural developments within Mesoamerica.

With the decline of Olmec influence after 600 BC the intensity of regional exchange seems to have decreased, and its 'international' flavour was displaced by the emergence of distinct regional styles. However, social differentiation and settlement nucleation persisted, particularly in the highland areas. Initially, with the gradual infilling of the landscape, communities remained small, but as the process continued settlements grew in size, especially in the prime agricultural areas. In the Valley of Mexico, from about 600 BC, a clear hierarchy of settlements can be observed, followed by the first evidence of ceremonial architecture.[7] The growth of these larger settlements took place at the expense of the smaller, marginal settlements, upsetting the broad distribution of agricultural settlement that was the product of infilling. Cuicuilco appears to have been the first major centre of this kind to appear in the Valley of Mexico. Slightly later, the site of Teotihuacán was established at the opposite end of the basin, and these two centres were a strong influence on Formative settlement. When Cuicuilco was destroyed by volcanic activity, Teotihuacán became the undisputed centre of the Valley of Mexico.

58.4: *Plan of Monte Albán. Although the plan of the centre was established in Formative times, most of the structures shown here were constructed during the Classic period and many were built on top of earlier structures. The South Platform is thought to have supported temples, while the complex of residences and public buildings was located on the North Platform.*

A similar trend is evident in the Valley of Oaxaca, where initially undifferentiated settlements gave way to the formation of a much larger, central site with ceremonial architecture, San José Mogoté, the importance of which was eclipsed in turn by the foundation of the great ceremonial centre of Monte Albán. This site, located on a high spur at the intersection of the three main branches of the Oaxaca Valley, clearly became the focus of the entire region after about 500 BC.

Correspondingly, from about 600 BC a number of changes took place in the Maya lowlands that foreshadowed Classic Maya civilization. Large centres, such as Tikal and Altar de Sacrificios, began to appear, and with them ceremonial architecture. There is evidence of increasing social differentiation, with the appearance of a growing trade in exotic materials and of elaborate burials, which were often associated with the ceremonial structures. A general infilling of the landscape occurred, and new areas in the Peten were colonized.[8] By the late Formative period site hierarchies had emerged, and trade with the Highland Maya was intensifying at sites such as Kaminaljuyú, which were in turn being affected increasingly by trade connections with central Mexico.

The Classic period

The Classic period, which represents Mesoamerican civilization at its height, saw the emergence of true states both in the Valley of Mexico and in the Maya lowlands. Major development was not limited to these areas, however: the Highland Maya site of Kaminaljuyú rose to its peak of importance, albeit under the domination of Teotihuacán, as did Monte Albán in Oaxaca, and sites such as El Tajín on the Gulf coast of Veracruz became increasingly significant.

By late Formative times the elements that were to produce the first empire in the Basin of Mexico were already present. Increasing population size, the intensifying use of hydraulic agriculture and the centripetal pull of settlement to Teotihuacán, particularly after the destruction of Cuicuilco, led to the rapid formation of a truly urban state, which at its height, between AD 400 and 700,

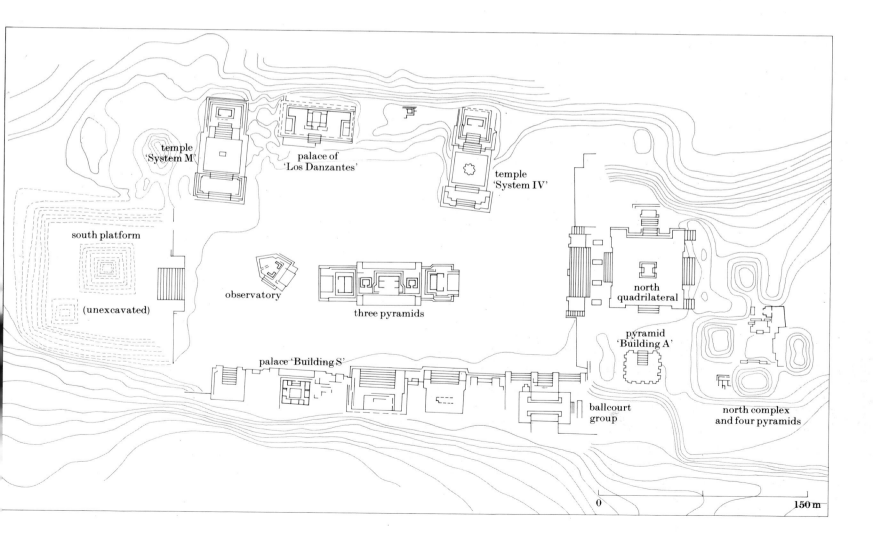

was inhabited by about 80 per cent of the population of the Valley of Mexico (approximately 100 000 people).[9] Civic planning and ceremonial construction took place on a scale beyond any known before in Mesoamerica.

The site of Teotihuacán covered about 20 square kilometres and was divided into four areas: the ceremonial complex itself, the residences of the elite, the market and residences of traders and craftsmen and the area where the agricultural population lived. The ceremonial complex encompassed more than a hundred shrines and pyramids, including the immense pyramids of the Moon and the Sun, the latter containing approximately one million cubic metres of fill.

In the absence of written records, it is difficult to determine with certainty the basis of social ranking in the city of Teotihuacán but it is probable that the city was controlled by religious leaders who also exercised civil authority. These leaders occupied a number of 'palaces' or elite residences within the city, such as Quetzalpapálotl, Xolalpan and Zacuala. Less privileged inhabitants lived in large, apartment-like compounds in which cramped windowless rooms were arranged around patios and courtyards.

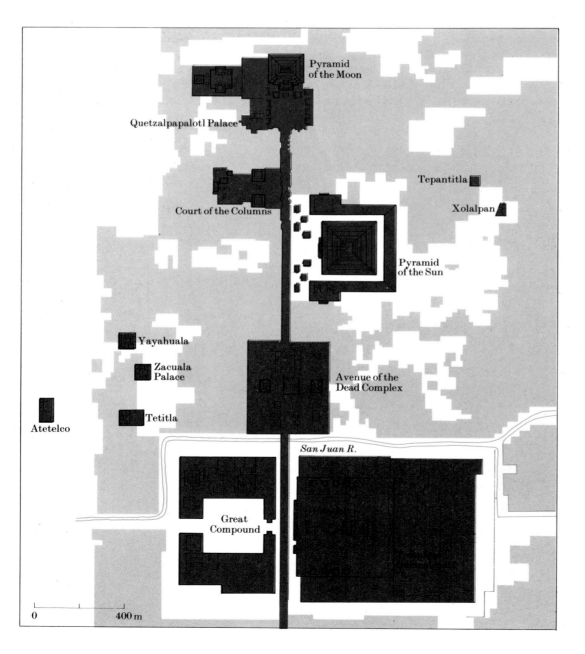

58.5: *Plan of Teotihuacán, encompassing the central ceremonial precinct of Teotihuacán and its surroundings. The Great Compound at the south of the precinct may have been the site of the central market. (Ritual buildings are shown in red, other built-up areas in grey.)*

58.6: *Stela F, Quirigua. This monument is typical of the style of Maya commemorative sculpture. It depicts an individual on its two faces, with hieroglyphic texts on both sides. The monument stands well over 7 metres high, and according to its text was erected in AD 761.*

Near the centre of the city there was a large open area known as the Great Compound, which was probably the site of Teotihuacán's central market.[10] Judging by later, Aztec parallels, this market may have distributed both local agricultural produce and utilitarian goods, and exotic foreign imports from the far corners of Mesoamerica. Commercial activity was clearly important to the city. Not only did local craftsmen, involved in the production of artifacts made of obsidian, marine shell, basalt and ceramics, live and work in their own *barrios* within the city, but foreign merchants from the Mayan areas and from Oaxaca also had permanent quarters there, an arrangement that was echoed in the Lowland Maya centre of Tikal and at Monte Albán in Oaxaca.

Teotihuacán exercised a profound influence over much of Mesoamerica during the Classic period, though the form that this influence took and the manner of its spread are still obscure. Perhaps the clearest example of Teotihuacán influence can be

observed at the Highland Maya site of Kaminaljuyú, where massive ceremonial constructions were erected in pure Teotihuacán style and the elite were buried with distinctly Teotihuacán ceramic forms and wares. There is evidence too of the appearance of the Teotihuacán rain deity, Tlaloc. Certainly, Teotihuacán dominated the city and controlled its public works and other functions. So marked is the Teotihuacán presence, in fact, that some investigators feel that Kaminaljuyú must have been invaded and occupied.

The collapse of Teotihuacán is as mysterious as that of the Olmec in the Formative period. In its final phase the population of the city fell to 70 000 and the population moved to the east of the main centres. In 700 the city was burned, and fifty years later there remained only a few hamlets in the area. There is no good evidence to suggest that a foreign invasion caused the collapse of Teotihuacán; but whatever the reason, within a very short period the greatest city of Classic Mesoamerica was abandoned.

The origins of Classic Maya civilization also lay in the later Formative period, when they exhibited close connections with the late Formative Izapa complex in Chiapas. However, the Classic Maya state contrasted sharply with the hydraulically based urban states of the Valley of Mexico. Agricultural production in the Maya lowlands remained largely extensive, and although water control was known (in the form of drainage projects, canal construction and, occasionally, irrigation), it did not represent a major component of agricultural intensification as it did in the Valley of Mexico. On the other hand, Mayan agriculture had a broader base: both maize and root crops were grown, and the breadnut (*ramón*) tree appears to have been planted in permanent orchards around each Mayan household.

Settlement in the Maya lowlands was well suited to the environment. In contrast to the carefully planned settlement at Teotihuacán, Maya habitations were organized into small clusters of two to five houses grouped around a small patio, which were inhabited, to judge by the evidence of the early historic period, by small patrilineages. These clusters of houses were distributed around local ceremonial centres, although settlement was denser in the areas immediately adjacent to the ceremonial centres themselves. Despite the less urban nature of Maya civilization, their centres performed the same administrative and regulatory functions as did their highland counterparts. These centres were organized in a strict hierarchy: small, local ones were subordinate to secondary centres, which were in turn dominated by super-centres, such as Tikal.[11]

The internal organization of Mayan society was similarly hierarchical; each ceremonial centre was ruled by a chiefly lineage. Leadership was strictly hereditary, though the husband of a daughter occasionally assumed the role of leader when no male heir was available.[12] Politically motivated marriages served both to perpetuate these lineages and to integrate the Mayan centres. Yet life was not always peaceful, as is evidenced by the discovery of defensive works at a number of Mayan sites and by the frequent depiction of captives on Mayan *stelae* and murals. The late Classic mural at Bonampak is particularly revealing; it depicts the richly clad Maya elite presiding over the torture of war captives.

Despite their relative isolation, the Maya were influenced significantly by the trade and politics of highland Mexico and the rest of Mesoamerica, particularly in the earlier half of the Classic period. The exchange network that had been initiated in the Formative period was extended, and trade intensified both in essential commodities such as salt, obsidian and grinding stones (for the preparation of maize flour), and in luxuries such as jade and cacao and exotic materials for the production of valuable artifacts. Unlike the intensive market system at Teotihuacán, however, trade among the Maya appears to have remained a prerogative of the elite, as it had been among the earlier Olmec.[13]

In the early stages of the Classic period the Maya were strongly influenced by Teotihuacán. In the lowland areas the influence appears to have been less direct than at the highland site of Kaminaljuyú, and seems to have been restricted largely to trade materials (particularly fine ceramics), the infiltration of certain Teotihuacán deities into the local art and an occasional structure in the style of Teotihuacán, which may signify the presence of a Teotihuacán trading colony. Among the lowland sites this influence appears to have been at its most dominant at the site of Tikal; it was much weaker at less important centres.

With the abandonment of Teotihuacán, the Lowland Maya reached their peak, spreading from their core region in the Peten westwards as far as Tabasco and southwards as far as Honduras. Maya architecture achieved its finest expression during this period, and numerous *stelae* and other glyphic writings have provided a wealth of information about Mayan dynastics.

The close of the Classic Maya period was sudden. Monumental construction and the recording of long count dates came to an abrupt end at one centre after another (the last known long count date is 909, carved on a jade ornament from an unknown site in Quintana Roo in the Yucatán). Various explanations have been offered, including invasions from central Mexico, environmental catastrophe, epidemic disease and combinations of all three, yet no hypothesis seems adequate to account for the rapid and widespread collapse of the Classic Maya civilization.

The Post-Classic

With the destruction of Teotihuacán and the collapse of the Classic Maya, Mesoamerica entered a period of cyclical conquest and collapse, marked by intensified competition between centres and a general increase in militarism. Aggressive Putún Mayan groups inhabiting southern Campeche and eastern Tabasco monopolized a marine trade in the coastal regions of the Yucatán from bases such as the island of Cozumel, and came to dominate much of northern Yucatán. During the same period the Highland Maya groups abandoned their valley settlements and moved to more defensible hilltop locations. In central Mexico centres such as Cholula, Xochicalco and Tula vied for supremacy in the vacuum left by the abandonment of Teotihuacán. Out of this competition arose the first secular and militaristic empire of Mesoamerica, that of the Toltec.

58.7: *The Temple of the Warriors and the Pyramid of Kukulcan, Chichén Itzá. These structures date to the Toltec occupation of Chichén Itzá and bear a strong resemblance to the architectural forms at Tula, while retaining a finer level of execution and finish characteristic of the Maya.*

The Toltec introduced full-scale warfare into pan-Mesoamerican culture and, along with it, an increased emphasis on human sacrifice. Military conquest was the basis of the rapid Toltec territorial expansion, which came to include a large part of Mesoamerica, including areas on the northern boundary that until this time had remained peripheral to the major cultural development in the south. Toltec influence also spread to the Yucatán, to sites such as Chichén Itzá, where it is clearly evident in the site's planning and architecture.

Yet the Toltec empire was not to last. By 1224 Chichén Itzá was abandoned and with it further mention of the Toltec in the Yucatán. Tula itself was violently destroyed in about 1168 by civil unrest, which was perhaps triggered by the severe climatic deterioration that desiccated much of north-central Mexico at this time and caused considerable friction among displaced populations.

After the destruction of Tula, Mesoamerica entered another interregnum, during which numerous smaller city-states, particularly the lakeside cities in the Basin of Mexico, competed for political and military dominance. During this time the Aztec, migrating from the northern frontier of Mesoamerica, attempted to settle in the densely populated Basin of Mexico, and eventually came to establish their city, Tenochtitlán, on a swampy island in Lake Texcoco in 1345. Over the next two hundred years the Aztec, through adroit political and military manoeuvring, emerged as the last native empire of Mesoamerica. In many respects Aztec civilization represented a continuation of cultural patterns dating to the Classic period, while others represented a direct outgrowth of Toltec developments.

The legacy of the Classic period is most clearly observed in Aztec agricultural practices and in the organization of trade. Aztec agriculture was the most intensive in the Basin of Mexico and supported a population greater than that of any previous period. Like the agriculture of Teotihuacán, Aztec agriculture relied on intensive water-control systems, including both irrigation and the drainage of lake margins. In addition, the Aztec made extensive use of *chinampas*, floating gardens that were formed by dredging rich silt from the lake bottom and piling it up to form raised surfaces in the shallow lake.

The Aztec also maintained the exchange system of Teotihuacán, with a distinct daily market of locally produced foodstuffs and commodities and a second market set aside for commerce in luxury items imported from outside the Aztec empire. Trade of the latter kind was conducted by the Pochteca, a hereditary class of professional merchants, who also served as an arm of Aztec foreign policy by acting as spies and *agents provocateurs* in advance of military undertakings. Many investigators now feel that the Aztec practice of local and foreign trading, and even the institution of the Pochteca, were established features of Classic-period Teotihuacán.[14]

Along with these inheritances from the Classic period, the Aztec preserved the Toltec traditions of human sacrifice and military conquest. The principal Aztec deities, Huitzilopochtli and Tezcatlipoca, required continual nourishment in the form of the blood and heart of sacrificial victims, who were obtained as captives or as

58.8: *Toltec colossal Atlantean figures. These figures, representing Toltec warriors in full battledress, supported the temple roof on top of Pyramid B at Tula, the Toltec capital. Each is approximately 4 metres high and is made of four sections that fit together.*

tribute from conquered regions. The worst excesses of sacrifice occurred in times of national rejoicing or catastrophe, and in one instance, the occasion of the dedication of the temple of Huitzilopochtli, some 20 000 individuals were sacrificed.[15]

It was, perhaps, the exigencies of commerce and the need for sacrificial victims that promoted Aztec militarism and the rapid expansion of the empire. Yet, although the Aztec were highly successful warriors, their social system lacked the cohesion necessary for the consolidation and administration of conquered territories. Such regions were forced to pay tribute to Tenochtitlán, both in local produce and in victims for sacrifice, but they retained their local leaders and identities and were not relocated or otherwise disrupted by the Aztec, as was the common practice of the contemporary Inca empire (see Chapter 59). Compliance with Aztec dictates was enforced solely by the threat of violence. Such a system predictably resulted in occasional revolts, especially given the demand for sacrificial victims, but it also meant that in times of crisis the Aztec could not rely on the continued obedience or support of vassal states. It was this aspect of Mesoamerican politics that the Spanish *conquistadores* successfully exploited, both by depriving Tenochtitlán of vital supplies and by enjoining Indian allies to rise against their former masters.

Hernán Cortes and a small army of just over five hundred soldiers landed on the Mexican Gulf coast on 12 March 1519 and, after burning their boats, set out for the capital of Tenochtitlán. By 13 August 1521 the last Aztec emperor, Cuauhtémoc, was Cortes' captive, the city of Tenochtitlán was in ruins and the Aztec empire had ceased to exist.

59. Andean South America: from village to empire

The Central Andean region of South America produced one of the world's major civilizations; in the century before the Spanish invasion of the region, the Inca state (Tawantinsuyu) became the largest native state in the New World. Besides its political achievements, the Central Andes is noted for early and elaborate road systems, the development of a complex agriculture, spectacularly fine textiles, monumental architecture and settlements of urban complexity and proportion. Geographically, the Andes is a vast and highly varied region, and its cultural history reflects this extensive regional diversity. Our understanding of the nature of Andean civilization and the course of its development is still preliminary; much remains to be discovered about it.

The Andean region

Andean South America is difficult to define precisely, in either a geographical or a socio-cultural context. Not only are the frontiers difficult to draw, but the shape and extent of the region, in cultural terms, have shifted somewhat through time. A rather broad definition is used here,[1] since it permits the inclusion of the wide range of developments that comprises native Andean history. This area embraces the entire Andean cordillera, paralleling the west coast of South America for virtually the entire length of the continent. It includes the coastal areas and the lands that border the cordillera to the east. In terms of modern political geography, it encompasses approximately the western half of Colombia, Ecuador, Peru and Bolivia (outside the tropical forest areas of those countries), the northern two-thirds of Chile and the north-west of Argentina. A narrower definition would limit the region essentially to the western parts of Peru and Bolivia – the area that represented the centre of Andean civilization in the final millennium before the European invasion.

Ecologically, the principal characteristic of the area is its diversity: the range is from complete desert to lush forests and grasslands, from warm valleys to frosty steppes. As much of the Andes lies within tropical latitudes, the major determinant of climate and vegetation is altitude. Differences in altitude of only a 100 metres or so produce substantially different ecologies, among which the *puna* and the *kechwa* are two of the most important. The *puna* is high grassland marked by drastic daily temperature variations. It was used primarily for pasturing llama

59.1: *The area of Andean civilization corresponds approximately to the Andean mountain range, the eastern foothills and the parallel Pacific coastal strip.*

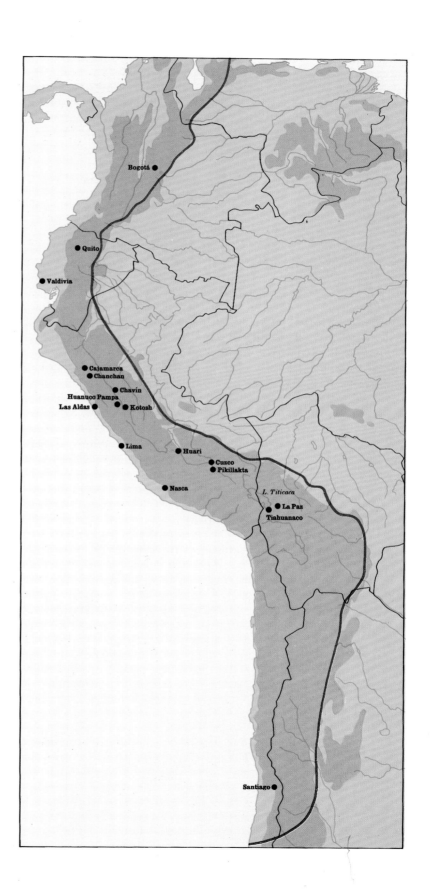

(*Lama glama*) and alpaca (*Lama pacos*) and for the cultivation of tubers, from which a series of storable food products was made. The best-known of these is *chuño*, which is prepared by alternate freezing and drying; the product has a long storage life. The warm *kechwa* valley slopes are areas of variable rainfall and maximum micro-ecological variation. They are suited to a variety of crops, many of which can be cultivated without irrigation, but irrigation was common, especially for maize. It was probably because of the suitability of the *kechwa* for maize agriculture that these regions had an importance far greater than was consistent with their geographical extent.

Longitudinal differences in the region are quite marked. The classic division of the central part of the Andes into desert coast, highlands and the forested eastern foothills (*montaña*) reflects this. While longitudinal differences are determined primarily by altitude, they are also affected by the cold waters of the Pacific to the west and the moist tropical forest region to the east. Besides producing the rich marine flora and fauna of the coastal waters, the cold Humboldt current is the major determinant of the desert climates of the coasts of Peru and northern Chile. Latitudinal differences are also substantial. For example, the altitude at which *kechwa* and *puna* regions occur varies from north to south. In the northern and southern Andes the altitudinal variations are of a different quality and somewhat less marked than they are in the central region. To the north the *puna* is replaced by the more humid *páramo*, which has different land-use characteristics. The currents off the coasts of Ecuador and Colombia are warm; as a result, the desert conditions of Peru and Chile are replaced by zones more closely resembling the tropical forests of the east.

Primary features of Andean civilization

Before exploring the history of civilization in the Andes, it is useful to review some of the characteristic features of the cultures that developed there.

The subsistence base in most of the region was agriculture, supplemented in varying degrees by hunting, collecting and (especially) fishing. On the coastal desert, as well as in parts of the *kechwa* of the highland valleys, agriculture was based on irrigation. The major cultivated crops in the highlands were the root crops, such as potato (*Solanum tuberosum*), mashua (*Tropaelum tuberosum*), ulluco (*Ullucus tuberosum*) and oca (*Oxalis tuberosa*). The high-altitude, grain-like quinoa (*Chenopodium quinoa*) was a major source of vegetable protein and other nutrients. Pastoralism was important, especially in the central and southern parts of the region. It was based on the llama, which was used primarily as a beast of burden, and the alpaca, which supplied wool. Of the domesticated animals, only the guinea pig (*Cavia porcellus*) appears to have been a significant source of food.

The radically different ecology of the arid coast produced a different subsistence economy based on a different set of products. The staple crops were varieties of maize, beans and squash. The coastal agricultural complex was related in part to the Meso-american crop complex (see Chapter 56). The nature of that relationship is still far from clear; it is not a case of an entire agricultural complex having been imported from another region, as several plants domesticated in the Andes were included. Cotton was an especially important plant on the coast and may have been domesticated there. Most cloth produced on the coast was made of cotton, although some of the finest examples depended on wool from the highlands that took dyes readily. A particularly important coastal resource was the rich marine fauna of the cold waters off the coasts of Peru and Chile, which contributed to the early establishment of elaborate permanent settlements in those areas. The exact role played by marine resources in the formation of complex coastal societies is a matter of dispute, but there is no doubt that fish formed a significant part of the subsistence economy throughout the span of native civilization.

One of the characteristics of complex societies is their ability to coordinate resources from diverse regions, to organize the specialized production of both subsistence and non-subsistence goods and to redistribute these over a broad geographical area. One of the most intriguing aspects of Andean cultural development is the economic coordination of a series of complementary units whose organization seems to set it apart from complex societies which developed in other parts of the world. The salient feature of this coordination of resources was the extensive, direct, socio-political control that was exercised over the production and exchange of goods rather than over trade, in which the focus of attention was the goods themselves. Production in various ecological zones was managed by a series of political units, which ranged in size from small ethnic groups of a few hundred families to enormous empires on the scale of that of the Inca. These socio-political units maintained outposts or colonies of their own members in various resource zones, creating an unusual pattern of dispersed and inter-digitated settlements that has been called the 'archipelago model'.[2] This pattern of economic organization is known mainly from the Inca period, when evidence of it is found in records written by the Spanish. It is a pattern more characteristic of the highlands than of the coast, but certain areas of the coast appear to have adopted it, at least in modified form.

The means by which goods moved between the various islands of a dispersed economic and political unit included the mechanisms of reciprocity, redistribution and mobilization exchange. The exchange of goods and services rested heavily on ethnic and kin ties and were reinforced by ceremony and hospitality. These forms of economic relationship are well known ethnographically; what is unusual in the Andean case is that they came to be used in the management of a large empire.

When the Andean is compared with other pre-industrial civilizations, it is perhaps the political achievement of the region that is most striking. This may be the consequence of the arrival of the Spanish during an unusual period when a single political entity held sway over an enormous region. The Inca empire, however, was a new phenomenon only in extent, not in political principle;

large states appear to have existed in earlier periods, and they were probably produced by similar politico-economic processes.

The factors that led to the rise of such polities are not fully understood. There were familiar ingredients, such as the ability to mobilize armies of conquest, elaborate road systems and a logistics base for both expansion and administration. However, there were other elements more closely related to the state's manipulation of certain aspects of the economy, especially its control over the distribution and production of luxury goods. There was also an evident relationship between the ability to form large political units and the system of economic complementarity that was common in parts of the region. The principles that permitted direct control over resources in various ecologies may have created a situation that encouraged political growth.

Settlements on an urban scale had appeared in the Andes by at least AD 1000. Among the largest and most intensively studied of these are Wari, Chan Chan and Cuzco, all of which were probably capitals of important states in different periods. Studies of Cuzco,[3] the Inca provincial sites of Huánuco Pampa[4] and Chan Chan[5] all suggest that many Andean cities were quite different from cities today. While they had monumental architecture and dense concentrations of buildings, and while they have provided evidence of both social stratification and economic specialization, much of the space in these impressive centres was given over to ceremonial activities and storage, and the permanent populations were probably not large. Unlike cities in Mexico, these Andean examples do not appear to have been major market centres; instead they fulfilled political and redistributive functions in the context of the political and economic organization suggested above. The earlier city of Wari is less well known than the others, but there are indications that, as a centre of trade and non-agricultural production with a large permanent population, it may have been closer to the usual model of a city.

Technology attained high levels of sophistication in several spheres. Besides the technologies of cultivation, elaborate means were developed of altering the landscape to increase production, including irrigation and terracing. The soils of the arid coastal valleys of the central Andes are exceptionally rich, and complex irrigation systems enabled them to be fully exploited. In the warm *kechwa* valleys of the highlands irrigation was frequently combined with terracing to increase both the yield and the amount of arable land. By the time the Europeans arrived the shape of some highland valleys had been literally transformed by terraces that incorporated irrigation canals: water was brought to dry hillsides, while the steps of the terraces increased the surface area. The new, flat surfaces also made cultivation easier and provided better control of drainage. Sunken fields in various parts of the coast tapped underground water from a high water-table, forming oases of cultivation in the desert. Ridged fields in high-altitude regions made possible the cultivation of poorly drained soils.

59.2: *The Nazca culture of the Peruvian south coast produced thin-walled vessels with stylized designs in brilliant polychromes. This one shows a swimming fisherman and dates from the early period of the culture.*

59.3: *The goldwork of the northern Andes was characterized by great regional diversity in style and technique. This nose ornament is from the Nariño culture on the border between Ecuador and Colombia.*

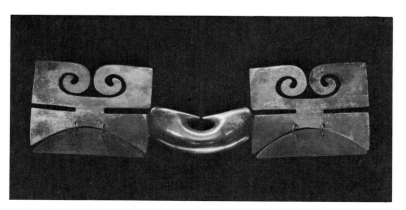

With a seasonally variable food supply, storage concerns are as critical as production itself. Storage was a special problem in *altiplano* areas because of the dependence on tubers rather than on more storable grains. By the time of the Spanish invasion a storage system was in place that was advanced both in technology and in organization. Storage depended largely on the exploitation of the natural advantages of high altitudes. Systems of ventilation and insulation combined with the cold night temperatures to create excellent conditions for tuber storage and for the production of *chuño*. The accumulation of significant stored surpluses depended on large-scale state organizations. The Inca, for example, amassed large quantities of food in storage centres along their road network.

In complex societies non-subsistence goods play a role nearly as important as that of food. These goods were symbols of status, and their production and distribution were intimately related to sociopolitical organization. Of all the arts and crafts, the greatest Andean achievements were in weaving. Textile traditions began very early, antedating pottery on the coast of Peru. By 500 BC the Paracas culture of the Peruvian south coast was making exquisite embroideries in complicated polychrome designs.

An accomplished metallurgy was also developed early. The northern Andes, especially the area that is now Colombia, perhaps produced the most distinguished pieces. The lost-wax process for casting hollow figures was used extensively there. In much of the Andes a form of 'depletion gilding' was developed, a process by which base metals were removed from the surface of alloys of gold, copper and other metals, leaving a layer of relatively pure metal.

Ceramics of high quality were produced in many parts of the region at various times. Among the most famous potters were those of the Nazca culture, on the south coast of Peru, and the Moche on the north coast. The Nazca made thin-walled vessels with stylized animal designs in bright polychromes. They also made ceramic pan pipes with tubes that appear to have been slip-cast. Moche ceramics are frequently modelled or painted with scenes of daily life and ritual.

The technology that was perhaps most important in supporting the large states so characteristic of the Andes was that of communication and logistics. The Inca recorded accounts and other information on a complex set of knotted cords called *khipu*. While true writing was not developed in the Andes, the *khipu* was an effective substitute, at least for most accounting and administrative purposes. Road systems go back at least to the time of the Moche on the north coast of Peru.

The development of agriculture and permanent settlement

The characteristics outlined above did not emerge rapidly but were the result of processes of development that spanned more than three millennia. Nevertheless, between about 3000 and 1500 BC a large number of changes occurred that provided the foundation for what followed. These were related on the whole to the establishment of subsistence and settlement patterns that would be elaborated, but not drastically altered, as Andean civilization developed.

The most significant of these new developments was the establishment throughout most of the region of settled life based on horticulture. In parts of the Peruvian coast these early stable settlements, such as that at Las Haldas in the Casma valley, depended heavily on marine fauna, but by 1500 BC the shift to an agricultural pattern of life had been made there as well. During this period weaving established itself as the principal Andean craft, and several other primary characteristics of the civilization were beginning to emerge (certain aspects of the 'archipelago' pattern of exploitation and exchange among various ecological zones may reach back to these early times).[6] The importance of feline and other animal representations in Andean religion probably date to this period, as does the use of drugs in religious contexts.

59.4: *This elaborate double-spouted vessel* (alcarraza) *is in the Calima style from the southern Cauca valley, Colombia. It is modelled in the shape of a group of houses linked by paths.*

Debate about the origins and spread of agriculture has been heated. While no general consensus has been reached on the broad range of questions related to agricultural origins, most Andeanists now agree on Mesoamerica as the source of maize and some other plants cultivated at low altitudes in the Andes. Most also believe that several local centres were involved in the domestication of the tubers and other specifically Andean cultivated crops. It is evident that the picture is a complex one; plants at various stages of domestication were increasingly incorporated into subsistence systems based largely on other resources. Dates and localities for the domestication of the Andean plants and animals are still insecure, but most were probably domesticated between 7000 and 5000 BC. Evidence tends to point to an important highland–tropical forest interaction in the domestication process.[7] Evidence of the domestication of the tubers and other high-altitude plants and animals is virtually non-existent; it is likely that these were domesticated in the central or southern highland regions, but their antiquity cannot be estimated with any precision.

An important conclusion to be drawn from the slender early evidence of domestication is that agriculture was not simply established in the core area of the central Andes, from where it diffused northward and southward. Early dates are now available from various latitudes. Many of these are of questionable reliability, but enough seem sound to indicate that domesticated plants were widely dispersed by quite early times. New evidence of very early stable settlements in lowland Ecuador are especially interesting, in that they suggest critical cultural developments in an area that was once regarded as 'intermediate' between the two great centres of high civilization in Mesoamerica and the central Andes.

Before about 3000 BC the role of cultivation seems to have been secondary. It was a minor component in a multitude of economies based on hunting, gathering and fishing. Shortly after 3000 BC parts of the Andes began to change rapidly. Large, stable settlements appeared, some of them organized around substantial buildings that seem to have served religious purposes. Agriculture

came to form the basis of subsistence; populations grew rapidly; the pace of change quickened markedly. By 2000 BC several centres with specialized religious architecture had appeared in the north and central highlands and on the central coast of Peru. Perhaps the most famous of these is Kotosh in the Huallaga valley, central Peru.

The origins and spread of ceramics have always figured prominently in discussions of early permanent settlements because pottery has tended to appear at about the same time as villages. In a sense, however, pottery is incidental to the early Andean sequence. It came later than weaving in most, if not all, of the region, and in parts of Peru it followed substantial non-residential architecture. The general location for the occurrence of the earliest pottery is the northern Andes, probably in what is now Colombia or Ecuador. Some scholars have attempted to trace the origins of Andean pottery to remote parts of the world. Stylistic similarities between the Valdivia pottery of Ecuador (about 3000 BC) and Jōmon ceramics from Japan have been particularly intriguing. However, simpler ceramics have now been found in levels underlying the Valdivia style, suggesting that the making of pottery was probably a local development.

The development of complex societies

Within a few centuries of the establishment of settled life in the Andes a new series of transformations began that changed the economic and social order, producing complex societies and, eventually, the enormous Inca empire.

The first suggestions of new, larger-scale societies came about 1000 BC with the spread of the Chavín art style. The spread of Chavín was accompanied by a series of innovations, including elaborate stone sculpture, new textile techniques and real monumental architecture. Varieties of the Chavín style are found in the north and central highlands and on the coast of Peru. In the south it extended at least to the Ica valley, leaving its imprint on the famous Paracas textiles of that region. The mechanisms that prompted the spread of Chavín are not understood. However, the iconography and contexts of the art tend to suggest religious associations. There is no direct evidence as yet of socio-economic stratification or of organized armed conflict and conquest on the scale usually associated with early state societies.

By about 100 BC the relative stylistic unity that had marked Chavín had been replaced by a series of strong regional developments. These new developments occurred in much of the central part of the region; once again, it is the Peruvian coast that is best

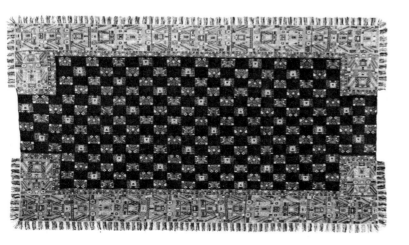

59.5: *Elaborate embroidered mantles were included in the rich tombs of the south coast of Peru. This example, made in the first centuries AD, is transitional between the Paracas and Nazca styles.*

known. In several of these cultures the arts reached their apex; beautiful objects were produced with a technological sophistication that was not equalled even during later periods.

There is a tendency to assume that the various regional cultures of this period were somehow qualitatively similar in spite of their great stylistic diversity. It has not been demonstrated, however, that similar principles of organization were involved in their development or that similar processes were propelling the regions in the same direction. Social stratification and militarism seem to have emerged at uneven rates; it is the Moche culture of the north coast of Peru that has provided the most marked evidence of these trends. However, the representational character of Moche art offers an insight into that culture and society not available in other regions: there are scenes of the elite being carried on litters, of warfare and of prisoners or captives.[8] The evidence also includes impressive fortifications, elaborate irrigation systems and roads. The monumental architecture most characteristic of Moche is the stepped pyramid, best represented by the 'Temple of the Sun' in the Moche valley. These pyramids apparently fulfilled religious and mortuary functions; religion served as an important foundation for Moche society. However, there is a great deal of evidence of social and economic differentiation and an administrative hierarchy, and there are indications that the territorial expansion of Moche was partly the result of conquest. Some scholars are not yet willing to grant Moche the status of a true state, but its pattern of growth was clearly parallel to that of a state. It seems likely that similar processes were under way in Nazca and elsewhere.

At roughly the same time new cultural manifestations were also emerging on the *altiplano* around Lake Titicaca. The focus of these developments was the site of Tiahuánuco with its megalithic stonework, represented most prominently by the so-called 'Gateway of the Sun'. Tiahuánuco was apparently both the ceremonial centre of an important religion and a population centre, although as yet no satisfactory estimate of its size has been advanced.

These regional elaborations appeared during a period of rapid population growth and competition between the various regions. The competition increasingly took the form of armed conflict; perhaps the inevitable result was ever larger units of political and military control to mediate regional disputes and to coordinate resources. The forces that first brought a large part of the central Andes under the control of a powerful state emanated from near Ayacucho, in the south-central highlands of Peru. The site of Huari was apparently its capital, and by about AD 700 it was a sizeable city. The style of Huari art shows a clear relationship with both Tiahuánuco and Nazca. The association with the former is particularly intriguing. It appears that aspects of Huari religion and iconography were derived from the Lake Titicaca region, although there is no evidence either for the early expansion of a Tiahuánuco political unit into central Peru or for later political control of the Lake Titicaca area by Huari.

Although religion remained an important factor in Huari expansion and consolidation, most Andeanists now feel that the growth of Huari involved military conquest and that the consolidation of its power included the establishment of a system of roads, administrative centres and state storehouses. It has also been suggested that people from the vicinity of Huari itself may have been moved to Pacheco, near Nazca,[9] which may indicate the colonization of remote areas. Such practices were adopted by the Inca, under whom they constituted essentially the adaptation of certain 'archipelago' principles of settlement at the level of, and for the purposes of, the state. These features suggest that Huari was an empire of the kind that the Inca would later create on an even larger scale.

The extent of Huari domination remains a matter of considerable debate. To the south it penetrated to the area of Cuzco, where the settlement of Pikillacta was built apparently as a Huari administrative centre. Control in the north seems to have included the area of Cajamarca and probably most of northern Peru. Huari domination of the Peruvian north coast has recently been contested. The situation was probably similar to that of later Inca times, when the nature of control differed greatly from region to region and is difficult to trace archaeologically in some areas. However the questions of the extent and nature of Huari domination are ultimately answered, the once-popular idea that urbanism originally spread in conjunction with Huari expansion now seems to be, at best, an over-simplification.

In about AD 800 the Huari empire disintegrated. The reasons for its collapse are not yet clear. It was replaced by a series of smaller states in a new pattern of regional autonomy. However, many of the smaller kingdoms that replaced Huari were perhaps more like Huari itself than its predecessors. They were characterized more by militarism and conflict than by the notable artistic achievements of pre-Huari times. Several of them conquered surrounding areas to assemble sizeable territorial units. The best-known (and perhaps the most powerful) of these kingdoms was Chimor,[10] on the Peruvian north coast. Chan Chan, its enormous capital constructed in mud brick, is one of the most impressive cities in the Andes.[11] Another large and wealthy kingdom was that of the Lupaca in the Lake Titicaca region.[12] The economy of the Lupaca was based on herding and highland root crops, but they maintained colonies in various distant areas, including the Peruvian south coast, which gave them access to a variety of ecologies.

The development of states and empires appears to have been largely a phenomenon of the central core of the Andean region. This picture may in part be the result of uneven data; the scale of societies that did not build substantial monuments of durable materials is frequently underestimated. Written records testify to sizeable political units in the northern Andes just before and at the time of the Spanish invasion. The Chibcha of Colombia and the Cañari of Ecuador are the most prominent examples. The southern Andes may not have had true states. The Auraucanians had controlled a large territory and proved formidable enemies to both the Inca and the Spanish, but their settlements appear to have been small and their military successes a product more of their mobility than of any permanent administrative organization.

Most of the northern and southern Andes and a significant part of the central Andes as well was thus populated by small, sedentary groups. Although not directly involved in the great imperial movements – at least not until they were overrun late in pre-Columbian times – these areas nevertheless developed complicated economies and political strategies of their own. They also made some remarkable advances in the arts and crafts, of which the metallurgical achievements of the northern Andes is the most striking example.

The Inca

During the fifteenth century the Inca brought much of the Andean area together in the New World's largest empire. When the Spanish arrived it extended from near the present Ecuador–Colombia border to south-central Chile and occupied much of the Andean regions of Bolivia as well. The degree to which incorporated areas were politically and economically controlled varied enormously, but the achievements of the Inca were astonishing considering the difficulty of communication and transport in the rugged Andean terrain without either the horse or the wheel. The basis of Inca success was not technological development; there is no evidence of major change in the way food or other goods were produced or in military tactics and communication. It is not yet established beyond doubt that the *khipu* was used prior to Inca times, but the remainder of the technological developments singled out at the beginning of this chapter were clearly in place at the outset of the expansion. The genius of the Inca lay in the creation of

59.6: *The Inca citadel of Machu Picchu, on the eastern frontier of the empire, is an extraordinary example of architectural harmony with a spectacular natural setting.*

an organizational structure that could hold a vast area together and extract from it the resources necessary to support armies of conquest and a sizeable state apparatus.

The Inca based their empire on organizational principles that, like their technology, were not really new. The key feature was a system of roads and administrative centres that provided an essential infrastructure for communication, conquest and control. More than 15 000 kilometres of roads and hundreds of way stations and administrative centres were integrated into an ambitious transport and administration network. The system frequently made use of existing roads and centres, but much of it represented new construction completed during the less than a hundred years between the beginning of the Inca expansion and the invasion of the Spanish. The storage facilities were especially impressive; for example, the food warehouses at the administrative city of Huánuco Pampa in central Peru had a capacity of nearly a million bushels (the equivalent of about 36 million litres).

In addition to their roads, massive armies and administrative infrastructure, the Inca employed other means to ensure the growth and maintenance of the state. The state's income was derived from labour obligations owed by its citizens. These obligations were modelled on practices of reciprocity common at the community level of Andean society.[13] The Inca, or his representative, was expected to provide hospitality and gifts in return for this labour. The state seems to have made substantial investments in land and facilities in order to fulfil its obligations. Increasing production of cloth and maize (as well as the beer brewed from it) by the state were particularly notable.[14] Such products were essential to royal hospitality and generosity – and therefore to a continuing (and growing) supply of labour and soldiers.

The political skills displayed by the Inca seem to have been a fairly pervasive feature of Andean civilization. Although there were marked regional differences, expansion and conquest appear to have been a more common approach to inter-zonal relations than trade, which accords with the 'archipelago' organization by which diverse ecologies were exploited. In much of the central Andean highlands at least, reliable access to essential products was achieved by the placing of members of each group in an area where they were available. Expansion and the management of large territories was thus almost inherent in the ecological system at various levels of society.

When and why did such a strategy come into being? It probably appeared early and was perhaps somehow related to the geographical distribution of critical natural resources. It may be that the steep gradient of the hillsides, which brings distinct ecologies very close to each other in parts of the Andes, encouraged direct control. Once such a system became successful and entrenched during early periods, it may have resisted change as distances increased. Indeed, the growth in politico-economic scale may have resulted in part from the advantages of coordinating resources from an ever greater region.

60. Tropical forest cultures of the Amazon basin

The tropical lowlands of South America are a vast low-lying area of over 3 000 000 square kilometres, covered with dense rain-forest and drained by the network of tributaries of the rivers Amazon and Orinoco. Hot, humid climatic conditions, with up to 300 centimetres of rain each year, cause vegetation to flourish and annihilate all but the most durable of archaeological materials. Rivers destroy and conceal archaeological sites as they change course in their confining valleys, eroding the remains of settlements built on river banks and covering others with layers of sterile alluvium. Few of the intact sites discovered so far have produced stratified evidence of multi-period occupation, and they rarely have depths of more than 1 metre. Despite these adverse conditions, excavation and research in Amazonia has revealed a complicated pattern of cultural development, indicating long-distance trade and migration from at least 2000 BC until the arrival of Europeans in the sixteenth century AD.

Amazonia is sometimes mistakenly thought to be flat and featureless. From the air the continuous green forest canopy is broken only by rivers, ox-bow lakes and small agricultural clearings called *chacras*. This apparent homogeneity is misleading, for although local relief may vary by only some 40 metres, the jungle cover conceals two distinct ecological zones. The Pre-Cambrian rocks of the Guianan and Brazilian shields and the old lacustrine sediments laid down during the Tertiary period, when the Amazon basin was an inland freshwater sea, form an upland area of poor soils cut by the major river valleys. This slightly higher area, the *terra firme*, covers approximately 90 per cent of the tropical lowlands. The remaining 10 per cent, known as the *várzea*, consists of the seasonally flooded bottom lands of the active flood plains of the river Amazon and its major tributaries, such as the Ucayali, the Putumayo, the Japurá, the Juruá, the Purús and the Madeira. The *terra firme* and *várzea* are areas of enormously differing agricultural potential: there are indications that each was exploited to a high degree by pre-Columbian indigenous societies.

Each year the soil of the *várzea* is rejuvenated by fertile flood-borne silts brought down from the Andes; it is therefore an area where continuous cultivation is possible. Observations of recent Indian groups have shown that high yields of manioc, *achira* (*Canna edulis*), sweet potatoes, peanuts, chili peppers, pineapples and avocados could be achieved without great effort. Intensive root-crop cultivation, especially of manioc, produces large quantities of food high in carbohydrates. Recent groups obtained proteins and vitamins from nuts and fruits, but most protein came from hunting and fishing. The rivers were (some still are) rich in fish, some of which weigh as much as 200 kilograms: formerly they were caught by spearing or trapping, by nets or by damming and poisoning stretches of river. Water fowl, cayman and turtle were also hunted, as were manatee (sea cow), capybara, coypu and other rodents.

Manioc, 'one of the most productive and least demanding crops ever developed by man',[1] was also cultivated by the Indian groups that inhabited the higher *terra firme* areas. Here the basic technique was to clear new *chacras* for planting as the soil under cultivation became exhausted after three or four harvests. Recent studies have indicated that manioc yields as high as 1.5–2 tonnes per hectare can be obtained from newly cultivated soil, but yields fall off rapidly with subsequent harvests. In any period, therefore, only a small part of an area utilized by a group was under cultivation. To take a single example: the Kuikuru, a tribe living in the *terra firme* of the Xingú river in the 1950s, cultivated fields within a radius of 6.5 kilometres from their village. At any one time they farmed only about 38 of the 5200 hectares potentially available, yet this provided ample carbohydrate food for the population of 145 and could have supported a larger group.[2] The major controlling factor in *terra firme* subsistence is the quantity of accessible protein. Much less fish is available from minor rivers; moreover, such rivers do not attract large reptiles and aquatic mammals. The protein resources of these higher areas are therefore far smaller than those of the *várzea*. There are few large land mammals in Amazonia; the tapir and peccary are not common, while monkeys, although numerous, tend to move away from populated areas where they are hunted.

Much of the initial approach to tropical forest cultures has been strongly influenced by recent ethnographical observations. These cultures are usually described as small-scale agricultural societies practising slash-and-burn (swidden) cultivation, with manioc as their staple crop.[3] Semi-permanent villages with populations of up to a few hundred people are often composed of large pole-and-thatch houses, each of which contains several families. The material culture of these groups is comparatively simple and based almost entirely on vegetable products of the forest. Characteristic artifacts are fibre hammocks, dugout and bark canoes, cotton textiles and hunting and fishing equipment such as blow guns, bows and arrows, nets and traps. Pottery is made by most groups and is used principally in the processing of manioc for storage and consumption. Stone tools are rare; the type most often found is a polished axe head. This picture of tropical forest culture is based essentially on observations of indigenous societies of the *terra firme* area. There has been a tendency to ascribe such societies to the earliest stage of an evolutionary model of cultural development in South America, as they lacked the political, religious and economic sophistication of the circum-Caribbean chiefdoms and the Andean civilizations.

While there has long been a tendency to consider Amazonia a cultural backwater, there are early accounts that indicate the existence of far larger social organizations. Accounts of *conquistadores* and missionaries in the sixteenth and seventeenth centuries describe the continuous villages built on the *várzea* of the middle and lower Amazon by the Omagua and Tapajós tribes and the great stores of food they had accumulated. One such account records: 'There was not from village to village one crossbow shot . . . and there was one settlement that stretched for five leagues without there intervening any space from house to house . . . there was a great deal of meat and fish and biscuit . . . enough to feed an expeditionary force of one thousand men for one year.'[4]

Populations of Omagua and Tapajós villages are estimated to have numbered between 300 and 2500 inhabitants. They had powerful chiefs, priests and temples and produced decorated pottery and textiles that impressed their European observers. Clearly, such societies do not fit the accepted definition of tropical forest cultures. It has, therefore, been suggested that their more developed state was due to influences from the higher cultures of the Andes, either through the immigration of Andean groups or more indirectly. A contrary interpretation suggests that the *várzea* areas had potential for the production of large food surpluses that favoured the development of stratified societies with specialist craft groups.

The Omagua and Tapajós were almost destroyed soon after European contact by disease and slave-raiding. Their valuable land along the main rivers was quickly taken over by European colonists, and the remnants of indigenous groups were pushed into the poorer *terra firme* areas, which were probably already being utilized by agricultural and hunting groups similar to the Kuikuru. The process of European control thus obscured the true dimensions of indigenous society; it forced highly developed groups away from the fertile *várzea* and obliged them to return to the less advanced systems that were necessary to sustain life in the *terra firme*.

60.1: *The active flood plains of the Amazon and its tributaries were the cradle of tropical forest culture. Influences spreading from this zone can be traced to Kotosh and Chavín in the Peruvian Andes and to the Pacific coast of Ecuador.*

present limit of forest area

annually flooded plain

The archaeological framework

Archaeology in the tropical lowlands of South America is still largely an attempt to untangle the many ceramic styles that are known, to date them and to build up an area-wide chronology. Changes and developments in the prehistoric economy must be inferred from the ceramic evidence, as organic materials such as animal bone and plant remains are seldom preserved. The most significant food sources, root crops, are soft and fleshy and do not set seeds, so there is no possibility of grain impressions.

In examining pottery remains, evidence for the cultivation of manioc is of great importance: where vessel forms can be reconstructed it is often possible to identify those used in the complex process by which manioc is made edible or brewed to make *chicha* beer. The general types of such vessels are known from the ethnographic record. Large, open-mouthed urns with rim diameters of about 40 centimetres were probably used as brewing vats for sweet manioc beer. Smaller bowls from the same ceramic complex were used for serving the gruel-like drink. The presence of these two types of pot therefore testifies to sweet manioc cultivation, and such evidence has been found in the Early Tutishcainyo phase of the upper Ucayali at Yarinacocha in Peru, tentatively dated to between 2000 and 1600 BC. A second type of manioc, the bitter variety that contains prussic acid, is recorded from the same area at a later date. To prepare the bitter manioc root for eating it must be grated and squeezed to extract the poisonous juice, which is caught in a large open vessel. The pulp is spread on flat pottery griddles and cooked over a fire to make rounds of unleavened bread, or turned into small pellets by being continuously stirred over heat. The baked clay platters, the cylindrical clay fire-dogs on which they rested and juice-collecting buck-pots have all been found in the Hupa-iya levels dated to about 200 BC at Yarinacocha. Small chalcedony and other stone 'teeth', set in wooden boards for grating the root in preparation for squeezing it, are also indications of the use of this type of manioc.

The pottery evidence is therefore important. The 'Horizon Style' classification that has been proposed,[5] which defines phases of similar stylistic development, is a convenient preliminary framework for describing the various pottery types found in this region. The four Horizon Styles – Zoned Hachure, Incised Rim, Polychrome, and Incised and Punctate – overlap and merge, both in geographical distribution and in time.

The earliest pottery found in Amazonia proper, though not directly dated there, is in the Zoned Hachure Horizon Style. It has links with the earliest ceramic complexes of the New World, such as Valdivia in Ecuador (3200 BC), Puerto Hormiga in Colombia (3000 BC), Mina in Brazil (3000 BC) and Monagrillo in Panama (2100 BC). These initial ceramics are characterized by their lack of painted decoration and by broad-line incision, excision and punctation, used alone or in combination. The earliest known

Date	NORTHERN ANDES OF PERU	RIO UCAYALI	RIO PASTAZA RIO NAPO	MIDDLE & LOWER AMAZON	MARAJÓ	LOWLAND BOLIVIA
		Shipibo				
1500				Santarém	Aruá	Rio Palacios
				Itacoatiara		
1000		Caimito	Napo	Tefé Guaríta	Marajoara	Masicito / Hernmarck
		Cumancaya				
		Nueva Esperanza		Caiambé / Japurá	Formiga / Acauan	
500	Higueras	Cashibocaño / Pacacocha	Tivacundo	Manacapurú	Mangueiras	Verlade
AD / BC	Kotosh Sajara-Patac	Yarinacocha / Hupa-iya	Yasuní	Paredão		
500	Kotosh Chavín	Shakimu				
1000	Kotosh Kotosh			Jauarí	Ananatuba	
1500		Late Tutishcainyo	Pastaza			
2000	Kotosh Waira-Jirca	Early Tutishcainyo				

60.2: *Major phases in Amazonian prehistory are defined entirely by ceramic complexes, as little else survives in the archaeological record. The time-depth of most of these pottery styles is uncertain, and future radiocarbon dates may well transform the tentative chronology.*

ceramics from the tropical forest area are from the Early Tutishcainyo phase at Yarinacocha. They are dated to between 2000 and 1600 BC by comparison with radiocarbon-dated sherds from the Waira–Jirca phase at Kotosh in the Peruvian Andes. The Early Tutishcainyo vessels have complex silhouettes with body flanges and are decorated with step-fret, rectilinear and curvilinear scrolls and other simple geometric designs incised into the surface of the vessel. The fields defined by the incised motifs are often filled with fine diagonal or criss-cross incised lines. Early Tutishcainyo may share a common ancestry with Valdivia. Definite evidence of sweet manioc cultivation (brewing vats and *chicha* bowls) has been found in Early Tutishcainyo levels, but there is no proof of the presence of bitter manioc.

Two sites in eastern Ecuador have produced confusingly different radiocarbon dates for Zoned Hachure Horizon Style ceramics in this area. A date of 2050 BC from the Pastaza phase agrees well with the dating of Early Tutishcainyo, but the vessel forms are mainly small open bowls unlike those from Yarinacocha. Sherds of the Yasuní phase excavated near Nuevo Rocafuerte are from vessels very similar to those of the Early Tutishcainyo. The shapes of carinated bowls and the use of rim and sub-labial flanges hint at close contact between groups on the rivers Ucayali and Napo, but the Ecuadorian examples are dated to 50 BC, almost two thousand years later than the Peruvian sherds. Intermediate dates for this pottery tradition have been obtained from the lower Amazon. At Jauarí incised Zoned Hachure pottery from a midden surrounding a pile-built house is dated to about 1000 BC. On the island of Marajó, at the mouth of the Amazon, excavations of Ananatuba-phase shell-middens dated to 980 BC have revealed traces of large communal houses occupied by incipient agricultural groups who still relied heavily on hunting and gathering.

The Incised Rim Horizon Style is characterized by bowls with wide, flat-topped rims carrying incised designs often based on chevrons and triangles. A new feature is the use of plastic decoration techniques: applied clay pellets and modelled animal-head ornaments on pots are very common. This ceramic style has been allocated to the first millennium AD,[6] though evidence from the central Ucayali indicates an earlier starting date. The Hupa-iya phase at Yarinacocha contains incised-rim and plastic-ornamented sherds at about 200 BC. Associated with this phase is the first tangible evidence of bitter manioc processing: small flat platters for baking manioc bread and buck-pots for collecting the poisonous juice extracted from the root. Spindle whorls also appear in the archaeological record.

The Incised Rim pottery style is very similar to that produced by Caribbean groups of the lower Orinoco between about 1000 and 800 BC. At this date the inhabitants of Ronquin Sombra and Barrancas were cultivating bitter manioc. It is possible that their agricultural knowledge and 'Barrancoid' ceramic style entered the Amazon basin from the Orinoco via the network of rivers leading to the river Negro.

Sites on the middle and lower Amazon also illustrate the strong association between Incised Rim Horizon pottery styles and bitter manioc cultivation. At Paredão on the river Negro manioc roasting plates were excavated from black-earth midden levels that also contained Incised Rim sherds, spindle whorls, pottery beads and large-collared burial urns decorated with zoomorphic *adornos* (small models in relief). The urns contained secondary inhumations (the bones, as opposed to the whole body, of the dead). Two radiocarbon dates from Paredão are AD 870 and 880, and a third date associated with a pottery style combining red-painted and modelled decoration is 450 BC. West of the confluence of the river Negro with the Amazon a large riverside village site of AD 425 has been located at Manacapurú. The settlement's midden area is approximately 2 kilometres long and 400 metres wide, indicating a sizeable population. Caiambé is another Incised Rim Horizon Style site on the middle Amazon, with radiocarbon dates of AD 630 and 640.

Early in the fifth century AD the Mangueiras phase succeeded the Ananatuba phase on the island of Marajó. The broad-line incised and hachured decorative motifs of the hunter–gatherer period were assimilated into the ceramic vocabulary of the Incised Rim Horizon potters. Sites of the Mangueiras period are much larger than those of the Ananatuba period and indicate much higher populations, which probably subsisted on bitter manioc. Tubular pipes, labrets and human figurines were found in Mangueiras middens.

The very attractive painted pottery of the Polychrome Horizon Style is late in date, from between AD 600 and 1300. Lidded urns, large plates and anthropomorphic burial urns for secondary inhumations were decorated with red-, black- and white-painted designs, many based on highly stylized interpretations of creatures such as the anaconda and the cayman. Broad- and fine-line elements dominate the designs, which were sometimes painted on a white-slipped background. Often incised, excised and modelled decorative techniques were used in conjunction with polychrome painting. On some anthropomorphic urns the limbs are shown in relief, the hands and feet are modelled in the round and facial features are shown by incised and excised lines. Polychrome ceramics are known from the whole length of the Amazon.

The Caimito complex of the central Ucayali has radiocarbon dates of AD 1350 and 1375. Vessel forms are very varied and include square-shaped, open dishes, anthropomorphic urns and pots with squarish cross-sections. This ceramic assemblage is very similar to that of the Napo phase found near Nuevo Rocafuerte and dated to AD 1168, 1179 and 1480. Early ethnohistorical records report that the river Ucayali and river Napo areas were colonized by the Cocama and Omagua tribes from the middle Amazon. The beautifully made and painted pottery is described in these accounts, and it seems certain that the Caimito and Napo phases represent this up-stream migration. These polychrome traditions persisted almost until the present day in ethnographic groups such as the Shipibo and the Cashibo.

Strangely enough, the pottery most similar to that of the Napo and Caimito phases comes from the extreme eastern end of the Amazon. Burial mounds of the Marajoara phase (dated to about AD 1200) on the island of Marajó contain secondary inhumations in anthropomorphic polychrome urns. The interplay of broad- and fine-line brushwork combined with incision and modelling techniques displayed on the urns is remarkably like that of the upper Amazon. Marajoara habitation sites consist of large, artificially constructed earthern mounds, often measuring 50 by 35 metres and raised 6 metres above the surrounding land. Multi-family houses were raised above flood waters and were occupied for several generations. *Tangas* (pottery pubic covers) have been found in Marajoara levels, as have labrets, clay stools, spindle whorls and figurines of seated humans. The political and social organization indicated by the size of earthworks and houses during the Marajoara period, and the technological and artistic sophistication of the pottery, have led some scholars to suggest a migration of Andean peoples or influences from Colombia to the mouth of the Amazon via the Napo and the Ucayali.[7]

There are many finds of polychrome pots from the middle Amazon, most of which are dated to between AD 1000 and 1300. Anthropomorphic burial urns are also found in this area, but they are decorated in a much bolder style and often show figures seated on stools. Other ceramic forms from excavations at Miracanguera, Maracá, Guarita, São Joaquin and Tefé display flanges and *adornos* that are 'Barrancoid' in feeling, though combined with polychrome painting. In lowland Bolivia the Upper Verlade and Hernmark ceramic styles (about AD 500 to 1000) that make use of polychrome painting and broad and narrow painted bands seem to have Amazonian affinities. The extensive raised, ridged and drained field systems of the Llanos de Mojos may be associated with these ceramic phases.

The Incised and Punctate Horizon Style occupies the period from AD 1000 to historic times. It is principally eastern in distribution; in the upper Amazon the Polychrome Tradition continued for many centuries and is represented in the pottery of the Cashibo and Shipibo peoples. The most famous sites at which Incised and Punctate Style ceramics have been found are Itacoatiara and Santarém. Both are dated to between AD 1200 and 1300. At Itacoatiara fine-line incision and punctated bands of decoration were arranged alternately on the exteriors of tall vessels and on the interior surfaces of shallow open bowls. The Santarém style is the most flamboyant and ornate in Amazonia. Bowls and jars are ornamented with a rococo profusion of *adornos* portraying birds, cayman, monkeys, frogs and humans. Some vessels have caryatid pedestal bases, and handles and flanges are often modelled into animal forms. These particularly impractical classes of vessel may have been used in connection with the funeral rites of the Tapajós tribe, with which the Santarém style has been linked.[8]

Interpretation

While these ceramic complexes summarize the major part of the archaeological information available from Amazonia, their inter-

pretation is contentious. The area may have been an underdeveloped backwater, receiving cultural influences from the civilized peoples of the Andes,[9] or it may itself have been a centre of innovation;[10] the evidence can be used to support either view of the prehistoric tropical forest cultures. If sites outside the tropical forest are examined carefully, there are indications that native Amazonian cultures did influence early groups in highland and coastal Peru and Ecuador. It has been suggested that close links between the tropical forest cultures and Chavín, an important ceremonial site in the northern Andes of Peru (see Chapter 59), show that much of Chavín culture had its roots in Amazonia.[11] The evidence is persuasive: many of the animals depicted in the complex iconography of Chavín – such as the harpy eagle, the jaguar, the constrictor snake (probably the anaconda) and the cayman – are species only found in the tropical lowlands. On the Tello Obelisk at Chavín itself the cayman is shown associated with manioc, bottle gourds, *achira* and chili peppers, all plants naturally alien to the highlands. If the dating of Early Tutishcainyo to about 2000 BC is correct, then the phase is ancestral to the Waira–Jirca complex at Kotosh, itself a crucial site in the development of Chavín culture. Long-distance trade and contacts between the tropical forest and the Pacific coast can be traced. Similarities between the evolution of Valdivia and Machalilla ceramics in coastal Ecuador with Tutishcainyo are remarkable. At about 1500 BC marine shells (*Spondylus*) were being traded across the Andes and into eastern Ecuador.[12]

These suggestions for the early date and significance of tropical forest culture support the theory of the area's dynamic influence on South American cultural history. Most of the evidence, however, comes from outside the forest. The true role of tropical forest culture will only be known when more has been discovered about the origins and development of prehistoric societies within the Amazon basin itself.

IX: Pattern and process

Archaeological research has accumulated a large body of evidence about the development of the human species and the nature of early societies. As well as piecemeal explanations of particular developments, this evidence demands a more general set of ideas to make sense of it. There is no ready-made philosophy that can accommodate the unique properties of the archaeological time-scale, which deals with a process whose rate of change is constantly accelerating, forming a bridge between the scale of evolutionary biology and that of history and anthropology. At an abstract level, however, archaeology resembles these other disciplines in dealing with problems involving growth, differentiation and the emergence of hierarchies. Archaeological theory is concerned with understanding three aspects of the subject: that of its primary material (the formation and interpretation of the archaeological record), that of the working of society on a small scale and its articulation with the environment and that of the larger processes that govern the emergence and disappearance of social forms. This section deals largely with the last of these concerns, surveying the broad sweep of the human past as reconstructed by archaeology. It is a small contribution to a comparative science of social development.

61. Interpretation and synthesis – a personal view

The results of recent archaeological research are impressive. While the full array of modern scientific methods and new approaches has only been tried in a fraction of its potential field of application, the past two decades have seen a remarkable increase in our understanding of events in the remote past. There now exists, even if only in outline, a coherent account of the major features of development over the whole span of human existence. Many of the pieces in the jigsaw puzzle have at last fallen convincingly into place.

The importance of this achievement goes beyond the individual technical accomplishments of its component discoveries. By filling in large gaps in our knowledge of such crucial periods as the early development of human culture, the beginnings of agriculture and the processes leading to the first civilizations, it has provided a continuous story of human development from the earliest times to the historical era. The long record of prehistory not only forms a bridge between the domain of biological evolution and that of history; it gives the opportunity to analyse the process of this development as a whole. This perspective places both ends of the story in a new relationship. It began with the unfolding of new properties that emerged during the later phases of mammalian evolution and ultimately produced the conditions that made industrial societies possible. It is the continuity between individual phases of development that is most striking: each new set of properties grows out of previously existing conditions. The whole process has a momentum that renders our division of it increasingly arbitrary and artificial.

In a real sense, therefore, the archaeological discoveries of the mid-twentieth century present an opportunity that has not existed before: that of analysing the human past in its own terms and over its entire length. The meaning of this shift in perspective becomes clearer if our present view of the past is contrasted with that which emerged in the later nineteenth century. Predisposed by the success of Darwinian biology to look for evolutionary patterns, social scientists tried to construct theories of social evolution that would explain the emergence of modern cultural institutions. As they lacked more than a rudimentary succession of tool types to fill the long period before written records, they sought to supplement this with evidence from contemporary societies around the world. Correctly observing the disparities and contrasts that existed between them, they erected a typology of social and technical forms that was then translated into the language of evolution to provide a sequence of developmental stages, from hunting through herding to agriculture and civilization. This succession of static types was inevitably punctuated by periodic revolutionary leaps as one stage followed another. The lack of genuine information about former conditions created an artificial model that not only underlay the writings of early anthropologists (who soon discarded it as irrelevant) but also sustained much of the interpretative study of archaeologists down to recent times.

While the attempt was a laudable one, and provided insights that could not have come from contemplation of the archaeological record alone, it has been both discredited and rendered unnecessary by recent advances. In the first place, the societies that were available for study by ethnographers can now be seen not as surviving examples of universal stages, but as specific creations of the recent past. Societies such as those of the Eskimo, the Bantu or the Polynesians arose within the same time-scale as the historical societies of Europe and Asia. No less than Classical Greece or Han China, they were products of the socio-economic changes of the later Postglacial. Moreover, many of the features observed by early ethnographers were, in fact, the outcome of already significant contact with Western colonialism, leading either to organizational change or to dislocation and collapse.

More fundamentally, however, the very process of comparison can be seen to have produced a misleading picture. Study of the end-products of evolution inevitably exaggerated the contrasts between the stages that different examples were supposed to represent. While there is undoubtedly a sharp difference between the population densities typical of recent hunting groups on the one hand and of farming societies on the other, the former exist only in relatively marginal habitats where agriculture has not penetrated, while the latter, in many cases, have already expanded nearly to the limits that their environment can support. It would be wrong to infer from this that the beginning of agriculture was marked by a massive and immediate growth in population: yet that is precisely the kind of conclusion that this form of argument inevitably produces. This is especially true of the periods of rapid change that are of particular interest. The economic and social characteristics of such periods were by their very nature unstable and transitional, and no ready-made models for them exist.

The effect of recent research has been to dissolve the neat, conventional divisions, to emphasize the continuous thread running through the whole process of man's development and to acknowledge that while each phase manifests revolutionary new possibilities, the transitions that separate them are phases of accelerated change rather than sharply delineated boundaries. The 'revolutions' of conventional archaeology are essentially no more than projections into the past of dichotomies evident in the contemporary world: hunter *versus* farmer, townsman *versus* peasant. They allow no scope for recognizing the historically unique qualities of the societies involved in the transitions and the early stages of development of new ways of life. A major concern of archaeology is now the reconstruction of extinct types of economy and social structure that could not be inferred from the study of ethnography or history alone.

It is not surprising, then, that nineteenth-century writers failed to produce a satisfactory theoretical synthesis for the long process of social evolution, as Darwin did for biological evolution and as

Marx attempted for the historical process. While both of the latter have thriving modern descendants, the premature theorizing of Morgan and his successors has proved an insufficient basis for current thought. The creation of such a body of theory is a task for our own times. It must be founded on the kind of evidence reviewed in this book; and it must offer some sort of overall perspective on the process of human development as it has emerged from recent archaeological work.

The evolution of culture

One of the most far-reaching reappraisals has resulted from a new time-scale for human evolution. While the appearance of fully modern forms of man is a relatively recent evolutionary episode, the beginnings of the process can now be seen to lie much deeper. The line that ultimately led to man began to differentiate as long ago as the Miocene, a period of major geological changes that produced mountain ranges like the Alps and led to the present configuration of the continents. The appearance of man was not a sudden event at the end of geological time, but a gradual unfolding of potentialities that developed out of a particular line of mammalian evolution in a period of unusual environmental change.

The evolution of the human species was thus only one aspect of the emergence of the modern mammalian fauna, including families like elephants or cattle. The reconstruction of human evolution shows that the appearance of an intelligent, bipedal, tool-making animal with the capacity for speech was the end-product of a series of changes that began with alterations in diet (reflected in the teeth), continued with alterations in posture and locomotion (the adoption of bipedalism) and only then produced significant changes in brain size and intelligence. It was a small initial change in feeding habits, associated with opportunities opened up by the reduction in forests, that created a situation in which more far-reaching changes could occur.[1]

The change in posture, which freed the hands for manipulating objects, was thus, in a sense, a by-product of alterations in diet and habitat, which in their turn ultimately made possible the development of tool-using, hunting and associated cultural behaviour. The development of the brain and the mental capacities that were later to be devoted to art, navigation and higher mathematics was similarly a by-product of the increasing coordination required for the development of tool-making and hunting. The patterns of social organization, involving cooperation and food-sharing, that emerged at this stage were ultimately to make life in cities and empires possible.

The older view of human evolution was characterized by an emphasis on speciation – the splitting up of the human line into a multitude of extinct species. The modern view, which takes into account the variability possible within a particular species, sees essentially a single line of evolution from the Pliocene to the present day. The exception to this, which is thrown into stark contrast as other supposed species have been amalgamated into the evolving human lineage, is the coexistence of at least two early hominids in East Africa at the beginning of the Pleistocene. The current interpretation sees one of these hominids becoming increasingly robust and ultimately becoming extinct, while the other developed further human attributes such as increasing brain size and an improved upright posture. It seems likely that what was happening here was the emergence of new capacities in only part of the late Pliocene hominid population and the gradual divergence of these advanced forms from their more slowly evolving contemporaries. The features – including tool-using – that differentiated the more advanced species led to the replacement of other forms that had not undergone this transition. This phenomenon, the expansion of more complex patterns of behaviour at the expense of less developed ones, is a recurring pattern; but this was the last occasion in the course of human evolution in which the process was manifested in biological terms, as the extinction of a species. Thereafter, the pace of development of cultural behaviour was more rapid than that of biological differentiation, and while regional populations might become extinct, these had not reached the stage of separate species. More commonly, however, advanced attributes were simply taken over by peripheral populations, either by genetic diffusion or by learning.

The lack of subsequent speciation is all the more remarkable in view of the enormous geographical expansion that took place during the Pleistocene. The spread of human populations, first to Europe and the southern part of Asia, then increasingly into northern Asia and ultimately to Australia and the New World, was accompanied by differentiation that went no further than the formation of races, geographical subspecies. While this expansion formed part of a general pattern of faunal mixing in the later Cenozoic, it contrasts with the spread of other families such as the elephants, which also extended their range from Africa to Asia and the New World but which underwent a considerable degree of speciation in the process. The unity of the human species in these circumstances reflects two important points: the increasing significance of cultural (rather than biological) adaptations and the maintenance of contacts between scattered human populations. The use of fire, clothing and shelters allowed the colonization of periglacial environments without major biological adaptation, taking man beyond the Arctic Circle by 60 000 years ago. While evolutionary changes were still taking place at this phase, they were generalized improvements in all-round capacity rather than specializations – changes of grade rather than line. The relatively mobile way of life, covering a wide variety of habitats, allowed continuing genetic and cultural exchanges among component populations. The striking similarities in handaxes from Britain and India, for instance, argues for some flow of communication, if only at a simple level. Equally, however, it probably reflects similarities in behaviour and way of life, indicating that although a diversity of habitats was being occupied, their variety was not being fully exploited.

The speed of biological and cultural changes in the Quaternary was undoubtedly related to the massive scale of environmental fluctuations that were by then taking place, affecting not only the glaciated areas but the tropics as well. This rapid development has parallels in other mammalian lines such as the sheep family, in which more complex patterns of social behaviour and communication emerged in response to the pressures and opportunities of repeated glaciation and deglaciation.[2] In the case of the human species, marked changes indicating a new threshold of development took place in the later part of the last glaciation, which led to the emergence of fully modern forms of man and their spread into America and Australia by sea.

Appreciation of the full significance of these developments has been one of the major achievements of recent archaeology. It has arisen largely from a recognition of the different patterns of variability in stone-tool assemblages between the Lower and Middle Palaeolithic on the one hand and the Upper Palaeolithic on the other. This was not just the introduction of new types of tool based on blades, but a more fundamental contrast.[3] In the former case the assemblages show neither the regional stylistic groupings nor the pattern of rapid directional change that are characteristic of the latter. The coincidence of these features with the appearance of anatomically modern populations, and the subsequent appearance of finds indicating trading and artistic activity, suggest that the final phase of biological evolution was now complete and that there was a new potential for cultural development. The intriguing suggestion that only at this stage was the full linguistic capacity of modern populations achieved accords well with the archaeological picture of an increased density and complexity of interaction, which involved regular territorial movements. It seems likely that the patterns of social organization characteristic of modern hunting populations, with complex networks of kinship links between local communities, only emerged at this time. This point thus marks the beginning of the phase of rapid development that led to agriculture, urbanism and industrialization.

The new emphasis on the changes of about 40 000 years ago gives a fresh perspective to subsequent developments. In many respects these represent the unfolding of the potential inherent in the existence of relatively dense populations of fully modern man, spread over the major habitable parts of the globe and organized in extensive social networks with regionally differentiated economies more closely adapted to their immediate surroundings. These were the preconditions for the more active manipulation of the natural environment, such as the intensive collection of certain plants and their spread beyond their natural habitats, that signals the beginnings of agriculture.

Although the most spectacular developments of the 30 000 years before the beginning of the Postglacial were associated with the florescence of big-game-hunting groups on the open plains and tundras, ultimately more significant changes were taking place elsewhere in areas like the Near East. These involved the use of a broad spectrum of resources, including the integration of a variety of seasonally available food sources such as birds, fish, snails and the small seeds of wild plants, and there was a global trend – accelerated where environmental change or human predation caused the extinction of the large mammals – towards the use of these resources. It is an open question whether the environmental changes of the Late-glacial and early Postglacial were purely incidental to the emergence of agriculture or played some causal role. It seems likely that, by bringing new stresses and opportunities, they accelerated trends already apparent. Certainly, it is a striking coincidence that evidence for early plant cultivation should appear in many parts of the world in the early Postglacial. It suggests that the increasing density of population was resulting in a degree of saturation that forced local communities to make use of labour-intensive methods of exploiting the particular resources of their immediate environment. This is not to say that 'agriculture' was the immediate solution to a global population crisis: only that more intensive means of obtaining food gradually became necessary, and that some of these had far-reaching consequences for future development.[4]

Agricultural origins

Views of the emergence of agriculture have changed radically since Childe first postulated a 'Neolithic Revolution'. The neat succession of 'Mesolithic' and 'Neolithic' cultures has proved inappropriate in describing early Postglacial developments, in which the beginnings of cultivation were essentially a part of a broader trend towards a more intensive exploitation of primary resources – the lower levels of the trophic pyramid. These small, locally common sources of food, such as seeds or shellfish, required labour-intensive collection and often represented unattractive foods that had previously been neglected in favour of larger game. In most cases (as with shellfish) this form of exploitation, which often necessitated a more sedentary pattern of existence, had no further consequences: but in the case of certain plant resources it opened up revolutionary possibilities.

Among the plants that it was worth while to collect intensively were those that had developed specialized storage organs in their seeds, roots or stems, usually as an adaptation to seasonal stress. Such plants generally occur in fairly restricted habitats but can be grown outside these if their dispersal is assisted and if they are protected from competition. Seeds especially (as opposed to roots) may have a relatively high protein content as well as carbohydrates and can form a major part of the diet. The grasses, in particular, underwent rapid genetic changes as a result of cultivation, leading to the emergence of more productive and adaptable forms that were of increasing importance in the subsistence economy.[5]

The various components of the agricultural complex – crops, livestock, cultivation technologies and permanent settlements – emerged in a slow process of development that started with the small-scale cultivation of plants in new habitats. The environments in which it is most profitable to grow such plants artificially are rich alluvial plains with a good supply of both nutrients and water. It was in such locations, therefore, that experiments with food crops were most successful. This led to a new pattern of population distribution, with higher densities in the fertile lowland valleys and plains. It allowed the formation of significantly larger, permanent communities, which in turn necessitated novel social structures as well as new technologies such as architecture. Further development came about as the crops were adapted to a wider range of habitats. It was at this point that the major characteristics of agricultural economies began to be evident, as regional population densities became significantly higher and other components, such as animal domestication and more advanced cultivation techniques like irrigation, were integrated into agricultural systems.

This process occurred in at least half a dozen regions in the subtropical and tropical areas of the globe, with explosive consequences for each of them. It was these areas that provided the foci of change for much of the Postglacial period. This is not to say that the intensification of subsistence methods did not take place elsewhere: only that the pace of change in these key areas was so rapid and their effects (such as the diffusion of new crops) so far-reaching that slower development in the same direction was often overtaken by the spread of successful forms of agriculture.

The role of animal domestication in these developments is less clear, but it seems that major changes in animal exploitation were probably a consequence rather than a cause of the village-based farming economy. Certainly, one of the surprises of recent work has been the fact that large, sedentary, cereal-growing communities such as Jericho were still dependent on hunting animals like gazelle for their meat. It was the integration of animals into a basically sedentary economy that necessitated new patterns of husbandry and selected certain 'social' species such as Old World sheep, which proved responsive to human management. The more advanced ungulate species of the northern hemisphere were better adapted to such manipulation than was the archaic fauna of Africa. Animal husbandry, too, had its emergent properties: certain species such as cattle and equids, as well as providing meat, could be used for traction and transport – the first use of non-human sources of energy. In some areas (notably parts of sub-Saharan Africa and the New World) domestic animals were less important and these changes did not take place. Animal-based economies were especially significant in the semi-arid belt of the Old World, however, where specialized forms of nomadic pastoralism developed.

A characteristic of Postglacial developments was thus the great diversity of contemporary economies, including those of intensive agriculturalists using irrigation and the plough, simple cultivators, pastoralists, intensive collectors, forest and steppe hunters, and specialized maritime hunter–fisher–gatherers. The basic pattern was a roughly zonal arrangement, with a central belt of increasingly complex agrarian societies surrounded by successively less intensive economies. The wider range of contacts in the northern hemisphere, however, produced a faster rate of change in peripheral groups than in the southern hemisphere, where comparatively archaic economies persisted in the more isolated landmasses of South America, southern Africa and Australia. The outer margin of the occupied area was still expanding – as in Polynesia and the Arctic – at the same time as crop and livestock complexes were spreading from nuclear areas at its centre.

The beginnings of complex society

The fastest rates of change occurred in the nuclear regions of western Asia, southern and eastern Asia, the sub-Saharan belt, Mesoamerica and the western Andes. These areas saw the appearance of more complex societies characterized by an unprecedented degree of social differentiation and hierarchical organization. While the greater range of contacts that grew up around them soon led to interaction between adjacent centres of development, the initial appearance of urban societies organized on the basis of states was an independent process in each area. These changes occurred, for the most part, in the river basins and valleys where there were the largest concentrations of population.

The problem of the origins of state societies has been widely discussed as a result of recent archaeological research, and many factors have been suggested as responsible. These include increases in local population density, the circumscribed nature of certain environments, the unequal distribution of resources, the growth of regional specialization in production, the need to control fluctuating and unpredictable resources, the greater organization required for irrigation, the effects of conquest and the requirements of defence, and the growth of long-distance trade. While all of these have some relevance, it is necessary to sort out the circumstances in which they became important and their role in each stage of the process.

A broad contrast may be drawn between local factors in the regions where state societies initially emerged and the later spread of such forms of social organization over larger areas of the globe. The long-distance trading networks that grew up between centres of established urban civilization were certainly responsible for the appearance of urban societies in areas like eastern Europe, south-east Asia or parts of Africa, where states emerged at the nodes of trade routes. Once initiated, the process of urban development had a contagious effect on surrounding areas, creating the conditions for further growth. However, within the areas of emergence of the so-called 'pristine states' – Mesopotamia, Egypt, the Indus valley, the Huang Ho, Mexico and Peru – the analytical problem is to identify the order in which the other factors became important. For instance, work on irrigation systems in several areas has suggested that early irrigation was relatively small-scale and could be organized on a village basis: it did not require a central authority to regulate and maintain it. While irrigation was a basic feature of each of the areas mentioned, it does not in itself explain the process of centralization.

As with the other processes of change discussed here, it seems likely that a model is required that postulates the importance of different factors at different times.[6] It is possible to suggest a sequence of changes in which different factors successively magnify the consequence of others to explain the rapid development of these areas.

A primary reason for the emergence of hierarchical societies is the unequal distribution of productive land. For small-scale societies with low population densities and a mobile way of life, such distinctions are not critical. Dense, sedentary communities that make more intensive use of their environment must inevitably take account of these inequalities. Fertile land gives its owners a higher return on expenditure than poorer land, producing a surplus for certain groups. In the relatively uniform environments of the temperate forest landscapes such contrasts were not acute at the level of simple agriculture, but in the linear oases of the Nile, the Euphrates and the Indus, for example, these local contrasts were marked.

Such fine-grain differences led to the existence of disposable surpluses among a limited sector of the population. These surpluses could not be consumed directly, any more than can the results of overproduction today: but they could be converted into real 'wealth' through their exchange for valuable imported items not available locally, and through their distribution in return for labour on monumental construction. Both activities enhanced the prestige and status of certain groups and promoted structural differentiation at a local level.

Once created, these local elites could take on new functions that had not been part of the reason for their initial emergence. They could alleviate local fluctuations in productivity through their access to surplus food; they could initiate local specialization by arrangement with neighbouring elites in areas of different productive potential; and they could bring a new organization to local production by means of a conscious policy of maximization and investment in new facilities. Such changes generated a potential for long-distance trade and a need for the acquisition of scarce raw materials, which brought with it an element of external aggression and a consequent need for systems of defence. These in turn strengthened the capacity for internal control through a monopoly of the use of force.

Such successions were not inevitable, but the conjunction of circumstances in the alluvial basins of the semi-arid zone rendered them highly probable; and once one or two such polities had emerged, they created others by reaction and precipitated a cellular structure over the whole region. While the details of the process may be different in each area, the essential characteristic of this model is that it takes account of a variety of factors that promoted similar types of social structure. Particular institutions may have come into being for a number of reasons; but once in existence they assumed new functions and led to similar patterns of development in different communities. Social hierarchies can cope with a variety of problems that could not be solved by less organized communities, but such hierarchies do not necessarily emerge as the direct response to those problems. It would be wrong to attempt to isolate a single universal factor behind the emergence of complex societies: but such societies have universal properties, of which one is the potential for further development.

The new archaeological picture has again emphasized the protracted and multilinear character of these developments. It has demonstrated the early existence of sites with special 'central' functions, like Tell es-Sawwan in the Old World, or Las Haldas and San José Mogote in the New World, long before the emergence of fully centralized states and 'civilizations'. It has been as unkind to the 'Urban Revolution' as to the 'Neolithic Revolution', in revealing them to be rooted in earlier trends and processes and to consist in the gradual accumulation of characteristic features rather than the sudden emergence of a whole complex.

The spread of urban life

The degree to which complex urban societies were responsible for influencing their less developed neighbours is still a matter of dispute. There has been a strong reaction against diffusion as an explanation of cultural change. In judging the impact of early urban societies on nearby farming populations, it is as well to bear in mind the following points.

First, the general convergence of global development in the Postglacial towards more intensive forms of food production, and its social consequences. The areas of early civilization were only the most advanced examples of a universal trend; some parallelism between developments in urban and non-urban areas is therefore only to be expected. Second, the association of certain types of advanced technologies with complex social structures is less close than was once assumed. The beginnings of metallurgy – including the production of alloys – has been convincingly demonstrated among pre-urban groups, notably in the Balkans and in Thailand. Similar observations apply to the construction of monumental tombs such as European megalithic monuments, which may be the products of small communities without hierarchical social structures. Third, among non-urban populations a number of spheres of intensive interaction emerged that were characterized by long-distance trade and an often surprising uniformity, over wide areas, in certain aspects of culture. Examples would include the Beaker phenomenon in Europe, Dong-son in south-east Asia, Hopewell in North America and perhaps Lapita in Polynesia. Again, these came about without significant external stimuli.

On the other hand, the scale of external contacts of the developing urban civilizations should not be underestimated. Impressive and irrefutable evidence of trading links, even of colonial activity, from the heartlands of Sumer and Elam has been revealed by recent discoveries at Habuba Kabira and Tepe Yahya, 1000 kilometres distant in either direction from the earliest urban centres. Trading contacts from northern Mesopotamia were undoubtedly significant in the genesis of urban states in Anatolia, as the demand for raw materials from the dense populations of the rich but stoneless and metal-less alluvial plain – met to a large extent by the export of manufactured textiles – affected an enormous hinterland around Mesopotamia. Once large urban populations were in existence, their trading and colonial activities may well have stimulated the formation of local elites in areas where they had an economic interest and may thus have recapitulated the chain of developments that lead to local states. Such processes would have been responsible for the appearance of advanced communities in the areas between the 'pristine states', for instance in the Levant and the Indo–Iranian borderland.

Study of long-distance contacts involves consideration of the modes of transport available at the time. Two important innovations that made large-scale interaction possible were the sailing ship and the use of pack animals. Both made their appearance in the Old World in the context of early urbanization before 3000 BC. Ships with sails were used on the great rivers of the Euphrates and the Nile and in the Persian Gulf and the eastern Mediterranean. Goods were also carried by pack donkeys to the trading colonies in surrounding areas. The range of these contacts, and the quantities of material that could be carried by these methods, allowed a rapid growth of trading networks and speeded the spread of urbanization.

How far, then, can the argument for local autonomy be taken? Can the emergence of literate civilizations in areas like the Aegean be seen as independent in the same sense as those of Egypt, Mesopotamia or the Indus?[7] To a certain extent it is a matter of definition, as even the last three shared a common basis of not only west Asiatic crops and livestock but also plough agriculture and perhaps irrigation practices. Nevertheless, it is meaningful to ask whether, given the same economic base, urban life would have arisen in the Aegean when it did without some immediate foreign stimuli.

The question cannot at present be answered directly, but there are grounds for arguing that it was part of a process of contagious spread rather than a simple, autonomous, local development. The appearance of literate communities and state organization in the western Old World did not occur in a random fashion, now in one place and now in another, but there is a clear pattern of successive additions to the network of urban civilizations linked by trade. The central Tigris/Euphrates–Levant–Nile arc was extended in the second millennium to include the Gulf, the Red Sea and the Aegean, and in the first millennium to encompass southern Arabia, the Caspian and Black Sea shores, the Adriatic and the western Mediterranean. In each case, the developing areas were contiguous with regions of older-established civilization. This strongly suggests that the process should be viewed as a whole, and that the timing of events on the edge of the area of urbanization must be related to the pattern of growth of trading contacts.

At a more detailed level there are clearly variations in the responses to such stimuli from neighbouring areas. It is instructive to compare the reactions of Cyprus and Crete, for instance, to increasing contacts within the eastern Mediterranean. In the former

area the result was a very limited degree of internal development, and urbanism was largely imposed from outside; in the latter, there was a flourishing local civilization with a strongly individual character. As with other problems in interpretation, therefore, the choice of an explanation in terms of diffusion or autonomous growth is largely a question of scale: at a gross level it may be useful to talk about diffusion, but this must be complemented by a more detailed analysis in local terms.

The foundation of the modern world

The existence of a number of complex societies, themselves interacting and generating further transformations at their edges, increased the disparity between the rapidly developing core of urban civilizations and more distant parts of the world. Increases in the scale of urbanization encouraged further change.

Under certain conditions larger political units emerged that included several of the earlier city-based states. Competition for resources by means of military expeditions was increasingly common, and the existence of bureaucracies capable of administering wider territories allowed a more permanent incorporation of conquered areas. The processes leading to the growth of empires represent another field for the construction of comparative models. Historical explanations based on the achievements of particular individuals must be complemented by a consideration of the economic and political basis that made possible the unification of larger areas.

New configurations of political power were most easily achieved where the area of urban societies was itself being enlarged. A common pattern is the phenomenon of 'peripheral takeover' – the conquest of an established urban core by a relatively marginal power. This can be seen in the case of the Assyrian, Persian, Aztec and, most notably, Macedonian empires.

The extension of imperial power into new areas was largely dependent on the existence of trade routes or local processes of urbanization. The area controlled by the Persian empire – about ten times the size of that acquired by the Egyptians – could be unified only because of the links already created by nomadic tribes in its arid hinterland. The northward extension of the Roman empire was possible because of the local emergence of Celtic states, themselves stimulated by trading contacts with the Mediterranean.

These larger political units allowed a much greater concentration of resources in particular areas and new levels of investment in the creation of transport systems and agricultural production. The 'Royal Road' from Susa to Sardis is testimony to the former, while the construction of massive new canal systems in Mesopotamia is a tribute to the latter. These were part of the general improvement in agricultural technology that also included *qanats* and extensive run-off concentration systems. An important contribution of recent archaeology has been the revelation of the scale of such rural development, which underlay the continued demographic growth and political development of the Near East.

The continuing process of state formation on the edges of the civilized world carried this form of social organization into new environmental zones, such as temperate Europe in the north and tropical Indo-China in the south. In southern and eastern Asia intensive rice cultivation, using the technique of transplanting in paddy fields and the creation of new rice-growing areas by terracing, supported a major growth in population there. The focus of Chinese civilization moved from the millet-growing areas of the north along the Yellow River to the southern rice-growing area of the Yangtze, while local states emerged in the flood plains, river valleys and deltas of south-east Asia and southern and eastern India. Maritime trading networks were important in stimulating urban growth and the associated intensification of food production. This linked the urban civilizations of this region in a continuous chain from the China Sea to the Mediterranean, opening up the way to new influences such as Islam.

Equally significant were developments in the great arid areas of North Africa and central Asia. The growth of long-distance trade routes in these regions, based on the use of the camel, created new links between the societies of Eurasia and opened up contacts with sub-Saharan Africa. The latter resulted in the formation of a belt of states that mirrored the emerging kingdoms of northern Europe. They were distributed in a line across the southern margin of the Sahara, in the area that had earlier seen the appearance of an indigenous African agriculture. The fact that complex societies appeared here at this date undoubtedly reflects outside stimuli across trans-Saharan trade routes, though it is quite probable that local states would have appeared in this region in time, as a result of indigenous development, had this process not been accelerated by outside contacts. Such may have been the case, indeed, with native states further south such as Zimbabwe.

The area of urban societies in the western Old World thus took on a new shape: the inner ring of states around the Mediterranean was complemented by an outer ring linking the trade routes that reached out like spokes from its centre. Yet it was a relatively marginal area in this overall pattern that emerged as the focus of developments that were to affect the whole of the world.

In an archaeological perspective the emergence of temperate Europe as a centre of innovation was the culmination of processes going back into prehistory. The fertile but relatively uniform environments of inland Europe did not have the stark contrasts that had earlier precipitated social differentiation in areas of more complex ecology such as the Near East. On the other hand, the rich forest soils could support a much more continuous density of population than could the more restricted areas of cultivation available in the latter. The Near East is, in a sense, one large oasis, created by the belt of Tertiary mountains that interrupts the arid zone and catches the winter Mediterranean rainfall. Its capacity to sustain population growth was limited when irrigation systems reached their maximum extent with a pre-industrial technology. There are signs that many parts of it had reached such limits by the early centuries of the Christian era and, indeed, that these

limits were actually contracting because of environmental deterioration such as salination and the silting up of irrigation works. Temperate Europe, on the other hand, was increasingly opened up by forest clearance in the later prehistoric period, and the process of internal colonization is a major theme of early medieval history. Successive improvements in plough technology allowed a continuing increase of agrarian population. Such a subsistence base could sustain further economic growth and the productivity required to support towns and cities. Although individual centres were perhaps small by comparison with Near Eastern ones, the overall density of population in the whole region was much higher.[8]

While present-day experience in the Third World demonstrates that density of population is not an automatic guarantee of economic growth and technical development, the difference between the two cases is that in Europe population growth and technological change went hand in hand, each stimulating the other. Europe's manufacturing and industrial base grew at the same time as its rise in population and its acquisition of overseas colonial territories. Technological developments – for instance, in waterpowered machinery and in sailing vessels – provided solutions to critical problems in the process of expansion. By the time that the agricultural area at home could no longer be extended, there were both foreign sources of supply and industrial solutions to the dilemma of increasing production, based on coal, steel and steam power.

The explanation of change

The replacement of the model of a static series of 'stages of development', separated by periodic revolutionary bursts, by one that stresses the dynamic character of prehistoric and early historic societies has important implications for the types of explanation that are appropriate in archaeology. In the nineteenth-century perspective, and still surviving in the views of Gordon Childe and Leslie White, was the idea of technological innovation as the crucial breakthrough, lifting societies from one level to the next. The re-evaluation prompted by ecological ideas suggested that societies are in general resistant to change, which often implies an increased workload and declining standards of living for the majority. It substituted for technology the idea of inexorable population growth, forcing the adoption of more intensive methods of production. In essence, however, it retained the basic structure of previous explanations by postulating a single driving force that carried development across successive thresholds of change.

In the ecological model the appearance of new levels of social organization or technology was seen as a rational response to problems posed, for instance by population growth or environmental change, and as having given rise to an inevitable succession of increasingly well organized or well adapted types of society. Since regional specialization and social hierarchies permit higher levels of population and production through organization and the rationalization of the economic process, these were seen as the logical consequences of population pressure. As the course of human prehistory and history demonstrates an overall trend towards greater densities of population and more hierarchical societies, they were regarded as causally connected.

Recent work on the critical transition periods in human development has not supported this model. In several cases it has been demonstrated that characteristic features emerged only in the later stages of the transition. Population growth is as often a consequence as a cause of change. More complex forms of organization did not necessarily emerge as the natural solution to problems of gaining a living, but often as unexpected by-products of other changes. There is no 'first cause' of cultural change, like technology or population, that can be isolated and given primacy. A variety of factors may have been responsible for realizing the possibilities inherent in existing patterns and for opening up a new range of possibilities as a result.

This should not cause a retreat into a particularist ideology that treats all change as a unique conjunction of accidental circumstances. What it does is to require explanations to be formulated at the appropriate level. There is a logic to the development of economic and social systems – the trend from big-game hunting to small-game hunting and plant collection, for instance, or from largely autonomous village communities to centrally controlled empires – that explains the order of certain developments, but not why particular transitions actually occurred. To explain the beginnings of agriculture, for example, requires an answer that takes account of several different time-scales: the existence of modern populations and of an economy already based on intensive collecting, the spread of wild cereals as a result of Postglacial climatic changes, the practice of re-sowing in alluvial habitats, and so on. The overall pattern, on a scale of thousands of years, may display a trend that, with hindsight, it is tempting to interpret in a rationalizing, purposive way; but to account for the actual course of development, in terms of centuries, it is necessary to invoke small-scale effects related to particular situations. Thus while the model may at one level appear deterministic, with finer resolution it becomes opportunistic.

In summary, therefore, the capacity for continuing change is inherent in human social organization and technology. The increasing scale of environmental fluctuation that has characterized the last few million years has constantly necessitated adjustments of various kinds. The cumulative nature of human culture, adding new elements and producing new configurations of old ones, has permitted these responses to follow a pattern of progressively more complicated social and technical forms. Population, while not in itself forcing such changes, has often acted like a ratchet – easier to move in one direction than another. Increasingly, this process has developed its own momentum, both through secondary, man-induced environmental change and because of successively more complex interactions within society itself. The more complex the pattern, the faster such changes could take place and the larger the scale of their effects.

While this chapter began by reasserting the independence of archaeology, it is appropriate that it should end on a less self-sufficient note. A social historian of the nineteenth century has recently written of the archaeology of that period: 'Subjects which had hitherto indulged an amiable but essentially unadventurous curiosity were now raising profound and deeply disturbing questions about the origin, nature and duration of human life.'[9] Study of the archaeological record constantly poses new problems of general significance. So today the questions raised by recent archaeological discoveries and reinterpretations can only find answers in a wider intellectual context. With a better grasp of his own subject matter, the archaeologist can turn with more confidence to debate its meaning with biologists, anthropologists and historians. To understand the great transformations of human society requires all the resources of modern scientific inquiry.

PART THREE

X: Frameworks: dating and distribution

The archaeologist requires a three-dimensional imagination, as much to grasp the disposition of ancient cultures in time and space as to visualize a buried site. Maps and time-charts are the plans and sections of the historical process. They are a guide to the patterns that underlie and make sense of the complexity of the real world. Although there are wide disparities in our knowledge of different parts of the globe, it is especially important to appreciate the process as a whole and the interrelationships within it.

To understand the reconstruction of the prehistoric past, however, requires some acquaintance with the methods that are used in dating it. While this book does not attempt to give a comprehensive guide to the scientific techniques employed by the archaeologist, the use of chronometric dating is so basic to the ordering of prehistoric developments that an extended account of it is included here. Few recent innovations have affected so fundamentally our view of the past. It has given an accurate perspective to the archaeological panorama.

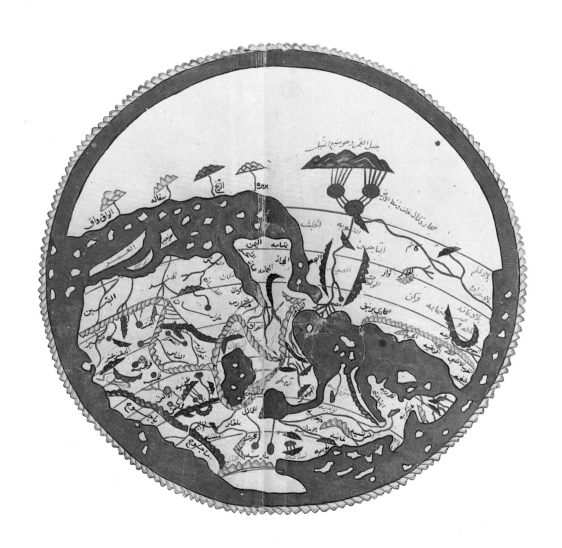

62. Dating and dating methods

Methods of establishing the relative age of excavated objects and monuments on the basis of their stratigraphy, associations or typology are fundamental to archaeology. Unless these methods can be directly related to a calendrical system, however, the archaeologist has no means of knowing the absolute age of his material. Fortunately, the physical sciences have come to the aid of archaeology in this respect by providing the means, mostly based on the rate of decay of radioactivity, by which absolute ages can be determined.[1]

As yet, no single absolute dating method covers the whole of the period with which human palaeontology and archaeology are concerned, nor do the individual methods cover their respective time-scales with the same precision. The coverage afforded by particular methods (and some of their limitations) is summarized in Figure 62.1. These methods are considered here approximately chronologically; the discussion begins with those appropriate to dating within the Pleistocene before moving on to the methods applicable to later prehistory.

Methods applicable to the earlier part of the archaeological time-scale

The continuous slow accumulation of sediment on the floor of the oceans over geological time has created the record from which much of the former history of the Earth has been reconstructed. The rate of accumulation of sediment on the ocean floor is slow, averaging about 1 centimetre per thousand years, but a very considerable depth of deposit formed over the two million years or so of the Pleistocene. In general this constitutes a much more continuous record than that provided by the deposits formed over the same period of time on land, where erosion has tended to destroy the record. Studies of the changes with temperature in the ratio of the stable isotopes of oxygen (^{18}O and ^{16}O) in foraminifera preserved in continuous cores of sediment recovered from the deep oceans have revealed the pattern of alternating glacials and inter-glacials during the Pleistocene (see Chapter 8). (Nearly all natural elements are mixtures of several isotopes. The isotopes of an element all have the same atomic number and identical chemical properties, but they have different atomic masses and slightly different physical behaviour.)

As the record obtained from the ocean floor is almost continuous, it is potentially a useful source for correlations with contemporaneous events on land. At the same time, ocean cores can also preserve a record of changes in, or reversals of, the Earth's magnetic field, and they may also contain long-lived radioactive elements of the uranium series that enable them to be dated absolutely. Using some or all of these properties, cores can be made to yield characteristic isotope or magnetic 'signatures'

rather similar to the more precise signatures revealed by the pattern of annual rings in some trees. Indeed, a numbered sequence of oxygen isotope stages, using even numbers to indicate glacials and odd numbers for inter-glacials, has already been established, and the more recent (uppermost) end of some cores may be within the radiocarbon age range.

The absolute dating of sediments, based on the rate of decay of long-lived naturally radioactive elements of the uranium series such as thorium (^{230}Th) or protactinium (^{231}Pa), depends on the low solubility of these daughter elements of uranium, which are precipitated in sediments unsupported by their parent elements (^{238}U and ^{235}U respectively). Possible sources of error are variations over time in the concentrations of these elements, their subsequent migration after deposition and variations in the rate of accumulation of sediment.

A method applicable to some terrestrial materials is the counting of fission tracks. These are linear dislocations about 20 microns in length that are found in certain materials, in particular volcanic glasses such as obsidian, and also in some man-made glasses, and represent damage caused by the spontaneous fission of the large, unstable atoms of uranium (^{238}U) present in minute amounts in these materials. Tracks may be observed directly in thin sections of such materials under the electron microscope but can be made more conveniently visible under an optical microscope by etching the sections with hydrofluoric acid, which attacks the tracks and enlarges them. Irradiation of a sample of the material in a nuclear reactor with a known flux of neutrons to induce fission of ^{235}U (which unlike ^{238}U does not undergo spontaneous fission) can be used to estimate the total amount of uranium present. From this, and from the known rate of fission of ^{238}U, the age of the material being examined can be calculated, the accuracy attainable being mainly dependent on the number of tracks counted. Fission-track dating has one of the most comprehensive age ranges of all dating methods, but unfortunately the range of archaeological materials to which it can be applied is very limited.

Perhaps the most important of all the strictly chronometric methods (that is, methods of dating that permit age to be assessed in years) applicable to the earlier part of the Pleistocene is the potassium/argon (K/Ar) method, by means of which the earliest known hominid remains from East Africa have been indirectly dated. This method depends on the decay of ^{40}K, the naturally radioactive isotope of the widely distributed element potassium, to the non-radioactive inert gas argon, and is applicable in particular to volcanic rocks, in which the K/Ar 'clock' was set to zero when they were formed. The time taken for a given amount of radioactivity to decay to half its initial value is known as its 'half-life'; half the radioactivity remains after one half-life, a quarter remains after two half-lives, and so on. The curve representing radioactive decay thus tends towards but never quite reaches zero. Each radioactive element has a definite and characteristic half-life, which may lie anywhere in the range from fractions of a second to millions of years. As the half-life of ^{40}K is very long (1300 million years) the K/Ar method has been applied to the problem of dating the Earth's oldest rocks, lunar rocks and other extra-terrestrial materials. The potassium content (and hence the original ^{40}K content) of suitable rock samples can be easily measured by standard laboratory techniques such as flame photometry, but the amount of radiogenic argon must be measured with a sensitive mass spectrometer after melting the rock sample to recover the gas. Loss of argon by diffusion since rocks were formed and contamination by atmospheric argon lead to under- and over-estimation of age respectively. For these reasons samples for measurement must be very carefully selected; by no means all rocks of volcanic origin are suitable for dating in this way. Potassium/argon dates for beds over- and underlying the important fossil hominid sites in East Africa, such as Olduvai, have nevertheless provided the main framework for the absolute dating of early man and his hominoid precursors.[2]

In most circumstances the reliable lower limit of K/Ar dating is about 250 000 years before the present, and no other widely applicable method currently exists to bridge the gap between that time and the present upper limit of radiocarbon dating of about 50 000 to 70 000 years. In this respect the relatively recently developed amino-acid method of dating described below is of great potential interest.

Amino-acid dating

Certain assymetric organic molecules exhibit the property of stereoisomerism; that is, they can exist in two alternative structural forms. The chemical composition of these two forms is identical, but the arrangement of the atoms in one form is a mirror image of their arrangement in the other. The two kinds of molecules are known respectively as laevo- (L) and dextro- (D) forms, or enantiomers, according to the direction in which solutions of these substances rotate a beam of polarized light. Of the two only the L enantiomer is synthesized within living systems. Molecules formed within living organisms, such as the amino-acids in protein, nevertheless slowly undergo spontaneous change from the L to the D form, a process known as racemization. This occurs to a measurable extent during the lifetime of the organism, and it has been suggested that racemization of amino-acids in protein within the enamel or dentine of teeth could be used to test claims of great longevity in humans. Amino-acids derived from the protein collagen can survive in bone and other hard tissues for very long periods of time and have even been found in trace amounts in some vertebrate fossils more than 300 million years old. By measuring the extent of racemization of a selected amino-acid (such as aspartic acid) in bone from an archaeological context, and as the rate at which the racemization process occurs is known, the age of the bone can be determined. Fortunately from the archaeological point of view, the study of proteins and amino-acids has long been of great importance to biology, medicine and allied fields, with the result that sensitive analytical procedures for examining these substances are well established. Advanced

analytical equipment has been developed and mixtures of amino-acids can be separated readily in the laboratory and their individual racemization constants determined. Aspartic acid has a relatively fast rate of racemization, and the half-life of the reaction at 20°C has been ascertained from laboratory measurements to be 15 000 years. Other amino-acids (for example, alanine and iso-leucine) have slower rates of racemization at the same temperature, and by using these the range of the method can be extended further back in time.

In practice, the range of the amino-acid method is of the order of 1000 to 1000 000 years, so that it promises to bridge very usefully the gap between radiocarbon and potassium/argon dating. Bone very often survives for long periods of time on archaeological sites (as witnessed by the survival of early hominid remains), often in the absence of other datable materials, and another advantage of the amino-acid method is that only fairly small samples of a few grams or so are required. As with other methods of dating, problems such as contamination by more recent material may arise, of course; a more serious limitation, however, is that the rates of racemization of amino-acids, like the rates of all other chemical reactions, are proportional to temperature. This may limit the range of sites to which the method can be applied mainly to those where the temperature (and, to a lesser extent, the physico-chemical environment) has been both moderate and fairly constant. Comparison of the dates obtained by another method such as radiocarbon dating for material from the same site may help to resolve the temperature problem.

Radiocarbon dating

Of all the physical methods of age measurement now available to archaeology radiocarbon dating holds pride of place, although some thirty years have elapsed since it was first introduced. The reasons for this ascendancy are simple enough, for the method is applicable to a wide range of materials commonly found on archaeological sites; it can be applied anywhere in the world; and it covers the last 50 000 years or so of man's development – roughly, that is, the entire period of modern man's history. This is not to say, however, that radiocarbon dating is entirely without limitations. Certainly, all the technological difficulties that were originally associated with the method have essentially been solved; indeed, an entirely new method of radiocarbon dating (using a particle accelerator) is almost within reach. However, partly as a result of these improvements in technique over the years, it has become apparent that the relationship between radiocarbon and calendar years is not a simple one for all periods of past time; in other words, it is necessary to calibrate the radiocarbon time-scale. It is towards the further understanding of this problem, which itself has great intrinsic interest from the geophysical point of view, that much of the effort of the world's hundred or so radiocarbon dating laboratories is now directed.[3]

The possibility of devising a dating method based on radiocarbon, natural ^{14}C, was first investigated by Professor W. F. Libby and his colleagues at the Institute for Nuclear Studies in Chicago in the late 1940s. Libby's original idea was based partly on contemporary knowledge of nuclear processes that occur in the Earth's atmosphere leading to the production of ^{14}C atoms, partly on intuitive speculation about the fate of these ^{14}C atoms, and largely on a now classic experimental investigation that he described in detail in his book *Radiocarbon Dating*.[4] For this work Professor Libby received the Nobel Prize for Chemistry in 1960, and it is a great tribute to his original percipience that in the time that has elapsed since the method was first developed and its use became widespread it has undergone serious modification in only one respect – that of the gradual recognition of the need for calibration of the radiocarbon time-scale already mentioned above.

The principles upon which the method of radiocarbon dating rest are fairly straightforward. Atoms of ^{14}C are formed in the upper atmosphere of the Earth, mainly in the stratosphere (the top 20 per cent of the atmosphere), through the interaction of neutrons with nitrogen atoms. The neutrons are produced at higher atmospheric levels still by the flux of high-energy cosmic radiation arriving from interstellar space (nitrogen is, of course, the major constituent of the Earth's atmosphere). In quantitative terms the amount of ^{14}C produced is small, on average about two ^{14}C atoms per square centimetre of the Earth's surface per second. This process is presumed, reasonably enough, to be long-established, perhaps for a period of the order of a thousand million years, so that an

equilibrium has long been reached in which the production of ^{14}C is matched by its loss by radioactive decay. Newly formed ^{14}C atoms are rapidly oxidized to carbon dioxide and become uniformly distributed by atmospheric mixing within perhaps a year or two, a very short time compared with the average lifetime of an individual ^{14}C atom of 8300 years. Thus, on a global scale ^{14}C is distributed uniformly throughout the separate parts of the so-called exchange reservoir: the atmosphere, the oceans and the living world (biosphere).

Carbon dioxide, on which ultimately all living organisms depend, forms only 0.033 per cent by volume of the Earth's atmosphere, and a very small proportion of this, about one molecule in ten million million, is 'labelled' with ^{14}C. The natural level of ^{14}C in living organisms is therefore very low, the specific radioactivity due

62.1: *Some of the more important scientific dating methods available to the archaeologist, the ranges of time over which these different methods extend and some of their inherent limitations. The time-scale given along the horizontal axis is a logarithmic one, which permits the comparison, in a single diagram, of methods that cover very long periods of time (such as potassium/argon dating) with those limited to a few thousands of years or less.*

METHOD	SOME LIMITATIONS
palaeomagnetism	requires specialized samples
potassium/argon	age range not generally useful to archaeology
uranium/thorium decay	not often applicable to archaeological sites
fission-track	requires specialized samples
amino-acid analysis	early stages of development
radiocarbon	calibration of the time-scale
dendrochronology	regional
thermoluminescence	mainly pottery
archaeomagnetism	requires specialized samples
bone analysis (U, F & N)	relative only
obsidian hydration	limited distribution

10^2 YEARS	10^3	10^4	10^5	10^6	10^7

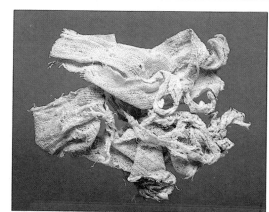

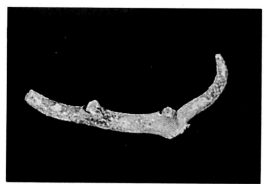

62.2: *A range of typical materials suitable for use as samples for radiocarbon dating, comprising wood, rope, reed and linen from Ancient Egyptian contexts. With the exception of the wood sample, all these are 'short-lived' materials that have been used to investigate the differences between radiocarbon ages and known historical dates (here obtained from inscriptional evidence).*

62.3: *Miner's pick of red deer antler, from a Neolithic flint mine at Grime's Graves, Norfolk, England. It provides a good example of a well-preserved bony material from a highly calcareous environment suitable for radiocarbon dating. Only the organic content of such material, the protein collagen, is used for radiocarbon measurement.*

62.4: *Linen from a Dynasty I tomb at Tarkhan, Egypt, showing the effect of pre-treatment to remove possible age contaminants before samples are converted into a pure chemical form for radiocarbon measurement. The sample on the left is untreated; that on the right has been subjected to prolonged washing in successive dilute solutions of acid and alkali, the minimum treatment necessary for most ancient sample materials before they can be dated.*

to ^{14}C being about 13.5 disintegrations per minute per gram of carbon in living tissue. Green plants are the base of the terrestrial food chain, and photosynthesis, the process through which such plants assimilate carbon dioxide, is the route by which ^{14}C enters the biosphere as a whole. With a few special exceptions (for example, terrestrial and freshwater molluscs or plants living in hard-water lakes, which may incorporate old or 'dead' carbon), all living organisms are in equilibrium with the concentration of ^{14}C in the atmosphere. When death occurs uptake of ^{14}C ceases and the ^{14}C in surviving tissue such as bone or wood, charcoal or other plant remains decays at a constant rate. Accepting the validity of the other assumptions of the method already discussed above, only two other pieces of information are needed to estimate the age of once-living material from the measurement of its residual ^{14}C content. These are, first, the length of the half-life (that is, the time taken for a unit amount of ^{14}C to decay radioactively to half that amount) and, second, the so-called contemporary assay, or ^{14}C activity, of living tissue, for which wood of known age is taken as a representative standard. Implicit in this is the idea that the contemporary assay has always been the same, that the concentration of ^{14}C in the atmosphere has always been constant; as will be seen in more detail in the section on calibration, it is now known that this assumption is erroneous. There have been substantial variations in the ^{14}C concentration of the atmosphere in the past, and it is these that have made calibration of the radiocarbon time-scale necessary, but the principle of comparing the activity of ancient material with that of a modern standard is not affected by this. In practice, two changes brought about by man have made it difficult to establish a modern reference standard directly. The very large amount of fossil fuel (coal and, more recently, oil, which are too old to contain any measurable ^{14}C) that has been burnt since the mid-nineteenth century has diluted the ^{14}C activity of the atmosphere, so that modern wood is not truly representative of the present-day level in age terms. Since the early 1960s this effect has been over-compensated for by artificial ^{14}C from nuclear-weapon testing. Use of wood pre-dating AD 1850 as a standard would overcome these problems, but an artificial modern standard known as NBS oxalic acid, distributed by the American National Bureau of Standards, is generally used, as it can conveniently be made available to all laboratories.

The half-life of ^{14}C is taken to be 5570 ± 30 years, the figure Libby first used as the best estimate then available. Since that time the value of 5730 ± 40 years has been shown to be a more accurate estimate, but a large number of dates (more than 40 000) based on the original value has been published, and it continues to be used as the basis for the 'conventional' radiocarbon dates published in the authoritative journal *Radiocarbon*. The underestimate of age (3 per cent) that results from the use of the conventional Libby half-life is generally smaller than the error in absolute age due to natural ^{14}C variations, and as calibrated dates take both these variations and the new half-life value into account, the issue is not one of primary importance.

The materials used as samples for radiocarbon dating, some

examples of which are shown in Figures 62.2 and 62.3, are predominantly those that were once a part of living organisms. This is certainly true of the large majority of archaeological samples, but for some geological and other applications natural carbonates in one form or another have sometimes been used. The interpretation of the ^{14}C activity of the latter materials in age terms is not straightforward, however. Normally samples consist of the organic materials commonly found on many archaeological sites, such as charcoal, wood, seeds and other plant remains, and human or animal bone. It is obviously of critical importance that the materials on which dating is based should be contemporaneous with the site or horizon under examination: substantial errors could result from a mistaken reliance on the age of large timbers or charcoal, as these could be considerably older than the site itself. Short-lived materials are therefore to be preferred as samples for radiocarbon dating, but these in turn may, if they comprise as little as one season's growth, reflect possible short-term ^{14}C variations. It thus appears that samples taken from wood that grew for between ten and twenty years are likely to give the most dependable results.

All sample materials have to be pre-treated for the removal of possible age contaminants (see Figure 62.4) before conversion into a pure chemical form suitable for the measurement of their ^{14}C

62.5: *Laboratory high-vacuum line, in which the preparative chemistry is carried out that is required to convert the original (pre-treated) sample material (charcoal, wood, collagen, etc.) into a standard pure chemical form for radiocarbon measurement. This procedure is necessary because of the very low levels of ^{14}C even in recent living material and the weak radiation that ^{14}C emits.*

activity. Pre-treatment of charcoal and wood generally entails very thorough washing with dilute acid and alkali to remove carbonates and humic substances that may have penetrated the samples during their period of burial. A further precaution that is sometimes taken with wood is to separate and use only the cellulose. Similarly, only the protein fraction of antler or bone, the collagen, is used, the carbonate in whole bone being liable to undergo exchange, generally leading to an erroneously recent date. Other materials may require more specialized pre-treatment, but in every case it is a vital preliminary step in the series of laboratory processes leading up to the final age determination.

As ^{14}C occurs at very low levels in nature, the activity of samples cannot be measured directly. Special measurement, or so-called counting procedures, have to be used, and these are described in the outline below. First it is necessary to convert the pre-treated samples into a standard form for measurement. The form chosen, a pure gas or a pure organic liquid, depends on the method of measurement in use, but the laboratory procedures are much the same for both. These consist of chemical syntheses carried out by standard techniques in high-vacuum systems, such as that shown in Figure 62.5, which permit the maintenance both of high standards of purity and of near-quantatitive yields from the chemical reactions employed.

The final sample that is to be measured may take various forms. Most commonly gases, monatomic or diatomic in carbon such as carbon dioxide and methane or acetylene respectively, or an organic liquid containing a high proportion of carbon such as benzene (92 per cent C), are used. The choice depends on which of the two preferred methods of measuring ^{14}C for radiocarbon dating, gas counting or liquid scintillation counting, is favoured by a particular laboratory. Although these methods differ in principle, both measure the same fundamental process, that is, the radioactive decay of ^{14}C atoms. Figure 62.6 summarizes the features of these two methods and their respective advantages and limitations.

Dates are calculated from the ratio of the net count rate of the unknown sample to that of the modern standard, taking into account the decay constant of ^{14}C (derived from the half-life) and the exponential form of the radioactive decay curve. The activity of both the sample and the standard are first corrected for possible fractionation (misleading discrimination in favour of the heavier ^{14}C atoms) of carbon isotopes in nature (and, usually to a limited extent, in the laboratory) by measuring the ratio of the stable carbon isotopes (^{13}C/^{12}C) with a mass spectrometer. Usually this effect is small but it could have a significant effect on the age of some samples if no correction were made. The net count rate is obtained by subtracting the background count of the counter system, that is, the residual count in the presence of a 'dead' sample containing no ^{14}C. This background derives mainly from radioactivity in the surroundings and in the materials from which the counter itself is constructed. The background cannot be eliminated completely, but careful design and the optimization of the counter system can keep its level low and relatively constant. The

GAS COUNTER	LIQUID SCINTILLATION SPECTROMETER
Massive shielding needed (several tonnes of lead or steel free from radioactive impurities).	Very little shielding required (typically a few kilograms of lead). Background largely eliminated by electronic means.
Counter purpose-built and of specialized construction.	Suitable counters are available commercially.
Chemistry of sample preparation fairly straightforward but high standard of gas purity required.	Sample preparation chemistry more complicated but purity requirements less stringent.
Prepared samples difficult to store permanently.	Once prepared, samples can be easily stored for possible remeasurement.
Counting of any one sample continuous over 1–2 days; background of counter cannot be measured during this period.	Sample and background (or standards) can be counted alternately at short intervals. In general larger samples can be counted.
Counters have to be pumped out to high measurements to avoid 'memory effects'.	Instantaneous changing of samples resulting in more continuous counting and higher productivity.
Better performance with very old or small samples. Age limit about 56 000 years.	Except in refined systems the age limit is generally about 40 000 years or less. Minimum sample size 1 gram of carbon.
Control of background important.	Less subject to external sources of background variation.
Control of counter environment important. Specially constructed building with underground counting room ideally required.	Counter can operate in open laboratory. No special ambient temperature control or air conditioning requirements.
	Scintillation spectrometers are perhaps marginally more suited to computer control processing and storage of counting data.

62.6: *The table lists some of the more important comparisons between the two preferred methods of measuring* ^{14}C *for radiocarbon dating. The new and much more specialized method of measuring radiocarbon ages, using a particle accelerator, will undoubtedly become increasingly important, especially for small or very old samples and perhaps in authenticity work, but it is unlikely to supersede these two established methods for most other purposes.*

background of the counter determines the age limit that can be attained by a system; an arbitrary measure of this is the so-called figure of merit of the system, the ratio of the background to the square of the net modern count rate. The higher this figure, the better the system is in terms of its age range. In practice, the need to measure samples older than, say, 40 000 years seldom arises, but the performance of a system with younger samples will be much better if it also has the inherent capacity for accurate measurement of much more ancient material. There is, nevertheless, great interest in measuring older material in some laboratories, though until recently the only way of extending the age limit beyond the 40 000–50 000 years that most laboratories can expect to reach has been by means of isotopic enrichment. In this process the sample (in the form of carbon monoxide or methane) is continuously recycled over a period of weeks through thermal diffusion columns, advantage being taken of the tendency of the heavier ^{14}C atoms to diffuse less readily than the atoms of ordinary ^{12}C. Eventually a sample of gas is obtained in which the ^{14}C concentration has been increased a small number of times, extending the measurable age range using conventional counting methods by several half-lives up to about 70 000 years. Relatively large samples are needed and the process, requiring equipment that few laboratories possess, is costly and time-consuming. The contamination of such samples with even small amounts of more recent material poses a severe problem.

A more recent and ambitious development that shows great promise has been the direct measurement of atoms of ^{14}C in a particle accelerator, disregarding their radioactivity altogether. This method of dating is founded on the separation that can be effected when ions (that is, atoms stripped of some of their outer electrons) are accelerated through large electric and magnetic fields. Under these conditions ions of different mass are constrained to follow slightly different curved paths; they can be collected separately and their numbers determined by measuring the electric charge they carry. The massive and costly machines in which these processes can be made to occur are the specialized tools of the high-energy physicist and are built for purposes more recondite than that of radiocarbon dating. Nevertheless, experiments with these machines have shown that $^{14}C/^{12}C$ ratios can be determined directly with sufficient precision for dating purposes, and machines are now being built exclusively for dating use. Some difficult problems will undoubtedly have to be surmounted, but it may not be too optimistic to state that the method will be firmly established in use during the next few years, although on grounds of cost alone it is unlikely ever to supplant existing methods. The great attraction of the accelerator method is that only very small samples are needed – of the order of a few milligrams of pretreated material, or about one-thousandth of the present minimum requirement. This will allow of very thorough chemical pretreatment even of small samples, which is a very important consideration with ancient material. The time taken to make the measurement will generally be much less than that required by the decay method and, using improved methods of sample enrichment, a far greater age limit (more than 100 000 years) may be attainable. The solution of a whole range of problems associated with materials not now amenable to radiocarbon dating – for example, Neanderthal skeletal material – will be within reach for the first time if all these advantages can be realized.

Radioactive decay is a random process in the sense that a radioactive atom may decay at any instant. As a result, there is a limit to the accuracy that radiocarbon dates, or indeed any measurements of radioactivity, can attain, depending on the number of observations that are made (the number of radioactive breakdowns or counts recorded within a finite period). The errors of such measurements are expressed as the standard deviation, or sigma (σ), which is numerically equal to the square root of the number of counts. As a standard practice dates are published with errors equivalent to $\pm 1\sigma$.

Disregarding systematic and sampling errors, which laboratories naturally strive to keep to a minimum, a series of measurements of the same sample will be found to have a so-called Gaussian or normal distribution, such that about 66 per cent of the measurements will fall within $\pm 1\sigma$. If the error limits are widened to $\pm 2\sigma$, 95 per cent of the observations will fall within these limits, and 99 per cent will fall within $\pm 3\sigma$. It is not usually practicable to make measurements to within accuracies greater than ± 1.0–0.5 per cent, and the error quoted with a date is (or should be) the combined error of the measurements of the unknown sample, the background and the modern reference standard. Doubling or trebling the quoted errors to increase the confidence that can be placed in a particular date would generally tend to reduce the usefulness of the result, since the limits of error would become too wide. Instead it is recognized that when a date is quoted with an error of $\pm 1\sigma$ there is one chance in three that the true value may lie outside the quoted limits. Thus, as has sometimes been said, a single date is no date at all. Confidence can be greatly increased, however, when the date is part of an internally consistent stratigraphic or other series, or when it agrees closely with other dates for similar archaeological assemblages.

Calibration

A consideration quite apart from further refinement of the methodology of radiocarbon dating is that of calibration of the radiocarbon time-scale. The methodology has already advanced to the point where, assuming that the material comprising the sample is correctly associated and free from contamination, the accurate determination of a radiocarbon age is largely a matter of routine. It is now accepted, however, that the results of all such physical measurements, no matter how precise they may be as measurements, cannot be interpreted simply as dates in calendar years. This is because the rate of production of ^{14}C in the atmosphere has not always been constant in the past, with the result that radiocarbon years are not directly equivalent to calendar years, at least over the greater part of the last eight millennia or so and

62.7: *Bristlecone pine* (Pinus aristata) *native to mountainous areas of the south-western United States. These trees grow at altitudes above about 3000 metres and are very long-lived, some examples being more than 4000 years old. Their extreme longevity and the pattern of annual growth rings that they exhibit in response to climatic stress (mainly differences in rainfall) render them uniquely important to dendrochronological studies, and they have played a prominent role in the calibration of the radiocarbon time-scale. Conservation of these trees is also becoming a matter for concern.*

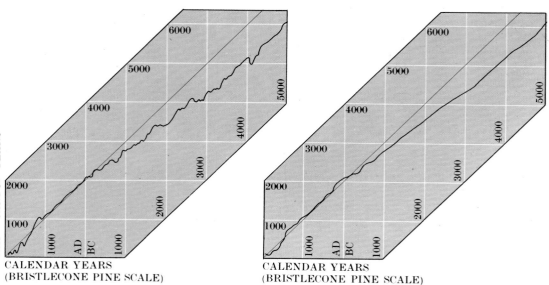

CALENDAR YEARS
(BRISTLECONE PINE SCALE)

CALENDAR YEARS
(BRISTLECONE PINE SCALE)

62.8: *Generalized curves illustrating the relationship between radiocarbon and calendar years, based on measurements of bristlecone pine wood of known age. The deviation from the 1:1 relationship (the 45° line) that radiocarbon and historical dates would have if radiocarbon and calendar years were directly equivalent appears to be due to a gradual change in the intensity of the Earth's magnetic field, which has affected in turn the production of* ^{14}C *in the atmosphere. The shorter-term 'wiggles' may be due to modulation of this overall trend by changes in solar activity. The smooth curve is a best fit through the data on which the irregular curve is based for tentative calibration purposes.*

s first tested, good agreement
...s and the historical dates for
... from Ancient Egyptian con-
...re precise and more dates were
... became apparent that there
...een the dates that were being
...ected from historical evidence.
...l in the period before about the
...adiocarbon dates appeared too
...d years, by comparison with
...est comparative material avail-
able, reeds used as bonding between mud-brick courses of tombs of
the Egyptian Dynasty I, about 3100 BC, appeared to be as
much as 600 years, or about 12 per cent, too young. The implications for older prehistoric material of this apparently increasing
divergence were as disturbing as the corollary that radiocarbon
years could no longer be regarded as absolute, constant units of
time.

The underlying cause of the increased amount of ^{14}C appears to
have been a gradual increase in the flux of cosmic radiation reaching the upper atmosphere. Most probably this was due to a corresponding reduction in intensity of the Earth's magnetic field, which
deflects radiation arriving from outer space. The fundamental
cause of such changes in the Earth's field is unknown. Other factors,
such as the increased amount of water in the oceans following the
end of the last glaciation and perhaps changes in solar activity, may
also have had a minor effect on the overall change in the concentration of ^{14}C in the biosphere.

Fortunately, an independent means of investigating and
quantifying this effect was available. Since the 1920s work had
been in progress in America on the variation in width, in response
to climatic stress, of the annual growth rings of some of the longer-
lived species of pine trees native to the south-west United States.
From the characteristic pattern of different ring widths, resulting
mainly from seasonal differences in rainfall, timber from trees of
overlapping age could be matched to build up a continuous
sequence – a procedure known as dendrochronology (see below).
Starting from living trees and working back through timber from
archaeological sites, a regional chronology extending back some
2000 years was achieved. More important, from the point of view
of radiocarbon dating, work on the bristlecone pine (*Pinus aristata*),
a species growing above about 3000 metres in the White Mountains
of California (Figure 62.7), revealed that some individual trees
were of truly astonishing age.

Ring counting of samples taken with a borer from one living
specimen showed it to be 4600 years old, far older than trees such
as the giant redwoods (*Sequoia gigantea*), previously thought to
hold the record for longevity. Intensive work at the University of
Arizona has now resulted in the establishment of a continuous
bristlecone chronology extending back 8200 years and accurate to
within one year, and the search for older material continues. The

original impetus for this work was the study of the record of past
climate preserved by these very old trees; their role in providing
the key to the problem of the calibration of the radiocarbon time-
scale was unforeseen.

Radiocarbon measurements of samples of bristlecone pine wood,
taken at intervals of approximately twenty-five years, have now
been made, principally at the laboratories of the universities of
Arizona (Tucson), California (La Jolla) and Pennsylvania (Philadelphia). This has resulted in the publication of a calibration curve
– or, more correctly, a number of similar calibration curves – from
which radiocarbon dates may be converted into dates in calendar
years (Figure 62.8). A considerable number of bristlecone calibration curves and tables has now been published, some of which are
perhaps more authoritative than others. All are based on essentially the same measurements; they differ mainly in the way in
which the laboratories or authors concerned have treated these
data statistically. Very generally, the results obtained from the use
of the curves and tables published by the three principal laboratories involved in calibration studies (and other more generalized
curves derived directly from these) do not differ greatly. The
calibrated dates so obtained are more accurate in absolute terms
than the corresponding radiocarbon dates, although their individual errors will be somewhat larger than those of the original raw
dates. This is due to the statistical errors, and perhaps to minor
systematic errors as well, inherent in the radiocarbon measurements upon which the bristlecone curve itself is based. For all
these reasons it is necessary to state which curve or set of tables
has been used in arriving at a calibrated date.

Leaving this latter consideration to one side, it is certain that the
overall trend of natural radiocarbon variations over the last eight
millennia is faithfully reflected by the bristlecone data. Superimposed on this main trend there appear to be some short-term
'wiggles' or kinks in the curve, and there is much greater uncertainty about the exact position and size of these fluctuations.
Their interest is twofold, since if they are real (and there are some
flat regions in the curve), they may impose a limitation on the resolution that radiocarbon dating can achieve; conversely, there may
also be regions where the curve changes more rapidly and radiocarbon dating is correspondingly more sensitive. Another possibility offered by the wiggles is the recognition of their characteristic
signature in a series of dates for individual rings in prehistoric
timber, which could then be matched very precisely with the
bristlecone curve. Obviously, the success of this last possibility
would depend on finding suitable preserved samples, and rather
precise measurements and rigorous statistical analysis of the
results are prerequisites.

The rapid mixing of the Earth's atmosphere (and the consequent
uniformity of the distribution of ^{14}C) has been demonstrated.
Nevertheless, the bristlecone pine is a rather specialized tree growing in an atypical environment, so that it has been considered desirable to repeat the radiocarbon measurements on a comparable
series of tree rings from other species from a different latitude and

nearer sea level. This work is now in progress, using wood comparable in age to the bristlecones from trees preserved in Irish peat bogs and elsewhere. The results obtained so far support the bristlecone data, though apparently without reproducing some of the smaller variations or kinks in the bristlecone curve. A good general agreement is indeed to be expected, for radiocarbon dates obtained for materials from Ancient Egypt agree substantially with the expected historical dates when corrected from the bristlecone data.

Apart from further elucidation of the problems of calibration, the next major advance seems likely to depend on the successful development of the accelerator method, by means of which the first dates have already been obtained experimentally. This method, using only milligram quantities of sample, offers the possibility of obtaining dates more rapidly than present methods, with a probable upper age limit of about 100 000 years. Cost is likely to restrict these installations to a few fortunate institutions, but the existence of even one or two such facilities would open up an entirely new range of possible applications.

Dendrochronology

The use of tree-ring analysis as a means of dating was first seriously suggested in 1837 by the mathematician Charles Babbage, inventor of the calculating machine. Earlier writers, including Leonardo da Vinci, had considered the same idea, but Babbage was the first to propose that the recognized pattern of variations in the width of the annual growth rings in some trees could be used to cross-date trees of overlapping age so that a chronology could be compiled. This was, in the words of the late Professor Zeuner, 'a remarkable case of vision in science',[5] for the idea remained latent for almost a hundred years until revived by the pioneer work of the astronomer A. E. Douglass in the American south-west in the early part of this century. Since then it has become the basis of the modern rigorous science of dendrochronology.

Dendrochronology has two distinct uses, both of which depend on the same underlying principle: the building of a sequence or master chronology by cross-dating (see Figure 62.9). These uses are, first, the measurement of elapsed time in order to obtain a precise date and, secondly, the study of past climate as recorded by the annual variations in width of tree rings. The first of these uses is almost exclusively archaeological, but the second may also provide information about the pattern of past environmental change of very considerable relevance to archaeological studies.[6]

In transverse section the annual rings of trees such as conifers exhibit two distinct bands, an inner light band and an outer dark band that terminates abruptly, defining the season's growth. This results from the change in density of the cellular structure of the wood due to seasonal variation in the rate of growth. Many broadleaved trees exhibit this same effect, and some, such as oaks, can also be used for dendrochronology. Factors controlling growth, such as rainfall or temperature, vary on average from season to season; ring widths vary accordingly. Not all species of trees, or even individual trees of any one species, respond equally to these factors, however. Those that show marked variations are termed sensitive, while those that do not are known as complacent trees. Only the former can be used for cross-dating purposes, and

62.9: *The use of the pattern of annual ring-widths to build a continuous tree-ring chronology by linking overlapping growth patterns from one tree to another. For the purposes of this diagram the overlapping timber sections have been shown with the same spacing between rings; in reality the exact spacing of rings varies from tree to tree, but the pattern of relative ring widths can still be matched from one tree to another.*

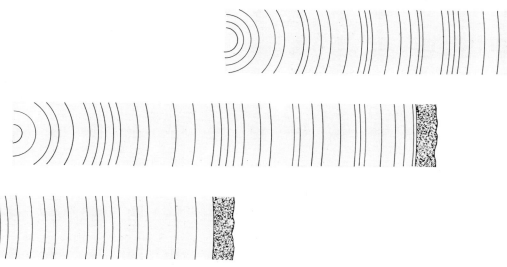

even then there may be difficulties in correlating trees of the same age from different or even neighbouring regions. Master chronologies must obviously be built from trees of the same species, and the possibility of the occurrence of abnormalities, such as double rings or rings not forming a complete circumference, has to be guarded against. Obviously, the application of dendrochronology to archaeological sites is critically dependent on the preservation of suitable ancient material, either as dry or waterlogged wood or as unbroken charcoal. For the purpose of absolute dating, comparisons must be made with a master chronology for the same species that starts at the present day or some known felling date; the initial establishment of this master chronology is usually the most difficult step. Floating chronologies – that is, sequences of ancient material that are continuous over a period but lack a known date – can sometimes provide much useful interim information as to sequence and duration prior to the establishment of a complete chronology. They can also sometimes be dated approximately by radiocarbon, and this serves to illustrate the contrast between these two dating methods, since radiocarbon measurements always carry some irreducible error, whereas the ideal dendrochronology is accurate to within one year.

Both for the initial building of a master chronology and for the dating of preserved ancient specimens, cross-sections of timber are preferable to radial samples or cores. Only cores may be taken, using specially designed borers, from living trees, particularly from uniquely important long-lived ones such as bristlecones, the conservation of which is a matter of great concern. Samples both ancient and modern usually have to be surfaced and polished by sanding, or have to be carefully scraped, to reveal the cellular structure, so that the rings can be counted and their widths accurately measured with the aid of a low-power microscope. Ring widths can be plotted for comparative purposes as absolute or relative measurements. Relative measurements that allow for differential growth effects as the radius of the tree increases are generally more useful. Many different methods of measuring and plotting ring widths have been developed, and advanced statistical techniques are used to compare the measurements of material of hitherto unknown date with the master chronology in order to ascertain the confidence with which a fit can be made.

Dendrochronology has made and continues to make many useful contributions to the archaeology and later history of parts of Britain, Europe and North America, but probably its most dramatic achievement has been the 8200-year bristlecone pine chronology described above in the section on calibration. That still older material is preserved has been demonstrated by radiocarbon measurements, and it seems probable that the bristlecone chronology will eventually be extended much further back in time, probably to more than 10 000 years ago. Work is in progress on oaks preserved in Holocene river gravels in Europe and on trees preserved in peat bogs and other deposits in the British Isles, and this may eventually lead to complete chronologies rivalling that of the bristlecone in length. The intrinsic scientific interest of this ancient

sub-fossil material and the different kinds of record that it preserves (and also that of living bristlecones) extends far beyond the confines of archaeology.

Thermoluminescence

The dating method known as thermoluminescence (TL) is based, like several of the other methods considered here, on radioactivity. This relationship is indirect, however, since the TL effect depends on what is known as the defect solid state. In the structure of the crystal lattice of most minerals there are defects or imperfections known as traps. Electrons may be stored in these as a result of energy transferred by various means, among the most important of which is the passage of alpha or beta particles or of gamma radiation from either natural or artificial radioactive sources. Energy stored in this way can be released in the form of an emission of light or 'glow' when heat is applied (hence the term thermoluminescence). Minerals exhibiting the property of TL are found in the clay fabric of most pottery bodies, which generally also contains very small amounts of the natural radioactive elements potassium-40 (^{40}K), thorium and uranium. Clays suitable for making pottery are usually of ancient origin; most will have accumulated TL over a long period of time, in some instances to the

62.10 *Roman pottery lamp (approximately 8 centimetres in diameter), showing in its base the small amount of sample required for thermoluminescence (TL) dating. The hole from which the sample has been drilled is about 2 millimetres in diameter and 2–3 millimetres in depth, corresponding to 50–100 milligrams of powdered sample. The TL method is thus essentially a non-destructive means of dating pottery and other fired ceramic materials. Individual sherds of ancient pottery, which are usually more dispensable than more complete objects, may be either drilled in the same way or carefully crushed to provide a sample for TL dating.*

point of saturation. The high temperatures used for firing pottery have the effect of annealing out the geologically acquired TL, so that the TL 'clock' is effectively reset to zero at the time of the manufacture of a fired ceramic object. In principle, then, if the TL acquired over archaeological time by a particular piece of ancient pottery is measured, and if its susceptibility to a known dose of radiation and its radiation history can be ascertained, the time that has elapsed since its manufacture can be calculated.

Two TL dating methods for pottery have been developed, known as the fine-grain and inclusion method respectively. In the former a sample is usually drilled out from the pottery object or sherd (see Figure 62.10), and particles in the size range 1–8 microns are sedimented from this sample as a uniform thin layer on an aluminium disk about 1 centimetre in diameter. In the inclusion method a sherd is carefully crushed, quartz inclusions in the range 100–150 microns sieved out and residual fine clay and other impurities removed by means of a magnetic separator. The resulting crystalline inclusions are then etched with hydrofluoric acid to remove the surface layers from the quartz and to dissolve unwanted minerals such as feldspars. Several samples are prepared for each sherd, some being needed for artificial irradiation with a known dose, and the disks or inclusions are heated, or 'glowed out', under carefully controlled conditions in a specially designed glow-oven in which the TL output from the samples is detected by a sensitive photomultiplier. TL is plotted against temperature on a chart recorder to give curves such as those shown in Figure 62.11.

Of the two the fine-grain method tends to be favoured because the preparation of samples is much easier and because quite frequently pottery contains too little quartz for the successful application of the inclusion method, or the quartz that it does contain proves to have poor TL properties. Fine grains can, however, exhibit 'anomalous fading' of the TL, leading to erroneously low estimates of age.

In practice, there are many potential difficulties in making TL measurements and even greater problems in their interpretation. These difficulties arise principally from uncertainties in the radiation dose received by the samples, their so-called radiation history, and from the complicated response to known doses of radiation of the material of some clay bodies, in which marked non-linearity or fading effects may sometimes be observed. The natural radiation dose is received from alpha, beta and gamma radiation from within the body of the pottery and from the surrounding environment, including a small contribution from cosmic radiation. These sources of radiation are effective over different ranges. Alpha particles are the least penetrating (about 25 microns) and contribute only negligibly to the dose received by quartz inclusions from which the outer surface has been removed with hydrofluoric acid, as described above. The dose received by fine grains, however, is largely made up from this source. Beta and gamma radiation is effective in inducing TL over ranges of about 2 millimetres and 30 centimetres respectively, so that in the inclusion method it is the environmental dose that is most important. For the most accurate dating by either method it is very desirable to be able to measure the environmental dose by direct dosimetry in the field. This may be done by placing capsules containing substances known as TL phosphors, such as calcium fluoride, which are much more sensitive to radiation than is pottery, in the appropriate deposits for up to a year, after which they may be recovered and measured. From this a close approximation to the annual dose received by the pottery can be obtained. Finally, the radioactivity of the pottery itself must be measured (for example, by alpha counting of a thick powdered sample) and the total potassium content measured by flame photometry or some other convenient analytical technique to enable the ^{40}K to be estimated. Loss from the pottery of the radioactive gases thoron and radon, which are part of the thorium and uranium decay series, complicates the dosimetry still further.

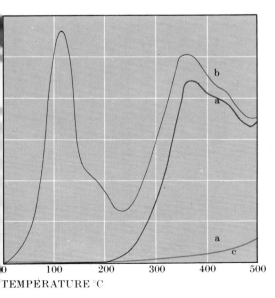

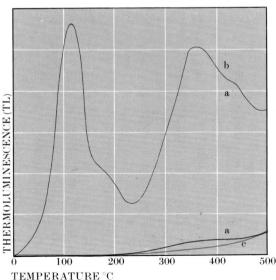

THERMOLUMINESCENCE (TL)

TEMPERATURE °C

TEMPERATURE °C

62.11: *The typical form of T L glow curves from ancient and modern samples, in which light output (vertical axis) is plotted against temperature (horizontal axis) and compared with the output resulting from an artificial radiation dose; the background 'black body' curve is derived from infra-red radiation emitted by the glow-oven heating plate.*

The overall result of these various uncertainties is that TL dates can at best achieve an absolute accuracy of within about ± 5 per cent at present. Fortunately, this is of little consequence as far as the other chief application of TL is concerned, the authentication of ceramic objects.[7] Usually in this application no information at all is available about the environmental radiation dose that the object has received, since most such objects are unprovenanced and a date is attributed on stylistic grounds. The only information about the dose received must come from direct measurement of the radioactivity of the object itself, as described above. If the TL age derived from this information and from interpretation of the glow curves approximates to the age postulated on stylistic grounds, it is usually possible to deduce that the object is genuine. If it lacks a natural TL glow curve, however, it will most probably be a spurious modern copy (see Figure 62.12).

TL can be applied to materials other than pottery and refractory materials such as burnt brick. In some circumstances the burnt clay of hearths may be suitable for TL measurements, so that samples that are potentially much older than the earliest pottery can be dated. This raises the possibility that useful comparisons may be made between TL and radiocarbon dates (and perhaps also archaeomagnetic measurements) beyond the present limit of the bristlecone calibration, although, as has been seen, the precision of TL dating is very considerably less than that of radiocarbon dat-

ing. A particularly interesting application of TL from the archaeological and scientific points of view is the possibility of dating burnt stones, in particular flint or chert, by applying the same principles as those on which the dating of pottery is based. The main differences are that flint contains very little natural radioactivity; that the environmental dose, which is more difficult to determine with accuracy, is a most critical factor; and that it has to be sliced to provide samples for measurement. There is evidence that flint was sometimes heat-treated by early man to make it easier to work. More important, flint waste or artifacts that have been recognizably burnt, presumably accidentally in most instances, are frequently found *in situ* in Palaeolithic deposits where the stratigraphy and typology are unequivocal. The age of such material often extends beyond the present furthest limit of radiocarbon dating, but the upper limit of TL dating for flint before the material becomes saturated, appears to be of the order of a million years or so. Dating of burnt flint by TL may therefore offer an independent means of closing the important gap that exists at present between the upper limit of radiocarbon dating (50 000–70 000 years BP) and the lower limit of the potassium/argon method (about 250 000 years BP). At present the use of TL for dating flint or other burnt stone materials worked by early man is still at the research stage, and many difficult problems relating to the dosimetry and TL properties of these materials are still to be overcome.

62.12: *Two terracotta figures attributed on stylistic grounds to the Six Dynasties period of China (AD 220–589), which illustrate the use of TL dating of unprovenanced objects for the purpose of establishing authenticity (see also Fig. 62.10). The otherwise convincing seated human figure (approximately 20 centimetres high) was shown to be modern, whereas the result of TL measurement on the ox-drawn cart (about 40 centimetres high) was consistent with its presumed historical age.*

Magnetic dating

The Earth's magnetic field is made up of two principal components. The larger of the two is the dipole field, which gives rise to the north and south magnetic poles, aligned at an angle of about 11° to the Earth's axis of rotation. A secondary, non-dipole, component is superimposed on this main field, and this varies from place to place on the Earth's surface. These magnetic fields arise from electrical currents generated in the molten iron- and nickel-rich interior of the Earth, and when the configuration of this molten region and the convection currents flowing within it vary, changes in the direction and intensity of the magnetic field occur. The two principal components of these changes, that is, direction and intensity, can be utilized for dating purposes.

Objects of fired clay preserve a stable record of the magnetic field at the time of firing, which is only liable to be seriously altered by exposure to extremely severe chemical weathering or by re-firing. The source of this so-called thermoremanent magnetism is grains of haematite and magnetite contained within the clay, which behave as small dipoles. During cooling following the firing of an object or structure these grains become magnetically aligned with the direction of the Earth's field prevailing at the time at that particular location. Thus, the material of fixed structures such as kilns or of objects that must have been fired in a particular orientation can be used to determine the direction of the Earth's field at various times in the past at particular points on the Earth's surface. The direction of the Earth's field varies at any given time from one point to another, but measurements taken from structures of known age and fixed alignment provide the basis for constructing a curve of the changes in the Earth's magnetic field with time that is applicable over a radius of several hundred miles. From this other objects or structures of fired clay from the same region can be dated by measurement of their remanent magnetism, providing that their orientation at the time of firing is also known or can be inferred. At present this method of dating can be applied to fired clay materials over the last 2000 years or so, but its use is confined to rather limited areas, where the detailed past history of the Earth's field is already well known or can be recovered.

The preserved record of the past intensity of the Earth's magnetic field may also provide useful dating evidence and has the advantage that no directional information is required. The laboratory procedures used to measure magnetic intensity necessitate the heating of the object or sample under investigation, which may not always be permissible as far as pottery and other artifacts are concerned. Where no such limitation applies intensity measurements have considerable potential value and interest, particularly in view of the apparent correlation between changes in the intensity of the Earth's magnetic field and natural ^{14}C variations over the last eight millennia (see section on calibration).

Complete or partial reversals of the Earth's dipole field have also occurred at intervals over geological time, the record of these being preserved in volcanic and sedimentary rocks. Complete reversals of long duration are known as epochs, those of shorter duration as events and incomplete reversals as excursions; most of those so far identified have been given names that are often used in a chronological sense as synonyms for particular intervals of time. Examples are the Matuyama epoch (2.43–0.69 million years ago, according to potassium/argon dating), the Jaramillo event (about 0.9 million years ago) and the Mungo excursion (about 30 000 years before the present). Where such reversals can be recognized in continuous sequences of material (for example, in deep ocean cores) their potential value for dating purposes on the basis of terrestrial correlations is considerable.

Relative dating

In contrast to absolute methods of dating based on directly measurable physical processes, such as the decay of radioactivity or the annual growth of tree rings, are three methods of relative dating. Two of these are based on chemical analysis and one on accumulated radioactivity. These methods are applicable to antler, bone and teeth (including ivory) and depend on an estimation of the elements nitrogen, fluorine and uranium these materials contain (Figure 62.13). Although these methods are independent of one another, it is often advantageous to apply all three simultaneously. The most important point to emphasize at once, however, is that these three relative-dating methods are entirely empirical. The concentration of nitrogen, fluorine or uranium in, for example, fossil bone is very dependent on local conditions of preservation, so that the analysis of bone from a particular site cannot necessarily be compared with that of similar bone of the same age from any other site. Analysis of these elements therefore provides only a very general indication of the age of buried antler, bone or teeth and cannot ever be truly chronometric.

The nitrogen method depends on the gradual loss of this element from these materials as a result of the breakdown of their organic component collagen into its constituent amino-acids, which are in turn leached away by moisture, especially under acid soil conditions. Fresh bone contains about 4–5 per cent of nitrogen, and the proportion is reduced fairly uniformly in progressively older bone, but the rate of decrease depends on the conditions of burial. Nitrogen is lost most rapidly when bone is buried under aerobic conditions (conditions in which free oxygen from the air is present) with active movement of soil water, whilst the loss may be negligible in bone sealed in some impermeable clays or under travertine (calcareous rock) in cave deposits. Under such conditions bone of Pleistocene age may be found to have retained a high nitrogen content, whereas bone of this age from open sites would normally be expected to contain little or no nitrogen. The nitrogen method is most useful for distinguishing bones of different age when these are found in apparent stratigraphic association in the same deposit, and for bones too recent to be amenable to reliable fluorine or uranium analysis. Conversely, it can sometimes be used as a cross-check on these two methods for bones of supposed Pleistocene age.

Since the carbon/nitrogen ratio of the organic content of unburnt bone is known to be about 2.5:1, nitrogen analysis can be used to indicate the amount of bone needed for radiocarbon age measurement, without the need for direct analysis of organic carbon. This may be a particularly important consideration where valuable fossil material is to be sacrificed for radiocarbon dating, and in some radiocarbon laboratories nitrogen analysis is carried out on all samples of bone or antler as a routine procedure. Very small samples, a few tens of milligrams (removed by drilling with a dental burr), are needed for the estimation of nitrogen either by the classic micro-Kjeldahl method or by micro-combustion, so that most specimens can be sampled without serious damage.

The discovery that fossil teeth may contain appreciable amounts of fluorine was made in the early nineteenth century but received little notice until its principles were reinvestigated and extended to bone by the French mineralogist Adolphe Carnot in the 1890s.

62.13: *A generalized illustration of the relationship of the three methods for the relative dating of bone, showing how nitrogen decreases with the lapse of time as fluorine and (more slowly) uranium build up in buried antler, bone and teeth. These three methods cannot be used in a strictly chronometric way, as the differing conditions of the physico-chemical environment at each particular site may affect the rate at which changes in the concentration of these elements occur in buried material, but in favourable circumstances indications of value can be obtained for relative dating purposes or for assessing the contemporaneity of fossil material.*

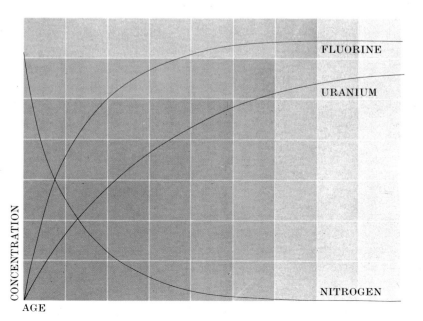

Although Carnot established the basis of the fluorine-dating method, his work too remained in obscurity until it was resurrected by K. P. Oakley in the late 1940s. Since then hundreds of samples of fossil antler, bone and teeth have been analysed for their fluorine content.[8] The principle of the method is that fluoride ions in solution in ground-water gradually replace the hydroxyl group of the mineral hydroxyapatite, of which antler, bone and teeth are largely composed.

The fluorapatite resulting from this exchange process contains amounts of fluorine up to a theoretical maximum of 3.8 per cent and is more stable chemically than the original hydroxyapatite, so that under all the conditions in which fossil skeletal material survives at all the change is irreversible. Antler, bone and dentine absorb fluorine uniformly, but the harder enamel of teeth usually proves more variable. The rate of uptake by the first three materials is such that the method cannot generally be applied to material more recent in age than early post-Pleistocene. Further, it cannot be successfully applied to material that has been buried under conditions of tropical weathering or where there is an unusually high concentration of fluorine in the environment, as in some volcanic regions, or (since the method depends on percolation of water) to fossil material sealed under travertine or recovered from situations where exceptionally arid conditions have long persisted.

Samples of about 100 milligrams are required for chemical analysis. To overcome the problem of the differing density of compact and cancellous (porous) tissue, and as a check on possible

contamination from mineral sources, the results are expressed as a fluorine/phosphate ratio (denoted by $100F/P205$) rather than simply as a percentage of fluorine. Fluorine may also be estimated from the measurement of line separation in the X-ray diffraction pattern of apatite. This may have advantages over the chemical method when a long series of samples is to be analysed, although a number of independent estimations using conventional chemical analysis are needed as a control.

One example of a particularly successful application of the fluorine method of relative dating is the confirmation of the recent date of the Piltdown hominoid remains compared with the antiquity of the extinct fauna from the same assemblage. Another is the indication given by fluorine analysis of the relatively recent date of the Galley Hill skeleton (later shown by radiocarbon to be of late Neolithic/early Bronze Age date) found in the same gravels as the truly Middle Pleistocene Swanscombe man (Figure 62.14).[9]

Relative dating by measurement of uranium also depends on the gradual accumulation of this element as a result of water percolation through the deposits in which skeletal remains have been buried. As with fluorine, the rate of accumulation of uranium in fossil antler, bone and teeth (probably by the replacement of calcium ions in hydroxyapatite) depends on both its abundance in the containing deposits and on the hydrological regime. In clays and limestones the natural concentration of uranium is low, but it is usually somewhat higher in sands and gravels. By contrast with the nitrogen and fluorine methods, in which chemical analysis is used for the estimation of the elements, the concentration of uranium is measured by radiometric assay, making direct use of its natural radioactivity, a property not possessed by nitrogen or fluorine. In fact, it is difficult to measure the amount of uranium in fossil material in any other way, since it is a rare element in nature and the concentration found in antler, bone or teeth is typically several orders of magnitude less than that of fluorine.

The concentration of uranium in fossil material can be estimated by counting beta particles and comparing the results with a uranium standard of known activity. A simple end-window Geiger counter, enclosed in a lead shield against natural radioactivity in the surrounding environment, can be used for this purpose. The small residual background count obtained from the counter in the absence of a sample must be subtracted from measurements of both the samples and the standard. Counting periods extend over a few hours or days, and the net count rate of each sample after subtraction of the background is expressed as equivalent parts per million of uranium oxide (e. U_3O_8 ppm). These measurements are, of course, subject to the same statistical laws as those that govern other radioactivity measurements, as explained in the section on radiocarbon dating. The concentrations of other natural radioactive elements such as ^{14}C and ^{40}K that may be present in the samples are too low to interfere with the measurement of uranium. Specimens small enough to fit inside the counting chamber can be assayed directly, although for more standardized results and for larger specimens it is necessary to drill out a sample

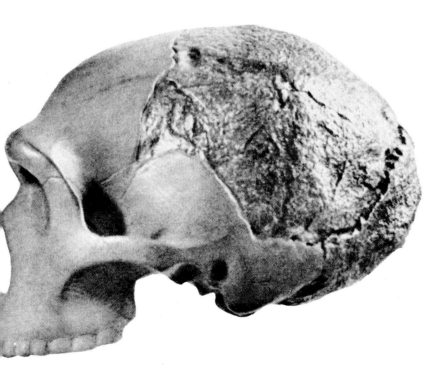

62.14: *Comparison of human skulls from two sites in England, Galley Hill (left) and Swanscombe (right; restored). The Galley Hill skull, found in 1888, came from the same terrace of the Thames as that in which the Swanscombe remains were later found. Relative dating based on fluorine and nitrogen analyses indicated that the Galley Hill skull and incomplete skeleton, though long held to be of primitive appearance (note, for example, the pronounced brow ridges), was a much later intrusive burial; radiocarbon dating of collagen extracted from the humerus confirmed that it was no more than 3600 years old. On the other hand, the Swanscombe skull, found nearby in the same stratigraphic horizon, is a most important human fossil of the Middle Pleistocene, transitional between* Homo erectus *and* Homo sapiens *and dating to the later part of the penultimate inter-glacial some 250 000 BP; the analysis showed that it had a high fluorine and uranium and a negligible nitrogen content.*

weighing about 1 gram.

The low natural level of uranium in most environments, and its slow accumulation in fossil material, limit the method to the Pleistocene, so that it cannot be applied to Postglacial remains. This means, however, that uranium measurements can be used to distinguish more recent intrusive remains from contemporaneous elements in Pleistocene deposits, particularly sands and gravels.

In summary, the principle use of these three methods of relative dating is to distinguish fossil antler, bone and teeth of Pleistocene or early post-Pleistocene age from more recent material. The three methods are valuable accessories to absolute methods of dating such as radiocarbon, as they are essentially non-destructive; damage to material of palaeontological importance to which they may be applied is minimal. This may be a particularly important consideration where human remains are concerned. For all three methods material of known age (preferably recent) from the same site is needed for comparison, since the concentration of nitrogen, fluorine and uranium in buried material depends very much on localized conditions. Similarly, the comparison of specimens of unknown and known age should be made between like materials; for example, bone should be compared with bone and teeth with teeth. Even then, because of such factors as individual variations in density or the state of preservation of these materials, a spread of results is normally to be expected. Pleistocene material can nevertheless readily be distinguished from recent material where no other indications exist, and material within a considerable range of intermediate age can be distinguished from both the former. The results can assume even greater significance when two or more of the methods can be applied to the same specimen in combination and the relative concentration of two or more of the elements compared. Under the conditions outlined above in which these methods can be usefully applied, specimens with high nitrogen and low fluorine and uranium are recent and those with low nitrogen and high fluorine and uranium are ancient, although the nitrogen content alone may not always be an infallible guide.

Summary

The most striking feature of the dating methods applicable to archaeology that have been discussed here is their diversity. This is evident from the wide range of physical and chemical principles and techniques upon which the different methods are based. Nevertheless, new methods of dating yet to be discovered may eventually broaden this already wide basis even further. The most important point, however, is not so much the breadth of the disciplines to which the different methods owe their origins as the way in which they can be marshalled to attack particular dating problems. From the support that the different methods offer each other accurate archaeological chronologies have emerged that could not have been arrived at in any other way. The logical extension of this already very considerable achievement is the further refinement of these time-scales for the whole span of human history, from the earliest times to the start of written records and beyond.

63.Comparative chronologies

In order to give an overall view of the developments discussed in earlier chapters of this book, the succession of major social and cultural phases is here presented in the form of charts. These charts are no substitute for the full accounts of regional developments provided in individual chapters and are not intended to include all, or even a majority, of the names that appear in those chapters. They are designed to give a visual impression of major developments and their interrelationships: the spread of human populations at the *erectus* and *sapiens* stages; the parallel inception of agriculture in different areas and the way in which this gave rise to native states and empires; and the contemporary development of new ways of life such as pastoralism and maritime adaptations. Although such diagrams necessarily involve arbitrary selection and juxtaposition, in conjunction with the global maps in Chapter 64 they are an essential aid in appreciating continuity and the relationships between different areas of the world.

The first three charts cover the entire world, and the following five are divided by major regions. A quasi-logarithmic scale has been used to accommodate the increasing rate of change in later periods: dates given are BP (before the present). The colours in the key below indicate the principal contrasts in economic and social development represented in each chart.

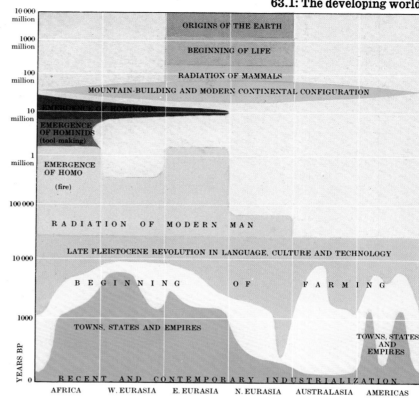

63.1: The developing world

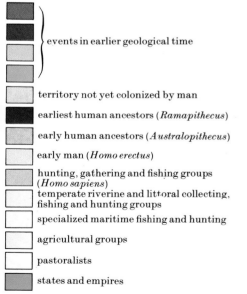

events in earlier geological time

territory not yet colonized by man

earliest human ancestors (*Ramapithecus*)

early human ancestors (*Australopithecus*)

early man (*Homo erectus*)

hunting, gathering and fishing groups (*Homo sapiens*)

temperate riverine and littoral collecting, fishing and hunting groups

specialized maritime fishing and hunting

agricultural groups

pastoralists

states and empires

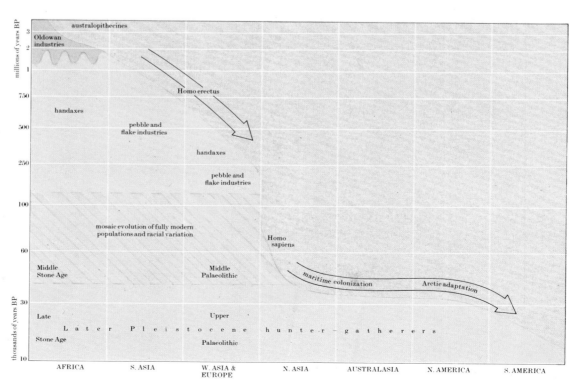

63.2: The Pleistocene world

63.3: The Holocene world

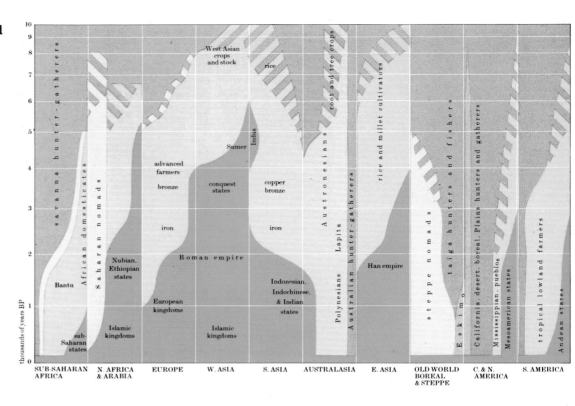

63.4: Western Asia and Europe

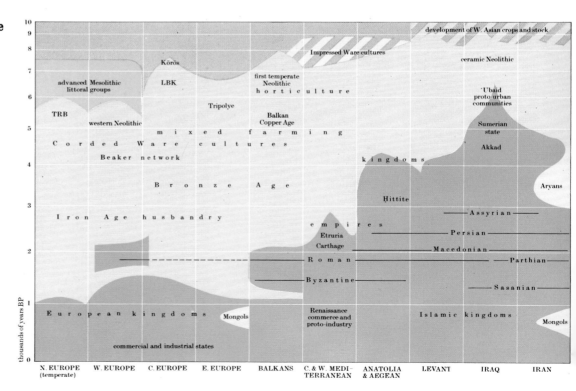

63.5: Africa

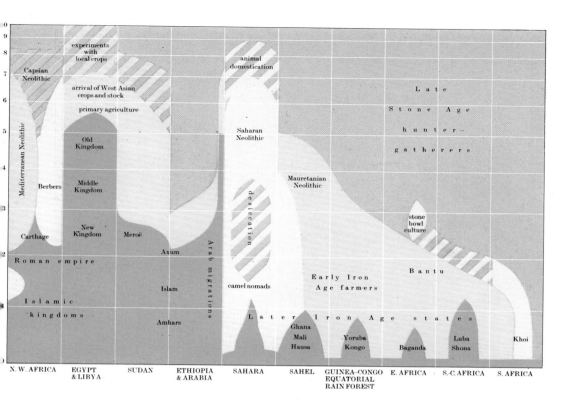

63.6: South Asia and Australasia

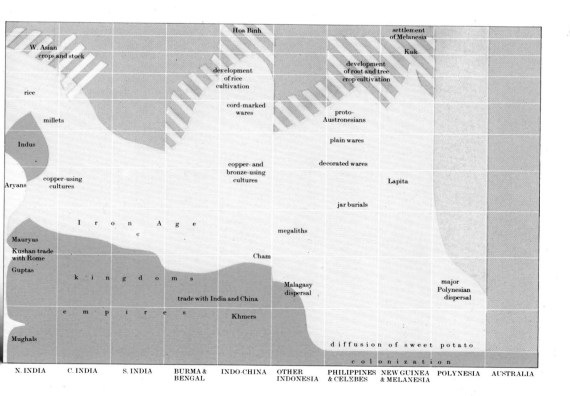

63.7: North and East Asia

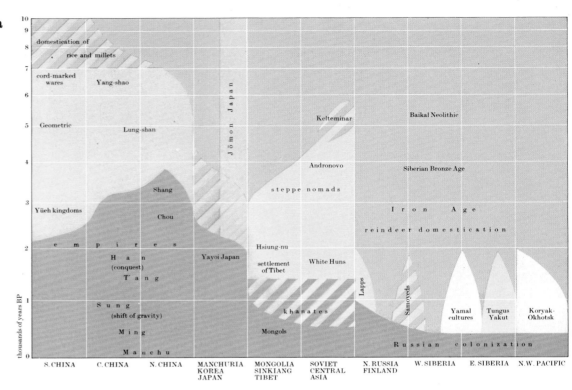

63.8: The Americas

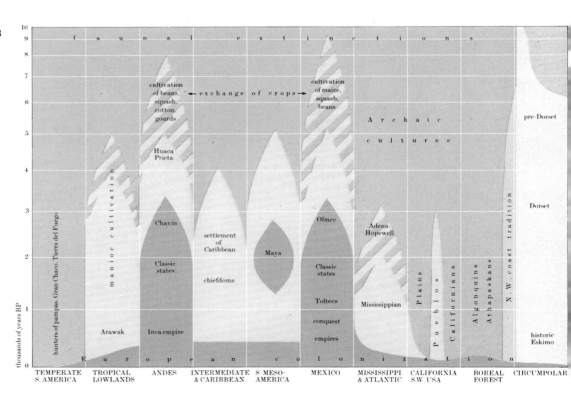

64.Chronological atlas

The following maps provide a global view of processes previously considered by region and area. The projection of the series of world maps has been chosen to emphasize zonal and regional relationships, and for each major period one or two subsidiary maps highlight elements in more detail. The colours of the world maps are a guide to the principal contrasts in economic and social development at each period (see key below), and the whole series illustrates the emergence of such patterns on a world scale.

The maps begin in the Pliocene, as ice caps were beginning to form. Further expansion of ice sheets in the Pleistocene led to a global lowering of sea levels, which exposed areas of the continental shelf; the spread of early human populations is shown against a background of fluctuating ice margins and temporary land bridges. The Postglacial saw intensive collecting and fishing economies and the development of agriculture. The spread of crops and stock produced new areas of farming and pastoralism, while states and empires were created in the urbanized heartlands. The continuing colonization of outlying regions took place as complex societies were appearing over an increasing area of the Earth's surface.

The map below provides a summary of the colonization of the world during the periods covered by the series of maps on the following pages and shows the spread of human populations from Africa to Asia and so to the New World and Australasia.

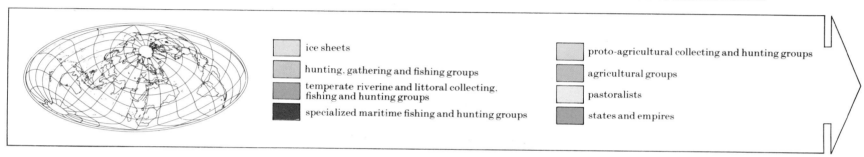

- ice sheets
- hunting, gathering and fishing groups
- temperate riverine and littoral collecting, fishing and hunting groups
- specialized maritime fishing and hunting groups
- proto-agricultural collecting and hunting groups
- agricultural groups
- pastoralists
- states and empires

64.1: The colonization of the world c. 3 000 000 BP to AD 1500

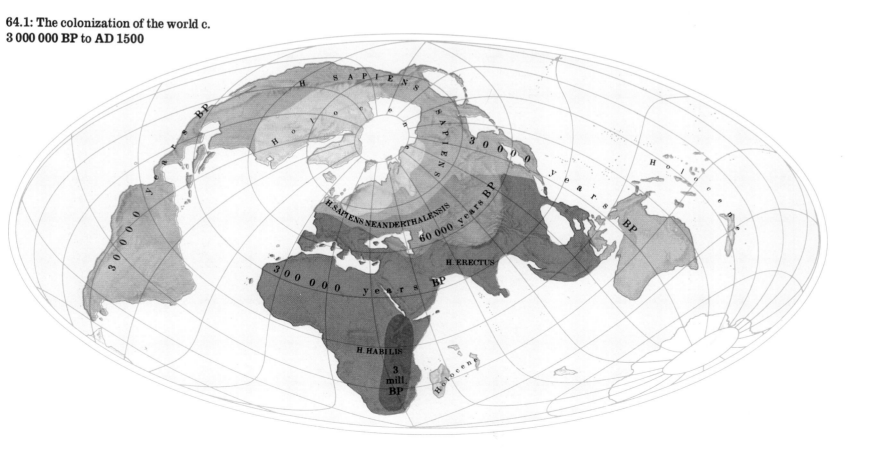

64.2: The world c. 3 million years BP

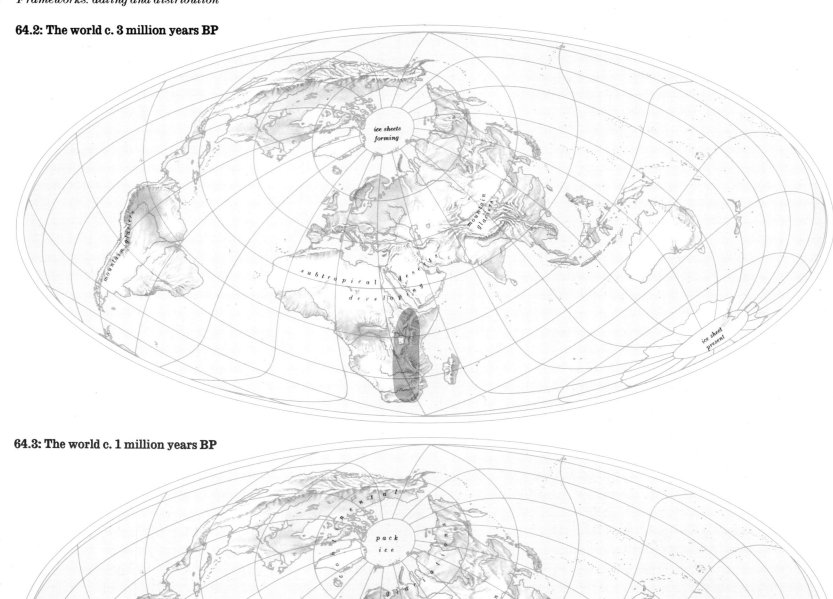

64.3: The world c. 1 million years BP

64.4: The world c. 300 000 BP

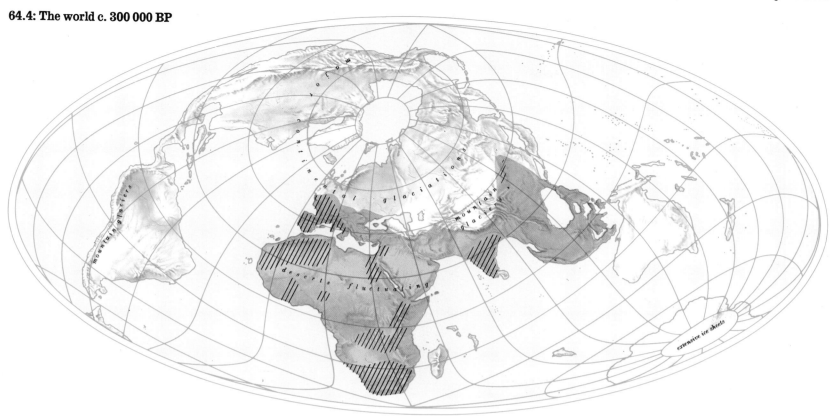

64.5: Early stone-tool industries

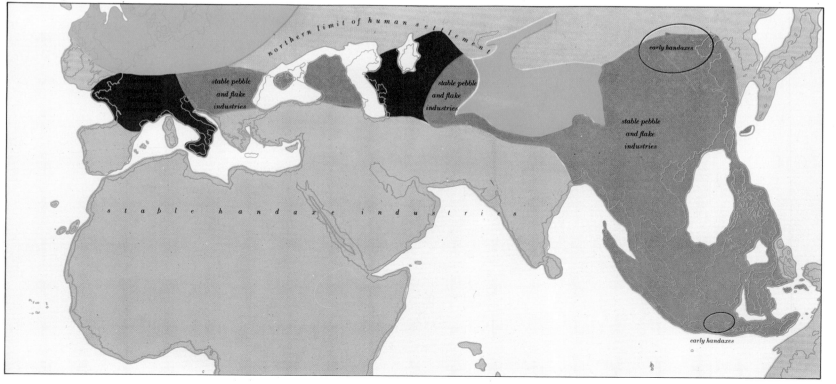

64.6: The world c. 60 000 BP

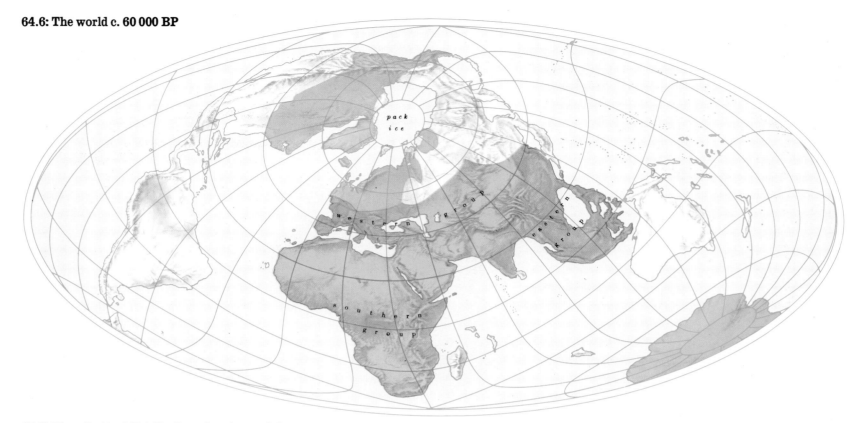

64.7: Hypothetical distribution of major racial groups

64.8: The world c. 30 000 BP

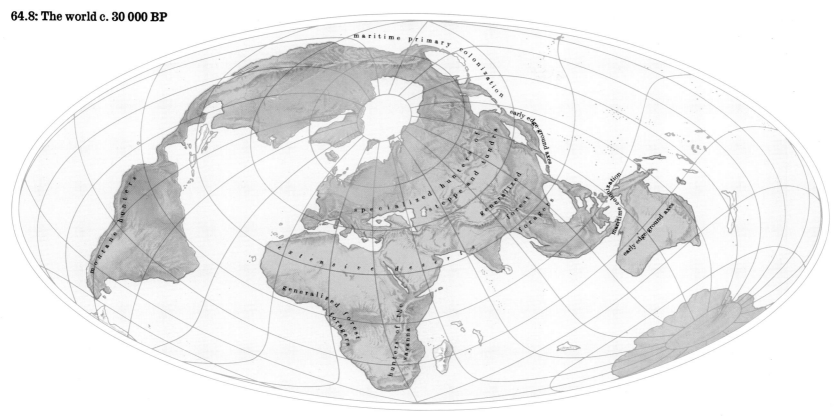

64.9: Circumpacific colonizations

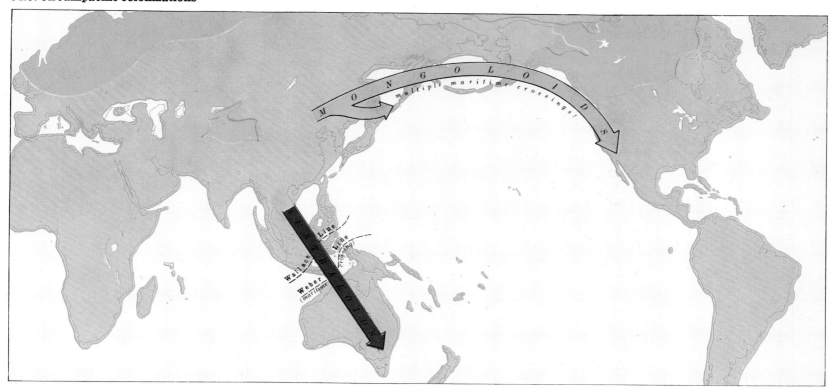

64.10: Holocene ecological opportunities

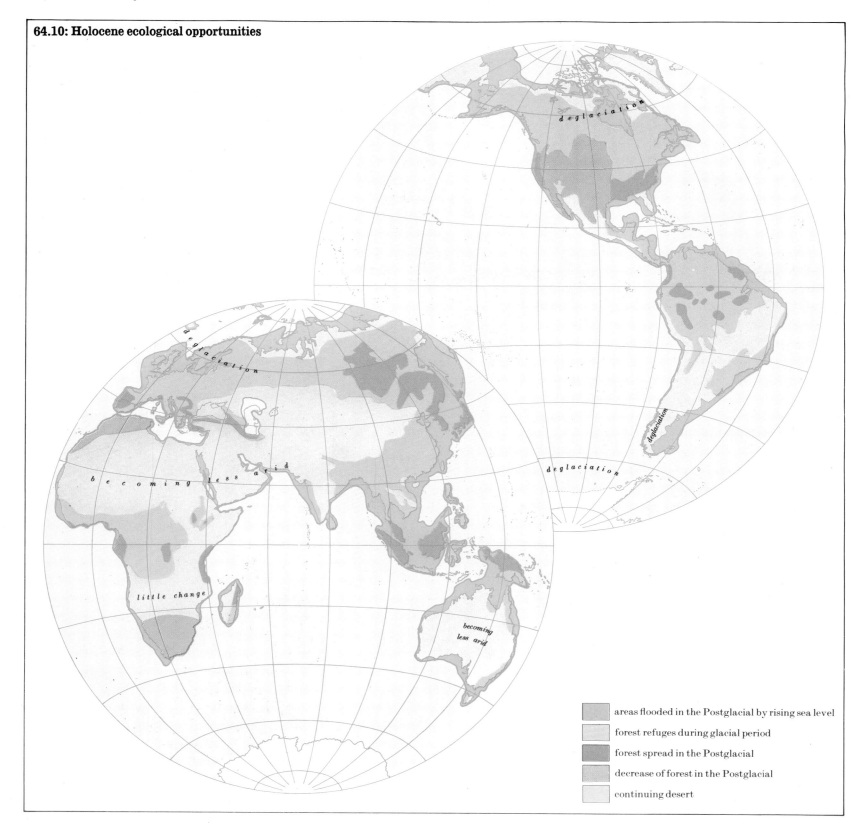

areas flooded in the Postglacial by rising sea level

forest refuges during glacial period

forest spread in the Postglacial

decrease of forest in the Postglacial

continuing desert

64.11: The world c. 10 000 BP

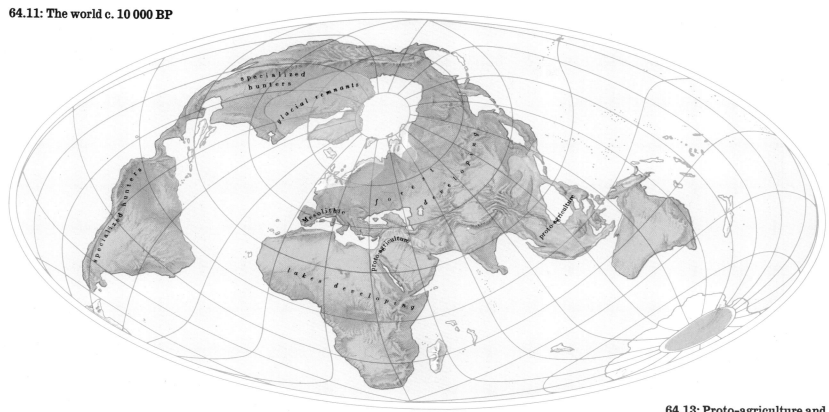

64.12: The emergence of agriculture in western Asia

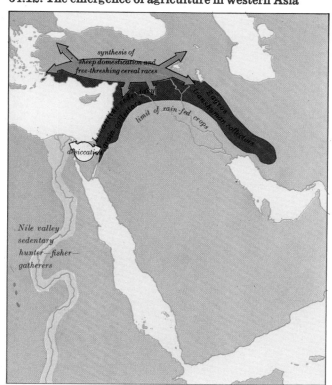

64.13: Proto-agriculture and maritime adaptation in south-east Asia

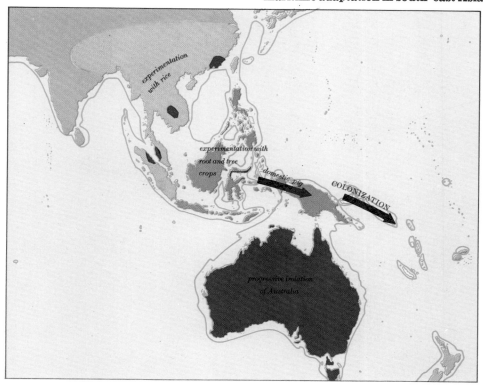

64.14: The world c. 6000 BP

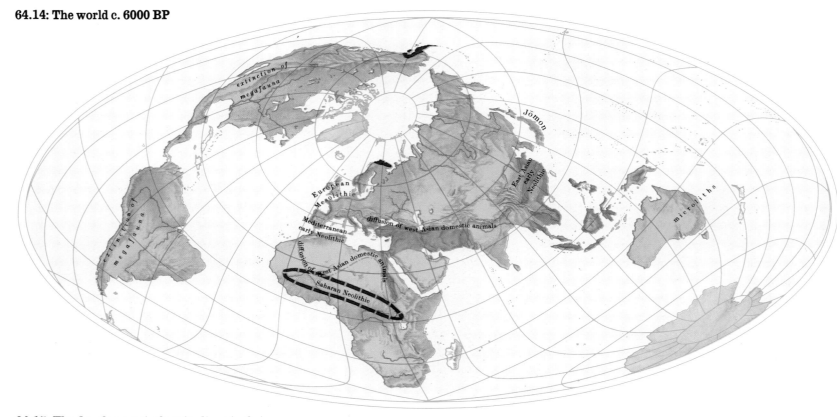

64.15: The development of agriculture in Asia

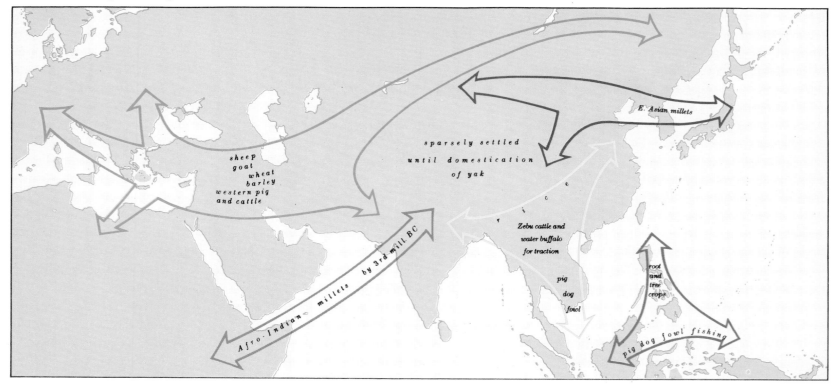

64.16: The world c. 4000 BC

64.17: The development of states in western Asia

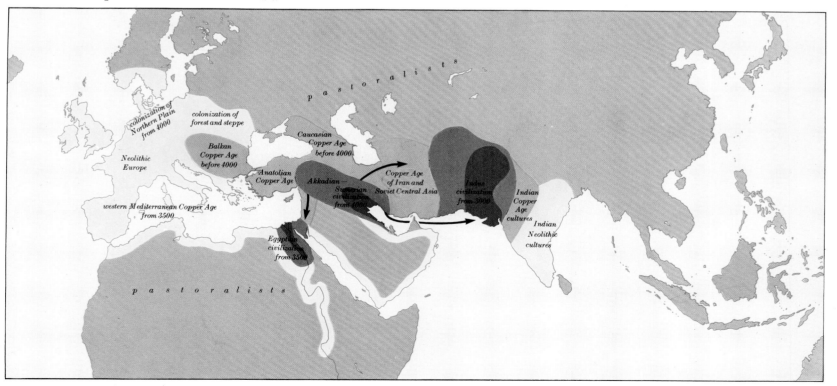

64.18: The world c. 2000 BC

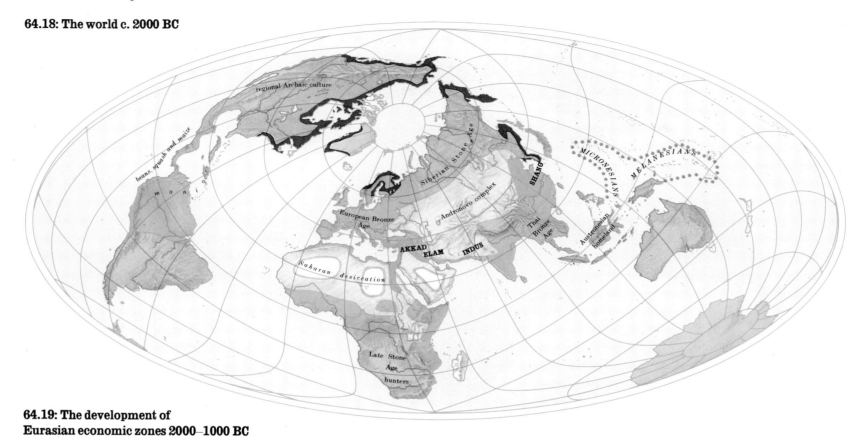

**64.19: The development of
Eurasian economic zones 2000–1000 BC**

64.20: The world c. 1000 BC

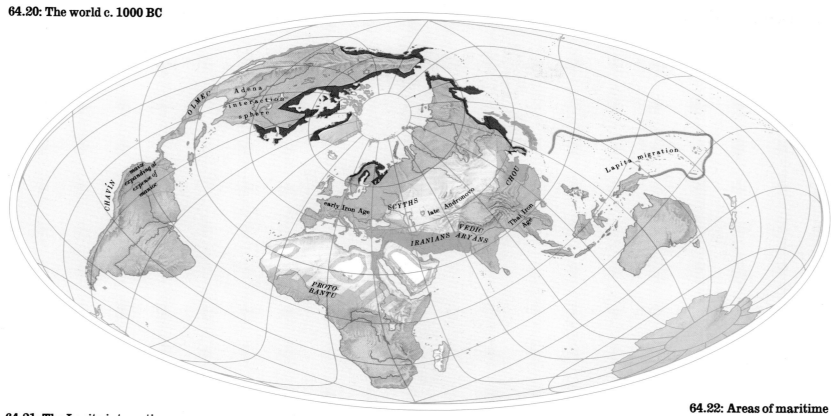

64.21: The Lapita interaction area

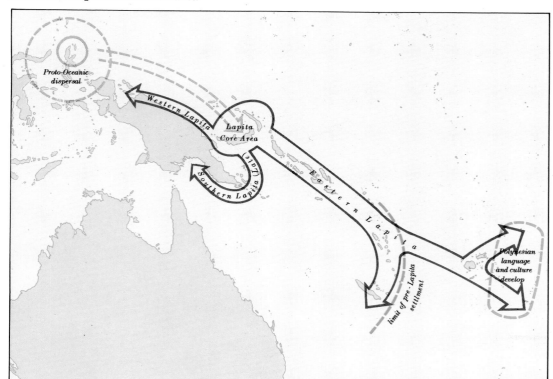

64.22: Areas of maritime adaptation in the circumpolar region

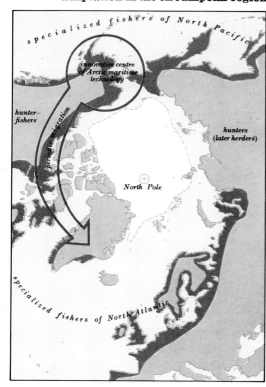

64.23: The world c. 500 BC

64.24: The origins of New World agriculture

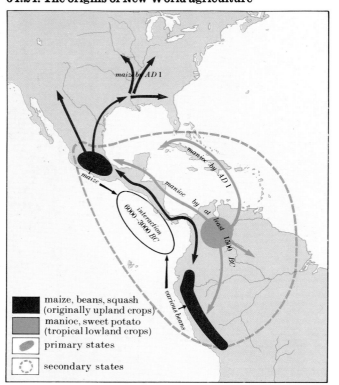

64.25: Eurasia in the first millennium BC

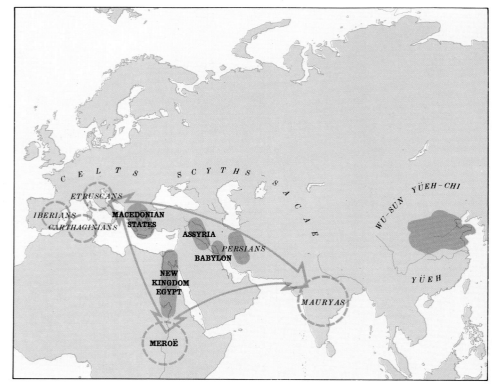

64.26: The world c. AD 1

64.27: Agricultural development in sub-Saharan Africa

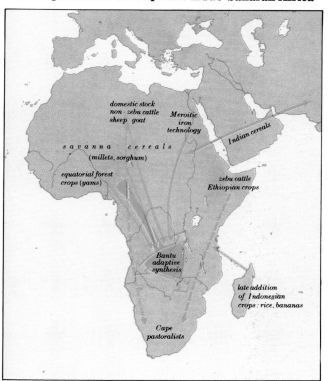

64.28: China in the later first millennium BC

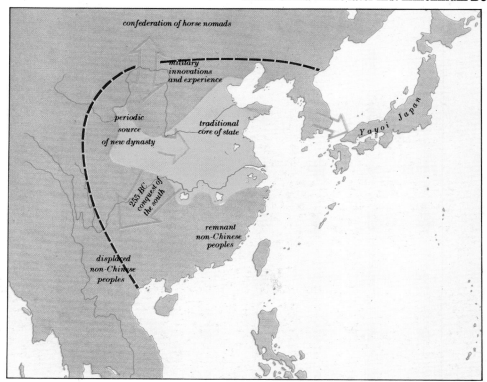

64.29: The world c. AD 500

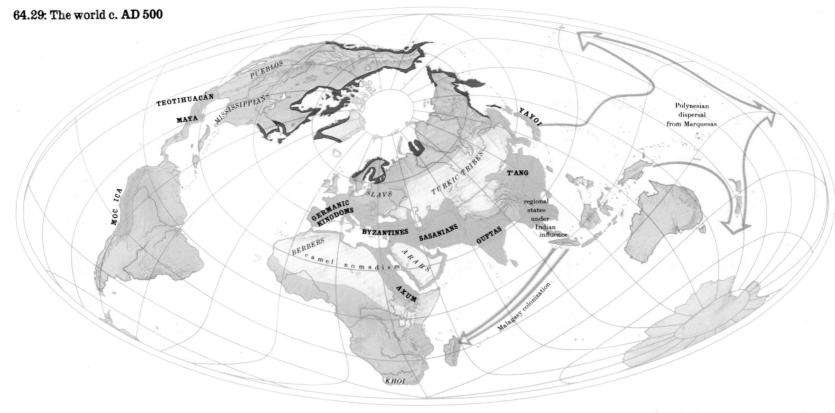

64.30: Polynesian dispersal to AD 500

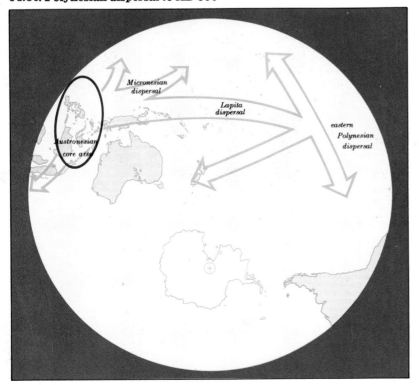

64.31: The Mediterranean economic axis

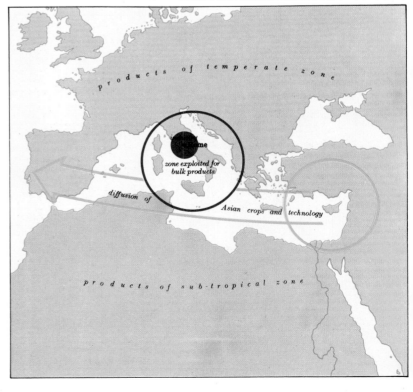

64.32: The world c. AD 1000

TOLTECS

TIAHUANACO

THULE (modern Eskimo migration)

VIKINGS

reindeer domestication

TUNGUS

MONGOLS MANCHU

MEDIEVAL STATES

KIEV PRINCIPATE

BULGARS

TURKS

KHAZARS

UIGHURS

KHITANS

Yak domestication

TIBETANS

SUNG

ALMORAVIDS

FATAMIDS

CALIPHATE

GHAZNAVIDS

MAGADHA

THAI

PAGAN

KHMER

GHANA

HAUSA

KANEM

DARFUR

LUNDA LUBA

BUSHMEN

64.33: South and East Asian states

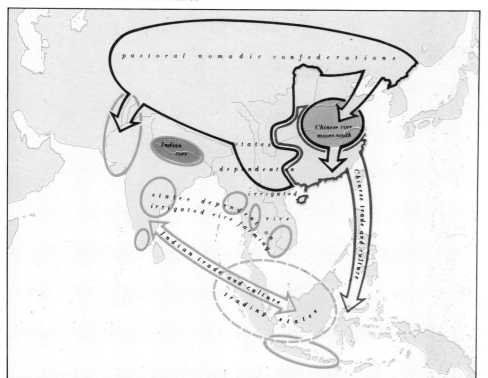

pastoral nomadic confederations

Chinese core moves south

Indian core

states

dependent on

irrigated

states dependent on irrigated rice farming

Chinese trade and culture

Indian trade and culture

trading states

64.34: The development of New World states

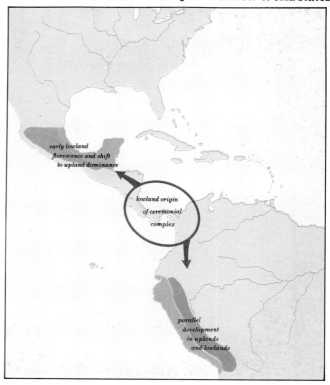

early lowland florescence and shift to upland dominance

lowland origin of ceremonial complex

parallel development in uplands and lowlands

64.35: The world c. AD 1500

CALIFORNIA
INDIANS
ATHAPASKANS

ALGONQUINS

YUKAGHIR

AZTEC
EMPIRE

CARIBS

ARAWAK

reindeer herders

MONGOL KHANATES

MING

MEDIEVAL
STATES

PAPUANS

INCA EMPIRE

TUPI-GUARANI

OTTOMAN
EMPIRE

TUAREG

ABORIGINES

MIDDLE-BELT AFRICAN STATES

AMHARA
GALLA
SOMALI

COPPERBELT
STATES

ZIMBABWE

64.36: The expansion of seaborne trade c. 1500

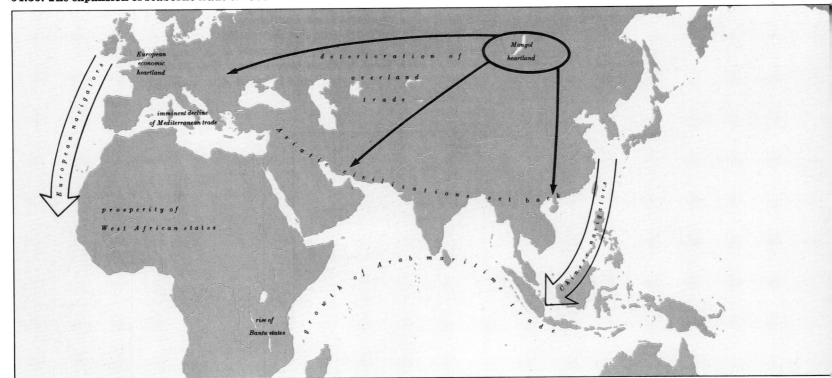

Bibliography

Chapter 1: The origins and growth of archaeology

1 Andrea Palladio, *Le Antichitá di Roma* (1554).
2 For example, J. Stuart and N. Revett, *Antiquities of Athens* (1762–1816) and *Antiquities of Ionia* (1769–97).
3 *Itinerarium Curiosum* (1724).
4 *Antiquities of Cornwall* (1754).
5 *Skandinaviska Nordens Orinvånare* (1838–43).
6 *Ledetraad til Nordisk Oldkyndighed*, which was translated by John Lubbock and appeared in English in 1848 under the title *A Guide to Northern Antiquities*.
7 *Danmarks Oldtid* (1842).
8 *Das Grabfeld von Hallstatt* (1868).
9 Oscar Montelius, *La civilisation primitive en Italie* (1895), *Die Chronologie der ältesten Bronzezeit in Norddeutschland und Scandinavien* (1898–1900).
10 *Die Altgermanische Tierornamentik* (1904).
11 'On the Principles of Classification Adopted in the Arrangement of His Anthropological Collection, by Colonel A. Lane-Fox', *Journal of the Anthropological Institute*, 4 (1875), a report on a paper given in 1874.
12 *Skandinavska Nordens Orinvånare*.
13 *Anthropology: An Introduction to the Study of Man and Civilization* (1881).
14 *Ursprung der Familie, des Privateigentums und des Staates* (1884).
15 *The Theory of the Earth* (1795).
16 *Principles of Geology* (1830–3).
17 *Précis d'un système hiéroglyphique* (1824).
18 M. Pope, *The Study of Decipherment* (London, 1975).
19 S. Lloyd, *Foundations in the Dust* (London, 1947).
20 Lloyd, *Foundations in the Dust*.
21 Sir Arthur Evans, *The Palace of Minos at Knossos* (London, 1921–35).
22 E. G. Squier and E. H. Davis, *Ancient Monuments of the Mississippi Valley* (1848).
23 A. Kidder, *Introduction to the Study of South-Western Archaeology* (New York, 1924).
24 H. Spinden, *Ancient Civilizations of Mexico and Central America* (1928).

Chapter 2: The revolution in archaeology

1 L. H. Morgan, *Ancient Society* (Cleveland, Ohio, 1877).
2 V. G. Childe, *Man Makes Himself* (London, 1936).
3 J. H. Steward, *Theory of Culture Change* (Urbana, Ill., 1955).
4 L. H. White, *The Evolution of Culture* (New York, 1959).
5 K. Polanyi, C. M. Arensberg and H. W. Pearson (eds), *Trade and Market in the Early Empires* (New York, 1957).
6 M. D. Sahlins, *Stone Age Economics* (Chicago/New York, 1972).
7 E. Service, *Social Organization: An Evolutionary Perspective* (New York, 1962).
8 W. W. Taylor, *A Study of Archaeology* (Menasha, Wis., 1948).
9 G. R. Willey, 'The Virú Valley Program in Northern Peru', *Acta Americana*, 4 (1946).
10 R. J. Braidwood and B. Howe, *Prehistoric Investigations in Iraqi Kurdistan*, Studies in Ancient Oriental Civilisation, 31 (Chicago, 1960).
11 J. G. D. Clark, *Excavations at Star Carr* (Cambridge, 1954).
12 L. R. Binford, *An Archaeological Perspective* (New York/London, 1972).
13 D. L. Clarke, *Analytical Archaeology* (London, 1968).
14 P. Haggett, *Locational Analysis in Human Geography* (London, 1965).
15 R. B. Lee and I. DeVore (eds), *Man the Hunter* (Chicago, 1968).
16 W. T. Sanders and B. J. Price, *Mesoamerica: The Evolution of a Civilisation* (New York, 1968).
17 K. V. Flannery, 'The Origins of Agriculture', *Annual Review of Anthropology*, 2 (1973).
18 E. S. Higgs, *Palaeoeconomy* (Cambridge, 1975).
19 J. E. Dixon, J. B. Cann and A. C. Renfrew, 'Obsidian and the Origins of Trade', *Scientific American*, March (1968).
20 S. Streuver and G. L. Houart, 'An Analysis of the Hopewell Interaction Sphere', in E. M. Wilmsen (ed.), *Social Exchange and Interaction*, Anthropological Papers of the University of Michigan Museum of Anthropology, 46 (Ann Arbor, Mich., 1972).

21 R. McC. Adams and H. J. Nissen, *The Uruk Countryside* (Chicago, 1972).
22 J. Friedman and M. J. Rowlands (eds), *The Evolution of Social Systems* (London, 1978).

Chapter 3: Investigation in the field

1 G. J. Gumerman, 'The Reconciliation of Theory and Method in Archaeology', in C. L. Redman (ed.), *Research and Theory in Current Archaeology* (New York, 1973).
2 L. R. Binford, 'A Consideration of Archaeological Research Design', *American Antiquity*, 29 (1964).
3 M. B. Schiffer and G. J. Gumerman (eds), *Conservation Archaeology* (New York, 1977).
4 For example, J. W. Mueller (ed.), *Sampling in Archaeology* (Tucson, Ariz., 1975); S. Plog, 'Relative Efficiencies of Sampling Techniques for Archaeological Surveys', in K. V. Flannery (ed.), *The Early Mesoamerican Village* (New York, 1976).
5 For further discussion of this subject, see F. T. Plog, 'Settlement Patterns and Social History', in M. Leaf (ed.), *Frontiers of Anthropology* (New York, 1974).
6 R. Palmer, 'Aerial Archaeology and Sampling', in J. F. Cherry, C. S. Gamble and S. J. Shennan (eds), *Sampling in Contemporary British Archaeology* (Oxford, 1978).
7 For instance, A. Clark, 'Archaeological Prospecting: A Progress Report', *Journal of Archaeological Science*, 2 (1975).
8 See, for example, A. J. Ammerman and M. W. Feldman, 'Replicated Collection of Site Surfaces', *American Antiquity*, 43 (1978).
9 Sir Mortimer Wheeler, *Archaeology from the Earth* (London, 1954).
10 For a detailed account of this approach, see P. Barker, *Techniques of Archaeological Excavation* (London, 1977).
11 See, for example, the contributions in Cherry, Gamble and Shennan, *Sampling in Contemporary British Archaeology*.
12 D. L. Clarke, 'A Provisional Model of an Iron Age Society and its Settlement System', in D. L. Clarke (ed.), *Models in Archaeology* (London, 1972).
13 M. B. Schiffer, *Behavioral Archeology* (New York, 1976).
14 See also R. A. Gould (ed.), *Explorations in Ethnoarchaeology* (Albuquerque, New Mexico, 1978).
15 R. Bradley, 'Prehistoric Field Systems in Britain and North-West Europe: A Review of some Recent Work', *World Archaeology*, 9 (1978).
16 D. H. Thomas, 'A Computer Simulation of Great Basin Shoshonean Subsistence and Settlement Patterns', in Clarke, *Models in Archaeology*.

Chapter 4: Analysis and interpretation

1 C. H. Waddington, *Tools for Thought* (St Albans, 1977).
2 D. L. Clarke, *Analytical Archaeology* (London, 1968); C. Renfrew, *The Emergence of Civilization* (London, 1972).
3 K. V. Flannery (ed.), *The Early Mesoamerican Village* (New York, 1976).
4 Renfrew, *The Emergence of Civilization*.
5 R. Thom, *Structural Stability and Morphogenesis* (Reading, Mass., 1975).
6 I. Hodder (ed.), *Simulation Studies in Archaeology* (Cambridge, 1978).
7 Clarke, *Analytical Archaeology*.
8 M. B. Schiffer, *Behavioral Archeology* (New York, 1976).
9 I. Hodder and C. Orton, *Spatial Analysis in Archaeology* (Cambridge, 1976).
10 Hodder and Orton, *Spatial Analysis in Archaeology*.
11 Flannery, *The Early Mesoamerican Village*.
12 D. L. Clarke, 'A Provisional Model of an Iron Age Society and its Settlement System', in D. L. Clarke (ed.), *Models in Archaeology* (London, 1972).
13 M. D. Sahlins, *Stone Age Economics* (Chicago, 1972); E. R. Service, *Primitive Social Organization* (New York, 1962); C. Smith, *Regional Analysis* (New York, 1976).
14 Flannery, *The Early Mesoamerican Village*; Renfrew, *The Emergence of Civilization*.
15 L. R. Binford, *An Archaeological Perspective* (New York/London, 1972).
16 J. Doran and F. Hodson, *Mathematics and Computers in Archaeology* (Edinburgh, 1975).
17 D. P. S. Peacock (ed.), *Pottery and Early Commerce* (London, 1977).
18 Hodder and Orton, *Spatial Analysis in Archaeology*.
19 G. Dalton, *Tribal and Peasant Economies* (New York, 1967).
20 G. Clark, 'Traffic in Stone Axe and Adze Blades', *Economic History Review*, 2nd series, 18 (1965).

21 Smith, *Regional Analysis*.
22 R. A. Gould (ed.), *Exploration in Ethnoarchaeology* (Albuquerque, New Mexico, 1978).

Chapter 5: Economic archaeology
1 A. C. Renfrew, *Before Civilization: The Radiocarbon Revolution and Prehistoric Europe* (London, 1973).
2 S. Payne, 'Partial Recovery and Sample Bias: The Results of some Sieving Experiments', in E. S. Higgs (ed.), *Papers in Economic Prehistory* (Cambridge, 1972).
3 H. N. Jarman, A. J. Legge and J. Charles, 'Retrieval of Plant Remains from Archaeological Sites by Froth Flotation', in Higgs, *Papers in Economic Prehistory*.
4 D. Grayson, 'Minimum Numbers and Sample Size in Vertebrate Faunal Analysis', *American Antiquity*, 43 (1978).
5 R. W. Dennell, 'The Economic Importance of Plant Resources Represented on Archaeological Sites', *Journal of Archaeological Science*, 3 (1976).
6 J. F. Cherry, C. S. Gamble and S. J. Shennan (eds), *Sampling in Contemporary British Archaeology* (Oxford, 1978).
7 E. S. Higgs and M. R. Jarman, 'The Origins of Agriculture: A Reconsideration', *Antiquity*, 43 (1969).
8 J. G. D. Clark, *World Prehistory in New Perspective*, 3rd edn (Cambridge, 1977).
9 W. van Zeist, 'On Macroscopic Traces of Food Plants in Southwestern Asia', *Philosophical Transactions of the Royal Society London*, B, 275 (1976).
10 D. Sturdy, 'Some Reindeer Economies in Prehistoric Europe', in E. S. Higgs (ed.), *Palaeoeconomy* (Cambridge, 1975).
11 G. N. Bailey, 'Shell Middens as Indicators of Post-Glacial Economies: A Territorial Perspective', in P. Mellars (ed.), *The Early Postglacial Settlement of Northern Europe* (London, 1978).
12 C. Vita-Finzi and E. S. Higgs, 'Prehistoric Economy in the Mount Carmel Area of Palestine: Site Catchment Analysis', *Proceedings of the Prehistorical Society*, 36 (1970).
13 P. J. White and J. F. O'Connell, 'Australian Prehistory: New Aspects of Prehistory', *Science*, 203 (1979).

Chapter 6: Historical archaeology
Classical authors whose works are cited may be consulted in Loeb Classical Library editions (London), which provide facing text and translation. References (for example, 6.3.5) are to book, chapter and line or section of the Greek or Latin text, a convention that is observed in most editions.
1 G. Alföldy, *Noricum* (London, 1974).
2 M. H. Crawford, 'Money and Exchange in the Roman World', *Journal of Roman Studies*, 60 (1970); C. M. Kraay, 'Hoards, Small Change and the Origin of Coinage', *Journal of Hellenic Studies*, 84 (1964).
3 Caesar, *de Bello Gallico*, 6.3.5.
4 Appian, *Celtica*, 12; Athenaeus, *Deipnosophists*, 4.3.7.
5 E. A. Thompson, *The Early Germans* (Oxford, 1965).
6 Diodorus, 5.26.3.
7 D. Nash, *Settlement and Coinage in Central Gaul c. 200–50 BC*, British Archaeological Reports, S 39 (Oxford, 1978).
8 Nash, *Settlement and Coinage in Central Gaul*.

Chapter 7: Recent advances and current trends
1 L. R. Binford and S. R. Binford, 'A Preliminary Study of Functional Variability in the Mousterian of Levallois Facies', *American Anthropologist*, 68 (1966); M. B. Schiffer, *Behavioral Archaeology* (New York, 1976).
2 L. R. Binford, General Introduction to L. R. Binford (ed.), *For Theory Building in Archaeology* (New York, 1977).
3 J. G. D. Clark, *World Prehistory in New Perspective*, 3rd edn (Cambridge, 1977).
4 T. K. Earle and J. E. Ericson (eds), *Exchange Systems in Prehistory* (New York, 1976).
5 D. P. S. Peacock (ed.), *Pottery and Early Commerce* (London, 1977).
6 J. W. Mueller (ed.), *Sampling in Archaeology* (Tucson, Ariz., 1975); J. F. Cherry, C. S. Gamble and S. J. Shennan (eds), *Sampling in Contemporary British Archaeology* (Oxford, 1978).
7 R. J. Braidwood and B. Howe, *Prehistoric Investigations in Iraqi Kurdistan*, Studies in Ancient Oriental Civilisation, 31 (Chicago, 1960).
8 F. Hole, K. V. Flannery and J. A. Neely, *Prehistory and Human Ecology of the Deh Luran Plain*, Memoirs of the Museum of Anthropology (Ann Arbor, Mich., 1969); F. Hole, *Studies in the Archaeological History of the Deh Luran Plain*, Memoirs of the Museum of Anthropology, University of Michigan, 9 (Ann Arbor, Mich., 1977).
9 R. S. MacNeish, 'Food Production and Village Life in the Tehuacán Valley, Mexico', *Archaeology*, 24 (1971); R. S. MacNeish, T. C. Patterson and D. L. Browman, *The Central Peruvian Interaction Sphere*, Papers of the Robert S. Peabody Foundation for Archaeology, 7 (Andover, Mass., 1975).
10 K. V. Flannery (ed.), *The Early Mesoamerican Village* (New York, 1976).
11 A. J. Ammerman and L. L. Cavalli-Sforza, 'The Wave of Advance Model for the Spread of Agriculture in Europe', in C. Renfrew and K. L. Cooke (eds), *Transformations: Mathematical Approaches to Culture Change* (New York, 1979).
12 J. Forrester, *Urban Dynamics* (Cambridge, Mass., 1969); K. L. Cooke and C. Renfrew, 'An Experiment in the Simulation of Culture Changes', in Renfrew and Cooke, *Transformations*.
13 S. B. Shantzis and W. W. Behrens, 'Population Control Mechanisms in a Primitive Agricultural Society', in D. L. Meadows and D. H. Meadows (eds), *Towards Global Equilibrium, Collected Papers* (Cambridge, Mass., 1972); D. H. Hosler, J. A. Sabloff and D. Runge, 'Simulation Model Development: A Case Study of the Classic Maya Civilization', in N. Hammond (ed.), *Social Processes in Maya Prehistory* (London, 1977).
14 J. Friedman and M. J. Rowlands, 'Towards an Epigenetic Model of the Evolution of "Civilisation"', in J. Friedman and M. J. Rowlands (eds), *The Evolution of Social Systems* (London, 1978).
15 C. Renfrew, 'Trajectory Discontinuity and Morphogenesis: The Implications of Catastrophe Theory for Archaeology', *American Antiquity*, 43 (1978).
16 K. Polanyi, C. M. Arensberg and H. W. Pearson (eds), *Trade and Market in the Early Empires* (New York, 1957).
17 C. S. Peebles and S. M. Kus, 'Some Archaeological Correlates of Ranked Societies', *American Antiquity*, 42 (1977).
18 H. H. Pattee (ed.), *Hierarchy Theory* (New York, 1976); G. A. Johnson, 'Information Sources and the Development of Decision Making Organisations', in C. L. Redman (ed.), *Social Archaeology: Beyond Subsistence and Dating* (New York, 1978).
19 K. V. Flannery, 'The Cultural Evolution of Civilisations', *Annual Review of Ecology and Systematics*, 3 (1972).

Chapter 8: Ice Age environments
1 G. J. Kukla, 'Pleistocene Land–Sea Correlations I: Europe', *Earth-Science Reviews*, 13 (1977); K. K. Turekian (ed.), *Late Cenozoic Glacial Ages* (New Haven, Conn., 1971).
2 A. B. Pittock, L. A. Frakes, D. Jenssen, J. A. Peterson and J. W. Zillman, *Climatic Change and Variability: A Southern Perspective* (Cambridge, 1978).
3 R. M. Cline and J. D. Hays, 'Investigation of Late Quaternary Paleoceanography and Paleoclimatology', *Geological Society Memoir No. 145* (1976).
4 K. W. Butzer and G. Ll. Isaac, *After the Australopithecines* (The Hague, 1976).
5 Butzer and Isaac, *After the Australopithecines*.
6 CLIMAP Project Members, 'The Surface of the Ice-Age Earth', *Science*, 191 (1976); Cline and Hays, 'Investigation of Late Quaternary Paleoceanography and Paleoclimatology'.
7 J. Gribben (ed.), *Climatic Change* (Cambridge, 1978); Pittock *et al.*, *Climatic Change and Variability*.
8 D. Q. Bowen, *Quaternary Geology* (Oxford, 1978).
9 Turekian, *Late Cenozoic Glacial Ages*.
10 Bowen, *Quaternary Geology*; K. W. Butzer, *Environment and Archaeology* (London, 1971); A. S. Goudie, *Environmental Change* (Oxford, 1977); F. W. Shotton (ed.), *British Quaternary Studies: Recent Advances* (Oxford, 1977).
11 Butzer and Isaac, *After the Australopithecines*.
12 G. M. Woollard, 'Grand Pile Peat Bog: A Continuous Pollen Record for the Last 140 000 Years', *Quaternary Research*, 9 (1978).
13 M. Sarnthein, 'Sand Deserts during Glacial Maximum and Climatic Optimum', *Nature*, 272 (1978).
14 Goudie, *Environmental Change*.
15 Cline and Hays, 'Investigation of Late Quaternary Paleoceanography and Paleoclimatology'.
16 Goudie, *Environmental Change*.

Chapter 9: Man and the primates
1 J. R. Napier and P. Napier, *A Handbook of Living Primates* (London, 1967);

E. Delson and P. Andrews, 'Evolution and Interrelationships of the Catarrhine Primates', in W. P. Luckett and F. S. Szalay (eds), *Phylogeny of the Primates: An Interdisciplinary Approach* (New York, 1975).

2 M. Goodman and R. E. Tashian, *Molecular Anthropology* (New York, 1976).

3 W. E. Le Gros Clark, *History of the Primates* (London, 1970).

4 D. R. Pilbeam, *The Ascent of Man* (New York, 1972).

5 P. Andrews, 'A Revision of the Miocene Hominoidea of East Africa', Geology Series, *Bulletin of the British Museum (Natural History)*, 30 (1978).

6 P. Andrews and J. A. H. Van Couvering, 'Palaeoenvironments in the East African Miocene', in F. S. Szalay (ed.), *Approaches to Primate Palaeobiology* (Basle, 1975).

Chapter 10: Early man

1 B. Cooke, 'Faunal Evidence for the Biotic Setting of Early African Hominids', in C. Jolly (ed.), *Early Hominids of Africa* (London, 1978); R. E. Moreau, 'The Distribution of Tropical African Birds as an Indicator of Past Climatic Changes', in F. C. Howell and F. Bourliere (eds), *African Ecology and Human Evolution* (Chicago, 1963).

2 B. H. Baker, P. A. Johr and L. A. J. Williams, 'Geology of the Eastern Rift System of Africa', Geological Society of America, Special Paper 136 (New York, 1972).

3 M. G. Leakey and R. E. F. Leakey (eds), *Koobi Fora Research Project*, Vol. 1: *The Fossil Hominids and an Introduction to their Context* (Oxford, 1978); M. D. Leakey, *Olduvai Gorge*, Vol. 3: *Excavations in Beds I and II, 1960–1963* (Cambridge, 1971); R. L. Hay, *Geology of the Olduvai Gorge* (Berkeley, Calif., 1976).

4 F. C. Howell, 'Overview of the Pliocene and Earlier Pleistocene of the Lower Omo Basin, Southern Ethiopia', in G. Ll. Isaac and E. R. McCown (eds), *Human Origins: Louis Leakey and the East African Evidence* (Menlo Park, Calif., 1976); Y. Coppens, F. C. Howell, G. Ll. Isaac and R. E. F. Leakey (eds), *Earliest Man and Environments in the Lake Rudolf Basin: Stratigraphy, Palaeoecology and Evolution* (Chicago, 1976).

5 D. C. Johanson *et al.*, 'Geological Framework of the Pliocene Hadar Formation (Afar, Ethiopia) with Notes on Palaeontology Including Hominids', in W. W. Bishop (ed.), *Geological Background to Fossil Man* (Edinburgh, 1978).

6 M. D. Leakey and R. L. Hay, 'Pliocene Footprints in the Laetolil Beds at Laetoli, Northern Tanzania', *Nature*, 278 (1979).

7 Cooke, 'Faunal Evidence for the Biotic Setting of Early African Hominids'.

8 H. M. McHenry, 'Fossils and the Mosaic Nature of Human Evolution', *Science*, 190 (1975).

9 P. V. Tobias, 'African Hominids: Dating and Phylogeny', in Isaac and McCown, *Human Origins*.

10 Leakey and Hay, 'Pliocene Footprints in the Laetolil Beds at Laetoli, Northern Tanzania'.

11 Johanson *et al.*, 'Geological Framework of the Pliocene Hadar Formation (Afar, Ethiopia)'.

12 D. C. Johanson and T. D. White, 'A Systematic Assessment of Early African Hominids', *Science*, 203 (1979).

13 R. E. F. Leakey, 'Evidence for an Advanced Plio/Pleistocene Hominid from East Rudolf, Kenya', *Nature*, 242 (1973).

14 A. Walker and R. E. F. Leakey, 'The Hominids of East Turkana', *Scientific American*, 239 (1978).

15 L. S. B. Leakey, P. V. Tobias and J. R. Napier, 'A New Species of the Genus *Homo* from the Olduvai Gorge', *Nature*, 202 (1964).

16 M. D. Leakey, 'The Early Hominids of Olduvai Gorge and the Laetolil Beds', in P. V. Tobias and Y. Coppens (eds), *The Oldest Hominids*, Colloque VI, IX Congrès de l'Union Internationale des Sciences Préhistoriques et Protohistoriques (Nice, 1976).

17 Walker and Leakey, 'The Hominids of East Turkana'.

18 H. Roche and J.-J. Tiercelin, 'Industries lithiques de la formation Plio-Pleistocen d'Hadar: campagne 1976', in R. E. F. Leakey and B. A. Ogot (eds), *Proceedings of the VIII Pan-African Congress of Prehistory and Quaternary Studies* (Nairobi, 1979).

19 J. Chavaillon, 'Evidence for the Technical Practices of Early Pleistocene Hominids', in Coppens *et al.*, *Earliest Man and Environments in Lake Rudolf Basin*; H. V. Merrick, 'Recent Archaeological Research in the Plio-Pleistocene Deposits of the Lower Omo Valley, Southwestern Ethiopia', in Isaac and McCown, *Human Origins*.

20 Leakey, *Olduvai Gorge*, Vol. 3: *Excavations in Beds I and II, 1960–1963*.

21 J. Chavaillon, 'Chronologie archéologique de Melka-Kunturé (Ethiopie)', in Leakey and Ogot, *Proceedings of the VIII Pan-African Congress of Prehistory and Quaternary Studies*; J. W. K. Harris and J. A. J. Gowlett, 'Evidence of Early Stone Industries at Chesowanja, Kenya', in Leakey and Ogot, *Proceedings of the VIII Pan-African Congress of Prehistory and Quaternary Studies*.

22 G. Ll. Isaac, 'The Activities of Early African Hominids: A Review of Archaeological Evidence from the Time Span Two and a Half to One Million Years Ago', in Isaac and McCown, *Human Origins*.

23 R. B. Lee, 'What Hunters Do for a Living, or How to Make Out on Scarce Resources', in R. B. Lee and I. DeVore (eds), *Man the Hunter* (Chicago, 1968).

24 V. M. Sarich, 'A Molecular Approach to the Question of Human Rights), in P. Dolhinow and V. M. Sarich (eds), *Background for Man* (Boston, Mass., 1971).

25 D. C. Johanson, 'Ethiopia Yields First "Family" of Early Man', *National Geographic*, December 1976.

26 A. E. Mann, *Paleodemographic Aspects of the South African Australopithecines* (Philadelphia, 1975).

27 G. Ll. Isaac, 'The Food-Sharing Behaviour of Protohuman Hominids', *Scientific American*, 238 (1978).

Chapter 11: The handaxe makers

1 L. H. Keeley, 'The Functions of Paleolithic Flint Tools', *Scientific American*, 237 (1977).

2 H. de Lumley, 'Une cabane acheuléenne dans la Grotte du Lazeret (Nice)', *Memoires de la Société Préhistorique Française*, No. 7 (1969).

3 H. de Lumley, 'Cultural Evolution in France in its Paleoecological Setting During the Middle Pleistocene', in K. W. Butzer and G. Ll. Isaac (eds), *After the Australopithecines* (The Hague, 1975).

4 G. Ll. Isaac, *Olorgesailie: Archaeological Studies of a Middle Pleistocene Lake Basin in Kenya* (Chicago, 1977).

5 M. D. Leakey, *Olduvai Gorge*, Vol. III: *Excavations in Beds I and II, 1960–63* (Cambridge, 1971).

6 P. Biberson, *Le paléolithique inférieur du Maroc atlantique* (Rabat, 1961).

7 H. J. Deacon, 'Demography, Subsistence and Culture During the Acheulian in Southern Africa', in Butzer and Isaac, *After the Australopithecines*.

8 J. D. Clark, *The Prehistory of Africa* (London, 1970); J. D. Clark, 'A Comparison of Late Acheulian Industries of Africa and the Middle East' in Butzer and Isaac, *After the Australopithecines*, G. Ll. Isaac, 'Stratigraphy and Cultural Patterns in East Africa During the Middle Ranges of Pleistocene Time', in Butzer and Isaac, *After the Australopithecines*.

9 F. Wendorf and A. E. Marks (eds), *Problems in Prehistory: North Africa and the Levant* (Dallas, Texas, 1975).

10 M. Kretzoi and L. Vértes, 'Upper Biharian (Intermindel) Pebble-Industry Occupation Site in Western Hungary', *Current Anthropology*, 6 (1965).

11 L. G. Freeman, 'Acheulian Sites and Stratigraphy in Iberia and the Maghreb', in Butzer and Isaac, *After the Australopithecines;* de Lumley, 'Cultural Evolution in France'; J. J. Wymer, *Lower Palaeolithic Archaeology in Britain, as Represented by the Thames Valley* (London, 1968).

12 G. Bosinski, *Die mittelpaläolithischen Funde im westlichen Mitteleuropa*, in H. Schwabedissen (ed.), *Fundamenta*, Reihe A, Band 4 (Cologne, 1967).

13 R. G. Klein, 'Chellean and Acheulian on the Territory of the Soviet Union: A Critical Review of the Evidence as Presented in the Literature', in J. D. Clark and F. C. Howell (eds), *Recent Studies in Paleoanthropology*, American Anthropologist Special Publication, 68 (1966).

14 H. D. Sankalia, *Prehistory and Protohistory of India and Pakistan* (Poona, 1974).

15 H. L. Movius, Jr, 'The Lower Palaeolithic Cultures of Southern and Eastern Asia', *Transactions of the American Philosophical Society*, 38 (1949).

Chapter 12: The development of human culture

1 K. Butzer, *Environment and Archaeology*, 2nd edn (Chicago, 1971); B. Frenzel, 'The Pleistocene Vegetation of Northern Eurasia', *Science*, 161 (1968); A. McIntyre *et al.*, 'Glacial North Atlantic 18 000 Years Ago: A CLIMAP Reconstruction', *Geological Society of America Memoir*, 145 (1976).

2 R. Klein, 'Middle Stone Age Man–Animal Relationships in Southern Africa: Evidence from Die Kelders and Klasies River Mouth', *Science*, 190 (1975).

3 R. Klein, 'The Mousterian of European Russia', *Proceedings of the Prehistoric Society*, XXXV (1969).

4   Klein, 'The Mousterian of European Russia'.
5   R. Klein, *Ice Age Hunters of the Ukraine* (Chicago, 1973).
6   J. D. Clark, *The Prehistory of Africa* (New York, 1970).
7   For example, J. D. Clark, *Kalambo Falls Prehistoric Site*, Vol. II (Cambridge, 1974).
8   R. Klein, 'The Ecology of Early Man in Southern Africa', *Science*, 197 (1977).
9   G.-J. Bartstra, *Contributions to the Study of the Paleolithic Padjitan Culture of Java (Indonesia)*, Pt I (Leyden, 1976); H. D. Sankalia, *Prehistory and Proto-history of India and Pakistan* (Poona, 1974); H. R. van Heekeren, *The Stone Age of Indonesia* (The Hague, 1972).
10   K. P. Oakley, *Frameworks for Dating Fossil Man*, 2nd edn (Chicago, 1968); J. M. Treistman, *The Prehistory of China* (New York, 1972).
11   K. C. Chang, *The Archaeology of Ancient China*, 3rd edn (New Haven, Conn., 1977); L. G. Freeman, 'Paleolithic Archeology and Paleoanthropology in China', in W. Howells and P. Tsuchitani (eds), *Paleoanthropology in the People's Republic of China* (Washington, DC, 1977).
12   F. Bordes, *The Old Stone Age* (New York, 1968).
13   J. González Echegaray and L. G. Freeman, *Vida y muerte en Cueva Morín* (Santander, 1978).
14   F. Bordes, 'Mousterian Cultures in France', *Science*, 134 (1961); Bordes, *The Old Stone Age*; F. Bordes, *A Tale of Two Caves* (New York, 1972).
15   P. Mellars, 'Sequence and Development of Mousterian Traditions in South-western France', *Nature*, 205 (1965).
16   L. R. Binford, 'Interassemblage Variability: The Mousterian and the "Functionalist" Argument', in C. Renfrew (ed.), *The Explanation of Culture Change: Models in Prehistory* (Pittsburgh, Pa., 1973); L. R. Binford and S. R. Binford, 'A Preliminary Analysis of Functional Variability in the Mousterian of Levallois Facies', *American Anthropologist*, 68 (1966); L. G. Freeman, 'The Nature of Mousterian Facies in Cantabrian Spain', *American Anthropologist*, 68 (1966).
17   H. de Lumley (ed.), *La préhistoire française*, 3 vols (Paris, 1976); González Echegaray and Freeman, *Vida y muerte en Cueva Morín*.
18   L. G. Freeman, 'An Analysis of some Occupation Floor Distributions from Earlier and Middle Paleolithic Sites in Spain', in L. G. Freeman (ed.), *Views of the Past* (The Hague, 1978); González Echegaray and Freeman, *Vida y muerte en Cueva Morín*.
19   Klein, 'Middle Stone Age Man–Animal Relationships in Southern Africa'; L. G. Freeman, 'The Significance of Mammalian Faunas from Paleolithic Occupations in Cantabrian Spain', *American Antiquity*, 38 (1973).
20   D. Garrod, L. Buxton, E. Smith and D. Bate, 'The Excavation of a Mousterian Rock Shelter at the Devil's Tower, Gibraltar', *Journal of the Royal Anthropological Institute*, 58 (1928); J. Waechter, 'The Excavation of Gorham's Cave, Gibraltar, 1951–54', *Bulletin of the Institute of Archaeology*, 4 (1964); T. P. Volman, 'Early Archaeological Evidence for Shellfish Collecting', *Science*, 201 (1978). Klein, 'Middle Stone Age Man–Animal Relationships in Southern Africa'.
21   González Echegaray and Freeman, *Vida y muerte en Cueva Morín*.
22   Klein, *Ice Age Hunters of the Ukraine*.
23   Bordes, *A Tale of Two Caves*.
24   de Lumley, *La préhistoire française*.
25   G. Camps, *Les civilisations préhistoriques de l'Afrique du Nord et du Sahara* (Paris, 1974).
26   L. Vértes, *Tata* (Budapest, 1964).
27   F. Harrold, 'A Survey and Formal Analysis of Middle and Upper Paleolithic Burials from Europe and Southwest Asia', unpublished Master's dissertation, University of Chicago.
28   B. Vandermeersch, 'Les sépultures néandertaliennes', in de Lumley, *La préhistoire française*.
29   P. Beaumont, H. de Villiers and J. Vogel, 'Modern Man in Sub-Saharan Africa prior to 49 000 Years BP: A Review and Evaluation with Particular Reference to Border Cave', *South African Journal of Science*, 74 (1978).
30   W. W. Howells, *Evolution of the genus* Homo (London, 1973).

Chapter 13: Later Pleistocene hunters
1   H. V. Vallois, 'The Social Life of Early Man: The Evidence of Skeletons', in S. L. Washburn (ed.), *The Social Life of Early Man* (Chicago, 1961).
2   R. G. Klein, *Ice Age Hunters of the Ukraine* (Chicago, 1973).
3   P. B. Beaumont, H. de Villiers and J. C. Vogel, 'Modern Man in Sub-Saharan Africa prior to 49 000 Years BP: A Review and Evaluation with Particular

Reference to Border Cave', *South African Journal of Science*, 74 (1978).
4   D. R. Brothwell, 'Upper Pleistocene Human Skull from Niah Caves, Sarawak', *Sarawak Museum Journal*, 9 (1960).
5   G. Clark, *The Stone Age Hunters* (London, 1967); D. de Sonneville-Bordes, 'The Upper Paleolithic: c. 33 000–10 000 BC', in S. Piggott, G. Daniel and C. McBurney (eds), *France Before the Romans* (London, 1973).
6   B. Klima, 'The First Ground Plan of an Upper Paleolithic Loess Settlement in Middle Europe and its Meaning', in R. J. Braidwood and G. R. Willey (eds), *Courses Toward Urban Life* (Chicago, 1962).
7   C. S. Chard, *Northeast Asia in Prehistory* (Madison, Wis., 1974).
8   R. G. Klein, 'Stone Age Exploitation of Animals in Southern Africa', *American Scientist*, 67 (1979).
9   W. E. Wendt, ' "Art Mobilier" from the Apollo 11 Cave, South West Africa: Africa's Oldest Works of Art', *South African Archaeological Bulletin*, 31 (1976).
10   R. G. Klein, 'The Pleistocene Prehistory of Siberia', *Quaternary Research*, 1 (1971); Yu. A. Mochanov, 'Stratigraphy and Absolute Chronology of the Paleolithic of Northeast Asia', in A. L. Bryan (ed.), *Early Man in America from a Circum-Pacific Perspective* (Edmonton, 1978).
11   R. G. Morlan, 'Early Man in Northern Yukon Territory: Perspectives as of 1977', in Bryan, *Early Man in America*.
12   P. S. Martin, 'Paleolithic Players on the American Stage: Man's Impact on the Late Pleistocene Megafauna', in J. D. Ives and G. R. Barry, *Arctic and Alpine Environments* (London, 1975).

Chapter 14: The arrival of man in Australia
1   J. B. Birdsell, 'The Recalibration of a Paradigm for the First Peopling of Greater Australia', in J. Allen, J. Golson and R. Jones (eds), *Sunda and Sahul: Prehistoric Studies in Southeast Asia, Melanesia and Australia* (London, 1977).
2   J. P. White and J. F. O'Connell, 'Australian Prehistory: New Aspects of Antiquity', *Science*, 203 (1979).
3   Birdsell, 'The Recalibration of a Paradigm for the First Peopling of Greater Australia'.
4   S. Bowdler, 'The Coastal Colonization of Australia', in Allen, Golson and Jones, *Sunda and Sahul*.
5   Bowdler, 'The Coastal Colonization of Australia'.
6   J. M. Bowler, 'Recent Developments in Reconstructing Late Quaternary Environments in Australia', in R. L. Kirk and A. G. Thorne (eds), *The Origin of the Australians* (Canberra, 1976).
7   J. M. Bowler, G. S. Hope, J. N. Jennings, G. Singh and D. Walker, 'Late Quaternary Climates of Australia and New Guinea', *Quaternary Research*, 6 (1976).
8   J. Chappell and B. G. Thom, 'Sea Levels and Coasts', in Allen, Golson and Jones, *Sunda and Sahul*.
9   R. Jones, 'Fire Stick Farming', *Australian Natural History*, 16 (1969).
10   Kirk and Thorne, *The Origin of the Australians*.

Chapter 15: The beginnings of agriculture in the Near East and Europe
1   H. E. Wright, 'Environmental Change and the Origin of Agriculture in the Old and New Worlds', in C. Reed (ed.), *The Origins of Agriculture* (The Hague, 1977).
2   W. C. Brice (ed.), *The Environmental History of the Near and Middle East since the Last Ice Age* (London, 1978).
3   D. Zohary, 'The Progenitors of Wheat and Barley in Relation to Domestication and Agricultural Dispersal in the Old World', in P. Ucko and G. Dimbleby (eds), *The Domestication and Exploitation of Plants and Animals* (London, 1969).
4   F. Wendorf and A. Marks, *Problems in Prehistory: North Africa and the Levant* (Dallas, Texas, 1975).
5   J. Cauvin, *Les premiers villages de Syrie–Palestine du IXème au VIIème millénaire avant JC* (Paris, 1978).
6   D. L. Clarke, 'Mesolithic Europe: The Economic Basis', in G. Sieveking, I. Longworth and K. Wilson (eds), *Problems in Economic and Social Archaeology* (London, 1976).
7   K. Kenyon, 'Ancient Jericho', in C. C. Lamberg-Karlovsky (ed.), *Old World Archaeology: Foundations of Civilization* (San Francisco, 1972); M. Hopf, 'Plant Remains and Early Farming in Jericho', in Ucko and Dimbleby, *The Domestication and Exploitation of Plants and Animals*.
8   Cauvin, *Les premiers villages de Syrie–Palestine*; A. T. M. Moore, 'The Excavations of Tell Abu Hureyra in Syria: A Preliminary Report', *Proceedings*

of the Prehistoric Society, 41 (1975).

9 J. Mellaart, *The Neolithic of the Near East* (London, 1975).
10 J. Dixon, J. R. Cann and A. C. Renfrew, 'Obsidian and the Origins of Trade', in Lamberg-Karlovsky, *Old World Archaeology*; K. V. Flannery, 'The Ecology of Early Food Production in Mesopotamia', *Science*, 147 (1965).
11 D. R. Theocharis (ed.), *Neolithic Greece* (Athens, 1973).
12 J. Mellaart, *Çatal Hüyük: A Neolithic Town in Anatolia* (London, 1967).
13 J. Oates and D. Oates, 'Early Irrigation Agriculture in Mesopotamia', in Sieveking *et al.*, *Problems in Economic and Social Archaeology*.
14 V. M. Masson and V. I. Sarianidi, *Turkmenia Before the Achaemenids* (London, 1972).
15 Theocharis, *Neolithic Greece*.
16 M. Gimbutas, *Neolithic Macedonia*, Monumenta Archaeologica: Institute of Archaeology (Los Angeles, 1976).
17 R. Tringham, *Hunters, Fishers and Farmers of Eastern Europe 6000–3000 BC* (London, 1971).

Chapter 16: The emergence of cities in the Near East

1 D. Oates and J. Oates, 'Early Irrigation Agriculture in Mesopotamia', in G. de G. Sieveking *et al.* (eds), *Problems in Economic and Social Archaeology* (London, 1976).
2 I. M. Diakonoff, 'Socio-Economic Classes in Babylonia and the Babylonian Concept of Social Stratification', *München Ak-Abh. phil.-hist.* (1972); A. L. Oppenheim, *Ancient Mesopotamia* (Chicago, 1964).
3 J. Oates, 'Religion and Ritual in Sixth-Millennium BC Mesopotamia', *World Archaeology*, 10 (1978).
4 J. Oates, T. E. Davidson, D. Kamilli and H. McKerrell, 'Seafaring Merchants of Ur?', *Antiquity*, 51 (1977).
5 G. A. Johnson, 'Locational Analysis and the Investigation of Uruk Local Exchange Systems', in J. A. Sabloff and C. C. Lamberg-Karlovsky (eds), *Ancient Civilization and Trade* (Albuquerque, New Mexico, 1975).
6 H. J. Nissen, 'Grabung in den Quadraten K/L XII in Uruk/Warka', *Baghdader Mitteilungen*, 5 (Berlin, 1970).
7 J. Oates, 'Mesopotamian Social Organization: Archaeological and Philological Evidence', in J. Friedman and M. J. Rowlands (eds), *The Evolution of Social Systems* (London, 1977).
8 R. Moorey, 'The Late Prehistoric Administrative Building at Jamdat Nasr', *Iraq*, 38 (1976).
9 T. Jacobsen, 'Early Political Development in Mesopotamia', *Zeitschrift für Assyriologie*, N.F. 18 (1957).
10 H. Weiss and T. C. Young, Jr, 'The Merchants of Susa', *Iran*, 13 (1975).
11 C. C. Lamberg-Karlovsky, 'Foreign Relations in the Third Millennium at Tepe Yahya', *Le Plateau Iranien et l'Asie Centrale des origines à la conquête islamique* (Paris, 1977).
12 D. Schmandt-Besserat, 'The Earliest Precursor of Writing', *Scientific American*, 238 (1978); P. Amiet, 'Glyptique susienne', *Mémoires de la Délégation Archéologique en Iran*, XLIII (Paris, 1972).
13 R. McC. Adams and H. J. Nissen, *The Uruk Countryside* (Chicago, 1972).

Chapter 17: Mesopotamia and Iran in the Bronze Age

1 S. N. Kramer, *The Sumerians: Their History, Culture and Character* (Chicago, 1963).
2 Robert McC. Adams, *Land Behind Baghdad: A History of Settlement on the Diyala Plains* (Chicago, 1965); Robert McC. Adams and J. Nissen, *The Uruk Countryside: The Natural Setting of Urban Societies* (Chicago, 1972).
3 I. J. Gelb, 'Thoughts about Ibla: A Preliminary Evaluation', *Syro-Mesopotamia Studies*, 1 (1977).
4 Robert McC. Adams, *The Evolution of Urban Society: Early Mesopotamia and Prehispanic Mexico* (Chicago, 1966); I. M. Diakonoff, 'Structure of Society and State in Early Dynastic Sumer', *Monographs of the Ancient Near East*, 1 (Los Angeles, 1974); A. Falkenstein, 'The Sumerian Temple City', *Monographs in History: Ancient Near East*, 1 (Los Angeles, 1974).
5 P. Matthiae, *Ebla: Un impero ritrovato* (Turin, 1977).
6 Gelb, 'Thoughts about Ibla'.
7 S. Lloyd, *The Archaeology of Mesopotamia: From the Old Stone Age to the Persian Conquest* (London, 1978); A. L. Oppenheim, *Ancient Mesopotamia: Portrait of a Dead Civilization* (Chicago, 1964).
8 H. Frankfort, *Cylinder Seals* (London, 1939); A. Moortgat, *The Art of Ancient Mesopotamia* (London, 1969).

9 Oppenheim, *Ancient Mesopotamia*.
10 C. L. Woolley, *Ur Excavations VI: The Buildings of the Third Dynasty* (London, 1974).
11 Lloyd, *The Archaeology of Mesopotamia*.
12 G. G. Cameron, *History of Early Iran* (Chicago, 1936); W. Hinz, 'Persia c. 2400–1800 BC', *Cambridge Ancient History*, Vol. I (2) (Cambridge, 1971).
13 L. Le Breton, 'The Early Period at Susa: Mesopotamian Relations', *Iraq*, 19 (1957).
14 S. N. Kramer, *Enmerkar and the Lord of Aratta* (Philadelphia, 1952).
15 C. C. Lamberg-Karlovsky, 'Third Millennium Modes of Exchange and Modes of Production', in J. A. Sabloff and C. C. Lamberg-Karlovsky (eds), *Ancient Civilization and Trade* (Albuquerque, New Mexico, 1975).
16 W. Hinz, 'Persia c. 1800–1500 BC', *Cambridge Ancient History*, Vol. II (1), (Cambridge, 1973).
17 R. H. Dyson, 'The Archaeological Evidence of the Second Millennium BC on the Persian Plateau', *Cambridge Ancient History*, Vol. II (1), (Cambridge, 1973).
18 K. Bittel, *Hattusha, the Capital of the Hittites* (Oxford, 1970).
19 O. R. Gurney, *The Hittites*, 2nd edn (London, 1954); J. G. MacQueen, *The Hittites and Their Contemporaries in Asia Minor* (London, 1975).
20 O. R. Gurney, *Some Aspects of Hittite Religion* (Oxford, 1977).
21 H. A. Hoffner, 'The Hittites and Hurrians', in D. J. Wiseman (ed.), *Peoples of Old Testament Times* (Oxford, 1973).
22 Oppenheim, *Ancient Mesopotamia*.
23 M. Liverani, 'The Amorites', in Wiseman, *Peoples of Old Testament Times*.
24 J.-R. Kupper, *Les Nomades en Mesopotamie au temps des rois de Mari* (Paris, 1957); M. B. Rowton, 'Dimorphic Structure and the Problem of the 'Apiru-'Ibrim', *Journal of Near Eastern Studies*, 35 (1976), and earlier articles cited there.
25 Adams, *Land Behind Baghdad*.
26 A. L. Oppenheim, 'The Seafaring Merchants of Ur', *Journal of the American Oriental Society*, 74 (1954).
27 W. F. Leemans, *Foreign Trade in the Old Babylonian Period as Revealed by Texts from Southern Mesopotamia* (Leyden, 1960).
28 Oppenheim, *Ancient Mesopotamia*; J. Oates, *Babylon* (London, 1979).
29 Lloyd, *The Archaeology of Mesopotamia*.
30 A. Parrot, *Mission archéologique de Mari II: Le Palais*, 3 vols (Paris, 1958–9).
31 J. A. Brinkman, *Materials and Studies for Kassite History*, Vol. I (Chicago, 1976).
32 Lloyd, *The Archaeology of Mesopotamia*.

Chapter 18: Egypt and the Levant in the Bronze Age

1 K. W. Butzer, *Early Hydraulic Civilization in Egypt* (Chicago, 1976); B. G. Trigger, *Beyond History: The Methods of Prehistory* (New York, 1968), ch. 6.
2 W. B. Emery, *Archaic Egypt* (Harmondsworth, 1961).
3 I. E. S. Edwards, *The Pyramids of Egypt* (New York, 1961); W. S. Smith, *The Art and Architecture of Ancient Egypt* (Baltimore, Md., 1958).
4 W. C. Hayes, *The Scepter of Egypt*, Vol. I, 2 vols (New York, 1953–9); I. E. S. Edwards, 'The Early Dynastic Period in Egypt', in I. E. S. Edwards, C. J. Gadd and N. G. L. Hammond (eds), *The Cambridge Ancient History*, Vol. V (1) Pt 2 (Cambridge, 1971), chs XX, XXI.
5 J. Van Seters, *The Hyksos* (New Haven, Conn., 1966).
6 Hayes, *The Scepter of Egypt*; G. Steindorff and K. C. Seele, *When Egypt Ruled the East* (Chicago, 1942).

Chapter 19: The Aegean and western Anatolia in the Bronze Age

1 C. W. Blegen, *Troy and the Trojans* (London, 1963).
2 C. Renfrew, *The Emergence of Civilization: The Cyclades and the Aegean in the Third Millennium BC* (London, 1972).
3 K. Branigan, *Aegean Metalwork of the Early and Middle Bronze Age* (Oxford, 1974).
4 K. Branigan, *The Tombs of Mesara* (London, 1970).
5 J. L. Caskey, 'The Early Helladic Period in the Argolid', *Hesperia*, 29 (1960).
6 P. Warren, *The Aegean Civilizations* (Oxford, 1975).
7 J. W. Graham, *The Palaces of Crete*, reprint (Priceton, N. J., 1969).
8 G. Cadogan, *Palaces of Minoan Crete* (London, 1976).
9 M. P. Nilsson, *The Minoan–Mycenean Religion and its Survival in Greek Religion*, 2nd edn (Lund, 1950); B. Rutkowski, *Cult Places in the Aegean World* (Warsaw, 1972).

10 S. Marinatos and M. Hirmer, *Krete, Thera und das mykenische Hellas*, 2nd edn (Munich, 1973).
11 O. T. P. K. Dickinson, *The Origins of Mycenaean Civilization* (Göteborg, 1977).
12 G. Mylonas, *Mycenae and the Mycenaean Age* (Princeton, N. J., 1966).
13 J. Chadwick, *The Mycenaean World* (Cambridge, 1976).

Chapter 20: Early agricultural communities in Europe

1 A. G. Sherratt, 'Resources, Technology and Trade: An Essay in Early European Metallurgy', in G. Sieveking, I. Longworth and K. Wilson (eds), *Problems in Economic and Social Archaeology* (London, 1976).
2 A. G. Sherratt, 'Plough and Pastoralism: Aspects of the Secondary Products Revolution', in N. Hammond, I. Hodder and G. Isaac (eds), *Patterns in the Past* (David Clarke Memorial Volume) (Cambridge, 1979).
3 B. Sielmann, 'Die Frühneolithische Besiedlung Mitteleuropas', in J. Lüning (ed.), *Die Anfänge des Neolithikums vom Orient bis Nordeuropa* (Cologne/Vienna, 1972).
4 J. Guilaine, *Premiers bergers et paysans de l'Occident Méditerranéen* (The Hague/Paris, 1976).
5 H. Todorova, *The Eneolithic in Bulgaria*, British Archaeological Reports, 1 (Oxford, 1978).
6 A. C. Renfrew, 'The Autonomy of the South-East European Copper Age', *Proceedings of the Prehistoric Society*, 35 (1969).
7 B. Gramsch, 'Zum Problem des Uebergangs vom Mesolithikum zum Neolithikum', in F. Schlette (ed.), *Evolution und Revolution im Alten Orient und in Europa* (Berlin, 1971).
8 A. G. Sherratt, 'Plough and Pastoralism'.
9 A. C. Renfrew, *The Emergence of Civilization: The Cyclades and the Aegean in the Third Millennium BC* (London, 1972).
10 J. Kruk, *Studia Osadnicze nad Neolitem Wyżyn Lessowych* (Warsaw, 1973).
11 H. Behrens, *Die Jungsteinzeit im Mittelelbe-Saale-Gebiet* (Berlin, 1973).
12 *Glockenbeckersymposion Oberried 1974* (Bussum-Haarlem, 1976).
13 M. Gimbutas, *Bronze Age Cultures in Central and Eastern Europe* (The Hague/Paris, 1965).
14 J. M. Coles and A. Harding, *The Bronze Age in Europe* (London, 1979).

Chapter 21: Agricultural origins in East Asia

1 Kwang-chih Chang, 'The Beginnings of Agriculture in the Far East', *Antiquity*, 44 (1970).
2 I. C. Glover, 'The Hoabinhian: Hunter-Gatherers or Early Agriculturalists in South-East Asia?', in J. V. S. Megaw (ed.), *Hunters, Gatherers and First Farmers Beyond Europe* (Leicester, 1977).
3 C. S. Chard, *Northeast Asia in Prehistory* (Madison, Wis., 1974).
4 Chard, *Northeast Asia in Prehistory*.
5 Kwang-chih Chang, *The Archaeology of Ancient China*, 3rd edn (New Haven, Conn., 1977).
6 Chang, *The Archaeology of Ancient China*.
7 W. Watson, *Cultural Frontiers in Ancient East Asia* (Edinburgh, 1971).
8 Chang, *The Archaeology of Ancient China*.
9 Glover, 'The Hoabinhian'.
10 C. F. Gorman, 'The Hoabinhian and After – Subsistence Patterns in Southeast Asia During the Late Pleistocene and Early Recent Periods', *World Archaeology*, 2 (1971).
11 Chang, *The Archaeology of Ancient China*.
12 Nguyen Phuc Long, 'Les nouvelles recherches archéologiques au Vietnam', *Arts Asiatiques* (special issue), XXXI (1975).
13 H. Th. Verstappen, 'On Palaeoclimates and Landform Development in Malesia', *Modern Quaternary Research in Southeast Asia*, 1 (1975).
14 H. R. van Heekeren, *The Stone Age of Indonesia*, 2nd edn (The Hague, 1972).
15 van Heekeren, *The Stone Age of Indonesia*.

Chapter 22: Early agriculture and the development of towns in India

1 F. R. Allchin and D. K. Chakrabarti (eds), *A Source Book of Indian Archaeology*, Vol. I (Delhi, 1979).
2 W. A. Fairservice, *The Roots of Ancient India* (Chicago, 1975); S. P. Gupta, 'Baluchistan and Afghanistan: Refuge Areas or Nuclear Zones?', in D. P. Agrawal and D. K. Chakrabarti (eds), *Essays in Indian Protohistory* (Delhi, 1979).
3 M. R. Mughal, *Present State of Research on the Indus Valley Civilization* (Karachi, 1973).

4 D. K. Chakrabarti, 'Size of the Harappan Settlements', in Agrawal and Chakrabarti, *Essays in Indian Protohistory*.
5 B. B. Lal, 'Kalibangan and the Indus Civilization', in Agrawal and Chakrabarti, *Essays in Indian Protohistory*; Sir Mortimer Wheeler, *The Indus Civilization* (Cambridge, 1968).
6 D. P. Agrawal, *The Copper-Bronze Age in India* (Delhi, 1971).
7 G. F. Dales, 'The Mythical Massacre at Mohenjodaro', *Expedition*, 6 (1964).
8 B. Allchin and R. Allchin, *The Birth of Indian Civilization* (Harmondsworth, 1968); H. D. Sankalia, *Prehistory and Protohistory of India and Pakistan* (Poona, 1974).
9 D. K. Chakrabarti, 'The Beginning of Iron in India', *Antiquity*, 50 (1976).

Chapter 23: East Asia in the Bronze Age

1 N. Barnard, 'The First Radiocarbon Dates from China: Revised and Enlarged', *Monographs on Far Eastern History*, 8 (Canberra) (1975).
2 Kwang-chih Chang, *The Archaeology of Ancient China*, 3rd edn (New Haven, Conn., 1977); Ping-ti Ho, *The Cradle of the East* (Hong Kong/Chicago, 1975).
3 P. Wheatley, *The Pivot of the Four Quarters* (Chicago, 1971).
4 Ho, *The Cradle of the East*.
5 N. Barnard and S. Tamotsu, *Metallurgical Remains of Ancient China* (Tokyo, 1975).
6 Wheatley, *The Pivot of the Four Quarters*.
7 W. Meacham, 'Continuity and Local Evolution in the Neolithic of South China', *Current Anthropology*, 18 (1977).
8 M. von Dewall, 'The Tien Culture of South-West China', *Antiquity*, 40 (1967).
9 D. Bayard, 'The Chronology of Prehistoric Metallurgy in North-East Thailand: Silābhūmi or Samṛddhābhūmi?', in R. B. Smith and W. Watson (eds), *Early South-East Asia* (Oxford, 1979).
10 C. Gorman and P. Charoenwongsa, 'Ban Chiang: A Mosaic of Impressions from the First Two Years', *Expedition*, 18 (1976).
11 P. Bellwood, *Man's Conquest of the Pacific: The Prehistory of Southeast Asia and Oceania* (Auckland, 1978).

Chapter 24: The final stages of hunting and gathering in Africa

1 R. R. Inskeep, *The Peopling of Southern Africa* (Cape Town, 1978).
2 H. J. Deacon, *Where Hunters Gathered*, South African Archaeological Society Monographs, No. 1 (Claremont, Cape, 1976).
3 Deacon, *Where Hunters Gathered*.
4 T. Shaw, *Nigeria: Its Archaeology and Early History* (London, 1978).
5 J. E. G. Sutton, 'The Aquatic Civilization of Middle Africa', *Journal of African History*, 15 (1974).
6 J. Woodburn, *Hunters and Gatherers: The Material Culture of the Nomadic Hadza* (London, 1970).
7 M. G. Bicchieri (ed.), *Hunters and Gatherers Today* (New York, 1972).
8 R. Story, 'Some Plants used by the Bushmen in Obtaining Food and Water', *Botanical Survey Memoir*, 30 (Pretoria, 1958).
9 J. E. Parkington, 'Seasonal Mobility in the Late Stone Age', *African Studies*, 31 (1972).

Chapter 25: Agricultural origins in Africa

1 J. V. S. Megaw (ed.), *Hunters, Gatherers and First Farmers Beyond Europe* (Leicester, 1977); J. R. Harlan, J. M. J. de Wet and A. B. L. Stemler (eds), *Origins of African Plant Domestication* (The Hague, 1976).
2 G. P. Murdoch, *Africa: Its Peoples and Their Culture History* (New York, 1959).
3 D. W. Phillipson, *The Later Prehistory of Eastern and Southern Africa* (London, 1977).
4 H. Epstein, *The Origin of the Domestic Animals of Africa*, 2 vols (New York, 1971).

Chapter 26: The Assyrian empire

1 M. T. Larsen, *The Old Assyrian City-State and its Colonies* (Copenhagen, 1976).
2 J. N. Postgate, 'Some Remarks on Conditions in the Assyrian Countryside', *Journal of the Economic and Social History of the Orient*, 17 (1974).
3 J. N. Postgate, *Taxation and Conscription in the Assyrian Empire* (Rome, 1974); J. E. Reade, 'The Neo-Assyrian Court and Army – Evidence from the Sculptures', *Iraq*, 34 (1972).
4 T. Jacobsen and S. Lloyd, *Sennacherib's Aqueduct at Jerwan* (Chicago, 1935); David Oates, *Studies in the Ancient History of Northern Iran* (London, 1968); J. E. Reade, 'Studies in Assyrian Geography', *Revue d'Assyriologie*, 72 (1978).

5 M. E. L. Mallowan, *Nimrud and its Remains* (London, 1966).
6 G. Loud and C. B. Altman, *Khorsabad*, Vols I, II (Chicago, 1936, 1938).
7 W. Andrae, *Das wiedererstandene Assur*, 2nd edn (Leipzig, 1977).
8 R. D. Barnett and W. Forman, *Assyrian Palace Reliefs* (London, n.d.).
9 A. Parrot, *Assur* (Paris, 1961).
10 J. N. Postgate, 'The Economic Structure of the Assyrian Empire', in M. T. Larsen (ed.), *Power and Propaganda: A Symposium on Ancient Empires* (Copenhagen, 1979).

Chapter 27: Late Period Egypt and Nubia
1 Herodotus, II, 77.
2 K. A. Kitchen, *The Third Intermediate Period in Egypt* (Warminster, 1973); Sir Alan Gardiner, *Egypt of the Pharaohs* (Oxford, 1961), chs XII, XIII; W. S. Smith, *The Art and Architecture of Ancient Egypt* (Baltimore, 1958); J. Boardman, *The Greeks Overseas* (Harmondsworth, 1964).
3 W. Y. Adams, *Nubia: Corridor to Africa* (Princeton, N. J., 1977), ch. 10.

Chapter 28: The Levant in the early first millennium BC
1 M. Weippert, *The Settlement of the Israelite Tribes in Palestine* (London, 1971).
2 N. K. Sanders, *The Sea Peoples* (London, 1978).
3 A. Dupont-Sommer, *Les Araméens* (Paris, 1949).
4 S. Moscati, *The World of the Phoenicians* (London, 1968).
5 J. Bright, *A History of Israel* (London, 1962); S. Herrmann, *A History of Israel in Old Testament Times* (London, 1975).
6 K. M. Kenyon, *Archaeology in the Holy Land* (London, 1970); D. Winton Thomas (ed.), *Archaeology and Old Testament Study* (Oxford, 1967); S. M. Paul and W. E. Denver (eds), *Biblical Archaeology* (Jerusalem, 1973).
7 T. A. Busink, *Der Tempel Salomos* (Leiden, 1970).
8 D. Ussishkin, 'King Solomon's Palaces', *Biblical Archaeologist*, 36 (1973).
9 Y. Yadin, *The Art of Warfare in Biblical Lands* (London, 1963).
10 J. W. Crowfoot and G. M. Crowfoot, *Early Ivories from Samaria* (London, 1938).
11 R. W. Bulliet, *The Camel and the Wheel* (Cambridge, Mass., 1975).
12 S. Moscati, 'L'expansion Phénico-Punique dans la Méditerranée occidentale', *Proceedings of the Second International Congress of Studies on Cultures of the Western Mediterranean* (Algiers, 1976).
13 I. J. Gelb, *A Study of Writing* (Chicago, 1969).

Chapter 29: Iron Age Greece and the eastern Mediterranean
1 V. R. d'A. Desborough, *The Greek Dark Ages* (London, 1972).
2 A. M. Snodgrass, *The Dark Age of Greece: An Archaeological Survey of the Eleventh to the Eighth Centuries BC* (Edinburgh, 1971).
3 J. N. Coldstream, *Geometric Greece* (London, 1977); A. M. Snodgrass, *Archaeology and the Rise of the Greek State*, Inaugural Lecture (Cambridge, 1977).
4 R. M. Cook, *Greek Painted Pottery*, 2nd edn (London, 1972).
5 J. G. Landels, *Engineering in the Ancient World* (London, 1978).
6 M. M. Austin and P. Vidal-Naquet, *Economic and Social History of Ancient Greece* (London, 1977).
7 C. M. Kraay, *Archaic and Classical Greek Coins* (London, 1976).
8 J. J. Coulton, *Greek Architects at Work: Problems of Structure and Design* (London, 1977).
9 J. Boardman, *Greek Sculpture: The Archaic Period* (London, 1978).
10 C. G. Starr, *The Economic and Social Growth of Early Greece 800–500 BC* (New York, 1977).
11 J. Boardman, *The Greeks Overseas*, 2nd edn (Harmondsworth, 1973).
12 J. Boardman, *Athenian Black Figure Vases* (London, 1974); J. Boardman, *Athenian Red Figure Vases: The Archaic Period* (London, 1975).
13 R. E. Wycherley, *The Stones of Athens* (Princeton, N.J., 1978).
14 A. Burford, *Craftsmen in Greek and Roman Society* (London, 1972); R. J. Hopper, *Trade and Industry in Classical Greece* (London, 1979).
15 R. E. Wycherley, *How the Greeks Built Cities*, 2nd edn (London, 1962).

Chapter 30: Iran under the Achaemenians and Seleucids
1 D. Stronach and M. Roaf, 'Excavations at Tepe Nush-i Jan: A Third Interim Report, Part 1', *Iran*, XVI (1978).
2 J. Hansman, 'An Achaemenian Stronghold', *Acta Iranica*, 6 (1975).
3 H. W. Bailey, 'Nasā and Fasā', *Acta Iranica*, 6 (1975).
4 E. F. Schmidt, *Persepolis I* (Chicago, 1953).
5 C. Nylander, 'Achaemenid Imperial Art', in 'Power and Propaganda: Sym-

posium on Ancient Empires', *Mesopotamia*, VII (1979); M. Roaf, 'A Mathematical Analysis of the Styles of the Persepolis Reliefs', in M. Greenhalgh and V. Megaw (eds), *Art in Society* (London, 1979).
6 R. T. Hallock, *Persepolis Fortification Tablets* (Chicago, 1969).
7 Herodotus V. 53.
8 P. Briant, 'L'élevage ovin dans l'empire achéménide', *Journal of the Economic and Social History of the Orient*, XXII (1979).
9 D. Stronach, *Pasargadae: A Report on the Excavations Conducted by the British Institute of Persian Studies from 1961 to 1963* (Oxford, 1978).
10 A. D. H. Bivar, 'The Achaemenids and the Macedonians: Stability and Turbulence', in G. Hambly (ed.), *Central Asia* (London, 1969).
11 R. McC. Adams, *Land behind Baghdad: A History of Settlement on the Diyala Plain* (Chicago, 1965).
12 R. J. Wenke, 'Imperial Investments and Agricultural Developments in Parthian and Sasanian Khuzestan: 150 BC to AD 640', *Mesopotamia*, X–XI (1975–6).
13 M. A. Dandamayev, *Persien unter den ersten Achämeniden* (Wiesbaden, 1976).
14 E. Badian, 'Some Recent Interpretations of Alexander', in 'Alexandre le Grand, image et réalité', *Entretiens sur l'Antiquité Classique*, XXII (1976).
15 H. Luschey, 'Der Löwe von Ekbatana', *Archaeologische Mitteilungen aus Iran*, N.F. 1 (1968).
16 J. Ferguson, *The Heritage of Hellenism* (London, 1973); M. Mealeau, 'Mesopotamia under the Seleucids', in P. Grimal (ed.), *Hellenism and the Rise of Rome* (London, 1968).
17 G. M. Cohen, *The Seleucid Colonies: Studies in Founding, Administration and Organisation* (Wiesbaden, 1978).
18 A. Labrousse and R. Boucharlat, 'La fouille du palais du Chaour á Suse en 1970 et 1971', *Cahiers de la Délégation Archéologique Française en Iran*, II (1972).

Chapter 31: The emergence of Arabia
1 D. B. Doe, *Southern Arabia* (London, 1971).
2 T. G. Bibby, *Looking for Dilmun* (New York, 1969).
3 M. Tosi, 'The Dating of the Umm an-Nar Culture and a Proposed Sequence for Oman in the Third Millennium BC', *Journal of Oman Studies*, 2 (1976).
4 K. Frifelt, 'A Possible Link Between the Jemdat Nasr and the Umm an-Nar Graves in Oman', *Journal of Oman Studies*, 1 (1975).
5 B. de Cardi, S. Collier and D. B. Doe, 'Excavations and Survey in Oman 1974–1975', *Journal of Oman Studies*, 2 (1976); B. de Cardi, S. Roskam and D. B. Doe, 'Excavations and Survey in Oman 1975–1976, *Journal of Oman Studies*, 3 (1977); D. B. Doe, 'Gazetteer of Sites in Oman', *Journal of Oman Studies*, 3 (1977).
6 K. Frifelt, 'Evidence of a Third Millennium Town in Oman', *Journal of Oman Studies*, 2 (1976).
7 A. F. L. Beeston, 'Pliny's Gabbanitae', *Proceedings of the Seminar for Arabian Studies*, 2 (1972); A. F. L. Beeston, 'Kingship in Ancient South Arabia', *Journal of Economic and Social History of the Orient*, 15 (1972).
8 F. V. Winnett, 'The Place of the Minaeans in the History of Pre-Islamic Arabia', *Bulletin of the American Schools of Oriental Research*, 73 (1939).
9 D. B. Doe, *The Monuments of South Arabia* (London, 1980).

Chapter 32: The Hellenistic world
1 R. Lane Fox, *Alexander the Great* (London, 1972).
2 R. E. Wycherley, *How the Greeks Built Cities*, 2nd edn (London, 1962).
3 P. M. Fraser, *Ptolemaic Alexandria* (Oxford, 1972).
4 P. Bernard, 'Ai Khanoum on the Oxus', *Proceedings of the British Academy*, 53 (1968) (Bernard's excavation reports published annually in *Comptes rendus de l'Académie des inscriptions et belles lettres* are also essential reading); L. Robert, 'De Delphes à l'Oxus', *Comptes rendus de L'Académie des inscriptions et belles lettres* (1968).
5 A. H. M. Jones, *The Cities of the Eastern Roman Provinces*, 2nd edn (Oxford, 1971).
6 M. I. Rostovtzeff, *Caravan Cities* (Oxford, 1932).
7 Wycherley, *How the Greeks Built Cities*.
8 J. M. Cook, *The Troad* (Oxford, 1973).
9 E. W. Marsden, *Greek and Roman Artillery: Historical Development* (Oxford, 1969); F. E. Winter, *Greek Fortifications* (London, 1971).

Chapter 33: First-millennium Europe before the Romans

1 S. Piggott, *Ancient Europe* (Edinburgh, 1965), chs 8 and 9.
2 N. Sandars, *Prehistoric Art in Europe* (Harmondsworth, 1968), chs 7, 8 and 9.
3 S. Moscatti, *The World of the Phoenicians* (London, 1968), sect. 3.
4 B. Rowlett, 'The Iron Age North of the Alps', *Science*, 161 (1968).
5 D. Ridgeway, 'The First Western Greeks', in C. F. C. Hawkes (ed.), *Greeks, Celts and Romans* (London, 1973).
6 J. Boardman, *The Greeks Overseas* (London, 1964).
7 M. Pallotino, *The Etruscans* (London, 1977).
8 A. Arribas, *The Iberians* (London, 1967).
9 F. R. Hodson and R. M. Rowlett, 'France from 600 BC to the Roman Conquest', in S. Piggott, G. Daniel and C. McBurney (eds), *France Before the Romans* (London, 1973).
10 W. Kimmig, 'Early Celts on the Upper Danube: The Excavations at the Heuneburg', in R. Bruce Mitford (ed.), *Recent Excavations in Europe* (London, 1975).
11 Boardman, *The Greeks Overseas*.
12 A. A. Formazou *et al.*, 'The Most Important Recent Archaeological Finds in European Russia', in Bruce Mitford, *Recent Excavations in Europe*.
13 V. Megaw, *The Art of the European Bronze Age* (Bath, 1970).
14 A. Ross, *Everyday Life of the Pagan Celts* (London, 1970).
15 T. Powell, *The Celts* (London, 1967).
16 V. Diacovicu, *Treasures from Romania* (London, 1971).
17 A. Alfoldi, *Noricum* (London, 1975).
18 F. Benoit, 'The Celtic *oppidum* of Entremont', in Bruce Mitford, *Recent Excavations in Europe*
19 B. Cunliffe, *Iron Age Communities in Britain* (London, 1975).
20 M. Todd, *The Northern Barbarians 100 BC–300 AD* (London, 1975).
21 Formazou *et al.*, 'The Most Important Recent Archaeological Finds'.

Chapter 34: The western Mediterranean and the origins of Rome

1 J. Boardman, *The Greeks Overseas* (Harmondsworth, 1964); D. B. Harden, *The Phoenicians* (London, 1962).
2 B. H. Warmington, *Carthage* (London, 1960).
3 M. Guido, *Sardinia* (London, 1963).
4 A. Ciasca *et al.*, *Mozia* I, II, III, Studi Semitici (Rome, 1964–73); J. I. S. Whitaker, *Motya* (London, 1921).
5 A. Blanco and J. M. Luzon, 'Pre-Roman Silver Miners at Riotinto', *Antiquity*, 43 (1969).
6 Guido, *Sardinia*.
7 D. Ridgway, 'The First Western Greeks: Campanian Coasts and Southern Etruria', in C. F. C. Hawkes and S. Hawkes (eds), *Greeks, Celts and Romans* (London, 1973).
8 Boardman, *The Greeks Overseas*.
9 J. B. Ward-Perkins, *Cities of Ancient Greece and Italy: Planning in Classical Antiquity* (New York, 1974).
10 D. Adamesteanu, 'Le suddivisioni di terra nel Metapontino', in M. I. Finley (ed.), *Problèmes de la terre en Grèce ancienne* (Paris, 1973).
11 M. Pallottino, *The Etruscans* (London, 1975).
12 Ward-Perkins, *Cities of Ancient Greece and Italy*.
13 N. Alfieri and P. E. Arias, *Spina* (Florence, 1958).
14 J. B. Ward-Perkins, 'Etruscan Engineering: Road-Building, Water Supply and Drainage', in M. Renard (ed.), *Hommages à Albert Grenier*, Collection Latomus, 58 (Brussels, 1962).
15 M. Torelli, 'Graviaca (Tarquinia): Scavi nella città etrusca e romana', *Notizie degli Scavi* (1971).

Chapter 35: Rome and its Empire in the West

1 E. Gjerstad, *Early Rome*, Vols I–IV (Lund, 1956–63).
2 R. Chevallier, *Roman Roads* (London, 1976).
3 F. E. Brown, *Cosa*, I, Memoirs of the American Academy at Rome, 20 (Rome, 1951).
4 J. B. Ward-Perkins, *Cities of Ancient Greece and Italy: Planning in Classical Antiquity* (New York, 1974).
5 T. W. Potter, *The Changing Landscape of Southern Etruria* (London, 1979).
6 M. H. Crawford, *The Roman Republic* (London, 1978).
7 D. Earl, *The Age of Augustus* (London, 1968).
8 J. Wacher, *The Towns of Roman Britain* (London, 1975).
9 Ward-Perkins, *Cities of Ancient Greece and Italy*.

10 Earl, *The Age of Augustus*.
11 R. Duncan-Jones, *The Economy of the Roman Empire* (Cambridge, 1974).
12 E. M. Wightman, *Roman Trier and the Treviri* (London, 1970).
13 K. D. White, *Roman Farming* (London, 1970).
14 Potter, *The Changing Landscape of Southern Etruria*.
15 R. Agache, *La Somme pré-romaine et romaine* (Amiens, 1978).
16 A. Boëthius and J. B. Ward-Perkins, *Etruscan and Roman Architecture* (Harmondsworth, 1970).
17 G. Webster, *The Roman Imperial Army* (London, 1969).
18 D. Baatz, *Der Römische Limes*, 2nd edn (Berlin, 1975); H. Schönberger, 'The Roman Frontier in Germany: An Archaeological Survey', *Journal of Roman Studies*, 59 (1969).
19 A. H. M. Jones, *The Later Roman Empire* (Oxford, 1964).
20 P. Brown, *The World of Late Antiquity* (London, 1971).

Chapter 36: The Roman Empire in the East

1 M. H. Crawford, 'Rome and the Greek World: Economic Relationships', *Economic History Review*, 30 (1977); K. Hopkins, *Conquerors and Slaves: Sociological Studies in Roman History*, Vol. I (Cambridge, 1978).
2 E. Badian, *Roman Imperialism in the Late Republic* (Oxford, 1968); E. Badian, *Publicans and Sinners* (Oxford, 1972).
3 F. Millar, *The Roman Empire and its Neighbours* (London, 1967); M. I. Rostovtzeff, *Social and Economic History of the Roman Empire*, 2nd edn (Oxford, 1957).
4 D. Magie, *Roman Rule in Asia Minor* (Princeton, 1950); R. Syme, 'Flavian Wars and Frontiers', *Cambridge Ancient History*, Vol. XI (Cambridge, 1936).
5 B. M. Levick, *Roman Colonies in Southern Asia Minor* (Oxford, 1967).
6 A. H. M. Jones, *The Greek City from Alexander to Justinian* (Oxford, 1940).
7 J. B. Ward-Perkins, 'Quarrying in Antiquity', *Proceedings of the British Academy*, 57 (1972).
8 Magie, *Roman Rule in Asia Minor*.
9 Rostovtzeff, *Social and Economic History of the Roman Empire*.

Chapter 37: The growth of a Chinese empire

1 Kwang-chih Chang, *The Archaeology of Ancient China*, 3rd edn (New Haven, Conn./London, 1977); Cheng Te-k'un, *Archaeology in China*, Vol. III – *Chou China* (Cambridge, 1963); W. Watson, *China Before the Han Dynasty* (London, 1961).
2 M. Loewe, *Everyday Life in Early Imperial China During the Han Period 202 BC–AD 220* (London, 1968).
3 H. Bielenstein, 'Lo-yang in Later Han Times', *Bulletin of the Museum of Far Eastern Antiquities* (Stockholm), No. 48 (1976).   x
4 Wang Yü-ch'üan, *Early Chinese Coinage* (New York, 1951).
5 W. Watson, *The Genius of China* (London, 1973).
6 M. Loewe, *Records of Han Administration*, Vols I, II (Cambridge, 1967).
7 J. Needham, *Science and Civilisation in China*, Vols I– (Cambridge, 1954–); *Historical Relics Unearthed in New China* (Peking, 1972).
8 W. Watson, *Ancient Chinese Bronzes* (London, 1962).
9 M. Medley, *A Handbook of Chinese Art for Collectors and Students* (London, 1964).
10 S. H. Hansford, *Chinese Carved Jades* (London, 1968).
11 K. H. J. Gardiner, *The Early History of Korea* (Canberra, 1969).
12 J. E. Kidder, Jr, *Japan Before Buddhism* (London, 1959).

Chapter 38: The rise of the nomads in central Asia

1 V. M. Masson and V. I. Sandriani, *Central Asia* (London, 1972).
2 G. F. Korobkova, 'Orudiya truda i khozaistvo neoliticheskikh plemen Srednei Azii', *Materialy i Isledovaniya po Arkheologii SSSR*, 158 (monograph) (Leningrad, 1969).
3 A. Sherratt, 'Plough and Pastoralism: Aspects of the Secondary Products Revolution', in N. Hammond, I. Hodder and G. Isaac (eds), *Patterns in the Past*, David Clarke Memorial Volume (Cambridge, 1979).
4 G. Dahl and A. Hjort, 'Having Herds', *Studies in Social Anthropology*, 2 (monograph) (Stockholm, 1976).
5 T. Sulimirski, *The Sarmatians* (London, 1970).
6 Masson and Sandriani, *Central Asia*.
7 S. I. Rudenko, *Frozen Tombs of Siberia* (London, 1970).
8 V. I. Tsalkin, 'Drevnee zhivotnovodstvo plemen Vostochnoi Evropy i Srednei Azii', *Materialy i Isledovaniya po Arkheologii SSSR*, 135 (monograph) (Moscow, 1966).

Chapter 39: India before and after the Mauryan empire
1 B. B. Lal, 'Excavations at Hastinapur', *Ancient India*, 10 (1954), 11 (1955).
2 K. A. Chaudhury, *Ancient Agriculture and Forestry in Northern India* (Bombay, 1977).
3 A. Bose, *Social and Rural Economy of Northern India* (Calcutta, 1942–5).
4 R. Thapar, *Ancient Indian Social History: Some Interpretations* (New Delhi, 1978).
5 P. L. Gupta, *Coins* (New Delhi, 1969).
6 N. Wagle, *Society at the Time of the Buddha* (Bombay, 1966); Bose, *Social and Rural Economy of Northern India*.
7 V. Smith, *The Early History of India* (Oxford, 1924).
8 R. Thapar, *Asoka and the Decline of the Mauryas* (London, 1961).
9 E. Hultzsch (ed.), *Corpus Inscriptionum Indicarum*, (London, 1888–1925).
10 Gupta, *Coins*; A. K. Narain, *The Indo-Greeks* (Oxford, 1957).
11 B. Rowland, *The Art and Architecture of India* (Harmondsworth, 1959).
12 J. Marshall, *Taxila*, Vols I–III (Cambridge, 1951).
13 P. L. Gupta, *Roman Coins from Andhra Pradesh* (Hyderabad, 1965).
14 H. Sarkar and B. N. Misra, *Nagarjunakonda* (New Delhi, 1966).
15 B. K. Gururaja Rao, *The Megalithic Culture in South India* (Mysore, 1972); A. Sundara, *The Early Chamber Tombs of South India* (Delhi, 1975).
16 R. Champakalakshmi, 'Archaeology and Tamil Literary Tradition', *Puratattva* (Bulletin of the Indian Archaeological Society), 8 (1975–6).
17 R. E. M. Wheeler, A. Ghosh and K. Deva, 'Arikamedu: An Indo-Roman Trading Station on the East Coast of India', *Ancient India*, 2 (1946).
18 R. S. Sharma, 'Decay of Gangetic Towns in Gupta and Post-Gupta Times', *Proceedings of the Indian History Congress*, 33rd Session (Muzaffarpur, 1972); R. S. Sharma, *Indian Feudalism* (Calcutta, 1965).
19 A. S. Altekar, *Catalogue of the Gupta Gold Coins in the Bayana Hoard* (Bombay, 1954).
20 Rowland, *The Art and Architecture of India*.

Chapter 40: South-east Asia: civilizations of the tropical forests
1 R. B. Smith and W. Watson (eds), *Ancient South-East Asia* (Oxford, 1979).
2 Smith and Watson, *Ancient South-East Asia*.
3 D. G. E. Hall, *A History of South-East Asia*, 3rd edn (London, 1968); G.-W. Wang, 'The Nanhai Trade', *Journal of the Malayan Branch, Royal Asiatic Society*, 31 (1958); P. Wheatley, *The Golden Khersonese* (Kuala Lumpur, 1961); O. W. Wolters, *Early Indonesian Commerce* (Ithaca, N. Y., 1967).
4 L. Malleret, *L'archéologie du Delta du Mekong*, 4 vols (Paris, 1959–63).
5 Aung Thaw, *Report on the Excavations at Beikthano* (Rangoon, 1968).
6 Smith and Watson, *Ancient South-East Asia*.
7 H. G. Q. Wales, *Dvāravāti, the Earliest Kingdom of Siam* (London, 1969).
8 G. Coedes, *The Indianized States of Southeast Asia* (Honolulu, 1968); B. P. Groslier, *Angkor, homes et pierres* (Paris, 1968).
9 P. Dupont, *L'archéologie Mône de Dvāravāti* (Paris, 1959).
10 J. Boisselier, *La statuaire du Champa* (Paris, 1963); A. J. B. Kempers, *Ancient Indonesian Art* (Amsterdam, 1959); S. J. O'Connor, *Hindu Gods of Peninsular Siam, Artibus Asiae* Supplementum, 28 (1971–2).
11 Tha Hla and Nyi Nyi, 'Report on the Field Work at Hmawza (Sri-Ksetra) and Prome', *Journal of the Burma Research Society*, 41 (1958).
12 Dupont, *L'archéologie Mône de Dvāravāti*; Smith and Watson, *Ancient South-East Asia*; Wales, *Dvāravāti, the Earliest Kingdom of Siam*.
13 J. Boisselier, *La statuaire Khmère et son évolution*, 2 vols (Paris, 1955); B. P. Groslier, *Indochina, Archaeologia Mundi* Series (Cleveland, Ohio, 1966).
14 Boisselier, *La statuaire du Champa*.
15 Smith and Watson, *Ancient South-East Asia*.
16 Kempers, *Ancient Indonesian Art*.
17 G. H. Luce, *Old Burma – Early Pagan*, 3 vols, *Artibus Asiae* Supplementum, 26 (1969).

Chapter 41: Imperial China and its neighbours
1 Jane Gaston Mahler, *The Westerners among the Figurines of the T'ang Dynasty of China* (Rome, 1959); *Han T'ang pi-hua* (Peking, 1974); *T'ang Yung-t'ai kung-chu mu pi-hua chi* (Peking, 1963); *T'ang Li Hsien mu pi-hua* (Peking, 1974).
2 A. Wright, *The Sui Dynasty* (New York, 1978).
3 *Cambridge History of China*, Vol. III (Cambridge, forthcoming).
4 *A Selection of Archaeological Finds of the People's Republic of China* (Peking, 1976). Brief summaries of reports contained in three Chinese professional

journals are given in the *Revue Bibliographique de Sinologie*, whose published volumes cover the period 1955–65, and some archaeological reports are now being translated into English in *Chinese Studies in Archaeology* (from 1979 onwards).

Chapter 42: Forest cultures of south and south-east Asia
1 J. I. Miller, *The Spice Trade of the Roman Empire* (Oxford, 1969).
2 E. E. McKinnon, 'Research at Kota Cina, a Sung-Yüan Period Trading Site in East Sumatra', *Archipel*, 14 (1977).
3 B. Bronson, 'Exchange at the Upstream and Downstream Ends: Notes Towards a Functional Model of the Coastal State in South-East Asia', in K. L. Hutterer (ed.), *Economic Exchange and Social Interaction in South-East Asia*, Michigan Papers on South-East Asia, 13 (Ann Arbor, Mich., 1977).
4 B. A. V. Peacock, 'The Later Prehistory of the Malay Peninsula', in R. B. Smith and W. Watson (eds), *Early South-East Asia* (Oxford, 1979).
5 B. Allchin, *The Stone-Tipped Arrow* (London, 1966).
6 Al Rashid, 'Malaysian Prehistory: A Review', in D. P. Agrawal and A. Ghosh (eds), *Radiocarbon and Indian Archaeology* (Bombay, 1973).
7 C. von Fürer-Haimendorf, *The Chenchus* (London, 1943).
8 C. von Fürer-Haimendorf, *The Reddis of the Bison Hills: A Study in Acculturation* (London, 1945).
9 F. Lebar, G. C. Hickey and J. K. Musgrave, *Ethnic Groups of Mainland South-East Asia* (New Haven, Conn., 1964).
10 F. Lebar (ed.), *Ethnic Groups of Insular South-East Asia*, 2 vols (New Haven, Conn., 1972).
11 J. Peterson, *The Ecology of Social Boundaries* (Urbana, Ill., 1978).

Chapter 43: Parthian and Sasanian Iran
1 A. Christensen, *L'Iran sous les Sassanides* (Copenhagen, 1944); M. A. R. Colledge, *The Parthians* (London, 1967); N. C. Debevoise, *A Political History of Parthia* (Chicago, 1938); R. Ghirshman, *Iran, Parthians and Sassanians* (London, 1962); G. Herrmann, *The Iranian Revival* (Oxford, 1977); L. Vanden Berghe, *Archéologie de l'Iran Ancien* (Leiden, 1966).
2 G. Frumkin, *Archaeology in Soviet Central Asia* (Leiden, 1970); Ghirshman, *Iran, Parthians and Sassanians;* Herrmann, *The Iranian Revival.*
3 John Hansman and David Stronach, 'Excavations at Shahr-i Qumis, 1967', and 'A Sasanian Repository at Shahr-i Qumis', *Journal of the Royal Asiatic Society* (1970), and 'Excavations at Shahr-i Qumis, 1971', *Journal of the Royal Asiatic Society* (1974).
4 R. Ghirshman, *Terrasses sacrées de Bard-è Néchandeh et Masjid-è Solaiman, L'Iran du Sud-Ouest du VIIIe siècle avant n. ère au Ve siècle de n. ère* (Paris 1976).
5 L. Waterman, *Preliminary Report upon the Excavations at Tel Umar, Iraq* (Michigan, 1931), and *Second Preliminary Report* (Michigan, 1933).
6 W. Andrae and H. Lenzen, *Die Partherstadt Assur* (Leipzig, 1933).
7 E. J. Keall, 'Qaleh-i Yazdigird: The Question of its Date', *Iran*, XV (1977).
8 O. Reuther, 'Sasanian Architecture', in A. U. Pope (ed.), *A Survey of Persian Art* (London/New York, 1938).
9 R. Naumann, D. Huff and R. Schnyder, 'Takht-i Suleiman, Bericht über die Ausgrabungen 1965–1973', *Archaeologischer Anzeiger*, 1 (1975).
10 R. McC. Adams, *Land Behind Baghdad: A History of Settlement on the Diyala Plains* (Chicago/London, 1965).
11 R. McC. Acams and H. J. Nissen, *The Uruk Countryside: The Natural Setting of Urban Societies* (Chicago/London, 1975).
12 R. J. Wenke, 'Imperial Investments and Agricultural Developments in Parthian and Sasanian Khuzestan: 150 BC to AD 64', *Mesopotamia*, X–XI (1975–6).
13 E. Haerinck, 'Typology and Distribution Pattern of Ceramics in Iran from ca. 250 BC to ca. 225 AD', *Proceedings of the Fifth Annual Symposium on Archaeological Research in Iran* (Tehran, 1977).

Chapter 44: Byzantium: an empire under stress
1 A. H. M. Jones, *The Later Roman Empire* (Oxford, 1964).
2 C. Foss and P. Magdalino, *Rome and Byzantium* (Oxford, 1977).
3 D. Claude, *Die byzantinische Stadt im 6. Jh.* (Munich, 1969); C. Foss, *Byzantine and Turkish Sardis* (Cambridge, Mass., 1976); C. Foss, 'Late Antique and Byzantine Ankara', *Dumbarton Oaks Papers*, 31 (1978); J. Liebeschuetz, *Antioch* (Oxford, 1972); H. Thompson, 'Athenian Twilight', *Journal of Roman Studies*, 49 (1949).

4   R. Janin, *Constantinople byzantine* (Paris, 1964).
5   C. Foss, *Ephesus After Antiquity* (Cambridge, 1979).
6   Jones, *The Later Roman Empire*.
7   J. P. Sodini, 'L'artisanat urbain à l'époque paléochrétienne', *Ktema* (forthcoming).
8   G. Tchalenko, *Villages antiques de la Syrie du nord* (Paris, 1953).
9   Claude, *Die byzantinische Stadt in 6. Jh.*,
10 R. Krautheimer, *Early Christian and Byzantine Architecture* (Harmondsworth, 1975).
11 J. Hussey (ed.), *Cambridge Medieval History*, Vol. IV (Cambridge, 1966–7); G. Ostrogorsky, *History of the Byzantine State* (Oxford, 1968).
12 C. Foss, 'The Persians in Asia Minor and the End of Antiquity', *English Historical Review*, 90 (1975).
13 Foss, 'The Persians in Asia Minor'; Foss, *Byzantine and Turkish Sardis*; J. Koder and F. Hild, *Hellas und Thessalia* (Vienna, 1976).
14 Foss, *Ephesus After Antiquity*.
15 Foss, *Ephesus After Antiquity*.
16 C. Foss, 'Late Antique and Byzantine Ankara'.
17 N. Thierry, *Nouvelles églises rupestres de Cappadoce* (Paris, 1963).
18 Krautheimer, *Early Christian and Byzantine Architecture*.

Chapter 45: The expansion of the Arabs
1   A. H. Hourani and S. M. Stern, *The Islamic City* (Oxford, 1970).
2   L. Boulnois, *La Route de la Soie* (Paris, 1963); D. S. Richards, *Islam and the Trade of Asia* (Oxford, 1970).
3   D. Whitehouse, 'Maritime Trade in the Arabian Sea: The Ninth and Tenth Centuries', *Proceedings of the Fourth International Conference on South Asian Archaeology* (Naples, 1979).
4   A. Creswell, *Early Muslim Architecture* (Oxford, 1932–40); G. Mitchell, *Architecture of the Islamic World* (London, 1978).
5   Arts Council of Great Britain, *The Arts of Islam* (London, 1976).
6   A. Lane, *Early Islamic Pottery* (London, 1947).

Chapter 46: Barbarian Europe in the first millennium
1   H. Beck *et al.*, *Reallexikon der Germanischen Altertumskunde* (Berlin, 1973–). (The production of this invaluable survey has only recently begun; it has reached Vol. IV.)
2   I. Dienes, *The Hungarians Cross the Carpathians* (Budapest, 1972).
3   J. Engel (ed.), *Grosser Historischer Weltatlas*, Pt 2: *Mittelalter*, 2nd edn (Munich, 1978); D. Talbot Rice (ed.), *The Dark Ages* (London, 1965).
4   H. Jankuhn *et al.* (eds), *Das Dorf der Eisenzeit und des Frühen Mittelalters* (Göttingen, 1977).
5   M. Barley (ed.), *The European Town* (London, 1977).
6   D. M. Wilson (ed.), *The Northern World* (London, 1980).
7   M. Todd, *The Northern Barbarians 100 BC–AD 300* (London, 1975); R. Hachmann, *The Germanic Peoples* (London, 1971); H. Eggers *et al.*, *Kelten und Germanen in Heidnischer Zeit* (Baden-Baden, 1964).
8   Hachmann, *The Germanic Peoples*; Eggers *et al.*, *Kelten und Germanen in Heidnischer Zeit*; L. Musset, *The Germanic Migrations* (trans. E. and C. James) (London, 1975).
9   Eggers *et al.*, *Kelten und Germanen in Heidnischer Zeit*; P. Foote and D. M. Wilson, *The Viking Achievement* (London, 1970); B. Almgren (ed.), *The Viking* (Gothenburg, 1975); J. Graham-Campbell and D. Kidd, *The Vikings* (London, 1980).
10 M. Gimbutas, *The Slavs* (London, 1971); J. Herrmann (ed.), *Die Slaven in Deutschland* (Berlin, 1974); Z. Vana, *Einführung in die Frühgeschichte der Slawen* (Neumunster, 1970).

Chapter 47: The rise of temperate Europe
1   M. L. Parry, *Climatic Change, Agriculture and Settlement* (Folkestone, 1978).
2   B. K. Roberts, 'Village Plans in County Durham: A Preliminary Statement', *Medieval Archaeology*, 16 (1972).
3   W. Janssen, 'Some Major Aspects of Frankish and Medieval Settlement in the Rhineland', in P. H. Sawyer (ed.), *Medieval Settlement: Continuity and Change* (London, 1976).
4   G. Duby, *The Early Growth of the European Economy: Warriors and Peasants from the Seventh to the Twelfth Century* (London, 1974).
5   E. M. Jope, 'The Regional Cultures of Medieval Britain', in I. L. Foster and L. Alcock (eds), *Culture and Environment* (London, 1963).

6   A. E. Herteig, ' "Bryggen": Economic and Cultural Aspects', in A. E. Herteig, H.-E. Liden and C. Blindheim, *Archaeological Contributions to the Early History of Urban Communities in Norway* (Oslo, 1975).
7   H. Clarke and A. Carter, *Excavations in King's Lynn 1963–1970* (London, 1977).
8   P. Rahtz and D. Bullough, 'The Parts of an Anglo-Saxon Mill', in P. Clemoes (ed.), *Anglo-Saxon England 6* (Cambridge, 1977).
9   F. A. Aberg (ed.), *Medieval Moated Sites* (London, 1978).
10 C. Platt, *Medieval England: A Social History and Archaeology from the Conquest to AD 1600* (London, 1978).
11 I. Kershaw, 'The Great Famine and Agrarian Crisis in England 1315–1322', *Past and Present*, 59 (1973).
12 Parry, *Climatic Change, Agriculture and Settlement*.
13 Platt, *Medieval England*.

Chapter 48: The urbanization of eastern Europe
1   J. Poulík, *Mikulčice* (Prague, 1975).
2   W. Hensel, *Anfänge der Städte bei den Ost- und Westslawen* (Bautzen, 1967), pp. 50–61.
3   L. Leciejewicz, 'Early Medieval Sociotopographical Transformations in West Slavonic Urban Settlements in the Light of Archaeology', *Acta Poloniae Historica*, 34 (1976).
4   S. Georgieva, 'Etudes archéologiques des cités du bas Moyen Age en Bulgarie', *Actes du 1er Congrès Internationale des Etudes Balkaniques et Sud-Est Européenes*, Vol. II (Sofia, 1969).
5   N. Dubrović, *Urbanizam kroz vekove*, Vol. I: *Jugoslavija* (Belgrade, 1950); B. Krekić, *Dubrovnik in the 14th and 15th Centuries* (Norman, Okla., 1972).
6   P. P. Tolochko, *Istorichna topografiia Kieva* (Kiev, 1970).
7   B. A. Kolchin and V. L. Yanin (eds), *Arkheologicheskoe izuchenie Novgoroda* (Moscow, 1978).
8   M. G. Rabinovich, *O drevnei Moskve* (Moscow, 1964).

Chapter 49: Northern forest cultures and the Arctic Fringe
1   G. Gjessing, 'Circumpolar Stone Age', *Acta Arctica*, 2 (1944).
2   G. Clark, *The Earlier Stone Age Settlement of Scandinavia* (Cambridge, 1975).
3   A. A. Semyontsev, 'Radiocarbon Dates of the Institute of Archaeology, III', *Radiocarbon*, 14 (1972).
4   Yu. A. Krasnov, 'Rannee zemledelyie i zhivotnovodstvo v lesnoi polose vostochnoi Evropy', *Materialy i Isledovaniya po Arkheologii SSSR*, 174 (monograph) (1971); K. L. Paaver, *Formirovaniye Teriofauny i Izmenchivost Mlekopytayushchikh Pribaltiki v Golotsene* (Tartu, 1965).
5   M. Zvelebil, 'Settlement and Subsistence in North-Eastern Europe', in P. Mellars (ed.), *Early Post-Glacial Settlement of Northern Europe* (London, 1978).
6   P. Simonsen, 'Varanger-funnene II: fund og udgravninger på fjordens sydkyst', *Tromsø Museum Skrifter*, 7 (Oslo) (1961).
7   R. S. Vasilyevski, *Proischozhdeniye i Drevnaya Kultura Koryakov* (Novosibirsk, 1971).
8   C. R. Chard, *North-East Asia in Prehistory* (Madison, Wis., 1974).
9   G. T. Vainshtein, *Istoricheskaya Etnografiya Tuvintsev* (Moskva, 1972).
10 V. N. Chernetsov and W. Moszynska, *Prehistory of Western Siberia* (Montreal, 1974).
11 P. Hajdu, *Finno-Ugrian Languages and Peoples* (London, 1975).
12 A. P. Okladnikov, *Yakutia* (Montreal, 1970).

Chapter 50: The prehistory of Oceania: colonization and cultural change
1   J. P. White, *Ol Tumbuna* (Canberra, 1972).
2   S. Bulmer, 'Settlement and Economy in Prehistoric New Guinea: A Review of the Archaeological Evidence', *Journal de la Société des Océanistes*, 31 (1975).
3   D. E. Yen, 'The Southeast Asian Foundations of Oceanic Agriculture: A Reassessment', paper given at IX Congrès de l'Union Internationale des Sciences Préhistoriques et Protohistoriques (Nice, 1976).
4   J. Golson, 'No Room at the Top: Agricultural Intensification in the New Guinea Highlands', in J. Allen, J. Golson and R. Jones (eds), *Sunda and Sahul: Prehistoric Studies in Southeast Asia, Melanesia and Australia* (London, 1977).
5   A. Pawley and R. Green, 'Dating the Dispersal of Oceanic Languages', *Oceanic Linguistics*, XII (1973).
6   P. S. Bellwood, *Man's Conquest of the Pacific* (Auckland, 1976).
7   R. C. Green, 'New Sites with Lapita Pottery and their Implications for an Understanding of the Western Pacific', *Working Papers in Anthropology*, 51 (Auckland, 1978).

8 J. M. Davidson, 'Western Polynesia and Fiji: Prehistoric Contact, Diffusion and Differentiation in Adjacent Archipelagos', *World Archaeology*, 9 (1977).
9 Bellwood, *Man's Conquest of the Pacific*.
10 B. Biggs, 'Implications of Linguistic Subgrouping with Speical Reference to Polynesia', in R. C. Green and M. Kelly (eds), Studies in *Oceanic Culture History* (1972); G. Law, 'The Likelihood of Multiple Settlement in Eastern Polynesia; A Stochastic Model', manuscript, University of Auckland; M. Levison, R. G. Ward and J. W. Webb, *The Settlement of Polynesia: A Computer Simulation* (Minneapolis, Minn., 1973).
11 J. T. Clark and J. E. Terrell, 'Archaeology in Oceania', *Annual Review of Anthropology*, 7 (1978).
12 J. E. Terrell, 'Perspective on the Prehistory of Bougainville Island', unpublished Ph.D. thesis, Harvard University.
13 G. J. Irwin, 'The Development of Mailu as a Specialized Trading and Manufacturing Centre in Papuan Prehistory: The Causes and Implications', *Mankind*, 11 (1978).
14 M. D. Sahlins, *Social Stratification in Polynesia* (Seattle, 1958).
15 I. Goldman, *Ancient Polynesian Society* (Chicago, 1970).
16 T. Earle, 'Economic and Social Organization of a Complex Chiefdom: The Halelea District, Kaua'i, Hawaii', *Anthropology Papers*, 63, Museum of Anthropology, University of Michigan.
17 B. Malinowski, *Argonauts of the Western Pacific* (London, 1922).
18 Irwin, 'The Development of Mailu as a Specialized Trading and Manufacturing Centre in Papuan Prehistory'.

Chapter: 51: Holocene Australia
1 D. J. Mulvaney, *The Prehistory of Australia*, rev. edn (Harmondsworth, 1975).
2 A. P. Kershaw, 'Record of the Last Interglacial–Glacial Cycle from North-eastern Queensland', *Nature*, 272 (1978).
3 R. Jones, 'The Tasmanian Paradox', in R. V. S. Wright (ed.), *Stone Tools as Cultural Markers* (Canberra, 1977).
4 J. Kamminga, 'A Functional Study of Use-Polished Eloueras', in Wright, *Stone Tools as Cultural Markers*.
5 H. Allen, 'The Bagundji of the Darling Basin: Cereal Gatherers in an Uncertain Environment', *World Archaeology*, 5 (1974).
6 S. Bowdler, 'The Coastal Colonization of Australia', in J. Allen, J. Golson and R. Jones (eds), *Sunda and Sahul: Prehistoric Studies in Southeast Asia, Melanesia and Australia* (London, 1977).
7 J. Golson, 'Australian Aboriginal Food Plants: Some Ecological and Culture-Historical Implications', in D. J. Mulvaney and J. Golson (eds), *Aboriginal Man and Environment in Australia* (Canberra, 1971).
8 R. A. Gould, *Australian Archaeology in Ecological and Ethnographic Perspective*, Warner Modular Publications, No. 7 (New York, 1973).
9 I. McBryde, 'Subsistence Patterns in New England Prehistory', *University of Queensland Occasional Papers in Anthropology*, No. 6 (1976).
10 J. M. Flood, 'Man and Ecology in the Highlands of Southeastern Australia: A Case Study', in N. Peterson (ed.), *Tribes and Boundaries in Australia* (Canberra, 1976).
11 Jones, 'The Tasmanian Paradox'.
12 D. J. Mulvaney, '"The Chain of Connection": The Material Evidence', in Peterson, *Tribes and Boundaries in Australia*.

Chapter 52: Iron Age Africa and the expansion of the Bantu
1 D. W. Phillipson, *The Later Prehistory of Eastern and Southern Africa* (London, 1977).
2 T. Shaw, 'Hunters, Gatherers and First Farmers in West Africa', in J. V. S. Megaw (ed.), *Hunters, Gatherers and First Farmers Outside Europe* (Leicester, 1976).
3 D. W. Phillipson, *The Prehistory of Eastern Zambia* (Nairobi, 1976).
4 R. R. Inskeep and T. M. O'C. Maggs, 'Unique Art Objects in the Iron Age of the Transvaal, South Africa', *South African Archaeological Bulletin*, 30 (1975).
5 Phillipson, *The Later Prehistory of Eastern and Southern Africa*.
6 P. de Maret, 'Sanga: New Excavations, More Data and Some Related Problems', *Journal of African History*, 18 (1977).
7 J. C. Miller, 'The Imbangala and the Chronology of Early Central African History', *Journal of African History*, 13 (1972).

Chapter 53: Early states in Africa
1 D. S. Robert, 'Les fouilles de Tegdaoust', *Journal of African History*, 9 (1970).

2 W. Filipowiak, 'Chronology of Niani in Radiocarbon Dating', *West African Journal of Archaeology* (forthcoming).
3 C. R. Flight, 'Gao, 1972', *West African Journal of Archaeology*, 5 (1975).
4 S. K. McIntosh and R. J. McIntosh, 'Excavation and Survey at Djenne-Djeno, Mali: Preliminary Results of the 1977 Field Season', *Proceedings of the Pan-African Congress on Prehistory, Nairobi, 1977* (Nairobi, 1979).
5 G. Connah, 'The Daima Sequence and the Prehistoric Chronology of the Lake Chad Region of Nigeria', *Journal of African History*, XVII (1976).
6 M. Posnansky, 'Aspects of Early West African Trade', *World Archaeology*, 5 (1973).
7 P. S. Garlake, 'Excavations at Obalara's Land, Ife', *West African Journal of Archaeology*, 4 (1974); F. Willett, *Ife in the History of West African Sculpture* (London, 1967).
8 T. Shaw, *Igbo Ukwu: An Account of Archaeological Discoveries in Eastern Nigeria* (London, 1970).
9 G. Connah, *The Archaeology of Benin* (Oxford, 1975).
10 N. Chittick, 'Discoveries in the Lamu Archipelago', *Azania*, 2 (1967).
11 P. S. Garlake, *The Early Architecture of the East African Coast* (Oxford, 1966).
12 N. Chittick, *Kilwa: An Islamic Trading City on the East African Coast* (Nairobi, 1974).
13 P. S. Garlake, *Great Zimbabwe* (London, 1973).
14 G. Barker, 'Economic Models for the Manekwani *zimbabwe*', *Azania*, 13 (1978).
15 P. S. Garlake, 'Pastoralism and *zimbabwe*', *Journal of African History*, 14 (1978).
16 B. M. Fagan *et al.*, *Iron Age Cultures in Zambia*, Vol. II (London, 1979).
17 M. Posnansky, 'Bigo bya mugenyi', *Uganda Journal*, 33 (1966).

Chapter 54: North America in the early Postglacial
1 J. D. Jennings, *Prehistory of North America*, 2nd edn (New York, 1974).
2 W. J. Wallace, 'Post-Pleistocene Archaeology 9000 to 2000 BC', in R. F. Heizer, *Handbook of North American Indians*, Vol. 8 (Washington, DC, 1978).
3 C. M. Aikens, 'The Far West', in J. D. Jennings (ed.), *Ancient Native Americans* (San Francisco, Calif., 1978).
4 W. R. Wedel, 'The Prehistoric Plains', in Jennings, *Ancient Native Americans*.
5 H. E. Wright, Jr, 'Late Quaternary Vegetational History of North America', in K. K. Turekian (ed.), *The Late Cenozoic Glacial Ages* (New Haven, Conn., 1971).
6 W. A. Ritchie and R. E. Funk, 'Aboriginal Settlement Patterns in the Northeast', *New York State Museum and Science Service Memoir*, 20 (New York, 1973).
7 R. I. Ford, 'Northeastern Archaeology: Past and Future Directions', *Annual Review of Anthropology*, 3 (1974).
8 J. B. Stoltman, 'Temporal Models in Prehistory: An Example from Eastern North America', *Current Anthropology*, 9 (1978).

Chapter 55: The colonization of the Arctic
1 D. D. Anderson, 'Akmak: An Early Archeological Assemblage from Onion Portage, North-West Alaska', *Acta Arctica* (Copenhagen), Fasc. 16 (1970); D. E. Dumond, *The Eskimos and Aleuts* (New York, 1977); R. E. Morlan, 'Early Man in Northern Yukon Territory: Perspectives as of 1977', in A. L. Bryan (ed.), *Early Man in America from a Circum-Polar Perspective*, Occasional Papers of the Department of Anthropology, University of Alberta, 1 (Edmonton, Alberta, 1978).
2 C. E. Borden, 'Origins and Development of Early North-West Coast Culture to about 3000 BC', *Archaeological Survey of Canada*, Paper No. 45, National Museum of Man Mercury Series (Ottawa, 1975); D. E. Dumond, 'Alaska and the North-West Coast', in J. D. Jennings (ed.), *Ancient Native Americans* (San Francisco, 1978).
3 D. D. Anderson, 'A Stone Age Camp Site at the Gateway to America', *Scientific American*, 218 (1968); E. Harp, Jr, 'Pioneer Cultures of the Sub-Arctic and the Arctic', in Jennings, *Ancient Native Americans*.
4 E. Harp and D. R. Hughes, 'Five Prehistoric Burials from Port aux Choix, Newfoundland', *Polar Notes*, 8 (1968); L. Oschinsky, *The Most Ancient Eskimos* (Ottawa, 1964).
5 J. L. Giddings, *Ancient Men of the Arctic* (New York, 1967); H. Larsen and F. Rainey, 'Ipiutak and the Arctic Whale Hunting Culture', *Anthropological Papers of the American Museum of Natural History*, 42 (1948).
6 Dumond, *The Eskimos and Aleuts*.
7 H. B. Collins, Jr, 'Archeology of St Lawrence Island, Alaska', *Smithsonian*

Miscellaneous Collections, 96 (1) (Washington, 1937).

8   R. McGhee, 'Speculations on Climatic Change and Thule Culture Development', *Folk*, 11/12 (1969–70).

9   Anderson, 'A Stone Age Camp Site'; J. P. Cook, 'Archeology of Interior Alaska', *Western Canadian Journal of Anthropology*, 5 (1975).

Chapter 56: Early agriculture in the Americas

1   W. Bray, 'From Foraging to Farming in Early Mexico', in J. V. S. Megaw (ed.), *Hunters, Gatherers and First Farmers beyond Europe* (Leicester, 1977).

2   E. S. Wing, 'The Use of Dogs for Food: An Adaptation to the Coastal Environment', in B. L. Stark and B. Voorhies (eds), *Prehistoric Coastal Adaptations: The Economy and Ecology of Maritime Middle America* (New York, 1978).

3   S. Webster, 'Native Pastoralism in the South Andes', *Ethnology*, 12 (1973).

4   J. Wheeler Pires-Ferreira, E. Pires-Ferreira and P. Kaulicke, 'Preceramic Animal Utilization in the Central Peruvian Andes', *Science*, 194 (1976); S. Wing, 'Animal Domestication in the Andes', in C. A. Reed (ed.), *Origins of Agriculture* (The Hague, 1977).

5   D. S. Byers (ed.), *Prehistory of the Tehuacán Valley*, Vol. I: *Environment and Subsistence* (Austin, Texas, 1967).

6   R. S. MacNeish, 'Preliminary Archaeological Investigations in the Sierra de Tamaulipas, Mexico', *Transactions of the American Philosophical Society*, NS 48 (1958).

7   K. V. Flannery, 'Archaeological Systems Theory and Early Mesoamerica', in B. J. Meggers (ed.), *Anthropological Archeology in the Americas* (Washington, DC, 1968); K. V. Flannery, 'The Origins of Agriculture', *Annual Review of Anthropology*, 2 (1973).

8   Flannery, 'The Origins of Agriculture'; J. Schoenwetter, 'Pollen Records of Guila Naquitz Cave'. *American Antiquity*, 39 (1974).

9   Flannery, 'The Origins of Agriculture'.

10 W. Bray, 'From Predation to Production: The Nature of Agricultural Evolution in Mexico and Peru', in G. de G. Sieveking, I. H. Longworth and K. E. Wilson (eds), *Problems in Economic and Social Archaeology* (London, 1976).

11 C. Niederberger, 'Early Sedentary Economy in the Basin of Mexico', *Science*, 203 (1979).

12 Webster, 'Native Pastoralism in the South Andes'.

13 J. V. Murra, 'El "control vertical" de un máximo de pisos ecológicos en la economía de las sociedas andinas', in John V. Murra (ed.), *Visita de la provincia de Léon de Huánuco (1562) por Iñigo Ortiz de Zuñiga*, Vol. II (Huánuco, 1972).

14 T. F. Lynch, 'The South American Paleo-Indians', in J. D. Jennings (ed.), *Ancient Native Americans* (San Francisco, 1978).

15 R. S. MacNeish, T. C. Patterson and D. L. Browman, 'The Central Peruvian Prehistoric Interaction Sphere', *Papers of the R. S. Peabody Foundation for Archaeology*, 7 (1975); R. S. MacNeish, 'The Beginning of Agriculture in Central Peru', in Reed, *Origins of Agriculture*; B. Pickersgill, pers. comm.

16 M. N. Cohen, 'Population Pressure and the Origins of Agriculture: An Archaeological Example from the Coast of Peru', in Reed, *Origins of Agriculture*; M. E. Moseley, *The Maritime Foundations of Andean Civilization* (Menlo Park, Calif., 1975).

17 D. W. Lathrap, J. G. Marcos and J. A. Zeidler, 'Real Alto: An Ancient Ceremonial Centre', *Archaeology*, 30 (1977).

18 F. Engel, 'A Preceramic Settlement on the Central Coast of Peru: Asia Unit 1', *Transactions of the American Philosophical Society*, 53 (1963).

19 G. F. Carter, 'A Hypothesis Suggesting a Single Origin of Agriculture', in Reed, *Origins of Agriculture*; D. W. Lathrap, 'Our Father the Cayman, Our Mother the Gourd: Spinden Revisited, or a Unitary Model for the Emergence of Agriculture in the New World', in Reed, *Origins of Agriculture*.

20 C. O. Sauer, 'Age and Area of American Cultivated Plants', *Actas del 33 Congreso Internacional de Americanistas*, 1 (1959).

21 B. Pickersgill and C. B. Heiser, 'Origins and Distribution of Plants Domesticated in the New World Tropics', in Reed, *Origins of Agriculture*.

22 G. W. Beadle, 'The Origins of *Zea mays*', in Reed, *Origins of Agriculture*; Flannery, 'The Origins of Agriculture'.

23 D. Bonavia and A. Grobman, 'El origin del maiz Andino', in R. Hartmann and U. Oberem (eds), *Estudios Americanistas 1 – Homenaje a Hermann Trimborn* (St Augustin, 1978).

24 S. A. Chomko and G. W. Crawford, 'Plant Husbandry in Prehistoric Eastern North America: New Evidence for its Development', *American Antiquity*, 43 (1978); R. A. Yarnell, 'Native Plant Husbandry North of Mexico', in Reed, *Origins of Agriculture*.

Chapter 57: Agricultural groups in North America

1   J. B. Griffin, 'Eastern North American Archaeology', *Science*, 156 (1967).

2   J. B. Griffin, 'The Midlands and Northeastern United States', in J. D. Jennings (ed.), *Ancient Native Americans* (San Francisco, 1978).

3   J. D. Muller, 'The Southeast', in Jennings, *Ancient Native Americans*.

4   Griffin, 'Eastern North American Archaeology'.

5   P. Phillips, J. A. Ford and J. B. Griffin, 'Archaeological Survey in the Lower Mississippi Valley, 1940–1947', *Papers of the Peabody Museum of Archaeology and Ethnology, Harvard University*, 25 (1951); D. B. Smith (ed.), *Mississippi Settlement Patterns* (New York and London, 1978).

6   B. G. Trigger (ed.), *Northeast: Handbook of North American Indians*, Vol. 15 (Washington, DC, 1978).

7   D. J. Lehmer, 'Introduction to Middle Missouri Archaeology', *Anthropology Papers 1*, National Parks Service, US Department of the Interior (1971).

8   W. R. Wedel, *Prehistoric Man on the Great Plains* (Norman, Okla., 1961); W. R. Wedel, *The Central Plains Village Tradition: Handbook of North American Indians*, Vol. 10 (Washington, DC, in press).

9   E. W. Haury, *The Hohokam, Desert Farmers and Craftsmen: Excavations at Snaketown, 1964–1945* (Tucson, Ariz., 1976).

10 J. B. Wheat, 'Mogollon Culture Prior to AD 1000', *American Anthropological Association Memoirs*, 82 (1955).

11 W. D. Lipe, 'The Southwest', in Jennings, *Ancient Native Americans*.

12 C. C. Di Peso, *Casa Grandes, A Fallen Trading Center of the Gran Chichimeca, I–VIII* (Dragoon and Flagstaff, Ariz., 1974).

Chapter 58: Mesoamerica: from village to empire

1   J. H. Steward and L. C. Faron, *Native Peoples of South America* (New York, 1959).

2   P. Tolstoy, 'Settlement and Population Trends in the Basin of Mexico (Ixtapaluca and Zacatenco Phases)', *Journal of Field Archaeology*, 2 (1975).

3   R. B. Woodbury and J. A. Neely, 'Water Control Systems of the Tehuacán Valley', in R. S. MacNeish (ed.), *The Prehistory of the Tehuacán Valley* (Austin, Texas, 1972).

4   N. Hammond, 'The Earliest Maya', *Scientific American*, 236 (1977).

5   W. T. Sanders and B. J. Price, *Mesoamerica: The Evolution of a Civilization* (New York, 1968).

6   K. V. Flannery, 'The Olmecs and the Valley of Oaxaca: A Model for Inter-Regional Interaction in Formative Times', in E. Benson (ed.), *Dumbarton Oaks Conference on the Olmec* (Washington, DC, 1968).

7   J. R. Parsons, 'The Development of a Prehistoric Complex Society: A Regional Perspective from the Valley of Mexico', *Journal of Field Archaeology*, 1 (1974).

8   D. S. Rice, 'Middle Preclassic Maya Settlement in the Central Maya Lowlands', *Journal of Field Archaeology*, 3 (1976).

9   Parsons, 'The Development of a Prehistoric Complex Society'.

10 R. Millon, 'Extensión y Población de la Ciudad de Teotihuacán en sus Diferentes Períodos: Un Cálculo Provisional', *Teotihuacán, Onceava Meso Redonda* (Mexico, D. F., 1967).

11 J. Marcus, 'Territorial Organization of the Lowland Classic Maya', *Science*, 180 (1973).

12 W. A. Haviland, 'Dynastic Genealogies from Tikal, Guatemala: Implications for Descent and Political Organization', *American Antiquity*, 32 (1977).

13 L. A. Parsons and B. J. Price, 'Mesoamerican Trade and its Role in the Emergence of Civilization', in R. Heizer and J. Graham (eds), *Observations on the Emergence of Civilization in Mesoamerica*, Contribution of the University of California Archaeological Research Facility, 11 (Berkeley, Calif., 1971).

14 Parsons and Price, 'Mesoamerican Trade and its Role in the Emergence of Civilization'.

15 M. P. Weaver, *The Aztec, Maya, and Their Predecessors* (New York, 1972).

Chapter 59: Andean South America: from village to empire

1   L. G. Lumbreras, 'Documento de Trabajo, No. 1', *Críticas y Perspectivas de la Arqueología Andina* (Lima, 1979).

2   J. V. Murra, 'El "control vertical" de un máximo de pisos ecológicos en la economía de las sociedas andinas', in J. V. Murra (ed.), *Visita de la provincia de Léon de Huánuco (1562) por Iñigo Ortiz de Zuñiga* (Huánuco, 1972).

3   J. H. Rowe, 'What Kind of Settlement was Inca Cuzco?', *Nawpa Pacha*, 5 (Berkeley, Calif., 1967).

4   C. Morris and D. E. Thompson, 'Huánuco Viejo: An Inca Administrative

Center', *American Antiquity*, 35 (1970).
5 M. E. Mosley, 'Chanchan: Andean Alternative of the Preindustrial City', *Science*, 187 (1975).
6 T. C. Patterson, *America's Past: A New World Archaeology* (Glenview, Ill., 1973).
7 D. W. Lathrap, 'The Hunting Economies of the Tropical Forest Zone of South America: An Attempt at a Historical Perspective', in R. B. Lee and I. DeVore (eds), *Man the Hunter* (Chicago, 1968); D. W. Lathrap, *Ancient Ecuador* (Chicago, 1975).
8 C. Donnan, *Moche Art of Peru* (Los Angeles, 1978).
9 E. P. Lanning, *Peru Before the Incas* (Englewood Cliffs, N. J., 1967).
10 J. H. Rowe, 'The Kingdom of Chimor', *Acta Americana*, 6 (1948).
11 Mosley, 'Chanchan: Andean Alternative of the Preindustrial City'.
12 J. V. Murra, 'An Aymara Kingdom in 1567', *Ethnohistory*, 15 (1968).
13 J. V. Murra, *Formaciones Economicos y Politicos des Mundo Andino* (Lima, 1975).
14 C. Morris, 'Reconstructing Patterns of Non-Agricultural Production in the Inca Economy: Archaeology and Documents in Institutional Analysis', in C. Moore (ed.), *Reconstructing Complex Societies* (Cambridge, Mass., 1974).

Chapter 60: Tropical forest cultures of the Amazon basin
1 D. W. Lathrap, *The Upper Amazon*, in Glyn Daniel (ed.), Ancient People and Places Series, No. 70 (London, 1970).
2 R. L. Carneiro, 'Slash-and-Burn Cultivation among the Kuikuru and its Implications for Cultural Development in the Amazon Basin', in J. Wilbert (ed.), *The Evolution of Horticultural Systems in Native South America: Causes and Consequences* (Caracas, 1961).
3 J. H. Steward (ed.), *Handbook of South American Indians*, Vol. 3: *The Tropical Forest Tribes*, Bureau of American Ethnology, Bulletin 143 (Washington, DC, 1948).
4 Gaspar de Carvajal, 'The Discovery of the Amazon, According to the Account of Friar Gaspar de Carvajal, and Other Documents' compiled by José Toribo Medina and edited by H. C. Heaton, *American Geographical Society Special Publication*, 17 (New York, 1934).
5 B. J. Meggers and C. Evans, Jr, 'An Experimental Formulation of Horizon Styles in the Tropical Forest Area of South America', in S. K. Lothrop *et al.* (eds), *Essays in Pre-Columbian Art and Archaeology* (Cambridge, Mass., 1961).
6 Meggers and Evans, 'An Experimental Formulation of Horizon Styles'.
7 B. J. Meggers and C. Evans, Jr, 'Archaeological Evidence of a Prehistoric Migration from the Rio Napo to the Mouth of the Amazon', *University of Arizona Social Science Bulletin*, 27 (1959).
8 B. J. Meggers, *Amazonia: Man and Culture in a Counterfeit Paradise* (Chicago, 1971).
9 Meggers and Evans, 'Archaeological Evidence of a Prehistoric Migration'; Meggers, *Amazonia: Man and Culture in a Counterfeit Paradise*.
10 D. W. Lathrap, 'Our Father the Cayman, Our Mother the Gourd: Spinden Revisited, or a Unitary Model for the Emergence of Agriculture in the New World', in Charles A. Reed, *The Origins of Agriculture* (The Hague, 1977).
11 D. W. Lathrap, 'The Tropical Forest and the Cultural Context of Chavin', in Elizabeth Benson (ed.), *Dumbarton Oaks Conference on Chavin* (Washington, DC, 1971).
12 P. I. Porras, *Arqueología de la Cueva de los Tayos* (Quito, 1978).

Chapter 61: Interpretation and synthesis – a personal view
1 D. Pilbeam, *The Ascent of Man* (New York, 1972).
2 V. Van Geist, *Mountain Sheep* (Chicago, 1971).
3 L. R. Binford and S. R. Binford, 'A Preliminary Analysis of Functional Variability in the Mousterian of Levallois Facies', *American Anthropologist*, 68 (1966); reprinted in L. R. Binford, *An Archaeological Perspective* (New York/London, 1972).
4 M. N. Cohen, *The Food Crisis in Prehistory* (New Haven, Conn., 1977).
5 K. V. Flannery, 'The Origins of Agriculture', *Annual Review of Anthropology*, 2 (1973).
6 J. Friedman and M. Rowlands (eds), *The Evolution of Social Systems* (London, 1978).
7 A. C. Renfrew, *The Emergence of Civilization* (London, 1972).
8 R. Wilkinson, *Poverty and Progress* (London/New York, 1973).
9 J. W. Burrow, *Evolution and Society: A Study in Victorian Social Theory* (Cambridge, 1966).

Chapter 62: Dating and dating methods
1 M. J. Aitken, *Physics and Archaeology*, 2nd edn (Oxford, 1974); D. Brothwell and E. Higgs (eds), *Science in Archaeology*, 2nd edn (London, 1969); M. S. Tite, *Methods of Physical Examination in Archaeology* (London, 1972).
2 W. W. Bishop and J. A. Miller (eds), *Calibration of Hominoid Evolution* (Edinburgh, 1972).
3 I. U. Olsson (ed.), *Radiocarbon Variations and Absolute Chronology* (London, 1970); R. Burleigh, 'Radiocarbon Dating: Some Practical Considerations for the Archaeologist', *Journal of Archaeological Science*, 1 (1974).
4 W. F. Libby, *Radiocarbon Dating*, 2nd edn (Chicago, 1955).
5 F. E. Zeuner, *Dating the Past*, 4th edn (London, 1958).
6 H. C. Fritts, *Tree Rings and Climate* (London, 1976).
7 S. J. Fleming, *Authenticity in Art – The Scientific Detection of Forgery* (London, 1975).
8 K. P. Oakley, 'Analytical Methods of Dating Bones', in Brothwell and Higgs, *Science in Archaeology*; K. P. Oakley *et al.*, *The Catalogue of Fossil Hominids*, Parts I–III, British Museum (Natural History) (London, 1967–75); K. P. Oakley, 'Relative Dating of Fossil Hominids of Europe', *Bulletin of the British Museum (Natural History)*, Geology Series (in press).
9 C. D. Ovey (ed.), *The Swanscombe Skull: A Survey of Research on a Pleistocene Site*, Royal Anthropological Institute Occasional Paper No. 2 (London, 1964).

Further reading

PART ONE

I: The development of modern archaeology

R. M. Adams, *The Evolution of Urban Society* (Chicago, 1966).

L. R. Binford, *An Archaeological Perspective* (New York/London, 1972).

D. Brothwell and E. Higgs, *Science in Archaeology* (London, 1969).

K. Butzer, *Environment and Archaeology* (London, 1972).

V. G. Childe, *Man Makes Himself* (London, 1956).

J. G. D. Clark, *Prehistoric Europe: The Economic Basis* (London, 1952).

D. L. Clarke, *Analytical Archaeology*, 2nd edn (London, 1978).

D. L. Clarke (ed.), *Models in Archaeology* (London, 1972).

J. Deetz, *Invitation to Archaeology* (New York, 1967).

G. Daniel, *The Idea of Prehistory* (London, 1962).

G. Daniel, *150 Years of Archaeology* (London, 1975).

T. K. Earle and J. Erikson, *Exchange Systems in Prehistory* (London, 1972).

K. V. Flannery (ed.), *The Early Mesoamerican Village* (New York, 1976).

J. Friedman and M. J. Rowlands (eds), *The Evolution of Social Systems* (London, 1978).

R. A. Gould (ed.), *Explorations in Ethnoarchaeology* (Albuquerque, New Mexico, 1978).

R. F. Heizer, *Man's Discovery of his Past: Literary Landmarks in Archaeology* (Englewood Cliffs, N. J., 1962).

I. Hodder and C. Orton, *Spatial Analysis in Archaeology* (Cambridge, 1976).

F. Hole and R. F. Heizer, *An Introduction to Prehistoric Archaeology* (New York, 1965).

R. B. Lee and I. DeVore (eds.), *Man the Hunter* (Chicago, 1968).

A. C. Renfrew (ed.), *The Explanation of Culture Change: Models in Prehistory* (London, 1973).

J. A. Sabloff and C. C. Lamberg-Karlovsky (eds), *The Rise and Fall of Civilisation* (San Francisco, 1974).

J. A. Sabloff and G. R. Willey, *A History of American Archaeology* (London, 1978).

C. Vita Finzi, *Archaeological Sites in their Setting* (London, 1978).

E. Zubrow (ed.), *New World Archaeology* (Readings from *Scientific American*) (San Francisco, 1974).

PART TWO

II: Man the hunter

F. Bordes, *A Tale of Two Caves* (New York, 1972).

F. Bordes, *The Old Stone Age* (London, 1968).

K. Butzer, *Environment and Archaeology* (Chicago, 1971).

K. Butzer and G. Ll. Isaac, *After the Australopithecines* (The Hague, 1976).

J. M. Coles and E. Higgs, *The Archaeology of Early Man* (London, 1968).

L. G. Freeman (ed.), *Views of the Past* (The Hague, 1978).

A. S. Goudie, *Environmental Change* (Oxford, 1977).

J. Gribbin (ed.), *Climatic Change* (Cambridge, 1978).

F. C. Howell, *Early Man* (New York, 1971).

G. Il. Isaac, *Olorgesailie: Archaeological Studies of a Middle Pleistocene Lake Basin in Kenya* (Chicago, 1977).

R. Klein, *Ice Age Hunters of the Ukraine* (Chicago, 1973).

R. B. Lee and I. DeVore (eds), *Man the Hunter* (Chicago, 1968).

A. Leroi-Gourhan, *Préhistoire de l'art occidental* (Paris, 1965).

D. R. Pilbeam, *The Ascent of Man* (New York, 1972).

K. K. Turekian (ed.), *Late Cenozoic Glacial Ages* (New Haven, Conn., 1971).

P. J. Ucko and A. Rosenfield, *Palaeolithic Art* (London, 1967).

J. d'A. Waechter, *Man Before History* (Oxford, 1976).

III: The Postglacial revolution

R. McC. Adams, *The Evolution of Urban Society* (Chicago, 1966).

C. Aldred, *The Egyptians* (London, 1961).

B. Allchin and R. Allchin, *The Birth of Indian Civilisation* (Harmondsworth, 1968).

J. Bintliff, *Natural Environment and Human Settlement in Prehistoric Greece* (Oxford, 1977).

C. Redman, *The Rise of Civilization* (San Francisco, 1978).

J. Chadwick, *The Mycenaean World* (Cambridge, 1976).

W. A. Fairservis, *The Ancient Kingdoms of the Nile and the Doomed Monuments of Nubia* (New York, 1962).

W. A. Fairservis, *The Roots of Ancient India* (Chicago, 1975).

J. R. Harlan, J. M. J. de Wet and A. B. L. Stemler, *Origins of African Plant Domestication* (The Hague, 1976).

T. B. Jones (ed.), *The Sumerian Problem* (New York, 1969).

S. K. Kramer, *The Sumerians* (Chicago, 1963).

R. B. Lee and I. DeVore (eds), *Man the Hunter* (Chicago, 1968).

J. V. S. Megaw (ed.), *Hunters, Gatherers and First Farmers Beyond Europe* (Leicester, 1977).

S. Milisauskas, *Prehistoric Europe* (New York, 1978).

J. Oates and D. Oates, *The Rise of Civilisation* (Oxford, 1976).

A. L. Oppenheim, *Ancient Mesopotamia* (Chicago, 1964).

S. Piggott, *Ancient Europe* (Edinburgh, 1965).

A. C. Renfrew, *The Emergence of Civilisation: The Cyclades and the Aegean in the Third Millennium BC* (London, 1972).

C. A. Reed (ed.), *The Origins of Agriculture* (The Hague, 1977).

R. B. Smith and W. Watson (eds), *Early South East Asia* (Oxford, 1979).

A. Snodgrass, *The Dark Age of Greece* (Edinburgh, 1971).

D. R. Theocharis (ed.), *Neolithic Greece* (Athens, 1973).

P. J. Ucko and G. W. Dimbleby (eds), *The Domestication and Exploitation of Plants and Animals* (London, 1969).

E. Vermeule, *Greece in the Bronze Age* (Chicago, 1964).

W. Watson, *China* (London, 1961).

W. Watson, *Cutural Frontiers in Ancient East Asia* (Edinburgh, 1971).

P. Wheatley, *The Pivot of the Four Quarters* (Chicago, 1971).

Sir Mortimer Wheeler, *The Indus Civilisation* (Cambridge, 1968).

J. Yellan, *Archaeological Approaches to the Present* (New York, 1977).

IV: The early empires of the western Old World

E. Akurgal, *Civilisation and Ruins in Turkey*, 2nd edn (Ankara, 1973).

C. Burney, *From Village to Empire: An Introduction to Near Eastern Archaeology* (Oxford, 1977).

R. G. Collingwood and I. A. Richmond, *The Archaeology of Roman Britain* (London, 1969).

A. Rosalie David, *The Egyptian Kingdoms* (Oxford, 1975).

M. I. Finley (ed.), *Atlas of Classical Archaeology* (London, 1976).

S. S. Frere, *Britannia: A History of Roman Britain* (London, 1974).

E. Gjerstad, *Early Rome*, Vols I–IV (Lund, 1956–63).

P. Green, *Alexander of Macedon* (Harmondsworth, 1974).

A. W. Johnston, *The Emergence of Greece* (Oxford, 1976).

R. Ling, *The Greek World* (Oxford, 1976).

P. R. S. Moorey, *Biblical Lands* (Oxford, 1975).

N. Postgate, *The First Empires* (Oxford, 1977).

C. M. Robertson, *A History of Greek Art* (Cambridge, 1975).

M. I. Rostovtzeff, *Social and Economic History of the Hellenistic World* (Oxford, 1941).

H. H. Scullard, *The Etruscan Cities and Rome* (London, 1967).

R. Stillwell (ed.), *Princeton Encyclopedia of Classical Sites* (Princeton, N.J., 1976).

W. W. Tarn and G. T. Griffiths, *Hellenistic Civilisation*, 3rd edn (London, 1952).

M. Vickers, *The Roman World* (Oxford, 1976).

C. M. Wells, *The German Policy of Augustus* (Oxford, 1972).

V: Empires in the eastern Old World

B. Allchin and R. Allchin, *The Birth of Indian Civilisation* (Harmondsworth, 1968).
Kwang-chih Chang, *The Archaeology of Ancient China* (New Haven, Conn./ London, 1968).
N. Dyson-Hudson and W. Irons (eds), *Perspectives on Nomadism* (Leiden, 1972).
R. B. Ekvall, *Fields on the Hoof* (New York, 1968).
P. Fitzgerald, *Ancient China* (Oxford, 1978).
K. Jettmar, *Art of the Steppes* (London, 1967).
S. Legg, *The Heartland* (London, 1970).
J. Needham, *Science and Civilisation in China* (Cambridge. 1954–   ).
E. D. Phillips, *The Royal Hordes* (London, 1965).
S. U. Rudenko, *Frozen Tombs of Siberia* (London, 1970).
R. B. Smith and W. Watson (eds), *Early South East Asia* (Oxford, 1979).
T. Sulimirski, *Prehistoric Russia* (London, 1970).
T. Sulimirski, *The Samartians* (London, 1970).
Cheng Te-k'un, *Archaeology in China* (Cambridge, 1963).
R. Thapar, *A History of India*, Vol. I (Harmondsworth, 1972).
A. Toynbee (ed.), *Half the World* (London, 1973).
J. Treistman, *The Prehistory of China* (Newton Abbot, 1972).

VI: Old empires and new forces

J. H. Clapham and M. M. Postan (eds), *Cambridge Economic History of Europe* (Cambridge, 1942–63).
N. J. Dejevsky, 'Novgorod: the Origins of a Russian Town' in M. W. Barley (ed.) *European Towns: their Archaeology and Early History* (London, 1977).
N. J. Dejevsky, *The Medieval Towns of Russia: Their Growth and Study* (London, forthcoming).
J. Hayes, *Late Roman Pottery* (London, 1972).
D. Oates, *Studies in the Ancient History of Northern Iraq* (London, 1968).
A. Pope, *Survey of Persian Art from Prehistoric Times to the Present* (London, 1938).
D. Talbot Rice, *Byzantine Painted Pottery* (Oxford, 1930).
M. N. Tikhomirov, *The Towns of Ancient Rus* (Moscow, 1959).
M. W. Thompson, *Novgorod the Great* (London, 1967).
M. Todd, *The Northern Barbarians 100 BC–AD 300* (London, 1975).
L. White, *Medieval Technology and Social Change* (Oxford, 1962).
P. Wolff (ed.), *Guide International d'Histoire Urbaine*, Vol. I: *Europe* (Paris, 1977).
A. Zbierski, 'Archaeology on Spatial Change in Gdansk', *Acta Poloniae Historica*, 34 (1976).
B. Zientara, 'Socio-economic and Spatial Transformations in Polish Towns During the Period of Location', *Acta Poloniae Historica*, 34 (1976).

VII: On the edge of the Old World

B. Allchin, *The Stone-Tipped Arrow* (London, 1966).
J. Allen, J. Golson and R. Jones, *Sundra and Sahul: Prehistoric Studies in South East Asia, Melanesia and Australia* (London, 1977).
P. Bellwood, *The Polynesians* (London, 1978).
J. D. Clark, *The Prehistory of Africa* (London, 1970).
W. FitzHugh, *Prehistoric Maritime Adaptations of the Circumpolar Zone* (The Hague, 1975).
D. J. Mulvaney, *The Prehistory of Australia* (London, 1975).
D. J. Mulvaney and J. Golson, *Aboriginal Man and Environment in Australia* (Canberra, 1971).
D. W. Phillipson, *The Later Prehistory of Eastern and Southern Africa* (London, 1977).
T. Shaw, *Nigeria: Its Archaeology and Early History* (London, 1978).

VIII: The New World

G. Bankes, *Peru before Pizarro* (Oxford, 1977).
M. D. Coe, *Mexico* (London, 1962).
M. D. Coe, *The Maya* (London, 1966).
D..E. Dumond, *The Eskimos and Aleuts* (London, 1977).
J. D. Jennings, *Prehistory of North America* (New York, 1974).
J. D. Jennings (ed.), *Ancient Native Americans* (San Francisco, 1978).
J. D. Jennings and E. Norbeck, *Prehistoric Man in the New World* (Chicago, 1964).
S. Gorenstein (ed.), *North America* (New York, 1975).
S. Gorenstein, *Not Forever on Earth* (New York, 1975).
D. W. Lathrap, *The Upper Amazon* (London, 1970).
J. A. Sabloff and G. R. Willey, *A History of American Archaeology* (London, 1978).
W. T. Sanders and B. J. Price, *Mesoamerica: The Evolution of a Civilisation* (New York, 1968).
D. Snow, *The American Indians: Their Archaeology and Prehistory* (London, 1976).
R. E. Taylor and C. W. Meighan, *Chronologies in New World Archaeology* (New York, 1978).
M. P. Weaver, *The Aztecs, Maya and their Predecessors* (New York, 1972).
W. R. Wedel, *Prehistoric Man on the Great Plains* (Norman, Okla., 1961).
G. Willey, *An Introduction to American Archaeology* (New Jersey, 1966).
G. R. Willey, *An Introduction to American Archaeology* (New Jersey, 1966).

IX: Pattern and process

J. G. D. Clark, *World Prehistory*, 3rd edn (Cambridge, 1977).
D. L. Clarke, *Analytical Archaeologist,* (London, 1979).
M. Cohen, *The Food Crisis in Prehistory* (New Haven, 1977).
J. Friedman and M. J. Rowlands, *The Evolution of Social Systems* (London, 1978).
B. Spooner, *Population Growth: Anthropological Implications* (Cambridge, Mass., 1972).
J. H. Toulmin and J. Goodfield, *The Discovery of Time* (Harmondsworth, 1965).

PART THREE
X: Frameworks: dating and distribution

M. J. Aitken, *Physics and Archaeology* (Oxford, 1974).
G. Barraclough (ed.), *The Times Atlas of World History* (London, 1979).
D. Brothwell and E. Higgs (eds), *Science in Archaeology* (London, 1969).
S. J. Fleming, *Dating in Archaeology: A Guide to Scientific Techniques* (London, 1976).
J. Hawkes, *Atlas of Ancient Archaeology* (London, 1974).
H. Kinder and W. Hilgermann, *DTV Atlas zur Weltgeschichte*, Vol. I (Stuttgart, 1964), published in English as *The Penguin Atlas of World History*, Vol. I (Harmondsworth, 1974).
C. McEvedy (ed.), *The Penguin Atlas of Ancient History* (Harmondsworth, 1967).
C. McEvedy (ed.), *The Penguin Atlas of Medieval History* (Harmondsworth, 1961).
M. S. Tite, *Methods of Physical Examination in Archaeology* (London, 1972).
D. Whitehouse and R. Whitehouse, *Archaeological Atlas of the World* (London, 1975).
F. E. Zeuner, *Dating the Past* (London, 1958).

Index

Page numbers in *italics* refer to illustrations.

Acknowledgements

The sources for the illustrations that introduce Parts One, Two and Three and Sections I–X are as follows:

PART ONE: 'The Shaft-Grave Circle at Mycenae', from Henry Schliemann, *Mycenae: A Narrative of Researches and Discoveries at Mycenae and Tiryns* (New York and London, 1880). Ashmolean Museum, Oxford.

PART TWO: 'Group of Tasmanian Natives in front of Their Windbreak', from François Péron, *Voyage de Découvertes aux Terres Australes*, 2 vols (Paris, 1807–16). Pitt Rivers Museum, Oxford.

PART THREE: 'Une Porte d'Angcor Thom', from François Garnier, *Voyage d'Exploration de l'Indo-Chine* (Paris, 1873). Royal Geographical Society, London.

Section I: Detail from 'Panorama of the Monumental Grandeur of the Mississippi Valley', by John J. Egan. The St Louis Art Museum.

Section II: Map prepared by F. Alayne Street.

Sections III–VIII: Maps prepared by Andrew Sherratt.

Section IX: Detail from 'The Indian Village of Socoton', by John White. Reproduced by courtesy of the Trustees of the British Museum. Michael Holford Photographs, Loughton, Essex.

Section X: Map of the world by the twelfth-century Sicilian geographer, Idrisi. Bodleian Library, Oxford: MS Pococke 375.

For permission to reproduce or adapt plans and illustrations included in this book the publishers gratefully acknowledge the sources listed below. Every effort has been made to obtain permission to use copyright material; the publishers trust that their apologies will be accepted for any errors or omissions.

1.1: Bodleian Library, Oxford **1.3:** The Society of Antiquaries, London **1.4:** Griffith Institute, Ashmolean Museum, Oxford **1.5:** The Oriental Institute, University of Chicago **1.6:** Iraq Museum/State Antiquities and Heritage Organization, Baghdad **2.1:** Institut für Ur- und Frühgeschichte der Universität, Cologne **2.2:** Dr Larry Keeley **3.1:** Hayling Island Excavation; photograph G. Soffe **3.2:** National Monuments Record Air Photograph: Crown Copyright Reserved **4.1:** After Hodder and Orton **4.2:** After Clarke **5.1:** After MacNeish **5.2:** After Sturdy **5.4:** After Higgs and Vita-Finzi **9.4:** Peter Andrews **10.2:** J. W. K. Harris **10.3:** Cleveland Museum of Natural History, Ohio **10.6:** J. W. K. Harris **10.7:** P. R. Jones, Laetoli Research Project **10.8:** J. W. K. Harris **11.4:** L. G. Freeman **11.5:** L. G. Freeman **12.3:** L. G. Freeman **13.4:** After Boriskorskij **13.5:** After González Echegaray and Freeman **13.6:** L. G. Freeman **13.7:** Picturepoint, London **14.2:** Alan Thorne **14.3:** Alan Thorne **15.3:** AAA Photo, Paris; photograph André Picou **15.6:** After Theocharis **16.1:** After Buchanan **16.3:** State Antiquities and Heritage Organization, Baghdad **16.4:** Hirmer Fotoarchiv, Munich **16.5:** After Sürenhagen **16.6:** After Amiet **16.7:** Hirmer Fotoarchiv, Munich **16.8:** Hirmer Fotoarchiv, Munich; seal impression, after Amiet **17.1:** Ronald Sheridan's Photo-Library, Harrow, Middx **17.2:** After Darby **17.3:** After Woolley **17.4:** Hirmer Fotoarchiv, Munich **17.6:** After Parrot **17.7:** Hirmer Fotoarchiv, Munich **17.8:** Hirmer Fotoarchiv, Munich **18.1:** Ashmolean Museum, Oxford **18.5:** Robert Harding Associates, London **19.3:** Peter Warren **19.4:** After Pendlebury **19.6:** Peter Warren **19.7:** Peter Warren **20.1:** After Todorova **20.2:** Ashmolean Museum, Oxford **20.3:** Andrew Sherratt **20.4:** Andrew Sherratt **20.5:** After Lüning and members of SAP **21.3:** Chosuke Serisawa, Tokoku **21.4:** J. Edward Kidder, Tokyo **21.9:** Ian C. Glover **21.10:** Ian C. Glover **22.1:** Dilip Chakrabarti **22.2:** Dilip Chakrabarti **22.5:** After Sankalia **23.3:** Ian C. Glover **23.4:** Ian C. Glover **24.1:** Pitt Rivers Museum, Oxford **24.3:** Ray Inskeep **24.5:** Drawings, after Fagan and van Noten; photograph, Ray Inskeep **25.1:** After Shinnie **26.1:** Courtesy of the Trustees of the British Museum, London **26.3:** After Mallowan **26.4:** Courtesy of the Trustees of the British Museum, London **28.1:** Direction des Antiquités, Beirut **28.3:** The Israel Department of Antiquities and Museums, Jerusalem **28.4:** After Kenyon **29.1:** Ashmolean Museum, Oxford **30.1:** David Stronach **30.4:** After Adams **30.5:** David Stronach **31.1:** D. Brian Doe **32.1:** Pergamon-Grabung **33.1:** Prähistorische Abteilung, Naturhistorisches Museum, Vienna **34.4:** After Adamesteanu **34.5:** Hirmer Fotoarchiv, Munich **35.4:** After Cotton **36.2:** Sonia Halliday, Weston Turville, Bucks **36.5:** Stephen Mitchell **37.3:** Courtesy of the Trustees of the British Museum, London **39.2:** After Marshall **39.3:** ZEFA Photo Library, London; photograph K. Siewert **39.4:** ZEFA Photo Library, London; photograph Jens Herrmann **40.3:** Bennet Bronson **41.2:** After Gernet **42.3:** C. von Fürer-Haimendorf, London **42.4:** C. von Fürer-Haimendorf, London **43.1:** The John Hillelson Agency, London; photograph Georg Gerster **43.2:** Georgina Herrmann **43.4:** After Adams **44.2:** Clive Foss **44.3:** Clive Foss **44.4:** Clive Foss **45.3:** Iraq Museum/State Antiquities and Heritage Organization, Baghdad **45.4:** Staatliches Museum für Völkerkunde, Munich **46.2:** After Haarnagel **46.3:** After Herrmann **46.4:** Courtesy of the Trustees of the British Museum, London **46.5:** National Museum of Denmark, Copenhagen **46.6:** Universitets Oldsaksamling, Oslo **46.7:** After Roesdahl **46.8:** After Böhner **47.1:** French Government Tourist Office, London **47.2:** After Goodband; by kind permission of the County Archaeologist, Wakefield, W. Yorks **47.3:** After Duby **47.4:** J. Combier, Mâcon **47.5:** The British Library, London **47.6:** After Hanawalt **47.7:** Moated Sites Research Group, Liss, Hants **47.10:** Niedersächsische Staats- und Universitätsbibliothek, Göttingen **47.11:** Archives Photographiques, Paris/SPADEM **48.2:** After Rabinovich **48.3:** After Škorpil **48.4:** After Arzamasov and Dolgov **49.1:** Cambridge Museum of Archaeology, Cambridge **50.2:** G. J. Irwin **50.3:** G. J. Irwin **51.2:** Australian Information Service, London **51.5:** Alan Thorne **51.6:** Australian Information Service, London **51.7:** Australian Information Service, London **51.8:** Australian Institute of Aboriginal Studies, Canberra; photograph Robert Edwards **52.1:** Alan Hutchison Library, London **52.3:** Ray Inskeep **52.5:** Almasy, Neuilly-sur-Seine **53.1:** Peter Garlake **53.3:** Peter Garlake **53.4:** Peter Garlake **54.2:** After Ford **54.5:** David Baerreis **55.1:** Don E. Dumond **55.2:** Don E. Dumond **56.1:** Barbara Pickersgill **56.2:** Robert S. Peabody Foundation for Archaeology, Andover, Mass. **56.6:** Warwick Bray **58.3:** Werner Forman Archive, London **58.4:** After Stierlin **58.6:** Maudslay Collection, The British Museum, London **58.7:** Werner Forman Archive, London **58.8:** Werner Forman Archive, London **59.2:** American Museum of Natural History, New York **59.3:** American Museum of Natural History, New York **59.4:** Rudolf and Times Newspapers Limited, London **59.5:** American Museum of Natural History, New York **59.6:** American Museum of Natural History, New York **62.1:** After Fleming **62.2:** Courtesy of the Trustees of the British Museum, London **62.3:** Courtesy of the Trustees of the British Museum, London **62.4:** Courtesy of the Trustees of the British Museum, London **62.5:** Courtesy of the Trustees of the British Museum, London **62.7:** BBC Copyright Photograph, London **62.10:** Courtesy of the Trustees of the British Museum, London **62.12:** Courtesy of the Trustees of the British Museum, London **62.14:** Royal Anthropological Institute of Great Britain and Ireland **63.1–8:** Charts prepared by Andrew Sherratt **64.1–9, 11–36:** Maps prepared by Andrew Sherratt **64.10:** Map prepared by F. Alayne Street